USEFUL WEBSITES

www.alta.org   The American Land Title Association

www.ired.com   International Real Estate Digest

www.reals.com   This is a real estate directory for such subjects as commercial real estate, international real estate, and professional services.

www.homeglossary.com   This is an online real estate dictionary.

www.findlaw.com   A good source of legal information including real estate.

www.mortgagemag.com   Includes real estate related articles and links to sites covering Mortgage Banking, Legal Services, and Technology.

http://dictionary.law.com   Legal dictionary.

http://real-estate-law.freeadvice.com   Real estate law FAQs.

www.bai.org   Current market rates on various financial investments.

www.interest.com   Current average mortgage rates, a mortgage calculator, and basic information on home buying.

www.interestratecalculator.com   Various tools including a mortgage calculator.

www.bankrate.com   Source of interest rates for CDs and other investments, also provides tools and information on mortgages.

www.nahb.com   National Association of Home Builders

www.bankofamerica.com   National lender that provides mortgage rate information on their Web site.

www.pueblo.gsa.gov   FAQs on various real estate tools.

www.fanniemae.com   Federal National Mortgage Association

www.hud.gov   Department of Housing and Urban Development

www.freddiemac.com   Federal Home Loan Mortgage Corporation

www.mbaa.org   Mortgage Bankers Association of America

www.aba.com   America Banker Association

www.businessfinance.com/wraparound-mortgage.htm   Examples of wraparound loans.

www.fha-home-loans.com/buydown_fha_loan.htm   Discussion of how FHA Buydown Loans are structured.

www.mgic.com   Mortgage Guarantee Insurance Corporation

www.realtor.com   National Association of Realtors

www.fhfa.gov   Federal Housing Finance Agency

www.freddiemac.com/finance/cmhpi   Freddie Mac's Conventional Mortgage Home Price Index (CMHPI)

www.bestplaces.net   Statistics on places to live.

www.ers.usda.gov/data/unemployment   U.S. Department of Agriculture. This link includes median household income and unemployment data on every county in the United States.

www.statetaxcentral.com   Provides tax information for every state.

http://realestate.yahoo.com/homevalues   Tools and information on home buying.

www.owners.com/partners/mortgages.aspx   This site provides information and articles on buying a home and financing.

www.hud.gov/offices/hsg/hsgabout.cfm   Discussion of FHA.

www.va.gov   Veterans Affairs

www.bls.gov/cpi   Consumer Price Index site sponsored by the U.S. Department of Labor Bureau of Labor Statistics.

www.reis.com   Provides commercial real estate trends, analytics, market research, and news that support transactions by real estate professionals.

www.leasingprofessional.com   Source of information about leases including terminology, sample leases, and links to other sites.

www.globest.com   Provides current real estate news that is updated daily.

www.appraisalinstitute.org   The Appraisal Institute

www.naifa.com   National Association of Independent Fee Appraisers

http://nreionline.com   National Real Estate Investor

www.irei.com   Institutional Real Estate, Inc. provides current news and on the "research" page includes links to research reports provided by several institutional investment firms.

www.buildings.com   *Buildings* magazine

www.ncreif.com   The National Council of Real Estate Investment Fiduciaries

www.reiac.org   Real Estate Investment Advisory Council

www.gecapitalrealestate.com   GE Capital Real Estate

www.capmark.com   Capmark commercial real estate

www.irs.gov   The IRS Web site can be useful to find information on the taxation of real estate income property.

www.ciremagazine.com Certified Commercial Investment Manager's Commercial Investment Real Estate magazine Web site.

www.century21.com The Century 21 Web site has several articles related to buying and selling advice, as well as calculators.

www.eris.ca Site has a searchable environmental risk database for Canada.

www.environmental-expert.com Good information on different types of environmental risk and brownfields developments.

www.eda.gov Economic Development Administration

www.corenetglobal.org Corporate Real Estate Network/CoreNet Global

www.naiop.org National Association of Industrial and Office Properties

www.uli.org Urban Land Institute

www.bizloan.org Good resource for information about different types of loans used for project development. Includes glossary of terms.

www.axiometrics.com Axiometrics is a research firm providing fundamental real estate research for the apartment sector.

www.sldtonline.com An online publication dedicated to delivering news and perspectives to land development professionals, including developers, planners, surveyors, civil engineers, landscape architects, and construction professionals, enabling them to succeed in today's dynamic environment.

www.census.gov U.S. Census Bureau Web site.

www.icsc.org International Council of Shopping Centers Web site.

www.economy.com Economy.com is a provider of economic data.

www.bls.gov U.S. Department of Labor

www.bea.gov U.S. Department of Commerce— Bureau of Economic Development

www.nielsen.com/nielsenclaritas Claritas provides demographic and enhanced census data.

www.sppre.com A national consulting, development management, and real estate asset management company with the sole purpose of assisting government, university, and school district officials to structure and implement public/private real estate partnerships and optimize the value of their underutilized real estate assets.

www.ginniemae.gov Ginnie Mae/Government National Mortgage Association is within HUD and ensures mortgage funds are available throughout the United States.

www.frbservices.org The Federal Reserves System Financial Services Web site provides transaction capabilities and service information.

www.investinginbonds.org Information about investing in CMOs from the Bond Market Association.

www.reit.com National Association of Real Estate Investment Trusts

www.allegiancecapital.com A site designed for institutional investors and high net worth individuals. Provides information on various investment alternatives.

www.wilshire.com Wilshire Associates produces a number of indices including a real estate index.

www.investorwords.com An investing glossary

www.fiabci.com The International Real Estate Federation

www.china-window.com Information about the real estate market in China

www.epra.com European Public Real Estate Association

www.riskgrades.com Measures the risk of the world's financial assets.

www.naea.co.uk The National Association of Estate Agents

www.realestate-tokyo.com Offers information on the real estate in the Tokyo, Japan area.

www.crea.ca The Canadian Real Estate Association

www.cbre.com/global/research Provides U.S. office and industrial vacancy reports.

www.economy.com/freelunch A good source of free economic data.

www.nasdbondinfo.com Contains transaction information as reported to NASD.

www.intex.com Analytical Solutions for Structured Finance

www.investopedia.com An educational guide to investing and personal finance.

Real Estate Finance and Investments

Real Estate Finance and Investments

Fifteenth Edition

William B. Brueggeman, PhD

Corrigan Chair in Real Estate
Edwin L. Cox School of Business
Southern Methodist University

Jeffrey D. Fisher, PhD

Professor Emeritus of Real Estate
Kelley School of Business
Indiana University
President, Homer Hoyt Institute

McGraw Hill Education

REAL ESTATE FINANCE AND INVESTMENTS, FIFTEENTH EDITION

Published by McGraw-Hill Education, 2 Penn Plaza, New York, NY 10121. Copyright © 2016 by McGraw-Hill Education. All rights reserved. Printed in the United States of America. Previous editions © 2011, 2008, and 2005. No part of this publication may be reproduced or distributed in any form or by any means, or stored in a database or retrieval system, without the prior written consent of McGraw-Hill Education, including, but not limited to, in any network or other electronic storage or transmission, or broadcast for distance learning.

Some ancillaries, including electronic and print components, may not be available to customers outside the United States.

This book is printed on acid-free paper.

1 2 3 4 5 6 QVS/QVS 19 18 17 16 15

ISBN 978-0-07-337735-3
MHID 0-07-337735-X

Senior Vice President, Products & Markets: *Kurt L. Strand*
Vice President, General Manager, Products & Markets: *Marty Lange*
Vice President, Content Production & Technology Services: *Kimberly Meriwether David*
Managing Director: *James Heine*
Executive Brand Manager: *Charles Synovec*
Lead Product Developer: *Michele Janicek*
Product Developer: *Jennifer Upton*
Digital Product Developer: *Tobi Philips*
Director, Digital Content: *Douglas Ruby*
Digital Product Analyst: *Kevin Shanahan*
Director, Content Design & Delivery: *Linda Meehan-Avenarius*
Executive Program Manager: *Faye M. Herrig*
Content Project Manager: *Mary Jane Lampe*
Buyer: *Sandy Ludovissy*
Content Licensing Specialist: *Ann Marie Jannette*
Cover Designer: *Studio Montage*
Cover Image: *©Erica Simone Leeds*
Compositor: *SPi Global*
Typeface: *10/12 STIX MathJax Main–Regular*
Printer: *Quad/Graphics*

All credits appearing on page or at the end of the book are considered to be an extension of the copyright page.

Library of Congress Cataloging-in-Publication Data

Brueggeman, William B.
    Real estate finance and investments / William B. Brueggeman, Ph.D., Jeffrey
D. Fisher, Ph.D.—Fifteenth edition.
        pages cm
    ISBN 978-0-07-337735-3 (alk. paper)
    1. Mortgage loans—United States. 2. Real property—United States—Finance.
I. Fisher, Jeffrey D. II. Title.
    HG2040.5.U5B78 2016
    332.7'2—dc23

                                                    2015015605

The Internet addresses listed in the text were accurate at the time of publication. The inclusion of a website does not indicate an endorsement by the authors or McGraw-Hill Education, and McGraw-Hill Education does not guarantee the accuracy of the information presented at these sites.

www.mhhe.com

Preface

Introduction to *Real Estate Finance and Investments*

This book prepares readers to understand the risks and rewards associated with investing in and financing both residential and commercial real estate. Concepts and techniques included in the chapters and problem sets are used in many careers related to real estate. These include investing, development financing, appraising, consulting, managing real estate portfolios, leasing, managing property, analyzing site locations, managing corporate real estate, and managing real estate funds. This material is also relevant to individuals who want to better understand real estate when making their own personal investment and financing decisions.

The turmoil in world financial markets during the late 2000s, which was closely tied to events in the real estate market, suggests that investors, lenders, and others who participate in the real estate market need to better understand how to evaluate the risk and return associated with the various ways of investing and lending. This requires an understanding of the legal issues that can impact the rights of lenders and investors, the characteristics of the various vehicles for lending and investing in real estate, the economic benefits of loans and investments, and how local economies may affect the investment performance of properties as well as the goals of lenders and investors.

This book is designed to help both students and other readers understand these many factors so that they can perform the necessary analysis and make informed real estate finance and investment decisions. As the book's title suggests, we discuss both real estate *finance* and real estate *investments*. These topics are interrelated. For example, an investor who purchases a property is making an "investment." This investment is typically financed with a mortgage loan. Thus, the investor needs to understand both how to analyze the investment and how to assess the impact that financing the investment will have on its risk and return.

Similarly, the lender, by providing capital for the investor to purchase the property, is also making an "investment" in the sense that he or she expects to earn a rate of return on funds that have been loaned. Therefore, the lender also needs to understand the risk and return of making that loan. In fact, one of the risks associated with making loans secured by real estate is that, if a borrower defaults, the lender may take ownership of the property. This means that the lender also should evaluate the property using many of the same techniques as the investor purchasing the property.

Organization of the Book

From the above discussion it should be clear that many factors have an impact on the risk and return associated with property investments and the mortgages used to finance them. This is true whether the investment is in a personal residence or in a large income-producing investment such as an office building.

Part I begins with a discussion of the legal concepts that are important in the study of real estate finance and investments. Although a real estate investor or lender may rely heavily on an attorney in a real estate transaction, it is important to know enough to be able to ask the right questions. We focus only on those legal issues that relate to real estate investment and financing decisions.

Part II begins with a discussion of the time value of money concepts important for analyzing real estate investments and mortgages. These concepts are important because real estate is a long-term investment and is financed with loans that are repaid over time. This leads to a discussion of the primary ways that mortgage loans are structured: fixed rate and adjustable rate mortgage loans.

Part III considers residential housing as an investment and covers mortgage loan underwriting for residential properties. This is relevant for individuals making personal financial decisions, such as whether to own or rent a home, as well as for lenders who are evaluating both the loan and borrower.

Part IV covers many topics related to analyzing income property investments. We provide in-depth examples that include apartments, office buildings, shopping centers, and warehouses. Many concepts also may be extended to other property types. These topics include understanding leases, demonstrating how properties are appraised, how to analyze the potential returns and risks of an investment, and how taxes impact investment returns. We also consider how to evaluate whether a property should be sold or renovated. Finally, we look at how corporations, although not in the real estate business per se, must make real estate decisions as part of their business. This could include whether to own or lease the property that must be used in their operations, as well as other issues.

While the first four parts of this book focus on investing or financing existing properties, **Part V** discusses how to analyze projects proposed for development. Such development could include land acquisition and construction of income-producing property of all types to acquisition of land to be subdivided and improved for corporate office parks or for sale to builders of residential communities. This section also includes how projects are financed during the development period. Construction and development financing is very different from the way existing, occupied properties are financed.

Part VI discusses various alternative real estate financing and investment vehicles. We begin with joint ventures and show how different parties with specific areas of expertise may join together to make a real estate investment. We use, as an example, someone with technical development expertise who needs equity capital for a project. A joint venture is created with an investor who has capital to invest but doesn't have the expertise to do the development. We then provide a financial analysis for the investment including capital contributions from, and distributions to, partners during property acquisition, operation, and its eventual sale. In this section, we also discuss how both residential and commercial mortgage loan pools are created. We then consider how mortgage-backed securities are (1) structured, (2) issued against such pools, and (3) traded in the secondary market for such securities. This also includes a discussion of the risks that these investments pose. **Part VI** also includes a discussion of real estate investment trusts (REITs). These public companies invest in real estate and allow investors to own a diversified portfolio of real estate by purchasing shares of stock in the company.

Finally, in **Part VII,** we discuss how to evaluate real estate in a portfolio that also includes other investments such as stocks and bonds. This includes understanding the diversification benefits of including real estate in a portfolio as well as ways to diversify within the real estate portfolio (including international investment). This is followed by a new chapter on real estate investment funds that are created for high net worth individuals and institutional investors. We discuss different fund strategies and structures and how to analyze the performance of the funds relative to various industry benchmarks.

Wide Audience

From the above discussion, one can see that this book covers many topics. Depending on the purpose of a particular course, all or a selection of topics may be covered. If desired, the course also may emphasize either an investor's or a lender's perspective. Alternatively, some courses may emphasize various industry segments such as housing and residential real estate, commercial real estate, construction and development, mortgage-backed securities, corporate real estate, or investment funds. In other words, this book is designed to allow flexibility for instructors and students to cover a comprehensive range of topics or to focus only on those topics that are most important to them.

Changes to the Fifteenth Edition

In addition to updating material throughout the text, we are particularly proud to introduce a new chapter in this edition. Chapter 23 provides extensive coverage of real estate investment funds. These funds now play a major role in the ownership of both residential and commercial real estate. Typically, these funds are created by professional investment managers and private equity firms that offer opportunities to high net worth investors, pension plan sponsors, and other institutional investors to invest in professionally managed portfolios of real estate. How these funds are structured, operated, and evaluated are among the important topics covered in this new chapter.

Another important addition is a new concept box in Chapter 18 that summarizes the new SEC regulations resulting from the "JOBS Act" which allow for "crowd funding" to raise capital for real estate investments. The new regulations now allow the Internet to be used to reach investors which is expected to result in a significant increase in investment from individuals that was not previously available.

This edition also introduces a new cloud-based, lease by lease, discounted cash flow program. It is designed to do investment analysis and valuation of real estate income property investments, as discussed below.

Excel Spreadsheets and REIWise Software

This book is rigorous yet practical and blends theory with applications to real-world problems. These problems are illustrated and solved by using a blend of financial calculators, Excel spreadsheets, and specialized software designed to analyze real estate income property. Excel spreadsheets, provided on the book's Web site at **www.mhhe.com/bf15e,** are an aid for students to understand many of the exhibits displayed in chapters throughout the text. By modifying these exhibits, students also may solve many end-of-chapter problems without having to design new spreadsheets.

Students can also register online to get free access to a cloud-based real estate valuation program called REIWise. We chose this program for this edition of the book because it is very easy and convenient to use by anyone with an Internet connection (including iPads and other mobile devices). REIWise is used in several chapters to supplement the use of Excel spreadsheets when doing investment analysis and solving valuation problems. Once students (or professors) register, they will also have access to data files that replicate examples in the book. Students can register at the following website: **www.reiwise.com/edu.**

Internet Tools and Assets

Making informed real estate investment and financing decisions depends on being able to obtain useful information. Such information may include national and local market trends, interest rates, and properties available for acquisition, financing alternatives, and the opinions of experts concerning the outlook for various real estate sectors.

The Internet provides a rich source of information to real estate investors and lenders. Knowing how to find information on the Web is an important part of the "due diligence" that should be done before making any real estate investments. This edition includes a number of **Web App** boxes that provide exercises that require finding relevant information on the Internet. These Web App boxes provide practical examples of the types of data and other resources that are available on the Internet. The fifteenth edition also contains Web site references that students can use to research various real estate topics. In addition to research, these resources provide readers with an opportunity to remain current on many of the topics discussed in the book.

The book's Web site, located at **www.mhhe.com/bf15e,** contains additional helpful materials for students such as Web links, multiple-choice quizzes, Excel spreadsheets, and appendixes to the text. Using a password-protected instructor log-in, instructors can find a solutions manual, test bank, and PowerPoint presentations.

Supplements

Several ancillary materials are available for instructor use. These include:

- **Solutions Manual**—developed by Jeffrey Fisher and William Brueggeman
- **Test Bank**—developed by Scott Ehrhorn, Liberty University
- **PowerPoint slides**—developed by Joshua Kahr, Columbia University

Acknowledgments

We would like to thank several people who contributed to recent editions by either being a reviewer or providing feedback to us in other ways that helped improve the current edition:

Edward Baryla
East Tennessee State University

Robert Berlinger, Jr.
University Institute of Technology

Roy T. Black
Georgia State University

Thomas P. Boehm
University of Tennessee-Knoxville

Thomas Bothem
University of Illinois at Chicago

Wally Boudry
University of North Carolina-Chapel Hill

Grace Wong Bucchianeri
Wharton School, University of Pennsylvania

Brad Case
NAREIT

Ping Cheng
Florida Atlantic University

Joe D'Alessandro
Real Estate Insights

Ron Donohue
Homer Hoyt Institute

John Fay
Santa Clara University

Michael Fratantoni
Georgetown University

Eric Fruits
Portland State University

Deborah W. Gregory
University of Arizona

Arie Halachmi
Tennessee State University (USA)
Sun Yat-Sen University (China)

Barry Hersh
NYU-SCPS Real Estate Institute

Samuel Kahn
Touro College

Joshua Kahr
Columbia University

W. Keith Munsell
Boston University

Michael Schonberger
Rutgers University-New Brunswick

Tracey Seslen
University of Southern California

Rui Shi
L&B Realty Advisors

Carlos Slawson
Louisiana State University

Jan Strockis
Santa Clara University

Several people played an important role in providing comments to help revise the current edition. Brad Case with the National Association of Real Estate Investment Trusts (NAREIT) and Ron Donohue with the Homer Hoyt Institute helped revise the chapter on real estate investment trusts. Joe D'Alessandro and Rui Shi helped with the revision of the new chapter on real estate funds. Rhea Thornton with FNMA provided comments on the chapter that discusses underwriting residential loans. Susanne Cannon with Megalytics helped with a new insert on Crowd Funding. Heather Hofmann helped in the preparation and submission of the manuscript.

Much of the material in the current edition benefited from many people who provided input into previous editions. Youguo Liang at ADIA provided significant input on the structure of joint ventures. Charles Johnson and Aaron Temple helped with Web references. Jacey Leonard helped prepare the Excel templates for the previous edition that were used in this edition. Anand Kumar helped with Web references and spreadsheets. Ji' Reh Kore helped with research on recent trends impacting the real estate finance industry, as well as with the preparation of the Solutions Manual. Deverick Jordan and Diem Chau also helped with the Solutions Manual and with chapter exhibits. Nathan Hastings helped update the legal chapters and provided input on the ownership structures used for real estate.

We will miss the late Theron Nelson, who contributed to prior editions of the book, including creating the original version of several of the spreadsheet templates. We appreciate his contributions to this book and to the real estate profession.

Our thanks to the book team at McGraw-Hill Education for their help in developing the new edition: Chuck Synovec, Michele Janicek, Jennifer Upton, Melissa Caughlin, M Jane Lampe, James Heine, Lynn Breithaupt, Douglas Ruby, and Kevin Shanahan.

We also continue to be indebted to people who have contributed as authors to previous editions, especially the late Henry E. Hoagland, who wrote the first edition of this book, and the late Leo D. Stone, who participated in several editions. Finally, we thank all of the adopters of previous editions of the book, who, because of their feedback, have made us feel that we have helped them prepare students for a career in real estate.

William B. Brueggeman

Jeffrey D. Fisher

Brief Contents

x

Table of Contents

Chapter 11
Investment Analysis and Taxation of Income Properties   343

Chapter 12
Financial Leverage and Financing Alternatives   393

Chapter 1

Real Estate Investment: Basic Legal Concepts

This is not a book about real estate law; however, a considerable amount of legal terminology is used in the real estate business. It is very important to understand both the physical nature and property rights being acquired when making real estate investments. In this chapter, we survey many important terms pertaining to real estate. Additional legal terms and concepts will appear in later chapters of this book on a "need to know" basis.

Many of the legal terms currently used in the real estate business have evolved from English common law, which serves as the basis for much of the property law currently used in the United States. For example, the term *real* in real estate comes from the term *realty,* which has, for centuries, meant land and all things permanently attached (the latter would include immovable things such as buildings and other structures). All other items not considered realty have been designated as *personalty,* which includes all intangibles and movable things (e.g., automobiles, shares of stock, bank accounts, and patents). The term *estate* has evolved to mean "all that a person owns," including both realty and personalty. Hence, the portion of a person's estate that consists of realty has come to be known as *real estate*. However, in current business practice, although the term "realty" is sometimes used, we generally use the term *real estate* to mean land and all things permanently attached.

Understanding the distinction between realty and personalty is important because our legal system has evolved in a way that treats the two concepts very differently. For example, long ago in England, disputes over real estate usually involved issues such as rightful ownership, possession, land boundaries, and so forth. When such disputes were brought before the court, much of the testimony was based on oral agreements, promises, and the like, allegedly made between the opposing parties, and these disputes were difficult to resolve. Decisions that had to be rendered were extremely important (recall that England's economy was very heavily dependent on agriculture at that time) and affected people's livelihood. Court decisions may have required one of the parties to vacate the land plus turn over any permanent improvements that had been made (houses, barns, etc.) to other parties. As the number of disputes increased, a pragmatic solution evolved requiring that all transactions involving real estate be evidenced by a *written, signed contract* in order to be enforceable.[1]

Parallel developments included (1) a system, whereby land locations and boundaries could be more accurately surveyed and described in contracts and (2) an elaborate system

---

[1] This requirement was included as part of the *Statute of Frauds and Perjuries,* which was passed in England in 1677 with the intent of reducing the number of disputes and questionable transactions brought before the court.

of public record keeping, whereby ownership of all realty within a political jurisdiction could be catalogued. Any transactions involving realty could then be added to this record, thereby creating a historical record of all changes in ownership and providing notice of such changes to the general public and especially to any parties contemplating purchasing or lending money on real estate. Similar practices continue today in the United States as we require written contracts, requirements, survey methods, and public record systems detailing the ownership of real estate within all counties in every state. We should note that many transactions involving personalty are not subject to the same contractual requirements as real estate and that oral contracts may be enforceable.

When investing in real estate, in addition to acquiring the physical assets of land and all things permanently attached, investors also acquire certain *rights*. Examples of these rights include the right to control, occupy, develop, improve, exploit, pledge, lease, exclude, and sell real estate. These have come to be known as *property rights*. Hence, the terms *real property* and *real property rights* have evolved.[2] As a practical matter, in business discussions, the terms *real estate* and *real property* are sometimes used interchangeably. However, as we will see, many of the property rights acquired when investing in real estate are independent and can be separated. For example, real estate may be leased or pledged to others in exchange for rent or other consideration. This may be done without giving up ownership. Indeed, understanding the nature of property rights and how they can be bundled and creatively used to enhance value is one goal of this textbook. The reader should refer to Exhibit 1–1 for an outline of these concepts.

Property Rights and Estates

As pointed out above, the term **real estate** is used to refer to things that are not movable such as *land* and *improvements* permanently attached to the land, and **ownership rights** associated with the real estate are referred to as **real property**. Real property has also been contrasted with **personal property**.[3]

It is important to distinguish between physical real estate assets and ownership rights in real property because many parties can have different ownership rights in a given parcel of real estate. Our legal system offers ways for the person financing or investing in real estate to be creative and to apportion these various interests among parties.

We generally refer to **property rights** as the right of a person to the possession, use, enjoyment, and disposal of his or her property. With respect to its application to real estate, *interest* is a broad legal term used to denote a property right. The holder of an interest in real estate enjoys some right, or degree of control or use, and, in turn, may receive payment for the sale of such an interest. This interest, to the extent that its value can be determined, may also be bought, sold, or used as collateral for a loan.

The value of a particular parcel of real estate can be viewed as the total price individuals are willing to pay for the flow of benefits associated with all of these rights. An individual

---

[2] For nonrealty, the term *personal property* has evolved, and personal property rights would include the bundle of rights which are similar to those listed above but pertaining to personalty.

[3] We should also point out that there are some items known as *fixtures*. These are items that were once personal property but have become real property because they have either been attached to the land or building in a somewhat permanent manner or are intended to be used with the land and building on a permanent basis. Examples include built-in dishwashers, furnaces, and garage door openers. There is significant case law on the subject of fixtures. In practice, when properties are bought and sold, a detailed list of all items that could be considered as either personal property or as a fixture will be documented and included as a part of the contract for purchase and sale. This is done to reduce ambiguity as to the property being conveyed from the seller to the buyer.

EXHIBIT 1–1 **Basic Property Concepts Important in Real Estate Finance and Investment**

(1) The General Nature of Property	(2) Classification of "Things"	(3) Examples	(4) Property Ownership: Evolution of Legal Requirements/Evidence
Any "thing" that can be possessed, used, enjoyed, controlled, developed, or conveyed, or that has utility or value is considered to be property.	A. Real Property (Realty)	A. Land and all things permanently affixed (buildings, sidewalks, etc.). Immovables. Fixtures.	A. Written contracts, legal descriptions, surveys, deeds, wills, possession. Public notice.
	B. Personal Property (Personalty)	B. Intangibles and all movable things (e.g., autos, stocks, patents, furniture).	B. Contracts, oral or written, purchase orders/invoices, and so on.
Property Rights Rights that can be exercised by the property owner. These include possession, use, enjoyment, control, and the creation of estates in property.		C. Property owner leases the use of realty to tenant, creates a leasehold estate.	C. Written document (lease) describing realty and the terms of possession in exchange for rent.
Interests in Property Created by owners of real estate who pledge and encumber property in order to achieve an objective without giving up ownership.		D. Property owner pledges real estate as security for a loan.	D. Mortgage liens, easements, and so on.
		E. Property owner grants an easement to another party to cross land in order to gain access to another site.	

does not have to be an owner per se to have rights to some of the benefits of real estate. For example, a person who leases land, a **lessee,** may have the right to possession and exclusive use of a property for a period of time. This right of use has value to the lessee, even though the term of the lease is fixed. In exchange for the right to use the property, the lessee is willing to pay a rent for the term of the lease. A holder of a mortgage also has some rights as a nonowner in real estate pledged as security for a loan. These rights vary with state law and the terms of the mortgage, but, in general, the lender (or mortgagee) has a right to repossess or bring about the sale of a property if the borrower defaults on the mortgage loan. Although a lender may not possess or use the real estate, the mortgage document provides the lender with evidence of a **secured interest.** Obviously, this right has value to the lender and reduces the quantity of rights possessed by the owner.

It should be clear that some understanding of the legal characteristics of real estate is essential to analyzing the relative benefits that accrue to the various parties who have some rights in a particular property. In most real estate financing and investment transactions, we generally think in terms of investing, selling, or borrowing based on one owner possessing all property rights in the real estate. However, as we have discussed, all or a portion of these rights may be restricted or transferred to others. For example, a property owner may lease a property and pledge it as security for a mortgage loan. Remarkably, these parties generally enjoy their respective rights in relative harmony. However, conflicts arise occasionally concerning the relative rights and priorities among holders of these interests. The potential for such conflicts may also affect rents that individuals may be willing to pay or the ability to obtain financing from lenders and, ultimately, the value of property.

Definition of Estate

The term **estate** means "all that a person owns." The term *real estate* means all realty owned as a part of an individual's estate. The term *estates in real property* is used to describe the extent to which rights and interests in real estate are owned. A system of *modifiers* has evolved, based on English property law, that describes the nature or collection of rights and interests being described as a part of a transaction. For example, a *fee simple estate* represents the most complete form of ownership of real estate, whereas a *leasehold estate* usually describes rights and interests obtained by tenants when leasing or renting a property. The latter is also a possessory interest and involves the general right to occupy and use the property during the period of possession.

Two General Classifications of Estates

(1) Based on Rights: Estates in Possession versus Estates Not in Possession (Future Possession)

Two broad categories of estates can be distinguished on the basis of the *nature of rights accompanying the ownership of such estates.* An estate in possession (a present estate in land) entitles its owner to immediate enjoyment of the rights to that estate. An estate not in possession (a future estate in land), on the other hand, does not convey the rights of the estate until some time in the future, if at all. An estate not in possession, in other words, represents a *future* possessory interest in property. Generally, it does not convert to an estate in possession until the occurrence of a particular event. Estates in possession are by far the more common. When most people think of estates, they ordinarily have in mind estates in possession. Obviously, lenders and investors are very interested in the nature of the estate possessed by the owner when considering the purchase or financing of a particular estate in property.

(2) Based on Possession and Use: Freehold versus Leasehold Estates

Estates in possession are of two general types: freehold estates and leasehold estates. These types of estates are technically distinguished on the basis of the definiteness or certainty of their duration. A **freehold estate** lasts for an indefinite period of time; that is, there is no definitely ascertainable date on which the estate ends. A **leasehold estate,** on the other hand, expires on a definite date. Aside from this technical distinction, a freehold estate connotes ownership of the property by the estate holder, whereas a leasehold estate implies only the right to *possess* and *use* the property owned by another for a period of time.

Examples of Freehold Estates

It is beyond the scope of this chapter to review all the possible types of freehold estates. We will discuss two of the most common examples, however, to convey the importance of knowing the type of estate that is associated with a particular transaction.

Fee Simple Estate

A **fee simple estate,** also known as a *fee simple absolute estate,* is the freehold estate that represents the most complete form of ownership of real estate. A holder of a fee simple estate is free to divide up the fee into lesser estates and sell, lease, or borrow against them as he or she wishes, subject to the laws of the state in which the property is located.

Apart from government restrictions, no special conditions, limitations, or restrictions are placed on the right of a holder of a fee simple estate to enjoy the property, lease it to others, sell it, or even give it away. It is this estate in property which investors and lenders encounter in most investment and lending transactions.

Life Estates

It is possible to have a freehold estate that has fewer ownership rights than a fee simple estate. One example is a **life estate,** which is a freehold estate that lasts only as long as the life of the owner of the estate or the life of some other person. Upon the death of that person, the property reverts back to the original grantor (transferor of property), his or her heirs, or any other designated person. Most life estates result from the terms of the conveyance of the property. For example, a grantor may wish to make a gift of his or her property prior to death, yet wish to retain the use and enjoyment of the property until that time. This can be accomplished by making a conveyance of the property subject to a reserved life estate. A life estate can be leased, mortgaged, or sold. However, parties concerned with this estate should be aware that the estate will end with the death of the holder of the life estate (or that of the person whose life determines the duration of the estate). Because of the uncertainty surrounding the duration of the life estate, its marketability and value as collateral are severely limited.

Estates Not Yet in Possession (Future Estates)

The preceding discussion concerned estates in possession, which entitled the owner to immediate enjoyment of the estate. Here, we discuss estates not in possession, or **future estates,** which do not convey the right to enjoy the property until some time in the future. The two most important types of future estates are the reversion and the remainder.

Reversion

A **reversion** exists when the holder of an estate in land (the grantor) conveys to another person (a grantee) a present estate in the property that has fewer ownership rights than the grantor's own estate and retains for the grantor or the grantor's heirs the right to take back, at some time in the future, the full estate that the grantor enjoyed before the conveyance. In this case, the grantor is said to have a reversionary fee interest in the property held by the grantee. A reversionary interest can be sold or mortgaged because it is an actual interest in the property.

Remainder

A **remainder** exists when the grantor of a present estate with fewer ownership rights than the grantor's own estate conveys to a third person the reversionary interest the grantor or the grantor's heirs would otherwise have in the property upon termination of the grantee's estate. A remainder is the future estate for the third person. Like a reversion, a remainder is a mortgageable interest in property.

Examples of Leasehold Estates

There are two major types of leasehold estates: estates for years and estates from year to year. There are two other types, but they are not common.[4] Leasehold estates are classified on the basis of the manner in which they are created and terminated.

---

[4] *Estate at Will:* An estate at will is created when a landlord consents to the possession of the property by another person but without any agreement as to the payment of rent or the term of the tenancy. Such estates are of indefinite duration. *Estate at Sufferance:* An estate at sufferance occurs when the tenant holds possession of the property without consent or knowledge of the landlord after the termination of one of the other three estates.

Estate for Years: Tenancy for Terms

An **estate for years** is the type of leasehold estate investors and lenders are most likely to encounter. It is created by a lease that specifies an exact duration for the tenancy. The period of tenancy may be less than one year and still be an estate for years as long as the lease agreement specifies the termination date. The lease, as well as all contracts involving transactions in real estate, is usually written. Indeed, a lease is generally required by the statute of frauds to be in writing when it covers a term longer than one year. The rights and duties of the landlord and tenant and other provisions related to the tenancy are normally stated in the lease agreement.

An estate for years can be as long as 99 years (by custom, leases seldom exceed 99 years in duration), giving the lessee the right to use and control the property for that time in exchange for rental payments. To the extent that the specified rental payments fall below the market rental rate of the property during the life of the lease, the lease has value (leasehold value) to the lessee. The value of this interest in the property can be borrowed against or even sold. For example, if the lessee has the right to occupy the property for $1,000 per year when its fair market value is $2,000 per year, the $1,000 excess represents value to the lessee, which may be borrowed against or sold (assuming no lease covenants prevent it).

While a property is leased, the original fee owner is considered to have a *leased fee* estate. This means that he or she has given up some property rights to the lessee (the leasehold estate). The value of the leased fee estate will now depend on the amount of the lease payments expected during the term of the lease plus the value of the property when the lease terminates and the original owner receives the reversionary interest. Hence, a leased fee estate may be used as security for a loan or may be sold.

Estate from Year to Year

An **estate from year to year** (also known as an estate from period to period, or simply as a periodic tenancy) continues for successive periods until either party gives proper notice of its intent to terminate at the end of one or more subsequent periods. A "period" usually corresponds to the rent-paying period. Thus, such a tenancy commonly runs from month to month, although it can run for any period up to one year. Such estates can be created by explicit agreement between the parties, although a definite termination date is not specified. Since these estates are generally short-term (a year or less), the agreement can be, and frequently is, oral. This type of estate can also be created without the express consent of the landlord. A common example is seen when the tenant "holds over" or continues to occupy an estate for years beyond the expiration date, and the landlord accepts payment of rent or gives some other evidence of tacit consent.

If present tenants are to remain in possession after the transfer or sale of property, the grantee should agree to take title subject to existing leases. The agreement should provide for prorating of rents and the transfer of deposits to the grantee. Buyers of property encumbered by leases should always reserve the right to examine and approve leases to ensure that they are in force, are not in default, and are free from undesirable provisions.

Interests, Encumbrances, and Easements

An *interest* in real estate can be thought of as a right or claim on real property, its revenues, or production. Interests are created by the owner and conveyed to another party, usually in exchange for other consideration. In real estate, an interest is usually thought to be less important than an estate. For example, an owner of real estate in fee simple may choose to *pledge* or *encumber* his property as a condition for obtaining a loan (mortgage loan). In this case, the lender receives only a *secured interest,* but not *possession, use, and so on,* of the property. The nature of the secured interest is usually documented in a mortgage which explains the actions that a lender may take in the event that the loan terms are not met by the property owner. In the interim, the property owner *retains possession and use* of the property. Another example of the creation of an interest in real property occurs when an owner encumbers a property by granting an easement, or the right to ingress or egress his property, to another party.

An **easement** is a **nonpossessory interest** in land. It is the right to use land that is owned or leased by someone else for some special purpose (e.g., as a right of way to and from one's property). An easement entails only a limited user privilege and not privileges associated with ownership.[5] Examples of easements would be the following: property owner A allows property owner B to use a driveway on A's land to provide owner B with better access to his property. In some retail developments, owners A and B may execute reciprocal easements to allow access across both properties, thereby enhancing customer traffic flow and shopping opportunities.

Assurance of Title

When making real estate investments, buyers of property typically want assurance that they will become the legal owner of the property and that the seller is lawfully possessed and has the right to convey title. Exhibit 1–2 contains a basic flow diagram that should help the reader understand concepts relating to real estate ownership.

When considering the purchase of real estate, buyers must be in a position to assess the quantity and quality of ownership rights that they are acquiring. **Title assurance** refers to the means by which buyers of real estate "(1) learn in advance whether their sellers have and can convey the quality of title they claim to possess and (2) receive compensation if the title, after transfer, turns out not to be as represented."[6] Lenders are also concerned about title assurance because the quality of title affects the collateral value of the property in which they may have a secured interest. Before we examine the mechanisms used for title assurance, we must briefly review the concepts of title and deed.

The Meaning of Title

Title is an abstract term frequently used to link an individual or entity who owns property to the property itself. When a person has "title," he is said to have all of the elements, including the documents, records, and acts, that prove ownership. Title establishes the quantity of rights in real estate being conveyed from seller to buyer. The previous section briefly examined some of the various types of ownership rights and possessory interests that can be involved in a parcel of real estate. We saw, for example, that one person may hold title in fee simple ownership, convey title to a life estate to someone else, and convey the right to reversion upon termination of the life estate to yet another person. Hence, there are many possible combinations of rights and interests.

---

[5] When a property owner provides another with an interest such as an easement, the property owner is said to have encumbered the property. This may be transferred as a part of subsequent sales to successive owners unless it is defeated, or the owner of the interest releases or recognizes the interest to the property owner.

[6] Grant S. Nelson and Dale A. Whitman, *Real Estate Transfer, Finance and Development,* 2nd ed. (St. Paul, MN: West Publishing, 1981), p. 167.

EXHIBIT 1–2
Flowchart:
Ownership of Real
Property

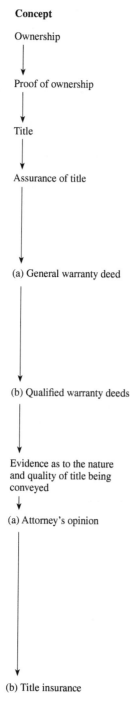

Concept	Discussion
Ownership	When a person or other legal entity has lawful possession of realty and real property rights they are said to have "ownership."
Proof of ownership	Proof is usually accomplished with documents such as deeds, contracts, wills, grants, property records, and/or evidence of continuous possession and use, and so on.
Title	When a person or entity has legal evidence, or "proof," of ownership, they are said to have "title" to a property. This evidence links ownership by a person to a specific property.
Assurance of title	When investing in real estate, the investor must be able to evaluate the quality and/or completeness of title that they will receive. This is important in the event that the buyer wants to obtain financing and/or resell the property in the future. As part of the contract negotiations, the seller usually agrees to convey title *and* to provide a warranty or guarantee.
(a) General warranty deed	When the seller conveys a *general warranty deed*, she warrants (1) that she is in lawful possession of the property and all property rights, (2) that no other individuals or entities have an ownership interest in the property, and (3) that the title is unencumbered or free of imperfections (with any specific exceptions noted: e.g., easements, leases, or liens). In the event that a buyer who relies on the seller's warranty incurs a loss because of title imperfections, the seller may be liable.
(b) Qualified warranty deeds	In cases when the seller is unsure of the quality of title or is unwilling to provide a general warranty deed, the seller may qualify assurance of title by conveying a "special warranty deed," a "bargain and sale deed," or a "quit claim deed."
Evidence as to the nature and quality of title being conveyed	How can the investor in a property be assured that the seller legally possesses the property and that the record of ownership is clear, or that the title is unencumbered?
(a) Attorney's opinion	An attorney reviews public property records and other evidence to ascertain whether or not the "chain of title" is "clear." When a title is clear, this usually means that all individuals who may have had an ownership interest in the property have conveyed or relinquished such interests in previous conveyances of title. When the *possibility* exists that other parties may have an ownership or other interest, these may be referred to as title "imperfections or defects." If an investor wants clear title, action must be taken to "cure" such defects. This is usually done by an attorney who will contact relevant parties in the chain of title and negotiate a release or conveyance of their interest, possibly in exchange for some consideration.
(b) Title insurance	More commonly, an insurance policy indemnifying against a loss due to possible title imperfections is purchased (usually by the buyer). This may be done because the seller's warranty may be effectively limited. This could happen if the seller files for bankruptcy or does not have the financial capacity to reimburse the buyer for losses due to title imperfections. Title insurance also may be used in lieu of an attorney's opinion because the latter protects the buyer only to the extent that the title search was done negligently by the attorney or her abstractor. Title insurance companies usually conduct a review of the title chain before issuing a title insurance policy.

An **abstract of title** is a historical summary of the publicly recorded documents that affect a title. The quality of the title conveyed from seller to buyer depends upon the effect these documents have upon the seller's rightful possession of his or her property.

Essentially, title exists only for freehold estates. A leasehold estate, on the other hand, is typically created by a contract (called a lease) between a person who holds the title (the **lessor**) and another person (the lessee), whereby possession of the property is granted by the owner to the other person for a period of time. The existence of leases on a property will, however, affect the nature of the rights that can be conveyed to a new buyer because lease terms are binding on the new owner unless waived by the lessee or, in some jurisdictions, unless title is acquired at a foreclosure sale. Because investors and lenders are concerned about the nature and extent of the rights they are acquiring or financing, leases encumbering the property can have a profound impact on a property's value.

Deeds

Usually title is conveyed from one person (the grantor) to another (the grantee) by means of a written instrument called a **deed.** (We use the term *grantor* instead of *seller* because title may also be transferred by the owner [grantor] to an heir [grantee] by means of a will; hence the terms *grantor* and *grantee.*) To be a valid conveyance of ownership interests in real property, all deeds must be in writing and meet certain other legal requirements of the state in which the property is located.[7]

Generally, a purchaser wants the deed to convey a good *and* marketable title to the property. A good title is one that is valid in fact; that is, the grantor does lawfully have the title he or she claims to have to the property. However, a good title, because of the lack of sufficient documentation or encumbrances on the property, may be unmarketable. A marketable title is one that is not merely valid in fact but is also "free from reasonable doubt," one that is "reasonably free from litigation," and "one which readily can be sold or mortgaged to a reasonably prudent purchaser or mortgagee (mortgage lender)."[8]

Encumbrances on a title, such as easements, leases, and mortgages (secured interests), do not automatically make it unmarketable. A purchaser may be willing to take title to the property subject to encumbrances. But the deed should note all encumbrances on the title so that a potential purchaser can rationally decide whether to purchase the property and to arrive at the appropriate price given any risks, costs, or restrictions posed by the encumbrances.

Methods of Title Assurance

There are three general ways in which a buyer has assurance that a title is good and marketable. First, the seller may provide a warranty as part of the deed. Second, there may be a search of relevant recorded documents to determine whether there is reason to question the quality of the title. This is usually done by an attorney and is accompanied by a legal opinion. Third, title insurance may be purchased to cover unexpected problems with the title.

---

[7] A deed is not the only way by which ownership rights in real property are conveyed. Titles are also transferred by wills, court decrees, and grants of land from the government to private persons. In addition, lawful title to property can be acquired by means of adverse possession. It should also be pointed out that although we use the terms *buyers* and *sellers* in this book, the more general terms *grantor* and *grantee* are frequently used in contracts or other documents in real estate. **Grantors** include sellers but also include property owners who may be transferring title by gift (not sale), by will, and so on. **Grantees** include buyers in a transaction but also may include persons who receive title by gift, as an heir in a will, and so on.

[8] *Black's Law Dictionary,* 7th ed. (St. Paul, MN: West Publishing, 1999).

General Warranty Deed

It is important to understand that any deed, no matter how complete the warranties contained therein, can only convey the quality of title that the grantor actually has to the property. This is why most buyers of real estate usually obtain independent assurance of the validity and marketability of the title from a third party. A **general warranty deed** is the most commonly used deed in real estate transactions and the most desirable type of deed from the buyer's perspective. It offers the most comprehensive warranties about the quality of the title. Essentially, the grantor warrants that the title he or she conveys to the property is free and clear of all encumbrances other than those specifically listed in the deed. As pointed out above, encumbrances listed in a deed could include easements and leases. Generally, the most significant covenants contained in such a deed are the following: (1) a covenant that the grantor has good (legally valid) title to the property, (2) a covenant that the grantor has the right to convey the property, (3) a covenant to compensate the grantee for loss of property or eviction suffered by the grantee as a result of someone else having a superior claim to the property, and (4) a covenant against encumbrances on the property other than those specifically stated in the deed. In a general warranty deed, these covenants cover all conveyances of the property from the time of the original source of title to the present.

Special Warranty Deed

A **special warranty deed** makes the same warranties as a general warranty deed except that it limits their application to defects and encumbrances that occurred only while the grantor held title to the property. Unlike the warranties in a general warranty deed, those in a special warranty deed do not apply to title problems caused or created by previous owners.

Bargain and Sale Deed

A **bargain and sale deed** conveys property without seller warranties. This is sometimes referred to as an "as is" deed. The buyer of property takes title with no assurances from the seller and must take the initiative to determine whether any imperfections exist and, if desired, how to cure such defects.

Sheriff's Deed-Trustee's Deed

A **sheriff's deed-trustee's deed** is a type of bargain and sale deed received by a buyer from a foreclosure or other forced sale because the sheriff or trustee is acting in a representative capacity. No warranties are added.

Quitclaim Deed

A **quitclaim deed** offers the grantee the least protection. Such a deed simply conveys to the grantee whatever rights, interests, and title that the grantor may have in the property. No warranties are made about the nature of these rights and interests or of the quality of the grantor's title to the property. The quitclaim deed simply says that the grantor "quits" whatever "claim" he or she has in the property (which may well be none) in favor of the grantee.[9]

---

[9] Quitclaim deeds are appropriately and frequently used to clear up technical defects or "clouds" on the title to a property. Where the record indicates a person may have any potential claim to the property, obtaining a quitclaim deed from him will eliminate the risk that such a claim will be made in the future.

Web App

The American Land Title Association (**www.alta.org**), founded in 1907, is the national trade association for the title insurance industry. ALTA members search, review, and insure land titles to protect home buyers and mortgage lenders who invest in real estate. ALTA is headquartered in Washington, DC. There is a "Consumer Information" link on this site that includes a discussion of common title problems. Outline the types of problems that can be encountered due to a problem with the title for a property.

Very few buyers of real estate rely solely on the guarantees of title provided in deeds of conveyance by the seller. The two methods that buyers employ most often to obtain assurance of title independently of the guarantees provided by the seller are an attorney's opinion of title and title insurance.

Abstract and Opinion Method

Obtaining a lawyer's opinion of title used to be the most common method of title assurance before the widespread availability of title insurance. Essentially, the abstract and opinion method is a two-step process. First, there is a search of the title record, which involves locating and examining all of the instruments in the public records that have affected the title of the property in question.[10] Second, when the title search is completed, a lawyer studies the relevant public records and other facts and proceedings affecting the title for the purpose of arriving at an expert opinion of the character of the title. Based upon this study of the abstract or the record, the lawyer will give his or her judgment whether the title is good and marketable. If the title is found to be "clouded," the opinion should state what defects or encumbrances were uncovered by an examination of the records, and it should also state what the lawyer thinks can and should be done to "cure" the defects uncovered.

Because a lawyer's responsibility is limited to what appears in the records, the lawyer cannot be held liable for any defect in the title not disclosed therein. Any liability borne by the lawyer is based upon proof of his or her negligence or lack of professional skill in the examination of the records. Rather than relying on the lawyer's opinion, the title insurance industry has evolved. Many lenders and investors now prefer title insurance, which reduces this risk.

The Title Insurance Method

Title insurance was developed to cure the inadequacies of title validation accomplished through an abstract and legal opinion. Title insurance does all that a carefully drawn abstract and a well-considered opinion by a competent lawyer are expected to do. In addition, it adds the principle of insurance to spread the risk of *unseen hazards* among many property owners.

Elimination of risk arising from unseen hazards in the public record has caused many investors and lenders to prefer this method of title assurance. In fact, title insurance is required for any mortgage that is traded in the secondary mortgage market. The title insurance process

---

[10] Most of the instruments that affect title to real estate are recorded, in accordance with the recording acts of the various states, at what is typically called the county recorder's office. But some instruments that affect title may be recorded in other places. The nature of these other places where records are filed varies from state to state.

starts with a careful analysis of the records. The information available to the commercial title insurance company may be even more complete than that found in the public records. Skilled technicians at title insurance companies examine all available evidence of the title to determine its character. If their conclusions warrant, the title company will insure the title to a property and assume risks that are not even disclosed in the public records or in its own files. In short, title insurance ensures that the title is good and marketable.

What title insurance is supposed to add to the abstract system and the opinion of skilled lawyers may be summarized as follows: (1) definite contract liability to the premium payer, (2) reserves sufficient to meet insured losses, (3) supervision by an agency of the state in which the title insurance company operates, and (4) protection to the policyholder against financial losses that may show up at any future time because of any kind of title defect, disclosed or hidden. Despite these advantages, the abstract and opinion method may still be used because of its lower cost. In general, one method, but not both, is used when purchasing property, to avoid the duplication of effort and cost.

Kinds of Title Insurance Policies

There are two kinds of title insurance policies. The **owner's policy** insures the interests of a new property owner. The **lender's (or mortgagee) policy** insures the interests of the mortgagee. The owner's policy is payable to the owner (or to the heirs of the owner); the lender's policy is payable to the mortgagee.

Both policies are paid for with a one-time premium. In many states, premiums are regulated by a state insurance commission, as are financial requirements to incorporate and continue to do business. The one-time premium for the owner's policy insures the owner for the entire period of time that she owns the property. The insurance premium may be paid by either the seller or the buyer, depending on the terms of the purchase contract, which are influenced by local custom and market conditions. It is almost universal practice for the borrower to pay the cost of the mortgagee's policy which will insure the lender for the term of the loan. In cases where properties are *refinanced* by the same owner, a title search may be required by a new lender. In these cases it may be possible to obtain a new title insurance policy from the same company at a *reduced cost.*

Recording Acts

All states have enacted statutes known as **recording acts.** Although the recording acts are not uniform among the states, these acts in general provide a publicly accessible system for assessing and establishing claims or interests in real estate as against all other parties. These statutes also provide a set of authoritative rules for resolving priority disputes among competing claimants to interests in real estate. As part of this system, procedures have been established for placing documents affecting claims to real estate interests on the public record and for maintaining these records to make information available concerning almost all interests in real estate. Once an instrument creating a claim on an interest in real estate has been duly recorded, the recording is deemed to give constructive notice of this interest "to the world." Constructive notice means that the recording acts deem a person to have whatever information is contained in the public records—information that could be obtained by a reasonably diligent investigation of the records whether or not the investigator actually has knowledge of the information recorded. Instruments affecting virtually all interests in real estate, including deeds, mortgages, assignments of mortgages, liens on real estate, land contracts, long-term leases, easements, restrictive covenants, and options to buy, are covered by recording acts.

Most recording acts say that in order to establish and preserve a claim to an interest in real estate that will take precedence in law against future claimants, the instrument creating that claim must be recorded in accordance with state law. These acts were designed in part to protect an innocent person who purchased an interest in real estate in good faith unaware that the interest had already been acquired by another. For example, if A conveyed to B, who did not record the instrument establishing his claim, and later A conveyed the same interest to C, who did record, C's claim would be superior to B's if C was unaware of the prior conveyance and paid valuable consideration to A. B's only claim would be to file a suit against A for fraud.

Mechanics' Liens

One cloud on the title which may not be disclosed by the public records is a **mechanics' lien.** In general, mechanics' liens give unpaid contractors, workers, and material suppliers the right to attach a lien on the real estate to which they added their labor or materials. To obtain the payment owed them, they may foreclose such liens by forcing a judicial sale of the encumbered property. They are then paid from the proceeds of the sale. Use of mechanics' liens exists in every state, although the nature of the statutes varies.

Mechanics' liens are permitted to be recorded "after the fact." In other words, state laws generally give contractors, laborers, or suppliers of materials a certain period of time following the completion of work or delivery of materials during which to file their lien. When the lien is filed, it "relates back" and takes priority over all liens filed after the time when materials were first delivered or work was first performed on the real estate. As a result, until the end of the time allowed for filing (generally 60 days), a purchaser of an interest in newly constructed or improved real estate cannot be sure that the interest will be unencumbered or that the interest will have the priority bargained for. As a precaution, lenders and purchasers of such real estate should require the seller to provide an *affidavit* stating that at closing, all moneys due to contractors and subcontractors have been fully paid. In the event that liens are filed after the closing, a breach of the seller's covenants in the affidavit can easily be proven, and the seller can be held liable for the discharge of those liens. In practice, owners of properties that are newly constructed or renovated should require contractors, workers, and material suppliers to sign a *lien waiver.* This is an acknowledgment that they have been compensated and that they agree to waive all lien rights. In many situations, if a lender is advancing funds for such work and material, a signed waiver will be required at each stage of construction before additional funds are released.

Limitations on Property Rights

Government Restrictions

Throughout this chapter, we have stressed the importance of property rights in real estate. We should also point out that although our form of government protects the rights of individuals to own real estate and to enjoy real property rights, these rights are not unrestricted. Government restrictions on private property rights do exist. Land use regulations are most prominent at the state and local level. The right to regulate emanates from the "police powers of the state," which are based on the protection of the health, safety, and general welfare of its citizens (societal considerations). As the population in an area grows, it may apply to the state to become incorporated as a city, township, or municipality. At this point, the state usually delegates some areas of land use regulation. Incorporated areas then may modify and expand land use controls and develop restrictions on land use. These items are usually enumerated in zoning ordinances and building codes. Common restrictions used to implement controls include zoning ordinances, allowable uses, height restrictions, parking requirements, and building codes, permits, and inspections. The state usually retains control over water or riparian rights, mineral rights, eminent domain, and the like, while the federal government regulates housing and loan discrimination, interstate land sales and securities, and environmental restrictions (pollution of water and air, and endangered species, as well as effects of property use and development on wet lands).

Private Deed Restrictions

In some cases, property owners may choose to incorporate certain **deed restrictions** that limit the use of property by all subsequent owners of that property. Property owners may use such restrictions to achieve personal or business objectives. One example of a personal objective would be to add a deed restriction explicitly prohibiting the sale or consumption of alcoholic beverages on the property forever. In the event that this restriction is violated, the restriction may stipulate that the title will revert to the owner who incorporated the restriction, or to his heirs. An example of a business objective that is commonly achieved through deed restrictions may involve subdivision of a large tract of land into smaller individual tracts to be sold to builders and developers. In order to assure the initial buyers of the subdivided tracts that subsequent buyers will build improvements that conform in quality and use, the owner of the initial larger tract may deed restrict each of the subdivided tracts. Such restrictions may require a minimum and/or maximum building size, minimum quality building materials, landscaping, and the like, thereby providing all owners with some assurance of conformity and general standards in design and building quality. However, resolution of any future violations of deed restrictions may prove to be problematic, particularly after a long period of time. In the first example, the original property owner or all of his heirs would have to bring an action against the current owner to regain title to the property if the deed restriction prohibiting the sale of alcohol were to be violated. In the case of the subdivision, usually a property owners association representing owners of the subdivided properties would have to bring legal action against the property owner who is in violation. In this instance, the court may require the owner in violation to cure the problem or pay the owners association for any loss in property value as opposed to forcing the sale of the property.

Conclusion

This chapter discussed legal considerations important in creating and defining various rights to real property. This is important in the study of real estate finance since it is these rights that are purchased, sold, and mortgaged. Thus, an understanding of the various rights associated with real estate is necessary to properly evaluate a real estate financial decision. Legal considerations affect the risk of receiving the economic benefit associated with one's property rights. For example, we have discussed the importance of having a marketable title. Any defects in the title may result in a loss of benefits to the owner and jeopardize the collateral value of the real estate for the mortgage lender. To some extent, this risk is controlled and minimized by the use of title assurance methods, including title insurance and the use of general warranty deeds.

Knowing the various ways of partitioning property rights may also result in maximizing the value of a particular property, since it allows parties with different needs (e.g., users, equity investors, and lenders) to have claims on the property rights that best meet those needs. Thus, the total value of all the rights associated with a property could exceed the total value of the property itself if there are no leases or other ways to separate rights.

Key Terms

abstract of title, *9*
bargain and sale deed, *10*
deed, *9*
deed restrictions, *14*
easement, *7*
estate, *4*
estate for years, *6*
estate from year to year, *6*
fee simple estate, 4
freehold estate, *4*
future estates, *5*
general warranty deed, *10*

leasehold estate, *4*
lender's (or mortgagee)
 policy, *12*
lessee, *3*
lessor, *9*
life estate, 5
mechanics' lien, 13
nonpossessory interest, *7*
owner's policy, *12*
ownership rights, 2
personal property, *2*
property rights, *2*

quitclaim deed, *10*
real estate, *2*
real property, 2
recording acts, 12
remainder, *5*
reversion, *5*
secured interest, *3*
sheriff's deed-trustee's
 deed, *10*
special warranty deed, *10*
title, *7*
title assurance, *7*

Useful Web Sites

www.alta.org—The American Land Title Association—Provides information related to title insurance.

www.ired.com—International Real Estate Digest—Provides information for most real estate professionals as well as real estate software and tools.

www.reals.com—This is a real estate directory for such subjects as commercial real estate, international real estate, and professional services.

www.findlaw.com—A good source of legal information, including real estate.

www.investorwords.com—InvestorWords.com provides all of the necessary keys for decoding what can often seem like an encrypted language, regardless of your investing experience. InvestorWords.com provides definitions for over 6,000 financial terms and includes 20,000 links between related terms. The glossary is completely free to use. It also provides a list of great investing and personal finance Web sites, but most of them assume you already have a certain level of experience, or even a certain vocabulary.

www.fiabci.com—This site is a good source for a comparison between legislation, professional standards, taxation, and licensing among different countries. It also gives a comparative snapshot of various requirements for commercial leases in several countries.

www.china-window.com/china_market/china_real_estate/index.shtml—This Web site gives information about the real estate market in China. It also gives useful information about the laws and regulations concerning real estate, different Web sites related to real estate in China, and contact information for different government agencies.

www.epra.com—This site is hosted by The European Public Real Estate Association (EPRA), which is a not-for-profit body established under Dutch law. This Web site gives quarterly review reports of developments in the European Real Estate Sector. It also provides different research reports published related to real estate.

Questions

1. What is the difference between real property and personal property?
2. What is meant by an estate?
3. How can a leased fee estate have a value that could be transferred to another party?
4. What is an abstract of title?
5. Name the three general methods of title assurance and briefly describe each. Which would you recommend to a friend purchasing a home? Why?
6. Would it be legal for you to give a quitclaim deed for the Statue of Liberty to your friend?

Chapter

Real Estate Financing: Notes and Mortgages

Financing can be a very important component of investing in real estate. In general, when investors desire to obtain financing, they usually pledge, or hypothecate, their ownership of real estate as a condition for obtaining loans. In many cases, investors also pledge personal property to obtain loans. What follows is an introduction to notes and mortgages, two legal instruments that are used frequently in real estate financing.

Notes

A **promissory note** is a document which serves as evidence that debt exists between a borrower and a lender, and usually contains the terms under which the loan must be repaid and the rights and responsibilities of both parties. Unless stated otherwise, the borrower is *personally liable* for payment of all amounts due under the terms of the note. (These loans are said to be made **"with recourse"** to the borrower.) While many loan provisions may be included, notes usually contain at least the following:

A. The *amount borrowed*—this is generally the face amount of the note, which is usually advanced in total when the loan agreement is executed. However, in cases involving construction loans, amounts could be advanced as a construction progresses, not to exceed a maximum amount.

B. The *rate of interest*—this could be a fixed rate of interest or an adjustable rate. If it is the latter, exactly how the rate may be adjusted (changed) will be specified.

C. The dollar amount, due dates, and number of payments to be made by the borrower— (e.g., $500 per month due on the first of each month following the closing date for 300 consecutive months).

D. The maturity date, at which time all remaining amounts due under the terms of the loan are to be repaid.

E. Reference to the real estate serving as *security* for the loan as evidenced by a mortgage document (to be discussed).

F. Application of payments, which are usually made first to cover any late charges/fees/penalties, then to interest, and then to principal reduction.

G. Default—occurs when a borrower fails to perform one or more covenants under the terms of the note. Default usually occurs because of nonpayment of amounts due.

H. Penalties for late payment and forbearance provisions—the latter specify any grace periods during which late payments can be made up (usually with penalties) without the lender declaring that the borrower is in default. The lender does not give up the right to declare that the borrower is in default at some future date by allowing a grace, or forbearance, period. Forbearance is used by lenders when they believe that borrowers will make up late payments. They allow time for borrowers to make up such payments when they believe that benefits from this course of action will exceed the time and the expense of declaring the loan in default and embarking on foreclosure proceedings and, perhaps, forcing the sale of the property.

I. Provisions, if any, for *unscheduled (early) payments* or the *full or partial prepayment* of outstanding balances—when included, this is usually referred to as a "prepayment privilege." It allows borrowers to make early payments, or to repay the loan, in part or fully before maturity. If allowable, the note will indicate whether future payments will be reduced or whether the loan maturity date will be shortened. This provision is a *privilege* and *not* a right because the dollar amount and number of payments to be made by the borrower are specified in (C). A prepayment provision is generally included in residential mortgage loans. However, when financing income-producing properties, it may be highly restricted and require payment of a fee or penalty.

J. Notification of default and the acceleration clause—in the event of past due payments, the lender must notify the borrower that he or she is in default. The lender *may* then accelerate on the note by demanding that all remaining amounts owed under the loan agreement be paid immediately by the borrower.

K. Nonrecourse clause—as noted above, when a borrower executes a note, he is personally liable, or the loan is made "with recourse." This means that if he defaults on the loan, the lender may bring legal action that may result in the sale of the borrower's other assets (stocks, bonds, other real estate) in order to satisfy all amounts past due under the terms of the note. In contrast, the "nonrecourse clause" is a provision in the note, whereby the lender agrees not to, or specifies conditions under which it will *not,* hold the borrower personally liable in the event of a default. In this case, the lender may only bring an action to force the sale of the property serving as security for the loan. The borrower is released of personal liability. This clause is very important to real estate investors and developers.

L. Loan assumability—this clause indicates under what conditions, if any, a borrower will be allowed to substitute another party in his place, who will then assume responsibility for remaining loan payments. This could occur if the borrower wishes to sell a property to another while allowing the new buyer to retain favorable financing terms that may have been previously negotiated. Lenders who deny borrowers this right can do so by expressly prohibiting it and/or by including a "due on sale" clause which requires that all remaining amounts due be paid upon sale of, or transfer of title to, the property. However, if the note provides that a new owner may assume the loan, the lender usually requires that the credit of the new owner be equivalent to that of the previous owner, or be acceptable to the lender. The note will also specify whether or not the original borrower remains personally liable or is released from liability when the loan is assumed by the new borrower.

M. The assignment clause—clause giving the *lender* the right to sell the note to another party without approval of the borrower.

    N. Future advances—provision under which the borrower may request additional funds up to some maximum amount or maximum percentage of the current property value under the same terms contained in the original loan agreement. These advances may be subject to an adjustment in the rate of interest.

    O. Release of lien by lender—lender agrees to release or extinguish its lien on the property when the loan is fully repaid.

The Mortgage Instrument

The following is a general discussion of mortgages. Much of this discussion applies to all mortgages. Provisions that are specific to residential and commercial properties and construction loans will be discussed as these topics are introduced. Utilization of mortgage financing has been the most common method of financing the purchase of real estate. This process usually entails the buyer borrowing funds from a lender and then using these and other funds to purchase a property. Funds are usually borrowed with the express intent of using the proceeds to acquire real estate that will serve as a security for a loan. However, loans also may be refinanced from time to time and a new mortgage is made serving as loan security. Real estate is generally regarded by lenders as excellent security for a loan, and lenders acquire a *secured interest* in the real estate with a mortgage.

Definition of a Mortgage

In its most general sense, the **mortgage document** is created in a transaction, whereby one party pledges real property to another party as security for an obligation owed to that party. A promissory note (discussed previously) is normally executed contemporaneously with the mortgage. This note creates the obligation to repay the loan in accordance with its terms and is secured by the mortgage. The elements essential to the existence of a mortgage are an *obligation* to pay or perform and a *pledge* of property as security for that obligation.[1] In general, when a loan is made by a seller to a buyer (borrower) to purchase real estate consisting of an existing property and improvement, it is referred to as a **purchase-money mortgage** (discussed in more detail later in this chapter). This is in contrast to construction loans, loans made to refinance existing loans, and so on.

Relationship of Note to Mortgage

Normally, the underlying obligation secured by a mortgage is evidenced by a separate promissory note. As pointed out in the discussion of notes, unless the note contains a nonrecourse clause, it provides evidence of the debt and generally makes the borrower (mortgagor) personally liable for the obligation. The mortgage is usually a separate document that pledges the designated property as security for the debt. Therefore, the lender (mortgagee) has two sources from which amounts borrowed can be repaid: (1) the borrower, who is personally liable and (2) the property that serves as security for the note. In case of default, the mortgagee may elect to disregard the mortgage and sue on the note. The judgment awarded the mortgagee as a result of a suit on the note may be attached to other property of the mortgagor which, when sold to satisfy the judgment lien, may enable the mortgagee to recover the amount of the claim more readily than if he or she foreclosed on the mortgage. In practice, the mortgagee will normally elect to *sue on the*

---

[1] The obligation secured by a mortgage need not be monetary. It may be, for example, an agreement to perform some service or to perform some other specified actions. An obligation which is not itself an explicitly monetary one must be reducible to monetary terms. In other words, a dollar value must be placed on it.

Web App

The Equal Credit Opportunity Act (ECOA) and the Fair Housing Act (FHA) protect you against discrimination when you apply for a mortgage to purchase, refinance, or make home improvements. Find out what your rights are under these acts. Go to a Web site like **www.findlaw .com** and use the search feature on the site to find information on mortgage discrimination. Alternatively, search for information on "mortgage discrimination" using one of the general search engines like **www. yahoo.com** or **www.google.com.** Give examples of what would be considered illegal discrimination by mortgage lenders.

note and foreclose on the mortgage simultaneously. Mortgages typically include clauses containing important **covenants** for both the mortgagor and mortgagee. These covenants are promises, duties, and responsibilities of the borrower, in addition to payments required under the terms of the note. These are frequently repeated in the promissory note, or the note may incorporate these covenants by reference to the mortgage.

Interests That Can Be Mortgaged

Most people are accustomed to thinking of a mortgage in relation to full, or fee simple, ownership. But any interest in real estate that is subject to sale, grant, or assignment— that is, any interest that can be transferred—can be mortgaged. Thus, such diverse interests as fee simple estates, life estates, estates for years, remainders, reversions, leasehold interests, and options to purchase real estate, among others, are all mortgageable interests as far as legal theory is concerned. Whether, as a matter of sound business judgment, mortgagees would be willing to lend money against some of the lesser interests in land is quite another question.

Minimum Mortgage Requirements

A mortgage involves a transfer of an interest in real estate from the property owner to the lender. Accordingly, the statute of frauds requires that it must be in writing. The vast volume of mortgage lending today is institutional lending, and institutional mortgages are standardized, formal documents. There is, however, no specific form required for a valid mortgage. Indeed, although most mortgages are formal documents, a valid mortgage could be handwritten. The requirements of a valid mortgage document are: (1) wording that appropriately expresses the intent of the parties to create a security interest in real property for the benefit of the mortgage and (2) other items required by state law.

In the United States, mortgage law has traditionally been within the jurisdiction of state law; by and large, mortgages continue to be governed primarily by state law. Thus, to be enforceable, a mortgage must meet requirements imposed by the law of the state in which the property offered as security is located.

Whether a printed form of mortgage instrument is used or an attorney draws up a special form, the following subjects should always be included:

1. Appropriate identification of mortgagor and mortgagee.
2. Proper description of the property serving as security for the loan.
3. Covenants of seisin and warranty.[2]

[2] A *covenant* is a promise or binding assurance. *Seisin* is the state of owning the quantum of title being conveyed.

4. Provision for release of dower rights.[3]

5. Any other desired covenants and contractual agreements.

All of the terms and contractual agreements included in the note can be included in the mortgage as well by making reference to the note in the mortgage document.

Although the bulk of mortgage law remains within the jurisdiction of state law, a wide range of federal regulations also are operative in the area of mortgage law. Moreover, in recent years the federal government has acted to directly preempt state law in a number of areas (e.g., overturning state usury laws,[4] overturning state restrictions on the operation of due-on-sale clauses, and establishing conditions for allowing prepayment of the mortgage debt and for setting prepayment penalties). This has been particularly true in legislation affecting residential mortgages. Commercial property lending and mortgages have generally been exempted from such federal legislation.

In addition, the federal government has exerted a strong but indirect influence on mortgage transactions by means of its sponsorship of the agencies and quasi-private institutions that support and, for all practical purposes, constitute the secondary market for residential mortgages. The Federal National Mortgage Association (FNMA) and the Federal Home Loan Mortgage Corporation (FHLMC) have adopted joint standardized mortgage forms for the purpose of facilitating secondary-market transactions on a nationwide basis. The joint FNMA-FHLMC uniform mortgage form has been so widely adopted by residential mortgage lenders that it has largely replaced the use of mortgage forms used by individual institutions. One reason for the popularity of this form with residential lenders is that it is readily acceptable by the major secondary market institutions, should the lender desire to sell the mortgage after it has been originated.

Important Mortgage Clauses

It is beyond the scope of this chapter to discuss all the clauses and covenants that might be found in a mortgage document. We will mention some of the more important clauses, however, so that the reader gains an appreciation of the effect these clauses may have on the position of the borrower and lender.

Funds for Taxes and Insurance

This clause requires the mortgagor to pay amounts needed to cover property taxes and property fire and casualty insurance, plus mortgage insurance premiums, if required by the lender, in monthly installments in advance of when they are due unless such payments are prohibited by state law. The purpose of this clause is to enable the mortgagee to pay these charges out of money provided by the mortgagor when they become due instead of relying on the mortgagor to make timely payments on his own. The mortgagee is thereby better able to protect his or her security interest against liens for taxes, which normally have priority over the first mortgage, and against lapses in insurance coverage. Such funds may be held in an escrow or trust account for the mortgagor.

Charges and Liens

This clause requires the mortgagor to pay all taxes, assessments, charges, and claims assessed against the property that have priority over the mortgage and to pay all leasehold

---

[3] *Dower* is the interest in a husband's real estate transferred by law to the widow after his death. The common law counterpart running in favor of the husband as a widower is called *curtesy.* Many states now have a statutory allowance from the decedent's estate in lieu of dower and curtesy.

[4] Usury laws prohibit charging unconscionable and exorbitant rates or amounts of interest for the use of money. A usurious loan is one whose interest rate exceeds that permitted by usury laws.

payments, if applicable. The reason for this clause is that the mortgagee's security interest can be wiped out if these claims, or liens, are not paid or discharged, since they generally can attain priority over the interests of the mortgagee. For example, if taxes and assessments are not paid, a first mortgage on the property can be wiped out at a sale to satisfy the tax lien, unless the mortgagee is either the successful bidder at the tax sale or pays the tax due to keeping the property from being sold at the tax sale.

Hazard Insurance

This clause requires the mortgagor to obtain and maintain insurance against loss or damage to the property caused by fire and other hazards, such as windstorms, hail, explosion, and smoke. In effect, this clause acknowledges that the mortgagee as well as the mortgagor has an insurable interest in the mortgaged property. The mortgagee's insurable interest is the amount of the mortgage debt.

Preservation and Maintenance of the Property

This clause obligates the mortgagor to maintain the property in good condition and to not engage in or permit acts of waste.[5] This clause recognizes that the mortgagee has a valid interest in preventing the mortgaged property from deteriorating to the extent that the collateral value of the property is impaired.

Transfer of Property or a Beneficial Interest in Borrower

This clause, known as the **due-on-sale clause,** allows the mortgagee to accelerate the debt (i.e., to take action to make the outstanding loan balance plus accrued interest immediately due and payable) when the property, or some interest in the property, is transferred without the written consent of the mortgagee. The purpose of the due-on-sale clause is to enable the mortgagee to protect his or her security interest by approving any new owner. The clause may also permit the mortgagee to increase the interest rate on the loan to current market rates. This, of course, reduces the possibility of the new owner assuming a loan with an attractive interest rate.

Borrower's Rights to Reinstate

This clause deals with the mortgagor's right to reinstate the original repayment terms in the note after the mortgagee has caused an acceleration of the debt. It gives the mortgagor the right to have foreclosure proceedings discontinued at any time before a judgment is entered enforcing the mortgage (i.e., before a decree for the sale of the property is given) if the mortgagor does the following:

1. Pays to the mortgagee all sums which would then be due had no acceleration occurred.
2. Cures any default of any other covenants or agreements.
3. Pays all expenses incurred by the lender in enforcing its mortgage.
4. Takes such action as the mortgagee may reasonably require to ensure that the mortgagee's rights in the property and the mortgagor's obligations to pay are unchanged.

Right of Entry: Lender in Possession

This clause provides that upon acceleration or abandonment of the property, the mortgagee (or a judicially appointed receiver) may enter the property to protect the security. The lender may collect rents until the mortgage is foreclosed. Rents collected must be applied first to the costs of managing and operating the property, and then to the mortgage debt,

---

[5] *Waste* is the abuse or destructive use of property which reduces the value and, therefore, the security for the loan.

real estate taxes, insurances, and other obligations of the mortgagor as specified in the mortgage.

Future Advances

While it is expected that a mortgage will always state the total amount of the debt it is expected to secure, this amount may be in the nature of a forecast of the total debt to be incurred in installments. In other words, a mortgage may cover **future advances** as well as current advances. For example, a mortgage may be so written that it will protect several successive loans under a general line of credit extended by the mortgagee to the mortgagor. In case the total amount cannot be forecasted with accuracy, at least the general nature of the advances or loans must be apparent from the wording of the mortgage.

As an illustration of a **mortgage for future advances,** sometimes called an **open-end mortgage,** consider the form of construction loans. Here, the borrower arranges in advance with a mortgagee for a total amount, usually definitely stated in the mortgage, that will be advanced, in stages, under the mortgage to meet the part of the costs of construction as it progresses. As the structure progresses, the mortgagor has the right to call upon the mortgagee for successive advances on the loan. All improvements become security under the terms of the mortgage as they are constructed.

Subordination Clause

By means of this clause, a first mortgage holder agrees to make its mortgage junior in priority to the mortgage of another lender. A **subordination clause** might be used in situations where the seller provides financing by taking back a mortgage from the buyer, and the buyer also intends to obtain a mortgage from a bank or other financial institution, usually to develop or construct an improvement. Financial institutions will generally require that their loans have first mortgage priority. Consequently, the seller must agree to include a subordination clause in the mortgage, whereby the seller agrees to subordinate the priority of the mortgage to the bank loan. This ensures that even if the seller's mortgage is recorded before the bank loan, it will be subordinate to the bank loan.

Assumption of Mortgage

When the mortgagor transfers his or her rights to another, the question arises, "Does the grantee (buyer) agree to become liable for payment of the mortgage debt and relieve the mortgagor (seller) of his or her personal obligation?" If this is the intention of both parties, the **assumption of the mortgage** by the grantee may accomplish the purpose. The deed, after specifying the nature of the mortgage which encumbers the property, will contain a clause to the effect that the grantee assumes and agrees to pay the amount of the obligations owed to the mortgagee as part consideration for the conveyance of title. Where an assumption is undertaken by the grantee, it should be couched in language that leaves no doubt about the intent.

An assumption agreement takes the form of a contract of indemnity. It shifts the responsibility for the payment of the debt from the grantor to the grantee. Thereafter, the grantor stands in the position of a surety (guarantee) for the payment of the debt. However, such an arrangement binds only the parties to it: the grantor and the grantee. Since the mortgagee is not ordinarily a party to such an agreement, he or she is not bound by it. As a consequence, the mortgagee may still hold the original mortgagor liable. Thus, if a property is sold with a loan assumption and the new owner defaults on the loan, the lender can hold the previous owner liable unless the previous owner was released from the debt.

Release of Grantor from Assumed Debt

When a mortgagor owning property grants that property to another and the grantee assumes the grantor's mortgage, the lender may or may not release the grantor from personal liability for the mortgage debt. The decision of release will depend on the value of the property as security, the grantee's financial capabilities, and other factors affecting the lender's attitudes toward the transaction. A mortgagee cannot be expected to release an antecedent mortgagor if the result will be to increase the credit risk unless the mortgagee is compensated in some way (e.g., a higher interest rate).

Acquiring Title "Subject to" a Mortgage

In contrast to the assumption of the personal obligation to pay the debt, grantees may not be willing to accept this responsibility. In this case, they may ask grantors to allow them to take title **"subject to" the mortgage.** So long as the grantees are financially able and think it will be to their advantage, they will keep up payments on the mortgage and observe its other covenants. Under normal conditions, if they purchased the property at a fair price, it will be to their advantage to avoid default on the mortgage to protect their own equity.

But should the grantees reach the conclusion that there is no longer any advantage to making further payments, or should they become financially unable to do so, they may default on their payments. By so doing, they run the risk of losing whatever equity they have in the property. However, grantees cannot be held personally liable for the amount of the debt that they assumed. Grantors are still personally liable and may be held liable for any deficiency judgment resulting from the foreclosure sale.

It is obviously riskier for grantors to sell property subject to the mortgage. Given a choice, they would generally prefer that responsible grantees assume the mortgage unless they are compensated for the additional risk they undertake as a surety (e.g., by receiving a higher price for the property).

Property Covered by a Mortgage

The property that is covered by the mortgage as security for the loan includes not only the land and any existing buildings on the land but also easements and fixtures. In addition, the mortgage agreement may provide that property covered by the mortgage also includes rights to natural resources (e.g., mineral, timber, oil and gas, and water or riparian rights) and even rights to rents and profits from the real estate. An easement that runs with the property is generally regarded by the law as being covered by the mortgage, regardless of whether the easement is created before or after the mortgage is executed. Such an easement, if in existence at the time the property is mortgaged, is covered by the mortgage even if it is not mentioned in the mortgage. Foreclosure of the mortgage will not extinguish this easement. An easement created subsequent to the recording of a mortgage, however, will be extinguished by the foreclosure.

Issues involving fixtures have generated a considerable amount of legal controversy. In general, a **fixture** is an item of tangible personal property (also referred to as *chattel*) that has become affixed to or is intended to be used with the real estate, so as to be considered part of the property. The law is in general agreement that fixtures are covered by the mortgage, with the exception of "trade fixtures"[6] installed by a tenant.

---

[6] Trade fixtures are personal property used by tenants in businesses. Such fixtures retain the character of personal property (e.g., shelves used to display merchandise).

A mortgage also will usually contain what is called an **after-acquired property clause** as part of its description of the type of property to be covered by the mortgage. This provision states in effect that property acquired subsequent to the execution of the mortgage that becomes part of the real estate *is included in the security* covered by the mortgage. After-acquired property includes additional improvements erected on the property or fixtures that become part of the property at any time in the future for as long as the debt remains outstanding. The courts have generally affirmed the validity of after-acquired property clauses, and the Uniform Land Transactions Act (ULTA) expressly accepts their validity.[7]

Junior Mortgages

In simple real estate financing transactions, such as those involving single residences, the character of the mortgage structure is easily defined. The senior or prior mortgage is usually called a **first mortgage.** All others are given the class name of **junior mortgages.** In any particular situation, there may be one or more junior mortgages or none at all. One junior lien, usually called a **second mortgage,** is sometimes used to bridge the gap between the price of the property and the sum of the first mortgage and the amount of money available to the purchaser to use as a down payment. Traditionally, second mortgages are short term and carry a higher rate of interest than first mortgages because of the additional risk associated with their junior status.

Recording of Mortgages

Unless the statutes of the state require it, recording is not essential to the validity of a mortgage because it is an agreement between the mortgagor and the mortgagee. The act of recording creates no rights that did not exist before, but it does give others notice of the existence and effect of the mortgage. A recorded mortgage protects its holder by giving him or her priority over the subsequent acts of the mortgagor. For example, if a mortgagee failed to record the mortgage, the mortgagor could mortgage the property to a second lender. If this second lender had no notice of the prior unrecorded mortgage, the second lender would have a lien prior to that of the original mortgagee. In general, the priority of successive liens is determined by the time they are accepted for record.

As we have discussed, the recording acts provide opportunities for the protection of holders of interests in property, but at the same time they place responsibilities upon them to make use of these opportunities. Failure to inspect the records for prior liens or to record the mortgage may result in loss to the mortgagee. In most states, *junior lienors* of record without notice of the existence of a senior mortgage will have priority over an unrecorded senior mortgage. Even subsequent recording of a senior mortgage lien will generally not elevate it to a higher priority.

Other Financing Sources

Seller Financing

A source of credit for a real property buyer is often the seller. If the seller is willing to take back a mortgage as part or full payment of the purchase price, it is referred to as **seller financing.** This type of financing is used when:

---

[7] For a discussion and case law materials related to after-acquired property clauses, see Grant S. Nelson and Dale A. Whitman, *Real Estate Transfer, Finance, and Development,* 2nd ed. (St. Paul, MN: West Publishing, 1981), pp. 633–39; see also Robert Kratovil and Raymond J. Werner, *Modern Mortgage Law and Practice,* 2nd ed. (Englewood Cliffs, NJ: Prentice Hall), pp. 114–17.

1. Third-party mortgage financing is too expensive or unavailable.
2. The buyer does not qualify for long-term mortgage credit because of a low down payment or difficulty meeting monthly payments.
3. The seller desires to take advantage of the installment method of reporting the gain from the sale.
4. The seller desires to artificially raise the price of the property by offering a lower-than-market interest rate on the mortgage, thereby creating more capital gains and less interest or ordinary income.[8]

Any mortgage given by a buyer to the seller to secure payment of all or part of the purchase price of a property is usually called a **purchase-money mortgage.** It can be a first mortgage, which might be the case if the seller is providing all of the financing necessary to consummate the transaction. It also could take the form of a second mortgage that is provided by the seller and is used to bridge the gap between an available first mortgage and the buyer's down payment. As such, it must be differentiated from mortgages given to secure a loan from a third party for the purchase of the property. The third-party lender (e.g., a financial institution) will normally want its mortgage to be a first mortgage. Thus, the purchase-money mortgage must either be recorded after the third-party loan or contain a subordination clause, as defined earlier.

Land Contracts

One form of financing real estate that has been widely used over the years is commonly referred to as a land contract. The term **land contract** has a variety of aliases, including real estate contract, installment sales contract, agreement to convey, and contract for deed. As the last term implies, the land contract seller promises to convey title at such time as the purchaser completes the performance of the obligation called for in the contract. Such performance usually means payment of the purchase price in stipulated installments, much the same way as under a note and mortgage.

It should be emphasized that a land contract is not a mortgage. Under the land contract, the sellers retain the title in their name. The deed record shows that the sellers are still the owners of the property, but the land contract is supposed to tie their hands to make sure that the sellers or their assigns ultimately transfer title to the vendees or their heirs or assigns.

The land contract may be used as a substitute for a purchase-money mortgage and would normally not be preferred if the latter were available. However, in cases where there is no down payment or a small down payment, and a very long period of time during which a buyer must make periodic payments to the seller, sellers of land may refuse to give a deed and take back a mortgage until a very substantial part of the purchase price has been paid.

Several points of comparison exist between purchase-money mortgages and land contracts. A land contract buyer does not have title to the property and therefore cannot control whether the property will be mortgaged subsequent to the execution of the land contract or be made subject to covenants, easements, or mechanics' liens in the future by the contract seller. Most land contracts contain a clause allowing the seller to mortgage property up to an amount equal to the buyer's indebtedness to the seller. The buyer would have this protection if mortgage financing were used because limits would be made explicit and the buyer would have title. Furthermore, the possibility of forfeiture of the land contract interest may exist without any of the procedural protections afforded mortgages.

---

[8] The use of this technique has been limited by the "unstated interest rule."

It is suggested that all such points of comparison should be considered in making the decision whether to buy or sell on land contract or to obtain mortgage financing. In general, land contracts are used in many of the same situations as purchase-money mortgages (e.g., where the buyer has difficulty obtaining third-party financing).

Recording of Land Contracts

State laws provide for the recording of conveyances of land and instruments affecting title. Land contracts generally are considered instruments affecting title and are consequently admissible to record. Recording land contracts is not essential to their validity; it merely gives notice of their existence to third parties.

Default

We have discussed the various property rights associated with real estate. Next, consider some of the problems that result when one of the parties does not fulfill a contractual obligation associated with its property right. The legal ramifications of these problems affect the financial security of other parties' rights and are thus an important aspect of real estate finance.

One of the most important risks in making a mortgage loan is that the borrower will default on the note in some way, so that the lender may not receive the expected mortgage payments. The risk associated with mortgage loans depends in part on the rights of the lender if and when such default occurs. Thus, it is important to understand the legal ramifications of mortgage default.

What Constitutes Default?

Default is a failure to fulfill a contract, agreement, or duty, especially a financial obligation such as a note. It follows that a **mortgage default** can also result from any breach of the mortgage contract. The most common default is the failure to meet an installment payment of the interest and principal on the note. However, failure to pay taxes or insurance premiums when due may also result in a default, which may precipitate an acceleration of the debt and a foreclosure action. Indeed, some mortgages have clauses that make specific stipulations to this effect. Even a failure to keep the security in repair may constitute what is commonly referred to as a *technical default*. However, because a breach of contract resulting in a technical default can usually be cured by a borrower, it seldom results in an actual foreclosure sale. Furthermore, it may be difficult for the mortgagee to prove that the repair clause in the mortgage has been broken unless the property shows definite evidence of the effects of waste. This means that even though there is a breach of contract, the mortgagee may postpone doing something about it. However, in the case of technical default accompanied by abandonment, the probabilities are that the mortgagee will act quickly to protect his or her interests against vandalism, neglect, and waste. This may occur even though the borrower may be current on the loan payments.

Alternatives to Foreclosure: Workouts

Foreclosure involves the sale of property by the courts to satisfy the unpaid debt. The details of this process are discussed later. Because of the time involved and the various costs associated with foreclosure (and possibly repair of any damage to the property), lenders often prefer to seek an alternative to actual foreclosure.

Although mortgage contracts normally indicate definite penalties to follow any breach therein, experience has shown that in spite of provisions for prompt action in case of a default in mortgage payments, many commitments are not met in strict accordance with the letter of the contract. Instead, whenever mortgagors get into financial trouble and are unable to meet their obligations, adjustments of the payments or other terms are likely to follow if both the borrower and lender believe that the conditions are temporary and will be remedied.

The term **workout** is often used to describe the various activities undertaken to deal with a mortgagor who is in financial trouble. Many times the parties make a workout agreement that sets forth the rules by which, during a specified period of time, they will conduct themselves and their discussions. The lender agrees to refrain from exercising legal remedies. In exchange the borrower acknowledges his or her financial difficulty and agrees to certain conditions such as supplying current detailed financial and other information to the lender and establishing a cash account in which any rental receipts from the property are deposited and any withdrawls are subject to lender approval.

Six alternatives can be considered in a workout:

1. Restructuring the mortgage loan.
2. Transfer of the mortgage to a new owner.
3. Voluntary conveyancy of the title to the mortgagee (lender).
4. A "friendly foreclosure."
5. A prepackaged bankruptcy.
6. A "short sale" with the lender agreeing to a sale price less than the loan balance.

Restructuring the Mortgage Loan

Loans can be restructured in many ways. Such restructuring could involve lower interest rates, accruals of interest, or extended maturity dates. If the original loan is nonrecourse to the borrower, the lender may want to obtain personal recourse against the borrower as part of the loan restructuring agreement. This makes the borrower subject to significantly more downside risk if the restructuring fails. The lender also may want a participation in the performance of the property to enhance the lender's upside potential as compensation for being willing to restructure the loan. For example, the lender could ask for a percentage of any increase in the income of the property over its current level.

Recasting of Mortgages

Once a mortgage is executed and placed on record, its form may change substantially before it is redeemed. It may be recast for any one of several reasons. A mortgage can be renegotiated at any time, but most frequently it is recast by changing the terms of the mortgage (either temporarily or permanently) to avoid or cure a default.

Where mortgage terms such as the interest rate, amortization period, or payment amounts are changed, mortgagees must exercise care to avoid losing their priority over intervening lienors. The mere extension of time of payment will not generally impair the priority of the extended mortgage. Courts, however, are watchful to protect intervening lienors against prejudice, and mortgages may lose priority to the extent that changes in the interest rate, payment amounts, or the amount of indebtedness place additional burdens on the mortgagor.[9]

---

[9] Recasting of mortgages to admit interests not present at the time the mortgages were executed is sometimes necessary. For example, the mortgage may make no provision for an easement of a public utility company that requires access to the rear of the site covered by the mortgage. Since the installation of the services of the utility will normally add to rather than subtract from the value of the security, the mortgagee will usually be glad to approve the change. Nevertheless, it will require a recasting of the mortgage to the extent indicated.

Extension Agreements Occasionally, a mortgagor in financial difficulty may seek permission from the mortgagee to extend the mortgage terms for a period of time. This is known as a mortgage **extension agreement.** A mortgagor may request a longer amortization period for the remaining principal balance or a temporary grace period for the payment of principal or interest payments or both. In responding to such a request, the mortgagee needs to consider the following issues:

1. What is the condition of the security? Has it been reasonably well maintained or does it show the effects of waste and neglect?
2. Have there been any intervening liens? These are liens recorded or attached after the recordation of the mortgage but before any modifications to it. If so, what is their effect upon an extension agreement? If such liens exist, it is possible that the extension of an existing mortgage may amount to a cancellation of the mortgage and the making of a new one. If so, this could advance the priority of intervening liens.
3. What is the surety status of any grantees who have assumed the mortgage? Will an extension of time for the payment of the debt secured by the mortgage terminate the liability of such sureties? The best way for mortgagees to protect themselves against the possibilities implied in these questions is to secure the consent of the extension agreement from all sureties to the extension. As parties to it, they can have no grounds for opposing it. But if they are not made parties to the extension—particularly if changes in the terms of the mortgage through the extension agreement tend to increase the obligations for which the sureties are liable—then care should be exercised to ensure that those sureties who refuse to sign the agreement are not released by the extension agreement. The possibility of foreclosure and a deficiency judgment against them may be a sufficient inducement to obtain their agreement to be parties to the extension.

The exact nature of an extension agreement depends upon the bargaining position of mortgagor and mortgagee. If mortgagors can refinance the loan on more favorable terms, they will probably not apply for an extension agreement. Alternatively, they may have to make changes that favor the mortgagee, such as an increase in the interest rate.

Alternative to Extension Agreements An alternative to an extension agreement has the mortgagee agree informally to a temporary extension without making any changes in the formal recorded agreement between the parties. If the mortgagor is unable to meet all monthly mortgage payments, these too may be waived temporarily or forgiven in whole or in part. For example, simply raising the question of such an agreement suggests that the mortgagor cannot pay the matured principal of the loan. Therefore, some informal arrangement may be made to permit the mortgagor to retain possession of the property in return for meeting monthly payments, which may or may not include principal installments. The use of this kind of informal agreement can be troublesome, but, in general, if it is reached, the amounts demanded will be adjusted to the present payment capacities of the borrower. Should the borrower's financial condition improve, the lender may again insist that the originally scheduled payments resume.

The use of such an alternative to a definite extension agreement may serve the temporary needs of both mortgagors and mortgagees. If the latter feel that the security amply protects their lien, the mortgagees can afford to be lenient in helping mortgagors adjust their financial arrangements during a difficult period. If the mortgagors also feel that any real equity exists in the property, they will wish to protect it if at all possible.

Transfer of Mortgage to a New Owner

Mortgagors who are unable or unwilling to meet their mortgage obligations may be able to find someone who is willing to purchase the property and either assume the mortgage liability or take the property "subject to" the existing mortgage. The new purchaser may be willing to accept the **transfer of mortgage** if he or she thinks the value of the property exceeds the balance due on the mortgage. In either case, the seller retains personal liability for the debt. However, if the seller is about to default and expects to lose the property anyway, he or she may be willing to take a chance on a new purchaser fulfilling the mortgage obligation. The risk is that the new buyer will default, and the seller will again have responsibility for the debt and get the property back.

Recall that if purchasers acquire the property "subject to" the existing debt, they do not acquire any personal liability for the debt. Thus, they can only lose any equity personally invested to acquire the property. This equity investment may be quite small where the sellers are financially distressed and face foreclosure. Thus, the buyers may have little to lose by taking a chance on acquiring the property subject to the mortgage. If it turns out to be a good investment, they will continue to make payments on the debt, but if they find that the value of the property is unlikely to exceed the mortgage debt within a reasonable time frame, they can simply stop making payments and let the sellers reacquire the property. Thus, we see that in this situation buyers of the property "subject to" a mortgage have in effect purchased an option. The equity that buyers invest is the payment for this option, which allows them to take a chance on the property value increasing after it is acquired. We can therefore see why purchasers might even give the sellers money to acquire a property subject to a mortgage even if the *current* value of the property is less than the mortgage balance.

For example, suppose that a property has a mortgage balance of $100,000. Property values in the area are currently depressed, and the owner believes that only $99,000 could be obtained on an outright sale. However, a buyer is willing to acquire the property at a price of $101,000 "subject to" the existing mortgage. Thus, $2,000 is paid for the option of tying up the property in hopes that property values rise above their current level.[10] If the property does not rise in value to more than $100,000 (less any additional principal payments that have been made), the purchaser could simply walk away, and the original owner again becomes responsible for the mortgage. If the property rises in value to more than $101,000, the purchaser stands to make a profit and would continue to make payments on the mortgage.

It should be clear that knowledge of various legal alternatives (e.g., being able to purchase a property "subject to" vs assuming a mortgage) can allow a buyer and seller to arrive at an agreement that best meets their financial objectives. Thus, legal alternatives can often be evaluated in a financial context.

Voluntary Conveyance

Borrowers (mortgagors) who can no longer meet the mortgage obligation may attempt to "sell" their equity to the mortgagees. For example, suppose that the mortgagors are unable to meet their obligations and face foreclosure of their equity. To save the time, trouble, and expense associated with foreclosure, the mortgagees may make or accept a proposal to take title from the mortgagors. If they both agree that the property value exceeds the mortgage balance, a sum may be paid to the mortgagors for their equity. If the value is less than the mortgage balance, the lenders may still be willing to accept title and release the mortgagors from the mortgage debt. This **voluntary conveyance** might be done because the cost of foreclosure exceeds the expected benefit of pursuing that course of action.

---

[10] The seller would receive $1,000 in cash, but since the seller had −$1,000 in equity, he or she receives the economic benefit of $2,000, which is also the difference between the price paid and the market value of the property.

When voluntary conveyances are used, title is usually transferred with a warranty or quitclaim deed from mortgagors to mortgagees. The mortgagors should insist upon a release to make sure that they are no longer bound under their note and mortgage, especially in situations where the mortgage balance is near or in excess of the property value. Otherwise, the mortgagors may find that they still have a personal obligation to pay the mortgage note. The conveyance to the mortgagees in exchange for a release from the mortgage debt is frequently referred to as giving **deed in lieu of foreclosure** of the mortgage. A deed in lieu of foreclosure has the advantage of speed and minimizes the expense of transferring the property and the uncertainty of litigation. It also avoids the negative publicity of foreclosure or bankruptcy. A deed in lieu of foreclosure does not cut off subordinate interests in the property. The lender must make arrangements with all other creditors. There are also potential bankruptcy problems. The transfer may be voidable as a preferential transfer. In addition to the legal questions involved in voluntary conveyances, the mortgagee frequently faces very practical financial issues as well. If there are junior liens outstanding, they are not eliminated by a voluntary conveyance. Indeed, their holders may be in a better position than before if the title to the property passes to a more financially sound owner. Unless in some manner these junior liens are released from the property in question—possibly by agreement with their holders to transfer them to other property owned by the mortgagor or even on occasion to cancel them—the mortgagee may find it necessary to foreclose instead of taking a voluntary conveyance because the title conveyed is subject to junior liens. Foreclosure provides the mortgagee with a lawful method of becoming free from the liens of the junior claimants.

Friendly Foreclosure

Foreclosure can be time consuming and expensive, and there can be damage to the property during this time period. A **"friendly foreclosure"** is a foreclosure action in which the borrower submits to the jurisdiction of the court, waives any right to assert defenses and claims and to appeal or collaterally attack any judgment, and otherwise agrees to cooperate with the lender in the litigation. This can shorten the time required to effect a foreclosure. This also cuts off subordinate liens and provides better protection in case of the borrower's subsequent bankruptcy. A friendly foreclosure normally takes more time than a voluntary conveyance but is less time consuming than an unfriendly foreclosure. This is discussed in more detail in the next section.

Prepackaged Bankruptcy

The mortgagee must consider the risk that the mortgagor will use the threat of filing for bankruptcy as a way of reducing some of his or her obligation under the original mortgage agreement. Bankruptcy can have significant consequences for secured lenders. To the extent that the collateral securing the debt is worth less than the principal amount of the debt, the deficiency will be treated as an unsecured debt. In a **prepackaged bankruptcy,** before filing the bankruptcy petition, borrowers agree with all their creditors to the terms on which they will turn their assets over to their creditors in exchange for a discharge of liabilities. This can save a considerable amount of time and expense compared with the case where the terms are not agreed upon in advance. The consequences of bankruptcy are discussed further in the last section of this chapter.

Short Sale

A **short sale** is a sale of real estate in which the proceeds from the sale fall short of the balance owed on a loan secured by the property sold. In a short sale, the mortgage lender agrees to discount the mortgage loan balance because of an economic or financial hardship on the part of the mortgagor. This is often done during periods when home prices have declined significantly and the financial hardship is more a result of market conditions than actions of the borrower.

In a short sale, the home owner/borrower sells the mortgaged property for less than the outstanding balance of the loan and then turns over the proceeds of the sale to the lender, usually in full satisfaction of the loan. In some cases, the lender may still pursue a deficiency judgment. The lender has the right to approve or disapprove a proposed sale. Typically a short sale is executed to prevent a home foreclosure, because the lender believes that it will result in a smaller financial loss than foreclosing. The decision to proceed with a short sale represents the most economical way for the lender to recover the amount owed on the property. In contrast to a foreclosure, if the borrower has been making payments up until the time the short sale is approved, the short sale may not adversely affect the borrower's credit report, because the lender has agreed to discount the loan. In the event that the property is sold for less than its outstanding low balance and the lender does not pursue a deficiency judgment, this may result in a "forgiveness of debt" by the lender and could be a "taxable event" for the owner/borowee.

Foreclosure

In practice, most mortgagees are not anxious to take property from mortgagors, particularly where the mortgagors have candidly communicated with the mortgagees concerning the default and have made realistic proposals to cure the default over a reasonable period of time. Because the management and disposal of property requires skills that are usually outside of the range of expertise of most lenders and therefore costly to acquire, mortgagees prefer to collect the amounts owed them and are likely to be lenient and patient when circumstances warrant it. Seldom do mortgagees insist upon the exact letter of their contract. Nor do they rush into court to insist upon **foreclosure** at the first evidence of default, but after patience and leniency have been extended to delinquent mortgagors, eventually a settlement becomes necessary and foreclosure proceedings are started.

Judicial Foreclosure

In general, the mortgagee possesses two types of remedies to protect his or her interests in case of default by the mortgagor. First, the lender may obtain **judicial foreclosure:** that is, to sue on the debt, obtain judgment, and execute the judgment against property of the mortgagor. In a judicial foreclosure, property subject to attachment and execution[11] is not limited to the mortgaged property. This judgment may be levied against any of the mortgagor's property not otherwise legally exempt[12] from execution.

Second, the lender may bring a foreclosure suit and obtain a decree of foreclosure and sale. If the sale of the mortgaged property realizes a price high enough to meet the expenses of the sale and the claims of the mortgagee and still leave a balance, this balance goes to the mortgagor. While foreclosure and sale of the property may be undertaken in two separate actions, they are usually pursued simultaneously in practice.

---

[11] *Attachment* is the act or process of seizing property of a debtor by court order in order to secure the debt of a creditor in the event judgment is rendered. *Execution* is the process of authorizing the sheriff or other competent officer to seize and sell property of the debtor in satisfaction of a judgment previously rendered in favor of a creditor.

[12] Most states provide by statute that a certain amount of a borrower's property shall be free from all liability from levy and sale as a result of the enforcement (execution) of a money judgment. These statutes typically provide that some amount of personal property and equity in a borrower's home not secured by a purchase-money lien shall be set off and free from seizure and sale in order to provide the borrower with a minimum amount of property to maintain his or her family on their road to financial recovery.

Redemption

Redemption is the process of canceling or annulling a title conveyed by a foreclosure sale by paying the debt or fulfilling the other conditions in the mortgage. It can be accomplished by paying the full amount of the debt, interest, and costs due to the mortgagee. The *equity of redemption*[13] must be asserted prior to foreclosure. Once the foreclosure sale has been confirmed, the mortgagor can no longer redeem the property, except in states that provide for a statutory period for redemption after foreclosure. The right to redeem after foreclosure is called the right of *statutory redemption,* which exists in about half of the states. Generally, the period for statutory redemption runs about six months to one year after the foreclosure sale. In a number of states, instead of granting the mortgagor a right to redeem after the foreclosure sale, state laws postpone the sale to provide a longer period of time to pay a debt that is in default.

Sales of Property

The advertising of the sale, the place where it takes place, and the method of sale are governed by state law. While details differ, the results are approximately the same in all states.

Fixing a Price

A mortgage foreclosure sale emanates from the assumption that a public auction is a satisfactory way to realize the best possible price in selling property. Hence, in some jurisdictions the highest bidder gets the property irrespective of its cost, the amount of liens against it, or any other consideration. Despite this requirement of a public sale, in most cases only the mortgagee or the mortgagee and a small number of bidders appear at the foreclosure sale and, as a result, the mortgagee is usually the successful bidder. The mortgagee can use his or her claims as a medium of exchange in the purchase, except for costs, which must be paid in cash. Others must pay cash for their purchases (which may be in the form of a loan obtained from another lender with an agreement granting to it the new mortgage), unless the successful bidder can arrange with the mortgagee to keep his or her lien alive by renegotiating or assuming the existing indebtedness. As a consequence, frequently only the mortgagee makes any serious bid for the property. Because lenders generally prefer to avoid owning and liquidating foreclosed properties, they will normally bid the full amount of their claim only where it is less than or equal to the market value of the security less foreclosure, resale, and holding costs. Rarely will lenders bid in excess of their claim in an attempt to outbid other buyers at the sale.

In a few states, an "upset" price is fixed in advance of the sale. This means that an appraisal by agents of the court fixes a minimum value for the property that must be reached in the bidding or the court will refuse to confirm the sale. This is not a common practice because it is quite difficult for the court to fix the price that the property must bring at the foreclosure sale. On the one hand, the court is interested in doing justice to the mortgagor. Since a deficiency judgment may be decreed in case the mortgagee is not completely satisfied from the proceeds of the sale, the lower the price, the larger the deficiency judgment. On the other hand, the mortgagee's rights also must be protected. If the court insists on too high a price, no sale would be effected, and hence the mortgagee would receive no satisfaction of his or her claims.

[13] The *equity of redemption* is the right of a mortgagor to redeem his or her property from default, the period from the time of default until foreclosure proceedings are begun.

Deed of Trust

The historical development of the law has commonly led, in some jurisdictions, to the finance of real estate by a **deed of trust** instead of a regular mortgage. There are three parties to a loan secured by a deed of trust. The *borrower* (creator of the trust) conveys the title to the property to be used as security to a *trustee,* who holds it as security for the benefit of the *holder of the note* executed by the borrower when the loan was made. The conveyance to the trustee is by deed, but the transfer is accompanied by a trust agreement, either as a part of the deed or in addition to it, setting forth the terms of the security arrangement and giving the trustee the power of sale in event of default.

The deed of trust is commonly used in Alabama, Arkansas, California, Colorado, the District of Columbia, Delaware, Illinois, Mississippi, Missouri, Nevada, New Mexico, Tennessee, Texas, Utah, Virginia, and West Virginia. Deeds of trust are not used extensively in other states because courts there have held that any conveyance of real estate given to secure a debt is a mortgage, irrespective of the form of the instrument used. This interpretation greatly restricts the trustee's power of sale, often requiring the expense and delay of a court process up to and including foreclosure. States imposing this restriction have sought to ensure that a reasonable sale price and all other appropriate benefits are obtained for both borrower and noteholder before the property is sold.

Where the deed of trust is used according to its terms, the trustee is authorized in case of default to foreclose the borrower's equity by a sale of the property at public auction. After a proper time period for advertisement, the trustee must account to both parties for the proceeds of the sale. The parties are entitled to their share as their interest may appear, after expenses of the sale, including compensation to the trustee, have been met. The deed of trust has the advantage of normally being more expeditious than a mortgage foreclosure.

Deed of Trust and Mortgage Compared

The deed of trust is such a mixture of trust and mortgage law that anyone using it should act under the counsel of a local real estate lawyer. In general, however, the legal rules surrounding the creation and evidence of the debt in the form of a note, rights of the borrower left in possession, legal description of the property, creation of a valid lien on after-acquired property, and recording are the same for mortgages and deeds of trust. Similarly, a property subject to a deed of trust may be sold subject to the deed of trust either with or without an assumption of the debt by the purchaser. Borrowers may sell their interest or borrow money using the interest as security. Technically, borrowers have a reversionary interest in the property, and title to the property reverts to them upon payment of the debt. In the event of failure or refusal of a trustee to execute a reconveyance when the borrowers repay their debt, the trustee may be forced to act by legal process, whereby the borrowers would obtain a court order forcing the trustee to act.

In California, where deeds of trust and mortgages are used side by side, several distinctions are made between the two instruments. While a mortgage may be discharged by a simple acknowledgment of satisfaction on the record, a reconveyance of title is considered necessary to extinguish a deed of trust.[14] Recording requirements for mortgages and deeds of trust also differ. Under the recording laws of most states, mortgage assignments may be, and in some states must be, recorded. Assignments of a deed of trust,

---

[14] Some states do not require reconveyance to extinguish a deed of trust. Instead, the secured beneficiary of the trust (noteholder) signs a request for release of the deed of trust, which is presented by the borrower to the trustee together with the canceled note and the deed of trust. The trustee issues a release of trust, which is then recorded at the appropriate office of public records for the county.

however, need not be recorded, and in some states are not eligible for recordation. The recording of the original deed of trust gives notice of the lien against the property, and only the trustee has the power to clear the record through a reconveyance of the property.

Nature of Title at Foreclosure Sale

The purchaser of property at a foreclosure sale is, in effect, the purchaser of the rights of the mortgagor whose interests are cut off by the sale. Even though the sale is conducted under court supervision, the court makes no representation concerning the nature of the title that a buyer will receive. Any title defects that existed prior to the foreclosure sale will continue with the title as it passes to the purchaser. If a junior lienor has been omitted in the suit for foreclosure, his or her claims will not be cut off by such suit. As long as lienor claims are not cut off, the purchaser acquires the property subject to those liens instead of a fee simple unencumbered.

Parties to Foreclosure Suit

When the holders of a senior mortgage bring suit to foreclose their mortgage, they must join in the suit all who share the mortgagor's interest. These include not only junior mortgage holders but judgment creditors, purchasers at an execution sale, and trustees in bankruptcy, if any. Failure to include all of these might improve their position with the foreclosure of the senior lien. For example, should the senior mortgagee become the successful bidder at the foreclosure sale, and should a junior lienor of record not be joined in the suit, it is possible that when the senior mortgagee takes title to the land, the junior mortgagee may acquire the position of a senior lienor. To avoid this possibility, every foreclosure action should be preceded by a careful search of the record to discover all junior lien claimants who should be joined in the foreclosure suit.

Should any junior lienors think that they have an equity to protect, they have the right to purchase the property at a foreclosure sale, paying off or otherwise providing for the interests of the claimants whose liens are superior to theirs. It might be, for example, that a senior mortgagee has a $50,000 lien on a property that a junior mortgagee with a $10,000 lien considers to be worth more than $50,000. If the junior lienor does not bid for the property, the senior mortgagee may bid it in for $50,000 (in the absence of other bidders) and cut off the junior lienor's equity, causing a loss to the junior lienor. By taking over responsibility for the senior mortgage, the junior lienor could bid up to $60,000 for the property without providing additional funds. In this event, it is not uncommon for a senior claimant to agree in advance upon the method of settlement of his or her claims. This may include an agreement to renew the senior mortgagee's claim, either with or without a reduction in the amount.

The purchaser at the foreclosure sale takes over the property free of the lien of the mortgage being foreclosed, but also free of all holders of junior liens who have been joined in the foreclosure action. If the senior mortgage holder or a third party purchases the property at a foreclosure sale, all such junior liens are of no further force or effect.

If junior lienholders bring suit for foreclosure, they should not join the senior lienholders in the suit. Instead, they should sue subject to the senior lien, but this means they are not obligated to pay off the senior lienholders. Junior lienholders may prefer to keep the senior mortgage alive. Holders of the senior lien may join the action voluntarily and sometimes do so to make sure that their interests are fully protected. They may wish to have the court determine the amount to be assumed by the purchaser which is due them. Or should there be any questions about the order of priority of this lien, senior lienholders may join the foreclosure action to have this question answered. Again, they may have a side agreement with the junior lienors to continue their mortgage unchanged in amount. In case the junior mortgage holders plan to buy the property at the foreclosure sale, they may prefer to pay off the senior lien as well. This must be done with the consent of the lienholders if they are not a party to the suit. This practice represents a redemption of the senior mortgage and follows the English maxim of "redeem up, but foreclose down." This concept is fairly obvious. It simply means that junior mortgagees must honor the prior position of senior mortgagees, but junior mortgagees may wipe out liens junior to theirs. For example, say a property now worth $100,000 is encumbered as follows:

First mortgage, A	$ 90,000
Second mortgage, B	20,000
Third mortgage, C	10,000
Total mortgage liens	$120,000

In a foreclosure action, mortgagee B has a buying power of $110,000 without raising additional funds if he is able to keep the first mortgage undisturbed, or if he refinances it. If he buys the property at the foreclosure sale for no more than $110,000, the third mortgage lien will be completely cut off by foreclosure.

Holders of junior liens destroyed in a foreclosure action are entitled to have the surplus of sale price over senior mortgage claims applied to their claims. If there is no surplus, they are entitled to a judgment for the full amount of their claims. From that time on, they are merely general, unsecured creditors of the mortgagor, unless the latter should own other real estate to which such judgments would attach.

Effect of Foreclosure on Junior Lienors

If a senior mortgage holder brings foreclosure suit and joins junior claimants in the suit, the question arises, "What happens to the claims of those cut off by the foreclosure sale?" Any surplus remaining after satisfying the costs of foreclosure and the claims of the senior lienor is distributed according to the priority rights of junior claims. Sometimes the distribution of this surplus is not as simple as it sounds. Frequent disputes concerning the order of priority require action by the court to establish the order of settlement.

Where a senior mortgage is properly foreclosed, it extinguishes the *lien* of the junior mortgage, but the *debt* secured by the mortgage is unaffected. Where there is no surplus from the foreclosure sale or where it is insufficient to meet all claims, the holders of such claims still maintain their rights to pursue the mortgagors on whatever personal obligation they have incurred by obtaining the mortgage. This legal right may or may not result in satisfaction of the claims of lienholders. Such obligations are not extinguished and may be enforced at some future time, should the mortgagors ever recover their economic status sufficiently to make pursuit of claims against them worthwhile.

Deficiency Judgment

While a sale of the mortgaged property may result in a surplus to which the mortgagor is entitled, it may on the contrary be sold at a price that fails to satisfy the claims of the mortgagee. Any deficit is a continuing claim by the mortgagee against the mortgagor. The mortgagor is personally obligated to pay the debt evidenced by the promissory note. Since mortgages may involve one or more specific properties, the mortgagee will normally look to such property to provide primary security for his or her claim, but any deficiency remains the obligation of the mortgagor. Any deficit remaining after a foreclosure and sale of the property is known as a **deficiency judgment.**

Deficiency judgments are unsecured claims—unless the mortgagor owns other real estate—and take their place alongside other debts of the mortgagor. Unlike the mortgage from which such judgment springs, the latter gives the holder no right of preference against any of the non–real estate assets of the debtor.[15] Hence, the value of deficiency judgments is always open to serious question. This is true in part because of the ways by which they can be avoided or defeated.

Debtors seeking to avoid the deficiency judgment may plan accordingly. Since such judgments attach only to real estate or other property that the debtors hold or may acquire in the future, the debtors may see that they do not acquire any future property interests or, if they do, they will be careful to have titles recorded in names other than their own.

Considerable sentiment exists in some quarters in favor of legislation to abolish deficiency judgments altogether, leaving mortgagees with only the property to protect their claims. Several states strictly limit the applicability of deficiency judgments. Of course, this increases the possibility that a borrower will walk away from a property if its market value falls below the loan balance.

Taxes in Default

Payment of property taxes is an obligation of the mortgagor. As such, taxes constitute a prior lien against the security. Transfers of title always take into account accrued but unpaid taxes. Mortgages commonly contain tax clauses giving the mortgagee the right to pay taxes not paid regularly by the mortgagor. The amounts so paid are then added to the claims of the mortgagee. While the lien of taxes gives tax-collecting authorities the right to foreclose in case of default, this right is seldom exercised on first or even second default. Instead, the taxing authority from time to time may pursue an alternative policy of selling tax liens with deeds to follow. Since tax liens constitute superior liens prior to the claims of mortgagees if the taxing authorities have observed statutory procedure, and since they customarily carry high effective rates of interest, mortgagees may prefer to maintain the priority claim of tax liens by paying delinquent taxes and adding them to their claims.

If foreclosure becomes necessary, mortgagees include all taxes they have paid. At the time of a foreclosure sale, the purchaser usually is expected to pay all delinquent taxes, thus making the tax status of the property current.

Tax Sales

Where mortgagees do not act to protect their interests against tax liens, sooner or later taxing authorities will bring pressure to collect delinquent taxes. In effect, if not in form, the **tax sale** procedure is intended to parallel that followed in the foreclosure of mortgages. At the time of the tax sale, the purchaser receives a tax certificate, which is then subject to redemption in nearly all states. The period of redemption is usually two or three years. If the property is not redeemed by the delinquent taxpayer within this period, the purchaser at the tax sale is then entitled to receive a deed to the property.

Tax titles are usually looked upon as weak evidence of ownership. The interest of the tax collector is to find someone willing and able to pay taxes for someone else in return for a claim against the property. The collector is not greatly concerned about passing good title. There is no suggestion of warranty. In addition to any defects in title regardless of delinquent taxes, the unconcern of the tax collector may in turn result in added clouds on the title. Among the latter, the following may occur:

---

[15] Deficiency judgments become a lien on all real estate owned by the judgment debtor in the county or counties where the judgment is entered. To the extent that there is equity in the real estate that is not exempt from execution, the judgment can be considered secured, and the creditor can enforce his lien through foreclosure and sale of the property to which the lien attaches.

1. Because of inaccurate description of the property or incorrect records of ownership, the notice of sale may be defective.
2. The property owner may have been denied due process or his or her day in court.
3. The line of authority for the sale may not be clear.
4. Irregularities and carelessness, even in minor procedural matters, may cause the tax sale to be invalidated.

All of these depend in part upon the recuperative powers of the delinquent taxpayers. If they have lost interest in the property or lack the financial resources to protect their interests, delinquent taxpayers may interpose no objections to the plans of the purchaser at the tax sale. Nevertheless, the risk is great enough to suggest caution and due attention even to minor details before purchasing tax liens.

In the absence of bidders at a tax sale—which might occur in periods of depression or in the sale of inexpensive vacant land—the property usually reverts to the state, the county, or some other local governmental unit. State and local units can be careless and neglect to take steps to realize a fair price when they dispose of property so acquired. A sale by the governmental unit, given full compliance with statutory requirements, normally offers a very short period of redemption after which the mortgagor and the mortgagee lose to the purchaser all rights to the property. Mortgagees should diligently monitor tax sale notices to ensure that their lien rights on property sold at tax sales are not affected.

Bankruptcy

Bankruptcy may be defined as a proceeding in which the court takes over the property of a debtor to satisfy the claims of creditors. The goal is to relieve the debtor of all liabilities, so that he or she may become financially solvent. The potential for bankruptcy under Chapters 7, 11, and 13 of the Bankruptcy Code affects the value of real estate as collateral. Lenders must be aware of the possibility that a borrower may file bankruptcy and must know how such a filing will change their positions. Both real estate investors and lenders must have a basic understanding of their rights in a bankruptcy proceeding to effectively negotiate with one another and resolve their differences short of a bankruptcy proceeding. It should also be stressed that in many states homestead laws protect certain residential and other property and may exclude such property from consideration in bankruptcy proceedings. Although a comprehensive examination of the Bankruptcy Code is beyond the scope of this text, several areas of bankruptcy law of particular importance to real estate investors and lenders are discussed below.

Chapter 7 Liquidation

The purpose of Chapter 7, or "straight bankruptcy," is to give debtors a fresh start by discharging all of their debts and liquidating their nonexempt assets. Chapter 7 is available to any person regardless of the extent of his or her assets or liabilities. A Chapter 7 petition can be filed voluntarily by a debtor or involuntarily by petitioning creditors, except that a farmer may not be forced into an involuntary proceeding.

Upon the filing of a Chapter 7 petition, the court appoints an interim trustee who is charged with evaluating the financial condition of the debtor and reporting at the first meeting of creditors whether there will be assets available for liquidation and distribution to unsecured creditors. The trustee's job is to oversee the liquidation of nonexempt assets and to evaluate claims filed by creditors. The ultimate objective of a Chapter 7 bankruptcy is the orderly liquidation of the debtor's assets and the distribution of the proceeds according to the legal rights and priorities of the various creditor claimants.

A lender whose loan to the debtor is secured by a mortgage on real estate will normally be paid in full if the value of the security exceeds the balance due under the mortgage. To foreclose on the mortgage and sell the debtor's property, the lender must first petition the bankruptcy court. If the debtor is not behind in the mortgage payments and desires to retain the property, he or she may do so by reaffirming the mortgage debt. This means that although the debtor's obligation to repay the debt has been discharged in bankruptcy, the debtor makes a new agreement after the discharge to repay the debt.

Chapter 11

An alternative to Chapter 7 is a Chapter 11 bankruptcy, which is available to owners of a business. While a Chapter 7 bankruptcy normally results in the liquidation of the debtor's assets, a Chapter 11 proceeding looks to the preservation of the debtor's assets while a plan of reorganization to rehabilitate the debtor is formulated. Within 120 days after filing a Chapter 11 bankruptcy petition, this plan of reorganization must be filed by the debtor with the court. The plan must classify the various claims against the debtor's assets and specify the treatment of the debts of each class. In a typical reorganization plan, the rights and duties of the parties are redefined in one of two ways. The plan may restructure the debt to provide for reduced payments over an extended period, or the plan may scale down the debt, reducing the debtor's obligation to an amount less than the full claim.

Once a plan is filed, the proponent of the plan, usually the debtor, must solicit creditor acceptance. Once holders of two-thirds of the total amount of the claims and a majority of the total number of claim holders assent to the plan, the court will analyze the plan and determine whether it meets the technical prerequisites for judicial confirmation. Even if one or more creditor classes dissent, the court can still confirm the plan if it meets certain statutory requirements. When the court decides that the bankruptcy plan is satisfactory in spite of the objections of creditors, the confirmation of the plan is known as **cramdown**.[16]

The cramdown provisions under Chapter 11 provide borrowers with the ability to restructure their secured (e.g., mortgage) and unsecured indebtedness by executing a plan of reorganization that outlines the mechanics for getting borrowers back on their feet and states how different classes of claims and interests will be treated. The cramdown provisions are essential to keeping the borrowers whole during a reorganization. Without a cramdown provision, secured lenders could continue to block the proposed reorganization by refusing to approve the plan and foreclose on the major assets of the borrower.

Under the Bankruptcy Code, a plan of reorganization may seriously impact secured lenders by impairing their claim. Despite this impairment, the plan may be confirmed by the court over the objections of the secured lenders. The law, however, makes some provision for secured lenders who do not approve the plan. One provision allows the borrower to keep the secured property but requires that the lender must receive present or deferred payments having a present value equal to the value of the collateral. A second provision calls for a sale of the collateral with the lender's lien attaching to the proceeds of the sale. A final catch-all provision requires the secured lender's realization of the "indubitable equivalent" of his or her claims.

Chapter 11 bankruptcy proceedings are of great concern to lenders who may find that their security is tied up for years during the reorganization of the debtor's financial affairs. Even lenders holding mortgages on a Chapter 11 debtor's personal residence may find that they are unable to foreclose on their liens where such a foreclosure would interfere with the

---

[16] During 2009, legislation was introduced in Congress that would allow federal judges to modify mortgages for property owners who have filed for bankruptcy and who are seeking to avoid foreclosure. This legislated form of cramdown could allow judges to reduce the mortgage balance or interest rate or change the loan maturity to avoid foreclosure.

debtor's plan of reorganization. In sum, the basic object of a Chapter 11 bankruptcy is to provide for a court-supervised reorganization, instead of a liquidation, of a financially troubled business.

Chapter 13

A Chapter 13 petition in bankruptcy, also known as a *wage earner proceeding,* represents an attractive alternative to the liquidation applied in Chapter 7. Like Chapter 11, a Chapter 13 proceeding envisions the formulation of a plan designed for the rehabilitation of the debtor. Such plans provide that funding of the plan will come from future wages and earnings of the debtor. Any debtor with regular income who has unsecured debts of less than $100,000 and secured debts of less than $350,000 qualifies for Chapter 13 relief. Thus, a Chapter 13 bankruptcy is the one most likely to be used by an individual.

The heart of Chapter 13 is the repayment plan, which is proposed by the debtor and, assuming it meets certain tests and conditions, is subject to confirmation by the court over objections of creditors. In a Chapter 13 plan, debtors propose to pay off their obligations and reorganize their affairs. The plan may call for payments over a three- to five-year period. Unlike a Chapter 7 or Chapter 11 bankruptcy that can be filed by debtors only every six years, a Chapter 13 plan can be filed immediately after completion of a prior bankruptcy liquidation or payment plan as long as it is filed in good faith.

During the period covered by the plan, creditors must accept payment as provided in the plan and may not otherwise seek to collect their debts. Assuming successful completion of the plan, debtors receive a discharge of all debts provided for in the plan other than long-term obligations for payments that continue beyond the period of the plan's duration. However, the plan may not modify the rights of mortgagees whose liens are secured only by property used by the debtors as their personal residence. This "preferred treatment" for such mortgagees under Chapter 13 is justified because the success of a reorganization plan could be jeopardized if foreclosure of this mortgage disrupts the affairs of the debtors by forcing them to seek other shelter. Although the plan may not "modify" the rights of secured lenders, lenders desiring to accelerate the balance of any indebtedness upon default to raise the interest rate should be aware of the borrower's right to cure a default in bankruptcy (by making arrangements to pay amounts currently in default over the period of the plan) and reinstate the mortgage. Thus, although a plan may not "modify" the rights of lenders whose debt is secured by liens on the debtor's personal residence, the filing of a Chapter 13 will likely prevent an imminent foreclosure and allow for repayment of arrearages existing on the date of the filing to be carried over a reasonable period of time. Where the plan calls for curing the arrearages and no modification of the schedule of current payments, courts will normally approve the plan because it does not materially affect the rights of such lenders.

Conclusion

This chapter has discussed the legal instruments and ramifications associated with financing real estate, such as default, foreclosure, and bankruptcy. The probability of one or more of these events occurring and the rights of the parties if it occurs ultimately affects the value of the various property rights. These legal considerations should be kept in mind as we discuss the risks associated with mortgage lending in later chapters. Clearly, the legal rights of borrowers and lenders affect the degree of risk assumed by each party and, thus, the value of entering into various transactions.

The availability of various legal alternatives can be viewed as a way of controlling and shifting risk between the various parties to a transaction. The probability of default or bankruptcy by a borrower and the legal alternatives available to each party affect the expected return to the lender from the loan. In later chapters we will discuss how the amount of the loan relative to the value of the property is used by the lender to control risk. The reader should keep in mind the fact that loan covenants as discussed in this chapter also control the risk.

Key Terms

after-acquired property
    clause, *24*
assumption of the mortgage, *22*
bankruptcy, *37*
covenants, *19*
cramdown, *38*
deed of trust, *33*
deed in lieu of foreclosure, *30*
deficiency judgment, *35*
due-on-sale clause, *21*
extension agreement, *28*
first mortgage, *24*
fixture, *23*

foreclosure, *31*
"friendly foreclosure," *30*
future advances, *22*
judicial foreclosure, *31*
junior mortgages, *24*
land contract, *25*
mortgage document, *18*
mortgage default, *26*
mortgage for future
    advances, *22*
open-end mortgage, *22*
prepackaged bankruptcy, *30*
promissory note, *18*

purchase-money
    mortgage, *18*
redemption, *32*
second mortgage, *24*
seller financing, *24*
short sale, *30*
"subject to" the mortgage, *23*
subordination clause, *22*
tax sale, *36*
transfer of mortgage, *29*
voluntary conveyance, *29*
"with recourse," *16*
workout, *26*

Useful Web Sites

www.alta.org—American Land Title Association—provides industry and government news, as well as an explanation of consumer interests in land titles.

www.mortgagemag.com—Includes real estate-related articles and links to sites covering mortgage banking, legal services, and technology.

http://dictionary.law.com—Legal dictionary.

http://real-estate-law.freeadvice.com—Many good FAQs about real estate law. Legal advice written by lawyers for nonlawyers.

Questions

1. Distinguish between a mortgage and a note.
2. What does it mean when a lender accelerates on a note? What is meant by forbearance?
3. Can borrowers pay off part, or all, of loans any time that they desire?
4. What does "nonrecourse" financing mean?
5. What does "assignment" mean and why would a lender want to assign a mortgage loan?
6. What is meant by a "purchase-money" mortgage loan? When could a loan not be a purchase-money mortgage loan?
7. What does default mean? Does it occur only when borrowers fail to make scheduled loan payments?
8. When might a borrower want to have another party assume his liability under a mortgage loan?
9. What does a deficiency judgment mean?
10. What is a land contract?
11. How can mechanics' liens achieve priority over first mortgages that were recorded prior to the mechanics' lien?
12. Name possible mortgageable interests in real estate and comment on their risk as collateral to lenders.
13. What is meant by mortgage foreclosure, and what alternatives are there to such action?
14. Explain the difference between a buyer assuming the mortgage and a buyer taking title "subject to" the mortgage.
15. What dangers are encountered by mortgagees and unreleased mortgagors when property is sold "subject to" a mortgage?
16. What is the difference between equity of redemption and statutory redemption?
17. What special advantages does a mortgagee have in bidding at the foreclosure sale where the mortgagee is the foreclosing party? How much will the mortgagee normally bid at the sale?
18. Is a foreclosure sale sometimes desirable or even necessary when the mortgagor is willing to give a voluntary deed?

19. What are the risks to the lender if a borrower declares bankruptcy?

20. What is a deficiency judgment and how is its value to a lender affected by the Bankruptcy Code?

Problems

1. Sedgewick arranged for an open-end construction loan from the Second National Bank not to exceed $50,000. The loan was closed and Sedgewick drew $30,000 initially. Three months later he drew the remaining $20,000. What is the bank's position concerning the possibility of intervening liens?

2. Last year Jones obtained a mortgage loan for $100,000. He just inherited a large sum of money and is contemplating prepaying the entire loan balance to save interest. What are his rights to prepay the loan?

3. Bob entered into a land contract to purchase real estate from Sam. The purchase price was to be paid over a 10-year period in monthly installments. At the end of five years, Bob defaulted, having failed to make his required payments. The contract provided that in event of default, the seller could declare a forfeiture after a period of 30 days and repossess the property. If the court should consider the land contract an equitable mortgage, what might be the rights of Bob and Sam?

4. Mr. Smith acquired a property consisting of one acre of land and a two-story building five years ago for $100,000. He also obtained an $80,000 mortgage loan from ACE Bank to provide financing to complete the purchase. This year, Mr. Smith constructed another building on the property with his own funds at a cost of $20,000. Mr. Smith has decided after completing the building to approach Duce Bank to borrow and mortgage the new building with a $16,000 loan. Is Duce Bank likely to provide the $16,000 in financing? What other options may Mr. Smith have to consider?

5. Ms. Brown purchased a property consisting of one acre of land and a building for $100,000 five years ago. She obtained an $80,000 mortgage loan from ABC Bank at that time. The building was very old and Ms. Brown has just had it torn down. She now wants to build a new building. Ms. Brown hopes to finance construction with ABC Bank and will call them soon to discuss financing the new project. How will ABC Bank evaluate the possibility of making another loan to Ms. Brown?

3

Mortgage Loan Foundations: The Time Value of Money

Financing the purchase of real estate usually involves borrowing on a long- or short-term basis. Because large amounts are usually borrowed in relation to the prices paid for real estate, financing costs are usually significant in amount and weigh heavily in the decision to buy property. Individuals involved in real estate finance must understand how these costs are computed and how various provisions in loan agreements affect financing costs and mortgage payments. Familiarity with the mathematics of compound interest is essential in understanding mortgage payment calculations, how loan provisions affect financing costs, and how borrowing decisions affect investment returns. It is also important for investment analysis calculations that we examine later in this text. This chapter provides an introduction to the mathematics of finance, sometimes referred to as the "time value of money," or TVM. It forms a basis for concepts discussed in financing single-family properties and income-producing properties, and in funding construction and development projects.

Compound Interest

Understanding the process of compounding in finance requires the knowledge of only a few basic formulas. At the root of these formulas is the most elementary relationship, **compound interest.** For example, if an individual makes a bank deposit of $10,000 that is compounded at an annual interest rate of 6 percent, what will be the value of the deposit at the end of one year? In examining this problem, one should be aware that any compounding problem has four basic components:

1. An initial deposit, or present value of an investment of money.
2. An interest rate.
3. Time.
4. Value at some specified future period.

In our problem, the deposit is $10,000, interest is to be earned at an annual rate of 6 percent, time is one year, and value at the end of the year is what we would like to know. We have four components, three of which are known and one that is unknown.

Compound or Future Value

In the preceding problem, we would like to determine what value will exist at the end of one year if a single deposit or payment of $10,000 is made at the beginning of the year and the deposit balance earns a 6 percent rate of interest annually. To find the solution, we must introduce some terminology:

PV = **present value,** or principal at the beginning of the year

i = the interest rate

I = dollar amount of interest earned during the year

FV = principal at the end of n years, or **future value**

n = number of years

In this problem, then, $PV = \$10,000$, $i = 6$ percent, $n =$ one year, and FV, or the value after one year, is what we would like to know.

The value after one year can be determined by examining the following relationship:

$$FV = PV + I_1$$

or the future value, FV, at the end of one year equals the deposit made at the beginning of the year, PV, plus the dollar amount of interest, I_1, earned in the first period. Because $PV = \$10,000$, we can find FV by determining I_1. Since we are compounding annually, FV is easily determined to be $10,600, which is shown in Exhibit 3–1.

Multiple Periods

To find the value at the end of two years, we continue the compounding process by taking the value at the end of one year, $10,600, making it the deposit at the beginning of the second year, and compounding again. This is shown in Exhibit 3–2.

EXHIBIT 3–1
Compound Interest Calculation for One Year

$$
\begin{aligned}
I_1 &= PV \times i \\
&= \$10,000(.06) \\
&= \$600
\end{aligned}
$$

Future value at the end of one year ($n = 1$ year) is determined as

$$
\begin{aligned}
FV &= PV + I_1 \\
&= \$10,000 + \$600 \\
&= \$10,600
\end{aligned}
$$

or

$$
\begin{aligned}
FV &= PV(1 + i) \\
&= \$10,000(1 + .06) \\
&= \$10,600
\end{aligned}
$$

EXHIBIT 3–2
Compound Interest
Calculation for
Two Years

$$\$10,600(.06) = I_2$$
$$\$636 = I_2$$

and value at the end of two years, or $n = 2$ years, is now

$$\$10,600 + I_2 = FV$$
$$\$10,600 + \$636 = \$11,236$$

Exhibit 3–2 shows that a total future value of $11,236 has been accumulated at the end of the second year. Note that in the second year, interest is earned not only on the original deposit of $10,000, but also on the interest ($600) that was earned during the first year. *The concept of earning interest on interest is an essential idea that must be understood in the compounding process and is the cornerstone of all financial tables and concepts in the mathematics of finance.*

From the computation in Exhibit 3–2, it should be pointed out that the value at the end of year 2 could have been determined directly from *PV* as follows:

$$FV = PV(1 + i)(1 + i)$$
$$= PV(1 + i)^2$$

In our problem, then, when $n = 2$ years

$$FV = PV(1 + i)^2$$
$$= \$10,000(1 + .06)^2$$
$$= \$10,000(1.123600)$$
$$= \$11,236$$

From this computation, the $11,236 value at the end of two years is identical to the result that we obtained in Exhibit 3–2. Being able to compute *FV* *directly* from *PV* is a very important relationship because it means that the future value, or value of any deposit or payment left to compound for any number of periods, can be determined from *PV* by simple multiplication. Therefore, if we want to determine the future value of a deposit made today that is left to compound for any number of years, we can find the solution with the general formula for compound interest, which is:

$$FV = PV(1 + i)^n$$

By substituting the appropriate values for *PV, i,* and *n,* we can determine *FV* for any desired number of years.[1]

Other Compounding Intervals

In the preceding section, the discussion of compounding applies to cases where funds were compounded only once per year. Many savings accounts, bonds, mortgages, and other investments provide for monthly, quarterly, or semiannual compounding. Because we will be covering mortgage loans extensively in a later chapter, which involve monthly compounding almost exclusively, it is very important that we consider the other compounding intervals.

[1] At this point, the reader may realize that these problems can be solved with a financial calculator or computer software. We will provide illustrations using notation and keystroke sequences that are consistent with the use of a financial calculator to solve many of the problems in this and other chapters in this book. The reader may choose to change this approach by using computer software in lieu of a financial calculator.

When compounding periods other than annual are considered, a simple modification can be made to the general formula for compound interest. To change the general formula:

$$FV = PV(1 + i)^n$$

where

$n =$ years

$i =$ annual interest rate

$PV =$ deposit

for any compounding period, we divide the annual interest rate (i) by the desired number of compounding intervals *within* one year. We then increase the number of time periods (n) by multiplying by the desired number of compounding intervals *within* one year. For example, let m be the number of intervals *within* one year in which compounding is to occur, and let n be the number of years in the general formula. Then, we have:

$$FV = PV\left[1 + \frac{i}{m}\right]^{n \cdot m}$$

Therefore, if interest is to be earned on the $10,000 deposit at an annual rate of 6 percent, *compounded monthly,* to determine the future value at the end of one year, where $m = 12$, we have:

$$FV = \$10,000\left[1 + \frac{.06}{12}\right]^{1 \cdot 12}$$

$$= \$10,000(1.061678)$$

$$= \$10,616.78$$

If we compare the results of monthly compounding with those from compounding annually, we can immediately see the benefits of monthly compounding. If our initial deposit is compounded monthly, we would have $10,616.78 at the end of the year, compared with $10,600.00 when annual compounding is used.

Another way of looking at this result is to compute an **effective annual yield (*EAY*)** on both investments. This is done by assuming that $10,000 is deposited at the beginning of the year and that all proceeds are withdrawn at the end of the year. For the deposit that is *compounded monthly,* we obtain:

$$EAY = \frac{FV - PV}{PV}$$

$$= \frac{\$10,616.78 - \$10,000.00}{\$10,000}$$

$$= 6.1678\%$$

The result can be compared with the effective annual yield obtained when *annual compounding* is used, or

$$EAY = \frac{\$10,600 - \$10,000}{\$10,000}$$

$$= 6\%$$

From this comparison, we can conclude that given the same nominal annual rate of interest, or 6 percent, the effective annual yield is higher when monthly compounding is used.

This comparison should immediately illustrate the difference between computing interest at a *nominal* annual rate of interest and computing interest at the same nominal annual rate of interest, *compounded monthly*. Both deposits are compounded at the same nominal annual rate of interest (6%); however, one is compounded 12 times at a monthly rate of (.06/12), or .005, on the ending monthly balance, while the other is compounded only once, at the end of the year at the rate of .06. It is customary in the United States to use a nominal rate of interest in contracts, savings accounts, mortgage notes, and other transactions. How payments will be made or interest accumulated (i.e., annually, monthly, daily) is then specified in the agreement. It is up to the parties involved in the transaction to ascertain the effective annual yield.

From the above analysis, one result should be very clear. Whenever the nominal annual interest rates offered on two investments are equal, the investment with the more frequent compounding interval within the year will always result in a higher effective annual yield. In our example, we could say that a 6 percent annual rate of interest compounded monthly provides an effective annual yield of 6.168 percent.

Other investments offer semiannual, quarterly, and daily compounding. In these cases, the basic formula for compound interest is modified as follows:

Nominal Annual Rate (%)	Compounding Interval		Modified Formula	Effective Annual Yield* (%)
6	Annually	$m = 1$	$FV = PV(1 + i)^{n \cdot 1}$	6.00
6	Semiannually	$m = 2$	$FV = PV\left[1 + \dfrac{i}{2}\right]^{n \cdot 2}$	6.09
6	Quarterly	$m = 4$	$FV = PV\left[1 + \dfrac{i}{4}\right]^{n \cdot 4}$	6.14
6	Monthly	$m = 12$	$FV = PV\left[1 + \dfrac{i}{12}\right]^{n \cdot 12}$	6.17
6	Daily	$m = 365$	$FV = PV\left[1 + \dfrac{i}{365}\right]^{n \cdot 365}$	6.18

*Also known as annual percentage yield (APY).

For example, if a deposit of $10,000 is made and an annual rate of 6 percent compounded daily is to be earned, we have:

$$FV = \$10,000\left[1 + \frac{.06}{365}\right]^{1 \cdot 365}$$
$$= \$10,000(1.061831)$$
$$= \$10,618.31$$

and the effective annual yield would be $\dfrac{\$10,618.31 - \$10,000}{\$10,000} = 6.1831$ percent. If the money was left on deposit for two years, the exponent would change to 2×365, and *FV* at the end of two years would be $11,274.86.

Many banks and savings institutions disclose what is referred to as the **APY (annual percentage yield)** on CDs, checking accounts, and so on. Conceptually, the effective annual yield shown here and the APY are generally the same. However, federal regulations require banks to include certain fees and penalties when applicable. Such fees could make the APY differ from the effective annual yield in our examples.

Throughout this book, we will follow the convention of using nominal rates of interest in all problems, examples, and exhibits. Hence, the term *interest rate* means a *nominal, annual rate of interest*. This means that when comparing two alternatives with *different* compounding intervals, the nominal interest rate should not be used as the basis for comparisons. In these cases, the concept of effective annual yield should be used when developing solutions.

Calculating Compound Interest Factors

Finding a solution to a compounding problem involving many periods is very awkward because of the amount of multiplication required. Calculators that are programmed with compound interest functions eliminate much of the detail of financial calculations. Another approach for finding solutions to compound interest problems can be used by calculating interest factors that can be used to solve many problems. *We will illustrate how these factors are calculated so the reader will understand the link between the mathematics of finance and calculators that have been programmed to provide solutions more efficiently. We also do this so that in the event that problems with many parts and multiple inputs must be solved, the reader may break the problem down and solve it in steps by using the necessary factors.*

To become familiar with the factors for various interest rates, recall that, in the problem discussed earlier, we wanted to determine the future value of a $10,000 deposit compounded at an annual rate of 6 percent after one year. Looking at the 6 percent column in Exhibit 3–3 corresponding to the row for one year, we find the interest factor 1.060000. When multiplied by $10,000, this interest factor gives us the solution to our problem.

$$FV = \$10,000(1.060000)$$
$$= \$10,600$$

The interest factor for the future value of $1, at 6 percent for one year, is 1.060000—the same result had we computed $(1 + .06)^1$, or 1.06 from the general formula for compound interest. In other words,

$$(1 + .06)^1 = 1.06$$

Calculators can be used to determine interest factors in Exhibit 3–3 for many combinations of interest rates and time periods. These factors allow us to find a solution to any compounding problem as long as we know the deposit (PV), the interest rate (i), and the number of periods (n) over which annual compounding is to occur. For example, by using keystrokes on a calculator, we can calculate the factor for 6 percent interest and one year as follows:

EXHIBIT 3–3
Interest Factors for an Amount of $1 at Compound Interest for Various Interest Rates and Compounding Periods

		Rate		
Year	6%	10%	15%	20%
1	1.060000	1.100000	1.150000	1.200000
2	1.123600	1.210000	1.322500	1.440000
3	1.191016	1.331000	1.520875	1.728000
4	1.262477	1.464100	1.749006	2.073600
5	1.338226	1.610510	2.011357	2.488320

$$PV = \$1$$

$$i = 6\%$$

$$n = 1$$

$$PMT = 0$$

Solve for FV $= 1.06$

Similarly, if we wanted the factor for 10 percent interest and four years, we would have:

$$PV = \$1$$

$$i = 10\%$$

$$n = 4$$

$$PMT = 0$$

Solve for FV $= 1.464100$

Question: What is the future value of $5,000 deposited for four years compounded at an annual rate of 10 percent?

Solution: $FV = \$5,000(1.464100)$
                    $= \$7,320.50$

As was the case with the interest factors for annual compounding, interest factors for *monthly* compounding for selected interest rates and years have been computed from the modified formula $PV(1 + i/12)^{n \cdot 12}$ and are compiled in Exhibit 3–4. To familiarize the student with these interest factors, in Exhibit 3–4 selected interest rates and periods have been chosen and factors have been calculated.

EXHIBIT 3–4
Interest Factors for an Amount of $1 at Compound Interest for Various Interest Rates and Compounding Periods

	Rate		
Month	6%	8%	
1	1.005000	1.006670	
2	1.010025	1.013378	
3	1.015075	1.020134	
4	1.020151	1.026935	
5	1.025251	1.033781	
6	1.030378	1.040673	
7	1.035529	1.047610	
8	1.040707	1.054595	
9	1.045911	1.061625	
10	1.051140	1.068703	
11	1.056396	1.075827	
12	1.061678	1.083000	
Year			Month
1	1.061678	1.083000	12
2	1.127160	1.172888	24
3	1.196681	1.270237	36
4	1.270489	1.375666	48

In our earlier problem, we wanted to determine the future value of a $10,000 deposit that earned interest at an annual rate of 6 percent, compounded *monthly*. This can be easily determined by choosing the factor for 6 percent and 12 months, or one year, in Exhibit 3–4. That factor is 1.061678. Hence, to determine the value of the deposit at the end of 12 months, or one year, we have

$$FV = \$10,000(1.061678)$$

$$= \$10,616.78$$

In other words, the interest factor for a 6 percent rate of interest compounded *monthly* for one year is 1.061678, which is the same result that we would obtain if we expanded $(1 + .06/12)^{1 \cdot 12}$ by multiplying, or

$$\left[1 + \frac{.06}{12}\right]^{1.12} = 1.061678$$

Question: What is the future value of a single $5,000 deposit earning 8 percent interest, *compounded monthly*, at the end of two years?

Solution: $FV = \$5,000\left[1 + \dfrac{.08}{12}\right]^{2 \cdot 12}$

$$= \$5,000(1.172888)$$

$$= \$5,864.44$$

Using Financial Functions: Calculators and Spreadsheets

Finding a solution to a compounding problem involving many periods may be greatly simplified with the use of a calculator. Calculators programmed with compound interest functions eliminate the need for financial tables for many problem situations. Spreadsheets such as Excel are programmed with functions that allow users to input financial variables and solve. We will present alternative solutions to most of the time value of money problems in the remainder of this text using a general function that corresponds to the format of a financial calculator. Refer to your specific calculator manual to confirm whether all operations are similar. Unless specified otherwise, the solutions assume that payments are made at the *end* of each period, and that money spent is $(-)$ and money received is $(+)$. When solving problems, we will use the following format:

$n =$ number of years, unless stated otherwise

$i =$ interest rate per year, unless stated otherwise

$PV =$ present value

$PMT =$ payments

$FV =$ future value

Solutions will follow the format above, with the unknown variable being solved listed last. Most calculations are carried out to at least six decimal places, then final monetary amounts are rounded back to two decimal places.

For example, in the problem discussed earlier, we wanted to determine the future value of a $10,000 deposit compounded at an annual rate of 6 percent after one year.

With the advent of technology, calculations involving the TVM and related concepts in mortgage lending, valuation, and investments have been greatly simplified. Many TVM and related concepts involve equations with exponents, which can make derivations and solving for solutions cumbersome. Professionals in the field of finance have come to use either, or both, *financial calculators* and *computer software* (Excel) that are programmed and allow computations to be made much quicker and efficiently.

What follows is a glossary of functions that are used frequently in the chapters that follow. The reader should become familiar with these functions and the notation.

PMT (n, i, PV, FV)—Function to calculate level payments (annuity) that occur over a specified time period that have a specified present value and may include a final payment in the future.

PV (n, i, PMT, FV)—Function to calculate the present value of level payments (annuity) and/or an amount to be received at a single point in time in the future.

FV (n, i, PV, PMT)—Function to calculate the future value of an annuity and/or level payments (annuity) that occur over a specified time period.

i (n, PV, PMT, FV)—Function to calculate the interest rate (also an IRR) that would be achieved on an investment made in the present that will have level payments over time and/or a future value at the end of the specified investment period (*n*).

n (i, PV, PMT, FV)—Function to calculate the number of periods (*n*) required to repay a loan (*PV*) at a specified rate of interest (*i*) for various future values (zero, non zero).

Notes:

1. Values for variables in these functions must be adjusted for frequency of receipts and disbursements as well as compounding and discounting intervals within a year.

2. In the most basic applications, these variables are assumed to be constant with respect to time. In those problems requiring that some variables (e.g., *PMT*) be allowed to vary from period to period, we will provide the proper approach to modify functions and solve for solutions as needed.

3. It will become apparent to the reader after solving TVM and related problems that a recurring pattern occurs. This pattern usually involves one equation containing *five* variables: *i, n, PV, FV*, and *PMT*. Most problems provide values (inputs) for *four* of these variables, leaving one unknown for which a solution is being sought. (See glossary of functions above where the variable listed to the left of the parenthesis is the unknown.) This notation should enable the reader to identify the unknown variable more readily.

Solution:		Function:
$n = 1$ year		FV (n, i, PV, PMT)
$i = 6\%$		
$PMT = 0$		
$PV = -\$10,000$		
Solve for FV $= \$10,600$		

(Note that this solution is the same as what would have been obtained had we calculated the factor 1.060000 shown in Exhibit 3–3. However, when a calculator is used, the intermediate step in which interest factors are calculated is eliminated.)

The same problem compounded monthly would follow the format listed below. Note: Several calculators include a function for a number of periods. In such cases, the number

Web App

What rate can you earn on your savings today? Go to a Web site like **www.bankrate.com** that has interest rates on certificates of deposit (CDs) and see what the current rate is for a five-year CD. Assuming you have $10,000 today, how much will that accumulate to after five years at the rate you found on the Web site?

of periods and interest are typically stated on an annual basis, and the number of periods is entered separately.

Solution:	Function:
n = 12 (1 year × 12 periods per year)	FV (i, n, PV, PMT)
i = .5% (6%/12 periods per year)	
PMT = 0	
PV = −$10,000	
Solve for FV = $10,616.78	

(Note that this solution is the same as what would have been obtained had we calculated the factor 1.061678 shown in Exhibit 3–4.)

The same problem *compounded daily* would look like this.

Solution:	Function:
n = 365 (1 year × 365 periods per year)	FV (i, n, PV, PMT)
i = .0164 (6%/365 periods per year)	
PMT = 0	
PV = −$10,000	
Solve for FV = $10,618.31	

Question: What is the future value of $5,000 deposited for four years *compounded annually* at a rate of 10 percent?

Solution:	Function:
n = 4 years	FV (PV, i, n, PMT)
i = 10%	
PMT = 0	
PV = −$5,000	
Solve for FV = $7,320.50	

Question: What is the future value of a single $5,000 deposit earning 8 percent interest, *compounded monthly,* at the end of two years?

Solution:	Function:
n = 24 (2 years × 12 periods)	FV (PV, i, n, PMT)
i = .666% (8%/12 periods)	
PMT = 0	
PV = −$5,000	
Solve for FV = $5,864.44	

Present Value

In the preceding section, we were concerned with determining value at some time in the *future;* that is, we considered the case where a deposit had been made and compounded into the future to yield some unknown future value.

In this section, we are interested in the problem of knowing the future cash receipts for an investment and of determining how much should be paid for the investment at *present.* The concept of **present value** is based on the idea that money has time value. Time value simply means that if an investor is offered the choice between receiving $1 today or receiving $1 in the future, the proper choice will always be to receive the $1 today because this $1 can be invested in some opportunity that will earn interest, which is always preferable to receiving only $1 in the future. In this sense, money is said to have *time value.*

When determining how much should be paid *today* for an investment that is expected to produce income in the *future,* we must apply an adjustment called **discounting** to income received in the future to reflect the time value of money. The concept of present value lays the cornerstone for calculating mortgage payments, determining the true cost of mortgage loans, and finding the value of an income property, all of which are very important concepts in real estate finance.

A Graphic Illustration of Present Value

An example of how discounting becomes an important concept in financing can be seen from the following problem. Suppose an individual is considering an investment that promises a cash return of $10,600 at the end of one year. The investor believes this investment should yield an annual rate of 6 percent. The question is how much should the investor pay *today* if $10,600 is to be received at the *end* of the year and the investor requires a 6 percent return compounded annually on the amount invested?

The problem can be seen more clearly by comparing it with the problem of finding the compound value of $1 discussed in the first part of this chapter. In that discussion, we were concerned with finding the future value of a $10,000 deposit compounded monthly at 6 percent for one year. This comparison is depicted in Exhibit 3–5.

In Exhibit 3–5 note that with compounding, we are concerned with determining the *future value* of an investment. With discounting, we are concerned with just the opposite concept; that is, what *present value* or *price* should be paid *today* for a particular investment, assuming a desired rate of interest is to be earned?

Because we know from the preceding section that $10,000 compounded annually at a rate of 6 percent results in a future value of $10,600 at the end of one year, $10,000 is the present value of this investment. However, had we not done the compounding problem in the preceding section, how would we know that $10,000 equals the present value of the investment? Let us again examine the compounding problem considered in the previous section. To determine future value, recall the general equation for compound interest:

$$FV = PV(1 + i)^n$$

EXHIBIT 3–5
Comparison of Future Value and Present Value

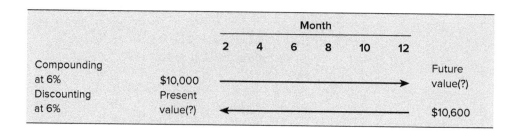

In our present value problem, *PV* becomes the *unknown* because *FV*, or the future value to be received at the end of one year, $n = 1$ year, is *known* to be \$10,600. Because the interest rate (i) is also known to be 6 percent, *PV* is the only value that is not known. *PV*, the present value or amount we should pay for the investment today, can be easily determined by rearranging terms in the above compounding formula as follows:

$$FV = PV(1+i)^n$$

$$PV = FV \frac{1}{(1+i)^n}$$

In our problem, then, we can determine *PV* directly by substituting the known values into the above expression as follows:

$$PV = FV \frac{1}{(1+i)^n}$$

$$= \$10,600 \frac{1}{(1+.06)^1}$$

$$= \$10,600 \frac{1}{1.06}$$

$$= \$10,600 \times (.943396)$$

$$= \$10,000$$

Note that the procedure used in solving for the present value is simply to multiply the future value, *FV*, by 1 divided by $(1 + i)^n$. We know from the section on compounding that in our problem $(1 + i)^n$ is $(1 + .06)^1$, which equals 1.06. Dividing 1 by 1.06 yields .943396. This result is important in present value analysis because it shows the relationship between future value and present value.

Because we see from Exhibit 3–5 that the discounting process is the opposite of compounding, to find the present value of any investment is simply to compound in a "reverse sense." This is done in our problem by taking the reciprocal of the interest factor for the compound value of \$1 at 6 percent, $1 \div 1.06$ or .943396, and multiplying it by the future value of the investment to find its present value. We can now say that \$10,600 received at the end of one year, when discounted by 6 percent, has a present value of \$10,000. Alternatively, if we are offered an investment that promises to yield \$10,600 after one year and we want to earn a 6 percent annual return, we should not pay more than \$10,000 for the investment (it is on the \$10,000 present value that we earn the 6 percent interest).

Calculating Present Value Interest Factors

Because the discounting process is the reverse of compounding, and the interest factor for discounting $1 \div (1 + i)^n$ is simply the reciprocal of the interest factor for compounding, a series of present value interest factors have been developed. Exhibit 3–6 contains a sample of factors to be used when discounting.

In our problem, we want to know how much should be paid for an investment with a future value of \$10,600 to be received at the end of one year if the investor demands an annual return of 6 percent. The solution can be found by calculating or selecting .943396 from the 6 percent column in Exhibit 3–6. The \$10,600 future value can now be multiplied by .943396, resulting in a present value (*PV*) of \$10,000. To help the reader understand

EXHIBIT 3–6
Interest Factors for the Present Value Reversion of $1 for Various Interest Rates and Time Periods

Year	Rate		
	6%	10%	15%
1	.943396	.909091	.869565
2	.889996	.826446	.756144
3	.839619	.751315	.657516
4	.792094	.683013	.571753
5	.747258	.620921	.497177
6	.704961	.564474	.432328
7	.665057	.513158	.375937

these concepts, this present value factor also may be determined using a financial calculator as follows:

Solution:	Function:
$n = 1$ year	$PV(n, i, PMT, FV)$
$i = 6\%$	
$PMT = \$0$	
$FV = \$1$	
Solve for $PV = .943396$	

Question: How much should an investor pay today for a real estate investment that will return $20,000 at the end of three years, assuming the investor desires an annual return of 15 percent interest on the amount invested?

Solution: $PV = \$20{,}000 \times \dfrac{1}{(1 + .15)^3}$

$= \$20{,}000(.657516)$

$= \$13{,}150.32$

The investor should pay no more than $13,150.32 today for the investment promising a return of $20,000 after three years if a 15 percent return on investment is desired.[2]

Expanding the Use of Calculators for Finding Present Values

As was the case with compounding, financial calculators allow us to calculate present value solutions *directly*, as they have been programmed to calculate factors internally and then complete the required operations to present a final answer. Our problem can be solved with a calculator as follows:

[2] An accepted convention in finance is that when one refers to a percentage return on investment, a nominal annual interest rate is assumed. If solutions are computed based on different compounding intervals within a year, such as monthly, the solution should be designated as an *annual rate of interest compounded monthly.* The latter solution may then be converted, if desired, to an effective annual yield, as shown previously.

Solution:

Function:

$$n = 3 \text{ years}$$
$$i = 15\%$$
$$PMT = 0$$
$$FV = \$20{,}000$$
Solve for PV $= -\$13{,}150.32$

PV (FV, PMT, n, i)

Because we can use the discounting process to find the present value of a future value when *annual* compounding is assumed, we can also apply the same methodology assuming *monthly* discounting. For example, in our illustration involving monthly compounding, the future value of $10,000 at an annual rate of interest of 6 percent compounded monthly was $10,616.80. An important question an investor should consider is how much should be paid today for the future value of $10,616.80 received at the end of one year, assuming that a 6 percent return compounded *monthly* is required?

We could answer this question by finding the reciprocal of the formula used to compound monthly, $1 \div (1 + i/12)^{1 \cdot 12}$, and multiply that result by the future value of $10,616.80 to find the present value (*PV*). We may calculate this factor with a calculator as:

Solution:

Function:

$$FV = \$1$$
$$PMT = 0$$
$$n = 12 \text{ months}$$
$$i = 6\% \div 12$$
Solve for PV $= .941905$

PV (FV, PMT, n, i)

Many factors have been calculated and included in the table shown in Exhibit 3–7.

In our problem, we want to determine the present value of $10,616.80 received at the end of one year, assuming a desired rate of return of 6 percent, compounded monthly. By going to the 6 percent column and the row corresponding to one year (12 months) and selecting the interest factor .941905, we can now multiply $10,616.80 × (.941905) = $10,000 and see that $10,000 is the maximum amount one should pay today for the investment.

Alternatively, if the reader is comfortable with the derivation of these interest factors and the discounting process, a solution may be found more directly with a calculator as follows:

Solution:

Function:

$$n = 1 \text{ year} \times 12 \text{ periods} = 12$$
$$i = 6\% \div 12 \text{ periods} = .5\%$$
$$PMT = 0$$
$$FV = 10{,}616.80$$
Solve for PV $= -\$10{,}000$

PV (n, i, PMT, FV)

EXHIBIT 3–7
Interest Factors for the Present Value Reversion of $1 for Various Interest Rates and Time Periods

Month	Rate		
	6%	8%	9%
1	.995025	.993377	.992556
2	.990075	.986799	.985167
3	.985149	.980264	.977833
4	.980248	.973772	.970554
5	.975371	.967323	.963329
6	.970518	.960917	.956158
7	.965690	.954553	.949040
8	.960885	.948232	.941975
9	.956105	.941952	.934963
10	.951348	.935714	.928003
11	.946615	.929517	.921095
12	.941905	.923361	.914238

Year	6%	8%	9%	Month
1	.941905	.923361	.914238	12
2	.887186	.852596	.835831	24
3	.835645	.787255	.764149	36
4	.787098	.726921	.698614	48

Question: How much should an investor pay to receive $12,000 three years (36 months) from now, assuming that the investor desires an annual return of 9 percent compounded *monthly?*

Solution: $PV = \$12,000(.764149)$
               $= \$9,169.79$

Solution:

$$n = 3 \times 12 = 36$$
$$i = 9\% \div 12 = .75\%$$
$$PMT = 0$$
$$FV = 12,000$$
$$\text{Solve for } PV = -\$9,169.79$$

Function:

$PV(n, i, PMT, FV)$

The investor should pay no more than $9,169.79 for the investment, or the present value (*PV*) of the investment is $9,169.79.

Compound or Future Value of an Annuity

The first section of this chapter dealt with finding the compound or future value of a *single deposit* or payment made only once, at the beginning of a period. An equally relevant consideration involves a series of equal deposits or payments made at equal intervals. For example, assume deposits of $1,000 are made at the *end* of each year for a period of five years and interest is compounded at an annual rate of 5 percent. What is the future value at the end of the period for a series of deposits plus all compound interest? In this case, the problem involves equal payments (*P*) or deposits made at equal time intervals. This series of deposits or payments is defined as an **annuity.** Because we know how to find the answer to a problem where only one deposit is made, it is logical and correct to assume that the same basic compounding process applies when dealing with annuities. However, that process is only a partial solution to the problem because we are dealing with a series of deposits that occur annually.

To compute the sum of all deposits made in each succeeding year and include compound interest on deposits only when it is earned, the general formula for compounded interest must be expanded as follows:

$$FV = P(1+i)^{n-1} + P(1+i)^{n-2} + \cdots + P$$

This may also be written as

$$FV = P \cdot \sum_{t=1}^{n-1} (1+i)^t + P$$

which simply means that we may take the constant payment or annuity *P* and multiply it by the "sum of" the series $1 + i$ expanded from time $t = 1$ to the period $n - 1$, plus *P*.[3] Hence, the symbol Σ represents the "sum of" that series and is simply a shortcut notation to be used in place of writing $1 + i$ repetitively.

In this expression, *FV* is now **future value of an annuity,** or the sum of all deposits, *P*, compounded at an annual rate, *i,* for *n* years. The important thing to note in the expression, however, is that each deposit is assumed to be at the *end* of each year and is compounded through year *n.* The final deposit does not earn interest because it occurs at the end of the final year. Since we are dealing in our example with a series of $1,000 deposits made over a five-year period, the first $1,000 deposit is compounded for four periods ($n - 1$), the $1,000 deposit made at the beginning of the second year is compounded for three periods ($n - 2$), and so on, until the last deposit, *P*, is reached. The last deposit is not compounded because it is deposited at the end of the fifth year.[4]

To compute the value of these deposits, we could construct a solution like that shown in Exhibit 3–8. Note that each $1,000 deposit is compounded from the end of the year in which the deposit was made to the end of the next year. In other words, as shown in our expanded formula above, the deposit at the end of year 1 is compounded for four years, the deposit made at the beginning of the second year is compounded for three years, and so on. By carrying this process out one year at a time, we determined the solution, or $5,525.63, when the compounded amounts in the extreme right-hand column are added.

Although the future value of $1,000 per period can be determined in the manner shown in Exhibit 3–8, careful examination of the compounding process reveals another, easier way to find the solution. Note that the $1,000 deposit occurs annually and never changes; it is constant. When the deposits are constant, it is possible to sum all of the individual interest factors (*IF*s) as 5.525631. By multiplying $1,000 by 5.525631, a solution of $5,525.63 is obtained, as shown at the bottom of the right-hand column in Exhibit 3–8.

---

[3] The formula shown here is the formula for an **ordinary annuity,** which assumes that all deposits are made at the *end* of each year. The final *P* in the expression means that the last payment is not compounded.

[4] The reader should be aware that this formulation is used for *ordinary annuities* or when payments or receipts occur at the end of a period. This is different from the formula for an **annuity due,** which assumes that deposits are made at the *beginning* of a period.

EXHIBIT 3–8

Interest Factors for the Future Value of an Annuity of $1,000 per Year Compounded at 5 Percent Annually

Year	Deposit		Interest Factor	Future Value	
1	$1,000	×	1.215506	=	$1,215.51*
2	1,000	×	1.157625	=	1,157.63*
3	1,000	×	1.102500	=	1,102.50
4	1,000	×	1.050000	=	1,050.00
5	1,000	×	1.000000	=	1,000.00
	Also 1,000	×	5.525631	=	$5,525.63*

*Rounded.

Use of Compound Interest Factors for Annuities

Because the *IF*s in Exhibit 3–8 can be *added* when annuities are being considered, a series of new interest factors have been calculated for various interest rates. A sample of these factors has been compiled in Exhibit 3–9.

In the problem at hand, to determine the future value of $1,000 deposited annually at 5 percent for five years, note that if we go to the 5 percent column in Exhibit 3–9 and obtain the *IF* that corresponds to five years, we can find the solution to our problem as follows:

$$FV = \$1,000(5.525631)$$
$$= \$5,525.63$$

This amount corresponds to the solution obtained from the long series of multiplications carried out in Exhibit 3–8.

As we have explained, for those readers who understand the compounding process and the equations discussed in the sections above, financial calculators programmed to perform and store the necessary steps for compounding annuities may be used to obtain an answer more directly as follows:

Solution:	Function:
$n = 5$	$FV(n, i, PV, PMT)$
$i = 5\%$	
$PV = 0$	
$PMT = -\$1,000$	
Solve for $FV = \$5,525.63$	

EXHIBIT 3–9

Interest Factors for the Accumulation of $1 per Period for Various Interest Rates and Time Periods

Year	Rate		
	5%	6%	10%
1	1.000000	1.000000	1.000000
2	2.050000	2.060000	2.100000
3	3.152500	3.183600	3.310000
4	4.310125	4.374616	4.641000
5	5.525631	5.637093	6.105100
6	6.801913	6.975319	7.715610
7	8.142008	8.393838	9.487171
8	9.549109	9.897468	11.435888

Question: What is the future value of $800 deposited each year for six years, compounded annually at 10 percent interest after six years?

Solution: $FV = \$800(7.715610)$

$\qquad\qquad = \$6,172.49$

Solution:	Function:
$n = 6$	$FV(n, i, PV, PMT)$
$i = 10\%$	
$PV = 0$	
$PMT = -\$800$	
Solve for FV $= \$6,172.49$	

The same procedure used for compounding annuities for amounts deposited or paid annually can also be applied to monthly annuities. A very simple modification can be made to the formulation used for annual annuities by substituting $i/12$ in place of i and adding the number of compounding periods per year (m) in the annual formulation, as follows:

$$FV = P\left[1 + \frac{i}{12}\right]^{n\cdot m - 1} + P\left[1 + \frac{i}{12}\right]^{n\cdot m - 2} + \cdots + P$$

or

$$FV = P \cdot \sum_{t=1}^{n\cdot m - 1}\left[1 + \frac{i}{12}\right]^{t} + P$$

However, in this formulation, $n\cdot m$ represents months. Deposits or payments, P, are made monthly and are constant in amount. Hence, the interest factors used to compound each monthly deposit may be added (as they were for annual deposits in Exhibit 3–8), and a new series for compounding monthly annuities can be computed. This has been done for selected interest rates and years.[5]

Question: An investor pays $200 per month into a real estate investment that promises to pay an annual rate of interest of 8 percent compounded *monthly*. If the investor makes consecutive monthly payments for five years, what is the future value at the end of five years?

Solution: $FV = \$200(73.476856)$

$\qquad\qquad = \$14,695.37$

[5] Like annual compounding, this formulation assumes that deposits are made at the *end* of each month, or that an *ordinary annuity* is being compounded.

Solution:

$$n = 5 \times 12 = 60 \text{ months}$$
$$i = 8\%/12 = .666\%$$
$$PV = 0$$
$$PMT = -\$200$$

Solve for FV $= \$14,695.37$

Function:

FV (n, i, PV, PMT)

In this case, the value of payments earning interest at an annual rate of 8 percent compounded monthly = $14,695.37.

Present Value of an Annuity

In the preceding section, our primary concern was to determine the future value of an annuity, or constant payments received at equal time intervals. In this section, we consider the **present value of an annuity,** or the series of annual income receipts the investment produces over time. Because an investor may have to consider a series of income payments when deciding whether to invest, this is an important problem. Recall that when dealing with the present value of a single receipt, or ending value, *PV,* we took the basic formula for compounding interest and rearranged it to determine the present value of an investment as follows:

$$FV = PV(1+i)^n$$

$$PV = FV \div (1+i)^n$$

$$PV = FV \cdot \frac{1}{(1+i)^n}$$

To consider the present value of an annuity, we need only consider the sum of individual present value for all payments/receipts. This can be done by modifying the basic present value formula as follows:

$$PV = PMT\frac{1}{(1+i)^1} + PMT\frac{1}{(1+i)^2} + PMT\frac{1}{(1+i)^3} + \cdots + PMT\frac{1}{(1+i)^n}$$

or this can be written as

$$PV = PMT \cdot \sum_{t=1}^{n} \frac{1}{(1+i)^t}$$

Note in this expression that each payment (*PMT*) is discounted for the number of years corresponding to the time when the funds were actually received. In other words, the first payment would occur at the end of the first period and would be discounted only one period, or $PMT \cdot [1 \div (1+i)^1]$. The second receipt would be discounted for two periods, or $PMT \cdot [1 \div (1+i)^2]$, and so on.

Assuming an individual is considering an investment that will provide a series of annual cash receipts of $500 for a period of six years, and the investor desires a 6 percent return, how much should the investor pay for the investment today? We can begin by considering the present value of the $500 receipt in year 1, as shown in Exhibit 3–10. Note that the present value of the $500 receipt is discounted for one year at 6 percent.

EXHIBIT 3–10
Present Value of $500 per Year (discounted at 6 percent annually)

Year	PMT	IF		Present Value
1	$500 ×	.943396	= $	471.70
2	500 ×	.889996	=	445.00
3	500 ×	.839619	=	419.81
4	500 ×	.792094	=	396.05
5	500 ×	.747258	=	373.63
6	500 ×	.704961	=	352.48
	Also $500 × 4.917324		=	$2,458.66†

†Rounded.

This is done because the income of $500 for the first year is not received until the end of the first period, and our investor only wants to pay an amount today (present value) that will assure a 6 percent return on the amount paid today. Therefore, by discounting this $500 payment by the interest factor for 6 percent, or .943396, the present value is $471.70. Note that the second $500 income payment is received at the end of the second year. Therefore, it should be discounted for *two* years at 6 percent. Its present value is found by multiplying $500 by the interest factor for 6 percent for two years, or .889996, giving a present value of $445. This process can be continued for each receipt for the remaining three years (see Exhibit 3–10). The present value of the entire series of $500 income payments can be found by adding the series of receipts discounted each month in the far right-hand column, which totals $2,458.66.

However, because the $500 series of payments is constant, we may simply sum all interest factors to obtain one interest factor that can be multiplied by $500 to obtain the same present value (see Exhibit 3–10). The sum of all interest factors for 6 percent is 4.917324. When 4.917324 is multiplied by $500, the present value, $2,458.66, found in the lengthy series of multiplications carried out in Exhibit 3–10, is again determined.

Now that the reader has been introduced to the equations and interest factors that result from these equations, a solution can be found directly using a financial calculator as follows:

Solution:	Function:
$n = 6$	$PV(n, i, FV, PMT)$
$i = 6\%$	
$PMT = -\$500$	
$FV = 0$	
Solve for $PV = \$2,458.66$	

Use of the Present Value of an Annuity Factors

As we have illustrated, the interest factors in Exhibit 3–10 may be summed, as long as the income payments are equal in amount and received at equal intervals. The sums of *IF*s for various interest rates have been compiled in table form and are listed in Exhibit 3–11. In our problem, we want to determine the present value of $500 received annually for six years, assuming a desired annual rate of return of 6 percent. How much should an investor pay for this total investment today and be assured of earning the desired return? We can solve this problem by computing the solution with a calculator or by looking at Exhibit 3–11, finding the 6 percent column, and looking down the column until we locate the *IF* in the row corresponding to six years, which is 4.917324. Thus,

EXHIBIT 3–11
Interest Factors for the Present Value of an Ordinary Annuity of $1 per Period for Various Interest Rates and Time Periods

Year	Rate			
	5%	**6%**	**10%**	**15%**
1	.952381	.943396	.909091	.869565
2	1.859410	1.833393	1.735537	1.625709
3	2.723248	2.673012	2.486852	2.283225
4	3.545951	3.465106	3.169865	2.854978
5	4.329477	4.212364	3.790787	3.352155
6	5.075692	4.917324	4.355261	3.784483
7	5.786373	5.582381	4.868419	4.160420
8	6.463213	6.209794	5.334926	4.487322

$$PV = \$500(4.917324)$$
$$= \$2,458.66$$

This solution corresponds to that obtained in Exhibit 3–10.

Question: An investor has an opportunity to invest in a rental property that will provide net cash returns of $400 per year for three years. The investor believes that an annual return of 10 percent should be earned on this investment. How much should the investor pay for the rental property?

Solution: $PV = \$400(2.486852)$
             $= \$994.74$

The investor should pay no more than $994.74 for the investment property. With that amount, a 10 percent return will be earned.

A more direct solution to this problem can be found by using a financial calculator as follows:

Solution:	Function:
$n = 3$	$PV\,(n,\,i,\,PMT,\,FV)$
$i = 10\%$	
$PMT = -\$400$	
$FV = 0$	
Solve for $PV = \$994.74$	

Based on the logic used in discounting annuities paid or received annually, the same procedure can be applied to cash receipts paid or received *monthly*. In this case, the formula used to discount annual annuities is simply modified to reflect monthly receipts or payments, and the discounting interval is changed to reflect monthly compounding:

$$PV = P\left[\frac{1}{1+\dfrac{i}{12}}\right]^1 + P\left[\frac{1}{1+\dfrac{i}{12}}\right]^2 + \cdots + P\left[\frac{1}{1+\dfrac{i}{12}}\right]^{12 \cdot n}$$

where payments (*P*) occur monthly, the exponents represent months running from 1 through *n·m*, and *PV* now represents the present value of an annuity received over *n·m* months.

Like annual discounting, computation of the present value of an annuity can be very cumbersome if one has to expand the above formula for each problem, particularly if the problem involves cash receipts or payments over many months. Hence, a series of interest factors have been computed by expanding the above formula for each monthly interval and adding the resulting interest factors (this was performed with discounting annual annuities in Exhibit 3–10). Like the annual tables, the factors in Exhibit 3–12 are labeled *Present Value of an Ordinary Annuity of $1 per Period* because the period in this case is one month. Hence, if an investor wants to know how much he or she should pay today for an investment that would pay $500 at the end of each month for the next 12 months and earn an annual rate of return of 6 percent compounded monthly on the investment, the investor can easily compute the solution with a calculator or determine it by consulting Exhibit 3–12. Looking to the 6 percent column and dropping down to the row corresponding to 12 months, you find the factor 11.618932. Multiplying $500 by 11.618932 results in $5,809.47, or the amount that the investor should pay today if a 6 percent rate of return compounded monthly is desired.

The calculator solution would be:

Solution:	Function:
$n = 12$ months	$PV\,(n,\,i,\,PMT,\,FV)$
$i = 6\% \div 12 = .005$	
$PMT = \$500$	
$FV = 0$	
Solve for $PV = \$5,809.47$	

EXHIBIT 3–12
Interest Factors for the Present Value of an Ordinary Annuity of $1 per Period for Various Interest Rates and Time Periods

Month	Rate 6%	Rate 8%	
1	.995025	.993377	
2	1.985099	1.980176	
3	2.970248	2.960440	
4	3.950496	3.934212	
5	4.925866	4.901535	
6	5.896384	5.862452	
7	6.862074	6.817005	
8	7.882959	7.765237	
9	8.779064	8.707189	
10	9.730412	9.642903	
11	10.677027	10.572420	
12	11.618932	11.495782	
Year			Month
1	11.618932	11.495782	12
2	22.562866	22.110544	24
3	32.871016	31.911806	36
4	42.580318	40.961913	48

Question: A real estate partnership predicts that it will pay $300 at the end of each month to its partners over the next six months. Assuming the partners desire an 8 percent return compounded monthly on their investment, how much should they pay?

Solution: $PV = \$300(5.862452)$
$$= \$1,758.74$$

Solution:	Function:
$n = 6$ months	$PV\ (n,\ i,\ PMT,\ FV)$
$i = 8\% \div 12 = .6666\%$	
$PMT = -\$300$	
$FV = 0$	
Solve for $PV = \$1,758.74$	

Accumulation of a Future Sum

The previous two sections have dealt with compounding and discounting single payments on annuities. In some instances, however, it is necessary to determine a series of payments necessary to *accumulate a future sum,* taking into account the fact that such payments will be accumulating interest as they are deposited. For example, assume we have a debt of $20,000 that must be repaid in one lump sum at the end of five years. We would like to make a series of equal annual payments (an annuity) at the end of each of the five years, so that we will have $20,000 at the end of the fifth year from the accumulated deposits plus interest. Assuming that we can earn 10 percent interest per year on those deposits, how much should each annual payment be?

In this case, we are dealing with accumulating a future sum. Recall from Exhibit 3–5 that this means we will be compounding a series of payments, or an annuity, to achieve that future value. Hence, we can work with the procedure for determining future values by compounding as follows:

$$FV = \$20,000$$

$$PMT(6.105100) = \$20,000$$

$$PMT = \$20,000 \div 6.105100$$

$$= \$3,275.95$$

Solution:	Function:
$n = 5$	$PMT\ (n,\ i,\ PV,\ FV)$
$i = 10\%$	
$PV = 0$	
$FV = \$20,000$	
Solve for $PMT = -\$3,275.95$	

This computation merely indicates that when compounded at an annual interest rate of 10 percent, the unknown series of equal payments (*PMT*) will result in the accumulation of $20,000 at the end of five years. Given the interest factor for compounding an annual annuity at 10 percent from Exhibit 3–9, 6.105100, we know that the unknown payment (*PMT*), when multiplied by that factor, will result in $20,000. Hence, by dividing $20,000 by the interest factor for compounding an annual annuity, we can obtain the necessary annual payment of $3,275.95. The result tells us that if we make payments of $3,275.95 at the end of each year for five years, and each of those payments earns interest at an annual rate of 10 percent, a total of $20,000 will be accumulated at the end of five years.

We can see from the above computation that dividing $20,000 by 6.105100 is equivalent to multiplying $20,000 by (1 ÷ 6.105100), or .163797, and the same $3,275.95 solution results. The factor .163797 is referred to in real estate finance as a **sinking-fund factor (SFF),** which is also used in other applications in real estate. In the case of monthly payments, if we want to know what monthly payments would be necessary to pay off the $20,000 debt at the end of five years, taking into account that each payment will earn an annual rate of 10 percent compounded monthly, we can obtain a calculator solution as follows:

Solution:

$n = 5 \times 12 = 60$

$i = 10\% \div 12 = .008333$

$PV = 0$

$FV = \$20,000$

Solve for *PMT* $= -\$258.27$

Function:

$PMT\,(n,\,i,\,PV,\,FV)$

Required monthly payments would be $258.27.

Determining Yields, or Internal Rates of Return, on Investments

Up to now, this chapter has demonstrated how to determine future values in the case of compounding and present values in the case of discounting. Each topic is important in its own right, but each has also provided tools for determining an equally important component used extensively in real estate financing, that is, calculating rates of return or **investment yields.** In other words, the concepts illustrated in the compounding and discounting processes can also be used to determine rates of return, or yields, on investments, mortgage loans, and so on. These concepts must be mastered because procedures used here will form the basis for much of what follows in succeeding chapters.

We have concentrated previously on determining the future value of an investment made today when compounded at some given rate of interest, or the present investment value of a stream of cash returns received in the future when discounted at a given rate of interest. In this section, we are concerned with problems where we know what an investment will cost today and what the future stream of cash returns will be, but we do not know what **yield,** or **rate of return** (compounded), will be earned if the investment is made.

Investments with Single Receipts

In many cases, investors and lenders are concerned with the problem of what rate of compound interest, or investment yield, will be earned if an investment is undertaken. To illustrate the investment yield concept, assume an investor has an opportunity today to buy an unimproved one-acre lot for $5,639. The lot is expected to appreciate in value and to be worth $15,000 after seven years. What rate of interest (or investment yield) would be earned on the $5,639 investment in the property if it were made today, held for seven years, and sold for $15,000? Note from our previous discussion of compounding that the $15,000 also represents the receipt of a future cash flow or future value (*FV*).

To solve for the unknown rate, we can formulate the problem as follows:

$$PV = FV \cdot \frac{1}{(1+i)^n}$$

$$\$5,639 = \$15,000 \cdot \frac{1}{(1+i)^7}$$

We want to know the annual rate of compound interest, *i*, that, when substituted into the above equation, will make the $15,000 future receipt, or future value, equal to the $5,639 investment outlay, or present value, today.

One approach is to rearrange the above equation as follows:

$$\frac{1}{(1+i)^7} = \frac{5,639}{15,000}$$

$$(1+i)^7 = 15,000/5,639$$

$$1+i = 1.15$$

$$i = .15 \text{ or } 15\%$$

Another approach is to use trial-and-error to solve for *i*. A value for *i* is estimated; then the equation is solved to ascertain whether the future value, or $15,000, when discounted to present value, *PV*, will equal $5,639. When the correct value for *i* is found, the solution for present value should yield $5,639.

How do we begin the search for *i*? One way is to simply guess a solution. Let us try 10 percent. Mathematically we ask, if

$$PV = \$15,000 \frac{1}{(1+.10)^7}$$

is *PV* = $5,639?

Solving for *PV*, we have

$$PV = (\$15,000)(.513158)$$

$$= \$7,697$$

We note that $7,697 or *PV* is much *greater* than the desired *PV*, or $5,639. This means that the yield, or rate of compound interest earned on the investment, is *greater* than 10 percent. Hence, we must continue the discounting process by increasing *i*.

Our next "trial" will be 15 percent. Substituting, we have

$$PV = \$15,000 \frac{1}{(1+.15)^7}$$

$$= \$15,000(.375937)$$

$$= \$5,639.06$$

This time *PV* equals $5,639. This "guess" was correct. From this result, we have determined that the yield or internal rate of return, *i*, earned on the investment is equal to 15 percent.

We have, in essence, "removed" interest compounded at the rate of 15 percent for seven years from the $15,000 receipt of cash (the future value), leaving the initial deposit, or present value, of $5,639.

When trying to find the yield in which only one future value is involved, we can use an approach where the interest factor in the financial tables is first determined as follows:

$$\$5,639 = \$15,000 \, \frac{1}{(1+i)^7}$$

$$\$5,639.06 \div \$15,000 =$$

$$.375937 =$$

The above calculations show that the interest factor is .375937, but we still do not know the *interest rate*. However, we do know that the time period over which the investment is to appreciate in value is seven years. Because our solution is .375937 and the term of investment is seven years, the interest tables in Exhibit 3–6 (see p. 54) allow us to easily find the correct interest rate. Since the *FV* or cash return of $15,000 is a single receipt, we need only locate a factor for the present value reversion of $1 equal to .375937 in the row corresponding to seven years for some interest rate. We begin the search for the interest rate by choosing an arbitrary interest rate, say 6 percent. The 6 percent column in Exhibit 3–6 shows the factor in this column for seven years is .665057, which is larger than .375937. Moving to the 10 percent column, the factor for seven years is .513158, which is lower than the factor at 5 percent but comes closer to the solution that we are looking for. If we continue this trial-and-error process, the 15 percent column indicates that the factor for seven years is .375937; therefore, the interest rate we desire is 15 percent. We know this is the correct answer because $15,000 (.375937) = $5,639.06.

A more efficient approach to finding the yield or internal rate of return is to use a financial calculator. For calculators that have the capability to solve for yields such as required by the problem at hand, we have:

Solution:	Function:
$n = 7$	$i\,(n,\, PV,\, PMT,\, FV)$
$PV = -\$5,639$	
$PMT = 0$	
$FV = \$15,000$	
Solve for $i = 15\%$	

What does this interest rate, or yield, mean? It means that the $5,639 investment made today, held for seven years, and sold for $15,000, is equivalent to investing $5,639 today and letting it compound annually at an interest rate of 15 percent (note the correspondence between the terms *interest rate* and *yield*).[6] This fact can be determined with the following computation:

$$FV = \$5,639(2.660020)$$

$$= \$15,000$$

---

[6] We are now using the terms *yield* and *internal rate of return* for *i*, instead of the interest rate. It is generally accepted practice to use the terms yield or internal rate of return when evaluating *investments*. The term *interest rate* is generally used when *loan terms* are being quoted by lenders. The two concepts are very similar, but the reader should become accustomed to these differences in usage.

This calculation simply shows that $5,639 compounded annually at an interest rate of 15 percent for seven years is $15,000. Hence, making this investment is equivalent to earning a rate of return of 15 percent. This rate of return is usually referred to as the *investment yield* or the **internal rate of return.**

Solution:

$n = 7$

$i = 15\%$

$PV = -\$5,639$

$PMT = 0$

Solve for FV = $15,000

Function:

$FV(n, i, PV, PMT)$

The internal rate of return integrates the concepts of compounding and present value. It represents a way of measuring a return on investment, expressed as a compound rate of interest, over the entire investment period. For example, if an investor is faced with making an investment in an income-producing venture, regardless of how the cash returns are patterned, the internal rate of return provides a guide or comparison for the investor. It tells the investor what the equivalent compound interest rate will be on the investment being considered. In the example of the unimproved one-acre lot, the 15 percent yield or internal rate of return is equivalent to making a deposit of $5,639 and allowing it to compound annually at an interest rate of 15 percent for seven years. After seven years, the investor would receive $15,000, which includes the original investment of $5,639 plus all compound interest. With the internal rate of return known, the investor can make an easier judgment about what investment to make. If the 15 percent return is adequate, it will be made; if not, the investor should reject it.[7]

The concepts of the internal rate of return or yield, present value, and compounding are indispensable tools that are continually used in real estate finance and investment. The reader should not venture beyond this section without a firm grasp of the concepts that have been explained. These concepts form the basis for the remainder of this chapter and the chapters that follow.

Yields on Investment Annuities

The concepts illustrated for a single receipt of cash (when the unimproved lot was sold) also apply to situations where a *series* of cash receipts is involved. Consequently, a yield or internal rate of return also can be computed on these types of investments.

Suppose an investor has the opportunity to make an investment in real estate costing $3,170 that would provide him with cash income of $1,000 at the end of *each year* for four years. What investment yield, or internal rate of return, would the investor earn on the $3,170? In this case, we have a series of receipts that we wish to discount by an unknown rate to make the present value of the $1,000 annuity equal the original investment of $3,170. We need to find a solution for i in this problem, or the rate of interest that will make the present value of the $1,000 four-year annuity equal to $3,170. Recalling the notation for the present value of an annuity, we have

$$PV = PMT \cdot \sum_{t=1}^{n} \frac{1}{(1+i)^t}$$

[7] When comparing different investments, the investor must also consider any differences in risk. This topic is discussed in later chapters.

Substituting gives

$$\$3,170 = \$1,000 \sum_{t=1}^{n} \frac{1}{\left(1+i\right)^{t}}$$

Using our shorthand notation, we can express our problem as follows:

$$\$3,170 \div \$1,000 = \sum_{t=1}^{n} \frac{1}{(1+i)^{t}}_{t}$$

$$3.170000 = \sum_{t=1}^{n} \frac{1}{(1+i)^{t}}_{t}$$

Solution:

$n = 4$

$PV = -\$3,170$

$PMT = \$1,000$

$FV = 0$

Solve for i = 10%

Function:

$i\,(n,\,PV,\,PMT,\,FV)$

This procedure is similar to solving for the yield, or internal rate of return, on single receipts discussed in the preceding section, except that we are now dealing with an annuity. Using the same procedure as before, we solve for the interest factor for a four-year period that will correspond to some interest rate. To determine what the interest rate is, search the factors in Exhibit 3–11 (p. 62) in the four-year row until you find a column containing a factor very close to 3.1700. A careful search reveals that the factor will be found in the 10 percent column (the reader should verify this). Hence, based on this procedure, we have determined that the investment yield or internal rate of return (*IRR*) on the $3,170 invested is 10 percent. A more in-depth analysis of what the internal rate of return means is presented in Exhibit 3–13.

An important component of this analysis is, first, to determine if the investment outlay of $3,170 will be recovered from total cash inflows. In Exhibit 3–13 we can see that cash inflows (cash received in years 1–4) total $4,000. Therefore, in addition to recovering the investment of $3,170, $830 in additional cash flow will be received and we can say that the investment will be profitable, or that the investment yield (*IRR*) must be positive.

When the internal rate of return is computed, two additional characteristics are present (see Exhibit 3–13). One is the *recovery of capital* in each period, and the other is *interest earned* in each period. In other words, when the *IRR* is computed based on the $3,170 investment and the $1,000 received each year, *implicit* in the cash flows recovered each year during the four-year period is the *full recovery* of the $3,170 investment *plus* interest. Note also that the total interest/profit that will be received equals $830 or ($4,000 – $3,170). Our goal is to simplify this investment result by finding a rate of compound interest for this investment. This result can be compared with compound rates of interest in other investments that may have different investment and cash flow patterns. Comparing interest rates (*IRRs*) on various investments is easier than comparing cash flows. We also benefit because the time value of money (*TVM*) is taken into account. Hence, the 10 percent investment yield is really a rate of compound interest earned on an outstanding investment balance, after each capital recovery is taken into account, from year to year. Of the total $4,000 received during the four-year period, total interest earned is $830 and

EXHIBIT 3–13
Illustration of the Internal Rate of Return (IRR) and Components of Cash Receipts

	Year			
	1	**2**	**3**	**4**
Investment (balance)	$ 3,170	$2,487	$ 1,736	$ 910
IRR at 10%	317	249*	174*	91*
Cash received	$1,000	$1,000	$1,000	$1,000
Less: Cash yield at 10%	317	249	174	90*
Recovery of investment	$ 683	$ 751	$ 826	$ 910
Investment (beginning of year)	$ 3,170	$2,487	$ 1,736	$ 910
Less: Recovery of investment	683	751	826	910
Investment (end of year)	$2,487	$ 1,736	$ 910	$ 0

*Rounded.

capital recovery is $3,170. This is also equivalent to earning a 10 percent annual rate of compound interest on our investment.

Monthly Annuities: Investment Yields

A similar application for investment yields can be made in cases where *monthly* cash annuities will be received as a return on investment. For example, assume that an investor makes an investment of $51,593 and will receive $400 at the end of each month for the next 20 years (240 months). What annual rate of return, *compounded monthly,* would be earned on the $51,593?

Solution:

$$n = 20 \times 12 = 240$$
$$PV = -\$51,593$$
$$PMT = \$400$$
$$FV = 0$$

Solve for *i*
$$i\text{ (monthly)} = 0.5833\%$$
$$i\text{ (annualized)} = .005833 \times 12, \text{ or } 7\%$$

Function:
$$i\,(n,\ PV,\ PMT,\ FV)$$

As was the case with finding the *IRR* for investments with annual receipts, we find that the *IRR* is 7 percent compounded monthly on the $51,593 investment. Both the recovery of $51,593 and the $44,407 in interest were *embedded* in the stream of $400 monthly cash receipts ($96,000 in total receipts) over the 20-year period.

Equivalent Nominal Annual Rate (ENAR): Extensions

Earlier in this chapter, we dealt with the problem of determining equivalent annual yields in cases where more than one compounding interval exists within a year. In our example, we showed the effective annual yield for a $10,000 investment compounded annually, monthly, and daily to be 6, 6.17, and 6.18 percent, respectively (see p. 46). In many situations, we may already know the *effective annual yield (EAY)* and would like to know the *nominal annual rate of interest compounded monthly* (or for any period less than one year). For example, we considered a problem in which compounding occurred monthly based on a nominal annual rate of interest of 6 percent. Because compounding occurred in monthly intervals, the effective annual interest rate (6.17%) was larger than the nominal

In Exhibit 3–13, we introduced the IRR concept in the context of an investment with cash inflows of $1,000 per year, or a level annuity. In many situations investors must evaluate investments with cash inflows that *vary* from period to period. Investors in these situations also must know the IRR. However, when cash inflows vary, solving for the IRR is slightly more complicated. To illustrate, assume that we have an investment with these characteristics:

PV	Cash Flows (CF)			
Investment	Yr.1	Yr.2	Yr.3	Yr.4
$8,182	$1,000	$2,000	$3,000	$4,000

To solve for the IRR (i), we have:

$$PV = \frac{CF_1}{(1+i)^1} + \frac{CF_2}{(1+i)^2} + \frac{CF_3}{(1+i)^3} + \frac{CF_4}{(1+i)^4}$$

Substituting:

$$\$8,182 = \frac{\$1,000}{(1+i)^1} + \frac{\$2,000}{(1+i)^2} + \frac{\$3,000}{(1+i)^3} + \frac{\$4,000}{(1+i)^4}$$

Summing the cash inflows shows that a *total* of $10,000 will be received over four years; therefore, we know that because this total exceeds the PV of $8,182, the investment will be profitable and (i) will also be positive. (At this point, the reader should verify that the current value for (i) needed to make the right side of the equation equal to the PV of $8,182 is 7 percent.) However, as the reader may realize, solving for (i) is very cumbersome.

Introduction of the CF_j Function. Many financial calculators and software programs have been designed to more efficiently solve for IRRs when cash flows vary from period to period. These programs use a "trial and error" or "iterative" approach to solve for (i). This approach begins by first choosing a very large value for (i), substituting it in the above expression, and then solving for PV. The difference between the value *calculated* for PV and $8,182 is determined to ascertain how close this difference is to zero. The process continues by selecting values for (i) and recalculating PV. By using successively higher, then lower values for (i), PVs are calculated until an (i) is found such that the difference between the calculated PV and $8,182 is equal to zero.

With advances in electronic technology, these many calculations can be carried out very quickly by using the CF_j and n_j functions. This involves entering cash flows (CF_j) per period (n_j), then solving for (i). In our example, we would have:

Solution:

Enter CF		Enter n_j
$CF_j = -\$8,182$		$n_j = 1$
$CF_j = \$1,000$		$n_j = 1$
$CF_j = \$2,000$		$n_j = 1$
$CF_j = \$3,000$		$n_j = 1$
$CF_j = \$4,000$		$n_j = 1$
Solve for (i) = 7%		

When each cash flow is for a single period, we will use the following notation for the IRR function:

IRR (CF_1, CF_2, ..., CF_n)

For the above example, we would have IRR(-8182, 1000, 2000, 3000, 4000) = 7%.

rate (6%). Assuming that we wanted to know what the nominal annual rate of interest, compounded *monthly,* would have to be to provide a desired *EAY* of 6 percent, we can employ the following formula, where *ENAR* is the **equivalent nominal annual rate,** compounded monthly:

$$ENAR = [(1 + EAY)^{1/m} - 1] \cdot m$$

In our problem, we would have

$$ENAR = [(1 + .06)^{1/m} - 1] \cdot 12$$

$$= [(1 + .06)^{.083333} - 1] \cdot 12$$

$$= [1.004868 - 1] \cdot 12$$

$$= .0584106 \text{ or } 5.84106\% \text{ (rounded)}$$

To illustrate this concept, if we have investment A, which will provide an *effective annual yield* of 6 percent, and we are considering investment B, which will provide interest compounded monthly, we would want to know what the equivalent nominal annual rate (*ENAR*) of interest, *compounded monthly,* would have to be on investment B to provide the *same* effective annual yield of 6 percent. That rate would be an annual rate of 5.84106 percent, *compounded monthly.*

$$FV = \$1\left[1 + \frac{.0584106}{12}\right]^{12}$$

$$= \$1.06 \text{ (rounded)}$$

From our example, we know that the *EAY* is ($1.06 − $1.00) ÷ $1.00, or 6 percent. Hence, we now know that an investment of equal risk, with returns compounded *monthly,* must have an annual nominal rate of interest of at least 5.84106 percent to provide us with an equivalent, effective annual yield of 6 percent. Obviously, this application can be modified for any investment with different compounding periods by altering *m* in the above formula.

Solution:	Function:
n = 12 months	FV (n, i PV, PMT)
i = 5.84106 ÷ 12 = .486755%	
PV = −$1	
PMT = 0	
Solve for **FV** = $1.06	

Solving for Annual Yields with Partial Periods: An Extension

Many investments produce monthly cash flows but call for investment returns to be reported as an effective annual rate. However, many investments may be sold within a year (say, after five months into a calendar year). How can monthly cash flows within a year be expressed as an annual rate of interest? Consider the following example.

An investment is made in the amount of $8,000 and is expected to be owned for two years. The contract calls for investment returns to be reported as an effective annual rate. However, the investment is sold early and monthly cash flows of $500 are received for 17 months. What is the equivalent *annual* return on the investment? This can be determined as follows:

STEP 1:

Solution: Solve for monthly interest rate	Function:
n = 17 months	$i\,(n, PMT, PV, FV)$
PMT = $500	
PV = −$8,000	
FV = 0	

Solve for i = .682083%

STEP 2: The monthly interest rate of .682083% can now be used to determine the effective *annual rate* as follows:

Solution:	Function:
PV = −$1	$FV\,(PV, i, PMT, n)$
i = .682083%	
PMT = 0	
n = 12	

Solve for FV = 1.084991

STEP 3: The effective annual rate of interest would be:

$(FV/PV) - 1 = 1.084991 - 1.000 = .084991$ or 8.5% (rounded)

Therefore, this investment over a 17-month period has produced an equivalent *effective annual yield* (*EAY*) of 8.5 percent. (Note that this yield is also equivalent to a nominal annual rate, *compounded monthly,* which would be .682083 × 12 = 8.19 percent.)

Note on the XIRR

An alternative way of calculating an effective annual rate is to calculate what is referred to as the *XIRR.* The *XIRR* has been increasingly used in performance measurement because it is included in spreadsheet programs like Excel and can handle cash flow patterns that include partial years, as in the previous example, as well as cash flow patterns that are irregular and can occur any day of the year.

The *XIRR* is the rate that solves the following equation:

$$\sum P_j \big/ (1 + \text{rate})^{d_j/365} = 0$$

where P_j is the jth payment that is received d_j days after the starting date of the investment. Excel allows you to actually input calendar dates for each payment (cash flow), which is then converted to the number of days. The left side of the above equation simply discounts the cash flows to a present value using the effective annual rate as the discount rate. We need to find the rate that makes the *PV* equal to zero.

Using the previous example of $500 occurring monthly for 17 months, we assume that cash flows are now received on about the 30th of each month over the 17 months, as shown in Exhibit 3–14. Column 2 has the days as a fraction of 365. Recall that we calculated an effective annual rate of 8.5 percent in the previous example. We now prove that the *XIRR* calculation gives the same result by using 8.5 percent to see if the result is a zero present value.

Column 3 of Exhibit 3–14 uses the effective annual rate in the above *XIRR* formula because we want to show that this is the rate that makes the present value equal to $0, which it does, as can be seen by the sum of the final column. Each row in this final column indicates the present value of the payment received on that day of the year.

In the above example the cash flows occurred monthly. But cash flows can occur on any day of the year. In Excel, the actual date (e.g., February 12, 2012) would be used in the *XIRR* function to specify that a cash flow occurred on that date.

EXHIBIT 3–14
Proof of *XIRR*

		Rate 8.5%			
		(1)	(2)	(3)	(4)
Month	Days	Days/365	P	$(1 + rate)^{(days/365)}$	P/Column 3
0	0	0.000000	−8,000	1.000000	−$8,000.00
1	31	0.084932	500	1.006953	496.55
2	61	0.167123	500	1.013727	493.23
3	92	0.252055	500	1.020775	489.82
4	122	0.334247	500	1.027643	486.55
5	152	0.416438	500	1.034557	483.30
6	182	0.498630	500	1.041517	480.07
7	213	0.583562	500	1.048758	476.75
8	243	0.665753	500	1.055814	473.57
9	274	0.750685	500	1.063155	470.30
10	305	0.835616	500	1.070547	467.05
11	336	0.920548	500	1.077990	463.83
12	366	1.002740	500	1.085243	460.73
13	396	1.084932	500	1.092544	457.65
14	425	1.164384	500	1.099648	454.69
15	455	1.246575	500	1.107046	451.65
16	485	1.328767	500	1.114494	448.63
17	515	1.410959	500	1.121992	445.64
				Sum	.00

Conclusion

This chapter introduced and illustrated the mathematics of compound interest in financial analysis. Although this may be a review for many readers, a thorough understanding of this topic is essential in real estate finance. The concepts and techniques introduced in this chapter are used throughout the remainder of this text to solve a variety of problems encountered in real estate finance. In the following two chapters, we apply the mathematics of finance to the calculation of mortgage payments and the effective cost of various alternative mortgage instruments. Later, we apply the mathematics of finance to the analysis of income property investments. This chapter illustrated the use of financial tables, interest factors, and how these tables and factors can be found using a financial calculator. These tables were included to help the reader to understand the process of compounding, discounting, and finding internal rates of return by using interest factors. The tables are not necessary to solve any of the problems in the remainder of the book. In fact, an alternative calculator solution is also provided for many of the problems. The interest factor solutions are shown only so that the readers can see the mathematics behind the calculator solutions. As we move toward more advanced material, it is assumed that readers can obtain the solutions using a financial calculator or by using a spreadsheet program on a personal computer.

Key Terms

annual percentage yield (APY), 46
annuity, 57
annuity due, 57
compound interest, 42
discounting, 52
effective annual yield (EAY), 45

equivalent nominal annual rate (ENAR), 72
future value (FV), 43
future value of an annuity, 57
internal rate of return (IRR), 68
investment yield, 65
ordinary annuity, 57

present value (PV), 43
present value of an annuity, 60
rate of return, 65
sinking-fund factor (SFF), 65
yield, 65

Useful Web Sites

www.bai.org—Good source of current market rates on various financial instruments as well as discussion of ways to properly compare investments with different payment patterns.

www.interest.com—This site provides the current average mortgage rates, a mortgage calculator, and basic information on home buying.

www.bankrate.com—Source of interest rates for CDs and other investments.

Questions

1. What is the essential concept in understanding compound interest?
2. How are the interest factors (*IFs*) in Exhibit 3–3 developed? How may financial calculators be used to calculate interest factors in Exhibit 3–3?
3. What general rule can be developed concerning maximum values and compounding intervals within a year?
4. What does the time value of money (*TVM*) mean?
5. How does discounting, as used in determining present value, relate to compounding, as used in determining future value? How would present value ever be used?
6. What are the interest factors in Exhibit 3–9 and how are they developed? How may financial calculators be used to calculate interest factors in Exhibit 3–9?
7. What is an annuity? How is it defined? What is the difference between an *ordinary annuity* and an *annuity due*?
8. How must one discount a series of uneven receipts to find present value (*PV*)?
9. What is the sinking-fund factor? How and why is it used?
10. What is an internal rate of return? How is it used? How does it relate to the concept of compound interest?

Problems

1. Jim makes a deposit of $12,000 in a bank account. The deposit is to earn interest *compounded annually* at the rate of 6 percent for seven years.
   a. How much will Jim have on deposit at the end of seven years? (*Hint:* What is future value?)
   b. Assuming the deposit earned a 9 percent rate of interest *compounded quarterly,* how much would he have at the end of seven years?
   c. In comparing (*a*) and (*b*), what are the respective *effective annual yields?* (*Hint:* Consider the future value of each deposit after one year only.) Which alternative is better?

2. Would you prefer making a $25,000 investment that will earn interest at the rate of 6 percent *compounded monthly* or making the same $25,000 investment at 7 percent *compounded annually?* (*Hint:* Consider one year only.)

3. Jones can deposit $5,000 at the end of each six-month period for the next 12 years and earn interest at an annual rate of 8 percent, *compounded semiannually.* What will the value of the investment be after 12 years? If the deposits were made at the beginning of each year, what would the value of the investment be after 12 years?

4. Suppose you deposit $1,250 at the end of each quarter in an account that will earn interest at an annual rate of 10 percent *compounded quarterly.* How much will you have at the end of four years?

5. Suppose you deposit $2,500 at the end of year 1, nothing at the end of year 2, $750 at the end of year 3, and $1,300 at the end of year 4. Assuming that these amounts will be *compounded at an annual rate* of 15 percent, how much will you have on deposit at the end of five years?

6. Suppose you have the opportunity to make an investment in a real estate venture that expects to pay investors $750 at the end of each month for the next eight years. You believe that a reasonable return on your investment should be an annual rate of 15 percent *compounded monthly.*
   a. How much should you pay for the investment?
   b. What will be the total sum of cash you will receive over the next eight years?
   c. What do we call the difference between (*a*) and (*b*)?

7. An investor is considering an investment that will pay $2,150 at the end of each year for the next 10 years. He expects to earn a return of 12 percent on his investment, *compounded annually.* How much should he pay today for the investment? How much should he pay if the investment returns are received at the *beginning of each year?*

8. An investor can make an investment in a real estate development and receive an expected cash return of $45,000 at the end of six years. Based on a careful study of other investment alternatives, she believes that a 9 percent *annual return compounded quarterly* is a reasonable return to earn on this investment. How much should she pay for it today?

9. Walt is evaluating an investment that will provide the following returns at the end of each of the following years: year 1, $12,500; year 2, $10,000; year 3, $7,500; year 4, $5,000; year 5, $2,500; year 6, $0; and year 7, $12,500. Walt believes that he should earn 12 percent compounded annually on this investment. How much should he pay for this investment? What if he expects to earn an annual return of 9 percent *compounded monthly?* How much should he pay?

10. John is considering the purchase of a lot. He can buy the lot today and expects the price to rise to $15,000 at the end of 10 years. He believes that he should earn an investment yield of 8 percent *compounded annually* on his investment. The asking price for the lot is $7,000. Should he buy it? What is the internal rate of return *compounded annually* on the investment if John purchases the property for $7,000 and is able to sell it 10 years later for $15,000?

11. The Dallas Development Corporation is considering the purchase of an apartment project for $100,000. They estimate that they will receive $15,000 at the end of each year for the next 10 years. At the end of the 10th year, the apartment project will be worth nothing. If Dallas purchases the project, what will be its internal rate of return, *compounded annually?* If the company insists on an 8 percent return *compounded annually* on its investment, is this a good investment?

12. A corporation is considering the purchase of an interest in a real estate syndication at a price of $75,000. In return, the syndication promises to pay $1,000 at the end of each month for the next 25 years (300 months). If purchased, what is the expected internal rate of return, *compounded monthly?* How much total cash would be received on the investment? How much is profit and how much is return of capital?

13. An investment in a real estate venture will provide returns at the end of the next four years as follows: year 1, $5,500; year 2, $7,500; year 3, $9,500; and year 4, $12,500. An investor wants to earn a 12 percent return *compounded annually* on her investment. How much should she pay for the investment? Assuming that the investor wanted to earn an annual rate of 12 percent *compounded monthly,* how much would she pay for this investment? Why are these two amounts different?

14. A pension fund is making an investment of $100,000 today and expects to receive $1,600 at the end of each month for the next five years. At the end of the fifth year, the capital investment of $100,000 will be returned. What is the internal rate of return *compounded annually* on this investment?

15. A loan of $60,000 is due 10 years from today. The borrower wants to make annual payments at the end of each year into a sinking fund that will earn *compound interest* at an *annual rate* of 10 percent. What will the annual payments have to be? Suppose that the monthly payments earn 10 percent interest, *compounded monthly.* What would the annual payments have to be?

16. An investor has the opportunity to make an investment that will provide an effective *annual yield* of 12 percent. She is considering two other investments of equal risk that will provide compound interest *monthly* and *quarterly,* respectively. What must the equivalent nominal annual rate (*ENAR*) be for each of these two investments to ensure that an *equivalent annual yield* of 12 percent is earned?

17. An investment producing cash flows in the amount of $1,200 per month is undertaken for a period of 28 months. The investor pays $24,000 for the investment and the contract stipulates that investment returns must be reported on a basis equivalent with *annual compounding.* Given that the investment is sold after 28 months, what would be the equivalent *annual compound* rate of interest reported to the investor? What would be the annual rate *compounded monthly* for this investment?

18. An investment is expected to produce the following annual year-end cash flows:

    year 1: $5,000   year 4: $5,000
    year 2: $1,000   year 5: $6,000
    year 3: $0   year 6: $863.65

    The investment will cost $13,000 today.

    a. Will this investment be profitable?

    b. What will be the *IRR* (*compounded annually*) on this investment?

    c. **Prove** your answer in (*b*) by showing how much of each year's cash flow is *recovery of* the $13,000 investment and how much of the cash flow is *return on* investment. (*Hint:* See Exhibit 3–13 and Concept Box 3.2.)

Chapter  4

Fixed Interest Rate Mortgage Loans

This chapter deals with various approaches to pricing and structuring fixed interest rate mortgage loans. By *pricing* a loan, we refer to the rate of interest, fees, and other terms that lenders offer and that borrowers are willing to accept when mortgage loans are made. As a part of the pricing process, we also stress the supply and demand for loanable funds, the role of inflation, and how both affect the rate of interest. As to loan structuring, we review the many innovations in mortgage payment patterns that have evolved from changes in the economic environment.

Another major objective of this chapter is to illustrate techniques for determining the yield to the lender and actual cost to the borrower when various provisions exist in loan agreements. Lenders on real estate commonly include various charges and fees in addition to the interest rate as a condition of making a loan. These charges may include loan discounts, origination fees, prepayment penalties, or prepaid interest. In addition, various amortization or loan repayment schedules can be agreed upon by the borrower and lender to facilitate financing a particular real estate transaction. Because these provisions often affect the cost of borrowing, the methodology used to compute the yield to the lender (cost to the borrower) is heavily stressed.

Determinants of Mortgage Interest Rates: A Brief Overview

Changing economic conditions have forced the real estate finance industry to go through an important evolution. These changing conditions now require lenders and borrowers to have a better understanding of the sources of funds used for lending and the nature of how risk, economic growth, and inflation affect the availability and cost of mortgage funds.

When considering the determinants of interest rates on mortgage loans, we must also consider the demand and supply of mortgage funds. Most mortgage lenders are intermediaries, or institutions that serve as conduits linking flows of funds from savers to borrowers. Borrowers use the savings in the form of mortgage credit. The market rate of **interest** on mortgage loans is established by what borrowers are willing to pay for the use of funds over a specified period of time and what lenders are willing to accept in the way of compensation for the use of such funds. On the demand side of the market, it can be safely said that the demand for mortgage loans is a **derived demand,** or is determined by the demand for real estate.

When supplying funds to the mortgage market, lenders also consider returns and the associated risk of loss on alternative investments in relation to returns available on mortgages. Hence, the mortgage market should also be thought of as part of a larger capital market, where lenders and investors evaluate returns available on mortgages and all competing forms of investment, such as bonds, stocks, and other alternatives, and the relative risks associated with each. Should lenders believe that a greater return can be earned by making more mortgage loans (after taking into account the costs and the risk of loss) than would be the case if they invested in corporate bonds or business loans, more funds would be allocated to mortgage loans, and vice versa. Hence, lender decisions to allocate funds to mortgages are also made relative to returns and risk on alternative loans and investment opportunities.

The Real Rate of Interest: Underlying Considerations

When discussing market interest rates on mortgages, we should keep in mind that these interest rates are based on a number of considerations. We pointed out earlier that the supply of funds allocated to mortgage lending in the economy is, in part, determined by the returns and risks on all possible forms of debt and investment opportunities.

One fundamental relationship that is common to investments requiring use of funds in the economy is that they earn at least the **real rate of interest.**[1] This is the minimum rate of interest that must be earned by savers to induce them to divert the use of resources (funds) from present consumption to future consumption. To convince individuals to make this diversion, income in future periods must be expected to increase sufficiently from interest earnings to divert current income from consumption to savings. If expected returns earned on those savings are high enough to provide enough future consumption, adequate amounts of current savings will occur.

Interest Rates and Inflation Expectations

In addition to the real rate of interest, a concern that all investors have when making investment decisions is how *inflation* will affect investment returns. The rate of inflation is of particular importance to investors and lenders making or purchasing loans made at fixed rates of interest over long periods of time. Hence, when deciding whether to make such commitments, lenders and investors must be convinced that interest rate commitments are sufficiently high to compensate for any expected loss in purchasing power during the period that the investment or loan is outstanding; otherwise, an inadequate real return will be earned. Therefore, a consensus of what lenders and investors expect inflation to be during the time that their loans and investments are outstanding is also incorporated into interest rates at the time investments and loans are made.

To illustrate the relationship between the **nominal interest rate,** or the contract interest rate agreed on by borrowers and lenders, and real rates of interest, suppose that a $10,000 loan is made at a nominal or contract rate of 10 percent with all principal and interest due at the end of one year. At the end of the year, the lender would receive $11,000, or $10,000 plus $10,000 times (.10). If the rate of inflation during that year was 6 percent, then the $11,000 received at the end of the year would be worth about $10,377 ($11,000 ÷ 1.06).

---

[1] If the reader can visualize an investment portfolio containing investments in all productive activities in the economy based on the weight that any particular activity has to the total value of all productive activity in the economy, the rate of current earnings on such a portfolio would be equivalent to the real rate of interest. Such a rate would also be the rate required by economic units to save rather than consume from the current income.

Thus, although the nominal rate of interest is 10 percent, the *real* rate on the mortgage is just under 4 percent ($377 ÷ $10,000 = 3.77%). Therefore, we conclude that if the lender wanted a 4 percent real rate of interest, the lender would have to charge a nominal rate of approximately 10 percent to compensate for the expected change in price levels due to inflation.[2]

We can summarize by saying that the nominal interest rate on any investment is partially determined by the real interest rate *plus a premium* for the expected rate of inflation. In our example, the real rate of 4 percent plus an inflation premium of 6 percent equals 10 percent. Note that this premium is based on the rate of inflation *expected* at the time that the loan is made. The possibility that inflation will be more or less than expected is one of many risks that lenders and investors must also consider.

We should also point out that the nominal interest rate is usually expressed as an *annual* rate of interest. However, depending on the type of loan, the nominal rate could be an annual rate compounded daily, monthly, quarterly, annually, or continuously. We will explore the effects of compounding, accrued interest, and payment patterns in more detail throughout this chapter.

Interest Rates and Risk

In addition to expected inflation, lenders and investors are also concerned about various *risks* undertaken when making loans and investments. Lenders and investors are concerned about whether interest rates and returns available on various loans and investments compensate adequately for risk. Alternatively, will a particular loan or investment provide an adequate risk-adjusted return?

Many types of risk could be discussed for various investments, but they are beyond the scope of this book. Consequently, we will focus on risks affecting mortgage loans. Many of these risks are, however, present to greater and lesser degrees in other loans and investments.

Default Risk

One major concern of lenders when making mortgage loans is the risk that borrowers will default on obligations to repay interest and principal. This is referred to as **default risk,** and it varies with the nature of the loan and the creditworthiness of individual borrowers. The possibility that default may occur means that lenders must charge a premium, or higher rate of interest, to offset possible loan losses. Default risk relates to the likelihood that a borrower's income may fall after a loan is made, thereby jeopardizing the receipt of future mortgage payments. Similarly, a property's value could fall below the loan balance at some future time, which could result in a borrower defaulting on payments and a loss to the lender.

Interest Rate Risk

An additional complication in lending and investing arises from the uncertainty in today's world about the future supply of savings, demand for housing, and future

---

[2] Actually, the nominal rate of interest should be (1.06 × 1.04) − 1, or 10.24 percent, if a real rate of 4 percent is desired. For convenience throughout this text, we will *add* the real rate and premium for expected inflation as an approximation to the nominal interest rate. We should point out that the relationship of expected inflation and interest rates has long been a subject of much research. While we show a very simple, additive relationship in our discussion, there may be interaction between real interest rates and inflation. The specific relationship between the two is not known exactly. Hence, the student should treat this discussion at a conceptual or general level of interpretation.

levels of inflation. Thus, interest rates at a given point in time can only reflect the market consensus of what these factors are expected to be. Investors and lenders also incur the risk that the interest rate charged on a particular loan may be insufficient, should economic conditions change drastically *after* a loan is made. The magnitude of these changes may have warranted a higher interest rate when the loan was made. The uncertainty about what interest rate to charge when a loan is made can be referred to as **interest rate risk.**

For example, **anticipated inflation** may have been 6 percent at the time our $10,000 loan was made. But if *actual* inflation turns out to be 8 percent, this means the interest rate that should have been charged is 12 percent. In this case, we say that the anticipated rate of inflation at the time the loan was made was 6 percent. However, because **unanticipated inflation** of 2 percent occurred, the lender will lose $200 in purchasing power (2% of $10,000) because the rate of interest was too low. This does not mean that lenders did not charge the "correct" interest rate *at the time the loan was made.* At that time, the inflation was expected to be 6 percent. Therefore, to be competitive, a 10 percent interest rate had to be charged. However, the additional 2 percent was unanticipated by all lenders in the market. It is unanticipated inflation that constitutes a major component of interest rate risk to all lenders.

The possibility that too low an interest rate was charged at the time the loan was made is a major source of risk to the lender. Hence, a premium for this risk must also be charged or reflected in the market rate of interest. Interest rate risk affects all loans, particularly those that are made with fixed interest rates, that is, where the interest rate is set for a lengthy period of time when the loan is made. Being averse to risk, lenders must charge a premium to incur this risk.

Prepayment Risk

Some mortgage loans allow borrowers to prepay loans before the maturity date without a penalty. This, in effect, gives borrowers the *option* to prepay the loan, refinance, or pay off the loan balance if a property is sold. If loans are prepaid when interest rates fall, lenders must forgo the opportunity to earn interest income that would have been earned at the original contract rate. As funds from the prepaid loans are reinvested by lenders, a lower rate of interest will be earned. When interest rates increase, however, the loan is not as likely to be prepaid. The risk that the loan will be prepaid when interest rates fall below the loan contract rate is referred to as **prepayment risk.**

Other Risks

There are additional risks that lenders and investors consider that may vary by type of loan or investment. For example, the *liquidity* or *marketability* of loans and investments will also affect the size of the premium that must be earned. Securities that can be easily sold and resold in well-established markets will require lower premiums than those that are more difficult to sell. This is called **liquidity risk.**

Legislative risk is another risk associated with mortgage lending that also may result in a premium. It can refer to changes in the regulatory environment in which markets operate; for example, regulations affecting the tax status of mortgages, rent controls, state and federal laws affecting interest rates, and so on, are all possibilities that lenders face after making loans for specified periods of time. Lenders must assess the likelihood that such events may occur and be certain that they are compensated for undertaking these risks when loans are made.

A Summary of Factors Important in Mortgage Loan Pricing

We can now see that the interest rate charged on a particular mortgage loan will depend on the real interest rate, anticipated inflation, interest rate risk, default risk, prepayment risk, and other risks. These relationships can be summarized in general as follows:

$$i = r + p + f$$

In other words, when pricing or setting the rate of interest (i) on a mortgage loan, the lender must charge a premium (p) sufficiently high to compensate for default and other risks and a premium (f) that reflects anticipated inflation to earn a real rate of interest (r) that is competitive with real returns available on other investment opportunities in the economy. If lenders systematically *underestimate* any of the components in the above equation, they will suffer real economic losses.

Pricing decisions by lenders are rendered complex because mortgage loans are made at fixed interest rates for long periods of time. For example, if we assume that a mortgage loan is to be made with a one-year maturity, the interest rate charged at origination should be based on what the lender expects each of the components discussed above to be during the coming year. More specifically,

$$i_t = r_1 + p_1 + f_1$$

or the mortgage interest rate (i) at origination (time t) would be based on the lender's expectations of what the real rate of interest, the rate of inflation, and risk premiums (for risks taken in conjunction with making the mortgage loan over and above the level of risk reflected in the real rate of interest) should be for the term of the loan.

Understanding Fixed Interest Rate Mortgage (FRM) Loan Terms

As previously discussed in Chapter 2, there are many terms and options in mortgage loan agreements that are very important. We begin our analysis of fixed interest rate loans with a discussion of some of the most elementary terms:

- Loan amount
- Loan maturity date
- Interest rate
- Periodic payments

The *loan amount* identifies the amount borrowed and what the borrower is legally required to repay. The *loan maturity date* is the date by which the loan must be fully repaid. While these terms are relatively easy to understand, when analyzing and comparing various loan alternatives, the interest rate and its affect on periodic payments can be more complex and will be discussed further.

When dealing with fixed interest rate loans, in addition to the loan amount and maturity, lenders generally quote what is referred to as a *nominal annual rate of interest.* To elaborate, say a 30-year loan is made for $60,000 and the interest rate is 12 percent. That rate of interest is referred to as the *nominal rate because no reference is made as to how interest is to be calculated or how frequent payments will be.* If, in this case, *interest* is to be calculated *monthly* and *payments* are to be made *monthly,* one interpretation of the 12 percent *nominal interest rate* would be an annual rate of 12 percent interest *compounded monthly*. Recall from Chapter 3 that another way to interpret an annual rate of interest, compounded monthly, is to *calculate its equivalent annual rate of interest.* That is, a rate of interest *compounded annually* that would be equivalent to a loan with an annual rate of interest *compounded monthly.* This can be done in our example as follows:

STEP 1:

Solution: Find the *FV* of an amount   Function:
          that earns interest at an annual   *FV (PV, i, n)*
          rate *compounded monthly:*

$PV = -\$60,000$

$i = 12\%/12 = 1\%$ or $.01$

$n = 12$

Solve for *FV* $= \$67,609.50$

STEP 2: Find the equivalent annual interest rate *compounded annually*:

$FV = \$67,609.50$

$n = 1$

$PV = \$60,000.00$

Solve for *i* $= 12.6825\%$

In Step 1, using our approach outlined in Chapter 3, we consider a $60,000 deposit made today and compounded monthly for 12 months at 12 percent, leaving an *FV* of $67,609.50. We then solve for the *annual* compound rate equivalent in Step 2 by changing the compounding period to 1. This produces $i = 12.6825$ percent. In other words, a loan quoted with a 12 percent annual rate of interest compounded *monthly* is equivalent to a loan with an annual rate of 12.6825 percent compounded *annually*. The difference in these rates is due to the fact that when interest on a loan is compounded monthly and paid monthly, the incremental value is greater than receiving cash flows annually.[3] This is true even though the interest rate may be quoted as 12 percent in both cases. So, a loan with an annual rate of 12 percent compounded *monthly* is worth the equivalent of a loan with an annual rate of 12.6825 percent compounded *annually*. The latter can be thought of as an *effective* or *equivalent* annual rate of interest. Alternately, a loan with an annual rate of 12.6825 percent compounded *annually* is equivalent to a 12 percent annual rate compounded *monthly*.

So why do lenders quote *nominal* rates of interest (12% in our case)? If interest is to be compounded monthly (or for other periods), why not quote equivalent annual rates (12.6825% in our case)? If the latter approach was used, uniformity would be achieved because interest rates on all loans could be quoted based on an equivalent annual rate *regardless* of how frequently interest is calculated and payments are made (daily, monthly, quarterly, annually). The answer partially lies in the evolution of banking, financial instruments, simplicity when making interest calculations, and a general lack of knowledge (understanding) among people working in finance-related fields. *In the discussion that follows, and throughout this book, we will follow the practice used by lenders and use the nominal rate of interest for all mortgage loan examples. In most cases, interest will be calculated monthly and payments will be made monthly. However, the reader should be aware that interest could be calculated and payments made over very different time periods.*

---

[3] The reader may recall that we discussed this concept with annual percentage yield (APY) in Chapter 3.

Calculating Payments and Loan Balances—Fixed Interest Rate Loans

The Importance of Accrued Interest and Loan Payments

A very important concept that must be understood when calculating payments or outstanding loan balances for real estate loans is: (1) the relationship between *accrued interest* and *loan payments* for a given period and (2) how any differences between them will affect loan balances. For example, as discussed above, many loans require interest to be *accrued monthly* ($i/12$); that is, if a fixed interest rate mortgage (FRM) loan is made in an amount of $60,000 ($PV$) at a 12 percent interest rate and interest (i) is to be accrued monthly, the dollar amount of interest accrued as of the end of the first month would be calculated as:

$$\$60,000 \times (.12/12) = \$600$$

We should also point out that ($i/12$) is referred to as the **accrual rate.** The amount of interest *accrued* and *owed* to the lender at the end of the month will be $600.

The borrower and lender may also negotiate payments (PMT). The ratio of these payments to the loan amount is referred to as the **pay rate.** If the borrower and lender agree that payments (PMT) to be made at the end of each month are to be equal to accrued interest, then the monthly pay rate and the monthly accrual rate are the same.[4] This means that dollar payments (PMT) will be $600, or *exactly equal* to $600 accrued interest. When the monthly accrual rate and the monthly pay rate are equal, the outstanding loan balance remains unchanged. So, in our example, the loan balance would remain $60,000 at the end of the month. *We should again stress at this point that, in any given period, the pay rate and accrual rate do not have to be equal.*

Loan Amortization Patterns

In the previous section, we emphasized the relationship between accrued interest and payments on mortgage loans. We used the example of an interest-only loan which indicated that the pay rate and accrual rate were equal. When considering other loan types, we will see that the monthly accrual and pay rates are frequently *not* equal. There are many situations when lenders and borrowers consider *different* loan structures and vary the pay rate and accrual rate. In these cases, loan balances will be affected and will change depending on the difference between the two.

Differences between Accrued Interest and Payments

We now consider situations where the pay rate, and therefore, monthly *payments* are (1) greater than, (2) equal to, or (3) less than monthly accrued interest. We then consider the effect that each case has on loan balances. At this point in our discussion of **Constant Payment Mortgage (CPM)** loans, we will use examples for fixed interest rate loans that are classified in four very general ways:

Type of CPM Loan	Pay Rate	Loan Balance at Maturity
1. Fully amortizing	Greater than accrual rate	Fully repaid
2. Partially amortizing	Greater than accrual rate	Not fully repaid
3. Interest only	Equal to accrual rate	Equal to amount borrowed
4. Negative amortizing	Less than accrual rate	Greater than amount borrowed

[4] We will use *monthly time periods* for accrued interest and payments to limit the number of possible examples. The reader should be aware that accrual and payment periods do not have to be equal.

Notice that the first loan type, which we refer to as **fully amortizing,** means that the pay rate will *exceed* the accrual rate. This means that monthly payments will *exceed accrued interest* by an amount sufficient to pay the accrued interest due each month and *fully repay the loan by the maturity date.*

The second loan type, or the **partially amortizing loan,** refers to the case when the borrower and lender agree that, like the fully amortizing loan, the pay rate will result in a payment that will *exceed accrued interest,* but not by as much as the payment for the fully amortizing loan. Therefore, the loan will *not be fully repaid at maturity.* It will be only *partially repaid.*

The third loan type, or the **interest-only loan,** is sometimes called a **zero amortizing loan.** As we have discussed, in this case the pay rate will equal the accrual rate. Consequently, the loan balance at the end of each month will remain the same as the original loan amount. The *full, original, loan amount will have to be paid at maturity.*

Finally, the fourth loan type, or the **negative amortizing loan,** represents the case where borrowers and lenders agree that the pay rate will be *less than* the accrual rate. As a result, payments will *not* equal the amount of interest due and the loan balance will actually *increase* each month. At maturity, the *loan balance will be greater than the original loan amount.*

We will now illustrate payments for each category of loan. We also should note at this point that each category of loan will have constant, or level, monthly payments. We will discuss other monthly payment patterns later in this chapter.

Fully Amortizing, Constant Payment Mortgage (CPM) Loans

The most common loan payment pattern used in real estate finance during the post-depression era, and one which is still very prevalent today, is the fully amortizing, constant payment mortgage (CPM). (**Amortization** means the process of loan repayment over time.) The CPM loan payment pattern is used most extensively in financing single family residences and, to a lesser extent, income-producing properties such as multifamily apartment complexes and shopping centers. This payment pattern means simply that a level, or constant, monthly payment is calculated on an original loan amount at a fixed rate of interest for a given term. Each monthly payment includes interest and *some* repayment of principal. At the end of the term of the CPM loan, the original loan amount, or **principal,** is completely repaid, or has been fully amortized. The lender has earned and the borrower has paid a fixed rate of interest on the monthly loan balance.

To illustrate how the monthly loan payment calculation is made, we turn to our previous example of a $60,000 loan made at a 12 percent (nominal) rate of interest for 30 years. What are the constant monthly mortgage payments on this loan, assuming it is to be fully amortized at the end of 30 years? Based on our knowledge of discounting annuities from Chapter 3, the problem involves no more than finding the present value of an annuity and can be formulated as follows:

$$PV = \sum_{t=1}^{n} \left[\frac{PMT_t}{1 + \dfrac{i}{12}} \right]^t$$

where
PV = present value
PMT = payment
i = fixed nominal, interest rate on mortgage
n = number of months loan will remain outstanding

because *PMT* is a constant, this is also equivalent to:

$$PV = PMT \times \sum_{t=1}^{n} \frac{1}{\left(1 + \frac{i}{12}\right)^t}$$

and

$$PMT = \frac{PV}{\displaystyle\sum_{t=1}^{n} \frac{1}{\left(1 + \frac{i}{12}\right)^t}}$$

Solution:	Function:
$n = 30 \times 12 = 360$	$PMT\,(n, i, PV, FV)$
$i = 12\%/12 = 1\%$ or .01	
$PV = -\$60{,}000$	
$FV = 0$	
Solve for **PMT** = \$617.17	

In this case, we are interested in solving for *PMT,* or the constant monthly payment (annuity) that will fully repay the loan amount (*PV*) and earn the lender 12 percent interest compounded monthly. The required payment will be \$617.17.

Consider the fully amortizing loan pattern illustrated in Exhibit 4–1. The initial, relatively low principal reduction, shown in column 6, results in a high portion of interest charges in the early monthly payments. Note that the ending loan balance after the first six months (column 6) is \$59,894.36; thus, only \$105.64 has been amortized from the original balance of \$60,000 after six months. Interest paid during the same six-month period totals \$3,597.38. The explanation for the high interest component in each monthly payment is

EXHIBIT 4–1
Fully Amortizing
Loan Pattern

(1)	(2)	(3)	(4)	(5)	(6)
	Beginning	Monthly	Interest		Ending Loan
Month	Loan Balance	Payment	(.12 ÷ 12)	Amortization*	Balance
1	\$60,000.00	\$617.17	\$600.00	\$17.17	\$59,982.83
2	59,982.83	617.17	599.83	17.34	59,965.49
3	59,965.49	617.17	599.65	17.52	59,947.97
4	59,947.97	617.17	599.48	17.69	59,930.28
5	59,930.28	617.17	599.30	17.87	59,912.41
6	59,912.41	617.17	599.12	18.05	59,894.36
.	.	.	.	.	.
.	.	.	.	.	.
.	.	.	.	.	.
358	1,815.08	617.17	18.15	599.02	1,216.06
359	1,216.06	617.17	12.16	605.01	611.06
360	611.06	617.17	6.11	611.06	-0-

*Amortization increases each month by the factor $1 + i/12$; that is, $17.17(1.01) = 17.34$, and so on.

that the lender earns an annual 12 percent return (1 percent monthly) on the outstanding monthly loan balance. Because the loan is being repaid over a 30-year period, obviously the loan balance is reduced only very slightly at first and monthly interest charges are correspondingly high. Exhibit 4–1 also shows that the pattern of accrued interest in the early years of the loan reverses as the loan begins to mature. Note that during the last months of the loan, accrued interest declines sharply and amortization increases.

Interest, Principal, and Loan Balance Illustrated

Exhibit 4–2 (panel A) illustrates the loan payment pattern over time, by indicating the relative proportions of interest and principal in each monthly payment over the 30-year term of the loan. Exhibit 4–2 (panel B) shows the rate of decline in the loan balance over the same 30-year period. It is clear that the relative share of interest as a percentage of the total monthly mortgage payment declines very slowly at first. Note in panel A that halfway into the term of the mortgage, or after 15 years, interest still makes up $514.24 of the $617.17 monthly payment and principal the difference ($617.17 − $514.24 = $102.93). Further, the loan balance after 15 years (panel B) is approximately $51,424. Total mortgage payments of

EXHIBIT 4–2
Monthly Payment, Principal, Interest, and Loan Balances for a Fully Amortizing, Constant Payment Mortgage

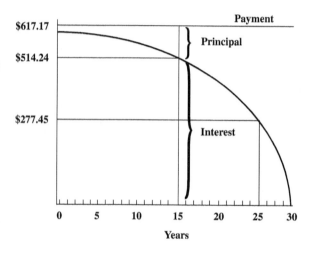

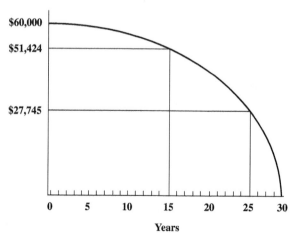

Prior to widespread use of financial calculators and spreadsheets, performing loan calculations had to be done manually. Therefore, a series of tables containing what were referred to as **loan constants** were developed. *These factors continue to be used* in the vocabulary of the lending industry. Equivalent to the pay rate discussed earlier in the chapter, these constants are simply the present value of a monthly annuity for various interest rates and time periods. These can be applied to any FRM loan to determine the constant monthly payment.

Related to our example, if we desired we could calculate the loan constant as:

Solution:

$PV = \$1$

$n = 360$

$FV = 0$

$i = 12\%/12 = 1\%$ or $.01$

Solve for PMT $= .01286$ (or loan constant)

Function:

$PMT\,(PV, n, FV, i)$

This constant, or payment, can be applied to any fully amortizing loan made at 12 percent for 30 years (360 months) to determine the monthly payment. The term *loan constant* continues to be used in lending negotiations, loan agreements, and other discussions between lenders and borrowers. The loan constant can be multiplied by any beginning loan amount to obtain the monthly mortgage payments necessary to amortize the loan fully by the maturity date.

Years	Months	Interest Rate 9%	10%	11%	12%
5	60	.020758	.021247	.021742	.022244
10	120	.012668	.013215	.013775	.014347
15	180	.010143	.010746	.011366	.012002
20	240	.008997	.009650	.010322	.011011
25	300	.008392	.009087	.009801	.010532
30	360	.008046	.008776	.009523	.010286

In the table above, we provide a sample of monthly mortgage loan constants (or pay rates) for various interest rates and loan maturities. Returning to our problem of finding the monthly mortgage payment for a $60,000 loan made at 12 percent for 30 years, we locate the 12 percent column and look down until we find the row corresponding to 30 years, where the loan constant is .010286 (rounded).* Loan constants are often stated on an annualized basis by multiplying the monthly loan constant by 12. In the above example, the annualized loan constant is $.010286 \times 12 = .123432$, or 12.34% (rounded). Note that this is greater than the interest rate of 12 percent. The difference is how the loan gets amortized. If the annualized constant was 12 percent, it would be an interest-only loan. Note that the annualized loan constant still assumes that payments are made monthly.

---

* Because of rounding (to six decimal places), the loan constant is .010286. When we multiply $60,000 by the rounded constant, we get a monthly payment of $616.16. The more exact solution is $617.17. Hence, readers should be aware that small discrepancies between their solutions and ours may occur when financial calculators are used, because calculator solutions may be rounded off to eight or more decimal places. We have attempted to carry out solutions to at least six decimal places before rounding.

EXHIBIT 4–3
Relationship between
Monthly Mortgage
Payments and
Maturity Periods:
Fully Amortizing
Loans

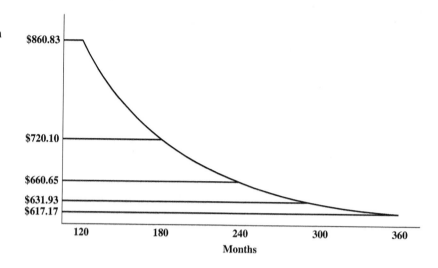

$111,090.60 ($617.17 × 180 months) have been made through the 15th year, with approximately $8,576 (or $60,000 − $51,424) of the loan repaid at that point. This pattern reverses with time. Note in panel A that after 25 years, interest makes up only $277.45 of the monthly payment, and the loan balance (panel B) has declined sharply to $27,745.

The Effect of Maturity on Monthly Payments—Fully Amortizing Loans

Exhibit 4–3 shows the effect of loan maturity on monthly payments for the base case mortgage loan. The exhibit shows the extent to which levels of constant monthly payments decline as maturities negotiated by the lender and borrower increase. In our base case example of a $60,000, fully amortizing, 30-year loan made at 12 percent interest, monthly payments would decline from $860.83 for a maturity period of *10 years* to $617.17 for a maturity of *30 years*. This indicates the importance of loan maturity and its effects when negotiating a loan structure.

Partially Amortizing, Constant Payment Mortgage (CPM) Loans

In many cases, loans may be structured to accomplish one or more goals. For example, the borrower may desire (1) a payment that is lower than what would be available with a fully amortizing loan and/or (2) a nonzero outstanding loan balance on the maturity date. This can be shown in the following example: A borrower and lender agree that a $60,000 loan made at 12 percent interest for 30 years will have a $40,000 balance (sometimes referred to as a **balloon payment**) on the maturity date. It will have constant monthly payments.

To solve for those payments, we modify the equation that was used to calculate the CPM with full amortization as follows:

$$PV = \sum_{t=1}^{n} \frac{PMT_t}{\left(1+\frac{i}{12}\right)t} + \frac{FV_n}{\left(1+\frac{i}{12}\right)^n}$$

The above equation differs in that the term *FV* is introduced and represents the desired outstanding balance (also frequently referred to as a balloon payment), at period *n*, or maturity.

The calculator solution for our problem can be modified as follows:

Solution:	Function:
$n = 12 \times 30 = 360$	$PMT\,(n, i, PV, FV)$
$i = 12\%/12 = 1\%$ or .01	
$PV = -\$60,000$	
$FV = \$40,000$	
Solve for $PMT = \$605.72$	

Note that the payment for the partially amortizing loan is $605.72, which is *less than* the $617.17 payment that we calculated for the fully amortizing loan. We should also point out that the loan constant, or pay rate, is $605.72 ÷ $60,000 = .010095. This is different from the *loan constant* that would apply if the loan was fully amortizing, which was $617.17 ÷ $60,000 = .010286.

It should be noted that the $605.72 payment also is slightly closer to the $600 accrued interest calculated earlier. This means that loan amortization will be only $5.72 at the end of month one. A more detailed schedule demonstrating the monthly relationships between payments, accrued interest, and the loan balance is shown in Exhibit 4–4.

EXHIBIT 4–4
Partially Amortizing
Loan Pattern

Month	Beginning Loan Balance	Monthly Payment	Interest ($.12 \div 12$)	Amortization	Ending Loan Balance
1	$60,000.00	$605.72	$600.00	$ 5.72	$59,994.28
2	59,994.28	605.72	599.94	5.78	59,988.50
3	59,988.50	605.72	599.88	5.84	59,982.66
4	59,982.66	605.72	599.83	5.90	59,976.76
5	59,976.76	605.72	599.77	5.95	59,970.81
6	59,970.81	605.72	599.71	6.01	59,964.79
.	.	.	.	.	.
.	.	.	.	.	.
.	.	.	.	.	.
358	40,605.03	605.72	406.05	199.67	40,405.35
359	40,405.35	605.72	404.05	201.67	40,203.69
360	40,203.69	605.72	402.04	203.69	40,000.00

Zero Amortizing, or Interest-Only—Constant Payment Mortgage (CPM) Loans

Another pattern for fixed interest rate and constant payment loans that is frequently used in real estate finance is referred to as the **interest-only loan.** As the name implies, constant monthly payments will be "interest only."

Solution:	Function:
$n = 360$	$PMT\,(n, i, FV, PV)$
$i = 12\%/12 = 1\%$ or .01	
$PV = -\$60,000$	
$FV = \$60,000$	
Solve for $PMT = \$600.00$	

Because the loan is interest only, the payment is simply equal to accrued interest or .12 ÷ 12 × $60,000 = $600. This means, of course, that the loan balance at the end of each month will remain at $60,000. The monthly pattern of accrued interest, payments, and loan balances for the interest-only loan are detailed in Exhibit 4–5.

EXHIBIT 4–5
Interest-Only Loan Pattern

Month	Beginning Loan Balance	Monthly Payment	Interest (.12 ÷ 12)	Amortization	Ending Loan Balance
1	$60,000.00	$600.00	$600.00	$0.00	$60,000.00
2	60,000.00	600.00	600.00	0.00	60,000.00
3	60,000.00	600.00	600.00	0.00	60,000.00
4	60,000.00	600.00	600.00	0.00	60,000.00
5	60,000.00	600.00	600.00	0.00	60,000.00
6	60,000.00	600.00	600.00	0.00	60,000.00
.	.	.	.	.	.
.	.	.	.	.	.
.	.	.	.	.	.
358	60,000.00	600.00	600.00	0.00	60,000.00
359	60,000.00	600.00	600.00	0.00	60,000.00
360	60,000.00	600.00	600.00	0.00	60,000.00

Negative Amortizing, Constant Payment Mortgage (CPM) Loans

A final category of fixed rate, constant payment loans to be discussed in this chapter is referred to as a **negative amortizing loan.** This pattern may occur when: (1) the borrower and lender agree that the loan balance at maturity will be *greater* than the initial loan amount; that is, $FV > PV$ or (2) payments are negotiated to be lower than the periodic interest due on the loan.

To illustrate the first case, if $60,000 is borrowed but the amount due at maturity will be $80,000, then monthly payments will be $594.28. This result can be obtained as shown in the calculator solution below.

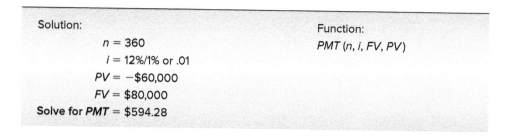

Solution:
$n = 360$
$i = 12\%/1\%$ or .01
$PV = -\$60,000$
$FV = \$80,000$
Solve for $PMT = \$594.28$

Function:
$PMT\,(n, i, FV, PV)$

We should also point out that the *pay rate,* calculated as $594.28 ÷ $60,000, is now equal to .009905. This is lower than the accrual rate, which is .12 ÷ 12, or .010000. When the pay rate used to determine monthly payments is *less* than the interest rate specified in the note, also referred to as the "accrual rate," negative amortization occurs. This is because payments are not large enough to meet monthly interest requirements. The difference between payments actually made and those that would be made on an interest-only loan deferred and becomes additional amounts owed by the borrower to the lender. These amounts must also earn interest. The rate at which they earn interest is usually the same as the interest rate on the note. In this example, it would be .12 ÷ 12, or .010000 per month. The monthly payment pattern, accrued interest, and loan balance for the negative amortizing loan are shown in Exhibit 4–6.

The second example for negative amortization loans is to set the desired payment pattern, and then to solve for the loan balance that will include negative amortization.

EXHIBIT 4–6
Negative Amortizing
Loan Pattern

Month	Beginning Loan Balance	Monthly Payment	Interest (.12 ÷ 12)	Amortization	Ending Loan Balance
1	$60,000.00	$594.28	$600.00	$(5.72)	$60,005.72
2	60,005.72	594.28	600.06	(5.78)	60,011.50
3	60,011.50	594.28	600.12	(5.84)	60,017.34
4	60,017.34	594.28	600.17	(5.90)	60,023.24
5	60,023.24	594.28	600.23	(5.95)	60,029.19
6	60,029.19	594.28	600.29	(6.01)	60,035.21
.	.	.	.	.	.
.	.	.	.	.	.
.	.	.	.	.	.
358	79,394.97	594.28	793.95	(199.67)	79,594.65
359	79,594.65	594.28	795.95	(201.67)	79,796.31
360	79,796.31	594.28	797.96	(203.69)	80,000.00

For example, in the above problem, if we assume that the loan is negotiated with monthly payments *preset* at $400, the loan balance at the end of year five could be calculated as:

Solution:	Function:
$PV = \$60,000$	$FV(PV, n, i, PMT)$
$n = 60$	
$i = 12\%/12$	
$PMT = \$400$	
Solve for $FV = \$76,333.93$	

Note that because the monthly payments have been set at $400, which is below the $600 in monthly interest being accrued, $200 per month in interest is *not being collected.* Over the 60-month period, this amount must be added to the loan balance and also must earn 12 percent interest compounded monthly. This results in a total of $16,333.93 being added to the loan balance. Note that the balance outstanding at the end of year 5 is now $76,333.93. When compared to the initial loan amount of $60,000, we can see that negative amortization has increased the loan balance by $16,333.93.

Summary and Comparisons: Fixed Interest Rate, Constant Payment Mortgage (CPM) Loans with Various Amortization Patterns

At this point, we have discussed four types of fixed interest rate, constant payment mortgage (CPM) loans, categorized by amortization pattern. Exhibit 4–7 (panel A), provides a diagram showing the four distinct monthly mortgage payments for our base case example (a $60,000 loan made at 12% for 30 years). Looking at the monthly loan balance pattern for each of the four cases, the reader should begin to understand the trade-offs involved when considering these different loan types. Furthermore, the strategy and objectives of borrowers should be apparent. Holding all else constant, *monthly payments* range from the highest amount when loans are *fully amortizing* to the lowest amount when they are *negatively amortizing.*[5] Moving to panel B, we can see that loan balances are

---

[5] Obviously, there are many combinations in between.

EXHIBIT 4–7

Base Case: Summary and Comparison of Monthly Payments and Loan Balances for Selected Fixed Interest Rate, Constant Payment Mortgage (CPM) Loan Patterns

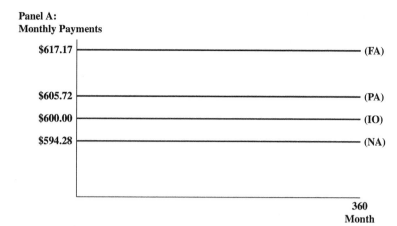

Panel A:
Monthly Payments

$617.17 —————————————————— (FA)

$605.72 —————————————————— (PA)

$600.00 —————————————————— (IO)

$594.28 —————————————————— (NA)

360
Month

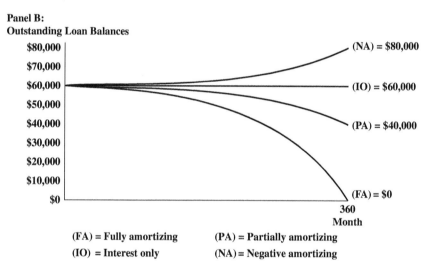

Panel B:
Outstanding Loan Balances

(NA) = $80,000

(IO) = $60,000

(PA) = $40,000

(FA) = $0

360
Month

(FA) = Fully amortizing   (PA) = Partially amortizing

(IO) = Interest only   (NA) = Negative amortizing

highest when payments are lowest and lowest when payments are highest. Risk is also considerably different under each of the four scenarios. It should be clear that if the *same property* is being financed by the *same borrower* in each case, risk will be greatest in the case involving the negative amortizing loan.

We should emphasize that we have deliberately kept our base case example the same throughout the chapter in order to emphasize the most important aspects of *mortgage loan mechanics* and *loan structuring*. Structuring mortgage loans in real estate financing is, in many cases, critical to the success or failure of a transaction; therefore, knowledge of the relationships discussed in this chapter should prove valuable to the reader. For instance, many of these concepts will prove to be beneficial in later chapters when applications involving structuring partnerships, mortgage-backed securities, and other financing vehicles and arrangements are considered. Another important observation should be made regarding the interest rate in our base case example, which has been kept constant. In reality, we would expect the interest rates on loans to increase as risk increases. Finally, there are additional factors that affect risk when structuring loans. These factors include varying loan maturities and varying the amount borrowed. Changes in these factors tend to increase or decrease risk, depending upon the type of payment and loan amortization patterns chosen.

Determining Loan Balances

Because most mortgage loans are repaid before they mature, mortgage lenders and real estate investors must be able to determine balances on mortgage loans at any time. As previously indicated, even though most loans are made for terms of 25 or 30 years, mortgages are usually repaid from 8 to 12 years after they are made. Therefore, it is very important to know what the loan balance will be at any time when financing real estate. There are many ways to find loan balances. We will demonstrate several approaches in this section.

To illustrate one approach, let us return to our base case example of the $60,000 fully amortizing loan made at 12 percent interest for a term of 30 years. After 10 years, the borrower decides to sell the property. To do so, the existing loan must be paid off. How much will have to be repaid to the lender after 10 years? We could construct a loan balance schedule as in Exhibit 4–1; however, this is time consuming and unnecessary. Finding loan balances can be accomplished in other ways. First, one can simply find the present value of the $617.17 payments at the 12 percent contract rate of interest *for the 20 years remaining until maturity.* For example:

Solution:	Function:
$n = 20 \times 12 = 240$	$PV(n, i, FV, PMT)$
$i = 12\%/12 = 1\%$ or .01	
$PMT = -\$617.17$	
$FV = 0$	
Solve for PV $= \$56,051.02$	

The unpaid balance after 10 years is $56,051.02. This exercise also points out another interesting fact. Because the payments include interest and a reduction of principal each month, by "removing" all interest from all remaining payments, it follows that only the principal can remain. Discounting the $617.17 monthly payments at an annual rate of 12 percent compounded monthly is a process that really amounts to "removing interest" from the payments. Hence, after "removing interest" by discounting, we ascertain that the unamortized or unpaid balance must be $56,051.02.

Another way of finding a loan balance using a financial calculator is to calculate future value (*FV*). This may be done by entering payments (*PMT*), the initial loan amount as a present value (*PV*), the number of periods (*n*) (e.g., months) that the loan has been amortized, and the interest rate (*i*). Future value (*FV*) then can be calculated as the outstanding loan balance.

Solution:	Function:
$PV = -\$60,000$	$FV(PV, n, i, PMT)$
$n = 10 \times 12 = 120$	
$i = 12\%/12 = 1\%$ or .01	
$PMT = \$617.17$	
Solve for FV $= \$56,050.24$ (difference due to rounding of payment)	

An alternative method for finding mortgage balances at any time in the life of the mortgage is to divide the interest factor for the *FV* of $1 per period, for the year in which the balance is desired, by the *FV* of $1 per period factor for the original term of the mortgage, and then subtract that result from 1. The result of this computation is the loan balance expressed as a percentage of the original amount.

Solution: % of loan balance: $1 - \dfrac{FV \text{ at } n = 10 \text{ year}}{FV \text{ at } n = 30 \text{ year}}$	Function: $FV(PV, n, i, PMT)$

STEP 1: *FV* at 10 years:

  $n = 120, i = 12\%, PMT = -1, PV = 0$
Solve for FV = $230.03869

STEP 2: *FV* at 30 years:

  $n = 360, i = 12\%, PMT = -1, PV = 0$
Solve for FV = $3,494.9641

STEP 3: % of loan outstanding

  $1 - (\$230.03869 \div \$3,494.9641) = 93.42\%$

This is a more general formula that can be used regardless of the original dollar amount of the loan or payments because it gives a solution in percentage form. In this case, we determine that approximately 93.42 percent, or $56,052, of the original loan balance ($60,000) is still outstanding. This solution is nearly the same result that we obtained by discounting. The difference is due to rounding.

It should also be noted that many financial calculators may be purchased with a loan amortization function preprogrammed in them. Finding a loan balance becomes simply a matter of inputting the loan information and pressing an amortization key.

Finding Loan Balances—Other Amortization Patterns

We now consider how to solve for loan balances when loans are prepaid at the *end of 10 years* for the other three CPM loan categories discussed in this section.

Solution:		
Partial Amortizing	**Interest Only**	**Negative Amortizing**
$PV = -\$60,000$	$PV = -\$60,000$	$PV = -\$60,000$
$i = 12\%/12$	$i = 12\%/12$	$i = 12\%/12$
$n = 120$	$n = 120$	$n = 120$
$PMT = \$605.72$	$PMT = \$600$	$PMT = \$594.28$
Solve for FV = $58,684	**Solve for FV = $60,000**	**Solve for FV = $61,316**

The reader should note that simply substituting the loan payment that we calculated previously for each loan amortization pattern and solving for *FV* yields the appropriate loan balance at the end of 10 years.

A Note on Interest Rates, Loan Yields, and Early Payoff

At this point, it is not unusual for some readers to wonder: Is the cost to borrowers or the yield[6] to lenders different if the loan is repaid early or prior to maturity? It should be stressed that *regardless of when loans are repaid,* either at maturity or any time prior to

[6] When the term *yield* is used in lending it is usually referred to from the lender's perspective, who evaluates loans on the basis of profitability. Also, in addition to interest, lenders frequently charge fees on loans and use the term *yield* to include interest and fees on loans that they make.

maturity, each loan pattern discussed here will yield 12 percent compounded monthly to the lender. Similarly, the cost for the borrower also will be an annual rate of 12 percent compounded monthly, *regardless of when the loan is repaid.* This is the case because each loan pattern is structured around an accrual rate of 12 percent. Thus, interest is accrued and will eventually be paid on all loan balances outstanding. This is the case for fully, partially, zero, or negative amortizing loans.

However, we also should stress that if *additional financing fees* are charged by the lender, the effective cost of borrowing to the borrower will usually be greater than the interest rate. Yields to the lender also will vary depending on when the loan is repaid. We now turn to the topic of loan fees and the cost of borrowing.

Loan Closing Costs and Effective Borrowing Costs

Loan closing costs are incurred in many types of real estate financing, including residential property, income property, construction, and land development loans. Closing costs that affect the cost of borrowing are additional finance charges levied by the lender. These charges constitute additional costs to the borrower and must be included as a part of the cost of borrowing. Generally, lenders refer to these additional charges as *loan fees.*

Loan fees can be classified into two categories: loan origination fees and loan discount fees. **Loan origination fees** are intended to cover expenses incurred by the lender for processing and underwriting loan applications, preparation of loan documentation and amortization schedules, obtaining credit reports, and any other expenses that the lender believes should be recovered from the borrower. Lenders usually charge these costs to borrowers when the loan is made, or "closed," rather than charging higher interest rates. They do this because if the loan is repaid soon after closing, the additional interest earned by the lender as of the repayment date may not be enough to offset the fixed costs of loan origination. For example, assume that the prevailing interest rate on a $60,000 mortgage is 12 percent and the lender believes that expenses equal to $1,000 will be incurred to close the loan. If the lender chose to increase the interest rate to 12.25 percent to recover these origination costs, an additional $150 (approximately) would be collected during the first year ($60,000 × .0025). If the loan was repaid after the first year, the lender would not recover the full $1,000 in origination costs. This is why lenders attempt to "price" these origination costs separately.

The second category of loan fees is **loan discount fees,** or **points.**[7] This charge also represents an additional finance charge, but its primary purpose is to *adjust the yield* on a mortgage loan. In the context of real estate lending, loan discounting amounts to a borrower and lender negotiating the terms of a loan based on a certain loan amount. The lender then discounts the loan by charging a fee, which will be deducted from the contract loan to the borrower. Payments made by the borrower, however, are based on the contract amount of the loan. For example, assume a borrower and lender agree on a $60,000 loan at 12 percent interest for 30 years. The lender actually disburses $58,200 to the borrower by including a loan discount charge of 3 percent (points), or $1,800. The borrower is required to repay $60,000 at 12 percent interest for 30 years. However, because the borrower actually receives $58,200 but must repay $60,000 plus interest, it is clear that the actual borrowing cost to the buyer is greater than 12 percent.

Why do pricing practices such as discounting exist? Many reasons have been advanced. One reason given by lenders is that mortgage rates tend to be somewhat "sticky" in upward

---

[7] Lenders in some areas of the country refer to loan discounts as "discount points" or simply "points." In conventional mortgage lending, the borrower usually pays this charge, which adds to financing costs. In this chapter, we are concerned with conventional lending situations where the borrower pays the loan discount as a part of origination fees.

and downward moves. For example, suppose that the prevailing rate is 12 percent and market pressures begin to push rates upward. However, instead of all lenders moving the rate to perhaps 12.25 percent, one or more lenders may continue to quote 12 percent as the loan rate. However, in lieu of raising the interest rate, these lenders may charge borrowers loan discount points. This practice is also referred to as the borrower **"buying down the interest rate"**. That is, instead of paying 12.25 percent interest, the borrower will buy down the interest rate to 12 percent by paying discount points to the lender.

Another reason points may be charged is because many mortgage loans are originated by lenders who have entered into contracts with investors to assemble or package, then sell them a specific number, or dollar amount, of such loans. Such contracts with investors may require that loans are to be sold to yield investors a *rate of interest* very close to the rate that lenders expect to charge borrowers. Therefore, in order for originating lenders to earn a profit, points are charged to borrowers to provide lenders with revenue for performing origination services prior to the delivery of loans to investors.

Another situation may provide lenders with an opportunity to replace revenue in a declining interest rate environment. In these cases, interest rates may begin to decline before the date that the loan is made to the borrower but after the date on which the lender and investor agree on the yield on the packaged mortgages to be sold. In this case, loans will be originated at a lower interest rate, and the lender will charge discount points in order to offset the decline in interest rates being charged to borrowers as the loans are being assembled or packaged.

A final reason for loan discount fees is that lenders believe that, in this way, they can better price the loan relative to the *risk* they take. For example, in the beginning of this chapter we referred to the risk premium component (*p*) of the interest rate. However, the risk for some individual borrowers is slightly higher than it is for others. Further, these loans may require more time and expense to process and control. Hence, discount points may be charged by the lender (in addition to origination fees) to compensate for the slightly higher risk.

The practice of using loan origination fees and discount points has historically prevailed throughout the lending industry. It is important to understand (1) how these charges affect borrowing costs and (2) how to include them in computing effective borrowing costs on loan alternatives when financing any real estate transaction.

Loan Fees and Borrowing Costs

To illustrate loan fees and their effects on borrowing costs in more detail, consider the following problem: A borrower would like to finance a property for 30 years at 12 percent interest. The lender indicates that an origination fee of 3 percent of the loan amount will be charged to obtain the loan. What is the actual interest cost of the loan?

We structure the problem by determining the amount of the origination fee [.03 × ($60,000) = $1,800]. Second, we know that the monthly mortgage payments based on $60,000 for 30 years at 12 percent will be $617.17. Now we can determine the effect of the origination fee on the interest rate being charged as follows:

Contractual loan amount	$60,000
Less: Origination fee	1,800
Net cash disbursed by lender	$58,200
Amount to be repaid:	
Based on $60,000 contractual loan amount, $617.17 for 30 years.	

In other words, the amount actually disbursed by the lender will be $58,200, but the repayment will be made on the basis of $60,000 plus interest at 12 percent compounded monthly, in the amount of $617.17 each month. Consequently, the lender will earn a yield on the $58,200 actually disbursed, which must be greater than 12 percent.

Using a financial calculator, we can calculate the **effective interest rate** for the loan, assuming it is outstanding until maturity, as 12.41 percent. This yield is obviously higher than the 12 percent contract, or nominal, rate of interest specified in the note or mortgage.

Solution:	Function:
$n = 30 \times 12 = 360$	$i\,(n, PMT, PV, FV)$
$PMT = -\$617.17$	
$PV = \$58,200$	
$FV = 0$	

Solve for

i (monthly) = 1.034324% monthly rate

i (annualized) = 1.034324% $\times$ 12 = 12.41% effective interest rate

This computation forms the basis for a widely used rule of thumb in real estate finance; that is, for every 2 percentage points in the origination fee charged to the borrower, the effective cost to the borrower, or investment yield earned by the lender, increases by approximately one-fourth of a percent above the contract rate. Note that in our solution, we obtained an effective rate of 12.41 percent, versus 12.375 percent using the approximation. While this estimate is close to the yield calculated in one example, we have assumed that the loan remains outstanding until maturity. However, most loans on the average are "prepaid" or paid off long before maturity. Hence, this rule of thumb, while helpful, generally provides a very rough estimate of the effective cost (yield) for most mortgage loans.[8]

We should point out that, in the above example, the 12.41 percent effective interest rate is an *annual rate of interest, compounded monthly*. Many analysts prefer to calculate the **effective annual interest rate** (recall that this is equivalent to an annual rate of interest, compounded annually). We can easily calculate this as follows:

STEP 1:	
Solution:	Function:
$i = 12.41\%$	$FV\,(PV, i, n)$
$PV = -\$60,000$	
$n = 12$	
Solve for FV = $67,884.47	

STEP 2:	
Solution:	
$FV = \$67,884.47$	
$n = 1$	
$PV = \$60,000.00$	
Solve for i = 13.14%	

[8] This rule of thumb will become very inaccurate if the payoff period is very short relative to the maturity and when the level of interest rates increases.

Because of problems involving loan fees and the potential abuse by some lenders of charging high fees to unwary borrowers, Congress passed the federal Truth-in-Lending Act to provide disclosure regarding the effects of loan fees to *consumers purchasing residences.** As a result of this legislation, the lender must disclose to consumers the **annual percentage rate** *(APR)* being charged on the loan. (We will deal with the *APR* more extensively in Chapter 8.) Calculation of the *APR* is generally done in the manner shown for calculating the effective interest rate, assuming that the loan is repaid at maturity. The *APR* in our chapter example would be disclosed to the borrower at closing as 12.41 percent. The *APR*, then, does reflect origination fees and discount points and treats them as additional income or yield to the lender regardless of what costs, if any, the fees are intended to cover. Other fees charged by the lender as a condition for obtaining the loan also may have to be included in the *APR.*†

* See Regulation Z of the Federal Reserve Board, 12 C.F.R., sec. 226, as amended.

† Generally, the *APR* disclosed to the borrower is the effective interest rate computed under the assumption that the loan will be outstanding until maturity. The lender *may* round the *APR* to the nearest quarter percent; however, it must fall in a range that is within one-eighth of 1 percent above or below the *APR* that is calculated based on federal guidelines as disclosed in Regulation Z. If the reader desires greater accuracy in these computations, consult *Computational Procedures Manual for Supplement 1 to Regulation Z of the Federal Reserve Board: Calculator Instructions* (Office of the Comptroller of the Currency, February 1978).

Note that because of the effects of (1) monthly compounding and (2) discount points, the *effective annual interest rate* is 13.14 percent, whereas the nominal interest rate is 12 percent and the effective interest cost is 12.41 percent (annual rate of interest compounded monthly) for the loan in our example.

Loan Fees and Early Repayment: Fully Amortizing Loans

An important effect of loan fees and early loan repayment must now be examined in terms of the effect on interest rate. We will show in this section that when loan fees are charged and the loan is paid off before maturity, the effective interest rate of the loan increases even further than when the loan is repaid at maturity.

To demonstrate this point, we again assume our borrower obtained the $60,000 loan at 12 percent for 30 years and was charged an $1,800 (3 percent) loan origination fee. At the end of *five years,* the borrower decides to sell the property. The mortgage contains a due-on-sale clause; hence, the loan balance must be repaid at the time the property is sold. What will be the effective interest rate on the loan as a result of both the origination fee and early loan repayment?

To determine the effective interest rate on the loan, we first find the outstanding loan balance after five years to be $58,598.16. To solve for the yield to the lender (cost to the borrower), we proceed by finding the rate at which to discount the monthly payments of $617.17 *and* the lump-sum payment of $58,598.16 after five years so that the present value of both equals $58,200, or the amount actually disbursed by the lender.

This presents a new type of discounting problem. We are dealing with an annuity in the form of monthly payments for five years *and* a loan balance, or single lump-sum receipt of cash, at the end of five years. To find the yield on this loan, we proceed as follows:

STEP 1: Solve for remaining balance:

Solution: Function:

$$n = 25 \times 12 = 300$$

$$i = 12\%/12 = 1\% \text{ or } .01$$ $PV(n, i, PMT, FV)$

$$PMT = -\$617.17$$

$$FV = 0$$

Solve for PV = $58,598.16 (remaining balance)

STEP 2: Next, solve for the interest payment, holding a 30-year loan, for five years, and
discounted by the loan origination fee:

Solution: Function:

$$n = 5 \times 12 = 60$$ $i(n, PMT, FV, PV)$

$$PMT = -\$617.17$$

$$PV = \$58,200$$

$$FV = -\$58,598.16$$

Solve for i (monthly) = 1.069%

Solve for i (annual)   = 1.069% $\times$ 12 = 12.82%

An Excel template is included on the Web site for this book that may be used to calculate
the same yield shown in this example (*www.mhhe.com/bf15e*).

This formulation simply says that we want to find the interest rate (i) that will make the
present value of both the $617.17 monthly annuity and the $58,598.16 received at the end
of five years equal to the amount disbursed, or $58,200. From the above analysis, we can
conclude that the actual yield (or actual interest rate) that we have computed to be
approximately 12.82 percent is higher than both the contract interest rate of 12 percent and
the 12.41 percent yield computed assuming that the loan was outstanding until maturity.
This is true because the $1,800 origination fee is earned over only five years instead of
30 years, which is equivalent to earning a higher rate of compound interest on the $58,200
disbursed. Hence, when this additional amount earned is coupled with the 12 percent
interest being earned on the monthly loan balance, this increases yield to 12.82 percent.[9]

Relationship between Yield and Time

Based on the preceding discussion, we can make some general observations about
the relationship of mortgage yields and the time during which mortgages are outstanding.
The first observation is that the effective interest rate on a mortgage will always be
equal to the contract rate of interest when no finance charges are made at the time of
loan origination or repayment. This follows because, as we saw in Exhibit 4–2, the
level payment pattern assures the lender of earning only a given annual rate of interest,
compounded monthly, on the monthly outstanding loan balance. Hence, the outstanding
mortgage balance can be repaid at any time, and the lender's yield (borrower's cost) will
not be affected. It will be equal to the contract rate of interest.

The second observation is that if origination or financing fees are charged to the
borrower, the following occurs: (1) the effective yield will be higher than the contract rate
of interest and (2) the yield will increase as repayment occurs sooner in the life of the

---

[9] If the loan is repaid in less than one year, the yield becomes larger and approaches infinity, should
the loan be repaid immediately after closing.

Web App

There are numerous companies offering mortgage rate information on the Internet, such as **www.bankrate.com.** Find a quote for a 15-year fixed rate mortgage on a $150,000 primary residence valued at $200,000. What are the current interest rate, discount points, and other lender fees for the loan you found?

Calculate the effective cost of the mortgage over the lifetime of the loan. Calculate the effective cost of paying off the mortgage after seven years. How do these rates compare to the stated *APR*? What accounts for the discrepancy between the effective rate and the *APR*?

EXHIBIT 4–8
Relationship between Mortgage Yield and Financing Fees at Various Repayment Dates

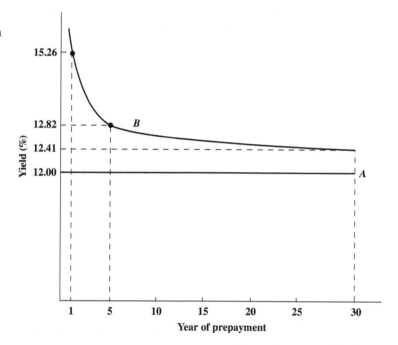

mortgage. These relationships can be explained by referring to Exhibit 4–8, where the two curves, *A* and *B,* represent the mortgage yield pattern under two assumptions. Line *A* represents the effective yield, or cost, when no financing fees are charged to the borrower. In our previous example, the yield would remain at 12 percent, equal to the contract rate of interest regardless of when the loan is repaid; hence, the horizontal line is over the range of 0 to 30 years. Curve *B* represents a series of loan yields computed under the assumptions that a 3 percent origination fee is charged to the borrower and that the loan is prepaid in various years prior to maturity. In our example, we note that the yield earned by the borrower is 15.26 percent if the loan is repaid one year after closing and that it diminishes and eventually equals 12.41 percent after 30 years. Hence, we can again conclude that if financing fees are charged to the buyer, the effective yield to the lender (cost to the borrower) can range from one that is extremely high if prepaid, say, after one year (the yield in that case would be approximately 15.26 percent) to a yield that would be considerably lower if repaid at maturity, or 12.41 percent. If a borrower knows when he or she expects to repay a loan, this method of computing the effective borrowing cost should be used. This is particularly important if the borrower is comparing alternative loans with different terms.

Prepayment Penalties

Many borrowers mistakenly take for granted that a loan can be prepaid in part or in full anytime before the maturity date. This is not the case; if the mortgage note is silent on this matter, the borrower may have to negotiate the privilege of early repayment with the lender. However, many mortgages provide explicitly that the borrower can pay a **prepayment penalty,** should the borrower desire to prepay the loan.

One rationale for a prepayment penalty is that the lender may be trying to recover a portion of loan origination costs not charged to the borrower at closing. This may have been done by the lender to compete for the loan by making initial closing costs lower for the borrower. Another reason for prepayment penalties is that the lender has agreed to extend funds for a specified time, 30 years in our present example. Early payment from the lender's view may represent an unanticipated inflow of funds that may or may not be readily reinvested in periods when mortgage rates are stable or are expected to decline. However, if interest rates undergo a sustained increase over long periods of time, lenders usually welcome early repayments since they may be able to loan out funds again at higher rates of interest.

Another reason for prepayment penalties is that they are not included in the computation of the *APR;* hence, they are not included in the *APR* disclosure to the borrower. Borrowers may not be able to determine the effect of these penalties on borrowing costs and, therefore, the penalties represent a technique lenders use to increase yields. Some states have begun prohibiting the enforceability of prepayment penalties to individuals financing residences if the loan has been outstanding more than some specified minimum number of years. Also, in areas where penalties are allowed, lenders may waive them if the buyer of a property agrees to originate a new loan with the same lender.

Because of the use of prepayment penalties, we want to know the effective mortgage loan yield (interest rate) when both a loan discount fee and a prepayment penalty are charged on the loan. To illustrate, we consider both the effects of the 3 percent loan discount and a 3 percent prepayment penalty on the outstanding loan balance for the $60,000, 30-year loan with a contract interest rate of 12 percent used in the preceding section. We assume the loan is the effective interest rate to the borrower (yield to the lender). To solve for the yield, mortgage funds actually disbursed in this case will be $60,000 minus the origination fee of $1,800, or $58,200. Taking the loan discount fee into account, we want to find the discount rate which, when used to discount the series of monthly payments of $617.17 plus the outstanding loan balance of $58,598.16 and the prepayment penalty of $1,758 (3% of $58,598.16), or a total of $60,356, will result in a present value equal to the amount of funds actually disbursed, $58,200.

Using a financial calculator, with a 3 percent origination fee, early payment in the fifth year, and a 3 percent prepayment penalty, we see that the effective yield on the loan will increase to about 13.25 percent.

Solution:	Function:
$n = 5 \times 12 = 60$	$i\,(n, PMT, FV, PV)$
$PMT = -\$617.17$	
$PV = \$58,200$	
$FV = -\$60,356$	
Solve for *i* (monthly) $= 1.10425\%$	
Solve for *i* (annually) $= (1.10425\% \times 12) = 13.25\%$	

In this case, the *APR* will still be disclosed at 12.375 percent, which reflects the loan discount only, not the prepayment penalty, and assumes the loan is repaid at the end of 30 years. The actual yield computed here of 13.25 percent is a marked difference from both the loan contract rate of 12 percent and the disclosed *APR* of 12.375 percent.

Charging Fees to Achieve Yield, or "Pricing" FRMs

In the preceding examples, we have developed the notion of the effective borrowing costs and yield from a given set of loan terms. However, we should consider how these are determined by lenders when "pricing" a loan. As we discussed earlier in the chapter, lenders generally have alternatives in which they can invest funds. Hence, they will determine available yields on those alternatives for given maturities and weigh those yields and risks against yields and risks on mortgage loans. Similarly, competitive lending terms established by other lenders establish yields that managers must consider when establishing loan terms. By continually monitoring alternatives and competitive conditions, management establishes loan offer terms for various categories of loans, given established underwriting and credit standards for borrowers. Hence, a set of terms designed to achieve a competitive yield on categories of loans representing various ratios of loan-to-property value (70% loans, 80% loans, etc.) are established for borrowers who are acceptable risks. These terms are then revised as competitive conditions change.

If, based on competitive yields available on alternative investments of equal risk, managers of a lending institution believe that a 13 percent yield is competitive on 80 percent mortgages with terms of 30 years and expected repayment periods of 10 years, how can they set terms on all loans made in the 80 percent category to ensure a 13 percent yield? Obviously, one way is to price all loans being originated at a contract rate of 13 percent. However, management may also consider pricing loans at 12 percent interest and charging either loan fees or prepayment penalties or both to achieve the required yield. Why would lenders do this? Because (1) they have fixed origination costs to recover and (2) competitors may still be originating loans at a contract rate of 12 percent.

To illustrate how fees for all loans in a specific category can be set, we consider the following solution:

STEP 1: Solve for payment

Solution: Function:

$$PV = -1$$ $$PMT \, (PV, i, n, FV)$$

$$i = 12\%/12 = 1\% \text{ or } .01$$

$$n = 30 \times 12 = 360$$

$$FV = 0$$

Solve for *PMT* = .010286

STEP 2: Solve for loan balance EOY_{10}

Solution: Function:

$$PV = -1$$ $$FV \, (PV, i, n, PMT)$$

$$n = 120$$

$$i = 12\%/12$$

$$PMT = .010286$$

Solve for *FV* = .934180

STEP 3: Solve for *PV*, $i = 13\%$

Solution: Function:

$$FV = .934180$$ $$PV \, (FV, i, n, PMT)$$

$$i = 13\%/12$$

$$n = 120$$

$$PMT = .010286$$

Solve for *PV* = .9453

The result $PV = .9453$ means that the net disbursement at loan closing should be 94.53 percent, or 94.5 percent (rounded), of the loan amount. Therefore, if the loan is priced by offering terms of 12 percent interest and a 5.5 percent origination fee ($100\% - 94.5\%$) and the loan is repaid at the end of 10 years (EOY_{10}), management will have its 13 percent yield.

Other FRM Loan Patterns—Declining Payments and Constant Amortization Rates

The **constant amortizing mortgage (CAM)** loan pattern represents yet another variation that may be considered in loan structuring. Payments on CAMs are determined first by computing a constant amount of each monthly payment to be applied to principal or monthly amortization. Interest is then computed on the monthly loan balance and added to the monthly amount of amortization. The total monthly payment is determined by adding the constant amount of monthly amortization to interest on the outstanding loan balance. Consider the following example of a CAM loan. A loan was made for $60,000 for a 30-year term at 12 percent (annual rate compounded monthly); payments were to be made monthly and were to consist of *both* interest and amortization (or reduction of principal), so that the loan would be repaid at the end of 30 years. However, amortization is determined by dividing the number of months or the term of the loan (360) into the loan amount ($60,000), resulting in a reduction of principal of $166.67 per month. Interest would be computed on the outstanding loan balance and then added to amortization to determine the monthly payment. An illustration of the payment pattern and loan balance is shown in Exhibit 4–9.

The computation in Exhibit 4–9 shows that the initial monthly payment of $766.67 includes amortization of $166.67, plus interest computed on the outstanding loan balance. The total monthly payment would decline each month by a constant amount, or $1.67 (.01 × $166.67). The loan payment and the balance patterns are shown in Exhibit 4–10. It should be kept in mind that in spite of the declining monthly payment pattern, the yield in the CAM remains at 12 percent interest. Like the fully amortizing, partially amortizing, interest only, and negative amortizing loans, the CAM is also a fixed interest rate mortgage loan. Its payments and balance pattern are simply structured differently than the loans in our previous examples.

The constant amortizing payment pattern is considered to be a very conservative loan structure because it places primary emphasis on the amortization of the loan. Nonetheless, it demonstrates yet another alternative that may be of value when structuring a loan. Or perhaps, it may be combined with another loan amortization pattern. It also demonstrates

EXHIBIT 4–9
Monthly Payments and Loan Balance (Constant Amortizing Loan)

(1) Month	(2) Opening Balance ×	(3) Interest (.12 ÷ 12)	(4) Amortization	(3)+(4) Monthly Payment	(2)−(4) Ending Balance
1	$60,000.00	$600.00	$166.67	$766.67	$59,833.33
2	59,833.33	598.33	166.67	765.00	59,666.66
3	59,666.66	596.67	166.67	763.34	59,499.99
4	59,499.99	595.00	166.67	761.67	59,333.32
5	59,333.32	593.33	166.67	760.00	59,166.65
6	59,166.65	591.67	166.67	758.34	58,999.98
.	.	.	.	.	.
.	.	.	.	.	.
360	166.67	1.67	166.67	168.34	–0–

EXHIBIT 4–10
Declining Loan
Payment and Balance
Patterns (Constant
Amortizing Loan)

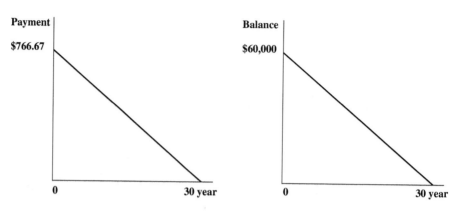

the range of alternative payment and amortization patterns available within the fixed interest rate class of mortgage loans.

Amortization Schedules and Callable Loans

A final variation in loan structuring to be included in this section is a commonly used provision in which an amortization schedule, if specified in the note, is different from the maturity date. For example, two parties may agree that a $100,000 fully amortizing loan will be made at 12 percent interest with monthly payments calculated based on a 30 year *amortization schedule*. However, both parties agree that the loan *will be,* or may be, **callable** at the lender's option, at the end of 10 years. In this case, payments can be calculated as follows:

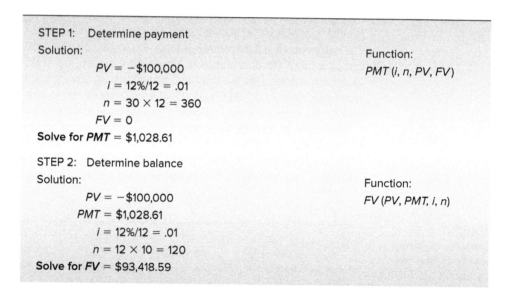

STEP 1:   Determine payment
Solution: Function:
$$PV = -\$100{,}000$$ $PMT\,(i, n, PV, FV)$
$$i = 12\%/12 = .01$$
$$n = 30 \times 12 = 360$$
$$FV = 0$$
Solve for **PMT** = $1,028.61

STEP 2:   Determine balance
Solution: Function:
$$PV = -\$100{,}000$$ $FV\,(PV, PMT, i, n)$
$$PMT = \$1{,}028.61$$
$$i = 12\%/12 = .01$$
$$n = 12 \times 10 = 120$$
Solve for **FV** = $93,418.59

If the loan is called at the end of 10 years, the amount due would be the balance at that time, or $93,418.59 (reader should verify). This loan structure is used by borrowers and lenders (1) to keep monthly loan payments lower than they would be if a fully amortizing loan was made for 10 years, (2) to keep the loan maturity relatively short at 10 years, and (3) to achieve some loan amortization even though the loan is paid after 10 years.

By now, the reader should be aware that depending on the objectives of the borrower and lender, loans can be *structured* to achieve many results. **Loan structuring** is usually described as a process of adjusting loan terms to calibrate loan payments, loan balances, amortization rates, and so on, to achieve desired results. Such results usually include lower monthly payments than would be available under a fully amortizing structure. However, it could also be that another objective is sought, such as having a desired loan balance at maturity.

"Reverse Mortgages"

Reverse mortgage loans[10] represent a very different type of mortgage loan. Instead of receiving the full loan proceeds at closing, the loan amount in a reverse mortgage is "taken down" as irregular periodic payments until such payments and accrued interest reach the agreed-upon loan amount. In real estate construction and development, these "take-downs" are also referred to as "draws." In recent years, reverse mortgages have also become important to the home-owning population as they approach retirement and seek ways to supplement their retirement income. For example, assume that a household owns a residential property worth $500,000 today. They would like to use the value of the property to supplement their retirement income with a reverse mortgage. A lender agrees to make a loan in an amount not to exceed $250,000 for a period of 10 years. However, instead of giving the borrower cash in the amount of $250,000, the lender agrees to let the borrower *take down the loan in monthly installments* over the life of the mortgage. The lender will charge an interest rate of 10 percent on the loan. What will be the maximum monthly payments that the lender will make to the borrower under these terms? We can solve for this as follows:

Solution:	Function:
$FV = -\$250,000$	$PMT\,(FV, i, n, PV)$
$i = 10\%/12$	
$n = 120$	
$PV = 0$	
Solve for PMT $= \$1,220.44$	

Looking at this example, note that the borrower can supplement his income by drawing $1,220.44 from the lender each month for 120 months, at the end of which time the lender will be owed a total of $250,000. If the property has retained its value of $500,000, the homeowner will have $250,000 in equity at the end of 10 years. If the borrower makes no more draws, the loan balance will continue to increase at 10 percent until the property is sold or the owner dies.

Exhibit 4–11 shows the monthly payment pattern and loan balances for our reverse mortgage example. To determine reverse mortgage loan balances, we reverse the procedure used in our previous FRM examples; that is, we solve for *future value* (*FV*) and not present value. As shown in the exhibit, instead of the declining loan balances that are characteristic of fully amortizing mortgage loans, reverse mortgage balances *increase* over time. For example, after three years our reverse mortgage loan balance would be:

Solution:	Function:
$i = 10\%/12$	$FV\,(i, n, PV, PMT)$
$PMT = \$1220.44$	
$n = 36$	
$PV = 0$	
Solve for FV $= \$50,992.21$	

[10]These are also known as home equity conversion mortgages (HECMs).

With the baby boomers advancing in age and many having a substantial amount of equity in residential housing, reverse mortgages, also known as home equity conversion mortgages (HECMs), have been developed. These loans are designed to help seniors "unlock" the equity by borrowing against property value, thereby supplementing their retirement income. Most mortgage loans are *federally insured* and require borrowers to consult with an approved reverse mortgage counselor. Borrowers should be aware of the following general qualifications:

- Applicant must be 62 years of age or older.
- The borrower must have title to the home and the home must be the borrower's primary residence.
- Borrowers can generally qualify as follows:

  —age 62,   50% of value, 10 years or expected life
  —age 72,   60% of value, 10 years or expected life
  —age 82,   70% of value, 10 years or expected life

- As is the case with other mortgage loans, reverse mortgages usually require certain up-front costs, including organization fees (points), mortgage insurance, loan servicing fees, an appraisal, and other closing costs.
- Draw-downs may be taken in one lump sum, monthly payments, or through a line of credit. This loan also may give the borrower the option of making draw-downs when desired. In this event, interest is charged at prevailing rates on the monthly outstanding balance.
- Interest rates may be fixed or floating (called adjustable rate mortgages, or ARMs).
- Borrowers must continue to maintain the residence and pay property taxes and hazard insurance.
- The sum of all draw-downs plus interest does not have to be paid back unless the homeowner permanently leaves the home or until death. In the latter event, title to the property would be obtained by the borrower's heirs. Typically, the property would then be sold and the loan balance repaid (just as would be the case without the reverse mortgage).
- Amounts received from a reverse mortgage are not subject to federal income taxes.
- All interest accrued under a reverse mortgage is not deductible until actually paid. This is usually when the loan is paid off in full.

Useful Web sites:

www.aarp.org/money/personal/reverse_mortgages
www.reversemortgage.org
www.hud.gov/buying/rvrsmort.cfm

The balance at the end of any year can be determined by changing the values for n and resolving for future value.

EXHIBIT 4–11
Reverse Mortgage Draw and Balance Patterns

Year	Draw per Month	Balance EOY
1	$1,220.44	$ 15,335.52
2	1,220.44	32,276.87
3	1,220.44	50,992.21
4	1,220.44	71,667.28
5	1,220.44	94,505.30
6	1,220.44	119,738.97
7	1,220.44	147,612.73
8	1,220.44	178,405.23
9	1,220.44	212,422.11
10	1,220.44	250,000.00

Conclusion

In this chapter, we discussed various approaches to pricing and structuring fixed interest rate mortgage loans. We saw that the price or interest rate on the loan depends on a number of factors, including various types of risk that affect mortgage lenders. It is important to keep these risk factors in mind in future chapters as we consider alternative mortgage instruments which are often designed in ways that alter risk characteristics. Although the focus of this chapter has been on residential mortgages, the concepts and calculations are equally important for commercial mortgages, which also are discussed in later chapters. We will find that the riskiness of the mortgage is also a factor in the risk and expected rate of return for investors in real estate income properties.

Key Terms

accrual rate, *83*
amortization, *84*
annual percentage rate (*APR*), *98*
anticipated inflation, *80*
balloon payment, *88*
buying down the interest
  rate, *96*
callable loans, *104*
constant amortizing mortgage
  (CAM), *103*
constant payment mortgage
  (CPM), *83*
default risk, *79*

derived demand, *77*
effective annual interest rate, *97*
effective interest rate, *97*
fully amortizing loan, *84*
interest, *77*
interest-only loan, *84, 89*
interest rate risk, *80*
legislative risk, *80*
liquidity risk, *80*
loan closing costs, *95*
loan constants, *87*
loan discount fees, *95*
loan origination fees, *95*

loan structuring, *104*
negative amortizing loan, *84, 90*
nominal interest rate, *78*
partially amortizing loan, *84*
pay rate, *83*
points, *95*
prepayment penalty, *101*
prepayment risk, *80*
principal, *84*
real rate of interest, *78*
reverse mortgage, *105*
unanticipated inflation, *80*
zero amortizing loan, *84*

Useful Web Sites

www.nahb.org—National Association of Home Buyers—Provides industry news, new home listings, and remodeling information.

www.bankrate.com—Provides mortgage rate information from numerous national lenders.

www.freddiemac.com/pmms/pmms30.htm—This is a good site for finding fixed rates and points for 30-year mortgages.

Questions

1. What are the major differences between the four CPM loans discussed in this chapter? What are the advantages to borrowers and risks to lenders for each? What elements do each of the loans have in common?

2. Define *amortization*. List the five types discussed in this chapter.

3. Why do the monthly payments in the beginning months of a CPM loan contain a higher proportion of interest than principal repayment?

4. What are loan closing costs? How can they be categorized?

5. In the absence of loan fees, does repaying a loan early ever affect the actual or true interest cost to the borrower?

6. Why do lenders charge origination fees and loan discount fees?

7. What is the connection between the Truth-in-Lending Act and the annual percentage rate (*APR*)?

8. What is the effective borrowing cost?

9. What is meant by a nominal rate of interest on a mortgage loan?

10. What is the accrual rate and payment rate on a mortgage loan? What happens when the two are equal? What happens when the accrual rate exceeds the payment rate? What if the payment rate exceeds the accrual rate?

11. An expected inflation premium is said to be part of the interest rate. What does this mean?

12. A mortgage loan is made to Mr. Jones for $30,000 at 10 percent interest for 20 years. If Mr. Jones has a choice between either a fully amortizing CPM or a CAM, which one would result in his paying a greater amount of total interest over the life of the mortgage? Would one of these mortgages be likely to have a higher interest rate than the other? Explain your answer.

13. What is negative amortization?

14. What is partial amortization?

Problems

1. A borrower obtains a fully amortizing CPM loan for $125,000 at 11 percent interest for 10 years. What will be the monthly payment on the loan? If this loan had a maturity of 30 years, what would be the monthly payment?

2. A fully amortizing mortgage loan is made for $80,000 at 6 percent interest for 25 years. Payments are to be made monthly. Calculate:

   a. Monthly payments.

   b. Interest and principal payments during month 1.

   c. Total principal and total interest paid over 25 years.

   d. The outstanding loan balance if the loan is repaid at the end of year 10.

   e. Total monthly interest and principal payments through year 10.

   f. What would the breakdown of interest and principal be during month 50?

3. A fully amortizing mortgage loan is made for $100,000 at 6 percent interest for 30 years. Determine payments for each of the periods *a–d* below if interest is accured:

   a. Monthly.

   b. Quarterly.

   c. Annually.

   d. Weekly.

4. Regarding Problem 3, how much total interest and principal would be paid over the entire 30-year life of the mortgage in each case? Which payment pattern would have the greatest total amount of interest over the 30-year term of the loan? Why?

5. A fully amortizing mortgage loan is made for $100,000 at 6 percent interest for 20 years.

   a. Calculate the monthly payment for a CPM loan.

   b. What will the *total* of payments be for the entire 20-year period? Of this total, how much will be the interest?

   c. Assume the loan is repaid at the end of eight years. What will be the outstanding balance? How much total interest will have been collected by then?

   d. The borrower now chooses to reduce the loan balance by $5,000 at the end of year 8.

      (1) What will be the new loan maturity assuming that loan payments are not reduced?

      (2) Assume the loan maturity will not be reduced. What will the new payments be?

6. A 30-year fully amortizing mortgage loan was made 10 years ago for $75,000 at 6 percent interest. The borrower would like to prepay the mortgage balance by $10,000.

   a. Assuming he can reduce his monthly mortgage payments, what is the new mortgage payment?

   b. Assuming the loan maturity is shortened and using the original monthly payments, what is the new loan maturity?

7. A fully amortizing mortgage is made for $100,000 at 6.5 percent interest. If the monthly payments are $1,000 per month, when will the loan be repaid?

8. A fully amortizing mortgage is made for $80,000 for 25 years. Total monthly payments will be $900 per month. What is the interest rate on the loan?

9. A partially amortizing mortgage is made for $60,000 for a term of 10 years. The borrower and lender agree that a balance of $20,000 will remain and be repaid as a lump sum at that time.

   a. If the interest rate is 7 percent, what must monthly payments be over the 10-year period?

   b. If the borrower chooses to repay the loan after five years instead of at the end of year 10, what must the loan balance be?

10. An "interest-only" mortgage is made for $80,000 at 10 percent interest for 10 years. The lender and borrower agree that monthly payments will be constant and will require *no* loan amortization.

    a. What will the monthly payments be?

    b. What will be the loan balance after five years?

    c. If the loan is repaid after five years, what will be the yield to the lender?

    d. Instead of being repaid after five years, what will be the yield if the loan is repaid after 10 years?

11. A partially amortizing loan for $90,000 for 10 years is made at 6 percent interest. The lender and borrower agree that payments will be monthly and that a balance of $20,000 will remain and be repaid at the end of year 10. Assuming 2 points are charged by the lender, what will be the yield if the loan is repaid at the end of year 10? What must the loan balance be if it is repaid after year 4? What will be the yield to the lender if the loan is repaid at the end of year 4?

12. A loan for $50,000 is made for 10 years at 8 percent interest and *no monthly payments* are scheduled.

    a. How much will be due at the end of 10 years?

    b. What will be the yield to the lender if it is repaid after eight years? (Assume monthly compounding.)

    c. If 1 point is charged in (*b*) what will be the yield to the lender?

13. John wants to buy a property for $105,000 and wants an 80 percent loan for $84,000. A lender indicates that a fully amortizing loan can be obtained for 30 years (360 months) at 8 percent interest; however, a loan origination fee of $3,500 will also be necessary for John to obtain the loan.

    a. How much will the lender actually disburse?

    b. What is the effective interest rate for the borrower, assuming that the mortgage is paid off after 30 years (full term)?

    c. If John pays off the loan after five years, what is the effective interest rate? Why is it different from the effective interest rate in (*b*)?

    d. Assume the lender also imposes a prepayment penalty of 2 percent of the outstanding loan balance if the loan is repaid within eight years of closing. If John repays the loan after five years with the prepayment penalty, what is the effective interest rate?

14. A lender is considering what terms to allow on a loan. Current market terms are 9 percent interest for 25 years for a fully amortizing loan. The borrower, Rich, has requested a loan of $100,000. The lender believes that extra credit analysis and careful loan control will have to be exercised because Rich has never borrowed such a large sum before. In addition, the lender expects that market rates will move upward very soon, perhaps even before the loan is closed. To be on the safe side, the lender decides to extend to Rich a CPM loan commitment for $95,000 at 9 percent interest for 25 years; however, the lender wants to charge a loan origination fee to make the mortgage loan yield 10 percent. What origination fee should the lender charge? What fee should be charged if it is expected that the loan will be repaid after 10 years?

15. A borrower is faced with choosing between two loans. Loan A is available for $75,000 at 6 percent interest for 30 years, with 6 points to be included in closing costs. Loan B would be made for the same amount, but for 7 percent interest for 30 years, with 2 points to be included in the closing costs. Both loans will be fully amortizing.

    a. If the loan is repaid after 20 years, which loan would be the better choice?

    b. If the loan is repaid after five years, which loan is the better choice?

16. A reverse mortgage is made with a balance not to exceed $300,000 on a property now valued at $700,000. The loan calls for monthly payments to be made to the borrower for 120 months at an interest rate of 11 percent.

    a. What will the monthly payments be?

    b. What will be the loan balance at the end of year 3?

    c. Assume that the borrower must have monthly draws of $2,000 for the first 50 months of the loan. Remaining draws from months 51 to 120 must be determined so that the $300,000 maximum is not exceeded in month 120. What will draws by the borrower be during months 51 to 120?

17. A borrower and a lender agree on a $200,000 loan at 10 percent interest. An amortization schedule of 25 years has been agreed on; however, the lender has the option to "call" the loan after five years. If called, how much will have to be paid by the borrower at the end of five years?

18. A fully amortizing CAM loan is made for $125,000 at 11 percent interest for 20 years.

    a. What will be the payments and balances for the first six months?

    b. What would payments be for a CPM loan?

    c. If both loans were repaid at the end of year 5, would the lender earn a higher rate of interest on either loan?

19. A $50,000 interest-only mortgage loan is made for 30 years at a nominal interest rate of 6 percent. Interest is to be accrued daily, but payments are to be made monthly. Assume 30 days each month.

    a. What will the monthly payments be on such a loan?

    b. What will the loan balance be at the end of 30 years?

    c. What is the effective annual rate on this loan?

20. **Comprehensive Review Problem:** A mortgage loan in the amount of $100,000 is made at 12 percent interest for 20 years. Payments are to be monthly in each part of this problem.

    a. What will monthly payments be if:

       (1) The loan is fully amortizing?

       (2) It is partially amortizing and a balloon payment of $50,000 is scheduled at the end of year 20?

       (3) It is a nonamortizing, or "interest-only" loan?

       (4) It is a negative amortizing loan and the loan balance will be $150,000 at the end of year 20?

    b. What will the loan balance be at the end of year 5 under parts a (1) through a (4)?

    c. What would be the interest portion of the payment scheduled for payment at the end of month 61 for each case (1) through (4) above?

    d. Assume that the lender charges 3 points to close the loans in parts a (1) through a (4). What would be the *APR* for each?

    e. Assuming that 3 points are paid at closing and the loan is prepaid at the end of year 5, what will be the effective rate of interest for each loan in parts a (1) through a (4) ?

    f. Assume conditions in a (1) except that payments will be "interest only" for the first three years (36 months). If the loan is to fully amortize over the remaining 17 years, what must the monthly payments be from year 4 through year 20?

    g. Refer to a (4) above, where the borrower and lender agree that the loan balance of $150,000 will be payable at the end of year 20:

       (1) How much total interest will be paid from all payments? How much total amortization will be paid?

       (2) What will be the loan balance at the end of year 3?

       (3) If the loan is repaid at the end of year 3, what will be the effective rate of interest?

       (4) If the lender charges 4 points to make this loan, what will the effective rate of interest be if the loan is repaid at the end of year 3?

21. **Excel.** Refer to the "Ch4 Eff Cost" tab in the Excel Workbook provided on the Web site. Suppose that another loan is available that is an 11 percent interest rate with 6 points. What is the effective cost of this loan compared to the original example on the template?

22. **Excel.** Refer to the "Ch4 GPM" tab in the Excel Workbook provided on the Web site. How would the loan balance at the end of year 7 change if the payments increase by 5 percent each year instead of 7.5 percent?

Inflation, Mortgage Pricing, and Payment Structuring

The fully amortizing, constant payment mortgage has been the most widely used mortgage instrument in the United States for some time. In more recent times, particularly during the 1970s and early 1980s, inflation and its effect on this "standard" mortgage instrument have caused problems for both lenders and borrowers. Because of these problems, a number of different mortgage instruments have been proposed as alternatives to the standard mortgage instrument. In this section, we outline the problems that inflation has brought for both borrowers and lenders who have relied on the standard mortgage instrument. Also included is a detailed description of the graduated payment mortgage. This mortgage is also a fixed interest rate mortgage and may be used in place of the constant payment mortgage, particularly during periods of rising interest rates.

Effects on Lenders and Borrowers

How does inflation relate to mortgage lending and cause difficulty for lenders and borrowers desiring to make constant payment loans with fixed interest rates? The answer to this question can be easily illustrated. Let us assume initially that a $60,000 loan is made at a time when no inflation is expected. The loan is expected to be outstanding for a 30-year period. Because there is no inflation, an inflation premium (f) is not required; hence, the lender will earn a return equivalent to the riskless interest rate (r), plus a premium for risk (p) over the period of the loan.[1] We assume that the interest rate charged under such assumptions would be 4 percent, representing a 3 percent real rate of interest and a risk premium of 1 percent over the period of the loan. Assuming a constant payment, fixed interest rate loan made in an inflationless environment, the lender would collect constant payments of approximately $286 per month, based on the loan constant for 4 percent and 30 years. This amount is shown in Exhibit 4A–1 as a straight line (RP) over the life of the loan and represents the series of *constant real payments* necessary to earn the lender a 3 percent fixed real return plus a 1 percent risk premium each year that the loan is outstanding.

Now assume that the same loan is made in an inflationary environment, where a 6 percent rate of inflation is expected

to prevail during each year that the loan is outstanding. The interest rate on the mortgage loan would now have to increase to approximately 10 percent for the lender to earn the same real return. This includes the base rate of 4 percent earned when no inflation was expected, plus an inflation premium of 6 percent.[2] Given that the standard mortgage instrument is to be used, the lender must now collect approximately $527 a month (rounded). This new payment pattern is shown in Exhibit 4A–1 as the horizontal line labeled *NP*, representing a constant series of nominal payments received over the term of the loan. Hence, included in the series of nominal payments are amounts that will provide the lender with a 4 percent basic rate of interest representing a real return and risk premium, plus a 6 percent inflation premium over the 30-year loan term.

In our example, an expected inflation rate of 6 percent caused an 84 percent rise in the monthly mortgage payments from $286 to $527, or $241 per month. Why is there such a significant increase in these monthly payments? The reason can be easily seen by again examining curve *NPD* in Exhibit 4A–1. This curve represents the real value of the monthly payments that the lender will receive over the 30-year loan period. It is determined by "deflating" the $527 nominal monthly payments by the rate of inflation.[3] The *NPD* curve is important because the lender, realizing that inflation is going to occur, expects that the constant stream of $527 payments to be received over time will be worth less and less because of lost purchasing power. Hence, to receive the full 10 percent interest necessary to leave enough for a 4 percent real return and risk premium over the life of the loan, more "real dollars" must be collected in the *early* years of the loan (payments collected toward the *end* of the life of the mortgage will be worth much less in purchasing power).

To illustrate, let us examine the deflated or real value of the $527 payments collected each month, as represented by the curve *NPD*. Note that for about the first 10 years of the loan life, the real value of these payments is greater than those for the 4 percent loan. However, after 10 years, the real value of these payments falls below the payments required on the 4 percent loan. However, even though the two payment streams differ, the real value of the nominal payment stream is equal to the required real payments at 4 percent, or $NPD = RP$.

---

[1] Actually the interest rate charged will be related to the expected repayment period that may occur before maturity. However, this will not alter the concept being illustrated. The figures chosen here are arbitrary. Some studies indicate that the real rate of interest has historically been in the 1 to 3 percent range and risk premium on mortgages in the 2 to 3 percent range.

[2] The nominal interest rate would actually be $(1 + .04)(1 + .06) − 1$, or 10.24 percent. However, as indicated earlier, we use 10 percent to simplify calculations.

[3] Deflating an income stream is done by computing the monthly inflation factor $.06 ÷ 12$, or $.005$, and multiplying $527(1 ÷ 1.005)^1$ in the first month, $527(1 ÷ 1.005)^2$ in the second month, and so on, until the end of year 30.

EXHIBIT 4A–1
Real and Nominal Values of Mortgage Payments

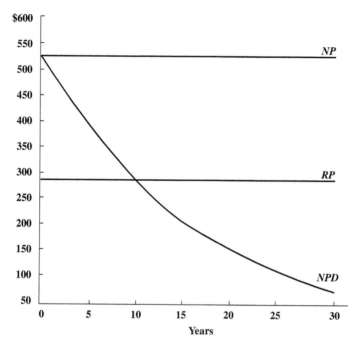

NP = Nominal payments
RP = Real payments
NPD = Nominal payments deflated

This means that from the stream of nominal $527 monthly receipts, the lender will ultimately earn the same real value as a stream of $286 payments or 4 percent on investment after deflating the nominal payments by the inflation rate. However, in order to earn the same real interest rate, the real value of the payment stream (*NPD*) must be greater than *RP* in the early years, since it will fall below *RP* in the later years. This relationship is referred to as *tilting* the real payment stream in the early years to make up for the loss in purchasing power in later years.

This **tilt effect** also has a considerable impact on the borrower. Recall that with no inflation the borrower faced a $286 payment; however, with inflation a $527 monthly payment is necessary. When the loan is first originated, the difference in the two payments is about $241 per month and represents an additional amount of real or current dollars that the borrower must allocate from current real *income* to meet mortgage payments.

Over time, this burden moderates. For example, by the end of the first year, the real value of the $527 payments deflated by the 6 percent rate of inflation would be about $497 per month and the borrower's real income will have increased by 3 percent, or by the real rate of growth in the economy. At that time, the borrower will have more real income to pay declining real mortgage payments. The important point is that even though the borrower's income is increasing in both real and nominal terms each year, it is not enough to offset the tilt effect in the early years of a loan. From this analysis, it becomes apparent from Exhibit 4A–1 why it is so difficult for

first-time home buyers to qualify for constant payment, fixed interest rate loans during periods of rising inflation. With the general rate of inflation and growth in the economy, borrower incomes will grow gradually or on a year-by-year basis. However, as expected inflation increases, lenders must build estimates of the full increase into current interest rates "up front," or *when the loan is made*. This causes a dramatic increase in required real monthly payments relative to the borrower's current real income.

One final observation about the tilt effect is that, as the rate of inflation increases, the tilt effect increases. In Exhibit 4A–2, we show the effect of an increase in inflation from 6 percent in our previous example to 8 percent per year. Note that nominal monthly payments increase from $527 to $617 per month, the latter figure based on an increase in the mortgage interest rate to 12 percent. The impact of the tilt effect on a constant payment loan when inflation is expected to be 8 percent can be seen relative to the effect when inflation was expected to be 6 percent. Note that when the $617 monthly payments are deflated at 8 percent (*NPD* @ 8%) for inflation, the burden of the real payments to be made by the borrower increases relative to the real payments required when inflation was 6 percent in the early years of the loan. The curve corresponding to monthly payments deflated at 8 percent indicates that the real value of monthly payments on the 12 percent mortgage exceeds the real value of payments on the 10 percent mortgage for about the first 10 years of the loan term. This is true even though the lender will earn a 4 percent real return on both mortgages after inflation. Further, if we again assume that the

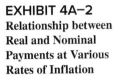

EXHIBIT 4A–2
Relationship between Real and Nominal Payments at Various Rates of Inflation

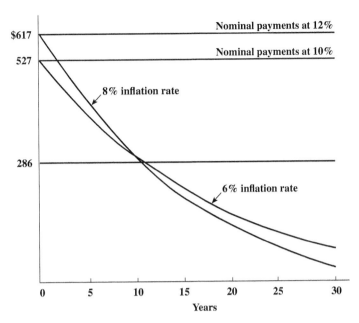

"average" borrower's real income will increase by 3 percent, regardless of the rate of inflation, as inflation increases from 6 percent to 8 percent, it is clear that the borrower will have to allocate even more current real income to mortgage payments. This indicates that in the early years of the mortgage, the burden of the tilt effect on borrowers increases as the rate of inflation increases. This increased burden is due solely to (1) the nature of the mortgage instrument, that is, a constant payment, fixed interest rate mortgage and (2) the rate of inflation. Further, the tilt effect makes it even more difficult for borrowers to qualify for loans based on their current income and make payments from current income. To partially overcome the tilt effect, lenders have designed a mortgage loan that retains a fixed rate of interest but includes a series of stepped-up payments that are lower in the earlier years, thereby better matching borrowers' incomes, and then rising over time. These loans are known as graduated payment mortgages (GPMs).

The Graduated Payment Mortgage (GPM)

In an attempt to deal with the problem of inflation and its impact on mortgage interest rates and monthly payments, lenders have instituted new mortgage instruments. One such instrument is the **graduated payment mortgage (GPM).** The objective of a GPM is to provide for a series of mortgage payments that are *lower* in the initial years of the loan than they would be with a standard mortgage loan. GPM payments then gradually increase at a predetermined rate as borrower incomes are expected to rise over time. The payment pattern thus offsets the tilt effect to some extent, reducing the burden faced by households when meeting

mortgage payments from current income in an inflationary environment.[4]

An example of the payment pattern for the graduated payment mortgage is illustrated in Exhibit 4A–3. The exhibit contains information on how payments should be structured for the 30-year, $60,000, fully amortizing loan used in our previous examples. GPMs can have a number of plans allowing for differences in initial payment levels, rates of graduation, and graduation periods. Exhibit 4A–3 contains information on one of the more popular payment plans in use today. This plan allows for a 7.5 percent rate of graduation in monthly payments over five years, after which time the payments level off for the remaining 25 years. Computing initial payments on a mortgage of this kind is complex and is illustrated at the end of this appendix.[5]

Looking at the information contained in Exhibit 4A–3, we see that for a standard constant payment mortgage (CPM) loan of $60,000 originated at 12 percent for 30 years, the required constant monthly payments would be $617.17. A GPM loan made for the same amount and interest rate, where the monthly payments are increased (graduated) at the end of each year at a predetermined rate of 7.5 percent, begins with

---

[4] The Federal Housing Administration initiated the first widely accepted graduated payment plan under its Section 245 program. For more detail, see the *HUD Handbook's* various issues.

[5] Although we discuss GPMs relative to single family lending, this type of loan also could be used to structure debt financing for income-producing properties where mortgage loan payments are designed to match income growth from rents collected over time.

EXHIBIT 4A–3
Comparison of GPM Payments and Constant Payments ($60,000, 30-Year Maturity, Fully Amortizing, at Various Interest Rates)

	Interest Rate				
	10%	11%	12%	13%	14%
Constant Payments	$526.54	$571.39	$617.17	$663.72	$710.94
GPM Payments Graduated (7.5% Annually)					
1	$400.22	$436.96	$474.83	$513.71	$553.51
2	430.24	469.73	510.44	552.24	595.03
3	462.51	504.96	548.72	593.66	639.65
4	497.19	542.83	589.87	638.18	687.63
5	534.48	583.55	634.11	686.04	739.20
6–30	574.57	627.31	681.67	737.50	794.64

EXHIBIT 4A–4
Comparison of Mortgage Payment Patterns (Loan Amount = $60,000, Maturity = 30 Years, Interest 12% *GPM* Add: 7.5% Graduation Rate, 5 years)

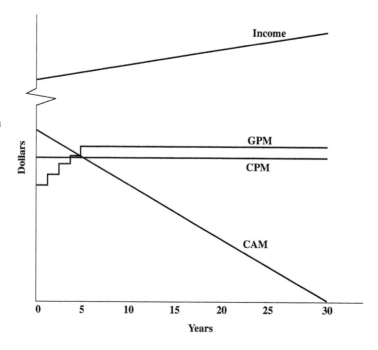

an initial payment of approximately $474.83. This initial payment will then increase by 7.5 percent per year to an amount equal to $681.67 at the beginning of year 6 and will remain constant from that point until the end of year 30. Compared with $617.17 in the constant payment mortgage, GPM payments are initially lower by $142.34 in the first year. The difference becomes smaller over time. The graduated payment level reaches approximately the same payment under the standard mortgage between the fourth and fifth years after origination. GPM payments exceed constant payments by $64.50 ($681.67 − $617.17) beginning in year 6. GPM payments then remain at the $681.67 level for the remaining 25 years of the loan term.

Exhibit 4A–4 provides a comparison of payment patterns for a graduated payment mortgage (GPM), a constant payment mortgage (CPM), and a constant amortizing mortgage (CAM). GPM payments are based on the 7.5 percent graduation plan. All three loans are assumed to be originated for $60,000 at 12 percent interest for 30 years. Note that the GPM is below that of the CPM for approximately five years, at which point the GPM payments begin to exceed CPM payments. The reason for this pattern should be obvious. Under either payment plan, the yield to the lender must be an annual rate of 12 percent compounded monthly, assuming no origination fees, penalties, and so on. Therefore, because the GPM payments are below those of the CPM in the early years, GPM payments must eventually exceed the level payment on the CPM loan to "make up" for the lower payments on the GPM in the early years. Hence, if the borrower chooses the GPM in our example, the payments will exceed those of a standard CPM mortgage from years 6 to 30.

The advantages of the GPM program are obvious from the borrower's standpoint. The initial payment level under the GPM plan shown in Exhibit 4A–4 is significantly lower than under the CPM plan. Further, in the early years, GPM payments correspond more closely to increases in borrower's income. Hence, the burden of the tilt effect requiring borrowers to allocate more current real dollars for mortgage payments from current real income in an inflationary environment is reduced somewhat with the GPM. Based on this analysis, it is easy to conclude that the GPM significantly reduces monthly payments for borrowers in the early years of the mortgage loan, corresponds more closely to increases in borrower income, and therefore may increase the demand for mortgage credit by borrowers.

When judged relative to the CAM, the CPM and GPM clearly provide for initial payments that are far below payments required for the CAM with the same terms. It is important to stress that higher rates of inflation have caused a modification in mortgage instruments over time. Even though all three mortgage instruments provide the same yield (12%),

changes in mortgage payments have clearly been structured to reduce initial payments. This has been done with the expectation that growth in real incomes and expected inflation will extend into the future, resulting in sufficiently high borrower incomes to repay the debt while reducing initial payments sufficiently to reduce the payment burden at the time of loan origination.

Outstanding Loan Balances: GPMs

Because the initial loan payments under GPM plans are usually lower than payments necessary to cover the monthly interest, the outstanding loan balance under the GPM will *increase* during the initial years of the loan. It will remain higher than that of the standard CPM mortgage until full repayment occurs at maturity. A comparison of loan balances for a GPM and a standard mortgage, based on the 12 percent, $60,000, 30-year terms used in our previous example, is shown in Exhibit 4A–5.

Exhibit 4A–6 indicates that the mortgage balance with the GPM *increases* until approximately year 5, when it begins to decline until it reaches zero in year 30. Hence, if a borrower sold this property during the first four years after making a GPM loan, more would be owed than originally borrowed. The loan balance increases during the first four years after origination because the initial GPM payments are lower than

EXHIBIT 4A–5
Loan Balances for Graduated Payment and Constant Payment Mortgages as Compared with Expected property Value

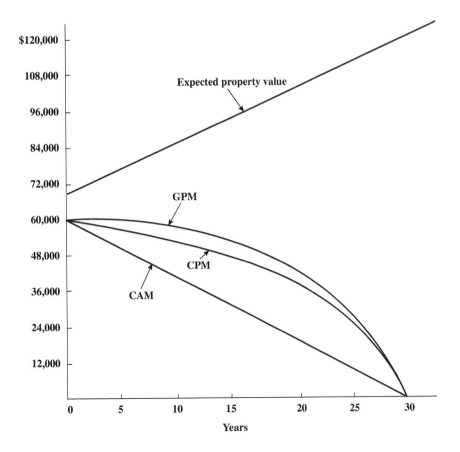

EXHIBIT 4A–6
Determining Loan Balance on a GPM ($60,000 Loan, 12%, 30 Years, 7.5 % Rate of Graduation)

www.mhhe.com/bf15e

Year	Beginning Balance	Required Monthly Interest Payment	GPM Payment	First Month Loan Amortization	Change in Balance	Ending Balance
1	$60,000.00	$600.00	$474.83	$125.17	$1,587.47	$61,587.47
2	61,587.47	615.87	510.44	105.43	1,337.12	62,924.59
3	62,924.59	629.25	548.72	80.53	1,021.32	63,945.91
4	63,945.91	639.46	589.87	49.59	628.93	64,574.84
5	64,574.84	645.75	634.11	11.64	147.62	64,722.46*
6	64,722.46	647.22	681.67	(34.45)	(436.91)	64,285.55

*Maximum balance. During the sixth year, the payments ($681.67) will exceed the required interest ($647.22), and loan amortization will begin.

the monthly interest requirements at 12 percent. Therefore, no amortization of principal occurs until payments increase in later periods. To illustrate, in our previous example, the interest requirements under a GPM after the first month of origination would be $60,000 × (.12 ÷ 12), or $600.00. The GPM payments during the first year of the loan are only $474.83, which are less than the monthly interest requirement of $600.00. The difference, or $125.17, must be added to the initial loan balance of $60,000, as if that difference represented an additional amount *borrowed* each month. This $125.17 monthly difference is **negative amortization.** Further, this shortfall in interest must also accumulate interest at the rate of 12 percent compounded monthly. Hence, during the first year, $125.17 per month plus monthly compound interest must be added to the $60,000 loan balance. This process amounts to compounding a monthly annuity of $125.17 at 12 percent per month and adding that result to the initial loan balance to determine the balance at year-end. The amount added to the loan balance at the end of the year will be the future value (*FV*) of $125.17 per month, compounded monthly at 12 percent or $125.17(12.682503) = $1,587.47.

Solution:
$$n = 12$$
$$i = 12\% \div 12 = 1\%$$
$$PMT = \$474.83$$
$$PV = -\$60,000$$
Solve for FV = $61,587.47 (loan balance)

Alternate Solution:
$$n = 12$$
$$i = 12\% \div 12 = 1\%$$
$$PMT = \$125.17$$
$$PV = 0$$
Solve for FV = −$1,587.47   (addition to annual loan balance)

The importance of the increasing GPM loan balance and negative amortization can be seen in relationship to the property value also (see Exhibit 4A–5). It is important to note the "margin of safety," or difference between property value and loan balance. This margin is much *lower* when a GPM loan balance is compared with that of a CPM. This makes a GPM loan riskier to the lender than a CPM, because more consideration must be given to *future* market values of real estate and *future* borrower income. For example, let us assume that the GPM borrower decides to sell a property after five years. When compared with the CPM, the lender will have received relatively lower monthly payments up to that point. Further, because of negative amortization, the proceeds from sale of the property must be great enough to repay the loan balance that has increased relative to the original amount borrowed. In short, with a GPM, the lender must now be more concerned about trends in real estate values because resale value will constitute a more important source of funds for loan repayment.

GPM Mortgage Loans and Effective Borrowing Costs

A closing note in this appendix considers the question of the effective interest rate and GPMs. In the absence of origination fees and prepayment penalties, the yield on GPMs, like yields on CAMs and CPMs, is equal to the contract rate of interest as specified in the note because the GPM, like the CPM, is a fixed interest rate mortgage. This is true whether or not the GPM loan, like CAM and CPM loans, is repaid before maturity. However, to the extent points or origination fees are charged, the effective yield on a GPM will be *greater* than the contract rate of interest, and it will increase the earlier the loan is repaid. When computing yields on GPMs originated with points, the same procedure should be followed as described with the standard CPM; that is, the interest rate making the stream of GPM payments equal to the funds disbursed after deducting financing fees is the effective cost of the loan. Where origination fees are charged on GPMs, the authors have computed results that are very close to those computed for standard mortgage loans with the same terms and origination fees. This is true regardless of the loan amount or rate of graduation on the GPM. In the GPM discussed above, for example, if 3 points are charged and the loan is repaid after five years, the effective rate would be about 12.78 percent, compared with 12.82 on a CPM with the same terms.[6] Is a borrower better off or worse off with a GPM or a CPM loan? Generally, if a standard loan and a GPM are originated at the same rate of interest and have the same fees, there will be little, if any, difference in their effective costs. However, because the graduated payment pattern reduces the tilt effect, the borrower is definitely better off with a GPM *if it can be obtained at the same interest rate* as the standard mortgage.

Would a GPM generally be available at the same interest rate as a standard CPM mortgage? It would appear that because of the additional risk taken by the lender—in the form of an increasing loan balance due to negative amortization in the early years of the loan and lower initial monthly cash flows received from reduced payments—the GPM lender would require a *higher risk premium* than the CPM lender. Hence, all things being equal, a slightly higher interest rate may be required on a GPM than on a CPM. This would tend to neutralize some of the positive features of the GPM compared with the CPM.

Graduated Payment Mortgages—Further Extensions

As explained in the chapter, the mechanics of determining monthly payment streams and loan balance are relatively straightforward for FRMs. However, when designing a GPM structure, the reader should be aware that the rate of graduation, number of years during which payments will graduate, term, and interest rate will vary, depending on the goals of the borrower and lender and the loan market that it is being designed to serve.

Perhaps, the most complex problem associated with a GPM is *establishing the initial monthly payment*. For example, in Exhibit 4A–3 monthly payments for various GPMs are illustrated. Each group of monthly payments was assumed to increase at the rate of 7.5 percent beginning in year 2. However, the reader may be wondering how the initial payment is determined and, perhaps more importantly, how one may go about designing a structure for payment patterns

requiring a graduated or stepped up repayment schedule. For example, in the case of our 12 percent GPM mortgage, we note that the initial payment would be $474.83. How was that payment determined?

To answer this question, we provide what appears to be a difficult solution. Upon closer examination, however, we will see that it is an application of the present value formulas that we have learned. It is important to recall that for the GPM, as was the case with the CAM, the present value of all payments discounted at the contract rate of interest will equal the initial loan amount. This concept is very important and must be kept in mind as we work through the problem at hand. What follows is a general formula for determining the initial monthly payment for a GPM:

$$PV = \left[MP_1 \cdot \sum_{t=1}^{12} \frac{1}{\left(1+i/12\right)^t} \right]$$

$$+ \left[MP_1(1+g)^1 \cdot \sum_{t=1}^{12} \frac{1}{\left(1+i/12\right)^t} \cdot \frac{1}{\left(1+i/12\right)^{12}} \right]$$

$$+ \left[MP_1(1+g)^2 \cdot \sum_{t=1}^{12} \frac{1}{\left(1+i/12\right)^t} \cdot \frac{1}{\left(1+i/12\right)^{24}} \right]$$

$$+ \left[MP_1(1+g)^3 \cdot \sum_{t=1}^{12} \frac{1}{\left(1+i/12\right)^t} \cdot \frac{1}{\left(1+i/12\right)^{36}} \right]$$

$$+ \left[MP_1(1+g)^4 \cdot \sum_{t=1}^{12} \frac{1}{\left(1+i/12\right)^t} \cdot \frac{1}{\left(1+i/12\right)^{48}} \right]$$

$$+ \left[MP_1(1+g)^5 \cdot \sum_{t=1}^{300} \frac{1}{\left(1+i/12\right)^t} \cdot \frac{1}{\left(1+i/12\right)^{60}} \right]$$

where

PV = loan amount

i = contract interest rate

MP_1 = monthly payments during year 1

g = rate of graduation in the monthly payment

While the computation appears to be complex, a relatively simple solution for MP_1 is obtainable for our $60,000, 12 percent, 30-year GPM with a graduation rate of 7.5 percent. Note that the expressions containing the $\sum$'s are simply the interest factors for the present value of an annuity presented in Chapters 3 and 4. The terms $1 \div (1 + i/12)^{12}$, $1 \div (1 + i/12)^{24}$, and so on are simply the factors also discussed in Chapters 3 and 4. These factors correspond to various 12-month intervals during which monthly payments will be greater than the previous 12-month period. However, in any given year, monthly payments (unknown) will remain constant during that year.

[6] Computations for the effective interest rate on GPMs are much more difficult than those for the CPM because the amount disbursed must be set equal to a series of seven "grouped cash flows" or annuities, representing different payments for 12 periods in each of the six years, with the final annuity payment covering years 6 to 30. Similarly, when finding loan balances, we may use for GPMs the same procedure demonstrated for CPMs; that is, the remaining payment streams would be discounted at the contract rate of interest and the present value would be determined. However, determining loan balances on GPMs may involve discounting a series of one or more annuities spanning many different 12-month intervals if any remaining CPM payments differ. For an illustration of how to calculate payments for GPMs see the following section.

EXHIBIT 4A–7
Worksheet for Solving for Initial *GPM* Payments

www.mhhe.com/bf15e

(1) Payment Period	(2) Payment	(3) Graduated Payment Factor	(4) Present Value of 12 Payments Received at End of Month each Year	(5) Present Value of (Col. 4) Received at End of each Year	(6) (3 × 4 × 5)
MP_1	$= MP_1(1.0)$	1.0	11.255077	—	11.255077
MP_2	$= MP_1(1 + .075)$	1.075000	11.255077	.887449	10.737430
MP_3	$= MP_1(1 + .075)^2$	1.155625	11.255077	.787566	10.243594
MP_4	$= MP_1(1 + .075)^3$	1.242297	11.255077	.698925	9.772473
MP_5	$= MP_1(1 + .075)^4$	1.335469	11.255077	.620260	9.323008
MP_{6-30}	$= MP_1(1 + .075)^5$	1.435629	94.946551	.550450	75.030751
				Total	126.362333

Hence, what we have in our base case example are six different groups of unknown monthly annuities, which, when discounted by the contract rate of interest on the mortgage (*i*), must equal the initial amount of the loan. This process is usually referred to as discounting *grouped cash flows* and is a problem encountered frequently in real estate finance.

Essentially, our problem involves finding MP_1, which is the only unknown. We know the loan amount ($60,000), the monthly interest rate ($i \div 12 = .01$), and the term of the loan (360 months). Further, we know that *MP* in years 2, 3, 4, 5, and 6 will be equal to MP_1, increased by $(1 + g)^1$, $(1 + g)^2$, $(1 + g)^3$, $(1 + g)^4$, and $(1 + g)^5$, respectively, where $g = .075$. Given this information, MP_1 can be found by assembling the information as shown in Exhibit 4A–7.

Looking at Exhibit 4A–7, we see that column 1 corresponds to the payments for years 1 to 30. Column 2 merely indicates that payments during each year will be increased at the rate of 7.5 percent per year, which is equivalent to compounding MP_1 (unknown) by 1.075 for each year's set of payments *beginning* in year 2. In other words, we are solving for payments in year 1 which will remain the same for 12 months, and then increase by 1.075 beginning in year 2. Hence, column 3 is simply the compound interest factor for the rate of graduation (7.5 percent) applied to MP_1.

In Exhibit 4A–7, column 4 contains the present value of 12 payments received at the end of the month each year at 12 percent. This factor is, in effect, being used to discount the six different series of monthly payments *within* the interval during which they will occur. For example, in each of the first five years, 12 monthly payments will be received and must be discounted for that 12-month interval, hence the factor 11.255077. From years 6 to 30, 300 payments will be received and must be discounted for that interval, hence the factor 94.946551.

Column 5 contains the present value of column (4) received at the end of each year, which must be used to discount each series of monthly annuities back to time period zero or present value. In other words, column 4

discounts the 12 monthly payments *within* the 12-month interval. Column 5 is necessary because each series of grouped payments is not received all at once; instead, the series received during the second year has a lower present value than the series received in the first year. Hence, each series must be discounted again by the column (5) factor for one year, the third year must be discounted for two years, and so on.

Finally, column 6 is simply the product of columns 3, 4, and 5. Note that these factors are additive because we have been able to express each series of payments (MP_2, MP_3, MP_4, MP_5, and MP_{6-30}) in terms of MP_1 because we know that each succeeding period's payment will increase by the same rate of graduation $(1 + g)$. Careful inspection of the equation shows that the compounding and discount rates in columns (4) and (5) and $1 + g$ may be factored, multiplied, and added. This is in essence what we have done in Exhibit 4A–7. Hence, the equation reduces to

$$MP_1(126.362333) = \$60,000$$

$$MP = \$474.83$$

Because we know that MP_2 will be 1.075 times greater than *MP*, we have $474.83(1.075)$ or 510.44, and so on. The reader may now complete the calculations and verify the payments in the 12 percent column in Exhibit 4A–3.

This formula and procedure have widespread application in real estate finance whenever one is faced with a series of payments which are scheduled to increase after given time intervals at any specified rate of increase.[7] The student is also encouraged to think about how the schedule and formula may change if different rates of graduation over different periods of time are desired.

---

[7] This procedure can be programmed into many financial calculators and spreadsheets. An explanation can usually be found in the manual accompanying calculators and spreadsheets under graduated payment mortgages and/or discounting grouped cash flows.

Regarding loan balances for GPMs, once the mortgage payments are known, balances can be determined at any time by finding the present value of the remaining payments. This is done by discounting those payments by the contract rate of interest, taking into account any grouped cash flows in the remaining series, and discounting them appropriately. As for effective interest rates, any origination fees should be subtracted from the loan amount (PV). Then, given the GPM payments and balance, a new series of compounding and discount rates such as shown in columns (4) and (5) in Exhibit 4A–7 at a rate greater than 12 percent would be used to discount the payments and balances until the present value of all cash inflows equals the net amount of funds disbursed.

Key Terms:

graduated payment mortgage (GPM), *113*
negative amortization, *116*
tilt effect, *112*

Questions

A–1. Why do level or constant monthly mortgage payments increase so sharply during periods of inflation? What does the tilt effect have to do with this?

A–2. As inflation increases, the impact of the tilt effect is said to become even more burdensome on borrowers. Why is this so?

Problems

A–1. A property is purchased for $70,000. The purchase is financed with a GPM carrying a 12 percent interest rate. A 7.5 percent rate of graduation will be applied to monthly payments beginning each year after the loan is originated for a period of five years. The initial loan amount is $63,000 for a term of 30 years. The homeowner expects to sell the property after seven years.

  a. If the initial monthly payment is $498.57, what will the payments be at the beginning of years 2, 3, 4, and 5?

  b. What would the payment be if a CPM loan was available?

  c. Assume the loan is originated with two discount points. What is the effective yield on the GPM?

A–2. Mr. Qualify is applying for a $100,000 GPM loan for 25 years at an interest rate of 9 percent. Payments would be designed so as to graduate at the rate of 7.5 percent for three years beginning with payments in the second year.

  a. What would the monthly payments be for Mr. Qualify in each of the first five years of the loan?

  b. What would the loan balance be on the GPM at the end of year 3?

  c. If the lender charged 4 points at origination, what would be the effective interest rate on this loan after five years?

A–3. **Excel.** Refer to the "Ch4 GPM" tab in the Excel Workbook provided on the Web site. How would the initial payment change if the payments increase by 5 percent each year instead of 7.5 percent?

eXcel
www.mhhe.com/bf15e

Chapter

Adjustable and Floating Rate Mortgage Loans

In the preceding chapter, we discussed fixed interest rate mortgage (FRM) instruments, giving particular attention to payment patterns. We saw how payment structures and amortization rates can be negotiated.

This chapter deals with a variety of mortgage loans with interest rates that are tied to a market rate, or index, and may change with market conditions. When used to finance single family residences, these loans are called **adjustable rate mortgages—ARMS.** When used to finance commercial properties, these mortgages frequently are called **floating rate loans.** Because both types of mortgages are very similar, we will not differentiate between them. In our discussion, we will use the term ARM more frequently. These instruments differ from fixed interest rate mortgages (FRMs) in that they are designed to adjust in one or more ways to changes in economic conditions. Rather than making mortgages with fixed rates of interest over long periods of time, these mortgages provide an alternative method of financing through which lenders and borrowers *share the risk* of interest rate changes, or **interest rate risk.** This enables lenders to match changes in interest costs with changes in interest revenue more effectively and thus provide borrowers with potentially lower financing costs.

In this chapter, we begin with a general discussion of the price level adjusted mortgage (PLAM). Although not widely used, the PLAM illustrates many of the problems that must be considered by lenders and borrowers in financial decision making. We then consider ARMs and issues relative to how they are "priced." As a part of the analysis of ARMs, we investigate the effects of limitations on (1) interest rate changes, (2) payment increases, and (3) negative amortization and the resultant effects on ARM loan yields. We also consider how these mortgages should be priced relative to FRMs and other ARMs made on different loan terms. At the conclusion of the chapter, we consider the shared appreciation mortgage (SAM), whose repayment terms are partially based on appreciation in property values.

One major issue faced by lenders and borrowers with FRMs is that the *interest rate is fixed on the date of origination and remains fixed until the loan is repaid.* Hence, from the day of origination, lenders are underwriting the risk of any significant changes in the implicit components of mortgage interest rates, that is, the real rate of interest (r), the risk premium (p), and the premium for expected inflation (f). To the extent that lenders underestimate any or all of these components at the time of mortgage origination, they will incur a financial loss. For example, assume that a fully amortizing mortgage loan for $60,000 is made for 30 years at 10 percent interest. This mortgage would require monthly payments of about $527 (rounded). Should such a loan be made, it must follow that the consensus of lenders at the time the loan is made is that a 10 percent rate of interest is sufficiently high to compensate them for all forms of risk bearing expected to occur over the time that the loan is expected to be outstanding. If over that time, one or more of the components of the mortgage interest rate (i) are significantly higher than was anticipated at the time of origination, lenders will suffer a loss.[1] If, for example, lenders make an inaccurate prediction of inflation and unanticipated inflation occurs, warranting a 12 percent interest rate instead of 10 percent, the magnitude of the loss to the lender over a 30-year period is determined as follows:

Solution:	Function:
$i = 12\%/12$	$PV\,(i, n, PMT, FV)$
$n = 360$	
$PMT = \$527$	
$FV = 0$	
Solve for PV $= \$51,\!190$	

The loss would be equal to $60,000 – $51,190 = $8,810. Hence, in this case, a 2 percent rate of **unanticipated inflation** would result in a financial loss of $8,810 or 14.7 percent of the loan amount. Based on this example, it should be easy to see the relationship between *interest rate risk* and potential losses to lenders. That there is always some additional risk because of the *uncertainty* about expected levels of each of the components of i is one of the reasons why a risk premium, *p,* is demanded by lenders. To the extent that this uncertainty about future levels of r and f increases, p will also increase, and vice versa.[2]

It should be noted that *losses incurred by lenders result in gains to borrowers.* Of course, one could argue that if interest rates declined, then lenders would gain. However, when this occurs, borrowers usually try to refinance their loans. This pattern implies that with fixed interest rate lending, risk bearing may not be "symmetric," or evenly balanced; that is, lenders bear the risk of loss when interest rates increase, which may not be equally offset by gains if interest rates decline because borrowers can usually prepay loans and will do so when interest rates decline. This problem has motivated lenders and borrowers to use interest rate caps and floors, interest rate swaps, "lockout," and/or prepayment prohibitions and/or penalties. These features and other options will be discussed in various chapters throughout this book.

[1] There are many reasons why lenders may inaccurately predict the components of i over the expected repayment period. Monetary growth may expand or contract, causing changes in the rate of inflation (f). General economic activity may expand (contract), resulting in a change in the general level of investment and employment, thereby affecting real interest rates and default risk (r and p).

[2] The reader should realize that there will always be some likelihood that expected levels of r and f will not always be accurate because of *unanticipated* changes. During some time periods, when economic conditions are stable, the uncertainty in these estimates is likely to be less, whereas in other periods, uncertainty may be greater. Hence, the *uncertainty* of these estimates is what causes interest rate risk and, in turn, larger or smaller risk premiums.

The Price Level Adjusted Mortgage (PLAM)

One *concept* that has been discussed as a remedy for the uncertainty problem for lenders is the **price level adjusted mortgage (PLAM).** Recalling from the discussion in the previous chapter on the determinants of mortgage interest rates, i (where r = expected real rate of interest; p = risk premium; and f = expected inflation), we displayed the following equation:

$$i = r + p + f$$

We also indicated that perhaps the most difficult variable in the equation to predict was a premium for expected inflation (f). To help reduce interest rate risk, or the uncertainty of inflation and its effect on interest rates, it has been suggested that lenders should *originate* mortgages at interest rates that reflect expectations of the real interest rate plus a risk premium for the likelihood of loss due to default on a given mortgage loan, or $r + p$.

After estimating initial values for r and p, the PLAM loan balance would be adjusted up or down by a *price index.* Payments would then be based on a new loan balance, adjusted for inflation. This would shift the risk of changes in market interest rates brought about by inflation (f) to borrowers and relieve lenders of the difficult task of forecasting future interest movements when originating loans. The lender would still bear the risk of any unanticipated change in r or p.[3]

PLAM: Payment Mechanics

An example of a PLAM loan would have payments based on a rate of interest consisting only of expectations for r and p for an expected maturity period. Payments would be adjusted periodically, based on the indexed value of the *mortgage balance* for the remaining loan term. To illustrate, assume that a mortgage is made for $60,000 for 30 years at an interest rate of 4 percent, or a lender's estimate of $r + p$. The lender and borrower may agree that the loan balance will be indexed to the consumer price index (CPI) and adjusted annually. Initial monthly payments would be based on $60,000 at 4 percent for 30 years, or approximately $286. After one year, the loan balance, based on a 30-year amortization schedule for the 4 percent interest rate, would be about $58,943. If it is assumed that the CPI increased by 6 percent during the first year of the loan, the *loan balance* at the end of year 1 would become $58,943 (1.06) or $62,480. This balance would be repaid over 29 remaining years. Monthly payments, beginning in the second year, would be based on the higher-indexed loan balance of $62,480 at the same 4 percent interest rate for 29 years or $304 per month. This process would continue each year thereafter: (1) computing the loan balance using an amortization schedule based on a 4 percent interest rate for the remaining term, (2) increasing the balance by the change in the CPI during the next year, and (3) computing the new payment over the remaining loan term.

Assuming inflation continued at an annual rate of 6 percent for the remaining loan term, Exhibit 5–1 shows the nominal payment and loan balance pattern every year for the PLAM loan. There are many patterns that should be pointed out in Exhibit 5–1. Note that

[3] Although we are treating each of these variables making up i as independent and additive, they may not be independent and may well interact with one another. For example, the risk premium (p) is partially dependent on the likelihood that a borrower's income and wealth will rise or fall, which may depend on changes in the economy and, hence, the underlying real rate of interest (r). Changes in income would affect the likelihood of default on a loan because of payments rising relative to income (which may rise or fall) or the loan balance exceeding the market value of the house. Similarly, we do not fully understand the relationship between inflation (f) and real growth (r) and the possible interaction between them. Hence, the reader should be aware that we are dealing with these influences in a conceptual way to illustrate the importance of each component, but we do not mean to imply that the specification of i is this simplistic.

EXHIBIT 5–1
Payments and Loan Balance Patterns, $60,000 PLAM, 4%, Inflation = 6% per Year, versus $60,000 CPM, 10% Interest, 30 Years

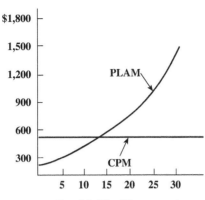

Panel A: Monthly payments

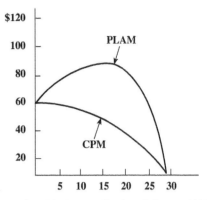

Panel B: Outstanding loan balances ($000s)

the PLAM payments shown in panel A increase at approximately the same rate as the change in the price level, or 6 percent over the life of the loan. This increase in payments continues over the life of the loan even though loan amortization begins to occur as the number of remaining years to maturity declines (see panel B). This pattern of rising payments occurs (1) because of the effect of the increasing price index on the loan balance and (2) because each succeeding year's payment is computed over a shorter remaining loan term.[4] It is also interesting to compare the payments on this PLAM to a $60,000, constant payment FRM made at 10 percent for 30 years. Payments on the FRM would be approximately $527, as compared to the initial PLAM payment of $286. Thus, it would appear that many more households could qualify to purchase housing with PLAMs when compared to CPMs.

The PLAM is not without problems, however. Panel B in Exhibit 5–1 shows that the loan balance on the PLAM increases to about 155 percent of the original loan amount, or from $60,000 to approximately $93,000, after 15 years. Housing is only one of many components making up the CPI. Hence, should prices of other goods represented in the CPI increase faster than house prices, or if house prices declined, indexing loan balances to the CPI could result in loan balances increasing faster than property values. When this occurs, borrowers have an incentive to default. This possibility would place a considerable burden on lenders because now, instead of dealing with inflation and fixed interest rate loans, they would have to establish adequate down payment levels for all borrowers, forecast future housing prices, and be assured that the value of the property that serves as collateral for the mortgage would always be greater than the outstanding loan balance. Hence, it is questionable whether the CPI is the proper index to use when adjusting PLAM balances.

A second problem with PLAMs has to do with the relationship between mortgage payments and borrower incomes. It would appear that the tilt problem, discussed in the appendix to Chapter 4, would be greatly reduced, because payments would be matched more closely with borrower incomes. However, this assumes that both the CPI, which is used to index the PLAM, and borrower incomes change in the same way. A desired ratio

---

[4] The reader should realize that the process of adjustments occurring at the end of each year can be viewed as an annual series of new mortgage loan originations. As such, payments may be modified based on different rates of interest or maturities, with the outstanding loan balance always representing the new amount being borrowed. Hence, it is possible for changes in interest rates or maturities to be renegotiated or varied by the lender and borrower at any time to moderate or increase monthly payments.

between mortgage payments and borrower incomes may be easy to maintain as long as incomes keep pace with increases in the CPI. Over the long run, this relationship may be possible as increases in income and mortgage payments "balance out." However, if inflation increases sharply, it is not likely that borrower incomes would increase at the same rate in the short run. During such periods, the payment burden may increase and households may find it more difficult to make mortgage payments. Because of this possibility and the need to develop a desired relationship to mortgage payments, lenders would have to estimate future income for households in different occupational categories and the relationship of that income to inflation. The problems of rising loan balances and payments just discussed make estimating the risk premium (p) that lenders must charge extremely difficult.

A third problem with PLAMs is that the price level chosen for indexation is usually measured on a historical, or ex post facto, basis. In other words, the index is based on data collected in the *previous period* but published currently. In as much as mortgage payments are to be made in the future, historic prices may not be an accurate indication of future prices. To illustrate, the change in the CPI may have been 10 percent during the past year (published currently). This figure would be used to index the outstanding mortgage balance, which will determine payments during the *next* year. If the rate of increase in the CPI subsequently slowed to 2 percent during the next year, it is easy to see that mortgage payments would be rising at a faster rate (10%) than current prices (2%) and, perhaps, faster than borrower incomes. Although borrower incomes may have increased by 10 percent in the previous year, the lag between realization of income in one period and higher payments in the next still presents a problem. This lag problem could become even more distorted in our example if the CPI were to decline and then increase. For this reason, many observers believe that if the PLAM programs were adopted extensively, the time intervals between payment adjustment periods would have to be shortened considerably. This time is called an *adjustment interval.*

In spite of the practical problems with implementing PLAMs, many PLAM features form the framework for understanding adjustable rate mortgages (ARMs). We now turn our attention to ARMs, which will be our focus for the remainder of this chapter.

ARMs and Floating Rate Loans: An Overview

Rather than using changes in the price level as a mechanism to adjust mortgage interest rates and payments, lenders are choosing a variety of mortgages with *interest rates* that are *indexed to other market interest rates.* By choosing indexes based on interest rates rather than on a price index, lenders partially avoid having to estimate real interest rates and risk premiums for the entire period that loans are expected to be outstanding. With ARMs, lenders are, in effect, making a loan, with terms that are updated to current interest rate levels at the end of each adjustment period. By using an interest rate index instead of an ex post measure of inflation based on the CPI or any other price index, lenders earn expected yields based on *expected future values* for r, p, and f over a future period of time. Because interest rates are a reflection of lender and borrower expectations of r, p, and f over specific future periods of time, revisions in ARM payments are always based on future expectations. Therefore, by tying the terms of a mortgage to an index of interest rates, payments are updated frequently. Hence, an ARM provides for adjustments that are more timely for lenders than a PLAM because values for r, p, and f are revised at *specific* time intervals to reflect market expectations of future values for *each* component of i between adjustment dates. For example, the value for f, or expected inflation, is based on an estimate of *future* prices rather than a past measure as exemplified in the CPI or other price indexes. Similarly, values for r and p

are based on the market's current assessment of risks in the prospective economic environment between adjustment dates.

Payment Basics Illustrated

We can begin to illustrate ARM mechanics with a simple example. An ARM for $60,000 with an *initial* interest rate of 10 percent is originated with a term of 30 years, but its payments are to be reset at the end of one year based on an interest rate determined by a specified index at that time. Based on these initial loan terms, monthly payments would be approximately $527 per month for the first year, and the balance at the end of the year would be $59,666. If the market index were to rise at the end of one year and change the interest rate on the ARM to 12 percent, payments would be determined based on the outstanding loan balance for 29 years as follows:

STEP A: Function:
Solution: Find loan balance at end of year 1: $FV(PV, n, i, PMT)$

$$n = 12$$
$$PMT = \$527$$
$$PV = \$60,000$$
$$i = 10\%/12$$

Solve for *FV* = $59,666

STEP B:
Solution: Find new payments at 12%:   Function:
$$n = 29 \times 12 = 348$$ $PMT(n, i, FV, PV)$
$$i = 12\%/12 = 1\%$$
$$PV = \$59,666$$
$$FV = 0$$

Solve for *PMT* = $616

Hence, the new 12 percent interest rate on the ARM at the end of the first year is an updated estimate of the components of *i* for the *coming year,* and payments will increase from $527 to $616 per month.

At least three general observations should be made concerning our simple example.

1. The use of ARMs does not completely eliminate the possibility of lenders realizing losses because of *interest rate risk.* In our first example, the yield to the lender on the ARM during the first year was 10 percent. If market rates move to 12 percent *the day after* the ARM is originated, the lender would sustain a 2 percent loss for the remaining 12-month period during year 1. Obviously, this loss would be eliminated if the adjustment period was reduced to one day, or the loss could be reduced to the extent the adjustment period was less than one year.

2. The longer the payment **adjustment interval,** the greater the interest rate risk to the lender. Hence, the expected yield to the lender on such a mortgage should be greater. This idea will be elaborated later in the chapter.

3. Finally, as the lender assumes *less* interest rate risk, the borrower incurs *more* interest rate risk, depending on the nature of the index chosen and the frequency of payment adjustments. This point can be appreciated if one compares an FRM, where the lender assumes that the full risk of future interest rate changes to an ARM with payments adjusting freely with

market conditions. Clearly, in the latter case the borrower would be assuming more interest rate risk and the lender less. Because the borrower assumes more risk, the *initial interest rate,* or *start rate,* on an ARM should generally be *less* than that on an FRM. Further, because the lender is shifting interest rate risk to the borrower, the lender should also expect, at the time of loan amortization, to earn a lower yield on an ARM over the term of the loan. These three factors are obviously considered by both lenders and borrowers as they negotiate such loans.

Other ARM Characteristics

The following list contains a description of some of the more important terms used when dealing with adjustable rate mortgages:

- *Index.* The **index** is the interest rate series (such as one from the list below) agreed on by both the borrower and the lender and over which the lender has no control. This index may be very short or long term in nature and will be used to reset the interest rate on an ARM on the reset date. Some commonly used indexes are:

  —Interest rates on one-year Treasury securities or Treasury indexes with a specific maturity (6 months, 10 years, etc.).

  —The average cost-of-funds index (COFI) for the 11th FHLB District.

  —The London Interbank Offered Rate (LIBOR) for various loan periods.

- *Margin.* A premium in addition to the index chosen for an ARM is known as the **margin,** or **spread.**

- *Composite rate.* The sum of the interest rate based on the index chosen plus the margin used to establish the new rate of interest on each reset date is called the **composite rate.** It can differ from the initial interest rate on the origination date.

- *Reset date.* The point in time when mortgage payments will be adjusted is called the **reset date.** This time period is usually six months or one year. However, it could be as long as every three to five years, or it could be as short as one month or less.

- *Negative amortization.* To the extent accrued interest in a given period exceeds the periodic payment, the difference may be compounded at current rates and added to the outstanding loan balance. When additions to the outstanding loan balance are allowed in the loan agreement, such amounts are referred to as **negative amortization** (see the discussion in the previous chapter).

- *Caps.* Maximum *increases* allowed in payments, interest rates, maturity extensions, and negative amortization (or loan balances) on reset dates are called **caps.**

- *Floors.* Maximum *reductions* in payments or interest rates on reset dates are called **floors.**

- *Assumability.* The ability of the borrower to allow a subsequent purchaser of a property to assume a loan under the existing terms is called **assumability.**

- *Discount points.* As with FRMs, these points or fees are also used with ARMs to increase the lender's yield.

- *Prepayment privilege.* Most *residential* borrowers usually have the option to prepay without penalty. However, because prepayment is a privilege and not a right, lenders may charge penalties if a loan is prepaid within a certain period of time.

- *Lockouts.* Many commercial mortgage loans prohibit repayment for a specified number of years. In these cases, should a borrower wish to prepay, a prepayment fee may have to be negotiated with the lender.

- *Conversion option.* The right of an ARM borrower to convert to an FRM. Depending on the agreement, this conversion option may be exercised by the borrower at will or only after a specific period of time. Lenders also may charge a fee for this option.

Clearly, many other combinations of the above provisions could be used to allocate interest rate risk between the lender and borrower.[5] Space does not allow for an in-depth analysis of all of these combinations. What we will provide, however, is a framework which should provide the necessary tools that can be used to analyze any given set of ARM or floating rate provisions.

Variations: ARM and Floating Rate Loans

3/1, 5/1, and 7/1 "Hybrid Loans"

Another frequently used category of ARMs is sometimes referred to as *hybrid* ARMs. This category combines elements of FRMs for periods of three, five, or seven years, after which interest rates are *reset* and the loan becomes an ARM. Subsequent payments are usually reset every year for the remaining maturity period. For example, a 3/1 hybrid would mean a three-year fixed rate after which the interest rate would become adjustable, tied to an index, *and would be reset each year thereafter.* ARM payments on such a loan, with a 30-year maturity and an initial rate of 6 percent, would begin with fully amortizing monthly payments like an FRM made for a period of 30 years. For the first three years, payments would be:

Solution:
Years 1–3:

$$PV = -\$100,000$$
$$i = 6\%/12$$
$$n = 360$$
$$FV = 0$$

Solve for PMT = $599.55

Function:
PMT (PV, i, n, FV)

---

[5] In *residential lending*, there are three additional terms that are commonly negotiated by borrowers and lenders. These include:

- *Expected start rate.* **The expected start rate** is based on the index chosen plus the margin on the loan closing date. Because the lender is assuming less interest rate risk than the borrower, it will almost always be lower than rates on FRMs.
- *Actual start rate, or initial interest rate.* **The actual start rate** is determined by competitive market conditions among lenders at the time ARM loan commitments are made. It may be the same as or lower than the expected start rate. When the initial, or actual, start rate is *lower* than the expected start rate, it is sometimes referred to as a "teaser rate."
- *Teaser rate.* When the actual start rate is very low when compared to the expected start rate, it is usually an indication that lenders are actively competing and are willing to offer a lower initial rate of interest **(teaser rate)** in order to attract borrowers. One additional issue that borrowers must determine is whether they are getting a true discount or whether the lower rate of interest will be deferred interest which will be added to the loan balance.

On the reset date at the end of three years, the reset rate would be based on the prevailing index and margin agreed on by the borrower and the lender. For example, at the end of three years, if the ARM rate has risen to 6.5 percent, payments for the first year thereafter (year 4) would be based on the balance at the end of year 3, or $96,084.

Solution:	Function:
Beginning of year 4 through year 30	$PMT\,(PV, i, n, FV)$
$PV = -\$96,084$	
$i = 6.5\%/12$	
$n = 324$	
$FV = 0$	
Solve for *PMT* $= \$629.88$	

In this example, for the first three years, payments would be the same as a $100,000 FRM made at 6 percent for 30 years, or $599.55. At the end of three years, the loan balance would be $96,084, the interest rate would be reset at 6.5 percent (assumption), and payments during year 4 would become $629.88. Payments would be recalculated on the reset date every year thereafter.

As discussed above, possible variations on a hybrid loan could consist of the payments in years 1 to 3 being interest only, with payments beginning in year 4 being based on the ARM index at the end of year 3. Because payments would be interest only, the loan balance beginning in year 4 would remain at $100,000. Payments beginning in year 4 would be recalculated based on the prevailing interest rate plus amortization of loan principal over 27 years. Payments would then be recalculated on each reset date at the beginning of each of the remaining 27 years.

Interest-Only ARM and Floating Rate Loans

Many floating rate loans are used to finance commercial properties. The **interest-only ARM** or floating rate loan requires that the borrower pay interest monthly. Interest payments vary in accordance with the underlying index and margin. For example, a $100,000 loan with an initial rate of 6 percent for 30 years and a one year reset period would require monthly interest-only payments as follows:

$$\text{Monthly payment} = \text{Loan amount} \cdot (\text{Interest rate} \div 12)$$

$$= \$100,000 \cdot (.06 \div 12)$$

$$= \$500$$

If, at the beginning of the next year (the reset date), the index has increased and the new interest rate becomes 8 percent, the new monthly payment becomes:

$$= \$100,000 \cdot (.08 \div 12)$$

$$= \$666.67$$

Note that in both cases, payments are interest only and do not include any amortization of principal. Now, consider the event that at the end of year 1, the borrower begins to

As has been pointed out, interest rates and monthly payments on ARMs are reset after expiration of a specific time interval (commonly one year). As has also been pointed out, the interest rate on the reset date will be based on the index chosen by the borrower plus a fixed margin. However, it is important to understand what is referred to as the *teaser rate*.

The *initial rate of interest* on an ARM is effective on the day that the ARM *closes* and is used to calculate monthly payments during the *first year*. To illustrate: On the date of closing the ARM loan, if one year treasuries are 4 percent and the margin is 2 percent, it would be logical to assume that the expected initial, or start, rate used to compute mortgage payments would be 6 percent. However, the initial rate *does not necessarily* have to be 6 percent. This is because at the point of origination, lenders are free to compete with other lenders by offering borrowers different initial interest rate points, other financing fees, and the like. For this reason, when the initial interest rate quoted on an ARM is *below* the prevailing market index rate plus the margin, it is sometimes referred to as a "teaser rate." Lenders use teaser rates to attract borrowers and compete for business with other lenders. However, the teaser rate will usually prevail only from the date of loan origination until the *first reset date*. On that date, the teaser rate ceases to exist and the interest rate and payments will be calculated based on the prevailing index plus the margin. Interest rates and payments will be reset each year thereafter based on the index plus margin for the remaining life of the loan.

In our example, if we assume that when the ARM is closed (with interest at the prevailing market rate of 6%), a teaser rate of 1.5 percent is offered by the lender, monthly payments for the *first year* would be:

Solution: Payments Based on Teaser Rate:

$$PV = -\$100{,}000$$
$$i = 1.5\%/12$$
$$n = 30 \times 12$$
$$FV = 0$$

Solve for *PMT* $= \$345.12$

Function:

$PMT\ (PV, i, n, FV)$

This payment is far lower than would be the case if the loan was originated at 6 percent interest. For example, "interest-only" payments would be $500 at 6 percent interest. Or, if the payment was based on a fully amortizing 30-year-loan schedule, it would be $607.32.

THE TEASER RATE AND THE ACCRUAL RATE

Recall in the above example that the teaser rate was set at 1.5 percent when the prevailing rate on one-year treasuries (4%) plus the margin would indicate that prevailing interest rates, or the expected start rate, should be in the range of 6 percent. It is also possible that the loan agreement may specify that during the first year, interest will *accrue* at 6 percent even though payments may be based on the teaser rate of 1.5 percent. If this is the case, the difference between the teaser rate and the accrual rate will be included in the loan balance with interest. Therefore, on the reset date, payments will be based on the outstanding loan balance which will have this difference, plus interest, added to the loan balance (negative amortization).

STEP 1:

Solution: Loan Balance EOY 1:

$PMT = \$345.12$

$i = 6\%$

$n = 12$ mos.

$PV = -\$100,000$

Solve for FV = $101,910.53 (balance)

Function:

$FV (PMT, i, n, PV)$

STEP 2:

Solution: New Payment on Reset Date at 6.5% Interest:

$PV = -\$101,910.53$

$i = 6.5\%$

$n = 29$ years

$FV = 0$

Solve for PMT = $651.43

Function:

$PMT (PV, i, n, FV)$

Note that if the loan agreement specifies that the difference between what the initial rate on the ARM would have been if payments were based on the market rate of 6 percent (the accrual rate) and the teaser rate of 1.5 percent will be accrued in the loan balance, then the loan balance on the reset date ($101,910.53) will be greater than the initial amount of the loan ($100,000.00) because of negative amortization. (This addition to the loan balance may be calculated as the difference in monthly interest accrued at 6 percent, or $500, less the amount paid, $345.12, or $154.88 compounded monthly at 6%.) This results in $1,910.53 being added to the loan balance. This provision may become even more important if the reset date is scheduled for two, three, or more years after the origination date. In this event, the loan balance may increase by an even greater amount because of more accrued interest (negative amortization).

PAYMENT SHOCK

In the above example we determined that when the ARM is originated at a 1.5 percent teaser rate, monthly payments are $345.12. As shown in our example, at the beginning of year 2, payments could increase to $651.43. This amounts to over an 80 percent increase in monthly payments. An increase of this magnitude is sometimes referred to as **payment shock.** This can occur if large increases in monthly payments occur on the reset date. This can happen when the index to which the ARM interest rate is tied has increased considerably. Payment shock can be even more serious for ARMs originated at teaser rates. Depending on the borrower's income, other assets, and the value of the property on the reset date, this shock could result in financial difficulty and force the borrower to default. *For this reason, use of a very low teaser rate to qualify a borrower based on their current ability to make monthly payments may create future problems when it is time for interest rates to be reset.*

make payments which will fully amortize the loan balance over the remaining 29 years. Now, instead of "interest-only" payments of $666.67, the new payments become:

Solution:	Function:
$PV = -\$100,000$	$PMT\,(PV, n, i, FV)$
$n = 29 \times 12 = 348$	
$i = 8\%$	
$FV = 0$	
Solve for *PMT* $= \$739.95$	

The payment at the beginning of year 2 would be $739.95, of which $73.27 would be applied to reduce principal. When monthly compound interest is applied to $73.27 at 8 percent, the loan amortization for the year is $912.20. (This can be seen by calculating $PMT = \$73.27$, $n = 12$, $i = 8\%$, and $FV = \$912.20$.) When this amount is subtracted from $100,000, it produces a loan balance at the end of year 2 of $99,087.79. It should be pointed out that with a floating rate loan (ARM), lenders and borrowers may choose to begin a full or partial amortization schedule at specified times. For example, at the end of year 3, "interest-only" monthly payments must stop and all further payments must begin to include principal so as to fully or partially amortize the loan balance at maturity.

Risk Premiums, Interest Rate Risk, and Default Risk

It is very difficult to determine how expected yields will vary among ARMs containing different repayment characteristics. However, for any given class of borrowers, the expected yield (cost) of borrowing with an ARM generally depends on the ARM provisions described in detail earlier: (1) the initial interest rate, (2) the index to which the interest rate is tied, (3) the margin, or spread, over the index chosen for a given ARM, (4) discount points charged at origination, (5) the frequency of payment adjustments, and (6) the inclusion of caps or floors on the interest rate, payments, or loan balances. The loan amount and each of the six characteristics listed will determine the cash outflow or amount loaned, expected monthly payments, and the expected loan balance for an expected time period from which an expected yield (internal rate of return) can be computed. In addition to understanding how each of the above relationships is likely to affect the expected yield (or cost of borrowing), further complications include understanding how combinations of these terms may *interact* over time and possibly amplify or reduce *default risk* to the lender.

While much has been said about benefits to lenders from shifting interest rate risk to borrowers, there are added risks that lenders must assume with ARMs. The combination of the six characteristics also affects default risk either (1) by interfering with the ability of the borrower to make mortgage payments or (2) by increasing the loan balance so that it is too high in relation to the value of the house, assuming that negative amortization is allowed. While we discuss lender underwriting standards used to gauge default risk in more detail in a later chapter, we also want to stress the importance of default risk in our present discussion.

A useful way to approach the relationships between interest rate risk and default risk for an individual and lender is to examine panel A of Exhibit 5–2. The exhibit shows the risk premium (*p*) demanded by the lender on the vertical axis and interest rate risk assumed by the lender on the horizontal axis. Looking at line A–B in the exhibit, we see that as more interest rate risk is assumed by the lender (less by the borrower), the lender will demand a higher risk premium. Hence, the interest rate risk curve is positively sloped. In the extreme, if the lender assumes all interest rate risk (point B), this would be equivalent to the amount

EXHIBIT 5–2
The Relationship between Interest Rate Risk, Default Risk, and Risk Premiums

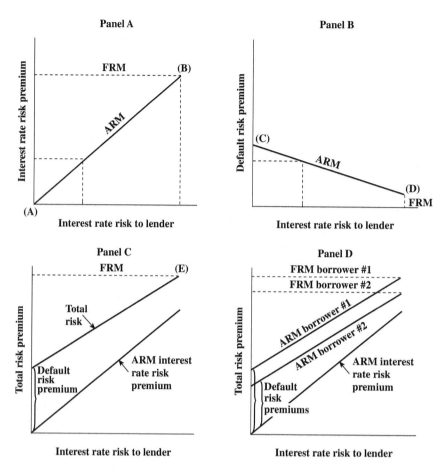

of interest rate risk assumed with an FRM. Note that when the lender assumes no interest rate risk, the borrower is assuming all interest rate risk. This is represented by the intersection of the interest rate risk line at the origin of the diagram (point A).

When interest rate risk assumed by the borrower increases (as would be the case with an ARM with *no cap* on payments or the interest rate), *default risk* assumed by the lender increases (see panel B). Default risk is greatest at point C, where there are no restrictions on ARM interest rates or payments, because the borrower faces a greater likelihood that unanticipated changes in interest rates may cause significant increases in payments ("payment shock") relative to income. Hence, the likelihood of default is greater when the borrower assumes all interest rate risk. However, as more interest rate risk is assumed by the lender, we should note in panel B that risk of borrower default declines because payment shock to the borrower is restricted when caps on payments or interest rates are used. In essence, by assuming more interest rate risk, the *lender* absorbs more shock, thereby reducing *borrower* default risk. This pattern is exhibited in panel B where the default risk curve is shown as negatively related to the risk premium demanded by the lender as interest rate risk to the lender increases. However, the level of default risk never declines below the risk assumed by the lender on a fixed rate mortgage (point D), which is also coincident with the lender's assumption of all interest rate risk (point B in panel A).

The total risk curve (see panel C of Exhibit 5–2) establishes the risk premium demanded by the lender for both risks (interest rate risk and default risk) assumed under various ARM terms. The total amount of risk assumed by the lender corresponds to various combinations of ARM terms, ranging from the assumption of all interest rate risk by the borrower (panel A, point A) to the assumption of all interest rate risk by the lender (panel A, point B), coupled with the amount of default risk incurred by the lender given different levels of interest rate risk (panel B). Hence, panel C shows the total risk premium the lender should earn, given levels of interest rate risk and default risk that correspond to various levels of interest rate risk. However, the total risk premium should not exceed the total premium that would be earned on an FRM (panel C, point E).

Panel D in Exhibit 5–2 shows the relationship between total risk and the risk premium demanded by the lender for *different borrowers.* Note that the amount of *interest rate risk* remains the same for each borrower; however, *default risk* differs. Hence, the premium charged by the lender on ARMs will vary, depending on the amount of default risk being assumed for each borrower, (1) or (2), and how that default risk interacts with expected changes in interest rate risk. We should point out that many other non-interest-rate factors can cause default such as loss of employment, divorce, and so on. We focus here only on how default risk changes with fluctuations in interest rates.

Exhibit 5–2 is appropriate only for specific borrowers, however. To date, the exact relationship between default risk and interest rate risk for many different classes of borrowers has not been studied extensively. Hence, you cannot generalize the example shown to all borrowers and lenders in the mortgage market. However, it is safe to say that ARM loans will only be made to an individual borrower as long as the expected benefits to the lender from shifting interest rate risk exceed the potential default losses. Similarly, as long as a given borrower is willing to undertake interest rate risk in exchange for paying a lower risk premium to a lender, the ARM will be acceptable to the borrower.

While Exhibit 5–2 graphically portrays the risk/return trade-off faced by lenders and borrowers, ARM terms may be structured in many ways to provide a trade-off between interest rate and default risk that is satisfactory to both. These terms could include many possible combinations of initial interest rates, margin, points, the index chosen, frequency of payment adjustments, caps on payments, and so on. We will explore various combinations of ARM terms later in this chapter.

From the above discussion, then, mortgage lending (borrowing) can be viewed as a process of *pricing risk,* with the expected yield being the return received (paid) by lenders (borrowers) for making loans with terms under which lenders and borrowers bear various amounts of risk. The terms utilized in construction of an ARM (e.g., initial rate, index, adjustment period, caps) are simply the "tools" at the disposal of borrowers and lenders to negotiate and allocate the amounts of interest rate and default risk being shared.[6]

Expected Yield Relationships and Interest Rate Risk

While the contracting process used by lenders and borrowers to allocate risk is a complicated one, there are some general relationships regarding interest rate risk and yields that can be employed in this process. The following general relationships regarding interest rate risk may be useful when comparing ARMs with FRMs and comparing ARMs containing different loan provisions with one another. The relationships focus on the effects of interest rate risk on ARM yields, given the conclusion that an ARM will never be made unless the expected benefit to a lender from shifting interest rate risk to a borrower exceeds expected losses from default risk. Proceeding with this assumption when evaluating ARM terms, interest rate risk, and expected yields to lenders, we should consider the following relationships:

1. At the time of origination, the *expected* yield on an ARM should be less than the *expected* yield on an FRM, to the extent that benefits to lenders from shifting interest

[6] If risk could be quantified, or reduced to some unit quantity such as dollars, an agreement could be devised that would specify exactly how much risk was being shared. However, because risk is an abstract concept, this is not possible. This is the reason why borrowers and lenders include various provisions in contracts to share risk under any set of unknown future economic conditions.

rate risk exceed increases in default risk to borrowers. Otherwise, the borrower and lender will always prefer an FRM. Coincident with the lower expected ARM yield, the *initial interest rate* on an ARM will *usually* be less than that of an FRM.[7]

2. Adjustable rate mortgages tied to short-term indexes are generally riskier to borrowers than ARMs tied to long-term indexes because the former are generally more variable than long-term interest rates. Therefore, the more risk-averse ARM borrowers will generally prefer ARMs tied to a longer-term index and they should be willing to pay more (a higher risk premium and expected yield to the lender). Less risk-averse borrowers will prefer a shorter-term index and will expect to pay less for taking additional interest rate risk. Borrowers who prefer no interest rate risk will choose a fixed rate mortgage and will pay the highest total risk premium to the lender.

3. Coincidentally with (2), ARMs with shorter time intervals between adjustments in payments are generally riskier to borrowers than those with longer time periods because, although an ARM may be tied to a short-term index, the adjustment period may not coincide with the index. For example, an ARM may be adjusted every *three* years based on the value of the *one-year* index at the time of adjustment. Hence, the more frequent the adjustment interval, the lower the interest rate risk to lenders because ARM payments will reflect current market conditions irrespective of the index chosen. Borrowers preferring no adjustment in payments will choose FRMs.

4. To the extent ARMs contain maximum caps on interest rate adjustments, the interest rate risk incurred by borrowers will be lower. Hence, the expected yield realized by lenders should be higher than if no restrictions were present. The expected yield will vary with the size of the limitations. When floors are used, the risk to the borrower is greater because of the limit placed on the decline in the interest rate used to compute ARM payments in any given year. Borrowers who prefer certainty in payments and interest rates will choose an FRM, which will always provide the highest *expected* yield to the lender.

5. If an ARM has negative amortization due to a payment cap, then the effect of changes in interest rates will not materially reduce interest rate risk to borrowers or the expected yield to lenders because any interest forgone because of limitations or caps will be deferred and become a part of the loan balance. Any amounts of negative amortization will also accrue compound interest and must be eventually paid by borrowers.

More Complex Features

In the preceding section, we described some general relationships regarding ARM loan terms, risk bearing, and what lenders (borrowers) should expect to yield (pay) over the life of the ARM contract, or repayment period. We must point out, however, that lenders and borrowers also negotiate certain *initial* loan provisions that (1) will be known at the point of origination and (2) will affect expected yields. Once the index frequency of payment adjustments, rates of payments, and negative amortization have been negotiated, the magnitude of the effect on lenders and borrowers will be determined solely by future market conditions. However, the initial terms on ARMs, or the loan amount, maturity, initial interest rate, margin, and discount points, are quantifiable and can be negotiated with complete certainty at the time the loan is made. These initial loan terms will reflect the net effect of (1) the amount of interest rate risk assumed by the lender as determined by the

---

[7] Although the initial interest rate on an ARM should generally be less than that of an FRM, in cases where short-term interest rates are greater than long-term rates and an ARM is tied to a short-term rate, it is possible that the initial rate on an ARM may be greater than an initial interest rate on an FRM. However, the *expected yield* on an ARM should be lower because yields are computed to maturity, which includes expected future interest rate patterns.

index chosen, adjustment period, any caps or negative amortization and (2) the amount of default risk assumed by the lender as determined by the amount of interest rate risk shifted to a specific borrower. Exhibit 5–3 contains a summary of hypothetical loan terms being quoted on three ARMs and one FRM.

EXHIBIT 5–3
Comparison of Hypothetical Loan Terms

Contents	ARM I	ARM II	ARM III	FRM
(*a*) Initial interest rate, or start rate	8%	9%	11%	14%
(*b*) Loan maturity	30	30	30	30
(*c*) Maturity of instruments making up index	1 year	1 year	1 year	—
(*d*) Percent margin above index	2%	2%	2%	—
(*e*) Adjustment interval, or reset date	1 year	1 year	1 year	—
(*f*) Points	2%	2%	2%	2%
(*g*) Payment cap	None	7.5%	—	—
(*h*) Interest rate cap	None	None	2%, 5%*	—
(*i*) Negative amortization	—	Yes	—	—

*2 percent maximum annual increase, 5 percent total increase over the loan term.

A careful review of these loans reveals considerable differences in terms. We note that the initial interest rate for ARM I is 8 percent, for ARM II it is 9 percent, and for ARM III it is 11 percent, while the fixed interest rate mortgage (FRM) is quoted at 14 percent. Why is this?

A quick review of the terms for ARM I shows that it has the same terms (*b*) to (*f*) as ARMs II and III; however, characteristics (*g*) to (*i*) reveal that future payments and interest rates are *unrestricted* since there are no caps on payments or interest rates. These terms may now be compared with ARM II, which has a cap of 7.5 percent between any adjustment period plus a provision for negative amortization. ARM III has an interest rate cap of 2 percent between adjustment periods and 5 percent over the life of the loan. When all three ARMs are compared, it is clear that the borrower is assuming more interest rate risk with ARM I than with any of the other ARMs. Hence, the expected yield on ARM I to the lender should be *less,* when compared with other ARMs, for an otherwise qualified borrower (i.e., a borrower with an acceptable level of default risk under all three ARM choices).

Because the *expected yield* should be *less* for ARM I, the *initial interest rate* will also generally be *lower* than each of the initial rates shown for the other ARM alternatives. Given that all ARMs are tied to the same index and have the same margin and discount points, the only way to "price" ARM I to achieve a lower expected yield is to *reduce* the initial interest rate relative to the other ARMs. ARM I should also have the largest discount, or spread, relative to the interest rate on the FRM. This would be expected because the borrower is bearing all interest rate risk; hence, the lender should expect to earn a lower risk premium and therefore a lower *yield* on ARM I when compared with the FRM (again, default risk is assumed to be acceptable for this borrower if ARM I is made).

Using a lower initial rate as an inducement for borrowers to accept more interest rate risk and unrestricted payments in the future is obviously only one of many combinations of terms that may be used to differentiate ARM I from ARMs II and III and from the FRM. For example, the lender could keep the initial rate on ARM I the same as that offered on ARM II, but reduce the margin on ARM I or charge fewer discount points, or both. Other terms, such as the choice of index, payment adjustment intervals, and so on, could also be varied with these three terms to accomplish the same objectives.

Moving to ARMs II and III in Exhibit 5–3, we note that both have initial interest rates that are greater than the initial rate on ARM I. The interest rate on ARM II is greater than that of ARM I because ARM II has a cap on payments that reduces payment uncertainty for the borrower.

When ARM III is compared to ARMs I and II, the interest rate risk assumed by the lender is clearly greater because payments are limited by interest rate caps. In this case, should market interest rates rise, the interest rate cap would restrict interest payments and not allow the lender to recover any lost interest. When compared with ARMs I and II, ARM III provides that more interest rate risk will be borne by the lender. Hence, it should be originated at a higher initial rate of interest.

Important note should be taken of other possibilities in Exhibit 5–3. If other terms, such as the index and adjustment interval, were to be changed, we would also expect changes in the initial loan terms. Suppose that in ARM I an index based on securities with longer maturities were to be chosen or payment intervals were longer than those shown. We would then expect either or all of the initial rate, index, or points to *increase* because of lower interest rate risk to the borrower; the risk is less because indexes tied to securities based on longer maturities are not as volatile as those based on shorter maturities. Obviously, the same would hold true for the other ARMs if a longer-term index and payment interval were used. Indeed, if such changes were made to the other ARMs, they would become more like an FRM. If longer-term indexes and lower caps were used on ARMs II and III, interest rate risk bearing would become greater for the lender; hence, the expected yield earned by the lender should approach that of an FRM as of the date of origination.

ARM Payment Mechanics

To illustrate how payment adjustments and loan balances are determined over the term for the ARMs in Exhibit 5–3, consider the example of a loan amount of $60,000 with a term of 30 years. We assume that the ARM interest rate will be adjusted annually. Hence, the first adjustment will occur at the beginning of the second year. At that time, the composite rate on the loan will be determined by the index of one-year U.S. Treasury securities, plus a 2 percent margin. If we assume (1) that the index of one-year Treasury securities takes on a pattern of 10, 13, 15, and 10 percent for the *next* four years, based on forward rates in existence at the time each ARM is originated and (2) that monthly payment and interest rate adjustments are made annually, what would payment adjustments, loan balances, and expected yields be for an ARM with these assumed characteristics?

No Caps or Limitations on Payments or Interest Rates

The first case to consider is ARM I, where payments are unrestricted or allowed to move up or down with the index without limit. What would be the payment pattern on such an ARM given that the expected distribution of future interest rates actually occurred? This unrestricted case, where no limitations apply to payments or interest, is straightforward to deal with.

The first four columns of Exhibit 5–4 contain the data needed for our computations. Note that we assume that the initial interest rate is 8 percent for the first year, but after the first year

EXHIBIT 5–4
Summary Data and
Results: ARM I
(Unrestricted Case)

(1) Year	(2) Index	+	(3) Margin	=	(4) Interest Rate	(5) Payments	(6) Balance[†]
1					8%*	$440.26	$59,499
2	10%		2%		12	614.25	59,255
3	13		2		15	752.27	59,106
4	15		2		17	846.21	58,990
5	10		2		12	617.60	58,639

*Initial rate.
[†]Rounded.

the index *plus* the 2 percent margin establish what the payment will be. From the beginning of year 2 through the beginning of year 5, the interest rates used to determine payments are 12, 15, 17, and 12, respectively, based on our assumptions. As previously pointed out, ARMs tied to the same index may vary with respect to the initial rate of interest, the margin, and, perhaps, discount points offered by lenders. These components are usually set by competitive conditions in the lending area and are the primary variables (along with caps or other restrictions) with which lenders compete when pricing loans. Lenders have no control over the index and, therefore, must rely on other components with which to compete when pricing the loan.

The payments column of Exhibit 5–4 is based on a series of relatively simple computations. They are carried out as though a new loan is originated at the end of each year based on a new rate of interest, as determined by the index plus the margin, applied to the outstanding loan balance.

The process of (1) computing the loan balance, based on the interest rate applicable during the year for which the balance is desired and (2) computing the new payment, based on any change in the index at the end of the appropriate adjustment interval, would continue after each adjustment interval over the remaining life of the loan.

STEP 1:

Solution: Determine First Year Payment:

$n = 30 \times 12 = 360$

$i = 8\%/12 = .66666\%$

$PV = \$60,000$

$FV = 0$

Solve for PMT $= -\$440.26$

Function:

$PMT\,(n, i, PV, FV)$

STEP 2:

Solution: Determine First Year Mortgage Balance:

$n = 29 \times 12 = 348$

$i = 8\%/12 = .66666\%$

$PMT = -\$440.26$

$FV = 0$

Solve for PV $= \$59,499$

Function:

$PV\,(n, i, PMT, FV)$

STEP 3:

Solution: Determine Second Year Payment:

$n = 29 \times 12 = 348$

$i = 12\%/12 = 1\%$

$PV = \$59,499$

$FV = 0$

Solve for PMT $= -\$614.25$

Function:

$PMT\,(n, i, PV, FV)$

STEP 4:

Solution: Determine Second Year Mortgage Balance:

$n = 28 \times 12 = 336$

$i = 12\%/12 = 1\%$

$PMT = -\$614.25$

$FV = 0$

Solve for PV $= \$59,255$

Function:

$PV\,(n, i, PMT, FV)$

Looking again at Exhibit 5–4, we carry out the computations using the hypothetical interest rate pattern. Assuming no restrictions or caps on interest rates or payments, we see considerable variation in monthly payments. Depending on interest rate changes, payments increase by over 39.5 percent and decline by as much as 27 percent during the first five years. For borrowers who have a strong aversion to interest rate risk and the coincident variability in payments, the unrestricted ARM, tied to a short-term instrument, may not be desirable. One final pattern should be noted in Exhibit 5–4: regardless of the interest rate pattern chosen, the loan is amortizing. The rate of amortization will differ, however, depending on the rate of interest in effect at each adjustment interval.

The default risk associated with ARM I should also be clear from Exhibit 5–4. Note that although the initial payment level is low, the variation in payments over the five-year period is great. Clearly, for a borrower to take this risk, the lender must view the borrower's future income or present and future wealth as sufficient to cover significant changes in monthly payments.

Payment Caps and Negative Amortization

We now consider ARM II where the lender and borrower have agreed that to moderate possible interest rate fluctuations in the future, there will be a payment cap, or a maximum rate at which *payments* can increase between adjustment intervals. This maximum rate of increase will be 7.5 percent per year. In this case, however, any difference between payments and interest that should be earned, based on unrestricted changes in interest rates, will be *added* to the loan balance. As previously discussed, this type of ARM contains both a *payment cap* and *negative amortization.*

Because this ARM allows for a payment cap and negative amortization, the receipt of more cash flow is pushed further into the future than in the unrestricted case. Therefore, interest rate risk to the lender is somewhat greater than with ARM I, so we assume that the initial rate on the mortgage is quoted to be 9 percent, while the margin will remain at 2 percent. Exhibit 5–5 contains computations of the payment and loan balance patterns for the ARM just described. As shown in the exhibit, based on an unrestricted change in our hypothetical pattern of interest rates, monthly payments in the second year would be $615.18, or 27.4 percent higher than the $482.77 payment required during the first year. A payment of $615.18 would obviously be greater than the 7.5 percent maximum allowable increase; hence, the payment would be capped at $518.98, or 7.5 percent more than $482.77. However, *because this ARM requires negative amortization,* the difference between interest charged during year 2, or 12 percent, and the amount actually paid will be added to the outstanding loan balance plus compound interest.

Negative amortization is computed by using the method shown for the graduated payment mortgage (GPM) in Chapter 4. Exhibit 5–5 contains a breakdown of interest and amortization for ARM II. Note that during the first year when loan payments are computed at 9 percent interest, monthly amortization occurs and the loan balance is reduced. After the first year, monthly payments must be computed *first* based on the unrestricted interest rate (column 3) to determine whether payments will increase at a rate greater than 7.5 percent. If uncapped payments would exceed 7.5 percent, then the payment cap (column 4) becomes operative and actual payments will be restricted to a 7.5 percent increase. The monthly interest that is *accruing* on the loan balance at the unrestricted rate is $(.12 \div 12)\$59,590 = \$595.90$ (column 6). However, the payment that will actually be made is $518.98. The difference, $76.92 (column 7), must be added to the loan balance with compound interest. Hence, the difference in year 2, $76.92 per month, is compounded at 1 percent per month (column 8), resulting in an increase of $975.54 in the loan balance.[8]

[8] Using a calculator: $PV = 0$, $PMT = \$76.92$, $i = 12\% \div 12$, $n = 12$: Solve for $FV = \$975.54$.

EXHIBIT 5–5
Determination of Payment Limits (Negative Amortization: ARM II, with Payment Cap = 7.5 Percent Annually)

(1) Beginning of Year	(2) Balance (Rounded)	(3) Uncapped Payment	(4) Payment Capped at 7.5 Percent
1	$60,000	$482.77	$482.77
2	59,590	615.18	518.98
3	60,566	768.91	557.90
4	63,128	903.79	599.74
5	66,952	700.96	644.72

(5) Monthly Interest Rate	(6) Monthly Interest (5) × (2)	(7) Monthly Amortization (4) − (6)	(8) Compounded Monthly Rate (End Year) from (5)	(9) Annual Amortization (7) × (8)
.09 ÷ 12	$450.00	$32.77	12.507596	$409.87
.12 ÷ 12	595.90	(76.92)	12.682503	(975.54)
.15 ÷ 12	757.08	(199.18)	12.860378	(2,561.53)
.17 ÷ 12	894.31	(294.57)	12.980582	(3,823.69)
.12 ÷ 12	669.52	(24.80)	12.682503	(314.53)

Payments in the third year of the ARM are determined by again establishing whether uncapped payments would increase by more than 7.5 percent. To determine this, we find that the loan balance, which includes the previous year's negative amortization, is $59,590 + $975.54 = $60,566 (rounded). The *unrestricted* interest rate of 15 percent for the remaining 336 months is used to compute the uncapped payment. Uncapped payments based on the unrestricted rate of 15 percent would be $768.91. This is a 48 percent increase from $518.98; hence, the payment will again be capped at a 7.5 percent increase, and negative amortization will be computed on the interest shortfall, compounded at 15 percent monthly, and added to the loan balance. This process is repeated for each adjustment interval over the life of the loan.[9] Actual loan balances with payments capped at 7.5 percent are shown in Exhibit 5–6.

Another observation regarding ARM II (see Exhibit 5–5) has to do with the increase in both the payment and loan balance during year 5 even though there is a significant decline in the interest index from 17 to 12 percent. This occurs because the loan balance has

EXHIBIT 5–6
ARM II: Loan Balances When Payments Are Capped at 7.5 Percent Annually (Negative Amortization Allowed)

Year	Index	Margin	Interest Rate	Beginning of Year Balances	Payments	Less: Annual Amortization	End of Year Loan Balances
1	—	—	9%*	$60,000	$482.77	409.87	$59,590
2	10%	2%	12	59,590	518.98	(975.54)	60,566
3	13	2	15	60,566	557.90	(2,561.53)	63,128
4	15	2	17	63,128	599.74	(3,823.69)	66,952
5	10	2	12	66,952	644.72	(314.53)	67,267

*Origination rate.

[9] ARMs with negative amortization provisions usually limit increases in the loan balance during the life of the loan because it is possible for the loan balance to increase to a level that exceeds the value of the property serving as security for the loan. Consequently, lenders and borrowers must agree that if a prespecified maximum is reached, the lender must either forgo further accumulation of interest in the loan balance or require that monthly payments be increased at that time.

increased, due to past negative amortization, to $66,952 at the end of year 4. Even though the interest rate declines to 12 percent, monthly interest will be $669.52, which is in excess of the maximum 7.5 percent increase from the $599.74 payment in the preceding year. Hence, payments would increase by 7.5 percent, even though interest rates have declined.

An *alternative* method that may be used to find loan balances for the ARM illustrated in Exhibits 5–5 and 5–6 is shown in the calculator sequence described below. Note in step 4 that even though payments due in year 2 have been increased by 7.5 percent to $518.98, they remain lower than the interest due which is $595.90 (the accrued rate of 12% ÷ 12, or 1% × $59,590.08). Furthermore, when the interest rate of 12 percent is used for *i* in the calculator sequence and the future value (*FV*) is solved for, the loan balance increases to $60,566 (rounded). When compared to the loan balance of $59,590 at the end of year 1, negative amortization of $975 (rounded) has occurred. This coincides with the amount shown in Exhibit 5–5 (column 9) during year 2 and consists of $76.92 per month compounded at a monthly rate of 12 percent (or 12% ÷ 12 = .01). The reader should read both Exhibits 5–5 and 5–6 and review the process involved to better understand the results from the alternative calculator solution shown below.

Alternative Solution for Determining Loan Balances and Negative Amortization for ARM in Exhibits 5–5 and 5–6:

STEP 1:

Solution: Determine Monthly Payments for Year (1):   Function:

$\quad$ PV = $60,000   PMT (PV, n, i, FV)

$\quad\quad$ n = 30 × 12 = 360

$\quad\quad$ i = 9%/12 = .75%

$\quad$ FV = 0

Solve for PMT = $482.77

STEP 2:

Solution: Determine Balance at the End of First Year: Function:

$\quad\quad$ PV = $60,000 (from above)   FV (PV, PMT, i, n)

$\quad$ PMT = $482.77 (from above)

$\quad\quad\quad$ i = 9%/12 = .75% (from above)

$\quad\quad\quad$ n = 1 × 12 = 12

Solve for FV = $59,590.08

STEP 3:

Solution: Determine Monthly Payments for Year (2):

$\quad$ PMT = $482.77 × 1.075 = $518.98

STEP 4:

Solution: Determine Balance at the End of Second Year: Function:

$\quad\quad$ PV = $59,590.08 (balance at end of first   FV (PV, PMT, i, n)
$\quad\quad\quad\quad$ year calculated above)

$\quad$ PMT = $518.98 (from above)

$\quad\quad\quad$ i = 12%/12 = 1%

$\quad\quad\quad$ n = 1 × 12 = 12

Solve for FV = $60,565.61

Repeat steps 2 through 4 for the remaining years.

Interest Rate Caps

The final case that we consider with ARMs is a common pattern in which interest rates are capped or limited (see Exhibit 5–7). In ARM III, the increase in interest rates is limited to 2 percent during any one adjustment interval (year in our example) and to a *total* of 5 percent over the life of the loan. If interest rates ever exceed these caps, payments are limited. Hence, the interest rate cap also acts as a payment cap because the maximum increase in interest rate determines the maximum increase in mortgage payments. This means that if the index plus the margin exceeds these caps, the lender will lose any amount of interest above the capped rates.[10] Exhibit 5–7 illustrates the payment mechanics of ARM III, where the interest rate quoted at origination, 11 percent, is higher than it is with ARMs I and II because the latter two have unrestricted interest rates, while ARM III has interest rate caps. Therefore, the lender is taking more interest rate risk with ARM III because of the possibility that the cap will be exceeded and interest will be lost. To compensate for this possibility, the lender will charge a higher initial interest rate and should expect to earn a higher expected yield.

The payment patterns shown in Exhibit 5–7 are determined from the loan balance established at the end of each adjustment interval. Payments are then computed based on the indicated rate of interest for the remaining term. Results of computations show that, compared with ARM I (the unrestricted case), payments on ARM III are higher initially, and then remain generally lower than payments on ARM I for the remaining term. Hence, borrowers would have to have more income to qualify for ARM III and default risk to the lender should be lower. The loan balances for both ARMs are about the same in year 5. ARM III payments begin at a higher level than those of ARM II, because of the higher initial rate of interest, and remain higher over the term of the loan. However, because of negative amortization, loan balances over time for ARM II are significantly higher than for ARM III.

Expected Yields on ARMs: A Comparison

In the preceding sections, we examined three kinds of ARMs with provisions commonly used in real estate lending. Other considerations are also important to lenders and borrowers. One important issue is the *yield* to lenders, or *cost* to borrowers, for each category of loan. Given the changes in interest rates, payments, and loan balances, it is not obvious what these yields (costs) will be.

EXHIBIT 5–7
Summary Data and Results: ARM III Interest Rates Capped at 2 Percent, 5 Percent (No Negative Amortization Allowed)

Year	Index + Margin	Capped Interest Rate	Payments	Balance
1		11%	$571.39	$59,730
2	12%	12	616.63	59,485
3	15	14	708.37	59,301
4	17	16	801.65	59,159
5	12	12	619.37	58,807

[10] In many cases, ARMs may contain floors as well as a cap. In our example, this would mean that a maximum reduction of 2 percent in the mortgage rate would be allowed, regardless of the decline in the index. These floors have limited effectiveness, however, because if a significant decline in the index occurs and the loan agreement allows for prepayment, borrowers may *refinance* with a new mortgage loan at a rate that is lower than the floor would allow.

Computing Yields on ARMs

To compare yields on ARMs, the yield (cost) to the lender (borrower) must be computed for each alternative by solving for the internal rate of return (IRR), or the rate of discount. This rate makes the present value of all expected mortgage payments and the loan balance in the year of repayment equal to the initial loan amount less discount points (or $58,800) for each alternative. To illustrate, consider the case of the *unrestricted* ARM I which is paid off in year 5. Using data from Exhibit 5–4, we compute the internal rate of return (or yield) as shown in Exhibit 5–8.

From the computations shown in Exhibit 5–8, we see that the solution is approximately 13.0 percent.[11] This means that even though the *initial* rate of interest was 8 percent and the forward rates of interest are expected to range from 8 to 17 percent over the five-year period, the *expected yield* (cost) is 13.0 percent. Hence, by computing the internal rate of return we have a result that can be compared among alternative ARMs.

Before comparing the results for each ARM considered, we examine the computational procedure used in Exhibit 5–8. Essentially, we are discounting a series of grouped cash flows. In the present case, we are dealing with five groups of monthly cash flows and a single receipt (the loan balance). Note that we discount each group of monthly cash flows by using the present value of a monthly annuity factor of 13 percent (column 3). However, this procedure gives us a present value for a *one-year group* of 12 monthly payments and does not take into account that the cash flows occurring from years 2 through 5 are not received during year 1. Hence, each of the grouped cash flows must be discounted again by the present value of $1 factor to recognize that the present value of each group of cash flows is not received at the same time. This is carried out in column 4. The loan balance, or $58,639, is then discounted as a lump sum.

Summary Observations: ARMs, Borrower, Lender, and Market Behavior

Recalling the graphic analysis of the risk premium and the relationship between interest rate and default risk in Exhibit 5–2, we now show how risk premiums demanded for ARMs I to III would fall on the total risk curve in Exhibit 5–9. This diagram basically indicates that in moving from ARMs I to III, interest rate risk to the lender increases. However, based on panel B in Exhibit 5–2, we recall that as interest rate risk increases to the lender, default risk

EXHIBIT 5–8
Computing the IRR for an Unrestricted ARM, Payoff at End of Year 5

(1) Year	(2) Monthly Payments		(3) PV Monthly Annuity 13%, 12 Months		(4) PV of $1 per Year, 13%, Years 1–5		(5) PV†
1	$440.26	×	11.196042	×	—	=	$4,929.39
2	614.25	×	11.196042	×	.878710	=	6,043.53
3	752.27	×	11.196042	×	.772130	=	6,503.22
4	846.21	×	11.196042	×	.678478	=	6,428.04
5	617.60	×	11.196042	×	.596185	=	4,122.43
5	$58,639.00	×	—	×	.523874	=	30,719.45
							$58,746.06*

*Desired *PV* = $58,800: *IRR* approximately 13 percent.
†Rounded.

[11] Using a financial calculator yields a solution of 13.0 percent. Also see Concept Box 3.2 in Chapter 3 for solving for the IRR. We will rely on this result in our discussion.

EXHIBIT 5–9
Ranking ARMs
Based on Total Risk

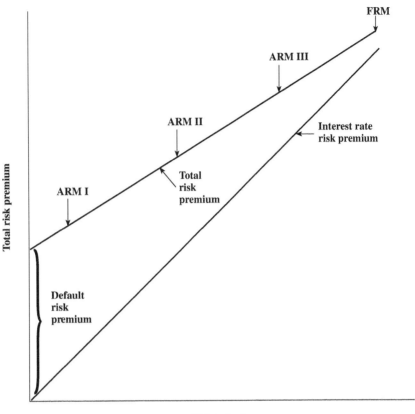

for a specific borrower declines due to interest rate changes. Following the market rule that benefits to the lender (from shifting interest rate risk to the borrower) *must exceed* expected default risk for the ARM to be originated, we see in Exhibit 5–9 that the total risk premium, and hence the expected yield to the lender, increases as we move from ARMs I to III. All expected ARM yields remain below that of the FRM, as they should.

We also know that, in general, the initial interest rate and expected yield for all ARMs should be lower than that of an FRM on the day of origination. The extent to which the initial rate and expected yield on an ARM will be lower than that on an FRM or another ARM depends on the terms relative to payments, caps, and so on. Terms that are more unrestricted and shift more interest rate risk to the borrower will generally have initial interest rates that are discounted furthest from FRMs. They will also be discounted from

Web App

Many lenders offer mortgage rate information online. Use a search engine like **www.yahoo.com** or **www.google.com** to find a lender offering an adjustable rate mortgage (ARM). Find out as many things as you can about how the mortgage works (e.g., What is the initial rate? What index is used for the adjustments? What is the margin over the index? How often does it adjust? What is the term of the loan? Are there any caps or floors on the loan? How does the rate on this ARM compare to the rate for a fixed rate mortgage? Which would you choose?)

ARMs containing caps on payment and interest rate increases. Hence, when a borrower is faced with selecting from a given set of ARMs with different terms and expectations of forward interest rates, an expected yield must be calculated before a comparison among adjustable rate mortgages and a fixed rate mortgage can be accomplished. While there is no guarantee that the *expected* yield calculated at origination will be the actual yield or cost of funds over the term of the ARM, the expected yield represents the *best estimate* of the cost of an ARM based on the information available at the time of origination.

Conclusion

In this chapter, we have shown how mortgage loan terms can be modified to incorporate variable interest rates. Loans with adjustable interest rates become necessary from time to time, depending on the rate of economic expansion and expected rates of inflation. In many situations, when the expected rate of inflation accelerates and becomes more uncertain, questions arise as to whether borrowers or lenders will bear the risk of future interest rate changes. During these times, fixed interest rate lending becomes very costly to borrowers because fixed interest rates and mortgage payments increase at a greater rate than borrower incomes. This imbalance between loan payments and borrower incomes motivates both borrowers and lenders to seek ways to modify loan agreements so that real estate purchases can be financed at loan payment levels that are commensurate with current borrower incomes. Adjustable rate mortgage (ARM) loans provide one solution to the imbalance problem. Through a variety of options, including the benchmark index chosen for ARM interest rates, the volatility of the index, frequency of payment adjustment, annual and over-the-loan-life interest rate caps, and negative amortization and other features, lenders and borrowers can negotiate loans and payment structures that result in interest rate risk-sharing agreements that are satisfactory to all parties.

Key Terms

actual start rate, *127*
adjustable rate mortgage (ARM), *120*
adjustment interval, *125*
assumability, *126*
caps, *126*
composite rate, *126*
The expected start rate, *127*

floating rate loans, *120*
floors, *126*
index, *126*
interest rate risk, *120*
margin, *126*
negative amortization, *126*
interest-only ARM, *128*
payment shock, *130*

price level adjusted mortgage (PLAM), *122*
reset date, *126*
spread, *126*
teaser rate, *127*
unanticipated inflation, *121*

Useful Web Sites

www.hud.gov—Department of Housing and Urban Development.
www.va.gov—Veterans Association Web site.
www.freddiemac.com—Federal Home Loan Mortgage Corporation.
www.mbaa.org—Mortgage Bankers Association of America.
www.aba.com—America Banker Association.
www.pueblo.gsa.gov/cic_text/housing/handbook/handbook.htm—Provided by U.S. Federal Reserve's Office of Thrift Supervision. Answers frequently asked questions about adjustable rate mortgages, describes how ARMs work, and provides a means of comparing two different loans.
www.fanniemae.com/homebuyers/index.html—Provided by Fannie Mae. Information, tools, and resources for consumers on getting a mortgage, buying, or refinancing a home.
www.freddiemac.com/pmms/pmmsarm.htm—This is a good site for finding monthly average commitment rate and points on a one-year adjustable rate mortgage.

Questions

1. In the previous chapter, significant problems about the ability of borrowers to meet mortgage payments and the evolution of fixed interest rate mortgages with various payment patterns were discussed. Why did not this evolution address problems faced by lenders? What have lenders done in recent years to overcome these problems?

2. How do inflationary expectations influence interest rates on mortgage loans?

3. How does the price level adjusted mortgage (PLAM) address the problem of uncertainty in inflationary expectations? What are some of the practical limitations in implementing a PLAM program?

4. Why do adjustable rate mortgages (ARMs) seem to be a more suitable alternative for mortgage lending than PLAMs?

5. List each of the main terms likely to be negotiated in an ARM. What does pricing an ARM using these terms mean?

6. What is the difference between interest rate risk and default risk? How do combinations of terms in ARMs affect the allocation of risk between borrowers and lenders?

7. Which of the following two ARMs is likely to be priced higher, that is, offered with a higher initial interest rate? ARM A has a margin of 3 percent and is tied to a three-year index with payments adjustable every two years; payments cannot increase by more than 10 percent from the preceding period; the term is 30 years and no assumption or points will be allowed. ARM B has a margin of 3 percent and is tied to a one-year index with payments to be adjusted each year; payments cannot increase by more than 10 percent from the preceding period; the term is 30 years and no assumption or points are allowed.

8. What are forward rates of interest? How are they determined? What do they have to do with indexes used to adjust ARM payments?

9. Distinguish between the initial rate of interest and expected yield on an ARM. What is the general relationship between the two? How do they generally reflect ARM terms?

10. If an ARM is priced with an initial interest rate of 8 percent and a margin of 2 percent (when the ARM index is also 8% at origination) and a fixed rate mortgage (FRM) with constant payment is available at 11 percent, what does this imply about inflation and the forward rates in the yield curve at the time of origination? What is implied if an FRM were available at 10 percent? 12 percent?

Problems

1. A price level adjusted mortgage (PLAM) is made with the following terms:

   Amount = $95,000

   Initial interest rate = 4 percent

   Term = 30 years

   Points = 6 percent

   Payments to be reset at the beginning of each year.

   Assuming inflation is expected to increase at the rate of 6 percent per year for the next five years:

   a. Compute the payments at the beginning of each year (*BOY*).

   b. What is the loan balance at the end of the fifth year?

   c. What is the yield to the lender on such a mortgage?

2. A basic ARM is made for $200,000 at an initial interest rate of 6 percent for 30 years with an annual reset date. The borrower believes that the interest rate at the beginning of year (*BOY*) 2 will increase to 7 percent.

   a. Assuming that a fully amortizing loan is made, what will the monthly payments be during year 1?

   b. Based on (*a*) what will the loan balance be at the end of year (*EOY*) 1?

   c. Given that the interest rate is expected to be 7 percent at the beginning of year 2, what will the monthly payments be during year 2?

    d. What will be the loan balance at the *EOY* 2?

    e. What would be the monthly payments in year 1 if they are to be interest only?

3. A 3/1 ARM is made for $150,000 at 7 percent with a 30-year maturity.

    a. Assuming that fixed payments are to be made monthly for three years and that the loan is fully amortizing, what will be the monthly payments? What will be the loan balance after three years?

    b. What would new payments be beginning in year 4 if the interest rate fell to 6 percent and the loan continued to be fully amortizing?

    c. In (*a*) what would monthly payments be during year 1 if they were interest only? What would payments be beginning in year 4 if interest rates fell to 6 percent and the loan became fully amortizing?

4. An ARM for $100,000 is made at a time when the expected start rate is 5 percent. The loan will be made with a teaser rate of 2 percent for the first year, after which the rate will be reset. The loan is fully amortizing, has a maturity of 25 years, and payments will be made monthly.

    a. What will be the payments during the first year?

    b. Assuming that the reset rate is 6 percent at the beginning of year (*BOY*) 2, what will the payments be?

    c. By what percentage will the monthly payments increase?

    d. What if the reset date is three years after loan origination and the reset rate is 6 percent, what will the loan payments be beginning in year 4 through year 25?

5. An interest-only ARM is made for $200,000 for 30 years. The start rate is 5 percent and the borrower will (1) make monthly interest-only payments for three years. Payments thereafter must be sufficient to fully amortize the loan at maturity.

    a. If the borrower makes interest-only payments for three years, what will the payments be?

    b. Assume that at the end of year 3, the reset rate is 6 percent. The borrower must now make payments so as to fully amortize the loan. What will the payments be?

6. A borrower has been analyzing different adjustable rate mortgage (ARM) alternatives for the purchase of a property. The borrower anticipates owning the property for five years. The lender first offers a $150,000, 30-year fully amortizing ARM with the following terms:

    Initial interest rate = 6 percent

    Index = 1-year Treasuries

    Payments reset each year

    Margin = 2 percent

    Interest rate cap = None

    Payment cap = None

    Negative amortization = Not allowed

    Discount points = 2 percent

Based on estimated forward rates, the index to which the ARM is tied is forecasted as follows: Beginning of year (*BOY*) 2 = 7 percent; (*BOY*) 3 = 8.5 percent; (*BOY*) 4 = 9.5 percent; (*BOY*) 5 = 11 percent.

    Compute the payments, loan balances, and yield for the unrestricted ARM for the five-year period.

7. An ARM is made for $150,000 for 30 years with the following terms:

    Initial interest rate = 7 percent

    Index = 1-year Treasuries

    Payments reset each year

    Margin = 2 percent

    Interest rate cap = None

    Payment cap = 5 percent increase in any year

    Discount points = 2 percent

    Fully amortizing; however, negative amortization allowed if payment cap reached

Based on estimated forward rates, the index to which the ARM is tied is forecasted as follows: Beginning of year (*BOY*) 2 = 7 percent; (*BOY*) 3 = 8.5 percent; (*BOY*) 4 = 9.5 percent; (*BOY*) 5 = 11 percent.

Compute the payments, loan balances, and yield for the ARM for the five-year period.

8. Assume that a lender offers a 30-year, $150,000 adjustable rate mortgage (ARM) with the following terms:

> Initial interest rate = 7.5 percent
>
> Index = one-year Treasuries
>
> Payments reset each year
>
> Margin = 2 percent
>
> Interest rate cap = 1 percent annually; 3 percent lifetime
>
> Discount points = 2 percent
>
> Fully amortizing; however, negative amortization allowed if interest rate caps reached

Based on estimated forward rates, the index to which the ARM is tied is forecasted as follows: Beginning of year (*BOY*) 2 = 7 percent; (*BOY*) 3 = 8.5 percent; (*BOY*) 4 = 9.5 percent; (*EOY*) 5 = 11 percent.

Compute the payments, loan balances, and yield for the ARM for the five-year period.

9. MakeNu Mortgage Company is offering a new mortgage instrument called the Stable Mortgage. This mortgage is composed of both a fixed rate and an adjustable rate component. Mrs. Maria Perez is interested in financing a property, which costs $100,000, and is to be financed by Stable Home Mortgages (SHM) on the following terms:

   a. The SHM requires a 5 percent down payment, costs the borrower 2 discount points, and allows 75 percent of the mortgage to be fixed and 25 percent to be adjustable. The fixed portion of the loan is for 30 years at an annual interest rate of 10.5 percent. Having neither an interest rate nor payment cap, the adjustable portion is also for 30 years with the following terms:

   > Initial interest rate = 9 percent
   >
   > Index = one-year Treasuries
   >
   > Payments reset each year
   >
   > Margin = 2 percent
   >
   > Interest rate cap = None
   >
   > Payment cap = None

   The projected one-year U.S. Treasury-bill index, to which the ARM is tied, is as follows: (*BOY*) 2 = 10 percent; (*BOY*) 3 = 11 percent; (*BOY*) 4 = 8 percent; (*BOY*) 5 = 12 percent.

   Calculate Mrs. Perez's total monthly payments and end-of-year loan balances for the first five years. Calculate the lender's yield, assuming Mrs. Perez repays the loan after five years.

   b. Repeat part (*a*) under the assumption that the initial interest rate is 9.5 percent and there is an annual interest rate cap of 1 percent.

10. A floating rate mortgage loan is made for $100,000 for a 30-year period at an initial rate of 12 percent interest. However, the borrower and lender have negotiated a monthly payment of $800.

    a. What will be the loan balance at the end of year 1?

    b. What if the interest rate increases to 13 percent at the end of year 1? How much interest will be accrued as negative amortization in year 1 if the payment remains at $800? Year 5?

11. **Excel.** Refer to the "Ch5 ARM No Caps" tab in the Excel Workbook provided on the Web site. Suppose that the index goes to 18 percent in year 5. What is the effective cost of the unrestricted ARM?

12. **Excel.** Refer to the "Ch5 ARM Int Cap" tab in the Excel Workbook provided on the Web site. Suppose that the index goes to 18 percent in year 5. What is the effective cost of this ARM? What cap affected the rate in year 5?

13. **Excel.** Refer to the "Ch5 ARM Pmt Cap" tab in the Excel Workbook provided on the Web site. Suppose that the index goes to 18 percent in year 5. What is the effective cost of the ARM? Does the payment cap keep the effective cost from rising?

www.mhhe.com/bf15e

Mortgages: Additional Concepts, Analysis, and Applications

In previous chapters, we have considered the analytics of various types of mortgages used in real estate finance. This chapter extends those concepts to various questions related to the analysis of mortgage financing. Questions raised include how to compare two loans with different loan terms (e.g., amount of loan, interest rate), how to decide whether to refinance or prepay a loan, and whether a loan assumption is desirable. We will also evaluate the effect of below-market financing on the sale price of a property. This is important because one must often pay a higher price for a property that appears to have favorable financing.

Incremental Borrowing Cost

We begin by considering how to evaluate two loan alternatives, where one alternative involves borrowing additional funds relative to the other. For example, assume a borrower is purchasing a property for $100,000 and faces two possible loan alternatives. A lender is willing to make an 80 percent first mortgage loan, or $80,000, for 25 years at 12 percent interest. The same lender is also willing to lend 90 percent, or $90,000, for 25 years at 13 percent. Both loans will have fixed interest rates and constant payment mortgages. How should the borrower compare these alternatives?

To analyze this problem, emphasis should be placed on a basic concept called the **marginal,** or **incremental, cost of borrowing.** Based on the material presented in earlier chapters, we know how to compute the effective cost of borrowing for one specific loan. However, it is equally important in real estate finance to be able to compare financing alternatives, whereby the borrower can finance the purchase of real estate in more than one way or under different lending terms.

In the problem at hand, we are considering differences in the amount of the loan and the interest rate. A loan can be made for $80,000 for 25 years at 12 percent, or $90,000 can be borrowed for 25 years at 13 percent interest. Because there are no origination fees, we know from Chapter 4 that the effective interest cost for the two loans will be 12 percent and 13 percent, respectively. However, an important cost that the borrower should compute is the cost to acquire the incremental or additional $10,000, should he choose to take the $90,000 loan over the $80,000 loan. At first glance, you may think that because the interest rate on the $90,000 loan is 13 percent, the cost of acquiring the additional $10,000 is also

13 percent. This is *not* so. Careful analysis of the two loans reveals that if the borrower wants to borrow the additional $10,000 available with the $90,000 loan at 13 percent, he also must pay an *additional* 1 percent interest on the first $80,000 borrowed. This increases the cost of obtaining the additional $10,000 considerably. The $90,000 loan has a larger payment due not only to the additional $10,000 being borrowed but also to the higher interest rate being charged on the entire amount. To determine the cost of the additional $10,000, we must consider how much the additional payment will be on the $90,000 loan compared with the $80,000 loan.[1] This difference should then be compared with the additional $10,000 borrowed. This can be done as follows:[2]

	Loan Amount		Loan Constant		Monthly Payments
Alt. II at 13%	$90,000	×	.0112784	=	$1,015.05
Alt. I at 12%	80,000	×	.0105322	=	842.58
Difference	$10,000		Difference		$ 172.47

We want to find the annual rate of interest, compounded monthly, that makes the present value of the difference in mortgage payments, or $172.47, equal to $10,000, or the incremental amount of loan proceeds received. Solving for *i,* we find:

Solution:

$n = 25 \times 12 = 300$

$PV = -\$10,000$

$PMT = \$172.47$

$FV = 0$

Solve for *i* $= 20.57\%$ (annual)

Function:

$i\,(n, PV, FV, PMT)$

A financial calculator indicates that the answer is 20.57 percent. Hence, if our borrower desires to borrow the additional $10,000 with the $90,000 loan, the cost of doing so will be more than 20 percent, a rate considerably higher than 13 percent. This cost is referred to as the marginal, or incremental, cost of borrowing. The 13 percent rate on the $90,000 loan can be thought of as a weighted average of the 12 percent rate on the $80,000 loan and the 20.57 percent rate on the additional $10,000. That is,

$$\left[\frac{80,000}{90,000} \times 12\%\right] + \left[\frac{10,000}{90,000} \times 20.57\%\right] = 12.95\% \text{ or } 13\% \text{ (rounded)}$$

The borrower must consider this cost when evaluating whether the additional $10,000 should be borrowed. If the borrower has sufficient funds so that the $10,000 would not have to be borrowed, it tells the borrower what rate of interest must be earned on funds *not* invested in a property because of the larger amount borrowed. In other words, by obtaining a larger loan ($90,000 vs $80,000), the borrower's down payment will be

---

[1] Although we use an $80,000 and a $90,000 loan in our example, the calculation can be generalized to other loans that are the same percentage of the property value.

[2] For single family residential properties, when loan amounts exceed 80 percent of the property value, private mortgage insurance is usually required by lenders. The cost of this insurance will affect the incremental borrowing costs and must be considered in the calculations. More will be said about private mortgage insurance in Chapter 8.

$10,000 less than it would have been on the $80,000 loan. Hence, unless the borrower can earn 20.57 percent interest or more on a $10,000 investment of equal risk on funds not invested in the property, he or she would be better off with the smaller loan of $80,000.

If the borrower does not have enough funds for a down payment to combine with the $80,000 loan and must borrow $90,000, the incremental borrowing cost is the cost of obtaining the extra $10,000. There may be alternative ways of obtaining the extra $10,000. For example, if the borrower could obtain a second mortgage for $10,000 at a rate *less* than 20.57 percent, this may be a better alternative than a $90,000 loan.[3] Therefore, the marginal cost concept is also an *opportunity cost* concept in that it tells the borrower the minimum rate of interest that must be earned, or the maximum amount that should be paid, on any additional amounts borrowed.

It should be noted that the 20.57 percent figure we calculated also represents the *return* that the lender earns on the additional $10,000 loaned to the borrower; that is, the *cost* of a loan to the borrower will reflect the *return* on the loan to the lender. Of course, keep in mind that the figures we are calculating do not take federal income tax considerations into account, which are also important in determining returns and costs (see the appendix to this chapter). For example, if the borrower is in a higher tax bracket than the lender, the after-tax cost to the borrower will be less than the after-tax return to the lender.

Early Repayment

We should also note that in this example, the incremental cost of borrowing will depend on when the loan is repaid. For example, if the loan is repaid after five years instead of being held for the entire loan term, the incremental borrowing cost increases from 20.57 percent to 20.83 percent. To see this, we modify the above analysis to consider that if the loan is repaid after five years, the amount that would be repaid on the $80,000 loan will differ from the amount that would be repaid on the $90,000 loan. Thus, in addition to considering the difference in payments between the two loans, we must also consider the difference in the loan balances at the time the loan is repaid. We can find the incremental borrowing cost as follows:

	Loan Amount		Loan Constant		Monthly Payments	Loan Balance after Five Years
Alt. II at 13%	$90,000	×	.0112784	=	$1,015.05	$86,639.88
Alt. I at 12%	80,000	×	.0105322	=	842.58	76,522.56
Difference	$10,000		Difference		$ 172.47	$10,117.32

To find the answer, we must find the interest rate that makes the present value of the monthly annuity of $172.47 and the differences in loan balances equal to $10,000. We can verify that the incremental borrowing cost is now 20.83 percent, the result of early repayment. As we will see in the next section, the impact of early payment may be greater when points are also involved on one or both of the loans.

[3] A lower effective cost for a second mortgage means that the borrower pays less interest each month. However, if the second mortgage has a term less than 25 years, the total monthly payments will be higher with the $80,000 first mortgage and a $10,000 second mortgage than with a $90,000 first mortgage. Thus, some borrowers may prefer to choose a higher effective borrowing cost to have lower monthly payments.

Solution:	Function:
$n = 5 \times 12 = 60$	$i\,(n, PV, PMT, FV)$
$PV = -\$10,000$	
$PMT = \$172.47$	
$FV = 10,117.32$	
Solve for i = 1.7360 (monthly)	
Solve for i = 1.7360 $\times$ 12 = 20.83% (annual)	

Origination Fees

It should be apparent that the concept of incremental borrowing cost is extremely import-ant when deciding how much should be borrowed to finance a given transaction. In the preceding section, the two alternatives considered were fairly straightforward; the only differences between them were the interest rate and the amount borrowed. In most cases, financing alternatives under consideration will have *different* interest rates as the amount borrowed increases and, possibly, *different* loan maturities. Also, loan **origination fees** will usually be charged on the loan alternatives. This section considers differences in loan fees on two loan alternatives. We will consider differences in loan maturities later.

The first case is the incremental cost of borrowing when loan origination fees are charged on two 25-year loan alternatives. For example, if a $1,600 origination fee (2 points) is charged on the $80,000 loan and a $2,700 fee (3 points) is charged on the $90,000 loan, how does this affect the incremental cost of borrowing? These differences can be easily included in the cost computation as follows.

Differences in amounts borrowed and payments:

	Loan	−	Fees	=	Net Amount Disbursed	Loan		Loan Constant		Monthly Payments
Alt. II at 13%	$90,000	−	$2,700	=	$87,300	$90,000	×	.0112784	=	$1,015.05
Alt. I at 12%	80,000	−	1,600	=	78,400	80,000	×	.0105322	=	842.58
			Difference	=	$ 8,900			Difference	=	$ 172.47

We want to find an annual rate of interest, compounded monthly, that makes the present value of the difference in mortgage payments, or $172.47, equal to $8,900, or the incremental amount of loan proceeds received. Using a financial calculator, we find that the exact answer is 23.18 percent. Hence, the marginal cost increases to about 23.2 percent when the effects of an additional $1,100 in origination fees charged on the $90,000 loan are included in the analysis. Thus, the borrower only benefits from an additional $8,900 instead of $10,000.

Solution:	Function:
$n = 25 \times 12 = 300$	$i\,(n, PV, FV, PMT)$
$PV = -\$8,900$	
$PMT = \$172.47$	
$FV = 0$	
Solve for i = 1.9316 $\times$ 12 = 23.18% (annually)	

As before, the marginal or incremental cost of borrowing increases if the loan is repaid before maturity. For example, if the loan in the above problem were repaid after five years, the incremental cost would increase to about 24.67 percent.

Incremental Borrowing Cost versus a Second Mortgage

The incremental borrowing cost obviously depends on how much the interest rate increases with the loan-to-value ratio. In the examples considered previously, the interest rate increased from 12 percent to 13 percent (a differential of 1%) when the loan-to-value ratio increased from 80 percent to 90 percent. When no points were charged and the loan was held until maturity, the incremental borrowing cost was 20.57 percent. The incremental borrowing cost would increase if the differential between the rate on the 80 percent loan and the 90 percent loan were greater than 1 percent. Conversely, the incremental borrowing cost would decrease if the differential were less than 1 percent.

Because borrowers have a choice between obtaining a 90 percent loan or an 80 percent loan plus a second mortgage for the remaining 10 percent, we would expect the incremental borrowing cost to be competitive with the rate on a second mortgage with the same maturity. In the example, if a second mortgage with a maturity of 25 years can be obtained with an effective borrowing cost that is much less than 20.57 percent, then the 90 percent loan is not competitive; it implies that the 1 percent yield differential between the 90 percent loan and the 80 percent loan is too great. Lenders would have to adjust the differential (or the second mortgage rate) so that the incremental borrowing cost is about the same as the effective cost of a second mortgage.

In Exhibit 6–1, we calculate the incremental borrowing cost for the alternatives discussed earlier, which assume that the loan is prepaid after five years. The exhibit shows how the incremental borrowing cost is affected by the interest rate differential on the 90 percent loan and the 80 percent loan. A 0 percent interest rate differential means that the contract interest rate, which is 12 percent, is the same for both loans. A 1 percent differential means the contract rate is 1 percent higher (e.g., 13% for the 90% loan).

When the interest rate differential is zero, the incremental cost is the same as the effective cost of the loan. For example, with no points the incremental cost is exactly 12 percent, the same as the interest rate for the 80 percent loan. As the interest rate differential increases, the incremental borrowing cost increases. The incremental cost increases by about the same rate for each loan.

Suppose that a second mortgage for 10 percent of the purchase price (on top of an 80% first mortgage) can be obtained with an effective cost of 20 percent with a 25-year maturity. This is added to Exhibit 6–1.[4] This implies that, to be competitive, the 90 percent loan should be priced so that its incremental cost over an 80 percent loan is 20 percent. Suppose that lenders expect the loan to be prepaid on average after five years and that they want to charge 2 points on an 80 percent loan and 3 points on a 90 percent loan as we have assumed in the previous examples. This implies that the interest rate differential should be about .50 percent or 50 basis points (see Exhibit 6–1). Alternatively, if lenders do not want to charge any points on either loan, the interest rate differential would have to be about 90 basis points.

Relationship between the Incremental Cost and the Loan-to-Value Ratio

In the previous section, we illustrated the calculation of the incremental borrowing cost for a 90 percent loan ($90,000) with a 13 percent interest rate versus an 80 percent loan

---

[4] To compare this rate with the incremental borrowing cost, this must be the effective cost of the loan, considering any points and the effect of prepayment.

EXHIBIT 6–1
Incremental Borrowing Cost versus Interest Rate Differential

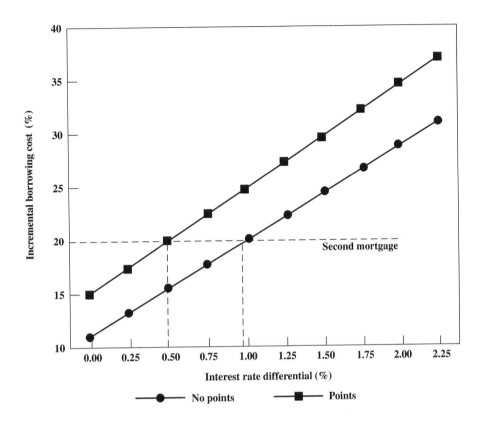

($80,000) with a 12 percent interest rate. Where there were no points and the loan was held until maturity, the incremental cost was 20.57 percent. The incremental borrowing cost is the amount that lenders require on the amount added to the loan that increases the loan-to-value ratio from 80 percent to 90 percent. As discussed previously, this incremental return should be competitive with the return required for a second mortgage for 10 percent of value. The incremental borrowing cost represents the return that lenders require at the margin for lending additional funds, that is, increasing the loan-to-value ratio, whether this is done with a larger first mortgage or a second mortgage.

In the previous examples, we used the difference in interest rates for the entire loan amount (e.g., the rate on an 80% loan vs. the rate on a 90% loan) to calculate the implied cost of the incremental 10 percent loan. In theory, however, it is the incremental cost of the extra amount loaned that must reflect the equilibrium required rate of return for the level of default risk associated with the additional amount loaned. As the loan-to-value ratio increases, the level of default risk also increases. Thus, we would expect the incremental borrowing cost to rise with the loan-to-value ratio. This, in turn, pulls up the average cost of the entire loan. Exhibit 6–2 shows the relationship between the rate for the incremental amount borrowed (incremental borrowing cost) and the average rate for the entire loan (effective rate for a loan with a particular loan-to-value ratio). To compare the results with the previous examples, the calculations in the exhibit are based on a loan term of 25 years, the assumption that the loan is held until maturity, and no points. Loans are assumed to be made in increments of 10 percent of value. The average and incremental rates are the same for a loan-to-value ratio of 10 percent because this is the first incremental loan amount. The incremental rate then increases as the loan-to-value ratio increases. The incremental rate rises faster than the average rate for the entire loan because the average rate for the entire loan is a weighted

EXHIBIT 6–2
Effect of Loan-to-Value
Ratio on Loan Cost

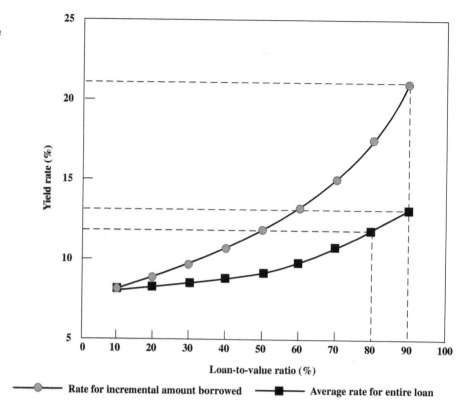

— Rate for incremental amount borrowed   — Average rate for entire loan

average of the incremental cost of each of the previous incremental costs. This is the familiar relationship between marginal and average costs; that is, the marginal cost pulls up the average cost as long as the marginal cost is greater than the average cost.

The exhibit indicates, for example, that the average cost for an 80 percent loan is 12 percent. The marginal cost of a 90 percent loan is about 21 percent. This implies that the average cost of a 90 percent loan can be approximated as a weighted average as follows:

$$\text{Average cost of 90\% loan} = (80/90 \times 12\%) + (10/90 \times 21\%)$$

$$\text{Average cost of 90\% loan} = 13\%$$

Note that these are the same numbers (rounded) as calculated in the previous section for the same loan when the loan had no points and was held until maturity.[5]

Because the incremental borrowing cost must be competitive with the rate for a second mortgage, the rate for the incremental amount borrowed shown in Exhibit 6–2 should also approximate the market rate for a second mortgage. Because it is inefficient for lenders to make loans with low loan-to-value ratios,[6] however, we may not actually observe quotes for loans at the lower end of the loan-to-value range; that is, a borrower may have to pay the same rate for any loan that is less than 60 percent of value. This means that the incremental cost and average cost might not actually begin to rise until the loan-to-value ratio exceeds 60 percent.

[5] This formula is an approximation because the relative weight of each loan actually changes slightly over time as the loans are amortized. Because each loan is amortized over 25 years, the loan-to-value ratio of the 80 percent loan must drop much faster than that of the 10 percent loan because both loan-to-value ratios must be zero at loan maturity.

[6] The transactions cost would be the same as loans with a higher loan-to-value ratio.

Web App

Private mortgage insurance is a way of getting a loan that is greater than an 80 percent loan-to-value ratio. Companies like Mortgage Guarantee Insurance Corporation (**www.mgic.com**) offer such loans. Paying for the insurance to get the additional loan (more than 80%) is analogous to paying a higher interest rate to get a higher loan-to-value ratio as discussed in the chapter. Go to the MGIC Web site and find out more about how private mortgage insurance works and the typical cost. How would you determine the incremental cost of a loan with private mortgage insurance versus one that did not require insurance?

Differences in Maturities

In the previous examples, the loan alternatives considered had the same maturities (25 years). How does one determine the incremental cost of alternatives that have different maturities as well as different interest rates? Do differences in maturities materially change results? We examine these questions by changing our previous example and assuming that the $90,000 alternative has a 30-year maturity and a higher interest rate. How would the analysis be changed? We first must compute the following information:

	Loan	Payments Years 1–25	Payments Years 26–30
Alt. III at 13%, 30 years	$90,000	$995.58	$995.58
Alt. I at 12%, 25 years	80,000	842.58	–0–
Difference	$10,000	$153.00	$995.58

In this case, we compute the monthly payment for a $90,000, 30-year loan at 13 percent interest, which is $995.58. However, there are two differences in the series of monthly payments relevant to our example. For the first 25 years, the borrower will pay an additional $153.00 per month for alternative III. For the final five-year period, years 26 through 30, the difference between payments will be the full $995.58 payment on alternative III because the $80,000 loan would be repaid after 25 years. In the above formulation, the second annuity of $995.58 runs for five years, but it is not received until the end of year 25 and therefore must also be discounted for 25 years. We cannot solve directly for the solution because there are two unknowns. Thus, we must use the procedures outlined in Concept Box 3.2 in Chapter 3 to calculate the yield (cost).

Solution:
Requires cash flow analysis:

$CF_0 = -\$10,000$
$CF_j = \$153.00$
$n_j = 300$ (years 1–25)
$CF_j = \$995.58$
$n_j = 60$ (years 26–30)

Function:
$IRR (CF_1, CF_2, \ldots CF_n)$

Solve for *IRR:* (monthly) = 1.5719% (annualized) = 18.86%

Because the desired present value is $10,000, the answer must be slightly less than 19 percent. Using a calculator[7] that can solve for an *IRR* with uneven, or grouped, cash flows, we find the solution is 18.86 percent. Hence, the marginal or incremental cost of borrowing the additional $10,000 given that (1) the interest rate increases from 12 percent to 13 percent and (2) the loan term increases from 25 years to 30 years will be about 18.86 percent. Compare this with the incremental cost of 20.57 percent in the first example, where no fees were charged but both maturities were 25 years. The reason the marginal cost is lower in this case is that although a higher rate must be paid on the $90,000 loan, it will be repaid over a longer maturity period, 30 years. Even though the borrower pays a higher rate for the $90,000 loan, there is a benefit to having a longer amortization period (and thus lower monthly payments) on the $90,000 loan.

Note that if the borrower expects to repay the loan before maturity, both the differences in monthly payments and loan balances in the year of repayment must be taken into account when computing the marginal borrowing cost. Also, should any origination fees be charged, the incremental funds disbursed by the lender should be reduced accordingly.

Loan Refinancing

On occasion, an opportunity may arise for an individual to refinance a mortgage loan at a reduced rate of interest. The fundamental relationships to know in any **loan refinancing** decision include at least three ingredients: (1) terms on the present outstanding loan, (2) new loan terms being considered, and (3) any fees associated with paying off the existing loan or acquiring the new loan (e.g., prepayment penalties on the existing loan or origination and closing fees on the new loan). To illustrate, assume a borrower made a mortgage loan five years ago for $80,000 at 15 percent interest for 30 years (monthly payment). After five years, interest rates fall, and a new mortgage loan is available at 14 percent for 25 years. The loan balance on the existing loan is $78,976.50. Suppose that the prepayment penalty of 2 percent must be paid on the existing loan, and the lender who is making the new loan available also requires an origination fee of $2,500 plus $25 for incidental closing costs if the new loan is made. Should the borrower refinance?

In answering this question, we must analyze the costs associated with refinancing and the benefits or savings that accrue because of the reduction in interest charges, should the borrower choose to refinance. The costs associated with refinancing are as follows:

Cost to refinance:	
Prepayment penalty: (2% × $78,976.50)	$1,580
Origination fees and discount points, new loan	2,500
Recording, etc., new loan	25
	$4,105

Benefits from refinancing are obviously the interest savings that result from a lower interest rate. Hence, if refinancing occurs, the monthly mortgage payment under the new loan terms will be lower than payments under the existing mortgage. Monthly benefits would be $60.87 as shown:

[7] Unlike the problems involving constant payments, this calculation requires a calculator that can accommodate inputs of various cash flows over time.

Monthly savings due to refinancing:	
Monthly payments, existing loan, $80,000, 15%, 30 years	$1,011.56
Less: Monthly payments, new loan, $78,976.50, 14%, 25 years	−950.69
Difference in monthly payments	$ 60.87

It is useful to know that total cash savings for the 25-year (300-month) period would be $60.87 × 300 or $18,261, which is greater than the $4,105 in refinancing costs. However, the $18,261 in savings will not be received immediately, so we must ask whether it is worth "investing," or paying out, $4,105 (charges for refinancing) to save $60.87 per month *over the term of the loan.* Perhaps, the $4,105 could be invested in a more profitable alternative? What rate of interest, compounded monthly, would an alternative investment have to earn in order to be equivalent to spending $4,105 to refinance? To analyze this question, we should determine what rate of return is earned on the investment of $4,105 for 25 years, given that $60.87 per month represents a savings. Using a financial calculator, we find that the yield on our $4,105 investment, with savings of $60.87 per month over 25 years, is equivalent to earning an annual rate of 17.57 percent compounded monthly. If another alternative equal in risk, which provides a 17.57 percent annual return, cannot be found, the refinancing should be undertaken. This return appears to be attractive because it is higher than the market rate of 14 percent that must be paid on the new loan. Thus, refinancing is probably desirable.

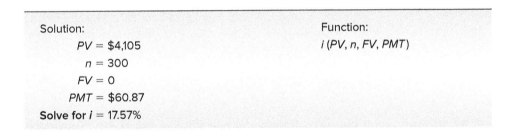

Solution:	Function:
$PV = \$4,105$	$i\,(PV, n, FV, PMT)$
$n = 300$	
$FV = 0$	
$PMT = \$60.87$	
Solve for $i = 17.57\%$	

Early Repayment: Loan Refinancing

If the property is not held for the full 25 years, the monthly savings of $60.87 do not occur for the entire 25-year term, and therefore the refinancing is not as attractive. If we assume that the borrower plans to hold the property for only 10 more years after refinancing, is refinancing still worthwhile? To analyze this alternative, note that the $4,105 cost will not change, should the refinancing be undertaken; however, the benefits (savings) will change. The $60.87 monthly benefits will be realized for only 10 years. In addition, since the borrower expects to repay the refinanced loan after 10 years, there will be a difference between loan balances on the existing loan and the new loan due to different amortization rates. We assume that there will be no prepayment penalty on either loan if they are prepaid 10 years from now.

Loan balance, 15th year—existing loan*	$72,275
Loan balance, 10th year—new loan†	71,386
Difference	$ 889

*Based on $80,000, 15 percent, 30 years prepaid after 15 years.
†Based on $78,976, 14 percent, 25 years, prepaid after 10 years.

The new calculation comparing loan balances under the existing loan and the new loan terms, should the new loan be made, shows that if refinancing occurs the amount saved with the lower loan balance will be $889. Hence, total savings with refinancing will be $60.87 per month for 10 years, plus $889 at the end of 10 years. Do these savings justify an outlay of $4,105 in refinancing costs? To answer this question, we compute the return on the $4,105 outlay as follows:

Solution:	Function:
$n = 10 \times 12 = 120$	$i\,(n, PV, FV, PMT)$
$PV = -\$4{,}105$	
$PMT = \$60.87$	
$FV = \$889$	
Solve for $i = 14.21\%$	

Because the loan is repaid early and the monthly savings of $60.87 will not be received over the full 25-year period, the yield is below the 17.57 percent yield computed in the previous example. The yield earned due to refinancing will be 14.21 percent per year for the 10-year period.

Obviously, this return is lower than the 17.57 percent computed under the assumption that the loan will be repaid after 25 years. This is true because the refinancing cost of $4,105 remained the same, while the savings stream of $60.87 was shortened from 25 years to 10 years. Although an additional $889 was saved because of differences in loan balances, it did not offset the reduction in monthly savings that would have occurred from year 10 through year 25. The relationship between the *IRR* and the number of years the loan is held after refinancing is illustrated in Exhibit 6–3. Note that the returns from

EXHIBIT 6–3
IRR **from Savings When Refinancing**

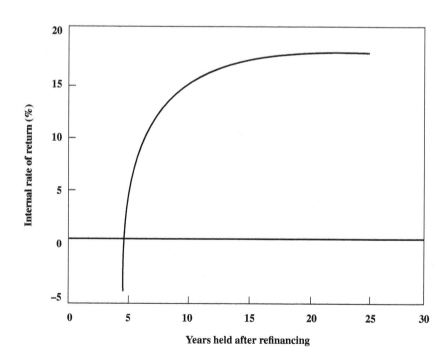

refinancing are negative if the loan is held for only five years after prepayment. The return rises sharply for each additional year the loan is held after prepayment until it is held for about 15 additional years. In analyzing refinancing decisions, then, we must compare not only costs and benefits (savings), but also the time period one expects to hold a property.[8]

Effective Cost of Refinancing

The refinancing problem can also be analyzed by using an extension of the effective cost concept discussed earlier. We know that points increase the effective cost of a loan. In our problem, the borrower would be making a new loan for $78,976.50 but must pay $4,105 in "fees" to do so. Although these fees include the prepayment penalty on the old loan, this can be thought of as a cost of making a new loan by refinancing, or the **effective cost of refinancing.** Thus, the borrower in effect receives $78,976.50 less $4,105, or $74,871.50. Payments on the new loan when made at 14 percent for 25 years would be $950.69. To find the effective cost where the loan is held to maturity, or 25 years, we proceed as follows:

Solution:	Function:
$n = 25 \times 12 = 300$	$i\,(n, PV, PMT, FV)$
$PV = -\$74{,}871.50$	
$PMT = \$950.69$	
$FV = 0$	
Solve for i = 14.86%	

Using a financial calculator, we obtain an interest rate of 14.86 percent. This can be interpreted as the effective cost of obtaining the new loan by refinancing. Since this cost is *less* than the rate on the old loan (15%), refinancing would seem to be desirable.[9] Thus, we arrive at the same conclusion we got when calculating the return on investing in refinancing.

Borrowing the Refinancing Costs

In the above analysis, we assumed that the borrower had to pay (as a cash outlay) the refinancing costs of $4,105. However, it is likely that if the borrower is going to the trouble of refinancing, he or she may also be able to borrow the refinancing costs.[10] How does this affect our analysis?

The borrower now gets a loan for the loan balance of $78,976.50 plus the fees of $4,105.00 for a total of $83,081.50. Payments at the 14 percent rate (assuming the interest rate is still the same) would be $1,000.10.[11] What do we compare this to now that the

---

[8] Obviously, the shorter the time period that the borrower expects to hold the property after refinancing, the lower the return on "investing" in refinancing. In fact if the period of time is relatively short, the return could be negative. Hence, if a borrower expects to sell a property within a short time after refinancing, it will be difficult to justify refinancing.

[9] Any points that had been paid on the old loan would not be relevant since they are a "sunk cost"; that is, they have already been paid and are not affected by refinancing. Thus, only the current interest rate on the old loan should be compared with the effective cost of the new loan.

[10] The borrower will probably have sufficient equity in the property to do so since, if the old loan was held for several years, the borrower has reduced the balance on the old loan and the property may have increased in value.

[11] If this approach were used to analyze the case where the loan was to be repaid early, the additional loan balance on the refinanced loan would have to be considered. This would reduce the benefit of the lower payments.

borrower has no cash outlay when refinancing? The answer is simple. These payments are still less than those on the old loan ($1,011.56). Given that the borrower has lower payments ($11.46) for 300 months without any cash outlay, it is desirable to refinance.[12]

We could, of course, also compute the effective cost of refinancing as we did in the previous section. In this case, the total amount of the loan is $83,081.50; however, the borrower, in effect, only benefits from $78,976.50 (the loan amount less the refinancing costs). Using the payment of $1,000.10 and assuming the new loan is held for the full loan term, we can calculate the effective cost as follows:

Solution:	Function:
$n = 25 \times 12 = 300$	$i\,(n, PV, PMT, FV)$
$PV = -\$78{,}976.50$	
$PMT = \$1{,}000.10$	
$FV = 0$	
Solve for $i = 14.81\%$	

Solving for the effective interest rate, we obtain an answer of 14.81 percent, which is virtually the same as we obtained in the previous section. The only reason the answer is slightly lower is that the origination fee on the new loan was assumed to remain at $2,500 even though the amount of the loan was increased to cover the refinancing costs.

Note that whether we calculate a return on investing in refinancing or the effective cost of refinancing, we arrive at the same conclusion. Often there are many ways of considering a problem that lead to similar conclusions. It is informative to look at a problem in several ways to gain skill in handling the wide variety of financial alternatives one may encounter. Knowing alternative ways of analyzing a problem also reduces the chance of applying an incorrect technique to solve it.

Other Considerations

Biweekly Payment Patterns—Interest Savings and Early Payoff

Generally speaking, when repaying mortgage loans, most borrowers prefer to make monthly payments. However, some borrowers consider **biweekly payments** which may (1) lower the amount of interest over the life of the loan and (2) repay the loan sooner. For example, if a borrower makes a fully amortizing $80,000 loan at 6 percent for 30 years and is considering a monthly versus a biweekly payment pattern, a comparison of payments would be as follows:

Solution:	
Monthly Payments (360)	**Biweekly Payments (26 *per year*)**
$PV = -\$80{,}000$	$\$479.60 \div 2$
$i = 6\%$	
$n = 360$	$PMT = \$239.80$
$FV = 0$	
Solve for $PMT = \$479.60$	

[12] If the interest rate was higher, then we would also want to consider the incremental cost of the additional $4,105, as considered earlier in the chapter.

The following shows:
(1) The number of payments needed to repay the biweekly loan, (2) the approximate number of years to maturity, and (3) approximate total interest savings over the life of the loan.

Solution:

Biweekly Mortgage Loan Payoff Period:	Total Interest Savings:	
$PV = -\$80{,}000$	Total monthly payments	$172,656
$PMT = \$239.80$	Total biweekly payments	$-152{,}752$
$i = 6\%/26^*$	Total interest savings	$ 19,904
$FV = 0$		
Solve for $n = 637$ payments (rounded)		
(approx. 24.5 years)		

*Annual rate of 6% compounded biweekly.

These calculations show that by choosing the biweekly payment pattern, the maturity period would be shortened from 30 years to about 24.5 years and *total interest saved* would be about $19,904. While it is clear that the borrower would definitely save by making biweekly payments, this does not always mean this would be the best choice. One way to think about this choice is to consider whether an alternative investment is available that is of equal risk and that will provide the borrower a return in excess of a 6 percent rate of interest, *compounded biweekly* ($i \div 26$). However, if such an alternative investment is unavailable, the borrower/investor would be better off "saving interest" by reducing interest costs and making the biweekly payments of $239.80. It should also be stressed that this analysis assumes that the borrower has sufficient cash flow to make *either* choice, that is, the biweekly or monthly loan payments. Unless enough cash flow is available to the borrower every two weeks, the biweekly payment pattern may not be a viable option to begin with.

Early Loan Payoffs

Another question that many borrowers ask is whether loans should be paid off early, or prior to maturity. For example, we assume that a borrower makes a fully amortizing loan for $80,000 at 6 percent interest for 30 years. He makes monthly payments for five years and suddenly receives a large amount of cash (e.g., inheritance) such that he may be able to repay the entire loan balance early. The question is should he do so? This question may be considered as follows:

Solution:

Loan Balance *EOY* 5:

$PMT = \$479.64$

$i = 6\%$

$n = 360$ months

$FV = 0$

Solve for $PV = \$74{,}443$

Function:

$PV\,(PMT, i, n, FV)$

Assuming that $74,443 becomes available to the borrower with which to repay this loan early, the question is should it be repaid? One issue to consider is the interest savings. This would be:

1.	Total payments equal $479.64 × 300 =	$143,892
2.	Less loan balance *EOY* 5	−74,443
3.	Interest saved by early repayment	$ 69,449

However, related questions would be whether or not the $74,443 available to repay the loan at the end of year 5 may be reinvested elsewhere and, if so, at what rate of interest. By paying off a loan early that has a 6 percent interest rate, the borrower is in effect "earning" a 6 percent return on the funds used to repay the loan.

1. *Reinvesting at a rate greater than 6 percent.* If this is possible, the borrower would be better off *not* paying off the loan. If the $74,443 available for early payment could be invested elsewhere, say at 7%, the borrower should not pay off the loan early. This way, a spread of 7 percent minus 6 percent, or 1 percent, could be earned on the $74,443.

2. *Reinvesting at a rate below 6 percent.* If this is the case, the borrower would obviously be better off repaying the loan at the end of year 5. For example, if interest rates have fallen to 5 percent, the borrower may repay the loan thereby saving 6 percent. Alternatively, he may choose to refinance the loan at 5 percent. This would provide *savings* based on a spread of 6 percent minus 5 percent, or 1 percent. However, even this choice would be preferable only if alternative investments are available to invest the $74,443 at rates in excess of 5 percent.

Early Loan Repayment: Lender Inducements

After a period of *rising interest rates,* borrowers may have a loan that has an interest rate below the market rate. Earlier, we considered the situation where interest rates have fallen. In such cases, the borrower may find it beneficial to refinance at a lower interest rate even if additional fees and penalties have to be paid to the lender. Where interest rates have risen considerably, the situation may be the opposite. Lenders and other entities that have issued debt in earlier periods may be willing to "pay" borrowers to induce them to repay the loan early. That is, a lender may offer a borrower a discount to pay off the balance of a below-market-interest-rate loan.[13] How much of a discount should be offered?

Suppose a borrower has a loan that was made 10 years ago. The original loan amount was $75,000 to be amortized over 15 years at 8 percent interest. The balance of the loan is now $35,348, and the payments are $716.74 per month. If the current market interest rate has *increased* to 12 percent, then the lender would like to have the loan paid off early so that funds could be loaned to someone else at the market rate. However, the borrower has no incentive to prepay the loan even if he or she has $35,348 available to do so. In this case, the bank may be willing to offer the borrower a discount to prepay the loan. Suppose the lender discounts the loan by $2,000, so that only $33,348 must be paid to the lender. Is this attractive to the borrower?

By accepting the discount, the borrower, in effect, earns a return on the funds used to repay the loan; that is, by making a payment of $33,348 to the lender, the borrower saves $716.74 per month. To calculate the return earned by prepaying the loan, we have:

---

[13] An analogy in corporate finance would include a corporation buying back its debt or "calling it" at market value.

Solution: Function:

$$n = 5 \times 12 = 60$$ $$i\,(n, PV, FV, PMT)$$

$$PV = -\$33{,}348$$

$$PMT = \$716.74$$

$$FV = 0$$

Solve for i = 10.50%

Using a financial calculator, we find the return to be about 10.5 percent. Thus, the interest savings represent a 10.5 percent return on the "investment" made to repay the loan.[14] Whether this represents an attractive proposition for the borrower depends on what alternatives he or she has for investing the $33,348.

In the preceding example, we assumed that the borrower had the funds ($33,348) to prepay the below-market-rate loan. Several other possibilities could be considered. One is that the borrower could refinance some or all of the loan at the market rate. Another is that the borrower wants to increase the loan balance by refinancing. In either case, the lender may still be willing to provide an inducement for the borrower to refinance since the existing loan is at a below-market rate. However, the approach taken to analyze the problem depends on whether, on balance, the borrower gives funds to the lender to reduce the loan balance in exchange for the lower payments or the borrower receives additional funds in exchange for an additional loan payment.

Market Value of a Loan

We have considered several problems in which the balance of a loan was determined after payments had been made for a number of years. The balance of the loan represents the amount that the borrower must repay the lender to satisfy the loan contract. (Any prepayment penalties must be added to the loan balance.) The loan balance may be interpreted as the "contract" or "book value" of the loan. However, if interest rates have changed since the origination of the loan, the loan balance will probably not represent the "market" value of the loan.

The **market value of a loan** is the amount that a new lender or investor would pay to receive the remaining payments on the loan. It can be thought of as the amount that could be loaned so that the remaining payments on the loan would give the lender a return equal to the current market rate of interest.

To find the market value of a loan, you simply calculate the present value of the remaining payments at the market rate of interest. For example, suppose that a loan was made five years ago for $80,000 with an interest rate of 10 percent and monthly payments over a 20-year loan term. Payments on the loan are $772.02 per month. To calculate the market value of the loan, we must find the present value of the remaining monthly payments of

---

[14] The above analysis does not consider the impact of federal income taxes. The IRS has ruled that when a lender discounts a loan such that the borrower does not have to repay the contract loan balance, the discount represents "loan forgiveness" and as such is considered taxable income. Thus, the borrower would have to pay taxes on the $2,000 discount. For an investor in the 40 percent tax bracket, the taxes would be $800. Thus, the net result is as if the borrower only received a discount of $2,000 − $800 = $1,200. This clearly reduces the benefit to the borrower to repay the loan. This forgiveness rule may also apply in cases where lenders accept a deed in lieu of foreclosure or take title to a property from a borrower when the loan balance outstanding exceeds the value of the property.

$772.02 by discounting at the *market rate of interest,* which we assume to be 15 percent. We do this in two steps:

STEP 1: Calculate present value of the remaining payments.

Solution:

$$i = 15\%$$
$$n = 180$$
$$PMT = \$772.02$$
$$FV = 0$$

Solve for PV = $55,161

Function:

$$PV(i, FV, PMT, n)$$

STEP 2: Calculate loan balance to determine % discount.

Solution:

$$PMT = \$772.02$$
$$i = 10\%$$
$$PV = \$80,000$$
$$n = 60$$

Solve for FV = $71,842

Function:

$$FV(i, PV, PMT, n)$$

Thus, the market value of the loan is $55,161, compared to a loan balance of $71,842. The $55,161 is the amount that the lender would receive if the loan were sold to another lender, investor, or the secondary market.[15] We could say that the above loan is selling at a "discount." The amount of the difference in this case would be $71,842 − $55,161 = $16,681. We could also say that the mortgage is selling at a discount of 23 percent of its "face" value.

The market value of the loan is lower than the contract loan balance in this example because interest rates have risen relative to the interest rate (10%) at which the loan was originated 10 years ago. However, the borrower is required to make payments based on 10 percent even though market rates have risen to 15 percent. This is one reason why adjustable rate mortgages have become more attractive to lenders (see Chapter 5). With an adjustable rate mortgage, the market value of the outstanding loan will not differ as much as a new loan originated at market rates of interest. Indeed, if the interest rate on the outstanding loan could be adjusted at each payment interval and there were no limitations (caps) on the amount of the adjustment, the contract rate on the loan would always equal the market rate. In this event, the loan balance and market value for such a loan would always be equal because future payments would be based on current rates of interest.

Effective Cost of Two or More Loans

Many situations exist when an investor may be considering a combination of two or more loans (e.g., a first and a second mortgage). One situation is the assumption of a loan that has a favorable rate of interest.[16] However, the amount of cash necessary for the buyer to

---

[15] It is informative to look at an alternative approach that yields the same answer. Suppose that we were to make a loan for $71,842 at the market rate of 15 percent for the remaining loan term of 15 years. The payment would be $1,005.49. This is $233.47 higher than the contract payment. If we discount this *difference* in payments for the 15-year period at the market rate, we get a present value of $16,681. Subtracting this difference from the loan balance results in the market value of the loan.

[16] Depending on negotiations between borrowers and lenders, it may be possible for properties to be sold on assumption. However, the right to sell on assumption may be precluded explicitly in the mortgage or by the lender not approving the new buyer. Lending practices vary widely, depending on the tradition and the economic conditions in a given area.

assume a mortgage may be prohibitive. This can occur when the seller has already paid down the balance of the loan and when the property has appreciated in value since it was originally financed by the seller. Thus, the buyer must use a second mortgage to bridge the gap between the amount available from the loan assumption and the desired total loan amount.

Suppose that an individual bought a $100,000 property and made a mortgage loan five years ago for $80,000 at 10 percent interest for a term of 25 years. Due to price appreciation, the market value of the property has risen in value over the past five years to $115,000. The amount of cash equity required by the buyer to assume the seller's loan would be $39,669, determined as follows:

Purchase price	$115,000
Seller's mortgage balance ($80,000, 10%, 25 years after 5 years)	75,331
Cash equity required to assume seller's loan	$ 39,669

If the buyer does not have $39,669 in cash, even though he or she desires an assumption, the transaction may not be completed. One alternative open to the buyer unable to make the large cash outlay may be to obtain a second mortgage. However, using a second mortgage will be justified in this case only if the terms of the second mortgage, when combined with the terms on the assumed mortgage, are such that the borrower is as well or better off than if the entire purchase had been financed with a new mortgage. If the entire purchase can be financed with a new $92,000 loan (80% of value) at 12 percent for 20 years, we must know how to combine a second mortgage with the assumed mortgage that determine whether the assumption would be as attractive as the new mortgage loan. Suppose a second mortgage for $16,669 ($92,000 − $75,331) could be obtained at a 14 percent rate for a 20-year term. To analyze this problem, we compute the combined mortgage payments on the assumed loan, and a second mortgage loan made for 20 years at 14 percent.

Monthly payment, assumed loan*	$726.96
Monthly payment, second mortgage loan†	207.28
	$934.24

*Based on original $80,000 loan, at 10 percent, for 25 years.
†Based on second mortgage loan of $16,669, at 14 percent, for 20 years.

The combined monthly payments equal $934.24. We now want to compute the effective cost of the combined payments that are made on the combined loan of $92,000.

Solution:

$n = 20 \times 12 = 240$

$PV = -\$92,000$

$PMT = \$934.24$

$FV = 0$

Solve for $i = 10.75\%$

Function:

$i\,(n, PV, PMT, FV)$

Using a financial calculator, we find an answer of 10.75 percent. This is the cost of obtaining $92,000 with the loan assumption and second mortgage. Since this is less than the cost of obtaining $92,000 with a new first mortgage at a rate of 12 percent, the borrower is still better off with the loan assumption and a second mortgage.[17] It is important to note, however, that the preceding analysis does not consider the fact that the seller may have *raised the price of the property* to capture the benefit of the assumable below-market-rate loan. Later in the chapter, we will consider this in our analysis.

Second Mortgages and Shorter Maturities

In most cases, second mortgages may not be available for a 20-year period. If a five-year term were available on a second mortgage loan at 14 percent interest, would the borrower still be better off by assuming the existing mortgage and taking a second mortgage? To answer this question, we must determine the combined interest cost on the assumed mortgage, which carries a rate of 10 percent for 20 remaining years, and the second mortgage, which would carry a rate of 14 percent for five years. This combined rate can then be compared with the current 12 percent rate for 20 years presently available, should the property be financed with an entirely new mortgage loan.

To combine terms on the assumable mortgage and second mortgage, we add monthly payments together as follows:

	Monthly Payments
Assumed loan*	$ 726.96
Second mortgage†	387.86
Total	$1,114.82

*Based on original terms: $80,000, at 10 percent, for 25 years.
†Based on $16,669, at 14 percent, for five years.

The sum of the two monthly payments is equal to $1,114.82. However, the combined $1,114.82 monthly payments will be made for only five years. After five years, the second mortgage will be completely repaid, and only the $726.96 payments on the assumed loan will be made through the 20th year.

Whether the combined mortgages should be used by the borrower can now be determined by again solving for the combined cost of borrowing. This cost is based on the monthly payments under both the assumed loan and second mortgage, for the respective number of months payments must be made, in relation to the $92,000 amount being financed. These costs are easily seen as the monthly payments of $387.86 on the second mortgage for *five years* and the monthly payments of $726.96 on the assumed mortgage for *20 years,* both discounted by an interest rate that results in the present value of $92,000.

We must find the interest rate that makes the present value of the combined monthly mortgage payments (grouped cash flows) equal to $92,000. Using a financial calculator, we find that the combined interest cost on the existing mortgage assumed for 20 years and

[17] It should be apparent that such a high interest rate can be paid on the second mortgage because $75,331, the amount assumed, carries a 10 percent rate and represents about 82 percent of the $92,000 to be financed, while the second mortgage of $16,669 represents only 18 percent. When weighted together by the respective interest rates, the total rate paid on the combined amounts is influenced more by the amount assumed at 10 percent. As an approximation of the average "blended" rate for the two loans, we have (.82 times 10%) + (.18 times 14%) = 10.72%, which is approximately the same as the answer we found using the present value factors above.

the second mortgage for five years is 10.29 percent. This combined package of financing must again be compared to the 12 percent interest rate currently available on an $80,000 mortgage for 20 years. Because the effective cost of the two combined loans is less than the market rate, this is the best alternative. It should be noted, however, that for the first five years the combined monthly payments of $1,114.82, should the assumption and second mortgage combination be made, would be higher than the payments with a new mortgage for $92,000 at 12 percent for 20 years, which would be $1,013.00 per month. Although this is offset by the lower $726.96 payments after five years, the borrower must decide which pattern of monthly loan payments fits his or her income pattern, in addition to simply choosing the loan alternative with the lower effective borrowing cost. A borrower may be willing to pay a higher effective cost for a loan (or combination of loans) that has lower monthly payments.

Solution:	Alternative Solution:
Requires cash flow analysis:	$CF_0 = \$92,000$
Initial flow $= -\$92,000$	$CF_j = \$1,114.82$
Flow 1 $= \$1,114.82$	$N_j = 60$
Number of times $= 60$ (years 1–5)	$CF_j = \$726.96$
Flow 2 $= \$726.96$	$N_j = 180$
Number of times $= 180$ (years 6–20)	
Solve for *IRR*:	**Solve for *i*** $= 0.8573\%$ (monthly)
IRR (monthly) $= 0.8573\%$	$= 10.29\%$ (annually)
IRR (annualized) $= 10.29\%$	

In recent years, there have been many new loans that combine features of second mortgage lending, consumer lending, and credit card debt. These are described in Concept Box 6.1.

Effect of Below-Market Financing on Property Prices

In many situations, an investor may have an opportunity to purchase a property and obtain financing at a below-market interest rate. We have previously discussed one case where the seller had a below-market-rate loan that could be assumed by the buyer. Below-market financing might also be provided by the seller with a *purchase money mortgage*. In this case, the seller provides some or all of the financing to the buyer at an interest rate lower than the current market rate. Indeed, this type of financing is common during periods of tight credit and high interest rates.

Obviously, below-market-rate loans have value to the buyer. However, because the informed seller also recognizes the value of this type of financing, we would expect the seller to increase the price of the property to reflect it. That is, the "price" of the property would be higher with below-market financing than with market rate financing.

We now consider how a buyer would analyze whether to purchase a property with below-market financing if the price is higher than that of an otherwise comparable property that does not have below-market financing. Suppose that a property can be purchased for $105,000 subject to an assumable loan at a 9 percent interest rate with a 15-year remaining term, a balance of $70,000, and payments of $709.99 per month. A comparable property without any special financing costs $100,000, and a loan for $70,000 can be obtained at a market rate of 11 percent with a 15-year term. Which alternative is best for the buyer? Note that we are assuming that the two loan amounts are the same. In analyzing this problem, we must

Many types of second mortgage loans are used by residential property owners to borrow additional funds after a property has been owned for some time and has appreciated in value. These loans are generally classified as **home equity loans** (HELs). Borrowers would want to consider these alternatives relative to refinancing existing loans. Generally, lenders usually require that borrower-homeowners have accumulated approximately 20 percent of equity in their properties in order to qualify for home equity loans. Borrowers must also qualify for financing based on income and credit history. Two of the more popular loans currently in use are home equity loans (HELs) and home equity lines of credit (HELOCs).

In the cases of both HELs and HELOCs:

1. Amounts received at closing are not taxable. Such amounts are increases in indebtedness and not a "taxable event" as may be the case if a property was sold at a gain.
2. Interest payments are generally tax deductible as long as the lender acquires a lien on the property.

HOME EQUITY LOANS

These loans usually provide borrowers with a *lump sum* amount at closing. In addition to the borrower's personal liability on the note, lenders also acquire a second mortgage lien on the property. Owner's equity is measured as the difference between the appraised value of the property at the time that the HEL is applied for, minus any loan balance owed on the first lien. For example, if a property is currently appraised to be worth $100,000 and it has an existing first lien in an amount of $40,000, the owner's equity would be $60,000. This $60,000 of equity serves as security for the home equity loan. In practice, because the security provided by second liens is inferior to first liens, HELs are riskier to lenders and will carry a higher rate of interest than that available for first-lien financing. Other characteristics of home equity loans are these:

1. Interest rates may be fixed or adjustable.
2. The loan agreement will specify a maturity period.
3. Payments are usually made monthly.
4. Loan payments may be fully amortizing, partially amortizing, or interest only. In the case of the latter two options, payments will be made for a specified number of months, at which point the loan must become either fully amortizing or the remaining balance at maturity must be repaid.

HOME EQUITY LINES OF CREDIT

Not to be confused with HELs, **home equity lines of credit** (HELOCs) are also available to borrowers. These loans have many characteristics that are similar to *consumer credit loans*. Although HELOCs also are secured by second liens, there are many features of HELOCs that differentiate them from HELs. For example:

1. Although the loan will be made for a specific maximum amount, that amount is not necessarily disbursed as a lump sum. Funds may be borrowed (drawn down) against the line as the consumer-borrower desires. However, when the loan balance reaches a maximum amount, no further draws may be made.
2. Like credit card payments, borrowers generally have some flexibility as to the amount of monthly payment that they choose to make. However, lenders will usually insist that monthly payments be at least some minimum amount. To the extent that borrowers choose to make payments that are less than the monthly interest due, the loan balance will increase (negative amortization). Any payments greater than monthly interest due will reduce the loan balance.
3. Interest rates are usually adjustable and, like ARM rates, are usually tied to a well-known interest rate index (e.g., the prime rate).

4. Like consumer credit card accounts, amounts borrowed and monthly loan payments will determine the loan balance, which may increase or decrease from month to month.

Although HELOCs are similar to many consumer credit loans, because of the added security provided by second liens, HELOCs should be available at interest rates below those of credit card debt. This is because credit card debit is usually unsecured and is totally dependent on a borrower's personal credit and capacity to repay.

In addition to the interest rate, HELOC borrowers should consider the following issues:

1. *Early termination fees.* Because these loans are more like a combination of consumer credit and an ARM, the interest rate is likely to be tied to an index. Consequently, at some future time, interest rates could increase dramatically and borrowers may want to switch to a fixed rate loan. In anticipation of this possibility, HELOC lenders may include a termination fee (similar to a prepayment penalty) in the loan agreement.

2. *Inactivity fees.* Because this loan may be used as a line of credit, if borrowers do not use the line or if they attempt to keep only a small loan balance without terminating the account to avoid the penalty described in (1) (while switching their financing to another lender), a monthly inactivity fee also may be included in the loan agreement. Also, like many credit card loans, there may be an annual renewal or administrative fee associated with this type of loan.

consider whether it is desirable for the buyer to pay an additional $5,000 in cash (additional equity invested) to receive the benefit of lower payments on the below-market loan. The calculations are as follows:

	Down Payment	Payment
Market rate loan	$30,000	$795.62
Loan assumption	35,000	709.99
Difference	$ 5,000	$ 85.63

Using a financial calculator, we find that making the additional $5,000 down payment would result in earning the equivalent of 19.41 percent because of the lower monthly loan payments. Alternatively, should the buyer decide not to pay the additional $5,000, he or she would have to find a return of 19.41 percent on the $5,000 in an investment with comparable risk. Because the 19.41 percent rate is higher than the 11 percent market rate, buying the house with below-market financing appears to be desirable.

Solution:

$$n = 15 \times 12 = 180$$
$$PV = -\$5,000$$
$$PMT = \$85.63$$
$$FV = 0$$

Solve for i = 1.6177% per month

= 19.41% per year

Function:

$i\ (n, PV, PMT, FV)$

Assuming a Lower Loan Balance

For simplicity, it was assumed in the above example that the balance of the assumable (below-market) loan was the same as the amount available for a new loan at the market rate. As discussed previously, an assumable loan may have a lower balance than a new market rate loan because the seller has paid down the loan and the property may have increased in value. Suppose the balance on the assumable loan in our example is only $50,000 and monthly payments are $507.13. The buyer, however, needs financing of $70,000, the amount that can normally be borrowed at market rates. The borrower may also obtain a second mortgage of $20,000 for 15 years at a 14 percent rate, with payments of $266.35 per month. Is it still desirable to assume the loan, take a second mortgage, and pay $5,000 more for the property? We can make the following calculations:

	Down Payment	Payment
Market rate loan	$30,000	$795.62
Loan assumption + second mortgage	35,000	773.48*
	$ 5,000	$ 22.14

*$507.13 on the $50,000 loan assumption plus $266.35 on the second mortgage.

The return is now -2.90 percent. The buyer is clearly better off by not paying $5,000 more for the property to assume the loan. How much more would the buyer be willing to pay? This is the subject of the next section.

Cash Equivalency

In the previous section, we considered how a buyer could analyze whether a premium should be paid for a property with a below-market-rate loan. We now extend that discussion to consider how much the buyer *could* pay to be indifferent to purchasing the property with a below-market-rate loan or one that must be financed at the market rate.

We will use the example from the last section, where a $70,000 loan could be assumed at a 9 percent rate with a remaining term of 15 years and payments of $709.99 per month. Recall that a comparable property with no special financing available would sell for $100,000 and could be financed at a market rate of 11 percent. How much more than $100,000 could the buyer pay if he or she chose to assume the 9 percent loan and still be as well off as if the property were purchased for $100,000 and financed with an 11 percent loan? We first find the present value of the payments that can be assumed using the *market* rate. This is the market value or **cash equivalent value** of the assumable loan. It represents the price at which the old loan could be sold to a new lender/investor.

Solution:

$n = 15 \times 12 = 180$

$i = 11\%/12 = 0.91666\%$

$PMT = \$709.99$

$FV = 0$

Solve for $PV = \$62,466.30$

Function:

$PV\,(i, n, FV, PMT)$

By assuming the existing loan balance, the buyer would obtain financing equal to $70,000.00 instead of $62,466.30 for the same $709.99 payment. Thus, the buyer receives a net benefit of $70,000.00 − $62,466.30 = $7,533.70. Therefore, the buyer could pay $7,533.70 more for the property, or $107,534 (rounded).

In the previous section, we calculated that the return to the buyer would be 19.41 percent if an additional $5,000 more, or $105,000, were paid for the property. It is possible to verify that by paying $107,534, the buyer's return would be exactly 11 percent, the same as the market interest rate on the loan.

Based on the above analysis, the property with an assumable loan could probably sell for as high as $107,534. The buyer would be paying a cash equivalent value of $100,000 for the property plus an additional **financing premium** of $7,534 to obtain the benefit of the below-market-rate loan. The value of the property remains $100,000. This is referred to as the cash equivalent value for the property. This differs from the *price* paid for the house, which includes the $7,534 financing premium. The recognition of this premium is important because if we knew that the property had actually sold for $107,534 but did not consider that it had an assumable below-market-rate loan, we would have an inflated opinion of value. Alternatively, the buyer would never want to agree to pay $107,534 for the property unless the 9 percent below-market financing could be obtained.

Note that the amount of cash (equity) invested in the property is $107,534, less the mortgage balance of $70,000, or $37,534. When $37,534 is added to the cash equivalent value of the loan of $62,466, we obtain the cash equivalent value for the property of $100,000.

Cash Equivalency: Smaller Loan Balance

In the previous section, we determined the indifference price for a property that had an assumable below-market-rate loan. The loan balance was the same as the buyer could obtain with a market rate loan. However, when loan assumptions occur, it is likely that the loan balance is significantly less than would normally be desired. We now modify the example in the last section by considering that the balance of the assumable 9 percent loan is only $50,000 and the buyer would have to borrow an additional $20,000 through a second mortgage to obtain the $70,000 needed. We assume that the second mortgage could be obtained at a 14 percent rate for a 15-year term. We continue to assume that a $70,000 new first mortgage (70% of the property value) could be obtained at an 11 percent rate with a 15-year term.[18] Now, how much could the buyer pay for the property and be indifferent to the two methods of financing?

We begin by finding the present value of the *sum* of the payments on the assumable loan ($507.13) plus payments on the second mortgage ($266.35), using the 11 percent market rate. The difference between the present value ($68,052.27) and the $70,000 available at the market rate is $1,947.73. Thus, the buyer would now pay only an additional $1,947.73 for the property to get the below-market-rate loan. Therefore, the property would probably sell for no more than $101,950 (rounded). This is considerably less than the $107,500 obtained where the assumable loan had a balance of $70,000 instead of $50,000. There are two reasons that the premium is less: First, because the balance of the assumable loan is less, the saving (from lower payments) is less. Second, because this balance is less than the amount of the loan that could be obtained at the market rate, the benefit from lower payments on the assumable loan is reduced by the necessity of obtaining a second mortgage at a higher interest rate than the rate on a new first mortgage. It is important to realize that when carrying out this analysis, the need for a second mortgage must be considered; otherwise, the benefit of the loan assumption is overstated.

[18] Even if an investor did not need a second mortgage, we can only evaluate the benefit of the loan assumption by comparing it with what is currently available in the market. Since market rates are usually based on a loan-to-value ratio of 70 percent or more, a second mortgage must be considered in the analysis.

Solution:

$$n = 15 \times 12 = 180$$
$$i = 11\%/12 = 0.91666\%$$
$$PMT = \$773.48$$
$$FV = 0$$
Solve for PV $= \$68,052.27$

Function:

$$PV\,(n,\, i,\, PMT,\, FV)$$

Cash Equivalency: Concluding Comments

In the previous two sections, we showed how to analyze the impact of below-market financing on the sale price of a property. It is important to recognize the relationship between the price at which a property sells and any special (e.g., below-market) financing that might be available. Although we have considered several examples of cash equivalency calculations, we have only introduced a few of the possible situations that could arise in practice. At least three additional situations could arise that would affect the analysis.

1. If the below-market financing is not transferable to a subsequent buyer, this means that a previous buyer may not benefit from the below-market-rate loan for its remaining term. This obviously affects any financing premiums that would be paid for properties.

2. Even if below-market loans were always assumable by subsequent buyers, the value of this type of financing over the remaining term of the loan to a subsequent buyer depends on the market rate of interest at the time of subsequent sales. These rates may be higher or lower than rates prevailing at the time that the present owner purchased the property. If market rates at the time the property is sold are no longer greater than the contract rate on the assumable loan, then the subsequent buyer would not pay a premium. Hence, the likelihood of subsequent sales and interest rates at such points in time adds an element of uncertainty to the benefit of assuming any loan and should tend to reduce the amount buyers are willing to pay for such loans.

3. Even if the buyer plans to own the property for a time period exceeding the loan term, interest rates could drop after the loan is assumed. Because borrowers can usually refinance when interest rates drop, a below-market-rate loan has less value if interest rates are expected to fall. In effect, the value of the below-market financing is reduced by the "option" to refinance if interest rates fall.

All of the situations discussed above tend to reduce the premium a buyer would pay for a below-market-interest-rate loan. Thus, our analysis is likely to indicate the *upper limit* on the premium associated with below-market-rate loans. The best way to verify the value of such premiums is by observing how much more buyers pay for below-market financing in contrast to properties without special financing.

Wraparound Loans

Wraparound loans are used to obtain additional financing on a property while keeping an existing loan in place. The wraparound lender makes a loan for a face amount equal to the existing loan balance plus the amount of additional financing. The wraparound lender agrees to make the payments on the existing loan as long as the borrower makes payments on the wraparound loan. Instead of making payments on the original loan in addition to payments on a second mortgage, the borrower makes a payment only on the wraparound loan.

Suppose a property owner named Smith has an existing loan with a balance of $90,000 and monthly payments of $860.09. The interest rate on the loan is 8 percent and the remaining loan term is 15 years. From the time Smith originally obtained this loan, the property has risen in value to $150,000. Smith's current loan balance is 60 percent of the current value of the property. He would like to borrow an additional $30,000, which would increase his debt to $120,000, or 80 percent of the property value.

Assume that the current effective interest rate on a first mortgage with an 80 percent loan-to-value ratio is 11.5 percent with a term of 15 years, and the current effective interest rate on a second mortgage for an *additional* 20 percent of value ($30,000) would be 15.5 percent for a term of 15 years.

A lender different than the holder of Smith's existing loan is willing to make a wraparound loan for $120,000 at a 10 percent rate for a 15-year term. Payments on this loan would be $1,289.53 per month. If Smith makes this loan, the wraparound lender will take over the payments on Smith's current loan; that is, Smith will pay $1,289.53 to the wraparound lender, and the wraparound lender will make the $860.09 payment on the original loan. Thus, Smith's payment would increase by $429.44 ($1,289.53 − $860.09) per month. Because the wraparound lender is taking over the payments on the old loan, Smith will actually receive only $30,000 in cash (the $120,000 amount for the wraparound loan less the $90,000 balance of Smith's current loan).

Is the wraparound loan a desirable alternative for Smith to obtain an additional $30,000? The rate on the $120,000 wraparound loan (10%) is less than the market rate (11.5%) on a new first mortgage for the entire $120,000. Thus, the wraparound loan would be more desirable than refinancing with a new first mortgage.[19] Why would the wraparound lender make a loan that has a lower rate than a new first mortgage? The answer is that the wraparound lender is primarily concerned with earning a competitive rate of return on the *incremental* funds loaned (i.e., the additional $30,000). It is the effective cost of the incremental funds loaned that the borrower also should be concerned about.

What is the cost of the incremental $30,000? This is analogous to determining the incremental borrowing cost of a loan that we discussed at the beginning of the chapter. That is, we want to know the incremental cost of the 80 percent wraparound loan versus the 60 percent existing loan. To get the additional $30,000 on the wraparound loan, the borrower must pay a 10 percent interest rate on the entire $120,000, not solely the additional $30,000. Because the rate on the existing $90,000 is only 8 percent, the incremental cost of the additional $30,000 is greater than 10 percent. The question is whether the incremental cost is more or less than the 15.5 percent rate for a second mortgage of $30,000.

The incremental borrowing cost of the wraparound loan can be determined by finding the interest rate that equates the present value of the additional payment with the additional funds received. Using a financial calculator, we find that the interest rate is 15.46 percent or about 15.5 percent. This is the same rate as that for a second mortgage, which is what we would expect. The wraparound lender can charge a lower rate on the wraparound loan and still earn a competitive rate on the incremental funds loaned because the existing loan is at a below-market rate. The wraparound rate of 10 percent is,

[19] It is assumed that there are no points on the wraparound loan so that the effective cost of the wraparound loan is 10 percent. The cost of a wraparound loan can be compared with the cost of a new first mortgage because both rates reflect the cost of a loan for $120,000.

in effect, a weighted average of the rate on the existing loan (8 percent) and the rate on a second mortgage (15.5%).[20] If the existing loan were at the market rate for a 60 percent loan, then the wraparound rate would have to be equal to the rate on an 80 percent loan, so that the wraparound lender would earn a rate of return on the incremental funds equal to a second mortgage rate.

Solution:	Function:
$n = 15 \times 12 = 180$	$i\,(n, PV, PMT, FV)$
$PV = -\$30{,}000$	
$PMT = \$429.44$	
$FV = 0$	
Solve for $i = 15.46\%$	

Is there any reason why the wraparound lender should be willing to make the loan at a rate that is more attractive than a second mortgage? The wraparound loan is, in effect, a second mortgage because the original loan is still intact. Furthermore, the loan-to-value ratio is increased by the same amount with the wraparound loan as it would be with a second mortgage. However, the wraparound loan has one advantage: The wraparound lender makes the payments on the first mortgage loan. Hence, control is retained over default in its payment, whereas if a second mortgage was made, the second mortgage lender would not necessarily be aware of a default on the first mortgage loan and might not be included in foreclosure action resulting from it. In a typical wraparound mortgage agreement, the wraparound lender is obligated to make payments on the original mortgage only to the extent that payments are received from the borrower, and the borrower agrees to comply with all of the covenants in the original mortgage except payment. Any default by the borrower will be realized by the wraparound lender, who may not want to see the property go into foreclosure. The wraparound lender may make advances on the first mortgage and add them to the balance on the wraparound loan, foreclose on its mortgage, or negotiate for the title to the property in lieu of foreclosure, while still making payments on the first lien. Thus, the wraparound lender may be willing to earn an incremental return that is slightly lower than a second mortgage rate.

It should be noted that the original mortgage may contain a prohibition against further encumbrances or a due-on-sale clause that may preclude use of a wraparound loan to access equity in, or finance the sale of, property. In the absence of these restrictions, the original lender may also be willing to work out a deal with Smith that would be attractive to both of them. For example, this lender might offer Smith a new first mortgage at the same 10 percent rate as the wraparound loan (rather than the 11.5% market rate on a first mortgage) if Smith agrees to borrow the additional $30,000 from the bank. Again, because the 10 percent rate applies to the entire $90,000 (not only the additional $30,000), the original lender can earn an incremental return of 15.5 percent on the incremental funds advanced. Thus, the existing lender can earn a competitive rate of return on the new funds and keep the existing borrower as a customer. The lender still earns only 8 percent on the

---

[20] The weighted average is $(90{,}000 \div 120{,}000 \times 8\%) + (30{,}000 \div 120{,}000 \times 15.5\%) = 9.875$ percent, or about 10 percent, which is the rate on the wraparound loan. Note that the weighted average is less than the 11.5 percent rate on a new $120,000 first mortgage, which indicates that the existing loan is at a below-market rate.

existing loan, but this would also be true if the borrower gets a second mortgage or a wraparound loan from a different lender. Thus, the original lender may be willing, in effect, to offer the same deal as a wraparound lender by charging a rate on a new first mortgage that is equal to the wraparound rate of 10 percent.[21]

Buydown Loans

The final type of loan situation we consider is the **buydown loan.** With a buydown loan, the seller of the property (frequently a builder) pays an amount to a lender to buy down, or lower, the interest rate on the loan for the borrower for a specific period of time. This may be done in periods of high interest rates to help borrowers qualify for financing. For example, suppose that interest rates are currently 15 percent and a purchaser of a builder's property has only enough income to qualify for a loan at a 13 percent fixed rate. Let us assume that the loan will be for $75,000 with monthly amortization based on a 30-year term. Payments based on the market rate of 15 percent would be $948.33 per month. Payments at a 13 percent rate would only be $829.65 per month. Based on the buyer's income, the buyer would qualify to make payments of $829.65 but not $948.33. Suppose that the builder wanted to buy down the interest rate from 15 to 13 percent, thereby enabling the bank to make the loan, so that payments are only $829.65 per month for the first five years of the loan term but will increase to $948.33 for the remaining loan term. To accomplish this, the builder would have to make up the difference in payments ($118.68 per month for the five-year period). If this difference were paid by the builder to the lender at the time the loan closed, the amount paid would have to be the present value of the difference in payments, discounted at the market rate of 15 percent. The builder would therefore pay $4,988.67 to the lender to buy down the loan. When coupled with the payments received from the buyer, the lender would earn a market rate of 15 percent and be willing to qualify the buyer.

Solution:	Function:
$n = 5 \times 12 = 60$	$PV(n, i, PMT, FV)$
$i = 15\% \div 12 = 1.25\%$	
$PMT = \$118.68$	
$FV = 0$	
Solve for $PV = \$4,988.67$	

The buydown has the advantage of allowing borrowers to qualify for the loan when their current income might not otherwise meet the lender's payment-to-income criteria. Based on our discussion of cash equivalent value, however, you should realize that the builder will probably have added the buydown amount to the price of the property. Thus, the borrower might be better off bargaining for a lower price on the property and obtaining his or her own loan at the market rate. Probably, the same home or a similar one could be obtained for $4,988.67 less without a buydown. The borrower is, in effect, paying $4,988.67 in "points" to lower the interest rate to 13 percent from 15 percent.

[21] This is often referred to as a "blended rate" because the 10 percent rate is a weighted average of the rate on the existing loan and the rate on the incremental funds loaned.

It should also be noted that many buydowns are executed with graduated payments for three or five years; that is, to continue with our current example, they may be initiated with monthly payments of $829.65 and step up each year by a specified amount until $948.33 is reached in the fifth year.

Some buydown programs are also used in conjunction with adjustable rate mortgages, where the initial rate of interest will be bought down. Because initial rates on ARMs are typically lower than those on fixed rate mortgages, this results in even lower initial payments, thereby allowing more buyers to qualify. However, this type of buydown practice has been discouraged because payments may increase considerably, particularly if there is an increase in the market rate of interest. In these cases, payments would rise because of higher market rates and because future payments have not been bought down.

Conclusion

This chapter has illustrated a number of problems concerning financing situations that borrowers and lenders might face. In today's era of creative financing, many other examples could be discussed. However, we have chosen examples that illustrate the main concepts and approaches to solving important problems. These can be applied to other situations that you might want to analyze. Thus, this chapter should be viewed as introducing various tools that can be used to handle problems relating to both residential and commercial properties.

To keep our analysis as straightforward as possible and focus on the key new concepts we wanted to introduce, we have used fixed rate mortgages in all our examples in this chapter. However, the analyses also apply to other types of mortgages, such as ARMs, and floating rate and other loans.

Key Terms

biweekly payments, *160*
buydown loan, *175*
cash equivalent value, *170*
effective cost of
 refinancing, *159*
financing premium, *171*

home equity line of
 credit, *168*
home equity loan, *168*
incremental cost of
 borrowing, *148*
loan refinancing, *156*

marginal cost of
 borrowing, *148*
market value of a
 loan, *163*
origination fees, *151*
wraparound loan, *172*

Useful Web Sites

www.businessfinance.com/wraparound-mortgage.htm—Examples of wraparound loans.

www.fha-home-loans.com/buydown_fha_loan.htm—Discussion of how FHA buydown loans are structured.

www.bankrate.com—Good source of rates and articles on different kinds of mortgages. Includes some useful mortgage calculators to choose between loan alternatives.

www.mgic.com—Mortgage Guarantee Insurance Corporation, a national provider of private mortgage insurance.

www.freddiemac.com/pmms/pmms30.htm—This is a good site for finding fixed rates and points for 30-year mortgages.

www.freddiemac.com/pmms/pmmsarm.htm—This is a good site for finding monthly average commitment rates and points on one-year adjustable rate mortgages.

www.ipd.com—This Web site provides objective measurement and analysis of various properties. The company that runs this Web site does not invest in the market and does not offer any direct investment advice, so it tends to be unbiased.

Questions

1. What are the primary considerations that should be made when refinancing?
2. What factors must be considered when deciding whether to refinance a loan after interest rates have declined?

3. Why might the market value of a loan differ from its outstanding balance?

4. Why might a borrower be willing to pay a higher price for a home with an assumable loan?

5. What is a buydown loan? What parties are usually involved in this kind of loan?

6. Why might a wraparound lender provide a wraparound loan at a lower rate than a new first mortgage?

7. Assuming the borrower is in no danger of default, under what conditions might a lender be willing to accept a lesser amount from a borrower than the outstanding balance of a loan and still consider the loan paid in full?

8. Under what conditions might a property with an assumable loan sell for more than comparable properties with no assumable loans available?

9. What is meant by the incremental cost of borrowing additional funds?

10. Is the incremental cost of borrowing additional funds affected significantly by early repayment of the loan?

Problems

1. A borrower can obtain an 80 percent loan with an 8 percent interest rate and monthly payments. The loan is to be fully amortized over 25 years. Alternatively, he could obtain a 90 percent loan at an 8.5 percent rate with the same loan term. The borrower plans to own the property for the entire loan term.

   a. What is the incremental cost of borrowing the additional funds? (*Hint:* The dollar amount of the loan does not affect the answer.)

   b. How would your answer change if two points were charged on the 90 percent loan?

   c. Would your answer to part (*b*) change if the borrower planned to own the property for only five years?

2. An investor has $60,000 to invest in a $280,000 property. He can obtain either a $220,000 loan at 9.5 percent for 20 years or a $180,000 loan at 9 percent for 20 years and a second mortgage for $40,000 at 13 percent for 20 years. All loans require monthly payments and are fully amortizing.

   a. Which alternative should the borrower choose, assuming he will own the property for the full loan term?

   b. Would your answer change if the borrower plans to own the property only five years?

   c. Would your answers to (*a*) and (*b*) change if the second mortgage had a 10-year term?

3. An investor obtained a fully amortizing mortgage five years ago for $95,000 at 11 percent for 30 years. Mortgage rates have dropped, so that a fully amortizing 25-year loan can be obtained at 10 percent. There is no prepayment penalty on the mortgage balance of the original loan, but three points will be charged on the new loan and other closing costs will be $2,000. All payments are monthly.

   a. Should the borrower refinance if he plans to own the property for the remaining loan term? Assume that the investor borrows only an amount equal to the outstanding balance of the loan.

   b. Would your answer to part (*a*) change if he planned to own the property for only five more years?

4. Secondary Mortgage Purchasing Company (SMPC) wants to buy your mortgage from the local savings and loan. The original balance of your mortgage was $140,000 and was obtained five years ago with monthly payments at 10 percent interest. The loan was to be fully amortized over 30 years.

   a. What should SMPC pay if it wants an 11 percent return?

   b. How would your answer to part (*a*) change if SMPC expected the loan to be repaid after five years?

5. You have a choice between the following two identical properties: Property A is priced at $150,000 with 80 percent financing at a 10.5 percent interest rate for 20 years. Property B is priced at $160,000 with an assumable mortgage of $100,000 at 9 percent interest with 20 years remaining. Monthly payments are $899.73. A second mortgage for $20,000 can be

obtained at 13 percent interest for 20 years. All loans require monthly payments and are fully amortizing.

a. With no preference other than financing, which property would you choose?

b. How would your answer change if the *seller* of Property B provided a second mortgage for $20,000 at the same 9 percent rate as the assumable loan?

c. How would your answer change if the seller of Property B provided a second mortgage for $30,000 at the same 9 percent rate as the assumable loan so that no additional down payment would be required by the buyer if the loan were assumed?

6. An investor has owned a property for 15 years, the value of which is now to $200,000. The balance on the original mortgage is $100,000 and the monthly payments are $1,100 with 15 years remaining. He would like to obtain $50,000 in additional financing. A new first mortgage for $150,000 can be obtained at a 12.5 percent rate and a second mortgage for $50,000 at a 14 percent rate with a 15-year term. Alternatively, a wraparound loan for $150,000 can be obtained at a 12 percent rate and a 15-year term. All loans are fully amortizing. Which alternative should the investor choose?

7. A builder is offering $100,000 loans for his properties at 9 percent for 25 years. Monthly payments are based on current market rates of 9.5 percent and are to be fully amortized over 25 years. The property would normally sell for $110,000 without any special financing.

a. At what price should the builder sell the properties to earn, in effect, the market rate of interest on the loan? Assume that the buyer would have the loan for the entire term of 25 years.

b. How would your answer to part (a) change if the property is resold after 10 years and the loan repaid?

8. A property is available for sale that could normally be financed with a fully amortizing $80,000 loan at a 10 percent rate with monthly payments over a 25-year term. Payments would be $726.96 per month. The builder is offering buyers a mortgage that reduces the payments by 50 percent for the first year and 25 percent for the second year. After the second year, regular monthly payments of $726.96 would be made for the remainder of the loan term.

a. How much would you expect the builder to have to give the bank to buy down the payments as indicated?

b. Would you recommend the property be purchased if it was selling for $5,000 more than similar properties that do not have the buydown available?

9. An appraiser is looking for comparable sales and finds a property that recently sold for $200,000. She finds that the buyer was able to assume the seller's fully amortizing mortgage which had monthly payments based on a 7 percent interest rate. The balance of the loan at the time of sale was $140,000 with a remaining term of 15 years (monthly payments). The appraiser determines that if a $140,000 loan was obtained on the same property, monthly payments at the market rate for a 15-year fully amortizing loan would have been 8 percent with no points.

a. Assume that the buyer expected to benefit from the interest savings on the assumable loan for the entire loan term. What is the cash equivalent value of the property?

b. How would your answer to part (a) change if you assumed that the buyer only expected to benefit from interest savings for five years because he would probably sell or refinance after five years?

10. A borrower is making a choice between a mortgage with monthly payments *or* biweekly payments. The loan will be $200,000 at 6 percent interest for 20 years.

a. How would you analyze these alternatives?

b. What if the biweekly loan was available for 5.75 percent? How would your answer change?

After-Tax Effective Interest Rate

The preceding chapters have dealt with numerous situations where financing alternatives were evaluated. In all cases, the analysis was made without considering that mortgage interest is tax deductible. An obvious question is whether consideration of federal income taxes affects the conclusions in our analyses. To gain insight into this question, we first consider the *after-tax effective cost of borrowing* with a standard fixed rate mortgage loan.

Example

Suppose that a borrower makes a $100,000 loan with annual payments at a 10 percent rate and a 10-year term. The loan is fully amortizing; however, payments are made on an annual basis to simplify the initial illustration. The annual loan payment is calculated as follows:

Solution:	Function:
PV = $100,000	PMT (PV, i, n, FV)
i = 10%	
n = 10	
FV = 0	
Solve for PMT = $16,275	

A loan schedule is calculated in Exhibit 6A–1 for the 10-year loan term. The pretax cost of this loan is simply 10 percent because there are no points or prepayment penalties. We now want to see the effect of interest being tax deductible. The tax benefit of the interest tax deduction is calculated by multiplying the loan interest each year by the borrower's tax rate. For example, the first year interest is $10,000. At a 28 percent tax rate, this means that the borrower can reduce taxes by $2,800 by deducting the interest.

The after-tax cost of the loan can now be found by subtracting the tax savings from the loan payment. The after-tax cost is calculated in Exhibit 6A–2.

To calculate the after-tax effective cost of borrowing, we need to find the annual compound interest rate that equates the after-tax payments to the initial amount of the loan ($100,000). Calculating this rate indicates an after-tax cost of borrowing of exactly 7.2 percent. This is verified in Exhibit 6A–3.

Adding the present value column in Exhibit 6A–3 results in a net present value of zero, which verifies that the after-tax cost is 7.2 percent.

Now that we have performed the calculations the "long way," you may wonder if the pretax and after-tax costs are in

EXHIBIT 6A–1 Loan Schedule

End of Year	Payment	Interest	Principal	Balance
1	$16,275	$10,000	$6,275	$93,725
2	16,275	9,373	6,902	86,823
3	16,275	8,682	7,592	79,231
4	16,275	7,923	8,351	70,880
5	16,275	7,088	9,187	61,693
6	16,275	6,169	10,105	51,588
7	16,275	5,159	11,116	40,472
8	16,275	4,047	12,227	28,245
9	16,275	2,825	13,450	14,795
10	16,275	1,480	14,795	0

EXHIBIT 6A–2 After-Tax Cost of Loan Payment

Year	Payment	After-Tax Value of Deduction*	After-Tax Payment
1	$16,275	$2,800	$13,475
2	16,275	2,624	13,650
3	16,275	2,431	13,843
4	16,275	2,218	14,056
5	16,275	1,985	14,290
6	16,275	1,727	14,547
7	16,275	1,444	14,830
8	16,275	1,133	15,141
9	16,275	791	15,484
10	16,275	414	15,860

*Interest times tax rate.

EXHIBIT 6A–3 Net Present Value of After-Tax Payments

Year	ATCF	PVIF*	Present Value
0	−$100,000	$1.00000	−$100,000
1	13,475	0.93284	12,570
2	13,650	0.87018	11,878
3	13,843	0.81174	11,237
4	14,056	0.75722	10,644
5	14,290	0.70636	10,094
6	14,547	0.65892	9,585
7	14,830	0.61466	9,115
8	15,141	0.57338	8,682
9	15,484	0.53487	8,282
10	15,860	0.49894	7,913
Total present value			0

*For a discussion of present value interest factors, see Exhibit 3–6.

some way related to the borrower's tax rate. There is a very simple relationship in this situation:

$$\text{After-tax effective cost} = (\text{Pretax effective cost})$$
$$\times (1 - \text{Tax rate})$$
$$= 10\% (1 - .28)$$
$$= 7.2\%$$

We see that the after-tax borrowing cost is inversely proportional to the complement of the borrower's tax rate; that is, if the tax rate is 28 percent, the complement of the tax rate is 72 percent and the after-tax cost is 72 percent of the pretax cost. (In effect, the entire interest cost is tax deductible.) This relationship will hold even if the loan is repaid early. The relationship also applies to loans with points if the points are deductible when they are paid. If the points cannot be deducted in the same year they are paid, the relationship will not hold exactly. Even where it does not hold exactly, it is usually a good approximation of the effective cost.[1] It should also be clear that the higher the borrower's tax rate, the greater the benefit of the interest tax deduction.

Monthly Payments

The above example assumed that the payments on the loan were made annually, for example, at the end of the year, which coincided with the time the borrower received the tax deduction. If the loan payments were monthly, would the answer differ significantly? If we assumed that the buyer realized tax benefits from the interest deductions monthly, then the answer would not change at all. It could be argued that taxes are paid only once each year (on April 15 of the following year!) and thus the tax deduction is not received at the exact time as the loan payment. However, knowing that the tax benefit from the interest deduction will affect tax forms at the end of the year may also mean that borrowers pay less estimated taxes during the year.[2] Furthermore, borrowers may have less taxes withheld from their monthly pay because they know that the interest will reduce their taxable income at the end of the year. Because of these possibilities, it may be more realistic to assume, when calculating the after-tax cost of financing, that interest deductions occur at different points in time than the mortgage payment. However, even if the tax deduction was not assumed to occur until the end of the year, it would not affect the calculated effective interest rate

significantly. Thus, for practical purposes, we can conclude that the after-tax effective monthly interest cost is equal to the pretax effective monthly cost multiplied by the complement of the investor's tax rate $(1 - \text{Tax rate})$.

Effect of After-Tax Interest Cost on Loan Decisions

We have seen that the after-tax effective interest rate is proportional to the borrower's tax rate. This will be true as long as the interest is tax deductible in the year it is paid.[3] When this is true, tax considerations will not affect any of the conclusions regarding selection from alternative mortgages because taxes affect each loan in a similar manner. Thus, we can still compare pretax effective interest costs when choosing a loan and be confident that tax considerations will not affect financing decisions. Similarly, we can compute the incremental borrowing cost, the effective cost of refinancing, and other decision criteria discussed in the preceding chapter on a pretax basis. We do not mean to imply that interest deductions for tax purposes are an unimportant consideration when deciding to borrow money. Clearly, a borrower should consider the tax deductibility of the interest payments as part of the cost of making borrowing decisions. The *higher* a borrower's tax rate, the lower the after-tax cost of borrowing. This affects one's willingness to borrow on investment real estate, as you will see later in the book when we evaluate financial leverage.

Negative Amortization Loans

We have seen that the after-tax effective cost of a loan is equal to the pretax effective cost multiplied by the complement of the investor's tax rate. This is true as long as all interest "charged" on the loan is tax deductible in the year that the interest is paid. By interest charged we mean the portion of each monthly payment which is *not* principal.

In the case of loans with negative amortization, interest charged will exceed the payment during some or all of the loan term. One example we have discussed is the graduated payment mortgage (GPM). We will now see how the after-tax effective cost is calculated for a loan with negative amortization. Consider a loan for $100,000 at a 10 percent interest rate with *annual* payments of $8,000 per year for the first five years, followed by payments of $12,000 per year until the entire balance is repaid.

Because interest charged is $10,000 (.10 × $100,000) the first year and the payment is only $8,000, negative amortization will be $2,000. This increases the balance of the loan to $102,000 after one year. The interest the second year

---

[1]For example, if points are charged on loans for *income* property, the relationship may not hold exactly. This is because the timing of the tax deduction for the points may not correspond with the actual payment of the points. Whereas the points are paid at the time the loan is closed, they must be amortized over the loan term for tax purposes. Points paid when purchasing an owner-occupied residence are generally deductible, although points paid when refinancing a residence must be amortized over the loan term.

[2]The IRS requires taxpayers to estimate their tax liability and in many cases quarterly payments must be made to the IRS.

[3]Some alternative mortgages such as the graduated payment mortgage have interest charged (due to negative amortization) which is not deductible in the year it is paid. This is discussed later in this appendix.

EXHIBIT 6A–4 **Loan Schedule**

Year	Beginning Balance	Payment	Interest	Amortization
1	$100,000	$ 8,000	$10,000	$(2,000)
2	102,000	8,000	10,200	(2,200)
3	104,200	8,000	10,420	(2,420)
4	106,620	8,000	10,662	(2,662)
5	109,282	8,000	10,928	(2,928)
6	112,210	12,000	11,221	779
7	111,431	12,000	11,143	857
8	110,574	12,000	11,057	943
9	109,631	12,000	10,963	1,037
10	108,594	12,000	10,859	1,141
11	107,453	12,000	10,745	1,255
12	106,198	12,000	10,620	1,380
13	104,818	12,000	10,482	1,518
14	103,300	12,000	10,330	1,670
15	101,630	12,000	10,161	1,837
16	99,793	12,000	9,979	2,021
·	·	·	·	·
·	·	·	·	·
·	·	·	·	·

is, therefore, $10,200 (.10 × $102,000). Proceeding in this manner, we can construct the loan schedule in Exhibit 6A–4.

From the exhibit, we see that negative amortization for the first five years increases the balance. In year 6, when the payments increase to more than the interest charged, the loan balance begins to decline. However, it takes until the end of year 15 before the balance decreases below the initial $100,000.

The question now is how much interest can the borrower deduct for tax purposes each year? Most borrowers, at least with owner-occupied homes, compute taxes on a "cash basis"; that is, their income and expenses for tax purposes are based on actual cash income and expenditures.[4] For these borrowers, *current tax regulations require that interest deductions may not exceed the amount of payment.* Thus, in our example, only $8,000 could be deducted each year during the first five years. Starting with year 6, we see that the payment exceeds the interest. What happens to the interest that could *not* be deducted during the first five years (due to the negative amortization)? The answer is that the borrower can continue to deduct the entire loan payment *until the loan balance is reduced to its initial balance,* in this case, $100,000. Thus, the borrower can deduct the $12,000 payment until year 14. In year 15, the borrower can deduct the $10,161 interest, plus the remaining negative amortization that will reduce the balance to $100,000, or $1,630. After year 15, interest is deducted at the applicable rate in the same manner used on any constant payment mortgage. Exhibit 6A–5 illustrates the relationship among the mortgage payment, interest charges, and loan balance in this example.

After-Tax Effective Cost

We now have the information we need to calculate the tax deductions and after-tax effective cost of the loan. We can create the schedule in Exhibit 6A–6.

We could compute the effective cost for the entire loan term or for repayment of the loan at any time prior to the end of the loan term. For purposes of illustration, we will

---

[4] The alternative is an "accrual basis," where an accrual-based accounting system is used to determine income and expenses.

EXHIBIT 6A–5 **Tax Deductions—Negative Amortization Loan**

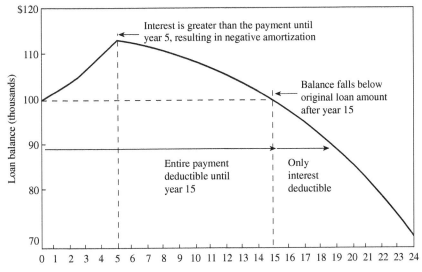

EXHIBIT 6A–6 **After-Tax Payments**

Year	Payment	Interest Deductions	Tax* Savings	After-Tax Payment
1	$ 8,000	$ 8,000	$2,240	$5,760
2	8,000	8,000	2,240	5,760
3	8,000	8,000	2,240	5,760
4	8,000	8,000	2,240	5,760
5	8,000	8,000	2,240	5,760
6	12,000	12,000	3,360	8,640
7	12,000	12,000	3,360	8,640
8	12,000	12,000	3,360	8,640
9	12,000	12,000	3,360	8,640
10	12,000	12,000	3,360	8,640
11	12,000	12,000	3,360	8,640
12	12,000	12,000	3,360	8,640
13	12,000	12,000	3,360	8,640
14	12,000	12,000	3,360	8,640
15	12,000	11,791	3,302	8,699

*28 percent tax rate.

compute the after-tax effective cost for repayment of the loan at the *end* of year 15, when the balance is $99,793. We have the following cash flows:

Year	After-Tax Cash Flow
0	−$100,000
1–5	5,760
6–14	8,640
15	108,492

The *IRR* for the above cash flows is 7.32 percent. Recall that the pretax effective cost was 10 percent; thus, we see that the after-tax effective cost is slightly higher than it would be for a fully amortizing loan, which would have an after-tax effective cost of exactly 7.2 percent. The higher after-tax effective cost for the negative amortization loan occurs because of the *deferral* of interest deductions. During the period of time that the loan balance is increased, less interest is deducted than is charged. The portion of interest that is not tax deductible during those years becomes deductible from the time the loan balance begins to fall until it reaches the original balance.

Conclusion

The tax deductibility of interest payments reduces the after-tax cost of debt. As long as the entire amount of interest charged in a given year is tax deductible that year, there is a very simple relationship between the pretax cost of a loan and the after-tax

cost. The after-tax cost is equal to the pretax cost multiplied by the complement of the borrower's tax rate. That is

$$\text{After-tax cost} = (\text{Pretax cost})(1 - \text{Tax rate})$$

If the entire amount of interest charged is *not* deductible, as was illustrated for negative amortization loans, the effective after-tax cost will be higher than it would be for the fully amortized loan. This results from the delay in receiving the tax deduction. However, even in this situation, multiplying the pretax cost times the complement of the borrower's tax rate provides a close approximation of the after-tax borrowing cost.

If all loans evaluated for tax purposes are treated about the same, taxes do not have to be considered in the analysis since they affect all loans in the same manner and thus "wash out" in the final analysis. Thus, the types of analyses discussed in previous chapters can still be made without explicitly considering taxes. However, tax deductibility of interest is still important when deciding whether to borrow in the first place since it reduces the cost of using debt to finance the purchase of real estate. This is particularly important when determining whether to borrow money for investment property since the after-tax cost of the funds borrowed must be compared with the after-tax return on the property (before considering borrowing money) to see whether it is favorable to use debt to finance the purchase.

Problems

1. A $100,000 loan can be obtained at a 10 percent rate with monthly payments over a 15-year term.

   a. What is the after-tax effective interest rate on the loan, assuming the borrower is in a 30 percent tax bracket and the loan is held only three years? Assume that the benefit of interest deductions for tax purposes occurs at the same time payments are made.

   b. Calculate the after-tax effective cost for the above loan, assuming that 5 points are charged and that the points are tax deductible at the time they are paid.

   c. How does the after-tax cost in part (b) compare with the pretax effective cost of the loan?

2. A mortgage for $100,000 is made with *initial* payments of $500 per month for the first year. The interest rate is 9 percent. After the first year, payments will increase to an amount that makes the loan fully amortizable over the remaining 24 years with constant monthly payments.

   a. Calculate the interest deductions for the loan for the first year.

   b. How much, if any, interest must be deferred until the second year?

   c. How much interest will be deducted in the second year?

Chapter 7

Single-Family Housing: Pricing, Investment, and Tax Considerations

In previous chapters, we covered the nature of real estate assets, property rights, a broad range of fixed and adjustable rate mortgage loans, and the loan underwriting process. In this chapter, we focus on single-family residential housing as an investment. In doing so, we provide an analysis of homeownership as an alternative to renting, the characteristics of supply and demand for housing, pricing, federal income tax treatment for homeowners, and investing in "distressed" properties. All of the topics in this chapter are essential for prospective investors in housing.

Overview

Homeownership has long been considered to be an important goal for many individuals in the United States. In addition to providing shelter, many view homeownership as an important investment vehicle that is important for personal wealth accumulation. Some have come to think of housing as both a consumption good (shelter) and an investment. As our economy has developed, many institutions have evolved to support the growth in the housing industry. These include financial institutions, developers and builders, mortgage lenders, real estate brokers, the property insurance industry, and many other service providers. Indeed, it has been estimated that housing and related services account for as much as 15 percent of total U.S. output. In addition, federal income tax policy has long favored homeownership by providing for the deductibility of mortgage interest and, under certain conditions, excluding capital gains from taxation when properties are sold. These tax incentives stem from the belief by members of Congress that homeownership encourages stronger social networks, better educational achievement rates, and lower crime rates. Consequently, they have continued to provide special tax incentives to encourage homeownership. What follows is a more detailed examination of factors that influence housing as an investment.

House Prices

One element related to considering housing as an investment is the rate of price appreciation (or depreciation) and what drives it. To begin our discussion, it is useful to review a list of important influences on price appreciation, as shown in Exhibit 7–1. Data for all of these concepts are available at the metropolitan statistical area (MSA) level for each metro

EXHIBIT 7–1
Economic Influences
on Housing Demand

Increases In	Direction of Impact on Demand
(1) Population growth	+
(2) Household formations	+
(3) Employment	+
(4) Household income	+
(5) Interest rates	−
(6) Federal income tax rates	−
(7) Cost of renting housing	+

area (see Web site references for the U.S. Census Bureau, U.S. Bureau of Labor Statistics and U.S. Department of Commerce/Bureau of Economic Analysis at the end of this chapter). The right-hand column in Exhibit 7–1 shows the direction of influence, holding all else constant, that each variable should have on housing demand. These influences should be interpreted based on *increases* in each variable. For example, increases in population, households, income, and employment, when considered individually, should affect the demand for housing positively. However, increases in interest rates would have a negative effect. Increases in federal income tax rates would have a negative effect. And if the cost of rental housing increases relative to house prices, demand should increase. Obviously, if the change for any of the variables in the above list were in the opposite direction, the impact on housing would be the reverse of what we have discussed (e.g., a decline in interest rates would have a positive effect on housing).

Finally, when attempting to forecast a trend in the above variables, we see two questions of fundamental importance: (1) What drives each variable? (2) Why do changes in the variables *vary by city?* In recent years, population growth has been greatly affected by immigration. It has been estimated that immigration accounted for as much as one-third of the total increase in population during the 1990s. It is also important to note that the growth rate in households paralleled the population increase. As already indicated, households tend to form as younger individuals leave home for college or employment.

Social trends have also tended to increase the number of households. These include delays in the average age at which marriages are occurring, the increasing number of divorces, and the number of people never marrying. These factors result in greater demand for separate, or individual, housing units. Increases in the average life expectancy have also resulted in households occupying housing units for longer periods of time. This, in turn, has reduced "housing turnover," or the inventory of existing housing units that would otherwise be available to younger household groups.

Other important industry data indicate that: (1) first-time home purchasers tend to be 28–32 years of age, (2) households tend to sell their first home and purchase a different home (upgrade) by age 40, and (3) potential purchases of vacation or second homes usually occur by age 48–52. Retirement homes are usually considered when households reach 60 years of age or older.

Income and Employment

While growth in population and households is a necessary condition for housing demand, employment is also an important driver of housing affordability. Recent data indicate that U.S. employment growth has averaged about 1.76 percent annually during the past 10 years. Sunbelt cities have enjoyed the greatest growth in employment. The share of the population employed also has increased as more women have joined the labor force. Many of these women represent single-parent households, which reinforces the demand for more housing units. Although we will discuss the economic base of cities later in the chapter, we should point out that there are differences in the nature of employment opportunities and the types of businesses that locate in various regions of the United States. The relative desirability of regions that attract businesses (1) affects the ability of households to earn income that they use to acquire housing and (2) also affects house prices. An important item to remember is that the quality and nature of employment and the salaries earned by the labor force also vary by metro area. So, while employment growth is important, the quality of jobs and the wages and salaries earned in these occupations are also important. There is a very strong association between house price appreciation and income/employment growth. Therefore, when viewing housing as an investment, we must remember that, for cities under consideration, basic research concerning these trends is very important.

Interest Rates

Many factors determine interest rates. The more important factors include the supply and demand for loanable funds as the economy expands and contracts and Federal Reserve policy in the course of its management of the monetary system. The Federal Reserve generally has a significant effect on interest rates, which in turn affects housing demand. Because real estate has a "high debt capacity" and many loans are made as a large percentage of property value, monthly payments may rise or fall substantially, depending on changes in interest rates. The effects of interest rate changes also tend to spill over into many areas of the housing industry. These areas include construction, land development, financing, brokerage, inspections, appraisals, and other housing-related service businesses. Because of these far-reaching influences, housing is a very important sector of the economy.

As indicated in Exhibit 7–1, *holding all else constant, increases* in interest rates tend to have a *negative* influence on housing demand. This relationship is somewhat intuitive because as interest rates increase, this is analogous to raising the cost on borrowed capital, thereby raising the cost of financing homeownership. Conversely, as interest rates *fall,* the effects on housing demand tend to be *positive.*

While the effects of interest rates on demand are relatively clear, the *magnitude* of the impact has become more complex to understand in recent years because of a greater variety of mortgage loan options. As discussed in Chapters 4 and 5, these options are no longer limited to fixed interest rate mortgages (FRMs). Adjustable rate mortgage (ARM) loans and many other types of loans now provide for different rates, loan amortization periods, and other features. In addition, some of the other terms of lending, such as financing fees, prepayment options, and the rigor with which lenders apply underwriting standards, tend to reinforce the direction of mortgage interest rates. For example, during periods of appreciating house prices and/or low interest rates, lenders may tend to be more flexible on such things as credit scores when underwriting. This tends to amplify the effect that interest rates otherwise may have on housing demand.

Renting versus Owning

Another important consideration when analyzing the demand for homeownership investment is the cost of renting. If individuals find that renting is more cost-effective than owning, homeownership may not be a good investment. What follows is a comparative analysis of the relative costs of owning versus renting the *same residence.* The goal of this exercise is to compile all cash flows associated with each form of occupancy, and then calculate the rate of return that will be earned on the funds used to make an equity investment (down payment) if the property is purchased. Alternatively, it is this rate of return that an investor would have to earn on the "down payment" saved if renting is chosen, to make renting the financial equivalent of owning.

The framework for making a comparison between renting and owning is presented in the example summarized in Exhibit 7–2. In this example, we have a property that could be

www.mhhe.com/bf15e

EXHIBIT 7–2 **Rent versus Own Analysis of a Personal Residence**

1. Property Information

		Loan Information	
Purchase price	$150,000	Loan-to-value ratio	80.00%
Initial rent	$12,000	Loan amount	$120,000
Rental growth rate	2.00%	Interest rate	7.00%
Property growth rate	2.00%	Loan term	30 years
Insurance	$500.00	Payments	12 per year
Maintenance	$500.00	Annual debt service (payment)	$9,580
Expense growth	2.00%	Annual loan constant	7.98%
Marginal tax rate	28.00%	Equity investment/down payment	$30,000
Property tax as % of value	1.50%	Selling expenses	7.00%

2. Annual Loan Schedule

End of year	0	1	2	3	4	5
Mo. Payments · 12		$ 9,580	$ 9,580	$ 9,580	$ 9,580	$ 9,580
Balance		118,781	117,474	116,072	114,569	112,958
Interest (year)		8,361	8,273	8,179	8,077	7,969
Amortization (year)		1,219	1,307	1,402	1,503	1,612

3. Property Data

	0	1	2	3	4	5
Property value	$150,000	$153,000	$156,060	$159,181	$166,365	$165,612
Rents		12,000	12,240	12,485	12,734	12,989

rented for $12,000 per year ($1,000 per month) or *purchased* for $150,000 with $30,000 down and financed with a fully amortizing mortgage loan of $120,000 at 7 percent interest for 30 years. Other costs associated with *owning* include maintenance, insurance, and property taxes. In our example, these expenses would not have to be paid if renting is chosen. All other expenses would have to be paid regardless of whether the property is owned or rented, such as utilities, and so on. Because they offset, they do not have to be included in our analysis. Other *assumptions* include (1) a federal income tax rate of 28 percent, (2) escalation in expenses, rents, and property value at 2 percent per year, and (3) a five-year period of analysis, at the end of which, the property would be sold (if owned). Selling expenses of 7 percent would have to be paid at that time.

Cash flows associated with our analysis are summarized annually for convenience and presented in Exhibit 7–3. Note that for the ownership alternative, cash flows must be developed both before and after taxes because, as indicated, owners of residential property are provided with special federal income tax treatment (see summary of tax provisions in Exhibit 7–4). This treatment is not available to renters; therefore, cash outflows for renters are the same on a before- and after-tax basis (see part C). Looking to Exhibit 7–3, note that in panel A, we have summarized *before-tax* cash outflows associated with owning. These total $12,830 during year 1. Included in these cash outflows are constant monthly mortgage payments of $798.33 · (12) or $9,580 each year. The tax treatment shown in part B includes allowable deductions for property taxes and mortgage interest. These deductions *reduce* the owner's federal income tax[1] payments and therefore reduce net outflows associated with homeownership. These deductions reduce taxes at a rate of 28 percent, or by a total of $2,971 in year 1. Interest deductions decline to $7,969 in year 5 because

---

[1] This assumes that the homeowner itemizes for tax purposes.

EXHIBIT 7–3   **Cash Flow Analysis—Rent versus Own Analysis of a Personal Residence**

	Year 1	Year 2	Year 3	Year 4	Year 5
A. Before-tax cash flows—owner:					
(1) Property taxes	$ 2,250	$ 2,295	$ 2,341	$ 2,388	$ 2,435
(2) Insurance	500	510	520	530	540
(3) Maintenance	500	510	520	530	540
(4) Mortgage payments (P&I)	9,580	9,580	9,580	9,580	9,580
(5) Cash outflows before taxes	$ 12,830	$ 12,895	$ 12,961	$ 13,028	$ 13,095
B. Tax deductions—owner:					
(1) Property taxes	$ 2,250	$ 2,295	$ 2,341	$ 2,388	$ 2,435
(2) Interest	8,361	8,273	8,179	8,077	7,969
(3) Total deductions	10,611	10,568	10,520	10,465	10,404
(4) Tax savings @ 28%	$ 2,971	$ 2,959	$ 2,945	$ 2,930	$ 2,913
C. Renter status:					
(1) Rents	$ 12,000	$ 12,240	$ 12,485	$ 12,734	$ 12,989
D. Net cash flows—owning:					
(1) Before-tax outlays (A.5)	$ (12,830)	$ (12,895)	$ (12,961)	$ (13,028)	$ (13,095)
(2) Tax savings (B.4)	2,971	2,959	2,945	2,930	2,913
(3) After-tax cash flows	(9,859)	(9,936)	(10,016)	(10,190)	(10,182)
(4) Rent saved (C.1)	$ 12,000	$ 12,240	$ 12,485	$ 12,734	$ 12,989
(5) After-tax cash flows—owning	$ 2,141	$ 2,304	$ 2,469	$ 2,635	$ 2,807
E. Before-tax cash flow—for sales occurring in years 1–5:					
(1) Property value	$153,000	$156,060	$159,181	$162,365	$165,612
(2) Less: Selling expenses	10,710	10,920	11,143	11,366	11,593
(3) Less: Mortgage payoff	118,781	117,474	116,072	114,569	112,958
(4) Before-tax cash flow sale	$ 23,509	$ 27,666	$ 31,966	$ 36,430	$ 41,061
F. After-tax cash flow—for sales occurring in years 1–5:					
(1) Property value	$153,000	$156,060	$159,181	$162,365	$165,612
(2) Less: Selling expenses	10,710	10,920	11,143	11,366	11,593
(3) Less: Basis	150,000	150,000	150,000	150,000	150,000
(4) Gain on sale	(7,710)	(4,860)	(1,962)	999	4,019
(5) Less: Exclusion	—	—	—	999	4,019
(6) Tax	0	0	0	0	0
(7) After-tax cash flow (E.4 − F.6)	$ 23,509	$ 27,666	$ 31,966	$ 36,430	$ 41,061
G. After-tax IRR on equity ($30,000) if sold:					
(1) ATIRR (D.5 + F.7)	− 14.50%	3.57%	9.63%	12.34%	13.71%

interest on the loan declines over time. The net annual after-tax cash outflows if owning is chosen are summarized in part D and are $12,830 (from part A) *less* $2,971 in *tax savings* (from part B), resulting in a net outflow of $9,859. If the property is owned, this also means that rent of $12,000 *does not have to be paid.* To complete the annual outflow in our analysis, we must consider rent savings if owning is chosen. This amounts to $12,000 the first year and when included in the analysis produces a net after-tax savings from

EXHIBIT 7–4 **Summary of Tax Provisions Important to Residential Housing**

I. Tax Treatment of Personal and Qualified Residences*

    A. *Interest Deductions and Qualified Residences.* Interest is deductible on "qualified residences." A taxpayer's qualified residences are a personal residence and *one* other residence. The second residence does not have to be used by the taxpayer during the taxable year to be a qualified residence if it is not rented during the year. If it is rented for part of a year, a specified amount of personal use is required (see II.A, below). Interest on three or more homes is not deductible, unless the home is a business or investment property not used personally by the taxpayer. Under certain conditions, mobile homes, boats, trailers, time-shares, and stock in a cooperative housing corporation may be a qualified residence.

    B. *Maximum Interest Deductions.* Interest on two types of home mortgage debt is deductible.

        (1) Interest is deductible on "acquisition debt," which is *secured debt* used to purchase, build, or substantially improve a qualified residence. Interest on acquisition debt is deductible as long as the debt does not exceed the cost of the residence and its improvements. The maximum amount of indebtedness upon which interest is calculated may not exceed $1,000,000 for couples filing jointly.

        (2) Interest is also deductible on "home equity debt." For couples filing jointly, the amount of indebtedness upon which interest is based can be up to the lesser of $100,000 or the amount of equity in the residence. Home equity debt must be secured by a qualified residence.

    C. *Points on Mortgage Loans.* The term *points* is used to describe certain charges paid, or treated as paid, by a borrower to obtain a home mortgage. Points may also be called loan origination fees, loan charges, loan discounts, or discount points. Points can be deducted in the year paid if *all* of the following tests are met:

        (1) The loan is secured by a qualified residence.

        (2) The funds you provided at or before closing, plus any points paid by the seller, were at least as much as the points charged.

        (3) If the loan was used to buy or build a home (qualified residence).

        (4) The points were computed as a percentage of the principal amount of the mortgage.

        (5) The amount is clearly shown on the settlement statement as points charged for the mortgage. The points may be shown as paid from either your funds or the seller's funds.

    If the above tests are *not* met, points must be deducted over the life of the loan.

    D. *Real Estate Taxes.* Property taxes must be a direct tax on interests in real property. The tax is deductible in the year paid only by the owner of the property upon which the tax was imposed and paid. Generally, prepaid real estate tax can be deducted in the year of the prepayment.

    E. *Capital Gain Exclusions.* For sales of a personal residence after 5/6/97, a homeowner may exclude from income $250,000 of gain, and a married couple may exclude up to $500,000 of gain realized on the sale.

        (1) Individual must have owned and used the home as a principal residence for at least two of the five years prior to the sale (the two years do not have to be consecutive).

        (2) Exclusion applies to only *one* sale every *two* years.

II. Tax Treatment of Second Residences

    A. *Interest Deductions.* All rules relating to personal residence interest deductions apply.

    B. *Points.* Points paid on loans secured by a second home are amortized and deducted over the life of the loan.

    C. *Sale of Second Residence:* Capital Gains Exclusion. Generally only one home (either the primary or secondary) that is used for a majority of the time during the year will be considered the principal residence and will qualify for the exclusion. Second homes do not qualify for the exclusion.

III. Tax Treatment of Second or Vacation Homes

    A. If the property is not rented and is owned for personal use only, then deductions are determined as though it is a non-primary, qualified residence (see: I.A above).

    B. If the property is owned for personal use and rented for 14 days or less per year, no rents or expenses must be reported.

    C. If the property is owned for *both* personal use and rented, all rental income must be reported and all expenses can be deducted. Personal use cannot exceed 14 days or 10 percent of the number of days for which it was rented (whichever is greater).

    D. If the property is owned for both personal use and rented, and the number of days of personal use exceeds 14 days or 10 percent of the number of days for which it was rented, then all rental income must be reported and deductions are limited to the amount of rental income. Any expenses in excess of rental income may be carried forward to offset income earned in future years.

---

* Generally based on Internal Revenue Code **P** 163(h)(4) and **P** 1.163-10T. The reader should not rely on this general discussion when making investments and/or tax elections. This discussion may not be complete, and the Internal Revenue Code is modified frequently.

homeownership of $2,141, as shown in part D. Note that savings in year 2 are $2,304 and so on. This analysis must be carried out for each year to assess (1) the net effects of increasing nondeductible expenses such as maintenance and insurance, (2) increasing rents, (3) increasing deductible expenses such as property taxes, and (4) declining deductible expenses such as the interest portion of payments on the mortgage loan.

Finally, we must consider the proceeds from sale of the property. We calculate this for each year in sections E and F of Exhibit 7–3. The before-tax cash flow in section E is simply the sale price, less selling expenses and the mortgage loan balance. After-tax cash flows must include any taxable gains on sale. The latter is based on the selling price, less selling expenses, less the tax basis for the residence which in this case is the original purchase price.[2] Should a sale occur, the tax consequences are shown to be zero in each of the first three years because the property appreciation rate is not sufficient to offset the selling expenses. Therefore, if the property is sold, the borrower would not recover the initial acquisition price and no taxable gain or deductible loss would result. It should be noted that, beginning in year 4, a $999 gain from sale results, as does a $4,019 gain in year 5. However, because of the capital gains exclusions that apply to residential real estate (see Exhibit 7–4), these capital gains are not taxable. The annual after-tax cash flows up to the year of sale and the cash flows produced from sale are combined, and internal rates of return are calculated and presented in section G of Exhibit 7–3. Note that if the property was sold at the end of year 1, the after-tax *IRR* on the $30,000 investment would be negative. This means that if the property is expected to be sold after only one year, renting may be the wiser choice. However, returns from ownership improve in years 2 through 5, as the annual after-tax cash flows and the property value increase.[3] The *IRR*s during those years indicate that in order to justify renting, an investor would have to earn from 3.5 percent to 13.7 percent on an after-tax basis on *other investments* equal in risk with the $30,000 equity saved to make renting equivalent to owning.

Other Considerations

After we summarize the cash flows associated with owning and renting, a number of additional questions arise. For instance, our example assumes a sale at the end of year 5. Inasmuch as people must have shelter, what should be done with the proceeds from sale after year 5? Will the investor choose to own or rent from the end of year 5 into the future? What if the owner chooses not to sell after year 5, but continues to own for the indefinite future—how should this possibility be analyzed? One guide that may help to answer these questions would be to first consider the likelihood that a sale may occur in a relatively short period of time. Generally, if frequent sales are likely to occur because of employment changes/relocation, renting should tend to become more desirable *unless* house appreciation rates and rents are increasing at significant rates in the area where the residence is located. In the latter case, when a sale occurs, a borrower would be more likely to recover selling expenses and save increasing rents that would otherwise have to be paid. On the other hand, if house prices are expected to remain flat or decline, a short period of occupancy would tend to make renting more favorable. Alternatively, other combinations that could make renting more favorable than owning would include (1) expected rents would have to decline, or (2) non-tax-deductible housing expenses (maintenance, insurance, etc.) would have to be expected to increase dramatically, or (3) the initial interest rate available on mortgage loans would have to be much higher than the 7 percent shown in our example.

---

[2] If any improvements or remodeling expenses have been incurred, these should be added to the original purchase price to establish the tax basis for the residence in the year of sale. "Fixing up" expenses immediately prior to sale may also be included.

[3] To calculate the after-tax *IRR* in year 2, one must find the interest rate (discount rate) that makes the present value of $2,141 in year 1 and $2,304 plus $27,666 at the end of year 2 equal to the equity outlay of $30,000.

As to periods beyond five years, it is apparent from Exhibit 7–3 that net benefits from homeownership continue to increase over time. While this pattern cannot be expected to continue with certainty, an examination of the importance of appreciation in house prices and equity investment may be helpful.

If one examines the cash flow analysis again in Exhibit 7–3, it becomes clear that advantages to homeownership are substantial because of house appreciation rates (E.1 and F.1) and the **capital gains exclusion.**

The Rent versus Own Decision—Other Issues

What has been presented above is a purely financial analysis of owning or renting the same place of residence. In the example, it was apparent that ownership was generally the favored choice, particularly if the property was to be owned and occupied for three years or more. One interesting question that may occur to the reader is: "Is there a level of *rent* at which benefits from homeowning are eliminated?" That is, at what level of rent would you be indifferent between renting and owning? This would be a level of rent that results in an after-tax *IRR* from owning that is just sufficient to compensate for capital invested as a down payment. We will assume that this is 5 percent. This is about the same as the after-tax cost of the loan [$7\% \times (1 - .28) = 5\%$ rounded].

We *recalculate* the net cash flows in Exhibit 7–3 by changing rent saved (part C) to $9,155 for the first year, which changes results in part D(4) and produces the following after-tax *IRR*s on the $30,000 equity investment:

Revised annual cash flows and after-tax *IRR* recalculation:

Year	1	2	3	4	5
After-tax *IRR*	−23.98%	−6.19%	.19%	3.27%	5.00%

From this analysis, it is apparent that if the same residence could be rented for $9,155 per year, then based on financial considerations only, the investor would be *indifferent* as to whether the property is owned or rented for five years. It could also be said that almost no advantage exists between the purely financial elements of owning and renting. The rent of $9,155 could be found by trial and error or using "Goal Seek" in Excel.

Historical Trends

Based on historical trends in the United States, approximately 67 percent of all residential housing is owned and 33 percent is rented. This suggests that homeownership is both strongly preferred and may be a good investment. However, there are other issues to consider. Renting could be favored in spite of financial returns on equity in residential ownership for a number of reasons. These include:

1. Need for flexibility because of frequent relocation of employment, family, or other reasons.
2. Lack of funds for a down payment.
3. Credit quality of the resident.
4. No desire to bear the risk of ownership and volatility in house prices.
5. A desire to shift maintenance, security, and management to others.
6. A desire to avoid volatility, or risk of loss because of "bubbles," in house prices. This may occur when house prices rise relative to rents to such an extent that the prospect of further appreciation in prices becomes problematic. In some housing markets affected by sharp increases in employment tied to higher cyclical industries, should contraction in employment occur in those industries, volatility in house prices may be affected.

To the extent that any or all of the above considerations are important to residents, they may be willing to forgo returns available from homeowning and pay an implicit premium or opportunity cost to maintain renter status. For this and other reasons, there are many investors and developers who develop, own, and manage *rental housing units.* We will deal with that type of real estate investment in a later chapter.

Analyzing Expected House Prices

There are many other facets of the housing market that are important when considering a purchase. When investing in housing, investors find it useful to measure the **expected rate of appreciation in house prices (EAHP).** This is calculated as:

$$\frac{HP_1 - HP_0}{HP_0} = EAHP\%$$

where HP_0 is the house price in year zero and HP_1 is the expected price at the end of year one. To illustrate, if $HP_0 = \$100,000$ and $HP_1 = \$103,000$, then the expected appreciation in house prices for one year is 3 percent, shown as:

$$\frac{\$103,000 - \$100,000}{\$100,000} = 3\%$$

To extend this analysis and provide more perspective for investors, a useful exercise is to consider the **expected appreciation rate on home equity (EAHE).** This concept can be calculated as follows:

$$\frac{HP_1 - HP_0}{HP_0(1 - L/V)} = EAHE\%$$

defining L/V as the **loan-to-value ratio.** Assuming a 3 percent house appreciation rate and an 80 percent loan-to-value ratio, the annual *equity* appreciation rate expected for a one-year period would be:

$$\frac{\$103,000 - \$100,000}{\$100,000 \,(.2)} = EAHE$$

$$\frac{\$3,000}{\$20,000} = 15.0\%$$

Alternatively, the expected average annual appreciation in home *equity* (EAHE) can be approximated from the average house price appreciation rate (EAHP) of 3 percent by multiplying it by the ratio of house price to equity (*HP/E*), which is $100\% \div 20\%$, or 5.0. Using this formulation, we have:

$$EAHP(HP/E) = EAHE$$

$$3\% \cdot 5 = 15.0\%$$

These calculations show that a 3 percent annual average rate of appreciation in house price results in a 15 percent appreciation rate on equity when 80 percent financing is used. This example can be thought of as a method of providing investors with an estimate of **unrealized equity gains,** which the owner has the option of realizing by: (1) selling the residence (although proceeds may be subject to federal income taxes—see Exhibit 7–4) or (2) refinancing, in which case there may be no federal income taxes to pay because refinancing is not a "taxable event." This example also clearly illustrates why investing in housing financed with mortgage loans has provided an extremely powerful financial incentive for households, particularly those interested in long-term wealth accumulation. Consider the research done by economists on the so-called "**wealth effect.**" This is the effect that expected appreciation in assets, including home equity, may have on consumer spending on other goods and services in the economy. This comes about as consumers feel more financially secure about their future economic well-being, because their stocks, bonds, and houses are rising in value. Where prices are declining, consumer spending also may decline as a result of a "reverse wealth effect."

Unrealized Annual Rates of Appreciation on Equity

The above calculations provide a good approximation in situations where rate of house appreciation is expected to be a constant or when a rough estimate is adequate for the reader. In cases where the rate of house price appreciation is expected to be different each year, or should a more exact calculation be needed, the above calculation may be modified as shown in the following example for a $100,000 property financed with an 80 percent loan.

End of Year	House Price	Appreciation Rate	Equity	Calculation	Annual EAHE
0	$100,000	—	$20,000	—	—
1	103,000	3%	23,000	3,000 ÷ 20,000	15.0%
2	105,060	2%	25,060	2,060 ÷ 23,000	9.0%
3	109,262	4%	29,262	4.202 ÷ 25,060	16.8%

Solution:

$n = 3$
$PV = -20,000$
$FV = 29,262$
$PMT = 0$
Solve for i = 13.55%

Function:

$i\,(n, PV, FV, PMT)$

As shown in the above example, average expected appreciation in home equity for the three-year time period is equivalent to an annual compounded rate of interest equal to 13.55 percent. See Concept Box 7.1, which contains very important data sources that are used frequently when forecasting house prices.

Regional Economic Influences on Property Values

An important concept in real estate analysis is the fact that the house prices are highly *dependent* on the regional or geographic area in which they are located. The demand for properties in local markets is highly influenced by the nature of the industries, businesses, and so on, that are attracted to a region. Business activity and its growth determine employment and income in a region, which influence the demand for all property types. In short, when a real estate analysis is undertaken, the *regional economic drivers* must be identified and a judgment must be made about whether these drivers will provide a source of growth or decline in a region. To determine the latter, trends must be established for the future global outlook for growth in those industries (e.g., computer technology, communication technology, medical-pharmaceutical, and tourism/recreation).

HOUSING STATISTICS

1. National Association of Realtors (NAR): www.realtor.org

A. Median House Prices

Essentially, prices on all *existing* housing units sold during each month (single-family, condominium, co-ops) are ranked from high to low. The midpoint, or median sale price, of all sales throughout the United States is selected and reported. A quarterly series also is reported by most metropolitan areas (MSA = metropolitan statistical area, as defined by OMB-2004).

Issues: When calculating appreciation rates based on median prices selected for specific time periods, some observers have questioned the *comparability* of housing units over different time periods. In addition to price changes, house size, lot size, and location of housing units also are believed to change over time. This makes the interpretation of price changes problematic, thereby limiting the usefulness of the appreciation data.

B. Pending Home Sales

This is an indicator of sales volume that is compiled *monthly* based on the number of signed contracts to purchase homes. Given that two to three months are required to obtain loan commitments and close the title, this "pre-final sale" series is used as a *leading indicator* for analysis of the housing industry. Data are available only for the United States and four major census regions.

C. Housing Affordability Index (HAI)

The HAI is a monthly series consisting of (1) *median family income* and (2) *median qualifying income* (income needed to make mortgage and housing expense payments on a median price house with a 20 percent down payment). The ratio of median family income to median qualifying income is then calculated and used as an indicator of the extent to which a housing purchase is affordable for median income families.

2. Federal Housing Finance Agency: www.fhfa.gov

A. Purchase-Only House Price Index (HPI)

The Federal Housing Finance Agency publishes the Purchase-Only HPI, which is a quarterly average series based on prices obtained from repeat, "purchase-only" transactions for the *same properties* over time for all MSAs in the United States An average for the United States also is calculated by weighting these prices by a population weighted index as compiled by the U.S. Census Bureau. By focusing on repeat sales of the same houses over time, this index attempts to maintain comparability of housing characteristics based on size, age, and so on.

B. All Transactions House Price Index (HPI)

In addition to data used to compile the quarterly Purchase-Only HPI, appraisal data from refinancing are included in this "All Transactions" HPI.

Issues: Both data sources are obtained from FHLMC-FNMA loan files. These files are based on *conforming loans*, or loans that conform to underwriting standards for these agencies. Because maximum loan limits are set by these agencies, mortgages made for amounts above those maximum loan limits are not included in either database. Therefore, house prices used to compile both indexes are useful only when analyzing transactions in the "conforming" segment of the housing market.

3. S&P Case-Shiller® Index: www.homeprice.standardandpoors.com

The S&P Case-Shiller® Index is a monthly house price index based on data obtained from repeat sales of the same housing units in 20 MSAs. A U.S. national home price index is also calculated. When computing price changes, a statistical technique is employed to use only paired sales of the same housing units over time. Houses are removed from the sample if any improvements, remodeling, or the like have been undertaken between sale dates. This methodology is used in an attempt to capture price changes on housing units with the same characteristics over time.

Issues: Data are a three-month moving average, published monthly and are available for up to 20 MSAs only.

Why do certain kinds of economic activity tend to "cluster" more in some regions and urban areas than others? We do not intend to provide an extensive discussion of the phenomena here as there have been volumes written on this subject by many regional economists. However, we do believe that an understanding of the underpinnings of this economic behavior is critical when thinking about the relative attractiveness of real estate investments. As we will stress in this chapter and in others, making an investment in a specific real estate asset cannot be separated completely from *making an investment in an economic region* because the real estate is permanently located in that region. Therefore, the need to know the forces that drive economic growth in an area is essential to the success of an investment.

Analogy with the Law of Comparative Advantage

This concept, stated very simply, says that some geographic regions have a comparative advantage over other regions in that certain goods/services can be produced more efficiently and profitably in that region than in other regions. This advantage may exist because of (1) natural advantages (e.g., seaport, minerals, low-cost energy, and beaches), (2) employee characteristics such as a highly trained, educated workforce (e.g., location of universities, workforce training in technical industries), and/or (3) proximity to many major consumer markets (e.g., transportation hub). Regional examples would include high-tech research and development (California, Seattle, Boston), oil and gas exploration (Houston), communication and computer assembly (Austin, San Diego), medical technology/clinics (Minnesota, Boston), and production of entertainment (Los Angeles). These industries tend to locate in certain geographic areas because land, labor, and capital can be combined cost-effectively or revenues can be enhanced by locating in those regions. This simple concept is very useful in real estate investing because when researching markets for real estate investment opportunities, those markets having industries with the highest likelihood of future growth will have a positive effect on house prices.

Identifying Regional Economic "Drivers" or Base Industries

One obvious way to identify the drivers of economic growth in an area is to identify **base,** or **driver, industries,** which are those businesses producing the greatest *profits.* Unfortunately, data pertaining to profits is difficult to collect on a regional basis because (1) much of it is private information and (2) for publicly owned firms, multiple operating divisions may make profits by region very difficult to break down. As a result, many analysts rely on *employment data* that are collected by the U.S. Department of Labor and by various agencies in all 50 states. The underlying logic for using employment data for real estate investment research is that expanding businesses will have expanding needs for labor. Identifying the number of those industries with a comparative advantage in that region will help to estimate the number of employees in these industries and, in turn, the number of housing units needed. While employment data are generally thought to be the best tool available for analysis, this method is not ideal because labor may not always be added in direct proportion to increases in revenues or the output of goods and services produced by a company. Furthermore, the method may tend to underestimate the importance of less labor-intensive businesses in a region that may be very profitable and pay high wages to fewer employees.

Economic Base Analysis—Location Quotients

One widely accepted approach in economic analysis for identifying driver industries in a region—the **economic base**—is to calculate what are referred to as **location quotients.** This is done very simply by using the following relationship:

$$\frac{\left(\dfrac{RE_j}{RE_{TOT}}\right)}{\left(\dfrac{USE_j}{USE_{TOT}}\right)} > 1.0?$$

Terms in this relationship are as follows:

RE = Regional employment

USE = U.S. employment

j = Industry classification

TOT = Total

For example, if we let j represent the computer assembly industrial classification, then this ratio will tell us if the proportion of regional employment (RE) in the computer assembly business (j) as a percentage of total employment in that region (RE_{TOT}) is greater or less than the proportion of those employed in industry j throughout the United States as a percentage of the total employment throughout the country. If this ratio is *greater* than 1.0, then industry j would be identified as a *base* or *driver industry* for a region because it employs a greater-than-proportionate amount of workers in that industry than is the case for the United States as a whole. Obviously, if the ratio is *less* than 1.0, then that industry would not be a base industry. Industry classifications with ratios less than 1.0 are usually referred to as *supporting industries.* Examples of the latter could be accounting firms, advertising firms, and so on. These supporting businesses are also important for real estate investment, particularly for retail establishments, personnel services, and similar firms, all of which must also lease operating space in properties.

Data classifications for various industries (designated above as *j*) have been developed and published by the U.S. Office of Management and Budget and are used by the U.S. Department of Labor. This department collects and categorizes data on all employees in the United States. Depending on the level of detail desired, all employment data are broken into several industry classifications. These classifications are referred to as North American Industry Classification System, or NAICS. The data are collected for over 300 metropolitan areas.

Employment Multipliers

This aspect of economic base analysis is conducted to determine how *total employment* in a region is affected by changes in *base employment.* After a complete analysis is conducted for every employment classification (*j*) in a region and all base employment has been identified with location quotients and totaled, employment in the remaining categories is totaled. Then, the ratio of *total* to *basic* employment is calculated. If, for example, total employment in a metropolitan area equals 1,000,000 and base employment or employment in classifications with a location quotient >1.0 totals 400,000, supporting employment would be 600,000. In this case, the total-employment to basic-employment multiplier would be 1,000,000 ÷ 400,000, or 2.5. Therefore, if a forecast called for an increase of 40,000 jobs in *all basic* employment categories, it may be the case that total employment would increase by 40,000 × 2.5, or 100,000, of which 60,000 would be supporting employment. Obviously, a real estate investor would like to know how many of the 100,000 expected new jobs would likely result in the construction of new houses, apartments, and office and warehouse space to provide for these workers. An examination of population data would shed light on the expected age distribution and sizes of households. It should be stressed that there can be instances where employment in base industries in a metropolitan area is expected to *decline.* In these instances, total employment rates would be expected to decline by an amount greater than declines in base industry employment.

This method of analysis is not without its shortcomings. Furthermore, this analysis usually provides a snapshot of employment at a point in time. In order to better understand employment relationships, economic base analysis should be done at various points in time so as to identify shifts and trends in an area's employment base.

Housing Supply: An Overview

When trying to complete the analysis of housing as an investment, we must also consider the supply side of the market. In general, the supply of housing is determined by the relative cost of land, labor, and capital (materials). Two barometers of housing activity that are monitored by investors are housing starts and sales of existing homes. Two observations should be made concerning these data. One is that the supply of new single-family housing and sales volumes for existing units are price elastic and highly volatile. The other is that both of the latter relationships are highly influenced by interest rates. Although we include interest rates in our discussion of housing supply, it is also very important on the demand side of the market, as it affects the financing cost that a household must pay from incomes earned primarily from employment.

Other influences on supply costs on a *more local level* include the existence of restrictions such as zoning, building codes, environmental factors, and the physical differences in land terrain and how these vary between locations. These latter influences have a significant impact on costs that builders incur when producing housing. Many of these influences are thought to result in a restriction on supply (new construction), which results in higher house prices. Some MSAs (such as San Francisco, Boston, and others) restrict development density by requiring adherence to very rigid building codes, requiring open space, assessing impact fees, and so on, all of which affect housing availability. Over the long run, this may cause house price appreciation and construction costs to be greater than in other metro areas. Any investor in the housing market must assess these supply-side factors when making housing choices. See Concept Box 7.2, which describes very important data sources that may be used to assess the supply of new housing units as well as sales and inventory.

1. National Association of Home Builders (NAHB): www.nahb.org

    A. A subscription-based data source that provides data for:

- Housing starts (single family and multifamily)
- New home sales
- New home sales price (average, median)

2. U.S. Department of Commerce/U.S. Census Bureau: www.census.gov

    A. Housing statistics published *monthly,* including:

- Housing construction permits
- Construction starts
- Housing units under construction
- Housing units completed

    B. Quarterly survey of housing vacancies

- 75 Metro areas

Comment: Many analysts make estimates of current housing supply conditions in local housing markets from data on (1) construction permits *approved*, (2) the number of permits actually *started*, (3) units *under construction*, and (4) *completions*.

After the timing in all stages of production and new home sales has been taken into account, the inventory of houses available for sale can be estimated. From these data, judgments can be made as to whether or not an excess supply condition may exist, how long any excess supply may persist, and implications for future house prices.

Submarkets: Neighborhoods/Municipalities

While the above discussion is important when trying to differentiate among MSAs, a number of other issues are important when trying to select housing among submarkets/municipalities *within* MSAs. A list of important considerations that should be analyzed when making such a selection is contained in Exhibit 7–5. Many of these attributes include services and goods that *must also be acquired* when the *housing investment is made.* Many of these attributes are referred to as **public goods** that are acquired along with housing. These factors have been studied over the years and deemed to be important in driving house price appreciation in different submarkets.

Capitalization Effects: Price Premiums

Many of the attributes in Exhibit 7–5 have been deemed important in explaining differences in house prices among neighborhoods and jurisdictions. However, it is difficult to generalize the extent (dollar amount) to which each factor affects price. There is a concept in the urban economics literature, called the **capitalization effect,** that relates to the quality of the public services that individuals receive *relative to the taxes* (usually property tax and fees) that are paid for these services when they choose to purchase housing in a particular neighborhood or municipality. To the extent that residents perceive that services received have a value greater than the taxes and fees paid for them, *net benefits* may exist. These net benefits are reflected or capitalized in house prices (land prices) because households are willing to pay for these net benefits which can only be obtained by purchasing housing in the location where the benefits are present. For example, if two otherwise identical houses are located in two different neighborhoods

EXHIBIT 7–5   **Public Goods and Other Attributes Affecting House Prices in Different Submarkets and Neighborhoods within Metropolitan Areas**

Description	Measurements/Indicators
1. Quality of school districts	SAT scores, percentage of HS graduates that go to college, library facilities
2. Crime rates/police/fire	Data relative to various crime categories per 1000 residents, response times
3. Parks/recreation	Relative to size of population, quality of programs
4. Housing market indicators	Number of listings, time on market prior to sale, percentage of asking price achieved by submarket
5. Quality of utilities	Cost and source of water, electric, gas, sewer. Any assessments related to each
6. Size of submarket	Population, percentage of nearby land area available for future development, and zoning related to such areas
7. Health care facilities	Number of physicians and beds per thousand residents
8. Building codes/zoning	Restrictions, regulation of construction quality, minimum lot sizes
9. Insurance rates	Premiums by location
10. Noise levels	Proximity to, and decibel levels of (airports, freeways, etc.)
11. Environmental	Open spaces, pollution, water, air, and so on
12. Transportation/access	Distance and travel time to major employment centers, airports

Web App

The Federal Home Loan Mortgage Corporation (Freddie Mac) and the Federal Housing Finance Agency publish house price indexes. These are available at **www.freddiemac.com/finance/cmhpi** and **www.fhfa.gov/default.aspx?page=14,** respectively. These indexes provide a measure of typical price inflation for houses within the United States. Values are calculated nationally, for each state, and for major MSAs.

Using one of these price indexes, select one of the MSAs and analyze the growth rate in home prices for the MSA versus the rest of the state and for the nation over the past five years. Are homes in the MSA growing at a slower or faster rate than the rest of the state and nation? If you were doing a rent-versus-own analysis as discussed in this chapter, what growth rate would you assume for home prices in the selected MSA?

or municipalities and one sells for a higher price, the question is, "Which combination of the above influences caused the buyer to pay a higher price?" Was it the net benefits from educational quality or some other public good? When housing is viewed this way, it becomes clear that many public good consumption choices are being made *simultaneously* with the housing decision.

Finally, there has also been discussion regarding the **optimal size of cities** or of jurisdictions. This concept has to do with the relationship between the size (population and geographic area) of separate political jurisdictions (townships, cities, etc.) and how cost-effectively they provide services such as education, police protection, and the like. Some argue that there may be cost savings in providing public services as cities (politically defined) get larger and annex surrounding areas. However, there may be a *limit* on size (in terms of both area and/or population) such that when this size is exceeded, (1) costs begin to rise relative to the quality of services delivered or (2) the quality of services begins to deteriorate. Thus, communities in which there exists a balance between size, efficiency, and scale of operations may be producing public services very cost-effectively. This efficiency may be reflected in lower property taxes for the flow of services being produced, which may, in turn, be capitalized in the prices of properties in such jurisdictions.

Pricing Property in Specific Submarkets/Locations

At some point in the acquisition process, after the prospective homebuyers have evaluated the regional drivers affecting house price appreciation, they must estimate whether a specific property in a specific location that is being considered for purchase is *competitively priced.* Prospective buyers want to be sure that they are not "overpaying" for a property. Also, lenders want assurance concerning the price of the property because it will be serving as security for repayment for the mortgage debt and, over time, it must remain sufficiently high to repay the outstanding loan balance in the event of default. While prospective buyer-investors may estimate a value for a property, lenders will usually require that an estimate of value be made by an *independent fee appraiser,* which is someone who specializes in performing appraisals for a fee. An appraiser must be unrelated to the parties to the transaction and must have no vested or financial interest in the property being appraised.

The objective of the appraisal is to establish a **market value,** usually meaning the most probable price that would be paid for a property under competitive market conditions. The reader should understand that this notion of *value* may be different from the *price* that an individual buyer may be willing to pay for the property. For example, one person's *individual preference* for attributes of a property being acquired may be such that she may be willing to pay a significantly higher price for a property than the *majority* of potential buyers in the market. Because the lender is more concerned about what the market price would be in the event of default, the appraiser must make an independent estimate of the most probable price that a property would bring if it were sold under competitive market conditions, where individuals other than the prospective buyer would be bidding. In a sense, the appraiser's estimate of value will help the lender determine whether the price being offered by the borrower-applicant is an "outlier," or a price that is significantly different from what would be paid by most buyers in the market for similar properties. (Although there are some differences in appraisal requirements used in conventional, FHA, and VA mortgage underwriting, the general approaches to estimating value are similar.)

To produce an estimate of value, the appraiser generally begins with an assessment of national, regional, and local economic conditions, stressing income, population, employment, and interest rate trends, which, as discussed above, form the determinants of demand for the property in question. Supply is examined by assessing the relative cost of land and the factors of production (wages, capital). Current market equilibrium conditions in the housing market are then considered by examining the current availability (inventory) of housing units, absorption rates, rental vacancies, and trends in rents to gauge the likelihood of any short-run price movement that may affect the estimate of value. Finally, the appraiser must identify the area-relevant location, or **submarket,** in which the property being valued is viewed as being competitive or substitutable with other properties. This submarket also may be thought of as a neighborhood because of the proximity of retail, educational, religious, and other facilities which may appeal to households with similar income, tastes, and preferences. This is important because, as will be seen, price and other data will be obtained on properties that have sold recently in this area. Submarket selection is very important as the appraiser seeks to eliminate any differences that could be attributable to school districts, police and fire services, libraries, and so on in the analysis. These data will serve as a basis for estimating the price for which the property in question is likely to sell.

When estimating the value for the specific property (usually referred to as the "subject property"), the appraiser usually relies on three approaches: the market, cost, and income capitalization approaches. In *residential appraisals,* only two approaches, cost and market, are usually thought to be reliable. The market, or **sales comparison,** approach involves selecting properties in the same submarket or in close proximity to the subject property.

Comparables are chosen from those properties that have sold most recently and where adjustments for dissimilarities (such as size of dwelling, lot, amenities) can be kept at a *minimum*. This approach is based on the principle that at the time of the appraisal, buyers should be willing to pay the same price for otherwise identical properties. By adjusting the sale price of comparable properties for dissimilarities, the appraiser is trying to make properties that have recently sold very comparable to the subject property. The adjusted price of the comparables can then be used to price the subject.

The **cost approach** involves estimating the cost to reproduce the structure (less depreciation), and then adding the value of the land (site) to it in arriving at a value. The rationale for this approach is that no knowledgeable buyer would pay *more* for a property than the cost at which it can be reproduced. Finally, the **income approach** is a process, whereby comparable residences that are currently renting for income are used to estimate the value of the subject. This process usually involves establishing a ratio between the selling price and income of such recently sold comparables. The rent is then adjusted for dissimilarities with the subject. A comparable rent for the subject is then established and the ratio of price to rent for comparables is used to convert the adjusted rent into a value for the subject. This latter approach is not frequently used when pricing owner-occupied residential properties because it is generally the least reliable method. This is because there are usually few comparable residences that are rented.

Based on these approaches, the appraiser makes a final estimate of value and reports it to the prospective homebuyer and the lender. The lender will review the report and, if in agreement with the approach used by the appraiser, will use the lower of appraised value or the market price in establishing the maximum loan amount. For a more detailed examination of each of these approaches, we now consider a problem example. In the example, we use the uniform appraisal form (see Exhibit 7–6, panels A and B) required by the Federal National Mortgage Association and Federal Home Loan Mortgage Corporation. Today most residential mortgages utilize this form because it is a part of the required documentation any lender would need if it wished to sell a loan to either of these entities after, origination.[4]

The Sales Comparison Approach

As previously indicated, when using this method, the appraiser estimates the value of a property by comparing the selling prices of properties similar to, and near, the property being appraised. Because no two properties are exactly alike, the appraiser adjusts the values of similar properties (called **comparable properties**) for dissimilarities. These differences are isolated, and adjustments are made by the appraiser, who, using her judgment and knowledge of current market conditions, establishes what the market value is for each major attribute of a comparable that is different from the subject property. Because the value of the subject property is unknown, the price of the *comparables* will be adjusted until all differences have been taken into account. If this process is carried out correctly, the adjusted value of the comparable properties may then be used to approximate the price of the subject property. When selecting the comparables, the appraiser must be careful to establish that the sales of the comparable properties were *arm's-length transactions*

---

[4] For more detailed information see *Underwriting Guidelines, Home Mortgages,* Federal Home Loan Mortgage Corporation. The sale of mortgages to institutions in the secondary mortgage market will be covered in a later chapter. While all residential appraisals are made using the three approaches to value discussed above, additional specifications concerning condition and construction quality of the dwelling being appraised are sometimes included in FHA and VA appraisals. While such specifications are too numerous to be considered here, the following sources provide additional information: for an overview of FHA appraisal policies, see *HUD Handbook 4150.1;* for VA policies, see VA Bulletins and Benefits Circulars.

EXHIBIT 7–6

(Panel A) Property Description

Property Description & Analysis **UNIFORM RESIDENTIAL APPRAISAL REPORT** **File No.** _____

SUBJECT

Property Address 482 Liberty Street	Census Tract 1005.00
City Anytown, USA. County ___ State ___ Zip Code ___	
Legal Description Lot 78,1st Section Happy Acres Farm	
Owner/Occupant John and Jane J. Jones	Map Reference 33-84
Sale Price $ 76,700 Date of Sale 3-01-96	
Loan charges/concessions to be paid by seller $ None	
R.E. Taxes $ 797.00 Tax Year ___ HOA $/Mo. None	
Lender/Client XYZ Federal Savings and Loan Assoc.	

LENDER DISCRETIONARY USE
Sale Price $ ___
Date ___
Mortgage Amount $ ___
Mortgage Type ___
Discount Points and Other Concessions
Paid by Seller $ ___
Source ___

PROPERTY RIGHTS APPRAISED
[x] Fee Simple
[ ] Leasehold
[ ] Condominium (HUD/VA)
[ ] De Minimis PUD

NEIGHBORHOOD

LOCATION	[ ] Urban	[x] Suburban	[ ] Rural
BUILT UP	[x] Over 75%	[ ] 25-75%	[ ] Under 25%
GROWTH RATE	[ ] Rapid	[x] Stable	[ ] Slow
PROPERTY VALUES	[ ] Increasing	[x] Stable	[ ] Declining
DEMAND/SUPPLY	[ ] Shortage	[x] In Balance	[ ] Over Supply
MARKETING TIME	[ ] Under 3 Mos.	[x] 3-6 Mos.	[ ] Over 6 Mos.

PRESENT LAND USE	%	LAND USE CHANGE	PREDOMINANT OCCUPANCY	SINGLE FAMILY HOUSING PRICE $(000)	AGE (yrs)
Single Family	80	Not Likely [x]	Owner [x]		
2-4 Family	10	Likely [ ]	Tenant [ ]	55 Low	10
Multi-family	10	In process [ ]	Vacant (0-5%) [ ]	80 High	20
Commercial	___	To: ___	Vacant (over 5%) [ ]	65 Predominant	15
Industrial	___				
Vacant	___				

NEIGHBORHOOD ANALYSIS

	Good	Avg.	Fair	Poor
Employment Stability		[x]		
Convenience to Employment		[x]		
Convenience to Shopping			[x]	
Convenience to Schools	[x]			
Adequacy of Public Transportation		[x]		
Recreation Facilities			[x]	
Adequacy of Utilities		[x]		
Property Compatibility		[x]		
Protection from Detrimental Cond.		[x]		
Police & Fire Protection			[x]	
General Appearance of Properties		[x]		
Appeal to Market		[x]		

Note: Race or the racial composition of the neighborhood are not considered reliable appraisal factors.
COMMENTS: shopping is approximately two miles away at I-75 and Colerain.City Park one mile north. Other recreational facilities of a private nature. Fire protection is voluntary unit. Other aspects average or better.

SITE

Dimensions 60x125x72x140	Topography Level
Site Area 8,745 Sq.Ft. Corner Lot Yes	Size Typical in neighborhood
Zoning Classification R-2 (Min.Size 7500 Sq.Ft.) Zoning Compliance Yes	Shape Typical in neighborhood
HIGHEST & BEST USE: Present Use Single family res. Other Use ___	Drainage Good
	View Average
	Landscaping Typical in neighborhood
	Driveway ___
	Apparent Easements ___
	FEMA Flood Hazard Yes* No x
	FEMA* Map/Zone ___

UTILITIES	Public	Other	SITE IMPROVEMENTS	Type	Public	Private
Electricity	[x]		Street	Macadem	[x]	
Gas	[x]		Curb/Gutter	Concrete	[x]	
Water	[x]		Sidewalk	Concrete	[x]	
Sanitary Sewer	[x]		Street Lights			
Storm Sewer			Alley			

COMMENTS (Apparent adverse easements, encroachments, special assessments, slide areas, etc.): None

IMPROVEMENTS

GENERAL DESCRIPTION		EXTERIOR DESCRIPTION		FOUNDATION		BASEMENT		INSULATION	
Units	1	Foundation	Concrete	Slab	Concrete	Area Sq. Ft.	1316	Roof	[x]
Stories	1	Exterior Walls	Brick	Crawl Space	None	% Finished	0	Ceiling	[x]
Type (Det./Att.)	Det.	Roof Surface	Cedar Shingle	Basement	Yes	Ceiling		Walls	[x]
Design (Style)	Rambler	Gutters & Dwnspts	Galv. Iron	Sump Pump	No	Walls		Floor	[x]
Existing	Yes	Window Type	Dbl.Hung Wood	Dampness	None	Floor	Concrete	None	
Proposed		Storm Sash	Yes	Settlement	None	Outside Entry	Yes	Adequacy	[x]
Under Construction		Screens	Yes	Infestation	None			Energy Efficient Items:	
Age (Yrs.)	10	Manufactured House	No					•R-38 Ceiling	
Effective Age (Yrs.)	10-12							R-19 Walls	

ROOM LIST

ROOMS	Foyer	Living	Dining	Kitchen	Den	Family Rm.	Rec. Rm.	Bedrooms	# Baths	Laundry	Other	Area Sq. Ft.
Basement												
Level 1	x	x	x	x		x		3	2			
Level 2												

Finished area above grade contains: 7 Rooms; 3 Bedroom(s); 2 Bath(s); 1645 Square Feet of Gross Living Area

INTERIOR

SURFACES	Materials/Condition
Floors	Hardwood/Good
Walls	Plaster
Trim/Finish	Wood
Bath Floor	Ceramic Tile
Bath Wainscot	Ceramic
Doors	

HEATING		KITCHEN EQUIP.		ATTIC	
Type	FWA	Refrigerator	[x]	None	
Fuel	Gas	Range/Oven	[x]	Stairs	
Condition	Good	Disposal	[x]	Drop Stair	[x]
Adequacy	x	Dishwasher	[x]	Scuttle	
COOLING		Fan/Hood	[x]	Floor	
Central	x	Compactor		Heated	
Other		Washer/Dryer		Finished	
Condition		Microwave	[x]		
Adequacy	x	Intercom			

IMPROVEMENT ANALYSIS

	Good	Avg.	Fair	Poor
Quality of Construction	[x]			
Condition of Improvements	[x]			
Room Sizes/Layout		[x]		
Closets and Storage		[x]		
Energy Efficiency	[x]			
Plumbing-Adequacy & Condition		[x]		
Electrical-Adequacy & Condition		[x]		
Kitchen Cabinets-Adequacy & Cond.		[x]		
Compatibility to Neighborhood		[x]		
Appeal & Marketability		[x]		

Estimated Remaining Economic Life 45 Yrs.
Estimated Remaining Physical Life 60 Yrs.

Fireplace(s) #

AUTOS

CAR STORAGE			HOUSE ENTRY	
Garage		Attached	Adequate	[x] House Entry
No. Cars 1	Carport [x]	Detached	Inadequate	Outside Entry
Condition None		Built-In	Electric Door	Basement Entry

Additional features Fireplace in living room; rear concrete covered patio (22x12);4 ft. high chain link fence around rear yard.

COMMENTS

Depreciation (Physical, functional and external inadequacies, repairs needed, modernization, etc.) _____
Additional insulation (floor and ceiling) and automatic thermostat were added in 1979

General market conditions and prevalence and impact in subject/market area regarding loan discounts, interest buydowns and concessions: _____

Freddie Mac Form 70 10/86 12Ch. AO Forms and Worms Inc.,® 315 Whitney Ave., New Haven, CT 06511 1(800) 243-4545 Item #111710 Fannie Mae Form 1004 10/86

between the buyer and seller. For instance, if a seller was under duress, as in a foreclosure situation, or if a sale was between relatives, such a sale would not be desirable for use as a comparable because the buyer may not have paid a fair market price for the property. Once the appraiser has determined that all comparable sales were arm's-length transactions, the appraiser's process of adjusting the comparable sales can begin.

EXHIBIT 7–6
(Panel B) Property Valuation

UNIFORM RESIDENTIAL APPRAISAL REPORT File No.

Valuation Section

Purpose of Appraisal is to estimate Market Value as defined in the Certification & Statement of Limiting Conditions.

COST APPROACH

BUILDING SKETCH (SHOW GROSS LIVING AREA ABOVE GRADE)
If for Freddie Mac or Fannie Mae show only square foot calculations and cost approach comments in this space

Measurements	No. Stories	=	Sq.Ft.
42x37	x 1		1,554
24x3.8	x 1		91
Total gross living area			1,645sq.ft

ESTIMATED REPRODUCTION COST - NEW - OF IMPROVEMENTS:

Dwelling 1,645	Sq. Ft. @ $ 38.09	=	$62,658
1,316	Sq. Ft. @ $ 7.89	=	10,383
Extras soft wtr.sys.;d/w. disp.			
range/oven;f/h; fireplace		=	3,240
Special Energy Efficient Items R-30 Insultn		=	500
Porches, Patios, etc. and fence		=	1,800
Garage/Carport 200 Sq Ft @ $ 6.50		=	1,300
Total Estimated Cost New		=	$79,881

	Physical	Functional	External
Less			
Depreciation 13,500		7,500	= $21,000

Depreciated Value of Improvements .... = $58,881
Site Imp. "as is" (driveway, landscaping, etc.) = $ 3,050
ESTIMATED SITE VALUE = $15,500
(If leasehold, show only leasehold value.)
INDICATED VALUE BY COST APPROACH = $77,431

(Not Required by Freddie Mac and Fannie Mae)
Does property conform to applicable HUD/VA property standards? [X] Yes [ ] No
If No, explain:

Construction Warranty [ ] Yes [X] No
Name of Warranty Program
Warranty Coverage Expires

SALES COMPARISON ANALYSIS

The undersigned has recited three recent sales of properties most similar and proximate to subject and has considered these in the market analysis. The description includes a dollar adjustment, reflecting market reaction to those items of significant variation between the subject and comparable properties. If a significant item in the comparable property is superior to, or more favorable than, the subject property, a minus (−) adjustment is made, thus reducing the indicated value of subject. If a significant item in the comparable is inferior to, or less favorable than, the subject property, a plus (+) adjustment is made, thus increasing the indicated value of the subject

ITEM	SUBJECT	COMPARABLE NO. 1		COMPARABLE NO. 2		COMPARABLE NO. 3	
Address	482 Liberty	478 Liberty St.		225 West 17th Street		110 East 16th Street	
Proximity to Subject		Adjacent		2 blocks West		3 blocks SE	
Sales Price	$ 76,700		$ 65,000		$ 73,500		$ 67,500
Price/Gross Liv. Area	$ 46.63	$ 46.43		$ 44.54		$ 42.19	
Data Source	Sales con-tract	Present Owner		Appraiser's Files		Selling Broker	
VALUE ADJUSTMENTS	DESCRIPTION	DESCRIPTION	+ (−)$ Adjustment	DESCRIPTION	+ (−)$ Adjustment	DESCRIPTION	+ (−)$ Adjustment
Sales or Financing Concessions		None	−	None	−	None	−
Date of Sale/Time	3-1-96	1-29-96	−	2-14-96	−	12-17-95	−
Location	Avg.Suburb	Similar		Similar		Similar	−
Site/View	Corner Lot	Inside Lot	1,950	Inside Lot	1,950	Corner Lot	−
Design and Appeal	Rambler-Avg.	Similar		Similar		Similar	−
Quality of Construction	Good	Good		Good		Good	−
Age	20 years	19 years		20 years		13 years	(3,250)
Condition	Good	Good		Good		Int.Paint Fair	950
Above Grade Room Count	Total 7 : Bdrms 3 : Baths 2	Total 6 : Bdrms 1 : Baths 1.5	7,500	Total 7 : Bdrms 3 : Baths 2	−	Total 7 : Bdrms 3 : Baths 1	
Gross Living Area	1,645 Sq. Ft.	1,400 Sq. Ft.		1,650 Sq. Ft.		1,400 Sq. Ft.	2,800
Basement & Finished Rooms Below Grade	80% Bsmt Area Unfinished	Full Bsmt Rec. Room	(1,950)	Full Bsmt,Rec Rm,½ Bath	(2,800)	50% Bsmt Unfinished	3,200
Functional Utility	Good	Good	−	Good		Fair	2,800
Heating/Cooling	Central	Central	−	None	2,500	Central	−
Garage/Carport	1Car att.C/P	Similar	−	2 Car att.Gar.	(4,000)	2 Car att.Gar.	(4,000)
Porches, Patio, Pools, etc.	Fence, Rear Patio	Fence, Rear Screen Porch	(1,200)	Fence, Rear Patio		No Fence,Rear Screen Porch	(500)
Special Energy Efficient Items	R-38 Ceiling Ins. Solar HW Heater	No solar HW Heater	3,900	No solar HW Heater	3,900	Inf.Insulatn, No solar HW Heater	4,600
Fireplace(s)	Living Room	Similar	−	No Fireplace	1,800	No Fireplace	1,800
Other (e.g. kitchen equip., remodeling)	Range/Oven Disp,Dish Washer	Similar	−	Similar	−	No Built-in Appliance	500
Net Adj. (total)		[X] + [ ] −	$10,200	[X] + [ ] −	$3,350	[X] + [ ] −	$ 8,900
Indicated Value of Subject			$75,200		$76,850		$ 76,400

Comments on Sales Comparison: Sale No. 1 is recent sale of smaller house next door to subject and indicated value reflects considerable net adjustments as does sale No. 3. Sale No.2 is most comparable to subject and required only a few moderate size adjustments consequently

INDICATED VALUE BY SALES COMPARISON APPROACH most weight is assigned to its indicated value. = $ 76,850

INDICATED VALUE BY INCOME APPROACH (If Applicable) Estimated Market Rent $ 650 /Mo. x Gross Rent Multiplier 116 = $ 75,400

This appraisal is made [X] "as is" [ ] subject to the repairs, alterations, inspections or conditions listed below [ ] completion per plans and specifications.

Comments and Conditions of Appraisal: Property is at the top of the neighborhood value, but at estimated value it is readily saleable.

RECONCILIATION

Final Reconciliation: Most weight is given to market approach as the comps.are recent sales and are fairly similar and in close proximity to subject. Less weight is assigned to cost approach due to the difficulty in reliably establishing depreciation. Least weight given to income approach.

This appraisal is based upon the above requirements, the certification, contingent and limiting conditions, and Market Value definition that are stated in

[ ] FmHA, HUD &/or VA instructions.
[ ] Freddie Mac Form 439 (Rev. 7/86)/Fannie Mae Form 1004B (Rev. 7/86) filed with client December , 19 95 [ ] attached.
I (WE) ESTIMATE THE MARKET VALUE, AS DEFINED, OF THE SUBJECT PROPERTY AS OF March 7, 19 96 to be $ 77,000

I (We) certify: that to the best of my (our) knowledge and belief the facts and data used herein are true and correct; that I (we) personally inspected the subject property, both inside and out, and have made an exterior inspection of all comparable sales cited in this report; and that I (we) have no undisclosed interest, present or prospective therein.

Appraiser(s) SIGNATURE _____ NAME _____
Review Appraiser SIGNATURE _____ (if applicable) NAME _____
[X] Did [ ] Did Not Inspect Property

Freddie Mac Form 70 10/86 12Ch.   Forms and Worms Inc.,® 315 Whitney Ave., New Haven, CT 06511 1(800) 243-4545   Fannie Mae Form 1004 10/86

To illustrate how the appraiser will adjust the comparable sales for any differences between the subject property and the comparable properties, Exhibit 7–6 contains a property description in panel A and an example of the three approaches to value used in the appraisal process in panel B. Note that panel A contains the identification of the property and a general description of the property. Section II of panel B provides an example of the sales comparison approach to value. Some of the items that the appraiser will have to adjust the comparable properties for are: (1) time since the comparable has been sold, (2) location, (3) view, (4) design appeal, (5) quality of construction, (6) age of the property, (7) condition, (8) size of rooms, (9) quality of interior finish, (10) functional utility, (11) type and condition of major systems such as central heat and air, and (12) sale or financing concessions.

When making these adjustments, the appraiser adds to, or subtracts from, the value of the *comparable properties* to reflect the differences in market value between the comparable and the subject property that are caused by different attributes. If the subject property is superior to the comparable property with regard to a particular attribute, then the appraiser will *add* to the value of the *comparable property*. If the subject property has attributes that are inferior to the comparable property, then the appraiser will *subtract* from the value of the *comparable property*. Recall that the value of the subject is unknown; hence, *adjustments must be made to the comparable properties*. After all adjustments have been made to the comparables, the adjusted values of the comparables should be approximately equal to the value of the subject.

The amount that the appraiser adds to, or subtracts from, the price of a comparable property is an estimate of the *market value* of attributes that are different when comparing the subject with comparable property. For example, in dealing with differences in the *site,* in panel B (middle) we see that comparables 1 and 2 are both "inferior" to the subject in the sense that the subject is a corner location and the comparables are not. Comparable 3 is also on a corner lot so no adjustment is made because this attribute is considered to be the same as the subject. The appraiser judges that such a difference is worth $1,950 in additional market value for the subject, and hence increases the prices of the *comparables* by $1,950. On the other hand, we note that comparable 2 has a two-car garage, whereas the subject has only a one-car garage. In this case, the price of the comparable 2 is adjusted *down* by the difference in the value of a two-car versus a one-car garage ($4,000). Again, the idea is to adjust the *comparables* until all positive and negative characteristics are priced and added to or subtracted from the comparables, leaving a residual value (after adjustments) that should be approximately equal in price to the bundle of characteristics contained in the subject property. The residual values of all comparables, after adjustments, should approach the value of the subject, which is unknown.

How does the appraiser estimate the value of these characteristics? Estimating is done on the basis of experience, judgment, and knowledge of how individual buyers and sellers tend to *price* these attributes in various neighborhoods, given the site and other property characteristics. In other words, the appraiser must be able to *identify* and *defend* the estimated increase or decrease in the total price of a property, given the addition or removal of one or more characteristics (garage, bedroom, bath, etc.). This may seem to be a difficult task; however, in many housing markets hundreds of properties are sold each week and the appraiser generally has access to these data. A process of comparison and continuous updating of information makes the estimation possible. It should be stressed that under the sales comparison approach to value, adjustments are *not* based on the *cost* of constructing improvements. All adjustments in value between the property being appraised and comparables must be made on the basis of how the appraiser believes the *market value* will be affected by the presence or absence of such attributes. This is because the *market* may not value attributes the same way that an individual may. For example, the cost of adding a swimming pool to a property in an area of small, older, lower-priced homes may not be recovered in the market price when the property is sold, even though the current owner may believe that the value of this addition is at least equal to its cost. In this case, the addition to *market value may not be equal to the cost of constructing the pool* because the appraiser may judge that buyers composing the market for the property are not willing to pay as much for such an improvement as the current owner. Hence, the swimming pool may be referred to as an **overimprovement** to the property, and its full cost may not be reflected in the sale price.[5]

To obtain the final estimate of value under the sales comparison approach, the appraiser gives a *qualitative* weight to the residual price for each comparable. The weight assigned to each price depends on how many adjustments were made to each comparable. If many adjustments were made to a comparable, it would be given less weight, and vice versa. The appraiser then assesses the final estimates for each comparable in relation to the qualitative weights (see the comments at the bottom of Panel B, Exhibit 7–6) given to each, and arrives at a final estimate of value. Summarizing from the above:

Summary	Comp. 1	Comp. 2	Comp. 3
Sales price	$65,000	$73,500	$67,500
Net adjustments	+10,200	+3,350	+8,900
Adjusted values of comps:	75,200	76,850	76,400

Based on the various adjustments to comparables and the appraiser's weighting of these estimates, a value of $76,850 is assigned to the property being appraised under the sales comparison approach.

An additional concern of appraisers when using the sales comparison approach to value is the possibility that a comparable sale price may contain financing benefits paid for by the seller of a property. The effects of **seller financing** may be present when the seller of a comparable is attempting to help the buyer qualify for a loan and has paid points or discount fees for the buyer, or has taken back a second mortgage at a below-market rate of interest, which usually reduces the borrower-buyer's monthly payments and cost of financing the property.[6] Sellers often recover such financing costs by charging a higher price for the property. If this property is used later by an appraiser as a comparable to estimate the value of another property, the use of its price may be inappropriate. This is a difficult situation for appraisers because unless they know the conditions of a property's sale, it will not always be clear whether the seller of a property has paid some of the buyer's financing costs. During times when interest rates are rising and buyers find it difficult to qualify, seller-paid financing is common. During these times, appraisers usually verify that a comparable transaction does not include seller financing by speaking directly with one of the parties to the transaction or the settlement agent before using the comparable in the appraisal process. If seller financing has been used in the transaction, the appraiser must reflect this in his estimate of value by estimating the cost of the seller financing and subtracting this amount from the comparable value.[7] In the example shown in Exhibit 7–6, panel B, we see that no seller financing was present in any of the comparable sales.

---

[5] Overimprovements occur when individuals make improvements that they may prefer and/or believe will add value to the property. However, buyers in the market may not agree and will not pay for the full cost of the improvement. Similarly, a homeowner can also make an underimprovement, for example, if too small a house is built on a large site. In this case, individuals may not be willing to pay as much for the property as they would have if the relationship between the site and the improvement had been in conformity with other properties in the market area. Many textbooks are available on appraising if you want to pursue the topic (see the Appraisal Institute for sources).

[6] "Seller financing" occurs periodically in residential transactions. This problem is more prevalent in periods of high interest rates, when buyers have a difficult time qualifying for a loan. In these situations, sellers may finance all or part of the purchase at below-market rates of interest or contribute in some way to the buyer's cost of financing. Appraisers must be aware of such a possibility and make adjustments in their estimate of value.

[7] This will be analyzed in detail in the next chapter.

The sales comparison approach gives the most reliable indication of value when there are a number of current sales of highly comparable properties and information about the circumstances surrounding the transaction is easy to obtain. When these conditions are in effect, appraisers prefer the sales comparison approach.

The Cost Approach

When using the cost approach, the appraiser establishes a *value for the land* on which the improvement is located, and then determines the *cost of reproducing the improvement* and adds the two. After adding the cost of the improvement and land value, the appraiser deducts an amount for any depreciation (if appropriate) that improvements have suffered since they were constructed. If the improvement has just been completed, the latter adjustment is usually unnecessary. This procedure is illustrated at the top of Exhibit 7–6, panel B.

In arriving at the estimate of land value, a procedure similar to that followed in the sales comparison approach is used. Comparable sites that have been recently sold are selected, and adjustments are made for differences in location, size, shape, and topography. In estimating the improvement cost, the appraiser will usually consult cost manuals for material, labor, and profit (overhead) as well as verify with local construction companies the costs associated with constructing improvements with specific physical and qualitative dimensions. Based on these sources, estimates of construction costs per square foot are made for living space, basements, garages, and second floors. Individual estimates are then made for fixtures (kitchen, bath, etc.), landscaping, and additional improvements (pool, porches, etc.).

In the event the improvement is not newly constructed, there are three types of *depreciation* that the appraiser will deduct from the cost estimate just described. The first is depreciation in the property's value resulting from normal wear and is referred to as *physical depreciation.* Examples of physical depreciation include curable items, such as worn carpeting or walls needing paint. Incurable items, which include items such as foundation settling, may detract from a property's appearance but do not necessarily affect the usefulness of the structure. The second is depreciation resulting from internal property characteristics that make the property less livable or marketable than it was when first constructed. This is referred to as *functional obsolescence.* Examples of incurable functional obsolescence may include excessive amounts of hallway space. Curable obsolescence includes the replacement of lighting fixtures. The third type of depreciation the appraiser will consider is called *external obsolescence.* It is caused by characteristics external to the property, such as changing land uses in a neighborhood that cause a structure to become obsolete before the actual building wears out. Examples of external factors that cause economic depreciation to occur include pollution, shifting land uses, or changing legal restrictions on land use.

The older a property becomes, the more difficult it is for the appraiser to estimate the amount of depreciation that should be used in the appraisal process. In the example shown in Exhibit 7–6, panel B, we see that the appraiser has estimated that for the subject property (which is 10 years old), physical depreciation amounts to $13,500, economic depreciation is $7,500, and no functional obsolescence was apparent. Based on the cost approach to value, we see that the appraiser assigns a value of $77,431 to the subject property.

The cost approach to value usually provides the most reliable estimate of value when comparable properties are newly constructed and require very few adjustments for depreciation. Appraisers also consider the cost approach when determining value if only a few transactions involving comparable properties exist and the sales comparison approach to value is difficult to use.

The Income Approach

The income approach, a third appraisal method, establishes the market value of property by determining how much an investor is willing to pay for the income stream that a property produces. Using this method, the appraiser attempts to establish the relationship between a property's sale price and the monthly income stream it would produce if rented. The appraiser typically uses rents and prices from recent sales of rental properties that are similar to the subject property and determines the ratio of sale price to monthly rental income. This ratio is referred to as the **gross rent multiplier.** The value of the subject property would then be estimated by judging what the subject property should rent for (again by looking at comparable rental units and adjusting for dissimilarities), and then multiplying this estimate by the ratio established from comparable sales.

In our example we see in the lower portion of panel B in Exhibit 7–6 that the appraiser has estimated that, if rented, the subject would bring $650 per month. Given that comparable properties have recently sold for 116 times their monthly rents, it is reasonable that the same relationship would also hold for the subject. Hence, a value of $75,400, or $650 × 116, is arrived at by using the income approach.

Typically the income approach is difficult to use because sales of very comparable single-family rental properties are rare in an area. Consequently, appraisers tend to rely on the sales comparison and cost approaches when establishing value. However, it should be stressed that for some properties, such as condominiums, where many units are frequently rented, the income approach may provide a reliable estimate of value.

Final Estimate of Value

The appraiser must reconcile the different estimates of value provided by the sales comparison, income, and cost approaches when making a final estimate of value. This is accomplished by using a qualitative weighting method, in much the same way as in the sales comparison approach. The appraiser assigns subjective weights to each of the three values based on the reliability of the data and the number of adjustments that had to be made in each technique. More weight would be given to the method requiring fewer adjustments where data are verifiable, current, and complete. In our example, we see that the final estimate of value is $77,000, which, as the appraiser points out, is closest to the sales comparison and cost approaches.

Property Appraisal and Actual Sale Price

In our example, the sale price of a property agreed on between a buyer and seller does not exactly correspond to the appraised value. For example, a buyer and a seller agreed on a price of $76,700 for the property (see panel A) and the appraised value was $77,000. When considering the value of a property when making loans, lenders will generally use $76,700, or the lower of sale price or appraised value, as the value on which the loan will be based, unless there is convincing evidence to change it.

Property Values over Time

A cardinal rule followed by lenders is that loan security, which is dependent on the value of a mortgaged property, should never fall below the outstanding loan balance at any time during the life of the mortgage. In other words, the lender wants to be assured that the market value of the property will always be higher than the loan balance in the event of default by the borrower.

An additional consideration for the lender when considering the relationship of the mortgage balance and property value over time will be the potential effect of any *increases* in the mortgage balance relative to property value. This may present problems in the case of mortgage programs in which the loan balance may, or will, increase after the time of loan origination. (Recall the discussion in Chapters 4 and 5 dealing with the possible effects of negative amortization.)

Investing in "Distressed Properties"

The term *distressed* is used to describe various events or circumstances that usually result in the sale of properties that otherwise might not occur. **Distressed properties** may present opportunities for investors to acquire properties at below current market prices. *However, these discounts usually exist for a reason; otherwise, owners would simply sell their properties at current market prices as the properties become distressed.* As we will discuss, there are many reasons why properties become distressed and why owners may be willing to sell them for a discount. In such instances, investors usually acquire properties and provide an infusion of cash and hope to eliminate problems that may range from structural damage to legal issues affecting the title to properties. By remedying these problems, investors expect that the property value will increase enough to provide them with a satisfactory investment return.

Some of the personal financial and/or legal situations affecting the owner that may explain why properties become distressed are listed below. One or more of these factors may be occurring simultaneously:

Borrower inability to make mortgage payments.

Market value of the property below the mortgage balance.

Delinquent property taxes/property tax liens.

Internal Revenue Service tax liens.

Civil judgments/bankruptcy/divorce.

Mechanics and/or construction loan liens.

Personal debts.

Estate settlements.

One very common reason why a distressed property becomes available is the borrower's inability to make mortgage payments. In this case, the borrower-owner of the property may not yet be formally in default, as the lender may be providing the borrower with a grace period on the loan, hoping that foreclosure proceedings can be averted.[8] However, if the borrower cannot "cure" the problem, it is possible that the lender may acquire title to the property directly from the owner (usually referred to as "deed in lieu of foreclosure"). By using this process, both parties may save time and foreclosure costs and avert an auction. However, if the lender and the borrower cannot agree on a deed transfer, the lender may have to foreclose. In these cases, the property may have to be sold at auction.

Another reason for default occurs in cases where property values fall below the outstanding loan balance. When this happens, properties are said to be "underwater" or "upside down." Situations like this can come about because owners may have overpaid for a property or overimproved a property relative to other comparable properties. Should property owners have difficulty making monthly loan payments on such an "underpriced" property, they may default.

Deterioration in local economic conditions, such as unemployment because of layoffs, plant closings, and the like, may lead to an increase in the number of distressed properties available for sale. Increases in unemployment may reduce household incomes and negatively affect the demand for housing. Such a market downturn may cause an extraordinary number of properties to become distressed and available for purchase.

There are also a number of events, usually unanticipated by homeowners, that may result in a distressed property situation. These events may not necessarily be related to the

---

[8] If the borrower's situation is believed to be temporary, a lender may also be willing to consider restructuring the terms of the loan. Such a loan restructuring is referred to as a *workout*.

condition of the property and could include liens because of unpaid income taxes or property taxes, judgments because of civil actions stemming from lawsuits or business failures, bankruptcy, divorce, default on personal loans and/or business loans, or the need to settle an estate. Property owners may be seeking a financial solution to these unrelated financial or legal problems and may be considering the sale of properties to raise funds.

In addition to the causes listed above, it should be stressed that real estate is not like financial assets such as stocks and bonds, many of which have very active and liquid markets where they can be traded. Real estate requires a considerably longer period of time to buy and sell. Trading residential properties with the attendant requirements to finance and close may require at least 60 to 90 days under normal circumstances. In cases involving distressed properties, it may take even longer. Furthermore, in cases where the current owner may have overpaid for a property, because of aggressive lending practices or poor estimates of price appreciation, buyers of distressed properties may have to carry properties until "repricing" occurs in a market environment that is changing. In these cases, investors are providing financing and taking "repricing" risk until the market stabilizes.

Financial Framework for Analyzing Distressed Properties

When analyzing an investment in distressed properties, investors usually consider a financial framework as shown in Exhibit 7–7. Note that items listed in Exhibit 7–7 are classified into three phases: (A) acquisition, (B) holding period, and (C) disposition. For the investment to be profitable (D), net cash inflow from the sale phase (C) must exceed costs expended in phases (A) and (B). When the exhibit is reviewed, a number of factors must be analyzed. Perhaps, the most important considerations have to do with thinking about the following general questions: (1) Why does the so-called distressed property situation exist? (2) Why cannot the current property owners remedy the things causing the problem and sell or rent the property themselves? (3) What services and investment will an investor have to make to restore the property value and justify its acquisition?

Acquisition Phase

Sources of Information for Identifying Distressed Properties

Banks and lenders maintain **REO (real estate owned) lists** that are usually made available upon request. These lists contain information on properties that lenders have acquired by deed in lieu of foreclosure or through foreclosure and auction. Because lenders are not in the business of investing and managing real estate, they are generally interested in selling such properties as soon as possible. REO lists also are maintained by the FHA, VA, and HUD.

EXHIBIT 7–7
Summary of Financial Considerations When Investing in "Distressed Properties"

A. Acquisition Phase	B. Holding Period Phase
Acquisition costs:	Interim costs:
Purchase price	Renovation costs
Market and legal research costs	Insurance, property taxes, and so on
Inspection costs	Interest on investor financing
Elimination of liens	Other ____
Other ____	Total costs during holding period
Total acquisition cost	

C. Disposition Phase	D. Profitability
Expected sale price	C − (A + B)
Less: Selling expenses	
Net cash from sale	

Properties are usually acquired by these agencies when a foreclosure occurs in conjunction with one of the FHA insurance, VA guarantee, and/or HUD affordable housing programs. These properties are usually advertised for sale or they may be auctioned to the public.

Many *individual* property owners advertise their desire to sell properties because of financial difficulty. One reason why this is done is so that they may try and avoid default and preserve their credit standing. The latter may be important to these individuals at some future time, if they re-enter the market to buy a property. At that time, they may have to apply for mortgage financing and will have to supply lenders with a credit history. Other sources of information include public announcements, by county property tax authorities, regarding properties that are being sold for delinquent taxes. Other auctions are announced by the Internal Revenue Service, which obtains court orders to auction properties that have been seized to satisfy tax liens.

Legal Research

A search of a property's title history is perhaps one of the most important activities that will require an expenditure by the investor. It often must occur prior to the acquisition of a property. This is very important because if the investor plans to eventually sell a distressed property, the next owner may require a general warranty deed to obtain title insurance and financing. Therefore, any legal issues must be known by investors *prior* to acquisition in order to estimate the cost of extinguishing liens and other factors affecting title. It should be pointed out that in some situations, when purchasing distressed properties, investors do not always receive a general warranty deed. For example, if an investor is purchasing a foreclosed property from a lender, the lender may be willing to provide the investor with only a "bargain and sale deed." This means that the lender will provide the investor with a title "as is." It is then up to the investor to decide if the title record is satisfactory. If the title record is not satisfactory, the investor may have to expend time and money to clear the title. In some other cases, lenders may be willing to give a "special warranty deed." This means that the lender will warrant the title against liens and encumbrances that occurred only during the period when the lender held title. No warranty is made by the lender regarding any liens or title imperfections *prior* to that time. In summary, unless the lender provides the investor with a general warranty deed, the investor may have to expend funds and negotiate with all lienholders and obtain releases, thereby clearing the title in order to sell the property at a later date.

The Auction Process

The auction process is important to understand (1) because of possible delays between the time that foreclosure and sale occur and (2) because other bidders are likely to be present at auction. Because of possible delays, investors must make a judgment as to if, or when, the property will actually be sold before expending funds on extensive legal or market research. It is important to note that each state has its own auction process that investors should understand. Generally, the auction process in the United States can be described under three categories. For example, in states following the *lien theory* of mortgages, foreclosures generally require a civil action (lawsuit) against the borrower-owner who is in default. A court hearing is held and a judicial declaration must be made terminating the property owner's equitable rights. This is followed by an order directing the sheriff to conduct an auction. In some cases, as a part of the civil action, delays may be requested by the borrower for many reasons. This may prolong the time from foreclosure to actual sale.

In states favoring the so-called *title theory* of mortgages, title is usually vested in the lender when the mortgage loan is made and reconveyed to the borrower when the loan is repaid. In addition to having title, the lender is empowered to take certain steps in the event that the borrower defaults. These steps generally include providing the borrower notice of default and acceleration on the note, and that the sale of the property will occur to satisfy the debt. However, during this process, the borrower may bring an action to enjoin the lender from proceeding to sell the property. Actions taken by the borrower to prohibit and/or delay sale obviously affect the likelihood of a timely acquisition by investors. In some states, the so-called *modified lien theory* of mortgages is followed. Under this system, when a loan is made, title is invested in an independent third party (trustee). The trustee receives a deed of trust containing instructions to be followed if the lender provides notice to the trustee that a mortgagor is in default. In this event, the trustee usually notifies the borrower that the deficiency must be cured by a certain date or the trustee will proceed to auction the property. This process is different from the procedures described above in that it does not require a civil action or a court hearing. In order to delay this process, borrowers may take legal action and request that the court instruct the trustee to delay the property sale.

In summary, under all three systems, there may be opportunities for borrowers to bring legal action to delay the foreclosure-and-sale process. These range from claims that the lender and/or trustee did not give the borrower proper notice of default, challenges regarding contractual provisions in the note and/or the mortgage agreement, delays because of other actions pending against the borrower, bankruptcies, and so forth. In short, if the sale of the property at auction is delayed, the investor (1) may expend time and money on title research, (2) may have to wait even longer until the auction actually occurs, and (3) may not be a successful bidder when the auction occurs. These examples represent some of the costs and risks associated with the business of investing in distressed properties.

Lenders at Auctions

When properties are sold at auction, lenders holding notes and mortgages will bid for properties. Lenders are usually allowed to bid an amount at least equal to the mortgage balance owed them without providing additional cash. If the amount owed to the lender is close to the current market value of a property, the lender may be the successful bidder and will add the property to its REO list. But if the market value of the property is greater than the loan balance, an investor may outbid the lender. In the latter event, the lender must be repaid in order for the lien to be extinguished.

In cases where the current property value is less than the amount owed, the lender may bid an amount equal to the property value and sue the borrower for the deficiency. In this case, the property becomes a part of the lender's REO list and the lender will try to sell the property for as much as possible. In summary, as a part of the acquisition phase, investors must do a considerable amount of legal and market research. They must also decide whether or not there will be delays before an auction actually occurs and whether or not they will be successful bidders. Finally, they also must determine the amount of time, effort, and cost that will need to be expended to "clear the title" to the property they are acquiring. Otherwise, they may expend a considerable amount of time and money and not make a successful acquisition of the property.

Other Issues—Equitable Rights

Prior to bidding for properties at auction, investors must also identify the extent to which previous owners may have any equitable rights *after* an auction is completed. For example, in some states, statutory provisions are made for "equitable rights of redemption." This generally means that even after auction occurs and a new investor acquires title to a property, it may be possible for the previous owner to *reacquire title.* Generally, this may be done if a previous owner pays all deficiencies plus any interest and penalties to the previous lender and the investor who obtained a property at auction.

In some other cases, courts of equity may award borrowers in default such redemption rights. Usually, such awards will be made based on the court's analysis of the extent to which a borrower has accumulated equity in a property prior to default (e.g., borrower defaults in the 29th year and 11th month of a 30-year mortgage). Obviously, investors interested in distressed properties in these situations must consider the likelihood that borrowers will be able to cure past deficiencies and reacquire title to such properties.

Buying at Auctions Conducted by Public Entities

When buying properties at auctions conducted by public agencies, investors should determine the nature of the title that they may receive if they make a successful bid. In some states, for example, if investors obtain title at an auction resulting from delinquent property taxes, the investor may receive from the county what is referred to as a "tax deed." These deeds may provide that if the previous property owner in arrears can cure the past-due taxes within a prescribed time period and pay the holder of the tax deed an additional amount of interest and/or penalties, they may reacquire title to the property. Even if the previous owner fails to cure the deficiency, the county tax authority may not provide the new investor with a general warranty deed. It may be the responsibility of the holder of the tax deed to institute appropriate legal action in the state where the property is located to assure possession of legal and marketable title.

To reiterate, the quality of title is usually *critical* to the success of investing in a distressed property. Typically, in order to successfully sell the property at a later time, the investor generally must eventually have a *marketable title*. That is, the investor must be able to convey a deed of sufficient quality so the next purchaser of the property is able to obtain mortgage financing from conventional financing sources. Since lenders usually insist that the borrower acquire title insurance and that the title record be free of liens, investors must *decide* if this requirement can be met during the acquisition phase, or *prior* to bidding at auction.

Market Research/Costs

Expenditures on market research must also be made by investors prior to making an acquisition. The goal of the research is to determine the value of comparable properties that are likely to compete with the distressed property when it is ready for sale. This must also be done to establish the extent to which the distressed property must be improved or renovated in order to compete against other properties for sale and to set a sale price upon disposition. In cases where the value of a property has fallen below its original purchase price, investors must estimate whether prices are likely to fall further, or if and when prices are likely to recover. This research is also important because it will help to establish the offer that an investor must make at auction or when purchasing properties from individuals or lenders.

Inspection Costs

In addition to legal and market research, property inspections should be made at the beginning of the acquisition phase when developing a bid for a property. Items that are usually inspected include:

- Land/building.
- Foundation.
- Drainage.

- Building quality and building code compliance.
- Environmental issues: lead paint, asbestos, and the like.

If problems are discovered, investors must estimate any outlays that must be made to remedy problems. These costs must be factored in during the acquisition phase and will affect the investment analysis made by the investor.

Holding Period Phase

Depending on what is required to achieve their investment objective, investors generally make outlays for various items during the period of ownership, including:

- Renovation costs.
- Interest or other financial carrying costs.
- Property taxes and insurance.

In many cases, investors will choose to finance their investment. Typical financing sources include:

- Assumption of outstanding mortgage debt.
- Personal loan or credit lines.
- Personal equity/other equity sources.
- First or second mortgages on other real estate owned.
- Home equity credit line on other real estate owned.

In some cases, the existing lender who has acquired a distressed property at auction or through a deed in lieu of foreclosure may be willing to finance the sale of a property to an investor. This may occur if the lender wants to dispose of a property and/or if the lender believes that it may avert a loss by allowing an investor to renovate and market a property.

As noted above, investors also may borrow by using their personal credit or by using other real estate that they may own as security for a loan. Such loans may be obtained by refinancing properties that they may own or by obtaining loans secured by second liens. In some cases, if investors plan on continuously bidding for a number of properties, lenders may be willing to provide credit lines to investors to acquire properties and to finance necessary improvements. See Exhibit 7–8 for an example of an investment analysis of a foreclosed property.

EXHIBIT 7–8
Example: Investment Analysis of a Foreclosed Property

ABC Bank has title to a 3,000-square-foot, three-bedroom, two-bath home situated on one-quarter acre of land. The bank acquired the property at auction for the loan balance owed by a previous owner and has added this property to its REO list. It has indicated that the asking price for the property is $200,000 and that it can convey a general warranty deed to the purchaser. GMI Sharpe Investors is considering the purchase of this property. An estimate of costs associated with the acquisition and expenses of owning the property for a period of one year is as follows:

Phase A. Acquisition fees:	
Legal counsel/research	$ 2,000
Inspection fee/report	500
Payoff of existing property tax lien	8,000
Total	$10,500

**EXHIBIT 7–8
(Continued)**

Phase B. Renovation costs:

Carpet	$ 6,000
Dry wall repair/paint	1,000
Countertops/cabinets	3,000
Utilities during renovation	200
Roof repair	8,000
Plumbing/electric	3,000
Property taxes (1 year) and insurance	4,000
Interest ($200,000 personal loan @ 7%)	14,000
Total	$39,200

Phase C. Sale phase:

Broker commission (est)	$ 6,000
Total	$ 6,000

Question

Assuming that GMI Sharpe acquires the property for $200,000, how much must the *property sell for* in order for Sharpe to achieve a 20 percent return (annual rate, compounded monthly) on its investment during this one-year period?

Cash Flow Analysis

Phase A: Acquisition		Phase B: Average Monthly Outflows	Phase C: EOY Sale	
Purchase Price	$ 200,000	$3,267	Sale Price: TBD	
Plus Acquisition fees	10,500			
Less: Loan	200,000		Less: Selling expenses =	$ 6,000
Equity	$ 10,500	$3,267	Repayment of loan =	$200,000

Present value analysis:

$$PV = -10,500$$
$$PMT = -3,267$$
$$n = 12 \text{ months}$$
$$i = 20\% \div 12$$

Solve for FV = ? (net cash flow needed in year of sale)

Solution/Interpretation

A sale price at the end of year 1 must be great enough to repay the $200,000 loan plus $6,000 in selling fees and have enough cash flow remaining to make the investment worthwhile. Solving for *FV* produces $55,808, which is the *net* cash flow after the loan repayment and selling fees ($206,000) that must be realized at the *EOY*1 in order to achieve a 20 percent return.

   This means that GMI Sharpe must be able to sell the property for at least $261,808 ($206,000 + $55,808) in order to repay the loan; pay all costs of acquisition, holding, renovation, and sale; and earn a 20 percent *IRR* (annual rate compounded monthly). The investor must conduct careful market research to determine whether any comparable properties have sold in this price range or when, if ever, properties are likely to sell in this price range.

Pre-foreclosure Investments

In some situations, unanticipated events that affect the property owner but that are not directly related to the property or market conditions may result in properties becoming distressed. As indicated earlier, there are many events that may require a homeowner to obtain funds to repay business creditors.* In turn, this may cause a homeowner to sell a property to raise funds to satisfy debts. In some cases, it may be possible for an investor to contract to purchase a property, whereby the seller delivers title on a future date and the investor immediately conveys title to a new buyer. In the meantime, the seller retains title and keeps existing loans alive. In the interim, the investor implements a necessary strategy to sell

EXHIBIT 7–8
(Concluded)

the property and acts as a middleman, taking title only briefly immediately before the property is sold. For example, the owner of a distressed property and an *investor* may agree on a specific selling price (or "strike price") and enter into an *option contract* to provide the investor title on or before a future date. This option may be exercised at the *investor's* option anytime between the date of the contract and the expiration date. The seller agrees not to abandon the property and also agrees not to enter into any other contracts that would encumber title to the property. The investor hopes to find a buyer before the expiration date of the option *and* simultaneously take title and sell the property and give title to a new buyer immediately. The funds received by the investor from the new buyer at closing are used to purchase the property from the seller who agrees to repay the outstanding debt. Title is then transferred from the previous owner to the new owner with the investor obtaining title only briefly at the closing when transferring title to the new owner.

* In some states, the debtor's homestead may be protected from bankruptcy judgments caused by business failures or personal debts. However, such homesteads are not usually protected if the borrower defaults on a mortgage loan secured by the homestead.

Other Approaches to Investing in Distressed Properties

Concept Box 7.3

A. OPTION CONTRACT WITH SIMULTANEOUS TITLE CLOSING

Typical terms and conditions:

1. Investor contracts with seller for seller to deliver a deed at the option of investor at any time up to one year from the contract date.
2. Investor does research on real estate values and must be convinced that the distressed property can be resold at favorable price. Investor determines the extent of liens. Investor may have to provide funds to clear title such as paying past-due property taxes prior to sale.
3. Investor may or may not agree to make monthly mortgage payments for seller during the option period. Investor usually obtains interim financing with a personal line of credit or home equity loan.
4. Seller agrees not to abandon the property, execute any contracts further encumbering the property, or make any physical modifications to the property in any way during the contract period.
5. When a new purchaser is identified by investor, investor exercises the option to buy the property. Seller then sells the property and delivers title to investor at the contract (strike price). Seller pays off mortgage debt with funds received from investor. Investor simultaneously sells property and transfers title to third party.

Summary—The investor does not take title until a new buyer is found. This usually saves the investor closing costs and financing fees. The risk is that no buyer will be found during the option contract period. Unless the option contract is extended, the investor loses all cash flows expended on research, monthly payments, and so on. The seller benefits in that foreclosure is avoided, thereby preserving credit. Assuming that the market price that the investor receives from the new owner exceeds the option price, the investor would keep any difference between the final sale price and option price as a return on investment. In the event that the market value does not exceed the option price, the investor may elect not to exercise the option. However, as long as the market value exceeds the strike price on the expiration date, the investor may elect to exercise the option in order to minimize losses. Another reason for this option approach, as opposed to an outright purchase of the property by the investor, is to avoid transactions costs that may have to be paid twice during a short ownership period. Recall that the investor plans to have the property sold within six months. Therefore, taking title and incurring various closing costs during a short ownership period may significantly reduce the investor's returns and make the required sale price higher and could make the transaction not feasible. The risk to the investor is the potential loss of all cash outlays during the acquisition and holding period should the property value upon sale not increase enough to recover these costs and achieve the desired return. A related question is this: Why does the homeowner need the investor? In many cases, homeowners may not have sufficient cash to make monthly payments, pay property taxes in arrears, clear up title problems, and so on. Furthermore, this homeowner remains in the property for six months and does not have to make payments on the mortgage, property taxes, or insurance. Finally, this homeowner may not want to default on the mortgage loan, thereby avoiding future bad credit issues. Additionally, other issues relating to employment, marital status, possible business failure, and so on, may have higher priority and preclude the homeowner from investing the time and effort needed to dispose of the real estate. There is another risk that must be considered by the investor in the event that the market value of the property exceeds the option price. In this case, it is imperative that the investor execute a very well-written option contract in order to avert any motivation by the seller to default on the option contract with the investor and attempt to sell the property independently.

B. CONTRACT FOR FUTURE DEED

In some cases an investor may purchase a property; however, in order to sell the property, the investor and a *buyer* may have to enter into a contract for a future deed. This situation develops when a buyer would like to purchase the property, but cannot do so because of insufficient credit and has difficulty in obtaining financing. The investor may be willing to provide financing, but does not want to convey title as yet in order to avoid legal and other costs should the buyer default on the loan. Both parties agree on a specific selling price ("strike price") and enter into an *option contract,* whereby the investor agrees to deliver title to the new owner at a future date. This option may be exercised at the buyer's option anytime between the date of the contract and the expiration date. The buyer agrees not to abandon the property and also agrees not to enter into any other contracts involving the property. The buyer also must make monthly rent payments, some, or none, of which may be credited toward the selling price.

Typical term/conditions:

1. Investor purchases property and takes title.
2. Investor enters into a contract with a potential buyer to purchase the property at a specified price by a specific date. Investor agrees to deliver and close title if terms and conditions of contract are met.
3. Investor obtains financing and may pay property taxes and hazard insurance to avoid liens and to protect title to property during the contract period.
4. Potential buyer makes monthly payments (rent) to investor. Buyer attempts to accumulate additional equity and or repair any credit problems.
5. As a buyer eventually qualifies for financing and executes the purchase option, investor delivers title and receives strike price from buyer.*

*The effect of federal income taxes is not included in this analysis.

Disposition Phase—Exit Strategies

The obvious strategy that can be used to complete an investment in distressed properties would be to sell the property upon completion of the holding period phase. However, if a sale cannot be achieved because of a change in market conditions or for other reasons, an investor could consider converting a distressed property into a rental property to earn income or, perhaps, using the property as a personal residence.

Conclusion

Readers should now have a general understanding of the determinants of house prices and appraisal procedures used for residential mortgage lending. We have provided techniques for determining the appreciation rates in house prices and on equity, as well as federal income tax treatment for homeowners and comparisons with the cost of renting. We have also reviewed the three approaches used by appraisers to estimate the market value of residential properties. Various issues involving housing bubbles and investing in distressed properties have been discussed. Lenders and investors should be familiar with these concepts and with the assumptions made by each and their effects on value.

Key Terms

base industries, *194*
capitalization effect, *197*
capital gains exclusion, *190*
comparable properties, *200*
cost approach, *200*
distressed properties, *207*
driver industries, *194*
economic base, *195*
expected appreciation rate on
   home equity (EAHE), *191*

expected rate of appreciation in
   house prices (EAHP), *191*
gross rent multiplier, *206*
income approach, *200*
loan-to-value ratio, *191*
location quotient, *195*
market value, *199*
optimal size
   of cities, *198*
overimprovement, *203*

public goods, *197*
REO (real estate owned)
   list, *208*
sales comparison, *199*
seller financing, *204*
submarket, *199*
unrealized equity gain, *191*
wealth effect, *192*

Useful Web Sites

www.nahb.org—National Association of Home Builders.

www.realtor.com—National Association of Realtors.

www.freddiemac.com/finance/cmhpi—Freddie Mac's Conventional Mortgage Home Price Index (FMHPI).

www.bestplaces.net—Statistics, including crime rates, on places to live.

www.ers.usda.gov/data/unemployment—U.S. Department of Agriculture. This link includes median household income and unemployment data on every county in the United States.

www.statetaxcentral.com/—Provides tax information for every state.

http://homes.yahoo.com/—This site provides information for home buying such as comparable sales, home valuation, and neighborhood demographics for an address the user enters.

www.owners.com/partners/mortgages.aspx—This site provides information and articles on buying a home and financing.

www.fairmark.com—This Web site is a good resource for finding tax-related policies. It can help in doing real estate analysis from a tax-saving perspective.

www.fhfa.gov—Federal Housing Finance Agency.

www.census.gov—U.S. Census Bureau. Publishes housing statistics monthly.

www.bls.gov—U.S. Bureau of Labor Statistics. Publishes employment data for the entire United States and by metropolitan areas.

www.bea.gov—Bureau of Economic Analysis in U.S. Department of Commerce. Provides data on income, RGDP, and other economic aggregates.

www.homeprice.standardandpoors.com—S&P/Case-Shiller® Home Price Index.

Questions

1. Why is the income approach to value often difficult to use on a single-family residential appraisal?
2. What are the differences between the cost and sales comparison approaches to appraising property?
3. What are the capital gains rules as applied to residential property owners?
4. List four important drivers of housing demand and price appreciation.
5. What are public goods? How may they be reflected in house prices?
6. When considering an investment in "distressed" properties, what are the two most important areas of research that should be undertaken?

Problems

1. You are considering an option to purchase or rent a single residential property. You can rent it for $2,000 per month and the owner would be responsible for maintenance, property insurance, and property taxes. Alternatively, you can purchase this property for $200,000 and finance it with an 80 percent mortgage loan at 6 percent interest that will fully amortize over a 30-year period. The loan can be prepaid at any time with no penalty.

   You have done research in the market area and found that (1) properties have historically appreciated at an annual rate of 3 percent per year, and rents on similar properties have also increased at 3 percent annually; (2) maintenance and insurance are currently $1,500.00 each per year and they have been increasing at a rate of 3 percent per year; (3) you are in a 26 percent marginal tax rate and plan to occupy the property as your principal residence for at least four years; (4) the capital gains exclusion would apply when you sell the property; (5) selling costs would be 7 percent in the year of sale; and (6) property taxes have generally been about 2 percent of property value each year.

   Based on this information you must decide:

   a. In order to earn a 10 percent *IRR* after taxes on your equity, should you buy the property or rent it for a four-year period of ownership?
   b. What if your expected period of ownership was to change to five years. Would owning or renting be better if you wanted to earn a 10 percent percent *IRR* after taxes?
   c. Approximately, what level of rents would make you *indifferent* between owning and renting for a four-year period? Assume that a 4.5 percent after-tax *IRR* would be the minimum you would need to earn on capital invested in the home.

2. You are considering the purchase of a property today for $300,000. You plan to finance it with an 80 percent loan. The appreciation rate on the property value is expected to be 4 percent annually for the next three years.

   a. Approximate the expected annual average rate of appreciation on *home equity* for the *next three years*.
   b. What if you now think that a $300,000 purchase price may be somewhat high and that if you pay this price, the expected appreciation rates in your house price will be as follows: year 1 = 0%, year 2 = 2%, and year 3 = 3%. How will your answer to part (a) change?

3. You are trying to estimate the value of a property that you are interested in buying. The subject property is located at 322 Rock Creek Road in a new suburb of a large metropolitan area. The property is like many others in the area, with three bedrooms, two baths, a living room, a den, a large kitchen, and a two-car garage. The residence has about 1,800 square feet of air-conditioned space and is of traditional design. The property is located on an interior lot with no potential flooding problems. The quality of construction appears to be about average for the market area.

Comparable properties in the area have the following characteristics:

	Comparable I	Comparable II	Comparable III
Address	123 Clay St.	301 Cherry Lane	119 Avenue X
Sale price	$85,000	$79,000	$75,000
Time of sale	6 months ago	7 months ago	13 months ago
Design	Modern	Traditional	Traditional
Parking	2-car garage	2-car carport	1-car garage
Location	Corner lot	Interior lot	Interior lot
Drainage	Good	Below average	Good
Bedrooms	Four	Three	Two
Baths	Two	Two	Two
Construction	Average	Average	Below average

You have come to some conclusions concerning what you believe the different attributes of the comparable properties are likely to be worth in the market area. Appreciation in house values in the area has been very low over the past eight months, and you think that any properties that have sold within that period would probably not require any adjustments for the time of sale. However, one of the comparable properties sold over a year ago, and you think it will require a $1,500 upward adjustment. You also believe that properties in the area that are located near the creek sell for about $1,200 less than other properties in the area because of a slower rate of runoff after heavy rains. Properties on corner lots generally sell for a premium of about $1,000. Houses with the fashionable modern design usually bring about $1,000 more than those that have traditional design characteristics. Because three-bedroom homes are considered desirable by buyers in the area, an additional fourth bedroom will generally only add about $1,200 in value to a property. However, properties that contain only two bedrooms are rather difficult to sell, and often bring $2,000 less than their three-bedroom counterparts when they are sold. Most homes in the area have a two-car garage, but when properties have a one-car garage, they usually sell for about $800 less. A two-car open carport generally reduces the value of the property by a similar amount, or $800. The inferior construction quality exhibited by comparable III should reduce its value by about $1,500.

a. You plan to complete the sales comparison approach to value and assign an estimate of value to the subject property. Give specific reasons for your choice of value.

b. Assume that the value of the lot the subject property is constructed on is $13,000. Air-conditioned space in the dwelling would cost about $36.00 per square foot to reproduce, and the garage would cost approximately $3,700 to reproduce. Complete the *cost* approach to value, assuming that, because the property is new, no depreciation of the structure is required.

4. An investor is considering the acquisition of a "distressed property" which is on Northlake Bank's REO list. The property is available for $200,000 and the investor estimates that he can borrow $160,000 at 8 percent interest and that the property will require the following total expenditures during the next year:

Inspection	$ 500
Title search	1,000
Renovation	13,000
Landscaping	800
Loan interest	12,800
Insurance	1,800
Property taxes	6,000
Selling expenses	8,000

a. The investor is wondering what such a property must sell for after one year in order to earn a 20 percent return (*IRR*) on equity. What other issues must he consider?

b. The lender now is concerned that if the property does not sell, he may have to carry the property for one additional year. He believes that he could rent it and realize net cash flow before debt service of $1,200 per month. However, he would have to make an additional $12,800 in interest payments on his loan during that time, and then sell. What would the price have to be at the end of year 2 in order to earn a 20 percent *IRR* on equity?

5. You have an opportunity to acquire a property from First Capital Bank. The bank recently obtained the property from a borrower who defaulted on his loan. First Capital is offering the property for $200,000. If you buy the property, you believe that you will have to spend (1) $10,500 on various acquisition-related expenses and (2) an average of $2,000 per month during the next 12 months for repair costs, and so on, in order to prepare it for sale. Because First Capital Bank would like to sell the property as soon as possible, it is willing to provide $180,000 in financing at 8 percent interest for 12 months payable monthly (interest only). Your market research indicates that after you repair the property, it may sell for about $225,000 at the end of one year. Furthermore, you will probably have to pay about $3,000 in fees and selling expenses in order to sell the property at that time.

   If you wanted to earn a 20 percent return compounded monthly, do you believe that this would be a good investment? If not, what counteroffer would you have to make First Capital in order to achieve the 20 percent return?

6. **Spreadsheet Problem.** Use the Ch7_Rent_vs_Own worksheet in the Excel workbook provided on the Web site. Determine the after-tax *IRR* for owning versus renting in each of the five years with the following changes in the original assumptions in the spreadsheet:

   a. The homeowner has a 15 percent marginal tax rate instead of 28 percent.

   b. Rents and property values will not increase over the five years.

   c. The loan amount is $105,000 instead of $120,000.

   d. The initial rent for year 1 is $15,000 instead of $12,000.

www.mhhe.com/bf15e

8

Underwriting and Financing Residential Properties

This chapter deals with the process of seeking long-term mortgage financing for owner-occupied residential properties. Here, we focus on two aspects of this process: loan *underwriting* and *closing*. When discussing the underwriting process, we consider borrower and property characteristics and how loan terms are established. We also consider the size of the loan relative to property value, loan payments relative to borrower income, and default risk undertaken by lenders. We discuss the use of mortgage insurance or guarantees that may be necessary to grant a given loan request in cases where the total risk of lending to a specific borrower is too great for a given lender to undertake. Insurance may be provided by private insurers, or, depending on the property and borrower characteristics, insurance or guarantees may be available from various government agencies.

We look at the loan-closing process in terms of the necessary accounting between the borrower, lender, seller, and other parties to a transaction in which transfer of title and a loan closing occur simultaneously, and we consider federal regulations that require certain practices from the lender regarding uniform disclosure of interest charges, closing statements, and collection of credit and other information about the borrower.

Underwriting Default Risk

The process of evaluating a borrower's loan request in terms of potential profitability and risk is referred to as **underwriting.** This function is usually performed by a loan officer at a financial institution or mortgage banking company. The loan officer performs this analysis based on information contained in (1) the loan application submitted by the borrower and (2) an appraisal of the property. This analysis is made in the context of a lending policy, or guidelines, that a particular institution specifies. In some cases, lenders will require that borrowers obtain **default insurance.** The borrower purchases this insurance policy to protect the lender from potential losses, should the borrower default on the loan. In such cases, the lender is not willing to bear the total risk of borrower default, or the loan may be sold to a third-party investor (recall the process of assignment of the note and mortgage discussed in Chapter 2). In the latter case, the lender must consider underwriting standards required by such investors; otherwise, the lender may lose the option of selling mortgages later. In deciding whether a loan application should be accepted or rejected, the loan officer follows some fundamental concepts in loan risk analysis.

Before beginning a detailed discussion of specific underwriting standards and policies, we first consider some basic relationships and terms used in mortgage underwriting. Two fundamental relationships that must be assessed by any lender when considering the risk of making a mortgage loan are the expected **payment-to-income ratio** and the **loan-to-value ratio.** The payment-to-income ratio is simply the monthly payment on the loan amount being applied for plus other housing expenses divided by the borrower's income. The loan-to-value ratio is the loan amount requested divided by the estimated property value.

The first ratio is important because the borrower will generally be personally liable on the note and must be able to make payments either as scheduled (in the case of a *fixed rate mortgage*) or as market conditions change interest rates (in the case of *adjustable rate mortgages*). Clearly, the greater the ratio of mortgage payment to income for a given borrower, the greater is the default risk. Hence, a higher risk premium must be earned by the lender. Similarly, because the property being acquired by the borrower also serves as security for the note, as the loan-to-value ratio increases, the likelihood of loss increases. This is because the property may not bring a sufficient price at a foreclosure sale to cover the outstanding loan balance, any past due payments, and foreclosure costs. Therefore, the major problems facing a lender when reviewing a loan request made by a borrower are: (1) assessing the many variables that affect default risk, (2) determining whether a fixed interest rate or adjustable rate mortgage can be made, and (3) if the total risk on a particular loan request is too great, deciding whether the loan should be refused or made with default insurance or guarantees from third parties.

Classification of Mortgage Loans

In previous chapters, we discussed and classified mortgage loans mainly in terms of interest rate risk, that is, whether a loan was a fixed rate mortgage (FRM) or an adjustable rate mortgage (ARM). While those chapters also included a basic discussion of default risk, specific methods and procedures for assessing borrower default risk are primary topics in this chapter.

Recall from the previous chapter that default risk was defined as a potential loss that could occur if the borrower failed to make payment on a loan. This failure could be caused by a borrower having insufficient income, or because the market value of the property fell below the outstanding mortgage balance, or both. There are several ways that default risk can be shared. Default risk may be fully assumed by the lender, shared by the lender and a third-party insurer, or fully assumed by a third-party insurer or guarantor. To facilitate discussion, we use the following classifications:

1. Conventional mortgages.
2. Insured conventional mortgages.
3. FHA-insured mortgages.
4. VA-guaranteed mortgage loans.

Conventional Mortgage Loans

Conventional mortgage loans are negotiated between a borrower and lender. From these negotiations, the loan-to-value ratio, interest rate (or ARM terms), and the payment-to-income ratio are established. The loan-to-value ratio establishes the borrower's down payment, or equity. Should the borrower default on the loan, both the lender and borrower may incur losses. Losses usually include any past due interest, costs of selling the property, and the extent to which the sale price is less than the mortgage balance. In the event of loss, the borrower absorbs such losses first to the extent of any equity. If losses exceed the amount of borrower equity, the lender will then incur a loss, which then becomes a claim against the borrower and (depending on state law) may be used to attach other assets owned by the borrower (recall the discussion of deficiency judgments in Chapter 2).

Typically, if the borrower desires a conventional loan, the maximum loan amount will be 80 percent of the value of the real estate being purchased. Location of the property—for example, in a platted subdivision with city utilities—is also a key factor. Because the lender must look to the sale of the property for repayment of the mortgage loan, should the borrower default, regulations governing the operation of most savings institutions generally require that for conventional loans, equity of at least 20 percent of value must be provided by the borrower. Therefore, such losses must exceed 20 percent of the original property value before the lender would suffer a loss. Much of the lending activity in the conventional loan market is affected by the Federal National Mortgage Association (FNMA) and the Federal Home Loan Mortgage Corporation (FHLMC). See Concept Box 8.1 for a brief discussion.

Insured Conventional Mortgage Loans

In many instances, borrowers do not have the necessary wealth to make a down payment of 20 percent of value when purchasing a property. However, if the income-earning ability of the borrower and the location of the property being acquired are satisfactory, lenders may be willing to grant a loan request *in excess of 80 percent of value* with a condition that the borrower purchase **mortgage insurance** against default risk. Many firms provide this insurance for a premium, which is paid by the borrower and is based on the amount of risk assumed by the mortgage insurer. A useful way of thinking about mortgage insurance is to view the borrower as negotiating for a larger loan from the lender, and then paying an insurer to assume the increase in default risk above that taken by the lender on a conventional loan. In other words, only the amount of the loan in *excess* of 80 percent of the property value at the time of loan origination is usually covered under the mortgage insurance policy. Therefore, if a mortgage is made for 95 percent of value and private mortgage insurance is purchased, the borrower would make an equity down payment of 5 percent of the property value and the mortgage lender would make a 95 percent loan. However, the lender would have 80 percent of the loan amount at risk and the mortgage insurer would insure any losses to the lender in an amount equal to 15 percent of the property value. Borrowers evaluating a 95 percent loan must weigh the incremental cost of the additional 15 percent by considering the combination of a possibly higher rate of interest plus the cost of mortgage default insurance. (Recall the discussion of incremental borrowing costs in Chapter 6.) This incremental cost may be compared to the cost of acquiring second-lien financing or the opportunity cost associated with borrowers making a greater down payment.

Mortgage insurers are private companies that operate by collecting premiums from borrowers based on the incremental risk being assumed as loan amounts rise above 80 percent. These premiums are pooled and the insurers maintain reserves that are used to pay claims to lenders, should mortgage defaults occur. These companies can usually take this additional risk at a premium that would be lower than individual lenders would have to charge because they insure many different borrowers making mortgage loans nationally, whereas individual lenders make loans to fewer individuals in fewer geographic regions.

The influence of FNMA and FHLMC (Fannie Mae and Freddie Mac) goes far beyond the standardization of documents (appraisal forms, etc.) noted in Chapter 7. As will be described in detail in later chapters dealing with mortgage-backed securities, these two government-sponsored enterprises (GSEs) dominate the secondary residential mortgage market in the United States.

These organizations (1) purchase mortgages from lenders, (2) create large mortgage pools (often in the billions of dollars), and then (3) using these pools as collateral, issue mortgage-backed securities, which are sold to investors such as pension funds, insurance companies, and overseas investors. In order to accomplish this securitization process cost-effectively and efficiently, FNMA and FHLMC have instituted many requirements that lenders must adhere to and that have resulted in considerable standardization in the mortgage lending process.

GSEs classify loans that they are willing to purchase as (1) *conforming* or (2) *nonconforming* mortgages. The conforming category specifies the loan amount that Congress has authorized as the maximum mortgage loan that these GSEs may purchase from lenders and for which the U.S. Treasury will provide credit backing. These loans also must meet the underwriting standards of FNMA/FHLMC. FNMA and FHLMC dominate the conforming loan market because of their GSE status, which includes possible market support at the option of the U.S. Treasury. Because of the implied market support by the Treasury, FNMA and FHLMC can borrow at lower rates of interest than other entities and can buy conforming loans at lower yields than their competitors.[†]

Nonconforming loans are: (1) loans made in amounts *greater* than the loan maximums set for conforming loans or (2) loans that do not meet the underwriting standards used for conforming loans. Because jumbo loans are made in larger amounts and are not backed with government guarantees, FNMA and FHLMC must compete for them with non-GSE lenders. Because of this competition, jumbo loans are usually made by many lenders at higher interest rates than those of conforming loans.

Two additional nonconforming loan categories are *subprime* and *ALTA* loans. As will be discussed further in the underwriting section of this chapter, **subprime loans** usually indicate situations where some aspect of a borrower's credit listing is deficient. The term ALTA stands for "alternative to *A* paper," where "*A* paper" is a low risk, conforming loan. When **ALTA loans** are underwritten, some aspect of the loan application cannot be verified, such as self-employment income. However, the borrower may have sufficient assets (cash, stocks, etc.) to be approved for a loan. ALTA loans also are sometimes referred to as "low doc" (low documentation) loans.

[†]For a description of the U.S. Treasury Preferred Stock Purchase Agreement, see: http://www.treasury.gov/press-center/press-release/pages/hp1131.aspx.

Consequently, mortgage insurers are able to diversify the additional default risk more effectively than a single lender can. A single lender could be more adversely affected, should an economic decline occur in a particular region.

When an insured conventional mortgage is made, the maximum loan that a borrower is likely to obtain will be 95 percent of value, although some lenders will go even higher. Because a greater potential for loss exists and much of the risk of loss is being assumed by the mortgage insurer, underwriting requirements that the lender uses to evaluate the borrower are likely to be heavily influenced by the insurer. Lenders must rigidly adhere to these standards when this type of loan is considered. Premiums will be based on the extent to which the loan-to-value ratio exceeds 80 percent for any given borrower.

FHA-Insured Mortgage Loans

A mortgage loan can also be insured by the **Federal Housing Administration (FHA).** Unlike conventional insurance, which protects the lender against some portion of the potential loan loss, FHA mortgage insurance insures the lender *completely* against any default losses. It should be stressed that *FHA does not make loans but provides insurance.* Because FHA accepts the entire risk of borrower default, it maintains strict qualification procedures before the borrower and property will be accepted under its insurance program.

The FHA was created in 1934 with the passage of the Federal Housing Act.[1] The original intent of the FHA was to stabilize the housing industry after the Depression of the early 1930s. It has also had a long-standing policy objective to make housing affordable to lower- and middle-income families. This has been accomplished by allowing such families to purchase homes with lower down payments than would be required under conventional lending standards. The FHA operates as an *insurance program,* collecting premiums from borrowers, usually as a part of their monthly payments. These premiums are pooled to create reserves for payment of lender claims. Because FHA mortgage loans are made with higher loan-to-value ratios than conventional uninsured loans and because the FHA assumes the entire risk of default, mortgage insurance premiums charged by FHA are usually higher than private mortgage insurance premiums. This is because private mortgage insurance is usually limited to a fixed percentage of the loan amount (e.g., 15%). FHA insures lenders against all losses caused by borrower default, and this could be greater or less than a fixed percentage of the loan amount originated.

Why is there a need for both FHA and private mortgage insurance? Regulations place loan maximums on FHA-insured mortgage loans which may not be sufficient for many borrowers who purchase higher-priced properties.[2] Hence, qualified borrowers will normally choose a conventional, privately insured loan when a larger loan is necessary to purchase higher-priced property with a low down payment. In general, borrowers with higher incomes, who desire to purchase higher-valued properties with low down payments, opt for private mortgage insurance because the loan amount can be greater than the maximum available under FHA at a lower insurance cost. FHA borrowers are likely to have lower incomes and purchase properties in lower price ranges, within the maximum loan limits set by FHA. Because of the borrowers' lower incomes, lenders may insist that the entire mortgage loan be insured; consequently, these borrowers will pay higher insurance premiums to FHA.

FHA extends insurance to buyers under a number of programs. The most common is Section 203b, which insures loans on one- to four-family detached residences. This program requires fixed interest rate financing with a term of between 15 and 30 years. Other FHA loan programs include Section 251, an ARM program; Section 234c, a condominium insurance program; and Section 245, a graduated payment mortgage insurance program.[3]

VA-Guaranteed Mortgage Loans

Qualified veterans who desire to purchase a residential property and who meet certain length-of-service tests may obtain a mortgage loan guarantee from the **Department of Veterans Affairs (VA).** The VA provides **guarantees** that compensate lenders for

---

[1] The National Housing Act of 1934, as amended.

[2] For a discussion of FHA maximum insurable loan amounts, see *HUD Handbook 4000.2* and subsequent revisions. FHA maximum insurable loan amounts depend on the geographic region in which the loan is made. These amounts also change from time to time.

[3] For a detailed listing of FHA mortgage insurance programs, see *HUD Handbook 4000.2.*

losses on loans made to veterans (borrowers). The amount of the guarantee varies with the home loan amount and the veteran's remaining entitlement. The amount of the guarantee varies over time and usually cannot exceed 25 percent of FNMA-FHLMC conforming loan limits. As is the case with the FHA program, VA does not make mortgage loans. It does, however, make direct loans to the public in connection with the sale of repossessions. *Unlike the FHA program, the VA provides a loan guarantee, not default insurance.* The certificate of guarantee is provided at no charge to the lender. Unlike FHA and private mortgage default insurance, the borrower does not pay any monthly or other insurance premiums for the VA guarantee. All losses incurred by VA under this program are paid by the U.S. government through its budget allocation to the Department of Veterans Affairs. Because of this guarantee, VA underwriting is very structured, particularly regarding appraisals and property inspections.

The amount of the loan that may be guaranteed is generally limited to the amount shown on the **Certificate of Reasonable Value (CRV).** Veterans also may use their VA home loan entitlement more than once. The amount of entitlement available to a borrower at any given time depends on the current guarantee maximum, amounts of previously used entitlement, plus any amounts restored from previously used entitlement. For example, if the current maximum entitlement is $36,000 and a borrower purchases a property for $80,000, the VA will issue a certificate of guarantee for 40 percent, or $32,000, leaving $4,000 of entitlement for future use by the borrower. If after a time the borrower meets the legal requirements for *restoration,* the $32,000 of previously used entitlement would be added back to the remaining entitlement, making the full entitlement $36,000 once more.

If the borrower sells the property on assumption to another qualified veteran borrower with entitlement who agrees to substitute his entitlement for the entitlement used by the original borrower on the loan, the original borrower's entitlement would be restored.

Many other influences affect the amount of entitlement for which a borrower may qualify, for example, when both husband and wife are qualified veterans.[4]

The Underwriting Process

Regardless of the type of mortgage (conventional, conventional insured, FHA, or VA), much of the underwriting process is common to all types of mortgage loans. The underwriter begins by collecting data to determine whether credit should be extended. The goal of this process is to determine whether the loan-to-value ratio, the payment-to-income ratio, assets of the borrower, and borrower credit history are acceptable to the lender or the lender and insurer. Next, we discuss (1) how borrower income is estimated and the relationship of that income to the proposed mortgage payments and other obligations of the borrower and (2) how the value of the property is established through an appraisal.

Borrower Income

The underwriting process usually begins with the underwriter obtaining the data needed to determine whether credit should be extended. An item of primary importance will be *borrower income.* To gather the necessary data regarding income, the borrower is requested

---

[4] For a discussion of VA loan guarantee eligibility requirements, see Title 38, U.S. Code, Section 3701.

to allow the lender to (1) verify place of employment, (2) verify wages (via W-2 forms, paycheck stubs, etc.), and (3) inquire as to whether employment is likely to continue into the future. Typically, where a borrower is employed on a full-time basis and obtains regular income from this employment, there is little problem in verifying income. In cases where a borrower's income is derived from more than a single source, the process of verifying the amount and the likelihood of that income continuing is more difficult.

Other possible income sources include these:

- Part-time employment
- Working spouse
- Rentals
- Alimony or child support
- Commissions
- Self-employment
- Bonuses
- Dividends or interest
- Retirement annuity
- Social Security
- Public assistance

Generally, two tests must be met before any of these sources will be included in establishing borrower income in the underwriting process. First, the underwriter must judge that the income is likely to continue. This usually means that a source of income must have already occurred continuously for a sufficient time for the underwriter to judge whether that income will continue. Second, the income must be verifiable, usually by reviewing the borrower's federal income tax returns for at least two years. When the income is nontaxable, such as distributions from retirement annuities, canceled checks or verification of deposits may be used to verify the existence of the income.

In addition to deciding what sources of income should be included, difficulties also arise when determining how much income should be used in the underwriting process. For example, the amount of income from a particular source may vary from period to period. When income is variable in nature, such as the earnings from commission sales positions, rentals, or self-employment, a borrower's income will generally be averaged over a period of at least two years from amounts shown on tax returns. Any expenses incurred in earning that income will be deducted from the amount of income earned.

When two individuals are employed, the question arises of what constitutes income. The general rule applied by the lender takes a long-run viewpoint; that is, it asks whether both individuals will remain employed indefinitely, or at least until the income of one is sufficient to meet the monthly mortgage payments. This question often presents difficulty when the value of the property and the loan amount being requested are high in relation to the income of only one of the earners. Obviously, the lender will have to exercise judgment about the future stability of the joint incomes. Generally, if both parties have been employed for several consecutive years, future income stability is more likely. If the intent of one of the parties is to end employment after a given number of years and this individual is presently employed in a professional activity with employment stability, both incomes may be included for the time both expect to remain employed. An estimate may be made as to what the primary worker's total income will be at the time the other party ceases employment.

Although income forms much of the basis for risk analysis by the lender, recent federal regulations have limited the extent to which lenders may obtain information or make inferences concerning a loan applicant's background. Regulation B of the Board of Governors of the Federal Reserve System provides guidelines that lenders must comply with when gathering information about potential borrowers.[5]

Verification of Borrower Assets

Another step in the data collection process is the *verification of borrower assets.* Assets of the borrower must at least be sufficient to close the transaction. This means that borrower assets must be sufficient to pay closing costs and make a down payment. Moreover, lenders usually do not allow borrowed funds to be used as the borrower's down payment. Thus, how long a borrower's assets have been on deposit will be used as an important indicator of whether the borrower is planning to use borrowed funds to make a down payment. Gifts, on the other hand, are usually allowed for all funds necessary to close. A gift letter stating that no repayment is required, signed by both the borrower and gift donor, is usually required. The lender will usually document the transfer of funds from the donor's account to the borrower's account. Any assets that are not required to close the lending transaction will reflect favorably upon the creditworthiness of the borrower.

Other assets of the applicant also play an important role in rating the loan quality by the lender. The rating is improved if the applicant has demonstrated a consistent ability to save as evidenced by savings accounts or investments in other property, ownership of life insurance (cash value), purchase of securities, and the like, as well as the ability to carry the obligations associated with the acquisition of these assets. For example, an older applicant whose remaining life expectancy is less than the term of the mortgage being sought may be granted a loan with the desired maturity, even though it exceeds the years of life expectancy remaining, if adequate life insurance exists to pay off the mortgage loan in the event death occurs before the loan is repaid. In most cases, the lender will request that the applicant sign a request allowing other financial institutions, investment companies, and credit agencies to disclose to the lender the nature and amount of the applicant's assets. These could include stocks, bonds, savings accounts, and any recent activity in the accounts.

Assessment of Credit History

Typically, the underwriter will also make a judgment about the acceptability of the borrower's past payment history on other obligations. Credit reports from a central credit bureau, located

---

[5] (1) The use of sex, marital status, race, religion, age, or national origin in a credit underwriting procedure is prohibited. (2) Creditors may not inquire into birth control practices or into childbearing capabilities or intentions, or assume, from her age, that an applicant or an applicant's spouse may drop out of the labor force due to childbearing and thus have an interruption of income. (3) A creditor may not discount part-time income but may examine the probable continuity of the applicant's job.
(4) A creditor may ask and consider whether and to what extent an applicant's income is affected by obligations to make alimony or child support or maintenance payments. (5) A creditor may ask to what extent an applicant is relying on alimony or child support or maintenance payments to repay the debt being requested, but the applicant must first be informed that no such disclosure is necessary if the applicant does not rely on such income to obtain the credit. Where the applicant chooses to rely on alimony, a creditor shall consider such payments as income to the extent the payments are likely to be made consistently. (6) Applicants receiving public assistance payments cannot be denied access to credit. If these payments and security provided for the loan meet normal underwriting standards, credit must be extended. (7) An individual may apply for credit without obligating a spouse to repay the obligation, as long as underwriting standards of the lender are met. (8) A creditor shall not take into account the existence of a telephone listing in the name of an applicant when evaluating applications. A creditor may take into account the existence of a telephone in the applicant's home. (9) Upon the request of an applicant, the creditor will be required to provide reasons for terminating or denying credit.

in most cities, will give a history on a borrower's payment habits for up to 10 years. Such things as slow payment of past borrower obligations may reflect unfavorably upon the loan applicant. Many examples of adverse credit experience will surely cause the loan application to be rejected. However, a brief interruption in an otherwise acceptable credit history caused by explainable events such as divorce or interruption in income will sometimes be overlooked by the underwriter if an explanation is provided—assuming that the borrower has recovered financially from the adverse circumstances that caused this problem. Even bankruptcy may not automatically cause a loan application to be rejected if there were extenuating circumstances and the borrower has had several years of acceptable history since the problem occurred. For developments in analysis and **credit scoring,** see Concept Box 8.2.

Estimated Housing Expense

Determining the housing expense used to establish the payment-to-income ratio that a borrower is proposing to undertake is relatively straightforward. The following is a list of items that are likely to be included in the estimate of monthly housing expense:

- Principal and interest on the mortgage being applied for.
- Mortgage insurance (if any).
- Property taxes.
- Hazard insurance.
- Condominium or cooperative homeowners association dues (if applicable).

The underwriter will have to estimate many of these items because their exact amounts will not be known at the time of underwriting. Very often, the lender may require that the borrower pay monthly, prorated installments toward mortgage insurance, hazard insurance, and property taxes, in addition to the mortgage payment. Judgment concerning the risk associated with making the mortgage loan will depend upon the total cost of home ownership relative to borrower income. If this total cost of home ownership is too high, then an applicant's loan application may be rejected. Specific examples of how these expenses are estimated and related to income will be discussed later in the chapter.

Other Obligations

In most cases, borrowers will have other obligations in addition to the mortgage loan being applied for. Obvious examples include auto loans, credit card accounts, other mortgage debts, or alimony and child support payments. The underwriter will request that the borrower disclose all debts at the time of application, and then verify these commitments by obtaining a credit report with the approval of the borrower. Courthouse records in the borrower's county of residence also may be checked to determine whether there are any judgments outstanding against the borrower for unpaid debts. Another item on the credit report of importance to the underwriter will be whether the borrower has ever filed for bankruptcy.

Compensating Factors

It is possible that the underwriter will find other favorable factors about the borrower that can offset certain unfavorable factors during the underwriting process. Typically, it is considered favorable for a borrower to have liquid assets that could be used to make monthly mortgage payments should the borrower's income be interrupted. Another favorable factor is if the borrower is employed in a field in which his or her skills are in high demand and the likelihood is that the borrower's income will increase over time. These factors may prove sufficient to allow a borrower to devote more income to housing

The evolution of credit scoring models has had a profound impact on all areas of lending, including mortgage lending. When underwriting mortgage loans, lenders usually require that a credit report be obtained on borrowers. Most credit reports contain *credit scores.** This credit score is a three-digit credit rating that represents an estimate of an individual's financial creditworthiness as determined by a statistical model. Lenders use the borrower/applicant's credit score as *one of many inputs* in the underwriting process. The credit score attempts to quantify the likelihood that a prospective borrower will fail to repay a loan during a specified period of time. Credit scores have an important influence on (1) loan approval and (2) the interest rate that will be quoted on a loan. The maximum credit score is usually in the range of 850. High credit scores increase the probability that the loan will be approved and that it will be made at a lower interest rate than may be quoted to borrowers with lower credit scores. Scores below 600 to 700 may result in rejection of the loan application, unless the lender has additional compelling information, such as other assets owned by the loan applicant that may serve as security.

While the contents of credit-scoring models are private, it is generally believed that the major variables used in the models to determine the final credit score include the following (approximate weights are shown in parentheses):

A. Punctuality of past payments (35%).
B. Capacity used: the ratio of current debt (credit card balances, etc.) to total available credit card limits (30%).
C. Years of credit experience (15%).
D. Types of credit used (10%).
E. Recent searches for credit and/or the number of credit cards/accounts applied for recently (10%).

A. Punctual payment. A prompt payment history has a very positive effect on credit scores. Any payments reported more than 30 days late have a negative affect on credit scores. Any account placed in "collection status" (usually after it is six months past due) has a very negative effect on scores. (To increase credit scores, borrowers should strive to pay an amount greater than the minimum payment due each month on credit cards and installment loans. If possible, borrower should repay the outstanding loan/credit balance in full each month.)

B. Capacity used. Large total outstanding loan balances as a percentage of total credit limits available on all credit cards used by a borrower will generally have a negative effect on the credit score. Capacity used is calculated as the maximum credit balance used anytime during the billing cycle divided by the total credit limit available on credit accounts. When consolidating the credit card debt, borrowers should be aware that the capacity used ratio may increase if credit accounts are closed and outstanding credit balances are transferred as fewer accounts could result in a lower total credit limit.

C. Length of credit history experience. A lengthy experience with managing credit usually has a positive influence on borrower credit scores. Individuals with less credit experience will not score as well. This tends to favor older individuals with a long history of successful credit management.

D. Types of credit used. Loans made with consumer finance companies or other entities that make loans to high-risk individuals at high interest rates have a negative effect on scores.

E. Searches/inquiries. The number of applications, credit cards issued, and inquiries to credit bureaus regarding the status of the borrower's credit tend to have a negative impact on credit scores. Frequent inquiries regarding borrower credit reporting balances may also adversely affect scores.

* The basis for most credit scores is the so-called *FICO score*, developed by the Fair Issac Corporation and based on a statistical default risk model. Such models have been used by the three major credit reporting agencies (TransUnion, Equifax, and Experian). However, the suppliers of credit data (retailers, etc.) to these three agencies are not all the same. Consequently, depending on the credit reporting agency chosen, credit scores may differ for the same applicant.

- *Lock-in period and fee.* Most lenders will provide a firm interest quote usually for 30 days prior to closing. This "lock in" period is a commitment by the lender to make a loan at a specific rate of interest for a specified number of days, even though market interest rates may change prior to the actual loan closing. Some lenders may charge a fee to lock this rate in. Lock-in periods may also be extended to 45 or 90 days, usually for a higher fee.

- *Private mortgage insurance (PMI).* This is usually required for loans that are over 80 percent of value. However, borrowers who need loans in excess of 80 percent of value may consider a first lien for 80 percent, and then add a second lien for the additional amount needed. By keeping the first lien at or below 80 percent, borrowers may avoid PMI. However, interest rates on second liens are usually higher, and this higher rate must be compared to PMI premiums.

- *Option to eliminate PMI or FHA insurance after closing.* These requirements may be dropped, usually when loan-to-value ratios fall below 80 percent. This will reduce monthly payments by the amount of the monthly insurance premium. Elimination of this insurance will usually require a new appraisal conducted by an appraiser who must be approved by the lender.

- *Buying down interest rates.* This option may be compared with making larger down payments. As larger down payments are made, interest rates quoted on a loan should be compared to the interest rate available if the borrower buys down the rate from the lender.

- *Subprime loans.* When a deficiency is discovered (e.g., low credit score) during the underwriting phase of the loan application process, lenders may be willing to make a **subprime loan.** These loans are usually made at higher rates of interest than would otherwise be available and may also include prepayment penalties and significant penalties for late payments. Subprime borrowers may attempt to negotiate a provision in the loan that, if such a deficiency is cured (e.g., the borrower achieves a higher credit score) after closing, the interest rate will be reduced.

expenses, even if the borrower's proposed housing expense ratio is higher than for other borrowers with similar incomes. Of course, making a substantial equity down payment as part of the purchase price is considered favorable as well. When any or all of these conditions exist, it is possible that underwriting policies may be relaxed to some degree.

After all of the factual data described above have been determined, the loan underwriter will consider whether or not the loan in question should be granted. The process of making this evaluation varies, depending upon the kind of loan the borrower is seeking. The following examples of the underwriting process in conventional, insured conventional, FHA, and VA loan transactions should help to illustrate this point. For a list of other important issues and strategies, see Concept Box 8.3.

The Underwriting Process Illustrated

This chapter section illustrates how each of the four types of mortgage loans described above are generally underwritten by lenders. As indicated earlier, one goal of underwriting is to establish whether the risk of borrower default is acceptable and whether the loan should be granted. We will consider each type of mortgage (conventional, insured conventional, FHA, and VA) separately. In this section, we look at how the maximum mortgage amount is established, how it is related to property value, and how that relationship varies with each type of mortgage. We also discuss (1) proposed housing expenses and other obligations relative to borrower income, (2) the criteria used to establish acceptable relationships between expenses and income, which will serve as the basis for the lending decision, and (3) the role of appraisals in establishing the loan-to-value ratio.

To facilitate the discussion, we use the sample borrower information in Exhibit 8–1 to illustrate the underwriting process for each category of mortgage loans. Details about the underwriting criteria will be sufficient to allow generalizations beyond the cases used in our discussion.

Underwriting Standards—Conventional and Insured Conventional Mortgages

Looking at the data shown in Exhibit 8–1, we see that in addition to the verification of income and outstanding debts, the lender has estimated both property taxes and hazard insurance (fire, storm, etc.), which are also used in estimating housing expenses. These expenses establish the monthly payment-to-income ratio for the borrower-applicants. Looking at Exhibit 8–2, we see some of the general underwriting standards that lenders will apply in making the decision to grant or deny the loan request. In other words, after assembling the facts necessary to establish monthly housing expenses and other obligations, the lender will compute the necessary ratios and compare them to the general standards used by the lenders and mortgage insurers. This will help determine whether the default risk is acceptable, given the prevailing rate of interest. Lenders and insurers establish these underwriting standards, or maximum allowable ratios, based on loss experience from previously underwritten loans. Interpret these ratios as a general guide, however, because there may be other assets or compensating factors to be considered as part of the underwriting process.

Also note in Exhibit 8–2 that, in the case of ARMs, more stringent underwriting standards may have to be met in certain cases. This is because an increase in interest rates could result in either an increase in payments or an increase in the loan balance due to a

EXHIBIT 8–1	Name of borrower:
Sample Underwriting	Income:
Illustration:	
Borrower and	
Property	Debts:
Characteristics	

Name of borrower:	John and Jane J. Jones
Income:	$3,542 monthly from salaried employment of both spouses, $42,500 annually
Debts:	Installment obligation of $181 per month with 35 months remaining
	Credit card obligations, $50 per month with more than 12 months remaining
Sale price:	$76,700
Appraised value:	$77,000
Estimated property taxes:	$797 annually
Hazard insurance:	$552 annually
Desired mortgage:	FRM with a 30-year term, constant payment

[6] When the composite rate is higher than the initial rate at the time of origination, the initial, or start rate, is referred to as the *teaser rate*, because lenders may be using it as an incentive for borrowers to make ARMs. In some cases, the loan agreement may specify that at closing, any difference between the start rate and the composite rate represents accrued interest and is added to the loan balance. When the first payment adjustment occurs, payments will then increase if the composite rate remains higher than the initial rate. Should the composite rate increase substantially on the payment reset date, the increase in ARM payments may be substantial and is referred to as *payment shock* in the lending industry.

EXHIBIT 8–2
General Industry Standards for Underwriting Conventional and Insured Conventional Loans

	Conventional		Insured Conventional	
	FRMs	ARMs	FRMs	ARMs
Maximum ratios allowed (%):				
Loan-to-value	80%	80%	95%	90*–95%
Payment-to-income	28	25†–28	28	25†–28
Total obligations to income	36	33†–36	36	33†–36

*Conventional ARMs with loan-to-value ratios in excess of 90 percent are generally not available, although some lenders will loan in excess of 90 percent at a higher interest rate. Graduated payment mortgages (GPMs) are usually limited to 90 percent loan-to-value ratios because of scheduled negative amortization.

†Generally, the higher ratios are allowed; however, if the conventional ARM or GPM allows for the possibility of maximum increases in monthly payments beyond prescribed limits, the lower ratios must be met for the loan to be insured.

See: Bankrate.com for current information on underwriting standards.

payment cap and negative amortization. Lenders refer to cases where negative amortization is expected as *scheduled amortization* and usually take it into account when underwriting the ARM by requiring a *lower* loan-to-value ratio. If payments are likely to be adjusted because the composite rate (current ARM index plus margin) at the time of origination is higher than the initial interest rate, the underwriter will probably consider the scheduled payment increase when reviewing the payment-to-income ratio.[6] Note that conventional GPMs are usually underwritten on the basis of scheduled amortization, which is known at the time of origination, and the loan-to-value ratio is usually restricted to 90 percent. Also, in the case of ARMs, initial maximum payment-to-income ratios may be lowered if the mortgage agreement provides for the possibility of monthly payments exceeding prescribed maximums. For example, if an ARM is made with a payment cap greater than 15 percent annually, or if the interest rate cap exceeds 2 percent annually or 5 percent over the life of the mortgage, lower ratios will usually be required. This latter restriction also applies to GPMs.

When computing these ratios for the conventional and insured conventional cases, we take relevant information from Exhibit 8–1 and compute the necessary ratios shown in Exhibit 8–3. Note that in the two cases being considered, the insured conventional loan is larger (95% vs. 80%) and is made at a higher interest rate. Also, the insured loan requires a monthly mortgage insurance premium, and the conventional loan does not. The ratios calculated and shown at the bottom of the exhibit indicate that the borrower would probably qualify for either a conventional loan or an insured conventional loan, given that those ratios fall well below the maximum ratios allowed under the general underwriting standards shown in Exhibit 8–2. Whether the borrower will prefer the conventional or insured conventional loan depends on the amount available for a down payment (20% or 5% of appraised value) and whether the borrower wants to pay additional interest and insurance charges. The latter choice also depends on whether the borrower has sufficient funds to make either down payment requirement.[7] If the borrower could afford to make either down payment, the borrower must decide whether the difference (15%) can be reinvested at a rate of interest in excess of the added interest and insurance charges. (A procedure that may be used to choose between loans that differ in amount and interest rates was presented in detail in Chapter 7.)

[7] Examples of various closing costs to be discussed later in the chapter include origination fees, appraisal fees, credit report fees, and transfer taxes.

EXHIBIT 8–3
General Approaches to Computation of Borrower Qualification (Conventional and Insured Conventional Loan Examples)

	Conventional	Insured Conventional
Loan amount requested	$61,360	$72,865
Terms	FRM 30 years 9.25%	FRM 30 years 9.5%
Loan-to-value ratio	80%	95%
Borrower income (A)	$ 3,542	$ 3,542
Housing expenses:		
Principal and interest	$ 505	$ 613
Property taxes	66	66
Hazard insurance	46	46
Mortgage insurance	—	21
Housing expense (B)	617	746
Add:		
Installment debt*	181	181
Credit cards	50	50
Total obligations (C)	$ 848	$ 977
Housing expense ratio (B ÷ A)	17%	21%
Total obligation ratio (C ÷ A)	24%	28%

*Usually defined as an obligation with at least 11 remaining monthly payments. However, any obligation that in the judgment of the underwriter requires a large monthly outlay relative to income may be included, even if the number of remaining payments is less than 11.

Underwriting Standards—FHA-Insured Mortgages

If the borrower in our example is considering an FHA-insured mortgage, a similar approach is used to underwriting, with some notable exceptions. To begin our general discussion of FHA underwriting, we point out that unlike the conventional underwriting process, which provides for loan amounts as a percentage of appraised value (80%, 95%, etc.), FHA has a specific procedure that is used to establish the *maximum insurable loan amount* for which it is willing to issue an insurance binder.[8] This process is generally described in Exhibit 8–4.

It should be stressed that FHA has historically established its own standards for both of these qualifying ratios (see bottom of the exhibit), which it uses uniformly for FRM, GPM, and ARM loans. This practice of computing ratios based on *current income* at the time of loan origination is followed even though monthly payments with a GPM or ARM may change in future periods.

As in the case of conventional lending, the underwriter is likely to take into account other assets, credit history, and offsetting factors when deciding to accept or reject a loan application. Qualifying ratios used as standards in determining the adequacy of borrower income are based on FHA's loss experience in the operation of its insurance fund. Our hypothetical borrower-applicants, then, would likely qualify for an FHA-insured loan. FHA uses one additional underwriting test, however, which is discussed in the next section.

Underwriting Standards—VA-Guaranteed Mortgages

The underwriting process followed by the Veterans Administration (VA) differs considerably in its approach to establishing the adequacy of borrower income in relation to the loan request. The VA procedure stresses the notion of **residual income,** which is a process, whereby gross income is reduced by all monthly outlays for housing, expenses, taxes, all debt obligations, and recurring job-related expenses (see Exhibit 8–5). The difference, or

[8] The maximum loan-to-value limits are subject to change at any time.

Web App

First-time homeowners often use FHA loans to finance their home. Go to **www.fha-home-loans.com** and find out the *current* requirements to qualify for an FHA loan. They may differ slightly from that described in the book be- cause the underwriting requirements frequently change. Summarize the types of loans that are currently available. What is the highest loan-to-value ratio that you could obtain?

EXHIBIT 8–4
General Approach in the Determination of Maximum Loan Amount and Borrower Qualification Ratios (General FHA Example)

SECTION I. Maximum Loan Amount Calculation

First Calculation

Lower of price or appraised value	$76,700
Plus: Closing cost allowance*	1,350
Acquisition cost	$78,050
97 percent of the first $25,000	$24,250
95 percent of the remainder	50,397
Maximum loan amount under first calculation	$74,647

Second Calculation

Lower of price or appraised value	$76,700
Times: Maximum loan-to-value ratio—Value > $50,000	97.75%
Maximum loan amount under second calculation	$74,974
Maximum loan amount†—lesser of the first or second calculation	$74,647
Plus: Financed mortgage insurance premium† of 2.25 pecent‡	1,679
Amount financed	$76,326

SECTION II. Computation of Qualifying Ratios

Gross income (monthly) (A)	$ 3,542
Housing Expense	
Principal, interest, and up-front mortgage insurance premium	
($76,326, 9.5%, 30 years)	$ 642
Property taxes	66
Hazard insurance	46
Annual mortgage insurance premium‡	31
Total housing expense (B)	$ 785
Other Obligations	
Installment debt§	$181
Credit cards	50
Total obligations (C)	$ 1,016

Qualifying Ratios (percent)	Applicant Ratios (%)	FHA Maximum Ratios (%)
Housing expense ratio B/A	22	29
Total obligations ratio C/A	29	41

*The FHA may provide a closing cost allowance in determining the loan amount. Limits on this amount vary by region.
†The maximum loan amount may not exceed limits set by FHA regulations. These limits vary by city and change over time.
‡The mortgage insurance premium is composed of two components, an up-front insurance premium, which may be financed or paid in cash, and an annual fee, which varies in terms of amount and term according to the loan-to-value ratio. See U.S. Department of Housing and Urban Development *Mortgagee Letter 94–14* and revisions for a complete discussion on mortgage insurance premiums.
§Usually, debt with 10 installments remaining. However, the underwriter can increase or decrease the number of installments depending on the total number of obligations outstanding and the relationship to borrower income.

EXHIBIT 8–5
Determination of Borrower Qualification (General VA-Guaranteed Loan Example)

Residual income technique		
Gross income		$3,542
Less federal income taxes		602
State income taxes		106
Social Security taxes		266
All debts*		231
Maintenance		58
Utilities		134
Principal and interest payment†		657
Property taxes		66
Hazard insurance		46
Job-related, or child care expense		50
Residual income		$1,326
Minimum residual income for family of:‡	1	424
	2	710
	3	855
	4	964
	5	999
	6	1,079
	7	1,159

*Usually includes obligations with six monthly installments remaining; however, the underwriter may include any obligations considered material relative to the borrower's income.
†Based on a loan amount of $78,138 at 9.5 percent for 30 years (rounded).
‡Residual income figures are determined by the region of the country and the loan amount.

residual income, is then examined to establish whether VA deems it adequate for supporting the borrower's family.

A few items are of particular importance. The mortgage loan amount is equal to the sale price, $76,700, plus a funding fee ranging from .5 percent to 3.0 percent of the loan request to help the borrower fund closing costs (to be discussed).[9] Because the loan request is equal to or less than the maximum loan amount, it would qualify for a guarantee.[10] In addition, because the VA is providing a *guarantee,* no monthly mortgage insurance premium is required of the borrower. Based on the borrower-applicant information in Exhibit 8–1, with a family size of two and no minor dependents, our hypothetical borrowers should qualify for a VA-guaranteed loan. They would also meet the supplemental test as used as a secondary underwriting tool by the FHA.

[9] VA has typically allowed the funding fee (which is paid to VA) to be included in the veteran's loan amount. However, the VA monitors what it considers to be excessive closing costs when considering whether to extend its guarantee.

[10] The down payment plus VA guarantee are subject to change at any time, depending on congressional action. VA loans also may be assumable. There are two types of assumptions: (1) nonqualifying assumptions, where the buyer may or may not be a veteran or qualify with VA before assuming the loan and (2) qualifying assumptions, where the buyer assumes the loan with VA approval. When a VA mortgage loan is assumed, the buyer is not required to be a veteran and is not charged for the mortgage guarantee. If, however, the buyer is a veteran and the seller can induce him to substitute his guarantee for the guarantee used by the seller, then the seller's VA entitlement can be restored and used again. Also, in many instances, increases in VA guarantees provided for by Congress are retroactive. As a result, a veteran who used his maximum VA guarantee in one period may have an additional VA guarantee in a subsequent period.

Underwriting and Loan Amounts—A Summary

It is useful at this point to summarize some pertinent data before moving on to the next topic, closing costs. Exhibit 8–6 provides a summary breakdown of some of the more important characteristics considered thus far. The first item to be noted is that although we begin with the same appraised value in all cases, the loan amount will vary by mortgage category. This variation is based on the fact that we have assumed that a loan-to-value ratio of 80 percent is to be used in the case of the conventional loan and a 95 percent loan is to be made in the insured conventional loan case with any additional closing costs to be paid by the borrower in both cases. In the FHA case, the loan amount is higher because of the higher loan-to-value ratio allowed by FHA (97% and 95% of portions of the loan request) *and* because a closing cost allowance may be financed under this program. In the case of the VA, the loan amount is 100 percent of the lower of price or appraised value, plus an allowance for closing costs. Also note that an additional term, *amount financed,* is used in the exhibit. This is the amount upon which the monthly interest and principal will be calculated. In two of the cases it is equal to the loan amount. In the FHA case, the amount financed includes the total insurance premium, or 2.25 percent of the loan balance (or an additional $1,679), that the lender is also financing and that must be repaid as a part of monthly principal and interest on the total loan amount. In the case of the VA loan, the funding fee also may be borrowed, making the amount financed greater than the loan amount.

Other items of importance in Exhibit 8–6 are the interest rates and notes regarding insurance costs. In our example, we have assumed that the interest rate on the conventional loan will be 9.25 percent, or lower than the rate charged in the other three cases. This is because the amount of funds being loaned is lower than in the other cases. Another important item about interest rates in the exhibit is that all of these rates are competitively determined through negotiation between borrower and lender and will change over time. Do not infer from our example that there is a fixed spread between interest rates on conventional and other loan types. These illustrations are used as *examples only.* Similarly, we assume the terms of the mortgages to be 30 years. While FHA and VA loans are available in 15- to 30-year terms, 30-year loans are used most frequently under these programs. Conventional mortgages, however, are frequently made from 15 to 30 years. Finally, keep in mind that in developing the estimates of housing expenses, total obligations, and other expenses used in underwriting, we have assumed the same estimates in many of our examples for similar expense categories (utilities, maintenance, debts, etc.). In reality, these estimates may differ, depending on the specific regulations, policies, cost manuals, and guidelines that the various insurers and lenders involved in the

EXHIBIT 8–6
Summary of
Underwriting Results

	Conventional	Insured Conventional	FHA Insured	VA Guaranteed
(a) Lower of price/ appraised value	$76,700	$76,700	$76,700	$76,700
(b) Loan amount	$61,360	$72,865	$74,647	$76,700
(c) Amount financed	$61,360	$72,865	$76,326	$78,234
(d) Interest rate	9.25%	9.5%	9.5%	9.5%
(e) Term	30 years	30 years	30 years	30 years
(f) Insurance fee	N.A.	*	†	N.A.

* For example: .8 percent of loan at closing, .35 percent per year, payable monthly.
† Two components: an up-front mortgage insurance premium that may either be financed or paid at closing and a monthly insurance premium that varies according to the loan term, loan-to-value ratio, and date of loan closing.

underwriting process use.[11] While there are many other peculiarities associated with underwriting each type of loan, we have attempted to limit the administrative and regulatory detail and to focus on the major differences between underwriting approaches and regulations in order to help the reader understand the more important attributes of the process.

The Closing Process

When a property is being acquired, all interested parties gather, execute, and exchange the documents necessary both to *close the buyer's loan* and to *transfer title to the property* from the seller to the buyer. Generally, such closings are attended by (1) the buyer and seller (perhaps each with legal counsel), (2) any real estate brokers involved, and (3) the settlement agent. The settlement agent is usually a representative of a title insurance company, if such insurance is being purchased, or a representative of the lender, if no title insurance is purchased. The purpose of the closing, then, is (1) to make final settlement between the buyer and seller for costs, fees, and prorations associated with the real estate transaction prior to the transfer of title and (2) to finalize the loan agreement between the buyer/borrower and the lender.

To summarize the disbursements, charges, and credits associated with the closing, a settlement of closing statement is prepared by the settlement agent. This statement summarizes the expenses and fees to be paid by the buyer and seller, and it shows the amount of funds that the buyer must pay and the amount of funds that the seller will receive at closing. The loan and title closing occur simultaneously because the new lender wants assurance that his lien is established (1) as soon as the seller's lender is repaid and that lien is canceled and (2) when the buyer's title company provides title insurance, thereby providing assurance that there are no outstanding liens and/or imperfections in the title being transferred to the buyer. In this event, the new lender will have first lien on the property.

Fees and Expenses

Expenses associated with loan closings must be paid either by the buyer or by the seller, depending on negotiations between the buyer and seller and to some extent on custom in a particular lending area. There is no generally established practice in the area of expense settlement, and in many cases payment of any, or all, expenses is negotiated between the buyer and the seller. What follows is an identification of various expenses associated with real estate closings, followed by an illustration of a settlement statement.

Financing Costs

These charges are generally paid by the buyer/borrower to the lender and are made in connection with services performed by the lender when underwriting and approving the loan. What follows is an extensive list of possible charges that may be made by the lender.

1. Loan application fee. Charge made for processing the borrower's loan application.
2. Credit report fee. Charge made for compilation of the borrower's credit statement.
3. Loan origination fee. Charge which compensates the originator of a mortgage loan for handling paperwork, preparing mortgage documents, and dispensing funds to the borrower.

---

[11] FHA and VA closing cost estimates may vary regionally, or even locally, and are updated continuously. In some instances, an appraiser may even make specific estimates of utilities and maintenance items for a given property.

4. Lender's attorney's fees. For preparing loan documents—mortgage/note; also for examining title documents presented to the lender.
5. Property appraisal fee required by the lender. (In many cases, this fee is paid directly by the buyer outside of the closing.)
6. Fees for property survey and photos when required by the lender. (This fee may also be paid by the buyer/borrower directly to the surveying company outside of closing.)
7. Fees for preparation of loan amortization schedule by the lender from the borrower.
8. Loan discount points. Additional charge paid to the lender to increase the loan yield (per discussion in Chapter 4).
9. Prepaid interest. Interest charged from the date of closing until the date that interest begins accruing under the terms of the note. The latter date usually coincides with the day of the month that the borrower and lender prefer to make payments, which may be different from the day of the month that the closing occurs.

Prorations, Escrow Costs, and Payments to Third Parties

Property Taxes, Prorations, and Escrow Accounts

Because the dates on which property taxes are due to a particular governmental unit rarely coincide with the title closing date, a *portion* of the annual property taxes is usually prorated between the buyer and the seller. For example, if a county collects taxes due on January 1 of each year, and the loan-closing is April 1, the seller should pay taxes (January through March), because the seller owned the property for part of the next tax period. A proration of taxes is usually made at closing by refunding to the buyer that portion of the taxes that the buyer will be responsible for on the next January 1st, but related to the period that the seller owned the property. In this way, the seller pays taxes up until the closing date.

Depending on the loan-to-value ratio in the transaction, the lender may require that an escrow account be established. An escrow account is a non-interest-bearing account into which are deposited prorated taxes from the seller and into which the borrower prepays a monthly share of property tax along with the monthly mortgage payment. These funds are accumulated until taxes are due; then, a disbursement is made by the lender to pay the tax bill when due. In addition to these monthly payments, the lender may also require that two additional monthly payments be prepaid and escrowed at closing. This is done to ensure the lender of a "cushion," or reserve, in the event that the borrower falls behind in payments or is in default. This provision assures the lender that no tax liens will be attached to the property as a result of the borrower's failure to pay property tax, and is usually required in cases where the loan-to-value ratio exceeds 80 percent.[12]

Mortgage Insurance and Escrow Accounts

When mortgage default insurance is made a requirement of obtaining a loan, it will be paid in one of two ways. Either the full policy premium will be paid by the borrower at closing, or, if the borrower plans to make premium payments over time, the premium for the first year will be prepaid by the borrower at closing and then disbursed to the insurer. The premium for the second year is also determined at closing, and the borrower will be required to prepay an amount equal to two monthly premiums into escrow. Monthly

---

[12] A lender may require that escrow accounts be established on any mortgage regardless of the loan-to-value ratio, but loans with loan-to-value ratios above 80 percent will always require escrow accounts; see Title 12 CFR, Section 54532(b)(6).

premium payments are then prepaid into escrow each month after the closing. In this way, when the annual policy premium comes due each year after closing, the lender will always have a full year's premium for payment plus premiums for two additional months in escrow. The escrow or reserve may be needed, should the borrower fall behind in mortgage payments and default becomes a possibility. The escrow ensures that the default insurance policy will not lapse, should the borrower be in danger of default. This is the objective of requiring a default insurance policy, and the lender wants to be certain that it does not lapse and coverage is not lost while the loan is about to go into default. In most cases, mortgage insurance will no longer be required by the lender after the loan balance falls below 80 percent of its original balance, and under certain other conditions.[13]

Hazard Insurance and Escrow Accounts

Hazard insurance against property damage is required by the lender as a condition for making the loan, and the mortgage usually carries a provision to that effect. For loans made in excess of 80 percent of value, however, the lender usually requires evidence that the borrower has obtained a commitment or "binder" showing that the premium for the first year will be collected by the date of closing. An escrow account will also be established for pro rata payments made by the borrower toward the next annual premium due on the policy renewal date. In other words, like the collection of property taxes and mortgage insurance premiums, the lender collects monthly installments equal to 1/12 of the annual premium, along with the mortgage payment, and credits the insurance payment to the borrower's escrow account. When the policy renewal date arrives, the lender then disburses the 12 monthly payments accumulated to the property insurance company. In this way, the lender is certain that the property is always insured against damage. This in turn insures the loan collateral. In addition to these requirements, the lender will also require that two months' premiums be prepaid at closing and escrowed. In this way, the lender has a hazard insurance reserve with which to pay premiums, should the borrower default.

Mortgage Cancellation Insurance and Escrow Accounts

Mortgage cancellation insurance is usually optional, depending on whether the borrower desires it. Essentially, it amounts to a declining term life insurance policy which is taken out at closing and runs for the term of the mortgage. Because the outstanding loan balance declines as monthly payments are made on a fully amortizing mortgage, the insurance coverage also declines with the loan balance. In the event of the borrower's death, the insurance coverage is equal to the outstanding loan balance. The mortgage loan is repaid with insurance proceeds. Premiums are usually paid monthly and are added to the monthly mortgage payment. The lender then disburses those payments to the life insurance company. Although mortgage cancellation insurance is usually bought at the borrower's option, if the borrower's age is a critical factor in the lender's loan analysis, purchase of such insurance may be necessary to obtain the loan.

---

[13] Mortgage insurance may no longer be required by the lender: (1) after the borrower pays the mortgage down to less than 80 percent of its original loan amount, (2) if the property appreciates in value such that the outstanding loan-to-current-value ratio falls below 80 percent, (3) if permitted by the loan agreement, borrowers are allowed to prepay or make a partially amortizing payment reducing the loan balance to less than 80 percent of value, or (4) in some cases, when the mortgage loan reaches the midpoint of its amortization schedule. Assuming that it is allowed in the mortgage insurance policy, the borrower should request that monthly premiums no longer be required at that time.

Title Insurance, Lawyer's Title Opinion

Premiums are charged by the title insurance company to search, abstract, and examine title to a property and to issue an insurance policy that indemnifies the buyer against loss arising from claims against the property. Attorneys may perform a similar service for a fee and render an opinion as to the validity of the title held by the seller and whether it is merchantable. Normally, *either* the full premium for the insurance policy or the fee for the title opinion is paid at closing. Depending on the policy of the lending institution and government regulations, either title insurance or an attorney's opinion is required as a condition for granting a loan.

Release Fees

Release fees are associated with canceling outstanding liens, such as the seller's mortgage lien, mechanics' liens, and so on, and for services rendered by third parties in negotiating and obtaining such releases.

Attorney's Fee

When incurred by the buyer or seller, legal fees may be paid directly by each party outside of the closing or may be included in the closing.

Pest Inspection Certificate

A pest inspection may be made at the insistence of the lender or buyer. In some states, such as Florida, an inspection is required before title is transferred. The inspection fee may be paid directly or included in the closing settlement.

Real Estate Commission

When a seller of a property engages the service of a real estate agent to sell a property, the seller usually pays the commission for such service at the closing.

Statutory Costs

Certain costs may be imposed by a local or state government agency and must be paid before deeds can be recorded. These costs include:

1. Recording fees. Fees paid for recording of the mortgage and note in the public records.
2. Transfer tax. A tax usually imposed by the county on all real estate transfers.

Requirements under the Real Estate Settlement and Procedures Act (RESPA)

RESPA is a law passed by Congress to provide a uniform set of procedures and documents for buyer/borrowers of residential real estate. It includes many provisions; however, only those directly associated with the closing are covered here. The essential aspects of RESPA fall into seven areas that are used here to facilitate discussion:

1. Consumer information.
2. Advance disclosure of settlement costs.
3. Title insurance placement.
4. Prohibition of kickbacks and referral fees.
5. Uniform settlement statement.
6. Advance inspection of uniform settlement statement.
7. Escrow deposits.

Consumer Information

Under provisions in RESPA, lenders are required to provide prospective borrowers with an information booklet containing information on real estate closings and RESPA when a loan application is made.

Advance Disclosure of Settlement Costs

At present, the lender is required to mail to the borrower within *three days after* the time of application a *good faith* estimate of certain closing costs for which information is available. The lender must provide information on the basis of actual costs known at that time,[14] or estimates based on past experience in the locality where the property is located.

The estimates provided by the lender generally cover costs in the following categories: (1) title search, (2) title examination and opinion, (3) title insurance, (4) attorney's fee, (5) preparation of documents, (6) property survey, (7) credit report, (8) appraisal, (9) pest inspection, (10) notary fees, (11) loan closing service fee, (12) recording fees and any transfer tax, (13) loan origination fees, (14) discount points, (15) mortgage insurance application fees, (16) assumption fees, (17) mortgage insurance premiums, (18) escrow fees (fees charged for setting up escrow accounts), and (19) prepaid mortgage interest.

In addition, it is suggested, but not required, that the lender disclose (1) hazard insurance premiums and (2) escrow deposits for mortgage insurance, hazard insurance, and property taxes, if these amounts are known at the time of the advance disclosure. In practice, it would be difficult for the lender to know these latter two amounts three days after the borrower has applied for a loan. Although these two items are not likely to be estimated by the lender at the time of the advance disclosure, they will be charged to the borrower at the time of closing.

The form of the advance disclosure may vary from lender to lender and still remain within the requirements of the act. Typically, the disclosure will be made in dollar amounts which will be estimates of the cost of settlement services which are to be performed. However, it is also acceptable for the lender to disclose *ranges* for settlement costs. For instance, a loan origination fee could be stated as ranging from $1,500 to $2,000 in the lending area where the settlement is to occur. However, the lender may not disclose a range if a *specific party* is required by the lender to provide a settlement service. In this case, a specific dollar amount is required. Also, the lender is under no requirement to redisclose if the estimates of settlement services provided to the borrower change prior to the time of closing.

Title Insurance Placement

Under RESPA, a seller may not require that a buyer use a specific title insurance company as a condition of sale. This regulation is aimed primarily at developers who may have obtained a very favorable title insurance rate on undeveloped land, with the understanding that after development, buyers would be required to place the title insurance with the same company. This part of the act prohibits such requirements and ensures the freedom of the buyer to place title insurance with any title company.

Prohibition of Kickbacks and Referral Fees

Under RESPA, no person can give or receive a kickback or fee as a result of a referral. If any person refers a buyer-borrower to any specific party involved in the closing (lender, title company, attorney, real estate broker, appraiser, etc.) and receives a fee for the referral, receipt of such a fee violates the act. RESPA also prohibits fee splitting by parties associated

---

[14] See: Public Law 95-522 as amended. Under RESPA, the lender is only required to disclose exact amounts of settlement costs when the lender requires a specific third party to provide a settlement service. If the borrower is free to choose providers of services, the lender need only disclose a range of what an acceptable fee for the service might be. See the consumer information booklet on RESPA obtainable from the U.S. Department of Housing and Urban Development.

with the closing unless fees are paid for services actually performed. This latter part of RESPA has probably caused more confusion than any other provision of the act because of the vagueness of the term "services actually performed." However, the intent was to prohibit any circumvention of payments that would have been normally called referral fees by simply splitting fees.

Uniform Settlement Statement

Under RESPA provisions, a uniform settlement statement must be used by the settlement agent at closing. The responsibility for preparation of this statement lies with the lender, and it must be delivered to the borrower and seller at closing. Other closing statements, such as a company form, can also be used for closing purposes, if desired, but the uniform settlement statement must be completed.

This statement is uniform in the sense that the same form must be used in all loan closings covered under RESPA. This form, coupled with the information booklet received by the borrower when the loan application is made, which defines and illustrates costs on a line-by-line basis, should enable the borrower to make a better judgment concerning the reasonableness of the closing costs to be paid.

Advance Inspection of Uniform Settlement Statement

Not only must a uniform settlement statement be used at the closing, but the borrower has the right to inspect this statement one day prior to closing. At that time, information on the additional closing costs not required to be disclosed when the loan application is made must be disclosed to the borrower. These costs include hazard insurance premiums and any required escrow deposits, whatever their intended use is to be.

All of these costs must be disclosed to the extent that they are known to the lender on the day prior to closing. Also, the good faith estimates of other closing costs made when the loan application was completed by the borrower must be revised, if necessary, to reflect actual costs at that time. Both groups of costs must be entered on the uniform disclosure statement for inspection by the borrower.

Although the borrower has the right to advance disclosure, under RESPA the borrower is deemed to have *waived* the right of advance inspection unless a request is made in writing to see the settlement statement on or before the business day prior to settlement. If no request has been received, the lender is under no obligation to prepare the advance disclosure statement.

Escrow Deposits

RESPA limits the amount that a creditor may require the borrower to pay as an initial deposit into the escrow account. The maximum that a lender may require from the borrower as an escrow deposit is one-sixth of the annual amount to be paid on the borrower's behalf. For example, if the lender forwards premiums on the borrower's hazard insurance annually, then the maximum escrow deposit that the borrower can be required to make is one-sixth (two monthly premiums) of the annual hazard insurance premium. Lenders are not allowed to earn or pay the borrower interest on the initial deposit or monthly payments made into the escrow account.

Settlement Costs Illustrated

To help the reader understand how settlement costs are allocated between buyer and seller, we present an example involving the acquisition of the property used in our base example. We demonstrate first how closing costs are determined for a *conventional loan*. The basic information for the closing transaction is shown in Exhibit 8–7. Essentially, these costs must be disclosed to the borrower on a settlement statement, shown in Exhibit 8–8.

EXHIBIT 8–7
Information for
RESPA Closing
Statement

Buyer: John and Jane J. Jones
                         482 Liberty Street
                         Anytown, USA

Seller: Ralph and Pearl Brown
                         200 Heavenly Dr.
                         Anytown, USA

Lender: ABC Savings and Loan Association
                         Anytown, USA

Settlement agent: Land Title Company
                         Anytown, USA

Loan application date: March 1—conventional loan

Advance disclosure date: March 3

Borrower may request advance copy of actual settlement statement on March 24

Actual settlement date (closing date): March 25

I.   Buyer and seller information:

a.	Purchase price	$76,700.00
b.	Deposit	1,000.00
c.	Real estate tax proration (taxes to be paid by buyer-owner January 1) $797	
	Taxes owed by seller Jan. 1–March 24, or (83 days ÷ 365)* $797	181.24

II.   Buyer-borrower and lender information:

a.	Amount of loan (9.25% interest, 30 years, conventional loan)	61,360.00
b.	Prepaid interest March 25–31 (7 days) or (.0925 ÷ 365) times	
	$61,360 times 7 =	108.85
c.	Property tax (escrow) (2 months @ $66.42 per month)	132.84
d.	Loan origination fee (1%)	614.00
e.	Loan discount (1%)	614.00
f.	Application fee	50.00
g.	Appraisal	125.00
h.	Credit report	45.00
i.	Hazard insurance (escrow)	92.00
j.	Title insurance: Land Title Company	350.00
k.	Land Title Company closing fee	75.00

III.   Transaction between buyer-borrower and others:

a.	Recording fees	31.00
b.	Lender's title insurance—Land Title Company	100.00

IV.   Transactions between seller and others:

a.	Release statement seller's mortgage	5.00
b.	Payoff seller's mortgage (Anytown State Bank)	21,284.15
c.	Real estate brokerage fee (6%) (Bobbie Broker)	4,602.00

As shown in Exhibit 8–7, closing costs are separated into four categories, the first three of which involve the buyer. These are the amounts to be paid to, or received from, the seller, lender, and third parties. The fourth category involves costs that must be paid by the seller to third parties. Most items have been previously explained; however, a few computational procedures deserve mention.

In Section I of Exhibit 8–7, note that a property tax adjustment is made for the 83 days that the property has been owned by the seller during the current tax year. Since the buyer must pay $797 in total taxes at year end, a refund for part of this tax is $181.24 payable by the seller to the buyer at closing. An additional $132.84, representing two months of prepaid property taxes, will also be collected and escrowed by the lender. Prepaid interest for

EXHIBIT 8–8
Settlement Statement

I. Amount Due from Buyer:		II. Amount Due to Seller:	
(A) Purchase price	$76,700.00	Sale price	$76,700.00
Plus: Settlement charges	2,337.69	Less: Property tax proration	181.24
Less: Property tax proration	181.24	Less: Payoff of existing loan	21,284.15
Less: Earnest money	1,000.00	Less: Settlement charges*	4,607.00
Less: Mortgage loan	61,360.00	Net amount due to seller	$50,627.61
Net amount due from buyer	$16,496.45		

Buyer's Share of Settlement Charges:		*Seller's Share of Settlement Charges:	
Loan origination fee	$ 614.00	Broker commission	$ 4,602.00
Loan discount	614.00	Recording fee	5.00
Appraisal fee	125.00		
Credit report	45.00		
Mortgage insurance application fee	50.00		
Interest (7 days @ $15.55)	108.85		
2 months premium—escrow	92.00		
2 months property tax—escrow	132.84		
Title insurance (lender)	100.00		
Recording fee	31.00		
Closing fee	75.00		
Title insurance	350.00		
Total	**$ 2,337.69**	**Total**	**$ 4,607.00**

seven days will be collected by the lender, as monthly payments are scheduled to commence on May 1 (Section II). Interest included in the first, regular payment on May 1 spans the period of April 1–30; hence, interest for March 25–31 (inclusive) must be paid at closing. The reader should also note that two monthly installments for hazard insurance are to be prepaid by the buyer and escrowed by the lender. Finally, the lender is also requiring evidence of a binder for a one-year hazard insurance policy at closing. The amounts shown in Exhibit 8–7 are summarized on the uniform settlement statement in Exhibit 8–8. As previously indicated, this statement must be used by lenders to disclose closing costs in most residential transactions.

Federal Truth-in-Lending (FTL) Requirements

In addition to disclosure requirements affecting settlement costs under RESPA, disclosure requirements under the federal Truth-in-Lending Act, which deals with the cost of mortgage credit, have been a requirement affecting lenders since 1968.[15] The intent of FTL legislation is to require that lenders disclose to borrowers financial information contained in loan agreements in a uniform manner. This is required so that borrowers can compare the cost of different loan agreements. It should be stressed that FTL legislation does not attempt to regulate the cost of mortgage credit, but it mandates uniform disclosure of the cost of credit. Truth-in-lending legislation generally requires that lenders disclose financial information contained in mortgage loan agreements to individuals purchasing one- to four-family residences. Commercial real estate transactions are generally excluded. The FTL disclosures must be made by lenders *three days after* application for a mortgage is made

[15] USC 1601; Stat. 146; Pub. L. 90-321 (May 29, 1968) as amended.

by the borrower. Recall that this time requirement is the same as the RESPA disclosure for closing costs. However, unlike the RESPA disclosure, which contains estimates, the FTL disclosure, particularly the annual percentage rate (APR), must be accurately disclosed according to FTL guidelines. The APR as calculated by the lender *may* be rounded up or down to the nearest one-quarter of a percent. However, after rounding, it must fall within the nearest one-eighth of a percent of the APR calculated based on FTL calculation requirements. Furthermore, if market interest rates and, hence, the APR change from the time of application until the loan is closed, the lender must make additional disclosures prior to the date of loan closing.

Truth-in-Lending Sample Disclosure

Exhibit 8–9 contains a description of disclosures that must be made under FTL regulations. Referring to Exhibit 8–9 will aid the reader in establishing which financing costs are included under each disclosure item.

Establishing the APR under Federal Truth-in-Lending Requirements

The APR is the most important required disclosure under FTL, because not only must it be disclosed to loan applicants, but it must also be used when the lender advertises specific loan programs. Accuracy of calculation is also important because in the case of fixed rate, constant payment mortgages, the stated APR may vary from the true APR by only one-eighth of a percent. The calculation performed to determine the APR is essentially the same as the internal-rate-of-return calculation developed in previous chapters.

The information provided in Exhibit 8–10 makes determining the APR for a conventional mortgage fairly straightforward. The APR is determined in three steps. First, we consider the amount financed, shown in the exhibit as item (f). This item is the mortgage loan of $61,360, *less* (a) the loan origination fee of $614, (b) the loan discount fee (points) of $614, and (c) prepaid interest charges of $109, or a net amount advanced of $60,023. Second, we consider the buyer/borrower's monthly payments of $504.79 (based on the amount borrowed of $61,360 at 9.25% interest for 30 years), shown in the exhibit as item (b). As the final step, we solve for the interest rate that makes the present value of the monthly payments equal to the amount financed. This is done as follows:

Solution:	Function:
$PV = -\$60,023$	$i\,(PV, PMT, n, FV)$
$PMT = \$504.79$	
$n = 360$	
$FV = 0$	
Solve for i = .791827 (monthly)	
Solve for i = .791827 × 12 = 9.50% (annually)	

Determining the APR on the conventional insured mortgage is more difficult. This is because of multiple, uneven payments that occur as annual premiums for mortgage insurance change at the end of each year. Exhibit 8–11 illustrates the payment pattern on a conventional insured mortgage, where the annual mortgage insurance premium is based as a percentage of the outstanding loan balance each year. The schedule indicates that monthly mortgage insurance payments should stop during the 16th year, or when the loan balance reaches 80 percent of the original loan amount. The reader should also recall our discussion regarding other conditions under which mortgage insurance payments may no longer be required. To find the APR, 30 groups of 12 monthly payments listed in the exhibit

EXHIBIT 8–9 FTL Disclosure Requirements (Numerical Disclosures, FRM)

Disclosure Item	Description
Annual percentage rate	The effective cost of credit to the borrower on an annual basis as determined by an actuarial method prescribed in the act.
Finance charges	The sum of (1) all interest paid over the term of the loan including discount points, (2) loan application fees,* (3) *required* mortgage insurance or guarantee, credit life or disability, and hazard insurance,† (4) loan origination fees, (5) discount points, (6) escrow charges made for establishing an escrow account, (7) prepaid mortgage interest, (8) assumption fees, and (9) fees for the preparation of an amortization schedule, when *paid for by the borrower.*
Amount financed	The mortgage amount less any of the finance charges described above that are paid at closing.
Total of payments	The borrower's total monthly payment over the loan term, including interest and principal reduction and fees for required mortgage insurance or credit life insurance, but typically excluding charges for property taxes and hazard insurance.
Amount of payments	The dollar amount of borrower monthly payments. When the monthly payment varies due to the cost of mortgage insurance, typically the highest and lowest payment amounts will be disclosed. When payment increases are known, as would be the case on a GPM, all payment amounts must be disclosed to the borrower.
Number of payments	For a constant payment, fixed rate mortgage, the term of the mortgage times 12. For a GPM, the number of times a borrower must make a payment must be disclosed.
Security interest	The lender must describe the nature of any interest that will be acquired in the borrower's property, should the loan be granted. Typically, the lender must describe any assets which he places a lien against.
Assumption policy	The lender must inform the borrower whether the mortgage is assumable by a subsequent purchaser of the property and whether the loan terms might change at the time of assumption.
Variable rate	If the interest rate on the mortgage is not fixed, the lender must disclose this fact.
Filing fees	The lender must disclose any statutory fees for filing liens against loan assets.
Late charge	The lender must disclose the existence and amount of any late payment fees.
Payment due date	The date after which the lender will charge late fees.
Prepayment policy	Whether or not a penalty will have to be paid, should the borrower repay the loan before the term has expired. The amount of any penalty need not be disclosed.
Hazard insurance	The lender must disclose whether insurance is required.
Mortgage insurance	Premium amount of any such insurance if the lender either requires or offers it for sale to borrowers.

*When an application fee is charged to all applicants, rather than just to applicants who receive loan approval, this fee need not be included in the finance charge.
†Credit life or disability insurance need not be disclosed with the finance charge unless it is required by the lender. Hazard insurance is included in the finance charge only when the lender requires that a specific insurer be used.

must be discounted until the present value equals the amount financed. The procedure for discounting grouped cash flows has been presented in an earlier chapter, and the student should refer again to that material. The APR on the mortgage used in the example and the payment pattern shown in Exhibit 8–10 is 10.19 percent (calculation not shown).

ARMs and Truth-in-Lending Disclosure

In addition to the required disclosure for an FRM outlined in Exhibit 8–9, slightly more disclosure is required when a borrower applies for an ARM. Additional items that must be disclosed are listed in Exhibit 8–12. The intent of the additional disclosure on ARMs is to illustrate to the borrower the effect of an increase in the composite rate (the index plus the margin) on monthly payments and the loan balance. However, determining the APR

EXHIBIT 8–10
Federal Truth-in-Lending Disclosure Requirements (FRM Transactions)

	Conventional	Conventional Insured
(a) Prepaid finance charges		
Loan origination fee	$ 614	$ 729
Discount fee (points)	614	729
Prepaid interest	109	133
Prepaid mortgage insurance	–0–	583
Prepaid finance charge	$ 1,337	$ 2,174
(b) Payment amount		
Constant	$ 504.79	N/A
Highest		$ 633.94
Lowest		$ 612.69
(c) Number of payments	360	360
(d) Total of payments (c times b)	$ 181,724	$ 223,919
(e) Total finance charge*	121,701	153,228
(f) Amount financed		
(1) *First method:*		
Original loan balance	61,360	72,865
Less:		
Prepaid finance charge	(1,337)	(2,174)
Amount financed	$ 60,023†	$ 70,691†
(2) *Second method:*		
Total payments	$ 181,724	$ 223,919
Less:		
Total finance charge	$ 121,701	153,228
Amount financed	$ 60,023	$ 70,691
(g) APR	9.5%	10.19%

*This amount includes all interest and mortgage premiums, as well as all prepaid finance charges.
†Based on amount financed.

is more difficult on an ARM. The difficulty arises because, as discussed in the previous chapter, future interest rates on ARMs are *unknown*.

Because the future pattern of interest rates is unknown, the method required when determining the APR on an ARM requires that the margin plus index *at the time of origination* be used as the assumed interest rate over the remaining term of the loan. An example should help clarify this point. We make the following assumptions:

Conventional ARM

$60,000 loan amount

2 percent annual interest rate cap

5 percent over the life of the mortgage cap

5 percent initial rate

7 percent index at origination

2 percent margin

30-year term

$1,200 prepaid finance charge

$59,498.76 balance at the end of year 1

Negative amortization is allowed

EXHIBIT 8–11
Mortgage Insurance Premiums (Conventional Insured Mortgage)

Year	Mortgage Balance Beginning of Year	Annual Mortgage Insurance Premium	Monthly Mortgage Insurance Payment	Borrower Monthly Mortgage Payment	Current Mortgage Balance as a Percentage of the Original Mortgage Balance
Closing	$72,865.19	$582.92	$21.25	$633.94	100.00%
1	72,865.19	255.03	21.12	633.81	100.00
2	72,415.87	253.46	20.98	633.67	99.38
3	71,921.96	251.73	20.82	633.51	98.71
4	71,379.03	249.83	20.64	633.33	97.96
5	70,782.22	247.74	20.45	633.14	97.14
6	70,126.17	245.44	20.24	632.93	96.24
7	69,405.01	242.92	20.01	632.70	95.25
8	68,612.28	240.14	19.76	632.45	94.16
9	67,740.87	237.09	19.48	632.17	92.97
10	66,782.98	233.74	19.17	631.86	91.65
11	65,730.02	230.06	18.83	631.52	90.21
12	64,572.55	226.00	18.46	631.15	88.62
13	63,300.21	221.55	18.05	630.74	86.87
14	61,901.59	216.66	17.61	630.30	84.95
15	60,364.17	211.27	17.11	629.80	82.84
16	58,674.15	205.36	0.00	612.69	80.52
17	56,816.41	0.00	0.00	612.69	77.97
18	54,774.29	0.00	0.00	612.69	75.17
19	52,529.50	0.00	0.00	612.69	72.09
20	50,061.91	0.00	0.00	612.69	68.70
21	47,349.43	0.00	0.00	612.69	64.98
22	44,367.73	0.00	0.00	612.69	60.89
23	41,090.11	0.00	0.00	612.69	56.39
24	37,487.19	0.00	0.00	612.69	51.45
25	33,526.70	0.00	0.00	612.69	46.01
26	29,173.13	0.00	0.00	612.69	40.04
27	24,387.48	0.00	0.00	612.69	33.47
28	19,126.87	0.00	0.00	612.69	26.25
29	13,344.15	0.00	0.00	612.69	18.31
30	6,987.52	0.00	0.00	612.69	9.59
31	0.00	0.00	0.00	–0–	0.00

EXHIBIT 8–12
Federal Truth-in-Lending Additional Required Disclosures for ARMs

- Index.
- Margin.
- Composite rate at the time of origination.
- Adjustment period.
- Payment caps at each adjustment period (if any).
- Payment caps over the term of the loan (if any).
- Interest rate caps over the life of the loan (if any).
- Interest rate caps at each adjustment period (if any).
- Whether composite rate increases will affect payment amounts, the loan balance, or both.
- An example of the effect that an increase in the composite rate would have on payment amounts or the loan balance or both (depending upon payment and rate caps, as well as any limits on negative amortization the loan may feature).

The following illustrates the calculation of an APR on the ARM loan described above:

(A) Payment year 1:

Solution:

$$PV = -\$60,000$$
$$n = 360$$
$$FV = 0$$
$$i = 5\%$$

Solve for PMT = $322.09

Function:

$PMT\,(PV, n, FV, i)$

(B) Payments year 2 through 30:

Solution:

$$PV = -\$59,114.78$$
$$n = 348$$
$$FV = 0$$
$$i = 9\%$$

Solve for PMT = $478.92

Function:

$PMT\,(PV, n, FV, i)$

Solving for the APR:

Solution: (Note: *CF*s are grouped *PMT*s for 12 months, then 348 months)

$$PV = -\$58,800 \text{ (60,000 less points)}$$
$$CF_j = \$322.09$$
$$n_j = 12$$
$$CF_j = \$478.92$$
$$n_j = 348$$
$$FV = 0$$

Solve for i = 0.733437 (monthly)

Solve for i = 0.733437 × 12 = 8.80% (annually)

Recall that disclosure of the APR on a fixed rate mortgage must be accurate to one-eighth of a percent; however, on an ARM, the APR may vary as much as one-fourth of a percent from the actual APR.

It should be stressed that this method of computing the APR on an ARM will almost certainly *not* reflect the true cost of funds to the borrower. Clearly, a decrease or increase in the index over the loan term would cause the stated APR to be incorrect. Moreover, the lender is not required to redisclose the APR at closing. As a result, the borrower should be aware that using the APR for an ARM for comparison with FRMs or ARMs with substantially different terms is not advisable. Indeed, the usefulness of an APR for an ARM is quite limited since it assumes that the composite rate (9%) in existence at the time that the loan is originated will be the same at the end of the first adjustment interval and for every succeeding period for the term of the loan.

Key Terms

ALTA loans, *223*
Certificate of Reasonable Value (CRV), *225*
conventional mortgage loans, *221*
default insurance, *220*
Department of Veterans Affairs (VA), *224*

Federal Housing Administration (FHA), *224*
FHA-insured mortgages, *224*
guarantees, *224*
loan-to-value ratio, *221*
mortgage insurance, *222*
mortgage insurers, *222*

payment-to-income ratio, *221*
residual income, *233*
subprime loans, *223*, *230*
underwriting, *220*
VA-guaranteed mortgage loans, *224*

Useful Web Sites

www.hud.gov—U.S. Department of Housing and Urban Development. Includes the Federal Housing Administration (FHA), which is now part of HUD. See www.hud.gov/offices/hsg/hsgabout.cfm for discussion of FHA.

www.fha-home-loans.com—Excellent site for information about FHA loans, including the current requirements to qualify.

www.mortgageprofessor.com—Excellent site for questions and answers on many aspects of mortgage lending.

www.freddiemac.com—Federal Home Loan Mortgage Corporation.

www.homeloans.va.gov—Veteran's Administration. Includes information on VA-guaranteed loans.

www.fanniemae.com—Federal National Mortgage Association.

Questions

1. What is the legislative intent of federal truth-in-lending disclosures, and what specific disclosures are required under the act?

2. When would the cost of credit life insurance be included in the finance charge and APR calculations for federal truth-in-lending disclosures?

3. What assumption about the future composite rate of interest on an adjustable rate mortgage is made when determining the APR for federal truth-in-lending disclosures?

4. List the closing cost items which require RESPA disclosure. What items may be excluded from disclosures under the act? What form can these disclosures take?

5. What types of fees and conditions are prohibited under RESPA?

6. For what items may a lender require escrow accounts from a borrower?

Problems

1. A loan with the following terms is being made:

   Fixed rate, constant monthly payment. Closing date February 9th.

   9% interest rate. Prepaid interest due at closing.

   $70,000 mortgage loan amount.

   $1,500 loan discount points to be paid by the buyer/borrower to the lender.

   25-year term, monthly payments, fully amortizing.

   a. Calculate the APR for federal truth-in-lending purposes.

   b. Do you think that the APR calculated in (a) reflects the likely return that the lender will receive over the term of the loan? List specific reasons that the lender's actual return might be different from the APR.

2. You are a new loan officer with Alpha Mortgage, and the manager of the loan department has just presented a problem to you. He is unable to complete the APR calculation on an adjustable rate mortgage which a borrower applied for yesterday. The loan features initial payments based on a 10 percent rate of interest, while the current composite rate on the loan is 13 percent. No discount points have been paid by any party to the transaction, and any difference between borrower payments and the interest payment required at the composite rate will be accrued in the mortgage balance in the form of negative amortization. The mortgage amount desired by the borrower is $65,000 for a 30-year term, but a one-time mortgage insurance premium of $2,400 is being funded as a part of the loan amount, making the total loan balance $67,400. The borrower is paying $1,600 in prepaid finance charges at closing.

   a. Determine the APR, assuming that the ARM is made with a 2 percent annual and 5 percent over-the-life interest rate cap.

   b. In what way does the APR disclosure aid the borrower in understanding the terms of this specific loan agreement? What are some of the problems with the APR calculations on ARMs?

3. On August 20, Mr. and Mrs. Cleaver decided to buy a property from Mr. and Mrs. Ward for $105,000. On August 30, Mr. and Mrs. Cleaver obtained a loan commitment from OKAY National Bank for an $84,000 conventional loan at 10 percent for 30 years. The lender informs Mr. and Mrs. Cleaver that a $2,100 loan origination fee will be required to obtain the loan. The loan closing is to take place September 22. In addition, escrow accounts will be required for all prorated and prepaid property taxes and hazard insurance; however, no mortgage insurance is necessary. The buyer will also pay a full year's premium for hazard insurance to Rock of Gibraltar Insurance Company. A breakdown of expected settlement costs, provided by OKAY National Bank when Mr. and Mrs. Cleaver inspect the uniform settlement statement as required under RESPA on September 21, is as follows:

I. Transactions between buyer-borrower and third parties:

a.	Recording fees—mortgage	$ 30.00
b.	Real estate transfer tax	225.00
c.	Recording fees/document prep.	200.00
d.	Hazard insurance—one-year policy—Rock of Gibraltar Ins. Co.	420.00
e.	Peggy Prudent—attorney	150.00
f.	Inspections	50.00
g.	Title insurance fee (Landco Title Co.)	400.00
h.	Landco Title Co.—closing fee	125.00

II. Transactions between seller and third parties:

a.	Release statement—seller's mortgage	5.00
b.	Payoff—seller's mortgage (Home State Bank)	32,715.00
c.	Real estate brokerage fee (6% Fast Deal Realty)	6,300.00

III. Buyer-borrower and lender information:

a.	Amount of loan	$ 84,000.00
b.	Prepaid interest is owed from closing through September 30, which equals nine days (inclusive). Regular payments to begin on November 1. [.10 × 84,000) ÷ 365] · 9	207.12
c.	Property tax escrow—two months required	133.33
d.	Loan origination fee	2,100.00

IV. Buyer and seller information:

a.	Purchase price	$105,000.00
b.	Deposit paid by Cleaver to Ward (paid in escrow to OKAY National Bank)	1,500.00
c.	Real estate tax proration (taxes to be paid by buyer to county next January 1: $800 per year). Seller owns property from January 1 to September 22, or 264 days. Buyer owes for remaining 101 days. Therefore, a refund for part of the $800-per-year real estate tax (for 101 days) is due to buyer from seller or ($800 ÷ 365) × 101 days.	$ 221.37

Required:

a. What are the amounts due from the borrower and due to the seller at closing?

b. What would be the disclosed annual percentage rate as required under the Truth-in-Lending Act?

c. When will the first regular monthly mortgage payment be due from the borrower?

Income-Producing Properties: Leases, Rents, and the Market for Space

In this chapter our focus is on income-producing properties. We begin by identifying the major property types and the economic forces that affect their value. We will consider supply and demand relationships, location analysis, and the competitive nature of the real estate business. We will then turn to a discussion of the importance of leases in defining the contractual relationship between the owner of the property and the tenant using the space. Leases impact the income potential and riskiness of income property investments.

Property Types

We begin with Exhibit 9–1, which outlines the major classifications used to identify and group different types of real estate. The two major categories used to classify property are residential and nonresidential. Residential properties include *single-family houses* and *multifamily properties* such as apartments. Condominiums and co-ops are also included as residential properties.

In general, residential properties are properties that provide residences for individuals or families. Although hotels and motels can also be thought of as providing residences for people, they are considered to be transient or temporary residences and thus are not categorized as residential property. In the discussion that follows, we use the same categories, which are logical from an economic perspective because factors that affect the supply and demand for hotels and motels are quite different from those that affect the residential properties used as a residence.

Single-family dwellings are usually thought of as individual, detached units developed in subdivision tracts. Other variants include cluster home developments, where owners share "green space" in outdoor areas, and "zero lot line" developments, which contain single-family and detached units. They may be owner occupied or rental properties.

EXHIBIT 9–1
Classification of Real Estate Uses

I. Residential

  A. *Single family*
    Detached
    Cluster developments
    Zero lot line developments

  B. *Multifamily*
    High rise
    Low rise
    Garden apartments

II. Nonresidential

  A. *Office*
    Major multitenant—(central business district) CBD
    Single or multitenant—suburban
    Single-tenant—build to suit
    Combination office/showroom
    Professional: Medical, specialized use

  B. *Retail*
    Regional shopping centers/malls
    Neighborhood centers
    Community centers
    Strip centers
    Specialty/lifestyle centers
    Discount/outlet centers

  C. *Hotel/motel*
    Business/convention
    Full service
    Tourist/resort:
      Limited service
      Extended stay
      All suites

  D. *Industrial/Warehouse*
    Heavy industrial
    Light industrial warehouse
    Office/warehouse
    Warehouse:
      Distribution
      Research and development (R&D)
      Flex space

  E. *Recreational*
    Country clubs
    Marinas/resorts
    Sports complexes

  F. *Institutional (special purpose)*
    Hospital/convalescent
    Universities
    Government
    Other

III. Mixed Use Developments
  Combinations of the above uses

The second major category of residential housing is multifamily housing. It is usually differentiated by location (urban or suburban) and size of structure (high rise, low rise, or garden apartments). High-rise apartments are usually found near the central business district (CBD) of cities because land costs are greater than in suburban areas. These are income-producing properties.

Nonresidential properties are typically broken down into six major subcategories: office, retail, industrial, hotel/motel, recreational, and institutional. As is the case for many of the categories, the same *building* can contain both office and retail space. In fact, the same building could contain residential as well as nonresidential uses of space. A combination of end uses in one property is usually referred to as a *mixed use development.* Thus, the categories being discussed should be viewed more as a convenient way of categorizing the use of space for the purpose of analyzing supply and demand, and thus investment potential for that space.

Office buildings range from major multitenant buildings found in the central business districts of most large cities to single tenant buildings, often built with the needs of a specific tenant or tenants in mind. An example of the latter would be a medical office building near a hospital.

Retail properties vary from large regional shopping centers containing over a million square feet of space to small stores occupied by individual tenants found in almost every town. As indicated earlier, it is also common to find retail space combined with office space, particularly on the first floor of office buildings in major cities.

Hotels and motels vary considerably in size and facilities available. Motels and smaller hotels are used primarily as a place for business travelers and families to spend a night. These properties may have limited amenities and will often be located very close to a major highway. Hotels designed for tourists who plan to stay longer will usually provide dining facilities, a swimming pool, and other amenities. They will also typically be located near other attractions that tourists visit. Hotels at "destination resorts" provide the greatest amount of amenities. These resorts are away from major cities, where the guests usually stay for several days or even several weeks. Facilities at these resort hotels can be quite luxurious, with several dining rooms, swimming pools, nearby golf courses, and so forth. Hotels that cater to convention business may be either a popular destination resort or located near the center of a major city. People who go to conventions usually want a variety of choices for dining and want to be able to "combine business with pleasure."

Industrial and warehouse properties include property used for light or heavy manufacturing as well as associated warehouse space. This category includes special-purpose buildings designed specifically for industrial use that would be difficult to convert to another use, buildings used by wholesale distributors, and combinations of warehouse/showroom and office facilities. Older buildings that were initially used as office space often "filter down" to become warehouse or light industrial space.

Recreational real estate includes uses such as country clubs, marinas, sports complexes, and so on. These are very specialized uses, usually associated with retail space that complements the recreational activity (e.g., golf shops). Dining facilities and possibly hotel facilities may also be present.

Institutional real estate is a general category for property that is used by a special institution such as a government agency, a hospital, or a university. The physical structure could be similar to other properties; government office space, for example, would be similar to other offices, and could in fact be in the same building. However, space used by institutions such as universities and hospitals is usually designed for a specific purpose and not easily adaptable for other uses.

Supply and Demand Analysis

In an earlier chapter, we discussed the importance of economic base analysis in assessing potential real estate investment. Market rents for properties depend on the economic base, as well as on the supply and demand for space by tenants. In this section, we look more closely at market forces that affect both the supply and demand for space and how these factors affect real estate investments.

Equilibrium Market Rental Rate

At any point in time, a fixed stock of space exists in the market in previously constructed buildings. Some of this space will be leased. The remaining space constitutes vacancies, or supply of space available for lease. The price at which an owner can lease the space depends on the market rental rate on comparable properties. The amount of existing space that building owners are willing to lease at different rental rates is expressed by a supply curve

EXHIBIT 9–2
Rental Market
Equilibrium

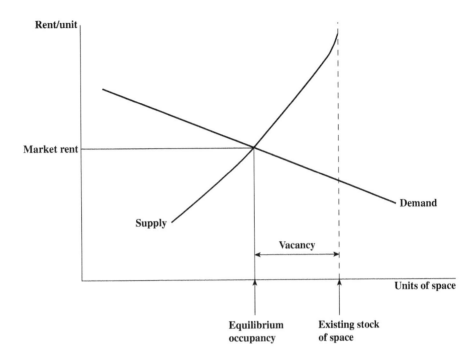

as illustrated in Exhibit 9–2. As the market rental rate rises, more space is supplied by the building owners. The maximum amount of space that can be leased at any given point in time is limited, however, to the existing stock of space.

At lower market rental rates, some of the existing space may not be made available for lease. This space may be deliberately held vacant by owners in anticipation of higher market rents in the future. Alternatively, they may prefer to convert the space to a different use rather than rent it under the existing use at the current market rate for that use. A certain amount of space will also always be vacant because of tenants moving and the time it takes for newly constructed space to be offered for lease. This stock of space will change over time due to construction of new buildings and demolition of existing buildings.

Exhibit 9–2 also shows the *demand* for space from users. As the rental rate falls, firms are more willing to use additional space in their operations rather than other factor inputs such as labor and capital. As shown in the exhibit, the intersection of the supply and demand curves determines the equilibrium market rental rate as well as the amount of space that is leased. The total space that is leased at a given point in time includes space that was leased in previous periods. The difference between the existing stock of space and the total amount leased at the market rate represents vacant space. This is a normal, or equilibrium, market vacancy rate.

The supply curve illustrated in Exhibit 9–2 depicts a short-run equilibrium for a period of time during which the total supply of existing space is fixed and does not increase due to new construction or decrease due to demolition. That is, the supply of space includes existing space that was constructed in the past based on an analysis of the rental market at that point in time. Changes in the market for space after an additional building is constructed can result in a change in the market rental rate. For example, suppose that the demand for office space increases because new firms are locating in the area and office employment is increasing. This is indicated by a shift in the demand curve from D to D' in Exhibit 9–3. Based on the supply curve for existing space offered for lease, the market rent would rise from R to R'. The increase in demand is likely to result in an increase in the construction of new space, however, because the profitability of developing new space

EXHIBIT 9–3
Increase in Demand and Supply

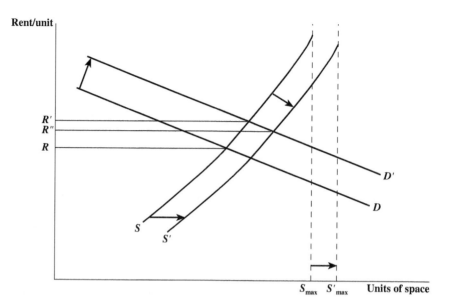

increases at the higher market rents and lower market vacancy rate. The amount of new space that is actually developed depends on the profitability of developing new space as well as the supply of land for development. As new space is developed and the stock of space increases, the maximum amount of space that can be offered for lease increases from S_{max} to S'_{max} and shifts the entire supply curve from S to S' as shown in Exhibit 9–3. Based on the new supply curve (after new space is constructed) equilibrium rents decrease from R' to R''. In other words, the rental rate does not rise as much as it would have in the absence of new construction. Depending on the quantity of space added by the new construction, it is possible that rental rates could fall below the level at which they were before demand increased if more space is developed than was needed to meet the increase in demand.

This analysis considered an increase in the demand for space, which was followed by an increase in the supply of space. A *decrease* in the demand for space causes an opposite movement in the demand curve and a reduction in the equilibrium market rental rate. This results in an increase in the vacancy rate. Because the stock of space already exists, the higher vacancy rate may persist until the demand for space increases. Some decrease in the existing stock may occur due to depreciation and demolition of older buildings, but this occurs over a long period of time.

Implications for Risk

In general, market rent depends on changes in the demand for space as well as expected changes in the supply of space as we discussed. Expected and unexpected changes in market rental rates over the entire economic life of a property affect the return and risk associated with investing in that property. Changes in the demand for space can result from a number of factors that affect the economic base of the area where the property is located. Changes in the supply of space can result from developers reacting to anticipated increases in the demand for space or a belief that they can attract a sufficient number of tenants from existing buildings to make their building profitable. The investor must evaluate how changes in the market rental rate due to changes in supply and demand can affect the income potential of a possible investment as well as the volatility in income. Even if the investment is an existing building that has already been leased, the income can be affected when the existing leases expire and are renewed at the market rental rate at that time. As we will see later in this chapter, *leases* can be structured to shift some of the risk from the owner/lessor to the user/lessee.

Local Market Studies of Supply and Demand

While it is useful to think of supply and demand relationships in the abstract, when real estate investments are made, a market analysis must usually be undertaken to determine the level of vacancies, rents, the amount of new construction under way, and when the property will be ready for occupancy. This is important because, as we will see later in this chapter, a forecast of rents, vacancies, and expenses must be made when a property is under consideration for investment. Exhibit 9–4 contains a summary of many of the variables that must be considered when undertaking a market study. All of these relationships are generally dependent on, or derived from, the types of employment generated by the economic base of the area and the levels of supporting employment discussed in the previous section. However, in order to consider the demand for space by type of property, more detail is necessary. When considering investments in apartment and retail properties, in addition to forecasting the number of new employees, investors need information on the quality of job creation indicated by the salaries and wages that will be earned by individuals in the area, as well as their ages, the size of their households, and other related information. This information will provide a better understanding regarding the *type* of apartments and retail merchandise desired, which will, in turn, indicate which submarkets are likely to benefit from economic growth.

EXHIBIT 9–4
Determinants of Supply and Demand—Major Property Types

Demand Influences:

Apartments:
Number of households, age of persons in households, size of household incomes, interest rates, home ownership, affordability, apartment rents, housing prices.

Office Space:
Categories of employment with very high proportions of office use include service and professional employment, including attorneys, accountants, engineers, insurance, real estate brokerages and related activity, banking, financial services, consultants, medical–dental, pharmaceutical, and so on.

Warehouse Space:
Categories of employment with high concentrations in warehouse use include wholesaling, trucking, distribution, assembly, manufacturing, sales/service, and so on.

Retail Space:
Demand indicators include household incomes, age, gender, population, size, and tastes/preferences.

Supply Influences:
Vacancy rates, interest rates and financing availability, age and combination of existing supply stock, construction costs, land costs.

Property Type		Typical Construction Periods
Apartments	Suburban garden walkup	6–18 months
	Urban mid-, high-rise	18–24 months
Office Buildings	Suburban low-rise	18–24 months
	CBD mid-, high-rise	24–48 months
Retail	Strip/standalone	6–12 months
	Neighborhood/community	12–24 months
	Enclosed malls	36–48 months
Warehouse	Suburban, single level	9–12+ months

Similarly, when considering investments in warehouses and office properties, a deeper understanding of the nature and kinds of employment produced by growth in the economic base will help in investment analysis. For example, when one considers employment growth in New York City, it is likely that much of the employment will be occurring in offices. On the other hand, if considering Detroit, a higher percentage of employment growth is likely to occur in industrial and warehouse properties. Exhibit 9–4 provides the reader with some idea of the variables that influence the demand for various property types.

For the supply side of each market, developers of each property type also carefully consider each of the same variables in Exhibit 9–4. However, they must also weigh the costs of financing and the economic benefits of acquiring land and undertaking development in other locations. The exhibit provides some idea as to the time required to develop various property types. Based on this information, it should be fairly clear that the supply of space available in any market tends to be fixed in the short run and, unlike many other goods and services, requires lead time to adjust to increases in demand. Furthermore, trying to establish the quantity of space that can be produced effectively relative to the size of a submarket is also important when completing an investment study.

Location and User-Tenants

After briefly examining a method for identifying the economic drivers affecting cities and regions, we now turn to a conceptual framework for determining how locations *within* a city are evaluated by businesses. It goes without saying that location is an important attribute in real estate. Successful real estate investors and developers must also realize that location as viewed by *user-tenants* is also important to recognize. We mean that successful real estate investors and developers should understand the *business operations* of potential *tenant-users and how certain locations will appeal to those users.* Recall that many users of real estate are business firms that operate to make a profit. Consequently, most real estate decisions made by these users are considered in terms of how leasing space in alternative locations will generate more profit by (1) increasing sales revenue, (2) reducing the cost of operations, or (3) some combination of both. A very basic illustration of the relationship between user profits and locations is shown in Exhibit 9–5.

As Exhibit 9–5 shows, if we evaluate three locations in Big City, it is clear that User A will realize more profit in location (1) because revenues are greater and its operating expenses are invariant to location. User A can afford to pay more rent per square foot in location (1) and potentially earn a greater profit than it would in locations (2) and (3). User B, on the other hand, will be best off in location (3) because its revenues are invariant to location, and its expenses will be lowest in that location. Location (2) appears to be suboptimal for both Users A and B and may also be appealing to businesses that are different from Users A and B.

Because profitability will vary by location, the above analysis also implies that User A and other users, either who are in competition with User A or who operate businesses in which location significantly affects *sales revenue* (examples could be retailers, restaurants, or certain service providers), will tend to cluster near location (1) as they anticipate earning higher profits there. These firms will compete with one another by bidding for space in that location. The location will take on the characteristics of a *submarket* containing those tenant-users selling goods and services to consumers who are sensitive to the location.

On the other hand, User B, whose *expenses* are very sensitive to location, will choose location (3) because it will tend to lower costs and thus produce higher profits. Competitors of User B and firms that are not necessarily in the same business as User B but that have

EXHIBIT 9–5
Relationship between User Revenue, Expenses, and Profits per Square Foot by Location

	Locations in Big City, USA		
	(1)	(2)	(3)
User A:			
Revenue	$120	$100	$ 90
Less: Expenses	80	80	80
Profit	$ 40	$ 20	$ 10
User B:			
Revenue	$100	$100	$100
Less: Expenses	90	80	70
Profit	$ 10	$ 20	$ 30

similar operating cost structures will compete for space in and around location (3). Examples of user-tenants in this location might include wholesale distributors occupying large warehouses. Such distributors may charge the same price for products to all customers in a region; however, their delivery expenses will vary by location. Therefore, they will tend to choose a location in an area that will minimize delivery expenses.

This process of profit analysis and competition by many different firms for space in locations that tend to maximize profits produces certain general land-use results in real estate markets:

1. The process of firms competing for space will result in the highest rents possible for the most profitable locations and, ultimately, the highest land value and best development for a site (e.g., office, retail, warehouse, apartment, or hotel).

2. Locations will tend to be dominated by clusters of users with revenue or operating expense structures that relate in similar ways to a given location.

3. Locations with the greatest appeal to users will tend to produce higher rents and also to exhibit highest spatial *densities*. Developers will attempt to build multistory projects or cluster buildings on very desirable sites so that they may earn the highest rents per square foot. This process will tend to attract tenants whose operations can be conducted in relatively small amounts of space or in multistory structures while still enabling them to earn higher revenues and profits.

4. Some locations are competed for by firms that are most cost-sensitive. These firms tend to require large amounts of land and large facilities on which to conduct larger scales of operations at lower rents per square foot.

When viewing location in this way, we can begin to understand how and why land-use patterns and submarkets develop within urban areas. It should also help us understand why retail and high-rise office developments occur in some areas, while warehouses requiring large quantities of land on single levels occur in others. Of course, these patterns of land use are also affected by zoning and historic land-use patterns in urban markets. However, even the latter influences are subject to periodic changes.

In summary, a key concept to understand is that for most business users, real estate is considered to be an *operating input* that is used with labor to produce output. In other words, business firms in their operations combine labor and materials *with* real estate at a location to produce goods and services. For example, law, accounting, and advertising firms produce services for clients, and employees and real estate are major *inputs* in the *production* of their client services that are sold from a specific location. Retailers may combine large quantities of merchandise and salespersons on land and in buildings to produce a merchandise/service mix that appeals to customers. Further, the distribution of their goods and merchandise may require a large quantity of land and warehouse buildings with relatively few employees to break down, re-sort, and deliver merchandise to customers. The point of these examples is that because business users view real estate as an input that affects operating expenses and/or revenues, the relationships between land and building space requirements, rent, the number of employees, and revenues should be viewed in the context of various locations. These resources tend to be combined by businesses so that they maximize profit. Land-use patterns follow this pattern of business location decision making.

The Business of Real Estate

Contrary to popular belief, the vast majority of real estate used by business firms is *leased* and not owned. This is true in spite of the vast number of buildings with signs that carry a name of a major corporation on the exterior.[1] Why is this the case? There are many important reasons:

1. Most tenants find leasing to be *more cost-effective than owning*. This is particularly true when their space requirements are less than the quantity of space they would have to purchase in order to satisfy their needs in a desired location. For example, assume that a user needs 20,000 square feet of space to operate profitably, and it must have such space in a specific location. However, only buildings with a minimum size of 100,000 square feet are available for purchase in that location. In this case, the user will usually opt to *lease* the 20,000 square feet of space as opposed to purchasing a 100,000-square-foot building. Leasing will usually be preferred because purchasing would include the responsibility for leasing the remaining 80,000 square feet of excess space to other users. Purchasing would generally not be optimal because:

   a. Owning would require a large commitment of capital to purchase the 100,000-square-foot facility. Such capital could be used in other business activities.

   b. A purchase would "put the user in the real estate business." That is, the tenant would have to take the risk of owning and also have the real estate business "know how" to lease, collect rents, maintain, and insure the additional 80,000 square feet of space that it does not use.

2. Even if a tenant could occupy the entire 100,000 square feet in a building, it might still choose to lease because:

   a. Owning would *reduce* operating flexibility. For example, if the firm decided to leave a metropolitan area and/or consolidate or expand in a different location in the same metro area, it might have to sell the entire property. This could take a considerable amount of time and tie up personnel and capital. If it had leased the property, it could move upon the lease expiration date or even negotiate a release from the owner/lessor.

   b. If it owns the property, the firm must operate, maintain, and repair the facility. These activities may result in the loss of focus on its core business activities. For example, a technology-consulting firm may be better off focusing all of its effort on consulting with clients and not have the worry of owning, operating, leasing, and managing the

---

[1] These signs usually identify major corporate tenants in a building, who are granted the right to erect a sign by the property owner in its lease agreement.

building that it occupies. Operating and managing properties is usually done more cost-effectively by firms that specialize in real estate operations.

c. If the firm decided to *size down* from using 100,000 square feet, as the owner of the building it would have to engage a broker to find an additional user or buyer for the excess space. Furthermore, it might have to renovate the space to suit the requirements of the new tenant. Again, this would mean undertaking unrelated real estate business activities.

In summary, the primary point is that history is replete with evidence of corporations that ventured away from their core businesses and engaged in real estate investment and development. Results have been mixed at best. The real estate industry includes economic functions that are *specialized in nature* and are separate and distinct from the operations of the many different business activities conducted by tenant-users. These noncore real estate business activities include the risks of (1) selecting the "right tract" of land and developing the "right amount" of space; (2) leasing that space to many different tenants; (3) hiring personnel, collecting rents, and maintaining the facility; (4) finding financing for the investment or development; and (5) doing continuous research about real estate markets in order to decide when to sell, raise or lower rents, renovate, and so on. These are a few examples of many of the functions requiring special skills that can be performed most cost-effectively by real estate firms that specialize in these activities. Business firm–users are best left to focus on their primary activities (e.g., lawyers, accountants, and advertising companies serving clients, and retailers serving their customers). These users will generally not be as effective in real estate development, investment, leasing, and so on, as those firms that specialize in these activities. It has been estimated that over 80 percent of all office buildings and retail properties is *leased* to tenants. This number is slightly lower for industrial/warehouse properties, of which 37 percent is estimated to be occupied by owners and 63 percent is leased to user-tenants. In summary, the reader should be aware that the real estate business is an activity that involves many firms that specialize in providing services to users. It is generally more cost-effective for users to lease their space requirements than to engage in the activities demanded by ownership.

One general exception to the above observations may occur if a single tenant-user requires its own facilities for its corporate headquarters or must have unique features such as high-tech labs, specialized computer installations, security, or other features that are unique. In these very special cases, ownership may be preferred to leasing.

The "Market" for Income-Producing Real Estate

Given the preceding discussion about (1) the general relationships between users seeking a location to maximize profits, (2) the general desirability among users to lease rather than own the space they need in their operations, and (3) the advantages in terms of cost-effectiveness of depending upon the real estate business/industry to perform the functions and risks associated with developing, owning, leasing, and maintaining land and buildings (as opposed to the tenant-user undertaking these responsibilities), it is clear that an enormous market for real estate services has emerged.

When we approach the subject of making real estate investments, we must understand how this competitive market operates and the nature of the negotiations between owners of real estate and tenant-users. It is also important to understand how owner-investors in real estate must differentiate between expenses associated with operating buildings and expenses that are related to the business operations of a tenant. Property expenses are usually allocated by owners to users, and property owners do not pay expenses associated with the operations of tenants.

It can be best summarized to say that in this market for real estate services, tenants are searching for locations that provide the highest profit (through either greater revenues or lower costs), and real estate investor-owners stand ready to take the risks of developing and/or leasing and operating real estate for tenant-users. Real estate owners engage in providing these services in exchange for rent. However, as will be seen below, the term *rent* is a very general term and, though important, is not adequate to explain how expenses are allocated between owners and renters. In order to estimate total occupancy costs for tenants and profits for owners, there are many other areas of negotiation between real estate owners and business-users of real estate or tenants in addition to rent. These may include additional rights and responsibilities of both parties that are usually contained in *leases*. Lease contents are important because they affect how much income may be produced from an investment property, the legal responsibilities, and any future options negotiated between owners and tenants that may ultimately affect the value of an investment.

Income Potential—Real Estate Assets

In this section, we consider four major property types: apartment, office, and retail buildings, and industrial/warehouses. Our goal is to familiarize the reader with the operating and lease characteristics for each and how forecasts of cash flow may be developed.

The term **market rent** refers to the price that must be paid by a potential tenant to use (lease) a particular type of space under then current market conditions. The rent depends on many factors, including (1) the outlook for the national economy, (2) the economic base of the area in which the property is located, (3) the demand for the type of space provided by the property in the location being analyzed, and (4) the supply of similar competitive space.

For example, the market rent on office buildings depends on the number of firms doing business in the area as well as the likelihood of new firms locating in the area, the number of employees these firms currently employ and are expected to employ in the near future, and the amount of space that the firm needs for its employees to do their job. These factors can be very difficult to estimate as they depend upon many uncertain and complex factors. The number of employees and amount of space per employee that is needed by a particular type of firm may be quite different in the future than it was in the past, due to changes in the way the firm does business, especially with advances in technology.

Similarly, the market rent on apartments depends on the demographic makeup of the population and median income of families in the area in which the property is located, the cost and availability of homes or condominiums to purchase as an alternative to renting an apartment, and other factors. Market rents for retail space also depend on the demographic makeup of the population and the median income of families as well as the percentage of income they typically spend on various goods and services from retail establishments in a particular area. Real estate investors must also be very concerned with the *credit quality* of tenants. As a part of the leasing process, credit reports, bank references, and references from suppliers and customers are all important.

Real estate is a durable asset that has a relatively long economic life. The market rent at a given point in time is the price that users must pay for the use of a particular unit of space, for example, the rent per square foot of leasable area in a building. Market rents can change many times over the economic life of the building because of changes in the demand for space from potential users and/or changes in the supply of space as additions or deletions are made to the stock of available space. These changes are one source of volatility that will affect the rental income from properties over time. The value of a particular property at any point in time depends on the present value of the rental income expected from the building over its remaining economic life. Thus, real estate investors must consider how changes in the supply and demand for space might affect market rental rates over the economic life of the property.

Vacancy

As indicated previously, all space available in a building may not be leased at a particular time. This is because tenants may leave after their lease has expired (or breach their lease agreement before it expires!), or it could be that the space has never been rented, especially if it is in a newly constructed building. To project income for a property, it is therefore necessary to project how much of the space will be occupied by tenants during the anticipated holding period for the project. There should always be some allowance for vacant space, even in markets where leasing activity is strong, because as tenant turnover occurs it takes time to make space ready and to re-lease space to new tenants. Hence, there will always be some loss in rents, even in buildings occupied by a few larger tenants.

It is more difficult to project vacancy for newly constructed properties. While some leases may be signed before a project is completed, it is possible that *less than full occupancy* will be achieved immediately after construction is completed. In these cases, projections must be made as to how long it will take for remaining space to be "absorbed" by the market. That is, how long will it take for occupancy to reach a normal level? Obviously, the longer it takes for space to be rented, the less income the investor will receive during the initial years of the project. Because this affects cash flows in the early years of the holding period, it will also have a significant impact on the investment value of a property.

At this point it is useful to make a few additional observations. First, when dealing with an acquisition of a property and developing a pro forma statement that will be used in an investment analysis, it is important to stress that such a forecast should contain a summary of *cash flow only*. The focus on cash flow is stressed and should be differentiated from statements that stress accounting income determined in accordance with generally accepted accounting principles (GAAP). While the latter may be important when producing annual reports, taxes, and so on, it should *not* be used in making an analysis for acquisitions of properties. Second, the term *net operating income* (*NOI*) was discussed in the previous chapter and is used extensively in the real estate investment business. In this chapter, we also focus on *operating cash flow*, that is, a summary of all cash inflows and outflows. We make this distinction because when undertaking an investment analysis, we will usually have access to detailed rent and expense information from the seller of the property or his agent. We will usually make an inspection of the property and estimate the extent of needed outlays for tenant improvements that may be necessary as leases mature and the property is made ready for new tenants or outlays for major repairs after the property is inspected. As a result, we will be in a position to adjust *NOI* by making annual estimates of cash outflows for such items. In Exhibit 9–6, we list data sources that may be used to help compile appropriate benchmarks for operating expenses and other data that may be relevant when developing financial projections for various properties. In summary, when analyzing financial statements, the reader should pay particular attention to how treatments of outlays for

Web App

There are many online sites such as **www.reis.com** that offer summaries and outlooks on both national and regional rental markets. Find reports on the current state of either the apartment, office, warehouse, and retail properties for the city or region where you live or are interested in living. What is the outlook for this type of property in that area? What is happening to rents and vacancy rates?

EXHIBIT 9–6
Useful Data Sources for Income Property Research

Type of Property	Source
Apartment, condominium, cooperative	*Income and Expense Analysis: Apartments, Condominiums and Cooperatives* (Chicago: Institute of Real Estate Management, annually)
Office buildings	*Office Building Experience Exchange Report* (Washington, DC: Building Owners and Managers Association International, annually)
Shopping centers	*The Dollars and Cents of Shopping Centers* (Washington, DC: Urban Land Institute)
Industrial parks	*Site Selection Handbook* (Atlanta: Conway Publications, Inc.)

tenant improvements, repairs, and replacements are included in statements of cash flows. In this chapter, rather than using an average outlay for such items, we will make an estimate of cash outflows for the year in which the outlay is expected to occur.

Underwriting Tenants

Typically, income properties are leased to tenants for a specified period of time. The lease document assigns rights, duties, and responsibilities between the **lessor** (owner) and **lessee** (tenant) for the duration of the lease. The terms of the **lease** include legal considerations that are designed to protect the interests of both the lessor and the lessee and specify how rents and expenses are to be paid.

When negotiating for the use of space, the property owner will evaluate the financial capacity of the tenant. This investigation is extremely important because the lease is a contractual agreement that creates an asset for the property owner and a liability for the tenant. Leases may require significant rent payments for very long periods of time; therefore, the ability of the tenant to pay currently and in future periods is very important. Furthermore, to properly assess risk, the property owner must understand the nature of the tenant's business, its competitive position in the industry, and the health of the industry itself. Typically, when evaluating a tenant and a lease proposal, the owner considers the following information:

- Financial statements/income statement–balance sheet.
- Credit ratings.
- Any analyst reports on the firm/industry.
- Bank relationships.
- Existing obligations (debt, other leases).

Underwriting leases is a very important component of risk assessment, which ultimately affects cash flow produced by a property and hence its value. Furthermore, if a tenant defaults on a lease because of a business failure and petitions a court for bankruptcy protection, the tenant may be allowed to continue to occupy the space and pay little or no rent during reorganization.[2]

General Contents of Leases

As discussed earlier, the contents of the lease include the term "lessor," which usually refers to the owner of the property. Thus, we tend to use *lessor* and *owner* interchangeably.

---

[2] It should also be pointed out that from a *tenant's* point of view, the financial condition of the *property owner* is very important. Should the property owner encounter financial difficulty and enter bankruptcy, the ownership of the property may change and the operation/management may affect the quality of service to the tenant.

Similarly, the "lessee" is typically the tenant who occupies and uses the space and pays rent. Hence, the terms *lessee* and *user-tenant* are used interchangeably. While many terms may be included in lease agreements, elements that are commonly included in many leases are shown below:

1. Parties to the lease, namely, lessor and lessee. The date of the lease agreement, occupancy date, identification of area to be leased, and the length of the lease term.
2. The base or minimum rent and any methods that will be used to calculate and adjust future rent. Description of any concessions and other inducements to be provided to the tenant by the landlord.
3. Deposits and any indemnities and guarantees from third parties or co-signers.
4. Condition of the leased premises to be provided to the occupant on the move-in date, including any tenant improvements.
5. Allowable uses of the property, restrictions on occupancy, and prohibitions regarding future changes in the use of the property.
6. Any restrictions on assignment or subletting of any of the leased space by the tenant.
7. The use of common areas and facilities, such as lobbies, rest rooms, and parking lots.
8. Responsibility for maintenance and repair of the tenant's space and of the general premises.
9. Any restrictions on alteration or improvements to the property by the tenant.
10. Construction of any expansion in the future by the owner and provisions for affected tenants.
11. Eminent domain and any consideration to be given to the tenant should it affect the space rented, business operation, availability of parking, and so forth.
12. The responsibility for payment of specific expenses by the lessee and/or the lessor.
13. The extent to which the owner and/or the tenant must provide for fire and casualty insurance.
14. Any lease renewal options.
15. Estoppels.

Depending on the amount of space, length of the term, and financial implications for both owners and tenants, leases may range from very complex to relatively simple agreements. For large corporate users who may be leasing large amounts of space and who plan to move many employees and equipment to the space being leased, many conditions may be negotiated in lease agreements. On the other hand, leases may be relatively straightforward, as may be the case for apartment leases. While we do not exhaust all possible features that may be included in leases, Concept Box 9.1 provides the reader with more detail on the general contents of leases listed above. This additional detail gives some idea as to the range and the variety of items that may be included in leases that affect the future cash flows from rents, payment of expenses, options, and other factors affecting risk and return on investment. When evaluating a property for investment, the analyst must carefully review each lease. Indeed, some consider the major determinant of property value to be the present values of cash flows from all leases in effect when a property is acquired. When undertaking an investment analysis, leases in effect may have been executed recently or many years ago, and each lease will reflect market conditions prevailing at the time the agreement was made. Consequently, when an analysis is being done, it is important to identify any leases with onerous or overly restrictive terms, as this can have a major effect on property values. Lenders also carefully consider lease terms when evaluating properties as security for mortgage loans. In fact, if lenders consider any lease terms to be objectionable, they may require property owners to obtain from tenants a change in the lease agreement as a condition for obtaining financing.

The goal of this concept box is to expand the discussion of leases and how various clauses and options may affect the risk and/or cash flow to the investor. While the following list is not exhaustive, the reader should be aware that like any contract being negotiated, many features may be added to leases to meet the needs of both the owner and tenants.

1. *Parties to the lease.* If a corporation is a party to the lease, assurance that the person signing the lease is a corporate officer with the proper responsibility is important. The nature of the corporate entity and its relationship to a parent corporation or other entities should be investigated. Failure to do so may present delays in receipts and payments of cash flows if rents become delinquent or the lease is terminated and bankruptcy occurs. **Occupancy dates** may be important in leases on newly constructed property which the owner may not have finished by the move-in date. In these situations, *tenants* may want the option to *terminate* the lease. Similarly with retail leases, should the tenant delay occupancy for an unreasonably long period of time, the property *owner* may want to *terminate* the lease, particularly if the retail sales of other tenants appear to be adversely affected by the vacant space. When dealing with the right to terminate a lease, issues including forfeiture of deposits and other penalties may have to be considered.

2. *Rents.* As will be explained in the chapter, there are many ways to determine rents, ranging from rents that are flat, stepped-up, indexed, and so forth. *Concessions* also may be included that effectively lower rents. For example, the owner may provide a **free rent** period during which no rent is paid. These concessions or discounts tend to be used (1) when vacancy rates are high because the market is oversupplied with rentable space or (2) when demand for space is weak because of slow economic growth. In addition to free rent, other concessions may include a move-in allowance, buyouts of existing leases, designated free parking, and the like.

3. *Other guarantees.* Depending on the outcome of the underwriting, if the risk of default is considered to be a possibility, a prospective tenant may be required to find a third party to indemnify the lease payments (a co-signer) or obtain a **letter of credit** (LOC) for a fee from a bank. In an LOC, the bank guarantees that any rents in arrears will be paid to the property owner. Provisions for reductions in the amount of the LOC based on timely rent payments by the tenant may be included in the lease in order to reduce annual LOC fees paid by the tenant.

4. *The condition of the space* on the move-in date may be "as is," or the lease may require it to be "finished out" or renovated before the move-in date. In such cases, the lease may call for **tenant improvements** (TIs), which could include paint, lighting, carpets, wall coverings, and so on. The extent of TIs is negotiated and expressed as dollars per square foot of usable space that the owner will budget for a tenant. Any cost in excess of the agreed budget amount must be paid by the tenant. The dollar amount and the description of TIs that the owner will provide are described in a **work letter** which is prepared by the property owner. Also, the disposition of any of these improvements upon expiration of the lease is usually specified.

5. **Allowable uses** and prohibited uses are enumerated in all leases. These provisions usually prohibit tenants from making major changes in their use of the leased space. For example, a tenant could be prohibited from adding a retail business in space that has been leased in an office building.

6. **Subletting.** In the event that a tenant needs less space than originally leased, leases may allow the tenant to *sublet* to third parties with approval of the property owner. The owner generally agrees not to unreasonably withhold approval even though the tenant may be "in competition" with the property owner, who may also be trying to lease vacant space in a building. Even if subletting is allowed, most owners will require that the original lessee remain liable for rents on any sublet space for the remaining lease term.

7. **Business conduct.** All tenants are usually required to "obey the rules" regarding the use of common areas as indicated in the lease. In retail leases, this could mean a prohibition relating to the use of the mall way (common area) for special sales, promotions, signing, and so on.

8. *Owner services to be provided.* In most office leases, the property owner will agree to provide services such as cleaning, maintenance, and repairs. In the case of retail and warehouse properties, more discretion is given to the tenant regarding maintenance and alteration of space to conform to the operating needs of the tenant. However, the property owner usually retains the right to approve (1) alterations and (2) the selection of architects, contractors, materials, and the like.

9. If the property owner wants to expand and construct new rental space, many leases contain **"non disturbance" clauses,** which require the owner not to interfere with the tenant's business operations during an expansion or as any existing space is being renovated. When negotiating leases, tenants may require temporary relocation to other space, or the creation of special accommodations (e.g., private entries, exits) during construction.

10. Should the state or other government entity use **eminent domain** to condemn all or part of the owner's property (to acquire right-of-way, etc.), the lease may provide that the tenant receive a reduction in rent or other consideration, should *parking* or other factors affecting the tenant's business occur. Similarly, leases usually include provisions that address events, such as a fire or other occurrences, that result in the loss of business or damage to the tenant's space.

11. Leases vary considerably regarding **responsibility for expenses.** In some cases, the property owner agrees to provide and pay for some or all of the operating expenses. In other cases, property owners do not wish to take responsibility for many of those expenses because (1) they may be directly related to the tenant's business and should be paid by the tenant and (2) there is a risk that such expenses may suddenly rise. Consequently, many property owners prefer to either "pass through" or recover certain expenses from tenants (to be discussed).

12. Many leases require the building owner to provide comprehensive insurance in common areas of the property (lobby, parking, etc.). Tenants must also provide *evidence of insurance* covering the tenant's space.

13. As the lease expiration date approaches, tenants must give a *termination notice* to the owner as to whether the lease will be renewed or terminated. This is an important decision for both the tenant and the property owner. For the tenant, if the lease is not renewed, considerable cost to move the business and employees may be incurred. For the property owner, nonrenewal may entail finding a new tenant to occupy the vacated space, negotiating the rent, and paying "make-ready" expenses and leasing commissions. The renewal option is likewise complicated because in addition to the usual factors, it usually involves re-negotiation of a new rent for the next lease term. In order to reduce the uncertainty regarding the rent negotiation, many office, retail, and warehouse leases specify that a market survey of comparable properties will be conducted by at least two brokerage or research firms (one selected by each party). The survey will be made up to one year before and not less than three months before the lease expiration date. The results of the survey will serve as the basis to negotiate the new rent. In some cases, tenants may have a "most favored nation" clause in their lease. This gives the tenant the right to review the most recent leases executed by the property owner with other tenants in the building. Information on current rents and other terms are thereby provided to the tenant and may be used in negotiations. The landlord and tenant may also agree to arbitration if a new lease agreement cannot be completed.

14. **Estoppel certificates.** This provision allows a questionnaire to be sent to existing tenants seeking verification of (1) rents/expenses that the tenant is obligated to pay under lease terms, (2) any past-due amounts, and (3) any rents being withheld by the tenant because of disagreements with the owner. This clause is important because investors may want verification (1) that all rents and recoveries are, in fact, being collected from tenants and (2) that there are no disputes, lawsuits, and the like, between the current owner and tenants.

15. *Change in property ownership/bankruptcy.* This provision may give the tenant the right to terminate the lease in the event that the property is sold or the property owner enters bankruptcy.

Leases and Rental Income

The initial rent that must be paid under the lease contract is usually a specified dollar amount, which we refer to as the **minimum rent,** or **base rent.** However, the base amount may stay the same or change during the term of the lease.

There are many ways that rents can be adjusted over the term of a lease. Adjustments are usually dependent on the term of the lease, the amount of space being leased, and the type of property (e.g., retail vs warehouse). Some very general methods used to adjust rents are discussed below. The reader also should keep in mind that a combination of the methods discussed below may be used to adjust rents.

1. *Flat rents.* In some cases, rents may remain the same (or flat) for the term of the lease. This is commonly the case for apartment leases. Flat rents may also apply to other leases with relatively short terms, or when tenant/user turnover occurs frequently.

2. *Step-up rents.* Some leases include step-up clauses. These provide that rent will increase at the end of specified time intervals and in *specific amounts* during the term of the lease. Example: base rent will be $20 per square foot and will increase by $1 per square foot on the anniversary date of the lease for each of the next five years. Step-ups are used commonly in office, retail, and warehouse leases.

3. *Indexed rents.* Another way of adjusting rents is to use a specified index as a basis for the adjustment. This approach may be used in lieu of, or combined with, step-up provisions. The consumer price index (CPI) is commonly used when rents are indexed. That is, the base rental rate is adjusted periodically in accordance with changes in the CPI. Other indexes also can be used. For example, in New York City it is common to use *Porter's wage index* to adjust rents for office properties. Using price indexes like the CPI to adjust rents differs from step-up leases because the change in rents is not known until the date of the **CPI adjustment.** Furthermore, index adjustments shift the risk of unexpected changes in the rate of inflation to the tenant. As a result, tenants may negotiate caps, or upper limits, on the index. In return for using indexed adjustments in the lease, tenants may negotiate a lower base rent than would otherwise be the case if either flat or step-up provisions were used. The lease also may address adjustments when a decline in the index occurs (*deflation*). In such cases, a *floor,* or maximum reduction in rent, may be included. Indexed leases are used in office, retail, and warehouse leases.

4. *Rents adjusted based on revenue/sales performance.* In some retail leases, rents also may be fully or partially determined by an indicator of retail sales performance. For example, some leases in shopping centers may include a provision for rents to be partially based on the tenant's sales volume. This is referred to as a **percentage rent lease.** In such cases, a flat or step-up base rent is negotiated. Then an additional clause specifies that if the tenant's sales volume exceeds a certain amount (usually referred to as the "breakpoint"), additional rent will be paid based on some percentage of the tenant's sales over the negotiated breakpoint. The dollar amount by which the total rent exceeds the base rent is referred to as **overage rent.** In cases where a tenant's retail revenues decline, rents may revert to the base rent.

Leases and Responsibility for Expenses (Recoveries)

There are many ways in which property owners can structure leases in order to recover operating expenses. Lease contents can be varied to allow for different combinations of rent and expense payments. However, *it should always be kept in mind that competitive market conditions prevailing at the time that a lease is being negotiated will play a major part in determining: (1) rents and (2) who will bear the risk of paying some, or all, operating expenses.* Common patterns used to treat operating expenses in leases are described as follows:

1. *Gross (full-service) leases.* The tenant pays rent only, and the property owner provides all services and pays all operating expenses.

2. *Modified (full-service) leases.* The tenant pays rent that is lower than rent payable under a full-service lease. The owner provides all services but recovers from the tenant *specific expenses* identified in the lease (e.g., electricity). Such expenses tend to be highly variable in nature (e.g., energy related) and represent an expense risk that property owners may not be willing to assume. In many leases, total expenses for such items are usually determined for the entire property and then *prorated* on the basis of rentable square feet occupied by each tenant.

    a. *Direct pass throughs.* When some tenants, because of the nature of their business, use a greater amount of a service than other tenants occupying a property, owners usually attempt to link and "pass through" related expenses directly to those tenants. In these cases, owners may provide all services. However, instead of prorating expenses, owners will use submetering and other methods to assure that such costs are better matched to tenants relative to their usage.[3]

    b. *Non operating expense pass throughs.* Lease modifications are sometimes made when a property owner negotiates a pro rata "pass through" of certain, specific, *non operating* expenses to tenants. These non operating expenses are deemed "costs of doing business," but they are not manageable by the property owner. Examples of such **expense pass throughs** are property taxes and insurance. Many property owners believe that because these expenses are determined by external parties, such as public agencies and insurance companies, the property owner cannot "manage" them. Should there be a sudden increase in taxes or premiums, property owners argue that they cannot always recover them by increasing rents. This is particularly a concern in cases where long-term leases are involved. Consequently, many property owners maintain that such expenses should be "passed through" to tenants as a "cost of doing business."

3. *Leases with operating expense recoveries.* In many situations, particularly for leases involving large amounts of space, property owners may *not* want to execute either a full-service or modified full-service lease because they would continue to bear the risk of paying a substantial amount of the expenses required to operate the property. In these cases, tenants usually agree to pay lower rents than would be the case for a full-service or modified full-service lease, in exchange for agreeing to pay a greater range of operating expenses. Typically, in such leases, certain operating expenses will be identified as "recoverable." (See Concept Box 9.2.) These expenses will be totaled, prorated, and billed to tenants, usually based on the percentage of rentable area that the tenant occupies in a property.

Large Users of Leased Space

Typically, as individual tenants lease very large amounts of the total space available in a property, a greater share of operating expenses will be directly related and identifiable to the operation of that tenant. In these cases, rather than identifying recoverable expenses and then prorating and billing tenants, leases usually provide that such tenants pay all operating

---

[3] For example, if tenant (A) operates its business seven days a week or evenings, other tenants in a building will not want to bear any of tenant (A)'s share of operating expenses, even if based on a proration. In such cases, the property owner will generally find a way to link such expenses (electricity, security, HVAC, etc.) directly to the tenant.

In order to better understand what expenses are identified as recoverable expenses in leases, it may be useful to review the greater range of expenses usually associated with *owning* and *operating* a property.

Operating Expenses Typically Classified as Recoverable in Leases		Ownership Expenses Typically Not Classified as Recoverable in Leases
Cleaning	Water/sewer	Leasing commissions
Repairs	Security	Property accounting
Maintenance	Management	Administrative overhead
Landscaping	Real estate taxes	Financing fees
Electricity	Insurance	Capital outlays/tenant improvements
Business taxes	Depreciation allowance*	

*This allowance does not have to be the same as one of the depreciation methods prescribed by GAAP accounting principles. It may represent a rate of actual economic depreciation of the building, as estimated by the property owner.

As shown above, not all expenses incurred by a property owner are recoverable. Expenses incurred relative to marketing, leasing, advertising, concessions, capital expenditures/depreciation, are viewed as ownership expenses and therefore the *responsibility of the property owner*. These expenses relate more to the ownership of the property and are not directly related to services provided to tenants.

expenses directly. In many of these cases, the owner provides a reduced level of services or no services (cleaning, etc.) that would be provided under a full-service or modified full-service lease. Examples include:

1. *Single net leases.* The tenant pays rent and pays for all operating expenses identified in the lease.

2. *Double net or net, net leases.* As in the single net lease, the tenant pays rent and pays all operating expenses directly. In addition, the owner "passes through" non operating expenses such as property taxes and insurance costs to the tenant.

3. *Triple net or net, net, net leases.* As in the single and double net lease, in addition to paying operating expenses, taxes, and insurance, the tenant also agrees to pay certain recurring capital outlays for repairs, alterations, and modifications to the *interior* of the leased building space. (Triple net leases are commonly used by tenants occupying large amounts of space in warehouse/industrial properties or office buildings. In these cases, tenants may require the flexibility to modify, move fixtures, and reconfigure the interior space in order to operate their business efficiently. However, tenants usually must be willing to pay for the cost of doing so.) Property owners are usually responsible for the cost of certain *exterior* repairs (roof, walls, and other equipment) to the property.

4. **Common area maintenance (CAM).** In cases where a building is a part of a larger property development (e.g., a corporate campus or industrial/warehouse park), tenants may pay a pro rata share of expenses required to maintain "common areas" in the

After owners and tenants negotiate what expenses will be recoverable, tenants usually also agree to pay for increases in recoverable operating expenses after they take occupancy of the space. In order to establish a base line of recoverable expenses at the time the tenant takes occupancy, the lease will generally specify that tenants will pay only a share of increases in recoverable expenses *in excess* of what is referred to as an **expense stop.** This "stop" is usually calculated based on the total recoverable operating expenses *per square foot* of **rentable area** in the building that is incurred by the property owner during a specified *base year*.* The tenant agrees to pay only for increases in recoverable operating expenses per square foot *in excess* of this stop. For example, when a lease is negotiated, if the building owner has incurred recoverable operating expenses per rentable square foot of $7 for the entire building during the base period, this may be used as the "stop." If expenses subsequently increase to $8 per square foot during the *next period*, the tenant would pay only recoverable expenses in excess of the $7 stop, or $1 per rentable square foot. The owner would be responsible for the base level of such expenses, or $7. The $7 stop may remain the same during the term of the lease or it could be indexed.†

*The owner and tenant will usually negotiate whether the *base year* is defined to be the current year, the year before, or the year after the lease is signed. This may be important during periods when operating expenses have been increasing. Determining rentable area is discussed later in the chapter.

†One complication arises when establishing stops and operating expenses for new or renovated buildings that are not yet fully occupied. In these cases, operating expenses per square foot of rented area may be unknown, or disproportionately high until the building reaches normal occupancy levels. As such, tenants may insist that their share of operating expenses be based on some level of normal occupancy (say 95%), and not on current occupancy levels.

campus. These expenses could include maintenance/lighting of roads, landscaping, security, and so on, and are referred to as CAM charges. In *retail leases,* CAM charges for maintaining, heating, and cooling mallways, as well as maintaining parking lots, providing security, and the like, are very important. How these CAM expenses are prorated among tenants is also very important and will be discussed in more detail in the case examples that conclude this chapter.

Comparing Leases: Effective Rent

From the above discussion, we know that a number of provisions may affect how rents are determined and various expense recovery options that may be included in a lease. These provisions, in combination, determine the expected series of rental payments and the extent of risk that is borne by the owner/lessor versus the tenant/lessee over the term of the lease. Because of the large number of possible combinations of lease terms, cash flows may vary considerably from lease to lease, making it difficult to establish what the lease cost is, as well as making comparisons between leases difficult. Therefore, it is useful to calculate a single measure or **effective rent** that can be used for comparison of individual leasing alternatives. It should be stressed again that lease contents will vary based on competitive market conditions as tenants/users shop and compare space in various locations. Market conditions at the time leases are negotiated and renewed will determine rents, methods of rent adjustments, concessions, and the extent to which the property owner may pass through certain operating expenses and/or recover them from tenants. In order to compare the various possibilities, it is useful to calculate the effective rent for every lease at the time that it is being *negotiated* or *renewed.* To calculate the effective rent we will use the following procedure:

1. Calculate the present value of the expected net rental stream. The net rental stream is the amount of rent received minus operating expenses that the owner must pay after deducting any expense recoveries from the tenant. Note that the focus here is on the income to the *owner* of the property.
2. Calculate an equivalent level annuity over the term of the lease. An equivalent level annuity has the same present value as the original cash flow stream.

To illustrate, we will calculate the effective rent that would be collected by the lessor for different lease structures. Because of rent adjustments, the responsibility for payment of operating expenses can vary considerably for different lease structures, so the effective rent must be calculated *net* of any operating expenses that must be paid by the lessor. That is, any operating expenses that must be paid by the lessor will be subtracted from the rental income. A similar procedure would be used to calculate the effective rent paid by the lessee. In this case, the amount of operating expenses that the lessee is responsible for paying would be *added* to the rent each year.

The effective rent will be calculated for the following five alternatives for a five-year lease on 10,000 square feet of rentable space:

1. *Gross lease.* Rent will be $40.00 per rentable square foot each year. The lessor (owner) will be responsible for the payment of all operating expenses. Expenses are estimated to be $20.00 during the first year and will increase by $1.00 per year thereafter.
2. *Gross lease with expense stop.* Rent will be $38.00 per rentable square foot the first year with the lessor responsible for payment of recoverable operating expenses as identified in the lease, up to an expense stop of $20.00 per square foot. Lessee pays all expenses in excess of $20.00 per square foot. Expenses are estimated to be $20.00 during the first year and will increase by $1.00 per year thereafter.
3. *Gross lease with step up rents.* Rent will be $35.00 per rentable square foot and will increase by $2.00 per square foot each year thereafter. Operating expense will be $20.00 per square foot and will increase by $1.00 per year.
4. *Gross lease with step up rents and expense stop.* Rents will be $32.00 per square foot. Operating expenses will be $20.00, and will increase by $1.00 per year. The tenant will pay (the owner will recover) all increases in operating expense above a $20.00 expense stop.
5. *Gross lease with expense stop and CPI adjustment.* Rent will be $30.00 per rentable square foot the first year and increase by the full amount of any change in the CPI after the first year with an expense stop at $20.00 per square foot. The CPI will increase as shown in case (5) in Exhibit 9–7. Operating expenses are assumed to be $4 per square foot and will increase by 50 cents per year thereafter.

Based on the above assumptions, the average rent, the present value of the rental stream, and the effective rent for each lease alternative are shown in Exhibit 9–7. A 10 percent discount rate is used to calculate the present value and convert the present value into an effective rent. This rate should reflect the riskiness of the rental stream, as discussed below. The effective rent varies for each alternative. This is expected because the risk differs for each alternative.

To illustrate the determination of *effective rent,* the following calculations are shown for the first lease alternative:

Step 1. Find the *present value* of net rent assuming that a discount rate of 10 percent is appropriate.

$$PV = \frac{\$20.00}{1.10} + \frac{\$19.00}{(1.10)^2} + \frac{\$18.00}{(1.10)^3} + \frac{\$17.00}{(1.10)^4} + \frac{\$16.00}{(1.10)^5}$$

$$= \$68.95$$

Step 2. Calculate the equivalent level annuity with the same present value. The result is the *effective rent.* Either the present value or the effective rent may be used for comparisons. The effective rent amounts to an annualized equivalent of the present value and is more commonly used in practice.

Solution:	Function:
$PV = -\$68.95$	$PMT\,(PV, i, n, FV)$
$i = 10\%$	
$n = 5$	
$FV = 0$	
Solve for *PMT* $= \$18.19$	

The same calculation can be performed for each lease alternative, and the results are shown in Exhibit 9–7.

Based on the examples shown in Exhibit 9–7(A), property owners can now use **effective net rent,** to compare leases with major differences in rents and responsibility for operating expenses. We should point out that results for **net leases** or those leases with a total operating expense pass through to tenants can now also be considered. This can be done by examining the net rent component of each of the five cases in Exhibit 9–7(A). Because the <u>net rent</u> in each case is equal to the gross rent less all operating expenses (now being passed through to the tenant), the <u>net rent</u> would be the cash flow that should be of importance to property owners when evaluating net leases.[4]

Other Financial Considerations

In addition to rents and operating expenses, there are several other financial considerations that may be negotiated as a part of lease agreements. Depending on how competitive market conditions are when leases are being negotiated, owners and potential lessees may negotiate one or more of the following:

Concessions and/or tenant improvement allowances (TIs) including: moving allowances, free or discounted rent, buyouts of existing leases or lease termination fees, and other inducements that a property owner may use to lease space to a desirable tenant.

To illustrate how these considerations may be included in effective net rent calculations, we return to case 1 in Exhibit 9–7(A). Recall that we are considering a lease of

---

[4] We should point out that, in practice, net leases are often used in negotiations with tenants requiring large amounts of space. Gross leases tend to be used more often for multi-tenant users requiring smaller amounts of space. So, in practice, comparing gross and net leases may not occur frequently because of the differences in the types of tenants and their rentable area requirements.

EXHIBIT 9–7 (A) **Comparative Effective Rents—Hypothetical Scenarios**

Year	(0)	(1)	(2)	(3)	(4)	(5)
1. Gross Lease—Flat Rents						
Gross rent	—	40.00	40.00	40.00	40.00	40.00
Less: Operating expenses	—	20.00	21.00	22.00	23.00	24.00
Add: Recoveries	—	—	—	—	—	—
Net rent		20.00	19.00	18.00	17.00	16.00
Average net rent	18.00	—	—	—	—	—
Present value	68.95	—	—	—	—	—
Effective net rent	18.19	—	—	—	—	—
2. Gross Lease—Flat Rents with Expense Stop						
Gross rent	—	38.00	38.00	38.00	38.00	38.00
Less: Operating expenses	—	20.00	21.00	22.00	23.00	24.00
Add: Recoveries	—	—	1.00	2.00	3.00	4.00
Net rent	—	18.00	18.00	18.00	18.00	18.00
Average net rent	18.00	—	—	—	—	—
Present value	68.23	—	—	—	—	—
Effective net rent	17.99	—	—	—	—	—
3. Gross Lease with Step Up Rents						
Gross rent	—	39.00	41.00	43.00	45.00	47.00
Less: Operating expenses	—	20.00	21.00	22.00	23.00	24.00
Add: Recoveries	—	—	—	—	—	—
Net rent	—	19.00	20.00	21.00	22.00	23.00
Average net rent	21.00	—	—	—	—	—
Present value	78.89	—	—	—	—	—
Effective net rent	20.81	—	—	—	—	—
4. Gross Lease with Step Up Rents and Expense Stop						
Gross rent	—	37.00	39.00	41.00	43.00	45.00
Less: Operating expenses	—	20.00	21.00	22.00	23.00	24.00
Add: Recoveries	—	—	1.00	2.00	3.00	4.00
Net rent	—	17.00	19.00	21.00	23.00	25.00
Average net rent	21.00	—	—	—	—	—
Present value	78.16	—	—	—	—	—
Effective net rent	20.62	—	—	—	—	—
5. Gross Lease Rents Indexed to Expected CPI with Expense Stop						
CPI	—	N/A	5.0%	6.0%	6.0%	6.0%
Gross rent	—	35.00	36.75	38.95	41.29	43.77
Less: Operating expenses	—	20.00	21.00	22.00	23.00	24.00
Add: Recoveries	—	—	1.00	2.00	3.00	4.00
Net rent	—	15.00	16.75	18.95	21.29	23.77
Average net rent	19.15	—	—	—	—	—
Present value	71.02	—	—	—	—	—
Effective net rent	18.73	—	—	—	—	—

EXHIBIT 9–7 (B)
Commentary on
Effective Rents by
Type of Lease shown
in Exhibit 9–7(A)

Lease type	Effective Rents (PSF)	Comments
1. Flat Rent	$18.19	Owner receives flat rents totaling $40.00 PSF annually and is responsible for paying operating expenses. Owner (1) forgoes any opportunity to raise rents and (2) must absorb all current and future increases in operating expenses.
2. Flat Rent with Expense Stop	$17.99	Owner receives lower flat rents totaling $38.00 PSF annually. However, owner will "pass through" to the tenant all operating expenses in excess of the $20.00 PSF expense stop. Owner forgoes opportunities to raise rents, but shifts some of the risk of any increases in operating expenses to the tenant.
3. Step Up Rents @ $2.00 annually	$20.81	Owner receives lower initial rent of $39.00. However, rents will be "stepped up" by $2.00 PSF per year. As in case 1, owner absorbs any future increase in operating expenses.
4. Step Up Rents and $20.00 Expense Stop	$20.62	Owner receives lower initial rents of $37.00 PSF. However, owner will step up rents by $2.00 PSF each year. Owner also will shift all operating expenses in excess of $20.00 PSF to the tenant.
5. Rents Indexed to CPI and Expense Stop	$18.73	Initial rents are lowest under this scenario. To the extent that future rents are correlated with the CPI, the owner will shift the risk of future rent increases to the tenant. Also, the owner will shift increases in operating expenses in excess of the $20 stop to the tenant.

10,000 square feet of space. The present value per square foot is $68.95. When multiplied by 10,000 SF, a total present value of $689,500 is determined. We now consider a case where the property owner offers a lease with the following incentives: $15,000 moving allowance and $20,000 in additional tenant improvements (TIs). These concessions would total $35,000. This will reduce the present value in case 1 to $654,500 and reduce the present value to $65.45 per square foot. Solving for the equivalent ordinary annuity as before results in an effective rent of $17.25.

In some cases, free rent may also be used as an inducement. For example if in case 1, if our property owner was to offer a rent reduction to $30 PSF for the first two years of the lease, we would re-compute the effective rent by discounting at 10% for five years. This results in an effective net rent of $13.61.

Year	(0)	(1)	(2)	(3)	(4)	(5)
Net rent		$10.00	$9.00	$18.00	$17.00	$16.00
Present value	$51.69					
Effective net rent	$13.61					

When the concessions of $35,000 are included in addition to the discounted rent, the new present value would be ($51.59 × 10,000) − $35,000 = $480,900. This revised present value of $480,900 ÷ 10,000 = $48.09 per square foot. This results in an effective rent of $12.69.

From the preceding examples, it should be clear that the effective rent is a measure of the expected present value of cash flows to the lessor (cost to the lessee). However, it should be stressed that effective rents cannot be compared without considering differences in risk. The effective rent is useful, however, when it is desirable to compare the expected returns from different lease alternatives with a single measure. It also is superior to comparing average rents or total rents over the life of the lease.

Developing Statements of Operating Cash Flow

What follows is a general discussion of the *link* between lease provisions and how investors in income-producing real estate develop statements of cash flow. These statements are very important as they serve as a basis for estimating real estate values and performing an investment analysis. These statements reflect (1) lease terms, (2) market supply and demand conditions affecting rents, (3) the tenant's credit risk, and (4) how responsibility for certain expenses associated with operating a property will be divided between the property owners and the tenants. As has been described, lease terms vary considerably for apartments, office buildings, retail properties, and warehouses. Differences in lease terms must be translated, and models must be developed into statements of cash flow in order to assess investment risk and return for investment opportunities.

It is useful to think of net cash flow realized from an investment in an income property as a combination of the relationships shown in Exhibit 9–8. *Rental income* for a property is calculated based on rents specified *in every lease* made with individual tenants. As we have discussed, rents specified in leases may be flat, stepped up, indexed, or based on some level of business performance. Furthermore, because existing leases have been made in previous periods and for different maturity periods, some leases may be due to expire, or "rollover," after a property is acquired. Therefore, rentable income in any year is a reflection of leases executed in previous years as well as leases being executed currently. As Exhibit 9–8 shows, in addition to rent, many properties produce *other income* from other services provided (such as laundry facilities in apartments, cell towers atop office buildings, covered parking, etc.).

EXHIBIT 9–8
General Approach for Developing Pro Forma Statements of Cash Flow for Income-Producing Properties

Rental Income
Add: Other Income
Expense Recoveries
Less: Vacancy and Collection Losses
Concessions
Effective Gross Income
Less: Operating Expenses
CAPEX/Improve Allowance*
NOI (Net Cash Flow)*

*This item represents recurring cash outlays for repairs and improvements made in conjunction with the normal operation of a property. Such items may include outlays needed to improve operating efficiency or prepare space for new tenants. In cases where major outlays for capital improvements (new roof, parking lot, etc.) are needed, these items should be included in a supplemental statement showing such outlays as nonoperating capital outflows only for the years that they are expected to occur.

**The reader should be aware that in real estate investment analysis, cash flow is the relevant focus. Even though the term *net operating income* (NOI) will be used in the coming chapters, it is calculated as cash flow and not income as determined by generally accepted accounting principles (GAAP). The term *NOI* is used interchangeably with cash flow from operations.

The statement shown in Exhibit 9–8 also shows that expense recoveries are usually *added* to the rent and other income to produce gross cash inflow for the property. *As we have explained, depending on the lease terms, some operating expenses may be recovered from tenants. Depending on the types of leases negotiated, such as full-service leases, modified full-service leases, net leases, and so on, some tenants may pay a pro rata share of operating expenses, while other tenants may pay a higher base rent but not make any contribution to operating expenses. Expense recoveries also must be determined on a lease-by-lease basis.*

After other sources of income and expense recoveries are determined, cash inflow is then reduced by loss of rents because of vacancies and nonpayment of rents (because of tenant bankruptcy, etc.). In addition to these reductions, property owners may have provided tenants with **concessions,** such as move-in allowances or rent reductions for a specified period of time. These are inducements for new tenants to lease space or to keep old tenants who are renewing leases. After these allowances are deducted, the resultant *effective gross income* is the amount of cash flow available to the owner to pay operating expenses.

In addition to operating expenses, additional items requiring cash outlays include "make ready" expenses for new tenants and other expenditures. These items are likely to occur regularly and will depend on the rate of lease turnover and will require that expenditures be made. Exhibit 9–8 includes such an allowance (see: CAPEX/Improve allowance). As will be shown later, when doing an investment analysis, multiperiod statements of cash flow including operating cash flows and a separate statement for capital outlays should be developed.

From effective gross income, operating expenses and the CAPEX allowance are deducted, and the net result is the *net cash flow,* also referred to as *net operating income (NOI).* This concept represents the net cash inflow from operating the property over a normal operating cycle (usually one year). *NOI is a very important concept in real estate investment analysis.*

As we explained, the pro forma statement of cash flow shown in Exhibit 9–8 is very basic. As each major property type is considered in this chapter, pro forma statements of cash flow may be affected because of certain lease provisions that are important to each property type. We should also note that our explanation in this chapter is limited to basic pro forma statements *for only a one-year period.* As will be seen in later chapters, when doing an investment analysis, pro forma statements must be developed annually for longer periods of time. We now turn to an examination of how leases and cash flows may vary for office, retail, industrial/warehouse, and multifamily properties.

Case Example: Office Properties

Rent Premiums and Discounts for Office Space

Office space tends to be leased for three- to seven-year terms with tenants often having the option to renew leases for additional terms. Rents vary by location within office properties, and owners may charge *premium rents* for space with the following features and locations:

- Ground floor, transfer points, and space contiguous to elevator banks.
- Higher floors with unobstructed views.
- Building corners.

   Rent discounts may apply to office space in the following locations:

- Middle floors and locations not adjacent to the elevator bank.
- Offices with obstructed or less desirable views.
- Noncontiguous space occupied by one tenant (e.g., space on the second floor and space on the sixth floor).

   See Concept Box 9.3 for a listing of the typical provisions in office property leases.

Determining Lease Revenue

In order to determine revenue, the base rent per square foot of **rentable area** must be multiplied by the quantity leased to tenants. While this may seem to be a straightforward calculation, it is not always as easy as it seems. This is particularly true in buildings where multiple tenants use and share common space. We will provide a hypothetical example using an office building to give the reader some idea of how rentable space is determined. However, depending on the city in which a building is located, local practices may affect how these calculations will be done.

Rentable Area in a Building

It is useful to think about the rentable area in a building as the total area that could be rented to a *single tenant-user.* This would usually equal the total area on all floors and the lobby *but exclude* the nonrentable area, which usually includes the thickness of exterior walls, any columns or protrusions through the floors such as elevator shafts or structural supports, mechanical equipment closets, basements, and so on, needed by the owner to maintain or operate the building. It would *include* areas such as elevator landings, lobbies, or reception areas, restrooms, or any areas that could be used by a tenant and their visitors/clients (these latter areas are also referred to as *common areas*). To illustrate, if we assume that a building contains 250,000 square feet of gross building area and, of that area, 200,000 square feet *could be rented and occupied by one tenant,* and if we also assume that base rents are $20 per square foot, then the total rent would equal $20 times the rentable area of 200,000 feet, or $4,000,000 per year. The single tenant would make payments based on this amount prorated monthly by dividing by 12.

Multiple Tenants—Rentable Area per Floor—Load Factors

In cases where many tenants share a building, each tenant will occupy its **usable area** on a floor. For example, if four tenants share one floor equally and that floor has a total of 20,000 square feet of rentable area that is partitioned off into equal interior office spaces of 4,500 square feet each, then the total *usable* space on the floor is 18,000 square feet. However, there would have been 20,000 square feet of usable *area* if only one tenant leased the entire floor. Therefore, when multiple tenants *share* a floor, the difference between the total rentable area on a floor (or space that would be used if only one tenant occupied that floor) and usable area occupied by multiple tenants is a common area of 2,000 square feet. This space would be used by all four tenants and their clients/visitors. In this instance, the owner will prorate the 2,000 square feet of common area among the four tenant users to determine the *rentable area* for each tenant by using a **load factor,** which is calculated as follows:

$$\text{Load factor per floor} = \frac{\text{Rentable area per floor}}{\text{Usable area per floor}}$$

$$1.111 = \frac{20,000}{18,000}$$

Therefore, for a tenant with *usable area* of 4,500 square feet, *rentable area* for that tenant would be calculated as 4,500 × 1.111 = 5,000 square feet. The tenant would pay rent based on its *rentable area* of 5,000 square feet. If this relationship exists on each of the 10 floors in the building, the load factor for the building would be (200,000 ÷ 180,000) = 1.111.

However, it should be pointed out that loads may vary by tenant and by floor. For example, if a single tenant occupies an entire floor, then the useable area and the rentable area would be the same, or 20,000 square feet for that tenant on that floor.

Because of the cost and importance of space that firms use in their operations, many options and other features are considered by owners and tenants when negotiating leases. In addition to the basic provisions discussed earlier (see Concept Boxes 9.1 and 9.2), what follows is a sample of some features found frequently in office leases:

- *Tenant right of first refusal.* According to the **right of first refusal,** tenants may have the right to rent contiguous space and/or any space in the building when it becomes available.
- *Tenant right to "put back" space to property owner.* Tenant may have the right to decrease space rented in the event that tenant desires to reduce space needs.
- *Sale or merger* by a landlord shall give tenant the option to terminate the lease.
- *Access-egress.* Material modification in access/egress or parking on the site by the owner requires approval of tenant.
- *Purchase option.* The tenant has the first right to purchase the property, should the property owner desire to sell at some future date.
- *Signage.* The purpose of a **signage clause** is to grant one or more tenants the right to display a name inside and/or outside of the building. (For tenants that lease very large amounts of space, sometimes referred to as **anchor tenants,** signage may be offered as an inducement to lease space.) The size and designs of the signs are carefully controlled by the landlord, particularly when given exclusively to one tenant. Note: Other potential tenants may avoid leasing space in an office building featuring a competitor's name. There may be "prestige" issues involved, depending on the tenant mix in the building.
- *New lease approval.* Anchor tenants may want the right to approve any major lease agreements being negotiated by the property owner with new tenants so as to protect their image/identification with the building.
- *Overloading—use of space.* Tenant must keep the current and future number of employees per square foot at an agreed level (e.g., 250 sq. ft. of rentable space per employee).
- *Parking.* Property owner must reserve and/or keep a specified minimum number of spaces relative to rentable square feet currently in the building and relative to leasable space to be constructed in the future.

In many cases, the load factor *per floor* may be further adjusted for additional areas in the building. For example, a large office building may contain an "oversized" and elaborate lobby and may have other common areas (rooftop observations, etc.). In our example, if we assume that the 200,000 rentable square feet is distributed evenly over 10 floors (square building), and the first floor is a lobby and common area containing 10,000 square feet, then an owner *may also attempt* to prorate this lobby common area among all tenants in the building. One way that this might be done is to take the ratio of the other common area (lobby) of 10,000 square feet ÷ 200,000 square feet total rentable area which is 5 percent. The load factor for a floor (1.111) may then be increased by another 5 percent or $1.111 \times 1.05 = 1.1667$ (total load factor). Our tenant's rentable area would then be calculated as: Usable area × Total load factor or $4,500 \times 1.1667$ or 5,250 square feet. Assuming $20 per square foot base rents, the total rental revenue to the owner from this tenant would be:

$$\$20 \times (4,500 \times 1.1667) = \text{Rent per year}$$

$$20 \times 5,250 = \$105,000$$

For a single tenant occupying one entire floor, recall that the rentable and useable areas on that floor will be the same, or 20,000 square feet. Therefore, this single tenant would pay an annual rent based on the rentable area on the floor, increased by the load for other common areas in the building as follows:

$$\$20 \times 20{,}000 \text{ sq. ft.} \times 1.05 = \$420{,}000$$

Therefore, when tenants shop for office space in a multitenanted office building, they will not only be interested in the base rent per square foot. They will also be interested in how the *rentable area* is determined, including the *load factors* that will be applied to the usable area they occupy to determine the total rentable area. Rentable area is the quantity against which the base rent will be multiplied to determine rent payments. In many cases, when tenants compare buildings for possible occupancy, they compare total load factors as "efficiency measures." High load factors generally indicate a large amount of common area, and therefore *lower* "building efficiency." However, if an image-conscious tenant desires a premium, spacious area in which to receive its clients and large common areas, this qualitative consideration may offset low efficiency. It should also be pointed out that regardless of how load factors are calculated, these factors are negotiable between owners and tenants much in the same way as the commissions discussed above.

Pro Forma Statement of Cash Flow—Office Properties

In Exhibit 9–9, we provide an example of a pro forma statement of cash flow for Webster Office Plaza, a 17-story office property with 459,295 square feet of *rentable area*. Estimates of revenue used to compile this statement are based on a total of 65 leases, some of which include flat, step-up, and indexed rents. Based on the rentable area, and assuming full occupancy, a weighted average has been used to estimate total rent at $25.65 per rentable square foot, or $11,780,917 for the coming year. The property also should produce other income from some retail services, cell tower rents, and parking and storage fees. It should be noted that in the revenue section of the statement, an *expected expense recoveries from tenants* amount equaling $1,139,051 has been included. This amount was estimated by reviewing expense provisions in each of the 65 leases. Such a review should determine leases that (1) are "full service," and therefore do not provide for any operating expense recovery from tenants, (2) are modified full service, (3) provide for pass throughs for taxes and insurance, or (4) provide for operating expense recoveries, and if so, whether "stops" are applicable. Vacant space is estimated to be equivalent to 5 percent of gross rent. Also, as shown, concessions (moving allowances and rent discounts given to new tenants) are deducted from revenues. Effective gross income from all sources is $12,675,727.

Total expenses payable by the property owner are estimated to be $13.39 per rentable foot, for a total of $6,149,959. Additional deductions include $2,549,087 as a CAPEX/Improve allowance. These latter outlays include tenant improvement costs that have been negotiated as part of the tenant/improvement/"finish out" costs of preparing the space for new tenant occupancy and other outlays. After deducting operating expenses and the CAPEX/Improve allowance from effective gross income, the net operating income (NOI) for Webster Office Plaza is determined for the base year to be $3,976,681.

It should be stressed that this pro forma statement is intended to provide the reader with guidance as to how to construct a pro forma statement for the base year only. In order to perform a more comprehensive investment analysis of this property, a *multiyear forecast* for Webster must be made. This forecast would be made based on the terms in all 65 leases, including expected lease terminations, lease renewals, and lease extensions, as well as lease commissions. Future adjustments in rent, expenses, pass throughs, and recoveries also should be included. In addition, future major capital expenditures or outlays for major improvements, repairs, and replacements (roof, elevators, HVAC, etc.), and tenant improvements should be included for those years during which outlays are expected in such a multiyear forecast. Examples of a more comprehensive, multiyear forecast will be included in the next chapter.

EXHIBIT 9–9
**Pro Forma Statement
of Cash Flow—Base
Year Estimate**

Webster Office Plaza

Property Description

Webster Office Plaza
Rentable Area (RA): 459,295 sq. ft., 17 stories
Occupancy: 95%
Tenants: 65
Rentable sq. ft. per Tenant (avg.): 7,000

Parking: 2,000 spaces
Site Area: 10 acres
Elevators: 12

Revenue

Gross Rent ($25.65 base per sq. ft.* RA)		$11,780,917
Add: Expense Recoveries from Tenants	$1,139,051	
Add: Other Revenues		
Retail Services (Lobby)	10,000	
Cell Tower Rents	54,301	
Storage Fees	9,186	
Parking	381,215	
Less: Vacancy (5% of Gross Rent)	597,898	
Less: Concessions (Free Rent, etc.)	101,045	
Effective Gross Income		$12,675,727
Less: Operating Expenses		
Property Taxes	913,997	
Mgmt./Admin./Leasing Expenses	982,891	
Insurance	638,420	
Maintenance/Operations	987,484	
Utilities	1,731,542	
Janitorial/Cleaning	725,686	
Business & Other Taxes	169,939	
Total Operating Expenses	6,149,959	
CAPEX/Improve Allowance	2,549,087	8,699,046
Net Operating Income (NOI)		$3,976,681

*Rounded.

Case Example: Industrial and Warehouse Properties

Many of the same features in office leases apply to industrial properties and warehouses. Indeed, many buildings include a combination of office space and warehouse space. However, there are a few areas where these properties differ.

Leases for warehouse property tend to be highly individualized due to the special-purpose nature of the buildings. Tenants generally prefer longer-term leases ranging from 10 to 20 years. Long-term leases are preferred because many large warehouse users require equipment with high installation costs that cannot be moved easily or on short notice. Leases tend to contain significant pass-through clauses, or will usually be (1) *net,* (2) *net, net,* or (3) *net, net, net leases.* Rent premiums for industrial/warehouse properties might be added for properties with the following features:

- Located near entrances to industrial parks.
- Located near freeways, interstate highways, or rail access.
- Wide turning radius and access to loading docks.

Rent discounts for industrial/warehouse properties might be added for properties with the following features:

- Poor ingress/egress.
- Poor traffic circulation on the site.

When industrial and warehouse buildings are located in a large, campus-like development, common area charges may be included in leases. This occurs because of the expenses associated with maintenance, landscaping, upkeep, security, and the like, that may be performed in the common areas of the entire development for the benefit of all tenants but do not apply to any specific building. Because all tenants in all buildings benefit from these services, the owner may recover these expenses with a CAM (common area maintenance) charge.

Leases may provide that tenants can make outlays for leasehold improvements in order to improve efficiency. Such outlays are usually the responsibility of the tenant. Property owners usually retain the right to approve both the design and the contractor installing such improvements. How and if such improvements will be removed and the party responsible for the cost of doing so also should be addressed in the lease.

Pro Forma Statement of Cash Flow—Industrial/Warehouse Properties

In Exhibit 9–10, we provide a brief illustration of the pro forma cash flow for a distribution/warehouse with a total of 100,000 square feet of rentable area, 10 percent of which is office and showroom space. It will have a single tenant/user who has agreed to pay (a) $6.60 per square foot in rent and (b) a portion of additional operating expenses/fees related to maintenance and repair of the property equal to $1.00 per square foot per year. In this case, the lease agreement indicates that the tenant will pay all operating expenses, and utilities. The tenant agrees to pay the property owner an additional $1.00 per square

EXHIBIT 9–10
Pro Forma Statement of Cash Flow—Base Year Estimate

Hellis Distribution Facility		
Property Description		
Hellis Distribution Facility/Office/Showroom Building		
Rentable Area (RA): 100,000 sq. ft./10% Office/Showroom Space		
Lease: Single Tenant—5 Year Term—Net, Net		
Rent per sq. ft. : .55 per Month, $6.60 per Year		
Operating Expense Recovery from Tenant: $1.00 per sq. ft. per Year		
Revenue		
Rent (Base of $6.60 per sq. ft. × RA)		$660,000
Add: Expense Recovery from Tenant	$100,000	
Pass Throughs:		
Property Taxes	125,000	
Insurance	50,000	
Effective Gross Income		$938,000
Less: Operating Expenses		
Maint./Repair/Other Expenses	150,000	
Property Taxes	125,000	
Insurance	50,000	
Total Operating Expenses	325,000	
CAPEX/Improve Allowance	69,000	394,000
Net Operating Income (NOI)		$544,000

foot for operating expenses (maintenance, etc.) incurred by the owner, who will, in turn, make payments to service providers. As can be seen in the exhibit, operating expenses for general maintenance, repairs, and other expenses total $150,000. As a result, all expenses will not be recovered from the tenant, who is expected to pay an expense recovery totaling $100,000. The difference is the net amount of expenses that must be paid by the owner. However, property taxes and insurance will be billed, or "passed through" to the tenant, then paid by the owner. Other outlays shown in Exhibit 9–10 include: CAPEX/Improve allowance outlays for recurring expenses prior to occupancy of the warehouse.

As was the case for office properties (see Exhibit 9–9), this pro forma is for the base year only. A more thorough investment analysis would include multiyear pro forma statements reflecting changes in revenue and expenses based on the lease agreement and any expected capital outlays for repairs of exterior, structural items such as roofing, parking areas, driveways, and the like for the years in which such outlays are expected.

Case Example: Retail Properties

Retail properties derive much of their value from the landlord's ability to lease to a mix of tenants that attract shoppers. Key indicators of the success of a retail property include *sales per square foot of rentable space* and *customer traffic counts.* These factors are very important to retail property owners when trying to lease space to prospective tenants. When developing retail properties, owners usually complete a *trade area analysis.* This study uses the population, age, and income of potential customers in the trade area as an indicator of demand for goods and services.

Retail properties are subject to many changing trends, new concepts in retailing, fashions, and the like. In addition to rents and expenses, retail leases contain many provisions that affect how tenants may, and may not, operate their businesses. This is because most retailers will be operating their businesses adjacent, or in proximity, to other retailers. Furthermore, some tenants may have the right to approve leases being negotiated with competing retailers. Retail leases with some tenants may also exclude certain other tenants that may be deemed as incompatible or that may detract or interfere with the operations of existing retailers.

Cash flow from retail leases may vary greatly. In addition to the flat, stepped-up, and/or indexed base rents, landlords and tenants may negotiate some of the rent based on a tenant's sales volume. Furthermore, retail leases usually incorporate recoveries of certain operating expenses. One very important item regarding retail properties is the recovery of expenses related to maintaining common areas, or **CAM charges.** These expenses tend to be *very significant* and are very important to tenants in retail properties. Although much of our discussion applies to shopping malls, many of the concepts described here also apply to other types of retail properties.

The Retail Leasing Environment

Anchor Tenants versus In-line Tenants

When an investment in large retail properties is considered, understanding the nature of the business and importance of various tenants is important. A common distinction is made between *anchor* tenants and *in-line,* or *shop,* tenants. Anchor tenants usually include very large department stores or other retailers that achieve very high sales volumes and generate a considerable amount of customer traffic. In many cases, because they lease a very large amount of space, anchors receive large rent discounts and demand many special lease features. In-line tenants, on the other hand, tend to be smaller retailers that hope to generate retail sales as a result of participating in the high shopping traffic, part of which is produced by the anchor tenants. By combining primary, complimentary, and cross-shopping activity between anchor and in-line tenants, the property owner hopes to create a retail environment that tends to produce high total retail sales for all tenants per square foot of rentable space.

Rents

Another very important distinction between anchor and in-line tenants is the determination of rent. In general, when negotiating with property owners, anchor tenants can usually bargain more effectively than in-line tenants. In many cases, *anchor tenants will pay very low rents, or no rent at all.* In fact, if a particular anchor tenant is highly desirable, the property owner may be willing to lease space at very favorable rents *and* provide other incentives such as contributing funds to construct and finish out the space being leased by the anchor. In some cases, property owners may sell a portion of the property to an anchor tenant, thereby allowing the tenant to build, finish, operate, and control the retail space in accordance with the floor plan and dêcor that the anchor believes to be most desirable and successful. Alternatively, if the property is not sold, the landlord usually enters a long-term operating agreement with the anchor tenant.

In contrast to the low rents and very long-term leases made with anchor tenants, rents for in-line tenants tend to be driven by current market conditions. Rent typically consists of a *base rent* per square foot of rentable space for relatively short terms—say, three to five years (with renewal options). Furthermore, as is the case for many commercial properties, this base rate could be flat for the lease term, subject to specific, periodic step-ups, or indexed to the CPI. Leases are usually reviewed by the owner and tenant prior to the expiration date and renegotiated.

For some in-line tenants, an additional component of retail leases combines base rent with a so-called **percentage rent clause.** The rationale for this usually occurs when, in spite of high traffic counts and sales volumes, in-line tenants believe that the base rents being asked by the property owner are relatively high. In these cases, tenants may prefer to negotiate a lower base rent and agree to pay additional rents (referred to as **overage rents**) if their business in the retail property is successful. The additional rent is based on a percentage of the retail sales above some **breakpoint sales level.** Tenants may believe that this rent arrangement is consistent with the landlord's claims relative to sales per square foot and customer traffic count: If the retail environment is as good as the owner claims, then the owner should bear part of the tenant's business risk as a portion of the total rent determination.

A basic example of a percentage lease is as follows. Assume that for 1,000 square feet of rentable retail space, a property owner is asking a flat base rent of $38 per square foot (psf). However, instead of the $38 psf rent, the landlord may offer a *lower base rent* of $35 psf, plus *overage rent* equal to 8 percent of all gross sales revenue produced in excess of a breakpoint sales volume. Breakpoint sales levels and percentage rent factors are negotiated and vary by the type of retail tenant. For example, jewelry stores may have a relatively low breakpoint sales level and a high percentage rent factor, while a party goods store would have a relatively high breakpoint sales volume and low percentage rent factor. In our example, if the breakpoint sales level is negotiated to be $900,000 and the tenant produces gross sales of $1,000,000, then base rents plus *overage rents* would be as follows:

Base rent:		Total	Per Square Foot (psf)
$35 psf × 1,000 sq. ft.	=	$35,000	$35
Add overage rents:			
($1,000,000 − $900,000).08	=	8,000	8
Total base rent plus overage rents		$43,000	$43
Rent due beginning of each month	=	($43 × 1,000 sq. ft.) ÷ 12 = $3,583.33	

On the other hand, if sales volume for the in-line tenant in our example turned out to be less than the breakpoint sales volume of $900,000, base rents would remain $35 per square foot. Percentage leases also must specify what revenue items will be included in gross sales when determining breakpoint sales and overage rents. Returned merchandise, sales to employees, gift certificates, Internet sales, and revenue adjustments for sales taxes must all be clarified. Furthermore, documentation may be required of tenants and usually includes sales reports, financial statements based on tenant record retention, and sales tax receipts. The landlord also usually reserves audit rights.

CAM Charges—Recoveries

As indicated above, another very important component of retail leases is an expense recovery for common area maintenance (CAM). Most retail properties include a large amount of common area space that is used for mall walkways, parking, and nonshopping spaces that are used by all customers who visit the property. This space must be lighted, operated, maintained, and repaired, and security must be provided by the owner. Also, in an enclosed mall, common areas are usually heated and cooled. When rents on retail leases are negotiated, common area maintenance (CAM) charges based on specific expenses identified in the lease also are usually negotiated. With regard to CAM charges, it should be pointed out that in many situations anchor tenants pay less of these expenses than in-line tenants pay. CAM charges are usually charged to *in-line tenants* as follows:

CAM charges per square foot of rentable in-line space:

$$\frac{\text{(Total CAM expenses for the property} - \text{Contribution to CAM expenses paid by anchor tenants)}}{\text{(Total rentable area occupied by in-line tenants)}}$$

A general example of CAM charges might be as follows: (1) a retail mall contains 2 million square feet of space, of which 1.2 million is rentable area and 800,000 square feet is common area; (2) total CAM expenses are $3,000,000 for the year; and (3) anchor tenants occupy 700,000 square feet of rentable area and in-line tenants occupy 500,000 square feet. The owner of the mall has negotiated with four anchor tenants that they will pay $2 per rentable foot for CAM charges on a combined total of 700,000 square feet. The CAM charges for in-line tenants will be:

$$\frac{\$3,000,000 - \$1,400,000}{500,000} = \$3.20 \text{ CAM charges per rentable square foot (in-line tenants)}$$

It should be clear that when negotiating CAM charges with anchor tenants, the property owner may be taking on considerable risk. In many cases, property owners attempt to attract anchor tenants by providing very favorable leases, including relatively low rents and low CAM charges. However, in order to justify these favorable terms to anchor tenants, higher rents and CAM expenses may have to be negotiated with in-line tenants. Depending on the level of retail sales achieved, in-line tenants may not be able to afford relatively high rents and CAM charges. As a result, they may vacate the property at their first opportunity. Alternatively, the property owners may have to reduce rents to in-line tenants and may not achieve their expected rental revenue.

In addition to CAM charges, in some cases, retail property owners may pass through insurance and property taxes directly to all tenants based on the share of the rentable area that they occupy. In addition, all tenants will usually be required to belong to a retail merchants association and pay for various advertising and promotional costs. See Concept Box 9.4 for a discussion of retail property leases and operating characteristics.

Because of the nature of retail properties and the interaction of many vastly different businesses ranging from high fashion to restaurants, many features are unique to leases on retail properties. What follows is a list of some of the more important features that may affect risk and return.

- *Lease termination or kick out clause.* Because sales per square foot and customer traffic are so important to the success of retail property investments, both retailers and owners may include a **termination clause,** which specifies that the tenant must achieve a certain level of sales per square foot within a specific period of time (e.g., two years), otherwise either the property owner or the tenant may terminate the lease.

- *Co-tenancy clause.* The **co-tenancy clause** is a demand commonly made by tenants who require the continued presence of a certain anchor or other tenants as a condition of making a lease with the property owner. This occurs when a tenant has found that sales increase when certain co-tenants are present in retail malls. Furthermore, if any of these co-tenants terminate their leases, in-line tenants may: (1) require the property owner to find a comparable replacement within a specific time period, (2) renegotiate rent, or (3) terminate the lease.

- *Anchor tenant and lender approval of major leases.* In retail situations, large anchor tenants are usually very concerned about the quality, image, and visibility of potential in-line tenants, and they may demand the right to approve all major leases (e.g., 5,000 sq. ft. or more) being negotiated between property owners and (1) new in-line tenants and (2) other anchor tenants. Lenders may be concerned more from a financial perspective; that is, they may focus on the rents, CAM charges, and so on given to major tenants.

- *Signage.* A **signage clause** confers the right to display a name inside and/or outside of the building or in the mall ways. In the case of retail anchor tenants, unique signage may be offered as an inducement to lease space. Signage for in-line tenants will usually be specified as to size, color conformity, and so on.

- *Exclusivity clause.* An **exclusivity clause** limits the ability of the property owner to lease space in the building to competitors of existing tenants. Some exclusive retail shops insist upon an exclusive-use provision prohibiting any similar shop from leasing space anywhere in, or in proximity to, the building in order to protect sales.

- *Nondilution, or radius, clause.* When an exclusivity clause is provided to tenants, the property owner may require a **radius clause;** that is, the tenants must agree not to lease any additional space in the same market/trade area specifically defined (e.g., within a radius of five miles).

- *Excluded uses.* Many anchor tenants require that some uses be excluded within a specified number of feet from their leased space. These could include movie theaters, restaurants, health clubs, and so forth. The anchor tenant may believe that parking and/ or access to their location may be adversely affected by these uses.

- *Operating times.* All tenants must generally operate during specified times each day and on holidays. This precludes problems that may affect customer traffic due to nonuniformity in times of operation of the many tenants in a retail property.

Pro Forma Statement of Cash Flow—Retail Properties

Exhibit 9–11 provides an illustration for Shady Elm Community Shopping Center, a community center with 245,000 square feet of rentable space. It includes one 70,000 square foot grocery store and one 40,000 square foot home dêcor/furnishings store as *anchor tenants* and 30 other *in-line* or *shop tenants.* It includes an interior, covered, and air-conditioned mallway which provides 80,000 square feet of common area access for the entire center. Base rents are expected to average $16.73 per square foot; however, six

EXHIBIT 9–11
**Pro Forma Statement
of Cash Flow—Base
Year Estimate**

Shady Elm Community Shopping Center

Property Description
Shady Elm Community Shopping Center
Rentable Area (RA): 245,000 sq. ft.

Anchor Tenants: (2) Grocery/Home Furnishings		

Common Area: 80,000 sq. ft.   In-line/Shop Tenants: (30)
Parking: 2,500 spaces   Site Area: 19 acres

Revenue

Rent (Base of $16.73 per sq. ft. × RA)		$4,098,850
Add: Overage Rent (from % leases)	$ 308,700	
CAM and Other Expense Recoveries from Tenants	1,139,250	
Other Income (Kiosks, Outbuildings)	159,250	
Less: Vacancy (5% × RA × Base)	330,750	
Concessions	—	
Effective Gross Income		**$5,375,300**
Less: Operating Expenses		
Maintenance/Repair	584,700	
Mgmt./Admin./Leasing Expenses	340,000	
Property Taxes	1,050,000	
Insurance	66,000	
Other	35,000	
Total Operating Expenses	1,875,700	
CAPEX/Improve Allowance	315,000	2,190,000
Net Operating Income (NOI)		**$2,984,600**

tenants in the center have executed percentage rent leases. It is expected that these leases will produce *overage rents* of $308,700 during the base year. CAM expenses recoverable from tenants for maintenance of the 80,000 feet of mallway and other common area (parking lots, etc.) are expected to be $1,139,250, or about $4.65 per rentable foot. After considering rents, overage rents, other income, and CAM recoveries less vacancies, Shady Elm is expected to produce effective gross income of $5,375,300 during the base year. Total operating expenses to be paid by the owner are listed on the pro forma and are expected to be $1,875,700. Other items expected to be paid by the owner of Shady Elm include an allowance for tenant and capital improvements amounting to $315,000. After including all revenue items and deductions for operating expenses and a CAPEX/Improve allowance, NOI for the center is estimated to be $2,984,600.

In order to accomplish a more complete investment analysis of Shady Elm, a multiyear pro forma statement of cash flow based on a review of rents and expenses for all 32 leases, plus any expected capital expenditures (CAPEX) in years when outlays are expected to occur, would have to be made. We will provide a discussion of multiperiod pro forma cash flows in Chapter 10.

Case Example: Apartment Properties

Using the same general format shown in Exhibit 9–8, we consider a detailed determination of cash flows for apartment investments. For a number of reasons, investments in apartment properties are considerably different from office, retail, and warehouse investments. Leases are made for relatively short periods of time, the turnover of units may be very significant, and many state and federal consumer protection laws may apply. Exhibit 9–12 shows a pro forma statement of cash flow for apartment properties.

It should be noted that the *gross potential rental income* is calculated based on *full occupancy* of the mix of one- and two-bedroom units at an *average current rent* of $885.65 per month, producing $2,465,649 for the coming year. The "*loss to lease*" term is somewhat unique to estimating cash flows for apartments. It reflects the fact that leases on a number of units may have been made in previous periods and are different from current market rents being negotiated on new leases. The $61,036 loss to lease is determined by identifying the number of units with older leases made in prior periods. The difference in rents being collected on the older leases and rents that are currently being collected on new leases is determined and then multiplied by the number of older leases/units. From this amount, rents on vacant units and rent losses from nonpayment and rent discounts/concessions are then subtracted, producing net rental income of $1,937,861. Other income from nonrent sources (such as parking, storage, laundry facilities, etc.) is shown to produce an additional $111,080, and utility expense recoveries from tenants for water and heat provided by the property owner are also included, resulting in a total income from all sources of $2,248,941. Operating and leasing expenses are projected to be $990,380. After combining all items of income and expenses, *net operating income* is projected to be $1,012,466, after including a CAPEX allowance of $246,095 for replacements. Many other contents in apartment leases and other operating features affecting cash flows are detailed in Concept Box 9.5.

EXHIBIT 9–12
Waterfall Court Apartments— Summary Description

Name of Property: Waterfall Court Apartments		**Principal Amenities:** Direct-access garages with automatic garage door openers. Washer/dryer connections (full-size) in some units, swimming pool, limited access gates, parking spaces (400/some covered).	
Location: Suburbia, USA			
Improvement Description: A 232-unit garden apartment community located on a major north-south arterial road. The property was well constructed with a high level of amenities, including 100% direct-access garages. All buildings are two-story construction with 90% brick exteriors.		**Land Area Density:** 15 acres/15.5 units per acre	
		Unit mix:	
		1 bedroom—1 bath	104 units
		2 bedrooms—2 baths	128 units
		Avg. 1,000 sq. ft. per unit	
		Average monthly rent:	
Age: Seven years old		$885.65 per unit/.88 per square foot	

Gross Potential Rental Income (GPRI)		$2,465,649	
Less: Loss to Lease*		61,036	
Gross Rental Income		$2,404,613	
Less: Vacancy and Collection Loss		285,013	
Concessions and Adjustments		181,739	
Net Rental Income			1,937,861
Add:			
Other Income		111,080	
Recovery of expenses from tenants		200,000	311,080
Total Income			2,248,941
Less: Operating and Leasing Expenses			990,380
CAPEX/Improve Allowance			246,095
Net Operating Income (NOI)			1,012,466

*Loss to lease could be positive if current market rents have fallen relative to rents on older leases made prior to the present time.

1. *Leases.*
   a. Multiple occupants—all occupants are jointly and severely liable for rent. No subletting or substitution of tenants is allowed without approval of lessor. A fee may be charged for substitution of tenant on the lease.
   b. Lease termination—failure to pay rent, delay in taking occupancy, breach of lease agreement, breach of community rules. In some situations, the lessee may be able to terminate the lease and/or temporarily stop rent payments because of military duty or loss of employment.
2. *Collection losses* are usually due to nonpayment of rent, bankruptcy, abandonment of units, and so on.
3. *Concessions and adjustments.* Free rents, reduced rents for affordable housing requirements, discounts for corporate accounts, and so on.
4. *When leases expire* and the tenant does not give notice to vacate or renew, some states require that the lease automatically becomes "month to month," whereas other states may require that the lease be extended for a term equivalent to the original term of the lease. In some cases, if leases are not explicitly renewed, an additional "fee" may be added to the rent.
   a. *Fees* are usually charged for late rent payments and for NSF checks.
   b. *Deposits: security, damage, pets*—specified dollar amounts usually collected upon execution of the lease and the conditions under which all or part of amounts collected will be returned to the lessee (tenant).
   c. *Move out notice by tenants*—usually 30 days prior to move out date. Failure to provide notice results in an additional fee.
   d. *Additional income* may come from the following sources: lease cancellation fees, application fees, forfeited deposits, cable TV contract, laundry room, vending machines, garage rentals, clubroom rents, damage charges, and so on.
5. *Recoveries.* Heating/cooling, water, and special services provided to tenant by property owner.
6. *Repairs.* Owner takes responsibility for repairs of appliances, roof sprinklers, parking lot, equipment, glass, windows, key/lock, pool, HVAC, and all supplies. Turnover costs: all make-ready expenses (carpet and other cleaning, paint, countertop, tile/bath, etc.), property maintenance, security, administrative costs, and benefits.

Conclusion

The purpose of this chapter has been to familiarize the reader with lease provisions and operating characteristics generally representative of major property types. The illustrations have shown that regional economic conditions, market supply and demand, lease terms, tenant credit, investment risk, and the ability of property owners to pass through operating costs are all important considerations in income property analysis. Furthermore, the ability to modify and develop pro forma cash flow statements and to undertake a competitive market analysis serve as foundations for analysis and for estimating an investment value for properties being sought for acquisition. These latter topics will be the focus in the chapters that follow.

Key Terms

allowable uses, *266*
anchor tenant, *279*
base rent, *268*
breakpoint sales level, *284*
business conduct, *266*
CAM charges, *283*
common area maintenance
  (CAM), *270*
co-tenancy clause, *286*
concessions, *277*
CPI adjustment, *268*
effective rent, *271*
eminent domain, *267*
estoppel certificate, *267*
exclusivity clause, *286*

expense pass through, *269*
expense stop, *271*
free rent, *266*
industrial and warehouse
  properties, *254*
institutional real estate, *254*
termination clause, *286*
lease, *264*
lessee, *264*
lessor, *264*
letter of credit, *266*
load factor, *278*
market rent, *262*
minimum rent, *268*
non disturbance clause, *267*

nonresidential property, *253*
occupancy dates, *266*
overage rent, *268, 284*
percentage rent, *268*
percentage rent clause, *284*
percentage rent lease, *268*
radius clause, *286*
rentable area, *271, 278*
responsibility for expenses, *267*
right of first refusal, *279*
signage clause, *279, 286*
subletting, *266*
tenant improvements, *266*
usable area, *278*
work letter, *266*

Useful Web Sites

www.bls.gov/cpi—Consumer price index site sponsored by the U.S. Department of Labor, Bureau of Labor Statistics. This site gives information on different indexes and rates as well as news releases.

www.reis.com—Provides commercial real estate trends, analytics, market research, and news that support transactions by real estate professionals.

www.leasingprofessional.com—Source of information about leases, including terminology, sample leases, and links to other sites.

www.globest.com—Provides current real estate news that is updated daily.

www.naea.co.uk/—This site is hosted by the National Association of Estate Agents (NAEA), which is the United Kingdom's leading professional body for estate agency personnel, representing the interests of approximately 10,000 members who practice across all aspects of property services both in the United Kingdom and overseas. These include residential and commercial sales and lettings, property management, business transfer, and auctioneering.

www.realestate-tokyo.com—This site is a good source for residential and commercial real estate properties in Tokyo. It also offers information on apartments and houses to rent in the Tokyo area, properties for sale, offices for rent, and, in general, about life in Japan and the real estate market.

www.ipd.com—This site provides objective measurement and analysis of various properties. The company that runs this Web site does not invest in the market and does not offer any direct investment advice, so it tends to be unbiased.

www.snl.com/sectors/real-estate—This site provides fundamental financial data on more than 230 REITs, REOCS, and homebuilders. It gives detailed, descriptive property data, cost and performance data, and property mapping. It also is a good source for analyst coverage, FFO estimates, proprietary AFFO, and NAV consensus estimates.

Questions

1. How may the use of leases shift the risk of rising operating expenses from the lessor to the lessee?
2. What is the difference between base or face rents and effective rents?
3. What is meant by useable versus rentable space?
4. What are CAM charges?
5. What are (a) pass through expenses, (b) recoverable expenses, and (c) common area expenses? Give examples of each.
6. What is an estoppel? Why is it used?
7. What is meant by "loss to lease"? Explain.
8. What types of expenses would property owners pay when operating and maintaining common areas? Give examples for office, retail, and warehouse properties.

Problems

1. A building owner is evaluating the following alternatives for leasing space in an office building for the next five years:

   Net lease with steps. Rent will be $15 per square foot the first year and will increase by $1.50 per square foot each year until the end of the lease. All operating expenses will be paid by the tenant.

   Net lease with CPI adjustments. The rent will be $16 per square foot the first year. After the first year, the rent will be increased by the amount of any increase in the CPI. The CPI is expected to increase 3 percent per year.

   Gross lease. Rent will be $30 per square foot each year with the lessor responsible for payment of all operating expenses. Expenses are estimated to be $9 during the first year and increase by $1 per year thereafter.

   Gross lease with expense stop and CPI adjustment. Rent will be $22 the first year and increase by the full amount of any change in the CPI after the first year with an expense stop at $9 per square foot. The CPI and operating expenses are assumed to change by the same amount as outlined above.

   a. Calculate the effective rent to the owner (after expenses) for each lease alternative using a 10 percent discount rate.

   b. How would you rank the alternatives in terms of risk to the property owner?

   c. Considering your answers to parts (a) and (b), how would you compare the four alternatives?

2. As CFO for Everything.Com, you are shopping for 5,000 square feet of *usable* office space for 25 of your employees in Center City, USA. A leasing broker shows you space in Apex Atrium, a 10-story multitenanted office building. This building contains 300,000 square feet of gross building area. A total of 45,000 square feet is interior space and is nonrentable. The nonrentable space consists of areas contained in the basement, elevator core, and other mechanical and structural components. An additional 30,000 square feet of common area is the lobby area usable by all tenants. The 5,000 square feet of usable area that you are looking for is on the seventh floor, contains 28,000 square feet of rentable area, and is leased by other tenants who occupy a combined total of 20,000 square feet of usable space. The leasing broker indicated that base rents will be $30 per square foot of *rentable area*.

   a. Calculate total rentable area in the building as though it would be rented to one tenant.

   b. Calculate the load factor and common area on the seventh floor only.

   c. Calculate the rentable area, including the load factor for common areas on the seventh floor and the total rent per square foot that will be paid by Everything.Com for the coming year if it chooses to lease the space.

   d. Adjust (b) assuming that the owner adjusts the load factor for other common areas in the building.

   e. Calculate total rent per square foot, assuming that adjusted load factors are applied to usable area for both the common areas in the building lobby and on the seventh floor.

3. An owner of the Atrium Tower Office Building is currently negotiating a five-year lease with ACME Consolidated Corp. for 20,000 rentable square feet of space. ACME would like a base rent of $20 per square foot with step-ups of $1 per year beginning one year from now.

   a. What is the present value of cash flows to ATRIUM under the above lease terms? (Assumes a 10% discount rate.)

   b. The owner of ATRIUM believes that base rent of $20 PSF in (a) is too low and wants to raise that amount to $24 with the same step ups. However, now ATRIUM would provide ACME a $50,000 moving allowance and $100,000 in tenant improvements (TIs). What would be the present value of this alternative to ATRIUM?

   c. ACME informs ATRIUM that it is willing to consider a $23 PSF with the $1 annual step-ups. However, under this proposal, ACME would require ATRIUM to buyout the one year remaining on its existing lease in another building. That lease is $15 PSF for 20,000 SF per year. If ATRIUM buys out ACME's old lease, ACME will not require a moving allowance or TIs. What would be the present value of this proposal to ATRIUM? How does it compare with the alternative in (b)?

4. CAM charges for retail leases in a shopping mall must be calculated. The retail mall consists of a total area of 2.8 million square feet, of which 800,000 square feet has been leased to anchor tenants that have agreed to pay $2 per rentable square foot in CAM charges. In-line tenants occupy 1.3 million square feet, and the remainder is common area, which the landlord believes will require $8 per square foot to maintain and operate each year. If the owner is to cover total CAM charges, how much will in-line tenants have to pay per square foot?

5. A retail lease for 10,000 square feet of rentable space is being negotiated for a five-year term.

   Option A calls for a base rent of $25 per square foot for the coming year with step-ups of $1 per year each year thereafter. CAM charges are expected to be $3 for the coming year and are forecasted to increase by 6 percent at the end of each year thereafter.

   Option B calls for a lower base rent of $23 per square foot with the same step-ups and CAM charges, but the tenant must pay overage rents based on a percentage lease clause. The clause specifies that the tenant must pay 8 percent on gross sales over a breakpoint level of $900,000 per year. The owner believes that the tenant's gross sales will be $850,000 during the first year but should increase at a rate of 10 percent per year each year thereafter.

   a. If the property owner believes that a 12 percent rate of return should be earned annually on this real estate investment, which option is best for the owner of the retail center?

   b. What if sales are expected to increase by 20 percent per year?

6. You have been asked to develop a pro forma statement of cash flow for the coming year for Autumn Seasons, a 200-unit suburban garden apartment community. This community has a mix of 40 studio, 80 one-, and 80 two-bedroom apartments with current monthly rents of $550, $600, and $800, respectively. Leases with tenants are usually made for 12-month periods. Current rents are expected to remain fixed for the next six months. After that time, monthly rents for each apartment type should increase by $10 per unit and remain at those levels for the remainder of the year. Ten studios were leased three months ago for $500, 20 one-bedroom units were leased two months ago for $580, and 10 two-bedroom units were leased last month for $805. All other units have been leased recently at current rents. All of the previously leased units also are on 12-month leases. When those leases roll over, all are expected to be renewed at market rents upon rollover for an additional 12 months. Presently, 4 studios, 6 one-, and 6 two-bedroom units are vacant. This vacancy pattern should remain the same for the remainder of the year.

   Autumn Seasons anticipate that during the coming year, it will earn other income from laundry facilities, the awarding of an exclusive cable TV contract, parking, plus fees from net deposits, late fees, and so on of $200,000. Autumn Seasons expect to pay total turnover and operating expenses of $400 per month, per occupied unit during the next year. However, it expect to recover some of these expenses for heating and central cooling that it provide to tenants in an amount totaling $100 per month, per occupied unit. During the next year, it is also anticipated that $100,000 will be required for recurring, make ready expenses (carpet, paint, drywall repair, etc.) and another $250,000 will be required as an allowance for non recurring items including parking lot repairs, and so on. A total of $10,000 in fees will be paid to Apartment Locator Services, a company that provides marketing services and new tenants for Autumn.

   a. Prepare a statement of operating cash flow (NOI) for the coming year.

   b. Add to the (*a*) anticipated outlays for non recurring items and commissions. What will be net cash flow for the coming year?

7. You have been asked to develop a pro forma statement of cash flow for the coming (base) year for Summer Place Mall. The information given to you is listed below.

   Property Information:

   SUMMER PLACE MALL

Age of Improvement	10 years
Rentable Area (RA)	400,000 sq. ft.
Common Area (CA)	160,000 sq. ft.
Number of Tenants	40

Financial Information:

Avg. Base Rents	$20 per sq. ft.
Overage Rents (5 Tenants)	50,000 sq. ft. @ $8.00 per sq. ft.
CAM Expenses Recoverable from Tenants	$5.00 per sq. ft.
Average Lease Term	3.5 years
Vacancy	Equal to 10% of total rental revenue

Operating Expenses:

Maintenance/Repair	$1,200,000
Mgmt/admin./Leasing Expenses	$230,000
Property Taxes	$1,715,000
Insurance	$105,000
Other	–

Other Information:

Recurring CAPEX/Improve Allowance	$160,000

a. From the above data, develop a pro forma statement for a base year showing net operating income (NOI) for Summer Place.

b. If you plan to begin work on *future pro formas* for Summer Place, list at least five major factors that you would consider.

8. You have been asked to develop a pro forma statement of cash flow for Betts Distribution Center, an Internet-based order fulfillment/distribution/office/warehouse property. In addition to recoverable operating expenses, the new tenant will be billed for pass throughs including insurance and property taxes, which will then be paid by the owner. The information given to you is listed below.

Property Information:

BETTS DISTRIBUTION CENTER

Age of Improvement	8 years old
Rentable Space	200,000 sq. ft.
Single Tenant	10 year lease term, net, net

Financial Information:

Rent	$7.00 per sq. ft. (7-year term), flat
Recoverable Expenses from Tenant	$1.50 per sq. ft., fixed
Operating Expenses	$700,000
Property Taxes	$50,000
Insurance	$15,000

Other Cash Outlays:

Allowances for:

Recurring CAPEX/Improve Allowance	$60,000

a. Develop a pro forma statement for the Betts property for a base year showing net operating income (NOI).

b. If you plan to begin work on *future pro formas* for Betts, list at least five major factors that you would consider.

9. You have been asked to develop a pro forma statement of cash flow for West Office Plaza. The information given to you is listed below.

Property Information:

WEST OFFICE PLAZA

Rentable Area	300,000 sq. ft.
Age	8 years

# Stories	15
# Tenants	40

Financial Information:

Base Rent Avg.	$20 per sq. ft.
Other Income/Parking/Storage	$1.50 per sq. ft.
Expenses Recoverable from Tenants	$2.50 per sq. ft.
Current Vacancy	5%

Expenses:

Mgmt./Admin./Security/Ownership	$695,000
Property Taxes	$675,000
Insurance	$430,000
General Operations/Leasing Expense/Marketing	$667,000
Utilities	$1,159,100
Janitorial/Cleaning	$489,000
Business Taxes	$110,000

Other:

Recurring CAPEX/Improvement Allowance	$700,000

  a. Develop a pro forma statement of cash flow for a base year showing net operating income (NOI) for West Office Plaza.

  b. If you plan to begin work on *future pro formas* for West Office Plaza, list at least five major factors that you would consider.

www.mhhe.com/bf15e

10. **Spreadsheet Problem.** Refer to the effective rent example on page 276 in the book that is replicated in the Ch9 Eff.Rent tab in the Excel workbook provided on the Web site.

  a. Suppose that the CPI is expected to increase by 4 percent starting in year 2 and remain at 4 percent per year rather than the original pattern that is 2 percent in year 2, 3 percent in year 3, 4 percent in year 4, and 5 percent in year 5. What leases will be affected? What is the new effective rent on these leases?

  b. Suppose that in addition to the change in part (*a*), expenses increase by $1 per year instead of $.50. What leases will be affected? What is the new effective rent on these leases?

Chapter 10

Valuation of Income Properties: Appraisal and the Market for Capital

Introduction

Chapter 9 introduced property markets and discussed the supply and demand for space, leases, rents, and expense recoveries. It also introduced how concepts affecting users of real estate and locations interact to impact the value of income-producing property. Property value also depends on the cost and availability of capital for real estate investments. In this chapter, we will focus on various methods that can be used to estimate the market value of a property.

Valuation Fundamentals

Market value is a key consideration when financing or investing in income-producing properties. It is defined as follows:

> The most probable price which a property should bring in a competitive and open market under all conditions requisite to a fair sale, the buyer and seller each acting prudently and knowledgeably, and assuming the price is not affected by undue stimulus. Implicit in this definition is the consummation of a sale as of a specified date and the passing of title from the seller to the buyer under conditions, whereby:

> 1. The buyer and the seller are typically motivated;
> 2. Both parties are well informed or well advised, and acting in what they consider their best interests;
> 3. A reasonable time is allowed for exposure in the open market;
> 4. Payment is made in terms of cash in U.S. dollars or in terms of financial arrangements comparable thereto; and
> 5. The price represents the normal consideration for the property sold unaffected by special or creative financing or sales concessions granted by anyone associated with the sale.

A property's market value is also the basis for the *lending decision* because the property will be either the full or partial security for the loan. When making investment decisions, the investor will not normally want to pay more than the market value of the property. Similarly, the lender will not want to lend more than a proportion of the market value of the property because if the property must eventually be sold due to foreclosure of the loan, it would probably not sell for more than its market value. In the context of real estate finance, appraisal reports on properties are a part of the documentation required by lenders when considering whether to make mortgage loans. Because lenders and borrowers or investors use appraisals in decision making, they should be familiar with the generally accepted approaches to appraisal or valuation. There are many other instances when estimates of property values must be made after a property is acquired. These include valuations for insurance purposes, property tax assessments, investment performance reports for investors, and so on. These estimates may have to be made annually or even more frequently regardless of whether or not a property is sold. The purpose of this chapter is to explain the appraisal process and the three approaches ordinarily used in valuation.

Appraisal Process and Approaches to Valuation

An appraisal is an *estimate* of value. In making this estimate, appraisers use a systematic approach, referred to as the **appraisal process.** First, they ascertain the physical and legal identification of the property involved. Second, they identify the property rights to be appraised or valued. For example, the property rights being valued may involve fee simple ownership of the property or something other than fee simple such as a leased fee estate. Third, appraisers specify the purpose of the appraisal. Besides an estimate of market value for lending and investment decisions, appraisals are also made in situations involving condemnation of property, insurance losses, and property tax assessments. Fourth, appraisers specify the effective date of the estimate of value. Since market conditions change over time, the estimate must be related to a specific date. Fifth, appraisers must gather and analyze market data, and then sixth, apply appropriate techniques to derive the estimate of value. This process is the main concern of this chapter.

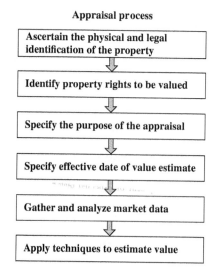

Appraisal process

| Ascertain the physical and legal identification of the property |
| Identify property rights to be valued |
| Specify the purpose of the appraisal |
| Specify effective date of value estimate |
| Gather and analyze market data |
| Apply techniques to estimate value |

In the appraisal process, a considerable amount of market data must be collected and analyzed. Market data on rents, costs, vacancies, supply and demand factors, expenses, and any other data considered to be an important influence on property values must be collected, summarized, and interpreted by the analyst when making an estimate of value. It is not the intent of this book to cover how to conduct market studies and collect data for making appraisals. In real estate finance, it is more commonly the case that lenders, borrowers, and investors will use the appraisal report to make lending and investment decisions. However, the user must understand the approach used by the appraiser in estimating value. By understanding these approaches, the user will be in a better position to decide whether the appropriate market data have been used and whether appropriate techniques have been used to estimate the value.

The role of appraisals cannot be overemphasized because appraised values are used as a basis for lending and investing. Methods and procedures used in establishing values are thoroughly reviewed and evaluated by lenders to prevent overborrowing on properties and by investors to avoid overpaying for properties. Lenders want to be assured that both the initial property value and the pattern of property value over time exceed the outstanding loan balance for any given property over the term of the loan.

In income property appraisals, at least two of three approaches are normally used: the *sales comparison approach,* the *income capitalization approach,* and/or the *cost approach.* We review the essentials of each approach here to provide insight into the process followed by appraisers in establishing the market value of income property.

Sales Comparison Approach

The **sales comparison approach** to value is based on data provided from recent sales of properties *highly comparable* to the property being appraised. These sales must be "arm's-length" transactions or sales between unrelated individuals. They should represent normal market transactions with no unusual circumstances, such as foreclosure, sales involving public entities, and so on. In short, when market value for a property is established, current transaction prices are important benchmarks to use because they indicate what investors have paid to acquire properties.

To the extent that there are differences in size, scale, location, age, and quality of construction between the project being valued and recent sales of comparable properties, adjustments must be made to compensate for such differences. Obviously, when this approach is used, the more differences that must be adjusted for, the more dissimilar are the properties being compared, and the less reliable the sales comparison approach. The *rationale for the sales comparison approach* lies in the principle that an informed investor would never pay more for a property than what other investors have recently paid for comparable properties. Selection of data on properties that are truly comparable along all important dimensions, and that require relatively minor adjustments because of differences in building or locational characteristics, is critical to the successful use of this approach.

In developing the sales comparison approach to valuation, the appraiser summarizes and uses sales transaction data on comparable properties from the market area analysis in the development of expected rents and value estimates for the property being appraised. Exhibit 10–1 illustrates an example of some of the data that could be used in the development of a sales comparison approach for a hypothetical small office building and three comparable properties.

Based on the data developed from the market area analysis shown in Exhibit 10–1, we see that the subject property being appraised is very comparable to three small office buildings that have recently sold. A careful analysis of the data reveals relatively minor deviations in gross square footage, location, front footage on major streets, construction type and quality, landscaping, and age of structures. The procedure that may be used to

EXHIBIT 10–1
Market Area Analysis and Sales Data (Sales Comparison Approach, Hypothetical Office Building)

Item	Subject Property	Comparable Properties		
		1	2	3
Sale date	—	Recent	1 year ago	2 years ago
Price	—	$355,000	$375,000	$413,300
Gross annual rent	—	$58,000	$61,000	$69,000
Gross square feet	13,300	14,500	13,750	15,390
Price per square foot*	—	$24.48	$27.27	$26.86
Rent per square foot*	—	$4.00	$4.44	$4.48
Proximity to subject†	—	2 miles	2.5 miles	3.5 miles
Frontage lineal feet	300	240	310	350
Number floors	2	2	2	2
Number elevators	1	1	1	1
Age	New	3 years	4 years	6 years
Exterior	Brick	Brick	Stucco	Brick
Construction§	Average	Average	Average	Average
Landscaping§	Average	Average	Average	Average

*Gross square footage (rounded).
†In this example, the subject property is considered to be at the best location, and locations further away are less desirable.
§Quality.

EXHIBIT 10–2
Adjustments from Comparables to Subject Property

	Comparable Properties		
	1	2	3
Sale price	$355,000	$375,000	$413,300
Square footage	14,500	13,750	15,390
Sale price per square foot	$ 24.48	$ 27.27	$ 26.86
Adjustments:			
Sale date	—	+4%	+7%
Square footage	−5%	−4%	−12%
Location	+7%	+12%	+15%
Frontage	+10%	−14%	−15%
Age of structure	+8%	+10%	+15%
Net difference	+20%	+8%	+10%
Adjusted price	$426,000	$405,000	$454,630
Adjusted price per square foot	$ 29.38	$ 29.45	$ 29.54
Estimated price per square foot for subject	= $ 29.50		
Indicated market value $29.50 × 13,300 square feet	= $392,350		

estimate value via the sales comparison approach is to attempt to adjust for the deviations between the property being appraised and the comparables. This adjustment can usually be accomplished in one of the two ways. The price per square foot paid for each comparable can be adjusted to determine the market value for the subject, or the relationship between gross rental income and sale price on the comparable can be applied to the subject with appropriate adjustment. Exhibit 10–2 shows how the price-per-square-foot adjustment could be carried out. In both cases, adjustments are based on the appraiser's judgment as to how the market value should be changed after doing a comprehensive analysis of how differences in property characteristics are being priced in the submarket.

Such adjustments on a square footage basis require adjustments for any major physical or locational deviations between the property being valued and the comparables recently sold. Adjustments on the square footage cost should be made *relative to* the property being valued; that is, the comparable data must be adjusted as though one wants to make the comparables identical to the subject property. Positive features that comparables possess relative to the subject property require negative adjustments, and negative features require positive adjustments. The appraiser makes all percentage adjustments based on the knowledge of current market values and how various favorable and unfavorable attributes of comparable properties would affect the value of the subject. When adjusting for age differentials, front footage, or differences in the percentage of leasable square footage, the appraiser must be able to estimate the value of such attributes and how the addition or deletion of those attributes affects the value of properties. *It should be stressed that the cost of these attributes should not always be added or subtracted to ascertain value. This is because buyers of properties establish what the value of each attribute of a property is and how each attribute interacts with others. Hence, the appraiser should be concerned with the effect that the addition or deletion of an attribute will have on total property value, holding all other attributes constant. In other words, the appraiser is concerned with the marginal change in value. This marginal change in value may not correspond to the cost of adding or deleting an attribute.* This is a subjective process and such adjustments should be justified with evidence based on recent experience with highly comparable properties; otherwise, serious errors can result.

In the above example, the price of each of the comparable properties was divided by the number of square feet of the building to adjust for differences in the size of the property. This adjustment was made under the assumption that the price for an office building is directly related to its size in square feet. In this case the price per square foot is considered a **unit of comparison.** Other examples of units of comparison are number of apartment units in an apartment building and number of cubic feet in a warehouse.

Income Approach

The **income approach** to property valuation is based on the principle that the value of a property is related to its ability to produce cash flow. When attempting to estimate value using this approach, the analyst must take into account the many market influences that affect cash flows as well as extracting data from the sale of competitive properties deemed comparable to the property being evaluated. In this section, three commonly used techniques are discussed. Two of the techniques, the *gross income multiplier* and *direct capitalization methods,* rely heavily on current market transactions involving the sale of comparable properties. These techniques resemble the sales comparison method discussed in the previous section in many ways. The focus of these techniques is to determine a market value that is consistent with prices being paid for comparable properties trading in the marketplace. However, rather than giving priority to adjusting for differences in value by adding and subtracting directly from the prices of comparable properties for physical and locational attributes, these two methods tend to focus first on the income-producing aspect of comparable properties relative to the prices at which they were sold. Adjustments are then made for physical and locational dissimilarities.

The third income capitalization technique discussed in this section is the *discounted present value method.* This method differs considerably from the gross income multiplier and direct capitalization techniques in that a forecast of future income production and expected investment return is used. The point of view utilized is more like that of an investor trying to value properties by using a technique that incorporates many of the same steps and information that he would use to make an investment decision. The following is a discussion of these three techniques.

Gross Income Multipliers

One technique used in conjunction with the income capitalization approach to valuation is to develop what are referred to as **gross income multipliers.** These are relationships between gross income and sale prices for all comparable properties that are applied to the subject property. This technique also requires that an estimate of the gross income be made for the subject property. The gross income multiplier (*GIM*) is defined as

$$GIM = \frac{\text{Sales price}}{\text{Gross income}}$$

or simply the ratio of sale price to gross income. Such multipliers can be developed for the properties comparable to the office building being valued in Exhibit 10–1. In this case, gross income can be considered a unit of comparison. From the data developed in Exhibit 10–3, we can see that the *GIM*s range from 5.99 to 6.15, which means that the comparable properties are sold for 5.99 to 6.15 *times* the current gross income. If the subject property is comparable, it too should sell for roughly a price that bears the same relationship to its gross income.

In arriving at a value for the subject property, the appraiser must develop an estimate of gross income based on the market data on comparables shown in Exhibit 10–3. For the comparable properties the gross income should be the annual income at the time the property is sold (i.e., what it will be during the first year for the purchaser). Similarly, gross income for the subject will be for the first year of operation after the date for which the property is being appraised.

Some appraisers use **potential gross income** (which assumes all the space is occupied) when developing *GIM*s. Others use **effective gross income,** which is based on occupied space (potential gross income less vacancies). The results should be similar if the appraiser is consistent for the comparable and subject properties. If there are significant differences in the vacancy rates among the comparable properties, then using effective gross income may be more appropriate. Of course, this may indicate that the properties are not really very comparable and may be in *different market segments.*

This method relies on gross income. Therefore, an additional assumption critical to the use of this method is that the operating expenses are about the same proportion of gross income for all properties. *In many situations, particularly when smaller, older properties are being valued, information regarding operating expenses may not be available.* If for some reason this assumption is not valid, then this technique should not be used.

Care should be taken here to ensure that significant changes in *lease agreements* are not expected to occur. For example, if a major increase in rent is expected on a comparable due to a lease expiration in the near future, this must be taken into account and adjusted for. In addition to comparability in physical attributes, location, and leases, it is also assumed that no material differences in operating expenses exist between comparables. If material differences do exist, this technique should not be relied on.

EXHIBIT 10–3
Development of *GIM*
(Comparable
Properties)

	Subject Property	Comparable Properties		
		1	2	3
Sale price	?	$355,000	$375,000	$413,300
Current gross income	$36,600	58,000	61,000	69,000
GIM	?	6.12×	6.15×	5.99×

From the range of *GIM*s shown in Exhibit 10–3, the appraiser also must select an appropriate *GIM* for the subject property. This is done by observing the range in *GIM*s for the comparable properties, as shown in Exhibit 10–3. Rather than simply averaging the *GIM*s in the table, the appraiser would normally give more or less weight to a particular comparable when choosing a rate to apply to the subject property. For example, the appraiser may believe that of the three comparable properties, the first one should be given the most weight because it was the most recent sale. Thus, the appraiser might believe that the *GIM* should be closer to that for the second and the third comparable properties. The experience and judgment of the appraiser are important parts of this process. Assuming that the appraiser chooses a *GIM* of six times as "appropriate" for the subject property, its indicated value would be $59,185 \times 6$ or $355,110.

Capitalization Rate

In cases where it is suspected that differences in operating expenses exist between comparables, the focus of the analysis should be shifted from gross income multipliers to *net operating income* (*NOI*). Additional information that may be used in this analysis and definitions of common income and expense items are summarized in Exhibit 10–4. This information centers on aspects of the net operating income-producing capability of the subject property and the three properties selected as comparables from market transactions data.

As shown in Exhibit 10–4, the price, rent, and operating expense ratios for the three comparable properties have been obtained from brokers who were involved in the sale of the comparable properties. (Data were obtained with the permission of the buyer and the seller of the comparable properties.) In each case, the **net operating income (NOI)** was obtained by subtracting operating expenses from rents reported on the comparables at the time of sale. The reader should note the definitions used to identify all items of rent, income, and expenses in Exhibit 10–5. After determining the *NOI,* it is then divided by the transaction price to obtain what is defined in the industry as the **capitalization rate** (sometimes referred to as the "cap rate" and designated as *R*) for the three comparable properties. This method is referred to as the **direct capitalization method**. Note that the cap rates or *R*s, for the three comparables range from .094 to .099.

Given that the *NOI* for the subject property is $366,000, we would like to determine its value using the following relationship:

$$\text{Value} = NOI \div R$$

By substituting $366,000 for *NOI* for our subject property and dividing by an *estimate* of *R* which we obtain from the comparable sales data, we hope to estimate the value for the office building that we are analyzing. The question is, which *R* should be selected from which comparable sale? Should we select an average of three *R*s, or put more weight on some of the comparables than others?

The best procedure to follow at this point is to choose an *R* based on a careful reexamination of the data in Exhibit 10–4 to determine the comparables that are *most* like the subject property. To complete this example, we see that cap rates for the three comparables range between .094 and .099. Assuming that comparable (2) is most similar and a slightly higher cap rate of .095 is chosen, the value for our subject may be estimated as follows:

$$\text{Subject property value} = \$366,000 \div .095$$

$$= \$3,852,631 \text{ or } \$3,853,000 \text{ (rounded)}$$

EXHIBIT 10–4
Income, Expense, and
Price Relationships

	Subject Property	Comparable Properties		
		1	2	3
Price	?	$3,078,000	$3,764,000	$4,112,000
Effective gross income	$600,000	503,000	610,000	690,000
% operating expense	39%	40%	42%	41%
NOI	366,000	301,600	353,800	407,100
NOI ÷ Price = (R)	?	.098	.094	.099

Definitions of Common Income and Expense Items

    Rental Income at Full Occupancy. An estimate of revenues expected to be received from existing tenants based on lease terms plus any vacant space priced at market rents.

+ **Other Income.** Examples may include revenues from parking, laundry and cable TV fees, application fees, net deposits, and so on.

= **Potential Gross Income (PGI).** Total cash flow possible from all sources and activities relative to the property ownership.

− **Vacancy and Collection Losses.** Estimated rent losses from unoccupied space or due to unpaid rents and losses from other sources.

= **Effective Gross Income (EGI).** All sources of potential income less vacancy and collection losses.

− **Real Estate Taxes.** Based on assessed value by the county and/or other tax assessing entities.

− **Insurance.** Property owners usually provide for insurance on the premises (building, parking lots, etc.) for property damage and for personal injury.

− **Utilities.** Cost of electric, water, and so on, that may be paid in full or part by property owners, depending on lease terms.

− **Repair and Maintenance.** Estimates of cash outlays for recurring items expected to be replaced within three years or less of economic use.

− **Salaries.** On-site employees who maintain, "make ready," and repair the property.

− **Administrative and General.** Allocations of costs for personnel and expenses from an off-site activity. That is, a real estate company with many properties under its ownership may allocate a percentage of certain costs (e.g., human resources, payroll, accounting) to the operating expenses of its individual properties.

− **Management and Leasing Expenses.** Supervisory on-site management employees who lease, collect rents, pay expenses, and so on. These may be the employees of the property owner or include payment by the property owner for services outsourced to other companies who specialize in property management and leasing and earn fees and commissions.

− **CAPEX/Improve Allowance.** Estimated cost of tenant improvements and expected outlays for replacement of capital items that are recurring but have a useful life less than that of the entire building improvement.

= **(NOI) Net Operating Income.** An annual estimate of the net operating income resulting from the compilation of all of the above items.

Further Interpretation—Application and Limitations

Essentially, this method uses income and expense data from current sales comparisons as market *benchmarks*. This only assures that if a price of $3,853,000 is paid for the subject property, this price appears to be reasonable, or "in line" with prices currently being paid for comparable properties. In this case, buyers of properties should not expect to pay less and sellers should not expect to receive more than this estimated market price. It should be stressed, however, that this approach to valuation *does not assure that this property will be a good investment if purchased.* It only assures the buyer that it is a competitive market price and that if the method is applied correctly, the buyer is probably not overpaying

When developing pro forma statements of cash flow, certain cash outlays must be reflected in the statements that are not coincident with the regular operating cycle* of a property. Even though these outlays are not *operating* expenses, they should be included in cash flow projections.

LEASING COMMISSIONS

As tenants vacate space and leases expire, property owners may engage brokers for marketing, providing property tours, and identifying potential tenants. Estimates of commissions for these brokerage services may vary from year to year, depending on tenant turnover. Estimates of such turnover and related expenses, which may be substantial, should be made in projections each year.

*An operating cycle for income-producing real estate is usually one year. During this time, rents are usually received, and operating expenses are paid monthly. Although certain expenses, such as insurance, property taxes, payments on maintenance contracts, and so on may not be paid monthly, all are usually paid within one year.

---

or underpaying for the property relative to what other investors have paid for similar properties. The question of *whether or not it is a good investment will depend on the future growth in rents, income, and property values.* These aspects are not specifically considered as a part of this or the gross income multiplier technique and, therefore, no conclusions can be drawn as to the *investment potential* of this property. That must be determined by estimating the future course of the economic base in the market in which the property is located—the leases, rents, expenses, major repairs, and so on. We will consider these factors when we address *investment analysis* in the next chapter.

EXHIBIT 10–5
Pro Forma Statement of Cash Flow— Subject Property

Rental Income		$615,000
Add: Other Income	$ 20,000	
Potential Gross Income		$635,000
Less: Vacancy and Collection Loss (5%)	$ 35,000	
Effective Gross Income		$600,000
Less: Operating Expenses		
Real Estate Taxes		40,000
Insurance	15,000	
Utilities	30,000	
Repair/Maintenance	20,000	
Administrative	20,000	
Management/Leasing Commissions*	30,000	
Salaries	20,000	
Total Operating Expenses	175,000	
CAPEX/Improve Allowance*	59,000	234,000
Net Operating Income (*NOI*)		$366,000

*The reader should be aware that, in practice, there is considerable non uniformity in how certain expenses are treated in the determination of *NOI*. This is particularly true for (1) *leasing commissions,* (2) allowances for *tenant improvements,* and (3) *major capital outlays* for items that may have a shorter useful life (e.g., 3–5 years) than the economic life of the property improvement (e.g., 50 years or more). These items can be material in amount and may vary considerably from year to year. Inconsistencies will depend whether or not these items are included in the determination of *NOI*. The choice of treatment may have a material effect on the estimate of property value because the level of *NOI* will be affected. Therefore, when valuing a property, the reader should always carefully review how these items were treated in determining *NOI* for the subject property and for all comparables used in the analysis. In our example, when determining *NOI*, we included these items. Leasing commissions, which are estimated based on lease maturities and turnover rates, were included as part of the $30,000 shown as management and leasing expenses. Also, we included outlays for tenant improvements (also based on lease expiration rates and tenant turnover) and expected capital expenditures in the $59,000 amount shown for CAPEX/Improve Allowance. For a detailed discussion, see Concept Box 10.1.

TENANT IMPROVEMENTS

Property owners usually negotiate an *allowance* with tenants toward the cost of making space ready for occupancy. Typically tenants must construct cubicles, wall partitions, carpet, and so on, before occupancy. Generally, the property owner will negotiate a specific dollar allowance toward the cost of these improvements with the tenant. As is the case for leasing commissions, tenant improvement costs may be material and will vary from year to year depending on lease turnover-renewal rates. In some cases, even when existing tenants renew leases, an amount may be negotiated for some improvements to "update" the leased space.

CAPITAL EXPENDITURE ALLOWANCE

Includes expenditures for *recurring* replacement of items such as hot water heaters, countertops, electric lighting fixtures, and so on. Major expenditures of *non-recurring* nature would include replacement of roofs, HVAC, parking lots, and so on.

Capitalization Rates—A Note of Caution

The above discussion of direct capitalization that concerns the relationship between value and *NOI* and cap rates derived from comparable sales is an important one. However, it must be stressed that when direct capitalization is used, properties chosen as comparables must be *truly comparable* to, and/or competitive with, the property under consideration for investment. The term *comparability* means very similar in quality, construction, size, age, functionality, location, and operating efficiency. It also means the properties are comparable in terms of lease maturities, lease options, rent escalators, and any other major lease attributes such as easements, title restrictions, and so on. While these attributes may be similar for many property investments, they may not be for many other investments. An example of the importance of the latter might be two office properties that have sold at the same time and that are locationally and functionally comparable. However, one office property may be leased by *four* tenants on a long-term lease basis with many lease options, and the other property may be leased to 30 small tenants with shorter-term average lease maturities and with many other different lease characteristics. It may be possible that the *NOI*s for the two properties were similar when they were sold. However, because of the differences in the *leases* and *attendant risk,* the prices for both, and therefore the cap rates, should be different. This also means that if an investor chooses to develop a cap rate (R) based on these two sales to use in pricing a property being considered for purchase, many adjustments will have to be made to reflect differences in the leases, in addition to any additional differences in physical, locational, and other attributes among the comparables. Making such adjustments is not always easy. As a result, assigning the "correct" cap rate is difficult and an incorrect one could result in a serious pricing error.

Another area of caution has to do with the treatment of nonrecurring outlays for any necessary replacement of building components that are of a nonoperating nature. Other items such as tenant improvements and commissions should also be accounted for. When making estimates of value based on the *NOI* obtained from the sales of comparable properties, the reader *must* determine whether or not, or how, outlays for tenant improvements and capital requirements were included in the data. *Industry practice varies on this issue.* Many appraisers estimate an *annual average outlay* for such items and adjust *NOI* downward by deducting such outlays much like an annual expense. In cases where properties are *highly comparable,* this practice may not materially affect the estimate of value as long as its treatment is consistent for all properties being used in the analysis. However, when properties used in this approach are somewhat dissimilar in that material differences in outlays of a nonrecurring nature are expected, then the reader must make adjustments for such items. If such adjustments are believed to be material and difficult to make, then this generally implies that the properties in question may really not be that comparable. Therefore, the results of this approach should be interpreted with caution.

When is it appropriate to use direct capitalization? Cap rates are important market benchmarks that are widely used in the real estate industry. However, it should be stressed again that estimating a property's value on a forecast of *NOI* for only one year and applying a cap rate generated from data collected on the sales of comparable properties can prove to be problematic.

Discounted Present Value Techniques

The **discounted present value method,** the final income capitalization technique, is based on the principle that investors will pay no more for a property than the present value of all *future NOIs*. Finding the value for a property that is expected to produce income over a very long economic life requires many assumptions and in-depth knowledge of discounted cash flow techniques and *approximations* that make finding present values over long economic lives manageable. It is also necessary to understand the assumptions underlying present value mechanics when such approximations are used. For these reasons, most professionals who value properties prefer to use direct capitalization or one of the sales comparison approaches when possible. However, this method is used by professionals when necessary. To illustrate this method, we use an apartment example. Our forecast of *NOI* is made for a time period during which we can foresee any material change in market supply or demand conditions that could affect rents. In short, we want to forecast and analyze cash flow over a period for which we have knowledge regarding existing tenants, lease terms, and supply and demand market conditions.

Forecasting NOI

Based on our knowledge of market supply and demand, lease terms, as well as income and expenses, we have made a forecast for the Hypothetical Hills apartment complex. We believe that a forecast for a 10-year period is appropriate and this forecast is shown in Exhibit 10–6. We believe that because Hypothetical Hills is relatively new and unique in terms of both location and design, there are very few comparable properties that have been sold recently with which to compare it. Therefore, the sales comparison method described in the preceding section may not produce a reliable estimate of value. In our forecast, we believe that vacancy rates for Hypothetical Hills will remain below average relative to other apartment properties. Furthermore, the sales comparison method would probably not be useful because our estimate that cash flows are expected to grow at an *above-average* rate ranging from 5 percent to 3 percent for the first eight years is not characteristic of growth expected for other apartment investment opportunities. *NOI* will then stabilize at

EXHIBIT 10–6 **Ten-Year *NOI* Forecast, Hypothetical Hills Apartments**					

Year	NOI	% Growth	Year	NOI	% Growth
1	$338,800	—	6	$416,127	3
2	355,740	5	7	428,611	3
3	373,527	5	8	441,469	3
4	388,468	4	9	450,299	2
5	404,007	4	10	459,304	2

a long-term rate of about 2 percent in year 9 and thereafter. We also believe that this 2 percent growth rate will eventually become consistent with long-run supply and demand conditions and those for competing apartment projects. Based on our forecast of cash flows and knowledge of market conditions, we conclude that other apartment properties are not as comparable as would be desired in order to use the sales comparison method.

Expected Future Capital Improvements

In the case of Hypothetical Hills, we do not expect any nonrecurring capital outlays during the forecast period.

Selection of a Discount Rate (r)

After estimating *NOI* over an expected period of analysis in the preceding section, step 3 in the present value approach to income capitalization requires the selection of a **discount rate** or **required internal rate of return** (*r*) over the investment period. Conceptually, this discount rate should be thought of as a required return for a real estate investment based on its risk when compared with returns earned on competing investments and other capital market benchmarks. For example, if the period of analysis is 10 years for our prospective real estate investment, the discount rate selected should be greater than (1) the interest rate on a 10-year U.S. Treasury bond, (2) the interest rate on a 10-year commercial mortgage loan, and (3) the weighted average of corporate bond rates, or the borrowing rates for tenants in the property being evaluated.[1] A risk premium for real estate ownership and its attendant risks related to operation and disposition should also be included to arrive at a reasonable discount rate. Exhibit 10–7 depicts the above discussion conceptually in terms of expected returns relative to the risk that may be expected on different asset classes. In the case of income-producing real estate, the diagram indicates that expected returns should be

EXHIBIT 10–7
Risk and Return Trade-Off by Type of Investment

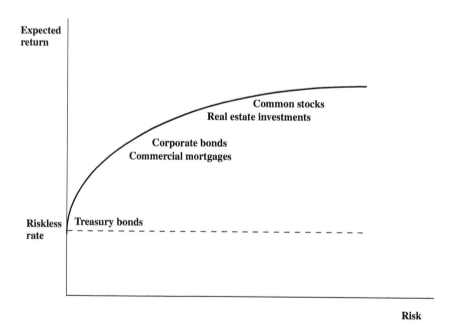

[1] This is because when properties are leased, tenants are, in a sense, substituting lease obligations created by renting for loans that would be used if tenants chose to build and finance properties using bank debt. Therefore, in addition to credit risks, because real estate investors take the added risk associated with operating real estate, they should earn a return greater than the interest rate that tenants would otherwise pay on mortgage debt. If real estate investors could not earn more than this rate, real estate investors would be better off being lenders and making loans to tenants.

above expected returns for Treasury bonds, commercial mortgages, and corporate bonds, but below expected returns on riskier common stocks. It should be stressed, however, that this conceptualization depicts the average returns for all income-producing real estate as a sector. Risk on individual properties may be higher or lower than risk relative to the "average" property; therefore, expected returns on individual properties may be greater or less than this average. In our example, after considering the risk on other competing properties, we have selected 12 percent as the internal rate of return that we should expect to earn if we invest in Hypothetical Hills.

Thus far, we have completed three of the *four* steps that we need in order to estimate present value, that is:

1. A forecast of *NOI*.
2. Selection of a relevant period of analysis or the **holding period** for the investment.
3. Selection of a discount rate or required rate of return (*r*) for the period selected in (2).

In the fourth step, we must deal with the present value of expected *NOI beyond the 10-year period* of analysis. We will represent these cash flows with a **reversion value** (*REV*) or *resale price*. Returning to our estimate of cash flow in Exhibit 10–6, note that we have estimated that *NOI* will *stabilize* from year 9 and beyond at a rate of 2 percent per year. In our example, we assume that the property value or *REV* will be established at the end of year 9. As you will see, this will require a cash flow forecast beginning in year 10 and a long-term growth assumption from that point until the end of the economic life of the property. In making this estimate for *REV,* we make the following major assumptions:

1. The demand for apartments in this market region will tend to grow in a stable, long-term relationship with growth in the U.S. economy.
2. There will be no *major* or *structural* changes in the determinants of supply and/or demand for apartments from year 10 and thereafter.

If these assumptions cannot be made, a year-by-year forecast of *NOI* beyond year 10 must be made until a period of stability is expected to be reached.

Using Approximations to Estimate Reversion Values

At this point, the reader is probably wondering how the value for *REV* will be estimated at the end of year 9, particularly for an asset such as Hypothetical Hills, a new apartment community that is expected to have a long economic life, perhaps 50 years or more. The following are three techniques that are used frequently to do this.

(A) Estimating REV by Developing a Terminal Cap Rate Based on Required Rate of Return (r) and Expected Growth in Long-Term Cash Flows (g) Clearly, forecasting cash flows each year from year 10 through 50 would not be practical. One approach that could be used is to *approximate* the present value of cash flow for the remaining economic life of the asset by using a **terminal cap rate** (R_T). This approach may be used only under very restrictive assumptions regarding the pattern of cash flow that is expected from the end of the holding period through the end of the useful life of the asset and its relationship to the *required rate of return* (*r*) that investors expect to earn over the entire period of investment. These are:

Case 1: $R_T = (r - g)$ when average *long-run growth* (*g*) in *NOI* is expected to be *positive.*

Case 2: $R_T = (r)$ when *long-run growth* (*g*) in *NOI* is expected to be level or zero.

Case 3: $R_T = (r + g)$ when average *long-run growth* (*g*) in *NOI* is expected to be negative or to decline.

Depending on the long-run scenario chosen for the remaining economic life *after* the holding period, an estimate for *g* must be selected in order to estimate *REV*. In our case, we have estimated that from *year 10 until the end of the economic life, NOI* will tend toward an average growth rate (*g*) of 2 percent per year. Based on this set of assumptions, the reversion value (*REV*) for Hypothetical Hills at the end of year 9, based on a 10-year projection period, can be approximated as follows:

$$REV_9 = (NOI_{10}) \div (r - g)$$

This means that the estimated resale price or reversion value REV_9 is equal to *NOI* in year 10, which is shown in Exhibit 10–6 as $459,304 divided by *r*, which is the 12 percent discount rate or required rate of return that we have selected, minus the stabilized or long-term expected growth rate in cash flow, designated as *g*, or 2 percent. The relationship (*r* − *g*) in period 9 is also referred to by industry practitioners as a *terminal* capitalization rate, designated as R_T.

$$REV_9 = NOI_{10} \div (R_T) \qquad \text{Note: } R_T = (r - g)$$

$$REV_9 = \$459,304 \div (.12 - .02) \qquad R_T = .10$$

$$REV_9 = \$459,304 \div .10, \text{ or}$$

$$REV_9 = \$4,593,040$$

Now that we have estimated the reversion value in year 9, or REV_9, which is the present value of expected cash flows from year 10 through the end of the expected economic life of the property, we can now estimate the present value for the property over its *entire economic life* beginning in year 1, as shown in Exhibit 10–8.

To summarize, the present value (*PV*) of estimated cash flows for this property can be illustrated as:

$$PV = PVNOI + PVREV$$

$$PV = 2,073,475 + 1,656,296$$

$$PV = \$3,729,771$$

This exercise completes our analysis, which, based on our assumptions, yields a present value, or property value *today*, of $3,729,771 for Hypothetical Hills. If an investor were to

EXHIBIT 10–8
Final Calculation of Present Value for Hypothetical Hills Apartments

End of Year	(a) NOI	(b) PVNOI @ 12%	(c) REV	(d) PVREV @ 12%	(e) (b + d) Total PV
1	$338,800	$302,500			$ 302,500
2	355,740	283,594			283,594
3	373,527	265,869			265,869
4	388,468	246,878			246,878
5	404,007	229,244			229,244
6	416,127	210,823			210,823
7	428,611	193,882			193,882
8	441,469	178,302			178,302
9	450,299	162,382	$4,593,040*	$1,656,296	1,818,676**

Note: *PV* of *NOI* Σ 2,073,475 + *PV* of *REV* $1,656,296   = $ 3,729,771

* Calculated as $450,299 $\times$ 1.02 = $459,304, and $459,304 $\div$ .10 = $4,593,040.
** In year 9, *NOI* of $450,299 and *REV* of $4,593,040 when discounted at 12% produce $1,818,676.

pay this price for the property and own it for nine years and then sell it for $4,593,040, she would earn an *IRR* of 12 percent on the initial investment of $3,729,771. We should again point out that using the *terminal cap rate* of R_T, or .10, produces an REV_9 of $4,593,040. This result is heavily dependent on the *NOI* continuing to grow at 2 percent per year from years 10 through 50 discounted at 12 percent.

(B) Estimating REV with a Terminal Cap Rate from Sales of Older "Comparable" Properties This second approach is based on the concept that over time, as properties age and depreciate, the production of income declines; therefore, the expected growth in *NOI* for an older property should be less than that of a new property. This also means that, *holding all else constant*, when compared to newly developed properties, a property that is 10 years old should sell for a lower price relative to its *NOI* (higher cap rate) than a new one (lower cap rate). *An analyst may be able to verify today that this is the case by comparing cap rates from the sale of older properties with cap rates on newer properties.* Holding all else constant, the current difference between cap rates on older properties and newer properties should reflect differences in the amount of economic depreciation, and therefore lower rents and income, that will occur in the future.

Referring again to our Hypothetical Hills example, recall that when we made our estimates of cash flows in Exhibit 10–6, we recognized that because of its somewhat unique attributes, the expected growth for Hypothetical Hills would be significantly higher than that of other properties for the first eight years. After that period, *NOI* would be expected to take on a long-run growth rate of about 2 percent. In other words, when making these estimates of *NOI*, we recognize that Hypothetical Hills will not be able to sustain above-normal growth relative to its competition forever. This is because (1) more competing properties will be developed, thereby increasing supply and reducing the ability of Hypothetical Hills to earn rent premiums and (2) Hypothetical Hills will be older and its functions and style are likely to become obsolescent. As a result, its uniqueness relative to the competition will diminish. Recognizing this likelihood, the analyst may choose to estimate the terminal cap rate for Hypothetical Hills directly by adjusting the going-in cap rate upward based on sales data for properties that are *now 10 years old, that are likely to be representative of how Hypothetical Hills will compete in the apartment market 10 years from now.* Below, we show data from the sale of three properties that are very comparable to Hypothetical Hills in every way except that these properties are *10 years older.* From these sales data, we can calculate cap rates from the sale price and *NOI* for these properties and consider them as a possible input for estimating the terminal cap rate for Hypothetical Hills.

	Sales of Otherwise Comparable Properties 10 Years Older than Hypothetical Hills		
	Comparable 1	Comparable 2	Comparable 3
Current *NOI*	$400,000	$425,000	$450,000
Current Sale Price	$4,000,000	$4,100,000	$4,300,000
Current Cap Rate (*R*)	0.100	0.104	0.105

Based on this information, sales indicate current cap rates ranging from .10 to .105. If the analyst, after reviewing all available data on sales of these older properties, *chooses* a "terminal" cap rate of .1025 as an indicative terminal cap rate for Hypothetical Hills, then the terminal cap rate to be used in estimating the reversion value (*REV*) would be:

$$NOI_{10} \div \text{Terminal cap rate} = REV$$
$$\$459,304 \div .1025 = \$4,481,014$$

Using a cap rate based on "comparable sales" of older properties for estimating *REV* in year 10 for Hypothetical Hills produces a *reversion value* of $4,481,014. When we find the discounted present value for *REV* in our analysis, we obtain $1,615,899. We can then calculate the *present value* of all cash flows as:

$$PV_0 = PVNOI + PVREV_n$$
$$PV_0 = \$2,073,475 + \$4,481,014 \left(\frac{1}{1 + .12}\right)^9$$
$$PV_0 = \$2,073,475 + \$1,615,899$$
$$PV_0 = \$3,689,374$$

Using this approach to estimating the terminal value for Hypothetical Hills, we estimate the present value for the property today to be $3,689,374.

Obviously, the major assumption being made is that conditions currently affecting the pricing of older properties relative to Hypothetical Hills today generally will be the same when Hypothetical Hills is sold nine years from now. If this is the case, then the terminal cap rate for Hypothetical Hills should be the same as current cap rates for older, otherwise comparable properties being sold in the marketplace at the present time. While making such an assumption is very problematic, one general principle follows from this example. This principle is that, holding all else constant, as a property loses its capacity to produce income as it ages, the "terminal" cap rate used to value a specific property should generally be *greater* than its **"going-in" cap rate**. (The going-in cap rate can be defined as the ratio of the first-year *NOI* to the current value.) In the above example, the "going-in" cap rate is $338,800/$3,689,374 or 9.18 percent. This is lower than the 10.25 percent terminal cap rate. To assume that significantly lower or higher terminal cap rates will exist for properties 10 years from now generally implies that (1) a general, exogenous economic influence or event (inflation, change in interest rates, risk premiums, etc.) will occur, *thereby affecting all property values* or (2) a more specific event will affect the value of the subject property relative to other properties (e.g., a major loss of employment in the submarket in which the subject property is located). In such cases, the analyst would have to justify and incorporate these changes in the analysis. Clearly, these assumptions should be considered carefully by an investor relying on this approach to value.

While the above discussion may be helpful to you in understanding terminal cap rates, this approach will only hold when other major influences affecting the value of properties, such as investor expectations regarding interest rates, economic growth, and so on, are not expected to change. If, at the time a property is being valued, investors expect interest rates, economic growth, rents, risk, and so on, to change for all properties, then these changes also must be included in the analysis. Therefore, it may be possible that, when combined with such economic changes, terminal cap rates may be *greater or less than* those indicated by older properties that have recently sold. We will address the combined effects of such influences later in this chapter.

(C) Estimating the Resale Price Based on an Expected Change in Property Values

An alternative that is sometimes used in *lieu of using a terminal cap rate (R_T)* to estimate the resale price of a property is to assume that *property values* will change at a specified compound rate each year. If, for example, we estimate that the long-run value of a property and its *net operating income* will increase by 2 percent per year, we can estimate the value of the property based on this assumption using the information below. Recall from Exhibits 10–6 and 10–8 that, based on our desired return of 12 percent, the present value of *NOI* over nine years for our property is expected to be $2,073,475. Using a more direct approach to determining *REV*, we use this information combined with an algebraic manipulation to determine the present value (*PV*) of the property as follows:

$$PV_0 = PVNOI + PVREV_n$$
$$PV_0 = \$2,073,475 + REV_n$$

Using this approach for value, we must estimate PV_0 and REV_n simultaneously. This must be done because both values, that is, the *current property value PV_0 and the future property value (REV_n), are unknown.* However, based on this approach, we are assuming that whatever the property value is at the present time, it will appreciate at an annual rate of (g) during the next nine years. Therefore, $REV_n = PV_0(1 + g)^n$. *In other words, we are saying that, instead of using a terminal cap rate, REV at the end of year 9 will simply be whatever the value of the property is today (PV_0) compounded at an expected appreciation rate of (g).* Previously, we have assumed that the long-run growth rate (g) will be 2 percent. Using 2 percent as the appreciation rate, we have:

$$REV_n = PV_0(1 + g)^n$$

then

$$REV_n = PV_0(1 + .02)^9$$

and

$$REV_n = PV_0(1.195093)$$

This simply states that REV in period (n) will be whatever the present value of the property is today, PV_0, compounded at a long-term growth rate of 2 percent annually for the next nine years. However, because we do not know PV today, we also do not know REV in year 9. However, if we assume that PV will appreciate at 2 percent per year, then the property will be 1.195093 greater in value than it is today. Using 12 percent as the discount rate of return and some simple algebra, we now can solve for PV, REV, and $PVREV$ as follows:

$$PV_0 = PVNOI + PVREV_n$$
$$PV_0 = \$2,073,475 + PV_0(1 + g)^n \left(\frac{1}{1 + .12}\right)^n$$

$$PV_0 = \$2,073,475 + PV_0(1.02)^9 \left(\frac{1}{1 + .12}\right)^9$$

$$PV_0 = \$2,073,475 + PV(1.195093) \left(\frac{1}{1.12}\right)^9$$

$$PV_0 = \$2,073,475 + PV(1.195093)(.360610)$$
$$PV_0 = \$2,073,475 + PV(.430962)$$
$$.569038 \, PV_0 = \$2,073,475$$
$$PV_0 = \$3,643,825$$

This calculation provides a present value, or estimated property value, of $3,643,825. Also, since we assume that REV will be equal to the present value, or today's value, compounded at 2 percent per year for nine years, then REV in year 9 must be today's value compounded at 2 percent for nine years, or $3,643,825(1.02)^9 = \$4,354,708$. We can now "prove" our approach as follows:

$$PV_0 = PVNOI + PVREV_n$$
$$PV = \$2,073,475 + \$4,354,708 \; \frac{1}{(1 + .12)^9}$$
$$PV = \$3,643,826$$

In summary, if we believe that (1) we will receive *NOI* from Hypothetical Hills as shown in Exhibit 10–8 each year in years 1–9, (2) the sale price (*REV*) at the end of year 9 will be equal to whatever the value of the property is today compounded at an appreciation rate of 2 percent, and (3) the desired rate of return is 12 percent, then the present value or the value of the property today will be $3,643,826.

Reconciliation of Estimates of REV and Present Value

We have provided three approaches to estimating *REV* for Hypothetical Hills, summarized as follows:

Method Used to Estimate *REV*	Estimated *REV* at the End of Year 9	Present Value of *REV* Today
A. Use terminal cap rate based on an assumed required return (*n*) and long term (*g*)	$4,593,040	$3,729,771
B. Use terminal cap rate based on cap rates from sale of older "comparables"	$4,481,014	$3,689,374
C. Use expected appreciation in property value	$4,354,708	$3,643,826

In summary, the three approaches that we have developed to estimate *REV* and resultant *PV* are compared above. Obviously, the reader should be aware that many assumptions have been made in the analysis. Nonetheless, when making estimates of property values using the discounted present value approach, these approaches provide both conceptual frameworks and techniques that may be useful. As we have shown, various estimates should be tried to ascertain whether or not convergence in the estimates of property value occurs. If not, the analyst should re-examine the assumptions and review the methods applied for logical consistency.

Land Values: Highest and Best Use Analysis

In this section, we raise the question, "What determines land values?" What causes land prices to move up and down? There is a framework underlying the process that should help us to better understand land markets and their relationship to supply, demand, vacancies, and rents. To illustrate, we consider an example of a new office building on a site that is expected to produce *NOI* of $500,000 for the coming operating year. The improvements are expected to last for 75 years and *NOI* is expected to *grow* each year by 3 percent and investors expect an *IRR* of 13 percent. We would value the property as:

$$PV = \frac{NOI_1}{r-g} \text{ or } \frac{NOI_1}{R}$$

$$PV = \frac{\$500,000}{.13 - .03} \text{ or } \frac{\$500,000}{.10}$$

$$PV = \$5,000,000$$

In our example, an office building on the site would produce $500,000 in year 1 and grow at 3 percent (*g*) per year thereafter. Investors in similar office buildings are expecting 13 percent (*r*) on their total investment and/or comparable office buildings are trading based on cap rates (*R*) of 10 percent, thereby producing a present value of $5,000,000. Now *assuming that a new building would cost $4,000,000 to construct,* the implied, or residual, land value would be $5,000,000 − $4,000,000, or $1,000,000. The idea here is that the **residual land value** is the difference between the total property value, which is driven by rents and cash flows, and the cost of constructing an improvement on a given site.

Volatility in Land Prices

It may be useful to introduce at this point the causes of land price volatility. Many readers can probably relate to times when land prices in certain areas increase suddenly, and then subside and perhaps increase again. One observation may be that it is simply investor speculation causing such price fluctuations. While this may be the case from time to time, it is more likely that a fundamental change in a location has occurred, or is expected to occur, thereby changing one of the variables in our present value equation. To illustrate, we return to our office property example discussed earlier and two alternative scenarios for expected *NOI*.

Recall that expected *NOI* for our office property was $500,000 and the land value was $1,000,000. Now assume that because of unanticipated demand, our initial estimate of rents and, hence, *NOI* increases by 10 percent to $550,000. Holding all else constant, the total property value would rise to $5,500,000. However, building construction costs would be unaffected in the short run and remain at $4,000,000, thereby producing a land value of $1,500,000. The latter value represents a 50 percent increase in land value given only a 10 percent increase in the expected *NOI*. Conversely, if *NOI* was initially overestimated and declined to $450,000, then the value would fall to $4,500,000 and cause land value to drop by 50 percent. Similarly, if in addition to the difference in initial *NOI*, other changes in our present value equation were to occur (such as higher or lower growth rates, *g*), the resultant effect on land value could be more pronounced. These changes in expected *NOI* and/or expected values for *r* and/or *g* are the basic causes of volatility in land prices.

"Highest and Best Use" Analysis—Vacant Site

One additional use of the land residual method of valuation is to establish the type of property improvement that should be developed on the land. In our example, we used an office project; however, would the land be better used for a retail, warehouse, or apartment project? The answer lies in determining what use will provide the *highest total land value*. This analysis is also called the **highest and best use** of the land. For example, in Exhibit 10–9, we provide estimates of *NOI* for each property type that *could* be constructed on the Albert tract. We assume that a market study has been conducted, that rents and expenses have been estimated, and that investors must have a rate of return consistent with the risk associated with the possible uses shown in Exhibit 10–9. Construction costs include labor, materials, architect and engineering fees, and any other costs to develop the building, including a profit to the developer.

The results in Exhibit 10–9 indicate that an apartment project would be the highest and the best use of the Albert tract. Such a development would be expected to produce a total property value of $4,500,000 and an implied land value of $1,500,000. Note that although retail produces a higher total property value ($7,500,000), its construction cost is higher. To develop a retail project and earn the required return, then, a developer

EXHIBIT 10–9   **Highest and Best Use Analysis—Albert Tract**      **www.mhhe.com/bf15e**

Use	(a) Year 1 *NOI*	(b) (*r* − *g*)	(c) *R*	(a ÷ c = d) Implied Property Value (*PV*)	(e) Construction Cost of Bldg.	(d) − (e) Implied Land Value (Residual)
Office	$500,000	.13 − .03	.10	$5,000,000	$4,000,000	$1,000,000
Retail	600,000	.13 − .05	.08	7,500,000	6,750,000	750,000
Apartment	405,000	.12 − .03	.09	4,500,000	3,000,000	1,500,000
Warehouse	400,000	.10 − .02	.08	5,000,000	4,000,000	1,000,000

would pay no more than $750,000 for the land. In summary, it is the *expected use* of the land and its future income that determine its value. As developers and investors envision what will bring the highest property value, competition for sites and prices paid based on expected site developments will ultimately determine land values. Land value is determined by its highest and best use, which is the use that results in the highest residual land value.

"Highest and Best Use" Analysis—Improved Property

In the last section, we determined that apartments seemed to be the highest and best use of a *vacant* site. In our example, the apartment scenario produced a residual land value of $1,500,000. This would be the maximum price that a developer would pay for the land if it were vacant. But what if the site was not vacant and there were already improvements on the site? For example, assume that there is an old warehouse on the site that is currently producing *NOI* of $192,000 per year. Because it is older, the *NOI* is expected to increase by only 1 percent per year, and investors currently require a 13 percent rate of return. Based on this information, the value of the old warehouse (land and building) would be $192,000/ (.13 − .01) = $1,600,000.

Should the old warehouse be torn down and apartments built? In this case, the answer is that the warehouse should *not* be torn down. An investor would be willing to pay $1,600,000 for the old warehouse, whereas a developer of apartments could only afford to pay $1,500,000 for the land. Thus, the apartment developer would be outbid. The existing building is currently adding $100,000 to the land value that would be lost if the building were to be demolished and the site left vacant.

However, now suppose that, instead of producing *NOI* of $192,000 per year, the warehouse property only produces *NOI* of $168,000. We would now have a value for the warehouse (land and building) of $168,000/(.13 − .01) = $1,400,000. This value is less than the value of the land if it was vacant and available to be developed. The apartment developer can afford to pay more for the land to develop apartments than an investor could pay for the existing warehouse. One additional consideration is the demolition costs. Since the land is not actually vacant, the developer would have to incur some costs to demolish the existing warehouse. But as long as these costs are less than $100,000, the warehouse should still be demolished. For example, suppose that the demolition costs were $50,000. The developer of apartments could pay $1,500,000 − $50,000, or $1,450,000 for the site. This is still more than the $1,400,000 that could be paid to keep the warehouse.

It should be clear that highest and best use analysis is a very important concept because it is the basis for determining the value of the land and how it will be optimally used. It also provides guidance as to whether existing improvements on the land should be kept or demolished.

Mortgage-Equity Capitalization

In our recent discussion, value was found by discounting the *NOI* and resale proceeds for the property. *The discount rate chosen was a "free and clear" discount rate; that is, it did not consider whether the property was to be financed, for example, or how much debt versus equity was used.* In effect, we discounted the entire income available from the property as though the investor were paying cash for the entire purchase price. We did not consider the possibility of financing and how that income may be split among holders of debt (mortgage lenders) and equity investors. When financing is considered, the discount rate used to value a property subject to debt must be consistent with this assumption; that is, the discount rate must reflect rates of return expected on equity invested. As we will see in Chapter 13, it must reflect the *risk* associated with financial leverage. We now discuss how the value of a property can be estimated by explicitly taking into consideration the requirements of the mortgage lender and equity investor—hence the term **mortgage-equity capitalization.**

This method for estimating value is based on the concept that total property value (*PV*) must be equal to the present value of expected mortgage financing (*M*) and the present value of equity investment (*E*) made by investors. That is,

$$PV = M + E$$

To illustrate, suppose that the *NOI* for a small income property is expected to be $50,000 for the first year. Financing will be based on a 1.2 *DCR* (debt coverage ratio) applied to the first-year *NOI,* will have an 11 percent interest rate, and will be amortized over 20 years with monthly payments. We will see in Chapter 11 that financing for real estate income property is frequently based on a target first-year debt coverage ratio. In our example, the *NOI* will increase 3 percent per year after the first year. The investor expects to hold the property for five years. The resale price is estimated by applying an 11 percent terminal capitalization rate to the sixth year *NOI.* Investors require a 12 percent rate of return on equity (yield rate) for this type of property. Note that the discount rate of 12 percent and terminal capitalization rate of 11 percent imply an average annual compound growth in income after year 5 (for the remaining economic life of the property) of 1 percent per year. This is less than the 3 percent growth assumed for the first five years. As we have discussed, growth rates and capitalization rates can change over time.

We first determine the annual debt service (*DS*) as follows:

$$DS = NOI_1 \div DCR$$

$$DS = \$50,000 \div 1.20 = \$41,667$$

This equation results in a monthly mortgage payment of $41,667 ÷ 12 = $3,472.22. The amount of the mortgage can be found by discounting the monthly payments at the mortgage rate of 11 percent over the 20-year term. The amount of the mortgage can be thought of as the value of the mortgage (*M*) assuming that 11 percent is the current market rate for the mortgage.

We can now project the cash flows over a five-year holding period as follows:

www.mhhe.com/bf15e

	Operating Years Year					
	1	2	3	4	5	6
NOI	$50,000	$51,500	$53,045	$54,636	$56,275	$57,964
DS	41,667	41,667	41,667	41,667	41,667	N/A*
Cash flow	$ 8,333	$ 9,833	$11,378	$12,969	$14,608	
Resale:						
Resale in year 5					$526,945	
Less mortgage balance					305,495	
Cash flow					$221,450	
Total cash flow	$ 8,333	$ 9,833	$11,378	$12,969	$236,058	

*Shown only to estimate the resale price at the end of the five-year holding period.

The present value of the cash flows in this example at a 12 percent discount rate is $165,566. This represents the value of the equity investors' interest in the property (*E*).

The total property value (*PV*) can now be found by summing the value of the mortgage (*M*) and the value of the equity (*E*). We have

$$PV = M + E$$

$$PV = \$336,394 + \$165,566$$

$$PV = \$501,960$$

The above value implies a going-in capitalization rate of about 10 percent ($50,000 ÷ $501,960). Note that this is less than the 11 percent rate used to estimate the resale price. As emphasized previously, the capitalization rate can change over time depending on the assumptions about how income will change after the property is sold.

We can also calculate the first-year equity dividend rate based on the above equity value. (Recall that the equity dividend rate is equal to the first-year cash flow to the equity investor divided by initial equity investment.) The equity dividend rate is equal to $8,333 ÷ $165,566, or about 5 percent. Also, the loan-to-value ratio implied by the estimated value is $336,394 ÷ $501,960, or 67 percent.

We must emphasize that in the above formulation, proceeds to be realized by the equity investor are discounted at an investment yield rate (*k*), which is not the same "free and clear" rate (*r*) that was used for discounting *NOI,* because the equity that an investor is willing to invest in a project is equal to the discounted value of all cash returns to be realized on *equity* investment and not *total* investment. When attempting to estimate *E,* an estimate must be obtained for *k,* or the before-tax internal rate of return (*BTIRR*) investors expect to realize on their equity over the entire period of investment. In the previous cases, no leverage was assumed. Hence, the discount rate, *r,* reflects the required return on a total investment, or "all cash" basis, because the investor did not use any debt financing. For this reason we would also expect *k* to be greater than *r* because of the increased risk to the equity investor when financing is used.

As indicated previously, determining the mortgage interest rate and other mortgage terms and what percentage of value lenders would be willing to lend on a particular property is relatively straightforward. However, estimating the internal rate of return on equity (*k*) that investors expect to earn over an expected period of ownership is more complex. We do not normally know what cash flows were being estimated by an investor when a comparable property was purchased. Furthermore, *k* based on *historical data* may not be indicative of *future* trends. A few general guidelines, however, can be followed when estimating *k*.

1. We know that the risk premium should be *greater* for an equity investor than it would be for the mortgage lender. This equity position is riskier because the equity investor takes more risk than the mortgage lender since all debt-service (*DS*) requirements must be paid from *NOI* before the equity investor realizes any *BTCF* (before-tax cash flow). Also, because the property serves as security for the loan, the lender has first claim against proceeds from the sale of a property; that is, the mortgage balance must be paid from the proceeds from sales before any cash is received by the equity investor. Hence, the equity investor is in a residual position, or one in which the claims of the lender must be met before the equity investor receives any return.

2. We know that the rate of return required by an equity investor (*k*) should be higher than that for the entire property (*r*) because of the risk associated with financial leverage.

3. When the required investment yield on equity is estimated for a particular project, yields on other investments such as corporate bonds and stock can serve as a point of reference for estimation. Of course, adjustments must be made for differences in risk between the property being valued and any benchmark or average yields developed from other markets.

Reconciliation: Sales Comparison and Income Capitalization Approaches

Based on the preceding discussion, it is obvious that both the sales comparison and income capitalization approaches to valuation have positive and negative aspects in their respective applications. Therefore, it is probably a good policy to use both approaches to valuing properties when possible. This is because comparable market data are *always beneficial* in a valuation analysis. When the sales comparison method is used, cap rates reflect what investors are *currently paying* for comparable properties. Any property currently for sale should tend to sell for a price that is *similar* to prices paid for highly comparable properties that have recently sold. This will be true no matter what the present value method produces based on forecasts of cash flows, holding periods, discount rates, and reversion values. On the other hand, much of the time, properties that have sold recently are not always *truly comparable* to properties available for purchase. Consequently, the exclusive use of direct capitalization, even when adjusted for different property attributes, is not always well advised. For these reasons, a careful analysis using both the present value approach and sales comparisons can be helpful.

Exploring the Relationships between Changing Market Conditions, Cap Rates, and Property Values

Thus far, we have illustrated the *mechanics* or approaches to valuation by using case examples. Investors who are active in real estate valuation and investing must always try to interpret changing market conditions and the effect that these changes are having on cap rates and property values. In other words, as analysts track the sales of properties they may observe that cap rates ($NOI \div V$) from these transactions may be increasing or decreasing. What does this mean? What causes cap rates to rise and fall? In this section, we introduce certain changes in market conditions and try to interpret the effects of those changes on property values and cap rates.

Scenario 1. Effects of Changes in "Going-In" Cap Rates in Response to Supply and Demand

To illustrate what effects short-run conditions of excess *supply and demand,* or real market forces, may have on cap rates both in the current time period as well as in future time periods, we consider scenarios relative to a base case. Exhibit 10–10 summarizes these cases. In the base case, we assume that market supply and demand *are currently in balance,* and that long-term growth in rents and *NOI* is expected to be 3 percent and that investors expect returns of $r = 12$ percent. *To simplify the discussion and for purposes of illustration, we are assuming that NOI and cash flows in all examples that follow are equal.* Returning to our discussion, we show *NOI* to be $100,000 in year 1, which is expected to grow at 3 percent per year. At the end of year 5, we show *REV,* which is based on year 6 *NOI,* divided by ($r - g$), or $115,927 \div (.12 - .03) = $1,288,082$. Because of the short period of analysis in our example, we do not consider the possible influence of economic depreciation on the terminal cap rate. However, if the period of analysis were longer, or if the analyst believed that economic depreciation would occur, then it should be considered. Note that in panel B, these base case assumptions produce a *present value* of $1,111,111, and a going-in cap rate (R) of .09. This result is consistent with the condition of market equilibrium, or when supply and demand are thought to be in balance. Furthermore, investors have no reason to believe that market imbalances are likely for the foreseeable

EXHIBIT 10–10   Scenario 1: Short-Run Relationships between Supply and Demand, Investor Returns, and "Going-In" Cap Rates

					Year		
Panel A: Market Scenario							
		(1)	(2)	(3)	(4)	(5)	(6)
Base Case: Market in	NOI	$100,000	$103,000	$106,090	$109,273	$ 112,551	$115,927
balance, g = 3%	REV					1,288,082	
Case A: *Excess supply*	NOI	100,000	100,000	100,000	103,000	106,090	109,273
	REV					1,214,141	
Case B: *Excess demand*	NOI	100,000	105,000	110,250	115,762	119,235	122,812
	REV					1,364,578	

Panel B: Expected Result

			Commentary
Base Case:	NOI	$ 100,000	*Market supply/demand in balance.* Long-term growth in NOI = 3% and
	PV @ 12%	$1,111,111	investor expected return (r) = 12%.
	Cap rate (R)	.090	
Case A:	NOI	$ 100,000	*Excess supply* expected for three years. Rents remain flat, and then increase
	PV @ 12%	$ 1,054,776	to long-term growth of 3% in year 4 and thereafter. Therefore, property values
	Cap rate (R)	.095	would be expected to *fall* and cap rates would be expected to *rise* relative
			to the base case.
Case B:	NOI	$ 100,000	*Excess demand* causes NOI to rise at above normal growth (5%) for four
	PV @ 12%	$1,166,989	years. Rents then revert to long-term growth (3%) beginning in year 5 and
	Cap rate (R)	.086	thereafter. Therefore, property values would be expected to *rise* and cap
			rates would be expected to *fall* relative to the base case.

future. They believe that future growth is expected to produce real increases in *NOI* at the rate of 3 percent per year, and investors in properties such as the one illustrated expect to continue to earn a return of 12 percent. We now consider a change in cap rates brought on by *unexpected changes* that bring on market conditions of excess supply and demand.

In case A, we show the effects of an unexpected change in short-run conditions relative to the base case. This is a condition of *oversupply* which we now expect to last for three years and during which time rents are expected to be flat. Note that *NOI* remains at $100,000 for three years. Then, demand increases and *NOI* resumes a long-run growth pattern of 3 percent per year beginning in year 4. This assumption, in turn, produces the results shown in panel B for case A. Note that under conditions of three years of excess supply (holding all else constant), *present value declines* to $1,054,776 and *cap rates (R) rise* to .095. Obviously, *R* is now greater than .09 shown in the base case. *In short, conditions of excess supply produce rising cap rates.* Therefore, market conditions should show comparable property values falling because of higher market cap rates.

In case B, we show the effects of an unexpected short-run condition of *excess demand* that lasts for a period of four years, after which supply adjusts and a long-term growth pattern at 3 percent per year is restored. Such a condition could be brought about by a sudden increase in employment in a market, thereby increasing demand relative to supply. Note in panel B, case B, that present value increases to $1,166,989 and *cap rates fall* to .086 relative to results in the base case. Therefore, when demand exceeds supply of available rental space, this tends to reduce cap rates and increase property values.

In summary, the goal of this exercise is to demonstrate the effects of changes in market conditions on property values and cap rates. *Holding all else constant, excess supply tends to drive PV down and cap rates up.* Investors are discounting lower rents and, therefore, future cash flows are brought on by excess supply and are only willing to purchase properties at lower prices and higher cap rates. Conversely, *excess demand tends to drive PV higher and cap rates lower* as investors discount higher than normal cash flows, thereby producing higher property values and lower cap rates.

Scenario 2: Effects of Changes in Capital Market Conditions on "Going-In" Cap Rates

In the previous section, we illustrated the effects of how *real* market influences, that is, the *supply* of new space available for occupancy and the *demand* for such space, affect both property values and capitalization rates. In this section, we use the same base case to illustrate the effects of changes in the market for capital or *financial markets,* primarily through changes in interest rates, on property values and capitalization rates. In Exhibit 10–11, case C, we show the effect of an unanticipated *increase* in long-term interest rates that also causes expected returns (r) to increase from 12 percent to 13 percent. Note that this increase is assumed to occur *holding all else constant.* This means that future rents, *NOI,* and so on, remain unaffected. The results of this increase in interest rates are shown in panel B, where present value declines to $1,000,000 relative to the base case of $1,111,111 and cap rates rise to .10 from .09 in the base case.[2]

EXHIBIT 10–11   **Scenario 2: Relationship between Changes in Interest Rates, Investor Returns, and "Going-In" Cap Rates**

				Year			
Panel A: Market Scenario							
		(1)	(2)	(3)	(4)	(5)	(6)
Base Case:	NOI	$100,000	$103,000	$106,090	$109,273	$ 112,551	$115,927
	REV					1,288,082	
Case C: Interest Rates	NOI	100,000	103,000	106,090	109,273	112,551	115,927
Rise, r = 13%	REV					1,159,274	
Case D: Interest Rates	NOI	100,000	103,000	106,090	109,273	112,551	115,927
Fall, r = 11%	REV					1,449,093	

Panel B: Expected Result

			Commentary
Base Case:	NOI	$ 100,000	Base case: Market supply/demand in balance. Long-term growth in
	PV @ 12%	$ 1,111,111	NOI = 3% and investor expected return r = 12%.
	Cap rate (R)	.09	
Case C:	NOI	$ 100,000	Relative to the base case, property values *decline* because of a higher
	PV @ 13%	$1,000,000	discount rate (13%) and cap rates *rise.*
	Cap rate (R)	.10	
Case D:	NOI	$ 100,000	Relative to the base case, property values *rise* because of lower discount
	PV @ 11%	$1,250,000	rates (11%) and cap rates *fall.*
	Cap rate (R)	.08	

[2] Of course, in reality, the *exact* effect on present value may be different than what we have depicted. The reader should view this exercise more in terms of *direction of impact,* not in terms of exact dollar magnitudes.

In case D, we consider a decrease in interest rates and therefore required returns of 11 percent relative to the 12 percent used in the base case. Again, holding all else constant, property values *rise* ($1,250,000) relative to the base case ($1,111,111) because *NOI* remains the same, while investors' expected returns fall to 11 percent. Also, cap rates fall from .09 in the base case to .08.

The conclusions to be drawn here are that, holding all else constant, *rising* interest rates generally result in higher required returns (*r*) and higher cap rates. This, in turn, results in lower property values than would otherwise be the case if interest rates had not changed. Conversely, when interest rates *decline,* required returns also decline and property values rise. This tends to produce *lower cap rates.*

Scenario 3: Effects of Combining: (1) Changes in Capital Market Conditions and (2) Supply-Demand Influences on "Going-In" Cap Rates

In Exhibit 10–12, we consider the effects of an unanticipated increase in *interest rates,* coupled with market conditions consisting of real market changes, including short-run excess supply and short-run excess demand. The base case shows that both real and financial market forces affecting supply and demand are currently producing a balanced market. However, in case E, because of an increase of 1 percent in long-term interest rates, investors now expect to earn 13 percent. When coupled with a market condition of excess supply, the combined results produce a major *decline in property values* and a significant *increase in cap rates.* Note that this combination of excess supply and rising interest rates produces the lowest present values when compared to all other scenarios. This is because investors demand greater returns on real estate investments in a market that is being oversupplied by developers. This produces flat rents and *NOI* that are discounted by a larger discount rate. Case F, which depicts a combination of rising demand and rising interest rates, tends to produce a slightly lower *PV* and higher cap rate than in the base case because the condition of excess demand is producing both higher rents and *NOI;* however, these higher cash flows are being discounted at a higher discount rate because of rising interest rates.

Cases G and H shown in Exhibit 10–12 show the effects of falling interest rates under conditions of excess supply and demand, respectively. In these cases, the combination of excess demand and falling interest rates (case H) produces the greatest effect, resulting in dramatically lower cap rates relative to the base case and all other cases. Case G also produces a favorable result in terms of lower cap rates; however, the excess supply condition produces a present value that is somewhat lower than that shown in case H because of lower rents.

A Closing Note on Cap Rates and Market Conditions

In the above scenarios, we may summarize as follows:

Lower market cap rates (higher property values) tend to be brought about by:

1. Unanticipated increases in the demand for real estate relative to supply.
2. Unanticipated decreases in interest rates.
3. Both (1) and (2).

Higher market cap rates (lower property values) tend to be brought about by:

1. Unanticipated increases in the supply of real estate relative to demand.
2. Unanticipated increases in interest rates.
3. Both (1) and (2).

EXHIBIT 10–12   **Scenario 3: Relationship between Excess Supply/Demand Conditions, Interest Rates, Investor Returns, and "Going-In" Cap Rates**

Panel A: Market Scenario

		Year					
		(1)	(2)	(3)	(4)	(5)	(6)
Base Case:	*NOI*	$100,000	$103,000	$106,090	$109,273	$ 112,551	$115,927
	REV					1,288,082	
Case E: Oversupply and 13% return	*NOI*	100,000	100,000	100,000	103,000	106,090	109,273
	REV					1,092,727	
Case F: Excess demand and 13% return	*NOI*	100,000	105,000	110,250	115,762	119,235	122,812
	REV					1,228,120	
Case G: Oversupply and 11% return	*NOI*	100,000	100,000	100,000	103,000	106,090	109,273
	REV					1,365,909	
Case H: Excess demand and 11% return	*NOI*	100,000	105,000	110,250	115,762	119,235	122,812
	REV					1,535,150	

Panel B: Expected Result

			Commentary
Base Case:	*NOI*	$ 100,000	Market supply and demand are in balance. Long-term growth in
	PV @ 12%	$1,111,111	*NOI* = 3% and the investor expected return = 12%.
	Cap rate (*R*)	.09	
Case E:	*NOI*	$ 100,000	Oversupply *and* rising interest rates cause property values to *decline* and
	PV @ 13%	$ 949,957	cap rates (*R*) to *increase* relative to the base case.
	Cap rate (*R*)	.105	
Case F:	*NOI*	$ 100,000	Although excess demand exists, when combined with rising interest rates,
	PV @ 13%	$1,049,424	property values *rise* although by not as much as in the base case.
	Cap rate (*R*)	.095	
Case G:	*NOI*	$ 100,000	Falling interest rates exert a *positive* effect on property values; however,
	PV @ 11%	$1,185,780	this effect is offset to some extent by an oversupplied market. The result is
	Cap rate (*R*)	.084	*slightly higher* property values and *slightly lower* cap rates relative to the base case.
Case H:	*NOI*	$ 100,000	Both falling interest rates and excess demand combine to produce the
	PV @ 11%	$1,313,977	most *positive* effect on property values and dramatically *lower* cap rates
	Cap rate (*R*)	.076	relative to the base case.

There are obviously *many other factors* that contribute to increases and decreases in cap rates. These could include changes in the risk associated with a given property or could be due to changes in neighborhood characteristics and/or many other factors.

A Word of Caution—Simultaneous Effects of Real Market Forces and Interest Rates on Property Values

It should be stressed that the above illustrations were developed under strict assumptions regarding the timing and duration of conditions of excess supply and demand as well as the extent and duration of interest rate changes. These examples were developed to demonstrate the effects of changes in market conditions on property values and cap rates by using the benefit of numerical examples. In practice, projections of these relationships are difficult to make, as are the forecasts of the dollar magnitude of such changes on property values. There are many combinations of real market forces and interest rates that may be considered. Furthermore, we have not considered the possible *interaction* between changes in any one of these market forces on other market influences. For example, the effects of changes in interest rates may persist for a long period of time and affect the *long-term* growth in supply and demand and the pattern in *NOI* far beyond three years. Nonetheless, we believe that understanding these relationships is useful.

In practice, investors must know how to incorporate these relationships into forecasts. When valuing specific properties, the investors must consider:

1. Current market supply and demand conditions and how long such conditions will last.
2. The effects of such conditions on rents and *NOI*.
3. The future course of interest rates that may be affected by more global, non–real estate specific influences such as global economic growth and inflationary pressures.
4. The contents of leases that have been executed on the property being evaluated and whether conditions in (1), (2), and (3) will materially affect rents, expenses, and tenant default rates.

Leases: Valuation of a Leased Fee Estate

The previous examples in this chapter assumed that the properties being valued could be leased at current market rents. In these cases, it can be said that properties are valued as **fee simple estates.** However, in many situations when properties are being considered for purchase, there are existing leases in place that have below (or above) market rents. Such properties are purchased as **leased fee estates.** Similarly, when valuing properties and selecting comparable properties from recent sales, we find that many of these properties will also have existing leases. When such comparables are used, it is very important to investigate whether or not existing leases are present and the contents of such leases. Failure to investigate these cases can result in serious errors when estimating value.

For example, let us assume that property A has an existing net lease with payments for the next five years at $400,000 per year. At the end of the five-year period, the lease is scheduled to expire and rents could then be negotiated on a year-to-year basis at market rates. Alternatively, property B, which is exactly comparable to A, can be expected to produce net rent of $500,000 per year with an escalation of 3 percent per year because it has no existing leases, and market rents can be earned each year. Assuming this to be the case, we have:

PV	Cash Flow—Year 5					
	(1)	(2)	(3)	(4)	(5)	REV$_5$
Property A = $4,461,296	$400,000	$400,000	$400,000	$400,000	$400,000	$5,627,540
Property B = $4,908,366	500,000	515,000	530,450	546,364	562,754	5,627,540

We should also note that the reversion value at the end of year 5 (REV_5) is assumed to be the same in both cases because the lease on property A will have expired and the rents can be adjusted up to market rates at the end of that year and every year thereafter, thereby making the reversion value the same as in case B from year 6 into the future. Therefore, from year 5 on, cash flows are assumed to be the same in both cases and will produce the same *REV* at that time. We assume that the same required return of 13 percent is to be earned on both properties. However, note that both the present value and "going-in" cap rates for both sales are very different. After discounting, we show a value of $4.46 million for A versus $4.91 million for B, or a difference of about $450,000. Furthermore, the cap rates are .09 for property A and .102 for property B, respectively. One point to be made, then, is that if a property is under consideration for purchase (say, property C) and it is highly comparable to both properties A and B, but very little information is available on the existing leases for A and B, then using cap rates from either sale could produce very different estimates of value. Indeed, if the *NOI* for property C was $450,00, then depending on which cap rate was chosen, the estimated value could range from ($450,000 ÷ .09), or $5,000,000, to ($450,000 ÷ .102), or $4,411,765. This would be a difference of $588,235. *Therefore, it is important when selecting comparable properties for valuation purposes to be certain that, in addition to the physical and locational characteristics of the properties, the contents of existing leases on such comparables are also very similar to the lease contents of the property under consideration for purchase.*

Cost Approach

The rationale for using the **cost approach** to valuing (appraising) properties is that any informed buyer of real estate would not pay more for a property than what it would cost to buy the land and build the structure. For a new property, the cost approach ordinarily involves determining the construction cost of building a given improvement, then adding the market value of the land. In the case of existing buildings, the appraiser first estimates the cost of replacing the building. This estimate is reduced by estimating any **physical deterioration, functional obsolescence,** or **external obsolescence** (discussed below) in arriving at the estimated value of the building. This approach is procedurally identical to the cost approach detailed in Chapter 7 for residential financing. In the case of income-producing property, however, structural design and equipment variations and locational influences make the cost estimation process much more complex. Consequently, the cost approach may at times be difficult to apply, particularly if the property is not new.

Many techniques can be used in conjunction with the cost approach to value. The technique chosen to estimate value will generally depend on (1) the age of the structure being valued, (2) whether the structure is highly specialized in design or function, and (3) the availability of data to be used for cost estimating. Generally, if a project is in the proposal stage, cost data will be developed from plans and drawings by an appraiser or estimator. Cost estimation services are available for appraisers from the Marshall and Swift Company and the Boeckh Division of the American Appraisal Company.

If a project is in the proposal stage, specifications for material and equipment will have been set out in detail, usually making it possible to arrive at a relatively accurate cost estimate. Exhibit 10–13 contains a breakdown of hard and soft costs for a hypothetical office-warehouse complex in the proposal stage of development. The cost breakdown shown in Exhibit 10–13 is based on categories that generally correspond to how various subcontractors would make bid estimates on improvements. This procedure is quite common for new, nontechnical construction.

In addition to the hard-cost categories shown in Exhibit 10–13 for our hypothetical office-warehouse complex, we see two additional categories. One represents a soft-cost category, which includes estimated outlays for services and intangible costs necessary when designing and developing a project. The other category represents land cost. Estimates of land value are made from comparisons with other recent land sales. The sales

EXHIBIT 10–13
Cost Breakdown—
Hypothetical
Office-Warehouse
Complex (73,500
Square Feet: 8,000
Office; 65,500
Warehouse; 3 Land
Acres; Projected
Economic Life,
50 Years)

Component	Cost	PSF
	Hard Costs	
Excavation—back fill	$ 31,500	
Foundation	47,250	
Framing (steel)	160,500	
Corrugated steel exterior walls	267,750	
Brick facade (front)—glass	51,000	
Floor finishing, concrete	61,000	
Floor covering, offices	17,500	
Roof trusses, covering	115,040	
Interior finish, offices	57,400	
Lighting fixtures, electrical work	83,400	
Plumbing	114,500	
Heating–A/C	157,500	
Interior cranes, scales	139,060	
Loading docks, rail extension	96,000	
On-site parking, streets, gutters	176,000	
Subtotal	$1,575,000	$21.43
	Soft Costs	
Architect, attorney, accounting	$ 200,000	
Construction interest	125,000	
Builder profit	250,000	
Subtotal	$ 575,000	
Comparable land cost (from comparable land sale)	$ 350,000	
Value per cost approach	$2,500,000	$34.00

chosen to estimate value should be **comparable properties** to the land underlying the improvement being valued.

In cases where the project to be appraised includes an *existing* improvement, the detailed cost breakdown shown in Exhibit 10–13 is more difficult to use because the appraiser must estimate physical and economic depreciation on the component parts. Generally, when the cost approach to value is used for an existing improvement, the cost to replace the improvement is estimated and adjusted downward for depreciation caused by (1) physical deterioration, (2) functional or structural obsolescence due to the availability of more efficient layout designs and technological changes that reduce operating costs, and (3) external obsolescence that may result from changes outside of the property such as excessive traffic, noise, or pollution. These three categories of depreciation are very difficult to determine and, in many cases, require the judgment of appraisers who specialize in such problems. Adjusting downward for depreciation is especially difficult for industrial properties, special-use facilities such as public buildings, and properties that are bought and sold infrequently.

To illustrate how adjustments must be made to reflect physical, functional, and economic depreciation, we consider a different property, a 15-year-old office-warehouse complex. The improvement, if constructed today and "costed out" at *current prices* using a procedure similar to that shown in Exhibit 10–13, would be $1,750,000. However, because the structure is 15 years old, certain adjustments must be made for necessary repairs, changes in design technology, and depreciation, as shown in Exhibit 10–14.

EXHIBIT 10–14
Estimates of Depreciation and Obsolescence on Improved Property

Replacement cost estimate	$1,750,000
1. Physical deterioration	
a. Repairable (curable)	
Interior finish	25,500
Floor covering	5,200
Lighting fixtures	17,000
Total	$ 47,700
b. Nonrepairable (incurable)	
15 years divided by 50 years (age to economic life)	30%
2. Functional obsolescence	
Layout design (inefficiency)	
Increasing operating cost (annually)	$ 15,600
3. External obsolescence	
Loss in rent per year*	4,000
Site value by comparison	$ 200,000

*Portion attributable to the building.

The essence of the cost approach for existing properties is first to price the improvement at its current **replacement cost.** Then, that amount is reduced by any costs (1) that can be expended to upgrade the improvement or to cure obvious deterioration due mainly to needed maintenance or (2) that correspond to the economic loss associated with nonrepairable (or incurable) factors due to changes in design or layout efficiency that may make newer buildings less expensive to operate.

Hence, in our example, the appraiser estimates that a purchaser of the property would have to incur a cost of $47,700 simply to replace worn-out items, the result of deferred maintenance and replacement (curable physical deterioration). However, because the structure is 15 years old and the economic life was 50 years when the building was constructed, the appraiser estimates that structural nonrepairable or incurable depreciation due to wear and tear (incurable physical deterioration) would represent about 30 percent of current reproduction cost. This percentage was developed in the example by the ratio of age to economic life, or 15 divided by 50. This estimate assumes that the building will wear out evenly (at a rate of 2% per year—100% divided by 50 years) over its 50-year life. Because 15 years have passed, based on these assumptions, the building would be 30 percent depreciated. *Estimates of physical depreciation are not always based on these simple assumptions. Many structures may wear out faster or slower over time. In such cases, the appraiser should consider the* **effective age** *of the property rather than its actual age.*

As for functional obsolescence in our example, the appraiser estimates that operating costs will be $15,600 higher on the existing structure when compared with a completely new building. The higher costs could be caused, for example, by the lack of suspended ceilings in an older structure, by posts and columns that might affect traffic and storage patterns, or by an older conveyor system designed into the initial structure. This $15,600 additional annual expense could represent added costs in manpower, machinery, and so on, due to functional inadequacies. This additional expense is treated as a discounted annuity because the increase in operating costs is expected to be $15,600 per year for the next 35 years. Assuming the buyer could earn 10 percent annually on other investments, the adjustment for functional obsolescence would reduce the total operating costs to a present value of $150,449. It is assumed that the owner could invest in a similar real estate venture or an investment of equal risk and earn 10 percent on total investment. This was discussed in more detail in our consideration of the income capitalization approach earlier in the chapter.

Finally, the appraiser estimates $4,000 per year for external obsolescence. This cost accounts for environmental changes, such as pollution, noise, neighborhood changes, and other *external* influences that result in lower rents (or higher expenses) when present. Estimates for these characteristics must be obtained from comparable sites where none of these external influences are present. Because the land value is being estimated separately from the building value, the effect of economic obsolescence on the land value will already be accounted for in the estimated land value. Thus, during the adjustment for the effect of locational obsolescence on the *building* value, the estimated rent loss should represent only that portion of the total rent loss (land and building) that applies to the building. For example, the appraiser might estimate that the rent for the entire property will be $5,000 per year less due to the locational obsolescence. However, if there were separate leases on the building and the land, the appraiser might expect that the building would rent for $4,000 less, whereas the land would rent for $1,000 less. This loss in building rent is capitalized and used to reduce the building value. In our example, we assume this rent loss to be $4,000 per year. As was the case with functional obsolescence, this loss in income will also be discounted at 10 percent. The discounted value of this loss is $38,577. In practice, this estimate is extremely difficult to make. The appraiser must often use considerable judgment as to what the total rent loss would be and how much would be allocated to the building.

Adjustments to the replacement cost estimate for the existing improvement in our example are shown in Exhibit 10–15. Note that any repairable or curable depreciation or obsolescence should be subtracted from the replacement cost estimate before any reduction is made for nonrepairable or incurable costs (30% in our example). In other words, even after adjusting for the curable items, productivity loss due to functional obsolescence and structural depreciation would still exist. The estimate for those incurable items must be made based on the assumption that all curable items are repaired.

In summary, the cost approach is most reliable where the structure is relatively new and depreciation does not present serious complications. However, when adjustments have to be made for depreciation and obsolescence, and when it is difficult to find comparable land sales, the cost approach is less desirable. This usually occurs where older, improved properties are being valued. However, where there are very few sales and market data are scarce, the cost approach to valuing older properties may be the only method available.

EXHIBIT 10–15
Adjustment of
Replacement Cost
Estimate

Replacement costs at current prices	$1,750,000
Less: Repairable physical depreciation	47,700
Subtotal	$1,702,300
Nonrepairable (incurable) physical depreciation, 30%	510,690
Functional obsolescence (incurable):	
$15,600(*PV,* 10%, 35 years)	
$15,600(9.644159)	150,449
Economic-locational obsolescence:	
$4,000(*PV,* 10%, 35 years)	
$4,000(9.644159)	38,577
Add: Site value (by comparison)	200,000
Value per cost approach	$1,202,584
or (rounded)	$1,200,000

Valuation Case Study—Oakwood Apartments

Oakwood Apartments is a luxury apartment complex. It is being appraised for an investor who has contracted to purchase the property and needs to obtain financing. The bank has had its own staff appraisers estimate the value of the property but wants an independent appraiser to also provide an estimate using a "limited appraisal" that focuses on the income approach.

The bank has provided Exhibit 10–16, which summarizes information about the property. The appraiser has confirmed the expected rent per unit with the present owner, and she has also done an analysis of comparable apartment communities that is summarized in Exhibit 10–17.

Oakwood consists entirely of two-bedroom units. A competitive analysis indicates that Oakwood is very similar to comparables 1 and 2 even though they each have some one- and three-bedroom units. It appears that owners of apartment buildings with a greater proportion of two-bedroom units are able to get a higher average monthly rent per unit. Comparable 3 is more densely developed with one-bedroom apartments, and its parking ratios are lower than all others. It appears that the average rent for Oakwood is reasonable relative to the competition. In addition to rent, other cash flows may be realized from laundry facilities. Comparable 2 sold for $100,000 per unit, and comparable 1, which is

EXHIBIT 10–16
Property Information—Oakwood Apartments

Name of Property:
Oakwood Apartments
Location:
Suburbia, USA
Improvement Description:
A 95-unit luxury garden apartment community located on a major north-south arterial. The property is newly constructed and has a high level of amenities, including 100% direct-access garages. All buildings are of two-story construction with 90% brick exteriors.
Lender:
Bank of USA
Rent and Income Escalation = 3%

Principal Amenities:
Direct access garages with automatic garage door openers. Swimming pool and heated spa, fitness center, business center, jogging trail, limited-access gates, 200 parking spaces-some covered.
Land Area/Density:
4.75 acres
Unit Type:
95 two-bedroom units
1,100 square feet with two bedrooms and two baths
Age:
Three years old
Average Current Monthly Rent:
$1,250.00 plus other income of $120 per unit per year

EXHIBIT 10–17
Oakwood Apartments: Comparables

| | Oakwood | Comparables/Competitors | | |
		(1)	(2)	(3)
Units per acre	20	20.0	21.0	25.0
Unit mix:				
1BR/1Bath	–0–	10%	10%	60%
2BR/2Bath	100%	85%	80%	40%
3BR/2Bath	–0–	5%	10%	–0–
Parking spaces/unit	2.10	2.00	1.95	1.50
Age	3 years	3 years	3 years	5 years
Condition/amenities	Excellent	Excellent	Good	Good
Avg. monthly rent per unit	$1,250	$1,150	$1,100	$950
Price per unit	—	$110,000	$100,000	$90,000
Gross rent multiplier	—	95.65	90.91	94.74

most like Oakwood, sold for $110,000 per unit. Although the appraiser is not doing a formal sales comparison approach, she notes that a price of $110,000 per unit would suggest a value of Oakwood of $110,000 × 95 units = $10,450,000. The gross rent multipliers of two of the comps are around 95 but the third is around 91. The average would be around 93.8. Using this multiplier would suggest a value for Oakwood Apartments of 93.8 × $1,250 × 95 units = $11,139.000 (rounded to nearest thousand).

The appraiser has determined that the number of units per acre (usually set by zoning) is currently the maximum allowable. This may be important if zoning laws have changed and now allow development of 20 or more units per acre. The average number of parking spaces (2.10) per unit, or 400 spaces, seems reasonable relative to the competition, and the appraiser has determined that the amenity package is appropriate relative to rental rates and to what the competition is currently offering in the way of exercise and recreation facilities, TV cable/satellite services, high-speed Internet connectivity, washer/dryer hookups, and so on.

On-site expenses will include salaries for on-site personnel who maintain and "make units ready" for tenants in the community. An operating risk that must be considered by apartment investors is the relatively short nature of lease maturities, the potential tenant turnover, and downtime due to vacancies. Experience in large metropolitan areas indicates that as many as 60 percent of apartments in a given property may turn over each year. In making cash flow projections, analysts must consider turnover-related losses in revenue because of vacancies, in conjunction with recurring repairs and maintenance expenses involved in making units ready for new tenants. For Oakwood Apartments, these items are included in repair and maintenance expense. A management fee for oversight of all leasing, rent collection, tenant relations, and so on, and office expenses for payroll, insurance, tax property, and other bookkeeping services necessary for operations have also been estimated. These items should be validated from payment records and/or the appropriate agency or vendors.

Vacancy is expected to be 5 percent of potential income, and credit loss due to tenants who default on their lease is expected to be an additional 1 percent of potential income. The property is to be valued using an 11 percent discount rate and assuming the property will be sold after five years. The resale price will be estimated by using a 9 percent terminal capitalization rate applied to year 6 *NOI.* The rate reflects lower growth expectations after year 5. Selling costs when the property is sold will be 5 percent of the sale price.

Rents are expected to increase at the expected inflation rate of 3 percent per year. Additional revenue of $120 per unit is expected from the laundry machines that are included in a laundry area of the apartment complex. This income will also increase at 3 percent per year.

Contrary to most other property types, tenants occupying apartment properties usually sign leases with maturities of either 6 or 12 months. Furthermore, tenants usually pay for their own utilities, insurance, and so on, which usually relieves the investor of making payments for these items and recovering expenses from tenants. However, there are utility costs for common areas in the apartment community that must be paid by the owner.

Expenses next year are projected as follows:

Real estate taxes	$87,000
Office expenses (accounting administrative)	$20,000
Insurance	$150 per unit
Repairs and maintenance	$550 per unit
Advertising	$8,000
Utilities	$45,000
Miscellaneous expenses	$15,000

Expenses are projected to increase at the inflation rate of 3 percent per year.

In addition to the above expenses, a property management firm is paid 12 percent of effective gross income (rents less vacancy and credit loss) to find tenants, sign leases, handle tenant relations, and oversee repairs and maintenance.

Based on the assumptions above, cash flows for Oakwood Apartments are projected in Exhibit 10–18.

NOI is projected through year 6 since year 6 is used to estimate the resale price. Exhibit 10–19 shows the projected resale price by applying the 9 percent terminal capitalization rate to the year 6 *NOI* and subtracting the selling costs of 5 percent of the sale price.

Exhibit 10–20 shows the present value of the NOI over the five-year holding period plus the present value of the resale calculated above. Present values are based on an 11 percent discount rate. The total value is $10,573,934, or $10,574,000 (rounded). This is just slightly more than the replacement cost of $10,000,000 and in the range estimated by using the price per unit and gross rent multiplier from the comparable sales which was from $10,450,000 to $11,139,000

e**X**cel

EXHIBIT 10–18 **Projection of Net Operating Income for Oakwood Apartments**

Year	1	2	3	4	5	6
Income:						
Market Rent from Lease Renewals	$1,425,000	$1,467,750	$1,511,783	$1,557,136	$1,603,850	$1,651,966
Laundry income	$11,400	$11,742	$12,094	$12,457	$12,831	$13,216
Potential Gross Income (PGI)	$1,436,400	$1,479,492	$1,523,877	$1,569,593	$1,616,681	$1,665,181
Less: Vacancy	$71,250	$73,388	$75,589	$77,857	$80,193	$82,598
Less: Credit Loss	$14,250	$14,678	$15,118	$15,571	$16,039	$16,520
Effective Gross Income (EGI)	$1,350,900	$1,391,427	$1,433,170	$1,476,165	$1,520,450	$1,566,063
	$85,500	$88,065	$90,707	$93,428	$96,231	$99,118
Expenses:						
Real Estate Taxes	$87,000	$89,610	$92,298	$95,067	$97,919	$100,857
Office Expenses	$20,000	$20,600	$21,218	$21,855	$22,510	$23,185
Insurance	$14,250	$14,678	$15,118	$15,571	$16,039	$16,520
Repairs and Maintenance	$52,250	$53,818	$55,432	$57,095	$58,808	$60,572
Advertising	$8,000	$8,240	$8,487	$8,742	$9,004	$9,274
Management	$162,108	$166,971	$171,980	$177,140	$182,454	$187,928
Utilities	$45,000	$46,350	$47,741	$49,173	$50,648	$52,167
Miscellaneous Expenses	$15,000	$15,450	$15,914	$16,391	$16,883	$17,389
Total expenses	$403,608	$415,716	$428,188	$441,033	$454,264	$467,892
Net operating income (NOI)	$947,292	$975,711	$1,004,982	$1,035,132	$1,066,185	$1,098,171

EXHIBIT 10–19
Projection of Resale Proceeds for Oakwood Apartments

Resale	$12,201,901
Selling cost	610,095
Net resale	$11,591,806

EXHIBIT 10–20
Present Value of *NOI* and Resale Proceeds

PV of *NOI*	$ 3,694,762
PV of resale	6,879,172
Total value	$10,573,934

Thus, based on the income approach, the appraiser will provide the bank with an estimated value for Oakwood Apartments of $10,574,000.[3]

REIWise Solution

REIWise is a cloud-based program that is used for investment analysis and valuation real estate income properties like apartments, office buildings, shopping centers, and industrial properties. We will show how it replicates our apartment example in this chapter, and in Chapter 11 we will show how it replicates an office building example.

Students using this textbook have a free subscription to REIWise while enrolled in the course. The program can be used with any web browser on desktops, laptops, and mobile devices such as an iPad. All you need is an Internet connection. To get your free subscription, see www.REIWise.com/edu. The appendix to this chapter will show the inputs to REIWise necessary to replicate the Oakwood Apartments example.

Exhibit 10–21 shows one of the REIWise screens that shows the projected cash flows for Oakwood. The NOI is the same as we projected previously.

Exhibit 10–22 shows the estimated values from REIWise as if sold during each of the five-year holding periods shown. The results are shown as if the property was sold during each of the possible holding periods shown but we will focus on year 5. The result for a five-year holding period is exactly the same as we calculated earlier.

EXHIBIT 10–21
REIWise Screen for Oakwood Apartments

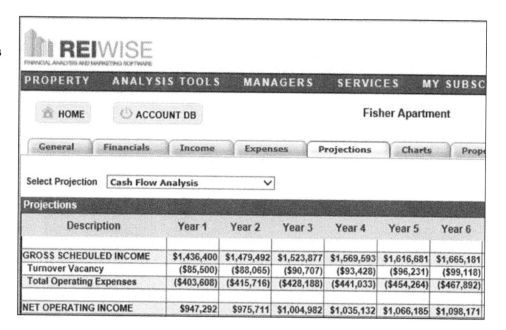

---

[3]Rounding the number conveys the fact that a high degree of precision is not possible given the nature of the assumptions that must be made in the appraisal process.

EXHIBIT 10–22
REIWise Screen for
Oakwood Apartments

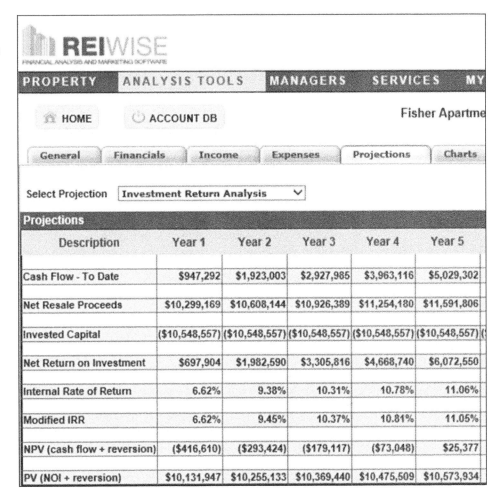

Description	Year 1	Year 2	Year 3	Year 4	Year 5
Cash Flow - To Date	$947,292	$1,923,003	$2,927,985	$3,963,116	$5,029,302
Net Resale Proceeds	$10,299,169	$10,608,144	$10,926,389	$11,254,180	$11,591,806
Invested Capital	($10,548,557)	($10,548,557)	($10,548,557)	($10,548,557)	($10,548,557)
Net Return on Investment	$697,904	$1,982,590	$3,305,816	$4,668,740	$6,072,550
Internal Rate of Return	6.62%	9.38%	10.31%	10.78%	11.06%
Modified IRR	6.62%	9.45%	10.37%	10.81%	11.05%
NPV (cash flow + reversion)	($416,610)	($293,424)	($179,117)	($73,048)	$25,377
PV (NOI + reversion)	$10,131,947	$10,255,133	$10,369,440	$10,475,509	$10,573,934

Web App

There are many sites that provide articles related to the current real estate investment climate. Go to a site like Institutional Real Estate, Inc. (**www.irei.com**) or one that you find by using a search engine like Google (**www.google.com**) to search for a phrase like "real estate capital market trends" and find an article related to the current investment climate. Summarize the current investment climate either for the national market or for a particular property type and/or location. Can you find examples of recent deals that provide insights into the investment climate?

Conclusion

We have demonstrated three approaches to valuation along with many of the techniques used in conjunction with each. Many combinations of approaches and techniques to valuation could be used; approaches and techniques should be chosen that best complement the data available for estimation. Stated another way, *the availability and quality of data should always dictate the methods and approaches chosen for valuation.* If perfect information were available, then theoretically the same value would result regardless of the method chosen, be it cost, market, or income capitalization. Even with imperfect information, the three approaches to value should correspond to some extent, which is the reason appraisal reports will typically contain estimates of value based on at least two approaches to determining value. While this procedure helps to corroborate the opinion of value, in the final analysis, it is up to the user of the report to interpret, understand, and critically analyze the assumptions, techniques, and methods used to estimate value. Appraisals are only estimates of market value based on market conditions and information available at the time of the appraisal. Economic conditions are subject to much uncertainty, and appraisals should be interpreted and used in light of that uncertainty. Lenders and investors should be familiar with the techniques used by appraisers and with the assumptions made in developing the estimate of value. The appraisal should be viewed as a complement, not a substitute, for sound underwriting or investment analysis by the particular lender or investor.

Key Terms

appraisal process, *296*
capitalization rate, *301*
comparable properties, *324*
cost approach, *323*
direct capitalization
    method, *301*
discount rate, *306*
discounted present value
    method, *305*
effective age, *325*
effective gross income, *300*
external obsolescence, *323*

fee simple estate, *322*
functional obsolescence, *323*
"going-in" cap rate (R), *310*
gross income multipliers, *300*
highest and best use, *313*
holding period, *307*
income approach, *299*
leased fee estates, *322*
mortgage-equity capitalization,
    315
net operating income
    (*NOI*), *301*

physical deterioration, *323*
potential gross income, *300*
replacement cost, *325*
required internal rate of
    return, *306*
residual land value, *312*
reversion value, *307*
sales comparison
    approach, *297*
terminal cap rate (R_T), *307*
unit of comparison, *299*

Useful Web Sites

www.appraisalinstitute.org—The Appraisal Institute gives information on appraisal education, products, news, and conferences.

www.naifa.com/consumerassistance—The National Association of Independent Fee Appraisers, which includes a link to a discussion of the appraisal process.

http://nreionline.com—National Real Estate Investor—a good source of current trends.

www.irei.com—Institutional Real Estate, Inc., provides current news and the research page includes links to research reports provided by several institutional investment firms.

www.buildings.com—*Buildings Magazine* Web site. Good source of articles on buildings and trends affecting the value of buildings.

www.crea.ca—This site, home page for The Canadian Real Estate Association, gives the average housing prices in different Canadian cities and provinces. It also gives recent news related to real estate in Canada.

www.cbre.com/global/research—This site gives U.S. office and industrial vacancy reports. Its Insight Reports section gives information about conditions and forces that shape the United States and Canadian real estate market in industrial, office, and retail areas. Its Global Market View report helps in finding commercial real estate trends including prime office yield and rent, availability and vacancy in the office, industrial, and retail sectors for Asia Pacific, Europe, North America, Latin America, and the Caribbean.

www.realestate-tokyo.com—This site is a good source for residential and commercial real estate properties in Tokyo. It also offers information on apartments and houses to rent in the Tokyo area, properties for sale, offices for rent, and, in general, life in Japan and the real estate market.

www.naea.co.uk—This site is hosted by The National Association of Estate Agents (NAEA), which is the United Kingdom's leading professional body for estate agency personnel, representing the interests of approximately 10,000 members who practice across all aspects of property services both in the United Kingdom and overseas. These include residential and commercial sales and lettings, property management, business transfer, and auctioneering.

www.epra.com—This site is hosted by The European Public Real Estate Association (EPRA), which is a not-for-profit body established under Dutch law. This Web site gives quarterly review reports of developments in the European real estate sector. It also provides different research reports published related to real estate.

www.demographia.com—This site is a very good resource for finding relevant demographic information about different markets spread across the world. Some of the main features of this site are that it gives international housing affordability rankings, different surveys, different economic reports, and different trends related to real estate. It's also a good source to find regulations and policies related to real estate.

www.fedstats.gov—This federal government-sponsored site is a very good resource for finding relevant demographic information about different states in the United States. This site is a gateway to statistics for more than 100 U.S. federal agencies.

www.city-data.com—This site gives very descriptive and interesting profiles of all U.S. cities. It has tens of thousands of city photos not found anywhere else, hundreds of thousands of maps, satellite photos, stats about residents (race, income, ancestries, education, employment, etc.), geographical data, state profiles, crime data, housing, businesses, birthplaces of famous people, political contributions, city government employment, weather, hospitals, schools, libraries, houses, airports, radio and TV stations, zip codes, area codes, user-submitted facts, similar cities list, and comparisons to averages. In sum, it is a very good site for doing real estate analysis.

Questions

1. What is the economic rationale for the cost approach? Under what conditions would the cost approach tend to give the best value estimate?

2. What is the economic rationale for the sales comparison approach? What information is necessary to use this approach? What does it mean for a property to be comparable?

3. What is a capitalization rate? What are the different ways of arriving at this rate for an appraisal?

4. If investors buy properties based on expected future benefits, what is the rationale for appraising a property based on current cap rates without making any income or resale price projections?

5. What is the relationship between a discount rate (or *IRR*) and a capitalization rate? What causes differences between them?

6. What is meant by a unit of comparison? Why is it important?

7. Why do you think appraisers usually use three different approaches when estimating value?

8. Under what conditions should financing be explicitly considered when estimating the value of a property?

9. What is meant by depreciation for the cost approach?

10. When may a "terminal" cap rate be lower than a "going-in" cap rate? When may it be higher?

11. In general, what effect would a *reduction in risk* have on "going-in" cap rates? What would this effect be if it occurred at the same time as an unexpected increase in demand? What would the effect on property values be?

12. What are some of the potential problems with using a "going-in" capitalization rate that is obtained from previous property sales transactions to value a property being offered for sale today?

13. When estimating the reversion value in the year of sale, why is the terminal cap rate applied to *NOI* for the year *after* the holding period?

14. Is a cap rate the same as an *IRR*? Which is generally greater? Why?

15. Discuss the differences between using (1) a terminal cap rate and (2) an appreciation rate in property value when estimating reversion values.

Problems

1. Zenith Investment Company is considering the purchase of an office property. It has done an extensive market analysis and has estimated that based on current market supply/demand relationships, rents, and its estimate of operating expenses, annual *NOI* will be as follows:

Year	NOI
1	$1,000,000
2	1,000,000
3	1,000,000
4	1,200,000
5	1,250,000
6	1,300,000
7	1,339,000
8	1,379,170

A market that is *currently oversupplied* is expected to result in cash flows remaining *flat* for the next three years at $1,000,000. During years 4, 5, and 6, market rents are expected to be higher. It is further expected that beginning in year 7 and every year thereafter, *NOI* will tend to reflect a stable, balanced market and should grow at 3 percent per year indefinitely. Zenith believes that investors should earn a 12 percent return (*r*) on an investment of this kind.

a. Assuming that the investment is expected to produce *NOI* in years 1–8 and is expected to be owned for seven years and then sold, what would be the value for this property today? (*Hint:* Begin by estimating the reversion value at the end of year 7. Recall that the expected *IRR* = 12% and the growth rate (*g*) in year 8 and beyond is estimated to remain level at 3%.)

b. What would the terminal capitalization rate (R_T) be at the end of year 7?

c. What would the "going-in" capitalization rate (*R*) be based on year 1 *NOI*?

d. What explains the difference between the "going-in" and terminal cap rates?

2. Ace Investment Company is considering the purchase of the Apartment Arms project. Next year's *NOI* and cash flow is expected to be $2,000,000, and based on Ace's economic forecast, market supply and demand and vacancy levels appear to be in balance. As a result, *NOI* should increase at 4 percent each year for the foreseeable future. Ace believes that it should earn at least a 13 percent return on its investment.

a. Assuming the above facts, what would the estimated value for the property be now?

b. What "going-in" cap rates *should* be indicated from recently sold properties that are comparable to Apartment Arms?

c. Assuming that in part (*a*) the required return changes to 12 percent, what would the value be now?

d. Assume results in part (*c*). What should the investor now be observing regarding the price of "comparable" sales? What market forces may be accounting for the differences in value between (*a*) and (*c*)?

3. Acme Investors is considering the purchase of the undeveloped Baker Tract of land. It is currently zoned for agricultural use. If purchased, however, Acme must decide how to have the property rezoned for commercial use and then how to develop the site. Based on its market study, Acme has made estimates for the two uses that it deems possible, that is, office or retail. Based on its estimates, the land could be developed as follows:

	Office	Retail
Rentable square feet	100,000	80,000
Rents per square foot	$24.00	$30.00
Operating expense ratio	40%	50%
Avg. growth in *NOI* per annum	3%	3%
Required return (*r*)	13%	14%
Total construction cost per square foot	$100	$100

Which would be the highest and best use of this site?

4. Ajax Investment Company is considering the purchase of land that could be developed into a class A office project. At the present time, Ajax believes that the site could support a 300,000 rentable square foot project with average rents of $20 per square foot and operating expenses equal to 40 percent of that amount. It also expects rents to grow at 3 percent indefinitely and believes that Ajax should earn a 12 percent return (*r*) on investment. The building would cost $100 per square foot to build:

   a. What would the estimated property value *and* land value be under the above assumptions?

   b. If rents are suddenly expected to *grow* at 4 percent indefinitely, what would the property value and land value be now? What percentage change in land value would this be relative to the land value in (*a*)?

   c. Instead of (*b*), suppose that rents will grow by only 1 percent because of excessive supply. What would land value be now? What percentage change would this be relative to the land value in (*a*)?

   d. Suppose that the land owner is asking $12,000,000 for the land. *Under assumptions in part (a)* would this project be feasible?

   e. If the land *must* be acquired for $12,000,000, returning to the assumptions in (*a*), how much of a change in the following would have to occur to make the project feasible? (Consider each item one at a time and hold all other variables constant.)

      (1) Expected return on investment (*r*).

      (2) Expected growth (*g*) in cash flows.

      (3) Building cost.

      (4) Rents.

5. Armor Investment Company is considering the acquisition of a heavily depreciated building on 10 acres of land. It expects to rent the building as a storage facility and expects to collect cash flows equal to $100,000 next year. However, because depreciation is expected to increase, Armor expects cash flows to decline at a rate of 4 percent per year *indefinitely*. Armor expects to earn an *IRR* on investment return (*r*) at 13 percent.

   a. What is the value of this property?

   b. Assume that after five years the building could be demolished and the land could be redeveloped with a strip retail improvement. The latter would produce *NOI* of $200,000 per year, grow at 3 percent per year, and cost $1 million to build. Investors currently earn a 10 percent *IRR* on such investments. How would this affect your estimate of value in (*a*)?

6. Athena Investment Company is considering the purchase of an office property. After a careful review of the market and the leases that are in place, Athena believes that next year's cash flow will be $100,000. It also believes that the cash flow will rise in the amount of $7,000 each year for the foreseeable future. It plans to own the property for at least 10 years. Based on a review of sales of properties that are *now* 10 years older than the subject property, Athena has determined that cap

rates are in a range of .10. Athena believes that it should earn an *IRR* (required return) of at least 12 percent.

 a. What is the estimated value of this office property (assume a .10 terminal cap rate)?

 b. What is the current, or "going-in," cap rate for this property?

 c. What accounts for the difference between the cap rate in (*b*) and the .10 terminal cap rate in (*a*)?

 d. What assumptions are being made regarding future economic conditions when using current comparable sales to estimate terminal cap rates?

7. An investor is considering the purchase of an existing suburban office building approximately five years old. The building, when constructed, was estimated to have an economic life of 50 years, and the building-to-value ratio was 80 percent. Based on current cost estimates, the structure would cost $5 million to reproduce today. The building is expected to continue to wear out evenly over the 50-year period of its economic life. Estimates of other economic costs associated with the improvement are as follows:

Repairable physical depreciation	$300,000 to repair
Functional obsolescence (repairable)	$200,000 to repair
Functional obsolescence (nonrepairable)	$ 25,000 per year rent loss

The land value has been established at $1 million by comparable sales in the area. The investor believes that an appropriate opportunity cost for any deferred outlays or costs should be 12 percent per year. What would be the estimated value for this property?

8. ABC Residential Investors, LLP, is considering the purchase of a 120-unit apartment complex in Steel City, Pennsylvania. A market study of the area reveals that an average rental of $600 per month per unit could be realized in the appropriate market area. During the last six months, two very comparable apartment complexes have sold in the same market area. The Oaks, a 140-unit project, sold for $9 million. Its rental schedule indicates that the average rent per unit is $550 per month. Palms, a 90-unit complex, is presently renting units at $650 per month, and its selling price was $6.6 million. The mix of number of bedrooms and sizes of units for both complexes is very similar to that of the subject property, and both appear to have normal vacancy rates of about 10 percent annually. All rents are net as tenants pay all utilities and expenses.

 a. Based on the data provided here, how would an appraiser establish an estimate of value?

 b. What other information would be desirable in reaching a conclusion about the probable value for the property?

9. The *NOI* for a small income property is expected to be $150,000 for the first year. Financing will be based on a 1.2 *DCR* applied to the first year *NOI,* will have a 10 percent interest rate, and will be amortized over 20 years with monthly payments. The *NOI* will increase 3 percent per year after the first year. The investor expects to hold the property for five years. The resale price is estimated by applying a 9 percent terminal capitalization rate to the sixth-year *NOI.* Investors require a 12 percent rate of return on *equity* (equity yield rate) for this type of property.

 a. What is the present value of the equity interest in the property?

 b. What is the total present value of the property (mortgage and equity interests)?

 c. Based on your answer to part (*b*), what is the implied overall capitalization rate?

10. Sammie's Club wants to buy a 320,000-square-feet distribution facility on the northern edge of a large midwestern city. The subject facility is presently renting for $4 per square foot. Based on recent market activity, two properties have sold within a two-mile distance from the subject facility and are very comparable in size, design, and age. One facility is 350,000 square feet and is presently being leased for $3.90 per square foot annually. The second facility contains 300,000 square feet and is being leased for $4.10 per square foot. Market data indicate that current vacancies and operating expenses should run approximately 50 percent of gross income for these facilities. The first facility sold for $9.4 million, and the second sold for $7.9 million.

    a. Using a "going-in" or direct capitalization rate approach to value, how would you estimate value for the subject distribution facility?

    b. What additional information would be desirable before the final direct rate (*R*) is selected?

11. Refer to the highest and best use analysis in Exhibit 10–9. Suppose that the warehouse income would grow at 3 percent per year instead of 2 percent. Does this change the highest and best use of the site? If so, what is the new implied land value?

12. You are an analyst with Perception Partners and have been asked to make pricing recommendations regarding the acquisition of Rose Garden Apartments. This project was built five years ago and contains 250 units in a suburban market area. The broker that brought the project to your attention indicates that the asking price will be $27,000,000. She has also provided the attached information based on a market survey showing data from three sales of comparable apartment properties that have occurred in a one-mile radius of Rose Garden during the past six months (see table below).

    Perception believes that market returns (*IRR*) should be in a range of 8 percent (compounded annually) for this type of investment. Perception (1) plans to own the property for five years and then sell it and (2) believes that rents will grow at 3 percent per year. At the present time,

	Rose Garden	Comparable 1	Comparable 2	Comparable 3
Age	5	6	7	10
Acres	14	10	8.75	12.5
# Units	250	200	175	250
Units per acre	17.9	20.0	20.0	20.0
Price		$20,000,000	$16,625,000	$21,000,000
Bedroom / Bathroom:	$ Rent / # Units / SF:	$ Rent / # Units / SF:	$ Rent / # Units / SF:	$ Rent / # Units / SF:
1 / 1	830 / 75 / 780	820 / 60 / 770	791 / 53 / 740	775 / 75 / 750
1 / 1.5	850 / 50 / 810	835 / 40 / 800	810 / 35 / 780	795 / 50 / 775
2 / 2	1,040 / 100 / 960	1,030 / 80 / 950	1,000 / 70 / 920	970 / 110 / 900
3 / 2	1,270 / 25 / 1,180	1,250 / 20 / 1,170	1,200 / 18 / 1,130	1,170 / 15 / 1,100
Weighted average	962 / × / 898	950 / × / 888	925 / × / 864	888.5 / × / 842
Rentable area (SF)	224,500	177,600	150,130	210,500
Vacancy	5%	5%	5%	5%
Operating expense	40%	40%	40%	45%
Gross rent	$2,886,000	$2,280,000	$1,928,076	$2,665,500
GIM		8.77	8.62	7.88
Net income	$1,645,000	$1,300,000	$1,099,000	$1,393,000
Cap rate		0.0650	0.0661	0.0663
Wt. Avg month rent/unit	$962	$950	$918	$889
Rent per sq. ft.	$12.855	$12.838	$12.843	$12.663
Price per unit		$100,000	$95,000	$84,000
Price per sq. ft.		$112.61	$110.74	$99.76
Quality	Excellent	Very good	Average	Average
Location	Excellent	Desirable	Desirable	Slightly less desirable
Parking spaces per unit	2.00	1.75	1.60	1.50
Security gate	Yes	Yes	Yes	No
Washer/dryer	Yes	Yes	Yes	Not in 1 / 1
A/C	Yes	Yes	Yes	Yes
Built-ins	Yes	Yes	Yes	Yes
Covered parking	Yes	Yes	No	No
Free cable TV	No	No	Yes	Yes
Fireplaces	No	No	Yes	No
Exercise room	No	No	No	Yes
Swimming pool/BBQ	Yes	Yes	Yes	Yes

Perception believes that the sale price that it hopes to achieve at the end of year 5 should be based on a "*going-out*" cap rate that will be .005 greater than the "*going-in*" cap rate. The property is to be acquired on an "*all cash*" basis.

  a. Prepare an analysis of Rose Garden with the three comparable properties. Based on this analysis, do you think that the "going-in" cap rate today for Rose Garden should be *higher* or *lower* than the cap rates shown for the comparables?

  b. If Rose Garden is acquired for $27,000,000, what would be the "going-in" cap rate at that price? How does this compare to cap rates for the comparables?

  c. If Rose Garden is acquired for $27,000,000, would the 8 percent required return be achieved over the five-year period of ownership?

13. An investor is considering the purchase of a small office building. The *NOI* is expected to be the following: year 1, $200,000; year 2, $210,000; year 3, $220,000; year 4, $230,000; year 5, $240,000. The property will be sold at the end of year 5 and the investor believes that the *property value* should have appreciated at a rate of 3 percent *per year* during the five-year period. The investor plans to pay all cash for the property and wants to earn a 10 percent return on investment (*IRR*) compounded annually.

  a. What should be the property value (*REV*) at the end of year 5?

  b. What should be the present value of the property today?

  c. How can the value at the end of year 5 be estimated today if the present value today is unknown?

  d. Based on your answer in (*b*), if the *building* could be reproduced for $2,300,000 today, what would be the underlying value of the *land*?

14. **Spreadsheet Problem.** Refer to the Ch10_Mort Eq Cap tab in the Excel Workbook provided on the Web site. This replicates the example discussed on page 315 of the book.

www.mhhe.com/bf15e

  a. Suppose that there is an aggressive lender that is willing to allow the debt coverage ratio (*DCR*) to be as low as 1.0. Keep all other assumptions, including the loan interest rate and equity discount rate (before-tax equity yield), the same. How does this affect the amount that can be borrowed and the property value?

  b. Refer to part (*a*). Is it reasonable to assume that the loan interest rate and equity discount rate would be the same? If not, would you expect each to be higher or lower? Why?

15. **Spreadsheet Problem.** Refer to the Ch10_H&BU tab in the Excel Workbook provided on the Web site, which replicates the highest and best use analysis example in the chapter.

www.mhhe.com/bf15e

  a. Suppose that the construction cost is $3.5 million for office, $6.5 million for retail, $2.5 million for apartment, and $3.5 million for warehouse. How does this change the highest and best use of the site and the land value?

  b. Use the same construction costs as part (*a*) but assume that office income would increase by 4 percent per year instead of 3 percent per year. Does this change the highest and best use of the site and the land value?

16. **Spreadsheet and ARGUS Problem.** Use the Oakwood Apartments.SF file provided on the book Web site to use with ARGUS. This replicates the Oakwood Apartments example in the book. This same example is also solved with Excel in the Ch10_Apartment tab in the Excel Workbook provided on the Web site. Suppose that investors required only a 9 percent rate of return (discount rate) instead of 11 percent and the terminal cap rate used to estimate the resale price was 8 percent instead of 9 percent.

www.mhhe.com/bf15e

  a. Use the Excel template to see how your answer would change.

  b. Use ARGUS to see how your answer would change.

REIWise Inputs and Output for Apartment Analysis

In the chapter, we showed sample output from REIWise that had the same answer for Oakwood Apartments as we discussed in the text. In this appendix, we show the inputs to the program to get these results.

Exhibit 10A–1 shows the general inputs for Oakwood Apartments. This includes the purchase price and resale information. The value of the land was made equal to the purchase price in this example just not to have any tax depreciation calculated since we are doing a before tax analysis. But a significant portion of the value would still be in the building. We are just not separating that out for this analysis. The resale price will be based on a cap rate applied to the NOI one year after the holding period (year 1 for the new buyer). The discount rate will be used to calculate a value for the property.

EXHIBIT 10A–1
General Inputs

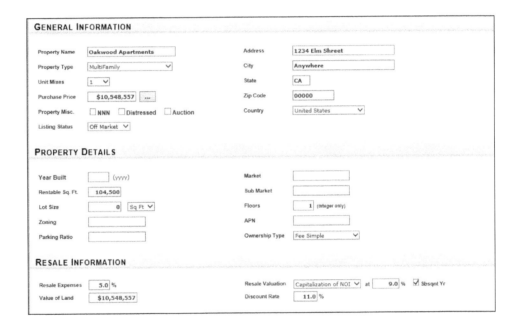

GENERAL INFORMATION

Property Name	Oakwood Apartments	Address	1234 Elm Shreet
Property Type	MultiFamily	City	Anywhere
Unit Mixes	1	State	CA
Purchase Price	$10,548,557 ...	Zip Code	00000
Property Misc.	☐ NNN ☐ Distressed ☐ Auction	Country	United States
Listing Status	Off Market		

PROPERTY DETAILS

Year Built	(yyyy)	Market	
Rentable Sq. Ft.	104,500	Sub Market	
Lot Size	0 Sq Ft	Floors	1 (integer only)
Zoning		APN	
Parking Ratio		Ownership Type	Fee Simple

RESALE INFORMATION

Resale Expenses	5.0 %	Resale Valuation	Capitalization of NOI at 9.0 % ☑ Sbsqnt Yr
Value of Land	$10,548,557	Discount Rate	11.0 %

Exhibit 10A–2 shows the rental income. For Oakwood Apartments there is only one rental type but in other cases there could be more than one with different rental information and vacancy for each. There is also input for miscellaneous income such as the laundry income in this example.

Exhibit 10A–3 shows the inputs for the expenses including property management which is a percent of gross operating income in this case. An allowance for replacement reserves was not included in this example and none of the expenses are reimbursable by the tenant. In an office building example in the next chapter we will see an example of expense reimbursements.

EXHIBIT 10A–2
Rental Income

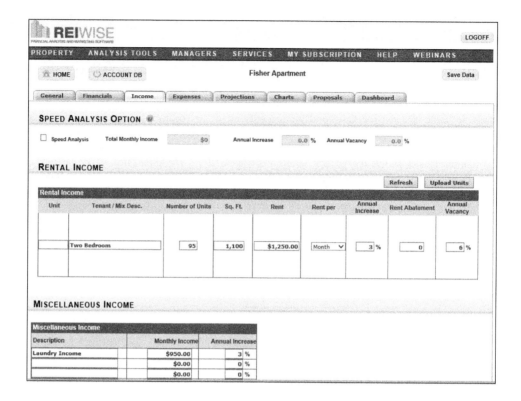

EXHIBIT 10A–3
Expenses

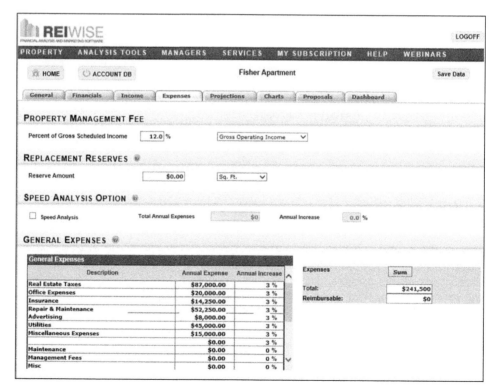

Exhibit 10A–4 repeats the output for the NOI each year of the holding period that was in the chapter and Exhibit 10A–5 includes the value that is calculated based on sale in each of the possible holding periods as was also shown in the chapter. Again, we are focusing on the value for a five year holding period in this case.

EXHIBIT 10A–4
Projected NOI

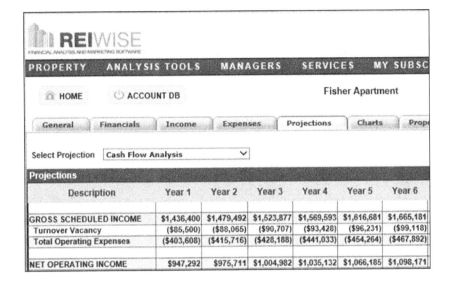

Description	Year 1	Year 2	Year 3	Year 4	Year 5	Year 6
GROSS SCHEDULED INCOME	$1,436,400	$1,479,492	$1,523,877	$1,569,593	$1,616,681	$1,665,181
Turnover Vacancy	($85,500)	($88,065)	($90,707)	($93,428)	($96,231)	($99,118)
Total Operating Expenses	($403,608)	($415,716)	($428,188)	($441,033)	($454,264)	($467,892)
NET OPERATING INCOME	$947,292	$975,711	$1,004,982	$1,035,132	$1,066,185	$1,098,171

EXHIBIT 10A–5
Projected Returns and Present Values

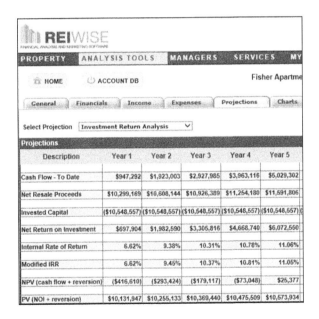

Description	Year 1	Year 2	Year 3	Year 4	Year 5
Cash Flow - To Date	$947,292	$1,923,003	$2,927,985	$3,963,116	$5,029,302
Net Resale Proceeds	$10,299,169	$10,608,144	$10,926,389	$11,254,180	$11,591,806
Invested Capital	($10,548,557)	($10,548,557)	($10,548,557)	($10,548,557)	($10,548,557)
Net Return on Investment	$697,904	$1,982,590	$3,305,816	$4,668,740	$6,072,550
Internal Rate of Return	6.62%	9.38%	10.31%	10.78%	11.06%
Modified IRR	6.62%	9.45%	10.37%	10.81%	11.05%
NPV (cash flow + reversion)	($416,610)	($293,424)	($179,117)	($73,048)	$25,377
PV (NOI + reversion)	$10,131,947	$10,255,133	$10,369,440	$10,475,509	$10,573,934

Exhibit 10A–6 shows one of several charts that are automatically created by REIWise that an analyst could incorporate into his or her report. In this case the trend in gross income and expenses. This is done automatically for 20 years even though we have indicated that the property will be sold after five years.

EXHIBIT 10A–6
Graph of Gross Income and Expenses

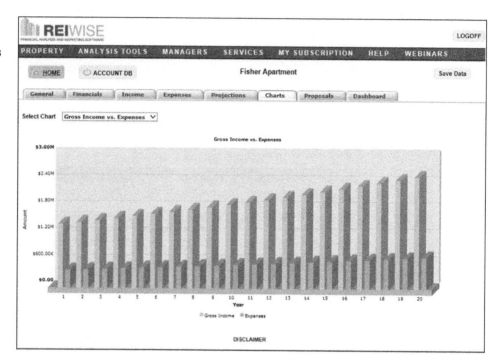

Chapter 11

Investment Analysis and Taxation of Income Properties

The investor must consider many variables when acquiring income properties, among them market factors, occupancy rates, tax influences, the level of risk, the amount of debt financing, and the proper procedures to use when measuring return on investment. Lenders are concerned with many of the same questions because these factors affect the value and marketability of the properties being used as collateral for loans. In addition, lenders are concerned with whether properties they finance will generate enough cash flow to cover the loan payments. This chapter provides the framework for analyzing additional issues addressed in many of the remaining chapters in this text.

Motivations for Investing

We have seen that there are many different categories of income property. We now consider why investors and lenders choose investments in one or more of these properties. We first consider the equity investor. The term **equity** refers to funds invested by an "owner," or the person acquiring the property. The particular form of ownership could be any of the freehold estates discussed in Chapter 2. That is, equity funds could be invested in a fee simple estate, a leased fee estate, a leasehold estate, and so forth. We contrast equity funds with debt, which is provided by a lender with the real estate used as collateral for the loan as discussed in Chapter 2.

What motivates the investor to make an equity investment in income properties? First, investors anticipate that market demand for space in the property will be sufficient to produce net income after collecting rents and paying operating expenses. This income constitutes part of an investor's return (before considering taxes and financing costs).

Second, the investor anticipates selling properties after holding them for some period of time. (A discussion regarding how long a property will be held is discussed in Chapter 14.) Investors often expect prices to rise over the holding period, particularly in an inflationary environment. Thus, any price increase also contributes to an investor's return.

A third reason for investing in real estate is to achieve diversification. By this we mean that most investors want to hold a variety of different types of investments such as stocks, bonds, money market funds, and real estate.

A final reason for investing in real estate, which may be more important to some investors than others, is the preferential tax benefits that may result. Because of favorable tax treatment of real estate, historically investors have paid little or no taxes on returns from real estate investments for many years. Although many of these favorable tax benefits have been eliminated over the years, an understanding of real estate tax law is still important. Investors must be able to understand changes in such laws and interpret their impact on rents and real estate values. As tax laws change, investor decisions regarding purchase prices, how much financing should be used, and when to sell the property are also affected.

Motivations for Investing in Income Properties

1. Rate of return.
2. Price appreciation.
3. Diversification.
4. Tax benefits.

Real Estate Market Characteristics and Investment Strategies

Based on our discussion of economic base analysis and local supply and demand analysis in previous chapters, it should be evident that expected market conditions are important when making estimates of future cash flows. For example, if supply and demand for a given property type are considered to be out of balance and these conditions are expected to persist, the effects on vacancies and rents should be taken into account in forecasts of cash flows. If done properly, estimates of value and investment returns will reflect these expectations. What follows is a description of (1) the cyclical nature of the real estate market and (2) a description of various *investment styles* that are widely used in all segments of the investment community (stocks, bonds, real estate, etc.). As the reader will come to realize, descriptions used to identify these "styles of investing" usually correspond to some underlying expectations regarding market conditions. We *do not advocate* any one or any combination of such investment styles. Nonetheless, these terms and descriptions are widely used by investment professionals to help classify and describe conditions in investment markets, and the reader should be aware of what they are.

The "Real Estate Cycle"

It may be useful at this point to discuss the **"real estate cycle,"** that is, the cyclical nature of the real estate industry as background material for the more specific investment styles and strategies we will discuss. Some underlying facts regarding the real estate industry are: (1) it is a very large market, in terms of both the number of properties and square footage, (2) it is highly competitive, and (3) ownership is highly fragmented, that is, no one owner or developer controls a significant share of the real estate market in major cities in the United States.

It is also a fact that when local real estate owners and investors sense that vacancy rates are declining and rents are rising, it generally implies that the amount of leaseable space is also declining. As a result, more development may be feasible. Consequently, developers begin to conduct highest and best use studies for specific sites and also analyze markets to determine if additional space, if developed, can be leased profitably. Because many competing developers may sense this opportunity simultaneously, they may all begin to obtain financing and develop at once in order to satisfy the demand. Even though there may be a definite need for additional space, the potential for overdevelopment will exist as each developer rushes to deliver additional space to the market before competitors. There is no way to determine exactly how much space should be developed because the depth and

EXHIBIT 11–1
The "Real Estate Cycle"

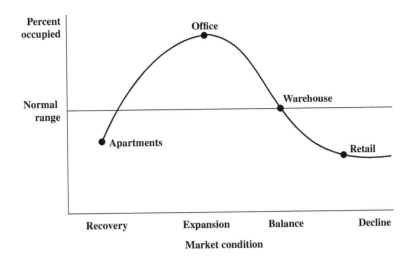

extent of demand are difficult to predict. As a result, the real estate industry is sometimes said to be prone to periodic *cycles* of "overdevelopment." Because of the highly competitive nature of the industry and its difficulty in forecasting demand, there are certain times when excess supply is unintentionally produced, thereby increasing vacancy rates, reducing rents, and causing volatility in property values.

The cyclical nature of this market pattern is shown in Exhibit 11–1, which shows a *hypothetical cycle* for all property types relative to a "normal" level of occupancy for each property type. All points above the normal occupancy range for each property type indicate a condition of high occupancy and rising rents. This is a condition when further development is likely. All areas below the normal range indicate a condition of low occupancy and the potential for declining rents, a condition not suitable for development.[1] To illustrate, based on the pattern shown in Exhibit 11–1, apartment properties are in a recovery phase of the cycle after experiencing a condition of either excess supply or lack of demand. As implied in the exhibit, this property class is expected to continue to "recover" as the occupancy rate improves and demand increases relative to supply.

On the other hand, office properties are shown to be in a condition of high occupancy due to either excess demand or a shortage of rentable space. This market imbalance is expected to result in rising occupancy and higher rents. Therefore, this market segment may be expected to undergo future development. Warehouse properties appear to be in a well-balanced condition. No material change in occupancy or rents is expected and, as a result, no unexpected amount of development is likely. Retail properties, however, are in a declining occupancy phase of the cycle due to either an excessive amount of space for lease or lack of demand. The graph also indicates that retail occupancy is expected to decline further.

In summary, Exhibit 11–1 is intended to provide a framework of the supply/demand balance for each property type at one point in time. Based on the current stage in this cycle, investors considering investing in apartments should anticipate a period of vacancies and soft rents in cash flow projections even though this market is in recovery. Office property investors should expect to enjoy a period of low vacancies and higher-than-normal rents. However, these investors should also expect more office development and, therefore,

[1] It should not be inferred from this exhibit that the normal level of occupancy shown in the graph is exactly the same for each property. This is a conceptual exhibit and is intended to depict general market conditions.

competition that will eventually result in rents, occupancies, and cash flows trending back to normal levels. Warehouse investors should not expect material changes in vacancies or rents. Retail property investors, on the other hand, should expect deteriorating conditions to continue and should forecast a continuing decline and an eventual turning point in cash flow forecasts. The time period associated with the cycle in Exhibit 11–1 is very difficult to forecast. It may be expected to exist only for a short period and must be continuously reevaluated (1) as new construction is being completed or (2) as the market experiences an unanticipated surge in demand for space. While the illustration in Exhibit 11–1 is very simplistic, it does serve as a starting point for investors in understanding the nature of the supply/demand balance by property type and should help the reader understand the general strategies that follow.

Investment Strategies

Thus far, we have approached the subject of pricing and investing in properties by stressing that investors should carefully make forecasts of future cash flows given the expected market supply and demand and capital market conditions. This section contains a summary of some strategies or styles that are followed by real estate investors and portfolio managers. These styles are chosen with the intent of realizing superior investment performance. Think about these styles in conjunction with the discussion of the real estate cycle and formulate a critique of each approach. Exhibit 11–2 provides you with a general perspective on real estate market cycles and investment strategies. It should be obvious that many of these strategies overlap and may include combinations of one or more strategies. For example, an investor may combine a sector strategy with a timing strategy in that sector. Nevertheless, becoming familiar with these strategies may be helpful in understanding much of the industry terminology that is used when describing the current state of a real estate market and the motivations of those seeking real estate investments.

EXHIBIT 11–2
Investment Styles Used by Real Estate Investors

A. Investing in Core Properties

This style is based on a goal of acquiring existing, seasoned, relatively low-risk properties that are at least 80 percent leased to tenants with good credit. These properties may also be acquired as a foundation for building a larger portfolio. The goal is to realize a relatively stable cash flow with returns that are competitive with comparable properties. No major change in the operation of the property or major capital improvements would be expected.

B. Investing in Core "Plus" Properties

This strategy combines core investment with a strategy to make minor changes in the management of the property with a releasing program or by making some limited and specific capital improvements. These latter changes tend to be very specific and are targeted toward increasing rents and outperforming competing properties in the same submarket.

C. Property Sector Investing

The **sector investing** style is based on the belief that over the long term, based on economic and demographic research, one *property type* will outperform other property sectors. For example, if research shows that prospects for the office sector are excellent and that this sector will outperform the retail, apartment, and warehouse property sectors over the long term, then an investor would specialize in office properties as a preferred sector investment. After the sector is chosen, then, based on market research, specific properties in specific cities and locations would be acquired. (This style is analogous to mutual funds that are created to invest only in stocks in specific industry sectors, such as the computer industry, energy, and health care companies.)

EXHIBIT 11–2
Continued

D. Contrarian Investing

The **contrarian investing** strategy is based on the premise that some major economic, technological, or other event will make the investment outlook for a given property type poor and "out of favor" among investors. Contrarians believe that investors tend to overreact to negative news and tend to oversell out-of-favor properties. For example, investors may believe that shopping on the Internet may have a very negative effect on retail properties; other investors may believe that outsourcing to overseas manufacturers may reduce the demand for industrial warehouse properties in the United States. If the majority of investors believe that these investments will perform poorly and sell them, a contrarian may wait until these properties become available at very low prices, and then *purchase* them with the expectation that after other investors realize that this property sector has been oversold, a price recovery will occur.

E. Market Timing

The **market timing** strategy is based on the belief that with an understanding of the stage of each property type in the real estate cycle and future economic conditions, some investors have the ability to predict when to buy or sell properties. For example, in Exhibit 11–1, if investors believe that occupancy and rents will definitely improve and that the apartment market has definitely passed the bottom of its cycle and is in a recovery phase, then apartments would become a target investment for a "market timer." Similarly, if further decline is expected in the retail property sector in a given market *because of excess supply,* a market timer may attempt to "time or wait" to enter this market when it appears the excess supply of space is about to be eliminated, and then acquire properties in the hope of realizing a profit as market prices cycle upward. (Note that this strategy may be different from that of contrarians, who tend to respond to external events such as e-commerce, while timers tend to emphasize current supply/demand or cyclical conditions in their evaluation of property markets.) Many market timers also believe that they should sell when a specific property type reaches a cyclical peak and buy a different property type in a *different* phase of the cycle. This variant of timing is sometimes referred to as a property sector *rotation strategy.*

F. Growth Investing

The **growth investing** strategy is based on "discovering," through research, those properties in markets that are likely to experience significant or above-average *appreciation in value.* Investors in these properties believe that economic conditions favor demand for specific property types in specific growth markets. This investment style is heavily dependent on the value of market research and the ability to understand changes in the economic environment/technology, and its effects on all real estate sectors. For example, growth in e-commerce and technology may be expected to *favor* warehouse properties in specific strategic geographic locations. A growth investor would search those strategic locations to invest in warehouse properties. These properties would be purchased with the expectation that as more investors discover these markets and properties, they will make investments and drive prices up, thereby producing superior appreciation in property values. Investors using the strategy should expect to bear more risk than average as these markets are apt to be more volatile as they expand and contract in concert with the industries that are driving the demand for space.

G. Value Investing

The **value investing** strategy is based more on a "tried and true" performance approach where research is directed toward finding those properties that have been "overlooked" by investors. Using careful research efforts, value investors try to identify properties with the ability to produce greater-than-expected income and appreciation. For example, investors may prefer to invest in office properties that are located in central business districts and leased on a long-term basis to many large corporate tenants. In this case, rental income is more assured as tenants are large tenants with good credit histories.

EXHIBIT 11–2
Continued

Because many leases may be about ready to expire, the ability of landlords to increase rents may be good. In trying to execute this strategy, investors attempt to focus on properties that have been overlooked by other investors and, therefore, appear to be undervalued.

H. Strategy as to Size of Property

This strategy is based on a preference for a subsector within a property type because investor/owners believe that they can better understand the operation of tenant-users and, therefore, better understand the demand for space in that subsector. As a result, such property owners tend to specialize in one property sector believing that it may be more cost-effective to lease and manage that property type. For example, an investor/owner may choose to invest *only* in neighborhood or community size retail shopping centers and not invest in larger regional malls. Or, an investor may prefer to invest in small, low-rise suburban office buildings rather than high-rise buildings located in central cities. They believe that a better understanding of these property subsectors and the tenants in these market sectors will be more profitable than would be the case if they invested in larger, more complicated, properties.

I. Strategy as to Tenants

This strategy is based on a preference for properties leased to multiple tenants or leased to a single or very few tenants. In the former case, owners may prefer to take the risk of higher tenant turnover because the ability to adjust rents to market levels more frequently is also greater. On the other hand, many investors may prefer properties that are leased to single tenants. These properties may be less risky because of low tenant turnover and the creditworthiness of tenants. These properties may be preferred even though they may not offer the opportunity for frequent adjustment in rents.

J. Arbitrage Investing

The **arbitrage investing** strategy is based on the ability of investors to recognize differences in prices that buyers are willing to pay for the same real estate investments in different markets. For example, this strategy has been used by investors who buy properties directly in *private* market transactions and then earn a profit by creating a publicly traded entity, such as an REIT, and issuing stock to the public. In this case, positive arbitrage profits are realized when the total market value of the REIT stock sold to the public exceeds the acquisition cost of the individual properties plus the cost of issuing stock. This strategy may also be reversed by purchasing all shares of a REIT and "taking it private," and then selling properties to private investors at higher prices than reflected in share prices of the REIT.

K. Turnaround/Special Situation

Turnaround investing strategies are generally based on the belief that successful investments can be made by investors who see opportunities by changing or modifying the use of existing properties. For example, investors may:

1. Acquire underperforming or undermanaged properties. After a period of more intensive leasing, renovation, and property management, these properties can be sold one at a time, such that the total amount received when all properties are sold exceeds the initial total cost.
2. Acquire "real estate rich" firms that own an extensive amount of real estate in their business. These firms may not realize that the market value of their real estate is not fully reflected in the value of their business operation. In this case, investors realize that the value of the business and the value of the real estate are separable. Consequently, a gain may be earned by acquiring the firm and then selling its real estate. The necessary space to run the business could then be leased. If successful, the value of the real estate and the value of the business after separation would be greater than the previously combined entity.

EXHIBIT 11–2
Concluded

L. Opportunistic Investing
This strategy involves acquiring properties from investors in financial difficulty or properties needing renovation, upgrading, or repositioning. The success of this investment plan is usually dependent on:

1. The ability to purchase properties at a discount.
2. Management understanding of the opportunity and how to upgrade, modify, or perhaps reposition the property (e.g., from office use to retail use). The success of such an investment may also be dependent on an exit strategy such as:
   a. Market acceptance of the repositioned assets.
   b. The ability of buyers to obtain financing to purchase such assets.

M. Investing in "Trophy" or "Blue Chip" Properties
This strategy is based on a "blue chip" approach to investing; that is, only very visible, well-located properties (**trophy properties**) should be the targets for acquisition. While similar to the value investing strategy discussed above, investors in trophy assets believe that properties with some unique historical, architectural, or locational attribute (e.g., Empire State Building, Rockefeller Center, Transamerica Tower, Mall of America, Watergate Apartments) will prove to be excellent investments for the long term.

N. Development—"Value Add"
This strategy usually involves the acquisition of land, design of the building, and a leasing program to reach stable occupancy. By embarking on this riskier strategy, investors believe that more value creation may occur through development, design, leasing, and so forth, thereby leading to superior investment returns than would be the case with investing in existing properties.

Market Analysis

Investors and appraisers perform a **market analysis** to evaluate the supply and demand for the type of property that they are evaluating as an investment. The demand for space comes from potential tenants who desire to use the space for their business. The supply of space comes from investors who have purchased or developed buildings and are willing to make that space available for rent. This is often referred to as the *space market,* as discussed previously in Chapter 9.

In Chapter 9, we discussed the different drivers of the demand for space for different property types. To illustrate market analysis, we will consider the market for office space in a hypothetical city. The key driver for office space comes from employment by companies that use a high proportion of office space, such as those in the finance, insurance, and real estate industries, as well as other service industries (e.g., lawyers, accountants, engineers, etc.). Data from the U.S. Bureau of Labor Statistics (*http://data .bls.gov*) are typically used to determine historical trends in office employment.

Exhibit 11–3 shows the historical employment in the office sector for a hypothetical city for the past 20 years, including the current year (0), which we assume is just ending. We see that the employment growth rate (in the last column) has varied over time, as typically happens due to the business cycle. Employment growth was strong in the early years and then slowed, becoming negative for several years due to a recession. It has been improving since then, although employment growth for the current year (0) appears to be trending downward.

Exhibit 11–4 graphs the historic employment growth rate. As employment growth increases, the demand for space increases and vice versa. Businesses typically use a certain amount of **space** (square feet) **per employee.** For example, historically the amount of

EXHIBIT 11–3
Historical Office
Employment

End Year	Beginning of Year Office Employment	Change in Office Employment	End of Year Office Employment	Change in Employment (%)
−19	22,800	1,000	23,800	4.39%
−18	23,800	1,200	25,000	5.04
−17	25,000	1,400	26,400	5.60
−16	26,400	600	27,000	2.27
−15	27,000	408	27,408	1.51
−14	27,408	208	27,616	0.76
−13	27,616	0	27,616	0.00
−12	27,616	−216	27,401	−0.78
−11	27,401	−435	26,966	−1.59
−10	26,966	−222	26,744	−0.82
−9	26,744	0	26,744	0.00
−8	26,744	500	27,244	1.87
−7	27,244	700	27,944	2.57
−6	27,944	1,000	28,944	3.58
−5	28,944	1,100	30,044	3.80
−4	30,044	1,250	31,294	4.16
−3	31,294	816	32,110	2.61
−2	32,110	600	32,710	1.87
−1	32,710	560	33,270	1.71
0	33,270	306	33,576	0.92

office space per employee tends to average about 250 square feet.[2] Thus, for each additional office employee, there will be a need for 250 additional square feet of office space. The number of square feet per employee may vary depending on whether the property is a high-rise downtown building, a suburban office building, and so on.

Exhibit 11–5 shows the historical amount of office space occupied in our hypothetical city. For larger cities in the United States, data such as these are usually available from organizations such as the Building Owners and Managers Association (BOMA) or large real estate brokerage companies.

EXHIBIT 11–4
Historic Employment
Growth Rate

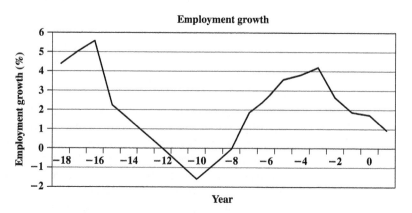

[2] Given advances in electronic/communication technology, this average has probably declined as less physical space is required per employee "on site." Tenants may now rely more on data centers, "cloud computing," and other technologies, which reduce the amount of square footage per employee required in some buildings. An increase in demand for alternative structures which "house" these technologies is now occurring in more remote locations. These properties typically make space available at a lower rent, and therefore lower costs to users.

EXHIBIT 11–5
Occupied Office
Space

End Year	Beginning of Year Occupied Space	Absorption	End of Year Occupied Space
–19	5,700,000	250,000	5,950,000
–18	5,950,000	300,000	6,250,000
–17	6,250,000	350,000	6,600,000
–16	6,600,000	150,000	6,750,000
–15	6,750,000	–35,000	6,715,000
–14	6,715,000	–87,041	6,627,959
–13	6,627,959	–138,082	6,489,877
–12	6,489,877	–132,849	6,357,027
–11	6,357,027	–154,802	6,202,225
–10	6,202,225	–184,831	6,017,394
–9	6,017,394	0	6,017,394
–8	6,017,394	248,720	6,266,114
–7	6,266,114	300,720	6,566,834
–6	6,566,834	235,000	6,801,834
–5	6,801,834	408,720	7,210,554
–4	7,210,554	300,000	7,510,554
–3	7,510,554	356,470	7,867,024
–2	7,867,024	310,552	8,177,575
–1	8,177,575	140,000	8,317,575
0	8,317,575	–91,352	8,226,224

The term *absorption* refers to the amount of space that was leased by tenants for the year, that is, "absorbed" by the market. Note that in some years the absorption was negative, indicating that less space was being occupied at the end of the year than at the beginning of the year. This often happens during the contraction phase of the business cycle, when companies are reducing the number of employees.

If we divide the total amount of space that was occupied at the end of each year by the number of office employees working at the end of the year, we can determine what the historical usage of space per employee was for each year. Exhibit 11–6 shows the results.

From Exhibit 11–6 we see that the amount of space per employee does vary over the business cycle. As the economy weakens, businesses tend to reduce the amount of space per employee in order to save rent and reduce operating costs. When the economy gets stronger, businesses tend to increase the number of employees and provide more space per employee. This may be the result of adding more computers and equipment so as to be competitive with other employers. This is important when attempting to forecast the amount of office space needed in the future, as we will consider later in this section.

The term "net absorption" is sometimes used to describe the amount of absorption less the amount of new space supplied to the market. Supply of space is covered in the next section.

Supply of Space

We now consider the supply of office space that is available for occupancy in the market. Exhibit 11–7 shows the historical inventory of space available in the market. This includes space that has been added through new construction and space that has been subtracted due to the demolition of obsolete buildings that were no longer the highest and best use of the site.

To this point, we have determined the annual amount of space occupied, or demand for space (Exhibit 11–6) as well as the existing inventory of space, or supply (Exhibit 11–7). Using these two data series we can calculate the amount of vacant space in the market and the vacancy rate. This is shown in Exhibit 11–8.

EXHIBIT 11–6
Space per Employee

End Year	End of Year Occupied Space	End of Year Office Employment	End of Year Space per Employee (sq. ft.)
−19	5,950,000	23,800	250
−18	6,250,000	25,000	250
−17	6,600,000	26,400	250
−16	6,750,000	27,000	250
−15	6,715,000	27,408	245
−14	6,627,959	27,616	240
−13	6,489,877	27,616	235
−12	6,357,027	27,401	232
−11	6,202,225	26,966	230
−10	6,017,394	26,744	225
−9	6,017,394	26,744	225
−8	6,266,114	27,244	230
−7	6,566,834	27,944	235
−6	6,801,834	28,944	235
−5	7,210,554	30,044	240
−4	7,510,554	31,294	240
−3	7,867,024	32,110	245
−2	8,177,575	32,710	250
−1	8,317,575	33,270	250
0	8,226,224	33,576	245

Market Rents

Now that we have seen how supply, demand, and the occupancy (or vacancy) rates have changed over time, we can relate these changes to rental rates over the same time period. Exhibit 11–9 shows the market rent trends and occupancy rates. We can see that rental rates

EXHIBIT 11–7
Supply of Office Space

End Year	Beginning of Year Office Supply	New Construction	Demolition	End of Year Office Supply
−19	6,500,000	400,000	0	6,900,000
−18	6,900,000	300,000	0	7,200,000
−17	7,200,000	100,000	0	7,300,000
−16	7,300,000	50,000	0	7,350,000
−15	7,350,000	0	0	7,350,000
−14	7,350,000	0	0	7,350,000
−13	7,350,000	25,000	20,000	7,355,000
−12	7,355,000	75,000	0	7,430,000
−11	7,430,000	50,000	0	7,480,000
−10	7,480,000	50,000	0	7,530,000
−9	7,530,000	100,000	0	7,630,000
−8	7,630,000	200,000	0	7,830,000
−7	7,830,000	300,000	0	8,130,000
−6	8,130,000	400,000	50,000	8,480,000
−5	8,480,000	300,000	0	8,780,000
−4	8,780,000	250,000	0	9,030,000
−3	9,030,000	100,000	0	9,130,000
−2	9,130,000	100,000	0	9,230,000
−1	9,230,000	50,000	0	9,280,000
0	9,280,000	0	0	9,280,000

EXHIBIT 11–8
Historic Occupancy and Vacancy Rates

End Year	End of Year Occupied Space	End of Year Office Supply	End of Year Occupancy Rate (%)	End of Year Vacancy Rate (%)
−19	5,950,000	6,900,000	86.23%	13.77%
−18	6,250,000	7,200,000	86.81	13.19
−17	6,600,000	7,300,000	90.41	9.59
−16	6,750,000	7,350,000	91.84	8.16
−15	6,715,000	7,350,000	91.36	8.64
−14	6,627,959	7,350,000	90.18	9.82
−13	6,489,877	7,355,000	88.24	11.76
−12	6,357,027	7,430,000	85.56	14.44
−11	6,202,225	7,480,000	82.92	17.08
−10	6,017,394	7,530,000	79.91	20.09
−9	6,017,394	7,630,000	78.86	21.14
−8	6,266,114	7,830,000	80.03	19.97
−7	6,566,834	8,130,000	80.77	19.23
−6	6,801,834	8,480,000	80.21	19.79
−5	7,210,554	8,780,000	82.12	17.88
−4	7,510,554	9,030,000	83.17	16.83
−3	7,867,024	9,130,000	86.17	13.83
−2	8,177,575	9,230,000	88.60	11.40
−1	8,317,575	9,280,000	89.63	10.37
0	8,226,224	9,280,000	88.64	11.36

and the growth in rents appear to be highly correlated with occupancy rates. Exhibit 11–10 illustrates this graphically by showing both the occupancy rate and rental growth over time. The average occupancy for the past 20 years is also shown. We can see how rental growth is higher as occupancy is above average and lower, sometimes even negative, when occupancy is below average. This is an example of the real estate cycle discussed at the

EXHIBIT 11–9
Market Rent Trends and Occupancy Rates

End Year	End of Year Occupancy Rate (%)	Rent ($)	Rental Growth (%)
−19	86.23%	4.76	—
−18	86.81	5.38	13.12%
−17	90.41	6.31	17.16
−16	91.84	7.70	22.10
−15	91.36	9.44	22.55
−14	90.18	10.74	13.82
−13	88.24	12.07	12.31
−12	85.56	13.02	7.87
−11	82.92	12.84	−1.37
−10	79.91	12.43	−3.15
−9	78.86	11.29	−9.20
−8	80.03	10.33	−8.50
−7	80.77	9.72	−5.92
−6	80.21	9.48	−2.46
−5	82.12	9.22	−2.70
−4	83.17	9.03	−2.09
−3	86.17	9.33	3.28
−2	88.60	10.40	11.51
−1	89.63	11.86	14.00
0	88.64	13.33	12.45

EXHIBIT 11–10
Historic Market Rent Growth and Occupancy Rates

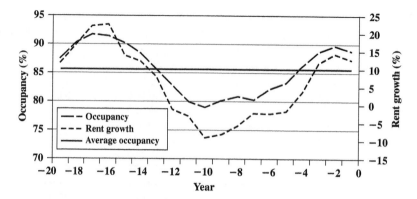

beginning of the chapter. As noted, different property types and different markets may be at different points in their cycle at any given point in time. Therefore, this type of analysis is usually done for a particular property type and for a given market or submarket (e.g., a suburban office in Chicago).

Forecasting Supply, Demand, Market Rents, and Occupancy

Thus far, we have considered only historical relationships. Of course, what we are really interested in is what the *future* supply and demand will be for this market and how it might impact market rents and vacancy rates.

We have previously discussed how rent growth is highly correlated to occupancy rates. Occupancy depends on the demand for space from office employment coupled with the supply of space in existing buildings from new construction, less demolitions. Although market forecasting can be quite challenging, we must estimate demand based on expected employment growth for the foreseeable future and supply as the expected amount of new space likely to be added to the market. We also must consider whether any changes to the amount of space per employee are likely.

To help with this analysis, many economic consulting firms provide projections of employment growth and other economic data at the metropolitan level. (One example is *www.economy.com*.) Knowing where the property type is in its market cycle (e.g., current occupancy relative to the average) may also be helpful.

To illustrate, in Exhibit 11–11 we present a forecast of office employment and space per employee. Exhibit 11–12 shows expected new supply as well as projected occupancy rates based on the employment projections and space per employee. Estimates of new supply

EXHIBIT 11–11
Forecast of Employment and Space per Employee

Year	Beginning of Year Office Employment	Change in Employment	End of Year Office Employment	Change in Employment (%)	End of Year Space per Employee (sq. ft.)
1	33,576	100	33,676	0.30%	245
2	33,676	500	34,176	1.48	240
3	34,176	1,000	35,176	2.93	235
4	35,176	500	35,676	1.42	240
5	35,676	400	36,076	1.12	245
6	36,076	300	36,376	0.83	245
7	36,376	200	36,576	0.55	245
8	36,576	200	36,776	0.55	250
9	36,776	100	36,876	0.27	250
10	36,876	100	36,976	0.27	250

EXHIBIT 11–12
Forecast of Supply, Absorption, and Occupancy Rates

Year	Beginning of Year Office Supply	New Construction	End of Year Office Supply	Beginning of Year Occupied Space	Absorption	End of Year Occupied Space	End of Year Occupancy Rate (%)
1	9,280,000	0	9,280,000	8,226,224	24,500	8,250,724	88.91%
2	9,280,000	0	9,280,000	8,250,724	−48,382	8,202,342	88.39
3	9,280,000	50,000	9,330,000	8,202,342	64,118	8,266,460	88.60
4	9,330,000	400,000	9,730,000	8,266,460	295,882	8,562,342	88.00
5	9,730,000	500,000	10,230,000	8,562,342	276,382	8,838,724	86.40
6	10,230,000	400,000	10,630,000	8,838,724	73,500	8,912,224	83.84
7	10,630,000	200,000	10,830,000	8,912,224	49,000	8,961,224	82.74
8	10,830,000	200,000	11,030,000	8,961,224	232,882	9,194,106	83.36
9	11,030,000	200,000	11,230,000	9,194,106	25,000	9,219,106	82.09
10	11,230,000	200,000	11,430,000	9,219,106	25,000	9,244,106	80.88

tend to come from talking to local developers, knowing what building permits have been issued, and knowing the amount of construction that typically takes place during different stages of the real estate cycle. These forecasts are for illustrative purposes only. As can be seen in Exhibit 11–11, employment increases each year, but the growth is very low after the first three years, suggesting that there will not be much employment growth in this area over the next 10 years. As a result, there will be little growth in the demand for office space.

We can use the historical relationship between rental growth and occupancy, combined with our projection of occupancy, to estimate rental growth. In Exhibit 11–13, we have plotted rental growth versus occupancy rates using Excel. We also have added a trend line to the chart, along with the equation for the trend line (an option in Excel). The same trend line would result from a regression of rental growth versus occupancy rates. Based on this analysis, we see that rental growth could be estimated as $2.2718 \times$ occupancy − 1.8831. Therefore, if occupancy increases by 100 basis points, then rental growth is likely to increase by about 227 basis points. This example is intended only as an illustration of one possible way of estimating rental growth. Forecasting can be an art as well as a science. The fact that the future cannot be known with certainty is one element of the risk that must be considered when selecting an appropriate discount rate to value the property.

That said, using the approach described above, we project the rental growth rates and the rents shown in Exhibit 11–14. Although we may not assume that rents will be exactly as shown in Exhibit 11–14, this provides some guidance as to a reasonable rental rate projection. For example, the average rent growth for the next 10 years is estimated to be about 5½ percent per year. Although we could simply forecast rents to grow at this rate over the

EXHIBIT 11–13
Rental Growth versus Occupancy Rates

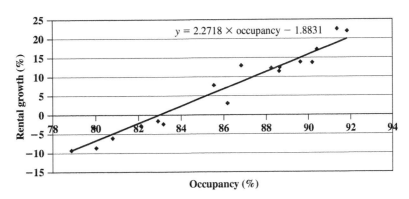

$y = 2.2718 \times$ occupancy − 1.8831

EXHIBIT 11–14
Rent Forecast

Year	End of Year Occupancy Rate (%)	Predicted Rent Growth (%)	Rent ($)
1	88.91%	13.67%	$15.16
2	88.39	12.49	17.05
3	88.60	12.97	19.26
4	88.00	11.61	21.50
5	86.40	7.97	23.21
6	83.84	2.16	23.71
7	82.74	−0.33	23.63
8	83.36	1.06	23.88
9	82.09	−1.81	23.45
10	80.88	−4.58	22.38

next 10 years, this ignores the fact that we are projecting higher rental growth during the first five years than in the latter five years. Similarly, we have some idea as to what the occupancy (or vacancy) rate will be in the market and can use that as a basis for what might be the vacancy rate for a new project that we might develop or for what might happen when leases expire and need to be renewed in the future on an existing project.

In the next section, we will draw upon the analysis in this section to discuss forecasting cash flows for a particular office building.

Making Investments: Projecting Cash Flows

We will now look more closely at how investors and lenders project expected cash flows when they consider investing in income-producing properties. This will be followed by a discussion of various performance measures used to determine the attractiveness of a particular property.

Office Building Example

To illustrate how to make a projection of income, we consider the possible purchase of an office building by an investor for $8.5 million. Construction of the Monument Office Building was completed two years ago. The lead tenant is a bank that signed a five-year lease, which started when the building was completed two years ago. A law firm signed a five-year lease one year ago and a mortgage broker just signed a five-year lease on the remaining space. A summary of the existing leases is shown below.

	Summary Lease Information—Monument Office Building			
Tenant	Square Feet	Rent (per square foot)	Base Rent	Remaining Lease Term (years)
Bank	70,000	$14.00	$ 980,000	3
Law firm	10,000	14.50	145,000	4
Mortgage broker	16,000	15.00	240,000	5
Total	96,000		$1,365,000	

Note: Additional assumptions about the tenant's responsibility for increases in operating expenses (expense stops) will be discussed later.

Additional assumptions are as follows:

Leaseable square feet area: 96,000.

Management costs 5.00 percent of base rent plus expense reimbursements
Current market rent (per square foot): $15.

Market rents are assumed to have been projected based on a market analysis as discussed in the previous section. The projected market rents are as follows:

Year	1	2	3	4	5	6
Market Rent Projection	$15.00	$15.50	$16.00	$16.75	$17.50	$18.00

This is the rent that is projected to apply during the year indicated, for example, for leases beginning in year 4, the market rent will be $16.75 per square foot. Market rents could vary for different spaces in the building. For example, space that has a better view will often command a higher rent. In our example we have assumed that all space will have the same market rent. The rent offered to an existing tenant on a lease renewal may also differ from that offered to a new tenant because an existing tenant may not ask the owner to pay for improvements to the space (tenant improvements). Also, there may be less or no commissions that have to be paid to a broker on a lease renewal compared to a new lease. Finally, if the owner has to find a new tenant that can take time and result in some vacancy. So the rent offered to an existing tenant might be lower than that offered a new tenant. In our example, we will assume that the market rent would be the same whether the tenant renews or a new tenant must be found. But we will assume that there is some vacancy once leases start coming up for renewal to account for the possibility an existing tenant will not renew.

Base Rent

From this summary we see that the total **base rent** is $1,365,000. Note that the base rent for the bank ($14) that was signed two years ago is less than the current market rent of $15 per square foot. Similarly, the base rent for the law firm ($14.50) signed one year ago is less than the current market rent of $15 per square foot. The market rent has increased over the past two years.

www.mhhe.com/bf15e

Year	1	2	3	4	5	6
Bank	$ 980,000	$ 980,000	$ 980,000	$1,172,500	$1,172,500	$1,172,500
Law firm	145,000	145,000	145,000	145,000	175,000	175,000
Broker	240,000	240,000	240,000	240,000	240,000	288,000
Total base	$1,365,000	$1,365,000	$1,365,000	$1,557,500	$1,587,500	$1,635,500

Market Rent

Market rent for our example is $15 per square foot during the first year. This is also the base rent for leases signed that year. Market rents were projected to increase each year based on a separate market analysis as discussed earlier. Leases will be assumed to be renewed at the market rent projected for the year of renewal.

It appears that a tenant will face much higher rents when the lease is renewed because the new lease is based on a market rate that is projected to increase over the term of the lease. However, we will see in the next section that the amount of expenses for which the tenant must reimburse the owner when the lease is renewed may also be reduced.

In the case of the bank, the initial base rent is $980,000, which is projected to remain constant until the lease expires in the third year. The base rent in year 4 is projected to be $1,172,500[3] based on the $16.75 projected market rent in year 4.

[3] $16.75 times 70,000 square feet = $1,172,500.

Expense Stops

Office leases commonly include a provision that protects the owner from increases in operating expenses beyond what they were during the year the lease was signed because of extraordinary expenses that may be related to the operation of one or more tenants or unexpected inflation in expenses. In our example, each lease for the office building has an **expense stop.** As briefly discussed in Chapter 9, these stops place an upper limit on the amount of operating expenses that will have to be paid by the owner. Any operating expenses in excess of the stop must be paid by the tenant. The amount of the stop is usually based on (1) the tenant's pro rata share (percent of total rentable area), (2) categories of expenses that the lessor and lessee agree will be included in the stop, and (3) the actual amount of operating expenses at the time the lease is signed.

For a newly developed property, the tenant and the property owner usually negotiate the amount of the stop. For older properties, the owner generally provides the prospective tenant with operating expense statements, and the stop will be based on the tenant's pro rata share of the actual expenses on such statements.

In the office building example, the lessor and lessee agree that the stop will include all operating expenses. However, the owner of the property will incur property management expenses that will not be chargeable to the tenants. All amounts in excess of the expense stop must be paid by the tenant in addition to the base rent specified in the lease. For example, if the expense stop in the lease is $4.00 per square foot and current expenses are $4.45 per square foot, then in addition to rent, the tenant must pay the owner 45 cents per square foot as an expense reimbursement. The reason for an expense stop is obviously to assure the owner that net income in subsequent years will be at least equal to the initial net income. Using expense stops is particularly important in leases containing fixed base rents (those without CPI adjustments). If expense stops are not used, operating expenses may rise during the term of the lease and net income will decline. The particular expenses passed through to the tenants are negotiable and vary with market conditions. In our example, we have assumed that all expenses except management will be passed through. Tenants are usually reluctant to allow these expenses to be passed through because they are the responsibility of the building owner, and any attempt to pass these through to tenants may be viewed, as excessive.

None of the leases in our example have CPI adjustments as mentioned in Chapter 9. CPI adjustments are more common during periods of relatively high inflation and are often combined with expense passthrough as we do have in this example. Although expense passthroughs protect the owner from increases in expenses due to inflation, this will just serve to keep the NOI constant. That is, owner's portion of expenses will remain constant but if rents are also constant, NOI will be flat in an inflationary environment until leases can be renewed at a higher market rent. CPI adjustments allow the NOI to increase by adjusting the rent upward based on any increase in the CPI during the previous year. When used in conjunction with an expense stop, the adjustment to rents is often a portion, for example, 50 percent of any increase in rents because any erosion in NOI due to the impact of inflation on expenses is already accounted for with the expense passthrough.

Expense stops in the existing lease are assumed to be as follows:

Lease	Stop
Bank	$4.00
Law firm	4.25
Brokerage	4.45

Panel A of Exhibit 11–15 shows the current expenses for the office building and the estimated annual increase in the expenses.

We can see from panel A of Exhibit 11–15 that the projection of total operating expenses subject to expense stops is $427,200 or $4.45 per rentable square foot. Panel B shows projections for the increase in each expense category. Future rates of increase depend on estimates of how each cost is expected to change. In our example, utilities (heat and air conditioning) are expected to increase at a higher rate than the other items. We assume that property taxes will be level for two years, but then will increase when property values are reassessed. We expect property taxes to be level again for at least four years after the reassessment.

Panel C of Exhibit 11–15 uses the information on expense projections and expense stops to project expense reimbursements. Note that in year 1 the first two tenants will be making expense reimbursements to the owner because actual expenses are $4.45 per square foot, which exceeds the $4.00 and $4.25 expense stops in their leases. Also note that no expense reimbursement is projected for the year that leases are renewed because the stops included in lease renewals will be based on actual expenses at that time.

Net Operating Income

Based on the rental information and expense information in Exhibit 11–15, we can project the **net operating income (NOI)** for the office building. Exhibit 11–16 projects the net operating income for the next six years. Recall that we assumed management expenses to be 5 percent of base rent plus expense reimbursements. Note that the income from expense passthroughs

EXHIBIT 11–15
Summary of Operating Expenses— Monument Office Building

www.mhhe.com/bf15e

Panel A: Operating Expenses			
	Dollars	**Dollars per Square Foot**	
Property tax	$148,800	$1.55	Increase 2.00% per year
Insurance	14,400	0.15	Increase 4.00% per year
Utilities	120,000	1.25	Increase 5.00% per year
Janitorial	76,800	0.80	Increase 3.00% per year
Maintenance	67,200	0.70	Increase 3.00% per year
Subtotal (before mgt)	427,200	4.45	(before management expenses)

Panel B: Projection of Reimbursable Expenses per Year						
Year	1	2	3	4	5	6
Property tax	148,800	151,776	154,812	157,908	161,066	164,287
Insurance	14,400	14,976	15,575	16,198	16,846	17,520
Utilities	120,000	126,000	132,300	138,915	145,861	153,154
Janitorial	76,800	79,104	81,477	83,921	86,439	89,032
Maintenance	67,200	69,216	71,292	73,431	75,634	77,903
Total before management	427,200	441,072	455,456	470,373	485,846	501,896
Per square foot	4.45	4.59	4.74	4.90	5.06	5.23

Panel C: Projected Expense Reimbursement						
Year	1	2	3	4	5	6
Bank	$31,500	$41,615	$52,103	$0	$11,282	$22,985
Law firm	2,000	3,445	4,943	6,497	0	1,672
Brokerage	0	2,312	4,709	7,196	9,774	0
Total	$33,500	47,372	61,756	13,693	21,056	24,657

EXHIBIT 11–16   **Projected Net Operating Income**   www.mhhe.com/bf15e

Year	1	2	3	4	5	6
Base income	$1,365,000	$1,365,000	$1,365,000	$1,557,500	$1,587,500	$1,635,500
Plus reimbursements	$ 33,500	$ 47,372	$ 61,756	$ 13,693	$ 21,056	$ 24,657
Total potential income	$1,398,500	$1,412,372	$1,426,756	$1,571,193	$1,608,556	$1,660,157
Less vacancy	0	0	0	78,560	80,428	83,008
Effective gross income	1,398,500	1,412,372	1,426,756	1,492,633	1,528,128	1,577,149
Less operating expenses:						
Reimbursable expenses	427,200	441,072	455,456	470,373	485,846	501,896
Nonreimbursable expenses	69,925	70,619	71,338	78,560	80,428	83,008
NOI	$ 901,375	$ 900,681	$ 899,962	$ 943,700	$ 961,855	$ 992,245

is included in the base that is used to calculate the management fee. As noted earlier, any vacancy might be deducted before calculating the management fee. That is, the management fee would be based on **effective gross income (EGI).** But in this example the management fee is not being reduced by vacancy. Vacancy could be a result of poor management, and thus it may make sense to just compensate the manager on what is actually collected. On the other hand, vacancy can also be a result of market conditions under which the manager has no control and that is when the manager may have to work the hardest to try to attract tenants.

Management expenses are not reimbursable in these leases. The management expense may be incurred by the owner or paid to a property management company. In either case it is not passed on to the tenant, so the owner has an incentive to control management expenses. Our example projects vacancy at 5 percent of the base rent, beginning in the fourth year when the first lease is renewed.

Expected Outlays for Replacements and Capital Improvements

As discussed in Chapter 9, the analyst should also consider outlays of a recurring nature for the replacement of items that wear out in the normal operating cycle of a property. These items may be included in operating expenses. In the case of capital outlays for major, nonrecurring items such as roof replacement, parking garage construction, and so on, these should be shown as an additional deduction from *NOI* in the year that the outlay will occur.

In our example, Monument Office Building is not expected to require any major capital outlays during the six-year projection made in Exhibit 11–16. It is also assumed that there will be no additional expenditures for tenant improvements (TIs) or leasing commissions when the leases have to be renewed. If the existing tenants do not renew, there may have to be money spent to reconfigure the space for the new tenant and there may also be leasing commissions to a broker to find a new tenant. But in this case, we have assumed that these costs will not be incurred.

Exhibit 11–17 shows the output for the NOI from REIWise which is a cloud-based DCF program available to students using this textbook. Note that the answers are the same as we have been discussing. See the preface to the book for information on how to obtain REIWise. The appendix to this chapter will provide additional information on how to use REIWise to replicate the office building investment analysis in this chapter.

Estimated Sale Price

To calculate measures of investment performance over an investment holding period, we must also estimate what our property might sell for. We first need to choose a holding period

EXHIBIT 11–17
REIWise Operating Data Report for Monument Office Building

Select Projection	Annual Property Operating Data ∨					
Projections						
Description	Year 1	Year 2	Year 3	Year 4	Year 5	Year 6
Rental Income	$1,365,000	$1,365,000	$1,365,000	$1,557,500	$1,587,500	$1,635,500
Expense Reimbursements	$33,500	$47,372	$61,756	$13,693	$21,056	$24,657
GROSS SCHEDULED INCOME	$1,398,500	$1,412,372	$1,426,756	$1,571,193	$1,608,556	$1,660,157
General Vacancy	$0	$0	$0	($78,560)	($80,428)	($83,008)
GROSS OPERATING INCOME	$1,398,500	$1,412,372	$1,426,756	$1,492,633	$1,528,128	$1,577,149
Expenses						
Property Management Fee	($69,925)	($70,619)	($71,338)	($78,560)	($80,428)	($83,008)
Property Tax	($148,800)	($151,776)	($154,812)	($157,908)	($161,066)	($164,287)
Insurance	($14,400)	($14,976)	($15,575)	($16,198)	($16,846)	($17,520)
Utilities	($120,000)	($126,000)	($132,300)	($138,915)	($145,861)	($153,154)
Janitorial	($76,800)	($79,104)	($81,477)	($83,921)	($86,439)	($89,032)
Maintenance	($67,200)	($69,216)	($71,292)	($73,431)	($75,634)	($77,903)
TOTAL OPERATING EXPENSES	($497,125)	($511,691)	($526,794)	($548,933)	($566,274)	($584,904)
NET OPERATING INCOME	$901,375	$900,681	$899,962	$943,700	$961,855	$992,245

over which to analyze the investment. For now we will choose five years. When estimating a sale price, investors commonly use two general procedures. The first procedure is to estimate a rate at which property values in general are expected to increase in the area. This is sometimes related to expected inflation rates, although office buildings in some areas may do better or worse than the overall inflation rate for the economy depending on employment.

Two problems are associated with using this approach to estimate the resale price. First, it is based on the assumed purchase price, which we may decide is not what the property is really worth once we complete our analysis. Second, it assumes that the resale price depends on how the historical value (purchase price) changed over time rather than looking forward to what will happen in the future. The approach to estimating a resale price discussed next addresses these issues.

A second way of estimating a resale price is to use the "terminal" capitalization rate concept discussed in an earlier chapter. Recall that the "going-in" capitalization rate (cap rate for short) is defined as the ratio of the first-year *NOI* to the purchase price. For our office building example, the cap rate based on the purchase price is 10.6 percent.[4] This ratio expresses the relationship between the purchase price of the property and the *NOI* that the purchaser expects to receive during the first year of ownership. The investor may find that, in general, office buildings that have recently been purchased by other investors have similar rates.

When estimating a sale price in the future, investors often add a slight premium to current (going-in) capitalization rates to reflect any depreciation, obsolescence, and the uncertainty of income in the future when the property will be sold. However, as discussed in Chapter 9, we have to consider other factors such as whether interest rates are expected to be higher or lower at the time of sale or if expected growth in income and property value will be higher or lower in the years after sale. All these factors impact what the cap rate will be for comparable properties at the time of sale and must be considered when projecting a terminal cap rate to estimate the resale price.

Because we are only looking at a five-year holding period in this example, the property will not be significantly older and we will assume that economic conditions (interest rates,

[4] Recall from the previous chapters that this is sometimes referred to as the "going-in" cap rate because it applies to the rate at the time of purchase.

property value growth rates, etc.) will be similar in five years.[5] Therefore, we will assume a terminal cap rate that is the same as the going in cap rate of 10.6%. Using *NOI* of $992,245 in year 6 and a capitalization rate of 9.6 percent results in an estimated resale price of $9,360,805.[6]

Clearly, the analyst must use some judgment at this point regarding what is a reasonable estimate for the resale price. We are simply pointing out some of the considerations that might go into the investor's thought process. No single precise methodology can be rigidly followed. It is also common to round off the numerical estimate to convey the subjective nature of the estimate.

Introduction to Investment Analysis

In general, when we refer to **investment analysis** in real estate, we are referring to analyzing a particular property to evaluate its investment potential. This analysis should also help answer other important questions: Should the property be purchased? How long should it be held? How should it be financed? What are the tax implications of owning the investment? How risky is the investment?

We will provide the analytic tools to answer these questions in the next several chapters. However, we can now begin to answer the first question: Should the property be purchased at a price of $8.5 million? To illustrate how we might approach this question, we continue with the pro forma statements from the Monument Office Building example.

Internal Rate of Return (IRR)

In our previous discussion of the Monument Office Building, we calculated the net operating income (*NOI*) for the property as well as the projected resale price. These numbers, along with the proposed purchase price, can be used to calculate the **internal rate of return (IRR)** for the property.

Exhibit 11–18 shows the cash flows used to calculate the *IRR*. Recall that this is the rate that makes the present value of the projected cash flows equal to the initial investment. In this case, the *IRR* is 13.46 percent. This is the return on the entire property. It does not consider the effect of borrowing money. Thus, it would be referred to as an "unleveraged *IRR*." Financing is discussed in the next section of this chapter.

EXHIBIT 11–18 **Calculation of *IRR*** www.mhhe.com/bf15e

Year	0	1	2	3	4	5
Purchase price	($8,500,000)					
Net operating income (*NOI*)		$901,375	$900,681	$899,962	$943,700	$ 961,855
Sales price						9,360,805
Cash flow	($8,500,000)	$901,375	$900,681	$899,962	$943,700	$10,322,659
IRR	13.46%					

[5] This assumes that no significant changes will occur in the market for office space during the six-year period that would change the relationship between *NOI* and value. The capitalization rate could change if a change in the supply and demand for office space affects the market rental rates or if the rate of return required by investors in office space changes.

[6] Recall that when a capitalization rate is used to estimate the resale price, it is often referred to as a *terminal capitalization rate*.

Present Value

The IRR for Monument Office Building (calculated above) is 13.46 percent. Suppose that the investor requires a 14 percent rate of return? How much would he be willing to pay? To answer this question, we discount the cash flows (*NOI* and sale price) at a 14 percent discount rate. The purchase price is not included in these cash flows because we are calculating how much the investor is willing to pay. Using a financial calculator or spreadsheet, the reader should be able to verify that the present value of the cash flows above, when discounted at 14 percent, is $8,011,000 (rounded to nearest thousand dollars). At a purchase price of $8,500,000 the property would have a net present value (*NPV*) of $8,011,000 − $8,500,000 or −$489,000.

Introduction to Debt Financing

In many cases, an investor will pay for a property by combining his own money (equity) with a loan (debt). In Chapter 12, we will discuss reasons why investors often find that a combination of equity and debt is desirable for real estate ownership. For now we will focus on how the use of debt affects the cash flows a real estate investor expects to receive.

To illustrate, we again return to our previous example of the Monument Office Building. Let us assume that an investor can obtain a loan for 70 percent of the property value at a 10 percent interest rate to be amortized over 20 years with monthly payments. The amount of the loan will be (.70 × $8,500,000) or $5,950,000. Monthly payments would be $57,418.79 or $689,025 per year. Traditional investment analysis computes loan payments based on monthly payments (assuming that is the way the payments will be made), but all cash flows are summarized on an annual basis for financial projections.

Exhibit 11–19 shows a summary loan schedule for the property for the first five years. From this point on projections will be made for five years under the assumption that the property will be sold after five years. The reason for projecting *NOI* for an *additional* year will become apparent when we discuss estimating the sale price of the property at the end of the five-year holding period.

Exhibit 11–20 shows the results of including the financing costs in the calculation of cash flows to the equity investor. Subtracting debt service from *NOI* results in before-tax cash flow from operations (*BTCF_o*). *BTCF_o* is also referred to as the **equity dividend** because it represents the cash flow that will actually be received by the investor each year, analogous to a dividend on common stocks.

EXHIBIT 11–19
Summary Loan Information

	1	2	3	4	5
Payment	$ 689,025	$ 689,025	$ 689,025	$ 689,025	$ 689,025
Mortgage balance	5,851,543	5,742,776	5,622,620	5,489,883	5,343,245
Interest	590,569	580,259	568,869	556,288	542,388
Principal	98,457	108,767	120,156	132,738	146,637

EXHIBIT 11–20
Estimates of Before-Tax Cash Flow

	Year				
	1	2	3	4	5
Net operating income (*NOI*)	$901,375	$900,681	$899,962	$943,700	$961,855
Less debt service (DS)	689,025	689,025	689,025	689,025	689,025
Before-tax cash flow	$221,350	$211,656	$210,937	$254,675	$272,829

Measures of Investment Performance Using Ratios

Equity Dividend Rate

The **equity dividend rate** is calculated by dividing the *BTCF* (also referred to as the equity dividend) in the first year by the initial *equity investment*. The investor's initial *equity* in the project *is equal to the purchase price less* the amount borrowed. Thus, the equity is $8,500,000 − $5,950,000 = $2,550,000. The equity dividend rate is therefore $212,350/ $2,550,000 = 8.33 percent. This is a rough measure of current return on equity. Note, however, that it is not an investment yield because it does not take into account future cash flows from operation or sale of the property. For the equity investor, the difference between the equity dividend rate and an investment yield, or *IRR*, is an important one. We will discuss this later in the chapter.

Debt Coverage Ratios

To obtain financing on the property, the lender must be satisfied that it is a good investment. One consideration obviously is the rate of return the lender will receive over the term of the loan, which depends on factors such as the interest rate charged, points, and so forth, as discussed earlier in this text. But the lender's rate of return is only one consideration. The lender will also evaluate the riskiness of the loan. One widely used indication of the riskiness of the loan is the degree to which the *NOI* from the property is expected to exceed the mortgage payments. The lender would like a sufficient cushion so that if the *NOI* is less than anticipated (e.g., from unexpected vacancy), the borrower will still be able to make the mortgage payments without using personal funds.

A common measure of this risk is the **debt coverage ratio (DCR)**. The *DCR* is the ratio of *NOI* to the mortgage payment. When *NOI* is projected to change over time, the investor typically uses first-year *NOI*. For the office building example, the projected *NOI* in year 1 is $901,375. The mortgage payment (debt service) is $689,025. These figures result in a debt coverage ratio of 1.31. Lenders typically want the first-year debt coverage ratio to be at least 1.2 so NOI could drop by about 20 percent before there is not enough to cover the mortgage payment.

We see that this project has a debt coverage of about 1.3 for the first year. Thus, it meets the minimum debt coverage ratio typically required by lenders.

Before-Tax Cash Flow from Sale

When the property is sold, the mortgage balance must be repaid from the sale proceeds. Repayment results in before-tax cash flow from sale (*BTCF_s*). After the fifth year, the mortgage balance is $5,343,245. Subtracting this from the sale price of $9,360,805 results in before-tax cash flow (*BTCF_s*) of $4,017,559. We can summarize the process as follows:

Estimates of Cash Flows from Sale in Year 5	
Sale price	$ 9,360,805
Mortgage balance	− 5,343,245
Before-tax cash flow (*BTCF_s*)	$ 4,017,559

Internal Rate of Return to Equity Investor

Recall that the initial equity investment is $2,550,000, found by subtracting the $5,950,000 loan amount from the $8,500,000 purchase price. We have also already calculated the before-tax cash flow to the equity investor. Exhibit 11–21 presents the cash flows.

You should confirm that this process results in an *IRR* of 17.11 percent, which we will refer to as the *BTIRR* since it is a before-tax *IRR*. This is the before-tax yield that the

EXHIBIT 11–21
Before-Tax Cash Flow Summary— Monument Office Building

Year	0	1	2	3	4	5
Before-tax cash flow	($2,550,000)	$212,350	$212,656	$210,937	$254,675	$4,290,389

investor may expect to earn on equity over the investment period. This considers the effect of the loan on the investor's return.

Is the return adequate? The answer to this question depends on what the investor can earn on comparable investments, such as similar office buildings or even other real estate investments with similar risk characteristics. We have discussed comparing capitalization rates and price per square foot with comparable properties. Similarly, we could also ask what rate of return we would expect to earn had we bought another property at the price paid by another investor. This may give us some idea of what returns other investors are expecting. Of course, we would have to make our own projections of *NOI* and resale price unless the other investor told us exactly what he was thinking. We would also make similar projections and *IRR* calculations for other properties that are for sale, using their asking price. That is, we should earn a return that is at least as good as the return we could earn on other properties that are for sale that have similar risk characteristics.

Another test of the reasonableness of the BTIRR is to compare it with the effective interest cost of any mortgage financing that could be obtained to purchase the property. Normally, we would expect the return on the property to be greater than the effective cost of financing on the property, because the investor accepts more risk than the lender. The lender assumes less risk because a lender would have first claim on income and proceeds from sale of the property should there be a default. For example, we should expect that the IRR for the office building (BTIRR of 17.11%) would be more than the 10 percent mortgage interest rate. Otherwise, the investor would be better off lending on real estate rather than investing in it. We will discuss approaches to measuring and evaluating risk to investors and show how debt affects that risk and return for equity investors in Chapter 13.

Summary of Investment Analysis Calculations

Exhibit 11–22 shows a summary of the calculations for the Monument Office Building example. The performance measures in Exhibit 11–22 should all be compared with other investment alternatives. The comparison will give a good indication of whether acquisition of the office building is a good investment. However, these measures may still not be sufficient to allow us to decide whether we should purchase the investment because we have not yet considered how *federal income taxes* might affect the results. We also need to know more about the *riskiness* of the investment so that we can be reasonably sure that we are comparing the performance measures outlined in Exhibit 11–22 with alternatives of comparable risk, as we discuss in the next section. We will also want to know whether we should borrow more or less money, and whether there are other, better ways of financing the property. Chapter 12 covers financing alternatives. Being able to obtain a loan on the property also depends on the appraised value an independent appraiser presents. This value may be more or less than the investor is willing to pay.

EXHIBIT 11–22
Summary of Monument Office Building Investment Analysis Measures

Capitalization rate	10.60%
IRR on property (unleveraged)	13.46%
IRR on equity (*BTIRR*)	17.11

When making pro forma cash flow projections for real estate income properties, the analysts must be realistic about the assumptions being made. The following abuses common in pro forma cash flow projections are based on an article in *Real Estate Review* by Vernon Martin:

1. Mismatched growth rates between rental income and expenses.
2. Failure to consider rental concessions and effective rents.
3. Absence of lease-by-lease analysis in properties encumbered by long-term leases.
4. Projection for expense recovery income that increases at the same growth rate as other expenses for a property encumbered by gross leases with expense stops.
5. Projections for vacancy and collection losses that are not synchronized with market conditions.
6. Omitting outlays for nonoperating expenses such as tenant improvements and leasing commissions.
7. Unsupported use of terminal capitalization rates that are lower than "going-in" capitalization rates. Terminal capitalization rates should be related to the property's age and remaining economic life.
8. Underestimation of selling expenses.
9. Use of an inappropriate internal rate of return (discount rate).
10. Failure to recognize capital outlays for renovations needed to maintain a property.

If the appraised value is too low, it will be difficult to finance the property with the amount of debt that we have assumed in our projections.

It should be obvious that we have only begun to do the in-depth analysis the potential acquisition of our office building requires. Whether investors consider all of these issues in practice depends on their level of sophistication. Our objective will be to cover all the issues that *should* be considered to be certain of making an intelligent investment decision.

Taxation of Income-Producing Real Estate

Earlier in this chapter, we introduced investment analysis of income-producing property. We calculated measures of investment performance such as the *IRR* and *NPV*. However, these calculations did not consider the effect of federal income taxes on the investment and financing decision; consequently, we referred to the analysis thus far as a before-tax analysis. We now extend investment analysis to include the effect of federal income taxes, which is referred to as an after-tax analysis.

Our discussion of taxes is intended only as a general overview of how taxes affect after-tax rates of return for real estate income property. Tax laws change frequently, and many complexities in the tax law are beyond the scope of this chapter. It is important, however, to have a sense of how tax laws influence investment decisions and how possible tax law changes may affect the desirability of real estate relative to other investments.

This chapter does *not* deal with real estate held as a *personal residence* by individuals. Special rules apply to the taxation of personal residences. For example, personal residences cannot be depreciated for tax purposes. We also assume that the property is not held for resale to others. Individuals holding property for resale to others in the ordinary course of business are referred to as **dealers,** *not investors.* Examples of individuals or firms with *dealer* status would be developers who develop lots for resale, builders of houses for resale, or others who do not intend to hold real estate as an investment, but rather for immediate resale. Real property held for resale by a dealer is *not depreciable* for tax purposes. (Depreciation rules are discussed later in the chapter.)

In this chapter, we only consider property "held for use in a trade or business." *Most income-producing real estate investments are included in this category.* An owner acquires real estate with the intent to operate, modify, or do whatever is necessary to produce income in a trade or business. Individuals in other occupations who own and operate rental properties are also in this category, although they must be actively engaged in the management of the property. Investors in a partnership, corporation, or trust may also hold property for use in a trade or business.[7] Real estate used in trade or businesses includes land and improvements, such as income-producing rental properties and commercial properties that are subject to depreciation. This category of real estate is the primary focus of the chapter.

Owners of real estate used in the production of income in a trade or business report income from rents and may deduct expenses incurred in operating the property, such as maintenance, repair, and utilities. They may also deduct property taxes, interest on mortgage loans made to acquire property, and interest on loans made in the operation of the business. In addition, they are allowed deductions for depreciation, and when properties are sold, certain capital gain and loss provisions (discussed in a later section) also apply.

Taxable Income from Operation of Real Estate

We have discussed at length how to calculate net operating income (*NOI*) for income-producing property. Recall that the calculation of *NOI* involves deducting expenses associated with *operating* a property, such as property taxes, insurance, maintenance, management, and utilities. Then, subtracting the mortgage payment from the *NOI* results in before-tax cash flow from operating the property ($BTCF_o$). We will now see that **taxable income** from operating real estate income property differs from $BTCF_o$ for two main reasons.[8] First, only the *interest* portion of a loan payment, not the total payment, is deductible from *NOI* for tax purposes. Second, the tax code allows owners to deduct a **depreciation allowance** from *NOI*. Thus, taxable income from operating a real estate income property can be stated as follows:

$$\text{Taxable Income} = NOI - \text{Interest} - \text{Depreciation Allowance}$$

The amount of interest deductible in a given taxable year equals the total interest paid to the lender during that year. We have discussed the separation of loan payments into principal and interest in considerable detail in earlier chapters.[9] We have not covered calculating depreciation allowances for tax purposes yet, and we will discuss this subject in the following section.

Depreciation Allowances

Physical assets like buildings suffer from physical depreciation over time that, *ceteris paribus,* reduces their economic value. Because buildings must ultimately be replaced, and because tax law allows investment in improvements to be recovered before income produced from the improvement is taxed, the investor may take a deduction for capital recovery (depreciation) from net operating income prior to the determination of taxable income. Otherwise, net operating income and taxable income would be overstated by an amount equal to the annual decrease in value due to economic depreciation. Thus, in theory, investors should only be taxed on the income net of this economic allowance for depreciation. This is the theoretical basis for tax depreciation.

---

[7] Real estate used for the production of income in a trade or business is categorized as Section 1231 assets. Capital equipment (such as machinery) purchased by businesses that use such assets in the production of income are also designated as Section 1231 assets.

[8] Additional differences will be shown in later chapters.

[9] You may want to review the appendix to Chapter 6 at this time.

However, because of inflation, changes in supply and demand, and other economic factors that also affect the value of real estate, it is difficult to know what portion of any net change in value is caused by physical depreciation. Further, our tax system has historically provided for depreciation allowances that are greater than any actual decline in the economic value of the property. As we will see, to the extent that tax depreciation *allowances* exceed *actual* economic depreciation, investors realize tax benefits. Exhibit 11–23 summarizes the methods for computing depreciation allowances that various tax laws in effect in recent years have allowed.

It should be obvious from the exhibit that tax policy on depreciation allowances has varied considerably. As indicated, this is because, historically, Congress has provided for allowances in excess of economic depreciation to stimulate investment in real estate in the belief that this policy would increase construction and, hence, the supply of rentable space in the economy. Unfortunately, it may also have contributed too much of the overbuilding that occurred during the early 1980s. As shown in the exhibit, the Tax Reform Act (TRA), which was passed in 1986, lengthened depreciable life from its length during the period from 1981 to 1986. Increasing the depreciable life of real estate is one of the several features in the 1986 law that reduced the favorable tax treatment that real estate had enjoyed previously. Later in this chapter, we will see that depreciation is one source of tax benefits to investors in real estate.

Depreciable Basis

The amount that can be depreciated for real estate improvements depends on the **depreciable basis** of the asset. The basis for a real estate investment is generally equal to the *cost* of the improvements (unless inherited or acquired by gift). *Cost* is generally defined to include the acquisition price of the improvements plus any installation costs associated with placing them into service. The cost of any capital improvements to the property made during the ownership period is also included in the basis when such outlays are made. Only improvements can be depreciated, not the cost of land. In this chapter, we focus on the tax treatment for existing properties. (Differences for properties that will be *developed and constructed* are discussed in a later chapter.)

EXHIBIT 11–23
Depreciation Rules for Real Estate*

Years	Depreciable Life	Methods Allowed
1969–1980	Useful life, approximately 30–40 years	Accelerated or straight line[†]
1981–1983	15 years	ACRS based on 175% of straight-line depreciation[‡]
1984–1985	18 years	ACRS based on 175% of straight-line depreciation[‡]
1986	19 years	ACRS based on 175% of straight-line depreciation[‡]
1987–1992	27.5 years for residential	Straight line
	31.5 years for nonresidential	Straight line
1993–1997	27.5 years for residential	Straight line
	39 years for nonresidential	Straight line

*Some real estate investments also include personal properties such as furniture and fixtures. Personal property can be depreciated over a much shorter time period than the real property (e.g., eight years under the current tax law).

[†]Investors generally selected accelerated depreciation methods that ranged from 125 percent to 200 percent of straight-line depreciation, depending on whether the property was residential or nonresidential, new or existing.

[‡]Because of severe "recapture" rules that affected investors who used accelerated depreciation on nonresidential real estate, most investors used straight-line depreciation in nonresidential real estate during this period.

EXHIBIT 11–24
2014 Marginal Ordinary Income Tax Rates for a Married Taxpayer Filing Jointly

Taxable Income	Marginal Tax Rate
$0–$18,150	10%
18,151–73,800	15
73,801–148,850	25
148,851–226,850	28
226,851–405,100	33
405,101–457,600	35
Over 457,600	39.6

Loan Points

Points paid in connection with obtaining a loan to purchase, refinance, or operate a real estate income property investment must be deducted ratably over the term of the loan. For example, suppose an investor secures a loan for $800,000 to purchase an office building. The loan is to be amortized over a 25-year term but has a term of 10 years with a balloon payment due at the end of the 10th year. Suppose two points, or $16,000, are paid on the loan. For tax purposes, the $16,000 would have to be amortized over 10 years, or $1,600 per year. If the investor sells the property before the points are fully amortized (year 10 in this example), the balance can be expensed in the year of sale. Thus, in the above example, if the property is sold and the loan is repaid after five years, $8,000 could be expensed against ordinary income.

Tax Liability and After-Tax Cash Flow

Once we have calculated taxable income, we can calculate the tax liability that results from operating the property. The tax liability is calculated by multiplying the taxable income by the investor's marginal tax rate. The **marginal tax rate** is the rate which the *additional* income from the investment under consideration will be taxed. In general, we can think of it as the investor's tax bracket. The tax rate that corresponds to a particular tax bracket is the rate that applies to an *additional* or *marginal* dollar of income that falls in a particular bracket. For investment decisions, we want to know how the additional income from adding the particular investment under consideration will affect the investor's taxes. Thus, we are interested in knowing what marginal tax rate (or rates) applies to the investment. For example, suppose that the individual to whom the rates in Exhibit 11–24 apply already has taxable income of $100,000. Furthermore, suppose that a real estate investment would produce taxable income of $10,000. According to the exhibit, the additional $10,000 of income would be taxed at a 25 percent rate, resulting in $2,500 in taxes.

Taxable Income from Disposal of Depreciable Real Property

In establishing whether a taxable **capital gain** or loss has occurred when a property is sold, we must determine the gross sales price. The gross sales price is equal to any cash or other property received in payment for the property sold, plus any liabilities against the property assumed by the buyer. Any selling expenses (e.g., legal fees, recording fees, and brokerage fees) may then be deducted to establish *net sales proceeds*. To determine gain or loss, subtract the *adjusted basis* of the property from net sales proceeds. The adjusted basis of a property is its *original basis* (cost of land and improvements, acquisition and installation fees) plus the cost of any capital improvements, alterations, or additions made during the period of ownership, less accumulated depreciation taken to date. Any excess of the net sales proceeds over the adjusted basis results in a taxable gain, and any deficit results in a taxable loss.

In the case of depreciable real estate held for use in trade or business, *net* gains on the sale are treated as long-term capital gains. The tax rate on long-term capital gains is often less than the rate on ordinary income. For example, the 1993 Tax Reform Act set the maximum capital gain tax rate at 28 percent even if the investor is in a higher tax bracket for ordinary income. In 1997, the capital gain tax rate was lowered to 20 percent for that portion of the gain due to any increase in the value of the property and 25 percent for that portion of the gain due to depreciation taken (recapture) during the seller's holding period. It is currently 15 percent for the portion of gain due to any increase in the property value and 25 percent for the gain due to depreciation recapture.

After-Tax Investment Analysis

We now consider the effect of federal income taxes on the office building investment analysis example introduced earlier in this chapter. As a starting point for our discussion, Exhibit 11–25 summarizes the calculation of before-tax cash flow for Monument Office Building.

After-Tax Cash Flow from Operations

We have estimated *before-tax* cash flows from the investment and now must determine the increase or decrease in the investor's taxable income as a result of undertaking it. Because taxes will either increase or decrease as a result of the investment, the increase or decrease must be added to or subtracted from before-tax cash flows to determine cash flow on an *after-tax* basis. To do this, we must consider how much taxable income is produced each year from operations and then consider taxes in the year that the property is sold. Exhibit 11–26 shows the calculation of taxable income and after-tax cash flow from operating the property. In Exhibit 11–26, we see that we can find taxable income by subtracting interest and depreciation from the *NOI*. Note that only the interest, not the total loan payment, is tax deductible. In our example, interest was based on having a $5,950,000 loan amortized over a 20-year term with monthly payments based on a 10 percent interest rate. Exhibit 11–27 reproduces the summary loan schedule from earlier in this chapter (Exhibit 11–19).

Depreciation

Taxable income is also affected by an allowance for *depreciation*. As discussed earlier in the chapter, residential properties may be depreciated over 27.5 years, and nonresidential

EXHIBIT 11–25 **Estimates of Before-Tax Cash Flow from Operations and Sale**

	Year				
	1	**2**	**3**	**4**	**5**
Cash flow from operations:					
Net operating income (*NOI*)	$901,375	$900,681	$899,962	$943,700	$ 961,855
Less: debt service (DS)	689,025	689,025	689,025	689,025	689,025
Before-tax cash flow	$212,350	$211,656	$159,894	$183,920	$ 190,856
Estimates of cash flows from sale in year 5:					
Sale price					$9,360,805
Less: mortgage balance					5,343,245
Before-tax cash flow (*BTCF*$_s$)					$4,017,559

EXHIBIT 11–26   **Taxable Income and After-Tax Cash Flow from Operations**

	End of Year				
	1	2	3	4	5
Taxable income:					
Net operating income (*NOI*)	$901,375	$900,681	$899,962	$943,700	$961,855
Less: interest	590,569	580,259	568,869	556,288	542,388
Depreciation	177,537	185,256	185,256	185,256	185,256
Taxable income (loss)	133,269	135,166	145,836	202,156	234,210
Tax (savings) at 36%	$ 52,893	$ 65,899	$ 79,207	$ 84,073	$101,270
After-tax cash flow:					
Before-tax cash flow	$233,725	$259,542	$285,121	$286,054	$319,925
Less: tax	46,644	47,308	51,043	70,755	81,974
After-tax cash flow	$165,705	$164,348	$159,894	$183,920	$190,856

EXHIBIT 11–27
Summary Loan Information

	End of Year				
	1	2	3	4	5
Payment	$ 689,025	$ 689,025	$ 689,025	$ 689,025	$ 689,025
Mortgage balance	5,851,543	5,742,776	5,622,620	5,489,883	5,343,245
Interest	590,569	580,259	568,869	556,288	542,388
Principal	98,457	108,767	120,156	132,738	146,637

real property must be depreciated over 39 years. Both must be depreciated on a straight-line basis.[10] Also recall that only the improvements, not land, can be depreciated. Thus, we need to know what portion of the $8.5 million purchase price of the office building represents building improvements as opposed to land. For our case example, we assume that land cost requirements are 15 percent of the purchase price or $1,275,000, leaving improvements of $7,225,000. Dividing improvement cost by 39 results in an annual depreciation deduction of $185,256. The first year is for $11\frac{1}{2}$ months due to the IRS assuming a "mid-month" convention.[11] So, the depreciation is multiplied by 11.5/12 to get the first month depreciation of $177,537.

Recall that depreciation allowances represent recovery of capital and do not represent an actual cash outflow for the investor (that occurs when the property is acquired). The deduction only affects taxable income and not operating cash flows. In our example, taxable income is $146,925 in year 1. Assuming the investor is in a 35 percent tax bracket, the increase in tax liability as a result of owning the property will be $46,644 (.35 × $133,269). Subtracting this from before-tax cash flow results in after-tax cash flow of $165,705 in year 1.

[10] In the case of mixed use properties (those with both residential and nonresidential uses), if *one* of the uses produces 80 percent of revenues, the total improvement may be depreciated over the tax life corresponding to that use.

[11] The IRS publishes tables that taxpayers must use to calculate depreciation deductions. The tables assume that the investor purchases the property in the middle of the month, and they prorate the first-year depreciation according to the actual month of the year the property is purchased. We are simply dividing by 39 years.

Note that taxable income is *positive* during each year in this example. If the taxable income were negative (i.e., a tax loss), additional assumptions would have to be made regarding the investor's ability to use the losses to offset other taxable income. We discuss negative taxable income later in this chapter.

After-Tax Cash Flow from Sale

Exhibit 11–28 illustrates how sale of the property affects the investor's taxable income. When determining the investor's capital gain from sale of the property, we should keep in mind that the investor will have depreciated the property for five years. Hence, the investor's *cost basis* in the property will be reduced. In our example, depreciation was $177,537 the first year and then $185,256 per year for the next four years, resulting in total depreciation (accumulated depreciation) of $918,563. Subtracting the accumulated depreciation from the original cost basis of the property (cost of the land and improvements) results in an adjusted basis of $7,581,437. (Adjusted basis is also sometimes referred to as the *book value* of the property.) The difference between the adjusted basis ($7,581,437) and the sale price ($9,360,805) is the capital gain, $1,779,368. As discussed earlier, the portion of this gain due to price appreciation (sale price less original cost basis) has a maximum capital gain tax rate of 15 percent. The portion of the gain due to depreciation taken over the holding period (accumulated depreciation) has a maximum tax rate of 25 percent. Thus, the capital gain tax in this example can be calculated as follows:

Price appreciation ($9,360,805 − $8,500,000)		$ 860,000
Accumulated depreciation		918,563
Total gain		$1,779,368
Tax on price appreciation	$860,805 × .15 =	$ 129,121
Tax on accumulated depreciation	918,563 × .25 =	229,641
Total capital gain tax		$ 358,761

Subtracting tax from the before-tax cash flow results in **after-tax cash flow** from sale of $3,658,798.

After-Tax *IRR*

Using the information from Exhibits 11–26 and 11–28, we may now calculate the **after-tax** *IRR*. Exhibit 11–29 summarizes the cash flows along with the before-tax cash flows for comparison. As we might expect, the after-tax *IRR* of 13.38 percent is lower than the before-tax *IRR*, which is 17.11 percent as shown in Exhibit 11–29. However, although

EXHIBIT 11–28
After-Tax Cash Flow from Sale in Year 5

www.mhhe.com/bf15e

Sale price		$9,360,805
Less mortgage balance		5,343,245
Before-tax cash flow ($BTCF_s$)		4,017,559
Taxes in year of sale		
Sale price	$9,360,805	
Original cost basis	$8,500,000	
Accumulated depreciation	918,563	
Adjusted basis	$7,581,437	
Capital gain	$1,779,368	
Tax on gain*		358,761
After-tax cash flow from sale ($ATCF_s$)		$3,658,798

EXHIBIT 11-29 **Cash Flow Summary** www.mhhe.com/bf15e

	End of Year				
	1	2	3	4	5
Before-tax cash flow	($2,550,000)	$212,350	$211,656	$210,937	$254,675	$4,290,389
After-tax cash flow	($2,550,000)	$165,705	$164,348	$159,894	$183,920	$3,849,654
Before-tax *IRR* (*BTIRR*)	17.11%				
After-tax *IRR* (*ATIRR*)	13.38%				

the investor's tax rate was 35 percent, the after-tax *IRR* is not 35 percent lower than the before-tax *IRR*. Rather, it is about 22 percent lower ($1 - 13.38/17.11 = 21.80\%$).

Effective Tax Rate

In the previous section, we indicated that the after-tax *IRR* is 22 percent lower than the before-tax *IRR,* even though the investor had a 35 percent marginal tax rate. In this case, we would say that the **effective tax rate** on income from this investment would be about 22 percent. Why is the effective tax rate on this investment lower than the marginal tax rate? The reason is that investors can reduce taxable income each year by the amount of depreciation deductions even though the property is not really decreasing in value. In fact, in this example it is increasing in value. Although depreciation allowances also reduce the adjusted basis of the property each year and will eventually result in an increase in taxes paid on the capital gain in the year of sale, the "time value of money" makes lower taxes paid on income each year a benefit to the investor. Furthermore, recall that the portion of capital gain due to price appreciation was only taxed at 15 percent, and the portion due to depreciation recapture was taxed at 25 percent. Thus, the investor is able to defer taxes until the property is sold, and convert (through depreciation deductions) some of the ordinary income to capital gains, which are taxed at a lower rate for investors than ordinary income.

Exhibit 11–30 shows the output from REIWise as if the property was sold after holding periods of one year, two years, and so on through five years. We see that the IRR for year 5 is exactly as shown above. The appendix to this chapter will show more output from REIWise.

A Note about Passive Losses

Starting with the Tax Reform Act of 1986, income and loss from all sources, including real estate, has to be divided into three categories as follows:

1. **Passive income** (or loss): Income or loss from a trade or business where the investor does not materially participate in the management or operation of the property. Material participation is defined as "involvement in the operations of the activity on a regular, continuous, and substantial basis." Investment in rental real estate is considered to be a passive activity. Hence, even if an investor materially participates in the operation of the

EXHIBIT 11–30

REIWise Resale Analysis

Select Projection	Investment Return Analysis ⌄				
Projections					
Description	Year 1	Year 2	Year 3	Year 4	Year 5
Cash Flow - To Date	$165,699	$330,044	$489,935	$673,853	$864,706
Net Resale Proceeds	$2,601,823	$2,659,189	$3,082,782	$3,314,787	$3,658,810
Invested Capital	($2,550,000)	($2,550,000)	($2,550,000)	($2,550,000)	($2,550,000)
Net Return on Investment	$217,522	$439,233	$1,022,717	$1,438,640	$1,973,516
Internal Rate of Return	8.53%	8.53%	12.57%	12.78%	13.38%

property, income and losses earned from such activity are categorized as passive income or loss. Income (or loss) received by a limited partner in a partnership is considered passive by definition.

2. **Active income** (or loss): Salaries, wages, fees for services, and income from a trade or business in which the investor materially participates. However, even if a taxpayer materially participates, income or loss from rental activity is not considered active income. Thus, income from rental housing, office buildings, shopping centers, and other real estate activities in which a taxpayer is a landlord is not classified as active income (or loss). This income or loss is classified as *passive income.* However, the operation of a hotel, other transient lodging, or a nursing home is *not* a rental activity, and therefore its owners will have active income if they materially participate.

3. **Portfolio income** (or loss): Interest and dividend income from stocks, bonds, and some categories of real estate that are classified as *capital assets.* As stated earlier in the chapter, most real estate investments are classified as being held for a trade or business and not as capital assets. Examples of portfolio income from real estate activity include dividends received on shares in a real estate investment trust (REIT) or income received on long-term land leases or net leases on real estate where the owner does not materially participate in its operation.

These income classifications are very important because, in general, passive losses cannot be used to offset income from another category (special exceptions are discussed in the next section). This stipulation is referred to as the *passive activity loss limitation* (PAL). Prior to the 1986 Tax Reform Act, many investors purchased real estate that was held as a trade or business by a limited partnership in which the individual investor (limited partner) did not materially participate. These investments often produced (and may still be producing) tax losses that the investor used to offset other taxable income. The passive activity loss limitation prevents investors from offsetting taxable income with passive losses. Passive losses produced from real estate investments and other passive activities now must be used to offset passive income earned during the tax year. Any remaining or unused passive losses must be "suspended" and carried forward to offset any passive income earned in future years.

When an investment producing passive income is *sold* and a capital gain occurs, any unused or suspended losses from that activity (1) must first be used to offset any capital gain from the sale of that activity, (2) must then be used to offset any other passive income produced from other passive activities during that year, and (3) can then be used to offset *any income,* including active and portfolio income earned during that year. To the extent that unused losses remain, they may be carried forward into succeeding years as capital losses, not subject to passive loss rules. For Section 1231 property, any remaining losses would be deductible as ordinary losses.

In cases where the sale of a passive activity, such as real estate, produces a capital loss *and* unused suspended losses from previous years also remain, the unused passive losses may be used to offset any other sources of income (active, passive, or portfolio). Of the capital loss portion, $3,000 of the loss may be used to offset any other source of income that year. Any excess must be carried forward to the next taxable year as a capital loss. It would no longer be subject to passive loss rules, and the excess as well as any unused passive losses may be deducted from ordinary income as a Section 1231 loss.[12]

Special Exceptions to PAL Rules

One special exception to the PAL rules that was included in the 1986 Tax Reform Act (TRA) applies to individual rental property owners (other than limited partners). These investors are allowed to offset active income with up to $25,000 of passive activity losses (to the extent such losses exceed income from passive activities) from rental real estate activities in which the individual *actively* participates. Active participation is less restrictive than the material participation standard referred to earlier and requires less personal involvement. In general, the individual must own a 10 percent or greater interest in the activity and be involved in management decisions, such as selection of tenants and determination of rents, or must arrange for others to provide services (e.g., a property manager to manage the property on a day-to-day basis).

The TRA phases out this special rule for individuals with adjusted gross incomes between $100,000 and $150,000. It reduces the $25,000 loss allowance by 50 percent of the amount of the individual's adjusted gross income when such income for the taxable year exceeds $100,000. Thus, individuals with an adjusted gross income of $120,000 would only be allowed to use up to $15,000 of any passive losses to reduce active income. An individual with adjusted gross income in excess of $150,000 would receive no loss allowance.

The Tax Act of 1993 introduced a second exception to the PAL rules that provides relief for real estate brokers, sales associates, and other real estate professionals who can demonstrate "material involvement in the real estate business."[13] These individuals are eligible to deduct unlimited real estate losses (1) if more than half of all personal services they perform during the year are for real property trades or businesses in which they materially participate and (2) if they perform more than 750 h of service per year in those real estate activities.

Web App

The Web site for *Commercial Investment Real Estate* magazine is part of the Web site for the Certified Commercial Investment Managers (CCIM) Institute. It includes the ability to do a keyword search of articles at

www.ciremagazine.com/search.php. Find a recent article related to investment in commercial real estate and provide an executive summary of the article. Explain how it relates to the material in this chapter.

[12] For further explanation, see P. Fass, R. Haft, L. Loffman, and S. Presant, *Tax Reform Act of 1986* (New York: Clark Boardman, 1986).

[13] Material involvement generally means that the taxpayer is involved in real estate operations on a regular, continuous, and substantial basis. Limited partners (discussed in Chapter 18) do not materially participate because active involvement could cause them to lose their limited liability status.

Conclusion

This chapter has introduced concepts and techniques important in the analysis of real estate income property. We discussed ways of projecting cash flows for an investor and ways of evaluating those cash flows with various measures of investment performance. The performance measures discussed in this chapter (*IRR, NPV, DCR*, etc.) will be used throughout the remainder of the text.

Although the techniques in this chapter provide a good initial analysis of a project, as demonstrated by the office building example, many questions remain to explore in more depth. For example, how will taxes affect the performance of the property? Are there alternative ways of financing the property that would be better? The remaining chapters in this part of the text will cover these and other questions.

Another area this chapter covered was the key tax considerations that affect real estate investment decisions. These considerations include determining the appropriate marginal tax rate, rules for depreciating real property, calculation of taxable income from operation of the property, and calculation of capital gain. These tax considerations will enter into different types of analyses that we will address in many of the remaining chapters of the text. In several cases we will be applying the tax rules introduced in this chapter to see how they affect investment. We will consider issues such as, what is the optimal time to dispose of a property? and, is it profitable to renovate a building? Additional tax considerations, such as the taxation of limited partnerships and development projects, will also be introduced in future chapters. Remember, however, that tax laws are subject to revisions that can have a substantial impact on the calculation of taxable income and taxes for real estate income property. Thus, this chapter is not intended to be a substitute for a comprehensive analysis of how current and future tax laws may affect a specific investor. It does, however, point out the general issues that investors should take into consideration regardless of the specifics of the tax law in effect at a particular point in time.

Key Terms

active income, *374*
after-tax cash flow, *372*
after-tax *IRR*, *372*
arbitrage investing, *348*
base rent, *357*
capital gain, *369*
contrarian investing, *347*
dealers, *366*
debt coverage ratio
  (*DCR*), *364*
depreciable basis, *368*
depreciation allowance, *367*

effective gross income
  (*EGI*), *360*
effective tax rate, *373*
equity, *343*
equity dividend, *363*
equity dividend rate, *364*
expense stop, *358*
growth investing, *347*
internal rate of return (*IRR*), *362*
investment analysis, *361*
marginal tax rate, *369*
market analysis, *349*

market timing, *347*
net operating income (*NOI*), *359*
passive income, *373*
portfolio income, *374*
"real estate cycle," *344*
sector investing, *346*
space per employee, *349*
taxable income, *367*
trophy properties, *349*
turnaround investing, *348*
value investing, *347*

Useful Web Sites

www.ncreif.com—The National Council of Real Estate Investment Fiduciaries (NCREIF) is an association of institutional real estate professionals who share a common interest in their industry. This site provides real estate information on standards, index, membership, and resources.

www.reiac.org—This is the Real Estate Investment Advisory Council Web site, whose purpose is to provide for the exchange of ideas, concerns, and experiences between people who conduct commercial real estate transactions within the structure of a nonprofit organization.

www.gecapitalrealestate.com—GE Capital Real Estate. This site offers information on a wide variety of real estate financial products that the company offers.

www.irs.gov—The IRS Web site can be useful to find information on the taxation of real estate income property. The main page has a search engine to search the IRS Web site.

www.ciremagazine.com—Web site for the Certified Commercial Investment Manager's *Commercial Investment Real Estate* magazine. Great source of articles related to investing in commercial real estate.

www.fiabci.com—This site is a good source for a comparison of the legislation, professional standards, taxation, and licensing in different countries. It also gives a comparative snapshot of various requirements for commercial leases in several countries.

www.china-window.com/china_market/china_real_estate/index.shtml—This Web site gives information about the real estate market in China. It also gives useful information about the laws and regulations concerning real estate, different sites related to real estate in China, and contact information for different government agencies.

www.city-data.com—This Web site gives very descriptive and interesting profiles of all U.S. cities. It has tens of thousands of city photos not found anywhere else, hundreds of thousands of maps, satellite photos, stats about residents (race, income, ancestries, education, employment, etc.), geographical data, state profiles, crime data, housing, businesses, birthplaces of famous people, political contributions, city government employment, weather, hospitals, schools, libraries, houses, airports, radio and TV stations, zip codes, area codes, user-submitted facts, similar cities list, and comparisons to averages. In sum, it is a very good site for doing real estate analysis.

Questions

1. What are the primary benefits from investing in real estate income property?
2. What factors affect a property's projected *NOI?*
3. What factors would result in a property increasing in value over a holding period?
4. How do you think expense stops and CPI adjustments in leases affect the riskiness of the lease from the lessor's point of view?
5. Why should investors be concerned about market rents if they are purchasing a property subject to leases?
6. What is meant by *equity?*
7. What are the similarities and differences between an overall rate and an equity dividend rate?
8. What is the significance of a debt coverage ratio?
9. What is meant by a *tax shelter?*
10. How is the gain from the sale of real estate taxed?
11. What is meant by an *effective tax rate?* What does it measure?
12. Do you think taxes affect the value of real estate versus other investments?
13. What is the significance of the passive activity loss limitation (PAL) rules for real estate investors?

Problems

1. An office building has three floors of rentable space with a single tenant on each floor. The first floor has 20,000 square feet of rentable space and is currently renting for $15 per square foot. Three years remain on the lease. The lease has an expense stop at $4 per square foot. The second floor has 15,000 square feet of rentable space and is leasing for $15.50 per square foot and has four years remaining on the lease. This lease has an expense stop at $4.50 per square foot. The third floor has 15,000 square feet of leasable space and a lease just signed for the next five years at a rental rate of $17 per square foot, which is the current market rate. The expense stop is at $5 per square foot, which is what expenses per square foot are estimated to be during the next year (excluding management). Management expenses are expected to be 5 percent of effective gross income and are not included in the expense stop. Each lease also has a CPI adjustment that provides for the base rent to increase at half the increase in the CPI. The CPI is

projected to increase 3 percent per year. Estimated operating expenses for the next year include the following:

Property taxes	$100,000
Insurance	10,000
Utilities	75,000
Janitorial	25,000
Maintenance	40,000
Total	$250,000

All expenses are projected to increase 3 percent per year. The market rental rate at which leases are expected to be renewed is also projected to increase 3 percent per year. When a lease is renewed, it will have an expense stop equal to operating expenses per square foot during the first year of the lease. To account for any time that may be necessary to find new tenants after current leases expire and new leases are made, vacancy is estimated to be 10 percent of *EGI* for the last two years (years 4 and 5).

a. Project the effective gross income (*EGI*) for the next five years.

b. Project the expense reimbursements for the next five years.

c. Project the net operating income (*NOI*) for the next five years.

d. How much does the *NOI* increase (average compound rate) over the five years?

e. Assuming the property is purchased for $5 million, what is the overall capitalization rate ("going-in" rate)?

2. You are an employee of University Consultants, Ltd., and have been given the following assignment. You are to present an investment analysis of a new small residential income-producing property for sale to a potential investor. The asking price for the property is $1,250,000; rents are estimated at $200,000 during the first year and are expected to grow at 3 percent per year thereafter. Vacancies and collection losses are expected to be 10 percent of rents. Operating expenses will be 35 percent of effective gross income. A fully amortizing 70 percent loan can be obtained at 11 percent interest for 30 years (total annual payments will be monthly payments * 12). The property is expected to appreciate in value at 3 percent per year and is expected to be owned for five years and then sold.

a. What is the investor's expected before-tax internal rate of return on equity invested (*BTIRR*)?

b. What is the first-year debt coverage ratio?

c. What is the terminal capitalization rate?

d. What is the *NPV* using a 14 percent discount rate? What does this mean?

e. What is the profitability index using a 14 percent discount rate? What does this mean?

3. (Extension of problem 2) You are still an employee of University Consultants, Ltd. The investor tells you she would also like to know how tax considerations affect your investment analysis. You determine that the building represents 90 percent of value and would be depreciated over 39 years (use 1/39 per year). The potential investor indicates that she is in the 36 percent tax bracket and has enough passive income from other activities so that any passive losses from this activity would not be subject to any passive activity loss limitations. Capital gains from price appreciation will be taxed at 20 percent and depreciation recapture will be taxed at 25 percent.

a. What is the investor's expected after-tax internal rate of return on equity invested (*ATIRR*)? How does this compare with the before-tax *IRR* (*BTIRR*) calculated earlier?

b. What is the effective tax rate and before-tax equivalent yield?

c. How would you evaluate the tax benefits of this investment?

d. Recalculate the *ATIRR* in part (*a*) under the assumption that the investor *cannot* deduct any of the passive losses (they all become suspended) until the property is sold after five years.

4. **Excel.** Refer to the Monument Office example. Assume the capital gain tax rate is lowered to 5 percent for all capital gain (price increase and depreciation recapture). How does this affect the investor's after-tax *IRR*?

5. Small City currently has 1 million square feet of office space, of which 900,000 square feet is occupied by 3,000 employees who are mainly involved in professional services such as finance, insurance, and real estate. Small City's economy has been fairly strong in recent years, but employment growth is expected to be somewhat lower during the next few years, with projections of an increase of just 100 additional employees per year for the next three years. The amount of space per employee is expected to remain the same. However, a new 50,000 square-foot office building was started before the recession and its space is expected to become available at the end of the current year (one year from now). No more space is expected to become available after that for quite some time.

   a. What is the current occupancy rate for office space in Small City?

   b. How much office space will be absorbed each year for the next three years?

   c. What will the occupancy rate be at the end of each of the next three years?

   d. Based on the above analysis, do you think it is more likely that office rental rates will rise or fall over the next three years?

Appendix A

Approaches to Metro Area Market Forecasting:

Basic Concepts and Data Sources

In Chapters 9 and 10, we discussed the importance of leases and cash flows. In this chapter, we illustrated how to estimate the amount of space tenants need, using office space as an example. In this appendix, we elaborate on the types of industries, businesses, and tenants that are important to the economic base, or the desired amount of space by tenants, in a local market. We provide a basic discussion of economic drivers that affect the economic base, which in turn affects rents. This is done for each of the major types of space: office, warehouse, retail, and multifamily.

Office Markets

As discussed in this chapter, the demand for office space is a *derived demand*. When making leasing decisions, users (tenants) consider how much space is needed for their operations, which in turn is affected by the sales of their products and services to customers. Therefore, as sales to customers and clients increase or decrease, tenants may demand more or less space for operations. Thus, *the demand for office and warehouse space is derived from sales of products and services produced by tenants.*

When forecasting the demand for space, access to revenues and sales data for all firms doing business in a given market would be ideal. Unfortunately, these data are not available either regionally or locally. Therefore, when considering investments and forecasting cash flows, a *proxy variable* that is believed to be highly correlated with the demand for office space is constructed and used as an indicator of demand.

As discussed earlier in this chapter, the proxy variable most commonly used for the case of office properties is office employment. Data on office employment are not collected as a specific data series. They must be compiled from total payroll employment and other data collected from the U.S. Department of Labor (*http://www.dol.gov/*). Payroll employment data, which are collected and classified based on the NAICS, or North American Industrial Classification System (*http://www.census.gov/eos/www/naics/*), are used to develop an estimate of office employment. As shown in Exhibit 11A–1, these data files are classified by major industry classifications that are then broken down further into subcategories.[1] Data are available for all metropolitan areas in the United States.

---

[1] Data are available for the United States and major metro areas. Further breakdowns (level 3) are also available. In addition, data are available by income/salary ranges for occupation categories. These data are published after a considerable time lag, however.

EXHIBIT 11A–1
NAICS Employment Classifications

Employment Classifications (Level 1)	Employment Classifications (Level 2)
(1) Resources, Mining, and Construction	* Natural Resources and Mining * Construction
(2) Manufacturing	* Nondurable Goods * Durable Goods
(3) Trade, Transportation, and Utilities	* Wholesale Trade * Retail Trade * Transportation and Utilities
(4) Information	* Publishing Industries (Except International) * Motion Picture and Sound Recording * Broadcasting (Except Internet) * Telecommunications * ISPS, Search Portals, and Data Processing * Other Information Services
(5) Financial Activities	* Finance and Insurance * Real Estate, Rental, and Leasing
(6) Professional and Business Services	* Professional and Tech Services * Administration and Waste Services
(7) Education and Health Services	* Education * Health Care and Social Assistance
(8) Leisure and Hospitality	* Art, Entertainment, and Recreation * Accommodations and Food Services
(9) Other Services (except public administration)	* Repair and Maintenance * Personal and Laundry Services * Membership Association and Organizations
(10) Government	* Federal Government

When forecasting the need for office space, it is important to realize that *some industry sectors tend to have a greater percentage of workers concentrated in office buildings as compared to other industry sectors*. For example, surveys have shown that well over 80 percent of employees in the finance, insurance, real estate, legal, and accounting NAICS industry sectors occupy office space. Other important industry sectors include those employing architects, lobbyists, consultants, engineers, and advertising executives. On the other hand, fewer employees in the manufacturing industry sectors occupy office space. Therefore, demand for office space will tend to be greater in cities with a higher concentration of financial services employment (e.g., New York City) than in cities with more manufacturing employment (e.g., Detroit).

There are many *techniques* that may be used to forecast demand for office space for a given market. One very basic approach begins by forecasting total employment (*TE*) in the U.S. economy (see U.S. Department of Labor, payroll employment, *www.dol.gov*). We start with the historical data set for TE_{US}. We then establish its relationship to total output, or real gross domestic product (*RGDP*) for the United States (see the U.S. Bureau of Economic Analysis, *www.bea.gov*, and the U.S. Department of Commerce, *www.commerce.gov*). The goal is to establish the amount of total U.S. employment required to produce *RGDP*, the total output of goods and services produced in the U.S. economy. The resulting equation is:

Step 1: $\quad TE_{US} = f(RGDP_{US})$

This notation simply means that total employment in the United States (TE_{US}) depends on or is a *function of* real gross domestic product in the United States ($RGDP_{US}$). We will assume for simplicity that this is a linear function that can be expressed by a simple equation for a straight line that has an intercept (α) and a slope (β).[2] To determine what the equation is, we use simple linear regression. That is, we regress TE_{US} on $RGDP_{US}$ and obtain the equation:

$$\widehat{TE}_{US} = \alpha + \beta\left(RGDP_{US}\right)$$

We then use estimates[3] of $RGDP_{US}$ to forecast $\widehat{TE}_{US}$. The $\wedge$ symbol in the above equation simply means that we are estimating TE for the United States based on a statistical relationship.

In step 2, we compile historical data for OE_{HC} (office employment in Hypothetical City) based on payroll employment in those NAICS codes that we believe have the greatest correspondence to office employment (OE).

We then regress OE_{HC} on TE_{US}. The resulting equation may be used to forecast office employment in Hypothetical City based on forecasts of TE_{US} for the desired forecast period:

Step 2: $\qquad OE_{HC} = \alpha + \beta\ (TE_{US})$

In step 3, we consider the *historic ratio* of OE_{HC} to the existing total stock of office space in Hypothetical City.[4] This can be calculated for past years from the annual total existing stock of office space and the total amount of office employment in Hypothetical City, or *Office Space*$_{HC} \div OE_{HC}$. The result is the *historic ratio of office space per office employee,* or $HOSPOE_{HC}$. This ratio in Hypothetical City may now be used to determine the amount of additional space required, should $\widehat{OE}_{HC}$ increase in future periods based on its relationship with increases in total U.S. employment, as shown in step 2. This assumes that the past, historic ratio of *HOSPOE*, explained in step 3 in Hypothetical City, is indicative of the future relationship.

In our example for Hypothetical City, the amount of office space demanded per office employee during the next period would be:

$$\widehat{OE}_{HC} \times HOSPOE_{HC} = \text{Amount of future office space} \atop \text{demanded in HC}$$

The analyst would then conduct a survey to determine the *actual amount of office space under construction in Hypothetical City* and scheduled for completion during the forecast period.[5] By comparing the amount of space under construction with the forecasted amount of demand, a judgment can be made as to whether the new supply will be greater or less than forecasted demand. From this, judgments

can be made regarding the likely course for vacancy rates and rents in Hypothetical City's office market.

Related Considerations

In addition to this very basic approach to forecasting total demand for office space in Hypothetical City, some additional questions relative to the use of data that the analyst must consider are: (1) How far back in time should data be collected? (2) Should data be compiled quarterly or annually? (3) Should seasonal factors be considered? (4) Is demand for *HC* for future periods likely to be related to total U.S. employment in the same way? (5) How far in the future should the forecast extend? (6) Are there leads or lags between this demand and the time required for additional supply to be constructed? (7) Are there any efficiencies brought about by electronic innovation (computers, cell phones, texting, teleconferencing, etc.) that may change the future relationship between office space and office employment relative to the past?

Considerations relative to *submarkets* or *smaller areas* within Hypothetical City are more difficult to estimate. Unlike employment variables, data measuring the differences of transportation—mass transit use, parking, proximity to airports, and transit hubs, all of which may affect demand for office space—may not be collected systematically. Data inputs for these influences are usually dealt with by conducting surveys from time to time. These influences are important and should be considered as "conditioning" or important "context" influences when doing research.

Warehouse/Distribution Markets

Related to the use of NAICS codes to identify employment in industry sectors closely related to office employment, another application of this approach is used frequently to estimate the demand for warehouse/distribution space. A *proxy variable* that is believed to be highly correlated with the sales and output of firms likely to lease significant volumes of warehouse space in a given market is usually constructed from payroll employment data and NAICS classifications. Industry sectors commonly used to focus more directly on warehouse-related employment include import-export, wholesale-retail, transportation, and manufacturing, as well as research and development activities. Employment in these sectors tends to expand and contract with businesses that include distribution/assembly/order fulfillment and shipping operations. As was the case with office employment

---

[2] Greek letters are typically used when equations are estimated from statistical analysis.

[3] Estimates for future growth in *RGDP* are usually available from research centers at major universities or from proprietary economic forecasting firms. Firms of note include Economy.com and Haver Analytics.

[4] Annual data for the stock of office space are usually obtainable from major office brokers in most metro areas.

[5] Forecasts may be made for various time periods. Forecast periods commonly used may be one, two, or three years. Forecast periods are commonly selected by the estimated time required to complete construction of buildings under way.

(*OE*), a data series closely related to those activities can be constructed from NAICS codes. Warehouse-related employment (*WE*) can be determined using total payroll employment data that are available for all major metro areas in the United States. Expected demand for warehouse space may be estimated following the steps used in the office market discussion relative to $RGDP_{US}$ and TE_{US} by substituting WE_{HC} in place of OE_{HC}. Based on the forecasted change in WE_{HC}, the demand for warehouse space may then be based on the historic ratio of warehouse space (obtained by broker surveys) per warehouse employee (*WE*). Given the expected change in $\widehat{WE}$, the demand for space may then be compared to warehouse space actually under construction to judge whether or not vacancy rates and rents for warehouse space in Hypothetical City are likely to increase or decrease.

Related Considerations

Many of the same issues discussed regarding forecasting office space are relevant for the warehouse market. Additional major considerations include trends in outsourcing (overseas) manufacturing, import-export activity, energy-fuel costs, the relative costs of rail, air, truck, and alternative/combined modes of transporting goods/inventory, as well as research and development activities. Data-reflecting activities and trends in these influences are important and should be incorporated, when possible, in forecasts.

Multivariate Analysis—Unique Regional Features in Office/Warehouse Markets

In the above formulations for Hypothetical City, we have basically asserted that the need for office and warehouse space in Hypothetical City is driven by growth in total employment in the United States. In short, we are establishing a systematic relationship between past employment growth in *HC* and its relationship to U.S. employment growth. We are also assuming that the pattern between *HC* and the United States will continue during the forecast period.

In some circumstances, the analyst may be able to improve the forecast for a local or regional market by *adding one or more additional variables* to the analysis. These variables must (1) be important enough to differentiate a local market (Hypothetical City) from U.S. total employment and (2) actually improve the accuracy of the forecast.[6] An example can be used for Houston, Texas, where the energy industry is a major driver of local employment. Hence, in addition to the TE_{US}, we use another variable, *WT* (the price of West Texas Intermediate crude oil) to represent an additional driver of local office employment. When forecasting office employment in Houston (*OE_H*) which is a major center for energy production, distribution, refining, and so forth, we may consider:

$$OE_H = f(TE_{US} \; WTI)$$

In other words, office employment in Houston (*OE_H*) is related to total U.S. employment (TE_{US}) and the price of West Texas Intermediate crude oil (*WTI*) (or some other proxy variable for energy prices). (See: U.S. Energy Information Administration, *www.eia.doe.gov*.) Regressing these relationships, we have:

$$\widehat{OE}_H = \alpha + \beta_1 \left(TE_{US} \right) + \beta_2 \left(WTI \right)$$

If this observation about energy prices is accurate, our forecast for office employment in Houston is likely to be more accurate than would be the case if the forecast did not include *WTI*. Similar applications could be made in metro areas such as New York City, where instead of *WTI*, the exchange rate between the U.S. dollar and other currencies (a proxy variable that reflects the extent of international capital flows) has been suggested to be an important explanatory variable.

Modifying forecasts by including additional variables is not without problems, however. This is because values for those variables (*WTI*, exchange rates, etc.) also must be forecasted in addition to TE_{US} when attempting to forecast future *OE*. Nonetheless, these additional variables reinforce the idea that employment in many local markets is affected not only by drivers of U.S. economic growth but also by unique features in the *economic base* of metro areas. If these factors are sufficiently different from drivers of total employment in the United States, including additional variables in the metro area forecasts may be warranted.

Retail Markets

Although the demand for retail space also is a *derived demand,* the *drivers* are very different than those discussed in relation to the office and warehouse sectors. Generally, income, consumer spending, and/or population growth tend to be important drivers of demand for retail shopping space.

Population Growth

One ratio that is carefully considered by many analysts when considering the demand for retail space in local markets is *retail space per capita*. This ratio can be interpreted as the amount of retail space per person in the local market being analyzed. At the most basic level of analysis, this indicator suggests that all individuals consume by shopping directly (or indirectly for minor children, dependents, etc.). Therefore, population growth is an extremely important driver for space needed by retail business establishments. One approach that may be used to begin a forecast of the desired amount of total retail space for Hypothetical City:

Step 1. Conduct a survey to establish total retail space (*TRS*) in Hypothetical City.[7]

---

[6] Regarding accuracy in forecasting, see an elementary statistics textbook for tests of significance, "goodness of fit," and other topics.

[7] Data for total retail space are usually available from local brokers, property managers, and so on. Population data are available from the U.S. Census Bureau, *www.census.gov*.

Step 2. Calculate the annual ratio of $TRS_{HC} \div Population_{HC} =$ Historical retail space per capita ($HTRSPC_{HC}$).

Step 3. Establish the statistical relationship between POP_{HC} and POP_{US} or:

$$POP_{HC} = f(POP_{US})$$

Then, given expected growth in POP_{US}, we get expected $\hat{POP}_{HC}$ as:

$$\hat{POP}_{HC} = \alpha + \beta \left(POP_{US} \right)$$

Then, using the historic ratio $HTRSPC_{HC}$ calculated in step 2, we multiply the increase in population for Hypothetical City and thereby obtain an estimate for the desired amount of total retail space, or:

$$HTRSPC_{HC} \times \hat{POP}_{HC} = \hat{TRS}_{HC}$$

We can then compare $\hat{TRS}_{HC}$ to the actual amount of existing retail space, plus space under construction in Hypothetical City, to determine the likelihood of vacancy and rent (cash flows) increasing or decreasing for the forecast period.

Multivariate Analysis: Unique Regional Features in Retail Markets

Depending on the nature of the market being analyzed, the simplified approach using population could be modified by considering changes in income, age groups, immigration, and other characteristics important to retail shopping in a local market.

Income Variables

Very important income concepts that are closely followed by retail property analysts include:

1. *Personal income.* Personal income measures the income of households from wages and salaries, fringe benefits, profits from self-employment, rent, patents, copyrights, royalties, interest, dividends, and other sources. Personal income data are available for all major metro areas in the United States (see Bureau of Economic Analysis, *www.bea.gov*, and the U.S. Department of Commerce, *www.commerce.gov*).

2. *Changes in the distribution of personal income.* An increase in the concentration of income earned by a smaller percentage of the population in an area may imply greater demand for luxury goods and specialty retail.

3. *Concentration of income by age group.* Personal income also may be measured by age group. For example, higher income, older households versus lower income, younger households may be an important distinction for retail shopping in some local markets.

Consumer Spending Variables

In addition to demographics and income, *consumer spending* is also followed closely by retail analysts. Consumer spending can be classified in three general ways based on data collected by the U.S. Department of Commerce (*www.census.gov/retail*):

1. *Personal consumption expenditures (PCE).* This is the broadest measure of spending and consists of consumer expenditures on all goods and services. This includes spending on durable and nondurable goods (utilities, autos, appliances, gasoline, food, medical, education, etc.).

2. *Retail sales.* This category is more specific and includes all consumer spending on goods and services purchased from *retail establishments*. This concept is narrower in focus than *PCE* in that utilities, transportation, and other services not purchased in retail establishments are excluded. Data collected for this concept are available for all major metro areas. Demographics are important to the retail sales category of consumer spending. For example, a greater concentration of older residents (retirees) versus younger age groups affects retail shopping patterns. For example, consider Palm Beach, Florida (older) versus Dallas, Texas (younger).

3. *General merchandise, apparel and accessories, furniture, and other sales (GAFO).* This concept includes those retail sales *most likely* to be purchased from establishments in shopping centers (particularly apparel) or in "stand-alone stores." Because this retail activity is most closely related to activities at malls, and similar retail establishments, it is very closely followed by investors in retail properties.

Submarket Analysis—Retail Trade Areas

After considering retail demand at the metro level, in cases where the analysis is focused on a specific location (submarket), retail analysts rely heavily on what is referred to as *trade area analysis*. This analysis is usually applied in one of two ways. In the first application, developers and/or investors may have an interest in a particular site or property and want to evaluate its potential retail demand. In this case, they collect and evaluate data corresponding to the population, income, age, gender, and education of households *living in proximity to the site or property in question*.[8] This information helps the analyst evaluate the appropriate retail mix of shops (grocery, bank, electronics, etc.) that will tend to maximize value.

The second application is used by retailers. This application usually involves *data mining*. *Data mining* involves analyzing attributes in locations where retailers have established successful operations. Economic/demographic characteristics in these successful locations and the corresponding trade areas are then used to identify potential sites and properties for future operations.

---

[8] Usually, such an analysis would be done in a one-, three-, or five-mile radius.

Multifamily Housing Markets

The demand for multifamily housing is generally related to several very important influences. A very important driver to begin a forecast is the number of households occupied by the 20- to 34-year-old age range. Research has shown that individuals ranging from 20 to 34 years of age represent the largest percentage of renters among all age groups. As the average age of a household exceeds 34 years, the percentage of renters tends to decline. This is because a greater percentage of older householders prefer to own rather than rent. To begin our forecast of multifamily housing units ($MFHU_{HC}$), we first obtain historical data for the number of multifamily units and the number of households in the 20- to 34-year-old age (AGE) group in Hypothetical City. We establish the functional relationship as:

$$MFHU_{HC} = f(AGE_{HC})$$

We then estimate the basic statistical relationship as:

$$\widehat{MFHU}_{HC} = \alpha + \beta_1\left(AGE_{HC}\right)$$

Future values for AGE are readily obtainable for all metro areas from the U.S. Census Bureau (*www.census.gov*).

Multivariate Analysis: Other Drivers of Multifamily Demand

Other important drivers of the demand for multifamily housing include:

1. *Income.* As average household income rises in a local market, holding all else constant, the demand for renter housing tends to fall relative to owned housing. This is because higher income households tend to prefer to own housing rather than rent.

2. *Price of single-family housing (or affordability).* As the price of single-family housing increases, holding all else constant, affordability of homeownership declines and the demand for multifamily housing tends to increase.

3. *Interest rates.* As interest rates rise, fewer households qualify for mortgage loans and therefore households tend to rent rather than own.

Essentially, the above discussion indicates that the demand for multifamily housing units (*MFHU*) in Hypothetical City is related to the number of households in the 20 to 34-year-age group (U.S. Census Bureau, *www.census.gov*), average personal income (*PI*) (U.S. Department of Commerce, *www.commerce.gov*), affordability of single-family housing (National Association of Realtors, *www.realtor.org*), and interest rates (Federal Reserve System Board of Governors, *www.federalreserve.gov*). Historical data needed for forecasting may be obtained from each source (link) indicated.

After making this $MFHU_{HC}$ forecast, the analyst may then determine whether the *actual total number of multifamily units, plus those under construction* in Hypothetical City are greater or less than the number forecasted. A judgment can then be made as to the impact on vacancies and rent (cash flows).

Other Considerations and Influences

In addition to the very basic and general approach to forecasting multifamily housing demand, there are several other trends that analysts may consider in regard to this property sector. These include:

Market Segments

* Age-restricted housing (seniors)
* Assisted living communities
* Retirement housing
* Recreational centered (golf, health)
* Downtown (conversions, lofts, etc.)
* Suburban (garden style)

Demographic Refinements

* Rural-to-urban migration
* Immigration
* Marriages
* Divorce rates

Supply Considerations: All Income-Producing Property Types

Thus far, we have illustrated some very general approaches to forecasting *demand* for the four major property types. When considering drivers affecting the *supply* of existing space and the construction of new space by developers in the office, warehouse, retail, and multifamily sectors, *forecasting becomes even more complex and, generally, less reliable.* Generally, the supply side for each property type is driven by many of the same factors. These include construction costs (*ConCost*) (i.e., the price of land, labor, and materials), interest rates (*i*) on construction loans, and existing vacancies (*VAC*). Given these factors, general function for supply (*S*) could be:

$$S = f(ConCost, i, VAC)$$

Generally, when vacancies decline, developers expect rents to increase. They then weigh construction and interest costs relative to expected rents to determine whether the construction of additional space may be profitable. However, additions to the supply of space are not continuous. This means that the scale of projects (e.g., 1,000 apartment units or 1,000,000 sq. ft. of space) tends to be "lumpy" and varies considerably as to the time required to acquire, finance, build, and lease. Large amounts of space being constructed in a multiphased and multiperiod process complicate forecasting. For this reason, investors and developers usually (1) supplement statistical estimation with actual market surveys of occupied space rents and units under construction for each property type and (2) continually monitor building permits, zoning, hearings, and so forth. Examples of other issues likely to vary by market area and affect supply include:

* Building codes
* Zoning restrictions
* Impact fees
* Inspections
* Historic significance
* Environmental impact
* Adequacy of infrastructure
* Terrain

Appendix B

REIWise Office Example

REIWise is a cloud-based DCF program that is designed specifically to solve investment analysis and valuation problems such as the office building analysis discussed in this chapter. Although this type of analysis can be done in Excel, it can become cumbersome to modify Excel templates for all the different ways that leases are structured including different start and end dates, different expense passthrough terms, and so on. A username and password to use REIWise, while using this textbook in a course, can be obtained by registering at the following web site: www.REIWise.com/edu.

In this appendix, we will show the inputs for REIWise to replicate the office building investment analysis example in the chapter and then illustrate a few additional analyses that can be done such as solving for the value of the property given a discount rate as was discussed in the previous chapter on valuation of income properties.

Exhibit 11B–1 shows the basic inputs for the Monument Office building example in Chapter 22. Most should be self-explanatory. There are only three tenants in this example but we have reserved inputs for three additional tenants. Users can also easily change the input for the number of tenants to add as many as needed.

We have specified a starting date for the analysis of July 2014. This will be important because as we will see, a starting date is also input for each lease. The property type input (office) is important because that determines many of the other inputs available for the analysis. For example, the inputs for apartments are based on unit types rather than leases. The discount rate will be used to estimate a property based on the present value of the NOI and projected resale (before considering financing and federal income taxes). Note that the terminal cap rate to estimate the resale price is indicated to apply to the subsequent year, that is, one year after the end of the holding period which is the way we discussed it is typically done.

Exhibit 11B–2 shows additional inputs for any capital reserves, financing, and tax information. There are no capital

reserve accounts being set up in this example. There is a loan as indicated in the loan details with the monthly payment calculated. The investor's tax rate is also specified for ordinary income and for capital gains. There is a drop-down menu to determine whether the passive loss rules apply to this property as discussed in the chapter. A state income tax can also be specified although there is none in this example.

Exhibit 11B–3 shows the basic inputs for the three tenants including the number of square feet in the lease, the base rent, and the starting date for the lease. The lease start date was not specified since the leases are already in effect. What is important for these three leases in the termination date and as we will see the inputs for expense stops and what happens when the existing leases terminate.

The speed analysis at the top is an alternative way of entering data in situations where a more detailed lease-by-lease analysis is not deemed necessary. These inputs should be self-explanatory.

The rent abatement input is for situations where there is a free rent period during the initial term of the lease. We will look at the term increases inputs next that are available after clicking on this entry.

Exhibit 11B–4 shows additional lease information for the bank. When the existing lease expires at the end of the remaining three-year term, it will be replaced by a new lease with a five-year term. There will be an increase of $2.75 from the contract rent on the existing lease to take it to the market rent we have projected for year 4 when the new lease starts. Recall that the base rent is $14 per square foot and the market rent for year 4 is projected to be $16.75. The increase of $2.75 will also apply on subsequent lease renewals but they are beyond our analysis holding period.

We could use this input screen to specify any increases in rent for the existing lease during its current lease term. For example, the lease could have a rent step which increases the rent after the third year of the lease which, since this lease started two years ago, would be the current year (year 1 of our

EXHIBIT 11B–1 **REIWise Basic Inputs**

ANALYSIS DATE

Analysis Date	07/2014 (mm/yyyy)	Auto Update	☐

GENERAL INFORMATION

Property Name	Monument Office	Address	
Property Type	Office ⌄	City	
Number Tenants	6 ⌄	State	
Purchase Price	$8,500,000 ...	Zip Code	
Property Misc.	☐ NNN ☐ Distressed ☐ Auction	Country	United States ⌄
Listing Status	Off Market ⌄		

PROPERTY DETAILS

Year Built	(yyyy)	Market	
Rentable Sq. Ft.	96,000	Sub Market	
Lot Size	0 Sq Ft ⌄	Floors	1 (integer only)
Zoning		APN	
Parking Ratio		Ownership Type	[select] ⌄

RESALE INFORMATION

Resale Expenses	0.0 %	Resale Valuation	Capitalization of NOI ⌄ at 10.60 % ☑ Sbsqnt Yr
Value of Land	$1,275,000	Discount Rate	14.0 %

EXHIBIT 11B–2 **REIWise Loan and Tax Inputs**

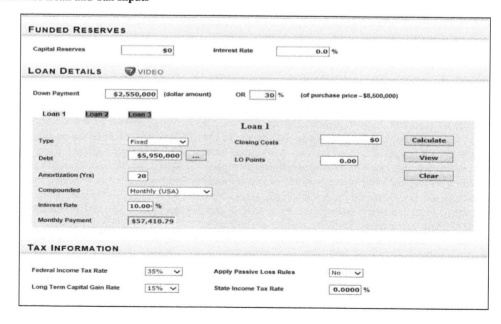

FUNDED RESERVES

Capital Reserves	$0	Interest Rate	0.0 %

LOAN DETAILS ▼ VIDEO

Down Payment $2,550,000 (dollar amount) OR 30 % (of purchase price – $8,500,000)

Loan 1   Loan 2   Loan 3

Loan 1

Type	Fixed ⌄	Closing Costs	$0	Calculate
Debt	$5,950,000 ...	LO Points	0.00	View
Amortization (Yrs)	20			Clear
Compounded	Monthly (USA) ⌄			
Interest Rate	10.00 %			
Monthly Payment	$57,418.79			

TAX INFORMATION

Federal Income Tax Rate	35% ⌄	Apply Passive Loss Rules	No ⌄
Long Term Capital Gain Rate	15% ⌄	State Income Tax Rate	0.0000 %

EXHIBIT 11B–3 REIWise Leasse and other Income

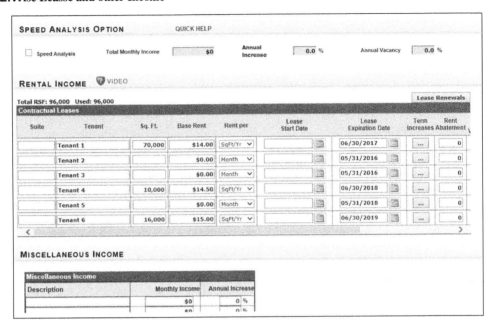

EXHIBIT 11B–4 **REIWise Lease Renewal and Lease Reimbursements**

REIWISE

Select Lease	Bank	CLOSE

LEASE RENEWAL DETAILS   QUICK HELP

Term (years)			
Rent Abatement	0	Tenant Improvements	$0.00
Turnover Vacancy	0 %	Leasing Commissions	0.00 %

LEASE RENEWAL RENT INCREASES   QUICK HELP

Term to Term Increase Type	SqFt/Year
Term to Term Increase Amount	$2.75 (every 5 years)
Within Term Increase Type	percent of base

	2	3	4	5	6
Within Term Increase Amount	0.00	0.00	0.00	0.00	0

LEASE REIMBURSEMENTS

Reimbursement Type	Base Stop Amount
Amount	$280,000

analysis). But in this example, there are no rent steps or CPI adjustments that would increase the rent during the lease term.

The bank lease does have an expense passthrough provision to pass through any increase in expenses above a rent stop which for this lease is $4 per square foot. Multiplying this by the 70,000 square feet for the bank's lease, results in an expense stop of $280,000. If the reimbursable expenses (all but management in this example) exceed $4.00 per square foot, then the excess will be passed through to this tenant based on 70,000 square feet.

The inputs for the other two leases (not shown) would be the same as for the bank except that the increase to market rent at the end of these two leases works out to be $3.00 for each lease. The insurance company goes from a base rent of $14.50 to $18.50 for year 5 and the broker goes from $15.00 to $18.00 in year 6. We only have a five-year holding period but recall that year 6 is used to estimate the resale price with a terminal cap rate.

Exhibit 11B–5 shows the assumptions for the operating expenses including any reserve allowance for replacement of longer lived items like a roof replacement. There are different options for how the expenses work. For this example, the management fee is a percent of base rent plus any reimbursable expenses. Another option in the drop down menu (not shown) is to have the management fee based on a percent of effective gross income (EGI).

There is no replacement allowance in this example. Note the speed analysis option for entering expenses. But in this case, we need to specify more details about each expense such as its growth rate. We can also specify whether each expense is reimbursable or not. In this case, all expenses (except management) are reimbursable.

The final input allows you to specify a specific year in which you expect capital expenses to occur such as repaving a driveway. This could be an alternative to or in addition to any reserve allowance already specified. In this example, we have not anticipated capital expenditures during the projected holding period.

Exhibit 11B–6 is allows you to enter a global vacancy rate. It is a minimum vacancy rate that applies for the years specified that allows for unexpected vacancy. For example, in our analysis, we assumed the tenants would renew. But if they do not, there will be some vacancy until a new tenant if found. The individual lease inputs allowed us to specify an expected vacancy due to the time to renew that lease. But we have chosen the alternative way of accounting for this possible vacancy by indicating that there will be a 5 percent vacancy rate starting in year 4 when the first lease is projected to be based on a renewal or new tenant. The same rate will apply for subsequent years.

Exhibit 11B–7 shows the projected NOI for years 1 to 6. Again, we have a five year holding period but year 6 NOI is needed to estimate the resale price. Actually, REIWise automatically does the projections for 20 years, but we are only interested in the projections up to year 6.

EXHIBIT 11B–5 REIWise Expense Assumptions

PROPERTY MANAGEMENT FEE

| Percent of Gross Scheduled Income | 5.0 % | Base Rent & Reimbursables ▾ | Reimbursable ☐ |

REPLACEMENT RESERVES

| Reserve Amount | $0.00 | Sq. Ft. ▾ |

SPEED ANALYSIS OPTION

| ☐ Speed Analysis | Total Annual Expenses | $0 | Annual Increase | 0.0 % |

GENERAL EXPENSES

| General Expenses | | | |
Description	Annual Expense	Annual Increase	Reimbursable
Property Tax	$148,800.00	2 %	☑
Insurance	$14,400.00	4 %	☑
Utilities	$120,000.00	5 %	☑
Janitorial	$76,800.00	3 %	☑
Maintenance	$67,200.00	3 %	☑
Handy Man	$0.00	0 %	☑
Janitorial	$0.00	0 %	☑
Legal	$0.00	0 %	☑
Maintenance	$0.00	0 %	☑

Expenses	Sum
Total:	$427,200
Reimbursable:	$427,200

CAPITAL EXPENSES

| Capital Expenses | | |
Description	Expense Amount	Year Expended
	$0	1
	$0	1

EXHIBIT 11B–6   **REIWise Vacancy Assumptions**

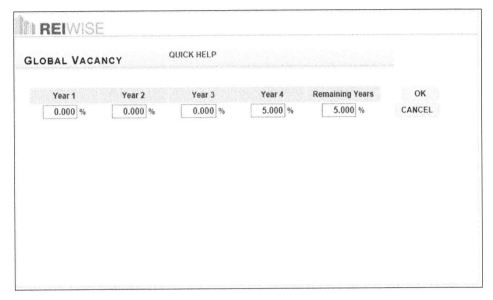

Exhibit 11B–7 shows the projections for resale. The projections are shown for each possible holding period up to year 5 in the exhibit but we are only interested in the one for year 5. Note the IRR of 13.38 percent, which is the same as we showed in the chapter for the after tax leveraged IRR for a five-year holding period.

Exhibit 11B–8 also has a row with the PV of NOI and Reversion. As suggested, this is the present value of just the NOI and reversion which are both before considering financing and before considering federal income taxes. This is based on the discount rate that was entered which, in this case, was 14 percent. The number for year 5 of $8,011,186 indicates that this is what should be paid for the property if the investor wants a 14 percent IRR. This is less than the purchase price because the actual IRR of 13.38 percent is less than 14 percent.

Exhibit 11B-9 shows the details of the calculation of after-tax cash flow from sale each possible year. Again, in

this case, we focus on the results for a five-year holding period. These are the cash flows used to get the cash flow from resale (net resale proceeds) in Exhibit 11B-8.

Finally, REIWise includes a number of charts that provide additional visual insight for analysts. Three of these are shown in Exhibits 1B–10 through 1B–12, and should be self-explanatory.

We encourage readers to register for use of REIWise while enrolled as a student. You will find it to be easy to use and a complement to use of spreadsheets. Learning to use a program like REIWise will also make it easy to understand any other DCF programs that are on the market because the concepts are generally the same in all the programs. What we like about REIWise is its ease of use for an initial exposure to lease-by-lease DCF programs and the ability to use it as long as you have an Internet connection—even from many mobile devices such as iPads.

EXHIBIT 11B–7   **REIWise NOI Projections**

Select Projection | Annual Property Operating Data ⌄

Projections

Description	Year 1	Year 2	Year 3	Year 4	Year 5	Year 6
Rental Income	$1,365,000	$1,365,000	$1,365,000	$1,557,500	$1,587,500	$1,635,500
Expense Reimbursements	$33,500	$47,372	$61,756	$13,693	$21,056	$24,657
GROSS SCHEDULED INCOME	$1,398,500	$1,412,372	$1,426,756	$1,571,193	$1,608,556	$1,660,157
General Vacancy	$0	$0	$0	($78,560)	($80,428)	($83,008)
GROSS OPERATING INCOME	$1,398,500	$1,412,372	$1,426,756	$1,492,633	$1,528,128	$1,577,149
Expenses						
Property Management Fee	($69,925)	($70,619)	($71,338)	($78,560)	($80,428)	($83,008)
Property Tax	($148,800)	($151,776)	($154,812)	($157,908)	($161,066)	($164,287)
Insurance	($14,400)	($14,976)	($15,575)	($16,198)	($16,846)	($17,520)
Utilities	($120,000)	($126,000)	($132,300)	($138,915)	($145,861)	($153,154)
Janitorial	($76,800)	($79,104)	($81,477)	($83,921)	($86,439)	($89,032)
Maintenance	($67,200)	($69,216)	($71,292)	($73,431)	($75,634)	($77,903)
TOTAL OPERATING EXPENSES	($497,125)	($511,691)	($526,794)	($548,933)	($566,274)	($584,904)
NET OPERATING INCOME	$901,375	$900,681	$899,962	$943,700	$961,855	$992,245

EXHIBIT 11B–8   **REIWise Investment Summary**

Select Projection | Investment Return Analysis ⌄

Projections

Description	Year 1	Year 2	Year 3	Year 4	Year 5
Cash Flow - To Date	$165,699	$330,044	$489,935	$673,853	$864,706
Net Resale Proceeds	$2,601,823	$2,659,189	$3,082,782	$3,314,787	$3,658,810
Invested Capital	($2,550,000)	($2,550,000)	($2,550,000)	($2,550,000)	($2,550,000) |($
Net Return on Investment	$217,522	$439,233	$1,022,717	$1,438,640	$1,973,516
Internal Rate of Return	8.53%	8.53%	12.57%	12.78%	13.38%
Modified IRR	8.53%	8.69%	12.65%	12.88%	13.44%
PV (NOI + reversion)	$8,244,184	$8,016,665	$8,100,331	$8,022,517	$8,011,186

EXHIBIT 11B−9 **REIWise Resale Price Estimates**

Select Projection	Resale Analysis	⌄				

Projections

Description	Year 1	Year 2	Year 3	Year 4	Year 5	Year 6
Projected Property Value	$8,496,994	$8,490,209	$8,902,831	$9,074,102	$9,360,805	$9,345,095
Resale Expenses	$0	$0	$0	$0	$0	$0
Proceeds b/f Debt Payoff	$8,496,994	$8,490,209	$8,902,831	$9,074,102	$9,360,805	$9,345,095
Basis at Acquisition	$8,500,000	$8,500,000	$8,500,000	$8,500,000	$8,500,000	$8,500,000
Depreciation	($177,518)	($362,767)	($548,016)	($733,265)	($918,514)	($1,103,763) (
Adjusted Tax Basis	$8,322,482	$8,137,233	$7,951,984	$7,766,735	$7,581,486	$7,396,237
Resale Tax Gain (Loss)	$174,513	$352,977	$950,847	$1,307,367	$1,779,319	$1,948,858
Resale Tax Benefit (Cost)	($43,628)	($88,244)	($197,429)	($269,432)	($358,749)	($402,705)
Loan Principal Balance	($5,851,543)	($5,742,776)	($5,622,620)	($5,489,883)	($5,343,245)	($5,181,253) (
Net Resale Proceeds	$2,601,823	$2,659,189	$3,082,782	$3,314,787	$3,658,810	$3,761,137

EXHIBIT 11B−10 **REIWise Equity Graph**

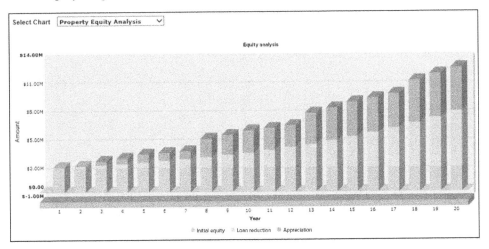

EXHIBIT 11B–11 REIWise Income and Cash Flow Graph

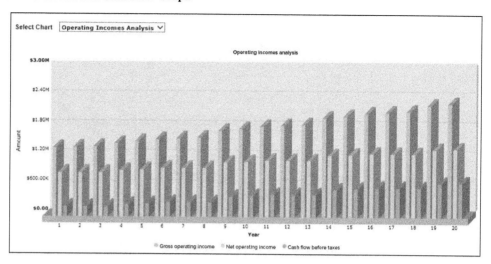

EXHIBIT 11B–12 REIWise Income and Expense Flow Graph

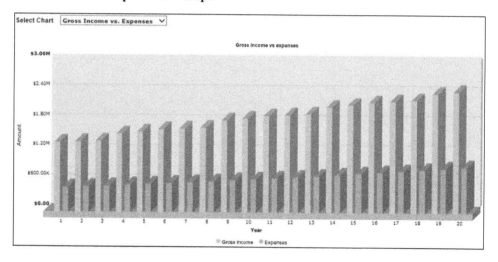

12

Financial Leverage and Financing Alternatives

In Chapter 6, we introduced a number of issues related to analyzing financing alternatives. Important concepts from that chapter include the effective cost of borrowing (before and after tax) and the incremental cost of borrowing additional funds. We also discussed how to evaluate whether a loan should be refinanced when interest rates decline. Although this discussion focused on *residential* property, all of the above concepts also apply to the analysis of income property.

The three preceding chapters have dealt with analyzing investment returns and risk on income property. In that analysis, we introduced financing and alluded to its effect on the before- and after-tax cash flow to the equity investor.

The purpose of this chapter will be to extend the discussion of debt from the earlier chapters in three additional ways. First, we consider how the level of financing affects the investor's before- and after-tax *IRR*. Second, we consider important underwriting procedures used by lenders when financing is sought by investors. Third, we consider several different financing alternatives that are used with real estate income property. Since it is impossible to discuss all the varieties of loans that are used in practice, we will concentrate on the primary alternatives and focus our discussion on concepts and techniques that you can apply to any type of financing alternative that you might consider.

Introduction to Financial Leverage

Why should an investor use debt? One obvious reason is simply that the investor may not have enough equity capital to buy the property. On the other hand, the investor may have enough equity capital but may choose to borrow anyway and use the excess equity to buy other properties. Because equity funds could be spread over several properties, the investor could reduce the overall risk of the portfolio. A second reason to borrow is to take advantage of the tax deductibility of mortgage interest, which amplifies tax benefits to the equity investor. The third reason usually given for using debt is to realize the potential benefit associated with financial leverage. **Financial leverage** is defined as benefits that may result for an investor who borrows money at a rate of interest lower than the expected rate of return on total funds invested in a property. If the return on the total investment invested in a property is greater than the rate of interest on the debt, the return on equity is magnified.

To examine the way financial leverage affects the investor's rate of return, we consider investment in a small commercial property with the following assumptions:

Purchase price	
Building value	$ 85,000
Land value	15,000
Total value	$100,000
Loan assumptions	
Loan amount	$ 80,000
Interest rate	10.00%
Term	Interest only
Income assumptions	
NOI	$12,000 per year (level)
Income tax rate*	28.00%
Depreciation	31.5 years (straight line)[†]
Resale price	$100,000
Holding period	5 years

*Used to illustrate this example only. Tax rates are subject to change.

[†]Recall from Chapter 11 that the Tax Act of 1993 allows residential property to be depreciated over 27.5 years and nonresidential property to be depreciated over 39 years. These rates are subject to change, however, and we use 31.5 years in this example for illustration only.

Using those assumptions, we obtain the cash flow estimates shown in Exhibit 12–1.

Exhibit 12–2 shows the cash flow summary and *IRR* calculations for the cash flows in Exhibit 12–1. From Exhibit 12–2 we see that the before-tax *IRR* (*BTIRR*) is 20 percent and the after-tax *IRR* (*ATIRR*) is 15.40 percent with an 80 percent loan. We now consider how these returns would be affected by a change in the amount of debt. Exhibits 12–3 and 12–4 show the cash flow and return calculations for the example assuming that *no loan* is used.

From Exhibit 12–4 we see that both the *BTIRR* and *ATIRR* have fallen. That is, both returns are higher with debt than without debt. When this occurs, we say that the investment has **positive (favorable) financial leverage.** We now examine the conditions that result in positive financial leverage more carefully. To do so, we first look at the conditions for positive leverage on a *before-tax* basis (the effect of leverage on *BTIRR*). Later, we examine the relationship on an *after-tax* basis (the effect of leverage on *ATIRR*).

Conditions for Positive Leverage—Before Tax

In the example when no debt was used, the *BTIRR* was 12 percent. We will refer to this as the *unleveraged BTIRR,* since it equals the return when no debt is used. In the case where 80 percent debt was used, the *BTIRR* increased to 20 percent. Why does this increase occur? It occurs because the *unleveraged BTIRR is greater than the interest rate paid on the debt.*[1] The interest rate on the debt was 10 percent, which is less than the 12 percent unleveraged *BTIRR*. We could say that the return on investment (before debt) is greater than the rate that has to be paid on the debt. This differential (12% vs 10%) means that positive leverage exists that will magnify the *BTIRR* on equity.

This relationship is formalized in a formula that estimates the return on equity, given the return on the property and the mortgage interest rate[2]:

$$BTIRR_E = BTIRR_P + (BTIRR_P - BTIRR_D)\,(D/E)$$

[1]More precisely, the unleveraged *IRR* is greater than the effective cost of the loan. Recall that the effective cost of a loan reflects points, prepayments, and other factors that affect the borrower.

[2] This is an approximation when the ratio of debt to equity changes over time.

EXHIBIT 12–1   **Cash Flow Estimates for Commercial Building**

		Estimates of Cash Flow from Operations			
			Year		
	1	**2**	**3**	**4**	**5**
A. Before-tax cash flow:					
Net operating income (*NOI*)	$12,000	$12,000	$12,000	$12,000	$12,000
Less debt service (*DS*)	8,000	8,000	8,000	8,000	8,000
Before-tax cash flow	$ 4,000	$ 4,000	$ 4,000	$ 4,000	$ 4,000
B. Taxable income or loss:					
Net operating income (*NOI*)	$12,000	$12,000	$12,000	$12,000	$12,000
Less interest	8,000	8,000	8,000	8,000	8,000
Depreciation	2,698	2,698	2,698	2,698	2,698
Taxable income (loss)	1,302	1,302	1,302	1,302	1,302
Tax	$ 364	$ 364	$ 364	$ 364	$ 364
C. After-tax cash flow:					
Before-tax cash flow (*BTCF*)	$ 4,000	$ 4,000	$ 4,000	$ 4,000	$ 4,000
Less tax	364	364	364	364	364
After-tax cash flow (*ATCF*)	$ 3,636	$ 3,636	$ 3,636	$ 3,636	$ 3,636

		Estimates of Cash Flows from Sale in Year 5		
Sale price				$100,000
Less mortgage balance				80,000
Before-tax cash flow (*BTCF$_s$*)				$ 20,000
Taxes in year of sale				
Sale price			$100,000	
Original cost basis		$100,000		
Less accumulated depreciation		13,492		
Adjusted basis			86,508	
Capital gain			$ 13,492	
Tax from sale				3,778
After-tax cash flow from sale (*ATCF$_s$*)				$ 16,222

where

$BTIRR_E$ = Before-tax *IRR* on equity invested

$BTIRR_P$ = Before-tax *IRR* on total investment in the property (debt and equity)

$BTIRR_D$ = Before-tax *IRR* on debt (effective cost of the loan considering points)

D/E = Ratio of debt to equity

Using the numbers for our example, we have

$$BTIRR_E = 12.00\% + (12.00\% - 10.00\%) \times (80\% \div 20\%)$$

$$= 20.00\%$$

This formula indicates that as long as $BTIRR_P$ is greater than $BTIRR_D$, the $BTIRR_E$ will be greater than $BTIRR_P$. This situation is referred to as favorable, or positive, leverage.

EXHIBIT 12–2
Cash Flow Summary
and *IRR*

	End of Year					
	0	**1**	**2**	**3**	**4**	**5**
Before-tax cash flow	$-20,000	$4,000	$4,000	$4,000	$4,000	24,000
After-tax cash flow	-20,000	3,636	3,636	3,636	3,636	19,858
Before-tax *IRR* (*BTIRR*) = 20.00%						
After-tax *IRR* (*ATIRR*) = 15.40%						

EXHIBIT 12–3   **Cash Flow Estimates (No Loan)**

	Estimates of Cash Flow from Operations				
	Year				
	1	**2**	**3**	**4**	**5**
A. Before-tax cash flow:					
Net operating income (*NOI*)	$12,000	$12,000	$12,000	$12,000	$12,000
Less debt service (*DS*)	0	0	0	0	0
Before-tax cash flow	$12,000	$12,000	$12,000	$12,000	$12,000
B. Taxable income or loss:					
Net operating income (*NOI*)	$12,000	$12,000	$12,000	$12,000	$12,000
Less interest	0	0	0	0	0
Depreciation	2,698	2,698	2,698	2,698	2,698
Taxable income (loss)	9,302	9,302	9,302	9,302	9,302
Tax	$ 2,604	$ 2,604	$ 2,604	$ 2,604	$ 2,604
C. After-tax cash flow:					
Before-tax cash flow (*BTCF*)	$12,000	$12,000	$12,000	$12,000	$12,000
Less tax	2,604	2,604	2,604	2,604	2,604
After-tax cash flow (*ATCF*)	$ 9,396	$ 9,396	$ 9,396	$ 9,396	$ 9,396

	Estimates of Cash Flows from Sale in Year 5		
Sale price			$100,000
Less mortgage balance			0
Before-tax cash flow (*BTCF$_s$*)			$100,000
Taxes in year of sale			
Sale price		$100,000	
Original cost basis	$100,000		
Less accumulated depreciation	13,492		
Adjusted basis		86,508	
Capital gain		$ 13,492	
Tax from sale			3,778
After-tax cash flow from sale (*ATCF$_s$*)			$ 96,222

Whenever leverage is positive, the greater the amount of debt, the higher the return to the equity investor. From this result many investors conclude that they should borrow as much as possible. (We will see later that this conclusion is not necessarily valid when risk is considered.) The graph in Exhibit 12–5 illustrates the effect of different loan-to-value ratios on the *IRR* for our example.

EXHIBIT 12–4
Cash Flow Summary and *IRR* (No Loan)

	Cash Flow Summary End of Year					
	0	**1**	**2**	**3**	**4**	**5**
Before-tax cash flow	$-100,000	$12,000	$12,000	$12,000	$12,000	$112,000
After-tax cash flow	-100,000	9,396	9,396	9,396	9,396	105,618

Before-tax *IRR* (*BTIRR*) = 12.00%
After-tax *IRR* (*ATIRR*) = 8.76%

EXHIBIT 12–5
Before- and After-Tax Positive Leverage

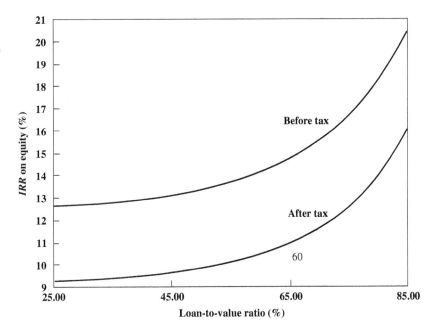

While the relationships in Exhibit 12–5 are relatively straightforward, the amount of debt that may be used is limited. What are the limits? First, for various amounts of debt, the debt coverage ratio may exceed the lender's limits, as discussed in Chapter 11. Because the *NOI* does not change when more debt is used, increasing the amount of debt increases the debt service relative to the *NOI*. Second, at higher loan-to-value ratios and declining debt coverage ratios, risk to the lender increases. As a result, the interest rate on additional debt will also increase. Indeed, at some point $BTIRR_P$ may no longer exceed $BTIRR_D$ (leverage will no longer be positive). Third, additional borrowing has additional risks for the equity investor. We will deal with the effect of leverage on risk more formally later in this chapter. However, we can point out now that leverage works both ways in the sense that it can magnify either returns or losses. That is, if the loan offers **negative (unfavorable) financial leverage,** or $ATIRR_D > BTIRR_P$, the use of more debt will magnify losses on equity invested in the property. We saw earlier that $BTIRR_P$ must exceed $BTIRR_D$ for the leverage to be favorable. Suppose that the interest rate is 14 percent instead of 10 percent. This results in negative leverage because the unlevered $BTIRR_E$ (12%) is now less than the 14 percent cost of debt. Exhibit 12–6 illustrates the effect that different loan-to-value ratios will have on the before- and after-tax *IRR*s. Note that when $BTIRR_P$ is less than $BTIRR_D$, the $BTIRR_E$ is also less than $BTIRR_D$ and declines even further as the amount borrowed (debt-to-equity ratio) increases. The next section develops this relationship more formally.

EXHIBIT 12–6
Before- and After-Tax Negative Leverage

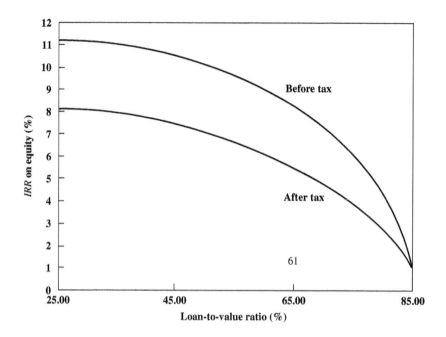

Conditions for Positive Leverage—After Tax

Looking at the after-tax *IRR* (*ATIRR*) in Exhibits 12–2 and 12–4, we see that $ATIRR_P$ (on total investment) is 8.76 percent and *ATIRR* on equity invested is 15.4 percent. Thus, the investor has favorable, or positive, leverage on an after-tax basis. That is, the expected after-tax *IRR* is higher if we can borrow money at a 10 percent rate as assumed in the example. How can leverage be favorable if the unlevered *ATIRR* (8.76%) is less than the cost of debt (10%)? The reason is because interest is tax deductible; hence, we must consider the after-tax cost of debt. Because there are no points involved in this example, the after-tax cost of debt is equal to the before-tax cost times $(1 - t)$, where t is the tax rate. Thus, the after-tax cost of debt is

$$.10(1 - .28) = 7.2\%$$

In the previous section we showed a formula to estimate the return on equity, given the return on the property and the mortgage interest rate. That formula can be modified to consider taxes as follows:

$$ATIRR_E = ATIRR_P + (ATIRR_P - ATIRR_D)\,(D/E)$$

where

$ATIRR_E$ = After-tax *IRR* on equity invested

$ATIRR_P$ = After-tax *IRR* on total funds invested in the property

$ATIRR_D$ = After-tax *IRR* on debt (effective after-tax cost of the loan)

D/E = Ratio of debt to equity

Using the above equation, we have

$$ATIRR_E = 8.76\% + (8.76\% - 7.2\%)\,(80\% \div 20\%)$$

$$= 15.00\%$$

Our example in Exhibit 12–7 assumes that the mortgage loan is made at a fixed rate of interest. As seen in Chapter 5, there are many transactions that are financed with *floating interest rate loans*. These loans are frequently made when financing commercial real estate. However, should borrowers *not* want a floating rate, **interest rate swaps** may be used to achieve the equivalent of a fixed interest rate. Banks that are willing to make only a floating rate loan are usually willing to execute a swap transaction for the borrower for a fee. The market for interest rate swaps is very large and involves many participants.

In our example, the borrower seeks to swap a floating rate for a fixed rate with a *counterparty* who is seeking to swap a fixed rate for a floating rate. Typically, the borrower selects a *notional amount* (in our example, $80,000) and pays a fee to the bank plus the spread (price) at which a counterparty with a similar credit rating is willing to execute the swap with the borrower. The amount is notional in the sense that it is only used to calculate what the interest would be based on this amount.*

This transaction is referred to as a "swap" because, in essence, the two parties to the swap trade payments. The borrower with the fixed rate mortgage pays a floating rate, and the counterparty with the floating rate pays a fixed rate. In actuality, only the *difference* in interest rates is exchanged between the parties. This transaction is usually referred to as a "plain vanilla swap" because it is the most frequent type of swap transaction. We also should point out that there is some probability that each party to the swap could default on their obligation or enter bankruptcy. Either or both parties can insure against default by the counterparty by purchasing a *credit default swap*, or "insurance."

In addition to interest rate swaps, foreign currency swaps for real estate development in other countries and other more complex transactions may be executed in the market for swaps. Finally, in addition to swaps, other alternatives may be used for hedging floating interest rate loans, such as buying and selling interest rate futures and/or options on futures. However, the latter strategies usually involve U.S. government securities with risk that is not directly correlated with commercial real estate risk. As a result, these transactions usually provide less efficient hedges than swaps.

*The swap in our example may be executed in amounts greater or less than $80,000. To the extent that it is lower, the borrower is underhedged and is bearing some risk, and to the extent that it is greater, the borrower is overhedged and may be expecting to profit, should interest rates increase.

Hence, the approximation is 15 percent versus the actual *ATIRR* of 15.40 percent, as shown in Exhibit 12–2. The formula is an approximation because the debt-to-equity ratio increases over the holding period. That is, although the initial debt-to-equity ratio is 4.0 ($80,000 ÷ $20,000), when the property is sold, the debt is still $80,000, but the equity is $16,222 ($ATCF_S$ of $96,222 less the loan of $80,000), resulting in a debt-to-equity ratio of 4.93. Thus, the average *D/E* for the holding period is greater than the initial *D/E* of 4 that we used in the formula. However, using the initial *D/E* is still a good approximation. And the pivotal point for leverage is still the after-tax cost of debt. That is, for leverage to be favorable on an *after-tax* basis, the after-tax return on total funds invested must exceed the after-tax cost of the debt. For example, in our illustration, if the $ATIRR_P$ was less than 7.2 percent, leverage would be unfavorable.

It is useful to summarize the various *IRR* calculations we have made for the office example. Exhibit 12–7 shows the before- and after-tax *IRR* with and without a loan. It is important to understand the difference between each of these returns. When using the term *return* (or *IRR*), it is obviously very important to specify whether that return is before tax or after tax, and whether it is based on having a loan (a *leveraged* return) or not having a loan (an *unleveraged* return).

EXHIBIT 12–7
Summary *IRR*
Measures

	$BTIRR_E$	$ATIRR_E$
No loan*	12.00%	8.76%
80% loan	20.00%	15.40%

*Note that $IRR_E = IRR_P$ when there is no loan.

Break-Even Interest Rate

In the previous discussion, we saw that the relationship between the after-tax *IRR* on the property (before debt) and the after-tax cost of debt determines whether leverage is favorable or unfavorable. It is sometimes useful to determine the maximum interest rate that could be paid on the debt before the leverage becomes unfavorable. This is referred to as the **break-even interest rate** and represents the interest rate at which the leverage is neutral (neither favorable nor unfavorable). By examining the after-tax leverage equation in the previous section, we see that the point of neutral leverage can be expressed as follows:

$$ATIRR_D = ATIRR_P$$

Based on this relationship, we want to know the interest rate that will result in an after-tax cost of debt that is equal to the after-tax *IRR* on total funds invested in the property. In general, recall from Chapter 6 that the after-tax cost of debt, $ATIRR_D$, can be estimated as follows:

$$ATIRR_D = BTIRR_D(1 - t)$$

Solving this for the before-tax cost of debt, we have

$$BTIRR_D = \frac{ATIRR_D}{1 - t}$$

Because the break-even point for leverage occurs when $ATIRR_D = ATIRR_P$, we can substitute $ATIRR_P$ for $ATIRR_D$ in the above equation and obtain a break-even interest rate:

$$BTIRR_D = \frac{ATIRR_p}{1 - t}$$

For our example, the break-even interest rate (*BEIR*) would be

$$\frac{8.76\%}{1 - .28} = 12.17\%$$

This means that regardless of the amount borrowed or the degree of leverage desired, the maximum rate of interest that may be paid on debt and not reduce the return on equity is 12.17 percent. To demonstrate this concept further, Exhibit 12–8 shows the after-tax *IRR* for interest rates ranging from 10 percent to 16 percent for three different loan-to-value ratios. Note that for interest rates above the break-even interest rate of 12.17 percent, the after-tax *IRR* for an equity investor ($ATIRR_E$) is less than the after-tax *IRR* on total investment ($ATIRR_P$), which is 8.76 percent. Conversely, for interest rates below the break-even interest rate, the after-tax *IRR* for the equity investor is greater than the after-tax *IRR* on the property.

Exhibit 12–9 graphs the information in Exhibit 12–8 and shows the break-even interest rate. Again note that the break-even interest rate remains 12.17 percent regardless of the amount borrowed (i.e., 60%, 70%, or 80% of the property value).

If an investor borrowed funds at an effective interest rate that was just equal to the break-even interest rate, leverage would be neutral; that is, it would not be unfavorable or favorable. However, at the break-even interest rate $ATIRR_P$ is exactly equal to $ATIRR_D$

EXHIBIT 12–8
Effect of Interest Rates on the After-Tax *IRR* on Equity

Interest Rate (%)	$ATIRR_E$ (%) Loan to Value		
	60%	70%	80%
10.00	10.83	11.86	13.73
10.50	10.36	11.16	12.61
11.00	9.89	10.45	11.48
11.50	9.41	9.73	10.32
12.00	8.92	9.01	9.16
12.50	8.44	8.27	7.98
13.00	7.95	7.53	6.78
13.50	7.45	6.79	5.57
14.00	6.95	6.03	4.34
14.50	6.45	5.27	3.10
15.00	5.95	4.50	1.85
15.50	5.44	3.73	0.58
16.00	4.92	2.94	−0.70

EXHIBIT 12–9
After-Tax *IRR* versus Interest Rates

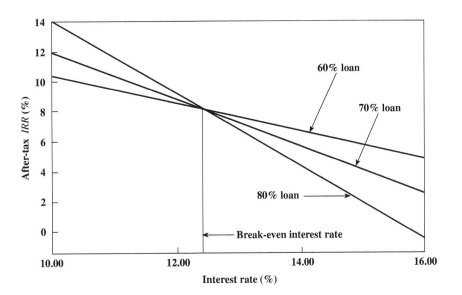

(by definition), which means that $ATIRR_E$ will exactly equal $ATIRR_D$. That is, the investor earns the same after-tax rate of return as a lender in the same project. But borrowing at the break-even interest rate will not provide a risk premium for the equity investor. Equity investors normally require a risk premium because they bear the risk of variations in the performance of the property. We will show this situation more formally below, in the section titled "Risk and Leverage."

Leverage and the Incremental Cost of Debt

As mentioned earlier in this chapter, as the amount of debt increases, lenders may charge a higher interest rate to obtain additional financing. Recall that in Chapter 6 we discussed the concept of the **incremental cost of debt,** which involves determining the actual cost of additional financing (e.g., getting a 90% loan instead of an 80% loan).

In the example we have been using in this chapter, an 80 percent loan was available at a 10 percent interest rate. Because this rate was less than the unleveraged return of 12 percent, we had favorable leverage, which resulted in a leveraged return of 15.4 percent.

Now suppose that the investor can obtain an 85 percent loan as an alternative to the 80 percent loan, but at a 10.25 percent interest rate instead of a 10 percent rate. Should the investor obtain the additional financing?

First, it might be noted that the 10.25 percent rate is still less than the 12 percent unleveraged return. Thus, there is still favorable leverage on *all* the funds being borrowed. But are the *additional* funds obtained from the 85 percent loan versus the 80 percent loan contributing to the favorable leverage? Or are these funds making it less favorable than it would have been with the 80 percent loan?

To get some insight into this, let us first calculate the incremental cost of the 85 percent loan. This is an interest-only loan, so the calculation of the incremental cost is fairly simple. Interest on the 85 percent loan is .1025 × $85,000, or $8,712.50. Interest on the 80 percent loan is .10 × $80,000, or $8,000. Thus, we have to pay an additional $712.50 in order to borrow an additional $5,000. Since it is interest only, we can simply divide the $712.50 by $5,000 to obtain the incremental cost of 14.25 percent. Thus, *additional* funds cost 14.25 percent. But what do we compare this to?

It is important to realize that we are now comparing the 85 percent loan with the 80 percent loan. As noted above, with the 80 percent loan we have a leveraged return of 15.4 percent for the example we have been analyzing. It is this return that the additional leverage is being applied to. That is, we are earning 15.4 percent before borrowing the *additional* money. To have favorable leverage on this additional money, the incremental cost of this additional money has to be less than 15.4 percent (not the original unleveraged return of 12%). Since the return before borrowing the additional money (15.4%) is greater than the incremental cost of debt (14.25%), there is positive leverage on the incremental funds. Thus, the leveraged return should increase even more if the additional funds are borrowed. The reader should verify that using an 85 percent loan with a 10.25 percent interest rate results in a leveraged *IRR* of 21.92 percent, which is higher than the original 20 percent leveraged return with the 80 percent loan at a 10 percent interest rate. (A good way to do this is to use the Excel spreadsheet provided with the book, which includes a tab with the leverage example.)

As we will discuss in the next section, the risk also increases as we borrow additional money. But at least we know that the additional leverage is positive. If it was not, then the investor might be better off just getting the 80 percent loan, since the additional funds would be reducing the leverage. Because the additional funds still contribute to positive leverage, the question is whether the additional return is a sufficient compensation for the additional risk.

Risk and Leverage

We have seen how favorable financial leverage can increase $BTIRR_E$ and $ATIRR_E$. We also have seen that increasing the amount of debt magnifies the effect of leverage. It is no wonder that many people conclude that they should borrow as much as possible (look at the number of "no money down" seminars and advocates of using "OPM," or other people's money). The point of the following discussion is to emphasize that *there is an implicit cost associated with the use of financial leverage.* This cost comes in the form of *higher risk.* To illustrate, consider the following investment opportunity:

Total project costs (land, improvements, etc.) will be $1 million. In our initial example, the investor does not use debt to finance the project. Three possible scenarios for a project are as follows:

Pessimistic—*NOI* will be $100,000 the first year and decrease 2 percent per year over a five-year holding period. The property will sell for $900,000 after five years.

Most likely—*NOI* will be level at $110,000 per year for the next five years, and the property will sell for $1.1 million.

Optimistic—*NOI* will be $120,000 the first year and increase 5 percent per year for five years. The property will then sell for $1.3 million.

The investor thinks probability for the pessimistic scenario is about 20 percent, for the most likely scenario, 50 percent, and for the optimistic scenario, 30 percent.

Using the preceding information, we have computed (calculations not shown) $BTIRR_P$ for each scenario, the expected $BTIRR_P$, the variance of the $BTIRR_P$, and the standard deviation of the $BTIRR_P$. The results are as follows:

| | Unleveraged | | | | | |
	(1) Estimated $BTIRR_P$	(2) Expected $BTIRR_P^*$	(3) Deviation (1) − (2)	(4) Squared Deviation	(5) Probability	(6) Product (4)(5)
Pessimistic	7.93	13.06	−5.13	26.31	0.20	5.26
Most likely	12.56	13.06	−0.50	0.25	0.50	0.12
Optimistic	17.31	13.06	4.25	18.07	0.30	5.42
					Variance	10.81
				Standard deviation = $\sqrt{10.81}$ = 3.29		

*7.93(.2) + 12.56(.5) + 17.31(.3) = 13.06%.

We now assume that the same investment is financed with a loan for $900,000, which is obtained at a 10 percent interest rate for a 15-year term. What will be the expected $BTIRR_E$ and the standard deviation of the $BTIRR_E$? The results are as follows:

| | Leveraged | | | | | |
	(1) Estimated $BTIRR_P$	(2) Expected $BTIRR_P^*$	(3) Deviation (1) − (2)	(4) Squared Deviation	(5) Probability	(6) Product (4)(5)
Pessimistic	−5.09	26.49	−31.58	997.36	0.20	199.47
Most likely	25.99	26.49	−0.50	0.25	0.50	0.13
Optimistic	48.38	26.49	21.89	479.13	0.30	143.74
					Variance	343.34
				Standard deviation = $\sqrt{343.34}$ = 18.53		

*− 5.09(.2) + 25.99(.5) + 48.38(.3) = 26.49%.

Note that under the most likely and optimistic scenarios, estimated *IRR*s are higher with the loan (leveraged) than with no loan (unleveraged), indicating that these cases offer favorable leverage. In the pessimistic case, however, the estimated return is lower, indicating that if that scenario occurs, leverage will be very unfavorable. Looking at the range in expected $BTIRR_P$, however, which is higher with the loan, one might think that it is still a good idea to borrow. Note, however, that the standard deviation is considerably higher in the levered case, 18.53 percent versus 3.29 percent. Thus, the investment is clearly riskier when leverage is used. (This would also be true regardless of whether the leverage is favorable or unfavorable.) The point is that the decision to use leverage cannot be made by only looking at $BTIRR_P$ and $BTIRR_E$. The investor must ask whether the higher expected return with leverage is commensurate with the higher risk. Alternatively, the investor should ask if there is a way to realize the higher return with less risk, such as another investment in a different property or in the same property but with a different way of financing. The impact of financial leverage on risk will be discussed further in the next chapter.

Underwriting Loans on Income Properties

Chapter 8 dealt with residential underwriting and lending. However, there are many additional issues that must be addressed by lenders when loan applications from investors in *commercial* and *multifamily* properties are evaluated. We focus only on the areas of major concern in the explanation that follows.

Market Study and Appraisal

When someone applies for debt financing, lenders usually require that the application be accompanied by a *market study* that includes an analysis of the economic base (see Chapter 7) and prospective employment growth for the city or region in which the property is located. Also included should be an analysis of the submarket showing vacancy rates and rents on competing properties, as well as any new construction and the expected demand by renters. In short, the lender must be assured that occupancy and rent will be adequate to support mortgage loan payments.

In addition to a market analysis for higher value properties, the loan application must be accompanied by an *appraisal* of the property being financed. This appraisal will usually be done by a third party (i.e., not the lender or the borrower), who will use one or more of the sales comparison, income capitalization, or cost approaches to value discussed in detail in Chapter 10. Each approach used to estimate value will be carefully reviewed by the lender, who may change any assumptions that are viewed to be too aggressive or otherwise inconsistent with the lender's assessment of the market, and a property value for lending purposes will be established. The loan will be secured by a mortgage on the property; therefore, the lender must be certain that the value of the property is sufficient to repay the loan in the event that the investor defaults and the property must be sold.

Borrower Financials

In addition to the mortgage security provided by the property, unless stated otherwise the borrower/investor will provide additional loan security in the form of personal liability on the note. Therefore, the lender will require a set of personal financial statements, or in the case of a corporate borrower, a set of corporate financial statements. The lender will consider the borrower's ability to pay, should income from the property be insufficient to pay debt services. However, in many cases borrowers and lenders may agree that a **nonrecourse clause** will be included in the note. This clause releases the borrower from personal liability and makes the property the sole source of security for the loan. To obtain a nonrecourse provision, lenders will usually require an additional fee and/or a higher interest rate as compensation for this lesser amount of loan security. From the standpoint of the borrower, this nonrecourse provision can be viewed as a **put option.** If default occurs and the value of the property is lower than the outstanding loan balance, the investor may "put," or give, the property security to the lender. The borrower/investor would lose any equity that existed when the loan was closed, plus the fee paid for the nonrecourse loan. These amounts can be thought of as the cost of the investor's option.

In case of default, assuming that the loan cannot be restructured in a workout agreement, the borrower would give the lender the deed to the property. This is sometimes referred to as *deed in lieu of foreclosure,* although depending on the state in which the property is located, the lender may have to go through a legal process to assure that title has been transferred to the lender and that the lender will be able to sell and transfer title to another investor.

The Loan-to-Value Ratio

Most lenders usually require that the loan amount being applied shall not exceed more than 75 percent to 80 percent of the value of the property. Therefore, should a borrower default on such a loan, the property serving as security for the loan would have to *decline* in value by 20 percent to 25 percent from the date of closing before the outstanding loan balance owed to the lender would be jeopardized. As a result, lenders tend to consider this range in the **loan-to-value ratio** to be important in underwriting.

The Debt Coverage Ratio

An additional underwriting benchmark widely used by lenders to limit default risk is the debt coverage ratio. This ratio measures the extent that the *NOI* from the property is expected to exceed the mortgage payments. The lender would like a sufficient cushion so that if the *NOI* becomes less than anticipated (e.g., from unexpected vacancy or a decline in rents), the borrower will still be able to make the mortgage payments without using personal funds.

The **debt coverage ratio** (*DCR*) is the ratio of *NOI* to the mortgage payment. For example, in Exhibit 12–1 the *NOI* projected in year 1 is $12,000 and the interest-only mortgage payment (debt service) is $8,000; these figures result in a debt coverage ratio of 1.50. Lenders typically want the debt coverage ratio to be at least 1.20. In this way, the operating income could decline by as much as 20 percent before the mortgage payment is in jeopardy. This 20 percent cushion is likely to be sufficient for most lenders. In the case shown in Exhibit 12–1, the cushion is 50 percent, which is far greater than 20 percent. Therefore, this property should easily meet the *DCR* target desired by the lender. However, one additional question of interest to the investor would be, "How high can the loan-to-value ratio be in order to reduce the loan-to-value ratio to 1.20?" The answer can be found as follows:

$$\frac{NOI}{\text{Desired } DCR \text{ target}} = \text{Max debt service}$$

$$\frac{\$12,000}{1.20} = \$10,000$$

This calculation indicates that a total of $10,000 *could* be expended on debt service while maintaining the desired debt coverage ratio of 1.20. The maximum loan amount will depend on the interest rate that the lender charges for loans greater than 80 percent. For example, if the lender required 11 percent for interest-only loans greater than 80 percent, then the maximum loan amount would be based on the debt service required at 11 percent interest while maintaining a debt coverage ratio of 1.20. This can be calculated as:

$$\frac{\text{Maximum debt service}}{\text{Mortgage loan constant}^3} = \text{Max loan amount}$$

$$\frac{\$10,000}{.11} = \$90,909$$

---

[3] We are using an interest-only loan in our example, so the mortgage loan constant is simply the loan interest rate. In cases where the loan is amortizing, the denominator should be the mortgage loan constant that corresponds to the appropriate interest rate and amortization period, expressed on an annual basis, that is 12 times the monthly loan constant discussed in Chapter 4.

However, this would amount to a loan of over 90 percent of the property value, which is far in excess of the more typical 75 percent to 80 percent loan-to-value benchmark. In this example, even though a $90,909 loan at 11 percent interest would meet the 1.20 debt coverage ratio requirement, it is unlikely that a lender would agree to such a loan because it is far in excess of 80 percent. Furthermore, the marginal cost of funds to the borrower to obtain such a high leverage loan would also be very high. This cost can be approximated as follows:

$$\frac{(\$90,909 \times .11) - (\$80,000 \times .10)}{(\$90,909 - \$80,000)} = 18.3\% \text{ incremental cost}$$

Obviously, the cost of obtaining incremental financing of $10,909 is very expensive. Furthermore, it would increase the $BTIRR_E$ only very slightly to 21 percent while significantly increasing risk to the investor. Recall our leverage formula:

$$BTIRR_P + (BTIRR_P - BTIRR_D) \; D/E = BTIRR_E$$

$$12\% + (12\% - 11\%) \times .90 = BTIRR_E$$

$$21\% = BTIRR_E$$

This compares to a 20 percent $BTIRR_E$ at a loan-to-value ratio of 80 percent. Therefore, if the greater amount of leverage were used, the investor would only achieve a 1 percent higher return while risking 10 percent more equity if the 90 percent loan were made.

In short, when lenders underwrite loans, they assess risk by using benchmark, or target, debt coverage ratios and loan-to-value ratios. They attempt to maintain a balance in the risk of default due to (1) an unanticipated decline in property value relative to the amount loaned or (2) significant deterioration in the debt coverage ratio. While these targets may vary depending on market conditions at the time of application, the above example should illustrate the trade-offs faced by lenders and borrowers when different amounts of leverage are considered.

Other Loan Terms and Mortgage Covenants

In addition to underwriting considerations relative to loan-to-value and debt coverage ratios, there are many other requirements that lenders may insist upon as a condition for making a loan. Many of these general requirements were discussed previously in Chapter 2. Recall that the lender will require the borrower to maintain and insure the property and pay property taxes and will not allow a sale of the property on an assumption of the loan by a third party without lender approval.

In commercial lending situations, the lender will also require notification of any material changes that may affect the value of the property. Some **covenants** that may be included in the mortgage document are as follows:

1. Lender must approve all new major leases made for space exceeding a specified amount of square footage (e.g., 5,000 sq. ft.).
2. Lender must approve any modification to existing leases.
3. Lender must approve any additional construction or modifications to the structure and/or site.
4. Borrower must supply periodic updates of property operating and/or cash flow statements.
5. Borrower must supply an annual property appraisal.
6. Borrower must notify the lender of any lawsuits brought by tenants or outside entities, any regulatory violations (e.g., environmental, building code), eminent domain actions, insurance claims filed by the borrower, and so on.

7. Borrower must notify lender of any major capital expenditures to correct structural or other property defects.
8. Lender will have the right to visit and inspect the property.

This list is meant to be illustrative and not exhaustive of the notifications and approvals that a lender may require. The lender's goal is to be assured that *after the loan is closed,* no material deterioration in (1) the value of the property (the mortgage security) and/or (2) the income-producing ability of the property has occurred. (In the case of loans made *with recourse,* the lender will also require that personal financial statements be provided periodically to the lender.) In the event that any of these covenants/requirements are not met by the borrower, the lender will usually notify the borrower that he is in default, and unless the violation of the covenant is corrected, the lender will accelerate on the note and institute foreclosure proceedings.

Lockout Period and Prepayment Penalties

Finally, two additional topics that should be discussed here are the lockout clause and prepayment penalties. The **lockout clause** *prohibits* the borrower from prepaying the loan within a specified period of time (usually 7 to 10 years). It is used because if the borrower were to sell the property or want to refinance within the lockout period, the lender would receive funds earlier than anticipated and face the prospect of having to reloan such funds at an interest rate that may be lower than the rate at which the loan was made. Similarly, if the loan has a 15-year maturity, the lender may also want protection against prepayment *after* the lockout period but before the loan matures, while still providing the borrower with an option to prepay. To accomplish this, the lender will charge a penalty usually referred to as a **yield maintenance fee** (*YMF*). A *YMF* may be calculated as follows. Assume that a loan in the amount of $10,000,000 is made at 8 percent interest only with a 15-year maturity and a lockout period of 10 years. At the time the loan is closed, the risk-free rate of interest (10-year Treasury bond) is 6 percent. Therefore, the loan *spread* over Treasuries is 2 percent (8 – 6%).

We now assume that at the end of year 11, the borrower wants to consider prepaying this loan. However, the risk-free interest rate for a four year Treasury obligation has fallen to 5 percent at the time of prepayment. Therefore, assuming that the lender and borrower had originally agreed that in the event of prepayment, the lender must continue to earn a minimum of 8 percent for the remaining four years (hence the term *yield maintenance*), the borrower must pay the *difference* between the lender's lowest potential reinvestment rate (which is the prevailing risk-free rate of 5% plus the 2% spread, or 7%) and the 8 percent original yield. Therefore, the yield maintenance fee (*YMF*) to be calculated and paid when the loan is repaid at the end of year 11 (month 132) would be:

Solution:	Function:
$n = 48$ months	$PV(n, i, PMT)$
$i = (8\% - 7\%)/12$	
$PMT = \$8,333$	
Solve for PV $= \$341,336$	

This means that in order for the borrower to prepay this loan after the lockout period (sale of property, refinancing, etc.), the borrower must pay the lender a fee of $341,336 upon prepayment. In this case, if the lender collects the fee of $341,336 plus the $10,000,000 loan balance and makes a new loan for $10,000,000 at 7 percent interest (a 2% spread over the prevailing risk-free rate of 5%) for four years, the lender will earn a yield of 8 percent over 15 years. This result would be the same to the lender as though the original loan had remained outstanding for 15 years.[4]

Alternatives to Fixed Rate Loan Structures

Loans on real estate income property can be structured in a variety of ways to meet the needs of the borrower and the lender. Lenders generally want the loan to be structured in such a way that the income generated by the property is expected to be sufficient to cover the mortgage payments each year. This relationship is often achieved by setting a minimum debt coverage ratio such as 1.20. At the same time, borrowers generally want to have a relatively high loan-to-value ratio.[5]

The income from real estate income property may be expected to increase substantially over the investment-holding period for several reasons. First, in an inflationary environment, income may be expected to rise—especially when the lease is structured to allow the lease payments to increase each year.[6] Second, the income for a building that was just developed may be expected to increase for several years because of the time required to lease the new space. Third, the income may be expected to increase because the property has below-market leases at the time it is purchased. If these leases will expire during the investment-holding period, the investor may project that income will rise as the leases are renewed at the higher projected market rate.

When the income from the property is expected to increase over time, it becomes difficult to structure a conventional (fixed rate, level payment) mortgage loan such that the loan-to-value ratio is high and the debt coverage ratio exceeds the minimum during the initial years of the loan term. This is because the present value of property includes the higher expected *future increases* in income, whereas the debt coverage ratio is based on the *current* income. The difference between future income and current income has an especially strong impact in an inflationary environment because fixed rate mortgages include a premium for expected inflation, as discussed in Chapter 4. Because the payments on a conventional mortgage are level, the expected inflation results in higher payments during the first year of the loan term. These higher initial payments result in a mismatch between the level payments on the mortgage and the income from the property, which is expected to increase each year to offset the effect of inflation. This mismatch is greatest during the first year of the investment-holding period and results in a low and often unacceptable debt coverage ratio.

Because of the problems discussed, the mortgage may have to be structured so that the initial payments are lower but the lender receives additional compensation in the future to ensure a competitive rate of return. This compensation can come in a variety of ways. For example, the mortgage payments could increase over time (like a graduated payment mortgage). Or the lender could receive a portion of the proceeds from sale of the property (like a shared appreciation mortgage). Sometimes the lender receives an option to purchase

---

[4] Obviously, there is some risk that the lender may not be able to maintain the 2 percent spread when making a new loan after prepayment. Therefore, when determining the calculation for *YMF*, the lender and borrower may also have to negotiate the spread that will be added to the risk-free rate for the remainder of the loan period.

[5] Although financial risk increases with the loan-to-value ratio, investors are often willing to incur this additional risk either because they have limited funds to invest and want to minimize their equity investment or because they desire the higher expected rate of return as part of their investment strategy.

[6] For example, an office building lease could include a CPI adjustment and/or expense stops, as discussed in Chapter 11.

the property at a specified exercise price, which allows the lender to earn a greater return if the value of the property exceeds the exercise price when acquired by the lender.[7]

The remaining part of this chapter will focus on the analysis of alternative loan structures such as the ones mentioned above. We will examine how these structures affect the payment pattern, and the way that the loan structure affects the risk and expected rates of return to both the borrower and the lender.

Participation Loans

We begin our discussion of financing alternatives by introducing **equity participation loans,** also referred to as *participations* or *equity kickers.* Actually, the term *equity participation* is somewhat a misnomer because the lender does not actually acquire an ownership interest in the property. Rather, in return for a lower stated interest rate on the loan, the lender *participates* in some way in the income or cash flow from the property. Thus, the lender's rate of return depends, in part, on the performance of the property.

The amount of participation can be determined in many ways. For example, the lender might receive a percentage of one or more of the following: (1) potential gross income, (2) net operating income (*NOI*), and (3) cash flow after regular debt service (but before the participation). In addition, there might be a participation at the time the property is sold based on total sale proceeds or the appreciation in property value since it was purchased.

A participation in cash flows often begins for newly developed properties after some pre-agreed amount of leasing and rental achievement is reached. For example, the participation might be based on a percentage of all *NOI in excess* of $100,000. In the case of existing properties, the break-even point is typically set so that the participation begins after the first operating year. For example, *NOI* might be expected to be $100,000 during the first year. Thus, the lender would receive a participation only when *NOI* increases to more than $100,000, which might occur in the second year.

In return for receiving a participation, the lender charges a lower stated interest rate on the loan—how much lower depends on the amount of participation. Participations are highly negotiable, and there is no standard way of structuring them.

Lender Motivations

Why would a lender be willing to make a participation loan? As we will discuss, the lender will want to structure the participation in such a way that the lender's rate of return (including the expected participation) is at least comparable to what the return would have been with a fixed interest rate loan (no participation). Whether the lender will accept a lower expected return with the participation or demand a premium depends on how risky the participation loan is perceived to be relative to a fixed interest rate loan. Clearly, some uncertainty is associated with a participation because receipts depend on the performance of the property. At the same time, however, the lender does not participate in any losses. The lender still receives some minimum interest rate (unless the borrower defaults). Furthermore, the participation provides the lender with a hedge of sorts against unanticipated inflation because the *NOI* and resale prices for an income property often increase as a result of inflation. Thus, to some extent a participation protects the lender's "real" rate of return.

---

[7] The exercise price of the option is the price that the lender must pay for the property. It is normally greater than the value of the property when the loan is made but could be less than the value of the property at the time the option can be exercised.

Investor Motivations

Why would an investor-borrower want a participation loan? As indicated above, participation loans are often structured so that the lender's participation is based on income or cash flow above some specified break-even point. Hence, the participation may be very little or zero for one or more years. During this time period the borrower will be paying less than he would have with a straight loan. Lower initial payments may be quite desirable for the investor since *NOI* may be lower during the first couple of years of ownership, especially on a new project that is not fully rented. Thus, the investor may have more cash flow during the early years of a participation loan than with a straight loan. Increased early cash flow also increases the debt coverage ratio. That is, the investor may be better able to meet debt service during the initial years of the loan with a participation.

At this point, you may be wondering about the case in which an investor accepts a participation loan with a lower rate and a participation that does not kick in for a couple of years and then sells the property before the participation kicks in. This problem is avoided by having a **lockout period** during which the property cannot be sold or refinanced without a prepayment penalty to compensate the lender.

Participation Example

To illustrate a participation loan, we assume that an apartment project that an investor is considering for purchase is projected to have *NOI* of $100,000 during the first year. After that the *NOI* is projected to increase 3 percent per year. The property can be purchased for $1 million. This price includes a building value of $900,000, which will be depreciated over 27.5 years. The property value is projected to increase 3 percent per year over a five-year holding period. The investor is in the 28 percent tax bracket for ordinary income and capital gains.

The lender has offered the following alternatives:

- A conventional, fixed rate, constant payment loan for $700,000 at a 10 percent interest rate (with monthly payments) over a 15-year term.
- A loan for $700,000 at 8 percent interest with monthly payments over 15 years and a participation in 50 percent of any *NOI* in excess of $100,000, plus a participation in 45 percent of any gain (Sale price − Original cost) when the property is sold.

Note that the *amount* of the loan for the two alternatives is the same. This is important because otherwise financial leverage would cause differences in risk. At this point, we want to focus on analyzing different ways of *structuring* the debt independently of the decision about the *amount* of debt, which we have already discussed.

Exhibit 12–10 shows the estimated cash flows for the conventional loan. Note that the debt coverage ratio (*DCR*) during the first year of the conventional loan is only 1.11. This is lower than many lenders would find acceptable. Recall that lenders typically require a minimum *DCR* of 1.2. Thus, the borrower may have difficulty borrowing $700,000 with a conventional loan. Of course, the amount of the loan could be reduced to increase the debt coverage ratio. As we will see, however, a participation loan may be structured to alleviate the *DCR* problem.

Exhibit 12–11 shows the estimated cash flows for the participation loan. The cash flow patterns differ significantly due to the different nature of the participation. Note that the participation loan offers lower payments (debt service plus participation payments) during the early years. This is because of the lower interest rate on the participation loan plus the fact that the participation does not start until the second year. Also, the part of the payments due to the lender from the participation loan does not come until the property is sold.

Despite the difference in payment patterns, the before-tax *IRR* ($BTIRR_E$) is virtually the same for both the conventional loan and the participation loan as a result of the terms for this particular participation loan.

EXHIBIT 12–10 Cash Flow Estimates for Conventional Loan

	Estimates of Cash Flow from Operations Year				
	1	2	3	4	5
A. Before-tax cash flow:					
Net operating income (*NOI*)	$100,000	$103,000	$106,090	$109,273	$112,551
Less debt service (*DS*)	90,267	90,267	90,267	90,267	90,267
Cash flow before participation	9,733	12,733	15,823	19,006	22,284
Participation	0	0	0	0	0
Before-tax cash flow	$ 9,733	$ 12,733	$ 15,823	$ 19,006	$ 22,284
B. Taxable income or loss:					
Net operating income (*NOI*)	$100,000	$103,000	$106,090	$109,273	$112,551
Less interest	69,045	66,823	64,368	61,656	58,660
Participation	0	0	0	0	0
Depreciation	32,727	32,727	32,727	32,727	32,727
Taxable income (loss)	−1,772	3,450	8,995	14,890	21,164
Tax	$ −496	$ 966	$ 2,519	$ 4,169	$ 5,926
C. After-tax cash flow:					
Before-tax cash flow (*BTCF*)	$ 9,733	$ 12,733	$ 15,823	$ 19,006	$ 22,284
Less tax*	−496	966	2,519	4,169	5,926
After-tax cash flow (*ATCF*)	$ 10,229	$ 11,767	$ 13,305	$ 14,837	$ 16,358

Estimates of Cash Flows from Sale in Year 5			
Sale price			$1,159,274
Less mortgage balance			569,216
Before-tax cash flow (*BTCF$_S$*)			$ 590,058
Taxes in year of sale:			
Sale price		$1,159,274	
Original cost basis	$1,000,000		
Accumulated depreciation	163,636		
Adjusted basis		836,364	
Capital gain		$ 322,910	
Tax from sale			90,415
After-tax cash flow from sale (*ATCF$_S$*)			$ 499,643

	Cash Flow Summary End of Year					
	0	1	2	3	4	5
BTCF	$−300,000	$9,733	$12,733	$15,823	$19,006	$612,342
ATCF	−300,000	10,229	11,767	13,305	14,837	516,001

Before-tax *IRR* = 18.37%
After-tax *IRR* = 14.30%

*It is assumed that the investor is not subject to passive activity loss limitations. For simplicity, the same tax rate is used for ordinary income and all capital gains.

EXHIBIT 12–11 **Cash Flow Estimates for Participation Loan**

	Estimates of Cash Flow from Operations Year				
	1	2	3	4	5
A. Before-tax cash flow:					
Net operating income (*NOI*)	$100,000	$103,000	$106,090	$109,273	$112,551
Less debt service (*DS*)	80,275	80,275	80,275	80,275	80,275
Cash flow before participation	19,725	22,725	25,815	28,998	32,276
Participation	0	1,500	3,045	4,636	6,275
Before-tax cash flow	$ 19,725	$ 21,225	$ 22,770	$ 24,362	$ 26,001
B. Taxable income or loss:					
Net operating income (*NOI*)	$100,000	$103,000	$106,090	$109,273	$112,551
Less interest	55,090	53,000	50,736	48,284	45,629
Participation	0	1,500	3,045	4,636	6,275
Depreciation	32,727	32,727	32,727	32,727	32,727
Taxable income (loss)	12,183	15,773	19,582	23,625	27,919
Tax	$ 3,411	$ 4,417	$ 5,483	$ 6,615	$ 7,817
C. After-tax cash flow:					
Before-tax cash flow (*BTCF*)	$ 19,725	$ 21,225	$ 22,770	$ 24,362	$ 26,001
Less tax	3,411	4,417	5,483	6,615	7,817
After-tax cash flow (*ATCF*)	$ 16,314	$ 16,809	$ 17,287	$ 17,747	$ 18,183

Estimates of Cash Flows from Sale in Year 5			
Sale price			$1,159,274
Less mortgage balance			551,364
Cash flow before participation			607,910
Less participation in gain from sale			71,673
Before-tax cash flow (*BTCF$_S$*)			$ 536,237
Taxes in year of sale:			
Sale price		$1,159,274	
Participation		71,673	
Original cost basis	$1,000,000		
Accumulated depreciation	163,636		
Adjusted basis		836,364	
Capital gain		$ 251,237	
Tax from sale			70,346
After-tax cash flow from sale (*ATCF$_S$*)			$ 465,891

	Cash Flow Summary: Investor End of Year					
	0	1	2	3	4	5
Before-tax cash flow	$−300,000	$19,725	$21,225	$22,770	$24,362	$562,238
After-tax cash flow	−300,000	16,314	16,809	17,287	17,747	484,074

Before-tax *IRR* = 18.36%
After-tax *IRR* = 14.07%

EXHIBIT 12–11 **Cash Flow Estimates for Participation Loan (Concluded)**

	Cash Flow Summary: Lender					
	0	**1–12**	**13–24**	**25–36**	**37–48**	**49–60**	**60**
Loan amount	$ − 700,000						
Debt service		$6,690	$6,690	$6,690	$6,690	$6,690	
Participation		0	125	254	386	523	$ 71,673
Loan balance							551,364
Total $	$ − 700,000	$6,690	$6,815	$6,944	$7,076	$7,213	$623,037

Lender's *IRR* = 10.17%

For a participation loan to be attractive to the lender, the expected rate of return to the lender, which is also the effective cost of the loan, must be attractive relative to the interest rate available on conventional loans. In this case, the lender's *IRR*, considering both debt service and participation payments, is 10.17 percent.[8] This *IRR* is nearly the same as the *IRR* for the conventional loan, which is 10 percent (the same as the interest rate on the loan because there are no points).

Although the lender's *IRR* is also about the same for each alternative, note that the *DCR* for the first year is 1.25 for the participation loan, whereas it is only 1.11 for the conventional loan. Recall that lenders typically require a *DCR* of at least 1.2. Thus, the participation loan might be much more acceptable to the lender. The investor may also prefer this payment pattern because the pattern of debt service (regular mortgage payment plus the participation) is a better match with the pattern of *NOI*. In an inflationary environment, the nominal increase in *NOI* will be greater than the real increase in *NOI*. Recall our discussion in Chapter 4 of problems associated with a constant payment mortgage in an inflationary environment. A participating mortgage helps alleviate the tilt effect by allowing the nominal debt service to start at a lower amount than necessary for a conventional loan, and then increase in nominal terms as a function of the nominal increase in the *NOI*.

Note that because part of the lender's return depends on the likelihood of income being produced by the property, the participation payments are referred to as *contingent* interest. Because the contingent interest is contingent on the performance of the property and its ability to produce income, this interest is also tax deductible, as shown in Exhibit 12–11. Thus, one feature of a participation loan is that the entire participation payment is tax deductible, whereas only the interest portion of a conventional loan is deductible. However, because the amount of participation is lower during the early years in this case, the present value of the interest deductions on the conventional loan is greater than the present value of the deductions for interest and participation payments on the participation loan. This results in an after-tax *IRR* ($ATIRR_E$) that is lower for the participation loan even though the before-tax *IRR* ($BTIRR_E$) is virtually the same for each loan alternative. Exhibit 12–12 summarizes the *IRR*s for each financing alternative and shows the *DCR* for each case (based on first-year cash flows).

From the foregoing analysis, it appears that the participation loan is a viable alternative to the conventional loan. The lender receives virtually the same *IRR*, and the *DCR* is higher.

---

[8] This *IRR* is found by calculating the interest rate that equates the amount of the loan ($700,000) with the present value of *both* the debt service paid each year ($80,275) *plus* the participation paid each year *plus* the loan balance and participation paid at the end of the holding period. The cash flows differ each year due to the participation. The answer we calculated (10.17%) was based on the assumption that the debt service and participation were paid monthly.

EXHIBIT 12–12		Before-Tax *IRR*	After-Tax *IRR*	DCR	Lender's *IRR*
Summary of Returns	Conventional loan	18.37%	14.30%	1.11	10.00%
to the Lender and	Participation loan	18.36	14.07	1.25	10.17
Investor					

The expected *BTIRR* for the investor is also virtually the same for each loan, and the expected *ATIRR* is only slightly less. Furthermore, the borrower might have difficulty obtaining the conventional loan due to the low *DCR*.

Sale-Leaseback of the Land

Up to this point in the chapter we have considered alternative ways of financing acquisition of a property (land and building). We have assumed that the investor finances both the land and building with the same loan. It is possible, however, to obtain financing on the building only (e.g., with the building as collateral for the loan). The investor may obtain a separate loan on the land or finance it with a land lease. That is, the investor would own the building but lease the land from a different investor. If the investor already owns the land, she can sell it with an agreement to lease the land back from the purchaser. This is referred to as a **sale-leaseback of the land.** Either way, the investor is, in effect, financing the land.

To illustrate the use of a sale-leaseback of the land, we will use the same example used in the previous section. We now assume that the land could be sold for $100,000 and leased back at an annual payment of $7,800 per year for 25 years. The building would be financed for $630,000 (70% of the *building* value) at a 10 percent rate and a 15-year term. The amount of equity invested is therefore equal to the purchase price ($1 million) less the price of the land ($100,000) less the amount of the loan on the building ($630,000), resulting in equity of $270,000. Exhibit 12–13 shows the cash flows for this alternative. Note that the resale price is now lower because only the building is being sold.[9]

An investor may find a sale-leaseback an attractive financing alternative for several reasons. First, it is, in effect, a way of obtaining 100 percent financing on the land. For example, a loan on the entire property (land and building) for 70 percent of the value also amounts to a 70 percent loan on the land. With the sale-leaseback, the investor receives funds in an amount equal to 100 percent of the value of the land. Instead of a mortgage payment on the land, the investor would make lease payments on the land. Note, however, that the investor may lose the building at the end of the lease unless he or she has an option to purchase the land at the end of the lease. Any such option would have to be based on the market value of the land at the time the option would be exercised. Without this option, the rate of appreciation on the building could be less while the land is being leased, because eventually the building will go to the land owner.

A second benefit of a sale-leaseback is that lease payments are tax deductible. Recall that only the interest, not the principal portion of the payment, is tax deductible with a mortgage.

Third, while the building can be depreciated for tax purposes, the land cannot be depreciated. Thus, the investor may deduct the same depreciation charges whether or not he owns the land. Because, as discussed above, less equity is required with a sale-leaseback of the land, the sale-leaseback results in the same depreciation for a smaller equity investment.

[9] We assumed that the building will still increase in value 3 percent per year, the same rate that we assumed the property value (land and building) would grow. Obviously, the building value may grow at a slower rate than the land, with the 3 percent growth rate for the property being a weighted average of the land and building growth rates. Using a rate of 3 percent for the building, the sale price is ($900,000)(1.03)^5 = $1,043,347. As noted above, the rate of building appreciation may be less because the building will revert to the land owner at the end of the land lease. In this case, the event is still 45 years in the future, so we have not lowered the appreciation.

EXHIBIT 12–13 **Cash Flow Estimates for Sale-Leaseback of the Land**

www.mhhe.com/bf15e

	Estimates of Cash Flow from Operations				
	Year				
	1	2	3	4	5
A. Before-tax cash flow:					
Net operating income	$100,000	$103,000	$106,090	$109,273	$112,551
Less debt service	81,240	81,240	81,240	81,240	81,240
Less land lease payment	7,800	7,800	7,800	7,800	7,800
Before-tax cash flow	$ 10,960	$ 13,960	$ 17,050	$ 20,233	$ 23,511
B. Taxable income or loss:					
Net operating income (*NOI*)	$100,000	$103,000	$106,090	$109,273	$112,551
Less interest	62,140	60,140	57,931	55,490	52,794
Land lease payment	7,800	7,800	7,800	7,800	7,800
Depreciation	32,727	32,727	32,727	32,727	32,727
Taxable income (loss)	−2,668	2,332	7,632	13,255	19,230
Tax	$ −747	$ 653	$ 2,137	$ 3,711	$ 5,384
C. After-tax cash flow:					
Before-tax cash flow (*BTCF*)	$ 10,960	$ 13,960	$ 17,050	$ 20,233	$ 23,511
Less tax	−747	653	2,137	3,711	5,384
After-tax cash flow (*ATCF*)	$ 11,707	$ 13,307	$ 14,913	$ 16,521	$ 18,126

		Estimates of Cash Flows from Sale in Year 5
Sale price		$1,043,347
Less mortgage balance		512,295
Before-tax cash flow (*BTCF_S*)		$531,052
Taxes in year of sale:		
Sale price		$1,043,347
Original cost basis	$900,000	
Accumulated depreciation	163,636	
Adjusted basis		736,364
Capital gain		$ 306,983
Tax from sale		85,955
After-tax cash flow from sale (*ATCF_S*)		$ 445,097

	Cash Flow Summary					
	End of Year					
	0	1	2	3	4	5
Before-tax cash flow	$−270,000	$10,960	$13,960	$17,050	$20,233	$554,563
After-tax cash flow	−270,000	11,707	13,307	14,913	16,521	463,223

Before-tax *IRR* = 19.16%
After-tax *IRR* = 14.98%

Finally, the investor may have the option to purchase the land back at the end of the lease. This option provides the investor the opportunity to regain ownership of the land if desired.

Whether or not the sale-leaseback is a desirable financing alternative depends on the "cost" of obtaining funds this way. One of the obvious costs is the lease payments that must be made. Another aspect of the cost is the "opportunity cost" associated with any appreciation in the value of the land over the holding period. That is, by doing a sale-leaseback, the investor gives up the opportunity to sell the land at the end of the holding period along with the building.

Effective Cost of the Sale-Leaseback

Calculating the effective cost of the sale-leaseback (before-tax return to the investor who purchases the land) is similar to calculating the cost of other financing alternatives. However, we must consider the opportunity cost of the proceeds from sale of the land.

When the land is sold at the time of the sale-leaseback, the building investor receives $100,000. During the five years of the holding period, the investor makes lease payments of $7,800. At the end of the five-year holding period, the investor receives $115,927 *less* than if he had not done the sale-leaseback (see Exhibit 12–13). That is, the entire property could be sold for $1,159,274 without the sale-leaseback (see Exhibit 12–11). In other words, if the sale-leaseback is used, the building alone will sell for $1,043,347 at the end of the holding period, for a difference of $115,927. We can now solve for the effective cost as follows:

Solution:	Function:
$n = 5 \times 12$ or 60	$i\,(n, PV, PMT, FV)$
$PV = \$100,000$	
$PMT = \$7,800/12$	
$FV = \$115,927$	
Solve for i = 10.25%	

The resulting yield is 10.25 percent. Thus, the cost of the sale-leaseback of the land (return to the purchaser-lessor of the land) is 10.25 percent, which is about 25 percentage points more than the return from the conventional loan. At the same time, the building investor's return on equity invested is greater than that for a straight loan. Furthermore, the lender for the building loan is still receiving the 10 percent return that would have been available on a straight loan on the land and building, and the building lender's risk is slightly less if the land lease is subordinated to the building loan.

Interest-Only Loans

Loans on real estate income properties are sometimes structured such that no amortization is required for a specified period of time, for example, three to five years. This is referred to as an **interest-only loan** because the monthly payment is just sufficient to cover the interest charges. Because the loan is not amortized, the balance of the loan does not change over time. At the end of the interest-only period, the loan is either amortized over the remaining loan term or the balance of the loan is due as a **balloon payment.** Lenders for income-producing properties refer to these loans as **bullet loans** because they are short term and require little or no amortization. Since the loan does not fully amortize, the term *balloon payment* refers to payment of the loan balance at maturity. Most of these loans are refinanced at maturity based on appraised values at that time.

To illustrate an interest-only loan, we use the same basic assumptions as in the previous two examples (a $700,000 loan at 10% interest) but assume that the investor makes interest-only payments for the first five years of the loan with a balloon payment due in year 5 when the property is sold. Exhibit 12–14 illustrates the after-tax cash flows. In contrast to

EXHIBIT 12–14 **Cash Flow Estimates for Interest-Only Loan**

	Estimates of Cash Flow from Operations Year				
	1	**2**	**3**	**4**	**5**
A. Before-tax cash flow:					
Net operating income	$100,000	$103,000	$106,090	$109,273	$112,551
Less debt service	70,000	70,000	70,000	70,000	70,000
Before-tax cash flow	$ 30,000	$ 33,000	$ 36,090	$ 39,273	$ 42,551
B. Taxable income or loss:					
Net operating income (*NOI*)	$100,000	$103,000	$106,090	$109,273	$112,551
Less interest	70,000	70,000	70,000	70,000	70,000
Depreciation	32,727	32,727	32,727	32,727	32,727
Taxable income (loss)	−2,727	273	3,363	6,546	9,824
Tax	$ −764	$ 76	$ 942	$ 1,833	$ 2,751
C. After-tax cash flow:					
Before-tax cash flow (*BTCF*)	$ 30,000	$ 33,000	$ 36,090	$ 39,273	$ 42,551
Less tax	−764	76	942	1,833	2,751
After-tax cash flow (*ATCF*)	$ 30,764	$ 32,924	$ 35,148	$ 37,440	$ 39,800

	Estimates of Cash Flows from Sale in Year 5		
Sale price			$1,159,274
Less mortgage balance			700,000
Before-tax cash flow (*BTCF$_s$*)			$ 459,274
Sale price		$1,159,274	
Original cost basis	$1,000,000		
Accumulated depreciation	163,636		
Adjusted basis		836,364	
Capital gain			322,910
Tax from sale			90,415
After-tax cash flow from sale (*ATCF$_s$*)			$ 368,859

	Cash Flow Summary End of Year					
	0	**1**	**2**	**3**	**4**	**5**
Before-tax cash flow	$−300,000	$30,000	$33,000	$36,090	$39,273	$501,825
After-tax cash flow	−300,000	30,764	32,924	35,148	37,440	408,659
Before-tax *IRR* = 18.98%						
After-tax *IRR* = 14.94%						

the conventional loan (Exhibit 12–10), the after-tax *IRR* increases slightly from 14.30 percent to 14.94 percent. This increase is due to the higher cash flows during the operating years, which, in present value terms, more than offset the lower after-tax cash flow from sale due to the larger loan balance. Another benefit of the interest-only loan is that the debt coverage ratio increases to 1.43 versus 1.11 for the conventional loan. The rate of return to the lender would still be 10 percent because the lender earns interest on the outstanding balance of the loan at this rate. Of course, the lender might require a slightly higher interest rate if the loan is viewed as riskier because it is not amortized for five years.

Accrual Loans

In the previous example we analyzed a loan with interest-only payments. In that case the monthly payment just covered the interest payment and the amortization was zero. Sometimes loans are structured so the payments for a specified number of years are lower than the amount that would be required to cover the monthly interest charge. These loans, when made on income properties, are referred to as **accrual loans** and they have negative amortization. The structure of these loans is similar to the graduated payment mortgage as illustrated in Chapter 4 for residential loans.

Loan payments are sometimes calculated by using a rate to calculate the loan payment (referred to as the **pay rate**) that is different from the rate used to calculate the interest charged (referred to as the **accrual rate**). The pay rate is used in place of the interest rate when calculating monthly payments. The pay rate is not the same as the loan constant. The accrual rate is the interest rate that the borrower is legally required to pay on the loan. If the payment rate is less than the accrual rate, the loan will have negative amortization. To illustrate, we now assume that a loan is obtained with a payment rate of 8 percent and an accrual rate of 10 percent. To further lower the payments, the payments are based on a 30-year amortization term although the loan will be due in 15 years with a balloon payment. All other assumptions remain the same as in the previous examples. Exhibit 12–15 illustrates the cash flows for this loan. The annual debt service (12 times the monthly loan payment) is now $61,636 versus $90,267 for the conventional loan. (The annual loan constant is 8.81%.) The lender's yield is still 10 percent because the lender earns interest on the outstanding balance at the accrual rate. The lender may view a negative amortization loan as riskier and might charge a higher accrual rate relative to a conventional loan. The debt coverage ratio has increased from 1.11 for the conventional loan to 1.62 for the negative amortization loan because of the lower annual debt service. Note that the loan balance reaches $753,972 in year 5 as a result of negative amortization. (Recall that the monthly interest differential between the 8% pay rate and the 10% accrual rate must be compounded at 10% and added to the loan balance.)

In many cases, loan payments may be structured based on the pay rate with no amortization. Regardless of whether amortization is required or not, when loans are structured with a pay rate that is lower than the accrual rate, a loan payment that is less than the amount of interest due on the outstanding loan balance usually results. This shortfall (**negative amortization**) causes the loan balance to increase. However, the lender will still require either that the loan be repaid at the end of a specified time period or that the loan begin to amortize at some point. These requirements can be met in a variety of ways. Frequently, negative amortization loans have a term of about 7 to 10 years; hence, the loan balance, which includes accrued interest, will be repaid at that time. Alternatively, when loans have longer terms, say 10 to 15 years, the pay rate increases after a specified number of years. At that point, the pay rate may be increased so that the loan will be amortized over the remaining loan term. Sometimes loan agreements are structured so that the pay rate increases each year for a certain number of years. For example, the loan may require that the pay rate begin at 8 percent the first year, and then increase by .5 percent each year until the 10th year, at which point the pay rate remains at 12.5 percent until the loan is fully amortized.

Structuring the Payment for a Target Debt Coverage Ratio

One of the primary motivations for structuring loans with negative amortization is to increase the debt coverage ratio without reducing the loan amount. As previously discussed, lenders typically require a loan to have a minimum debt coverage ratio (*DCR*). In the above example, the conventional loan had a *DCR* of 1.11. Suppose that the lender required a minimum debt coverage ratio of 1.25. The negative amortization loan discussed above

EXHIBIT 12–15   **Cash Flow Estimates for Negative Amortization Loan**

www.mhhe.com/bf15e

| | Estimates of Cash Flow from Operations | | | | |
| | Year | | | | |
	1	2	3	4	5
A. Before-tax cash flow:					
Net operating income	$100,000	$103,000	$106,090	$109,273	$112,551
Less debt service	61,636	61,636	61,636	61,636	61,636
Before-tax cash flow	$ 38,364	$ 41,364	$ 44,454	$ 47,637	$ 50,915
B. Taxable income or loss:					
Net operating income	$100,000	$103,000	$106,090	$109,273	$112,551
Less interest*	70,394	71,311	72,324	73,444	74,680
Depreciation	32,727	32,727	32,727	32,727	32,727
Taxable income (loss)	−3,121	−1,038	1,039	3,102	5,144
Tax	$ −874	$ −291	$ 291	$ 869	$ 1,440
C. After-tax cash flow:					
Before-tax cash flow (*BTCF*)	$ 38,364	$ 41,364	$ 44,454	$ 47,637	$ 50,915
Less tax	−874	−291	291	869	1,440
After-tax cash flow (*ATCF*)	$ 39,238	$ 41,655	$ 44,163	$ 46,768	$ 49,475

Estimates of Cash Flows from Sale in Year 5

Sale price		$1,159,274
Less mortgage balance		753,972
Before-tax cash flow (*BTCF$_S$*)		$ 405,302
Sale price	$1,159,274	
Original cost basis	$1,000,000	
Accumulated depreciation	163,636	
Adjusted basis	836,364	
Capital gain	$ 322,910	
Tax from sale		90,415
After-tax cash flow from sale (*ATCF$_S$*)		$ 314,887

| | Cash Flow Summary | | | | |
| | End of Year | | | | |
	0	1	2	3	4	5
Before-tax cash flow	$300,000	$38,364	$41,364	$44,454	$47,637	$456,217
After-tax cash flow	−300,000	39,238	41,655	44,163	46,768	364,362

Before-tax *IRR* = 19.27%
After-tax *IRR* = 15.25%

*The table assumes that interest can be deducted on an accrual basis for tax purposes.

resulted in a *DCR* that exceeded this minimum. Another way of determining the mortgage payment is to calculate the mortgage payment necessary to have a specified debt coverage ratio during the first year. To do so, we can simply divide the *NOI* by the specified debt coverage ratio. For example, the mortgage payment that results in a *DCR* of 1.25 during the first year is $100,000 ÷ 1.25 = $80,000. This amount is greater than the payment for the negative amortization loan discussed above, but less than the payment on the conventional loan. In this case the payment would not result in negative amortization because it is sufficient to cover the required interest payment. However, the loan amortization period is not sufficient to fully amortize the loan. For full amortization to occur, the loan has to be extended beyond 30 years. Hence, it is likely that the lender would require a balloon payment on or before the 30th year. Alternatively, the lender could shorten the amortization period by increasing payments each year or after a specified number of years. One possibility is to recalculate the payment each year to maintain a constant debt coverage ratio over time. For example, the above loan may have a payment during year 2 of $103,000 ÷ 1.25 = $82,400, and so on, until the loan begins to amortize sufficiently to be repaid at the end of the term. At that point, loan payments would remain fixed.

Convertible Mortgages

A **convertible mortgage** gives the lender an option to purchase a full or a partial interest in the property at the end of some specified period of time. This purchase option allows the lender to convert its mortgage to equity ownership, hence the term *convertible mortgage.* The lender may view a convertible mortgage as a combination of a mortgage loan and purchase of a call option, or as a right to acquire a full or partial equity interest for a predetermined price on the option's expiration date.

To illustrate, we assume that the property evaluated in the previous examples will be financed with a $700,000 (70% of value) convertible mortgage that allows the lender to acquire 65 percent of the equity ownership in the property at the end of the fifth year.[10] The loan will be amortized over 30 years with monthly payments. We assume the interest rate on the loan to be 8.5 percent versus 10 percent for the conventional loan. The lender is willing to accept the lower interest rate in exchange for the conversion option. The 150-basis-point difference in interest rates between the conventional mortgage and the convertible mortgage represents the "price" that the lender must pay for the option associated with the convertible loan.[11]

Exhibit 12–16 illustrates the after-tax cash flows for the investor under the assumption that the property is financed with the convertible mortgage described above and that the lender exercises the option to purchase a 65 percent interest in the property at the end of the fifth year. We would expect the lender to exercise this option because 65 percent of the estimated sale price ($753,528) is greater than the mortgage balance at the end of the fifth year ($668,432). That is, the option is "in the money" at the time it can be exercised. For comparison with the previous examples, we also assume that the investor will sell the remaining 35 percent interest in the property.

Lender's Yield on Convertible Mortgages

The lender's yield on a convertible mortgage depends on the interest rate charged on the mortgage as well as any gain on conversion of the mortgage into an equity position. If the mortgage is not converted, the lender's yield will equal the interest rate on the loan.[12] The interest rate is the lower limit of the yield, assuming that the borrower does not default on the mortgage. In the example on the next page, the lender's yield on the convertible

---

[10] Generally, the Internal Revenue Service requires that the loan-to-value ratio on the date of financing must be greater than the conversion ratio. This is because if the conversion ratio is greater, the IRS considers the option to be "in the money." Although the lender may have to wait to exercise the conversion option, the lender may have the right to sell or assign the convertible mortgage before the exercise date.

[11] That is, rather than pay an amount up front for the call option, the lender accepts a lower interest rate on the mortgage loan.

[12] Of course, the yield would be higher if points were also charged on the loan.

EXHIBIT 12–16 **Cash Flow Estimates for Convertible Mortgage**

www.mhhe.com/bf15e

	Estimate of Cash Flow from Operations Year				
	1	**2**	**3**	**4**	**5**
A. Before-tax cash flow:					
Net operating income	$100,000	$103,000	$106,090	$109,273	$112,551
Less debt service	64,589	64,589	64,589	64,589	64,589
Before-tax cash flow	$ 35,411	$ 38,411	$ 41,501	$ 44,684	$ 47,962
B. Taxable income or loss:					
Net operating income	$100,000	$103,000	$106,090	$109,273	$112,551
Less interest	59,297	58,829	58,320	57,766	57,163
Depreciation	32,727	32,727	32,727	32,727	32,727
Taxable income (loss)	7,976	11,443	15,043	18,779	22,661
Tax	$ 2,233	$ 3,204	$ 4,212	$ 5,258	$ 6,345
C. After-tax cash flow:					
Before-tax cash flow (*BTCF*)	$ 35,411	$ 38,411	$ 41,501	$ 44,684	$ 47,962
Less tax	2,233	3,204	4,212	5,258	6,345
After-tax cash flow (*ATCF*)	$ 33,178	$ 35,207	$ 37,289	$ 39,426	$ 41,617

	Estimate of Cash Flow from Sale in Year 5
Exchange of 65% interest in property for loan balance*	$000,000
Sale of remaining 35% interest in the property	405,746
Before-tax cash flow (*BTCF*$_S$)	$405,746
Sale price	$1,159,274
Original cost basis	$1,000,000
Accumulated depreciation	163,636
Adjusted basis	836,364
Capital gain	322,910
Tax from sale	90,415
After-tax cash flow from sale (*ATCF*$_S$)	$315,331

	Cash Flow Summary End of Year					
	0	**1**	**2**	**3**	**4**	**5**
Before-tax cash flow	$300,000	$35,411	$38,411	$41,501	$44,684	$453,708
After-tax cash flow	−300,000	33,178	35,207	37,289	39,426	356,948

Before-tax *IRR* = 18.40%
After-tax *IRR* = 13.06%

*The lender receives 65 percent of the property in exchange for the loan balance. The net cash flow to the investor is zero.

mortgage is greater than the 8.5 percent interest rate on the loan because of the gain on conversion of the mortgage balance into an equity position. This gain occurred because the conversion option included with the mortgage was assumed to be "in the money" on its exercise date. Thus, the mortgage lender receives mortgage payments of $5,382.39 per month, plus a 65 percent interest in the property worth $753,528 at the end of the fifth year. The lender's effective yield is calculated as follows:

Solution:	Function:
$n = 5 \times 12$ or 60	i (n, PV, PMT, FV)
PV = $700,000	
PMT = $64,589/12	
FV = $753,528	
Solve for i = 10.40%	

Using a financial calculator we obtain a yield of 10.40 percent. This is the lender's before-tax rate of return on the convertible mortgage.[13] The yield can also be interpreted as the borrower's effective borrowing cost for the convertible mortgage (before tax).

Comparison of Financing Alternatives

Exhibit 12–17 shows a summary of performance measures for each of the financing alternatives evaluated in this chapter. In this case, the accrual loan results in the highest return to the investor on both a before- and an after-tax basis. This loan also has the highest debt coverage ratio. Thus, it would appear to be the most attractive from the borrower's point of view. This result, however, is based on the assumption that the lender is willing to charge the same interest rate (10%) as a conventional loan. Although the debt coverage ratio is lower for the negative amortization loan, the loan balance *increases* over time, thereby *decreasing* equity in the property and *increasing* the default risk. Thus, we might expect the lender to charge a higher interest rate on the negative amortization loan.

Based on the above discussion, it is not surprising that the interest-only loan results in a lower return to the investor than the negative amortization loan but a higher return than the conventional loan. It requires lower payments than the conventional loan but higher payments than the accrual (negative amortization) loan. Considering the differences in default risk, we would expect lenders to charge a slightly higher rate on the interest-only loan than the conventional loan, but not as high as for the accrual loan.

The before- and after-tax returns to the investor for the sale-leaseback of the land are the second highest of the financing alternatives even though the effective borrowing cost for the sale-leaseback is slightly higher than for the conventional loan (10.25% vs 10.00%). Note, however, that less equity ($30,000) is required when the land is leased rather than

EXHIBIT 12–17
Comparison of Financing Alternatives

	$BTIRR_E$	$ATIRR_E$	DCR	IRR_D*
Conventional mortgage	18.37%	14.30%	1.11	10.00%
Participating mortgage	18.36	14.07	1.25	10.17
Sale-leaseback of land	19.16	14.98	1.12†	10.25§
Interest-only mortgage	18.98	14.94	1.43	10.00
Accrual mortgage	19.27	15.25	1.62	10.00
Convertible mortgage	18.40	13.06	1.55	10.40

*Based on monthly cash flows for debt service and participation payments.
†Includes land lease payment with debt service. The *DCR* is 1.23 when land lease payments are not included.
§This is the yield to the purchaser of the land who provides the sale-leaseback financing. The yield (*IRR$_D$*) on the building loan is 10 percent.

[13] It should be noted that the borrower has a taxable gain when the mortgage balance is converted into an equity interest in the property. This would have to be considered if the lender's after-tax yield were being calculated.

owned because the land lease is, in effect, equivalent to a 100 percent loan on the land. Thus, the amount of financing for the land has increased from 70 percent (in the case of a conventional mortgage) to 100 percent of the land value. This increases the amount of financial leverage and financial risk. Thus, the investor should expect to earn a slightly higher rate of return with a sale-leaseback than with a conventional mortgage loan.

Another reason that the investor's return is higher with the sale-leaseback of the land is that the payments on the land lease are less than the debt service would be if a loan were made on the land. Furthermore, a significant portion of the cost of the sale-leaseback to the borrower is because of the opportunity rate, or increase in land value, which is given up. This opportunity cost is not incurred, however, until the property is sold.

The debt coverage ratio for the sale-leaseback is 1.12, which is about the same as a conventional loan. To be consistent with the other examples, we calculate this ratio with the land lease payments added to the mortgage payments. We use the combination of mortgage and land lease payments because the land lease payment is a substitute for mortgage debt service.

The participation loan allows the lender to share in any increase in the net operating income from the property as well as any increase in the value of the property. This type of loan, then, is similar to the convertible mortgage in the sense that the lender receives an additional return if the property performs well, that is, if its income and value increase. Although the participation loan does not allow the lender to obtain an equity position, part of the lender's interest is contingent on the performance of the property. In both cases the lender accepts a lower contract interest rate in exchange for a "piece of the action" on the upside. In the above examples, the convertible mortgage results in a higher return to the lender than the participation loan and a lower after-tax return to the investor. At the same time, the lender would view the convertible mortgage as having greater risk than the participation loan. This is because the participation payments are expected sooner as *NOI* increases in the second year, whereas the gain from conversion does not occur until the fifth year.

If we assume that all the mortgages discussed above are nonrecourse to the borrower,[14] as is often the case, the lender bears the downside risk of receiving the property through default. In effect, the borrower has an option to "put" the property to the mortgage lender if the value decreases below the mortgage balance. Thus, with a convertible loan, and to some extent with a participation loan, the lender bears both the upside and downside risk of property ownership. Consequently, the expected return on each loan structure should be commensurate with this risk.

We approached the analysis of different financing alternatives by considering each one independently. However, features of the different financing alternatives are often combined. For example, a convertible mortgage could also include a participation in *NOI* during the operating years as well as interest-only or negative amortization features.

The above discussion provides a structure for thinking about the risk and return trade-offs for different financing alternatives. These alternatives allow the investor and lender to structure the financing so that the risk and return for the property are shared acceptably. The expected rate of return to each party must be commensurate with the risk. To a large extent, structuring the loan in different ways simply determines how that risk is shared between the borrower and the lender. Different tax status for the borrower and lender, however, may provide gains to both with some loan structures. For example, the lender may have a lower marginal tax rate than the investor, which would make the tax depreciation allowance associated with ownership of the property more valuable to the investor than to the lender. Thus, a participation loan that allows the investor to retain all of the ownership and tax depreciation may be more desirable than a convertible mortgage with the same before-tax cash flows to each party. Alternatively, the lender may desire to

[14] Recall that this means that the borrower incurs no personal liability in the event of loan default.

eventually own the property. By using a convertible mortgage, the investor would receive all the tax benefits of depreciation until the mortgage is converted into equity. In return for allowing the investor to capture these tax benefits and for taking the risk of buying the ownership option under a convertible mortgage, the lender would expect to earn a return higher than the interest rate on a more conventional loan structure. Thus, both parties may gain by attempting to structure the transaction in an optimal manner.

Other Financing Alternatives

An alternative to using a second mortgage to obtain additional financing is to use what is referred to as a **mezzanine loan.** A mezzanine loan bridges the gap between the first mortgage debt on the property and the equity investment. It differs from a second mortgage in that it is not secured as a mortgage on the property. Rather, it is secured by the investor's equity in the property. This means that instead of following the normal foreclosure procedure in the event of default on the mezzanine loan, the mezzanine lender would engage in legal proceedings that would give them an equity interest in the property.

The mezzanine lender usually enters into an intercreditor agreement with the first-mortgage lender to have the right to take over the first mortgage in the event of default. The first-mortgage lender is willing to enter into this agreement because it gives them another party to look to for payment on the first mortgage. This can also result in more rapid control of the property by the mezzanine lender because equity in the corporation or partnership is a personal asset and can be seized through a legal process that does not require as much time as foreclosure on a mortgage that is in default.

Another financing alternative is to issue **preferred equity** in addition to the regular or common equity. Preferred equity is an equity interest in the property but it has debtlike characteristics because preferred equity investors have a claim on cash flows from the property that comes before that of the regular (common) equity investors. For example, preferred equity investors may receive an 8 percent preferred return on equity invested, which means that they receive an 8 percent return on their investment before the regular equity investors receive any cash flow. This return may be cumulative, which means that if the preferred investors do not receive their 8 percent return in a given year, any shortfall carries over to succeeding years and must be paid before the regular equity holders receive any cash distributions. After payment of the preferred return, the remaining cash flows are often split between the preferred equity investors and regular equity investors. Preferred equity holders might also receive a preferred portion of the resale proceeds before the regular equity investors receive any of the cash flow from sale. This can take the form of a preferred *IRR*, which means that the preferred equity investors receive enough cash flow from the sale to achieve a specified *IRR* before any cash goes to the regular equity investors. The preferred *IRR* would be based on all cash flows distributed to the preferred investors, including any cash flows received from operating the property before it is sold. The idea is that cash flow is distributed so that the preferred equity investors first receive enough cash from the sale so that over the entire holding period the preferred investors receive a specified *IRR* on their original equity investment.

Preferred equity is somewhat analogous to mortgages with participations, discussed previously in this chapter. Although it is considered a form of equity, from the regular equity investor's perspective it serves as an additional source of financial leverage.

Conclusion

This chapter illustrated the concept of financial leverage and discussed the conditions for favorable leverage on both before-tax and after-tax bases. We also showed that the use of financial leverage in the hopes of increasing the rate of return on equity is *not riskless*. That is, increasing the level of debt increases the riskiness of the investment, as we illustrated by showing that debt increases the variance of the rate of returns. Thus, when investors use leverage, they must consider whether the additional risk is commensurate with the higher expected return (assuming positive leverage).

Financial leverage deals with the *amount* of financing. The chapter also discussed several financing alternatives, including different types of participation loans and a sale-leaseback of the land. We also considered the effect of each of these alternatives on the investor's cash flows, rates of return, and the debt coverage ratio, and we calculated the effective cost of each alternative. These calculations are used to determine which type of financing alternative is most appropriate (the *structure* of the debt).

It is impossible to discuss all the possible types of financing alternatives. However, the concepts discussed in this chapter should help you analyze any alternative encountered in practice.

Key Terms

accrual loans, *418*
accrual rate, *418*
balloon payment, *416*
break-even interest rate, *400*
bullet loans, *416*
convertible mortgage, *420*
covenants (in mortgage agreements), *406*
debt coverage ratio, *405*
equity participation loans, *409*
financial leverage, *393*

incremental cost of debt, *401*
interest-only loan, *416*
interest rate swaps, *399*
loan-to-value ratio, *405*
lockout clause, *407*
lockout period, *410*
mezzanine loan, *424*
negative amortization, *418*
negative (unfavorable) financial leverage, *397*

nonrecourse clause, *404*
pay rate, *418*
positive (favorable) financial leverage, *394*
preferred equity, *424*
put option, *404*
sale-leaseback of the land, *414*
yield maintenance fee, *407*

Useful Web Sites

www.century21.com/buyingadvice/buying101/mortgageoptions/otherconsid.jsp—This area of the Century 21 Web site has several articles related to different loan alternatives and concepts such as negative amortization.

www.gecapitalrealestate.com—The Web site for GE Real Estate provides information about a plethora of finance products, including higher-leverage loans and participating debt.

Questions

1. What is financial leverage? Why is a one-year measure of return on investment inadequate in determining whether positive or negative financial leverage exists?

2. What is the break-even mortgage interest rate (*BEIR*) in the context of financial leverage? Would you ever expect an investor to pay a break-even interest rate when financing a property? Why or why not?

3. What are *positive* and *negative* financial leverage? How are returns or losses magnified as the degree of leverage increases? How does leverage on a before-tax basis differ from leverage on an after-tax basis?

4. In what way does leverage increase the riskiness of a loan?

5. What is meant by a participation loan? What does the lender participate in? Why would a lender want to make a participation loan? Why would an investor want to obtain a participation loan?

6. What is meant by a sale-leaseback? Why would a building investor want to do a sale-leaseback of the land? What is the benefit to the party that purchases the land under a sale-leaseback?

7. Why might an investor prefer a loan with a lower interest rate and a participation?

8. Why might a lender prefer a loan with a lower interest rate and a participation?

9. How do you think participations affect the riskiness of a loan?

10. What is the motivation for a sale-leaseback of the land?

11. What criteria should be used to choose between two financing alternatives?

12. What is the traditional cash equivalency approach used to determine how below-market-rate loans affect value?

13. How can the effect of below-market-rate loans on value be determined using investor criteria?

Problems

1. An investor would like to purchase a new apartment property for $2 million. However, she faces the decision of whether to use 70 percent or 80 percent financing. The 70 percent loan can be obtained at 10 percent interest for 25 years. The 80 percent loan can be obtained at 11 percent interest for 25 years.

   NOI is expected to be $190,000 per year and increase at 3 percent annually, the same rate at which the property is expected to increase in value. The building and improvements represent 80 percent of value and will be depreciated over 27.5 years (1 ÷ 27.5 per year). The project is expected to be sold after five years. Assume a 36 percent tax bracket for all income and capital gains taxes.

   a. What would the *BTIRR* and *ATIRR* be at each level of financing (assume monthly mortgage amortization)?

   b. What is the break-even interest rate (*BEIR*) for this project?

   c. What is the marginal cost of the 80 percent loan? What does this mean?

   d. Does each loan offer favorable financial leverage? Which would you recommend?

2. You are advising a group of investors who are considering the purchase of a shopping center complex. They would like to finance 75 percent of the purchase price. A loan has been offered to them on the following terms: The contract interest rate is 10 percent and will be amortized with monthly payments over 25 years. The loan also will have an equity participation of 40 percent of the cash flow after debt service. The loan has a "lockout" provision that prevents it from being prepaid before year 5.

   The property is expected to cost $5 million. *NOI* is estimated to be $475,000, including overages, during the first year, and to increase at the rate of 3 percent per year for the next five years. The property is expected to be worth $6 million at the end of five years. The improvement represents 80 percent of cost, and depreciation will be over 39 years. Assume a 28 percent tax bracket for all income and capital gains and a holding period of five years.

   a. Compute the *BTIRR* and *ATIRR* after five years, taking into account the equity participation.

   b. What would the *BEIR* be on such a project? What is the projected cost of the equity participation financing?

   c. Is there favorable leverage with the proposed loan?

3. A developer wants to finance a project costing $1.5 million with a 70 percent, 25-year loan at an interest rate of 8 percent. The project's *NOI* is expected to be $120,000 during year 1 and the *NOI,* as well as its value, is expected to increase at an annual rate of 3 percent thereafter. The lender will require an initial debt coverage ratio of at least 1.20.

   a. Would the lender be likely to make the loan to the developer? Support your answer with a cash flow statement for a five-year period. What would be the developer's before-tax yield on equity (*BTIRR*)?

b. Based on the projection in (*a*), what would be the maximum loan amount that the lender would make if the debt coverage ratio was 1.15 for year 1? What would be the loan-to-value ratio?

c. Assuming conditions in part (*a*), suppose that mortgage interest rates suddenly increase from 8 percent to 10 percent. *NOI* and value will now increase at a rate of 5 percent. If the desired *DCR* is 1.20, will the lender be as willing to make a conventional loan now? Support your answer with a cash flow statement.

4. Ace Development Company is trying to structure a loan with the First National Bank. Ace would like to purchase a property for $2.5 million. The property is projected to produce a first year *NOI* of $200,000. The lender will allow only up to an 80 percent loan on the property and requires a *DCR* in the first year of at least 1.25. All loan payments are to be made monthly, but will increase by 10 percent at the beginning of each year for five years. The contract rate of interest on the loan is 12 percent. The lender is willing to allow the loan to negatively amortize; however, the loan will mature at the end of the five-year period.

a. What will the balloon payment be at the end of the fifth year?

b. If the property value does not change, what will the loan-to-value ratio be at the end of the five-year period?

5. An institutional lender is willing to make a loan for $1 million on an office building at a 10 percent interest (accrual) rate with payments calculated using an 8 percent pay rate and a 30-year loan term. (That is, payments are calculated as if the interest rate were 8% with monthly payments over 30 years.) After the first five years the payments are to be adjusted so that the loan can be amortized over the remaining 25-year term.

a. What is the initial payment?

b. How much interest will accrue during the first year?

c. What will the balance be after five years?

d. What will the monthly payments be starting in year 6?

6. A property is expected to have *NOI* of $100,000 the first year. The *NOI* is expected to increase by 3 percent per year thereafter. The appraised value of the property is currently $1 million and the lender is willing to make a $900,000 participation loan with a contract interest rate of 8 percent. The loan will be amortized with monthly payments over a 20-year term. In addition to the regular mortgage payments, the lender will receive 50 percent of the *NOI* in excess of $100,000 each year until the loan is repaid. The lender also will receive 50 percent of any increase in the value of the property. The loan includes a substantial prepayment penalty for repayment before year 5, and the balance of the loan is due in year 10. (If the property has not been sold, the participation will be based on the appraised value of the property.) Assume that the appraiser would estimate the value in year 10 by dividing the *NOI* for year 11 by a 10 percent capitalization rate.

Calculate the effective cost (to the borrower) of the participation loan assuming the loan is held for 10 years. (Note that this is also the expected return to the lender.)

7. Refer to Problem 6. Assume that another alternative is a convertible mortgage (instead of a participation loan) that gives the lender the option to convert the mortgage balance into a 60 percent equity position at the end of year 10. That is, instead of receiving the payoff on the mortgage, the lender would own 60 percent of the property. The loan would be for $900,000 with a contract rate of 9 percent, and it would be amortized over 20 years. Assume that the borrower will default if the property value is less than the loan balance in year 10.

a. What is the lender's *IRR* if the property sells for the same price in year 10 as the previous example?

b. What is the lender's *IRR* if the property sells for only $1 million after 10 years?

c. What is the lender's *IRR* if the property sells for only $500,000 after 10 years?

8. A borrower and lender negotiate a $20,000,000 interest-only loan at a 9 percent interest rate for a term of 15 years. There is a lockout period of 10 years. Should the borrower choose to prepay this loan at any time after the end of the 10th year, a yield maintenance fee (*YMF*) will be

charged. The *YMF* will be calculated as follows: A treasury security with a maturity equal to the number of months remaining on the loan will be selected, to which a spread of 150 basis points (1.50%) will be added to determine the lender's reinvestment rate. The penalty will be determined as the present value of the difference between the original loan rate and the lender's reinvestment rate.

a. How much will the *YMF* be if the loan is repaid at the end of year 13 if two year treasury rates are 6 percent? What if two-year treasury rates are 8 percent?

www.mhhe.com/bf15e

9. **Excel.** Refer to the participation loan example in the chapter. Suppose that the participation was reduced to 25 percent of the *NOI* in excess of $100,000 but increased to 75 percent of the gain in value.

a. What is the investor's before- and after-tax *IRR?*

b. What is the lender's *IRR?*

Chapter 13

Risk Analysis

Introduction

In previous chapters, we have discussed how to calculate the *IRR, NPV,* and other measures of investment performance. Because of risk differences, comparing *IRR*s or *NPV*s when making choices among alternative investments is usually not possible. Indeed, such a comparison may be made only if we assume that the risk associated with the different investments being analyzed is the same. In this chapter, we provide some techniques for evaluating risk that enable us to make a more thorough comparison of alternatives. We start with a brief discussion of sources of risk and how they may differ among investment alternatives.

Comparing Investment Returns

To begin our discussion, we will briefly explore considerations that investors should take into account when comparing the investment returns on a specific real estate investment with the returns on other real estate investments and other investments generally.

After the investor has gone through a reasonably detailed analysis of an income-producing property, and after having developed measures of return on the investment, the investor must decide whether or not the investment will provide an adequate or competitive return. The answer to this question will depend on (1) the nature of alternative real estate investments, (2) other investments that are available to the investor, (3) the respective returns that those alternatives are expected to yield, and (4) differences in *risk* between the investment being considered relative to those alternative investments available to the investor.

In Exhibit 13–1, we have constructed a hypothetical relationship between rates of return and risk for various classes of alternative investments. The vertical axis represents the expected return,[1] and the horizontal axis represents the degree of risk inherent in each category of investment. Note that we are dealing with the average risk for an entire class of assets. There are obviously significant differences in risk within each class. For example, some bonds will be riskier than other bonds within the general bond category. Also, less variance occurs within some asset classes than others (e.g., Treasury bills are considered to be riskless). Assets within one category may have more risk than some of the assets in a higher-risk category. For example, some bonds are riskier than some stocks, even though as a *class,* stocks are riskier than bonds.

---

[1] To be most comparable, returns should be calculated on an after-tax basis, as discussed later in this chapter.

EXHIBIT 13–1
Risk and Return
(Alternative
Investments)

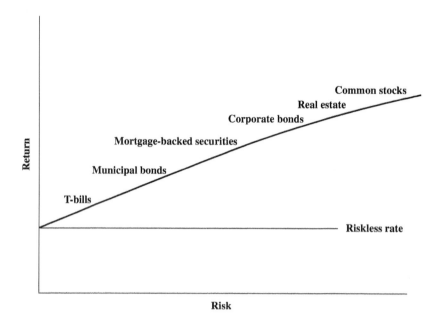

Risk, as presented in Exhibit 13–1, is considered only by class of investments in relative terms; that is, as one moves to the right on the axis, an investment is considered riskier and as one moves to the left, an investment is considered less risky. Hence, investments with higher risks should yield investors higher returns, and vice versa.

Note that, based on the risk-return "ranking" indicated in Exhibit 13–1, the security with the lowest return, U.S. Treasury bills, also has the lowest risk.[2] As we move out on the risk-return line in the exhibit, we see that expected before-tax returns on investments in real estate offer a considerably higher expected return but are also much riskier than investing in U.S. Treasury bills.

Types of Risk

What are the investment characteristics peculiar to real estate that make it riskier than investing in government securities? Similarly, what risk characteristics differentiate real estate investment from alternatives such as common stock, corporate bonds, and municipal bonds also shown in Exhibit 13–1? To answer this question we must consider the source of risk differences among various categories of investments. What follows is a brief summary of major investment risk characteristics that must be considered by investors when deciding among alternative investments.

Business Risk

Real estate investors are in the business of renting space. They incur the **business risk** of loss due to fluctuations in economic activity that affect the variability of income produced by the property. Changes in economic conditions often affect some properties more than others depending on the type of property, its location, and any existing leases. Many regions of the country and locations within cities experience differences in the rate of growth due to changes in demand, population changes, and so on. Those properties that are affected to a greater degree than others are therefore riskier. A property with a well-diversified

---

[2] Treasury bills are free from default risk although they are subject to some interest rate risk and inflation risk.

tenant mix is likely to be less subject to business risk. Similarly, properties with leases that provide the owner with protection against unexpected changes in expenses (e.g., with expense stops in the lease) have less business risk.

Financial Risk

The use of debt financing (referred to as financial leverage) magnifies the business risk. **Financial risk** increases as the amount of debt on a real estate investment is increased. The degree of financial risk also depends on the cost and structure of the debt. For example, a loan that gives the lender a participation in any appreciation in the value of the property in exchange for lower monthly payments may have less financial risk. Chapter 12 provided a discussion of financial leverage and the use of different types of loans such as participation loans. We will explore financial risk further later in this chapter.

Liquidity Risk

This risk occurs when a continuous market with many buyers and sellers and frequent transactions is not available. The more difficult an investment is to liquidate, the greater the risk that a price concession may have to be given to a buyer, should the seller have to dispose of the investment quickly. Real estate has a relatively high degree of **liquidity risk.** It can take from six months to a year or more to sell real estate income properties, especially during periods of weak demand for investment real estate such as occurred during the early 1990s. Special-purpose properties tend to have much more liquidity risk than properties that can easily be adapted to alternative uses.

Inflation Risk

Unexpected inflation can reduce an investor's rate of return if the income from the investment does not increase sufficiently to offset the impact of inflation, thereby reducing the real value of the investment. Some investments are more favorably or adversely affected by inflation than others. Despite **inflation risk,** real estate has historically done well during periods of inflation. This might be attributed to the use of leases that allow the *NOI* to adjust with unexpected changes in inflation. Furthermore, the replacement cost of real estate tends to increase with inflation. During periods of high vacancy rates, however, when the demand for space is weak and new construction is not feasible, the income from real estate does not tend to increase with unexpected inflation.

Management Risk

Most real estate investments require management to keep the space leased and maintained to preserve the value of the investment. The rate of return that the investor earns can depend on the competency of the management, known as **management risk.** This risk is based on the capability of management and its ability to innovate, respond to competitive conditions, and operate the business activity efficiently. Some properties require a higher level of management expertise than others. For example, regional malls require continuous marketing of the mall and leasing of space to keep a viable mix of tenants that draws customers to the mall.

Interest Rate Risk

Changes in interest rates will affect the price of all securities and investments. Depending on the relative maturity (short-term vs long-term investments), however, some investment prices will respond more than others, thereby increasing the potential for loss or gain, that is, the **interest rate risk.** Real estate tends to be highly leveraged, and thus the rate of return earned by equity investors can be affected by changes in interest rates. Even if an existing investor has a fixed-rate mortgage or no mortgage, an increase in the level of interest rates may lower the price that a subsequent buyer is willing to pay. Furthermore, yield rates that investors require for real estate tend to move with the overall level of interest rates in the economy.

Legislative Risk

Real estate is subject to numerous regulations such as tax laws, rent control, zoning, and other restrictions imposed by government. **Legislative risk** results from the fact that changes in regulations can adversely affect the profitability of the investment. Some state and local governments have more restrictive legislation than others—especially for new development.

Environmental Risk

The value of real estate is often affected by changes in its environment or sudden awareness that the existing environment is potentially hazardous. For example, while it used to be common to use asbestos to insulate buildings, asbestos in buildings is now perceived as a potential health hazard. A property may also become contaminated by toxic waste that has been spilled or previously buried on the site or an adjacent site. **Environmental risk** can cause more of a loss than the other risks mentioned because the investor can be subject to cleanup costs that far exceed the value of the property.

In the final analysis, a prospective investor in a specific real estate project must estimate and compute an expected return on the project and compare that return with expected returns on other *specific* real estate investments as well as all other investments. Any risk differentials must be carefully considered relative to any risk premium, or difference in expected returns, in all such comparisons. Investors must then make the final judgment as to whether an investment is justified.

Due Diligence in Real Estate Investment Risk Analysis

The term **due diligence** is used in the real estate investment community to describe the investigation that an investor should undertake when considering the acquisition of a property.[3] Although this process should be followed by any investor, it is particularly important when a firm is making investments on behalf of other investors. Essentially, due diligence is the process of discovering information needed to assess whether or not investment risk is suitable given a set of investment objectives. Exhibit 13–2 provides a general checklist of the areas that should be investigated along with some commentary regarding the importance of each. In most cases, a prospective investor will insist that any risks discovered in the due diligence process must be remedied by the current property owner as a condition of sale.

Sensitivity Analysis

We have discussed various types of risk that must be considered when evaluating different investment alternatives. Unfortunately, it is not easy to *measure* the riskiness of an investment. We will learn that there are different ways of measuring risk, depending on the degree and manner in which the analyst attempts to quantify the risk.

The performance of some properties will be more sensitive to unexpected changes in market conditions than that of other properties. For example, the effect of unexpected inflation on the net operating income for a property is affected by lease provisions such as expense stops and CPI adjustments. A property that is located in an area that has limited land available for new development is likely to be less sensitive to the risk that vacancy rates will increase as a result of overbuilding.

---

[3] The term is also used to describe investigations that should be undertaken in corporate mergers, formation of partnerships, and so on.

EXHIBIT 13–2   **Sample Due Diligence Checklist**

Areas of Review	Commentary
1. Rent roll analysis	Review to determine whether rent information and the payment history of tenants provided by the property owner are accurate and to discover whether there are any disagreements between tenants and landlord (e.g., withholding of rent) that may result in a future confrontation with tenants. Tenant creditworthiness and rent arrearages as well as bankruptcies are also important.
2. Lease agreement review Renewal option rights Expansion option rights First refusal rights Permitted uses Restrictive uses Tenant improvements Commissions Parking Signage	Review to determine the contents of leases as well as options that tenants possess and the responsibility and calculation of expenses. This may affect future expansion commitments relative to rents, expenses, expansions, and so on. Also, commitments made to tenants by the current owner regarding parking, future improvements, payment of commissions, rights to sublet, and to erect signs, and so on should be determined. Discover and review any amendments to existing leases.
3. Review of service and maintenance agreements Landscape, janitorial, trash removal, elevator, security, building systems, certificates of occupancy, mechanical, fire inspection, and so on	Review to establish the frequency and extent of any problems with building equipment and the steps taken to remedy/repair/replace by the owner. Chronic problems in this area could indicate future major expenses, problems obtaining insurance coverage, and so on. All equipment warranties should also be reviewed.
4. Pending or threatened matters review	Review to determine if there are any condemnation proceedings, tax suits, regulatory suits, governmental litigation, or private lawsuits that may affect the property.
5. Review of title/deed documents to determine: Nature and extent of easements Deed restrictions Quality of title Existence of liens • Financing liens • Mechanics' liens • Tax liens • Judgment liens	Examine title and deed documents to reveal any easements granted to other parties that could benefit or detract from the value of the property. This examination should also reveal any liens that may exist because of unpaid taxes, disputes over payments due to suppliers and contractors, and the existence of civil judgments against the current property owner.
6. Property survey Boundary lines Location of buildings, structures, and other improvements	Review to determine if any encroachments exist and if physical improvements are properly located on the site, or if they are in violation of any legal boundaries or site restrictions, including rights of way, setback requirements, and so on. This review should also address issues regarding the location of all rights of way, driveways, walkways, curbcuts, utility lines, streams, rivers, and ditches and the location of any setback lines and of all roads, streets, and highways bordering the property, showing access to and from these.
7. Government compliance Compliance with current zoning ordinances, permitted uses/grandfather provisions, including: • Parking ratios • Setback lines • Height limitations	Review to determine whether, the current and intended use of the property is allowed under zoning. Also, review to determine whether any grandfather provisions currently apply. Environmental concerns may include a number of issues, including the existence of toxic wastes, destruction of wetlands, trees, endangered species, and so on and whether a property lies in a designated special flood hazard area or the 100-year flood plain. This review is usually performed by an environmental engineering firm and requires an opinion letter.

(*continued*)

EXHIBIT 13–2 **Sample Due Diligence Checklist** **(Concluded)**

Areas of Review	Commentary
• Density limitations (*a*) Number of units (*b*) Floor area ratios • Environmental regulations: toxic waste/air quality	
8. Physical inspection Management files on repairs, maintenance, and warranties	Perform survey to determine the physical condition of the structure and if defects exist, whether needed repairs are covered by warranties. A report should be prepared assessing the existence of "as built" plans and specifications, the condition of building systems, structures, utilities, foundation, walls, and adequacy and availability of utilities. The presence of communication devices, such as satellite dishes, any variances from "as built" plans and specifications, and the existence of defects should be noted. This review should also indicate compliance with ADA (Americans with Disabilities Act) regulations.
9. Tax matters Property taxes • Assessed value • Special assessments • Payment history	Review to determine whether payment of all taxes and assessments is current as well as to discover any abatements or the existence of special local tax districts, and so on.
10. Insurance policies **11. Engineering studies** **12. Market studies** **13. List of personal property**	These reviews include the insurance claims history and any denial of insurance to the current property owner. The investor has a right to ask for any reports commissioned by the current property owner, such as market studies, engineering studies, and so on that may be relevant to the transaction. The investor may request a list of personal property that may be conveyed with the real property in order to avoid disputes.

One of the most straightforward ways of analyzing risk is to perform a **sensitivity analysis,** or a what-if analysis, of the property. This involves changing one or more of the key assumptions for which there is uncertainty to see how sensitive the investment performance of the property is to changes in that assumption. Assumptions that are typically examined in a sensitivity analysis include the expected market rental rate, vacancy rates, operating expenses, and the expected resale price.

A sensitivity analysis starts with a *base case,* that is, a set of assumptions to be analyzed that will provide a frame of reference for the sensitivity analysis. This set of assumptions usually represents the analyst's best estimate of the most likely situation.[4]

Once the base case set of assumptions has been identified, the analyst computes the *IRR, NPV,* and other measures of investment performance using this base set of assumptions. Then, the analyst varies the assumptions one or more at a time to see how each change affects the results. Usually the approach to changing assumptions is (1) to change a single assumption at a time or (2) to identify several scenarios in which more than one variable changes within a particular scenario.

Change a Single Assumption at a Time

The advantage of this approach is that it allows the analyst to isolate the impact of a specific input assumption. For example, in the office building analyzed in Chapter 11, we estimated

---

[4] In a statistical sense, the "most likely" case would be the one with the highest probability of occurrence. We will consider probabilities in more detail in a later section.

EXHIBIT 13–3
Sensitivity Analysis

Resale Price	Annual Change*	*BTIRR*
$ 7,300,000	−3.00%	6.69%
7,900,000	−1.45	10.74
8,500,000	0.00	14.23
9,100,000	1.37	17.32
9,700,000	2.68	20.08
10,300,000	3.92	22.60
10,900,000	5.10	24.91
11,500,000	6.23	27.05
12,100,000	7.32	29.05

*Compound annual rate of change from the purchase price of $8.5 million.

EXHIBIT 13–4
Monument Office Building Example: Sensitivity of *IRR* to Resale Price

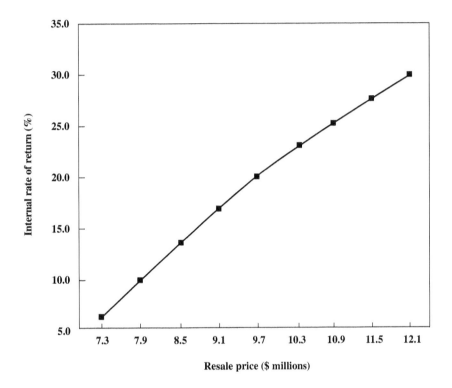

the *IRR* to be 20.08 percent under a specific set of assumptions that might be considered a base case. Included in these assumptions was an estimate that the property would sell for $9.7 million after five years. What if the property sells for more or less than this? How would a change in sale price affect the *IRR?* Exhibit 13–3 shows the *IRR* for a range of possible resale prices. This chart shows how sensitive the *IRR* is to a change in the resale price. Exhibit 13–4 graphs the results.

Scenarios

An alternative to changing a single variable at a time is to identify different **scenarios.** The base case assumptions might be viewed as a most likely scenario. Similarly, one could conceive of a pessimistic scenario in which the assumptions reflect a situation where things do not go as well as the most likely scenario. For example, vacancy might be higher, which in turn might mean that future market rents are lower and the resale price is lower. Scenario analysis allows the analyst to see how much investment performance is affected by a combination of negative or worst-case assumptions. Likewise, a set of optimistic assumptions could be identified to indicate how well the investment would perform if everything were to go well. We will illustrate the use of scenarios later in this chapter.

Partitioning the IRR

We have given a considerable amount of attention to the development of the internal rate of return on equity invested in real estate projects. While this measure of return is useful in helping the investor decide whether or not to invest in a project, it is helpful to "partition" that rate of return to obtain some idea as to the relative weights of the components of the return and some idea as to the timing of the receipt of the largest portion of that return.

To illustrate what we mean by **partitioning the *IRR***, recall that the internal rate of return on equity investment in real estate comprises two sources of cash flow: (1) cash flow from operations and (2) cash flow from the sale of the investment.

In Exhibit 13–5, we present the cash flow from operating the property ($BTCF_o$) and the cash flow from sale of the property ($BTCF_s$) for the office building example discussed in Chapter 11. Recall that the internal rate of return on equity for a five-year holding period was 20.08 percent. However, because both of the above-mentioned sources of cash flow make up the 20.08 percent internal rate of return, we have no way of knowing what proportion *each component bears to the total return.* A breakdown of each component would be useful to an investor concerned with how much of the return is made up of the cash flow from *operations* realized from the project and how much is due to proceeds from the *sale* of the property.

To consider these problems, it is a simple matter to reconsider the present value of the $BTCF_o$ and $BTCF_s$ in a slightly different manner, as shown in Exhibit 13–5. We should note that all cash flow components the investor expects to receive from the project are discounted to find the internal rate of return of 20.08 percent. Then, the *PV* of $BTCF_o$ and $BTCF_s$ are summed to get the total *PV* of $2,550,000 (rounded). The ratio of the *PV* of $BTCF_o$ and *PV* of $BTCF_s$ can now be taken to the total present value. These ratios now represent the respective proportion of the internal rate of return made up by cash flow (30%) and cash flow from appreciation and sale after five years (70%).

EXHIBIT 13–5
Partitioning the
***IRR*—Monument**
Office Building

PV of $BTCF_o$:

Year	Cash Flow	IFPV	Present Value
1	$ 233,725	0.832778	$ 194,641
2	259,542	0.693519	179,998
3	285,121	0.577548	164,671
4	286,054	0.480969	137,583
5	319,925	0.400541	128,143
Total			$ 805,035

PV of $BTCF_s$:

5	$4,356,755	0.400541	$1,745,057

PV of $BTCF_o$'	$ 805,035
PV of $BTCF_s$'	1,745,057
Total *PV*	$2,550,093 (rounded to $2,550,000)

Ratio of:
PV, $BTCF_o$ to Total *PV* = 31.6%
PV, $BTCF_s$ to Total *PV* = 68.4%

Why is partitioning an internal rate of return important? Because it helps the investor to determine how much of the return depends on annual operating cash flow and how much depends on the projected cash flow from resale. Generally, more certainty is associated with projecting cash flows that will occur during the operating years of the investment—especially when they are partially determined by existing leases. The resale price depends on expected cash flows that will occur beyond the current holding period. Thus, it would seem that the greater a proportion of the internal rate of return is made up of *expected appreciation in the future,* the greater the risk facing the investor. For example, the investment return for the office building example in Chapter 11 is 20.08 percent. This is made up of about 30 percent annual $BTCF_o$, and 70 percent $BTCF_s$. A second project might also require an investment of $2,550,000 and provide the investor with the same *IRR* of 20.08 percent. When the *IRR* is partitioned, however, we may find that the proportions of the return are much different—suppose 3 percent from annual $BTCF_o$ and 97 percent from $BTCF_s$. Hence, even though both investments have a 20.08 percent *IRR,* a much higher proportion of the return in the second case depends on future appreciation in property value.[5] Given this outcome, the investor may want to compare any differences in risk between projects more carefully because even though the two projects are estimated to yield the same *IRR,* the likelihood of significant risk differences between the two is strong.

Variation in Returns and Risk

Many of the sources of risk discussed in the chapter, such as business risk, financial risk, and so on, affect returns on real estate investment by making such returns more *variable.* Generally speaking, the higher the variability in returns, the greater the risk in a project. For example, consider the office building that we have been analyzing. Assume that we are considering two additional properties for investment, a hotel and an apartment building.

To illustrate, Exhibit 13–6 contains an estimate of the internal rate of return over a five-year investment period for the three properties under three different economic scenarios. Essentially, Exhibit 13–6 shows estimates of the *IRR* for all three investments under three general economic scenarios that could occur over the investment period.[6] That is, the investor would estimate rents and expenses for the three investment alternatives under three assumptions regarding economic conditions. Then, given the debt-service effects (and perhaps the tax effects) appropriate for each investment, the cash flow would be projected, as well as an estimate of the property value at the end of the investment period.

After computing the *IRR* under each case, the investor could then estimate the probability that each of the economic scenarios that affect the income-producing potential for each alternative will occur. The estimated *IRR,* when multiplied by the probability that a given economic scenario will occur, produces the expected return for each investment.

Based on the results in Exhibit 13–6, we see that the hotel property produces the highest expected return, 20 percent, compared to the 18.52 percent expected return for the office building and the 15 percent expected return for the apartment building. Does this mean that the hotel property should be selected over the office building and the apartment building? Not necessarily. At this point, the reader should recall our discussion of risk characteristics in the chapter and how each investment may be affected by those considerations. A property that provides a high expected return may also be riskier relative to investments with somewhat lower returns.

[5] Be aware that it is possible to have negative *BTCF* and still have a *positive IRR*. Hence, it is important to take the operating cash flows into account in addition to the *IRR*.

[6] The information in Exhibit 13–3 was used to select the rates of return for the office building. The pessimistic scenario assumes that the building is sold for $7.3 million and the optimistic scenario assumes that it is sold for $12.1 million.

EXHIBIT 13–6
Return and Risk
(Office, Apartment,
and Hotel Properties)

www.mhhe.com/bf15e

Office Building

	Return (R)	Probability (P)	R × P	R − Expected Return	P × (R − Expected Return)²
Pessimistic	6.17%	25.00%	1.54%	−12.35%	0.3812%
Most likely	19.64	50.00	9.82	1.12	0.0062
Optimistic	28.64	25.00	7.16	10.12	0.2559
Σ Expected return			18.52%	Variance	0.6434%
				Std. Dev.	8.02%

Apartment Building

	Return (R)	Probability (P)	R × P	R − Expected Return	P × (R − Expected Return)²
Pessimistic	10.00%	25.00%	2.50%	−5.00%	0.0625%
Most likely	15.00	50.00	7.50	0.00	0.0000
Optimistic	20.00	25.00	5.00	5.00	0.0625
Σ Expected return			15.00%	Variance	0.1250%
				Std. Dev.	3.54%

Hotel

	Return (R)	Probability (P)	R × P	R − Expected Return	P × (R − Expected Return)²
Pessimistic	5.00%	25.00%	1.25%	−15.00%	0.5625%
Most likely	20.00	50.00	10.00	0.00	0.0000
Optimistic	35.00	25.00	8.75	15.00	0.5625
Σ Expected return			20.00%	Variance	1.1250%
				Std. Dev.	10.61%

Summary

Property	Expected Return	Risk
Office	18.52%	8.02%
Apartment	15.00	3.54
Hotel	20.00	10.61

In dealing with the problem of comparing risk and return among investments, analysts can use some techniques to complement the qualitative considerations we have discussed. We now turn to a more quantitative discussion of the treatment of projected risk.

In trying to deal with all risk characteristics particular to an investment, some researchers and market analysts argue that in combination these risks (e.g., business risk, financial risk, and the other risks discussed in the chapter) serve to induce *variability in a project's rate of return.* In our above example, the hotel project is riskier than the office or apartment properties, and, in fact, if you closely examine the estimates of *IRR* under each economic scenario, you encounter a much *wider range* in possible *IRR*s with the hotel property compared to the other properties. In fact, if we diagramed the relationship between the probability of the possible economic states of nature and the expected *IRR* for each economic state of nature, we would have a pattern such as that shown in Exhibit 13–7. In that exhibit, we have plotted the probability of the state of the economy and expected *IRR* on each investment, given the state of the economy. We have "smoothed" the curves in the diagram between each probability point to show what the *IRR* would most likely be at points between those specifically estimated. The key concept to grasp from the exhibit is that even though the expected return for the hotel property is higher than that computed for the office building,

EXHIBIT 13–7
Probability Distribution of *IRR*s (Office, Apartment, and Hotel Properties)

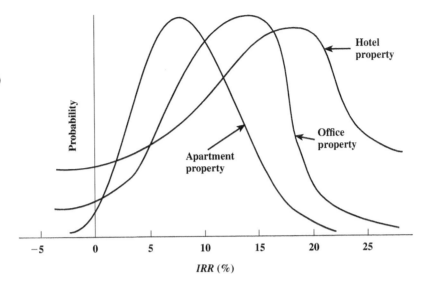

the range of expected returns for the hotel property is far greater than that for the office building. The narrowness in the range of outcomes for the office building relative to the outcomes for the hotel property indicates that there is *lower variability* in expected returns for the office building than for the hotel property. Many analysts consider *lower variability* in returns to be associated with *lower risk,* and vice versa. Therefore, by using a statistical measure of *variance,* the investor has an indication of the extent of the risk in an investment.

Measures of Variance and Risk

Computing the statistical variance in returns is a very simple procedure, as Exhibit 13–6 shows for the three properties. The *standard deviation about the mean return* for the hotel property is 10.61 percent, which is *greater* than that for the office building, which is only 8.02 percent, or for the apartment, which is 3.54 percent. This measure of *dispersion* tells us that the actual return for the apartment building is *more likely* to be *closer* to its expected return of 15.0 percent when compared to the hotel property or the office building. Because the standard deviation for the hotel property is 10.61 percent, the actual return for the hotel property is *less likely* to be closer to its expected return of 20 percent when compared to the office building or apartment property. Hence, if variation in returns is a good indicator of risk, then the hotel is clearly the riskiest of the three investments.

If the probability distribution of *IRR*s for the two investments being considered is normal, the standard deviation of returns for each investment also gives us valuable information. The standard deviation gives us a specific range within which we can expect the actual return for each investment to fall in relation to its expected return. For example, for the hotel property, 68 percent of the time we can expect its *actual* return to fall within + or − one standard deviation of its expected return of 20 percent. This means that 68 percent of the time we can expect the return on the hotel property to fall between 9.39 percent and 30.61 percent. We can expect its actual return to fall within + or − two standard deviations from its expected return approximately 95.5 percent of the time and + or − three standard deviations from its expected return approximately 99.7 percent of the time. In contrast, the actual return on the apartment building will fall in a much more narrow range of + or − one standard deviation from its expected return, or 15 percent + 3.54 percent = 18.54 percent and 15 percent − 3.54 percent = 11.46 percent, about 68 percent of the time, and so on.

Risk and Return

The relevance of these statistical measures, in addition to giving the investor a more quantitative perspective on dispersion and variance as proxies for risk, can also be related to the *IRR* in developing a measure of risk per unit of expected return. To do so for the investments, divide the standard deviation of the *IRR*s by the expected mean *IRR*. For the office building, this computation would be 8.02 ÷ 18.52, or .433; for the hotel property, it would be 10.61 ÷ 20.0, or .5305; and for the apartment it would be 3.54 ÷ 15, or .236. This statistic, called the *coefficient of variation,* is a measure of relative variation; that is, it measures *risk per unit of expected return.* In the case of the hotel property, the coefficient of variation is higher than that of the office building. The apartment has the lowest coefficient of variation. This suggests that return per unit of risk for the apartment building is not as high as it is for the office building and hotel. This comparison does not necessarily mean that the investor will decide not to accept the additional risk in exchange for the additional return; it depends on the investor's attitude toward risk. All investors are assumed to be *risk averse,* which means that they require a higher expected return as compensation for incurring additional risk. We cannot say, however, how much that return should be for a particular investor. If the returns for each of the three properties we have analyzed are based on market prices for each property, then the trade-off between risk and return reflects the price of risk in the market, which implies that investors would purchase each of the above properties based on their risk and return characteristics.

In Exhibit 13–8, we plot the expected return versus the risk (standard deviation) for each of the three properties. This exhibit is similar to Exhibit 13–1, which showed the risk and return trade-off for all assets. In fact, the part of the curve represented by Exhibit 13–8 can be thought of as a small slice from the portion of Exhibit 13–1 that passes through real estate as an asset class.

EXHIBIT 13–8
Risk versus Return

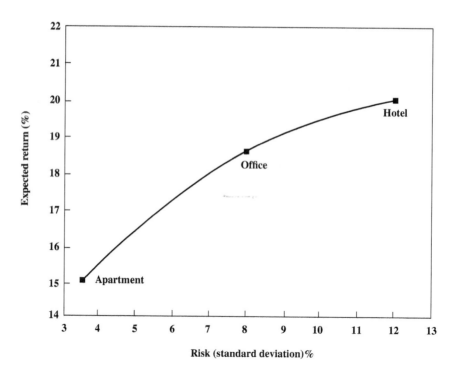

Portfolio Considerations

We have not considered the possibility of reducing risk (variance) by combining investments into a *portfolio.* By developing a portfolio of *different* investment properties, and also including stocks and bonds, the investor can significantly reduce risk through *diversification.* For example, economic events that result in the pessimistic scenario for the hotel property do not necessarily affect the apartment or office properties, and vice versa. Hence, the returns for the three properties may not be perfectly correlated. Diversifying among the three investment types rather than choosing only one can reduce the overall risk of the portfolio. Diversification lowers the variance of total returns from all investments in a portfolio because high and low returns tend to offset one another when combined, resulting in less variation about an expected mean return for the entire investment portfolio. In the context of Exhibit 13–8, then, the portfolio would have an expected return and variance that is to the left of the curve in the exhibit, in other words, less risk for the same expected rate of return. Chapter 22 discusses the role of diversification in reducing risk.

Retail Case Study—Westgate Shopping Center

Westgate Shopping Center is a neighborhood strip center that is 100,000 square feet. An investor is considering purchasing the property. He would hold the property for five years and expects to sell it based on a terminal cap rate of 10.5 percent applied to end-of-year-6 *NOI.* Selling costs would be 3 percent of the sale price. He hopes to get an 11 percent rate of return (before tax, unleveraged) over the five years.

Inflation over the next five years is expected to be 3 percent per year. In general, vacancy for similar shopping centers is about 5 percent, with credit loss an additional 1 percent. Although none of the existing tenants are expected to leave before the end of their lease, a 5 percent "general" vacancy rate will be assumed to allow for the possibility of losing a tenant before their lease expires.

Expenses for the center are projected as follows:

Real estate taxes are $40,000 the first year—increasing 2.5 percent per year.

Insurance is $.18 per square foot—increasing 3 percent per year.

Common area maintenance[7] is $.75 per square foot—increasing 3 percent per year.

Management fee will be 6 percent of effective gross income.

There are currently three tenants.

The first tenant is a drug store leasing 25,000 square feet. It has five years remaining on its lease. Its base rent is $12 per square foot and it will pay expense recoveries for real estate taxes, insurance, and common area maintenance on a net basis. At the expiration of its lease, the space is projected to be re-leased based on market rents at that time. Market rents are currently $12 per square foot and are projected to increase by 3 percent per year until the lease is renewed. The new lease is projected to have a five-year term with no expense recoveries.

The second tenant is a food store leasing 60,000 square feet. Its lease has 13 years remaining. Its base rent is $8.50 per square foot and it will pay expense recoveries for real estate taxes, insurance, and common area maintenance on a net basis. At the expiration of its lease the space is projected to be re-leased based on market rents at that time. Market rents are currently $9 per square foot and are projected to increase by 3 percent

---

[7] These are charges to maintain public areas such as walkways and parking.

per year until the lease is renewed. The new lease is projected to have a 10-year term with no expense recoveries.

The third tenant is a restaurant leasing 5,000 square feet. It has three years remaining on its lease. Its base rent is $15 per square foot and it will pay expense recoveries for real estate taxes, insurance, and common area maintenance on a net basis. This tenant also pays **percentage rent** based on its retail sales volume. It pays an **overage** percentage of 5 percent of retail sales in excess of $225 per square foot **breakpoint** sales volume. Its sales are currently $250 per square foot. At the expiration of its lease, the space is projected to be re-leased based on market rents at that time. Market rents are currently $16 per square foot for in-line space and are projected to increase by 3 percent per year until the lease is renewed. The new lease is projected to have a three-year term with no expense recoveries. In-line tenants would expect to receive tenant improvements,[8] which are currently $5 per square foot but are expected to increase 3 percent per year. Leasing commissions will be 4 percent per year of the base rent for the lease.[9]

There is also 10,000 square feet of vacant in-line space in the shopping center. It is projected that this space will be leased to two additional tenants. The first lease is expected to be signed this year, and the second, one year later. Each will be a three-year lease. Current market rents for in-line space are $16 per square foot. Leasing costs are 5 percent of the rent collected. Tenant improvement costs for the new tenants are expected to be $10 per square foot and the tenants will have expense recoveries on a net basis for real estate taxes, insurance, and common area maintenance. It is assumed that when these leases are renewed after three years they will be typical leases for in-line space. Exhibit 13–9 summarizes the key tenant assumptions.

Exhibit 13–10A shows the projected cash flow from operations. Rental income from existing leases, as well as market rent from lease renewals, is projected for each tenant. Total income also includes expense recoveries and overage rent for the restaurant. Income from lease up of

EXHIBIT 13–9
Westgate Shopping Center: Key Tenant Assumptions

Inputs	Tenant 1	Tenant 2	Tenant 3
Name	Drug Store	Food Store	Restaurant
Tenant size	25,000	60,000	5,000
Rent/sq. ft.	$12.00	$8.50	$15.00
Original lease term (years)	10	15	3
Market rent	$12.00	$9.00	$16.00
Market rent increase	3.00%	3.00%	3.00%
Sales volume/sq. ft.			$250.00
Sales annual change			3.00%
Breakpoint/sq. ft.			$225.00
Overage %			5.00%
Lease renewal term (years)	5	10	3
Lease renewal tenant improvement	$0.00	$0.00	$5.00
Lease renewal commissions	0.00%	0.00%	4.00%
Tenant improvement inflation	0.00%	0.00%	3.00%

[8] Recall that the leasing of a space to a new tenant often requires fixing up or "up fitting" the interior space to suit the tenant's need. Frequently, the landlord sets a standard base amount for up fit, and if the tenant exceeds the allowance, either the rent is increased or the tenant pays the overage amount directly to the building owner.

[9] Generally, the leasing of a space to a new tenant requires the payment of leasing commissions to an outside broker or to a leasing agent in the owner's firm. There are multiple options as to how the actual commission is calculated and paid. The typical method used is to multiply the first-year rent times a leasing commission percentage times the lease term.

vacant space is also included. Tenant improvements (TI) and leasing commissions also have to be paid for lease up of the vacant space and renewal of the restaurant lease (in-line space).

Exhibit 13–10B shows the projected cash flow from resale, and Exhibit 13–11 shows the unleveraged *IRR,* which is 10.48 percent.

Using the 10.48 percent *IRR* as a discount rate, we can partition the *IRR,* as shown in Exhibit 13–12. Based on this exhibit, we see that about 38 percent of the *IRR* is from cash flow from operations and about 62 percent is from the cash flow from resale.

eXcel

www.mhhe.com/bf15e

EXHIBIT 13–10A   **Westgate Shopping Center—Projected Cash Flow from Operations**

Year	1	2	3	4	5	6
Rental income:						
Drug store rent	$ 300,000	$ 300,000	$ 300,000	$ 300,000	$ 300,000	$ 0
Drug store market rent*	0	0	0	0	0	347,782
Drug store recoveries	33,250	34,198	35,172	36,175	37,206	0
Food store rent	510,000	510,000	510,000	510,000	510,000	510,000
Food store market rent	0	0	0	0	0	0
Food store recoveries	79,800	82,074	84,413	86,820	89,295	91,841
Restaurant rent	75,000	75,000	0	0	0	0
Restaurant market rent	0	0	84,872	87,418	90,041	92,742
Restaurant recoveries	6,650	6,840	0	0	0	0
Restaurant overage rent	6,250	8,125	0	0	0	0
Vacant space 1 rent	80,000	80,000	80,000	0	0	0
Vacant space 1 renewal rent	0	0	0	87,418	90,041	92,742
Vacant space 1 recoveries	6,650	6,840	7,034	0	0	0
Vacant space 2 rent	80,000	80,000	80,000	80,000	0	0
Vacant space 2 renewal rent	0	0	0	0	90,041	92,742
Vacant space 2 recoveries	0	6,840	7,034	7,235	0	0
Total income	$1,177,600	$1,189,915	$1,188,526	$1,195,066	$1,206,623	$1,227,849
Vacant space vacancy	80,000	0	0	0	0	0
General vacancy	58,880	59,496	59,426	59,753	60,331	61,392
Effective gross income	$1,038,720	$1,130,419	$1,129,100	$1,135,312	$1,146,292	$1,166,457
Management fee	62,323	67,825	67,746	68,119	68,778	69,987
Property tax	40,000	41,000	42,025	43,076	44,153	45,256
Insurance	18,000	18,540	19,096	19,669	20,259	20,867
CAM	75,000	77,250	79,568	81,955	84,413	86,946
Total expenses	195,323	204,615	208,435	212,818	217,602	223,056
NOI	$ 843,397	$ 925,804	$ 920,665	$ 922,494	$ 928,690	$ 943,401
Vacant space TIs	$ 50,000	$ 50,000	$ 0	$ 0	$ 0	
In-line space TIs	0	0	26,523	27,318	28,138	
Total TIs	$ 50,000	$ 50,000	$ 26,523	$ 27,318	$ 28,138	
Vacant space leasing commissions	$ 12,000	$ 12,000	$ 0	$ 0	$ 0	
In-line space leasing commissions	0	0	10,185	10,490	10,805	
Total leasing commissions	$ 12,000	$ 12,000	$ 10,185	$ 10,490	$ 10,805	
Cash flow from operations	$ 781,397	$ 863,804	$ 883,958	$ 884,686	$ 889,747	

*Market rent is from lease renewals.

EXHIBIT 13–10B
Westgate Shopping Center—Cash Flow from Resale

Cash flow from resale	
Resale	$8,984,768
Selling cost	$269,543
Net resale	$8,715,225

EXHIBIT 13–11
Westgate Shopping Center—Calculation of *IRR*

Year	0	1	2	3	4	5
Total cash flow:						
Cash flow	($8,500,000)	$781,397	$863,804	$883,958	$884,686	$9,604,972
IRR	10.48%					

EXHIBIT 13–12
Westgate Shopping Center—Partitioning the *IRR*

Partitioning the *IRR:*		
Using *IRR* as a discount rate:		
PV of cash flow from operation	$3,204,921	37.70%
PV of cash flow from resale	5,295,079	62.30
Total PV	$8,500,000	100.00%

Westgate Shopping Center Scenario Analysis

www.mhhe.com/bf15e

The investor also would like to know what his rate of return would be under a "pessimistic" scenario as follows:

- Market rents do not increase for the lease renewals of the existing tenants.
- Retail sales do not increase for the restaurant.
- The general vacancy rate is 10 percent instead of 5 percent to allow for the possibility of one tenant's defaulting on the lease.

Note that this will also result in a lower resale price because the year 6 *NOI* that is capitalized is lower.

Exhibit 13–13 shows the results. The *IRR* has dropped from 10.48 percent to 7.33 percent.

Lease Rollover Risk

In the previous chapters and in the Westgate Shopping Center example in this chapter, we made assumptions about what rate either the existing tenant or a new tenant would pay when the current lease expired. For simplicity, we assumed that what would happen at lease renewal was known with certainty.

In practice, there is uncertainty as to whether the existing tenants will renew their lease. Some may renew, while others may vacate. The difference can be significant. If the existing tenant renews the lease, then there will be no additional vacancy due to the tenant's leaving, and the owner may not have to pay any tenant improvements to get the tenant to renew (because the space already meets the tenant's needs). Also, if there is any commission paid to a broker for the lease renewal, it is often a lower rate than that which would have to be paid to find a new tenant. On the other hand, the owner may be willing, in order to avoid these additional costs and vacancy, to provide a discount from current market rents to get an existing tenant to renew the lease.

If the existing tenant does not renew the lease, there will often be some vacancy for several months until a new tenant is found to lease the space. Furthermore, the new tenant is likely to require money for tenant improvements as part of the deal, and commissions may have to be paid to a leasing agent.

EXHIBIT 13–13   Westgate Shopping Center—Pessimistic Scenario

Year	1	2	3	4	5	6
Rental income:						
Drug store rent	$ 300,000	$ 300,000	$ 300,000	$ 300,000	$ 300,000	$ 0
Drug store renewal rent	0	0	0	0	0	300,000
Drug store recoveries	33,250	34,198	35,172	36,175	37,206	0
Food store rent	510,000	510,000	510,000	510,000	510,000	510,000
Food store renewal rent	0	0	0	0	0	0
Food store recoveries	79,800	82,074	84,413	86,820	89,295	91,841
Restaurant rent	75,000	75,000	0	0	0	0
Restaurant renewal rent	0	0	80,000	80,000	80,000	80,000
Restaurant recoveries	6,650	6,840	0	0	0	0
Restaurant overage rent	6,250	6,250	0	0	0	0
Vacant space 1 rent	80,000	80,000	80,000	0	0	0
Vacant space 1 renewal rent	0	0	0	80,000	80,000	80,000
Vacant space 1 recoveries	6,650	6,840	7,034	0	0	0
Vacant space 2 rent	80,000	80,000	80,000	80,000	0	0
Vacant space 2 renewal rent	0	0	0	0	80,000	80,000
Vacant space 2 recoveries	0	6,840	7,034	7,235	0	0
Total income	$1,177,600	$1,188,040	$1,183,654	$1,180,229	$1,176,501	$1,141,841
Vacant space vacancy	80,000	0	0	0	0	0
General vacancy	117,760	118,804	118,365	118,023	117,650	114,184
Effective gross income	$ 979,840	$1,069,236	$1,065,289	$1,062,206	$1,058,851	$1,027,657
Management fee	58,790	64,154	63,917	63,732	63,531	61,659
Property tax	40,000	41,000	42,025	43,076	44,153	45,256
Insurance	18,000	18,540	19,096	19,669	20,259	20,867
CAM	75,000	77,250	79,568	81,955	84,413	86,946
Total expenses	191,790	200,944	204,606	208,432	212,356	214,728
NOI	$ 788,050	$ 868,292	$ 860,683	$ 853,775	$ 846,495	$ 812,929
Vacant space TIs	$ 50,000	$ 50,000	$ 0	$ 0	$ 0	
In-line space TIs	0	0	26,523	27,318	28,138	
Total TIs	$ 50,000	$ 50,000	$ 26,523	$ 27,318	$ 28,138	
Vacant space leasing commissions	$ 12,000	$ 12,000	$ 0	$ 0	$ 0	
In-line space leasing commissions	0	0	9,600	9,600	9,600	
Total leasing commissions	$ 12,000	$ 12,000	$ 9,600	$ 9,600	$ 9,600	
Cash flow from operations	$ 726,050	$ 806,292	$ 824,560	$ 816,857	$ 808,757	
Cash flow from resale						
Resale					$7,742,180	
Selling cost					232,265	
Net resale					$7,509,915	

Year	0	1	2	3	4	5
Total cash flow						
Cash flow	($8,500,000)	$ 726,050	$ 806,292	$ 824,560	$ 816,857	$8,318,672
IRR	7.33%					

When we are projecting cash flows to perform a discounted cash flow analysis for investment analysis, as discussed in Chapter 11, or valuation of income properties, as discussed in Chapter 10, we need to make an assumption about what will happen when the existing lease expires. Because we do not know whether the existing tenant will renew or not, one way this issue is handled in practice is to make an assumption about the **renewal probability** at the end of existing leases. For example, if the renewal probability is 60 percent, this means that there is a 60 percent chance that the existing tenant will renew the lease and a 40 percent chance that a new tenant must be found.

Market Leasing Assumptions with Renewal Probabilities

Because most tenant leases will expire during the holding period used in a discounted cash flow analysis, some releasing forecast must be made as discussed above. Typically, this is handled by selecting a series of market base forecasts for the various types of spaces in a building. These forecasts are referred to as **market leasing assumptions.** The forecast could be as simplistic as those made in previous chapters, that is, that there is a 100 percent probability of renewal.

In more sophisticated analysis, the market leasing forecast typically includes different market rents for new versus renewal leases, renewal probabilities to reflect the likelihood that an existing tenant will sign a new lease, the number of months vacant until a new tenant is found if the existing tenant does not renew the lease, leasing commissions for new and renewal leases, and the amount of tenant improvements for new and renewal leases. There can be a single market leasing assumption that applies to the entire property or different market leasing assumptions for groups of leases or even for each individual lease.

Using only one market leasing assumption could satisfy a simple office building where all tenant spaces are similar. However, more complicated retail properties may require using multiple market leasing assumptions. For example, a community shopping center may require separate market leasing assumptions for large tenant spaces, medium-sized tenant spaces, and small spaces. It is unusual to have different assumptions for each lease, although a particular lease may have its own market leasing assumption if the analyst feels that it is unique or the analyst has a better idea of the likelihood of that tenant renewing or vacating at the end of the lease.

Market Rent

When a renewal probability is less than 100 percent and there is a difference between market rent for new and renewal tenants, the implied rent is the weighted average of the two. For example, suppose that the renewal probability is 60 percent and the market rent for a new tenant would be $18 but for a renewal tenant it would be $17. The implied new market rent when the lease is renewed would be

$$(.60 \times \$17) + (.40 \times \$18) = \$17.40$$

Months Vacant

Typically, when a lease expires and is not renewed, the building owner will suffer some downtime until a new tenant is found and therefore will experience vacancy for a period of time. This is sometimes referred to as **turnover vacancy.** When the renewal probability selected is 100 percent, the months of expected vacancy is zero. When a renewal probability is less than 100 percent, the implied **months vacant** is equal to $(1 - \text{renewal})$ times the months vacant entry. For example, if the renewal probability is 60 percent and the number of months vacant would be 10 if the tenant does not renew the lease, then this is equivalent to

$$10 \times (1 - .60) = 4 \text{ months vacant}$$

The number is typically rounded up to the nearest integer.

Leasing Commissions

As discussed earlier, the leasing commission rate may be lower for renewal tenants than new tenants. When a renewal probability is less than 100 percent and there is a difference between the leasing commission for new tenants and the leasing commission for renewal tenants, the implied rate is the weighted average of the two multiplied by the lease term. For example, if the renewal probability is 60 percent and the leasing commissions for new tenants and renewal tenants are 5 percent and 3 percent, respectively, then the implied leasing rate is

$$(.60 \times 3\%) + (.40 \times 5\%) = 3.80\%$$

Tenant Improvements

As discussed above, tenant improvement rates may differ for new and renewal leases. When a renewal probability is less than 100 percent and there is a difference between the tenant improvement for new leases and the tenant improvement for renewal leases, the implied rate is the weighted average of the two multiplied by the lease term. For example, if the renewal probability is 60 percent and the amount of tenant improvements would be $20 for a new tenant and $5 for a renewal tenant, then we have

$$(.60 \times \$5) + (.40 \times \$20) = \$11.00$$

Industrial Case Study—Worthington Distribution Center

Worthington Distribution Center is a 140,000-square-foot building that is currently being analyzed. It is assumed that it will be sold after five years based on a terminal capitalization rate of 9.75 percent applied to the year 6 *NOI*. Selling costs will be 5 percent of the resale price. The rate of inflation over the next five years is projected to be 3 percent per year. There are currently three tenants occupying the property.

An electrical supply company is leasing 50,000 square feet of space. It has three years remaining on its lease. It pays rent of $6 per square foot with no expense recoveries in the lease. It has already indicated that it may renew its lease at the end of the lease term at market rents.

The second tenant is a sign company that is leasing 42,500 square feet with two years remaining on its lease at a rent of $6.50, and there are no expense recoveries in the lease. This tenant is expected to vacate its space.

The third tenant is a computer distribution company leasing 47,500 square feet. It has four years remaining on its lease. Its rent is $5.75 with no expense recoveries. It is not certain at this time whether it will renew its lease or not. The renewal probability is estimated to be 70 percent.

The market rent is currently $7.00 per square foot for a new tenant and $6.50 per square foot for existing tenants who renew their lease. There would be no expense recoveries in either case. Market rents are projected to increase at the inflation rate of 3 percent from now until leases are renewed. The typical lease term for new leases (new or renewal) is five years. Tenant improvements would be $5 for new leases and $2 for renewal leases.

Leasing commissions would be 3 percent for either new or renewal tenants payable to the property manager. If a tenant does not renew the lease, the downtime is expected to be six months until a new tenant would start paying rent.

Expenses and capital expenditures associated with operating the property are projected as follows:

Real estate taxes of $23,000 the first year, increasing 2.5 percent per year.

Insurance of $.15 per square foot the first year, increasing 4 percent per year.

Common area maintenance charges of $.20 per square foot, increasing 3 percent per year.

Management fee of 5 percent of effective gross revenue paid to the property manager.

Roof repair of $45,000 in year 1.

What is the value of this property using a before-tax unleveraged discount rate of 10.5 percent?

Exhibit 13–14 summarizes some of the key assumptions outlined above. Note that it was assumed that tenant 1 would renew for sure, tenant 2 would vacate for sure, but tenant 3 would use a renewal probability based on market leasing assumptions.

Exhibit 13–15 summarizes the calculations for months vacant, market rent, leasing commissions, and tenant improvements based on weighting the new and renewal assumptions by the renewal probability. Note that the weighted numbers are as of the first year of the analysis. They will increase over time with the inflation assumptions.

Exhibit 13–16 shows the projection of cash flows for Worthington Distribution Center. For each tenant, the rent from the current lease, as well as the "market" rent from the lease renewal assumptions, is projected. Turnover vacancy is a result of tenant 2 vacating for sure and the 30 percent probability that tenant 3 will not renew.

Note that tenant improvements and leasing commissions as well as the capital cost associated with the roof replacement must be deducted from *NOI* to calculate the cash flow.

Finally, Exhibit 13–17 shows the cash flow from resale and property value calculations. The resale is based on applying the terminal cap rate to the year 6 *NOI*. Selling costs are deducted to arrive at the net resale of $8,863,598. The property value is then calculated by adding the present value of the annual cash flow plus the present value of the resale. The property value is $7,629,201.

EXHIBIT 13–14
Worthington Distribution Center—Key Assumptions

Building name	Worthington Distribution Center	
Address		
City	Anywhere	
State	USA	
Building size (sq. ft.)	140,000	
Analysis begin date	6/1/2000	
Holding period	5	
Discount rate	10.50%	
Terminal cap rate	9.75%	
Selling cost	3.00%	

Inputs	Tenant 1	Tenant 2	Tenant 3
Name	Electric Supply	Sign Company	Computer Dist.
Tenant size	50,000	42,500	47,500
Rent/sq. ft.	$6.00	$6.50	$5.75
Lease term (years)	3	2	4
At expiration	Renew	Vacate	Market

EXHIBIT 13–15
Worthington Distribution Center—Market Leasing Assumptions

	Lease Term	Renewal Prob.	Months Vacant	Market Rent	Leasing Commissions	Tenant Improvements
New	5	70.0%	10	$7.00	3.00%	$5.00
Renewal			0	6.50	1.00	2.00
Weighted			3	6.65	1.60	2.90

EXHIBIT 13-16   **Estimated Cash Flows for Worthington Distribution Center**

www.mhhe.com/bf15e

	Year					
	1	2	3	4	5	6
Income:						
Electric supply rent	$300,000	$300,000	$300,000	$ 0	$ 0	$ 0
Electric supply market rent	0	0	0	355,136	355,136	355,136
Sign company rent	276,250	276,250	0	0	0	0
Sign company market rent	0	0	315,618	315,618	315,618	315,618
Computer dist. rent	273,125	273,125	273,125	273,125	0	0
Computer dist. market rent	0	0	0	0	355,520	355,520
Total income	$849,375	$849,375	$888,743	$943,879	$1,026,274	$1,026,274
Turnover vacancy	0	0	263,015	0	88,880	0
Effective gross income	$849,375	$849,375	$625,728	$943,879	$ 937,394	$1,026,274
Expenses:						
Management fee	$ 42,469	$ 42,469	$ 31,286	$ 47,194	$ 46,870	$ 51,314
Property tax	23,000	23,575	24,164	24,768	25,388	26,022
Insurance	21,000	21,840	22,714	23,622	24,567	25,550
CAM	28,000	28,840	29,705	30,596	31,514	32,460
Total	$114,469	$116,724	$107,870	$126,181	$ 128,339	$ 135,345
Cash Flow:						
NOI	$734,906	$732,651	$517,858	$817,698	$ 809,055	$ 890,929
Tenant improvements	0	0	225,441	109,273	155,039	
Leasing commissions	0	0	47,343	17,757	28,442	
Total TI and LC	0	0	272,784	127,030	183,480	
Capital costs	45,000	0	0	0	0	
Cash flow	$689,906	$732,651	$245,074	$690,669	$625,575	
PV factors	0.90498	0.81898	0.74116	0.67073	0.60700	
Present value of cash flow	$624,350	$600,030	$181,640	$463,256	$379,724	

EXHIBIT 13-17
Worthington Distribution Center—Resale and Estimated Value

Resale Calculations:		Value:	
Resale	$9,137,730	PV resale	$5,380,203
Selling cost	274,132	PV cash flow	2,248,999
Net resale	$8,863,598	Value	$7,629,201
PV factor	0.60700		
PV resale	$5,380,203		

Risk and Leverage

As discussed earlier, "financial risk" is one type of risk that is due to the use of financial leverage. The use of financial leverage increases uncertainty as to what the equity investor's rate of return will be. This can be illustrated with an example that shows how leverage affects the expected return and the standard deviation of returns.

Assume that a property can be purchased for $100,000 and its initial *NOI* is $9,000. It will be sold after five years based on a 10 percent terminal capitalization rate applied to year 6 *NOI*. There are three possible scenarios for the investment as follows:

Scenario	*NOI* Growth	Probability (P)
Pessimistic	−3.00%	30%
Most likely	0.00	50
Optimistic	3.00	20

The *IRR* for each scenario is shown in Exhibit 13–18 on an unleveraged basis. The returns range from 4.33 percent to 10.21 percent. Exhibit 13–19 shows that the expected return is 6.98 percent and the standard deviation of returns is 2.06 percent.

Now assume that the investor finances the purchase with a 70 percent loan ($70,000) at a 6 percent interest rate and a 25-year loan term with annual amortization for simplicity. The leveraged return calculations are shown in Exhibit 13–20.

The returns now range from −.45 percent to 18.59 percent. For the pessimistic scenario, recall that the unleveraged return was 4.33 percent. With a loan at a 6 percent interest rate, there is negative leverage in this scenario. (Recall from the previous chapter that unfavorable leverage occurs when the unleveraged return is less than the cost of debt.) Thus, the leveraged return is lower than the unleveraged return under this scenario.

For the most likely scenario, the unleveraged return was 7.27 percent. Thus, the leverage is slightly positive and the leveraged return is 10.22 percent under this scenario.

EXHIBIT 13–18
Unleveraged Returns for Each Scenario

www.mhhe.com/bf15e

							Pessimistic	
Year	0	1	2	3	4	5	6
Purchase	−100,000						
NOI		9,000	8,730	8,468	8,214	7,968	7,729
Resale						77,286	
Total cash flow	−100,000	9,000	8,730	8,468	8,214	85,254	
IRR	4.33%						

							Most Likely	
Year	0	1	2	3	4	5	6
Purchase	−100,000						
NOI		9,000	9,000	9,000	9,000	9,000	9,000
Resale						90,000	
Total cash flow	−100,000	9,000	9,000	9,000	9,000	99,000	
IRR	7.27%						

							Optimistic	
Year	0	1	2	3	4	5	6
Purchase	−100,000						
NOI		9,000	9,270	9,548	9,835	10,130	10,433
Resale						104,335	
Total cash flow	−100,000	9,000	9,270	9,548	9,835	114,464	
IRR	10.21%						

EXHIBIT 13–19
Expected Return and Standard Deviation of Unleveraged Returns

Scenario	Return (R)	Probability (P)	(Return × Probability)	R − Expected R	P × (R − Expected R)²
Pessimistic	4.33%	30%	1.30%	−2.64%	0.0210%
Most likely	7.27	50	3.64	0.29	0.0004
Optimistic	10.21	20	2.04	3.23	0.0209
			Expected return	6.98%	
			Variance	0.04%	
			Standard deviation	2.06%	

For the optimistic scenario, the unleveraged return was 10.21 percent. The leverage is even more positive under this scenario, and the leveraged return is 18.59 percent.

We can also compute the expected return and standard deviation of the leveraged returns. This is shown in Exhibit 13–21.

The expected leveraged return is 8.69 percent, which is higher than the unleveraged return. This is because the *expected* unleveraged return of 6.98 percent exceeds the interest cost of 6 percent. It is important to note that the leverage relationship discussed in Chapter 12

EXHIBIT 13–20
Leveraged Returns for Each Scenario

Pessimistic

Year	0	1	2	3	4	5	6
Purchase	− 100,000						
Loan	70,000						
NOI		9,000	8,730	8,468	8,214	7,968	7,729
Payment		−5,476	−5,476	−5,476	−5,476	−5,476	
Resale						77,286	
Loan balance						−62,808	
Total cash flow	−30,000	3,524	3,254	2,992	2,738	16,970	
IRR	−0.45%						

Most Likely

Year	0	1	2	3	4	5	6
Purchase	− 100,000						
Loan	70,000						
NOI		9,000	9,000	9,000	9,000	9,000	9,000
Payment		−5,476	−5,476	−5,476	−5,476	−5,476	
Resale						90,000	
Loan balance						−62,808	
Total cash flow	−30,000	3,524	3,524	3,524	3,524	30,716	
IRR	10.22%						

Optimistic

Year	0	1	2	3	4	5	6
Purchase	− 100,000						
Loan	70,000						
NOI		9,000	9,270	9,548	9,835	10,130	10,433
Payment		−5,476	−5,476	−5,476	−5,476	−5,476	
Resale						104,335	
Loan balance						−62,808	
Total cash flow	−30,000	3,524	3,794	4,072	4,359	46,181	
IRR	18.59%						

EXHIBIT 13–21
Expected Return and
Standard Deviation
of Leveraged Returns

Scenario	Return (R)	Probability (P)	(Return × Probability)	R − Expected R	P × (R − Expected R)²
Pessimistic	−0.45%	30%	−0.13%	−9.14%	.25%
Most Likely	10.22	50	5.11	1.53	.01
Optimistic	18.59	20	3.72	9.90	.20
		Expected return	8.69%		
		Variance	0.46%		
		Standard deviation	6.77%		

also applies when using expected returns. That is, *if the expected unleveraged return exceeds the cost of debt, then the expected leveraged return will be positive.*

Also note that in Exhibit 13–21 the standard deviation for the leveraged returns (6.77%) is much higher than the standard deviation for the unleveraged returns (2.06%). This is because the variability of returns increases with the use of leverage. The return for the pessimistic scenario is more negative, and the return for the optimistic scenario is more positive.

It is also important to note that the risk and standard deviation of the leveraged returns will be higher than for the unleveraged returns regardless of whether the leverage is positive or negative. That is, even if the leverage is negative based on expected returns, the standard deviation of the leveraged returns will still be higher than the standard deviation of the unleveraged returns.

A "Real Options" Approach to Investment Decisions

Earlier in this chapter, we saw how to calculate the "expected value" or "expected return" on investments by taking into consideration the probabilities associated with different outcomes. This captures the uncertainty of future events when making investment decisions. This approach is often used to evaluate the expected return on an investment when we must decide whether to purchase the property at a specific price *today* where there is uncertainty as to what the performance of the investment will be in the future.

There are often situations, however, where we do not have to fully commit to invest all our capital at one point in time. For example, on a development project we could purchase the land today but wait for a while before deciding whether or not to begin construction of a building. The market may not be such that starting construction immediately is feasible, but the developer may think that there is a good chance that the market will improve over the next year or so such that development will be feasible. On the other hand, the market may not improve and the building should not be constructed. The developer may want to go ahead and purchase the land, however, so that he has the land tied up to be able to construct the building if the market does improve. The land might be available for sale today and the developer may be concerned that another developer will purchase the land if he doesn't.

In situations like this, the developer who purchases the land, but can wait to decide whether to start construction, is said to have a **real option** on the land. The option is to develop the building in the future. The developer does not have to decide to construct the building. The land can remain vacant (perhaps it is leased to a farmer so that it generates some income). Thus, the developer has an option either to construct or not to construct a building depending on economic conditions in the future.

It is important to note that we are *not* talking about the developer getting an option from the seller of the land to purchase the land after some point in time. This is also often done as a way of dealing with uncertainty as to whether the property should actually be developed or not—especially when the developer may need to get zoning changes or development approvals which he may not be certain of getting. This strategy involves the use of options by the developer to deal with risk. But what is important to realize is that purchasing the land outright without the use of an option from the seller still gives the developer an option to either develop or not develop the land. It is this option that is referred to as a *real option.*

The reason that it is important to recognize the existence of an option when land is purchased is because this affects the way we should analyze what we would be willing to pay for the land. To illustrate, we will use an example where we first ignore the option aspect of owning the land, and then we will return to the importance of considering the option.

Consider the following assumptions:

- The developer plans to start construction of a building in one year if at that point rent levels make construction feasible.
- The building will cost $800,000 to construct.
- During the first year after construction would take place, there is a 50 percent chance that *NOI* will be $130,000 and a 50 percent chance that *NOI* will be $70,000.
- In either case, *NOI* is expected to increase at 2 percent per year after the first year.

How much should the developer be willing to pay for the land if she wants a 12 percent return?

Traditional Approach to Land Valuation

Note that this looks very similar to the "highest and best use" analysis that was discussed in Chapter 9. In that chapter, we found the land value by first calculating the value of the property based on its *NOI* and then subtracting the construction cost of the building to get the residual land value. This process was applied to several possible uses of the site in order to determine the highest and best use which maximized the land value.

But in Chapter 9, we assumed that the *NOI* for each potential use was either certain or that the *NOI* was really the "expected" *NOI,* even though we did not explicitly consider probabilities for different *NOI* scenarios.

In this case the expected *NOI* is as follows:

$$\text{Expected } NOI = (.50 \times \$130,000) + (.50 \times \$70,000) = \$100,000$$

The capitalization rate would be 10 percent (12% discount rate less 2% growth rate for *NOI*). Thus, the value of the property after construction would be $100,000/.10 = $1,000,000. Subtracting the construction cost of $800,000 results in a value at the beginning of the first year (after construction is complete) of $200,000. Since construction will not begin for a year, we have to discount this back for one additional year at the 12 percent discount rate so that the value of the land today under this approach would be $200,000/1.12 = $178,571.

Assuming this use results in the highest land value and is the highest and best use of the site, we would expect the developer to pay $178,571 for the land.

Real Option Approach to Land Valuation

What we failed to consider in the approach above is that the developer *does not have to decide today* whether the building will be constructed in a year. The developer can buy the land (so he has the land tied up) but wait until the end of the year to find out what the *NOI* is at that time before making a decision.

If at the end of the year the *NOI* is $130,000, then the property would be worth $130,000/.10 = $1,300,000, which far exceeds the construction cost of $800,000, making the land worth $500,000. But if the *NOI* is $70,000 after a year, the property would be worth only $700,000, which is less than the construction cost of the building, so development would not be feasible. The land value would be zero, assuming no interim use like farming.

Thus, the developer is really looking at the following situation. There is a 50 percent chance that the *NOI* will be $130,000, that he will construct the building, and that the value of the property will be $1,300,000. There is also a 50 percent chance the land will be worth nothing after a year. But the land will not have a negative value after a year! The developer will just decide to keep it vacant. In fact, he still has the option to construct something on it at some future point in time, but for simplicity we will assume that it is worth nothing. The scenarios are summarized in the following diagram:

Real option

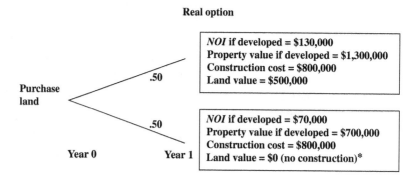

Purchase land		
.50	*NOI* if developed = $130,000 Property value if developed = $1,300,000 Construction cost = $800,000 Land value = $500,000
.50	*NOI* if developed = $70,000 Property value if developed = $700,000 Construction cost = $800,000 Land value = $0 (no construction)*

Year 0 — Year 1

*Land value is the maximum of Property value if developed—Construction cost, or zero.

Based on the above scenarios and probabilities related to the different possible land values after a year, the land value would be as follows after a year:

$$\text{Land value} = (.50 \times \$500,000) + (.50 \times \$0) = \$250,000$$

Discounting this back for one year to today at a 12 percent rate, we have

$$\$250,000/1.12 = \$223,214$$

Note that this implies a higher land value than we arrived at with the traditional approach considered earlier where the land was $178,571. The difference is $223,214 − $178,571 = $44,643. This difference represents the value of the option to wait to decide whether to construct the building. It is the value of the real option inherent in the ownership of vacant land with an option to develop the land in the future.

Web App

Environmental risk is of great concern to real estate investors because of the significant costs that can be associated with mitigating this type of risk. Visit one of the sites recommended in the "Useful Web Sites" for this chapter, such as **www.environmental-center.com,** or use a search engine like Google (**www.google.com**) and search for "environmental risk." Select a type of environmental risk and summarize the nature of the risk and why it is a concern for real estate investors.

Real Options Extensions and Strategy

The above example was simplified to illustrate the importance of thinking in terms of having options in real estate investments. In the above example, the value of the land was higher when this was considered. The developer most likely to purchase the land, and in turn determine the highest and best use of the site, will be the one that recognizes the value of this option.

There are many other situations where implicit options exist in real estate investments. Some additional examples are as follows:

Excess land purchased with a site that is not needed for the initial use is an option for future development. For instance, a developer for a shopping center may purchase more land than needed for the shopping center (including parking). This land might be developed into additional retail developments in the future, or even apartments or office space.

A development project can have different phases to the development. For example, a site might allow for three different apartment or condominium buildings but only one may be constructed initially. In this way, the developer can wait to see how well the first apartment building rents or sells before deciding to construct the additional buildings. Similarly, a land development project (discussed more in Chapter 17) can have different phases to the development so that roads, sewers, and so forth are first put in only for one phase and then additional funds committed only if the lots in the first phase sell well enough.

Having the ability to renovate a building is also an option. The building does not have to be renovated. It can be used "as is." So the owner/investor can wait to see whether the market will support a renovation before committing the funds. Purchasing the building under its current condition (before renovation) is analogous to purchasing the land.

These are just a few examples of the way that real options can exist in real estate investments. Considering these options can significantly affect how investors view the value of real estate investments. Furthermore, an astute developer can often create options in the way that he or she creates a development strategy. Projects should be designed to give the developer options to decide whether to commit additional funds at future points in time (such as the phasing examples discussed above) to maximize the expected value of the project and mitigate the risk.

Conclusion

This chapter discussed the importance of considering risk when analyzing investments. Rates of return for alternative investments cannot be directly compared if the investments have different degrees of risk. We introduced several methods the investor can use to attempt to evaluate the riskiness of a real estate investment, including sensitivity analysis, scenarios, partitioning the return, and the use of probability distributions to compute the expected return and standard deviation of returns.

We were able to look more closely at the effect of leverage (introduced in the previous chapter) on risk by seeing how leverage affects the expected return and standard deviation of returns. We saw that the standard deviation increases with leverage regardless of whether it is positive or negative.

Two case studies (an industrial property and a shopping center) were introduced to illustrate risk analysis as well as provide insight into some of the unique aspects of modeling cash flows for these property types. Previous chapters introduced apartment and office building investments.

The use of renewal probabilities was discussed to illustrate how to deal with the uncertainty regarding whether a tenant will renew the lease at the end of the lease term. We saw how this affects tenant improvements, leasing commissions, and vacancy rates at lease renewal.

Finally, the concept of real options was introduced as a way of thinking about the value of real estate investments where the investor has options after the initial investment is made as to whether additional funds should be invested in the project. We saw that having the option to delay or abandon any additional investment can increase the value of the investment. This was illustrated with the use of vacant land, the purchase of which gives the owner an option to either develop a building on the land in the future or keep the land vacant.

Although this is the only chapter that formally deals with risk, the concepts and techniques introduced in this chapter should be kept in mind throughout the remainder of this book.

Key Terms

breakpoint, *442*
business risk, *430*
due diligence, *432*
environmental risk, *432*
financial risk, *431*
inflation risk, *431*
interest rate risk, *431*
legislative risk, *432*

liquidity risk, *431*
management risk, *431*
market leasing
  assumption, *446*
months vacant, *446*
overage, *442*
partitioning the *IRR*, *436*
percentage rent, *442*

real option, *452*
renewal probability, *446*
scenarios, *435*
sensitivity analysis, *434*
turnover vacancy, *446*

Useful Web Sites

www.ecologeris.com—This site has a searchable environmental risk database for Canada.

Questions

1. What is meant by partitioning the internal rate of return? Why is this procedure meaningful?
2. What is a risk premium? Why does such a premium exist between interest rates on mortgages and rates of return earned on equity invested in real estate?
3. What are some of the types of risk that should be considered when analyzing real estate?
4. What is the difference between business risk and financial risk?
5. Why is the variance (or standard deviation) used as a measure of risk? What are the advantages and disadvantages of this risk measure?
6. What is meant by a "real option"?
7. What is meant by the term *overage* for retail space?
8. How does the use of scenarios differ from sensitivity analysis?

Problems

1. Two investments have the following pattern of expected returns:

	Investment A				
Year	1	2	3	4	4 (Sale)
BTCF	$5,000	$10,000	$12,000	$15,000	$120,000

	Investment B				
Year	1	2	3	4	4 (Sale)
BTCF	$2,000	$4,000	$1,000	$5,000	$180,000

Investment A requires an outlay of $110,000 and Investment B requires an outlay of $120,000.
    a. What is the *BTIRR* on each investment?
    b. If the *BTIRR* were partitioned based on $BTCF_o$ and $BTCF_s$, what proportions of the *BTIRR* would be represented by each?
    c. What do these proportions mean?

2. Mike Riskless is considering two projects. He has estimated the *IRR* for each under three possible scenarios and assigned probabilities of occurrence to each scenario.

State of Economy	Probability	Estimated *BTIRR* Investment I	Estimated *BTIRR* Investment II
Optimistic	0.20	0.15	0.20
Most likely	0.60	0.10	0.15
Pessimistic	0.20	0.05	0.05
	1.00		

Riskless is aware that the pattern of returns for Investment II looks very attractive relative to Investment I; however, he believes that Investment II could be more risky than Investment I. He would like to know how he can compare the two investments considering both the risk and return on each. What do you suggest?

3. An investor has projected three possible scenarios for a project as follows:

Pessimistic—NOI will be $200,000 the first year, and then decrease 2 percent per year over a five-year holding period. The property will sell for $1.8 million after five years.

Most likely—NOI will be level at $200,000 per year for the next five years (level *NOI*) and the property will sell for $2 million.

Optimistic—NOI will be $200,000 the first year and increase 3 percent per year over a five-year holding period. The property will then sell for $2.2 million.

The asking price for the property is $2 million. The investor thinks there is about a 30 percent probability for the pessimistic scenario, a 40 percent probability for the most likely scenario, and a 30 percent probability for the optimistic scenario.

a. Compute the *IRR* for each scenario.

b. Compute the expected *IRR*.

c. Compute the variance and standard deviation of the *IRR*s.

d. Would this project be better than one with a 12 percent expected return and a standard deviation of 4 percent?

4. Use the same information as in problem 3. Now assume that a loan for $1.5 million is obtained at a 10 percent interest rate and a 15-year term.

a. Calculate the expected *IRR* on equity and the standard deviation of the return on equity.

b. Contrast the results from (*a*) with those from Problem 3. Has the loan increased the risk? Explain.

5. A developer plans to start construction of a building in one year if at that point rent levels make construction feasible. At that time the building will cost $1,000,000 to construct. During the first year after construction would take place, there is a 60 percent chance that *NOI* will be $150,000 and a 40 percent chance that the *NOI* will be $75,000. In either case, *NOI* would be expected to increase at 2 percent per year after the first year. How much should the developer be willing to pay for the land if he wants a 12 percent rate of return?

Chapter

14

Disposition and Renovation of Income Properties

In the preceding chapters dealing with income properties, we have given much attention to measuring returns on investment in real estate and the extent to which financial leverage, federal income taxes, and other factors affect that return. Returns were always calculated based on a projected holding period for the property. In this chapter, we take a closer look at the factors that would affect an investor's decision to choose a particular holding period. We also consider alternatives to disposition, such as renovating and refinancing the property.

Disposition Decisions

An investor purchases a real estate investment based on the benefits expected to be received over an *anticipated* holding period. That is, the investor computes the various measures of investment performance based on expectations at the time the property is purchased. After the property is purchased, however, many things can change that affect the actual performance of the property. These same factors may affect the investor's decision as to whether the property continues to meet investment objectives. For example, market rents may not be increasing as fast as expected, thus reducing the investor's cash flow. Tax laws also may have changed. As we saw in Chapter 11, tax laws are frequently revised, which can affect potential new investors in a property differently than existing investors. Hence, investors should periodically evaluate whether it is time for **disposition,** that is, sale of the property.

Even if the investor's projections for a property are accurate, other factors may influence the investor to sell after a specified number of years. One important factor is the potential benefits associated with leverage that we have discussed in several previous chapters. Assuming that the mortgage on the property has positive amortization, the outstanding mortgage balance decreases each year and the investor's equity position increases. Although this **equity buildup** may appear desirable in the sense that the investor will get more cash from the property when it is sold, it also means that each year the investor has more funds tied up in the property. Any increase in the value of the property over time, whether anticipated or not, also contributes to an increase in the investor's equity buildup.

Equity buildup represents funds that the investor could place in another investment if the current property were sold. This is the *opportunity cost* of *not* selling the property. The proceeds that the investor could have received if the property were sold can be thought

458

of as the amount of equity investment made to *keep* the property for an additional period of time. But unless the property is refinanced, a greater portion of equity capital remains invested in relation to the cash flow being received from continuing to operate the property. Further, while the total mortgage payment (debt service) remains the same, the interest portion of the payment decreases each year, resulting in lower tax deductions. Hence, the investor is also losing the benefits of financial leverage each year.

A Decision Rule for Property Disposition

Next, we discuss the factors that investors should consider to determine whether to sell a property or retain ownership. This discussion is based on incremental, or marginal, return criteria that investors should utilize when faced with such decisions.

To illustrate the criteria that should be applied when making a decision to keep a property or sell it, we assume that an investor acquired a very small retail property five years ago at a cost of $200,000. The Apex Center was 15 years old at the time of purchase and was financed with a 75 percent mortgage made at 11 percent interest for 25 years. The investor uses straight-line depreciation with 80 percent of the original cost ($160,000) allocated to the building and 20 percent allocated to land. We assume that when originally purchased, the property could be depreciated on a straight-line basis over depreciable life of 19 years and that the investor has had a marginal tax rate of 50 percent over the past five years.[1] Exhibit 14–1 shows operating results during the *past* five years of operation.

If Apex were sold *today,* it is estimated that the property could be sold for $250,000. Selling costs equal to 6 percent of the sale price would have to be paid. Exhibit 14–2 shows

www.mhhe.com/bf15e

EXHIBIT 14–1   **Past Operating Results, Apex Center**

	Year				
	1	**2**	**3**	**4**	**5**
A. Before-tax cash flow:					
Rents	$ 39,000	$ 40,560	$ 42,182	$ 43,870	$45,624
Less operating expenses	19,500	20,280	21,091	21,935	22,812
Net operating income (*NOI*)	19,500	20,280	21,091	21,935	22,812
Less debt service (*DS*)	17,642	17,642	17,642	17,642	17,642
Before-tax cash flow	$ 1,858	$ 2,638	$ 3,449	$ 4,293	$ 5,170
B. Taxable income or loss:					
Net operating income (*NOI*)	$ 19,500	$ 20,280	$ 21,091	$ 21,935	$22,812
Less interest	16,441	16,302	16,146	15,973	15,780
Depreciation	8,421	8,421	8,421	8,421	8,421
Taxable income (loss)	−5,362	−4,443	−3,476	−2,460	−1,389
Tax	$−2,681	$−2,221	$−1,738	$−1,230	$ −695
C. After-tax cash flow:					
Before-tax cash flow (*BTCF*)	$ 1,858	$ 2,638	$ 3,449	$ 4,293	$5,170
Less tax	−2,681	−2,221	−1,738	−1,230	−695
After-tax cash flow (*ATCF*)	$ 4,539	$ 4,859	$ 5,187	$ 5,523	$ 5,865

[1] Tax laws change frequently. The purpose of this example is to illustrate how changes in the tax law and other factors affect disposition decisions. The intent is not to replicate a particular tax regime. See Chapter 11 for a summary of the tax law at the time of this revision.

EXHIBIT 14-2
Estimates of Cash
Flows from Sale
Today

Sale price		$250,000
Less sale costs (at 6%)		15,000
Less mortgage balance		142,432
Before-tax cash flow (*BTCF*)		$ 92,568
Taxes in year of sale:		
Sale price	$250,000	
Less selling expenses	15,000	
Original cost basis	$200,000	
Less accumulated depreciation	42,105	
Adjusted basis	157,895	
Capital gains tax at 28%	77,105	
Tax from sale		21,589
After-tax cash flow from sale (*ATCF$_s$*)		$ 70,979

the cash flows from sale of the property (if sold today). We assume that the capital gain from sale of the property is taxed at a maximum rate of 28 percent, the rate that the investor would have to pay if the property were sold today (a function of the tax law in effect at the time of sale). This rate could be different than what the investor expected when the property was originally purchased due to changes in the tax law.

Using the information in Exhibit 14–2, we can calculate the rate of return that the investor would have realized for the past five years if the property were sold. Exhibit 14–3 shows the cash flow summary.

We see that if the property were sold today, the investor would earn an ex post (historical) before-tax return (*BTIRR*) of 18.26 percent and an after-tax return (*ATIRR*) of 14.83 percent. But do these figures really help us decide whether to sell the property? For example, suppose that the investor had expected an after-tax return of 16 percent and now finds that sale of the property produces a return of only 14.83 percent. Does that mean the property should be sold? We really cannot say. All we can say is that the property did not perform as well as originally expected. It may be a good investment in the future.

If the historic return calculated above is also an indication of *future* performance, then it will likely be reflected in the price that the property can be sold for today. The current sale price of the property depends on expected *future* performance for a typical buyer. However, future performance does not necessarily have any relationship to historic returns.

IRR for Holding versus Sale of the Property

If we are to determine whether the investor should keep the property, we must evaluate the *expected future performance* of the property. The essential question facing the investor at this time is whether Apex should be sold and funds from the sale invested in another

EXHIBIT 14-3
Cash Flow Summary
Assuming Sale Today

	End of Year					
	0	**1**	**2**	**3**	**4**	**5**
Before-tax cash flow	$-50,000	$1,858	$2,638	$3,449	$4,293	$97,738
After-tax cash flow	-50,000	4,539	4,859	5,187	5,523	76,843

Before-tax *IRR* = 18.26%
After-tax *IRR* = 14.83%

property. Assuming that the investor believes that a reliable forecast for Apex can be made for the *next* five years, Exhibit 14–4 presents estimates of *ATCF* for years 6 to 10. The investor believes that rents and expenses will *not* continue to grow at the same 4 percent per year rate as for the past five years and projects them to increase at a 3 percent rate for the next five years. Note in the exhibit that depreciation charges remain at $8,421 per year based on *original cost* and the *original depreciation method*. Although our example will assume that a new buyer will be subject to a different depreciation rule, investors who already own a property prior to a tax law change are not usually required to change their method of depreciation. However, the investor's tax rate is now assumed to be 28 percent under the assumption that this is the rate that will be applicable for the next five years. Also note that mortgage payments and interest charges are still based on original financing.

If the forecast period is considered to be 5 years (10 years from the date of purchase), the investor must also compute $ATCF_s$. Using a 3 percent per year rate of price appreciation, the owner estimates that Apex should increase in value to $289,819 by then. Exhibit 14–5 computes an estimate of what $ATCF_s$ will be. Note that the mortgage balance and adjusted basis are based on a total period of 10 years, the time from the date of acquisition.

To fully analyze whether a property should be sold also requires investigation into (1) the alternative investments available in which cash realized from a sale may be reinvested and (2) the tax consequences of selling one property and acquiring another. Clearly, if the investor sells Apex and makes an alternative investment, that investment will have to provide a high enough return to make up for the return given up. The question is how much of an *ATIRR* must the alternative investment provide if Apex is sold?

If Apex is sold to acquire another property, the investor must pay capital gains taxes and selling expenses (if any) before funds will be available for reinvestment. Hence, when considering the sale of one property and the acquisition of another, the first task is to ascertain how much cash will be available for reinvestment. The estimated sale price for the Apex

EXHIBIT 14–4   **Estimated Future Operating Results: Apex Center (If Not Sold)**

eXcel
www.mhhe.com/bf15e

	Year (Since Purchase)				
	6	7	8	9	10
A. Before-tax cash flow:					
Rent	$47,450	$48,872	$50,340	$51,850	$53,404
Less expenses	23,725	24,436	25,170	25,925	26,702
Net operating income (*NOI*)	23,725	24,436	25,170	25,925	26,702
Less debt service	17,642	17,642	17,642	17,642	17,642
Before-tax cash flow (*BTCF*)	$ 6,083	$ 6,794	$ 7,528	$ 8,283	$ 9,060
B. Taxable income or loss:					
Net operating income (*NOI*)	$23,725	$24,436	$25,170	$25,925	$26,702
Less interest	15,565	15,325	15,056	14,757	14,423
Depreciation	8,421	8,421	8,421	8,421	8,421
Taxable income (loss)	−261	691	1,692	2,746	3,858
Tax	$ −73	$ 193	$ 474	$ 769	$ 1,080
C. After-tax cash flow:					
Before-tax cash flow (*BTCF*)	$ 6,083	$ 6,794	$ 7,528	$ 8,283	$ 9,060
Less tax	−73	193	474	769	1,080
After-tax cash flow (*ATCF*)	$ 6,156	$ 6,601	$ 7,054	$ 7,514	$ 7,980

EXHIBIT 14–5
Calculation of After-Tax Cash Flow from Sale after Five Additional Years

Sales price		$289,819
Mortgage balance		129,348
Selling expenses at 6%		17,389
Before-tax cash flow		$143,081
Taxes in year of sale:		
Sales price	$289,819	
Selling expenses	17,389	
Original cost basis	$200,000	
Less: Accumulated depreciation	84,211	
Adjusted basis	115,789	
Total taxable gain	$156,640	
Capital gains tax at 28%		43,859
After-tax cash flow from sale ($ATCF_s$)		$ 99,222

Center at this time is $250,000. However, the investor must consider how much cash will be available for reinvestment after payment of the mortgage balance, taxes, and selling expenses. We find that figure by computing *ATCF* as if the property were being sold *immediately,* as we did before. We saw in Exhibit 14–2 that if the property were sold today, the investor would net $70,979 after repayment of the mortgage and payment of capital gains taxes. Thus, $70,979 would be available for reinvestment, should the investor decide to *sell* Apex at this time. Note that capital gains tax rates are expected to remain at 28 percent for the next five years. Sale calculations should always be based on the tax laws that are expected to be in effect when the property is sold. In our case, for example, even though the property was *purchased* at a time when a 60 percent capital gains exclusion was available, because the property is being sold under the new tax law, the capital gains exclusion is no longer available. However, the maximum marginal tax has declined from 50 percent to 28 percent.

The owner must now consider whether or not the $70,979 can be reinvested at a greater rate of return (*ATIRR*) than the return that would be earned *if Apex were not sold.* In other words, we want to know what the *minimum ATIRR* would have to be on an alternative investment (equivalent in risk to Apex) to make the investor indifferent between continuing to own Apex and purchasing the alternative property.

The answer is relatively straightforward. We know that the cash available to reinvest is $70,979 if Apex is sold. Also, we know that if Apex is sold, the investor gives up *ATCF* for the next five years (Exhibit 14–2) and the *ATCF_s* of $99,222 (Exhibit 14–5) at the end of the five years. Hence, the $70,979 must generate a high enough *ATIRR* to offset the cash flows that would be lost by selling Apex. The cash flow summary and return calculation is as follows:

	Cash Flow Summary Year					
	5	6	7	8	9	10
After-tax cash flow	$−70,979	$6,156	$6,601	$7,054	$7,514	$107,202*
Internal rate of return = 15.60%						

*$99,222 + $7,980.

Therefore, the investor would have to earn an *ATIRR* greater than 15.60 percent on the funds obtained from the sale of the Apex Center. These funds must be used to purchase some alternative investment, *equal in risk,* to justify selling Apex. In this case, if an alternative investment is equal in risk to Apex and the investor estimates that the after-tax internal rate of return on equity ($ATIRR_e$) from that alternative would *exceed* 15.60 percent, then the sale of Apex and the acquisition of the alternative would be justified. If the $ATIRR_e$ on the alternative is expected to be less than 15.6 percent, then Apex should be retained.

Return to a New Investor

To examine how incentives for the current investor to hold the property can differ from the incentives for a new investor to invest in the same property, even if both have the same expectations for future rents and expenses, we will assume a new investor purchases the property at the current value. Recall that Apex is currently worth $250,000 and was financed five years ago with a $150,000 loan that is being amortized over 25 years with monthly payments at an 11 percent interest rate. To eliminate the effect of financing (leverage) on our comparison with the present owner, we assume that the new investor takes over the existing loan and does not obtain any additional financing. Therefore, the equity investment for the new investor is the purchase price of $250,000 less the mortgage balance being assumed of $142,432 or $107,568. Thus, the only difference for a new investor will be the effect of tax law. First, the new investor will have a new adjusted basis in the property. Assuming that the building is still 80 percent of the total value in year 5, the new investor will be able to depreciate 80 percent of $250,000 or $200,000, compared to depreciation for the present owner based on the original basis of $160,000. Second, a new investor must depreciate the property based on the tax law in effect at the time of purchase. We assume that the new investor would have to depreciate the property over a 31.5-year depreciable life, a much longer period than the 19-year schedule that would still apply to the present owner. In summary, the new investor gets an increased depreciable basis but must use a longer depreciable life. Note, however, that although this example assumes that the buyer would have a longer depreciable life than the existing investor, the reverse could also be true. Again, as noted in Chapter 11, depreciable lives for real estate have been shortened and lengthened frequently over time depending on the whims of Congress.

Exhibit 14–6 shows the projected cash flows and $ATIRR_e$. We see that a new investor would earn an $ATIRR_e$ of 9.1 percent. Although this may be a competitive return for a new investor, given opportunity cost, it is less than the current investor can earn (15.6%) by keeping the property, primarily because the existing investor can continue to use a depreciation schedule based on the old tax law. Thus, we see that tax law changes affect the relative benefits of existing versus new investments in the same property. If the tax law becomes *less* favorable, as it did in 1986, it tends to favor existing investors. If the tax law becomes *more* favorable, as it did in 1981 when *ACRS* was passed and depreciable lives were shortened considerably, then new investors tend to be favored. Thus, tax law changes tend to affect the turnover, or sale, of real estate. It is important that you understand these concepts since tax laws are always subject to change, and these changes affect the relative risk and return opportunities for new and existing investors.

Marginal Rate of Return

The return for selling versus holding the property calculated earlier (15.6%, using cash flows from Exhibits 14–4 and 14–5) is an $ATIRR_e$ based on holding the property for *five additional years*. We chose this period of time based on the assumption that if the property were sold, the funds would be placed in a similar investment, which would also be evaluated on the basis of a holding period of five additional years. A slightly different approach is to consider the return that would result from holding the property only *one* additional year. This return would be calculated the same way as above, but would project only one additional year of operating cash flow, and the $ATCF_s$ from sale after one year. We refer to this one-year $ATIRR_e$ as the **marginal rate of return**. For example, in the year that we are considering the

EXHIBIT 14–6
Projections for a New Investor

Calculation of After-Tax Cash Flow from Operations

	Year				
	6	**7**	**8**	**9**	**10**
Rent	$47,449	$48,873	$50,339	$51,849	$53,405
Less expenses	23,725	24,436	25,170	25,925	26,702
Net operating income	23,725	24,436	25,170	25,925	26,702
Less debt service	17,642	17,642	17,642	17,642	17,642
Before-tax cash flow	$ 6,083	$ 6,794	$ 7,528	$ 8,283	$ 9,060
Net operating income	$23,725	$24,436	$25,170	$25,925	$26,702
Less interest	15,565	15,325	15,065	14,757	14,423
Depreciation	6,349	6,349	6,349	6,349	6,349
Taxable income	1,811	2,763	3,764	4,818	5,930
Tax	$ 507	$ 774	$ 1,054	$ 1,349	$ 1,660
Before-tax cash flow	$ 6,083	$ 6,794	$ 7,528	$ 8,283	$ 9,060
Tax	507	774	1,054	1,349	1,660
After-tax cash flow	$ 5,576	$ 6,021	$ 6,474	$ 6,934	$ 7,400

Calculation of After-Tax Cash Flow from Sale after an Additional 5 Years

Sale price		$289,819
Less mortgage balance		129,348
Less selling expenses at 6%		17,389
Before-tax cash flow ($BTCF_s$)		$143,081
Taxes in year of sale		
Sale price	$289,819	
Less selling expenses	17,389	
Original cost basis	$250,000	
Less accumulated depreciation	31,746	
Adjusted basis	218,254	
Total taxable gain	$ 54,176	
Capital gains tax at 28%		15,169
After-tax cash flow from sale ($ATCF_s$)		$127,912

Cash Flow Year Summary

	5	**6**	**7**	**8**	**9**	**10**
ATCF	$−107,568	$5,576	$6,021	$6,474	$6,934	$135,312

Internal rate of return ($ATIRR_e$) = 9.10%

sale of the property, we can ask, "What will the marginal return be if the property is held one more year?" Then (assuming the property has not been sold) at the end of that additional year, we ask, "What is the marginal return for holding the property one more year?" This process can be continued until the property is actually sold (or renovated).

To illustrate calculation of the marginal return, we assume that *NOI* will actually increase 3 percent per year (the same rate used for our projections) over the next 10 years. We assume that the resale price will also actually increase 3 percent per year. Exhibit 14–7 shows the projected after-tax cash flows from operating the property over the next 10 years ($ATCF_o$). For each of the 10 years (years 6 through 15), the exhibit also shows the projected after-tax cash flow ($ATCF_s$) that would result *if* the property were sold at the end of that year.

Calculation of After-Tax Cash Flow from Operations
Year (After Purchase)

	6	7	8	9	10	11	12	13	14	15
Rent	$47,450	$48,872	$50,340	$51,850	$53,404	$55,006	$56,658	$58,356	$60,108	$61,910
Less expenses	23,725	24,436	25,170	25,925	26,702	27,503	28,329	29,178	30,054	30,955
NOI	23,725	24,436	25,170	25,925	26,702	27,503	28,329	29,178	30,054	30,955
Debt service	17,642	17,642	17,642	17,642	17,642	17,642	17,642	17,642	17,642	17,642
BTCF	$6,083	$6,794	$7,528	$8,283	$9,060	$9,861	$10,687	$11,536	$12,412	$13,313
NOI	$23,725	$24,436	$25,170	$25,925	$26,702	$27,503	$28,329	$29,178	$30,054	$30,955
Less interest	15,565	15,325	15,056	14,757	14,423	14,051	13,635	13,172	12,654	12,077
Depreciation	8,421	8,421	8,421	8,421	8,421	8,421	8,421	8,421	8,421	8,421
Taxable income	−261	691	1,692	2,746	3,858	5,032	6,272	7,586	8,978	10,457
Tax	$−73	$193	$474	$769	$1,080	$1,409	$1,756	$2,124	$2,514	$2,928
BTCF	$6,083	$6,794	$7,528	$8,283	$9,060	$9,861	$10,687	$11,536	$12,412	$13,313
Tax	−73	193	474	769	1,080	1,409	1,756	2,124	2,514	2,928
ATCF	$6,156	$6,601	$7,054	$7,514	$7,980	$8,453	$8,930	$9,412	$9,898	$10,385

Calculation of After-Tax Cash Flow from Sale

	6	7	8	9	10	11	12	13	14	15
Sale price	$257,500	$265,225	$273,182	$281,377	$289,819	$298,513	$307,468	$316,693	$326,193	$335,979
Mortgage balance	140,355	138,037	135,452	132,567	129,348	125,757	121,750	117,280	112,292	106,727
Selling expenses	15,450	15,914	16,391	16,883	17,389	17,911	18,448	19,002	19,572	20,159
BTCF	$101,695	$111,274	$121,339	$131,928	$143,081	$154,845	$167,270	$180,411	$194,330	$209,093
Original cost basis	$200,000	$200,000	$200,000	$200,000	$200,000	$200,000	$200,000	$200,000	$200,000	$200,000
Accumulated depreciation	50,526	58,947	67,368	75,789	84,211	92,632	101,053	109,474	117,895	126,316
Adjusted basis	$149,474	$141,053	$132,632	$124,211	$115,789	$107,368	$98,947	$90,526	$82,105	$73,684
Sale price	$257,500	$265,225	$273,182	$281,377	$289,819	$298,513	$307,468	$316,693	$326,193	$335,979
Selling expenses	15,450	15,914	16,391	16,883	17,389	17,911	18,448	19,002	19,572	20,159
Adjusted basis	149,474	141,053	132,632	124,211	115,789	107,368	98,947	90,526	82,105	73,684
Total taxable gain	$92,576	$108,259	$124,159	$140,284	$156,640	$173,234	$190,073	$207,165	$224,516	$242,136
BTCF	$101,695	$111,274	$121,339	$131,928	$143,081	$154,845	$167,270	$180,411	$194,330	$209,093
Capital gains tax	25,921	30,312	34,765	39,280	43,859	48,505	53,220	58,006	62,865	67,798
ATCF	$75,774	$80,962	$86,575	$92,648	$99,222	$106,340	$114,050	$122,405	$131,465	$141,295

We can use the information in Exhibit 14–7 to calculate the marginal rate of return (*MRR*) for each of the next 10 years. Each year, the marginal rate of return is based on the benefit of receiving $ATCF_o$ for one additional year and $ATCF_s$ at the end of the additional year. The cost of receiving this cash flow is $ATCF_s$ for the current year. Since only one year is involved, the return calculation is simply as follows:

$$MRR = \frac{ATCF_s \text{ (year } t + 1) + ATCF_o \text{ (year } t + 1) - ATCF_s \text{ (year } t)}{ATCF_s \text{ (year } t)}$$

Exhibit 14–8 shows what the *MRR* is for years 6 through 15, and Exhibit 14–9 plots those *MRR*s. We see that the *MRR* rises until year 10 and then begins to fall. Increasing rents and increases in the value of the property tend to increase the *MRR*. Equity buildup from the price appreciation and loan repayment, however, tends to lower the *MRR*. Also, because the depreciation deduction is fixed but rents are rising, the relative amount of tax benefits from depreciation decreases each year. After year 10, the effect of equity buildup dominates. How long should the property be held? The answer is that *the property should be sold when the marginal rate of return falls below the rate at which funds can be reinvested.* For example, suppose the investor believes that funds can be reinvested in a different property (with the same risk) at a rate of 15.5 percent. This means that the property should be sold in the 14th year, because the *MRR* falls below 15.5 percent after year 14.

EXHIBIT 14–8
Marginal Rate of Return for the Next 10 Years

Year	Marginal Rate of Return (%)
6	15.43%
7	15.56
8	15.65
9	15.69
10	15.71
11	15.69
12	15.65
13	15.58
14	15.49
15	15.38

EXHIBIT 14–9
Holding Period Analysis

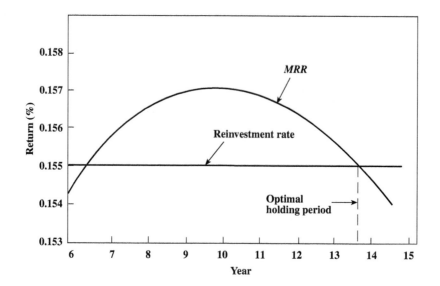

EXHIBIT 14–10
Holding Period
Analysis

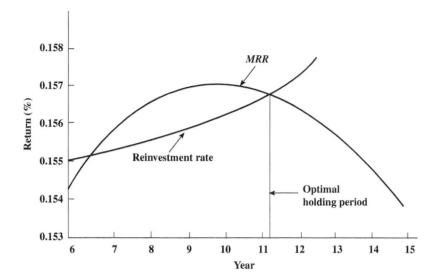

The above analysis assumes that the **reinvestment rate** remains constant throughout the next 10 years. It is not necessary to make this assumption. For example, the reinvestment rate may be expected to rise through time due to an increase in the general level of interest rates and yields on alternative investments. This increase could obviously change the optimal holding period, as illustrated in Exhibit 14–10. Because of the rising reinvestment rate, the **optimal holding period** in this case would be about 11 years.

Refinancing as an Alternative to Disposition

As we have discussed, after an investor has owned a property for a number of years, equity may build up as a result of an increase in the property value and amortization of the loan. Thus, the loan balance relative to the *current* value of the property will be lower than when the property was originally purchased. In this situation, the investor has less financial leverage than when the property was originally financed and may consider *refinancing* the property. Refinancing would allow the investor to increase financial leverage. Because refinancing at a higher loan-to-current-value ratio may provide additional funds to invest, it is, to some extent, an alternative to sale of the property.

If the investor's equity has increased due to an increase in the value of the property and amortization of the existing loan, then the investor should be able to obtain a new loan based on some percentage of the *current* property value. The current property value would normally be based on an appraisal of the property. Of course, points, appraisal fees, and other expenses may be incurred to obtain the new loan. However, no taxes have to be paid on funds received by additional borrowing, whereas taxes would have to be paid if the property were sold.

How should an investor decide whether it is profitable to refinance? To answer this question, we must first determine the cost of the additional funds obtained from refinancing. This is the topic of the next section.

Incremental Cost of Refinancing

In Chapter 6, we discussed the importance of considering the incremental borrowing cost when the borrower is faced with a choice between two different amounts of debt. Recall that when the interest rate is higher on the larger loan amount, the incremental cost of the additional funds borrowed is even higher than the rate on the larger loan because the higher rate has to be paid on all the funds borrowed, not just the additional funds.

The same concept applies to the analysis of refinancing. By refinancing, we obtain additional funds. If the interest rate on the new loan is higher than that on the existing loan, the incremental cost of the additional funds will be even higher than the rate on the new loan. To illustrate, we return to the Apex Center example introduced at the beginning of this chapter. Now, assume that Apex Center could be refinanced with a loan that is 75 percent of the current value of the property. Thus, the loan would be for 75 percent of $250,000 or $187,500. Suppose that the rate on this loan is 12 percent with a 25-year term. We can calculate the incremental cost of refinancing as follows:

	Current Balance	Monthly Payment	Balance after Five Years
New loan	$187,500	$1,975	$179,350
Existing loan	142,432	1,470	129,348
Difference	$ 45,068	$ 505	$ 50,002

The difference between the new loan amount of $187,500 and the existing loan balance of $142,432 represents the additional funds obtained by refinancing, $45,068. The incremental cost of these funds depends on the additional payment made after refinancing ($505) and the additional loan balance after five years ($50,002). Solving for the interest rate, we obtain 14.93 percent. We refer to this as the *incremental cost of financing.* To justify refinancing, the investor must be able to reinvest the proceeds from refinancing Apex Center in another project earning more than 14.93 percent before tax. Otherwise, favorable financing leverage would not result from use of the funds obtained by refinancing Apex Center.

Leveraged Return from Refinancing and Holding an Additional Five Years

Another way to look at this is to actually calculate the impact of refinancing on the investor's return from holding an additional five years after refinancing. We already determined earlier that if the property is held an *additional five years,* the after-tax *IRR* is 15.60 percent. We have just seen that the incremental cost of the additional financing is 14.93 percent before tax, which would be $14.93\% \times (1 - .28)$, or 10.75 percent after tax for an investor in the 28 percent tax bracket, as we have assumed. The return we are earning *before* borrowing more money is greater on an after-tax basis than the cost of the additional funds. Thus, the additional financing has favorable leverage. Readers may want to recall the discussion in Chapter 12 on leverage and the incremental cost of debt. We saw there that borrowing additional money contributes to positive leverage if the return before borrowing the additional funds is greater than the incremental cost of those funds. The same concept applies to funds obtained through refinancing.

We can now calculate the return if refinanced and held an additional five years in the same way we calculated the return for holding the property an additional five years. Recall that when we calculated this earlier in the chapter, the "initial investment" used in that analysis was the after-tax cash flow that would have been obtained if the property were sold. That initial investment is sometimes referred to as the *investment base.*

In the case of refinancing, the investment base is the after-tax cash flow that would have been received for the property less the additional funds obtained from refinancing. This is the amount of capital that is implicitly invested in the property immediately after refinancing. If the property were sold immediately after refinancing, the investor would receive these funds. By not selling, these funds are invested in the property. The investment base for the Apex Center is calculated as follows:

Price if sold today	$ 250,000
Less sale costs (at 6%)	15,000
Less mortgage balance before refinancing	142,432
Less additional funds obtained from refinancing	45,068
Less capital gain tax if sold today	21,589
Investment base	$ 25,911

The cash flows for the next five years, assuming the property is refinanced, will be as follows:

	Year				
	6	7	8	9	10
Rent	47,449	48,873	50,339	51,849	53,405
Less operating expenses	23,725	24,436	25,170	25,925	26,702
Net operating income	23,725	24,436	25,170	25,925	26,702
Less debt service	23,698	23,698	23,698	23,698	23,698
Before-tax cash flow	$ 27	$ 739	$ 1,472	$ 2,227	$ 3,005
Net operating Income	23,725	24,436	25,170	25,925	26,702
Less: Interest	22,432	22,271	22,090	21,887	21,657
Depreciation	8,421	8,421	8,421	8,421	8,421
Taxable income (loss)	(7,128)	(6,256)	(5,342)	(4,383)	(3,376)
Tax	(1,996)	(1,752)	(1,496)	(1,227)	(945)
Before-tax cash flow	27	739	1,472	2,227	3,005
Less tax	(1,996)	(1,752)	(1,496)	(1,227)	(945)
After-tax cash flow	$ 2,023	$ 2,491	$ 2,968	$ 3,454	$ 3,950

The cash flow from the sale of the property after five additional years will be as follows:

Sales price			$289,819
Sales costs			17,389
Mortgage balance			179,350
Before-tax cash flow			93,080
Sales price		$289,819	
Sales costs		17,389	
Org. cost basis	$200,000		
Accum dep	84,211		
Adj basis		115,789	
Capital gain		156,640	
Tax from sale			43,859
After-tax cash flow from sale			49,221

Now, we can calculate the returns from refinancing and holding the property five more years as follows:

	Year					
	5	6	7	8	9	10
Before-tax cash flow	(25,911)	27	739	1,472	2,227	96,085
After-tax cash flow	(25,911)	2,023	2,491	2,968	3,454	53,171
Before-tax *IRR* = 31.88%						
After-tax *IRR* = 22.31%						

We see that there was a significant increase in both the before-tax and after-tax *IRR*, as we expected based on our earlier comparison of the return before financing with the incremental cost of the funds obtained from refinancing. Either approach will indicate if the refinancing is desirable.

Refinancing at a Lower Interest Rate

The previous example assumed that the investor had to pay a higher interest rate when refinancing. The methodology would be the same if a lower rate could be obtained on the new loan. In this case, the savings associated with the lower interest rate would be reflected in a lower incremental cost of the additional funds obtained from refinancing. To illustrate, suppose that the rate on the loan used for refinancing Apex Center was at a 10.5 percent rate for 25 years. The incremental cost of refinancing would be as follows:

	Current Balance	Monthly Payment	Balance after Five Years
New loan	$187,500	$1,770	$177,321
Existing loan	142,432	1,470	129,348
Difference	$ 45,068	$ 300	$ 47,973

The incremental cost of refinancing in this case is 9.01 percent. Thus, the investor would achieve favorable financial leverage by investing the funds obtained from refinancing Apex Center in a project earning more than 9.01 percent.

Diversification Benefits

As we have pointed out, additional funds can often be obtained by refinancing a property because the property has increased in value since it was initially purchased and the loan balance has been reduced through amortization. The additional funds that are obtained from refinancing the property represent equity capital that can be reinvested in a second property. So refinancing enables the investor to increase the amount of property owned. Furthermore, the investor may be able to diversify investments further by owning more than two properties, especially if different property types can be acquired in different locations. For example, suppose that an investor currently owns a property that has a value of $1 million and an existing loan balance of $500,000. Equity in the project is therefore $500,000. By refinancing with a 75 percent loan, the investor has $250,000 to reinvest in a second project. Assuming that the investor could also obtain a 75 percent loan on the second project, she could purchase a second project that has a property value of $1 million. Note that the investor has the same total amount of equity capital invested ($500,000), but it is now being used to acquire *two* projects with a total value of $2 million. The investor has also incurred additional total debt of $1 million. Again, as stressed above, for refinancing to be a profitable strategy, the effective cost of this debt must be less than the unlevered return on the projects being financed.

Other Disposition Considerations—Portfolio Balancing

Thus far, we have analyzed whether an individual property should be sold based on the return that the *individual* property would earn if held versus the return from investing the funds in another project. An investor with a *portfolio* of properties also should take into consideration how sale of a property affects the mix of properties in the portfolio in terms of factors such as the property type (retail, office, industrial, apartment, etc.) and location.

We will see in Chapter 22 that portfolios are often constructed in a way that creates diversification benefits and reduces the risk of the portfolio. Thus, the decision to sell a property can affect the risk of the remaining portfolio if it means that the portfolio will be less diversified after the sale. This is not captured by just looking at the incremental return from holding the property that we evaluated earlier in this chapter. Portfolio analysis will be considered in depth in Chapter 22 but for now it is important to realize that there may be strategic considerations that an investor who holds a portfolio of properties will also consider, including the impact of a sale on the diversification of the portfolio. For example, if two properties are being considered for sale and both have about the same return if held, the property that contributes least to the diversification of the portfolio is a more likely candidate for sale. Similarly, the investor may be selling a property and replacing it with one that has about the same expected return as the one being sold but offers more diversification benefits so the risk of the portfolio is reduced by these transactions. For example, an investor may already have a portfolio that is overweighted with office properties relative to only a few retail properties. Hence, the investor may want to reduce exposure to office properties and increase exposure to retail properties to have a more balanced portfolio.

Although investing in different locations and property types may add diversification benefits, there are other factors that should be considered. For example, an investor would not want to invest in properties that are more difficult to manage if the investor lacks expertise in that property type or in properties that are not in an efficiently manageable location for the investor. Even though the investor may hire a property manager to handle the day-to-day operations of the property, the investor needs to provide some oversight and make longer-term decisions (e.g., whether to do renovation of the property) that may require that the investor have an understanding of the property and its location rather than rely completely on the expertise of the property manager. Thus, the balance between a diversified portfolio and efficient management must be taken into consideration in acquisition and disposition decisions. An investor may decide that certain properties in the portfolio are more difficult to manage than others and do not fit as well with the overall strategy for the portfolio. These properties should be sold and perhaps replaced with properties that are better aligned with the investor's portfolio strategy.

Tax-Deferral Strategies upon Disposition

In this section, we consider two tax-deferral strategies that may be considered when a property is sold. Instead of paying all of any capital gains tax due in the year of sale, these tax-deferral alternatives recognized in the Internal Revenue Code (IRC) may be used to defer such taxes into future years. In one case, when a property is sold, the buyer makes periodic payments to the seller after the year of sale. The contract of sale provides that, instead of paying the full price when the property is purchased, the buyer shall make payments over time, or in "installments." This transaction is referred to in the IRC as an **installment sale.**

A second alternative is referred to as a **like kind** or **tax-free exchange.** This alternative is typically used when a property owner wants to sell a property and then purchase another property within a specified period of time. Instead of paying a capital gains tax in the year of sale, the equity that the owner has in the property being exchanged is established and *carried over* as the equity in the acquired property. When the acquired property is eventually sold, the deferred capital gains taxes are paid at that time.[2] It should be pointed out that in this case, *like kind* refers to the exchange of real property for real property. The properties do not have to be the same type (e.g., an apartment property could be exchanged for an office property, land, or other type of real property). The general taxation concept behind the exchange is that because an investor continues to own real property after the exchange, the change in legal ownership does not warrant a *taxable event.* This is because the investor could have continued to own the exchanged property. Therefore, the fact that one property has been sold and a like kind property acquired amounts to an *equivalent investment.*

Both installment sales and tax-deferred exchanges are ways of deferring and perhaps reducing the total amount of capital gains tax that an investor would otherwise have to pay upon disposition of a property. In fact, the total capital gains tax may be reduced if, as gains are recognized over time, they may be combined with any future capital losses, thereby lowering total tax liability. For both installment sales and tax-deferred exchanges, the primary goal is to structure the sale such that the present value of after-tax cash flows— whether from an installment sale or a like kind exchange—is greater than it would be for an outright sale.

Installment Sales

When using an installment sale, a property is sold. However, rather than receiving the full sales price in the year of sale, the seller receives payments from the buyer in subsequent tax years. According to Internal Revenue Code **(IRC) Section 453 (1),** in general, the term *installment sale* means a disposition of property where at least one payment is received by the seller after the close of the taxable year in which the disposition occurs.[3]

An installment sale may include transactions in which the seller also provides financing and will receive interest payments for the amount financed, as well as installment payments due on the purchase price over time. It may include transactions in which a taxpayer-seller receives no monetary consideration in the year of sale and receives all proceeds from the sale at the beginning of the next tax year. The installment sale reporting provisions of the code allow the seller to match the payment of the tax due on the sale with the receipt of cash payments. This provision of the code is only available to investors who have assets

---

[2] That is, unless another like kind exchange is executed.

[3] It should be stressed that a sale of the property and a change in ownership (transfer of title) must occur in order to qualify as an installment sale. When a change in ownership will occur in a future period, or when ownership is *contingent* on an event or future consideration to be received by the seller, the transaction is generally disqualified from being an installment sale. The latter would be characterized as a *contract for deed* and is subject to different tax treatment not discussed here.

that are determined to be Section 1231 assets used in trade or business and Section 1221 investments.[4] It does not apply to assets that have been characterized as inventory.[5]

Base Case Example

As an example, we consider the following case. An investor is considering the sale of an office building for a price of $1,000,000. He currently owes $600,000 on a mortgage loan secured by this property. He has owned the property for five years and has deducted straight-line depreciation expenses on it each year, leaving an adjusted basis of $700,000. He is considering two choices. In scenario A, he sells the property for $1,000,000 and repays the $600,000 mortgage, thereby receiving cash flows of $400,000 in the year of sale. He also would have to recognize a capital gain of $300,000 and pay capital gains tax during the current year. In scenario B, he sells the property for $1,000,000; however, under this alternative, the buyer assumes the seller's $600,000 loan. Instead of the seller receiving $400,000 in the year of sale, the buyer makes a payment of $25,000 in the current year and agrees to make payments of $75,000 to the seller each year for five years. Although total cash receipts of $400,000 are eventually received by the seller, because payments are being made in installments, the IRC allows the capital gain of $300,000 (sale price of $1,000,000 less adjusted basis $700,000) to be deferred. In this case, taxes are calculated and paid by the seller as the buyer makes the initial installment of $25,000, then $75,000 during each of the next five years. The question that the investor faces is, Is the present value of receiving the installment payments and paying capital gains taxes each year over the five-year life of the installment sale greater than the net after-tax cash flow that would be realized from an outright sale of the property? To answer this question, we now consider the installment sales contract and IRC requirements.

Importance of the Profit Ratio

An installment sale is in essence a form of *seller financing.* The seller of the property is financing the sale by not receiving all of the money from the buyer at the time of sale. Some or all of the sale proceeds are paid over time as installment payments. In addition to the installment payments, interest is normally charged on the outstanding balance. The interest payments are treated as ordinary income. Capital gains are recognized as installment payments are made.

Because of the special tax status related to the installment sale, the IRC defines certain terms that are an integral part of the tax treatment and recognition. Two of these terms are the *profit ratio* and *contract price.* If the sale qualifies for installment sale reporting, the amount of the capital gain subject to tax each year is equal to the amount of the *installment payment*[6] multiplied by the *profit ratio.*

---

[4] Section 1231 property is depreciable property used in a trade or business, such as equipment, vehicles, and rental real estate. In general, if Section 1231 assets are held for the required period of time, capital gains treatment is available, while a loss is a deductible ordinary loss. Section 1221 investments generally include "nonbusiness" property such as stocks and bonds held as an investment. Readers should refer to the tax code for the specifics.

[5] This usually means that developers and builders cannot use installment sales because the land and property that they improve are generally classified as inventory. Therefore, for tax purposes, all sales must be reported based on contract prices. All sales must be reported in the current tax year regardless of the timing of the receipt of the payments from the sale, and all income is subject to ordinary tax rates.

[6] Installment payments are calculated before any interest being charged. It is analogous to a principal payment.

The **profit ratio** is defined as *gross profit* divided by the *contract price.* For the purpose of installment sale reporting, the IRC defines the **contract price** as the selling price minus any mortgages, debts, and other liabilities assumed or taken by the buyer. The contract price also generally equals the equity that the seller will eventually receive in principal payments over the life of the loan. Gross profit equals the total gain that the seller will report in the year of sale (sale price less selling costs less adjusted basis).

$$\text{Profit ratio} = \frac{\text{Gross profit}}{\text{Contract price}}$$

Whenever the profit ratio is less than 1, less than 100 percent of the principal received is reported as a gain. Using the information in the example described above, the profit ratio for the installment sale scenario can be determined as follows:

Sale price	$1,000,000
– Adjusted basis[7]	700,000
Gross profit	$ 300,000
Sale price	$1,000,000
– Seller's mortgage balance	600,000
Contract price	$ 400,000

$$\text{Profit ratio} = \$300{,}000 \div \$400{,}000$$
$$= 75\%$$

When thinking about the profit ratio, it is useful to consider what would happen if the property had been sold for cash. In that event, the seller would have reported a $300,000 gain, and after $600,000 was used to pay off the outstanding mortgage loan balance, the seller would have received $400,000 in cash (before tax). As a result, the profit ratio (as defined in the IRC) would be 75 percent ($300,000 ÷ $400,000 = 75%).

If, instead of receiving the entire $400,000 in cash at the time of sale, the seller receives the $400,000 as installment payments, the $300,000 gain will be recognized as installment payments made on the $400,000. By "installment payments," we mean payments that would be applied to repay the $400,000 to the seller. These payments could be considered "principal payments." The seller would also normally charge interest since he is in effect providing "seller financing." The profit ratio of 75 percent means that for each $1 of installment (principal) payments, 75 cents of gain will be recognized.

It should be pointed out that if the marginal tax rate of the taxpayer remains the same each year that installment payments are to be made, then the total tax due from a cash sale will be equivalent to the total tax due in an installment sale. The same amount of gain will be reported in either transaction. However, when using time value of money concepts, there may be benefits to the taxpayer in postponing the payment of taxes. Benefits also may be possible if the marginal tax rate becomes lower in a future period or if capital losses occur to offset reportable gains.

The installment sale described in our example above is structured such that the buyer agrees to assume the seller's loan for $600,000. The seller agrees to accept one payment of $25,000 at closing and to receive the remaining $375,000 in annual payments over the next

[7] *Adjusted basis* is defined as the cost of the property less any depreciation taken during the period of ownership.

five years. Therefore, in addition to the $600,000 in debt assumed by the buyer, the buyer, in effect, also receives $375,000 of seller financing. This is summarized as follows:

Payment from seller at closing	$ 25,000
Total amount of installment payments	375,000
Loan assumption by buyer	600,000
Sale price of property	$1,000,000

As discussed above, if the entire $400,000 in equity had been received by the seller at the time of sale, a $300,000 gain would have been recognized immediately. In the installment case, however, since only $25,000 was received by the seller in the year of sale, a gain would be recognized on only 75 percent of this amount, or $18,750. The remainder of the gain would be recognized over time as installment payments are made on the $375,000 financed by the installment sale.

Because the seller is financing $375,000, the seller will normally want to charge interest on the outstanding balance of the loan until it is repaid.[8] In our example, we will assume that the seller charges 10 percent interest on the unpaid balance of the seller financing and that this amount of interest will be added to installment payments each year. It is important to take the installment payments into consideration when comparing an installment sale with a cash sale, as we will do later, because the interest charged on the installment sale is one of the key differences between the two types of sales. Also, this interest income will be taxed as ordinary income.

After-Tax Sales Proceeds versus Future After-Tax Cash Flows from an Installment Sale

Continuing with our example, we now compare the amount of after-tax cash flow the seller would receive over time on an installment sale with the amount the seller would receive from an immediate cash sale. The after-tax cash flow from an immediate cash sale is calculated as follows:

Seller After-Tax Cash Flow: Year of Sale

Sale price	$1,000,000
− Mortgage	600,000
− Taxes	45,000*
Sale proceeds after tax	$ 355,000

*15% of $300,000. Recall that for an immediate sale, the entire $300,000 is taxed immediately at the 15 percent capital gains tax rate.

We now consider the after-tax cash flow from the installment sale. Sales proceeds after taxes based on the closing of the property sale are calculated as follows:

Principal payment received	$25,000
× Profit ratio	0.75
Gain to report	$18,750
× Tax rate	0.15
Tax liability	$ 2,813
After-tax cash flow	$22,188

[8] In fact, if interest is not charged, the IRS may "impute" interest and require the seller to pay ordinary income tax on this imputed interest. This is to prevent the seller from inflating the sale price of the property instead of charging interest. If the seller did this, the higher sale price, which is in effect prepaid interest, would result in a higher capital gains tax for the seller but no ordinary income tax from the interest. Thus, the seller would have converted ordinary income into a capital gain that is taxed at a lower rate.

Similarly, the tax liability and after-tax cash flow must be calculated when the installment payments are made during each of the next five years. *Recall that the seller will also receive interest income based on 10 percent of the $375,000 in seller financing. This interest will be taxed as ordinary income, which we assume is taxed at a 30 percent ordinary tax rate.* The after-tax cash flow for all five years is shown in Exhibit 14–11.

Exhibit 14–11 also shows that the present value (*PV*) of the after-tax cash flows has been calculated using a 7 percent discount rate. This rate was chosen because 10 percent interest was charged on seller financing (which is equivalent to equity that the seller would have retained in the property had it not been sold), with a 30 percent marginal tax rate, and so we assume that an appropriate after-tax discount rate would be $10\% \times (1 - .30) = 7\%$. This present value can be compared to the present value from an all-cash sale with all proceeds taxed in the year of sale. We previously calculated that amount to be $355,000.

We now see that in this case, the present value of the installment sale of $362,592 is greater than the present value of the all-cash sale of $355,000. Because the latter amount is received immediately, it is not discounted. Therefore, the analysis indicates that the investor is better off with an installment sale. The reader should recognize that results may vary considerably. Also, they depend on the interest rate charged, the investor's ordinary and capital gains tax rate, the size of installment payments, the number of years over which such is paid, and so on. Whether an installment sale or a cash sale is better depends on the circumstances for the particular investor and how the installment sale is structured.

EXHIBIT 14–11   **After-Tax Cash Flow from Installment Payments**

				Year			
	0	**1**	**2**	**3**	**4**	**5**	**Total**
A. Capital Gains Tax Recognition							
Installment payment	$ 25,000	$ 75,000	$ 75,000	$ 75,000	$ 75,000	$75,000	$400,000
× Profit ratio	75%	75%	75%	75%	75%	75%	
= Gain to report	$ 18,750	$ 56,250	$ 56,250	$ 56,250	$ 56,250	$56,250	$300,000
× Capital gains tax rate	15%	15%	15%	15%	15%	15%	
= Capital gains tax	$ 2,813	$ 8,438	$ 8,438	$ 8,438	$ 8,438	$ 8,438	$ 45,000
B. Interest and Tax on							
Seller Financing							
Beginning year balance	$400,000	$375,000	$300,000	$225,000	$150,000	$75,000	
Installment payment	$ 25,000	$ 75,000	$ 75,000	$ 75,000	$ 75,000	$75,000	$400,000
End of year balance	$375,000	$300,000	$225,000	$150,000	$ 75,000	$0	
Interest (10%)		$ 37,500	$ 30,000	$ 22,500	$ 15,000	$ 7,500	$112,500
× Ordinary income tax rate		30%	30%	30%	30%	30%	
Ordinary income tax		$ 11,250	$ 9,000	$ 6,750	$ 4,500	$ 2,250	$ 33,750
C. After-Tax Cash Flows							
Installment payment	$ 25,000	$ 75,000	$ 75,000	$ 75,000	$ 75,000	$75,000	$400,000
Less ordinary income tax	$ 0	$ 11,250	$ 9,000	$ 6,750	$ 4,500	$ 2,250	
Less capital gains tax	$ 2,813	$ 8,438	$ 8,438	$ 8,438	$ 8,438	$ 8,438	
After-tax cash flow	$ 2,188	$ 92,813	$ 87,563	$ 82,313	$ 77,063	$71,813	
Discount rate	7.00%						
Present value	$362,592						

Tax-Deferred Exchanges

Another strategy for deferring the recognition of capital gains when a property is sold is the use of a **tax-deferred exchange.** This is sometimes called a *tax-free* or *1031 exchange,* in reference to the applicable Internal Revenue Code (IRC) Section 1031. Under this provision, if an investor is willing to exchange a property for another within a requisite time period, he may *elect* to use tax treatment under IRC Section 1031. The gain that would normally be reported in the year of sale is not reported, and therefore no taxes are paid at that time. The gain postponed on the exchange is reported upon the eventual disposition of the property acquired.

In addition to deferring capital gains, an exchange may be used in conjunction with other investment strategies in order to:

- Adjust the geographic location of the investor's properties.
- Exchange one property for another that has different cash flow characteristics (e.g., a higher occupancy rate).
- Exchange one property for several properties in order to have a more diversified portfolio.
- Exchange one property for another that is less management-intensive (e.g., exchange an apartment property for a net leased medical office building).

IRC Section 1031

As will be seen, the investor must make certain fundamental considerations when evaluating whether or not to use a Section 1031 exchange strategy. Some of these considerations include:

- Whether the property being acquired can be identified and the exchange transaction completed within the time limits prescribed by the IRS.
- Whether the number of properties being acquired in the exchange (1) can be limited to a maximum of three or (2) if greater than three, whether the combined value of properties acquired can be limited to 200 percent of the fair market value of the property being exchanged.
- Whether the *current equity* in the property being exchanged is greater or less than the equity in the properties being acquired. This relationship may tend to reduce or eliminate the tax benefits derived from an exchange.
- Whether any nonreal property (personal property) is likely to be included in the exchange. In this event, such "unlike property" is considered personal property (referred to as "boot") and is subject to tax.

What follows is a very explicit discussion of like kind exchanges under IRC provisions.

According to **IRC Section 1031,** no gain or loss shall be recognized on the exchange of property held for productive use in a trade or business or for investment if such property is exchanged solely for property of like kind, which is to be held either for productive use in a trade or business or for investment. It should be stressed that only Section 1231 and Section 1221 assets qualify for an exchange; other assets exchanged do not qualify. The exchanger must give up equity in qualifying property and only receive equity in qualifying property. Similarly, the property that will be received in an exchange must be held by the exchanger as a Section 1231 or Section 1221 asset. Any real property held as Section 1231 or Section 1221 property may be exchanged for almost any other type of real property that is to be held as Section 1231 or Section 1221 property. For example, this allows the exchange of a multi-tenant retail center for a single-user big-box retail property; an apartment building for investment land; an office building for a retail center; or a

In the late 1970s, a taxpayer in the state of Oregon named Starker changed the way that tax-deferred exchanges are conducted by challenging the requirement that exchanges had to be simultaneous.

Starker owned thousands of acres of timberland in the Northwest that a lumber company wanted. He wanted to exchange land for other real property, but the problem he faced was finding replacement property, so that he could complete a simultaneous exchange. Unable to do so, and wanting to complete the transaction with the lumber company, both parties agreed to have Starker deed his land to the lumber company for a fixed price. The lumber company then agreed to spend the same amount of cash to acquire properties for Starker as he identified them. Over the next several tax years, the lumber company purchased properties identified by Starker and then deeded them to him, completing the exchange.

The problem in this plan, according to the IRS, was that Starker could not file his tax return for the year in which he gave up his timberland because he did not know if he had an exchange or a sale. Only after completing the acquisition of all replacement properties could he file his tax return. The IRS challenged this plan, saying that he did not qualify for exchange treatment under Section 1031 because he had not completed a simultaneous exchange.

Starker ultimately prevailed in his challenge and, as a consequence, IRC Section 1031 was modified to allow for the nonsimultaneous exchange of properties in qualifying tax-deferred exchanges. This was an important change, as it gave much more flexibility to investors considering the use of exchanges.

The successful argument Starker had in his favor was that he never received or controlled any non–like kind property. He did not receive cash from the transactions, as the lumber company always retained it. He had no control over the cash, except to tell the lumber company when to pay for the property he wanted to acquire. Because he gave up a deed to his property, received deeds to the replacement property, and never took constructive receipt of the cash, he was able to meet the requirements of exchanging solely for qualifying property.

AMENDMENT OF TIME FRAMES

Because of the outcome of the Starker case and similar cases, Congress has since amended Section 1031, and the IRS has issued regulations that provide guidance to taxpayers and real estate agents as to how to successfully complete a nonsimultaneous tax-deferred exchange. The taxpayer must acquire title on the property to be acquired within 180 days after selling the property to be exchanged.

REVERSE STARKER

A problem investors often face is that IRC Section 1031 also requires that the property to be acquired be identified within 45 days, and 45 days is not enough time to identify properties they want to acquire via an exchange. Also, investors are reluctant to enter into a sale agreement that results in such a restrictive timeline. Therefore, investors may want to identify the properties they want to acquire *prior* to having their existing property sold.

A strategy that is referred to as a "reverse Starker" occurs when the owner of property acquires the replacement property *first*, then sells the original property and claims that a tax-deferred exchange has been completed. This transaction, if done correctly, meets the time requirements of Section 1031; if the replacement property is owned by the investor prior to the sale of the original property, the 45-day and 180-day time limits have been met.

The taxpayer should consult a tax attorney or experienced tax professional when planning to take advantage of an installment sale and especially a reverse Starker strategy.

SAFE HARBOR RULES

During the exchange period, the taxpayer cannot receive property that is not considered like kind. Receipt of non–like kind property is considered cash and is not qualified for tax-deferred treatment.

So that the investor is not considered to be in constructive receipt of non–like kind property, the regulations give taxpayers several guidelines which are called *safe harbor rules*:

- A *qualified escrow account* is a type of escrow account wherein the escrow holder is not the taxpayer or a disqualified person (as defined in paragraph (k) of this section), and the escrow agreements expressly limit the taxpayer's rights to receive, pledge, borrow, or otherwise obtain the benefits of the cash or cash equivalent held in the escrow account.
- A *qualified trust* is a trust, wherein the trustee is not the taxpayer or a disqualified person, and the trust agreement expressly limits the taxpayer's rights to receive, pledge, borrow, or otherwise obtain the benefits of the cash or cash equivalent held by the trustee.
- A *qualified intermediary* is often used by the investor as an intermediary to facilitate the exchange. This is the most common way that exchanges are completed today. For a fee, the intermediary facilitates the delayed exchange by agreeing with the investor to acquire the property given up by the investor, acquire a replacement property identified by the investor, and then transfer that property to the investor.

The qualified intermediary does not have to actually take title to the replacement property. The transfer of the property may be by direct deed from the current owner to the present owner rather than through the intermediary. Requiring the deeding through the intermediary requires four deeds instead of two. When direct deeding is allowed, it requires twice the documentary tax and recording fees. It also reduces possible environmental liability.

multi-tenant office building for a single tenant office building.[9] A partnership may exchange the qualifying property it owns for other qualifying property and receive the tax-deferral promised in Section 1031. The partners, however, cannot exchange their partnership interests on a tax-deferred basis under the rules of Section 1031. The partnership interests owned by the investors are personal property. The partnership owns the real property.

Specific Time Frames Must Be Established

IRC Section 1031 (a) requires that the property be *identified* within 45 days and the exchange *completed* not more than 180 days after the title transfer of the exchanged property (or properties).

Property not acquired within the 180-day period is *not like kind property*. The 180-day period during which the taxpayer has to acquire a replacement property is further broken down into two time segments. The first section tells us that the taxpayer has 45 days to identify the property that is going to be acquired in the exchange.

Balancing Equities

To complete a successful tax-deferred exchange, the investor must, in effect, (1) give up equity in real property and (2) acquire equity in real property. Under the concept of *balancing equities,* if the equity given up is equal to the amount of equity acquired, then the equities are "balanced" and the exchange is totally tax deferred. For example, if the investor has a $500,000 property with no loan (free and clear) and exchanges it for a

[9] However, one limitation is that real property inside the United States and real property outside the United States are not considered like kind. Therefore, to qualify under Section 1031, either all the properties involved in the exchange must be located within the United States, or else all the properties in the exchange must be located outside the United States.

property purchased without a loan with a value of $500,000, it is clear that the investor gave up real estate equity equal to equity in the acquired property and did not receive unlike property. This would meet the requirement of exchanging solely real estate equity for real estate equity.

In many tax-deferred exchanges, however, equities will not be balanced. This occurs when the value of a property being exchanged is greater or less than the value of the real estate being acquired. In cases where the value of the property being acquired is *greater,* the gain on the exchanged property will be deferred and will reduce the basis of the acquired property. A *substitute basis* is then established and an allocation between land and improvement must be made to establish a depreciable basis. In these cases, when the acquired property is eventually sold, any gain on the sale will usually be greater because of the lower substitute basis of the acquired property. In cases where the value of the real estate being acquired is *less* than the value of the real estate being exchanged and the difference in values is a result of *unlike property* (this includes personal property, including cash, etc.), such unlike property must be recognized as a gain in the year of the exchange. A substitute basis for the acquired real estate is then established based on the value of the real estate acquired in the exchange. Finally, many exchanges may also include the assumption of mortgage debt by either or both parties as part of the exchange. In the event that there is a difference in the amount of debt being assumed, some relief of indebtedness may occur, benefitting one of the parties. When this occurs, a gain may have to be recognized in the year of the exchange. What follows are selected examples of transactions intended to help the reader better understand the concept of tax-deferred exchanges.

Recognized Gain

Ordinarily, if an investor sells a property for a gain, that gain must be reported in the year of sale and a capital gains tax must be paid. However, if an investor sold a commercial or investment property for cash, and all of the cash received was used to purchase another property, the investor may not have to recognize all of the gain from the sale. Section 1031 allows an investor to *transfer* equity from one property to another, thereby deferring some or all of the gain into a future period. Any gain that is not recognized is unrecognized gain.

For example, if an investor sold a property for $400,000 and had an adjusted basis of $160,000, the investor would have a recognized gain of $240,000 on a cash sale of the property.

Sale price	$400,000
− Adjusted basis	160,000
Recognized gain	$240,000
Sale price	$400,000
− Mortgage balance	0
Equity	$400,000

Substitute Basis What happens to the capital that is deferred in a qualifying exchange under Section 1031? The gain that is not reported in the disposition of the property relinquished becomes a basis adjustment in the property acquired. The basis in a property acquired in a tax-deferred exchange is called a **substitute basis.**

Using the previous example, suppose that the exchange is structured so that all of the realized gain can be deferred. Thus, it is unrecognized gain at the time of the exchange, meaning that no taxes are paid on it at that time. This unrecognized gain lowers the basis of the property acquired by the exchange. This is summarized as follows:

Market value of property given up	$400,000
– Basis	160,000
Realized gain	$240,000
Market value of property acquired	$500,000
– Unrecognized gain	240,000
Substitute basis	$260,000

The effect of this adjustment to basis is to build the $240,000 gain into the basis of the property acquired. For example, if the new property were sold the next day for $500,000, a $240,000 gain would be reported.

Allocation of Substituted Basis The substituted basis described above will be allocated between land and improvements for the purposes of depreciation deductions. If, in the above example, the property relinquished was raw land and the property acquired was a small apartment building with a ratio of 25 percent land and 75 percent improvement, $195,000 (75% of $260,000) would be depreciated for tax purposes.

Unlike Property (Boot) In many situations, the acquired property may not be exactly like kind. The term *unlike property* means property that is not real property. IRC Section 1031 requires that exchanges must be solely for like kind properties. If an exchange involves unlike property, this results in a taxable event.

When the investor receives unlike property in an exchange, gain will be recognized because the investor has not exchanged like kind property for like kind. Unlike property may be of various types and is sometimes, collectively, called **boot.** For example, if an investor exchanges undeveloped land for a hotel property, the latter may contain furniture and other personal property (unlike property). In this case, the personal property being acquired as part of the hotel acquisition is said to contain *boot.*

Cash Cash received in an exchange for unlike property must be reported as gain. For example, suppose that an investor exchanges a property based on the following facts:

Market value of property given up	$400,000
– Mortgage balance	200,000
Equity given up	$200,000
Market value of property acquired	$300,000
– Mortgage balance	200,000
Equity acquired	100,000
+ Cash acquired	100,000
Total equity acquired	$200,000

Note that in this exchange the investor acquired property that required $100,000 less equity and received $100,000 in cash. Thus, the investor received $100,000 of *unlike* property to balance equities. This $100,000 is boot, which means that $100,000 of gain must be recognized at the time of sale. If the *realized gain* on the original property were $300,000, then $100,000 of the gain would be taxed at the time of the exchange and $200,000 would be deferred.

Mortgage Relief If the investor owes less on the replacement property than on the property given up in the exchange, the investor is considered to have received *mortgage relief.* Consequently, when an investor's indebtedness is reduced as a part of the exchange, the requirement of having exchanged solely equity for equity has not been met. For example, suppose that we have the following facts for an exchange:

Market value of property given up	$400,000
– Mortgage balance given up	200,000
Equity given up	$200,000
Market value of property acquired	$300,000
– Mortgage balance acquired	100,000
Equity acquired	$200,000

Even though the equity given up equals the equity acquired, the investor has received mortgage relief because he owes $100,000 less after the transaction than before the transaction. This $100,000 is boot and will be reported as a gain at the time of the exchange, even though no cash changed hands. Although the same amount of equity went into the property being acquired, its value is $100,000 less, so it is as if the investor sold $100,000 of the original property, thus requiring taxation.

There are still other types of unlike properties that can result from an exchange. Readers should consult with a tax attorney or accountant before engaging in an exchange.

Unrecognized Gain

Once the recognized gain has been calculated and the amount of the unlike property (boot) to be received, if any, has been determined, the amount of unrecognized gain can be calculated. That is,

$$\text{Unrecognized Gain} = \text{Realized Gain} - \text{Boot}$$

For example, suppose that an investor would realize $250,000 of gain if a property were sold today for $700,000. In an exchange transaction, the investor transferred all of the equity to a new property except for $100,000 in cash. As a result, $150,000 of the gain would be unrecognized (deferred) and $100,000 of the gain (equal to the amount of unlike property or boot received) would be recognized.

Realized gain	$250,000
– Unlike property received	100,000
Unrecognized gain	$150,000

The goal in an exchange is to have an unrecognized gain that can be deferred to some future taxable disposition.

Economics of an Exchange

As we have discussed, the primary benefit of an exchange is to defer capital gains taxes. The question is whether the taxpayer is better off performing an exchange to acquire the second property or purchasing the second property in an outright sale. There are several factors to consider in comparing these two alternatives. First, in an exchange the substitute basis of the second property acquired through the exchange will be depreciated.

This basis is lowered by the amount of the deferred gain. Thus, there is less depreciation each year because of the lower basis of the second property. Second, because the gain on the exchanged property has been deferred, there will be larger capital gains upon sale of the second property. This is because the deferred gain will be recognized along with any additional capital gains from the sale of the property acquired through the exchange. So the question is whether or not the lower capital gains tax paid at the time of the exchange is offset by the present value of the reduced depreciation tax benefits each year after the exchange and the higher capital gains tax paid upon sale of the second property.

To illustrate, consider the following example. An investor owns a property that she wants to sell. She has identified a property that she would like to purchase and must decide whether or not to make an exchange.

The property can be sold today for $1,000,000. It has an adjusted basis of $600,000 that would result in a gain of $400,000 if sold. Assuming that a 15 percent capital gains tax rate would apply to the gain, the capital gains tax would be $60,000 if sold today. This is summarized as follows:

Sale price	$1,000,000
Adjusted basis	600,000
Gain	$ 400,000
Capital gains tax rate	15%
Tax	$ 60,000

Recall that with an exchange, the basis of the property acquired in the exchange is lowered by the amount of the deferred gain. It is this lower basis that is depreciated. In our example, this means that by doing the exchange, annual depreciation is lowered by $10,000 ($400,000/40) per year. If we assume that the investor has a 30 percent ordinary income tax rate, she will realize $3,000 ($10,000 × 30%) less in tax savings from depreciation each year if she does the exchange.

When the second property is sold, the deferred gain of $400,000 will be recognized. However, since the exchange results in less depreciation each year for the second property, the basis of the property acquired is lower than would have been the case if it had not been acquired in the exchange. In this case, depreciation is lowered by $10,000 per year for 10 years, for a total of $100,000. This offsets the difference in capital gain when comparing doing an exchange versus not doing an exchange. This difference in capital gain is summarized as follows:

Deferred gain from sale of first property	$400,000
Less: Additional accumulated depreciation if second property is acquired without an exchange 100,000	————
= Net amount of additional capital gain at sale for exchange versus no exchange $300,000	
× Capital gains tax rate	15%
Additional capital gains tax from exchange	$ 45,000

We can now calculate the economic benefit of doing an exchange versus an outright sale.

In year zero (time of exchange), we save $60,000 in taxes by doing the exchange. But each year we then have $3,000 less in tax savings ($ 10,000 × .30) from lower depreciation deductions as a result of doing the exchange instead of purchasing a new property. We also have an additional $45,000 in taxes at the time the second property is sold because of greater capital gains. Thus, we have:

$$PV = \$60,000$$
$$PMT = -\$3,000$$
$$FV = -45,000$$
$$n = 10 \text{ years}$$
$$\text{Calculate } i = 2.80\%$$

What does the 2.80 percent represent? In effect, this is the cost of "borrowing" $60,000 from the government by deferring the taxes with the exchange. The lower this cost, the more economical the exchange is for the investor. As long as the investor can earn more than 2.80 percent on his money each year until the second property is sold, the exchange is desirable.

Of course these results depend on assumptions such as the investor's ordinary income and capital gains tax rates, and whether the capital gains tax rate will differ when the second property is sold. So the results may differ with a change in these assumptions. For example, if the investor expects to have a lower capital gains tax rate when the second property is sold, the cost of the exchange will be even lower.

Finally, it should be noted that we did not consider the *NOI* and resale price for the property acquired in the exchange or how it might be financed. This is not necessary because the *NOI* and resale price are the same whether or not the second property is acquired in an exchange. The proper focus should be placed on the differences in tax treatment between the two alternatives.

Renovation as an Alternative to Disposition

Rather than selling one property to acquire another, the investor may consider the option of **renovation** of the property. For example, depending on economic trends in the local market and in the area where the property is located, the investor may consider improving a property by enlarging it or by making major capital improvements to upgrade quality and reduce operating costs. Alternatively, the investor may consider converting the improvement to accommodate a different economic use, such as converting a small multifamily residence to a small professional office building in an urban neighborhood (assuming zoning allows such a conversion).

The issue we address here is how to properly analyze such an option. To illustrate, we reconsider renovating the same property we analyzed in the first part of the chapter. Apex Center, which you recall is presently 20 years old, is owned by an investor who purchased it five years ago at a cost of $200,000. It was financed five years ago with a $150,000 loan at 11 percent interest for 25 years. We know that the property could be sold today for $250,000 if it is not renovated (Exhibit 14–2). We also know what the return will be if the property is held for five *additional* years and not renovated (Exhibits 14–4 and 14–5). We will now see how to evaluate the return associated with making an additional investment to renovate the property.

The owner is considering renovation that would cost $200,000. We initially assume that, because of the risk involved in the project, the bank will agree only to refinancing the present loan balance ($142,432) plus 75 percent of the $200,000 renovation cost, for a total loan of $292,432.[10] The new mortgage would carry an interest rate of 11 percent for 15 years.[11]

[10] The lender will often make a loan based on the present market value rather than on the existing loan balance, which was based on the market value at the time the loan was originally made, plus the cost of improvement. This is considered in the following section.

[11] Another alternative could be a second mortgage for $50,000. The procedure provided here would still be applicable to the problem.

If the owner, who is in a 28 percent tax bracket, undertakes the modernization project and wants to conduct an after-tax analysis of the investment proposal, the *additional* equity that the owner will have to invest in the property must be determined. This will equal the renovation cost less the additional financing (including both the financing for the renovation plus any existing financing on the remainder of the property). In this case, the lender would only provide additional financing to cover 75 percent of the renovation cost. However, it is also common on renovation projects to get an appraisal of what the entire property will be worth after the renovation and to borrow a percent of that value. This approach may allow the investor to get some equity out of the property.

In this case, the renovation cost is $200,000, and the additional financing amounts to 75 percent of the renovation cost, or $150,000. Thus, the *additional* equity investment is $200,000 − $150,000 = $50,000. What does the investor get in return for investing an additional $50,000 in the property? In general, renovation can have many benefits, including increasing rents, lowering vacancy, lowering operating expenses, and increasing the future property value.

Given the estimated cost of modernization and refinancing, the critical elements facing the investor are the estimates of rents, expenses, property values, and expected period of ownership. Obviously, the results of a planned renovation depend on such estimates, which require a careful market analysis and planning, as we have previously discussed. Assuming such a plan is carried out, the owner-investor's five-year projection for the modernized Apex Center is shown in Exhibit 14–12.

Looking at Exhibit 14–12, we should note that, based on the modernization plan, *NOI* in year 1 is estimated to increase from $23,725 without renovation (see Exhibit 14–4) to $45,000 with modernization. After the renovation, *NOI* is expected to increase at 4 percent per year instead of 3 percent. Debt service is based on the new $292,432 mortgage loan made at 11 percent for 15 years. The depreciation charge of $14,770 is computed by first calculating depreciation for the renovation expenditure, which increases the depreciable basis by $200,000. We assume that the renovation depreciates over 31.5 years based on the tax law in effect at the time. Thus, the renovation results in depreciation of $200,000 ÷ 31.5 = $6,349 per year. The depreciation for the existing building (the original depreciable basis) is not affected by the renovation. This depreciation is still $8,421 per year. Adding the original depreciation to the $6,349 depreciation resulting from the renovation results in the total depreciation of $14,770.

A five-year expected investment period has been selected for analysis. To estimate the resale price, the investor uses a 10 percent terminal capitalization rate applied to an estimate of *NOI* six years from now. This method is based on the assumption that the benefit of the renovation will be reflected in the future *NOI,* and a new investor purchasing the property after five years will purchase on the basis of *NOI* starting in year 11.

Now we are interested in determining how much the after-tax cash flow increases as a result of the renovation. That is, how much greater, if any, is the after-tax cash flow *after* renovation compared with the after-tax cash flow *before* renovation? The after-tax cash flow assuming no renovation is the same as determined in Exhibits 14–4 and 14–5 when we analyzed Apex Center assuming no sale. Exhibit 14–13 summarizes the after-tax cash flows for renovation versus no renovation.

From Exhibit 14–13, we see that after-tax cash flows are actually slightly less for the first two years if the property is renovated. After that, however, the after-tax cash flows are increasingly higher. And the after-tax cash flow from sale is higher if the property is renovated. Using the incremental cash flows, we can compute an *IRR* on the additional equity investment of 17.58 percent. This *IRR* means that the investor would earn 17.58 percent on the additional $50,000 spent to renovate the property. Whether this is a good investment depends on what rate the $50,000 could earn in a different investment of comparable risk.

EXHIBIT 14–12   **Projections for Apex Center after Renovation**

	Calculation of After-Tax Cash Flow from Operations Year					
	6	**7**	**8**	**9**	**10**	**11**
Net operating income (*NOI*)	$45,000	$46,800	$48,672	$50,619	$52,644	$54,749*
Less debt service	39,885	39,885	39,885	39,885	39,885	
Before-tax cash flow	$ 5,115	$ 6,915	$ 8,787	$10,734	$12,758	
Net operating income (*NOI*)	$45,000	$46,800	$48,672	$50,619	$52,644	
Less interest	31,766	30,827	29,779	28,609	27,304	
Depreciation	14,770	14,770	14,770	14,770	14,770	
Taxable income	−1,537	1,203	4,123	7,240	10,569	
Tax	$ −430	$ 337	$ 1,155	$ 2,027	$ 2,959	
Before-tax cash flow	$ 5,115	$ 6,915	$ 8,787	$10,734	$12,758	
Tax	−430	337	1,155	2,027	2,959	
After-tax cash flow	$ 5,545	$ 6,578	$ 7,632	$ 8,707	$ 9,749	

Calculation of After-Tax Cash Flow from Reversion		
Sale price		$547,494
Less selling costs at 6%		32,850
Less mortgage balance		241,290
Before-tax cash flow (*BTCF$_s$*)		$273,354
Taxes in year of sale		
Sale price		$547,494
Less selling expenses		32,850
Original cost basis	$400,000	
Accumulated depreciation	115,957	
Adjusted basis		284,043
Capital gain		$230,601
Capital gains tax at 28%		64,568
After-tax cash flow from sale (*ATCF$_s$*)		$208,786

*Projected *NOI* for year 11 is used to estimate the sale price at the end of year 10.

EXHIBIT 14–13
Incremental Analysis—Renovation versus No Renovation

	Year					
	5	**6**	**7**	**8**	**9**	**10**
ATCF assuming renovation		$5,545	$6,578	$7,632	$8,707	$218,585
ATCF assuming no renovation		6,156	6,601	7,054	7,514	107,202
Incremental cash flow	$−50,000	−611	−23	578	1,193	111,382
IRR on incremental cash flows = 17.58%						

It is important to realize that the 17.58 percent return we have calculated is not a return for the entire investment in Apex. It does not tell us anything about whether Apex is a good investment before renovation. That was the purpose of the analysis in the first part of the chapter. We are now assuming that the investor already owns Apex and wants to know whether an additional investment to renovate the property is a viable strategy.

Renovation and Refinancing

The previous example assumed that if the property were renovated, the additional financing would equal the existing loan balance of the property (before renovation) plus 75 percent of the renovation costs. When properties are renovated, the investor often uses that opportunity to refinance the entire property. For example, the existing loan balance on the Apex building is only 57 percent of the current value of the property ($142,432 ÷ $250,000). Thus, the investor may be able to borrow more than the renovation requires, especially if the investor plans to obtain a new loan on the entire property rather than a second mortgage to cover the renovation costs.

The total amount of funds that the investor will be able to borrow is usually based on a percentage of estimated value of the property after renovation is completed. This value would be based on an appraisal. If we assume that the *value* added by the renovation is equal to the *cost* of the renovation, then this value would be equal to the existing value of $250,000 plus the renovation cost of $200,000, or $450,000. If the investor can borrow 75 percent of this value, a loan for $337,500 could be obtained. Because the existing loan balance is $142,432, the net additional loan proceeds would be $195,068. Thus, the investor would have to invest only $4,932 of his own equity capital to renovate the property. Obviously, this is a highly leveraged situation, and the incremental rate of return should be significantly higher. Exhibit 14–14 shows the cash flows for Apex under the assumption that a loan is obtained for $337,500 at an 11 percent interest rate and a 15-year loan term.

Exhibit 14–15 shows the results of the incremental analysis. As indicated, only $4,932 must be invested to complete the renovation. However, because the new loan is much higher than the existing loan, the additional payments result in negative incremental cash flows for each of the years until the property is sold. Because of the higher value resulting from the renovation, a significant amount of additional cash flow occurs when the property is sold, resulting in an incremental *ATIRR* for the investor of 37.47 percent. Thus, the additional financing (leverage) significantly increases the incremental return from renovating the property. As we know, however, there is also more risk due to the additional debt. The investor must decide whether the additional return is commensurate with the additional risk. Some of the additional debt resulted from, in effect, bringing the original loan balance up to a 75 percent loan-to-value ratio. Thus, although the renovation cost is highly levered, total leverage on the property is at a typical level. The investor must consider all of these factors to make an informed investment decision.

Rehabilitation Investment Tax Credits

Investment tax credits are available for certain rehabilitation expenditures during the year (or when expenditures occur). Investment tax credits reduce the investor's *tax liability* (e.g., a dollar of tax credit generally reduces a dollar of taxes otherwise payable). Thus, a dollar of tax credit is usually more valuable to an investor than a dollar of additional deductions (e.g., depreciation) because an additional deduction reduces taxable income that would be taxed at the investor's marginal tax rate. For an investor in the 28 percent tax bracket, a dollar of deduction reduces taxes by 28 cents. However, a $1 tax credit reduces taxes by $1.

In general, the credits available for rehabilitation are as follows:

Category	Credit
Placed in service before 1936	10%
Certified historic structures	20%

www.mhhe.com/bf15e

EXHIBIT 14–14 After-Tax Cash Flow from Renovation with Refinancing

	Calculation of After-Tax Cash Flow from Operations					
	Year					
	6	7	8	9	10	11
Net operating income (*NOI*)	$ 45,000	$46,800	$48,672	$50,619	$52,644	$54,749*
Less debt service	46,032	46,032	46,032	46,032	46,032	
Before-tax cash flow	$−1,032	$ 768	$ 2,640	$ 4,587	$ 6,612	
Net operating income (*NOI*)	$ 45,000	$46,800	$48,672	$50,619	$52,644	
Interest	36,662	35,578	34,368	33,018	31,512	
Depreciation	14,770	14,770	14,770	14,770	14,770	
Taxable income	−6,432	3,548	−466	2,831	6,361	
Tax	$−1,801	$ −993	$ −131	$ 793	$ 1,781	
Before-tax cash flow	−1,032	$ 768	$ 2,640	$ 4,587	$ 6,612	
Tax	−1,801	−993	−131	793	1,781	
After-tax cash flow	$ 769	$ 1,761	$ 2,770	$ 3,794	$ 4,831	

	Calculation of After-Tax Cash Flow from Reversion Year 10	
Sale price		$547,494
Less selling costs (at 6%)		32,850
Less mortgage balance		278,477
Before-tax cash flow (*BTCF$_s$*)		$236,168
Taxes in year of sale		
Sale price	$547,494	
Selling costs	32,850	
Original cost basis	$400,000	
Accumulated depreciation	115,957	
Adjusted basis	284,043	
Capital gain	$230,601	
Capital gains tax at 28%		64,568
After-tax cash flow from sale (*ATCF$_s$*)		$171,599

*Projected *NOI* for year 11 is used to estimate the sale price at the end of year 10.

EXHIBIT 14–15
Incremental Analysis
Assuming
Refinancing

		Year				
	5	6	7	8	9	10
ATCF after renovation		$ 769	$ 1,761	$ 2,770	$ 3,794	$176,430
ATCF before renovation		6,156	6,601	7,054	7,514	107,202
Incremental cash flow	$−4,932	−5,387	−4,840	−4,283	−3,720	69,227
IRR on incremental cash flow = 37.47%						

The credit is available to the investor in the year the property is placed in service—when the property is open for tenants to occupy. The depreciable basis for the property is reduced by the *full* amount of the credit in the year it is deducted. For example, suppose that an investor spends $50,000 to rehabilitate a property that is a certified historic structure and meets the necessary requirements for a **rehabilitation investment tax credit.** The amount of tax credit will be $10,000 (20% of $50,000). The depreciable basis for the rehabilitation expenditures must be reduced by the amount of credit, or by $10,000. The depreciable basis will therefore be $40,000 ($50,000 − $10,000).

Certified historic structures have no age requirement. However, the building must be located in a registered historic district and approval must be obtained from the secretary of the interior. The rehabilitation must also be "substantial," which means that the amount of rehabilitation exceeds the *greater* of (1) the adjusted basis of the property prior to rehabilitation or (2) $5,000. (Note that this requirement favors investors who have owned the property for a long time and have a low adjusted basis.) Furthermore, at least 75 percent of the existing external walls of the building must have been retained (at least 50% still used as external walls) after the rehabilitation. Also, at least 75 percent of the building's internal structural framework must be retained.

If an investor takes a rehabilitation investment tax credit and disposes of the property during the first five years after the rehabilitated building has been placed in service, some of the credit will be recaptured. The amount of recapture as a percent of the original tax credit is as follows:

Year of Disposition	Recapture Percent
One full year after placed in service	100%
Second year	80
Third year	60
Fourth year	40
Fifth year	20

Low-Income Housing

A new **low-income housing tax credit** that was introduced with the Tax Reform Act of 1986 allows a tax credit to be claimed by owners of residential rental property providing low-income housing. The credits are claimed annually for a period of 10 years. The *annual* credit has a maximum rate of 9 percent for new construction and rehabilitation, and a maximum rate of 4 percent for the acquisition cost of existing housing. To qualify, the expenditure for construction or rehabilitation must exceed $2,000 per low-income unit. For the property to qualify for the credit, either (1) at least 20 percent of the housing units in the project must be occupied by individuals with incomes 50 percent or less of the area median income or (2) at least 40 percent of the housing units in the project must be occupied by individuals with incomes of 60 percent or less of area median income. The basis for project depreciation is *not* reduced by the amount of low-income credits claimed.

Web App

In addition to the federal tax credits discussed in the chapter, there are additional tax credits and other economic incentives available for renovation of certain types of property in most states. Research and summarize any state tax credits or other economic incentives available in a state that you select. Summarize the nature of the incentive and how you think it might encourage renovation of properties.

Conclusion

The primary purpose of this chapter was to answer the following two questions: (1) When should a property be sold? (2) Should a property be renovated? We saw that once a property has been purchased, the return associated with keeping the property might be quite different than the return originally estimated. The concept of a marginal rate of return helps evaluate whether a property should be sold or held for an additional period. The marginal rate of return considers what the investor could get in the future by keeping the property versus what he could get today by selling the property.

Alternative tax strategies should be considered when analyzing the disposition of property. Two important strategies that allow for the deferral of capital gains tax are *installment sales* and *exchanges*. A property can be sold in an outright (or all-cash) sale or an installment sale in which the seller receives a portion of the sale price in future years. The exchange process allows the exchange of one property for another without any gain being recognized at the time of sale. While sometimes called a *tax-free exchange,* what really occurs is that the gain, which is normally reported in a sale, is not reported in the year of disposition, and therefore no taxes are paid at that time. Rather, the gain postponed by the exchange is reported at the taxable disposition of the property acquired.

To determine whether a property should be renovated, we considered the incremental benefit associated with renovating the property versus not renovating the property. This approach is appropriate when the investor already owns the property and the question is whether an *additional* investment made to renovate the property is justified. If the investor does *not* already own the property, we must take a different approach. In this case, the investor will want to know the total rate of return associated with both purchasing and renovating the property. The investor will also want to know the return for purchasing the property but not renovating it, since it still might make sense to purchase the property but not renovate it.

From the above discussion, it should be obvious that the approach we take when analyzing an investment depends on the particular question that we are trying to answer. Poor investment decisions are often made because the analyst did not answer the right question.

Key Terms

boot, *481*
contract price, *473*
disposition, *458*
equity buildup, *458*
installment sale, *472*
IRC Section 453 (1), *472*
IRC Section 1031, *477*
like kind exchange, *472*

low-income housing tax
  credit, *489*
marginal rate of return, *463*
optimal holding period, *467*
profit ratio, *473*
rehabilitation investment tax
  credits, *489*
reinvestment rate, *467*

renovation, *484*
substitute basis, *480*
tax-deferred exchange, *477*
tax-free exchange, *472*

Useful Web Sites

www.globest.com—Provides current real estate news that is updated daily. Many articles will relate to disposition and renovation of properties.

www.eda.gov—The Economic Development Administration (EDA) provides grants for infrastructure development, local capacity building, and business development. This is a good site for resources related to economic development.

Questions

1. What factors should an investor consider when trying to decide whether to dispose of a property that he has owned for several years?
2. Why might the actual holding period for a property be different from the holding period that was anticipated when the property was purchased?
3. What is the marginal rate of return? How is it calculated?
4. What causes the marginal rate of return to change over time? How can the marginal rate of return be used to decide when to sell a property?

5. Why might the after-tax internal rate of return on equity ($ATIRR_e$) differ for a new investor versus an existing investor who keeps the property?

6. What factors should be considered when deciding whether to renovate a property?

7. Why is refinancing often done in conjunction with renovation?

8. Why would refinancing be an alternative to sale of the property?

9. How can tax law changes create incentives for investors to sell their properties to other investors?

10. How important are taxes in the decision to sell a property?

11. Are tax considerations important in renovation decisions?

12. What are the benefits and costs of renovation?

13. Do you think renovation is more or less risky than a new investment?

14. What is meant by the *incremental cost of refinancing?*

15. In general, what kinds of tax incentives are available for rehabilitation of real estate income property?

16. Why would an investor consider doing an exchange or an installment sale?

Problems

1. A property could be sold today for $2 million. It has a loan balance of $1 million and, if sold, the investor would incur a capital gains tax of $250,000. The investor has determined that if it were sold today, she would earn an *IRR* of 15 percent on equity for the past five years. If not sold, the property is expected to produce after-tax cash flow of $50,000 over the next year. At the end of the year, the property value is expected to increase to $2.1 million, the loan balance will decrease to $900,000, and the amount of capital gains tax due is expected to increase to $255,000.

   a. What is the marginal rate of return for keeping the property one additional year?

   b. What advice would you give the investor?

2. Refer to Problem 1. The owner determines that if the property were renovated instead of sold, after-tax cash flow over the next year would increase to $60,000 and the property could be sold after one year for $2.4 million. Renovation would cost $250,000. The investor would not borrow any additional funds to renovate the property.

   a. What is the rate of return that the investor would earn on the additional funds invested in renovating the property?

   b. Would you recommend that the property be renovated?

3. Lonnie Carson purchased Royal Oaks Apartments two years ago. An opportunity has arisen for Carson to purchase a larger apartment project called Royal Palms, but Carson believes that he would have to sell Royal Oaks to have sufficient equity capital to purchase Royal Palms. Carson paid $2 million for Royal Oaks two years ago, with the land representing approximately $200,000 of that value. A recent appraisal indicated that the property is worth about $2.2 million today. When purchased two years ago, Carson financed the property with a 70 percent mortgage at 10 percent interest for 25 years (monthly payments). The property is being depreciated over 27.5 years (1/27.5 per year for simplicity). Effective gross income during the next year is expected to be $350,000, and operating expenses are projected to be 40 percent of effective gross income. Carson expects the effective gross income to increase 3 percent per year. The property value is expected to increase at the same 3 percent annual rate. Carson is currently in the 36 percent tax bracket and expects to remain in that bracket in the future. Because Carson has other real estate investments that are now generating taxable income, he does not expect any tax losses from Royal Oaks to be subject to the passive activity loss limitations. If he sells Royal Oaks, selling expenses would be 6 percent of the sale price.

   a. How much after-tax cash flow ($ATCF_s$) would Carson receive if Royal Oaks was sold today (exactly two years after he purchased it)?

b. What is the projected after-tax cash flow ($ATCF_o$) for the *next* five years if Carson does *not* sell Royal Oaks?

c. How much after-tax cash flow ($ATCF_s$) would Carson receive if he sold Royal Oaks five years from now?

d. Using the results from (*a*) through (*c*), find the after-tax rate of return on equity ($ATIRR_e$) that Carson can expect to earn if he holds Royal Oaks for an additional five years versus selling it today.

e. What is the marginal rate of return (MRR) if Carson holds the property for *one additional year* (if he sells *next* year versus this year)?

f. Why do you think the MRR in (*e*) is higher than the return calculated in (*d*)?

g. Can you think of any other strategies that Carson could use to purchase Royal Palms and still retain ownership of Royal Oaks?

h. What is your recommendation to Carson?

i. *Optional for computer users.* What is the MRR for each of the next 10 years? How can this calculation be used to determine when Royal Oaks should be sold?

4. Richard Rambo presently owns the Marine Tower office building, which is 20 years old, and is considering renovating it. He purchased the property two years ago for $800,000 and financed it with a 20-year, 75 percent loan at 10 percent interest (monthly payments). Of the $800,000, the appraiser indicated that the land was worth $200,000 and the building $600,000. Rambo has been using straight-line depreciation over 39 years (1/39 per year for simplicity). At the present time Marine Tower is producing $90,000 in *NOI,* and the *NOI* and property value are expected to increase 2 percent per year. The current market value of the property is $820,000. Rambo estimates that if the Marine Tower office building is renovated at a cost of $200,000, *NOI* will be about 20 percent higher next year ($108,000 vs $90,000) due to higher rents and lower expenses. He also expects that with the renovation the *NOI* will increase 3 percent per year instead of 2 percent. Furthermore, Rambo believes that after five years, a new investor will purchase the Marine Tower office building at a price based on capitalizing the projected *NOI* six years from now at a 10 percent capitalization rate. Selling costs would be 6 percent of the sale price. Rambo is in the 28 percent tax bracket and expects to continue to be in that bracket. He also would not be subject to any passive activity loss limitations. If Rambo does the renovation, he believes that he could obtain a new loan at an 11 percent interest rate and a 20-year loan term (monthly payments).

a. Assume that if Rambo does the renovation, he will be able to obtain a new loan that is equal to the balance of the existing loan plus 75 percent of the renovation costs. What is the *incremental* return ($ATIRR_e$) for doing the renovation versus not doing the renovation? Assume a five-year holding period.

b. Repeat (*a*) but assume that Rambo is able to obtain a new loan that is equal to 75 percent of the *sum* of the existing value of the property ($820,000) plus the renovation costs ($200,000). (This assumes that after renovation the value of the property will at least increase by the cost of the renovation.)

c. Explain the difference between the returns calculated in (*a*) and (*b*). Is there a difference in the risk associated with each financing alternative?

d. What advice would you give Rambo?

5. **Excel.** Refer to the "Ch14 Renovation" tab in the Excel Workbook provided on the Web site. This worksheet calculates the incremental return if the Apex property is renovated as illustrated in the chapter. Suppose that the *NOI* after renovation is $42,000 instead of $45,000. How does this affect the after-tax incremental return?

6. **Excel.** Refer to the "Ch14 MRR" tab in the Excel Workbook provided on the Web site. Suppose both the *NOI* and property value growth rate are 5 percent instead of 3 percent. How would this change the marginal rate of return for years 1 to 10? Does the MRR increase or decrease for the first year? Does it decrease at a faster or slower rate over time?

7. An investor is considering selling a property that has an adjusted basis of $1.5 million for $2 million. The property has a loan balance of $1.75 million. She is exploring different disposition strategies. All capital gains would be taxed at 20 percent (whether from depreciation recapture or price appreciation) and ordinary income would be taxed at 35 percent.

   a. Suppose that the property is sold using an installment sale with the buyer assuming the loan and making a payment of $50,000 at the time of sale and then installment payments of $50,000 per year for the next four years. Interest at a rate of 10 percent would be charged on the unpaid balance due the seller. Is this better than a cash sale?

   b. Now suppose that the investor is considering doing a tax-deferred exchange rather than an installment sale. She would acquire a second property for $4 million and assume a loan for $3,750,000. She believes that the land would be about 20 percent of the purchase price and the building would be about 80 percent. If she does the exchange, she plans to sell the second property after five years. It would be depreciated over 30 years. Is the exchange strategy better than just selling the property for cash and then purchasing the second property?

Financing Corporate Real Estate

The focus of the previous chapters dealing with income properties has been that of an owner/investor who leases space to tenants. These tenants would generally be firms that use space as part of business operations. For example, a typical user could be a corporation that leases some, or all, of the space in an office building for use by its employees. Thus, the corporation uses the office space but does not own the building as an operating asset. This chapter analyzes real estate from the point of view of firms that are not real estate investors, but use real estate as part of business operations. Because so many of these "user firms" are corporations, their real estate activities are commonly referred to as **corporate real estate.**[1] However, this chapter is intended for any *user* of real estate assets and is not limited to corporations. Even though the primary business of these corporations is not real estate investment, they have to make many decisions regarding the use of real estate because real estate is typically an integral part of the firm's operations. For example, real estate is used for office space, warehouse space, manufacturing, and so on. In addition to using real estate, firms may choose to own real estate for a variety of other reasons, including these:[2]

- Owning, rather than leasing, space used in the operation of the business.
- Investing in real estate as one means of diversification from the core business.
- Retaining, rather than selling, real estate that may have been used previously in business operations.
- Acquiring real estate for future business expansion or relocation.

For these reasons, corporations are very significant users of commercial real estate in the United States. Corporate users control as much as 75 percent of all commercial real estate according to some estimates. On a book-value basis, moreover, roughly one-third of the total assets of Fortune 500 companies is estimated to be real estate. With such a large concentration of corporate wealth in commercial property, it is worth taking a closer look at the way that businesses or users of real estate should make real estate investment and financing decisions.

Benefits associated with ownership of real estate for a corporate user include many of the same benefits realized by investors. For example, a corporate owner that would

---

[1] Portions of this chapter are based on an article by William B. Brueggeman, Jeffrey D. Fisher, and David M. Porter, "Rethinking Corporate Real Estate," *Journal of Applied Corporate Finance,* 1991 (published by Continental Bank, Chicago).

[2] By "owning" real estate, we are referring to fee simple ownership in the property. A corporation may also have a leasehold interest in real estate that has value because the property is leased at a below market rate.

otherwise lease space saves lease payments, which is analogous to an investor earning lease income. By owning real estate, the corporation also receives the tax benefits from depreciation allowances. Furthermore, by owning real estate, the corporation retains the right to sell the property in the future. At that time, the property can be leased back from the purchaser if the firm still needs to use the space. Firms whose core business is not real estate investment, however, must consider additional factors. In particular, the user must consider the opportunity cost of capital invested in real estate, the impact that ownership of the real estate will have on corporate financial statements, and the corporation's ability to use space efficiently. These are some of the issues that this chapter will consider. We begin by considering how a corporate user should analyze whether or not to lease or own space necessary in its business operations.

Lease-versus-Own Analysis

Corporations can either lease or own space needed in business operations and may conduct **lease-versus-own analysis** to decide which option is superior. If a corporation owns space, it is essentially "investing" in real estate. When purchasing these assets, a corporation may decide to finance the purchase by taking out a mortgage secured by the property in addition to equity capital, or it may decide to use only equity capital. Alternatively, depending on the extent of debt already used to finance business operations, capital could consist of a combination of unsecured corporate debt and equity obtained from sale of stock or retained earnings.

If the firm leases space, on the other hand, it can use the space without investing corporate equity, freeing the equity capital for other investment opportunities available to the firm. Whether these investment opportunities are better than investing in the real estate depends on the after-tax rate of return and risk of these opportunities relative to that of the real estate.

Leasing versus Owning—An Example

To illustrate the decision to own rather than lease real estate that the corporation plans to use in its operations, consider the following example. Assume that the XYZ Corporation is considering opening an office in a new market area that would allow it to increase its annual sales by $1.5 million. The cost of goods sold is estimated to be 50 percent of sales, and corporate overhead would increase by $200,000, which does not include the cost of either acquiring or leasing office space. XYZ will also have to invest $1.3 million in office furniture, office equipment, and other up-front costs associated with opening the new office before considering the costs of owning or leasing the office space.[3]

XYZ could purchase a small office building for its sole use at a total price of $1.8 million, of which $225,000 (12.5%) of the purchase price would represent land value, and $1,575,000 (87.5%) would represent building value. The cost of the building would be depreciated over 31.5 years.[4] XYZ is in a 30 percent tax bracket. As an alternative to owning, an investor has approached XYZ and indicated a willingness to purchase the same building and lease it to XYZ for $180,000 per year for a term of 15 years. XYZ would pay all real estate operating expenses (absolute net lease), which are estimated to be 50 percent of the lease payments. XYZ has estimated that the property value should increase over the 15-year lease term, and the building could be sold for $3 million at the end of the 15 years.[5]

---

[3] Other costs might include sales training, relocating employees, and the like.

[4] For illustration only. The depreciable life would depend on the tax law in effect at the time of purchase.

[5] Even if the corporation still needs to use the space, it could sell the property and lease it back at the end of the lease term. Sale-leaseback is considered later in this chapter. The corporation could also decide to sell the building and relocate its sales office to another property that is leased or owned.

XYZ has also determined that if it purchases the property, it could arrange financing with an interest-only mortgage on the property for $1,369,000 (76% of the purchase price) at an interest rate of 10 percent with a balloon payment due after 10 years.[6]

Cash Flow from Leasing

Exhibit 15–1 shows the calculation of after-tax cash flow associated with opening the office building and obtaining use of the space by leasing. Recall that the initial cash outlay of $1.3 million is the up-front cost of setting up the office. After-tax cash flow of $196,000 is received each year for 15 years. We also assume that XYZ will close the office at the end of the lease, and that the furniture and equipment will have no residual value. An after-tax rate of return of 12.5 percent is assumed to be the opportunity cost, or after-tax reinvestment rate savings of $1.3 million, if XYZ chooses to lease rather than own the office building. This is the rate of return after tax that XYZ can compare with other investment alternatives of equal risk when considering whether it should invest the $1.3 million necessary to open the new office building.

Assuming that XYZ believes that it should open a new regional office, the next question is whether the firm should lease or own the property that will house the new operation. One way to answer this question is to calculate the after-tax cash flows and after-tax rate of return assuming that the space is owned rather than leased.

Cash Flow from Owning

Exhibit 15–2 shows the after-tax cash flow from opening the office building under the assumption that it is owned. The initial cash outlay of $1,731,000 includes the equity invested in the office building of $431,000 as well as the other up-front costs of $1.3 million.

EXHIBIT 15–1
After-Tax Cash Flow: Leasing Office Building

Cash Flow from Operations	
	Lease
Sales	$1,500,000
Cost of goods sold	750,000
Gross income	750,000
Less operating expenses:	
Business	200,000
Real estate*	90,000
Less: Lease payments	180,000
Taxable income	$ 280,000
Tax	84,000
Income after tax	$ 196,000
After-tax cash flow	$ 196,000

Summary of After-Tax Cash Flows		
	Outlay	**Cash Flow**
Year	0	1–15
	$−1,300,000	$ 196,000
IRR	12.50%	

*Operating expenses on the real estate (such as property taxes and insurance) that the tenant is responsible for paying under the net lease.

[6] For purposes of illustration, we assume the loan amount to be equal to the present value of the lease payments of $180,000 per year, discounted at the mortgage loan interest rate of 10 percent. This makes the financing comparable with leasing, as we will discuss later in the chapter.

EXHIBIT 15–2
After-Tax Cash Flow: Owning Office Building

Operating Years	
Sales	$ 1,500,000
Cost of goods sold	750,000
Gross income	750,000
Less operating expenses:	
Business	200,000
Building or property	90,000
Less: Interest	136,900
Depreciation	50,000
Taxable income	273,100
Less: Tax	81,930
Income after tax	191,170
Plus: Depreciation	50,000
Cash flow	$ 241,170

Sale at End of Lease		
Reversion		$ 3,000,000
Mortgage balance		−1,369,000
Reversion	$ 3,000,000	
Basis	−1,050,000	
Gain	$ 1,950,000	
Tax		−585,000
Cash flow		$ 1,046,000

Calculation of *IRR* Summary			
	Outlay	Cash Flow	Reversion
Year	0	1–15	15
Cash flow	$−1,731,000	$241,170	$ 1,046,000
IRR	12.95%		

During the first 15 years, the after-tax cash flow is $241,170. The after-tax cash flow from sale of the real estate is $1,046,000. The after-tax *IRR* under this scenario is 12.95 percent. This return is slightly higher than the after-tax rate of return of 12.50 percent if XYZ chooses to lease the space, as shown in Exhibit 15–1. This return suggests that owning is better than leasing. Note, however, that the 12.95 percent rate of return is the after-tax rate of return on *both* the funds invested in opening the office building ($1.3 million) and the additional equity invested in owning the building ($431,000). That is, this rate of return is for two combined investment decisions: (1) to open the office building and (2) to own the office building. Although the rate of return associated with owning the office building is greater than leasing it, the risk may also be greater, depending on the risk of holding the real estate as an investment.[7] To evaluate this risk further, we have to isolate the after-tax rate of return associated with making the investment in the real estate only.

[7] The decision whether or not to use the space for an office building should normally be made by considering the after-tax cash flow from leasing the space. This ensures that the decision to use the space is based on the market-determined cost of using the space. It also separates the benefits of owning the space from the benefits of using the space for a new sales office.

Cash Flow from Owning versus Leasing

Thus far, we have been dealing with two interrelated decisions. The first decision is whether the corporation should expand its operations by investing funds to *use* the additional office space. The second decision is how to pay for the use of the space. In the preceding analysis, we calculated the rate of return under two different assumptions about how the firm would pay for the use of the space. Assuming that the rate of return under one or both of these alternatives meets the firm's investment criteria, the firm should decide to use the space. It is not clear, however, whether the risk and rate of return are the same for both alternative ways of obtaining use of the space. In this example, both scenarios involve use of the same building with the same sales potential and non–real estate costs.[8]

As we have seen, however, the decision to own the space involves an additional equity investment in the property that is not required when leasing. To look more closely at the equity investment in the property that is included with the decision to own versus lease, we must consider the *difference* in the cash flow to the corporation if it leases the space rather than owns the space. Exhibit 15–3 replicates the after-tax cash flow under both the lease and own scenarios and computes the difference in these cash flows.

The first two columns of Exhibit 15–3 repeat calculations of the after-tax cash flows for owning and leasing, respectively. As we have discussed, these cash flows to the firm would result from using the office building based on each alternative. The $431,000 initial outlay now represents only the equity for investment in the property. During the first 15 years, the after-tax cash flow would be $241,170 per year if the property were owned, as compared to $196,000 per year if the property were leased—a difference of $45,170 per year. The firm would realize the $1,046,000 cash flow from sale if it chooses to own the project. When making the lease-versus-own decision, remember that the volume of sales and the operating costs associated with generating those sales will be the same whether the space is leased or owned. Therefore, the decision to lease or own should depend only on the *difference* in cash flows under the two alternatives. In other words, owning or leasing a building should in no way affect the XYZ's business operations. The difference in cash flows is shown in column 3 of Exhibit 15–3. By owning rather than leasing, XYZ should save $45,170 per year after taxes.[9] Furthermore, if XYZ owns the space, it will receive $1,046,000 at the end of the 15th year from sale of the office building.

Return from Owning versus Leasing

Recall that the equity investment required to own the property was $431,000. Based on this investment and the incremental cash flows of $45,170 per year and $1,046,000 in year 15 (owning vs leasing), the after-tax *IRR* is 13.79 percent. Whether this is sufficient to justify the additional investment in ownership versus leasing the space depends on the opportunity cost and risk associated with the investment of equity capital in the property. If XYZ believes that an after-tax rate of return of 13.79 percent is not sufficient to warrant the risk associated with owning the space, it should decide to lease rather than own the space. On the other hand, if XYZ thinks that 13.79 percent is an adequate return given the risk of owning and eventually selling the property after 15 years, then it should own.

---

[8] In practice, space that is available for leasing may not be available for purchase, so that the space that would be leased would not be the same as the space that would be owned. This could result in slightly different assumptions about the sales potential of each alternative. For simplicity, we have ignored this potential difference.

[9] Alternatively, by leasing rather than owning, the corporation must pay an additional $45,170 per year.

EXHIBIT 15–3
Lease-versus-Own
Analysis

Cash Flow from Operations

	Own	Lease	Difference (Own – Lease)
Sales	$ 1,500,000	$ 1,500,000	0
Cost of goods sold	750,000	750,000	0
Gross income	750,000	750,000	0
Operating expenses:			
Business	200,000	200,000	0
Real estate	90,000	90,000	0
Lease payments	0	180,000	–180,000
Interest	136,900	0	136,900
Depreciation	50,000	0	50,000
Taxable income	273,100	280,000	6,900
Tax	81,930	84,000	2,070
Income after tax	191,170	196,000	4,830
Plus: Depreciation	50,000	0	50,000
After-tax cash flow	$ 241,170	$ 196,000	$ 45,170

Cash Flow from Sale

Reversion/owning		$ 3,000,000
Mortgage balance		–1,369,000
Reversion	$ 3,000,000	
Basis	–1,050,000	
Gain	$ 1,950,000	
Tax		–585,000
After-tax cash flow		$ 1,046,000

Summary of After-Tax Cash Flows

	Outlay	Cash Flow	Reversion
Year	0	1–15	15
Own – Lease	$–431,000	$45,170	$1,046,000
IRR	13.79%		

Importance of the Residual Value of Real Estate

Leasing and owning are often viewed as two financing alternatives because lease payments substitute for debt payments as discussed above. As we saw in the above example, however, the debt liability that is comparable to a lease liability does not cover the portion of the purchase price that represents an investment in the right to the residual value. Hence, leasing property differs from equipment leasing, where the residual value can usually be assumed to be zero.

Generally, leasing or owning real estate differs from leasing or owning equipment because real estate may have a substantial residual value. The owner of the real estate has the right to the residual value and incurs the risk that the residual value will be different from the cost of the property at the time it was purchased. Thus, in addition to having use of the real estate during the term of the lease, *a corporation that chooses to own real estate has also made an investment in its residual value.* This means that deciding between owning and leasing real estate is not simply a choice between two financing alternatives. Although they are both ways of financing the use of the real estate over the lease term, ownership includes the right to the residual value of the property at the end of the lease term.[10] Leasing does not give the company any interest in the residual value of the property.[11] This residual value can be quite substantial if the property has retained its value or appreciated in value over the lease term, whereas with corporate equipment the expected residual value is so small in most cases that it can usually be ignored.

The residual value of the property is affected by changes in the supply and demand for real estate over the term of the lease and is usually more uncertain than the contract lease payments. Thus, the required rate of return from owning (discount rate) used to evaluate the incremental cash flows from owning versus leasing should probably be higher than the after-tax cost of corporate debt, although the rate of return may not have to be as high as the cost of capital used for the typical corporate investment.[12]

Estimating the Residual Value

Residual value—that is, the reversion value of land and improvements at the end of the lease term—is an important part of the decision to lease or own that causes confusion for corporate managers. Some analysts assume that the residual value of the real estate will be equal to the book value of the property, or the original acquisition cost less accounting depreciation at the expiration of the lease term. Others go to the extreme of assuming that there will be no residual value. Why? Because there will always be a need for a facility and the residual sale price received must be reinvested in a lease or on a new facility at that time.

Because real estate does not typically decline in value as fast as accounting depreciation and rarely has zero value at the end of a typical lease term, assuming no residual value biases the lease-versus-own decision toward leasing. However, it is just as incorrect to assume unrealistically high rates of appreciation that bias the analysis toward ownership. The correct approach is to make a realistic estimate of the residual value of the real estate and the uncertainty of the value estimate. This estimate should consider the *market value* of the real estate (as discussed in Chapter 10), not the investment value to the corporation.

By deciding to own, a corporation chooses, in effect, to bear a residual real estate risk that may be completely unrelated to its operating success. Real estate differs from other corporate assets in that, at the end of the lease term, the range of possible residual values runs from well below to well above the initial cost of the property. Over the life of a medium- to long-term lease, local, regional, and even international economic factors can cause the market values of corporate real estate to change significantly. By deciding to own rather than lease space, the company must bear the risk of any unexpected changes in the residual value of the real estate.

---

[10] Assume that the property in our lease-versus-own example is financed with a nonrecourse mortgage loan. The difference between owning and leasing (aside from the tax benefits) would be an option to keep the property if at the end of the lease its value exceeds the loan balance. If the value of the property is less than the loan balance, the corporation could default on the mortgage, and the property would revert to the lender just as it would to the lessor at the end of the lease. In this case, owning differs from leasing by including the investment made to purchase a call option on the residual value property. The exercise price of the option is the mortgage balance at the end of the lease term. Because we assumed the loan amount to be equal to the present value of the lease payments, the price paid for the call option is essentially the amount of equity that must be invested.

[11] Leases can also be structured to include a claim on the residual value of the property. For example, an "equity lease" gives the lessee an ownership interest in the building. The lessee might also have an option to buy the property at the end of the lease.

[12] The cost of capital typically used by corporations is a weighted average of the cost of corporate debt and equity capital. Because equity is more expensive than debt, the weighted average cost of capital is greater than the cost of debt. (See chapter appendix.)

Some analysts argue that the residual value of the real estate is irrelevant because the corporation needs to use space on an ongoing basis. That is, there will always be a need for a facility, and proceeds from the residual sale must be reinvested in a new facility at that time. But this approach ignores the fact that, by owning, the corporation retains ownership of an asset with value at the end of the typical lease term. At that time (when the lease ends) management may or may not decide to continue to *use* the same space. The corporation has the option to relocate if a change in the highest and best use of the site makes the space inefficient for continued use.[13] If the corporation decides to continue to use the space, it can then decide whether to continue to own the space or sell the space and lease it back.[14]

Regardless of what the firm decides to do in the future, the initial decision to own versus lease means that the firm has an asset with an expected market value when the initial lease term would have ended. If property values have risen, the corporation has an asset that is more valuable than when it was purchased. If property values have fallen, the asset is less valuable than when purchased. In either case, the corporation has an asset on the balance sheet that it would not have had if it had decided to lease. If the market capitalization rate for the property has remained fairly constant, any change in the market value of the property and market rental rates should be highly correlated. Thus, by owning, the corporation has in effect invested in an asset that has a rate of return that is correlated with changes in the corporation's cost of leasing the space. As suggested above, this may or may not be correlated with the return on the corporation's core business. If market values and rental rates rise, the opportunity cost of using the space will be greater in the future whether the space is leased or owned. The difference is that by having decided to own, the company has an asset that has appreciated in value and a gain on the value of the real estate. As noted, it can realize this historical gain by a sale and leaseback or by relocating.[15]

Alternatively, if the company had leased, it would still face higher lease costs but may or may not have invested funds in an asset that had increased in value. Of course, if rental rates fall, the company can now lease the space at a lower rate. But by owning instead of leasing, the company has also incurred a loss on the real estate.

The point is that by owning rather than leasing, the corporation has made an investment with a rate of return that depends on what happens to local real estate values. Own-versus-lease decisions must consider how the risk and expected return from the investment fit into the corporation's overall investment and financing strategy.

The Investor's Perspective

In the above analysis, we considered the incremental cash flow associated with owning versus leasing. The return from owning (and the cost of leasing) from the corporation's point of view was calculated to be 13.79 percent. If the corporation decides to lease the space, our analysis assumes that there is an investor willing to own the space and lease it to the corporation. What rate of return would the investor expect? This depends, of course, on how the investor finances the property and the investor's tax situation. For the sake of comparison, assume that the investor is in the same tax bracket as the corporation and that the property would be financed the same way. Exhibit 15–4 shows the projected after-tax cash flows from operating the property during the term of the lease and resale at the end of the lease.

---

[13] Options available to the corporation when the highest and best use of the space has changed are considered in a later section.

[14] Sale-leaseback is examined in more detail later in the chapter.

[15] If lease payments have risen as well as property values, the company may still be better off by continuing to own rather than selling and leasing back the space. This does not negate the fact that the return from owning the real estate may or may not have been greater than the return that the corporation could have earned from leasing instead of owning and investing the funds elsewhere.

EXHIBIT 15–4
Investment Analysis

Lease income	$ 180,000
Operating expenses (net lease)	0
Net operating income	180,000
Less: Depreciation	50,000
Less: Interest	136,900
Taxable income	−6,900
Tax	−2,070
Net operating income	180,000
Less: Debt service	136,900
Less: Taxes	−2,070
After-tax cash flow	45,170

Sale at End of Lease

Reversion		$ 3,000,000
Mortgage balance		−1,369,000
Reversion	$ 3,000,000	
Basis	−1,050,000	
Gain	$ 1,950,000	
Tax		−585,000
Cash flow		$ 1,046,000

Summary

	Outlay	ATCF	Reversion
Year	0	1–15	15
Cash flow	$−431,000	$45,170	$ 1,046,000
IRR	13.79%		

The rate of return for the investor is exactly the same as it was for the corporation. This should be no surprise because we have emphasized that the difference between owning and leasing is a real estate equity investment.

A Note on Project Financing

In the lease-versus-own analysis considered earlier, we assumed that the corporation took out a mortgage on the property. Rather than a mortgage, the corporation could have used unsecured corporate debt. Using a mortgage loan utilizing real estate as security substitutes for the use of unsecured corporate debt under the assumption that the corporation wants to maintain a constant proportion of total debt (e.g., mortgages on real estate, corporate bonds). However, corporations may find that the rate on a mortgage secured by the real estate is less than the rate it has to pay on a new issue of unsecured corporate debt. This is because the rate on a mortgage tends to reflect the risk of the real estate, whereas the risk for unsecured corporate debt reflects the risk of the corporation.

A corporation with a high credit rating may pay less for unsecured debt than for a mortgage because the rate on mortgage loans, particularly those made without recourse to the borrower, reflects the risk of default—the inability of the cash flows produced by the property to service the debt rather than the default risk associated with the borrower. That is, in the case of nonrecourse financing, the rate on the mortgage includes a risk premium to the lender because the borrower has the "option to default" in the event that the property value is less than the loan or cash flow cannot service the debt. In such cases, the financial community may consider debt based on the assets of the corporation less risky than the real estate, and, therefore, the unsecured corporate borrowing rate may be lower than that of a mortgage loan based solely on the real estate as security.

On the other hand, a corporation that has assets that are riskier than the real estate may have to pay more for unsecured corporate debt than the mortgage rate used to finance the acquisition of real estate when real estate is the only collateral for the debt.

If the corporation can obtain unsecured corporate debt at a lower rate than a mortgage on the property, we can assume the lower rate in the analysis in Exhibits 15–2 and 15–3. Alternatively, analysts sometimes calculate the incremental cash flows from owning versus leasing (as in Exhibit 15–3) *without explicitly considering the debt financing.* This type of analysis is analogous to calculating the return from owning the real estate (as in Exhibit 15–4) by using the cash flows before considering financing, that is, as if the property were unleveraged. In this case, the rate of return from owning (vs leasing) must be compared to the firm's weighted average cost of capital, which is an average of the firm's cost of debt and equity capital. This approach allows the cost of debt financing to be reflected in the required rate of return from owning the real estate rather than considering financing in the calculation of the cash flows.[16] As shown in the appendix to this chapter, this approach does not change the conclusion about the rate of return earned by investing in real estate. Analysts often argue that for lease-versus-own decisions, the rate of return on the incremental cash flows from owning versus leasing (when financing is not explicitly considered) should be compared with the corporation's cost-of-debt capital rather than a weighted average cost of debt and equity. This argument is based on the assumption that the lease liability (based on the present value of the lease payments) is equivalent to the amount of debt financing and that no additional equity would be invested in owning. This assumption is realistic for equipment leasing because equipment has no substantial residual value. However, as our example illustrated, even if we can borrow an amount equal to the present value of the lease payments, real estate requires an additional equity investment due to the expected present value of the residual.

Factors Affecting Own-versus-Lease Decisions

The above example provides insight into key financial factors that affect the decision to own or lease space. Additional matters, however, must be considered. Some of these are difficult to incorporate explicitly in a lease-versus-own analysis, but they may affect the final decision.

Space Requirements

Leasing is preferable when the company's space requirements are far less than the optimal development on a given site. In cases where the amount of space a corporate user desires is less than the optimal building scale that should be developed on a site, we expect (and typically find) corporate users leasing and developers (and their investment partners) assuming real estate risks. Even in cases where a corporate lessee will be the dominant tenant, it may be preferable for the corporate user to lease. For example, companies like IBM may be able to negotiate lease concessions (or a share of the developer's profits) that reflect the developer's use of the corporate credit when obtaining development financing.

Amount of Time Space Is Needed

In cases where the expected life of an asset far exceeds the company's projected period of use, companies will also generally choose to lease rather than bear the costs associated

---

[16] This approach is typically taken in corporate finance texts. The appendix to this chapter discusses the use of the weighted average cost of capital approach.

with selling an illiquid asset. This tendency can be explained, in part, by the comparative advantage of lessors in creating or locating alternative uses for such assets.

Risk Bearing

We have discussed the importance of the residual value of the real estate, which is affected by changes in local property values. Lease-versus-own analysis should carefully consider any relationship between the factors that influence the company's operating value and those driving local property markets. The aim of such consideration should be to determine whether other real estate investors have a comparative advantage in bearing the risk associated with local real estate markets. Pension funds, for example, generally hold unlevered portfolios of real estate diversified both by property type (offices, warehouses, etc.) and by geographic region. These funds, as well as real estate investment trusts (REITs), are likely to be able to diversify risks in property markets much more efficiently than all but the largest corporations. When a given real estate investment represents a large proportion of the company's total capital, the comparative advantage of other investors in bearing such risks may create a strong preference for leasing. For these reasons of relative risk-bearing capacity, larger companies with broadly dispersed operations are more likely to own than are smaller companies with geographically concentrated operations.

Management Expertise

Owning and managing real estate is not typically a primary part of a corporation's business activity. Thus, the corporation can be at a disadvantage when it comes to owning real estate. The corporation may not have the expertise to manage real estate assets. When property is owned rather than leased, managers may not be as aware of the true cost of using the space, leading to inefficient use of real estate. Leasing is favored when the company does not have a comparative advantage relative to developers and other investors in managing property and eventually selling it.

Maintenance

Companies are more likely to own assets whose values are highly sensitive to the level of maintenance. Lessors that own maintenance-sensitive buildings, unless protected by enforceable maintenance provisions,[17] are likely to charge higher lease rates to compensate for lower expected levels of maintenance undertaken by (particularly short-term) tenants. Therefore, unless corporate users find some means of reassuring lessors that maintenance is in the user's as well as the owner's best interest (perhaps through a very long-term lease), corporate users are likely to find it more economical to own.

Special Purpose Buildings

Companies are more likely to own buildings that have been "customized" for their operations, especially when those operations are unusual and the company has few competitors. To illustrate the case of customized corporate real estate, we typically observe corporations owning rather than leasing buildings outfitted for hi-tech, R&D operations.[18] (Bulk distribution warehouses, by contrast, are far more likely to be leased than owned.) The high

---

[17] Effective contracting may be very difficult to achieve even if a net lease is negotiated with the lessor because of time losses in monitoring, assessing blame, and resolving disputes over excessive equipment failures or other problems caused by poor building design or other flaws believed to be the responsibility of the lessor.

[18] The maintenance and specialization issues may in fact be closely related. For example, in an R&D facility requiring specific hardware in its design, technicians employed by the corporate entity may be better able to diagnose and respond to maintenance problems. In such cases, ownership would be preferable to constructing intricate provisions in lease contracts for the lessor to maintain such assets.

costs of relocating specialized corporate fixtures and machinery are an obvious incentive to own rather than lease. In the case of many single-tenant, **special purpose buildings,** the value of the real estate may well be far higher in its current corporate use than in any conceivable alternative use. To the extent this is the case, a lessor would be effectively holding a corporate security whose value depended almost entirely on the company's operating success. In such cases, corporate users would likely have a considerable advantage over real estate investors in bearing such firm-specific risk.

Tax Considerations

Tax considerations have historically played a major role in the standard lease-versus-buy analysis. It is less clear today than it was prior to 1986 whether corporations or individuals (through the medium of either partnerships or institutions) are the tax-favored owners of real estate.

The simple rule of thumb on taxes in lease-versus-buy decisions is as follows: If the lessor is in a higher tax bracket than the lessee, then leasing puts "ownership" of the asset in the hands of the party that can most benefit from the tax shelter provided by depreciation. From 1981 to 1986, two elements of the tax code together encouraged the ownership of real estate by individuals in high tax brackets: (1) depreciation lives were considerably shorter for real estate assets, thus increasing the depreciation tax shield and (2) the marginal tax rate for wealthy individuals (50%) was higher than the highest marginal tax rate for corporations (46%), and many companies had other tax shields that effectively lowered their marginal rate well below the statutory 46 percent rate. These two conditions, combined with the ability of partnerships to pass through operating losses directly to investors and avoid the double taxation of corporate dividends, created strong incentives for partnerships of high-tax individuals to own real estate and lease it to corporations. These tax incentives for corporations to sell real estate to individuals coupled with the market's perceived reluctance to reflect corporate real estate values in stock prices explain much of the real estate sales and sale-leasebacks that occurred during this time period.

The Tax Reform Act of 1986 in several ways substantially reduced the incentive for individuals to lease to corporations. First, it lengthened tax depreciation lives, thus lowering the tax shield. Second, the highest marginal tax rate for corporations (34%) is now slightly higher than that of wealthy individuals (31%). Third, individuals are subject to limitations on "passive" losses that restrict their ability to use accounting losses from real estate to offset other income. These tax law changes have leveled the playing field among partnerships, corporations, and tax-exempt entities such as pension funds as owners of real estate.[19] For this reason, taxes are far less likely today to be the deciding factor in corporate lease-versus-own decisions.

Access to Capital Markets

Real estate is very capital intensive. The cost of owning real estate is a function of the cost of obtaining debt and equity capital. As mentioned previously, corporations with a high credit rating may be able to obtain unsecured corporate debt and equity at a cost less than the cost of capital for the individual or institutional investor that would be willing to own and lease the real estate to the corporation. This would tend to make owning preferable because the lease rate must cover the owner's cost of capital. On the other hand, a corporation that has a high cost of capital relative to a potential lessor might find leasing more attractive than owning.

---

[19] In fact, some researchers now claim that, for tax purposes under certain conditions, corporations rather than partnerships may be the optimal organizational form for holding real estate. See Jeffrey D. Fisher and George Lentz, "Tax Reform and Organizational Forms for Holding Investment Real Estate: Corporations vs. Partnerships," *The American Real Estate and Urban Economics Association Journal* 17, no. 3, 1989.

Many corporate users with a significant presence in the retail sector choose to use sale-leasebacks as an integral, recurring part of their primary business operations. Firms that use this approach include: Walgreens, CVS, Mattress Firm, Dollar Tree, Dollar General, Lone Star Steakhouse, Tractor Supply, and many others.

These firms use sale leasebacks for several reasons. They can:

(1) exert significant control regarding the location, size, and design of their retail outlets.

(2) receive cash flow from the sale of these real estate assets, thereby redeploying funds for alternative uses and not "tying up" corporate capital in real estate assets.

(3) use the strength of their corporate credit rating when executing long-term leases which provides more secure rents for investors who purchase these properties.

This option also serves as an alternative to using corporate bond financing. Using bond financing could require that all properties be cross-collateralized as security for the bond offering. An economic failure of one or more of the retail properties could have significant negative effects when all properties are used as security for the bonds. Under a sale-leaseback arrangement, a negative event would result in a lease termination and a financial settlement for only those individual properties affected by the sale-leaseback.

If a property is mortgaged, we might expect the rate to be the same for the corporation or the investor, assuming that the rate is based on the risk of the real estate rather than the risk of the borrower. If the loan is made with recourse to the borrower, however, the mortgage rate for corporations and investors could differ.

Control

The corporation may want to control the real estate by owning the property for financial reasons not considered in the above example. For example, as the corporation does business at a particular site, it may build up goodwill that is difficult to transfer to another location. If the space is leased, the lessor may attempt to extract some of this firm-specific value from the corporation by charging a lease rate that is higher than the prevailing market rate. Owning the real estate ensures that the corporation retains goodwill at a reasonable cost.

Effect on Financial Statements

The decision to own versus lease space has an impact on the financial statements of the corporation, which, in turn, may affect the value placed on the corporation by investors and lenders and, consequently, the cost of capital for the corporation. These financial considerations can have a substantial impact on the decision to own versus lease. In fact, because of the nature of real estate versus other corporate assets, corporations are often at a disadvantage owning real estate versus other investors.

Looking again at Exhibit 15–3, note that by owning versus leasing, income after tax is only $4,830 higher during the first 15 years, even though the after-tax cash flow is higher by $45,170. Income based on accounting statements versus cash flows presents potential problems because investors may be aware only of the "earnings per share" reported by the corporation, not the cash flow. Furthermore, much of the benefit of owning in this example comes from the residual value of the real estate at the end of the lease term. This unrealized source of potential gain would not be reflected in the annual income statements. Another potential problem is that real estate is carried at book value on corporate balance sheets. Because book values are based on cost, they are equal to the original acquisition cost less accumulated depreciation. The investment community may not be aware of the market value of the real estate held by the corporation, or at least the real estate value is difficult to determine. Thus, many analysts argue that a corporation's stock price may not reflect the benefit of any above-average appreciation in any real estate assets that it owns.[20]

Indeed, unless real estate assets are valued periodically, corporate managers may not realize that the corporation's real estate is worth more than book value. Thus, they may use real estate inefficiently because they do not consider the true cost of the space. Corporations' inefficient use of real estate can lead to takeover attempts by investors who recognize the value of the real estate and the fact that it is not being put to its highest and best use. After such takeovers, the new owners sell real estate assets and shift operations to cost facilities elsewhere.

Another distortion in corporate balance sheets occurs when real estate is carried at book value but is financed with a mortgage based on its current market value. If this occurs, the proportion of financing (loan-to-market-value ratio) is lower than the loan-to-book-value ratio. Thus, a mortgage can increase a corporation's overall debt ratio, which is based on assets carried at book value. The debt ratio can make the corporation appear riskier to shareholders and result in a lower stock price because the assets of the firm may appear to be more highly levered than they actually are. Many have argued that this distortion partially accounts for premiums paid over the prevailing stock prices by investors who are aware of this difference when they seek to take over a firm.

Off-Balance-Sheet Financing

Because ownership of real estate often has an unfavorable impact on the company's financial statements, corporations often attempt to avoid showing real estate on the financial statements. They do this by using **off-balance-sheet financing.** Leasing may allow the corporation to get the real estate off the balance sheet if the lease meets certain criteria. If the lease is accounted for as an **operating lease,** the lease contract does not affect the corporation's balance sheet. If the lease is accounted for as a **capital lease,** however, the lease is recorded on the balance sheet as both a long-term asset and a long-term liability. Both are recorded on the balance sheet at an amount equal to the present value of the lease payments.[21] This obviously increases the corporation's debt-to-assets ratio. Thus, many corporations prefer to account for the lease as an operating lease. Under Financial Accounting Standards Board (FASB) guidelines, however, the lease must be accounted for as a capital lease if it meets any one of the four conditions.[22] A lease is a capital lease if it extends for at least 75 percent of the asset's life, if it transfers ownership to the lessee at the end of the lease term, or if it seems likely that ownership will be transferred to the lessee because of a "bargain purchase" option.[23] Finally, if the present value of the contractual lease payments equals or exceeds 90 percent of the fair market value of the asset at the time the lease is signed, then the lease is a capital lease.

In the past, many corporations used unconsolidated subsidiaries to provide a way to own real estate assets but report only the equity ownership interest (not the purchase price and the debt liability) and still report the earnings on consolidated financial statements. Corporations could use subsidiaries in this way when the subsidiary was considered to

---

[20] Investors may know that real estate has a higher value on average than its book value. But without details that as to the market value of the real estate for a specific company, the best they can do is to assume that the market value is higher than the book value by some arbitrary amount.

[21] This was one of the reasons that we assumed in the lease-versus-own example that the loan would equal the present value of the lease payments. FASB guidelines require that the discount rate be appropriate given the creditworthiness of the lessee. Recall that we assumed that the loan amount was equal to the present value of the lease payments discounted at the mortgage interest rate. A lease and a mortgage to the same corporation would be of comparable risk.

[22] FASB, *Statement of Financial Accounting Standards No. 13*, par. 7.

[23] A bargain purchase option gives the lessee the right to purchase the asset for a price less than the fair market value of the asset expected when the option is exercised.

engage in "nonhomogeneous," or unrelated, activities. Thus, if real estate was unrelated to the firm's core business, the corporation could use an unconsolidated subsidiary to own the real estate without affecting the consolidated balance sheet. FASB guidelines have since been revised, however, to severely restrict the use of unconsolidated subsidiaries for this purpose. Companies wanting to use unconsolidated subsidiaries to keep the real estate off the balance sheet must own less than 50 percent of the subsidiary, which means that they must give up control of the subsidiary.

The Problem of "Hidden Value"

The appreciation in value of some corporate real estate poses a critical problem for management. Many observers claim that: (1) because accounting conventions require companies to carry real estate assets on a "lower of cost or market" basis and (2) many properties contribute little to reported earnings, the value of corporate real estate is "hidden" from investors and, therefore, not fully reflected in stock prices. This is the problem of **hidden value.** To the extent that real estate values are not reflected in share prices, corporate management is vulnerable to the predations of raiders who are able to buy companies at bargain prices and then sell off the undervalued assets.

The perceived undervaluation of corporate real estate is leading corporate managers to take careful inventory of real assets and to evaluate their alternative uses. In some cases, this process has led to outright property sales accompanied by major relocations, in others to sale-leaseback, and in still others to a variety of asset-backed refinancing strategies designed to capture hidden values. At the same time, some companies are attempting to reduce occupancy costs as well as the potential for future hidden-value problems through the use of equity leases and joint ventures. Such methods allow corporations to participate in the appreciation of real estate projects in which they are major tenants, while avoiding the costs associated with a major capital commitment to real estate.

The case of real estate presents several special problems that may result in a discount in the share price. For one thing, the costs for outside investors to ascertain the values of such real estate may be large enough to warrant a large discount, especially if management (1) does not know the value of its own real estate or (2) does know but fails to communicate it to investors.

Second, investors may discount too heavily (if they consider it at all) the expected future value of real estate that produces no current operating cash flow—especially if they believe that management has no intention of selling or developing the real estate. For example, if prices of undeveloped land have risen dramatically but management does not inspire confidence that it has a plan to harvest such value, then investors may be justified in assigning low value to such growth options. Investors, after all, do not have the control necessary to realize hidden values.

Third, in the case of operating real estate, the fact that management persists in using assets with much-higher-valued alternative uses in marginally profitable operations would also warrant a large discount in the stock—again, provided management does not signal to the market its intent to sell or convert the asset.

Still another potential problem in valuing real estate arises even in the case of income-producing properties. Because accounting depreciation charges generally exceed true economic depreciation, the reported earnings of real estate companies typically understate the level of operating cash flow. And if the market responds mechanically to reported earnings, then it could systematically undervalue real estate assets, thus leaving companies prey to raiders concerned only about cash flow. But if markets do look through earnings to cash flow, as much as academic research suggests, then accounting conventions should not lead to the undervaluation of real estate.

On the other hand, as mentioned earlier, the ability of acquirers to take over asset-rich companies, write up the value of acquired real estate assets to market, and then depreciate their values over shorter lives (provided by the Economic Recovery Tax Act of 1981) clearly provided an artificial stimulus to takeover activity in the early 1980s. Such a stimulus was removed, however, with the Tax Reform Act of 1986.

To summarize, then, besides the possibility of market inefficiency, information and control problems could be responsible for large disparities between stock prices and perceived real estate values. First, in the case of large industrial companies with dispersed real estate assets, the costs to investors of ascertaining such values may be very large. Second, even if the market knows the value of such assets, the remaining uncertainty about whether management will take steps to realize the value of such real estate options, and about when such steps will be taken, could lead investors to heavily discount real assets in setting stock prices.

The Role of Real Estate in Corporate Restructuring

The business environment of the 1980s, which featured widespread deregulation, heightened international competition, and increased shareholder activism, forced American corporations to reexamine many aspects of their operations in the attempt to increase shareholder value (and, in some cases, to defend against raiders). By stepping up the urgency of management's search for efficiencies, these competitive forces produced an unprecedented number of mergers and acquisitions, divestitures, spinoffs, leveraged buyouts, and other major recapitalizations. Real estate assets were often a focal point in these restructurings.

As a consequence of this restructuring activity, corporate managements today are far more likely to question the traditional notion that corporations have a comparative advantage in owning real estate. It is important to remember that corporate real assets, while functioning as facilities in corporate operations, are part of local and regional property markets. And unless the company is a dominant force in a small local economy, the market value of those assets is typically governed by factors very different from those that drive the value of the firm's operating business. Developers and real estate investors are likely to be more alert to changes in property values, and to opportunities to take advantage of such changes, than a corporate management focused on operations.

Sale-Leaseback

An additional analysis that is relevant for a corporation that has owned real estate for some time is whether it should sell the real estate and lease it back from the new owner. This procedure would be attractive in cases where the company wants to sell the real estate but needs to continue to use the space because relocation is not practicable. In 1988, for example, Time, Inc., sold its 45 percent interest in its Rockefeller Center headquarters to the building's former co-owner, the Rockefeller Group, and then arranged a long-term lease.

Why might the corporation benefit from a sale-leaseback? In such cases, the corporation receives cash from sale of the property and, assuming that it still needs to use the real estate, leases the facilities back and makes lease payments. It also loses any remaining depreciation allowance on the book value of the building. However, it also removes the risk associated with the residual value of the property.

As discussed in the analysis of leasing versus owning, whether a corporation benefits from continuing to be an investor in the real estate will dictate whether to do a **sale-leaseback.** In fact, the analysis is very similar to that of leasing versus owning. There is one main difference: Because the corporation already owns the real estate, it has to consider the after-tax cash flow it receives from sale of the property (rather than the purchase price) as the amount of funds invested if it decides to continue to own the property.

The after-tax cash flow from sale will be less than the cost of purchasing the property if capital gains tax must be paid. Thus, the rate of return received on funds left in the property (if the company does not do a sale-leaseback) may be greater than would be the case if the company were deciding to own or lease the same property that it did not already own.

To see how we might analyze whether a corporation should sell and lease back space, we will extend the example we considered earlier in the lease-versus-own analysis. Suppose that

EXHIBIT 15–5
Sale-Leaseback

www.mhhe.com/bf15e

Original price: (5 years ago)			
Land	$ 225,000	12.50%	
Building	1,575,000	87.50%	
Total	1,800,000	100.00%	
Depreciation	31.5 years		
Tax rate	30.00%		
ATCF if sold today:			
Reversion		$ 2,000,000	
Mortgage balance		−1,369,000	
Reversion	$ 2,000,000		
Basis	−1,550,000		
Gain	$ 450,000		
Tax		−135,000	
Cash flow		$ 496,000	
Lease payment		$200,000 (15-year net lease)	
Operating expense		50.00% of lease payment	

	Own	Lease	Difference (Own − Lease)
Sales	$ 1,500,000	$ 1,500,000	$ 0
Cost of goods sold	750,000	750,000	0
Gross income	750,000	750,000	0
Operating expenses:			
Business	200,000	200,000	0
Real estate	100,000	100,000	0
Lease payments	0	200,000	−200,000
Interest	−136,900	0	−136,900
Depreciation	−50,000	0	−50,000
Taxable income	263,100	250,000	13,100
Tax	78,930	75,000	3,930
Income after tax	184,170	175,000	9,170
Plus: Depreciation	50,000	0	50,000
Less: Principal	0	0	0
Cash flow	234,170	175,000	59,170
Reversion			$ 3,000,000
Mortgage balance			−1,369,000
Reversion		$ 3,000,000	
Basis (after 20 years)		−800,000	
Gain		$ 2,200,000	
Tax			−660,000
Cash flow			$ 971,000
Year	0	1–15	15
Own − Lease	$ −496,000	$ 59,170	$ 971,000
IRR	14.10%		

five years ago, the corporation had decided to own rather than lease the real estate. Assume that it is now five years later and management is considering a sale-leaseback of the property. The property can be sold today for $2 million and leased back at a rate of $200,000 per year on a 15-year lease starting today. Exhibit 15–5 shows the after-tax cash flow if the property is sold today, taking into consideration that the company purchased the property five years ago for $1.8 million. Because it has depreciated the property over the past five years, the firm must pay capital gains tax of $135,000, making the after-tax cash flow from the sale today $1,865,000. By leasing instead of owning for the next 15 years, management must pay an additional $155,000 in after-tax cash flow each year.[24] Further, if the property is sold today, the firm will not receive the cash flow from sale of the property at the end of the lease. We assume that the property will be worth $3 million at the end of the 15-year lease.

As shown in Exhibit 15–5, the *IRR* from owning versus leasing is 14.10 percent. This is the *return from continuing to own* instead of leasing. Alternatively, the *IRR* can be viewed as the *cost of the sale-leaseback financing,* that is, the cost of obtaining $496,000 today by selling the property, then leasing it back. The return from continuing to own is slightly greater than in the original lease-versus-own example. Why? One reason is that taxes must be paid if the property is sold, which increases the benefit of continuing to own. Lease payments are also higher because market rents increased during the past five years. In this situation, there are more benefits from owning because the higher lease payments are now saved. Should the firm choose to lease, higher lease payments offset the higher price of the property that would be realized if the property were sold and reduce the benefit of owning relative to leasing.

A sale-leaseback also has implications for the corporation's financial statements. As we discussed, sale of the property results in capital gains tax. At the same time, however, it allows the corporation to report additional income because of the gain on the sale. Additional income results in an increase in reported earnings per share. Managers may have the incentive to do a real estate sale-leaseback to recognize a capital gain when they want to show an increase in earnings per share. Sale-leaseback for that reason is not necessarily in the best interest of the corporation, however.

A sale-leaseback, like any asset sale, removes an option for potential raiders to use real estate as a means of financing. Provided management can profitably reinvest the sale proceeds in its basic business or return the cash to shareholders, the opportunity for outside investors to profit from takeover by selling or refinancing the real estate is foreclosed. Furthermore, if the company leases with a short-term lease, it retains its option to relocate. But if a company simply sells and then commits itself to a long-term lease, the ownership transfer may offer no economic gain. The capital inflow from the sale may simply be offset over time by the higher rent charged by the new owner. Moreover, if the sale triggers a large tax liability payment, then the transaction could actually reduce shareholder value.

Assuming, however, that companies can shelter capital gains,[25] corporate shareholders could benefit from sale-leaseback to the extent that U.S. institutional or foreign investors are willing to accept lower yields than the returns required by corporate investors (again, adjusted for risk and leverage). In such cases, the sale proceeds to the company could exceed the present value of the new lease stream as well as any forgone tax savings from ownership.

Another potential benefit of sale-leaseback is its role as a "signaling" device. To the extent investors have been unable or unwilling to recognize real estate values, a sale-leaseback clearly demonstrates those values to the marketplace. Perhaps equally important, a sale-leaseback, especially when combined with stock repurchases, may also persuade investors that management has become more serious about its commitment to increasing shareholder value.

---

[24] Alternatively, by continuing to own, the corporation saves $155,000 in after-tax cash flow.

[25] Of course, there will always be cases where sale-leaseback may be used to recognize gains from the sale of assets to offset any loss carry-forwards that a corporation may want to utilize.

Web App

A type of off-balance-sheet financing called "synthetic leases" became popular in recent years as a way for corporations to structure leases on real estate that they leased. Many tech companies financed the construction or purchase of their corporate headquarters with these types of leases. Use a search engine to find either a company that has used this method or a site that discusses how these leases work. What were the major advantages and disadvantages of this lease structure? Are they still being used?

For companies in mature industries with limited investment opportunities, a sale-leaseback together with a large distribution to shareholders may add value by returning excess capital to investors.[26]

Still another possible benefit from sale-leaseback is to provide a source of capital that can be used to fund growth opportunities or to refinance existing high-priced debt. Fred Meyer, Inc., for example, recently sold and leased back 35 stores and a distribution center, thereby raising $400 million. Each store was leased for 20 years with a fixed-payment, net-lease rate, and an operating lease structure that allowed off-balance-sheet treatment. This transaction effectively enabled the company to capture the full market value of real estate assets, use the sale proceeds to retire some of its higher-yielding debt, and retain control of the assets by means of long-term leases.

Refinancing

One reason that the corporation might be considering a sale-leaseback as discussed in the previous section is to raise capital. An alternative might be to refinance the real estate with a mortgage, especially if unsecured corporate financing sources were initially used. As discussed earlier, mortgage financing may be a substitute for corporate debt if it is shown on the balance sheet and increases the corporation's debt ratio. Thus, the corporation must consider whether a mortgage on the real estate can be obtained at a lower cost than unsecured corporate debt. An additional option available to the corporation is refinancing with a hybrid mortgage, as discussed in Chapter 12.

Investing in Real Estate for Diversification

Corporations may view ownership of real estate as a way of diversifying their business activities, leading to the purchase of more real estate than it needs for its operations. For example, the corporation may decide to develop or purchase an office building that is larger than it needs for its own use. The rest of the office building is held as an investment.[27]

A corporation may also own space that was formerly used for the core business but is no longer needed. This excess space might be kept as an investment. In both of these cases, the question is whether the corporation has the expertise to own and manage investment real estate and whether the value of the company's stock will fully reflect the value

---

[26] This is the substance of Michael Jensen's argument known as the "agency costs of free cash flow." For a nontechnical explanation of this concept and its reflection in corporate restructuring activity, see Michael Jensen, "The Takeover Controversy: Analysis and Evidence," *Midland Corporate Finance Journal* 4, no. 2 (Summer 1986).

[27] If the corporation needs to expand, building ownership can be an advantage because, in effect, the corporation has the first option on space in the building it owns when another tenant's lease expires.

of the real estate investments. That is, would the real estate be considered more valuable if held by a different entity such as a real estate investment trust or a real estate limited partnership? These investment vehicles will be discussed further in later chapters. The point here is that corporations need to determine whether holding real estate as an investment is in the best interests of their shareholders. Shareholders may prefer to have the corporation own only assets related to its core business.

Conclusion

This chapter focused on the decision to own or lease real estate that is used by a corporation as part of its core business. We showed the decision to own versus lease real estate to be similar to the pure real estate investment decision we analyzed extensively in earlier chapters. A key difference, however, is the impact that ownership or sale-leaseback of real estate can have on the corporation's financial statements. Whether a particular corporation should own or lease depends on whether it has a comparative advantage owning real estate relative to other investors or investment vehicles.

CFOs, realizing the importance of property to their bottom line and share price, are increasingly giving corporate real estate more attention. Facilities managers today must justify ownership of real estate against a variety of alternatives that combine the operating control provided by ownership with reduced investment and greater flexibility. Corporations are more likely to accept such alternatives, which include a variety of leasing forms as well as joint-venture ownership, as ownership becomes unnecessary to maintaining operating control of real estate.

Key Terms

capital lease, *507*
corporate real estate, *494*
hidden value, *508*
lease-versus-own analysis, *495*

off-balance-sheet
    financing, *507*
operating lease, *507*
residual value, *500*

sale-leaseback, *509*
special purpose
    buildings, *505*

Useful Web Sites

www.reis.com—Provides commercial real estate trends, analytics, market research, and news that support transactions by real estate professionals.

www.corenetglobal.org—Corporate Real Estate Network, or CoreNet Global, is the premier organization for business leaders engaged in the strategic management of real estate for major corporations worldwide.

www.naiop.org—National Association of Industrial and Office Properties. Trade association for developers, owners, investors, and asset managers in industrial, office, and related commercial real estate.

www.equiscorp.com—UGL Equis is a global real estate company that focuses on managing corporate real estate.

Questions

1. What are the main reasons that corporations may choose to own real estate?
2. What factors would tend to make leasing more desirable than owning?
3. Why might the cost of a mortgage loan be greater than the cost of using unsecured corporate debt to finance corporate real estate?
4. Why might the riskiness of cash flow from the residual value of the real estate differ from the riskiness of cash flow from the corporation's core business? What would cause these cash flows to be correlated?
5. What would cause the rate of return for an investor that purchases real estate and leases it to the corporation to differ from the rate of return earned by the corporation on the incremental investment in owning versus leasing the same property?
6. Why might the decision to own rather than lease real estate have an unfavorable effect on the corporation's financial statements?
7. Why is the value of corporate real estate often considered "hidden" from shareholders?

8. How does the analysis of a sale-leaseback differ from the analysis of owning versus leasing?

9. Why is the cost of financing with a sale-leaseback essentially the same as the return from continuing to own?

10. Why might it be argued that corporations do not have a comparative advantage when investing in real estate as a means of diversification from the core business?

11. Why has real estate often been a key factor in corporate restructuring?

12. Why might refinancing be considered an alternative to a sale-leaseback?

13. What factors might cause the highest and best use of real estate to change during the course of a typical lease term?

14. Why should corporations have their real estate appraised on a regular basis?

15. What factors would tend to affect the value of a lease?

Problems

1. The ABC Corporation is considering opening an office in a new market area that would allow it to increase its annual sales by $2.5 million. The cost of goods sold is estimated to be 40 percent of sales, and corporate overhead would increase by $300,000, not including the cost of either acquiring or leasing office space. The corporation will have to invest $2.5 million in office furniture, office equipment, and other up-front costs associated with opening the new office before considering the costs of owning or leasing the office space.

    A small office building could be purchased for sole use by the corporation at a total price of $3.9 million, of which $600,000 of the purchase price would represent land value, and $3.3 million would represent building value. The cost of the building would be depreciated over 39 years. The corporation is in a 30 percent tax bracket. An investor is willing to purchase the same building and lease it to the corporation for $450,000 per year for a term of 15 years, with the corporation paying all real estate operating expenses (absolute net lease). Real estate operating expenses are estimated to be 50 percent of the lease payments. Estimates are that the property value will increase over the 15-year lease term for a sale price of $4.9 million at the end of the 15 years. If the property is purchased, it would be financed with an interest-only mortgage for $2,730,000 at an interest rate of 10 percent with a balloon payment due after 15 years.

    a. What is the return from opening the office building under the assumption that it is leased?

    b. What is the return from opening the office building under the assumption that it is owned?

    c. What is the return on the incremental cash flow from owning versus leasing?

    d. In general, what other factors might the firm consider before deciding whether to lease or own?

2. Refer to Problem 1. Suppose that five years ago the corporation had decided to own rather than lease the real estate. Assume that it is now five years later and management is considering a sale-leaseback of the property. The property can be sold today for $4,240,000 and leased back at a rate of $450,000 per year on a 15-year lease starting today. It was purchased five years ago for $3.9 million. Assume that the property will be worth $5.7 million at the end of the 15-year lease.

    a. How much would the corporation receive from a sale-leaseback of the property?

    b. What is the cost of obtaining financing with a sale-leaseback?

    c. What is the return from continuing to own the property?

    d. In general, what other factors and alternatives might the firm consider in order to decide whether to do a sale-leaseback?

3. Refer to Problem 1. ABC realizes that the benefits of leasing versus owning may be sensitive to many of the assumptions being made. The management wants to know how the return on the incremental cash flow from owning versus leasing is affected by different assumptions. (This problem is best done using a spreadsheet.)

    a. How would the return be affected by the corporation being in a zero tax bracket?

    b. How will the return be affected if the property value does not increase over time but remains constant?

    c. How would the return be affected if the mortgage were at an 8 percent (rather than 10%) interest rate?

4. **Excel.** Refer to the "Ch15 Lease_Own" tab in the Excel Workbook provided on the Web site. How does each of the following affect the *IRR* on the *ATCF* difference from owning versus leasing?

   a. The property can be leased for $175,000 instead of $200,000.

   b. A loan can be obtained at an 8 percent interest rate instead of 10 percent.

Appendix

Real Estate Asset Pricing and Capital Budgeting Analysis: *A Synthesis*

Introduction

As we have discussed beginning with Chapter 11, real estate income property is usually valued from the point of view of the equity investor. That is, we discount the cash flows (before or after tax) available to the equity investor based on explicit assumptions about the cost and terms of the mortgage used to finance the property. We use an after-tax discount rate to discount the after-tax cash flows. When analyzing the after-tax basis, the calculation of the after-tax cash flow to the equity investor reflects the tax deductibility of interest. The amount of equity an investor is willing to invest represents the value of the equity position. The amount of loan that a mortgage lender will lend on the property represents the value of the mortgage position. The total property value is the sum of the value of the mortgage and equity positions.

In contrast, the traditional capital budgeting procedures shown in corporate finance textbooks suggest that after-tax cash flows produced by the project *before deducting any financing costs* should be discounted by a weighted average cost of capital that considers after-tax cost of debt and equity. Tax deductibility of interest on debt is treated in one of the two ways: (1) the after-tax cost of debt is used when calculating the weighted average cost of capital or (2) the tax shield created by the interest deduction on debt is added back to the after-tax cash flow produced by the project. In this latter case, the before-tax cost of debt is used to calculate the weighted average cost of capital. In both of these approaches, the after-tax cost of equity is included in the weighted average cost of capital.

This appendix demonstrates that all three approaches mentioned above are consistent and result in the same property value when applied correctly.

Mortgage-Equity Approach

As we saw in Chapter 9, the term *mortgage-equity analysis* is often used in real estate to refer to the valuation of real estate income property by explicitly considering how the property will be financed. For simplicity, in this appendix, we assume that all cash flows are a level perpetuity, the loan is interest-only (no amortization), and there is no depreciation allowance.[1] In general, the value of the property can be found with the mortgage-equity approach as follows:

$$V = \frac{(NOI - r_dD)\,(1-t)}{R_e} + D$$

where

$V =$ Estimated property value

$D =$ Amount of debt

$NOI =$ Net operating income

$t =$ Tax rate

$r_d =$ Cost of debt (before tax)

$R_e =$ Cost of equity (after tax)

Example

Assume that *NOI* is $115,000 per year. A loan (D) is available for $800,000 with an interest rate (r_d) of 10 percent. The investor's tax rate (t) is 20 percent and the investor's required after-tax rate of return (R_e) is 14 percent.

Using the preceding formula, we have:

$$V = \frac{(115,000 - .10 \times 800,000)\,(1 - .20)}{.14} + 800,000$$

$$V = 200,000 + 800,000$$

$$V = 1,000,000$$

Weighted Average Cost of Capital—Alternative 1

Use of a weighted average cost of capital assumes that the project will have the same proportion of debt as in other projects. In the above example, debt represented 80 percent of

---

[1] Assuming that cash flows are not level and that the project is sold after a finite holding period or assuming that there is a depreciation allowance does not change any of the conclusions of this appendix.

property value. Assuming that another project is undertaken with the same proportion of debt, the weighted average cost of capital is as follows:

$$R_a = [D/V \times r_d \times (1 - t)] + [E/V \times R_e]$$

where

R_a = Weighted average cost of capital

E = Amount of equity

D/V = Proportion of debt

E/V = Proportion of equity

The value of the property is found as follows:

$$V = \frac{NOI\,(1 - t)}{R_a}$$

For the example considered earlier, we have:

$$V = \frac{115,000\,(1 - .20)}{[.80 \times .10 \times (1 - .2)] + (.20 \times .14)}$$

$$V = \frac{92,000}{.092}$$

$$V = 1,000,000$$

This is obviously the same answer as before.

Weighted Average Cost of Capital—Alternative 2

An alternative way of valuing the property is to adjust the after-tax cash flows available on the project for the tax shield associated with the deductibility of the debt. This tax shield is equal to the annual interest payment ($r_d \times D$) multiplied by the tax rate (t). In terms of the above symbols, the tax shield is equal to $r_d \times D \times t$. When the cash flows are adjusted by the tax shield, the cost of capital is calculated by using the before-tax cost of debt (r_d) rather than the after-tax cost. The after-tax cost of equity (r_e) is still used. In this case, the value can be expressed as follows:

$$V = \frac{(NOI)\,(1 - t) + (r_d \times D \times t)}{(D/V \times r_d) + (E/V \times R_e)}$$

Note that the numerator in the above formula is not the cash flow to the equity investor. It represents the cash flow on the

entire property plus an adjustment for the additional tax benefit associated with the debt.[2]

For the same example considered above, we have:

$$V = \frac{115,000\,(1 - .20) + (.10 \times 80,000 \times .20)}{(.80 \times .10) + (.20 \times .14)}$$

$$V = \frac{108,000}{.1080}$$

$$V = 1,000,000$$

Again, the answer is the same as before.

Conclusion

Use of the mortgage-equity approach is consistent with traditional capital budgeting procedures when valuing real estate. When using the mortgage-equity approach, the after-tax cost of equity is used in place of the weighted average cost of capital when discounting the cash flows produced after payment of interest. When using the traditional weighted average cost of capital calculation, an after-tax cost of debt and equity is used to discount before-tax cash flows. An alternative to the latter approach is to adjust the after-tax cash flow from the property by adding back an amount that represents the tax savings associated with the debt. When using this approach, a before-tax cost of debt must be used when calculating the weighted average cost of capital. In either case, the estimated value is the same as the mortgage-equity approach, which is typically used to value real estate.

We simplified the above analysis by assuming that cash flows were perpetuities and that the debt was not amortized. This approach implies that the proportion of debt and equity remains constant over time. Analysts argue that corporations can maintain a target proportion of debt in their capital structure by alternating between issuing debt and equity. Thus, it may not be appropriate to value a *particular* project based on the amount of debt or equity used to finance that project. However, mortgage loans are typically amortized and are usually secured by a specific property. Refinancing is expensive and, therefore, it is not feasible to maintain a constant proportion of debt from year to year. As this appendix points out, the value produced by the mortgage-equity approach is the same as that found with traditional capital budgeting techniques if consistent assumptions are made about the use of financing. However, because real estate is used as security for debt and refinancing to maintain a constant ratio of debt to assets is costly, using the mortgage-equity approach may be more appropriate because it allows financing to be considered explicitly.

---

[2] This adjustment does not necessarily assume that the use of debt adds to the value of the property relative to an unlevered property. It simply recognizes the fact that interest is tax deductible.

16

Financing Project Development

Introduction

This chapter deals with financing the development of income-producing real estate projects such as apartment complexes, office buildings, warehouses, and shopping centers. Developers of such projects face changing conditions in the national and local economies, competitive pressures from other developments, and changes in locational preferences of tenants, all of which influence the long-run profitability of developing and operating an income-producing property. Together, they affect the ability of the developer to acquire land, build improvements, lease space to tenants, and earn sufficient revenues to cover operating expenses.

Overview: The Planning and Permitting Process

Although this is not a textbook dealing with land planning, certain concepts and "terms of art" are important to understand when investing in a project development. By *project development,* we refer to the process of financing the acquisition of a tract of land with the intent of constructing a building, leasing, managing, and eventually selling the completed project. As a part of financing the acquisition of the land and estimating the nature and extent of development, certain regulatory terms and processes must be understood as these may affect (1) the size and the cost of the proposed development, (2) the price that an investor may pay to acquire the land, and (3) the price that a project may bring when it is sold. To introduce the reader to some of the basic development terms, we have provided Concept Box 16.1. At the top of the box is a very brief checklist of major concepts that are considered first when evaluating a tract of land for project development. These terms and selected others are then defined in the lower section of the box.

Permitting

The permitting process usually begins with an application which identifies the site, its location, and a preliminary design of the improvements to be constructed. This application is then used by public officials to verify compliance with its current zoning classification. If it complies, the permit is granted and the construction of the project may commence subject to building codes and inspections. If the permit is denied, the applicant will usually

The items in this checklist are usually the first items reviewed by a developer when evaluating a site for possible development.

1. Allowable uses per zoning classification.
2. Minimum lot size per zoning classification.
3. Maximum floor-to-area ratio (FAR).
4. Building bulk/density limits.
5. Setback/building line.
6. Building height limits.
7. Building footprint/envelope.
8. Parking ratios.
9. Circulation/road widths/other safety requirements.
10. Ingress/egress requirements.

IMPORTANT TERMS/PROJECT DEVELOPMENT

Setback/building line—requirement to construct building a specified number of feet (setback) from the right-of-way line or other landmark. This is to ensure conformity with adjacent buildings and/or provide clear visibility for pedestrians and/or motorists.

Right-of-way line—area designated for a public street or alley that is dedicated for traffic, public use, utilities, and so on. Public entities own this area and the general public has a right to use it. As a result, no improvements are generally allowed to be constructed on rights-of-way.

Building-related terms:

Footprint—the space/area included within the perimeter of a slab, wall, or exterior of a structure. It is the shape or outline of the primary building slab or foundation as it will be constructed on the site.

Envelope—the total outside perimeter of a structure, including footprints and any exterior patios, mallways, landscaping, and so on.

Facade—the exterior, usually the main entrance of a structure; approval of facades may be required as a part of the preservation of a historically important building or because of unique architecture, and so on.

Bulk—a three-dimensional space within which height, width, footprint, and number of structures/elevations/shapes are viewed in total relative to the land area upon which it will sit to determine land use intensity. This is then evaluated by planners relative to other structures in the area to assess the potential for congestion, noise, and so on, for the entire area.

Building codes—refer to required materials and methods used to construct improvements within a jurisdiction. Adherence to these codes is enforced by inspections before a certificate of occupancy (CO) is issued.

Permit—document executed by the director of planning authorizing the construction, restoration, alteration, repair, and so on of a structure and acknowledging that it conforms to requirements under the applicable zoning ordinance.

Floor-to-area ratio (FAR)—one of the more important tools used by city planners to control size and activity (use) desired within a geographic area. It is usually calculated as gross building area divided by square footage of land area. For example, an FAR of 3- to -1 would, for one acre of land (43,560 sq. ft.), provide that a structure with a gross building area of 130,680 sq. ft. may be developed (3 × 43,560 = 130,680). Obviously, the greater the FAR allowed for a site, the larger the project that may be constructed on that site, and vice versa.

Height restrictions—used to limit the vertical height of a structure to be constructed. Usually imposed by a zoning ordinance; however, also subject to FAA aircraft approach/landing requirements and FCC communication tower regulations. Suburban locations usually have lower restrictions than central business districts (CBDs), which usually allow both greater heights and FARs.

Allowable use—user activities permitted in a zoning classification, such as florist, travel agency, insurance agency, and so on. Usually based on SIC code classifications.

Impact fees—charged by public entities to cover added public sector expenses expected to be caused by a development, such as added traffic control, transportation issues, drainage, and so on.

Incentive zoning—used by city planners to accomplish community goals simultaneously with private sector development. Examples include the public sector granting a developer additional FAR, height, density, and so on, if a development includes multifamily housing or a public park.

Inclusionary zoning—that part of a zoning ordinance that *requires* that a specified type of development be included in order to obtain a permit for that site. An example would be the requirement that low-income housing units be included in a multifamily housing development in order for a permit to be granted.

Minimum lot size—per zoning classification. Examples include light industrial (usually no minimum), medium industrial (5 acres), heavy industrial (10 acres), single-family residential (1/4 acre per lots), and multifamily (20 units to the acre, that is 240 units requires 12 acres). This is used to assure some separation between large-scale developments.

Parking ratio—required number of parking spaces per square feet of gross building space or per number of apartment units. (e.g., one parking space per 1,000 sq. ft. of office space, or 1.5 spaces per apartment unit). Different ratios may apply to underground or elevated parking garages, surface parking, and shared parking (day–night) with other structures.

Site plans—drawing done to scale depicting the placement relative to right-of-way lines and setbacks of structures, circulation, parking, buffers, major landscaping, and so on, on a site.

Elevations/renderings—may first be conceptual or preliminary, then working, then final drawings of the improvements (buildings, etc.) to be constructed on a site. Will usually accompany the site plan as a part of presentation materials used for permitting, zoning, and financings.

Traffic counts—number of vehicle trips per hour past a specific site. Studies may be performed to ascertain the current traffic volume and the likely increase to be caused by a development. This study may be required as a part of an application for a permit, rezoning, or assessing impact fees by public entities.

Encroachment—occurs when the construction of improvements extends over a property line on to an adjacent property.

Property tax abatements—forgiveness of taxes for a specified number of years, which is used by city planners to attract development to certain locations. Examples would include property tax reductions for a hotel if constructed near a public convention center, sports facility, and so on.

Tax increment financing (TIF)—financing obtained for development of infrastructure and other public improvements usually adjacent to and required for a successful private development. Financing is based on added property value creation and dedication of future property taxes on the increase in value collected to repay the debt.

Special sales tax districts—special sales tax imposed on retail activities in an area which is dedicated to be used to finance public improvements/streets, and so on, in that area, or dedicated to pay interest on public bonds issued to construct facilities in the affected district.

Land-to-value ratio—calculated as dollar value of land to total project value (including land) anticipated upon completion of project. Used as a benchmark to evaluate whether the ratio of land acquisition price relative to total project value is comparable to that of other projects in the market.

Buffer/berm—construction of landscape/slope required to shield or block access, view, or noise from an adjacent property which may be a very different and/or nonconforming use.

Density transfer or transfer of development rights (TDR)—allowed in some jurisdictions, whereby one property owner can sell/transfer to another all or part of the development rights for his property, including allowable building height, density, and FAR, allowed under current zoning. This enables the acquiring entity more height and/or density for its development than what would otherwise be possible.

Mixed use development—usually a combination of office, retail, and/or hotel in a project; may also include recreation, sports facilities, and so on.

Inverse condemnation—results of a development that affect the value of nearby/adjoining land uses. Examples: building an airport, dam, power stations, and so on in an area that affects property values to a greater/lesser degree but may or may not require condemnation of the entire area via eminent domain.

Cumulative zoning—used in many jurisdictions to automatically allow *lower* density development than the maximum allowed under current zoning. For example, the most dense, noisy, and so on land use is usually heavy industrial zoning. Under cumulative zoning, land owners in an area zoned heavy industrial may develop less intrusive buildings, such as distribution centers, warehouses, and so on, *within* the heavy industrial classification. Other examples would allow single-family units (lower density) to be built within a multifamily zoning classification (higher density). However, more intrusive uses are not allowed in a less intrusive zoning classification (e.g., no multifamily development within an area zoned for a single family).

Stacking plan—a floor-by-floor template or layout used to diagram how much space will be available for lease per floor in a building and to track the location and quantity of space currently leased to tenants.

Circulation—minimum size of road widths, turnarounds needed to satisfy safety, fire, security requirements and.

Ingress/egress—number of entry and exits into and out of site. Capital requirements for off-site improvements.

clarify or amend the application and will ask the city planning staff/director to review it again. If denied again, the applicant usually has the right to a hearing before a subcommittee (zoning and planning) of the city council. A staff recommendation is usually made by the city planning department to this subcommittee regarding the application. It should be stressed that at each step in the process, the planning staff and the applicant engage in a series of negotiations (communications) in which problem areas of the proposed development are discussed. Modifications are usually offered by the applicant. However, in many cases this process fails and a series of appeals and/or reapplication is made by the developer. If the application continues to be denied, the applicant has the right to a hearing before the entire city council. The city council will usually vote to do the following: (1) approve the application, (2) deny and remand the application back to the planning staff, or (3) deny the application with prejudice (meaning that the specific application in question cannot be resubmitted by the developer again for approval).

The Development of Income-Producing Property

As the introduction points out, many types of income property may be developed, and each has its own special set of characteristics. Differences in market demand affect the economic feasibility of each of them. However, a few general concepts are common to all project developments.

The simplified diagram in Exhibit 16–1 shows the typical development process. With the possible exception of the management phase, this process is generally applicable to most categories of project development. Essentially, a developer (1) acquires a site, (2) develops the site and constructs building improvements, (3) provides the finish-out and readies the space for occupancy by tenants, (4) manages the property after completion, and (5) may eventually sell the project. How long after development the developer sells the project depends on the business strategy employed. The project has been an economic success if its market value exceeds the sum total of the land and development costs extended to complete it. It is in this sense that developers are said to "create value." That is, by combining land and building improvements, in any way that is highly valued by rent-paying tenants, the developer creates value in excess of the sum of the cost of individual components.

Developers' business strategies can be categorized in three general ways. First, many development firms undertake projects with the intention of owning and managing them for many years after completion. These developers view leasing and management as integral parts of their business in addition to the development function. Second, some developers expect to sell their developments after the lease-up phase, or when normal occupancy has been achieved. These developers usually sell projects to institutional investors such as insurance companies or other investment entities, or they may sell completely or in part to syndication firms that form limited partnerships. In these cases, even though they sell the project, development companies may continue to manage them. Third, some developers, particularly those involved in a combination of land development and the development of commercial property such as business parks and industrial parks, normally develop land and buildings for lease in a master-planned development. However, they may also **build to suit** for single tenants.

EXHIBIT 16–1
Phases of Real Estate Project Development and Risk

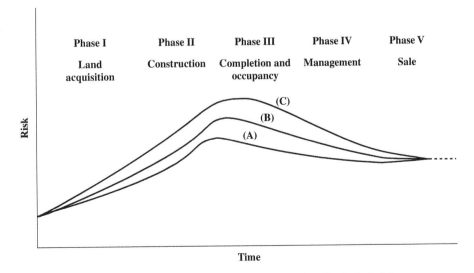

(A)   Greater than normal predevelopment leasing, completion ahead of schedule.
(B)   Normal predevelopment leasing, completion on schedule.
(C)   Lower than normal predevelopment leasing, completion behind schedule.

The point is that many developers intentionally *specialize* their business activities in one or more phases of the generalized diagram shown in Exhibit 16–1. Those developers intending to sell soon after lease-up rely heavily on external contractors, architects, real estate brokers, leasing agents, and property managers to accomplish much of phases II through V. Alternatively, very large, integrated development firms with activities in many regional markets find it profitable to provide most of the functions shown in the exhibit themselves, using external firms only when it is cost-effective to do so. For firms on both ends of the spectrum, however, it is possible that an unanticipated sale of a project may occur in any phase of development. Most developers are never averse to considering a serious offer to purchase a project at any time.

Market Risks and Project Feasibility

Exhibit 16–1 also depicts a typical risk scenario in a "normal" market, as represented by case (B), or one in which market rents are believed to be sufficient to justify development (a subject that we will elaborate upon later in the chapter). Risk begins with land acquisition and increases steadily as construction commences until expected cash flows from the leasing phase materialize. After lease-up is completed, occupancy takes place and the property management phase begins. At that point, project risk declines because tenants are committed to leases with terms of varying lengths. Assuming that the property is performing well, it is during phase IV that it may be described as a **seasoned property.** An example of a market scenario with less risk is shown as case (A), where market demand for space is increasing and predevelopment leasing, or leasing *prior* to project completion, is occurring at an "above normal" rate, thereby increasing expected cash inflows. The expected increase in cash inflows usually reflects a greater-than-anticipated demand for the type of space being developed and therefore a reduction in project risk. Obviously, if market demand and expected revenues were to decline or if the time required for the leasing phase were to be lengthened considerably, as in case (C), project risk would increase dramatically. Factors such as construction delays, price increases in materials, and interest rate increases cause changes in project risk.

Although regional and urban economics and employment are not the focus of this book, it should be clear that factors determining the demand for the type of space (e.g., office, retail, warehouse) being developed are critical to project risk. These factors may manifest themselves in current market indicators, such as vacancy rate levels, rent levels, or the extent of predevelopment leasing commitments from tenants. A very good understanding of the underlying economic base of an urban area or region is critical when assessing the viability of real estate development because not only is the demand for rental space important during development, but it is important long *after* development is completed. Demand may decline and rents may fall in markets at any time, and tenants may find more attractive space at lower rents. Simply because a project has been developed and leased up does *not* mean that it is no longer vulnerable to competition. As space in new developments is supplied to the market, owners of existing projects become subject to the possibility of a loss in tenants. Indeed, many developers are not willing to undertake this longer-term market risk and the intensive amount of property management necessary to retain tenants. As mentioned earlier, they may prefer to sell to institutional or other investors who are willing to specialize in real estate managing and leasing and bear that risk.

To illustrate a preliminary study dealing with how a project meets preliminary market tests regarding success or failure, we provide Concept Box 16.2, which reviews a feasibility analysis for an apartment project.

Contrasted with developers who generally sell projects shortly after lease-up, larger, more geographically diversified developers may be willing to manage projects in various regions. They view this risk in the context of a portfolio in which risks emanating from longer-term

I. Physical Feasibility:
1. *Goal:* To provide a preliminary development plan analysis to determine whether an apartment project can be built on a specific site in accordance with regulatory requirements and leased at current rental rates in order to justify land acquisition.
2. *Site:* 10 acres or 435,600 sq. ft.
3. *Asking price:* $2,800,000
4. *Basic project description/zoning:*
   a. Setback requirements: 15%
   b. Circulation requirements: 15%
   c. Maximum units per acre: 24 (based on a unit mix of 1-, 2-, and 3-bedroom apartments; weighted average = 900 sq. ft. per unit)
   d. Parking requirements: 1.5 spaces per unit @ 400 sq. ft. per space
   e. Open space, berms, landscape, support area: 1.0 acre (required) based on 240 units
   f. Maximum building height: 2 stories
5. *Physical feasibility* (in square feet):

a.	Gross land area	435,600
	Less: Setbacks	65,340
	Circulation	65,340
	Open space/support/other	43,560
b.	Area available for building development:	261,360
	Less: Surface parking, 240 units × 1.5 spaces × 400 sq. ft.	144,000
c.	Net surface area available for building	117,360
d.	Proposed total footprint areas for buildings, (240 units × 900 sq. ft.) ÷ 2 stories	108,000
	Excess (or deficiency) of square footage versus zoning requirements:	9,360

   Conclusion: It appears that the site can accommodate a 240-unit apartment project and comply with zoning requirements.

II. Financial Feasibility:

1.	Construction cost per unit: $80,000 × 240 units	$19,200,000
2.	Asking price for land:	2,800,000
	Total project cost:	$22,000,000[†]
3.	Gross revenue after lease-up and stabilization: Rent: $1.10 per sq. ft. @ 900 sq. ft. @ 240 units × 12 months	$ 2,851,200
	Less:	
	Average vacancy (5%)	142,560
	Operating expenses (35%)	997,920
	Net operating income	$ 1,710,720
4.	Return on total cost ($1,710,720 ÷ $22,000,000)	7.78%
5.	Approximate value based on NOI:	
	a. If cap rate = .078	$22,000,000
	b. If cap rate = .08	$21,384,000
	c. If cap rate = .07	$24,439,000

III. Conclusion: Project may be feasible if the investor/developer is willing to accept a total return on cost of 7.8%. If, upon completion, investors are pricing comparable projects at a cap rate of .08, this proposed project would not be feasible because value ($21,384,000) is less than cost ($22,000,000). If projects are being priced at cap rates of .07, the project would produce a sizable development profit of $2,439,000 (or $24,439,000 − $22,000,000).

[†]Includes all infrastructure (roads, drainage, utilities, sewer costs), land, and building costs.

economic growth and declines in individual regions can be sufficiently diversified to provide an adequate risk-adjusted return on their total property holdings. These firms may derive other benefits from continuing to perform the leasing and property management functions after development is completed. One benefit is that leads for future development opportunities may be obtained from the existing tenant base under management. These leads can take the form of (1) expansion of existing tenant facilities, (2) expansion opportunities in other cities as the businesses in which existing tenants are engaged need facilities to pursue growth opportunities elsewhere, and (3) development of different product types (e.g., the development of an office building for a satisfied tenant who currently leases warehouse space elsewhere).

Project Risks

The general market demand and leasing activity are not the only sources of risk that developers must consider in project development. Obviously, the location of the site to be acquired for the project development is an important consideration because its spatial proximity to other sites in an urban area will affect the cost of doing business for tenants or the demand for the product or service that tenants are selling. It follows that the better the spatial proximity, or location, as perceived by the tenant, the greater the value of the site. When developers acquire sites in a given market, the cost of acquisition is an important determinant of the quality and cost of building improvements. Generally, as the cost of a given site increases, the building improvements will be of higher quality and will cost more to develop. Further, as the price of the land increases, the site is likely to be more densely developed. These basic economic relationships partially explain why certain areas of cities, such as downtowns, are more densely developed with high-rise office buildings while suburban areas are less densely developed (e.g., warehouses on relatively low-cost suburban or agricultural land).

A few of the major components for which cost and quality can be differentiated include physical design, functionality in interior layout, quality of interior finish, density on the site and its adequacy of access and egress from transportation, amenities (dining, athletic, retail, etc.), landscaping, parking and circulation on the site, common areas, elevators, quality of heat, ventilation, and air conditioning (HVAC), and exterior finish (granite, aggregate, wood, etc.). Because of uncertainty about how the quantity and quality of services provided as a part of the development should be combined or "packaged" to meet demand, each of these elements presents a potential source of project risk.

Not all new projects are initially constructed as luxury "class A" space, which is usually complemented with higher-quality interior, exterior, and mechanical components. Indeed, many large national corporations seeking to expand facilities will have set policies regarding the quality of space necessary for various categories of employees. They may provide some employees involved with primary customer contacts (such as marketing) with relatively high-quality space; on the other hand, they may not see the need for such costly space for support services (accounting, computer, etc.). Indeed, if the majority of the expansion space will be required for support service, not only will the corporate tenant be looking for a facility with average finish and construction quality, but also the tenant may prefer a suburban location. Proximity to a residential location for its employees may be an extremely important corporate consideration, since a support facility does not usually involve customer contact. On the other hand, buildings that are to be occupied by tenants who have frequent face-to-face contact with customers (law firms, high-fashion retail shops) generally require facilities with significantly higher finish costs.

The point is that investors must examine the demand for space in terms of the characteristics of the demand by *end users* (tenants) in a given market. This demand, in turn, depends on the type of employment in the local market and the nature of the functions that tenants will perform. Only by understanding the local economy and the nature of employment can the developer anticipate demand accurately and produce or supply the quantity and quality of space in the proper combination to satisfy market demand.

Project Development Financing—An Overview

In phase I of Exhibit 16–1, the developer may use equity or combine equity with debt financing to acquire the land, perhaps after taking an option to purchase the land (to be discussed in Chapter 17). The developer may provide the equity capital, or it may come from a partnership between the developer and the landowner or other investors. Should the developer expect to move forward on the project immediately after land acquisition, he may negotiate a loan for the cost of constructing improvements, providing his equity requirements from one or a combination of the sources just described. Generally, the loan used for funds to construct the building and other site improvements is referred to as an **acquisition and development loan (ADL)** or as a **construction loan.** This loan usually comes from a commercial bank, a mortgage banking company, or, in some cases, a savings and loan association. It is generally based on a combination of (1) the appraised value expected upon completion; (2) the **hard costs** of construction (such as materials and labor for site improvements); and (3) **soft costs,** such as leasing costs, planning costs, and management. It may also include some of the costs of finishing the interior space for tenants through the lease-up stage. If the developer owns the land free and clear of debt, it may also be possible to obtain additional financing using the value of the land as security. Lenders prefer to make loans in amounts closely related to the cost of improvements. When possible, they prefer not to finance large amounts of soft costs or off-site improvements as these items *may not* be recovered in the event that the development encounters financial difficulty. However, in a rapidly expanding market, competition among lenders may result in more flexible lending policies. Also, in most cases when interim financing is sought, the developer is personally liable for the note. When construction is complete and the project is leased, the lender may fully or partially release the developer from personal liability. At this point the note becomes nonrecourse against the borrower/developer.

There are three general loan structures that are used to finance development.[1] Generally, the structure chosen will depend on what the developer expects to do with the property after construction and leasing are completed. In most cases, developers expect to do one of the three things:

1. The property may be sold upon completion and lease-up to investors who want to own real estate but who do not want to bear the risk of development and initial leasing. In this case, the difference between the developer's cost and the price received for the completed property represents profit to the developer. In this case, the developer will usually consider short-term financing structures.

2. The developer may retain ownership with the expectation that she will continue to manage, operate, and lease the property as an integral part of her business. Many developers maintain relationships with tenants and may have opportunities to develop and lease to them if future expansion becomes necessary. In this event, a developer will seek a longer-term financing structure. This may consist of two loans, a permanent loan and a construction loan.

3. A developer may consider the sale or refinancing of a property upon completion. This is an option that combines elements of (1) and (2) above. In this case, the developer may seek short-term construction financing, coupled with either an option, or a commitment, to extend financing for one or two years beyond the construction period. This allows additional time beyond construction to (1) prepare the property for sale or (2) provide actual financial data from operations to lenders. The latter may provide the opportunity for

[1] There are many possible loan structures. We focus on three commonly used forms in this chapter.

refinancing at more attractive interest rates as the project should be less risky to lenders. Many of these loans may have maturities ranging from five to seven years and are commonly referred to as **mini-perm loans.** However, the downside of this strategy is that interest rates may be higher than was the case when construction began and the developer may be forced to pay a higher interest rate than may have otherwise been available had a precommitment for a permanent loan been made at the beginning of the development process. If this strategy is chosen, the developer should also investigate the possibility of an interest rate swap or hedge against higher interest rates. After the lease-up stage is completed and normal occupancy levels are achieved, the interim loan will usually be repaid by using either proceeds from the sale of the property or funds obtained from a permanent mortgage loan. Permanent loans usually come from life insurance companies, pension funds, or, in some cases, large commercial banks.

In cases where a developer expects to have long-term ownership of a property, a commitment for permanent debt financing may be acquired *before* a commitment for the construction loan is obtained. Even in cases where developers expect to sell or refinance property when a project is completed, if leasing market conditions warrant it, the interim lender may require the developer to obtain a permanent loan commitment or to provide contractual evidence that he will sell the project to an identified buyer before the maturity date of the interim loan. Justification for such loan requirements may occur if the demand for space in a local market is expected to weaken, but the likelihood of sale of a project upon lease-up is high. Too much **speculative** and **open-ended construction lending** in a local market may result in significant overbuilding or an excess supply of space, which in turn may result in more vacancies and a reduction in rents. Property values may then decline, resulting in foreclosures.[2] In this case, a construction lender may want more assurance that the loan will be repaid from a sale or from a permanent loan committed to by another lender.

Lender Requirements in Financing Project Development

When developing income properties, the developer may find the process of obtaining financing more complicated because in some cases *two* lenders, construction and permanent, are involved. Hence, the developer must satisfy *two* sets of lending criteria. *While many components of these two criteria may be the same, some will be specific to each of the lenders.* A further complication is that the nature of the agreement reached with the permanent lender may affect the nature of the agreement that must be reached with the construction lender. When a permanent lender considers making a take-out commitment, that lender is literally "taking out" the construction lender and releasing that lender from any further lending responsibility to the developer. The take-out agreement may create a problem for a developer in that if the requirements of the commitment (lease-up requirements, lease approvals, etc.) are too stringent, it may be difficult to find a construction lender who is willing to comply. In this situation, the developer's financing options are narrower and considerable delay may result. Exhibit 16–2 will help you understand the process of obtaining project financing and the nature of the documentation that is generally required by both lenders.[3]

[2] Many observers believe that the availability of funds is the primary determinant of development activity. Indeed, these observers believe that if funds are available, developers will build regardless of general market indications because they are so optimistic that they believe that their individual projects will always succeed in spite of the nature of competition and local market conditions.

[3] The information contained in Exhibit 16–2 is not meant to be an exhaustive list of required documentation and requirements for obtaining loans. For a good treatment of legal considerations in construction lending, see Richard Harris, *Construction and Development Financing* (New York: Warren, Gorham, and Lamont, 1982).

EXHIBIT 16–2   General Submission and Closing Requirements for Project Development Loans

A. General requirements for a loan submission package.
  1. Project information.
     a. Project description—legal description of site, survey, photographs of site, renderings of building and any parking facilities, development strategy and timing.
     b. Site and circulation plan, identification of any easements, availability of utilities, description of adjacent land uses, soil tests.
     c. Plans for building improvements. Detailed list of amenities.
     d. Identification of architect, general contractor, principal subcontractors. Supporting financial data and past performance of parties. Copies of any agreements executed among parties. Description of construction and development procedures.
  2. Market and financial data.
     a. Full set of financial statements on the borrower and any other principal project sponsors, past development experience, list of previous project lenders.
     b. Pro forma operating statement. Detail on proposed leasing terms to tenants, including base rent, escalations, expense stops, renewal options, common area expense allocation, overage (retail leases), finish-out allowances, other commitments.
     c. Detailed cost breakdowns, including:
        • Any land acquisition costs.
        • Any necessary land development costs.
        • Any required demolition costs.
        • Direct or hard costs with breakdowns for excavation, grading, foundation, masonry, steel work, drywall or plastering, HVAC, plumbing, electrical, elevator, and other mechanical items, any special finish-out or fixtures.
        • Indirect or soft costs, including architects, engineering fees, legal fees, property taxes, interest-construction period, development fees, insurance and bonding fees, estimated contingency reserve, anticipated permanent loan fees.
     d. Any executed lease commitments or letters of intent from tenants detailing all terms of leases.
     e. Market study and appraisal, including all comparables and detached schedule of rents charged by competitors.
     f. Loan request, terms, anticipated interest rate, amortization period, anticipated participation options.
     g. Equity to be provided by developer and/or other sponsors (cash and/or land); anticipated financing of draws/repayment.
  3. Government and regulatory information.
     a. Statement as to zoning status.
     b. Ad valorem taxes, method of payment, reappraisal dates.
     c. All necessary permits, evidence of approved zoning variances, and so on (see list in Exhibit 17–2).
  4. Legal documentation.
     a. Legal entity applying for loan (evidence of incorporation, partnership agreement).
     b. Statement of land cost or contract evidencing purchase.
     c. Detail regarding deed restrictions, and so on (see Exhibit 17–2).
     d. Subordination agreements (see Exhibit 17–2).
     e. Force majeure provisions (events beyond the control of the developer such as an "act of God").
B. Additional information needed for interim loan package (if two loans are used).
  1. A copy of the permanent or standby commitment from the permanent lender. Details on the amount, rate, term, fees, options relative to prepayment, calls, and participation. Details on contingencies that the developer must meet before the commitment is binding (the chapter explains these contingencies).
  2. *Detailed* architectural plans and specifications.
  3. *Detailed* cost breakdown.
  4. All data relative to requirements listed in part A and *updated* as appropriate.
  Assuming that (1) upon review of all relevant materials in A and B, the interim lender makes a commitment and (2) the developer goes forward with the project, the next step will be to close the interim loan.

EXHIBIT 16–2 **General Submission and Closing Requirements for Project Development Loans (Concluded)**

C. Interim lender closing requirements.
   1. Project information: *final* drawings, cost estimates, site plan, and so on.
   2. Market and financial information: statement that no adverse change in borrower's financial position has occurred since application date.
   3. Government and regulatory information: all necessary permits, notification of any approved zoning variances, and so on (also see list in Exhibit 17–2).
   4. Legal documentation.
      a. Documentation indicating that the permanent lender has reviewed and approved all information in part A and all updates in part B.
      b. All documentation relative to contracts for general contractors, architects, planners, subcontractors. Evidence of bonding, conditional assignment of all contracts to interim lender. Agreements of all contractors to perform for interim lender. Verification of property tax insurance contracts, and so on (see list B in Exhibit 17–2 dealing with closing requirements in land development financing).
      c. Inventory of all personal property that will serve as security for the interim loan (particularly important for shopping centers and hotels).
      d. Any executed leases and approvals by permanent lender.
      e. Copies of ground leases and verification of current payment status by the lessor/owner.
      f. The interim lender will also insist on an assignment of all leases, rents, and other income in the event of default *and* a guarantee of loan payments by the borrower (personal liability). After review of all items indicated above, the interim lender will provide the borrower with a loan commitment detailing the terms of the loan, including amount, rate, term, fees, prepayment and call options, and any participations. However, the *permanent* lender may require certain agreements with the interim lender, including a buy–sell agreement or triparty agreement (discussed in chapter).
D. Permanent lender closing requirements. These requirements are necessary *if* the developer (1) completes construction and (2) satisfies all contingencies (including lease-up requirements) contained in the permanent loan commitment before the expiration date of the permanent commitment.
   1. Market and financial data.
      a. Statement of no material changes in financial status of borrower, or,
      b. A certified list of tenants, executed leases, and estoppel certificates indicating verification of rents currently being collected, any amounts owed, and any dispute relative to payments on finish-out cost agreements with the developer.
   2. Project information.
      a. Final appraisal of project value.
      b. Final survey of building on site.
   3. Government and regulatory information.
      a. Updates on currency of property taxes.
      b. Certificate of occupancy issued by building inspector.
      c. Other permit requirements (fire, safety, health, etc.).
   4. Legal documentation.
      a. Delivery of the construction loan mortgage (if assigned to the permanent lender).
      b. Architect's certificate of completion with detailed survey and final plans, and so on.
      c. Endorsements of all casualty and hazard insurance policies indicating permanent lender as new loss payee.
      d. Updated title insurance policy.
      e. Updated verification on status of ground rents (if relevant).
      f. An exculpation agreement, relieving the borrower of personal liability (if applicable).
      g. Lien releases from general subcontractors and verification of any payments outstanding and proposed disposition.

Loan Submission Information for Loan Requests—An Overview

While many of the items in section A of Exhibit 16–2 are self-explanatory, the initial submission to the *lender* will focus on what can be developed on the site; that is, it will provide a fairly detailed description of the size, design, and cost of the project. The submission will also provide a detailed market and competitive analysis, identify the team that will develop the project, and document all public approvals obtained or needed relative to zoning and permitting. Detailed pro forma operating statements and a set of financial statements from the borrower or borrowing entity will also be included. As just indicated, if the permanent lender gives the developer an indication of interest in financing the project, the permanent lender will request more detailed information, and the developer will be required to support the assumptions used in the pro forma operating statements from the market analysis and provide other data requested. Assuming that the developer provides data to the satisfaction of the lender, the lender usually issues an *intent* to provide financing, and the developer may proceed to work on much more detailed cost breakdowns, drawings, plans, and so on. This intent to finance is usually necessary before the developer invests additional funds in more detailed planning. However, this detailed planning must be completed before the permanent lender issues a *commitment.* The interim lender, who will be monitoring construction progress and compliance with plans and specifications, will certainly require detailed plans. The methods used to underwrite and analyze market and financial data will be covered in a case example later in the chapter.

The information in part A of Exhibit 16–2 will generally not be complete when the developer first approaches a permanent lender for funding, because in most cases the development concept and strategy will not be finalized. Keep in mind that the submission should contain as much information as possible; however, both lenders will have specific questions and requests for supporting data that the developer must provide. Hence, obtaining both permanent and construction financing should be viewed as a continuing process between all of the parties that may take several rounds of review by all concerned before any written commitments are made.

The Permanent or Take-Out Commitment

Assuming that an interim *and* a permanent loan are to be used, the permanent lender makes a commitment in writing and specifies *contingencies* (to be discussed in more detail below) that the developer-borrower must meet before the permanent lender's commitment becomes legally binding. When these contingencies are met, the permanent lender will provide funds for the developer to repay the construction loan. If any of the contingencies in the take-out commitment are not met, the permanent lender is not obligated to fund the permanent loan. In this event, the developer must seek another permanent loan, or the construction lender may have to continue to carry financing on the completed project, or the developer may face a foreclosure proceeding initiated by the interim lender when the interim loan expires. The intent of the take-out commitment, then, is to create a legally binding agreement between the developer and permanent lender, whereby the permanent lender fully intends to make a long-term loan on the property after the building is completed, satisfactory levels of leasing have been accomplished, and other contingencies have been satisfied.

Standby Commitments

Standby commitments may be obtained occasionally from a "standby" lender (1) when the developer cannot or does not want to pay fees to obtain a permanent loan commitment, (2) because the borrower expects to find a permanent loan commitment elsewhere after construction is under way and preleasing occurs on better borrowing terms, or (3) because the developer is planning to sell the project upon completion and lease-up and does not believe a permanent loan will be needed. Like the permanent loan, standby commitment funds are used to repay the construction loan. While standby commitments are similar to a permanent take-out loan in terms of the contingencies and other contents of the agreement, they differ from permanent take-outs in that neither the borrower nor the standby lender really *expects* the standby commitment to be used. However, because the developer-borrower wants to begin development, and the interim lender wants assurance of a take-out, the developer may have to find a standby commitment *at the insistence* of the interim lender. If the developer does not sell the project or if a permanent take-out cannot be found upon completion of the project, then the standby commitment will be used and the permanent loan will be closed with the lender who made the standby commitment.

Even though permanent lenders who offer standby commitments charge a commitment fee and are legally bound to deliver mortgage funds on the completion date, many banks are unwilling to make construction loans when a borrower has only a standby commitment because the commitment is made with a low expectation of being used. In many cases, should the borrower decide to use the commitment, the standby lender may be very inflexible concerning contingencies in it. For example, lenders who have issued standbys may look for "technical violations" of contingencies in the commitment (e.g., minor changes in construction plans and substitution of building materials that were not approved by the standby lender). One problem interim lenders face is determining when the developer and provider of permanent funding *intend* a commitment to be permanent and when they *intend* it as a standby. The agreement may not have explicit wording as to whether it is a take-out or standby commitment. Careful analysis of the permanent funding agreement the developer provides is important because if market conditions change, the developer and interim lender may consider the standby lender legally bound to provide funds, while the standby lender may balk because of the expectation that the project would be sold or long-term financing would be found on more attractive terms and the standby lender would not have to deliver.

Contingencies in Lending Commitments

When a developer obtains a permanent loan commitment prior to actual development and prior to obtaining a construction loan, the permanent lender usually includes **contingencies** in the commitment. In cases where an interim loan or mini-perm loan is to be used, many of these same contingencies must be satisfied before a lender is willing to release the developer from personal liability, thereby making the note *nonrecourse* against the borrower. As pointed out, if the developer does not fulfill the requirements under these contingencies, the permanent lender does not have to fund the loan. Common contingencies found in take-out commitments obtained from permanent lenders include these:

- The maximum period of time allowed for the developer to acquire a construction loan commitment.
- Completion date for the construction phase of the project.
- Minimum rent-up (leasing) requirements and approval of all major leases in order for permanent financing to become effective.
- Provisions for gap financing should the rent-up requirement not be met.
- Expiration date of the permanent loan commitment and any provisions for extensions.
- Approval of design changes and substitution of any building materials by the permanent lender.

Essentially, these items represent common contingencies that must be negotiated before a lender issues a permanent loan commitment. When financing is being sought on proposed projects, these contingencies are especially important because they establish that the permanent loan will be made when the developer has performed as promised.

These contingencies are indispensable to permanent lenders because they require that developers carry out certain responsibilities during development or prior to the expiration date of the permanent commitment. For example, the first two provisions in the preceding list require that the borrower have a specified amount of time in which to find an interim lender willing to make a loan to cover construction and development costs, and that the project be completed by a specific date. The permanent lender must rely on a local lender such as a bank to provide construction, or interim, funds and to monitor construction quality. Because large permanent lenders are usually life insurance companies, pension funds, and the like, they are not likely to be located in the city where the project is to be developed. The completion date contingency provides an incentive for developers to work as efficiently as possible toward completing construction and leasing the building space or face the possibility of losing the loan commitment.

As for leasing requirements, this contingency is used to help assure permanent lenders that local economic conditions that are being used to justify the appraised value and feasibility of the project are favorable. The permanent lender requires a provision such as this to shift some project risk to the interim lender, who should be very familiar with the local market and who specializes in construction lending in that market. The interim lender must carefully consider conditions in the local market because should the project not rent up to a specified percentage of occupancy by the expiration date, the rent-up contingency will not be met. This means that the permanent lender will not have to fund the commitment. Unless the permanent lender is willing to modify the terms of the permanent commitment, expiration would force the construction lender to extend its interim loan beyond the term originally intended and, perhaps, to become the permanent lender.

In many cases, the permanent lender may agree that if the occupancy requirement is not met, funds will be advanced on a pro rata basis or in proportion to occupancy achieved by the expiration date. Advances would then be made toward full funding as occupancy increases.

When a construction lender is unwilling to accept a pro rata funding take-out, however, the developer may have to find a third-party lender to stand by and provide a **gap financing** commitment. This commitment provides that the "gap" between any partial funding advanced by the permanent lender (because a rental achievement has not been met by the developer as of the date the permanent loan is scheduled to close) and the funds needed to repay the construction lender will be provided by a gap lender. The gap lender usually takes a second lien position and earns interest at a higher rate than both the interim and permanent lenders plus a nonrefundable gap commitment fee. Funds provided by the gap lender and permanent lender repay the interim lender. As the project leases up and the permanent lender releases more funds, the developer uses them to repay the gap lender.[4] The developer also uses gap lending when cost overruns in excess of both the construction and permanent commitments occur, or if a permanent loan commitment is less than the construction loan. In either instance, the gap lender will analyze the project and, if convinced that it is acceptable risk, may take a second lien position.

The last item in the preceding list of contingencies, that is, approval of construction and design changes, assures permanent lenders that developers will complete projects substantially as agreed—they will not substitute substandard materials and use shortcuts to save costs that may jeopardize project quality. Poor project quality could obviously affect the leasing success of a project and, therefore, the collateral security for the permanent loan. Consequently, interim lenders usually insist that they retain the right to approve all substitutions of material and design changes.

The Construction or Interim Loan

As indicated previously, before developers and lenders negotiate construction loans on income-producing properties, the developer may have already obtained a commitment for a permanent loan or a standby loan. The developer presents much of the same

---

[4] In some cases, as the expiration date for closing the permanent loan nears, the construction lender may agree to become a "gap lender" if the rental achievement is not met. The construction lender may do so to keep the permanent commitment alive, particularly if the borrower cannot find a third-party gap lender.

information about the proposed project used to obtain the permanent loan (shown in part A of Exhibit 16–2) as support for obtaining interim financing. The permanent lender is generally not interested in making the interim loan because construction lenders are knowledgeable about local market conditions and are able to monitor construction progress and disburse funds as phases of the project are completed. This activity in development lending requires knowledge of construction methods and materials, and the construction lender can usually perform it more cost-effectively. However, because of the contingencies the permanent lender requires of the developer, the construction lender must also evaluate the information in the permanent loan submission very carefully. In the event that the construction lender makes a commitment to fund the project's development and the developer does not meet the take-out contingencies, the permanent loan will not be funded and the construction lender will be forced to provide permanent funding for the project or call the construction loan due on the completion date, which could force the developer into bankruptcy.

In many cases, rather than negotiating a construction loan and a permanent loan, a developer may obtain a *single* loan from an interim lender and use it to finance construction and operations for a year or two beyond the lease-up stage. This variation, used in place of obtaining both a construction loan and a permanent loan, is the so-called **mini-perm loan.**[5] It was used extensively during the 1980s development boom throughout the United States as lenders aggressively competed against one another for a larger share of the construction loan market. Developers using this approach expected to either sell or refinance the project on very attractive terms at or before maturity. Lenders, primarily savings and loans and commercial banks, offered these loans as "one-stop shopping" that enabled developers to proceed without obtaining a permanent loan.

Methods of Disbursement—Construction Lending

Generally, the construction loan is secured by a mortgage for future advances or by an open-end mortgage. The construction lender usually requires a first lien on the land and all improvements as they are constructed on the site. Construction lenders follow the cardinal rule of never advancing loan funds in excess of the economic value of the property that serves as security for the loan. In other words, the construction lender never wants the developer "to get ahead" on a draw schedule by drawing down funds in excess of the cost of construction improvements made to date.

The most commonly used method to disburse funds for commercial development is the **monthly draw method.** This method is used extensively in the construction of larger-scale projects requiring sizable loans. The developer requests a draw each month based on the work completed during the preceding month. If an architect or engineer verifies to the lender that such work is in place, the lender disburses the funds. Again, the collateral value for the loan increases simultaneously with the disbursement of funds.

In some cases, the developer submits invoices to a title insurance company, if the lender is using one, which updates the title abstract between each draw and then approves payment on the invoices. As payments are made, contractors and subcontractors sign an agreement that they have been paid for work done to date.[6] This usually precludes them from filing mechanics' liens.[7]

---

[5] In cases where a mini-perm loan is negotiated, most of the material presented in the chapter is relevant, although some redundancy in documentation and other requirements is eliminated when *one* loan is used to finance a project.

[6] On very large-scale projects that will take an extensive period of time to finish and will involve many vendors and contractors, title companies frequently make disbursements and verify that no liens have been filed since the previous draw.

[7] Liens created during construction can cause problems for a developer in closing the permanent loan or selling the property when it is completed.

Interest Rates and Fees

As with many business loans, interest rates on construction loans are generally based on short-term interest rates that may vary considerably from period to period in response to current lending conditions. Most lenders, particularly commercial banks, usually rely on a system of floating interest rates on construction loans. Floating rates may be based on the bank's prime lending rate or the short-term interest rate charged on commercial loans to the bank's most creditworthy customers. However, some short-term loans may be based on either Treasury bill rates or the London Interbank Offering Rate (LIBOR). The lender normally evaluates a construction loan as to risk during the underwriting process, and the interest rate quoted on the loan reflects the short-term rate to which the loan will be tied *plus* a premium that is added to that rate. For example, an interest rate on a construction loan may be quoted as "two points over prime." This means that if the loan is tied to a 10 percent prime rate at closing, the interest rate charged on the construction loan will be 12 percent. Because the interest rate on construction loans is a "floating rate," the actual interest expense that the developer must pay can differ substantially from the amount budgeted or included in the loan request. In other words, the developer may bear the interest rate risk during the development period. The construction lender may also charge loan commitment fees.

Additional Information for Interim Loan Submission

Part B of Exhibit 16–2 summarizes some additional information required for an interim loan submission that generally supplements and updates the material provided to the permanent lender. The developer provides this additional information, *assuming* that the preliminary data supplied to the permanent lender are satisfactory and the developer has obtained a permanent take-out commitment. Much of the documentation required by the *construction lender* depends on the terms and conditions contained in the permanent loan commitment. Hence, the interim lender must be in a position to review the permanent, or take-out, commitment as well as the final set of development plans and updated information for each component of the loan submission listed in part A. Further, the interim lender will usually want assurance that the permanent lender will review all of these updates prior to closing the construction loan.

Requirements to Close the Interim Loan

Although this chapter focuses on financing, part C in Exhibit 16–2 lists general requirements the developer supplies to close the interim loan. Generally speaking, if the interim lender has expressed an interest to fund construction, the lender will issue a commitment letter containing all necessary requirements and documentation to close the loan.

Assignment of Commitment Letter

When a developer obtains commitments for two loans to finance a project, a legal obligation exists between the developer and each of the two lenders, but no legal obligation exists between the two lenders. To create such an obligation, the construction lender may require that the borrower obtain the right to assign the take-out commitment from the permanent lender to the interim lender. In this way, if the project is finished by the completion date and all contingencies are met, the construction lender can collect mortgage funds directly from the permanent lender, bypassing the developer. Also, should any disagreement occur between the developer and permanent lender, the construction lender, by obtaining assignment of the commitment, may pursue enforcement of the commitment directly with the permanent lender. Assignment of the commitment also limits the developer's ability to terminate the permanent loan commitment and seek another during construction.

Triparty Buy–Sell Agreement

In lieu of assignment of the take-out commitment, the developer, construction lender, and long-term lender may enter into a more formal agreement in which (1) the permanent lender agrees to buy the construction mortgage loan directly from the construction lender on the completion date, assuming all contingencies are met and (2) the two lenders agree about their duties and responsibilities. This formal agreement, known as a **triparty buy–sell agreement,** goes beyond the assignment of the take-out commitment and provides that the permanent lender will (1) notify the interim lender that the take-out commitment is in full effect, (2) indicate whether all necessary plans and documents have been reviewed and approved prior to closing the construction loan, and (3) provide the construction lender with notice of any violations in the terms of the loan commitment by the developer and the time available to cure such a violation.

The goal of this agreement is to create legal responsibilities between the borrower, the permanent lender, and the construction lender. In this way, both lenders are more likely to be better informed as to the progress that the developer is making and whether any problems are likely to occur when it is time to close the permanent loan. With this approach, the permanent lender also has more assurance that the permanent loan will be made at the agreed-upon rate of interest and other terms. Otherwise, when the permanent lender makes the take-out commitment, some question may remain about whether the developer has a mandatory commitment to close the permanent loan. Indeed, if the developer finds another commitment on more favorable terms, he may choose to forfeit any commitment fees and close with the new lender. In that case, since funding will be available to repay the construction loan, the original lender may not object. But, by using a triparty agreement, the construction lender agrees not to accept funding from any source other than the initial permanent lender.

The Permanent Loan Closing

After completion of the construction and lease-up period, assuming that all contingencies enumerated in the take-out commitment are met, the permanent loan will be closed and the construction lender is "taken out," or repaid, with funds advanced from the permanent lender. From this point, the borrower will begin to make monthly mortgage payments from rental revenues. Part D of Exhibit 16–2 lists some of the general requirements for the permanent loan closing. Keep in mind that even though the permanent lender may have made a take-out or permanent commitment, that commitment will not be funded until the loan is ready to be closed, or after the project has been completed. Hence, the permanent lender will be in a position to evaluate whether all building and material specifications, leasing, and so on have been carried out in conformance with what the developer promised when the permanent funding commitment was issued. Further, the permanent lender will also be in a position to ascertain whether all contingencies have been met before the permanent loan is closed.

A recent trend in the field of real estate finance has been to limit the liability of borrowers after all contingencies have been met, the permanent loan has been closed, and the project is operating normally. Liability can be limited by including an **exculpation,** or **nonrecourse, clause** in the permanent mortgage. Essentially, this clause limits the liability of borrowers by restricting the claim of lenders to proceeds from the sale of the real estate in the event of default. Because this relieves the developer of part of, or all, personal liability, it potentially reduces the lender's ability to recover losses in the event of default and foreclosure. This is a point that lenders and borrowers negotiate seriously. Liability limitations also place more underwriting emphasis on the quality of the property from the lender's perspective, since income produced from the property must repay the loan, and the property value must always be sufficiently high to repay the loan balance, should a property become financially troubled.

If an exculpation clause is not a part of the permanent loan, the permanent lender will want to be very careful to ascertain that no material change in the financial status of the borrower has occurred since the commitment date. No lender wants to be in a position of funding a developer heading toward bankruptcy. But "material change" can present a problem because the criteria used to ascertain what constitutes a material change may differ between the interim and permanent lenders, and the permanent lender may refuse to close the loan. In some cases, enhancements, such as letters of credit or third-party guarantees, may be required of the developer by either the interim lender or the permanent lender at the outset, in anticipation of potential problems.

Project Development Illustrated

Project Description and Project Costs

What follows is a case example of Rolling Meadows Center, a high-quality shopping center development located in an upper-income neighborhood proposed by Southfork Development Co. Southfork plans to develop, and then own and operate, Rolling Meadows for a long period of time. It plans to use both interim and permanent financing and has approached the Citadel Life Insurance Company to provide permanent financing. If Southfork planned to sell the shopping center after completion and lease-up, it might have elected to pursue a mini-perm loan. In either case, much of the underwriting analysis and contingencies that follow would be applicable. Exhibit 16–3 contains a breakdown of site size, floor-to-area ratio, parking, and anticipated construction and permanent financing. It also provides percentage breakdowns for building coverage, parking, and open space. The

EXHIBIT 16–3 **Project Description** **for Rolling Meadows** **Center**	

A.	Site and proposed improvements	
	Site area (in acres)	9.5
	Gross buildable area (*GBA*)	120,000 sq. ft.
	Gross leasable area (*GLA*)	110,000 sq. ft.
	Percent leasable area	91.67%
	Floor-to-area ratio (site area)	3.45
	Parking index	5 spaces/1,000 sq. ft. (*GLA*)
	Parking spaces	550
B.	Development period	12 months
C.	Site plan	
	Building coverage	29%
	Street parking	45%
	Open space/landscaping	26%
	Total	100%
D.	Loan information	
	Construction loan	
	Loan term	12 months
	% of construction loan drawn in the first four months	75%
	% of construction loan drawn in the last months	25%
	Interest rate	12%
	Construction loan fee	2%
	Permanent loan	
	Debt amortization	25 years
	Term of loan	10 years
	Interest rate	12%
	Permanent loan fee	3%
E.	Anticipated hold after completion	5 years

lender will review the percentage breakdowns to ascertain whether the density of the project development on the site is too high and whether parking is adequate. The lender will pay particular attention to the site plan and ease of traffic circulation on the site. Citadel will have access to comparative data for this project from previous project financing files and from industry statistics.[8]

Exhibit 16–4 breaks down development costs into land acquisition costs, off-site costs, hard costs, and soft costs. These costs are also broken down as a percentage of total cost and cost per square foot of gross building area (*GBA*).

Depending on the type of shopping center (e.g., strip, neighborhood, specialty, regional mall), lenders will want to know whether the relative breakdown of costs conforms to average breakdowns for recently developed neighborhood centers in comparable locations. Land costs that are too high or hard costs that are too low relative to land costs may mean that the total cost of developing an adequate mix of retail space of adequate quality may not be achievable at prevailing market rents. Similarly, common areas (difference between gross building area and gross leasable area) that are too large or too small may affect the ability to lease space and can be detrimental to profitability. The "correct" mix of location improvements, density, parking, circulation, and design is crucial to success.

In many cases, lenders will not fund any land acquisition costs or base loans as a percentage of appraised value. In other words, lenders prefer to make loans to cover improvement costs only, and the developer may be expected to contribute the land as equity. Further, lenders usually require a first lien on the land and all improvements made with the proceeds of the construction loan. They do so because loans based on appraised value alone may result in the lender advancing funds in excess of the market value of the property if the appraisal is in error. For example, if the lender agrees to lend 80 percent of the total project value and the appraisal (which you must realize is being done for a project that is still in the planning and design stages) results in an overestimate of value in the range of 130 percent of actual value upon completion, then the loan advances would equal 104 percent of actual value (80% of 130%). Further, if an overoptimistic assessment of future rental achievement caused the overestimate of project value, the developer may have difficulty servicing the mortgage debt. This difficulty obviously creates problems for the developer and for the interim lender who may be looking to a permanent lender to take out the construction loan. Recall that the take-out commitment may contain contingencies relative to leasing and rental achievement and may also contain a requirement that the final project appraised value exceed the permanent loan commitment by a specified percentage. If these provisions are not achieved, the interim lender and developer may have difficulty enforcing the take-out commitment.

We do not mean to say that lenders never consider appraised values in loan requests. Most lenders realize that the loan being requested must represent a reasonable percentage of appraised value. Reasonable percentage generally means that if the loan-to-value ratio for the proposed project is 80 percent, the lender anticipates that the improvement costs plus any other development costs that the lender is willing to fund should also be in the range of 80 percent. The funding percentage, in turn, implies that land values and other costs not funded in the loan should be in the range of 20 percent. In other words, the lender is looking for an equity contribution of 20 percent by the developer. If improvement costs were estimated to be 90 percent of value, for example, the lender may still be willing to fund only 80 percent of value. In this case, all improvement costs would not be funded. An alternative way of looking at the loan-to-appraised-value relationship is that a lender may, in our example, prefer to provide funds equal to the lower of either all improvement costs or 80 percent of project value.

---

[8] One important source of data is the Urban Land Institute's *Dollars and Cents of Shopping Centers.*

EXHIBIT 16–4
Summary of Cost Information for Rolling Meadows Center

	Cost	Percent of Total Cost	Cost per Sq. Ft. *GBA*
A. Land and site improvements:			
Site acquisition and closing costs	$ 2,500,000	20.9%	$20.83
On-/off-site improvement costs:			
Off-site improvements $ 250,000			
On-site improvements:			
Excavation and grading 50,000			
Sewer/water 150,000			
Paving 200,000			
Curbs/sidewalks 100,000			
Landscaping 100,000			
Total on-/off-site costs	$ 850,000	7.1%	$ 7.08
B. Construction costs:			
Hard costs:			
Shell structure $3,925,000			
HVAC 528,500			
Electrical 613,000			
Plumbing 221,580			
Project management fees 300,250			
Finish-out 1,400,600			
Graphics/signage 66,570			
Total hard costs	$ 7,055,500	58.9%	$58.80
Soft costs:			
Architect engineering $ 147,000			
Fees and permits 24,300			
Legal fees 26,900			
Construction interest 692,416			
Construction loan fees 180,028			
Permanent loan fees 270,042			
Leasing commissions 45,300			
Direct overhead 160,000			
Indirect overhead 30,800			
Total soft costs	$ 1,576,787	13.2%	$13.14
Total project costs	$11,982,287	100.0%	$99.85
Construction Loan Request:			
Total on-/off-site improvements	$ 850,000		
Total hard construction costs	7,055,500		
Soft costs	403,500		
Total costs to be financed	8,309,000		
Estimated interest carry	692,416		
Total loan amount	9,001,416		
Equity requirements	2,980,871		
Total project cost	$11,982,287		

Many lenders will not fund off-site improvements that are part of a loan request because other parties may have title to the land on which improvements will be made. Even if the developer has title to the off-site land, the construction lender may have difficulty acquiring satisfactory lien security on the land where the off-site improvements will be made. The ability to acquire funding of off-site costs depends on the lender's judgment as to how far in excess of the total loan amount the value of the project will be when completed.

Most lenders will fund all hard costs if they can be documented and are commensurate with the overall quality of the development. Lenders, however, vary in their willingness to fund many soft-cost items. They may not be willing to fund closing fees associated with the land acquisition, financing fees, planning and design fees, permitting fees, and/or any overhead charges the developer requests as a part of the project cost. This is because these changes represent fees for services or intangibles which may be regarded as difficult to recover in the event of default or bankruptcy should a property have to be auctioned or sold to repay the construction loan. Hard costs represent outlays for tangible improvements (e.g., bricks and mortar) and are thought to be better security than outlays for intangibles, even though the latter are necessary. In most cases, however, an estimate of construction interest carry is *included* in the loan request.

Construction Loan Request

Exhibit 16–4 also contains a breakdown of the *loan request.* Note that this particular loan request does not include land cost. Also note that it does not ask for financing for all soft costs. However, Southfork is requesting funding for some off-site improvements. The total loan request is $9,001,416, which represents about 75 percent of the $11,982,287 estimate of total project cost (land plus all other outlays). Also, note in Exhibit 16–4 that the request includes construction period interest as part of the loan. This is very common in construction lending because the project will not provide any rent or cash inflow during development. Therefore, the developer will usually be allowed to borrow the interest as one additional cost of construction. An estimate of *construction period interest* is made by computing the *monthly draw rate* for construction costs to be funded by the lender over the 12-month period. This is illustrated in Exhibit 16–5.

Note in the exhibit that the draw rates shown in column (a) are calculated by determining expected monthly draws for *direct costs* ($8,309,000). Also note that the estimated interest is $692,416. This consists of interest calculated at 12% ÷ 12 months, or 1 percent per month on the cumulative loan balance shown in column (c). Interest draws are computed on the outstanding monthly loan balance and are borrowed as a part of the construction cost draws at the end of each month. The developer makes cash interest payments (column d) to the bank each month. However, because all of the interest carry is *borrowed,* it becomes part of the loan balance, and because all monthly payments made by the developer are interest only, no reduction of principal occurs. In short, this pattern is analogous to an interest-only loan, discussed in previous chapters. The reader may recall that these loans require no reduction in loan principal because payments are computed to include interest payments only. Also note that the interest payments in column (d) are exactly offset by the interest draw in column (b). Thus, the net effect is as if there were no payment to the lender until the entire loan balance is repaid at the end of the construction period. This is analogous to a negative amortization loan with the loan balance increasing by the amount of interest accrued each month.

In summary, Exhibit 16–5 shows that the loan balance will increase each month by the amount of the project cost draws plus interest borrowed. The total ending balance, $9,001,416, will be equal to the total construction loan amount at the end of the 12-month period. This amount will be funded by the permanent lender, thereby taking out the construction lender at that time. In most cases, the permanent loan and the interim loan commitments are made for the same amount.

Even though developers may estimate costs very carefully, the *actual* costs of development and interest carry will differ from such estimates because of uncertainties in the rate at which work will progress and because interest rates may change. Hence, it is likely that the *actual* interest draw pattern will deviate from the *estimated* pattern. Once the $9,001,416 commitment amount is reached, however, the construction lender *is not*

EXHIBIT 16–5
Projected Loan Repayment Schedule for Rolling Meadows Center

	Loan Draws			Payments		
	(a)	(b)	(c)	(d)	(e)	(f)
End of Month	Project Costs	Construction Interest	Loan Balance	Interest	Principal Reduction	Ending Loan Balance
0	$ 0	$ 0	$ 0	$ 0	$ 0	$ 0
1	1,557,938	0	1,557,938	0	0	1,557,938
2	1,557,938	15,579	3,131,454	15,579	0	3,131,454
3	1,557,938	31,315	4,720,706	31,315	0	4,720,706
4	1,557,938	47,207	6,325,851	47,207	0	6,325,851
5	259,656	63,259	6,648,766	63,259	0	6,648,766
6	259,656	66,488	6,974,910	66,488	0	6,974,910
7	259,656	69,749	7,304,315	69,749	0	7,304,315
8	259,656	73,043	7,637,014	73,043	0	7,637,014
9	259,656	76,370	7,973,041	76,370	0	7,973,041
10	259,656	79,730	8,312,427	79,730	0	8,312,427
11	259,656	83,124	8,655,208	83,124	0	8,655,208
12	259,656	86,552	$9,001,416	$86,552	$9,001,416	$ 0
Total	$8,309,000	$692,416				

required to fund any more draws, and the permanent lender is not required to fund any more than the committed amount. If the developer does not want to bear the risk of unanticipated interest rate changes and the possibility of interest cost overruns, she can eliminate, or at least reduce, that risk for a fee by purchasing an interest rate swap.

If the developer does not want to bear the cost of eliminating interest rate risk, she will have to provide additional funds (perhaps by attracting more partners to the venture) or find a gap lender or equity partners. If actual costs exceed estimated costs because of material and labor cost overruns, unanticipated changes in interest rates,[9] a longer-than-anticipated lease-up period because of a declining market, and so on, and if the developer cannot find other sources of equity (through a partnership or similar arrangement) or a gap loan, and if the interim lender refuses to extend additional funds, the developer may face foreclosure.

Lenders and developers also use a draw, interest, and repayment schedule similar to that shown in Exhibit 16–5 as a tool for financial control. They may use this schedule in conjunction with field surveys completed by staff engineers to verify that the total percentage of *work in place* at the end of each month corresponds to the outstanding loan balance at the end of each month. If the lender feels that total funds drawn down are in excess of construction in place, the lender will not allow further draws until offsetting improvements have been made. Note that because the construction lender charges a 2 percent loan origination fee, the loan yield will be about 15.5 percent, as compared with the 12 percent rate of interest used to compute interest on the loan. This yield is calculated by finding the rate of discount that makes the present value of monthly outflows in months 1 through 12 plus the lump sum inflow also in month 12 equal to the loan fees charged at closing by the interim lender, or $180,028.

A final note regarding the draw schedule has to do with lenders' use of **holdbacks.** Generally, when project developers contract with various building contractors to perform work, developers hold back a percentage (10%) of each progress payment made to such

---

[9] Some developers use interest rate futures to hedge against interest rate risk when using floating interest rate loans.

contractors until all work is satisfactorily completed. Holding back payments assures the developer that all work has been completed in accordance with plans and specifications. When work is completed to the developer's satisfaction, the final payment is made to the contractors. Most lenders are aware of holdback practices and will in turn hold back a percentage (10%) of all loan draw requests from developers. Lender holdbacks prevent developers from drawing down funds at a faster rate than they must pay to contractors. Exhibit 16–5 does not take holdbacks into account. However, you should be aware of this practice and take holdbacks into account in the draw schedule if applicable.

Permanent Loan Request

Upon completion of the project, Citadel Life Insurance Company will replace the construction loan with **permanent financing,** assuming that all conditions in the construction loan and all contingencies outlined in the permanent financing commitment have been met. Remember, the permanent loan terms (outlined in Exhibit 16–6) were predetermined before construction began. Any additional development costs over $9,001,416 are Southfork's responsibility. For a 3 percent loan fee, Citadel Life Insurance Company will provide Southfork with a 10-year mortgage. Monthly payments will be $94,805 based on a 25-year amortization schedule at an interest rate of 12 percent.

Market Data and Tenant Mix

Exhibit 16–7 contains a breakdown of the expected tenant mix for Rolling Meadows Center and the space tenants are expected to occupy. For a neighborhood center, most lenders would expect at least one predevelopment lease commitment from a food chain and/or general merchandiser. Obviously, if favorable predevelopment lease commitments accompany the loan request, it is more likely that a commitment will be made. The other data in the exhibit are based on experience from U.S. data averages and with averages obtained from local market surveys. It should be stressed that exact comparability in tenant mix is not expected in each and every project submitted for review. However, past experience usually indicates that certain types of tenants are not compatible (e.g., auto parts and jewelry stores) in the same center, whereas other tenants are compatible (e.g., jewelry stores and furriers). A submission that indicates a lack of understanding regarding tenant mix may reveal developer inexperience. Further, the tenant breakdown should be realistic—if the developer projects too many "high-end" retail stores (which usually pay high rents), it may indicate overoptimism.

In addition to the data shown in Exhibit 16–7, the developer will have to provide more detail regarding the trade area expected to be served by the center, a competitive analysis of other centers, and proof that the addition of another center will not oversupply that market with retail space. Additional information relative to population growth, age, households, income, retail spending patterns, and so forth (not shown), in the trade area must also support the loan request. The importance of these data cannot be stressed enough.

EXHIBIT 16–6
Summary of Permanent Loan Terms

Total loan	$9,001,416
Debt amortization	25
Term of loan	10
Interest rate	12.00%
Debt service/month	$94,805
Debt service/year	$1,137,661
3% permanent loan fee	$270,042
Yield to permanent lender	12.55%

EXHIBIT 16–7
Market Survey Data—Shopping Centers (Tenant Information)

Classification	Number of Stores	% of Tenants*	Sq. Ft. of *GLA*	% *GLA*	U.S. Avg. %	Local Avg. %
General merchandise	1	3.57%	4,950	4.50%	5.60%	5.20%
Food	2	7.14	37,400	34.00	30.80	36.00
Food service	1	3.57	8,800	8.00	8.80	7.00
Clothing	3	10.71	7,700	7.00	5.00	6.00
Shoes	1	3.57	1,155	1.05	1.30	0.70
Home furnishings	1	3.57	1,100	1.00	2.60	2.30
Home appliances	1	3.57	990	0.90	2.40	1.00
Building materials	1	3.57	1,320	1.20	3.40	2.00
Automotive supplies	0	0.00	0	0.00	1.70	1.50
Hobby	1	3.57	2,035	1.85	2.70	2.50
Gifts and specialty	2	7.14	2,860	2.60	2.50	2.30
Jewelry and cosmetics	1	3.57	1,650	1.50	0.70	2.00
Liquor	1	3.57	1,430	1.30	1.50	1.50
Drugs	1	3.57	9,900	9.00	8.50	8.00
Other retail	6	21.46	12,100	11.00	4.40	6.00
Personal services	2	7.14	8,910	8.10	6.50	7.00
Recreational	1	3.57	2,200	2.00	3.50	3.00
Financial	1	3.57	3,300	3.00	4.10	3.00
Offices	1	3.57	2,200	2.00	4.00	3.00
Total	28	100.00%	110,000	100.00%	100.00%	100.00%

*Rounded.

Pro Forma Construction Costs and Cash Flow Projections

Another necessary ingredient in the submission of data to the permanent lender is a pro forma (estimate) of construction costs and net operating income. Exhibit 16–8 contains annual estimates for expenditures during the construction period for land acquisition, site improvements, hard costs, and soft costs. Total loan draws are based on the $9,001,416 loan request (including interest), for which financing is being sought, over the two-year development period. Note that the developer will require $2,950,071 from internal sources at closing to cover land acquisition and loan fees, plus an additional $30,800 to cover indirect overhead, or total equity of $2,980,871. Citadel Life Insurance Co. will review Southfork's financial statements (not shown) to determine whether it has the ability to provide such funding from internal sources.

EXHIBIT 16–8
Pro Forma Statement of Cash Flows—Construction Period

	Draws per Year		
	(0)	(1)	Total
Site acquisition and closing costs	$2,500,000		$ 2,500,000
Site improvements (on-/off-)		$ 850,000	850,000
Hard costs		7,055,500	7,055,500
Soft costs		434,300	434,300
Permanent loan fee	270,042		270,042
Construction loan fee	180,028		180,028
Construction interest		692,416	692,416
Total construction cash outflow	2,950,071	9,032,216	11,982,287
Less: Total draws	0	9,001,416	9,001,416
Total equity needed	$2,950,071	$ 30,800	$ 2,980,871

EXHIBIT 16–9   Pro Forma Statement of Cash Flows—Operating Period

Cash Flows (End of Year)	(2)	(3)	(4)	(5)	(6)
Income:					
Minimum rent	$1,650,000	$1,749,000	$1,853,940	$1,965,176	$2,083,087
Overage (5% of gross sales)	30,000	124,800	129,792	134,984	140,383
Tenant reimbursements					
Real estate taxes	137,500	143,000	148,720	154,669	160,856
Common area maintenance	385,000	400,400	416,416	433,073	450,396
Utilities	367,500	382,200	397,488	413,388	429,923
Insurance	33,000	34,320	35,693	37,121	38,605
Gross potential income	$2,603,000	$2,833,720	$2,982,049	$3,138,410	$3,303,249
Less: Vacancy allowance	780,900	141,686	149,102	156,920	165,162
Expected gross income	$1,822,100	$2,692,034	$2,832,947	$2,981,490	$3,138,087
Expenses:					
Management and leasing fees	$ 104,500	$ 93,690	$ 99,187	$ 105,008	$ 111,174
General and administrative	77,000	80,080	83,283	86,615	90,079
Real estate taxes	137,500	143,000	148,720	154,669	160,856
Common area maintenance	385,000	400,400	416,416	433,073	450,396
Utilities	300,300	312,312	324,804	337,797	351,309
Insurance	33,000	34,320	35,693	37,121	38,605
Other	27,500	28,600	29,744	30,934	32,171
Total expenses	$1,064,800	$1,092,402	$1,137,847	$1,185,215	$1,234,589
Net operating income	$ 757,300	$1,599,632	$1,695,099	$1,796,275	$1,903,498
Less: Debt service	1,137,661	1,137,661	1,137,661	1,137,661	1,137,661
Before-tax cash flow	$ –380,361	$ 461,971	$ 557,438	$ 658,614	$ 765,837
Ratios:					
Operating expense		40.58%	40.16%	39.75%	39.34%
Debt coverage ratio		1.41	1.49	1.58	1.67
Free and clear return		13.35%	14.15%	14.99%	15.89%
Return on equity		15.50%	18.70%	22.09%	25.69%
Vacancy-collection loss		5.00%	5.00%	5.00%	5.00%
Break-even occupancy rate		78.70%	76.31%	74.01%	71.82%

Exhibit 16–9 details the pro forma operating statement for Rolling Meadows Center. The lease-up or marketing effort should result in 70 percent occupancy during the second year and 95 percent thereafter. Southfork is estimating a base rent of $15 per square foot of gross leasable area, with average increases based on leases indexed to the CPI of 6 percent per year after the first year of operation (leases are expected to have terms ranging from one to five years). An overage provision requires tenants to also pay 5 percent of gross sales in excess of a base sales level each month.[10] In a retail operation, rent is usually divided into two components. The first is a minimum rent per square foot. The other component is called **percentage rent.** Developers frequently charge percentage rent, calculated as a percentage of the sales of a tenant in excess of a predetermined *breakpoint* or sales volume. As long as the tenant's sales are below the breakpoint, the owner receives only the minimum rent. When a tenant's sales increase above the breakpoint, the percentage rent rate is applied to the sales volume in excess of the breakpoint and is added to the

---

[10] Overages are common in retail leasing. The breakpoint is commonly determined by dividing the tenant's base rental amount (rate per square foot times rentable area) by the percentage rent negotiated between the owner and tenant. For further discussion, see *Shopping Center Development Handbook Series* (Washington, DC), published by the Urban Land Institute.

minimum rent, thus increasing the total rent. In this way, should the shopping center become very successful, the owner shares in the increased revenue produced by the tenants. The percentage rent shown in Exhibit 16–9 is estimated for all tenants in Rolling Meadows.

Tenant reimbursements are also shown in Exhibit 16–9. These amounts are based on negotiations between the owner and tenants and represent the amount of operating expenses over expense stops for which the tenant is responsible (recall the discussion of such stops in Chapter 11 for office buildings). Hence, base rents, percentage rents, and expenses for which tenants are responsible over some preagreed amount (stop) all represent gross income to the owner of Rolling Meadows.

Operating expenses are also detailed in Exhibit 16–9. These amounts represent the actual expenses that must be paid to operate Rolling Meadows. They are deducted from rents, overage, and tenant reimbursements. All leases are to be *net to the tenant,* with a direct pass-through for insurance and property taxes. Tenants will also be billed for their share of common area maintenance (parking lot, circulation space in center, etc.) and utilities. An additional premium will be added to the utility charge to provide for a replacement reserve on HVAC equipment.[11] Tenants will pay these expenses to Southfork as reimbursement. Southfork management will, in turn, pay any expenses to third parties as they become due. Southfork will also incur expenses of its own for property management, leasing commissions, and general and administrative expenses that will not be recoverable from tenants. These amounts are deducted from rents, overage, and tenant reimbursements. The projections assume that a sufficient number of leases will be signed at the end of the second year to warrant closing the permanent loan.

Pay particular attention to the ratios that appear at the bottom of Exhibit 16–9. These ratios, calculated beginning with data for year 3 when "normal" operation is anticipated, are used to evaluate the performance of the property. The permanent lender will review these and other ratios to ascertain whether they fall into acceptable underwriting ranges. We must stress again that market data supporting rents and overages, proof of estimates of operating costs from the management of comparable centers, realistic estimates of the lease-up rate, and lease terms that tenants are willing to accept in the retail market are all critical to the underwriting process.

The operating expense ratio, which is calculated by dividing total annual operating expenses by the effective gross income (*EGI*), indicates that at most, 40.5 percent of *EGI* from Rolling Meadows will go into servicing operating expenses. In contrast, Rolling Meadows's debt coverage ratio, or net operating income divided by debt service, exceeds 1.41. This ratio demonstrates the property's ability to meet its debt payments. The cash returns earned on the total investment will be positive and exceed the mortgage interest rate.[12] This free and clear return is calculated by dividing the net operating income by the total project costs. Return on equity, a second cash return measurement, is calculated by dividing before-tax cash flow by the total equity contributions. These returns do not include any appreciation in project value. Finally, the break-even occupancy rate approximates the level of occupancy required to service both the debt service and the operating expenses of a project. This ratio is calculated by dividing the annual debt service and operating expenses by the gross potential income. Assuming that the vacancy and collection loss of 5 percent is primarily due to vacancy, this implies an occupancy rate of 95 percent. Clearly, with occupancy projected to be 95 percent, Rolling Meadows easily meets its debt service and operating expense obligations.

---

[11] Note the difference in utility income to be collected from tenants and actual costs to be paid by Southfork management. This difference is a premium earned on selling utilities to the tenants. Depending on competition for space in the retail market, the developer may or may not be able to negotiate this premium.

[12] Total project cost is estimated at $11,982,287. When this amount is divided into *NOI,* a 13.35 percent return on total investment results.

Assuming that the permanent lender makes the take-out commitment, the developer will incorporate the actual amount of the loan commitment into the pro forma statements and seek out a construction lender.[13] During this time, the developer will refine and update cost and market estimates and provide more detailed construction plans in order to acquire interim financing. After the permanent financing commitment is acquired, however, all changes in design, cost, predevelopment lease agreements, and so on must be submitted to both the permanent and interim lenders for review.

Feasibility, Profitability, and Risk—Additional Issues

Most of the analysis that the interim and permanent lenders conduct focuses on the pro forma statements and market data supplied with the loan requests. This is because lenders are concerned about market conditions, rents, and the ability of the project to cover expenses and debt service. Southfork is equally concerned with these issues; however, it is also interested in knowing how well this project will perform as an investment, both before and after taxes. Also, from the standpoint of assessing risk, it needs to know how sensitive the estimates provided in the pro forma statements are to various assumptions made in the analysis. Much of what follows are analytic tools for assessing project performance. These tools may be used at any time during development as market data, building costs, interest rates, and so on, change. They also may be used to ascertain the maximum price that should be paid for the land *prior to its acquisition.* To illustrate these ideas, we will use the pro forma estimates presented thus far and change them by introducing sensitivity analysis.

Profitability before and after Taxes

For Southfork to assess the profitability of the Rolling Meadows Center before and after taxes, additional assumptions regarding the number of operating periods and the appreciation rate on the property value must be made. We have assumed that a sale will occur five years after construction.

Exhibit 16–10 summarizes estimates of before-tax cash flow (*BTCF*) during the development and operating periods, based on information contained in Exhibits 16–8 and 16–9. The before-tax estimate for *NPV* comprises all negative cash flows consisting of equity requirements at closing (land acquisition and loan fees), cash equity needed during development for costs not financed (indirect overhead), and cash requirements needed during year 2, or the lease-up phase. Positive cash flows are based on operations from years 3 through 6 plus cash flow from the sale of the project in year 6 (all figures are rounded).

Exhibit 16–11 contains estimates of before-tax cash flow when Rolling Meadows Center reevaluates its investment plans and instead of owning and operating, it decides to sell to Mony Mutual Realty Advisors, which acquires projects and manages them on behalf of pension fund sponsors. We see that after paying selling expenses and repaying the mortgage loan balance to Citadel, Southfork will have $7,104,160 in cash before taxes (*BTCF*s). The sale price for the project, $16,035,003, is based on the initial total project cost, $11,982,287 (Exhibit 16–8), compounded at an appreciation rate of 6 percent per year for five years.

---

[13] The actual take-out commitment will contain contingencies that may affect the pro forma statements presented here. Recall that all of the statements produced thus far are part of a *proposal* to the permanent lender. Should the lender decide to fund less than the total amount requested or insist on a higher lease-up requirement, among other things, those changes would have to be incorporated in the data submitted to potential interim lenders.

EXHIBIT 16–10 **Profitability Analysis for Rolling Meadows Center**

	Before-Tax Cash Flow						
	Year						
	0	1	2	3	4	5	6
Equity	$−2,950,071	$−30,800					
BTCF—operations			$−380,361	$461,971	$557,438	$658,614	$ 765,837
BTCF—sale							7,104,160
Total *BTCF*	$−2,950,071	$−30,800	$−380,361	$461,971	$557,438	$658,614	$7,869,997
BTIRR		21.33%					
BTNPV @ 21%	$	38,884					

	Taxable Income						
	Year						
	0	1	2	3	4	5	6
Net operating income			$ 757,300	$1,599,632	$1,695,099	$1,796,275	$1,903,498
Less:							
Interest			1,076,900	1,069,194	1,060,511	1,050,726	1,039,701
Depreciation:							
Capital improvements			256,769	256,769	256,769	256,769	256,769
Tenant improvements			256,769	183,406	131,005	93,575	77,979
Amortization:							
Leasing commissions			9,060	9,060	9,060	9,060	9,060
Construction loan fees		$ 180,028					
Permanent loan fees			27,004	27,004	27,004	27,004	27,004
Taxable income		$−180,028	$−869,202	$ 54,199	$ 210,750	$ 359,141	$ 492,985
Tax @ 28%		$ −50,408	$−243,377	$ 15,176	$ 59,010	$ 100,559	$ 138,036

	After-Tax Cash Flows						
Total *BTCF*	$−2,950,071	−30,800	$−380,361	$461,971	$557,438	$658,614	$7,869,997
Less: Ord. Tax	0	$−50,408	$−243,377	15,176	59,010	100,559	138,036
Cap. gain tax							1,713,304*
ATCF	$−2,950,071	$ 19,608	$−136,984	$446,795	$498,428	$558,055	$6,018,657
ATIRR		17.79%					
ATNPV @ 17%	$	96,077					

*See Exhibit 16–11.

From Exhibit 16–10, we can calculate an estimate for *NPV* before taxes based on all before-tax cash flows expected to occur from years 1 to 6, discounted at a required before-tax rate of 21 percent. This results in a positive *NPV* of $38,884. This 21 percent required rate of return represents a 9 percent risk premium over the mortgage interest rate that Southfork management believes would be a satisfactory return on its equity after recovery of all project costs, given the risk of the Rolling Meadows project.

The *after-tax internal rate of return* for Southfork is also presented in Exhibit 16–10. To arrive at net cash flow after tax during development and in each operating year, we need additional information to take income taxes into account.

EXHIBIT 16–11
Sale of Rolling
Meadows Center

	Before-Tax Cash Flow
Sale price	$16,035,003
Less:	
Selling expenses	320,700
Mortgage balance	8,610,143
Before-tax cash flow on the sale	$ 7,104,160

	Gain in Year of Sale
Sale price	$16,035,003
Less:	
Selling expenses	320,700
Adjusted basis	9,595,358
Total gain on the sale	$ 6,118,945

	After-Tax Cash Flow
Before-tax cash flow on the sale	$ 7,104,160
Less: Tax on gain @ 28%	1,713,304
After-tax cash flow on the sale	$ 5,390,856

Exhibit 16–12 provides the information about depreciation and amortization of various project costs that we need to estimate taxable income. Part A in Exhibit 16–12 contains a list of costs that must be capitalized as part of the improvement and depreciated. Of total depreciable costs, we see in part B that 90 percent are capital improvements and, therefore, subject to depreciation on a straight-line basis over 31.5 years.[14] Southfork estimates 10 percent of these costs to be tenant improvements, which are categorized as personal rather than real property. This category of improvement may be depreciated on a double-declining basis over seven years.[15] Part C contains a description of project soft costs that may be amortized. Because we assume two loans are being used to fund the project, we amortize loan fees over the respective terms of each loan.[16] Finally, we capitalize leasing commissions and write them off over the average of lease terms for the project.

We also need after-tax cash flow in the year of *sale* (*ATCFs*) to complete the computation of the after-tax *IRR*. From Exhibit 16–11, tax in the year of sale ($1,713,304) is the difference between the estimated net selling price less the adjusted basis times the 28 percent tax rate. As noted in Chapter 11, capital gains might be taxed at a lower rate than ordinary income. In this example, we assume that the same tax rate is used for ordinary income and capital gains. The adjusted basis is computed as the cost of land plus all improvements, or $11,982,287, less the sum of all depreciation and amortization taken over the seven-year period.[17] The adjusted basis, or cost to be recovered from the sale of

[14] See Chapter 11 for an explanation of depreciation methods. The depreciable life of 31.5 years used in this example is not necessarily representative of the current tax law. It is for purposes of illustration only.

[15] An explanation of double-declining-balance depreciation may be found in introductory accounting texts. Switching to straight-line is also allowed and carried out in the analysis here.

[16] The permanent loan fees are assumed to be paid when the commitment is obtained. However, amortization is assumed not to begin until the loan is closed at the beginning of the third year.

[17] In years prior to the 1986 Tax Reform Act, tax rates on capital gains and on ordinary income were different. Further, the tax treatment of construction period interest and property taxes and certain other fees also differed. Because of these differences, interest, taxes, and fees were capitalized from the improvement, and the unamortized balance in the year of sale was either deducted as an ordinary expense or added to the undepreciated basis. Stay informed about real estate taxation, particularly when analyzing project development, because the tax treatment of various cost categories changes frequently.

EXHIBIT 16–12
Depreciation and Amortization Schedule for Rolling Meadows Center

A. Depreciable costs:		
Site improvements (on-/off-)		$ 850,000
Hard costs		7,055,500
Soft costs:		
Architect engineering	$147,000	
Fees and permits	24,300	
Legal fees	26,900	
Construction interest	692,416	
Direct overhead	160,000	
Indirect overhead	30,800	
Total soft costs		$ 1,081,416
Total depreciable costs		$ 8,986,916

			Depreciation Period
B. Depreciation schedule:			
Capital improvements (90% of total)		$ 8,088,225	31.5 years
Tenant improvements (10% of total)		898,692	7 years
		$ 8,986,916	

			Amortization Period
C. Amortization schedule:			
Construction loan fees		$ 180,028	1 year
Permanent loan fees		270,042	10 years
Leasing commissions		45,300	5 years
Total depreciable/amortized costs		9,482,287	
Add: Land		2,500,000	
Total project costs		$11,982,287	

Adjusted Basis at the End of Year 6

Item	Total Cost	Less: Accumulated Depreciation/ Amortization	Adjusted Basis
Land	$ 2,500,000	$ 0	$2,500,000
Capital improvements	8,088,225	1,283,845	6,804,379
Tenant improvements	898,692	742,734	155,958
Permanent loan fees	270,042	135,021	135,021
Leasing commissions	45,300	45,300	0
Construction loan fees	180,028	180,028	0
Total	$11,982,287	$2,386,928	$9,595,358

the asset prior to computing the tax on the gain, is $9,595,358. We can then estimate the after-tax cash flow to be $5,390,856.

We can solve for the *ATIRR* shown in Exhibit 16–10 by setting the equity requirements at closing equal to *ATCF* in each year and in the year of sale and solving for the rate of interest that makes the after-tax *NPV* equal to zero. Note that although *BTCF* is negative in year 1, the after-tax cash flow is positive during that year because of the tax deductibility of loan fees. Those deductions result in a net loss, or an offset against any other active income earned by Southfork during that year. Hence, they *reduce* taxes, *save* cash, and offset negative *BTCF*. Taxes are calculated by assuming a tax rate of 28 percent,[18] and after-tax cash flows are determined and used to determine the *ATIRR,* which is 17.79 percent for Rolling Meadows. Note that this return is *not* equal to the *BTIRR* (shown in Exhibit 16–10) times 1 minus tax rate, or 21.33 percent (1 − .28 = 15.36%), because of the higher rates allowable for amortization of tenant improvements and fees (Exhibit 16–12) relative to the 31.5 year straight-line depreciation allowed for real property. Using an after-tax discount rate of 17 percent, we find that the after-tax *NPV* (*ATNPV*) is $96,077.

Sensitivity Analysis, Risk, and Feasibility Analysis

Based on the preceding analysis, we have concluded that if Southfork is satisfied that a 21 percent before-tax rate of return on equity is adequate to undertake the Rolling Meadows Center development, it will earn a positive *NPV.* This implies that the $2.5 million land acquisition price would be warranted, given estimates of construction costs, market rents, expenses, and the appreciation rate in property value. An interesting question that could be raised at this point is, "Suppose that market rents were estimated to be $12 per square foot instead of $15 and all other assumptions remained constant (quantity of space, construction costs, interest rates, appreciation rates, and operating expenses). Would the project still be feasible—would it cover all costs and provide the developer with a competitive return on equity?"

To consider this question, refer to Exhibit 16–13. This diagram represents the relationship between *BTNPV* (vertical axis) and market rents per square foot of leasable area (horizontal axis). Note that at the average rent of $15 per square foot assumed in our analysis, the *BTNPV* is slightly above zero (the discount rate is held constant at 21%). If, however, the market rent averaged $12 per square foot and all other assumptions remained the same, it is clear that the *NPV* would be negative. In that case, Southfork would not be interested in

EXHIBIT 16–13
BTNPV **of Rolling Meadows Center and Rents**

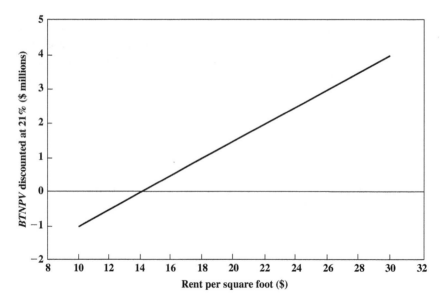

[18] We assume that Southfork is a sole proprietorship or a partnership whose owners are taxed at ordinary rates. We also assume that Southfork's owners have other passive income that they can use to offset the passive losses produced by this project (see Chapter 11 for a discussion of passive income).

Web App

Construction loans are available from a variety of lenders, including most commercial banks. There are numerous Web sites with information available from lenders offering construction loans. Use a search engine to find a site with information on current rates for construction loans. Summarize what the rate is and as much information as you can find about how the loan is structured.

EXHIBIT 16–14
BTNPV of Rolling Meadows Center and Land Cost

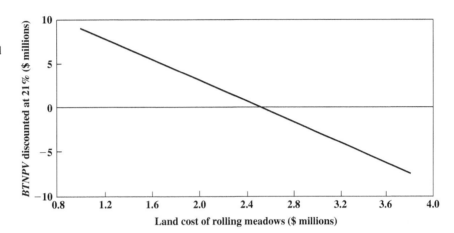

pursuing the development. An even more critical aspect of this analysis becomes clear if, after both loan commitments were made, construction went forward on the project and market rents *then* fell from $15 to $12 per square foot as the lease-up phase was under way. In this event, Southfork would be facing a negative *NPV* and would be committed to the development. If it was not able to produce more equity or to find additional investors to provide equity at that point, it would not be able to meet project expenses and debt service. At that point, the interim lender would be faced with the prospect that the permanent lender may not be compelled to honor its take-out commitment because the developer would not be able to meet rental requirements. The interim lender would have to negotiate the interim loan terms with the developer (sometimes referred to as a *workout*), or possibly foreclose. You can now begin to see how changing market conditions can affect project risk.

Another important consideration is apparent in Exhibit 16–14, where *BTNPV* is related to land cost (horizontal axis). Recall that we estimated a slightly positive *NPV* when we assumed that the land was acquired at $2.5 million. If Southfork was too optimistic and paid $3 million for the land, we can see from the diagram that the *NPV* would be negative (again, discounting at 21% and holding all other variables constant). On the other hand, if the land could be acquired for less than $2.5 million, the *NPV* would become more favorable. The value of this *sensitivity analysis* should be obvious at this point.[19] This analysis is also referred to as **feasibility analysis,** or a determination of whether a project is commercially feasible at prevailing market rents, land prices, and construction and financing costs.

[19] The same analysis may be carried out by changing other variables, such as construction costs, interest rates, or operating expenses one at a time to assess the impact on before-tax *NPV*.

Conclusion

This chapter dealt with financing the development of income-producing real estate such as apartment complexes, office buildings, warehouses, and shopping centers. Development projects include many risks in addition to those we have discussed in previous chapters for existing projects. We have seen that developers of such projects face changing conditions in the national and local economies, competitive pressures from other developments, and changes in locational preferences of tenants, all of which influence the profitability of developing and operating an income-producing property. All these forces combined affect the developer's ability to acquire land, build improvements, lease space to tenants, and earn sufficient revenues to cover operating expenses and repay both a construction and a permanent mortgage loan. This chapter illustrated the mechanics of construction loans, which differ from the permanent loans we have already discussed extensively because they involve draws over the construction period. The next chapter explores land development projects and extends the concepts of the present chapter to development and financing land for subdivisions.

Key Terms

acquisition and development
   loan (ADL), *525*
build to suit, *521*
construction loan, *525*
contingencies, *530*
exculpation (nonrecourse)
   clause, *534*

feasibility analysis, *549*
gap financing, *531*
hard costs, *525*
holdbacks, *539*
mini-perm loan, *526, 532*
monthly draw method, *532*
percentage rent, *542*

permanent financing, *540*
seasoned property, *522*
soft costs, *525*
speculative/open-ended
   construction lending, *526*
standby commitments, *529*
triparty buy–sell agreement, *534*

Useful Web Sites

www.uli.org—The mission of the Urban Land Institute is to provide responsible leadership in the use of land in order to enhance the total environment. This site also provides current issues for financial trends in the industry.

www.bizloan.org—Good resource for information about different types of loans used for project development. Includes glossary of terms.

www.census.gov—U.S. Census Bureau Web site.

www.icsc.org—International Council of Shopping Centers Web site.

www.economy.com—Economy.com is a provider of economic data.

www.bls.gov—U.S. Department of Labor Web site.

www.bea.gov—U.S. Department of Commerce—Bureau of Economic Development Web site.

www.claritas.com—Nielsen Claritas provides demographic and enhanced census data.

www.axiometrics.com—Axiometrics is a research firm providing fundamental real estate research for the apartment sector with an emphasis on the performance of portfolios owned by the publicly traded apartment REITs.

www.econdata.net—This site has around 1,000 links to socioeconomic data sources, arranged by subject and provider, pointers to the Web's premiere data collections, and its own list of the 10 best sites for finding regional economic data.

www.economy.com/freelunch—FreeLunch.com is the Web's best source of free economic data. Users can quickly and easily chart and download economic data. Moody's Economy.com data services teams in Asia, Europe, and the United States update FreeLunch.com's economic data as they are released by the primary source.

http://finance.yahoo.com—Yahoo Finance provides the subscriber with up-to-date information on finance. The site also features information centers in mutual funds, bill pay, banking, loans, insurance, retirement planning, and taxes.

Questions

1. What are the sources of risk associated with project development?
2. What are some development strategies that many developers follow? Why do they follow such strategies?
3. How can development projects be differentiated from one another in the marketplace?

4. Describe the process of financing the construction and operation of a typical real estate development. Indicate the order in which lenders who fund project development financing are sought and why this pattern is followed.

5. What contingencies are commonly found in permanent or take-out loan commitments? Why are they used? What happens if they are not met by the developer?

6. What is a *standby commitment?* When and why is it used?

7. What is a *mini-perm loan?* When and why is this type of loan used?

8. Third-party lenders sometimes provide gap financing for project developments. Why is this lending used? How does it work?

9. A presale agreement is said to be equivalent to a take-out commitment. What will the construction lender be concerned about if the developer plans to use such an agreement in lieu of a take-out?

10. Why do not permanent lenders usually provide construction loans to developers? Do construction lenders ever provide permanent loans to developers?

11. What is the difference between the assignment of a take-out commitment to the construction lender and a triparty agreement? If neither device is used in project financing, what is the relationship between lenders in such a case?

12. What is the major concern construction lenders express about the income approach to estimating value? Why do they prefer to use the cost approach when possible? In the latter case, if the developer has owned the land for five years prior to development, would the cost approach be more effective? Why or why not?

13. What do we mean by *overage* in a retail lease agreement? How might it be calculated?

14. What is *sensitivity analysis?* How might it be used in real estate development?

15. It is sometimes said that land represents "residual" value. This statement reflects the fact that improvement costs do not vary materially from one location to another, whereas rents vary considerably. Hence, land values reflect changes in rents (both up and down) from location to location. Do you agree or disagree?

16. Why is the practice of "holdbacks" used? Who is involved in this practice? How does it affect construction lending?

Problems

1. Review Concept Box 16.2. The investor-developer would not be comfortable with a 7.8 percent return on cost because the "margin for error" is too risky. If construction costs are higher or rents are lower than anticipated, the project may not be feasible.

   a. Based on the fact that the project appears to have 9,360 square feet of surface area in excess of zoning requirements, the developer could make an argument to the planning department for an additional 10 units, 250 units in total, or 25 units per acre. How would this affect financial feasibility? What could be included in such an argument? Why would a public regulatory institution be interested in increasing density to 25 units per acre? Why not?

   b. Instead of (a), suppose the developer could build a 240-unit luxury apartment complex with a cost of $83,000 per unit. What would such a project have to rent for (per square foot) to make an 8 percent return on total cost? What risk factors would the developer have to consider?

2. The CEO of Kuehner Development Co. has just come from a meeting with his marketing staff where he was given the latest market study of a proposed new shopping center, Parker Road Plaza. The study calls for a construction phase of one year and an operation phase of five years. The property is to be sold at the end of the fifth year of operation.

   Part I. *Construction Phase:*

   The marketing staff has chosen a 12-acre site for the project that they believe they can acquire for $2.25 million. The initial studies indicate that this shopping center will support a floor-to-area ratio of 36.35 percent and a 92.11 percent leasable area ratio. [This means that the gross building area (*GBA*) will be 190,000 sq. ft., and the gross leasable area (*GLA*) will be 175,000 sq. ft.]

   The head of Kuehner's construction division assures the CEO that construction can keep hard costs to $54 per square foot (*GBA*) and soft costs (excluding interest carry and all loan fees) to

$4.50 per square foot (*GBA*). The division has decided to subcontract all of the site improvements at a total cost of $750,000.

The Shawmut Bank has agreed to provide interim financing for the project. The bank will finance all of the construction costs and site improvements at an annual rate of 13 percent plus a loan commitment fee of two points. The construction division estimates that 60 percent of the total direct cost will be taken down evenly during the first six months of the construction phase. Kuehner expects to obtain permanent financing from the Acme Insurance Co. at an interest rate of 12 percent for 20 years with a 2.5 percent prepaid loan fee and a 10-year call. Kuehner is expected to make monthly loan payments.

a. What will be the total project cost for Parker Road Plaza (excluding loan commitment fees and interest carry)? What will be the total direct costs?

b. What will be the interest carry for the Parker Road Plaza project? What will be the total loan amount that Kuehner must borrow (including interest carry)? What will be the yield to the lender on this construction loan?

c. What is the total project cost and how much equity must be put into the project each year during the construction phase? (Kuehner will fund both loan commitment fees from project equity.)

Part II. *Operations and Final Sale Phase:*

Kuehner estimates that it can lease Parker Road Plaza for $18.50 per square foot (*GLA*) base rent with a 3 percent overage on gross sales in excess of $200 per square foot (*GLA*). The company expects rents to increase by 5 percent per year during the lease period and tenant reimbursements to run $8 per square foot (*GLA*) and to increase at the same rate as rents. Kuehner expects to have the shopping center 70 percent leased during the first year of operation. After that, vacancies should average about 5 percent per year. The vacancy losses should be calculated on the entire gross potential income, which includes minimum rents, percentage rents, and tenant reimbursements. Sales, which are expected to average $210 per square foot (*GLA*) for the first year of operation, should grow at 6 percent per year. The operating expenses are expected to average $14 per square foot of *GLA* for the first year and will increase at the same rate as the rents. Kuehner will collect an additional 5 percent of *EGI* as an annual management fee. The final sales price is expected to be $18.4 million and Kuehner will incur sales expenses of 2 percent. Two schedules provide necessary information about this phase of the project: (1) the gross potential income of Parker Road Plaza for the five-year operation period and (2) the schedule of amortization and depreciation expenses for the project.

d. What cash flows would Kuehner Development Co. earn before and after taxes for Parker Road Plaza if it were operated for five years (assuming the marginal tax rate to be 28% for ordinary income and capital gains)? What cash flows will Kuehner realize before and after taxes from the sale of the project after five years?

e. Assuming that Kuehner's before-tax required rate of return is 16 percent, should the company develop Parker Road Plaza? Justify your answer based on *BTNPV* and *BTIRR*.

Pro Forma Operating Statement—Parker Road Plaza					
Cash Flows (End of Year)	2	3	4	5	6
Income					
Minimum rent	$3,237,500	$3,399,375	$3,569,344	$3,747,811	$3,935,201
Overage (% of gross sales)	52,500	118,650	188,769	263,095	341,881
Tenant reimbursements (per *GLA*)	1,400,000	1,470,000	1,543,500	1,620,675	1,701,709
Potential gross income	$4,690,000	$4,988,025	$5,301,613	$5,631,581	$5,978,791

Item	Amortization Period
Construction loan fees	1 year
Permanent loan fees	10 years

	Depreciation Period
Capital improvements (90% of total)	31.5 years S/L
Tenant improvements (10% of total)	7 years DDB

3. As a financial advisor for the Spain Development Co., you have been given the construction and marketing studies for the proposed Timbercreek office project. Several potential sites have been selected, but a final decision has not been made. Your manager needs to know how much she can afford to pay for the land and still manage to return 16 percent on the entire project over its lifetime.

   The strategic plan calls for a construction phase of one year and an operation phase of five years, after which time the property will be sold. The marketing staff says that a 1.3-acre site will be adequate because the initial studies indicate that this site will support an office building with a gross leasable area (*GLA*) of 26,520 square feet. The gross building area (*GBA*) will be 31,200 square feet, giving a leasable ratio of 85 percent. The marketing staff further assures you that the space can be rented for $19 per square foot. The head of the construction division maintains that all direct costs (excluding interest carry and all loan fees) will be $2.4 million.

   The First Street Bank will provide the construction loan for the project. The bank will finance all of the construction costs, site improvements, and interest carry at an annual rate of 13 percent plus a loan origination fee of 1.5 points. The construction division estimates that the direct cost draws will be taken down in six equal amounts commencing with the first month after close. The permanent financing for the project will come at the end of the first year from the Reliable Co. at an interest rate of 11.5 percent with a 4 percent prepaid loan fee. The loan has an eight-year term and is to be paid back monthly over a 25-year amortization schedule. No financing fees will be included in either loan amount. Spain will fund acquisition of the land with its own equity.

   Spain expects tenant reimbursements for the project to be $3.25 per square foot and the office building to be 75 percent leased during the first year of operation. After that, vacancies should average about 5 percent of GPI per year. Rents, tenant reimbursement, and operating expenses are expected to increase by 3 percent per year during the lease period. The operating expenses are expected to be $9.50 per square foot. The final sales price is based on the *NOI* in the sixth year of the project (the fifth year of operation) capitalized at 9.5 percent. The project will incur sales expenses of 4 percent. Spain is concerned that it may not be able to afford to pay for the land and still earn 16 percent (before taxes) on its equity (remember that the land acquisition cost must be paid from Spain's equity).

   To consider project feasibility,

   a. Estimate the construction draw schedule, interest carry, and total loan amount for improvements. Determine total project cost (including fees) less financing and the equity needed to fund improvements.

   b. Estimate cash flows from operations and eventual sale.

   c. Establish whether a positive or negative *NPV* exists by discounting equity cash inflows and outflows in (*b*).

   d. What does the *NPV* mean in this case? If the asking price of the land were $195,000, would this project be feasible?

4. **Excel.** Refer to the "Ch16 Const" tab in the Excel Workbook provided on the Web site.

   a. What is the yield to the lender and the investor's after-tax *IRR* if 90 percent of the loan must be drawn during the first four months and 10 percent during the last eight months?

   b. Repeat (*a*) assuming that 60 percent of the loan is drawn the first four months and 40 percent the last eight months.

www.mhhe.com/bf15e

17

Financing Land Development Projects

As the last chapter indicated, real estate development is a very complex process to analyze, from the standpoint of both lenders and investors. This chapter deals with **land development,** which involves the acquisition of land with the intention of constructing utilities and surface improvements, and then reselling some or all of the developed sites to project developers or, in the case of housing, home builders. As described in the previous chapter, *project development* deals with the acquisition of a specific site, and then construction of an office building, shopping center, or other property type. This chapter contains a basic description of land development and financing. However, many attributes of real estate development are common to both types of development, so to avoid redundancy we do not repeat them here. After completing both chapters, you should have a general understanding of investment financing in the development process.

In this chapter, we provide insight into the land development process and how to determine the feasibility of land development projects. We discuss how to structure development loans, how to determine terms for disbursement and repayment, and how to make profitability projections. Structuring loan agreements and repayment schedules and estimating interest carry for land development projects are detailed and complex processes.

Characterization of the Land Development Business

When generalizing about the land development process, it is useful to think of the land developer as an individual with a general development concept. Before proceeding with the development, however, there must be evidence that the project is feasible or that market acceptance of the end product (single-family houses, offices, warehouses, etc.) is highly likely. This step is important even though the land developer may or may not be the developer of the final product. In other words, in the land development phase, the developer must anticipate and understand the demand for the final product (or products in the case of a mixed use land development, e.g., which may contain sites for sale to single-family builders, apartment developers, and/or shopping center developers). Demand for the end product obviously affects the demand for individual sites, lots, or pads within the land development. Every land acquisition decision must also be based on whether the tract of unimproved land on which the plan is to be executed is of sufficient size and contains adequate amounts of usable area to accommodate the development plan. While development plans will differ based on the general development concept, all plans include the subdivision, or platting, of sites within a tract of land to be acquired.

Decisions as to how to subdivide the larger development into lot sizes and how to price individual sites are based on expected end uses envisioned as a part of the general development concept.

In residential land development, it is common to find firms specializing in the acquisition of raw land in suburban fringe areas and developing sites for single-family detached units or for multiple uses, such as combinations of single-family units, multifamily apartments, and cluster housing. Based on the market segment in which the end use will likely sell, the land developer acquires land, develops a land use and traffic circulation plan, and then constructs streets, lighting, and subsurface improvements (utilities, drainage, sewer). The developer then subdivides individual sites, and sells smaller sites to builders and project developers. The developer may also retain some retail sites for later sale if the site has suitable highway frontage.

One point that must be stressed here is that land developers and builders or project developers may, or may not, be the same entities. Land developers may or may not have the expertise to undertake building construction and/or project development. These functions differ in their respective production technologies and market risks. However, a few large firms may engage in both activities. For example, where residential sites are being developed for entry level housing in lower price ranges, the land developer may also engage in some "tract" home building. On the other hand, when land is more expensive, the land developer usually sells lots to custom home builders and engages in little, if any, home building.

In business parks and industrial development, land developers (discussed in the previous chapter) may prepare sites for sale to project developers, but they usually retain some sites for project development of their own. For example, a major single tenant may want to have a building constructed in a business park. In this case, the park developer may design and **build to suit** a structure for the tenant and enter a long-term lease arrangement. Alternatively, the developer may construct a building on a site and sell it to the tenant on a **turnkey basis.** In business and industrial park development, the land developer may also construct some building improvements on a speculative basis to attract other tenants to the park. However, these developers usually stand ready to sell sites in the park to other project developers as long as those project developers abide by required development controls. These controls usually include construction of buildings of adequate quality, maintenance, landscaping, and so on. These controls are usually specified in deed restrictions and/or provisions in an agreement governing the operation of a business park owners association.

Another observation about land development is that the industry is highly fragmented, localized, and competitive. Many land development firms usually exist in a given urban market. They enter the market for raw land by contacting landowners or land brokers and obtaining information on tracts of land available for sale. These developers then engage consultants to conduct market studies to assess the demand for end uses that would ultimately be developed and price ranges for each use. The developer then completes a preliminary land plan, estimates the land development cost, and analyzes whether the tract can be purchased and developed profitably. This process is referred to as a **feasibility study.** It should be stressed that in many cases, the developer is more of a facilitator of the development process than a firm that undertakes all necessary functions in the land development process. Thus, many functions required to complete a land development project may be done by consulting firms (land planners, civil engineers, landscape architects) and contractors (roads and utility construction companies). In these instances, the developer owns the land, obtains the necessary financing, and implements the overall development plan but may not employ a staff that is directly involved in construction or design. The developer must also interact with public sector officials in obtaining various project approvals and changes in zoning when necessary, and then must market sites to project developers and/or builders.

The Land Development Process—An Overview

Exhibit 17–1 contains a general description of activities performed at various stages in the land development process. Generally, the process begins when a land broker, who represents the owner of a tract of land available for sale, contacts a developer. At this point (stage I), the developer conducts a very preliminary investigation of the site, the condition of the market, how a tract might be developed, and at what cost. Should sufficient interest exist to pursue negotiation, the developer usually negotiates an **option agreement** with the landowner. An option usually provides that the developer has the right, but no obligation, to purchase the land for a specific price at a future date. The developer pays an option price to the landowner, which is usually applied to the purchase price of the land if the developer purchases it (exercises the option). In the event that the developer decides not to purchase the land on the expiration date, the landowner may keep the money paid for the option.

Acquisition of Land—Use of the Option Contract

The developer usually negotiates an option contract because it takes time to accomplish various tasks and activities prior to the decision to actually purchase the land. Some of these activities are shown in stage II in the exhibit. Inasmuch as the developer's final decision to purchase depends on the information obtained from the activities indicated, the decision to purchase land obviously cannot be made quickly. Consequently, the developer would prefer to negotiate an option at the lowest price possible for the longest period of time possible in order to accomplish these tasks. Further, the developer will incur costs while carrying out the research about whether land should be purchased. The developer wants assurance that the land will not be sold while these costs are being incurred. On the other hand, if the landowner wants to sell as quickly as possible, an option with a short exercise period at the highest possible price would be preferred. While the option agreement provides the developer time to conduct research, it also ties up the land or precludes the landowner from selling it until

EXHIBIT 17–1 Land Development Process

Stage I Initial Contact by Land Broker	Stage II Option Period	Stage III Development Period	Stage IV Sales Period
• Site inspection	• Soil studies, engineering	• Purchase land	• Implement marketing program
• Preliminary market study	• Feasibility, appraisal, and design strategy	• Close on land development loan • Begin construction of improvements	• Additional coordination with builder
• Preliminary cost estimates	• Bidding and/or negotiating with contractors subject to closing • Submit plan for public approvals, submit package for financing	• Implement financial controls • Coordinate with contractors, consultants, public sector	• Implement design controls with builders • Implement facility management and/or begin homeowner association

the expiration date.[1] Consequently, the landowner may give up opportunities to sell the land during the option period with no assurance that the developer may actually close the transaction. Option periods can be very short (e.g., one month for small residential land developments) or as long as three years or more (e.g., regional shopping centers).[2]

Assuming that the developer obtains an option for an acceptable period of time and cost, some important activities must be undertaken before the expiration date, when the decision to acquire the land must be made. The site must be studied to establish how much of the surface area needs excavating and grading, and at what cost. These decisions are a function of the topography, drainage characteristics, soil condition, and subsurface characteristics. The market must be studied to estimate what the demand will be for a mix of lot sizes. (An example of a preliminary feasibility study is provided in Concept Box 17.1.) The supply of sites coming into the market in competing areas must also be considered. An estimate of the project's value upon completion of development must be made to determine whether it will be profitable or whether the market value will exceed the cost of the land plus all improvements, interest carry, and marketing costs. Improvement costs must be estimated by obtaining bids from contractors, consulting engineers, and land planners. These estimates must be based on an anticipated land development plan, which usually has to undergo several iterations before it (1) complies with the overall development concept that is intended to meet market demand and (2) meets the approval of various public agencies (city departments, planning commissions, city council, etc.). Results from all of these activities must then be interpreted and used to develop a loan submission request. Without approval from a lender, who may be asked to provide a large portion of the funds necessary to acquire the land and construct improvements, the project is not likely to go forward. (To provide very basic information on land use planning and some of the terms and concepts used when dealing with public officials, we have provided Concept Box 17.2.)

One aspect of the process depicted in stage II of Exhibit 17–1 should become clear at this point. The response time of the developer to accomplish these functions is critical and usually requires the commitment of other firms to the developer's timetable. If the developer cannot obtain the necessary approvals from public officials or find a lender, he may lose the cost of the option plus all fees and costs incurred while trying to accomplish the activities in stage II. If approvals and the loan commitment are not secured by the expiration date, the developer may try to negotiate an extension of the option period with the landowner. Failing that, the developer may have to raise equity from partners to acquire the land with the expectation that approvals and/or a loan will be obtained shortly after the option period expires and

---

[1] Because all terms of sale should be included in the option contract, in many cases a contract to purchase the land may be used instead of an option agreement. The contract would be executed with a closing date that would make it equivalent to the option period. All terms, conditions, contingencies, and so on would be negotiated and included in the sale contract at the time that the contract is executed. This approach usually eliminates contractual ambiguities between the buyer and seller that could arise if they used an option.

[2] Options with assignment clauses have also been used in land speculation. In these cases, the prospective land buyer obtains an option from the landowner with little or no expectation of purchasing the land (although he may not indicate this). The owner of the option hopes to find another buyer to purchase the land at a price higher than the exercise price prior to the expiration of the option. If he can do so, he realizes a gain. If he cannot find a buyer, the speculator loses the option price. This practice has been referred to as *flipping* a contract. In some cases, developers with options that have lengthy expiration dates inadvertently realize gains. These gains occur when, after developers undertake feasibility studies, they realize that land values have risen. In this case, they may engage a land broker or try to find a buyer prior to the option expiration date, or they may negotiate an extension period on the option with the landowner. In some instances, landowners face situations in which a subsequent offer of a higher price is received after an option has been given to a developer. In this case, if the new bidder wants to close the transaction prior to the expiration date of the option, the landowner may try to repurchase the option from the developer and hope that the new buyer and the developer do not meet and negotiate directly.

I. Physical Characteristics

1. *Goal:* To provide a preliminary development plan and financial analysis to determine whether a large-scale residential lot development can be built in accordance with regulatory requirements and sold at market prices sufficiently high enough to justify construction costs and the cost of land acquisition.
2. *Site:* 20 acres (871,200 sq. ft.).
3. *Asking price:* $1,000,000.
4. *Project description:* Nonlinear, curved layout for detached, single-family homes.
   a. Maximum lot density per zoning and/or deed restriction; must *average* four lots per acre, minimum lot size in the development = 6,000 sq. ft.; no maximum limits on lot size.
   b. *Circulation requirement:* 15% of land area for road/rights of way.
   c. *Open space* and/or required donation: 10% of land area. Retention ponds for surface water run off.
   d. *Net developable area:* 75% or 653,400 sq. ft.
   e. *Proposed lot mix/yield:* 80 lots.
   f. *Square footage by lot type,* including all setbacks to building lines: Type 1, 32 standard interior @ 6,000 sq. ft. each; Type 2, 32 premium interior @ 8,000 sq. ft. each; Type 3, 6 corners @ 12,837 sq. ft. each.

II. Financial Feasibility

1. Pricing based on market study:

Standard interior: $100,000 @ 32 lots	$3,200,000
Premium interior: $120,000 @ 32 lots	3,840,000
Corner lot: $130,000 @ 16 lots	2,080,000
Total sales revenue	$ 9,120,000

2. Less: Average development cost per lot (includes all circulation— roadways, drains, sewer, utility construction to property line of each lot): $70,025 @ 80 lots — $5,602,000
3. Less: Land asking price — 1,000,000
4. Potential gross profit — 2,518,000
5. Less: Administration, legal, commissions, advertising, and so on (12.5% of gross revenue) — 1,140,000
6. Potential net profit — $ 1,378,000

7. Margin on gross revenue: $1,378,000 ÷ $9,120,000 = 15%
   Return on total cost*: $1,378,000 ÷ $7,742,000 = 18% (rounded)
8. Conclusion: Project appears to be feasible; however, return projections do not include financing, discounting for the time schedule for construction, and the estimated time/sales rate for finished lots to builders.

*Development $5,602,000 + Land $1,000,000 + Adm $1,140,000

the land is acquired. Clearly, this approach can be risky because if the land is acquired, long delays may occur before financing and necessary approvals are obtained. Market conditions and costs can also change during this time, thereby increasing the risk of development.

Financing and Development

Assuming that the land developer successfully accomplishes all activities in stage II, the purchase and financing of the land, the construction of utilities, and surface improvements must occur next in stage III. As discussed earlier, the developer generally acts as a facilitator in coordinating, controlling, and paying for the construction of land improvements as funds are acquired from a lender. When financing the land acquisition and development process,

INTRODUCTION: ZONING AND LAND USE

Many communities adopt a *land use plan* developed by the city planning staff with input from all segments of the community: residents, businesses, nonprofit institutions, and so on. The plan generally identifies where all land uses will be located. These uses generally include industrial, residential, commercial (retail, office), and public land uses (parks, public buildings). Each general land use category is then *zoned* into more specific land use classifications; for example, residential zoning is usually subdivided into single family (R-1) and multifamily (R-2) with special uses (assisted living-convalescent, etc.). Within these zoning classifications, further subdivisions are made (e.g., R-2 multifamily could allow high-rise, garden walk-up, mid-rise structures). Requirements regarding the number of stories, elevators, maximum number of apartment units to the acre, parking ratios (or the number of parking spaces per unit), underground/garage parking allowances, and so on are also included. These classifications give the land use plan a sense of design, size, density, and traffic flow, as well as specifying where individuals will reside and seek employment and business, educational, public, and health services. Similar subcategories are detailed for each general land use classification (office, retail, industrial, etc.). This general land use plan is usually updated every 5 to 10 years in consultation with the community.

IMPORTANT TERMS USED IN LAND DEVELOPMENT

In the acquisition of land for development, various "terms of art" and concepts are important and must be well understood. These terms are used by developers, public officials, construction lenders, and others to describe the type of development to be undertaken. Many of these terms are very basic and are used to consider things like how many building lots may be developed on a site after allowing for streets, utilities, setbacks, and so on. These things must be understood as they may affect value. Many combinations of development patterns may also be considered to determine the most advantageous outcome for an investor. To that end, we have assembled a very basic list of terms and definitions which are contained below.

Plat—a map depicting the location of all individual tracts or lots and streets in a development. It generally evolves from a sketch to a preliminary concept, and then to a final, or approved, plat.

Assemblage—acquisition of many individual parcels of land with an intent to consolidate into one, single development tract.

Density—refers to the number of individual developable sites/lots proposed for development from a tract of land after allowing for desired lot sizes, setbacks, circulation requirements, and wetland-conservation areas/easements (if applicable).

Yield—usually refers to the area corresponding to square footage included in the number of lots expected to be developed as a percentage of the total square footage in a tract of land.

Grid and rectangular residential development—usually the most cost-effective method of land development, where streets, right of ways, and so on are laid out evenly in straight lines or in a grid pattern. Surface and infrastructure costs are usually lower than the cost for curvilinear development. However, traffic flow from a grid pattern is considered less safe and not as aesthetically pleasing as a curvilinear pattern.

Cluster development—allows for unbalanced lot development within a tract of land as long as a sufficient amount of green areas or open areas are provided. When developed, the *average density* per acre for all sites developed in the entire project must meet zoning requirements.

Circulation construction requirements—street widths, curb-cuts-turning radius, ingress and egress, load/stress specifications, and so on, as specified by jurisdictions in which the land is located. These requirements are necessary to accommodate general traffic flows and access by fire and emergency vehicles, and so on. Construction specifications must be met before dedication of streets, rights of way, and so on (transfer of maintenance, etc., from the developer to the public sector) takes place.

Dedication—transfer of ownership of right of ways, streets, parks, and so on, in land developments from private developers to public entities. At this point, maintenance of drainage, sewer, roads, and so on is the responsibility of the city. Property taxes from the new development are collected for these services.

Exclusionary zoning—ordinances adopted by jurisdictions resulting in certain structures/activities being *explicitly* excluded from an area or land development. Examples: exclusions of mobile homes from single-family residential areas. In some cases, exclusionary zoning may be illegal. For example, if minimum lot sizes are required and are deemed to be so unreasonably large so as to exclude low-income or minority families, this type of zoning may violate discrimination laws and be deemed *implicitly* biased and exclusionary.

Inclusionary zoning—requirement for "set aside space" to be used for low-income housing, retail use, public use, and so on as a condition for obtaining zoning approval for a large project.

Adverse impact—permit denied because of a negative influence emanating from the proposed site development. This could include inadequate drainage or sewage which would affect other properties.

Buildable area—amount of land remaining on a given tract of land after all zoning requirements, slopes, wetlands, and so on are subtracted from the gross land area, leaving the area upon which structures can be built.

---

a number of structures may be available to the developer; however, we will discuss only three of the more common alternatives here.

1. The developer may purchase the land for cash. The developer may then obtain a loan for the cost of improvements and interest carry.

2. The developer may purchase the land by making a down payment only. The seller finances all or a portion of the land sale by taking back a purchase-money mortgage from the developer. The developer then acquires a loan for improvements only. The seller of land (mortgagee) agrees to subordinate the lien represented by the purchase-money mortgage to the development loan, and the developer repays the seller's mortgage from funds as parcels are sold and after payments on the development loan are made.

3. The developer purchases the land by making a down payment and obtaining one loan based on a percentage of the appraised value of land plus improvements. The funds pay off the seller and construction improvements.

The extent to which developers use each of these techniques depends on conditions in the market for land and the price paid for the land. If the demand for developable land is strong, sellers may demand cash and may not be willing to sell "on terms" or take back purchase-money mortgages. However, during such times, lenders are generally more willing to provide funds for improvements and a part of the land acquisition price. During periods when demand is not as strong, sellers of land are more willing to finance a portion of the sale price; however, lenders are usually more cautious as uncertainty becomes more prevalent in the marketplace.[3]

Regardless of the financing technique used to acquire the land, lenders usually make loans for land improvements that allow developers to "draw down" funds in stages, usually

---

[3] It is difficult to generalize how much a lender is willing to provide to a land developer. If the developer does not own the land and is in the process of acquiring it for development, and if the lender is satisfied that the value of the land will not decline, the lender may be willing to make a land acquisition and development loan. Further, if the developer has considerable personal net worth and is personally liable on the loan, the lender may be more willing to advance a portion of the funds to acquire the land in view of the additional security behind the loan.

monthly, based on the percentage of development work completed and verified by the lender. The developer uses an open-end mortgage as security for the loan. Such loans are usually made on a floating rate basis. That is, the lender usually makes the loan at 2 percent or 3 percent above the prime lending rate. Hence, the developer bears the risk of an interest rate change during the development period. As previously indicated, the lender providing the funds for improvements will insist on obtaining first lien on the land being developed and first lien on all improvements as they are completed and as funds are disbursed.

Repayment of land development loans ultimately depends on the sale of the subdivided sites to builders or other developers. Because repayments depend on lot sales and lenders view such loans as very risky, they must accurately assess the risk of projects and the rate at which parcels will be sold in order to determine whether such loans can be repaid. Lenders closely analyze financial statements, appraisal reports, and market studies. In addition, as a development progresses, monthly inspections must be made to verify all work done before a draw can be made against a loan commitment.

As previously indicated, as the developer eventually obtains funds from the sale of individual parcels, a portion of the proceeds from each parcel sale must be used to repay loans used to make improvements and/or acquire the land. Developers and lenders usually negotiate amounts to be paid for each type of developed site in a project, which is referred to as a **release schedule.** When a developer sells a parcel and repays a lender or lenders, the developer obtains a release statement in which lenders waive all liens on the parcel to be sold. Clear title may then pass from the developer to the buyer of the parcel. Lenders use these release provisions as a control on development loans to ensure that repayment will occur as parcels are sold. Developers must also deal with risks of cost overruns, changes in market demand, and supply conditions that cause delays and increases in carrying costs (interest on loans, taxes, etc.) during this phase.

In stage IV, the final stage, promotion, marketing, and sales to builders or project developers occur. Generally, the developer will have designed a marketing program utilizing various media (newspapers, trade publications, etc.) to advertise the development to the builders and developers that are constructing improvements based on the nature of the land being developed (homesites, office parks, etc.).

Lender Requirements in Financing Land Development

While the focus of this chapter is on financial analysis and the feasibility of land development projects, some understanding of the financing process and interaction between lender and borrower is essential. A general understanding of the documentation requirements associated with the development process will also help the reader understand the nature of the liability and performance requirements created when projects are financed and developed. Exhibit 17–2 contains a general list consisting of (A) typical requirements for a land development loan submission to the lender, (B) requirements for closing the loan if the submission is approved, and (C) the final commitment and attendant terms of financing after closing. Be aware that this is a very general list of requirements and that each land development will have unique requirements of its own. Also, during the process of trying to finance a project and close a loan, the lender will raise other questions and require additional documentation and verification that the developer will have to supply during the application period. (Some of the material in Exhibit 17–2 is relevant to the land component of project development covered in Chapter 16. It was not included in Exhibit 16–2 to avoid redundancy.)

Much of the required information listed in Exhibit 17–2 deals with (1) the capacity of third parties (such as contractors and architects) to perform, (2) verification by public sector officials that the use and density of the proposed development conforms with both

Exhibit 17–2
General Loan
Submission and
Closing
Requirements—Land
Development and
Closing

A. General requirements for *loan submission* package—land development
  1. Project information
      a. Project description: all details for land use plan, aerials, soil reports, platting, circulation, amenities, renderings, environmental impact statement
      b. Survey and legal description of site showing property lines, easements, utility lines
      c. Preliminary plan for improvements and specifications
      d. Project cost breakdown
      e. Identification of architect, land planner, and general contractor with bank references and/or supporting data indicating their ability to complete the project if approved
  2. Market financial data
      a. Requested loan terms: amount, rate, maturity period, proposed release schedule (to be dealt with later in chapter)
      b. Financial statements of borrowers (including bank references) and development background
      c. Feasibility study, including market comparables, appraisals, pro forma operating statement (which will be dealt with later in chapter), schedule of estimated selling prices
      d. Projected loan closing date
  3. Government and regulatory information
      a. Statement of zoning status: current zoning status and disclosure of any zoning changes required before undertaking development
      b. Ad valorem taxes: any impending change in the method of levy, any pending reappraisal, and the current status of payment
  4. Legal documentation
      a. Legal documents, including corporate charters, partnership agreements (there should be no ambiguity as to the entity requesting the loan and where liability will rest)
      b. Statement of land cost and proof of ownership (deed) or impending ownership, as evidenced by an option or purchase agreement
      c. Detailed description of any deed restrictions or restrictive covenants regarding land use
      d. Subordination agreements: in the event of seller financing or debt financing used or to be used to acquire the land, evidence that such parties are willing to subordinate their liens to that of the development lender; if the land mortgages are to be repaid from advances from the development loan being requested, the exact amount should be stipulated, and the nature of any releases being obtained should be disclosed
B. General requirements for *loan closing*—land development
  1. Project information: land site plan containing platting, renderings, circulation, utility lines, landscaping, and so on.
  2. Market and financial data: statement that borrowers have had no adverse impact in financial condition since the initial loan submission
  3. Government and regulatory information
      a. Copies of all permits from all relevant agencies and jurisdictions; includes building permits, approved zoning variances needed, health, water, sewer, environmental impact statement, and so on.
      b. Availability of utilities: letters from appropriate municipal or county departments indicating extent of utilities available to the site. Any off-site utility extensions must be detailed and the extension cost disclosed
  4. Legal documentation
      a. Detail on contracts to be let with general contractor and all subcontractors, including size of contracts
      b. Evidence of contractor performance and payment bond

**Exhibit 17–2
(Continued)**

>   *c.* Agreement from general contractor, architect, and land planner to perform for the lender in the event of developer default
>   *d.* Evidence of all casualty, hazard, and other insurance policies naming the lender as loss payee
>   *e.* Evidence of all liability and workman's compensation coverage needed by the developer
>   *f.* Title insurance binder
> C. Final commitment and agreements
>   1. Loan commitment and terms: requirements for lender approval of draws, methods of calculating holdback requirements, prepayment options, and any extension agreement
>   2. Note and mortgage or deed of trust evidencing debt and lien status of lender
>   3. Borrower's personal guarantee for repayment of loan
>   4. Conditional assignment agreement covering all contracts made with architects, planners, and the general contractor to be assigned to the interim lender in the event of borrower default

appropriate zoning ordinances and the capacity of utilities on the site (the lender cannot rely on the developer to provide such information; the municipality or county must give an unambiguous statement on these issues because officials will have to provide permits to allow development to commence), and (3) verification that third parties are committed to bear unforeseen risks such as are indicated by the items listed in part 4 in category B. If the developer was unable to obtain any of these verifications, it would obviously be a signal to the lender that more factual information is necessary to support the loan application.

Detailed Cost Breakdowns

The developer usually must submit detailed cost estimates and plans for constructing the improvements. The lender generally verifies the cost breakdown for accuracy in accordance with construction plans and specifications. The lender will usually require verification of all costs on a monthly basis as development work progresses and as the lender disburses funds.

General Contracts and Subcontracts

Normally, lenders prefer that developers obtain fixed-price contracts from subcontractors. The lender may require these contracts as a means of protecting against cost overruns that may occur if material or labor prices rise during development.

Labor and Material Payment Bonds and Completion Bonds

Many lenders require that contractors purchase labor and material payment bonds and **completion bonds.** The first type of bond assures the lender that any unpaid bills for labor and material will be paid by the bonding company should a contractor default. The completion bond assures the lender that the bonding company will provide funds needed to complete the development in the event that a contractor defaults during construction.

Title Insurance

As a condition for obtaining a land development loan, the developer generally must purchase title insurance. Such insurance assures the lender that no liens superior to its lien exist on the property when construction commences.

Holdbacks

As we discussed in the previous chapter dealing with project development, land development loans may also provide for a **holdback** of a proportion of each disbursement payable to a developer. This occurs when the developer and/or a general contractor engage a number of subcontractors and hold back a portion of the funds due under subcontracts. The developer holds back these funds to be sure that subcontractors perform all work completely before receiving final payment. Consequently, the lender holds back from the developer so that no excess funds are made available to the developer during the period the developer is holding back from subcontractors.

Extension Agreements

Because it is possible that the loan will not be paid on time due to development problems or the slow sale of parcels, the lender usually requires an **extension agreement** clause in the initial loan contract. This clause specifies that an additional charge will be made for any extra time needed to repay the loan. This arrangement amounts to gap financing or additional interim financing, and the lender usually charges an extension fee in addition to interest on the outstanding loan balance if an extension is needed. In fact, these amounts may never be collectible. Indeed, if the project encounters extreme difficulty, the lender may have to foreclose and assume ownership of the development.

Residential Land Development Illustrated

To illustrate one of the many land development scenarios that are possible, we have chosen a medium-size residential land development project. However, many of the same *general* concepts and the framework for analysis apply to business/office parks and industrial/warehouse/distribution centers. Our illustration is based on the 50-acre Grayson tract, the availability of which has been brought to the attention of Landco Development Company by a land broker. Based on the combination of the description of the tract provided by the broker, Landco's knowledge of the area, and information obtained from the owner of the tract, a summary of important facts is provided in Exhibit 17–3.

Information in Exhibit 17–3 indicates that the tract is farmland at the fringe of suburban development 15 miles north of the central business district (CBD) with good proximity to highways. The present owner has recently had the property rezoned to allow for the development of single-family detached units. Most of the surface area may be developed; however, five acres consist of creek and floodplain. Current zoning provides for an *average* maximum development density of one single-family detached unit per 7,500 square feet of developable surface space (gross land area, less floodplain area, less circulation such as roads, alleys, etc). The terrain appears to present little, if any, problem to constructing

EXHIBIT 17–3
Data on Grayson Tract

Size of tract	50 acres
Asking price	$40,000 per acre, for a total of $2,000,000
Option	30-day "free look," $20,000 for next five months
Current zoning	Single-family detached, with a maximum average development density of 1 unit per 7,500 sq. ft. of developable area
Legal status	No deed restrictions or easements are currently indicated; no encumbrances exist
Site characteristics	Creek and floodplain comprise five acres of surface area. Terrain is gently rolling and moderately treed. A creek flows through the northeast quadrant, and the floodplain is contained within a channel to the edge of a steep embankment. The soil is stable with normal percolation.
Utilities	Water, sewer, electricity, and gas, all with adequate capacity, are extended to the site
Proximity	1,500 feet of highway frontage (state highway 66), 1 mile west of U.S. Interstate 166, 15 miles north of central business district (CBD)
Current use	Farmland in suburban fringe area

land improvements. The broker has indicated that the owner is willing to entertain an offer to sell the property for $2 million and will give the developer an option to purchase it for 30 days at no cost. At the end of such time, the developer may acquire another option for an additional five months at 1 percent of the price of the land, or $20,000. Should the purchaser exercise the option to purchase the land, credit for the option price would be applied toward the purchase of the land.[4]

Inasmuch as the owner is allowing a 30-day "free look" at the property, Landco has decided to expend effort to determine if the project is feasible and whether the $2 million asking price is justified. To accomplish this, Landco must complete a preliminary development plan and conduct a market study to assess the demand for residential sites and the competitive supply conditions, both currently and in the near future. If results from the land plan and market study appear positive, information will be compiled to apply for a loan commitment and public approvals.

Market Conditions and Site Plan

As previously indicated, this illustration is intended to focus on approaches that can be used to evaluate the economic feasibility of residential land development. Estimates used to make projections for such developments are heavily based on market and cost information. While we do not provide the reader with an in-depth discussion of how to conduct market studies and how to make cost estimates, we do not mean to imply that these are minor considerations when one is deciding whether to enter into a land development project. Indeed, these studies are extremely important, and you should consult other sources of information for additional insights into this process.[5]

Exhibit 17–4 provides a brief summary of important facts that should be the objective of market and engineering studies. These studies should be carried out during the option period, before acquiring the land and applying for financing. In addition to gauging how strong builder demand for lots is before committing to purchase the land, the developer must have a clear vision of the proposed development and how it will be viewed by buyers who have the choice of acquiring homes in competing developments.

Essentially, Landco's plan is to develop cluster-type housing sites and standard and oversized creek lots. The project will also include community facilities (pool, tennis courts). Five acres of the tract are not developable because they lie in a floodplain, and to the extent that competing land development projects do not have this loss in developable land, Landco may be at a competitive disadvantage unless (1) the loss of acreage is reflected in a lower acquisition price for the tract (holding all else equal) or (2) Landco can develop the creek area into a positive, complementary feature. If lots can be developed contiguous to the creek, they may command a premium price. This may fully or partially offset the loss of developable space in the floodplain. In any event, the developer must carefully consider how much of the land is developable relative to comparable sites and their respective prices when deciding whether the development is economically feasible. In Landco's case, the issue is whether the asking price for the Grayson land ($2 million) plus development costs will be too high relative to the market value of competing homesites.

One aspect of the site plan that must be considered when investing in and financing land development is the percent of land available for lot development. For example, gross acreage in our case is 50 acres. However, the amount of land actually available for development

---

[4] In many cases, the buyer may be able to use a letter of credit in lieu of a cash option payment to the seller. This approach, if acceptable to the seller, is usually a lower-cost alternative to the buyer, who may have a more profitable use for the funds during the option period.

[5] For an illustration, see John M. Clapp, *Handbook for Real Estate Market Analysis* (Englewood Cliffs, NJ: Prentice Hall, 1987).

EXHIBIT 17–4
Summary of
Market Data and
Development
Strategy: Grayson
Project

A. Market conditions	Based on a survey of three land developments under way in the area, absorption of building sites appears to be excellent. Builder surveys indicate a strong desire to purchase sites for future development. Average lot sizes in competing developments are approximately 8,700 sq. ft.
B. Lot mix and development plan	Landco plans to utilize the creek area to enhance the development by configuring the circulation pattern to accommodate larger lot sizes on both sides of the creek. The lots for cluster-type housing units would be placed adjacent to the highway frontage as a buffer. These would be complemented with heavy landscaping. Cul-de-sacs would be utilized where possible in the interior of the development. Lot sizes would range from 5,000 to 20,000 sq. ft. within the development, with the average lot size being 8,712 sq. ft.
C. Deed restrictions	Private deed restrictions would be used to ensure that detached housing units with a minimum of 2,000 sq. ft. would be constructed on each lot. Restrictions regarding setbacks, external finish materials (percent of brick and wood, roof composition), landscaping, fencing, and future additions to structures would continue to apply after completion of the development to ensure neighborhood quality.
D. Developable area	50 acres less 5 acres of creek and floodplain, less an additional 20 percent for circulation (alleys, streets, amenities, etc.), or 36 net acres. Lot yield should be 3.6 units per gross surface acre. Setbacks, lot lines, street and alley widths, and utility easements easily meet all city regulatory requirements.
E. Amenities	Clubhouse, two swimming pools, eight lighted tennis courts. A homeowners association will assume management upon completion and sell-out of development.
F. Construction of land improvements	Paving streets, curbing, water mains, hydrants, sewer, and all connections to be constructed in accordance with current city and county standards.
G. Development restrictions	Zoning allows an average of 1 unit per 7,500 sq. ft. of net developable area as the maximum density of development.

is equal to gross land area, less floodplain area, less circulation requirements. In our example, this would be $[(50 - 5) \times (1 - .20)] \div 50 = 72\%$, or 36 net acres of the total 50-acre tract. The lot yield in this case could be 180 lots ÷ 50 or 3.6 lots to the acre. This also means that an average of 8,712 square feet of developable land would be available per developed lot (36 acres × 43,560 sq. ft. per acre ÷ 180 lots).

The value in knowing these relationships lies in conducting comparative analysis with competing developments. Large differences in developable land and lot yields may indicate that a development would contain a housing pattern with relatively low density or that the site has soil, terrain, or other characteristics that make a significant part of it unusable. These ratios also give us a basis to compare the *density* of housing that will be built with competing projects. For example, if Landco's estimated gross and net lot yield are greater or less than lot yields in competing developments, Landco may be over- or underdeveloping the tract relative to competing developments. A more careful analysis of market data and a competitive analysis should reveal why this is the case.

For example, if a developer overpays for a site relative to the competition, she must attempt to recapture the higher land cost with more density (higher net lot yield). However, this strategy may not be successful because it depends on the price that builders (and eventually home buyers) are willing to pay for higher-density housing or smaller sites. Do not assume that developers always try to maximize net lot yield per acre. This approach may appear to be a more "efficient" utilization of land and provide the developer with more lots to sell, but market demand may prove that home buyers prefer larger lot sizes, wider streets and alleys (circulation), and a lower development density. Although this lower density may only be provided at higher prices, if household incomes and preferences will support the pattern, it would be a mistake to proceed with higher densities. On the other hand, if this tract were closer to the central business district, higher density might be acceptable to households that have preferences for smaller lot sizes with closer proximity to the city center. Hence, lot yield calculations should only be used as a tool to investigate why *deviations* from yields in comparable developments exist. Using them should provide a better understanding of the market segment that developers are appealing to. No absolute maximum or minimum rules apply.

Public agencies also use lot yield per acre to determine if the development adheres to zoning restrictions. As shown in Exhibit 17–4, we see that zoning provides that an *average* of one lot per 7,500 square feet of developable area is the maximum density allowed in this project. Landco projects that an *average* of 8,712 square feet per unit will be the maximum *average* density, which easily meets zoning restrictions. Notice that developers do not always design to the maximum density allowed by zoning regulations. In all cases, *market demand* and household preferences dictate what densities should be developed. As previously indicated, home buyers may prefer to pay higher prices for lower densities and corresponding increases in privacy (larger lots) and reductions in traffic and congestion. In this event, developers may take excessive risks if they attempt to increase densities, even if current zoning allows them to do so, and lower average lot prices for buyers could result.

To consider some of the market conditions Landco faces, refer to the competitive market analysis summary provided in Exhibit 17–5. For example, note that relative to Grayson, project A has about the same net development density, but it has no amenities or creek sites and it has a slightly lower average asking price per standard lot. Project B is larger in scale than Grayson, has much lower net density, larger average lot sizes, a slightly greater circulation requirement (because of hilly terrain), a slightly better amenity package, and bluff sites as a special feature. Its sites are priced higher in each category. Development C is largest in scale and has no special topographic features. It has a higher development density and more amenities than the Grayson project. Landco believes, based on this competitive analysis, that its price structure is justified (all other important characteristics, such as access to schools, shopping, churches, and so on, are thought to be equal).

From the above considerations, it should be apparent that estimating market demand and pricing the end product are very important. In cases where competing projects are very similar, pricing must be similar because the package of attributes being provided by each is the same. On the other hand, the more dissimilar projects are, the more variation in pricing is likely. In these cases, pricing must be based on the desirability of the relative attributes of each development. In these instances, pricing risk will be greater. Based on the estimated market prices for these lots, a preliminary estimate of the market value for the Grayson tract, *assuming all lots were completely developed and sold immediately,* would be $6,840,000.

Estimating Development Cost and Interest Carry

Landco has retained Robert Whole and Associates, an engineering firm, to estimate direct development costs based on the anticipated land plan Landco has presented.

EXHIBIT 17–5
Competitive Market Analysis Survey: Grayson Project

	Grayson	A	B	C
Gross acres	50	40	70	100
Number of lots	180	160	210	420
Density:				
Percent developable	72%	80%	75%	80%
Lot yield	3.6	4.0	3.0	4.2
Range in sq. ft./lot	5–20,000	5–10,000	5–25,000	5–22,000
Average sq. ft./lot	8,712	8,712	10,890	8,300
Circulation requirements	20%	20%	25%	20%
Amenities:				
Pools/cabanas	2	N/A	2	2
Tennis courts	8	N/A	10	12
Exercise rooms	N/A	N/A	1	2
Clubhouse	N/A	N/A	N/A	1
Other features	Creek sites	—	Bluff sites	—
Prices:				
Cluster	$19,000	N/A	$36,000	$19,000
Standard	45,600	40,000	48,000	40,000
Creek/bluff	47,500	N/A	60,000	N/A

	Number of Parcels	Price	Total	Total (%)
Cluster	54	$ 19,000	$ 1,026,000	15.0
Standard	90	45,600	4,104,000	60.0
Creek	36	47,500	1,710,000	25.0
Gross project value/Grayson tract			$6,840,000	100.0%

Construction period:	6 months
Approval period:	6 months
Likely financing terms:	$1,000,000 of the land acquisition cost, 100 percent of the improvement cost (subject to appraisal and feasibility analysis). Loan draws are to be made as improvements are completed, interest is to be paid monthly.
Interest rate:	12 percent, or prime rate of 10 percent plus 2 percent with 3 points to be paid at loan closing.

Exhibit 17–6 provides cost estimates. These costs are broken down into (A) land acquisition and development costs (hard and soft) and (B) operating expenses.

Land Acquisition and Development Costs

Many direct costs—and **acquisition and development costs**—must be evaluated when acquiring a site for land development. Site acquisition is only one part of these costs. A developer must also evaluate the hard costs, which include site preparation and utilities installation, and the soft costs, which include site engineering, public approval fees, construction interest, and loan fees. Not all soft costs will be financed by the lender; however, to the extent that Landco is able to borrow the land acquisition and development costs, interest carry will become a significant cost of the Grayson project, as it will take several years to complete.

Operating Expenses

Other items included in Exhibit 17–6 are expenses that the developer will incur for marketing, taxes, legal, and other outlays when the project is developed and parcels are ready for sale.

EXHIBIT 17–6
Grayson Project Cost Estimates

A. Land and development costs:		
Site acquisition and closing costs:		
50 acres @ $48,000 each		$ 2,400,000
Development costs:		
Hard costs:		
Grading/clearing	$ 390,000	
Paving	540,000	
Storm sewers	70,000	
Sanitary sewers	125,000	
Water	125,000	
Electricity	120,000	
Landscaping	90,000	
Other (signage, etc.)	90,000	
Amenities (pool, cabana, tennis)	390,000	
Subtotal—Hard costs		$ 1,940,000
Soft costs:		
Engineering	$ 110,000	
Direct overhead—Landco	80,000	
Public approvals, tap fees, etc.	90,000	
Miscellaneous direct costs	80,000	
Legal and accounting fees	100,000	
Contingencies	240,000	
Construction interest	451,052	
Construction loan fees (3%)	122,732	
Subtotal—Soft costs		$ 1,273,783
Total land, hard, and soft costs		$ 5,613,783
B. Other development expenses:		
Selling commissions (5%)	$ 342,000	
Property taxes	87,500	
General and administrative	210,000	
Marketing costs	100,000	
Total operating expenses		$ 739,500
Total project cost		$ 6,353,283

Landco Development Company has approached Mid City Savings Association regarding its 50-acre Grayson tract. Mid City has reviewed the project and believes it to be viable. It has agreed to finance $1 million of the land acquisition cost, all hard costs, $700,000 of soft costs, plus the interest carry on the project. The interest rate will be tied to the prime rate plus 2 percent. For the Grayson project, the interest rate will be 12 percent on the outstanding monthly loan balance. Landco also believes that the interest rate should remain the same during the development period.[6] As in the project development we discussed in the preceding chapter, financing interest carry as a part of a land development loan is very common, even though the developer will earn no income until much of the development is complete and lots are sold to builders. As long as the lender is convinced that the value added to the site from development exceeds the cost of the site plus the cost of improvements by more than the interest cost that will be incurred on the development loan, then making a loan that includes interest carry is feasible.

[6] The interest rate risk may be reduced by using interest rate swaps.

Draws and Revenue Estimates

Estimating the amount of interest carry is somewhat complicated because (1) the loan will be taken down in "**draws**," or stages, and interest will be calculated only as funds are drawn down; (2) the revenue from the sale of each type of site varies; (3) the rate of repayment of the loan depends on when parcels are actually sold; and (4) as indicated earlier, the interest rate is usually tied to a floating rate and, hence, is subject to change. Exhibits 17–7, 17–8, and 17–9 show the procedures used to estimate interest carry. Exhibit 17–7A contains a breakdown of the *loan request,* and Exhibit 17–7B contains a schedule of dollar draws and draw rates for direct development costs envisioned by Landco. Recall that Exhibit 17–5 shows that although the cluster lots represent 30 percent of the sites to be developed, they will produce only 15 percent of total revenue. Cluster lots produce less revenue because the individual sites are smaller; hence, the average cost of improving those sites is lower (not shown). Standard-size sites, which make up the majority of total sites, represent 50 percent of sites and will produce 60 percent of total revenue, whereas the creek sites represent only 20 percent of the sites but will produce 25 percent of total revenue. The latter sites are larger and require more than the average cost to develop.

EXHIBIT 17–7A
Estimate of Costs to be Funded by Loan Proceeds

Land costs financed		$1,000,000
Total hard development costs		1,940,000
Soft construction costs financed:		
Engineering	$110,000	
Direct overhead—Landco	80,000	
Public approvals, tap fees, etc.	90,000	
Miscellaneous direct costs	80,000	
Legal and accounting fees	100,000	
Contingencies	240,000	
Total soft construction costs		700,000
Total direct costs that will be financed		$3,640,000
Estimated interest carry (calculated in Exhibit 17–12)		448,109
Total loan amount		$4,088,109
Equity required:		
Total project cost		$6,353,283
− Total loan amount		4,088,109
Equity		$2,265,174

EXHIBIT 17–7B
Schedule of Estimated Monthly Cash Draws for Development Costs

Month	Amount	Rate (percent)
Closing*	$ 1,019,200	28.00%
1	655,200	18.00
2	655,200	18.00
3	655,200	18.00
4	218,400	6.00
5	218,400	6.00
6	218,400	6.00
Total	$3,640,000	100.00%

*$1,000,000 of land costs, plus an additional draw of $19,200 for direct costs incurred by Landco, to be funded at closing (28% of $3,640,000 = $1,019,200).

EXHIBIT 17−7C   Estimated Monthly Absorption Rate after Loan Closing

Month	Cluster*	Standard⁺	Creek§	Cumulative Unit Sales	Cumulative Sales Volume	Monthly Sales Revenue	Monthly Revenue Rate (Percent of Total)
Close	0	0	0	0	$ 0	$ 0	0.000000%
1–3	0	0	0	0	0	0	0.000000
4–6	2	2	0	12	387,600	129,200	1.888889
7–12	4	3	1	60	1,949,400	260,300	3.805556
13–18	3	6	3	132	4,788,000	473,100	6.916667
19–24	1	5	2	180	6,840,000	$342,000	5.000000
Total	54	90	36	180	$6,840,000	–	100.000000%

*Price per lot = $19,000.
⁺Price per lot = $45,600.
§Price per lot = $47,500.

EXHIBIT 17−8
Summary of Monthly Construction Draws and Sales Revenue

(a) Month	(b) Construction Draw	(c) Sales Revenue (Lot Sales)
Close	$1,019,200	0
1	655,200	0
2	655,200	0
3	655,200	0
4	218,400	$ 129,200
5	218,400	129,200
6	218,400	129,200
7		260,300
8		260,300
9		260,300
10		260,300
11		260,300
12		260,300
13		473,100
14		473,100
15		473,100
16		473,100
17		473,100
18		473,100
19		342,000
20		342,000
21		342,000
22		342,000
23		342,000
24		342,000
Total	$3,640,000	$6,840,000
Present value @ 12%	$3,569,554	$5,880,209

It might be inferred from this allocation that the project may be more profitable if more standard and creek sites were developed, which would also lower the total density of the development. However, market demand may not be high enough to sell more of these sites. The point is that the *relative demand* for each type of homesite is important in determining

EXHIBIT 17–9 **Loan Repayment Schedule Assuming Loan Payments Proportional with Lot Sales**

	Draws			Payments			
Month	(a) Construction Draw	(b) Interest	(c) Total Draw	(d) Payments Principal	(e) Interest	(f) Total Payments	(g) Ending Balance
Close 0	$ 1,019,200	$ 0	$ 1,019,200	$ 0	$ 0	$ 0	$ 1,019,200
1	655,200	10,192	665,392	0	10,192	10,192	1,684,592
2	655,200	16,846	672,046	0	16,846	16,846	2,356,638
3	655,200	23,566	678,766	0	23,566	23,566	3,035,404
4	218,400	30,354	248,754	78,430	30,354	108,784	3,205,728
5	218,400	32,057	250,457	78,430	32,057	110,488	3,377,755
6	218,400	33,778	252,178	78,430	33,778	112,208	3,551,502
7	0	35,515	35,515	158,014	35,515	193,529	3,429,003
8	0	34,290	34,290	158,014	34,290	192,304	3,305,279
9	0	33,053	33,053	158,014	33,053	191,067	3,180,318
10	0	31,803	31,803	158,014	31,803	189,817	3,054,108
11	0	30,541	30,541	158,014	30,541	188,555	2,926,635
12	0	29,266	29,266	158,014	29,266	187,280	2,797,887
13	0	27,979	27,979	287,193	27,979	315,172	2,538,673
14	0	25,387	25,387	287,193	25,387	312,580	2,276,866
15	0	22,769	22,769	287,193	22,769	309,962	2,012,442
16	0	20,124	20,124	287,193	20,124	307,318	1,745,373
17	0	17,454	17,454	287,193	17,454	304,647	1,475,633
18	0	14,756	14,756	287,193	14,756	301,950	1,203,196
19	0	12,032	12,032	207,610	12,032	219,642	1,007,619
20	0	10,076	10,076	207,610	10,076	217,686	810,085
21	0	8,101	8,101	207,610	8,101	215,710	610,577
22	0	6,106	6,106	207,610	6,106	213,715	409,073
23	0	4,091	4,091	207,610	4,091	211,700	205,554
24	0	2,056	2,056	207,610	2,056	209,665	$ 0
Totals	$ 3,640,000	$512,191	$ 4,152,191	$4,152,191	$512,191	$4,664,383	

the configuration of sites and prices that will maximize project value. For example, creek sites also will be most expensive to develop and consequently are priced highest. Cluster sites may be the only type of site amenable to the terrain on which the development of improvements must be constructed. In other words, the mix of all sites may be necessary to maintain an acceptable level of total development density, to utilize the sites along the creek, and to maximize the total project value.

Sales and Repayment Rates

Exhibit 17–7C provides an estimated schedule of how sales of the three categories of lots will occur and how funds will be drawn down for direct development costs for the Grayson project. Landco makes its sales estimates based on information obtained from market studies of competing projects and its own recent experience with similar projects. This sales estimate is necessary because the lender is to be repaid from revenue as lot sales occur. Exhibit 17–7C shows the revenue produced from the sale of each type of lot and the number of lots to be sold per month. These monthly revenue rates are important because as a parcel is sold, the lender will receive a partial repayment of the loan that corresponds to the revenue produced from each sale.

Exhibit 17–8 shows a summary of the monthly construction draws and monthly sales revenue, including the total and present value of the monthly amounts for each. We can use this information to calculate the percentage of each lot sale that needs to be paid to the lender so that the loan is repaid when the last lot is sold. (Later, we will discuss accelerating the payment schedule so that the loan is repaid before the last lot is sold.) In essence, what lenders will generally do is *match* the loan repayment with the revenue produced from each parcel sale. Then, as parcels are sold, the lender *releases* the lien held on that parcel as a part of the loan security, thus clearing the way for the developer to sell to a builder. The amount that the borrower pays the lender to obtain this release is referred to as the **release price.**

You might recall from early chapters of this book that the amount that the borrower receives on a loan (initial loan amount) is equal to the present value of the future payments, discounted at the interest rate on the loan. We can generalize this to say that the present value of the amounts the borrower receives over time (e.g., loan draws) must be equal to the present value of the future payments. In Exhibit 17–8, the two present values in the exhibit are not equal because the sales revenue includes both the amount necessary to repay the loan plus the amount that the developer will get to keep to cover his expenses and provide a return on equity invested. Therefore, if we take the ratio of the present value of the loan draws to the present value of the sales revenue, we get the percent of each dollar of lot sales revenue that needs to be used to repay the loan. Using the present values in the exhibit,

$$\% \text{ of revenue to lender} = \$3,569,554/\$5,880,209 = 60.7045\%$$

This means that whenever a lot is sold, the lender must receive 60.7045 percent of the sales revenue if the loan is to be repaid *exactly when the last lot is sold.* This can be used to determine the amount that must be repaid for each type of lot as follows:

Lot Type	Sale Price	% to Lender	Release Price
Cluster	$ 19,000	.607045	$ 11,534
Standard	45,600	.607045	27,681
Creek	47,500	.607045	28,835

The lender would normally contract for a fixed dollar amount rather than a percent of revenue to be repaid from each lot sale. This is because the lender does not want to be concerned about whether the developer will decide to cut the price on a lot at a later point in time in order to make a sale. More important, the lender will not want to wait until the last lot is sold to have the loan completely repaid. The lender does not want to incur the risk that a slowdown in lot sales or difficulty selling some of the lots will significantly delay loan repayment. Thus, the actual release price negotiated with the lender will normally be higher than the release prices shown above. Before we consider this, however, we will demonstrate that the release price above does repay the loan by the time the last lot is sold.

Exhibit 17–9 shows a loan repayment schedule based on the release prices calculated above. Note that, during months 1 through 3, the interest draw pattern in column (b) is based on the interest rate (12%) divided by 12 months, or 1 percent of the previous month's ending loan balance. Also, note that because the interest carry is *borrowed,* it is accumulated in the loan balance.[7] The ending monthly loan balance continues to increase until enough parcels are sold each month to provide a paydown of principal in excess of interest

---

[7] This is analogous to a negative amortization loan.

draws (month 7). However, monthly interest payments continue to be based on the preceding month's loan balance.[8]

Principal payments in Exhibit 17–9 are based on the projected lot sales and release prices calculated above. For example, in month 4, two cluster lots were sold for $11,534 and two standard lots sold for $27,681 for a total of $78,430. Note that the ending balance is exactly zero in month 24. This proves that the loan is repaid when the last lot is sold.

Release Schedule

Regarding the expected period that the loan will be outstanding, most lenders insist that the loan be repaid *prior* to the time expected for the borrower to sell all the parcels in the development. The lender usually does not want to take the risk associated with a possible slowdown in sales in the later stages of the project. In many land developments, choice parcels are sold early and less desirable ones may remain unsold as time passes. Because some parcels may be more difficult to sell, the lender wants assurance that the developer will take this added risk. Consequently, the lender will bargain for a faster rate of loan payments, thereby making sure that the loan will be repaid before all 180 parcels are sold.

Another reason for negotiating faster repayment rates is that since Mid City will put most of the "front-end" money into the development during the first six months, it wants assurance that the loan repayment will be given preference as sales proceeds are realized. Further, because the developer will realize some markup on each sale, the lender has some room to negotiate a satisfactory release schedule and still leave the developer with a reasonable amount of cash inflow.

Many land development loans set the repayment rate so that the loan is repaid when about 80 percent to 90 percent of total project revenue is realized. The exact schedule is negotiated based on how fast the lender wants the loan repaid, how much cash the developer must retain from each parcel sale to cover expenses not funded in the loan, and conditions in the loan market.

In Exhibit 17–10, the duration of the construction loan is estimated assuming that the lender wants to be repaid when approximately 83.33 percent of project revenues, or $5.7 million, is realized. This means that the lender wants to be repaid at a rate equal to

EXHIBIT 17–10
Determining the
Duration of the
Construction Loan

Month	Cluster	Standard	Creek	Monthly Cumulative Sales ($)	Monthly Sales Revenue	
4–6	6	6	0	$ 387,600	$ 129,200	
7–12	24	18	6	1,949,400	260,300	
13–18	18	36	18	4,788,000	473,100	
19	1	5	2	5,130,000	342,000	
20	1	5	2	5,472,000	342,000	
21	1	5	2	5,814,000	342,000	←Repaid during this month

[8] We show in Exhibit 17–9 that the developer actually receives interest draws in cash (column b). Then, the developer simultaneously makes a cash interest payment in the same amount (column c). Notice that the same loan balance would result if the lender provided a draw for the direct cost only (column a), *computed* interest on those draws as in column (b), added it to the loan balance (instead of actually paying out cash), reduced the loan balance as principal repayments occur (column d), and did not require cash interest payments from the developer (column e). If this pattern were followed, the ending balance would be the same and no cash disbursement for interest would have to be made by the lender or repaid by the developer. In the pattern just described, interest carry is simply being accrued in the loan balance.

120 percent of the rate at which monthly revenue is received (100%/83.33% = 120%). If the borrower and the lender agreed that the loan would be repaid over the entire life of the project (24 months), then 100 percent of the loan would be repaid when 100 percent of project revenues were received, as was illustrated in Exhibit 17–9. Accelerating the repayment rate by 16.67 percent means that for every $1 of sales revenue realized, the developer repays the loan by an amount 120 percent greater than would be the case if the loan were repaid over the entire life of the project. In our illustration, based on the cumulative sales revenue shown in Exhibit 17–7C, a total of 80 percent of project revenues will be received during month 21. Hence, the lender would like the loan to be repaid at that time.

Estimating Release Prices per Parcel Sold

We have already indicated that the lender will generally insist on a loan repayment rate in excess of the rate estimated for revenue to be earned. Indeed, in our example, we have indicated that the lender would like the loan to be repaid at 120 percent of the rate at which revenue will be received. However, as we have seen, when lenders and developers negotiate land development loans, they also usually assign a release price *to each parcel* in the development. When each parcel is sold, that release amount is paid to the lender, who then releases the lien, thereby assuring the buyer of an unencumbered title. In Exhibit 17–11, the release prices for the three types of lots in our example are calculated.[9]

Loan Request and Repayment Schedule

Exhibit 17–12 shows the revised loan schedule with the new release price. Note that the loan is now repaid in month 21 as we projected in Exhibit 17–10.[10] The exhibit indicates that the total interest carry will be $448,109. This is the amount that the developer must include in his loan request. If sales were to slow down, the loan balance would increase rapidly because *actual* interest draws would increase at a faster rate than *estimated* draws. If this slowdown occurred, the interest reserve of $448,109 might be depleted. Further, if the loan balance ever reached $4,088,109, the lender would not allow further draws. The developer would have to make interest payments from other sources. This is one reason why the loan request is a low percentage of gross project value ($4,088,109/$6,840,000) = 60% (rounded). Indeed, most lenders prefer to keep the loan-to-value ratio for land development projects in the range of 70 percent, so they have a better chance of recovering the loan balance, should the project go into default.

EXHIBIT 17–11
Calculation of the Release Price per Parcel

Lot Type	Release Price before Acceleration	Acceleration Factor	Acceleration Release Price
Cluster	$11,534	1.2	$13,840
Standard	27,681	1.2	33,217
Creek	28,835	1.2	34,602

[9] There are alternative ways of calculating the accelerated release price. Previous editions of this text used a slightly different approach. In this edition, we have simplified the approach while obtaining virtually the same answer. The point of any approach taken is simply to arrive at proposed release prices that are acceptable to both the lender and the developer.

[10] The reader should keep in mind that the approach in Exhibit 17–10 was an estimate to determine when the loan would be repaid to determine what release price to use. The actual month it is repaid may differ slightly when calculated using the more detailed projections in Exhibit 17–12 that actually calculate the interest, loan balance, and so on, every month.

EXHIBIT 17–12 **Accelerated Loan Repayment Schedule—Landco Development Company**

www.mhhe.com/bf15e

	Draws			Payments			
	(a) Construction	(b)	(c) Total	(d)	(e)	(f) Total	(g) Ending
Month	Draw	Interest	Draw	Principal	Interest	Payments	Balance
Close 0	$1,019,200	$ 0	$1,019,200	$ 0	$ 0	$ 0	$1,019,200
1	655,200	10,192	665,392	0	10,192	10,192	1,684,592
2	655,200	16,846	672,046	0	16,846	16,846	2,356,638
3	655,200	23,566	678,766	0	23,566	23,566	3,035,404
4	218,400	30,354	248,754	94,116	30,354	124,470	3,190,042
5	218,400	31,900	250,300	94,116	31,900	126,017	3,346,226
6	218,400	33,462	251,862	94,116	33,462	127,579	3,503,972
7	0	35,040	35,040	189,617	35,040	224,656	3,349,395
8	0	33,494	33,494	189,617	33,494	223,111	3,193,272
9	0	31,933	31,933	189,617	31,933	221,549	3,035,588
10	0	30,356	30,356	189,617	30,356	219,973	2,876,327
11	0	28,763	28,763	189,617	28,763	218,380	2,715,474
12	0	27,155	27,155	189,617	27,155	216,771	2,553,012
13	0	25,530	25,530	344,632	25,530	370,162	2,233,910
14	0	22,339	22,339	344,632	22,339	366,971	1,911,617
15	0	19,116	19,116	344,632	19,116	363,748	1,586,102
16	0	15,861	15,861	344,632	15,861	360,493	1,257,331
17	0	12,573	12,573	344,632	12,573	357,205	925,272
18	0	9,253	9,253	344,632	9,253	353,885	589,893
19	0	5,899	5,899	249,131	5,899	255,030	346,660
20	0	3,467	3,467	249,131	3,467	252,598	100,996
21	0	1,010	1,010	102,005	1,010	103,015	$ 0
22	0	0	0	0	0	0	
23	0	0	0	0	0	0	
24	0	0	0	0	0	0	
Totals	$3,640,000	$448,109	$4,088,109	$4,982,630	$448,109	$5,430,739	

Project Feasibility and Profitability

From the developer's viewpoint, the economic feasibility of the Grayson project is based on whether the market value of the sites after development will exceed the acquisition cost of the land, plus direct improvement costs, plus the interest carry and any other costs not included in the loan provided by Mid City. Exhibit 17–6, discussed previously, summarizes total costs, including closing costs and other costs that Landco must pay but that will not be funded in the loan for the Grayson project. The loan fees and interest carry *are included* in the total loan amount of $4,088,109. We can now do a more detailed projection of how the project costs will be incurred over time and how income will be generated over time from lot sales.

To investigate the developer's ability to carry this project until the loan is repaid and to establish whether the project is feasible for the developer to pursue and meet the expected return on investment, the lender must analyze a schedule of cash flows that the developer prepares. This statement should contain not only direct costs but also additional day-to-day operating expenses that the Grayson project may require. In this way, the lender can project the developer's cash position, better analyze the risk of loan default, and establish the profitability of the project. Exhibit 17–13 contains a quarterly summary of all cash inflows

EXHIBIT 17–13 Developer's Cash Flow   www.mhhe.com/bf15e

Quarter	Close	(1)	(2)	(3)	(4)	(5)	(6)	(7)	(8)
Inflow:									
Sales		$ 0	$ 387,600	$780,900	$780,900	$1,419,300	$1,419,300	$1,026,000	$1,026,000
Construction draw	$ 1,019,200	$1,965,600	655,200	0	0	0	0	0	0
Interest draw		50,604	95,717	100,466	86,274	66,985	37,687	10,375	0
Total inflow	$ 1,019,200	$2,016,204	$1,138,517	$881,366	$867,174	$1,486,285	$1,456,987	$1,036,375	$1,026,000
Outflow:									
Land purchase	$ 2,400,000								
Closing costs	100,000								
Loan fees	122,643								
Principal		$ 0	$ 282,349	$568,850	$568,850	$1,033,896	$1,033,896	$ 600,268	$ 0
Direct costs	19,200	1,965,600	655,200	0	0	0	0	0	0
Interest costs		50,604	95,717	100,466	86,274	66,985	37,687	10,375	0
General and admin.		26,250	26,250	26,250	26,250	26,250	26,250	26,250	26,250
Property tax					43,750				43,750
Sales expense		0	19,380	39,045	39,045	70,965	70,965	51,300	51,300
Total outflow	2,641,843	2,042,454	1,078,896	734,611	764,169	1,198,096	1,168,798	688,193	121,300
Net cash flow	$(1,622,643)	$ (26,250)	$ 59,621	$ 146,755	$ 103,005	$ 288,189	$ 288,189	$ 348,182	$ 904,700

Developer's *IRR* = 16.64% (*IRR* of quarterly cash flows multiplied by 4)
NPV @15.00% = $40,056

and outflows for Landco over the entire life of the project. The inflows are estimated based on the sales prices for each type of parcel, plus loan draws and equity required from the developer for the land purchase price and closing costs. The outflows include expenditures for direct development costs taken from the schedule of monthly draws (Exhibit 17–12). Loan repayments are taken from the schedule of loan repayments (Exhibit 17–12). Other operating expenses, including general and administrative expenses, sales commissions, and property taxes, have been estimated on a quarterly basis and included in the exhibit.

The developer will have negative cash flow during the first two quarters. Adding up these two negative cash flows results in a total of $1,648,893, which is the total equity that the developer is likely to need for the project. According to the loan repayment schedule detailed above, the developer will retain all cash flow from sale proceeds beginning in month 21 through month 24. Although some cash flow will be retained from earlier sales, clearly the developer will receive the greatest cash flow during the later quarters.

From the beginning of the development period until the 21st month, a question arises concerning the developer's ability to meet operating expenses and other cash outflow requirements not funded in the loan request from Mid City. The amount loaned to the developer covers only part of the land cost, direct costs, and interest carry. Other obligations, such as overhead and loan fees, must be paid during development. Sales commissions, property taxes, and general and administrative expenses were not funded as a part of the development loan and must also be covered from the cash retained by the developer from each parcel sale.

Exhibit 17–13 provides insight into Landco's ability to carry the cash needs of the entire project. At closing and in the first quarter, Landco will have negative cash flow. However, from the second through eighth quarters, cash flow will be positive. It is during such periods that estimates concerning costs, sales, rates, and repayment conditions become crucial to both Landco and Mid City. If the time needed for development exceeds initial estimates, if actual development costs exceed estimates, or if sales do not materialize as projected, Landco's cash flow position during these months will change dramatically. Similarly, if Mid City demands a release schedule calling for loan repayments that are too high, cash flow to Landco from sales revenue would be reduced, which might jeopardize Landco's ability to carry out the project and repay the loan. For this reason, Mid City must consider Landco's own financial resources in the event that any of these adverse factors materialize. Clearly, if Landco's cash position in this project becomes questionable, Landco will be expected to share in some of the risk by contributing working capital from its own resources to complete sale of the project successfully. To analyze Landco's ability to provide working capital, should it be necessary, Mid City will thoroughly review the company's income statement and balance sheet as well as possibly requiring additional loan security or guarantees from Landco beyond the land that serves as security for the loan.

Finally, according to Exhibit 17–13, Landco's cash flow does not materialize significantly until the later quarters of the project. This timing is in keeping with the way risk is taken during the project. Because the lender puts in front-end capital, it wants assurance of a high priority in the sales proceeds as the development matures. Consequently, Landco must wait until the lender's prior claim is satisfied before it realizes a return. However, from Landco's viewpoint, its equity in the project increases as value is added to the project as actual development occurs. Hence, most of its returns are appropriately deferred to the later stages of the project.

Project *IRR* and Net Present Value

Up to this point in the analysis, we have made some rough estimates as to the economic viability of the Grayson project. Recall that we estimated that the market value of the project if it were developed and all parcels were sold today would be $6,840,000, and we estimated costs to be $6,353,283, indicating that a margin between total revenues and total costs existed. Although such a margin exists, the cash inflows and outflows related to the development and subsequent sales *do not occur immediately.* Consequently, the *time value of money* must be taken into account. To do this for the Grayson project, we *estimate* that a risk premium of at least 3 percent over the borrowing rate of 12 percent, or 15 percent, would be the *minimum* before-tax return that Landco would be willing to accept on its equity investment at this time.[11] Applying this rate to the quarterly net cash flows shown in Exhibit 17–13 results in a net present value of $40,056. This figure indicates that the project is economically feasible and meets Landco's required return.[12] Stated another way, according to the assumptions used in our analysis, Landco can pay $2.4 million for the land and still earn a positive net present value. Finally, again using the cash flows in Exhibit 17–13, we see that the *IRR* for the project is 16.64 percent. As expected, since the *NPV* was positive, this exceeds Landco's required *IRR* of 15 percent.

Entrepreneurial Profits

In the preceding section, we noted that revenues produced by the Grayson project as projected by Landco would cover all costs, and the resultant cash flows, when discounted by the required rate of return (assumed to be 15% before taxes in the example), would provide a positive *NPV* of about $40,000. When such estimates are made, *all costs* associated with development, *particularly general overhead costs* relating to time spent by all Landco staff, executives, and other personnel, should be included (see Exhibit 17–6). The goal of the analysis is to produce an estimate of net cash flow that can be used to evaluate whether a required before-tax return of 15 percent (net of *all* relevant costs) will be earned on the $2,265,174 of equity Landco invests in the Grayson project. This required return should be viewed as a minimum rate of return that Landco must earn to justify allocating the equity to the project.

Some professionals in the real estate field may also include in their projections an estimate for developer profit, or **entrepreneurial profit** (say 10% or 15%), as an additional cost of development when projecting net cash flow. Net cash flow is then discounted by a required return on equity. When doing this, one must be careful to avoid "double counting"

[11] An annual rate of 15 percent, compounded quarterly, is the rate of return used for discounting. This discount rate represents the required return that Landco must earn as a development company or a going concern, *net of all direct and indirect costs* associated with this project. It represents a rate of return to the owners or shareholders of the Landco company.

[12] Because the project shows a positive net present value, Landco could pay slightly more than $2.4 million and still earn its required return. If the seller of the land, however, is satisfied with $2.4 million, Landco may be in a position to earn a higher return (assuming all projections materialize). Such a difference between what buyers and sellers are willing to pay and receive occurs because of differences in expectations concerning future development revenues, or because of differences in information (e.g., market knowledge) possessed by each party. You should now see that the exhibits presented in this chapter can be linked in a spreadsheet format, and with a computer, various "what if" scenarios or simulation analyses can be carried out.

profit by including a developer profit and discounting by a required return that includes a premium for taking development risk. We have included all costs relative to land, labor, and capital explicitly in our projections and have not included an estimate of markup or developer profit as an *additional* cost of development. Thus, the 16.64 percent projected return for this project includes compensation for Landco's entrepreneurial ability to develop the project.

Sensitivity Analysis

Given the analysis just concluded, because Landco estimated a positive *NPV,* the $2.4 million land price is justified. Indeed, the analysis shows that based on the assumptions used to make projections for the project, Landco could actually pay slightly more and still earn its desired return of 15 percent. However, Landco should also use sensitivity analysis to determine how sensitive this return is to lower market prices, larger development periods, cost overruns, higher interest rates, and the like, before acquiring the land. We discussed this analysis at the conclusion of the previous chapter. It applies to land development as well as to project development.

Conclusion

This chapter dealt with *land development,* which involves the acquisition of land with the intention of constructing utilities and surface improvements and then reselling some or all of the developed sites to project developers or, in the case of housing, home builders. Our discussion of land development extends many of the concepts introduced in the previous chapter that dealt with financing development projects. After completing both chapters, you should have a good understanding of the development process, including the mechanics of construction and land development loans.

Key Terms

acquisition and development costs, *568*	extension agreements, *564*	release schedule, *561*
build to suit, *555*	feasibility study, *555*	turnkey basis, *555*
completion bonds, *563*	holdbacks, *563*	
draws, *570*	land development, *554*	
entrepreneurial profits, *579*	option agreement, *556*	
	release price, *573*	

Useful Web Sites

www.uli.org—The mission of the Urban Land Institute is to provide responsible leadership in the use of land in order to enhance the total environment. This site also provides current issues for financial trends in the industry.

www.bizloan.org—This is a good resource for information about different types of loans used for project development. Includes glossary of terms.

www.census.gov—U.S. Census Bureau Web site.

www.icsc.org—International Council of Shopping Centers Web site.

www.economy.com—Economy.com is a provider of economic data.

www.bls.gov—U.S. Department of Labor Web site.

www.bea.gov—U.S. Department of Commerce—Bureau of Economic Development Web site.

www.claritas.com—Nielsen Claritas provides demographic and enhanced census data.

www.axiometrics.com—Axiometrics is a research firm providing fundamental real estate research for the apartment sector with an emphasis on the performance of portfolios owned by the publicly traded apartment REITs.

www.demographia.com—This site is a very good resource for finding relevant demographic information about different markets spread across the world. Some of the main features of this site are that it gives international housing affordability rankings, different surveys, different economic reports, and different trends related to real estate. It is also a good source to find regulations and policies related to real estate.

www.fedstats.gov—This federal government sponsored Web site is a very good resource for finding relevant demographic information for different states in the United States. This site is a gateway to statistics for more than 100 U.S. federal agencies.

Questions

1. How might land development activities be specialized? Why is this activity different from project development discussed in the preceding chapter?
2. What is an option contract? How is it used in land acquisition? What should developers be concerned with when using such options? What contingencies may be included in a land option?
3. What are some of the physical considerations that a developer should be concerned with when purchasing land? How should such considerations be taken into account when determining the price that should be paid?
4. In land development projects, why do lenders insist on loan repayment rates in excess of sales revenue? What is a *release price?*
5. What are the unique risks of land development projects from the developer's and lender's points of view?

Problems

1. Refer to Concept Box 17.1. A *revised* market study indicates the following: pricing for standard interior lots will probably be $103,000 each, premium interior lots $118,000, and corner lots $125,000; the average development cost per lot has been revised up to $71,000; administrative costs, and so on remain at 12.5 percent of gross revenue.

   a. Can the same 18 percent return on *total cost* continue to be maintained?

   b. Suppose that the developer wants a 21 percent return on cost. How much can be paid for the land?

2. Treetop Associated Group (TAG) is seeking financing for acquisition and development of 147 homesites. The land will cost $1.5 million, and TAG estimates direct development costs to be an additional $2.7 million. City Federal Bank will make a loan covering 40 percent of the land acquisition cost, 100 percent of direct improvement cost, and interest carry at 11 percent interest with a 3 percent loan origination fee.

   TAG has decided to split the development into *two* parcel types, standard and deluxe, with the standard parcels comprising 87 of the 147 total homesites. Also, TAG thinks that the deluxe sites will be priced at a $2,000 premium over the standard parcel price of $36,000. Total project revenue will be $5,412,000. After making a 60 percent down payment for the land and incurring closing costs of $50,000, TAG believes that the remaining development costs will be drawn down at $600,000 a month for the first three months and $300,000 a month for the next three months. Parcel sales are expected to begin during the fourth month after closing. TAG estimates that they will sell three standard parcels and four deluxe parcels a month for the remainder of the first year, and five standard parcels and two deluxe parcels per month for the second year.

   The company and the bank have agreed to a repayment schedule calling for the loan to be repaid at a rate 20 percent faster than the receipt of sales revenues; that is, the loan plus interest carry per parcel will be repaid when approximately 83.33 percent of all revenues are realized. Other costs to consider include sales expense (paid quarterly at a rate of 5% on parcels sold during the quarter), administrative costs of $7,500 per quarter, and property taxes of $19,000 at the end of each year.

   a. What will be the release price for each type of lot?

   b. Estimate the total loan amount including interest carry for TAG.

   c. Prepare a schedule based on (*b*) and the pattern of loan draws, showing when TAG will have the loan fully repaid. What will be the total cash payments on the project loan?

    d. What will total project costs be? What percentage of total project costs are being financed?

    e. What will be the *NPV* and *IRR* of this project if TAG's before-tax required rate of return is 15 percent? (*Hint:* Prepare a cash flow analysis on a quarterly basis over the life of the project.)

3. Lee Development Co. has found a site that it believes will support 75 homesites. The company also believes that the land can be purchased for $225,000, while direct development costs will run an additional $775,000. The Last National Bank of Texas will underwrite 100 percent of the improvements plus the interest carry. The loan would be made at 13 percent interest with a *3 percent loan origination fee.* Lee believes that the development will sell faster with two types of parcels, standard and deluxe, with the standard parcel comprising 57 of the total parcels.

    Lee's marketing staff believes that the deluxe sites can be sold for $24,000, while the standard sites should bring $13,500. Lee estimates that the direct cost draws will be taken down in four equal amounts during months 1 to 4. Other up-front fees include closing costs of $10,000 and a 3 percent loan fee (not covered by the loan). Lee's sales staff supervisor assures him that she can generate sales activity starting in the fourth month that will result in the sale of five standard parcels per month and four deluxe parcels per month for three months. For the next six months, activity should be seven standard parcels per month and only one deluxe parcel per month. The Last National Bank wants its money out of the project early and wants Lee to agree to a release price per parcel that will result in the loan being repaid at a rate 25 percent faster than sales revenue is expected to be earned. Other costs to consider include sales expense (paid quarterly on 5% of the sales price of parcels sold during the quarter), administrative costs of $11,000 per quarter, and property taxes of $7,000. None of these latter items are to be funded in the loan.

    a. Develop a total monthly sales schedule for Lee. What will be Lee's total revenue? How many months will it take Lee to fully repay the loan?

    b. What will be the total interest carry funded in the loan amount? What will be the release price for each type of lot? Compute the loan repayment schedule. What will be Lee's total cash payments to the Last National Bank?

    c. What will Lee's total equity requirement be? Should Lee undertake this project if its required return on equity is 18 percent? (*Hint:* Do a cash flow analysis on a quarterly basis for the life of the project.) What will be the *IRR* on the project?

www.mhhe.com/bf15e

4. **Excel.** Refer to Problem 3. Refer to the "Ch 17 Land Dev" tab in the Excel Workbook provided on the Web site. Change the assumptions in the file to solve Problem 3. Then, answer the following questions.

    a. Determine the release price based on a repayment schedule calling for the loan to be repaid at the following rates: 0 percent, 10 percent, and 30 percent faster than the receipt of sales revenues. (*Note:* the original problem assumes a rate 25% faster.)

    b. Develop a loan schedule to demonstrate that with 0 percent acceleration, the loan is paid off exactly when the last lot is sold.

    c. Calculate the lender's *IRR* (effective cost of the loan) for each of the rates in part (*a*).

18

Structuring Real Estate Investments: Organizational Forms and Joint Ventures[1]

Introduction

In Chapter 1, we discussed ways that ownership can be transferred from a seller to a buyer and ways of being sure that the title is valid. Many of the subsequent chapters have discussed the risk and return associated with the ownership of real estate. But so far we have not discussed the specifics of what legal form of ownership might have been used to acquire the property or properties. By *legal ownership entity,* we mean one that is recognized by the government and courts and has legal rights associated with it.

All legal ownership entities must be in one of the following forms: sole proprietorship, partnership, limited liability company (LLC), or corporation. In this section we discuss each legal entity, with an emphasis on how each may be used for real estate investment.

Sole Proprietorships

A **sole proprietorship** is an ownership entity consisting of a single person. No formalities or costs are necessary to create a sole proprietorship. It is created when an individual starts to do business. Income, expenses, gains, and losses from operations are reported on the individual's tax return, and there can be no management conflicts since there are no others involved in the business.

A sole proprietor has unlimited liability. The individual can lose more than just his or her equity investment, as courts can go after personal assets of the individual to satisfy a judgment. Sole proprietors also may find it difficult to raise capital or obtain financing for investments.

Sole proprietorships may be used for real estate investment because individuals can make investments without needing to form and maintain a company. There also may be tax advantages, because income and losses flow through to the investor's individual tax

[1] The authors appreciate the help of Youguo Liang, director of research for Prudential Real Estate Investors, in writing this chapter.

statement (e.g., the investor may be able to use any losses to offset other taxable income). However, sole proprietorships may not be the ideal ownership form for real estate, especially as the investments become more sophisticated, due to the associated personal liability, the difficulty in raising capital, and the inability to diversify among multiple properties or property type.

Partnerships

Partnerships provide a legal mechanism for more than one person to share in the ownership of one or more properties. The two main types of partnerships are general partnerships and limited partnerships.

General Partnerships

A **general partnership** is an ownership entity consisting of more than one person. Each member is a general partner and has equal rights to share in management responsibilities, unless specified otherwise in the partnership agreement. Members of general partnerships can be natural persons or other business entities. States regulate general partnerships, but no formalities or costs are required to create a general partnership. This is the default form of partnership that is created when two or more persons act as co-owners of a business for profit. Potential partners should consult with an attorney before undertaking any business activities to decide what form of ownership entity is desired and to avoid the unintentional creation of a general partnership when they may have preferred to form a different type of ownership vehicle. If a general partnership is desired, the attorney can help draft a partnership agreement, which can address such issues as profit and loss sharing, management responsibilities, and partnership termination.

A general partnership is a pass-through tax entity. The partnership reports information to the IRS on the income for the partnership but it does not pay taxes. The partnership files a tax return as a reporting function only. All income, gains, and losses from operations are reported on the individual partners' tax returns.

A significant disadvantage of a general partnership is that each partner has unlimited liability for any legal or financial responsibilities of the partnership. Each partner is an agent for the partnership, so if one partner is carrying on business, all other partners can be liable for such dealings with third parties. Further, each partner is liable in full for all outstanding debts of the partnership, regardless of the amount each individual has invested in the partnership.

Title to the property is held in the name of the partnership. Each partner owns an interest in the partnership, but not in the property itself. This may become an issue if liquidity is desired in the event of divorce, death, or financial difficulties involving one of the partners. Also, since an ownership interest in a general partnership is considered personal property, it is not eligible for a Section 1031 exchange (as discussed in Chapter 14).

A general partnership has a finite life and terminates upon the death, disability, or withdrawal of one of the partners, unless otherwise agreed to in the partnership agreement. If desired, the partnership agreement can specify a date on which the partnership will end. Investors should be certain that the life of the partnership is long enough to allow for the completion of the investment cycle, such as renovating and leasing up a property before disposition.

General partnerships are commonly employed by companies undertaking joint ventures and other strategic alliances, because such companies already enjoy limited liability as limited liability companies (LLCs), limited liability partnerships (LLPs), or corporations (discussed next). Adding another layer of limited liability through entity choice would not afford such companies any more protection than already exists, so they elect to form a general partnership because of its ease of administration and low cost of formation.

However, general partnerships are usually not recommended for groups of individuals that are seeking to form a business entity to invest in real estate, primarily because of the unlimited liability of each partner.

Limited Partnerships

A **limited partnership (LP)** is a legal ownership entity made up of at least one general partner and one or more limited partners. States generally regulate LPs, and the partnership must register as an LP to avoid the unintentional creation of a general partnership. The LP will have a partnership agreement that defines the responsibilities of each partner and how they share in the profits of the partnership. The registration and attorneys fees to create an LP can be costly and should be taken into account at the time of formation.

A key feature of the LP is the two different classes of partners. The general partners in the LP are responsible for all the business management for the partnership and are in essentially the same legal position as are partners in a general partnership, in that they assume unlimited legal and financial liability. The general partner makes decisions such as if and when to sell properties, refinance loans, and so on. In contrast, the limited partners are passive partners who do not participate in the day-to-day management and, as a result, have limited liability. Limited partners, like shareholders in a corporation, are only liable for the money they have at risk, and they bear no legal liability for the actions of general partners. The investment of limited partners is a passive activity and as such is impacted by the passive loss rules discussed in Chapter 11. There can be a conflict of interest between the general and limited partners because decisions such as when to sell a property can have different tax consequences for each and the limited partner has no say in this decision.

An LP is a pass-through tax entity. As with a general partnership, the partnership files a tax return but all income, gains, and losses from operations are reported on the individual partners' tax returns. Any cash distributions go to the partners without being taxed at the time of distribution.

Like general partnerships, the title to the property is held in the name of the LP. Each partner owns an interest in the partnership, but not in the property itself. Again, this may become an issue if liquidity is desired in the event of divorce, death, or financial difficulties involving one of the partners. Partnership interests often sell at discounts compared to their proportional interest in the underlying property. Because an ownership interest in a partnership is personal property, it is not eligible for a Section 1031 exchange.

An LP has a finite life, as opposed to a corporation. The partnership agreement must specify a date on which the partnership will end. Investors should be certain that the life of the partnership is long enough to allow for the completion of the investment cycle, such as completing a development project, leasing it up, and selling it.

LPs can be effectively used for real estate investments by having one or more general partners to manage the projects with the majority of the equity capital coming from passive investors who want limited liability as limited partners. An attorney should be consulted before forming any type of ownership entity, however, because the application of limited liability has extended to the point where even the general partners in an LP could be shielded from some liability by forming a limited liability partnership or limited liability company in lieu of an LP.

The economics of LPs will be discussed in more detail later in the chapter because they are often used for joint ventures and can be structured to allocate cash flows and tax benefits in different proportions to different partners to meet the needs of the parties involved.

Limited Liability Partnerships

A **limited liability partnership (LLP)** is a legal ownership entity regulated by the state. It is made up of any number of limited partners. LLPs are typically used by professional organizations such as attorneys or architects, and in some states, such as California and New York, only professional organizations are permitted to form LLPs. Like other partnership entities, the key document for the LLP is the partnership agreement. The registration and attorneys fees can be costly and should be taken into account at the time of formation.

As in a general partnership, each partner in the LLP is responsible for the business management of the partnership. The extent of limited liability may vary from state to state, but typically each partner is liable financially only for its own investment, and legally a partner will not be liable for the acts of other partners.

As with the other types of partnerships we have discussed, this partnership files a tax return as a reporting function only. All income, gains, and losses from operations are reported on the individual partners' tax returns. Any cash distributions go to the partners without being taxed at the time of distribution. Even though partners have limited liability, the passive loss rules do not apply because each partner has management rights.

Like all partnerships, title to the property is held in the name of the LLP. Each partner owns an interest in the partnership, but not in the property itself. As with the general and limited partnership forms, this may become an issue if liquidity is desired in the event of divorce, death, or financial difficulties involving one of the partners. Also, since an ownership interest in a partnership is considered personal property, it is not eligible for a Section 1031 exchange.

Unlike typical general or limited partnerships, an LLP generally has no definite term. The death or disability of a partner does not terminate the partnership, so in this respect it is more like a corporation. Because of the limited liability for each partner, an LLP can be an effective ownership entity for a group of real estate investors.

Limited Liability Companies

The **limited liability company (LLC)** is a relatively new legal form of ownership. In 1988, the IRS formally approved the LLC structure, and now every state has approved legislation to enable the formation and operation of LLCs. An LLC offers nearly every advantage of an LLP, especially in regard to the limited liability of partners. It also has the added management flexibility of allowing some members to be passive investors. However, an LLP may be preferred over an LLC if state laws offer more limited liability for LLPs than for LLCs, or if an existing general partnership is seeking to change entity status. Conversion from a general partnership to an LLP is an easier and a lower cost administrative process than changing to an LLC; and in some states, conversion from a general partnership to an LLC is a taxable event, whereas conversion to an LLP is not a taxable event. Another consideration is that there are mandatory insurance requirements for LLCs in some states, which could further add to the cost of maintaining the LLC.

In some states, one person can register as an LLC, while other states require at least two members. There is no limit to the number of members in an LLC. In order to register as an LLC, the company must file the articles of organization with the state. An operating agreement, outlining the relationships and responsibilities of the members, is essential for an LLC. Registration fees and attorney costs to set up an LLC can be significant. LLCs are often incorrectly referred to as limited liability *corporations* instead of limited liability *companies.* Laws covering LLCs differ among states. This may impact the ability of an LLC formed in one state to do business in another state in which it has not registered. Furthermore, because the LLC is a recent innovation, the law in relation to LLCs is relatively unsettled.

Two types of LLCs are available: (1) member-managed and (2) manager-managed. In both member- and manager-managed LLCs, all members, including managing partners, enjoy limited liability. Member-managed LLCs function much like LLPs, in that all members have an equal say in business operations and management decisions. All members have the authority to sign checks, enter contracts, and otherwise legally bind the LLC.

In a manager-managed LLC, a two-tier system is set up, much like a corporation. Managers are appointed to take care of the business operations of the LLC, while members are like shareholders in that they hold ownership interests but have no management responsibilities. Managers can be members of the LLC or outside managers. Responsibilities and duties of managers, including voting procedures, are specified in the operating agreement. Members of manager-managed LLCs can be active, day-to-day participants in the business, but they do not have a say in management decisions. It is possible for lenders to be made members of LLCs in exchange for more favorable financing terms, thus gaining a voice in how the LLC is run without taking on management responsibilities.

An LLC can elect to be taxed as a partnership, thus enjoying the benefits of pass-through taxation. Taxable income or losses are passed through to the individual investor and the LLC files an informational tax return only. LLCs also have a considerable amount of structural flexibility. Different classes of investors are allowed in an LLC, and there may be a disproportionate allocation of benefits among the different classes of members. There are no requirements for corporate boards, annual meetings, or other similar requirements of corporations. Some states, however, may require a franchise or capital values tax on LLCs, which in essence is the fee for limited liability and increased flexibility.

Like partnerships, title to the property is held in the name of the LLC. Each member owns interests in the LLC, but not in the property itself. This may become an issue, should liquidity be desired. Also, since an ownership interest in an LLC is considered personal property, it is not eligible for a Section 1031 exchange.

The flexibility of pass-through taxation, limited liability, and management structure have made the LLC an increasingly popular choice of ownership entity, especially for the ownership of commercial investment real estate. As the LLC has evolved and increased in management flexibility, it has generally replaced the LLP as the vehicle of choice for investors who are seeking limited liability and pass-through taxation. However, it may make more sense to form an LLP instead of an LLC when an existing general or limited partnership is attempting to change form to gain more limited liability, because in some states changing from a partnership to an LLC is a taxable event, while changing to an LLP is never a taxable event.

Corporations

The final ownership structure we will discuss is the corporation. There are two types of corporations that could be used for real estate: a C corporation and an S corporation.

C Corporations

A **C corporation** (C corp) is a legal and taxable entity that is owned by one or more shareholders and managed by directors. Shareholders can be natural persons or other business entities. C corp status is granted by individual states. The corporation files articles of incorporation and bylaws with the state. The bylaws specify the operating rules for the corporation. The incorporation and operation of a C corp can be expensive due to organization fees and other up-front costs that can be substantial. Other operational costs include required quarterly and annual reports to state and federal governments.

C corps offer limited liability for shareholders, who can only lose their equity investments. Shareholders are not responsible for the debts of the corporation. Another main advantage to C corps is their access to capital. Shares in a corporation are very liquid, much more so than real estate itself, especially with publicly traded C corps. Continuity of life is also available to a corporation, as its life does not end upon the death of any shareholder, director, or officer.

A disadvantage of a C corp is that it provides no option for pass-through taxation. The C corp is taxed on its income, and shareholders are subsequently taxed on any dividends received. Likewise, a C corp cannot pass losses on to individual shareholders. However, a C corp can shelter its own income. The ownership interest in a C corp is considered personal property and therefore is not eligible for the tax-deferral benefits of Section 1031 exchanges. C corps are not usually used as an ownership structure for group ownership in commercial real estate to be held as an investment because of the issues of double taxation and the inability of losses to pass through to investors.

S Corporations

An **S corporation** (S corp) is a legal entity that can be owned by an individual or group of investors. A corporation must elect to be an S corp at the time of incorporation and must have:

- No more than 100 shareholders
- No corporations as shareholders (shareholders must be individual persons)
- No nonresident alien investors
- No more than one class of stock

If these requirements are met, an S corp may elect to be taxed as a partnership, thus avoiding double taxation and allowing income, gains, and losses from operations to be passed through to individual investors. However, if one or more of the requirements fails to be met, the S corp's nontaxable entity status could be in jeopardy.

S corp status is granted by individual states. Like a C corp, an S corp must file its articles of incorporation and bylaws with the state. The incorporation of an S corp can be expensive, as organization fees and other up-front costs can be substantial. Operational costs also can be significant, as detailed records must be kept, including the accounting of each shareholder's capital account.

S corps offer limited liability for shareholders, who can only lose their equity investments. Shareholders are not responsible for the debts of the corporation. S corps typically also have good access to capital, and shares in an S corp are fairly liquid (although not as liquid as shares in a C corp due to the strict operating requirements of S corps). The ownership interest in an S corp is considered personal property and therefore is not eligible for the tax-deferral benefits of Section 1031 exchanges. Continuity of life is also available to an S corp, as its life does not end upon the death of any shareholder, director, or officer.

An S corp can be a good choice for real estate investment, especially because of pass-through taxation. An S corp can be used for the ownership of rental real estate when the corporation provides sufficient services. However, when the management of the rental property is passive in nature, as in the case of net leases, there is a risk that the S corporation may be subject to federal income tax. The corporation may have its status as an S corp terminated if, for three consecutive years, the passive income it collects exceeds 25 percent of its total gross receipts.

Joint Ventures

Joint ventures are formed by at least two parties with the intent of achieving a specific investment objective. Unlike many other business agreements, when the objective is achieved, the joint venture (JV) is usually terminated. While the range of possible real estate investment goals is very wide, joint ventures are formed, typically, around one or more of the following attributes:

1. *Risk sharing.* A single investor may be unwilling to undertake a real estate venture because of its size, location, capital requirements, and/or duration. However, by sharing the risk, two or more parties may be willing to undertake the venture.

2. *Combining expertise with capital.* Joint ventures are frequently formed as a way to pool equity capital from one or more sources, as well as a means of bringing parties with different expertise to the venture. For example, one joint venture partner with *development* expertise and/or the ability to manage the operations of the real estate investment may join the venture with other partners who may be willing to invest *capital* in the venture. A joint venture could also involve purchasing existing properties and operating them. In this case, one of the parties may be responsible for acquisition, leasing, and management, and the others may provide capital. In much of the discussion in this chapter, we will refer to the developer/operator as the partner responsible for the development and/or the operations of the property. We refer to the *investor-partner,* or *money-partner,* as the party who contributes much of the capital.

3. *Speculative objectives.* This may involve acquisition of a large tract of undeveloped land with the expectation that it will not be ready for development for many years. Indeed, the exact nature of the use, improvements, and so forth may be uncertain. Such a venture may not appeal to a single investor, whereas multiple investors may be interested.

Organizational Forms

Participants in joint ventures may include any combination of individual investors, partnerships, corporations, or trusts. However, a joint venture in and of itself is not a legal form of organization. In order to specify capital contributions, rights, duties, profit sharing, and the like, a joint venture agreement or a business entity must be created. The choice of organizational form used to accommodate these various groups of investors could be a partnership, corporation, or trust. In this chapter, we will focus on partnerships, which are frequently the vehicle of choice in real estate joint ventures.

Profit Sharing

Because the parties to a joint venture may contribute different things, and possibly in different proportions, a partnership must be structured such that it provides economic incentives for all parties. Differences in the tax status of investors also may affect the way partnerships are structured.

A joint venture can take on a number of different partnership forms. The most common is the *limited partnership.* As is the case with all partnerships, there must be at least one general partner and any number of limited partners. Generally, in real estate, limited partners are the investors that provide most of the equity capital, while general partners are usually responsible for managing the partnership assets and may contribute a relatively small portion of the required equity capital. Limited partners are generally very restricted in the management of a joint venture and their personal liability is limited, hence, the term *limited* partnership. This will be discussed in more detail later in this chapter. When determining how a joint venture is to be structured, potential investors usually consider the following factors:

- How much initial capital will the parties contribute and how will the parties contribute additional capital if needed in the future?
- How will the parties share in the annual cash flows to be produced from operating the property?
- How will the parties share in the cash flow received from sale of the property?

- Will some of the parties receive a preferred return? Will the preferred return be paid from annual cash flows and/or from sale?
- Will taxable income (or losses) and capital gain (or loss) be shared in the same proportion that operating cash flow is distributed?[2]
- Who will have control over the operation of the property and decisions involving capital improvements, approving leases to tenants, financing and possibly refinancing the property, and when to sell the property?

Initial Capital Contributions

As noted above, a joint venture is often motivated because one of the parties is in a position to invest capital and others may contribute expertise. An investor-partner may be a wealthy individual investor or perhaps a professional investment manager who raises funds from investors such as pension funds that want to invest in real estate but do not have the expertise to do so. The money-partner is usually more interested in diversification of investments and usually does not have the desire and/or expertise to develop or manage the properties.[3]

For example, the **initial capital contribution** may be distributed as follows: the money-partner may contribute 90 percent to 95 percent of the equity capital needed for a venture and a developer/manager may contribute the remaining 5 percent to 10 percent. Even though one partner may be providing the operating expertise, he is generally expected to contribute some capital in order to provide for some *alignment of financial interests* with the investor-partners. Returns to the developer/operator and the money-partner are usually "aligned" to some extent because both have some invested capital at risk in the venture. Because the developer/operator is supplying the day-to-day operational expertise, he will often receive a share of the cash flow in greater proportion to the initial investment. This usually provides further incentive for the developer/operator to make the investment successful. It should be pointed out that the developer/manager who is promoting the project may be approaching many money-partners in an attempt to find one who is interested. As such, the relationship between equity contributions, fees, and profit sharing will be competitively driven in the market for equity capital.

Sharing Cash Flow from Operations

One way to share cash flow from operating a property (*NOI* less debt service) is *in proportion* to the capital investment. For instance, if the developer contributes 10 percent of required equity, he will receive 10 percent of the cash flow. This is referred to as **noncumulative pari passu distribution** of the cash flows. However, it is more common for the money-partners and operating partners to share in cash flows and property appreciation disproportionately (a common example would have the investor-partners receiving a **preferred distribution** of cash flow and the developer-partners receiving a greater share in any property appreciation). For example, investor-partners may receive a **preferred return** calculated on an 8 percent yield on their initial investment. Consequently, if they invest $1 million in equity, as the property produces cash flow they receive the *first* $80,000 (or 8% of $1 million). After the capital distributions have been made to the investor-partners, the developer/operators *then* also receive cash equal to an 8 percent

---

[2] We will see that there can be "special allocations" that result in partners having a taxable income (or loss) as well as capital gains (or losses) that differ from the proportion of cash flow that they receive.

[3] Examples of money-partners could include pension funds and high-net-worth individuals who have access to capital but limited experience in sourcing, negotiating, and managing properties.

return on their initial investment *only if there are sufficient funds for distribution.* To the extent that funds are sufficient, any remaining cash flow may then be split in proportion to the initial contribution or based on some other agreed-upon percentage. For example, the remaining cash flow could be split evenly (50% to each party). In such cases, where the developer/operators may have invested only 5 percent of the capital but will receive an incentive of 50 percent of cash flow remaining after the initial distributions, they are said to be receiving a **promote.**

The 8 percent preferred return (used in the example) may be either cumulative or noncumulative. **Cumulative distribution** means that if total funds in any given year are insufficient to give the investor-partner his preferred yield, the liability to do so carries over to the next year. In these cases, in subsequent years, an investor would receive any funds that should have been paid in prior years before the developer/operator begins to receive any cash from current operations. It is also possible that all cumulative, preferred returns in arrears may be carried over into the next operating period with interest.

In addition to receiving a share of the net cash flow in one of the ways discussed above, the operating or development partner also may receive fees for providing these services. For example, a fee may be paid to the party overseeing the development of the project (e.g., the development fee might be 4% of the hard and soft costs).[4] A management fee also may be paid for overseeing the day-to-day management of the project once it is operating (e.g., the management fee might be 3.5% of effective gross income).[5] These fees reflect expenses for services performed and are unrelated to the amount of capital invested. Indeed, such fees would generally have to be paid to third parties if such work were outsourced by the joint venture partners.

Sharing of Cash Flow from Sale

The success of an investment may not be known until the property is actually sold. At that time an assessment can be made of whether the cash flow from operations and sale was sufficient to provide an adequate return to each party. Of course, factors including market rents and income earned by the property each year as well as interim appraisals of properties may provide some guidance as to whether the investment is likely to be successful. But until the property is actually sold, cash available for final distribution will not be known with certainty.[6]

Final distributions of cash flow from sales are usually made after repayment of any debt. In general, after repayment of debt, distributions are usually made such that all parties *first* each receive an amount *equal to their initial capital investment.* Any remaining cash flow from sale is usually distributed in predetermined proportions. There may also be what is referred to as an *IRR* **preference.** This means that one or more investors must receive cash flow that is sufficiently high to achieve a specified *IRR* on equity invested for the entire investment period before others share in cash flows from sale. In these cases, an investor will usually receive this preference in cash flow from sale after each party has received capital equal to their initial investment. To the extent that additional cash flow remains after the partner receives the *IRR* preference, it may be split in some predetermined proportion (e.g., 50% to each party).

A slight variation of the *IRR* preference distribution is referred to as an *IRR* **lookback.** In this case, any cash flow remaining after each party has received capital equal to their

---

[4] As discussed in Chapters 16 and 17, hard costs usually consist of the cost of material and labor, while soft costs include outlays for architects, engineers, appraisers, legal costs, and so on.

[5] Recall that effective gross income is defined as rents collected less vacancy and collection loss.

[6] Refinancing may also provide a source of cash flow until the property is sold—especially if property values have risen and more can be borrowed on the refinancing than is currently owed on the property.

initial investment will be split in a predetermined proportion, such as 50 percent to each party. However, this split may be subject to the condition that one or more partners must earn a specified *IRR* (such as 12%). If this is not achieved in the 50 percent split, then some of the cash that would have gone to all partners must be distributed so that partners who must earn an *IRR* lookback do so. The difference between the *IRR* lookback and the *IRR* preference is illustrated below.

Example

Investor Capital Inc. (ICI) has decided to enter into a joint venture with Property Developers Inc. (PDI) to develop and operate an office building. The project will require an initial equity investment of $50 million, with ICI investing $45 million and PDI investing the remaining $5 million.

For simplicity, we will assume that each party invests its capital and then participates in year-end cash flows from operations, which are projected as follows:

Time	Operating Cash Flows	Sale
Inception	($50,000,000)	
Year 1	$ 1,000,000	
Year 2	$ 2,000,000	
Year 3	$ 5,000,000	
Year 4	$ 6,000,000	
Year 5	$ 6,500,000	$75,000,000

It is further assumed that the property will be sold at the end of year 5 and that the net proceeds from the sale will provide $75 million to be distributed to the investors.

The joint venture partnership agreement specifies that ICI will receive a 5 percent *noncumulative,* preferred return on its $45 million in equity. This means that any shortfall is *not* carried over to the next year. However, this distribution must be paid before Property Developers Inc. receives *any* cash from operations. After ICI receives its preferred return, PDI will receive a 5 percent noncumulative return on its equity capital of $5 million. Any remaining cash flow will be split 50 percent to each party.[7] These annual returns are calculated by simply multiplying the 5 percent rate by the initial equity investment.

When the property is *sold,* proceeds from sale will first be used to provide ICI with a capital recovery equal to its initial equity investment. Next, PDI will receive an amount equal to its initial equity investment. ICI will then receive an amount sufficient to earn a 12 percent *IRR* on equity investment. All remaining cash proceeds are to be split 50–50.

Using the above assumptions, we summarize the total cash flows available to the JV partners. These are shown in Exhibit 18–1.

Summary of Cash Flows Distributed in Each Operating Year

As illustrated in Exhibit 18–2, the return for ICI must be calculated first to reflect a 5 percent preferred return, which is distributed before PDI receives any cash. Because the property is in its lease-up phase during the first two years, our example indicates that cash flow is not enough to provide a 5 percent preference return for ICI. Therefore, ICI will receive *all cash flow* and PDI will not receive any cash flow during years 1 and 2.

[7] It could be said that Property Development Inc. is receiving a "promote" of 40 percent because it invests only 10 percent of the capital but receives 50 percent of the remaining cash flow, which is 40 percent more.

EXHIBIT 18–1
Total Cash Flows
Produced by the JV

Year	Initial Equity Investment	Cash Flow from Operations	Cash Flow from Sale	Total Cash Flow Available to JV*
0	$-50,000,000			$-50,000,000
1		$1,000,000		1,000,000
2		2,000,000		2,000,000
3		5,000,000		5,000,000
4		6,000,000		6,000,000
5		6,500,000	$75,000,000	81,500,000

*The *IRR* would be 14.81 percent if a single party owned the entire investment.

EXHIBIT 18–2
Summary of Cash
Flows Distributed
from Operations

A. ICI

Year	Initial 5% Distribution	50% Share in Cash Flow Available after Initial Distribution to ICI and PDI	Total Distribution of Operating Cash Flows
1	$1,000,000	—	$1,000,000
2	2,000,000	—	2,000,000
3	2,250,000	$1,250,000	3,500,000
4	2,250,000	1,750,000	4,000,000
5	2,250,000	2,000,000	4,250,000

B. PDI

Year	Initial 5% Distribution	50% Share in Cash Flow Available after Initial Distribution to ICI and PDI	Total Distribution of Operating Cash Flows
1	—	—	—
2	—	—	—
3	$250,000	$1,250,000	$1,500,000
4	250,000	1,750,000	2,000,000
5	250,000	2,000,000	2,250,000

C. Reconciliation (ICI and PDI)

Year	Cash Available for Distribution	Cash Distributed to ICI	Cash Distributed to PDI
1	$1,000,000	$1,000,000	—
2	2,000,000	2,000,000	—
3	5,000,000	3,500,000	$1,500,000
4	6,000,000	4,000,000	2,000,000
5	6,500,000	4,250,000	2,250,000

During year 3, total cash flow from operations increases to $5,000,000. Therefore, ICI will receive a 5 percent return on its investment of $45 million, or $2,250,000, and PDI will also receive a return of 5 percent on its investment of $5 million, or $250,000. The remaining cash flow, or $2,500,000, is then split 50 percent, or $1,250,000, to each party.[8]

[8] It should be noted that if ICI were entitled to receive a "cumulative preferred return," it would receive $3,750,000 in year 3. This would consist of arrearages of $1,250,000 in year 1 and $250,000 in year 2, plus $2,250,000 due in year 3. Furthermore, the JV agreement may also be written such that all amounts in arrears are increased (compounded) by 5 percent or some other specified rate of interest each year.

Cash Flow from Sale

Next, we calculate the cash flows that each party will receive from sale of the property. First, each party must be able to receive a return of their initial investment, with Investor Capital Inc. having first priority to the capital. In this case, there is sufficient capital for both parties to receive their initial investment. Second, we determine how much cash flow Investor Capital Inc. should receive to earn a 12 percent preferred *IRR*. This is illustrated in Exhibit 18–3. The cash flow of $16,801,668 was calculated as the amount needed to make the *IRR* exactly 12 percent when added to the $45 million received as return on initial investment. This is how much of the cash flow from the sale that Investor Capital Inc. will receive before remaining cash flow is split between the parties.

After solving for the amount needed to produce the preference *IRR* for ICI (see Exhibit 18–3), we now determine how much cash flow remains to be split after ICI achieves its 12 percent preferred *IRR*. We have:

Total cash flow from *sale*	$75,000,000
Return of capital to Investor Capital Inc.	−45,000,000
Return of capital to Property Developers Inc.	− 5,000,000
Preferred *IRR* to Investor Capital Inc.	−16,801,668
Remaining cash flow to be split 50–50	$ 8,198,332, or $4,099,166 to each partner

Each party will now receive one-half of the $8,198,332 remaining cash flow from sale, or $4,099.166.

IRR to Each Joint Venture Party

After all cash flows are distributed, we can calculate the *IRR* for each partner. This is shown in Exhibit 18–4. We see that ICI will earn a 13.22 percent *IRR* and PDI will realize a 26.64 percent *IRR*. Note that ICI earns an *IRR* that is higher than its 12 percent *IRR* preference because of the additional 50 percent cash flow split received based on the final cash flow from sale. Also note that because of the "promote" received by Property Developers Inc., it will earn 26.64 percent *IRR*. (Recall that Property Developers Inc. invested only 10% of the initial equity capital but received 50% of cash flows both from operations and from sale after all preferences were paid to Investor Capital.)

EXHIBIT 18–3
Calculating the *IRR* Preference for ICI

Year	ICI's Share of Cash Flow from Operations	ICI's Return of Initial Investment from Sale Proceeds	Additional Cash Flow from Sale to Achieve 12% Preference *IRR*	Total Cash Received from or Distributed to ICI
0				$−45,000,000
1	$1,000,000			1,000,000
2	2,000,000			2,000,000
3	3,500,000			3,500,000
4	4,000,000			4,000,000
5	4,250,000	$45,000,000	**$16,801,668**	$66,051,668
				IRR = 12%

EXHIBIT 18–4
IRR **to Each Investor upon Termination of the Joint Venture**

Year	Investor Capital Inc.	Property Developers Inc.
0	$ −45,000,000	$ −5,000,000
1	1,000,000	0
2	2,000,000	0
3	3,500,000	1,500,000
4	4,000,000	2,000,000
5	$ 70,150,834*	$ 11,349,166†
IRR	13.22%	26.64%

*Year 5 operating cash flow: $4,250,000 + $45,000,000 + $16,801,668 + $4,099,166.
†Year 5 operating cash flow: $2,250,000 + $5,000,000 + $4,099,166.

It should be stressed that even though ICI earns a preferred return, because of its 50 percent split, PDI continues to have an incentive to make the investment successful. This example also illustrates the alignment of interest between PDI and ICI. Because PDI is responsible for the development and for operating the property, it has an incentive to make the investment as successful as possible. In our example, PDI earns in excess of a 26 percent return on its initial 10 percent equity contribution. ICI, which is the money-partner and a passive investor, earns a lower return, which is consistent with the lower risk exposure.

Variation on the Preferred *IRR*—"The Lookback *IRR*"

As discussed previously, an alternative way of handling preferences to investors (usually the equity partner, ICI in this case) is to provide for an *IRR lookback* rather than an *IRR preference*. Recall that the *IRR* preference required an allocation of cash flow to ICI in the year of sale sufficiently great to achieve a 12 percent *IRR*. All remaining amounts were then split 50–50 (see Exhibit 18–5).

With an *IRR* lookback, cash flows in the year of sale are split such that ICI receives a cash distribution only in an amount needed to achieve a 12 percent *IRR*. All excess cash flows are then distributed only to PDI. In the example above, this means that the additional cash flow to ICI would be limited to $66,051,493, which would provide ICI with exactly a 12 percent *IRR*. Note that in this case, PDI would receive all remaining cash flows in excess of $66,051,493, or $15,448,507. This increase in cash flow to PDI produces an *IRR* of 32.94 percent, which is higher than the 26.64 percent return based on an *IRR* preference to ICI. Although an *IRR* preference will always give the investor a return that is at least equal to or greater than what the return would be with an *IRR* lookback, there are reasons why ICI may prefer a lookback rather than a preference *IRR*. This could be the case when cash flows in the year of sale may be *lower* than expected. In this case, ICI may choose to take *less risk* by participating in *cash flows* in year of sale, emphasizing the recovery of its capital and earning a more secure, specific return *before* PDI receives *any* cash flows. Obviously, PDI would be taking more risk in this case; however, its return also may be higher (32.94% in Exhibit 18–5 vs 26.64% in Exhibit 18–4). It should be stressed, however, that if cash proceeds in the year of sale fall below the $45 million in equity contributed by ICI at commencement of the joint venture, ICI will receive *all* funds available from sale and PDI will receive nothing.

In recent years, the combination of debt and equity used to finance the acquisition and/or development of commercial real estate has come to be called the **"capital stack."** Distributions of cash flow to providers of debt and equity in the capital stack has come to be called a **"waterfall."** The latter also signifies how distributions will be prioritized among various providers of debt and equity.* A list of various combinations is as follows:

Debt and Equity Structure (aka "Capital Stack")	Cash Distributions to Debt and Equity Providers (aka "Waterfall")
Possible types of:	

Debt	**Interest Distributions**
First mortgage	Fixed, floating, interest only, accrual, and so on
Second mortgage/mezzanine debt	Subordinate to first mortgage
Participating mortgage	Contingent on cash flow
Convertible mortgage	Contingent on property value

Equity	**Residual Distributions**
Limited partners	Preference
	Look back
General partners	Promote
	Residual

*These terms became widely used when describing how distributions were made to different investor classes (tranches) in mortgage-backed security pools. (To be discussed in Chapters 19 and 20.) These terms have since been generalized and popularized when describing situations where cash is distributed to debt and/or equity investors based on a specific priority as described in investment agreements.

EXHIBIT 18–5
Investment Returns after 12 percent *IRR* Lookback to ICI upon Termination of the Joint Venture

Year	Investor Capital Inc.	Property Developers Inc.
0	$−45,000,000	$−5,000,000
1	1,000,000	0
2	2,000,000	0
3	3,500,000	1,500,000
4	4,000,000	2,000,000
5	$ 66,051,493	$ 15,448,507
IRR	12.00%	32.94%

Syndications

The concept of real estate **syndication** extends generally to any group of investors who have combined their financial resources with the expertise of a real estate professional for the common purpose of carrying out a real estate project. A syndication is not an organization form per se. It may take any of the legal business forms such as a corporation, limited partnership, or general partnership.

A syndicate can be formed to acquire, develop, manage, operate, or market real estate. Syndication can be viewed as a type of financing that offers smaller investors the opportunity to invest in ventures that would otherwise be beyond their financial and management capabilities. Syndicators benefit from the fees they receive for their services and the interest they may retain in the syndicated property. Many syndication firms are in the business of acquiring, managing, and then selling real estate projects. In order to acquire property, they bring in other investors with capital; this capital forms the equity base with which the property is acquired. Syndicators do not usually invest much of their own capital. Rather, they act more as agent-managers earning fees for acquiring, managing, and selling properties owned by the investors who have contributed capital to the syndication.

Developers who need additional equity capital to undertake a project often raise funds through syndications, either directly or by using a firm that specializes in raising capital by selling interests in the syndication. The syndication may become involved during the development and construction of the project or after the building is completed and leased. In the latter case, the syndication provides a means for the developer to remove equity from the project, especially if the value of the project upon completion and lease-up is greater than the construction cost. The developer also typically receives a development fee. This strategy allows the developer to focus on developing projects, earning a development fee, retaining some ownership in the project, and going on to the next development project.

In cases where one or a small number of projects are to be syndicated, investors often choose a **limited partnership.** For a smaller project that requires a limited number of investors, the capital for the partnership will usually be raised by what is referred to as a **private offering.** Syndicators must adhere to certain regulations when offering ownership interests in partnerships to investors.

In other cases a syndicator may desire to raise a large amount of funds to acquire many properties. The particular properties to be acquired may or may not be identified when the funds are raised. If not, the offering is referred to as a **blind pool.** A blind pool offering allows the syndicator discretion over what properties are purchased, subject to broad guidelines in an offering prospectus to investors. In cases where ownership interests will be sold to investors in many states, the syndication is usually undertaken through a **public syndicate.** This type of syndication is subject to numerous state and federal regulations that are discussed later in this chapter.

The purpose of this chapter is to familiarize students with basic approaches to understanding and evaluating investment in an ownership interest in a real estate syndication. This information is important for both potential investors and developers. The investor must evaluate how the rate of return and risk for investment in a share of a syndicate compares with other investment opportunities. The developer must evaluate how the *cost* of obtaining equity funds through syndication (in terms of what the developer must give up) compares with other financing alternatives.

The focus of our discussion in this chapter will be on the analysis of a *private* offering in which a *single* property is to be acquired by a limited partnership. The emphasis is on understanding how ownership of shares in a partnership that owns the property differs from direct ownership of the property, as we have assumed in previous chapters.

Use of the Limited Partnership in Private and Public Syndicates

Limited partnerships have often been used as vehicles for raising equity capital for real estate ventures. As discussed previously, they combine the limited liability feature of an investment in a corporation with the advantages of a general partnership, such as the ability to make special allocations of income and cash flow to the partners. An investor's liability is limited to his initial contribution plus any unpaid contributions he has agreed to make in the future. Thus, this investor is referred to as a **limited partner.** The responsibility for the management of the partnership rests with the **general partners,** who are frequently knowledgeable in real estate matters, thus providing the partnership with professional management.

The Tax Reform Act of 1986 removed many of the tax advantages associated with the use of limited partnerships relative to other forms of real estate ownership. For example, any tax losses resulting from investments in limited partnerships are subject to the passive activity limitation rules (see Chapter 11). These tax changes led to a significant decline in real estate syndicates' use of the limited-partnership form of ownership. It remains important to understand this ownership vehicle, however, since a large number of real estate limited partnerships still exist. Furthermore, a large number of the real estate investment trusts (REITs) formed during the early 1990s were structured so that the REIT was a general partner in a limited partnership. This structure allowed limited partners in existing syndications (including ones that were formed prior to the Tax Reform Act of 1986) to exchange their limited partnership interests for interests in the new partnership formed by the REIT as a "tax-free exchange." We discuss real estate investment trusts further in Chapter 21. The point here is simply that limited partnerships continue to play an important role in real estate finance.

Private Syndication Problem Illustrated

When a syndication with other investors is undertaken, it is essential for all parties, whether they are investors or lenders, to understand the framework in which the venture will operate. What follows is an analysis of a *private* real estate syndication formed to acquire and operate the Plaza Office Building. In this syndication, 35 individuals have been approached by Dallac Investment Corporation, which has agreed to act as the sole general partner in a *limited partnership.*[9] Dallac is trying to raise sufficient equity capital to undertake the purchase and has decided to use the *limited partnership* form of organization, which will limit the liability of all partners to their agreed-upon capital contribution to the venture.

The venture to be undertaken and relevant cost and financial data are summarized in Exhibit 18–6. Dallac has obtained an option to purchase the property and has a commitment

EXHIBIT 18–6
Plaza Office Building Acquisition Cost and Financing Summary

Cost breakdown		
Land	$ 525,000	
Improvements	3,475,000	(capitalized)
Points	60,000	(amortized over loan term)
Subtotal	$4,060,000	
Organization fee	20,000	(amortized over 5 years)
Syndication expenses	100,000	(capitalized but not depreciated)
Total funding required	$4,180,000	
Loan amount	$3,000,000	(71.77% of total funding)
Interest rate	12%	
Term	25 years	(monthly payments)
Points	$ 60,000	
Annual debt service	$ 379,161	

[9] For clarity, we will consider all 35 limited partners as a single entity. As we will discuss later in this chapter, when more than 35 investors become partners, it is generally considered a public offering.

for a nonrecourse loan from Prudent Life Insurance Company. The loan requires prior approval of any change in the general partner at any time in the future.

Financial Considerations—Partnership Agreement

Exhibit 18–7 summarizes the financial aspects of the partnership agreement and the equity requirements of the general and limited partners for this example. The partnership agreement governs the business relationship among the general and limited partners and is often long and rather involved. At a minimum, partnership agreements should specify how and in what proportions the equity will be initially contributed and whether assessments will be made, should a cash shortfall occur or should the improvement need substantial repair in the future. In this example, Dallac has agreed as general partner to contribute 5 percent of the required equity, with the 35 limited partners investing 95 percent.[10] There is no provision for future assessments of the limited partners. Since limited partners are not liable for future capital contributions, Dallac will have to address the issue of what happens in the event the property generates negative before-tax cash flow. Dallac could guarantee to cover negative before-tax cash flow (and will likely charge a fee for doing so), raise sufficient equity capital initially to cover future negative cash flows, arrange for additional borrowing, or reserve the right to raise new capital by admitting additional partners.

The partnership agreement should also specify how income or loss from operating the property and capital gain or loss from sale of the property should be distributed. In our example, profits, losses, and cash flow from operations will be distributed 5 percent to the general partner (Dallac) and 95 percent to the limited partners. However, gain (or loss)

EXHIBIT 18–7
Partnership Facts and Equity Requirements for Plaza Office Building Syndication

a. Organization: December, year 1
b. Number of partners: 1 general partner and 35 limited partners
c. Equity capital contribution: general partner, 5%; limited partners, 95%
d. Cash assessments: none
e. Cash distributions from operations: general partner, 5%; limited partners, 95%
f. Taxable income and losses from operations: general partner, 5%; limited partners, 95%
g. Allocation of gain or loss from sale: general partner, 10%; limited partners, 90%
h. Cash distributions at sale: Based on capital account balances (capital accounts will be explained in the following discussion)

Initial equity requirements	
Land and improvements	$4,000,000
Points on mortgage loan	60,000
Organization fee	20,000
Syndication fees	100,000
Total cash requirements	$4,180,000
Less mortgage financing	3,000,000
Equals equity requirements	$1,180,000
General partners (5%)	59,000
Limited partners (95%)*	$1,121,000

---

*As indicated earlier, it is common to allow limited partners to pay in their equity contribution over time. The general partner arranges for additional financing during this pay-in period, using the limited partners' notes as collateral. To keep this example manageable, we have not assumed such a pay-in.

[10] In this case, we assume that each limited partner invests an equal percentage of the cash required from each partner. In practice, however, partners could purchase different proportional interests. Also, in many syndications, the general partner may invest as little as 1 percent of the equity or no equity at all.

from sale of the property is to be allocated 10 percent to the general partner and 90 percent to the limited partners. As mentioned earlier, an important characteristic of a partnership is that all items of income and loss (including gain or loss from resale) and cash do not have to be distributed in the same proportion. This **special allocation** allows flexibility in the ability to allocate the benefits of the real estate investment between the general and limited partners. We will see that these allocations affect the rate of return to each of the partners and are, therefore, important considerations in the analysis of partnerships.

When special allocations are used to allocate items of income and cash flow in different proportions to different partners, it becomes important to know how to determine the amount of cash that should be distributed to each partner upon sale of the property. This final cash distribution must take into consideration the initial equity contribution, allocations of cash flow during the operating years of the property, and allocations of income (or loss) from operation and sale of the property. These items are accounted for in the partner's **capital account.** The nature and importance of the capital account will be discussed in more detail later in the chapter. For now, we point out that the partnership agreement specifies that the cash flow from sale of the property will be allocated according to the capital account balances at that time.

Operating Projections

Exhibit 18–8 summarizes Dallac's projections about operations. All projections in a syndication offering must be made carefully and prudently since any misrepresentation or failure to disclose all material risks of the investment may result in a lawsuit for rescission of the partnership or damages by investors, or an action by regulatory authorities.[11] Because of this scrutiny by public agencies and the potential for legal action by limited partners, many general partner–syndicators make very general projections regarding future results or provide only a description of the projects that will be invested in, along with some information on the business background of the general partner or partners.

In addition to projections for rental income, operating expenses, management fees, and the like, Dallac has also disclosed the method of depreciation to be used, the period over which loan fees and organization fees will be amortized, and when syndication fees will be

EXHIBIT 18–8
Plaza Operating and Tax Projections

Potential gross income (year 2)	$750,000
Vacancy and collection loss	5% of potential gross income
Operating expenses (year 2)	35% of effective gross income
Depreciation method	Straight line, 31.5 years*
Amortization of loan points	$60,000 over 25 years or $2,400 annually
Amortization of organization fees	$20,000 over 5 years or $4,000 annually
Projected growth in income	3% per year
Projected resale price after 5 years	$5,000,000
Limited partners' tax rate	28%
General partner's tax rate	28%

* As indicated in Chapter 11, depreciation rules change frequently. The depreciable like of 31.5 years in this example is for illustration only.

[11] In the case of public offerings, most states require that a prospectus be filed with the state securities and exchange commission, and such projections are carefully scrutinized before approval to offer the securities is granted. Interstate offerings must be filed with the U.S. Securities and Exchange Commission and undergo a similar examination. Review and examination of securities offerings by state or federal agencies in no way indicate approval or disapproval of the economic merits of the investment, but only that the offering substantially complies with the disclosure and other requirements for registration or exemption.

www.mhhe.com/bf15e

EXHIBIT 18–9   **Pro Forma Statement of Before-Tax Cash Flow for Plaza Office Building**

	\multicolumn{5}{c}{Year}
	(2)	(3)	(4)	(5)	(6)
Potential gross income	$750,000	$772,500	$795,675	$819,545	$844,132
Less vacancy and collection	37,500	38,625	39,784	40,977	42,207
Effective gross income	712,500	733,875	755,891	778,568	801,925
Less operating expenses	249,375	256,856	264,562	272,499	280,674
Net operating income	463,125	477,019	491,329	506,069	521,251
Less debt service	379,161	379,161	379,161	379,161	379,161
Before-tax cash flow (*BTCF*)	$ 83,964	$ 97,858	$112,169	$126,909	$142,091
Allocation:					
General partners	5%				
Limited partners	95%				
Distribution of *BTCF*:					
General partners	$ 4,198	$ 4,893	$ 5,608	$ 6,345	$ 7,105
Limited partners	$79,766	$92,965	$106,560	$120,563	$134,986

deducted for federal income tax purposes. Syndication fees cannot be deducted in the year in which payment occurs; they must be capitalized and amortized over a prescribed time period established by tax regulations. These expenses are important from the investor's perspective because the cash flow requirement occurs when the expenses are paid; however, their tax influence occurs over the period of years during which amortization occurs or when the item is appropriately deductible.

Statement of Before-Tax Cash Flow (*BTCF*)

An important projection to be considered when analyzing a partnership is the statement of cash flow. In addition to the $1,121,000 investment made by limited partners in December, or the end of year 1, the statement shown in Exhibit 18–9 summarizes the before-tax cash inflow (*BTCF*), or cash shortfalls, expected from the operation of the Plaza Office Building.

Another important aspect of the statement of before-tax cash flow deals with the distribution of cash to partners. In year 2, the project is expected to generate $83,964 in cash for distribution. Of this amount, $79,766 will be distributed to limited partners. This represents an equity dividend rate of about 7 percent.

Calculation of Net Income or Loss

To illustrate the tax effect of the projections made in Exhibit 18–8, we have constructed a statement of taxable income (or loss) in Exhibit 18–10 for the syndication-partnership investment in the Plaza Office Building. The exhibit shows that limited partners making a $1,121,000 (total for all partners) investment at the end of December would have a $12,502 taxable loss to report during year 2. The syndication loss is a passive loss, as discussed in Chapter 11, and subject to the passive activity loss limitation rules. In this example, we assume that each of the 35 partners has sufficient passive activity income from other investments (e.g., other real estate partnership investments that now have taxable income) to use the share of the loss (11,877 ÷ 35) in year 2. Beginning in year 3, investors would have to report taxable income, which would be subject to ordinary rates of taxation at that time.

eXcel

EXHIBIT 18–10 **Pro Forma Statement of Income (Loss), Plaza Office Building Syndication**

www.mhhe.com/bf15e

		Year			
	(2)	**(3)**	**(4)**	**(5)**	**(6)**
Net operating income	$ 463,125	$477,019	$491,329	$506,069	$521,251
Less					
Interest	358,910	356,342	353,448	350,187	346,512
Depreciation	110,317	110,317	110,317	110,317	110,317
Amortization					
Organization fee	4,000	4,000	4,000	4,000	4,000
Loan fee	2,400	2,400	2,400	2,400	50,400
Taxable income	$–12,502	$ 3,960	$ 21,164	$ 39,165	$ 10,022
Distribution					
General partners	5%				
Limited partners	95%				
Distribution					
General partners	$ –625	$ 198	$ 1,058	$ 1,958	$ 501
Limited partners	$–11,877	$ 3,761	$ 20,106	$ 37,207	$ 9,521

Calculation of Capital Gain from Sale

The calculation of capital gains and the resulting tax due from sale of the property is the same for a syndicated investment property sale as it is for the sale of property held by an individual. Exhibit 18–11 shows the calculation of the capital gain and its allocation to the general and limited partners pursuant to the partnership agreement, which provides that 10 percent of the gain be allocated to the general partner and 90 percent of the gain be allocated to the limited partner.

Capital Accounts

Capital accounts represent the partners' ownership equity in partnership assets. Capital accounts are maintained by *crediting* the account for all *cash contributed* to the partnership and all *income* and *gain* allocated to each partner. The account is then *debited* for *cash distributed* to the partner plus any loss allocated to the partner. Exhibit 18–12

EXHIBIT 18–11
Calculation of Capital Gain and Allocation to Partners

Calculation of Capital Gain from Reversion in Year 6		
Sale price		$5,000,000
Selling costs		250,000
Original cost basis	$4,100,000	
Less accumulated depreciation	551,587	
Adjusted basis		3,548,413
Total taxable gain		$1,201,587
Allocation of Gain		
General partners (10% of gain)		$ 120,159
Limited partners (90% of gain)		$1,081,428

EXHIBIT 18–12   Capital Accounts Prior to Distribution of Cash Flow from Sale

	End of Year					
	1	2	3	4	5	6
		Limited Partners				
Equity	$1,121,000					
Plus income	0	$ 0	$ 3,761	$ 20,106	$ 37,207	$ 9,521
Less loss	0	−11,877	0	0	0	0
Plus gain from sale	0					1,081,428
Less cash distributed	0	−79,766	−92,965	−106,560	−120,563	−134,986
Total for year	1,121,000	−91,643	−89,204	−86,455	−83,357	955,963
Balance	$1,121,000	$1,029,357	$940,153	$853,698	$770,341	$1,726,304
		General Partner				
Equity	$59,000					
Plus income	0	$ 0	$ 198	$ 1,058	$ 1,958	$ 501
Less loss	0	−625	0	0	0	0
Plus gain from sale						120,159
Less cash distributed	0	−4,198	−4,893	−5,608	−6,345	−7,105
Total for year	59,000	−4,823	−4,695	−4,550	−4,387	113,555
Balance	$59,000	$54,177	$49,482	$44,932	$40,545	$154,100

shows the capital account balances for the partners after accounting for the initial equity contribution, all income allocated from operating the property, all cash distributed while operating the property, and the allocation of gain from sale of the property. Thus, capital account balances include everything but cash proceeds from sale of the property because, according to the partnership agreement, the distribution of cash proceeds from sale of the property is to be based on the capital account balance.

The capital account balance at the end of year 1 is $1,121,000 for the limited partners and $59,000 for the general partner. This represents the initial equity contributions. In year 2, those balances are reduced by both the losses allocated and the cash distributed. Of course, the reason that cash is available for distribution at the same time losses are allocated is because losses are due to noncash deductions (depreciation and amortization), as discussed in Chapter 11. Note that beginning in year 3, income allocations increase capital accounts, but cash distributions reduce them. Finally, in year 6, capital accounts are increased by the gain from sale allocated to each partner. In an accounting sense, the balances in year 6 show what each partner has in the way of equity capital invested in the partnership at that time. This is important to know because cash proceeds from sale of the property will be distributed in accordance with these capital account balances. We will further discuss the importance of these capital accounts later.

Distribution of Cash from Sale of Asset

Exhibit 18–13 shows a breakdown of the cash distribution from the sale of the property. As indicated in the agreement, after selling expenses and the outstanding mortgage are paid, both the limited partners and the general partner will receive cash distributions from the

EXHIBIT 18–13
Cash Distribution
from Sale—Year 6

Sale price	$5,000,000
Less selling costs	250,000
Less mortgage balance	2,869,596
Before-tax cash flow	1,880,404
Distribution (based on capital account balances):	
General partners	154,100
Limited partners	1,726,304
Balance (should be zero)	$ 0

sale that are equal to their capital account balances. Capital account balances for all of the partners will be exactly zero after this distribution of cash because all prior allocations of income, cash flows, and losses have been accounted for in the partners' capital accounts (see Exhibit 18–12).

Calculation of After-Tax Cash Flow and *ATIRR* on Equity

After-tax cash flows from operations and reversion can be calculated and the *ATIRR* on the investment can be determined using the preceding exhibits and an assumed marginal tax bracket of 28 percent. This is done in Exhibit 18–14, where the initial equity investment is a cash outflow in year 1 and before-tax cash flows plus tax savings (or less taxes due) are cash inflows. After-tax cash flows from operations and reversion result in an *ATIRR* of 13.15 percent for limited partners and 22.24 percent for the general partner. The higher return to the general partner is due to the additional allocation of gain and, consequently, additional cash flow when the property is sold. That is, the general partner was allocated 10 percent of the gain from the sale, whereas the general partner contributed 5 percent of the equity and received 5 percent of the income and cash flow during the operating years. If the allocation of gain had also been 5 percent for the general partner, then the *ATIRR* would have been exactly the same for both general and limited partners. (This return would be 13.68%. Of course, the general and limited partners must also be in the same tax bracket for their after-tax returns to be the same.)

Given our analysis of Dallac, you should have a general framework in mind to consider potential investments involving limited partnerships. We should stress that the Dallac case example is meant to illustrate one possible way in which an investment can be structured. Indeed, many consider the field of real estate syndication financing and partnerships one of the most complex areas of federal tax law, subject to great variations in structuring terms among partners. Hence, much study of the law and federal taxation beyond the information presented here is required to gain expertise in the area.

However, you can keep in mind a few underlying generalizations when evaluating such investments. One generalization is that syndication arrangements are subject to the same economic influences that all investments are, that is, risk and return. Any real estate investment is capable of producing only so much income, regardless of whether or not it is syndicated. When syndicated under a limited partnership, cash flows and tax items from operating and the eventual sale of assets are simply split among different parties. The promoter of the syndicate, who in many cases becomes the general partner, will offer limited partners only what is necessary under current competitive conditions to induce them to invest in the project. Such a return must be commensurate with the risk and return available to investors from comparable syndication offerings or other investment opportunities. Hence, the *ratios* used to establish contribution of equity assessments, splitting of cash flows, and so on, should be structured in such a way that given reasonable projections of income and property value, investors will earn a competitive return as measured by the procedure described in this section of the chapter.

EXHIBIT 18–14   **Calculation of After-Tax Cash Flow and *ATIRR***

www.mhhe.com/bf15e

	End of Year					
	1	2	3	4	5	6
			General Partner			
Operation						
BTCF*	$−59,000	$4,198	$4,893	$5,608	$6,345	$7,105
Taxable income†	0	−625	198	1,058	1,958	501
Taxes (28%)	0	−175	55	296	548	140
ATCF	$−59,000	$4,373	$4,838	$5,312	$5,797	$6,965
Reversion						
BTCF‡						$154,100
Capital gain§						120,159
Taxes (28%)						33,644
ATCF						120,456
Total ATCF	$−59,000	$4,373	$4,838	$5,312	$5,797	$127,421
ATIRR = 22.24%						
			Limited Partners			
Operation						
BTCF*	$−1,121,000	$ 79,766	$92,965	$106,560	$120,563	$134,986
Taxable income†		−11,877	3,761	20,106	37,207	9,521
Taxes (28%)	0	−3,326	1,053	5,630	10,418	2,666
ATCF	$−1,121,000	$ 83,092	$91,912	$100,930	$110,145	$132,320
Reversion						
BTCF‡						$1,726,304
Capital gain§						1,081,428
Taxes (28%)						302,800
ATCF						1,423,504
Total ATCF	$−1,121,000	$ 83,092	$91,912	$100,931	$110,145	$1,555,824
ATIRR = 13.15%						

*From Exhibits 18–7 and 18–9.
†From Exhibit 18–10.
‡From Exhibit 18–12.
§From Exhibit 18–11.

Investors should be in a position to compare terms offered by competing syndicators given the risk and required equity investment, and to judge whether expected returns are adequate. However, keep in mind that the general partner must also earn a competitive return in order to profitably perform the economic function of syndicating. Essentially, syndicators view their role in the investment process more like that of an agent who seeks and finds properties for acquisition or development, finds equity investors, operates and manages properties during ownership by the syndication, and eventually disposes of them. Because syndicators perform these services, they must also be reasonably assured of being compensated. Hence, they attempt to charge *fees* for all services such as finding properties for purchase, renting facilities, promoting the sale of partnership interests, and managing and accounting for the partnership investment. Investors pay these fees in addition to legal and accounting costs of organizing the partnership.

Limited partners must consider the reasonableness of syndicators' fees and partnership fees, plus the general partner's share in cash flows and appreciation in property value, when comparing syndication alternatives. The primary concern of the limited partner is whether the general partner is "carving out" too much in fees and participation in future cash flows that would make the return on investment unattractive to limited partners. On the other hand, the general partner must be assured of earning a reasonable return for the risk and time involved in promoting the investment. Further, if the syndicator is attempting to earn all compensation from fees and is not taking some equity risk in the project, it may appear to a limited partner that the syndicator–general partner really has no stake in the project and has little concern over the long-run performance of the investment. If *expertise* in the operation and management of the investment is the part of the syndication that appeals to the limited partner, then the limited partner may be more satisfied if the general partner has a stake in the profits instead of receiving fees. Clearly, many facets of reimbursement must be considered, and the partners must reach some balance. Although fees to the general partner may ultimately reduce the limited partner's rate of return, these fees represent the cost of transferring certain risks and responsibilities to the general partner. Thus, the limited partner should not expect as high a return as in a situation where he must incur these risks and costs himself.

Partnership Allocations and Substantial Economic Effect

One of the advantages of a partnership, whether a limited partnership or a general partnership between a few individuals, is the ability to allocate profit and loss to different partners in different proportions than their equity contribution. However, certain guidelines must be followed to ensure that the benefits of these allocations will not be disallowed. Syndicates typically attempt to allocate the greatest amount of tax loss from the venture as quickly as possible to the individuals (usually limited partners) who have contributed capital to the partnership. In effect, it is these tax losses that the investors have purchased. Various means, such as disproportionate allocations of specific items (such as depreciation deductions), have been used to accelerate the allocation of losses to limited partners.[12] A partner's distributive share of each item of income, gain, loss, deduction, or credit is generally determined by the partnership agreement. However, for the IRS to accept the allocations as valid, the allocations must result in what is referred to as a **substantial economic effect.** Where the allocation in the partnership agreement lacks substantial economic effect, the item that is subject to the allocation will be reallocated by the IRS according to the partner's "interest in the partnership."[13]

In determining whether an allocation had a substantial economic effect on the partners, the courts have long inquired whether the allocation was reflected by an appropriate adjustment in the partners' capital accounts. The new proposed regulations governing special allocations adopt this view and provide rules for the proper maintenance of the partners' capital accounts.[14] As we have seen, capital accounts are used for accounting purposes and reflect the economic contribution of partners to the partnership. In general, the proposed regulations provide that if (1) an allocation to a partner is reflected in her capital account and the liquidation proceeds (cash flows from sale of the property) are distributed

---

[12] For a more inclusive discussion, see Richard B. Peiser, "Partnership Allocations in Real Estate Joint Ventures," *Real Estate Review* 13, no. 3, Fall 1983, pp. 46–54.

[13] A partner's "interest in the partnership" is determined by taking into account all of the facts and circumstances, including the partner's initial investment; interest in profits, losses, and cash flow; and distributions of capital upon liquidation.

[14] Treasury Regulation Section 1.704–1.

in accordance with the capital accounts and (2) following the distribution of the proceeds the partners are liable to the partnership (either pursuant to the partnership agreement or under state law) to restore any deficit in their capital accounts (by contributing cash to partners with positive capital account balances), the allocation has substantial economic effect and will be recognized by the IRS.

Capital Accounts and Gain Charge-Backs

Assume A and B form a partnership where A, the limited partner, contributes $100,000 and B, the general partner, contributes no cash. The partnership secures a $400,000 (10% interest only) nonrecourse loan and acquires AB Apartments for $500,000. Assume that the results from the first year of operations of AB Apartments are as follows:

Gross income	$ 70,000
Less vacancy and collection loss	−4,000
Effective gross income	$ 66,000
Less operating expenses	−21,000
Net operating income	$ 45,000
Less debt service (interest only)	−40,000
Before-tax cash flow	$ 5,000

Assume that tax depreciation the first year is $50,000. This results in taxable income as follows:

Net operating income	$ 45,000
Less depreciation	50,000
Less interest cost	40,000
Taxable income	$−45,000

Now assume that the partnership agreement provides that 90 percent of all taxable income, loss, and cash flow from operations is to be allocated to A and 10 percent to B. At the end of year 1, the capital accounts of A and B would appear as follows:

Capital Accounts after First Year of Operations		
	A's Capital Account	B's Capital Account
Initial equity contribution	$ 100,000	0
Less loss allocation	−40,500	$−4,500
Less cash flow distribution	−4,500	−500
Ending balance	$ 55,000	$−5,000

Assume that AB apartments is sold after year 1 for $550,000 with no expenses of sale. This results in a taxable gain as follows:

Sales price		$550,000
Purchase price	$500,000	
Depreciation taken	50,000	
Adjusted basis		450,000
Gain		$100,000

Cash proceeds from the sale would be as follows:

Sale price	$550,000
Less mortgage balance	400,000
Cash flow	$150,000

Now suppose that upon resale, taxable gains or losses are split 50–50 between A and B. Cash proceeds are distributed first to A in an amount equal to his original investment less any cash distributions previously received. Any remaining cash proceeds are split 50–50 between A and B. Exhibit 18–15 shows the impact this arrangement would have on the capital accounts of A and B. Notice that the *net* balance of the two capital accounts is zero (this will always be true if all items of income, cash, etc., are properly accounted for), but A's capital account is negative and B's is positive. As mentioned above, for an allocation to have a substantial economic effect, liquidation proceeds to be distributed must reflect the disparities in the partners' capital accounts. Where A's capital account is negative and B's is positive, A has in effect recovered his investment at the expense of B. If A is not obligated to restore the deficit in his capital account (by a $17,750 cash payment to B), he may not have borne the entire economic burden equivalent to his share of the depreciation deductions, and the allocations lack substantial economic effect. Therefore, in order for the allocations to be recognized, the capital accounts of the partners must be equalized before the partners in this example can split the remaining cash 50–50. Two acceptable methods of equalizing the capital accounts are discussed below.

The first method of equalizing capital accounts is to adjust the cash distribution to the partners. This adjustment would be done by allocating $17,750 less cash from sale to A and $17,750 more to B. The accounts would now be equal. The second method would be to credit A's capital account for an additional $17,750 in *gain from sale,* thereby reducing B's share of the gain proportionally. If more gain is allocated to A, capital account balances will be zero after cash is distributed.

Exhibit 18–16 illustrates a valid partnership allocation using the second approach, or **gain charge-back** method, and shows its impact on the capital accounts of A and B.

EXHIBIT 18–15
Capital Accounts after Sale of Building

	A's Capital Account	B's Capital Account
Balance prior to sale	$ 55,000	$ −5,000
Return of original equity		
Less previous cash distribution	$−95,500	NA
50% of gain	50,000	50,000
50% remaining cash proceeds	−27,250	−27,250
Ending balance	$− 17,750	$ 17,750

EXHIBIT 18–16
Capital Accounts after Sale of Building Using Gain Charge-Back

	A's Capital Account	B's Capital Account
Balance prior to sale	$ 55,000	$−5,000
Return of original equity		
Less previous cash distribution	$−95,500	
Gain charge-back	35,500	
50% of remaining gain*	32,250	32,250
50% remaining cash proceeds	−27,250	27,250
Ending balance	$ 0	$ 0

*Total gain from sale is $100,000. After the gain charge-back, $65,000 remains to be distributed.

Careful examination of the above example should make it clear that the requirement that capital account balances for both partners be zero after sale of the building is one way for the IRS to ensure that a partner who is allocated proportionately more losses for tax purposes is also either allocated more taxable gain at sale of the property or receives less cash. Otherwise, partnerships could be structured in such a way that the partners in higher tax brackets would receive most of the losses, whereas the partners in lower tax brackets would receive most of the gains! Furthermore, the partners in higher tax brackets would be willing to give up some of the cash flow in exchange for receiving the losses and not receiving the gains. The ending capital account balances would then most likely be negative for the partners in higher tax brackets and positive for partners in the lower tax brackets. While the partners may be perfectly happy with this arrangement, the government loses tax revenue. Thus, as we have emphasized, partnership agreements must provide for ending capital account balances to be zero to avoid challenge from the IRS.

Recall that in the case of the Plaza Office Building, the gain was first allocated to the capital accounts, and then the final cash flow was based on the capital account balances. This approach ensured that the capital account balances would be zero for both partners after all allocations and distributions to partners. The partnership agreement could have been structured in other ways for Plaza Office Building and still have resulted in zero capital account balances. For example, a specified percentage of the *cash* available from sale could first be distributed to each partner—the general partners in the Plaza Office Building might receive 10 percent and the limited partners 90 percent. Then, to ensure zero capital account balances, the allocation of gain could be based on the capital account balances. (In this case, the capital account balances would be negative after the distribution of cash. Allocation of gain to the partners would then eliminate the negative balance.) The point is that allocations of all items of income and cash flow cannot be made without some provision for ensuring that the capital account balances are zero after all allocations and distributions are made.

Use of the Limited Partnership in Private and Public Syndicates

Limited partnerships are widely used as vehicles for raising equity capital for real estate ventures. They combine the limited-liability feature of an investment in a corporation with the advantages of a general partnership, such as the ability to make special allocations of income and cash flow to the partners. An investor's liability (limited partner) is limited to the initial contribution plus any unpaid contributions agreed to in the future. Furthermore, the responsibility for the management of the partnership rests with the general partners who are frequently knowledgeable in real estate matters, thus providing the partnership with professional management.

In establishing the limited partnership, great care must be taken that the contractual terms identify it in effect as a partnership and not as an "association" as understood by the Internal Revenue Service. An association is taxed like a corporation. The six criteria for treatment like a corporation are:

1. Business association.
2. An objective to carry on the business and divide the gains therefrom.
3. Continuity of life.
4. Centralization of management.
5. Limited liability.
6. Free transferability of interest.

A corporation must have more corporate than noncorporate characteristics to be classified as a corporation for tax purposes. Criteria 1 and 2 are common to corporations and partnerships. Therefore, a business firm generally will be treated as a partnership if two of criteria 3 through 6 are absent.

Most limited partnerships have centralized management similar to that of corporations, so differentiation normally takes place in criteria 3, 5, and 6. Under the Uniform Partnership Act, after which most state statutes are patterned, the general partner has the power to dissolve the partnership at any time, thus denying it continuity of life. Otherwise, a terminal date may be provided in the partnership articles. The criterion of limited liability is negated by the very fact that one partner is a general partner with unlimited liability. Finally, free transferability of interests can be limited by requiring permission of the general or other limited partners to effect a change of ownership. This restriction has been deemed by the Treasury regulations as a legal curtailment of transferability of interests. By proper combination of these provisions, tax treatment as a partnership can be achieved.

Use of Corporate General Partners

The sole general partner of a limited partnership is often a corporation. The advantage of this arrangement lies in the limits on personal liability for the builder-sponsor of a project whose interest in the limited partnership is through a corporation. An incorporated general partner can also provide better continuity of management. To avoid "dummy" corporations as the sole corporate general partner, the Internal Revenue Service follows internal guidelines (called **safe harbor rules**) that impose certain ownership and minimum capital requirements. Limited partners may not own, individually or in the aggregate, more than 20 percent of the corporate stock. The net worth requirement of the corporate general partner depends on the total contributed capital of the partnership. If the contributed capital is less than $2.5 million, the corporate general partner must have a net worth at least equal to 15 percent of the total partnership capital, but not to exceed $250,000. Where the contributed partnership capital is $2.5 million or more, the corporate general partner must maintain at all times a net worth of at least 10 percent of the partnership capital.

Private versus Public Syndicates

An important way to classify syndicates is as **private** and **public.** Most private offerings are issued under Regulation D of the Securities Act of 1933 so as to be exempt from the registration requirements of that act. The Securities and Exchange Commission proposed Regulation D in 1982 to simplify and expand the exemptions from federal securities registration. It exempts syndicates from the registration requirement of the Securities Act, not from the full disclosure and antifraud provisions of securities laws. But that exemption can be significant—the costs of registration essentially eliminate all but the largest syndicated offerings, so exemption from registration under certain conditions facilitates small and medium-sized offerings. Compliance with the regulation does not by itself exempt syndications under *state* securities laws; many states, however, do have similar exemption statutes. Although Regulation D codifies and expands prior exemption statutes, it also defines important concepts, including that of the **accredited investor,** which is discussed in the following section. Anyone involved in making an offering pursuant to the regulation should read and understand it thoroughly to ensure careful compliance with its provisions.

Accredited Investors—Regulation D

If the securities are sold only to accredited investors, it is not necessary to provide investors with the information otherwise required to obtain an exemption under Regulation D. Accredited investors purchasing securities are also not counted in determining the maximum number of potential purchasers that may be solicited to retain exemption from Regulation D. Also, accredited investors do not need to meet the "sophistication and experience" requirements in financial and business matters that are applicable to other investors under the private placement exemption rule in Regulation D. General examples of criteria used to describe accredited investors include the following:

- Any director, executive officer, or general partner of the issuer of the securities being offered or sold, or a director, executive officer, or general partner of a general partner of that issuer.

- Any person who purchases at least $150,000 of the securities being offered, where the purchaser's total purchase price does not exceed 20 percent of the purchaser's net worth at the time of sale.

- Any natural person whose individual net worth, or joint net worth with that person's spouse, at the time of purchase exceeds $1 million.

- Any natural person who had an individual income in excess of $200,000 in each of the two most recent years and who reasonably expects an income in excess of $200,000 in the current year.

Private offerings are usually limited to 35 or fewer investors. A public offering, on the other hand, is characterized by rigorous compliance requirements of the federal and state securities divisions governing the sale of securities to the public. Numerous reports, brochures, prospectuses, and the like are required to qualify an issue for sale to the public. The minimum cost for a registration with the Securities and Exchange Commission is about $50,000 and can run as high as $300,000 to $500,000 for large syndications that register and sell shares in many states. Given the high cost of registering a public syndication under federal and state laws, it makes sense to have a public syndication for large transactions that raise a large amount of capital.

Certificates of participation in public syndicates have been sold in units as low as $500, $1,000, or $5,000. Minimum investments in private syndicates are usually 10 times this amount. Recently, public syndicates have reduced their investment minimums in an attempt to attract Individual Retirement Account and Keogh (self-employed retirement plan) money. The result has been that, instead of a few participants of substantial means and risk-taking ability, the syndicate membership may be composed of thousands of small investors. Individuals now have a chance to invest in prime real estate that would normally be beyond the reach of all but wealthy or institutional investors.

Caveats

In a large public syndication, the syndication general partners usually share very few of the risks. They may have originally bought property through another business entity and sold it to the syndicate at a profit. Through other companies that they may also own, they may receive substantial remuneration for the sale of securities to the public, management services, and so on. As the general partners, all earnings and capital gains not contracted to the limited partners accrue to their benefit. These activities may or may not be fully disclosed to potential investors. The role of general partners has been a matter of increasingly grave concern to state and federal securities sales regulators.

Crowd Funding: New Options for Raising Capital from Investors*

As noted in the chapter, raising equity to establish or expand a business by selling shares in it has been regulated by the Securities Act of 1933 and the Securities Exchange Act of 1934. This required registration with the Securities Exchange Commission (SEC), unless the offering was private and qualified for exemption under Regulation D, or the much less commonly used Regulation A.

Regulation D has been considered a "safe harbor" under the private offering exemption in the securities exchange act as long as the offering was to "accredited investors." States could not pre-empt the federal Regulation D exemption from registration. Recall that accredited investors are those whose earnings have been in excess of $200,000 (or $300,000 if combined with spouse's income) for the past two years or whose net worth excluding their residence is in excess of $1 million. A private placement is one that is not offered to the public but is only made available to people who had an established prior relationship with the issuer without registration. This meant that there could be no advertising to investors. Regulation D did allow a small number (up to 35) unaccredited investors as long as they were sophisticated investors and provided adequate disclosure about the risks of the offering. There could also only be a maximum of 500 investors including both accredited and unaccredited investors.

Regulation A permitted both accredited and unaccredited investors to purchase shares up to $5 million in a business that registers in the state or in multiple states under the "blue sky laws." One often cited example of the use of Reg A for real estate was the Fundrise redevelopment of a property on H Street in Washington, DC.[i] This was a small deal, with all of the funds raised locally so that it wasn't necessary to register in more than one state, but it heralded the changes in real estate equity funding that were on the horizon, and the firm has since become a leader in securing funds through internet offerings across the US. Although registration at the federal level was not required for Reg A, the SEC could still provide comments to the issuer that had to be addressed which could make the issuance time consuming and burdensome. With the relatively small amount of capital that could be raised under regulation A and the somewhat cumbersome state rules, Regulation A saw limited use by investors.

All of this changed, starting in 2012 when the Jumpstart our Business Startups Act (JOBS Act) passed in April 2012. (See following table that summarizes the options under the new regulations.) The legislation required that regulations to implement it would be drafted promptly, but that process dragged out until September 2013 before the Title II regulations came out for Regulation D (506C) investments, and then another eighteen months passed before the Title IV rules were issued governing the new "Reg A +" investments. It now looks like it will be 2016 before the draft rules on Title III Crowdfunding will actually become permanent. (The term "crowd funding" tends to be used more widely to refer to capital raised by reaching investors through the internet under the new regulations but true crowdfunding regulations are still in draft form as noted below.)

The rules reflect the delicate balance that the SEC has attempted to strike between policy and politics. The 1933 and 1934 Acts came into existence to protect consumers from the turmoil caused by the 1929 stock market crash, and the lack of transparency, outright fraud and misrepresentation. The underlying principal is that requiring disclosure will largely protect investors but that sophisticated investors need less protection than unsophisticated ones, and that enforcement of these protections belongs at the federal, not state, level.

*The authors thank Susanne Cannon with Megalytics, LLC for her assistance in the preparation of this insert. Investment Options under JOBS Act.

Investment Options Under New Regulations

Investor Qualification		Maximum Investment	Maximum Capital Raise	Proof of Status	Secondary Market
Accredited Investor	Title II, REG D (506c)	No limit	None, but only 2000 investors	Verification of Investor Status by issuer or platform	No, but a market is being developed
	Title IV, Reg A+	No Limit	Same as for unaccredited below	N/A	Yes
	Title III, Crowdfunding Draft Regulations	10% of income above $100,000	$1,000,000	Platform operator verifies	Only to accredited investor
Unaccredited Investor	Title IV, Reg A+ Tier 1	No Limit	$20 Million in 12 months; no limit on number of investors	No verification required	Yes
	Title IV, Reg A+ Tier 2	No more than 10% of income or 10% of wealth	$50 Million in 12 months, no limit on number of investors	No verification required	Yes
	Title III Crowdfunding Draft Regulations	$2,000 to $100,000 with Cap of 5% of income or net worth if income less than $100,000; Cap of 10% if income greater than $100,000	$1 Million in 12 months	Platform operator verifies	12 month prohibition on resale except to accredited investor

The table provides a simplified summary of the options for raising capital from accredited and unaccredited investors. The full rules for Regulation A+ can be found at the following URL: http://www.sec.gov/rules/final/2015/33-9741.pdf. And for Regulation D the rules can be found at: https://www.sec.gov/info/smallbus/secg/general-solicitation-small-entity-compliance-guide.htm.

A significant change is that businesses can use modern technology, i.e., the internet to advertise and try to reach accredited investors, and those investors now have several paths they can follow to make investments. Issuers must take reasonable care to verify that the investors are accredited.

Unaccredited investors have some new options now and will have the opportunity to make modest investments in small startup firms that they were previously prevented from investing in. The regulations created varying limits on the amount an investor can place, the total amount that can be raised, the liquidity of the shares, the sales mechanism and compensation scheme, disclosure and reporting requirements. A more detailed summary of the comparisons can be found at the following URL: http://www.duanemorris.com/alerts/SEC_adopts_regulation_a_plus_rules_5513.html. Note that Reg D now allows up to 2000 rather than 500 investors.

Under the new Reg A+ (tier 2) regulations, the limit on the amount of capital that could be raised increased to up to $50 million from the previous $5 million limit. The securities can be offered and sold publicly and state laws cannot preempt the federal regulations by providing further limitations. Also note that the same requirements apply for selling to accredited or unaccredited investors. Thus, in effect, there are not accredited investor requirements under the new Reg A+. These changes could result in a significant increase in the number of offerings under the new Reg A + compared to the previous Reg A rules.

Accredited investors may purchase shares in Reg D, Reg A+ or the new Title III crowdfunding opportunities when they become available. The most important changes in Reg D offerings are the ability to find investments and the requirement that they verify their status. Reg A+ has dramatic changes and are a sort of cross between Reg D and the anticipated true crowdfunding and more traditional public offerings. An excellent summary is available at the following URL: http://www.flastergreenberg.com/media/article/454_A_Regulation_A_Plus_Primer_final.pdf.

The issuer of the security is restricted in the sort of outreach to the investment community, who the sales persons are, how they are compensated, and the sorts of disclosure and reporting required. Part of this comes from the political backdrop that existed prior to the new rules, when Regulation A deals were small but governed by state securities authorities which didn't want to give up their power, and part comes from the sense that investors of modest means need special protections. The true crowdfunding rules have not been issued, but they will require either broker-dealers to sell the securities or the use of a yet-to-be-created entity called an internet "funding portal". The SEC has estimated that the cost to raise $1 million would range from $76,660 to $151, 660, and even very small capital raises would likely be at least $39,000.[ii] The draft rules are can be found at the following URL: https://www.sec.gov/rules/proposed/2013/33-9470.pdf and a more detailed summary of the draft rules can be found at http://www.whiteandwilliams.com/resources-alerts-Jumpstart-or-False-Start-SEC-Proposes-New-Rules-to-Implement-Crowdfunding-Provisions-of-the-JOBS-Act.html.

As an intriguing side note, over 20 states have created their own regulations for crowdfunding within the borders of their states and this adds both to the possibilities but also to the regulatory uncertainties for those seeking funding.

Beyond the regulatory structure there is the question of how these new mechanisms will work in the world of real estate investment. A wide array of choices has been emerging for investors. Investments are likely to have a wide range of risk and return expectations. Investments may have a time horizon from a few months to seven to 10 years. The size of investment can be as low as a thousand dollars or as high as $50,000 or more. The sponsor or issuer may be looking for a total equity investment, a total debt structure, or a hybrid in between, and may be proposing to do a ground-up development, one of the "fix and flip" housing deals so popular on television, or something that is a stabilized acquisition and operation deal. Property types range along a spectrum including hotel, retail, office, industrial, and housing.

There is expected to be tremendous growth in capital being raised under all these new regulations as it is becoming much easier to invest in real estate than was possible for many investors under the previous regulations. The new regulations allow promoters and investors to take advantage of the transparency and efficiency provided by use of the internet to facilitate the flow of capital from investors to investments. Companies like WealthForge (www.wealthforge.com) have emerged to make it even easier for promoters to use the internet to raise capital from accredited investors by providing the back-end infrastructure for crowd funding sites. Their solution takes potential investors through the Qualified Investor vetting process, tracks their progress through the investment process and processes the payments for those that end up investing. This allows individual companies without the regulatory expertise to "crowd fund" themselves by developing an "Invest" button that can be placed on any website. Therefore, a promotor of a deal could create a website for a property, add the WealthForge invest button and then steer potential investors to that website. This provides another alternative for investors in addition to finding the opportunity on a traditional crowd funding site.

Some of the most successful platforms offering real estate investments listed below.

Prodigy Network
www.prodigynetwork.com

RealtyShares
www.realtyshares.com

Realty Mogul
www.realtymogul.com

Patch of Land
https://patchofland.com

Fundrise
https://fundrise.com

CrowdStreet
www.crowdstreet.com

Endnotes

[i] http://www.citylab.com/work/2012/11/real-estate-deal-could-change-future-everything/3897/

[ii] http://venturebeat.com/2014/01/02/it-might-cost-you-39k-to-crowdfund-100k-under-the-secs-new-rules/

Regulation of Syndicates

The great flexibility of the limited partnership has led to abuses. In 1980, a statement of policy or guidelines that established standards for limited partnership offerings of real estate was adopted by the North American Securities Administrators Association (NASAA). State registration agencies, in those states where the guidelines are applicable, generally look with disfavor upon applications that do not conform to the standards contained in the guidelines. All states except California (which in some respects has even more stringent guidelines) belong to NASAA, but not all states have adopted the NASAA guidelines. However, a substantial number of states follow the guidelines, and although the guidelines are intended to *apply only to public syndicates,* many securities administrators look to them for guidance when considering requests for exemptions from registration. The guidelines address syndicates' investment policies, promoters' and managers' compensation, and investor suitability standards. It is in these areas that federal and state regulatory authorities have expressed their greatest concern.

Investment Objectives and Policies

Syndicates differ widely in the investment objectives they seek to accomplish and policies they follow to achieve them. If targeted syndicate investors are in a low tax bracket and seek current income (e.g., IRA and pension fund investors), the syndicate will acquire properties that produce the greatest cash flow. Some of these properties may be purchased for all cash. Other investors may not need current income and may seek properties (such as raw land in the path of urban growth) that offer the greatest potential for future capital gain. Still other investors may emphasize investments that generate tax shelters through high depreciation and mortgage interest deductions. The targeted investors for the syndicate will dictate the investment objectives and policies of the syndicator.

Until the late 1960s, syndicates normally raised capital to finance identifiable parcels, which were described in the prospectus or offering circular in detail so the investor could evaluate them before investing money. Such syndicates are referred to as "specified property" syndicates. Other syndicates raise capital before identifying any or all of the properties they will eventually own. They are known as **blind pool** syndicates and should be recognized as pure venture capital funds since no property descriptions or relevant economic or financial data are available to guide the investor. Specific investment criteria (e.g., type of property and geographic location) should be disclosed in the prospectus for such a blind pool syndicate, as well as the sponsor's background, experience, and previous results, because an investment in a blind pool is essentially an investment in the syndicator's track record and reputation. Investors in such offerings should carefully scrutinize the statement of investment objectives contained in the prospectus, as well as the background and track record of the syndicator. Syndicates' investment objectives generally vary around the following partial list of attributes:

- Fully identified properties.
- Blind pool investment.
- Use of leverage.
- Period of ownership expected before assets are sold.
- Land development investments to be allowed.
- Joint ventures with developers and other investors.
- Acquisition of foreclosed properties for resale.

Promoters' and Managers' Compensation

A major area of concern for syndicate investors is promotional and management fees. Keeping these fees to reasonable levels becomes especially difficult because of the many ways in which compensation can be paid. Syndicators often charge fees for providing services such as acquiring properties for the portfolio, managing them, guaranteeing investors a minimum cash flow, selling properties, or arranging refinancing. Obviously, up-front fees reduce the amount of funds available for investment in the actual real estate. Additional fees may also be charged on the "back end" out of proceeds from sale of the property.

Management fees have been based on gross assets, net assets, gross rentals, net income, and cash flow. Each method yields its own unique results depending on the fortunes of the syndicate operation. Unfortunately, projections of results are often based on hypotheticals without valid underlying assumptions. Bad projections distort judgments of appropriate compensation and the proper method for determining it. In all instances, full disclosure of conflicts of interest of principals, as well as all direct and indirect compensation payable by the partners to promoters, general partners, underwriters, and affiliates, should be made. This disclosure should describe the time of payment and amount of compensation, and it should detail the service rendered to earn it.

As we just pointed out, fees charged by syndicators and others promoting the syndicate vary widely. Because up-front fees reduce amounts available for investment, investors should look closely at deals where more than 20 percent of the equity raised is paid out in fees. Typical up-front fees include 7 percent to 10 percent for sales commissions to brokers selling syndicate interests, 1 percent to 3 percent for legal and accounting expenses, and 5 percent to 15 percent for organizational and financing fees.

Investor Suitability Standards

An outstanding weakness of a limited partnership interest as an investment is its lack of liquidity or marketability. Because of the restrictions on the assignability of the capital interest, a new partner must have the consent of the existing partners to acquire and enjoy the full interest of a selling partner. Furthermore, state-imposed requirements of financial responsibility of potential investors have made it more difficult to develop a secondary market for such interests. Even an issue of certificates of beneficial interest in a limited partnership is complicated because the limited partner selling an interest becomes a securities issuer and is subject to separate registration requirements. This lack of liquidity and marketability increases the riskiness of a limited partnership investment.

Another weakness of the syndicate is that many syndications have limited appeal to any but the investor in the high tax bracket. Yields other than from a tax shelter may be negligible. The low-income investor may acquire such a syndicate interest with too little appreciation of the weak economic viability of the venture. Minimum suitability standards for investors as recommended by the NASAA guidelines include either an annual gross income of $30,000 and net worth (exclusive of home, furnishings, and automobiles) of at least $30,000 or net worth of at least $75,000. Tax-oriented offerings may require higher standards, such as being in the highest federal income tax bracket, and high-risk offerings may impose higher income and net worth standards. In any case, the prospectus should clearly present the nature of the investor's expected return in the traditional sense, as well as the potential tax savings.

Federal and State Securities Authorities

The federal and state securities laws and regulations are relevant to any real estate syndication. Disclosure requirements under the Securities Act of 1933 and the Securities Exchange Act of 1934 make up the federal basis for civil liability and criminal fraud liability for principals and their professional counsels who fail to disclose full information about a public issue. Most state laws require securities salespersons to be registered in the local jurisdiction. These laws often go beyond the federal requirements in permitting the state commissioner to disqualify a securities offering on its merits, in addition to determining the required degree of disclosure of specific facts about the issue. Neglect by the issuer to qualify the issue may permit investors to rescind the whole transaction and demand their money back. Beyond these laws are the antifraud statutes that deal with fraudulent practices in connection with securities registration. Although the degree of applicability of federal or state laws and regulations differs with the characteristics of each issue, full and active compliance yields the best results for both the syndicator and investors.

Conclusion

Large real estate investments often require several investors to pool their capital in order to have sufficient equity to acquire the property. Different investors may bring different amounts of capital and expertise to the table. Therefore, an ownership agreement that takes this into consideration must be structured. This chapter discussed various ways that more than one investor can jointly acquire or develop real estate. The economics of these joint ventures were discussed, along with the legal ownership forms that can be used, such as general partnerships, limited partnerships, and corporations.

Although the focus of this chapter was on limited partnerships, the same concepts apply to simpler partnerships such as a general partnership that does not have limited partners. Finally, as noted in this chapter, most REITs formed in the past 10 years were structured such that the REIT is the general partner in a limited partnership that owns the properties. The limited partners are investors who exchanged their partnership interest in a syndication for a partnership interest in the limited partnership owned by the REIT. This is discussed further in Chapter 21.

Key Terms

accredited investor, *610*
blind pool, *597, 616*
capital account, *600*
capital stack, *596*
C corporation, *587*
cumulative distribution, *591*
gain charge-back, *608*
general partners, *598*
general partnership, *584*
initial capital contribution, *590*
IRR lookback, *591*
IRR preference, *591*

joint ventures, *588*
limited liability company (LLC), *586*
limited liability partnership (LLP), *585*
limited partners, *598*
limited partnership (LP), *585, 597*
noncumulative pari passu distribution, *590*
preferred distribution, *590*
preferred return, *590*

private offering, *597*
private syndicate, *610*
promote, *591*
public syndicate, *597, 610*
safe harbor rules, *610*
S corporation, *588*
sole proprietorship, *583*
special allocation, *600*
substantial economic effect, *606*
syndication, *596*
waterfall, *596*

Useful Web Sites

www.sppre.com—A national consulting, development, management, and real estate asset management company. Its sole purpose is to assist government, university, and school district officials in structuring and implementing public/private real estate partnerships and optimizing the value of their underutilized real estate assets.

Questions

1. What is the difference between an *IRR* preference and an *IRR* lookback?
2. What is the advantage of the limited partnership ownership form for real estate syndications?
3. How can the general partner–syndicator structure the partnership to offer incentives to limited partners?
4. Why is the Internal Revenue Service concerned with how partnership agreements in real estate are structured?
5. What is the main difference between the way a partnership is taxed versus the way a corporation is taxed?
6. What are special allocations?
7. What causes the after-tax *IRR* ($ATIRR_e$) for the general partner to differ from that of the limited partner?
8. What is the significance of capital accounts? What causes the balance in a capital account to change each year?

9. How does the risk associated with investment in a partnership differ for the general partner versus a limited partner?

10. What are the different ways that the general partner is compensated?

11. How do you think that Federal Income Tax Policy affects the desirability of investing in real estate partnerships?

12. What concerns should an investor in a real estate syndication have regarding general partners?

13. Differentiate between public and private syndications. What is an accredited investor? Why is this distinction used?

14. How are general partners usually compensated in a syndication? What major concerns should investors consider when making an investment with a syndication?

15. What is the main difference between organizing a real estate venture as a corporation versus a general partnership? How does a limited partnership have some of the characteristics of both?

Problems

1. ABC Fund has decided to enter into a joint venture with Newtown Development Inc. to develop and operate an office building that will require an initial investment of $100 million to cover all the development costs (hard and soft costs). There will be no debt financing for the joint venture. Each party invests its capital at the beginning of the first year and cash flow from operations is projected as follows:

Year 1	$ 2,000,000
Year 2	4,000,000
Year 3	9,000,000
Year 4	12,000,000
Year 5	14,000,000

It is expected that the property will be sold at the end of year 5 for $150 million.

ABC Fund will invest $45 million and Newtown Development Inc. will invest the remaining $55 million needed for the development costs. The $50 million development costs already include a developer fee to Newtown Development Inc. and the cash flow projections for each year above are net of a property management fee being paid to Newtown Development Inc.

ABC Fund will receive a 5 percent operating return that is noncumulative. That is, any shortfall is not carried over to the next year but is paid before Newtown Development Inc. receives any cash from operations. After ABC Fund is paid its preferred return, Newtown Development Inc. will receive a 5 percent operating return on its contributed capital. This is also noncumulative. Any remaining cash flow from operations is split 50–50 to each party.

When the property is sold, proceeds from sale will be distributed as follows:

First, repay the initial capital investment by ABC Fund.

Next, repay the initial capital investment by Newtown Development Inc.

Next, pay ABC Fund an 11 percent *IRR* preference on its investment.

Thereafter, split all proceeds 50–50.

Use the above assumptions to calculate the cash flows that each party will receive and its expected *IRR*.

2. Venture Capital Limited has formed a *private* real estate syndication to acquire and operate the Tower Office Building. Venture will act as the general partner and will have 35 individual limited partners. The venture to be undertaken and relevant cost and financial data are summarized as follows:

Cost breakdown

Land	$ 1,000,000	
Improvements	9,000,000	(capitalized)
Points	100,000	(amortized over loan term)
Subtotal	$10,100,000	
Organization fee	100,000	(amortized over 5 years)
Syndication expenses	100,000	(capitalized)
Total funding required	$10,300,000	

Financing

Loan amount	$ 8,000,000	
Interest rate	11%	
Term	25 years	(monthly payments)
Points	$ 100,000	

Partnership facts and equity requirements

Organization: December, year 1
Number of partners: 1 general partner and 35 limited partners
Equity capital contribution: General partner, 10%; limited partners, 90%
Cash assessments: None
Cash distributions from operations: General partner, 10%; limited partners, 90%
Taxable income and losses from operations: General partner, 10%; limited partners, 90%
Allocation of gain or loss from sale: General partner, 15%; limited partners, 85%
Cash distribution at sale: Based on capital account balances

Operating and tax projections

Potential gross income (year 2)	$1,750,000
Vacancy and collection loss	10% of potential gross income
Operating expenses (year 2)	35% of effective gross income
Depreciation method	Straight-line, 31.5 years
Projected growth in income	3% per year
Projected resale price after 5 years	$13,500,000
Limited partners' tax rate	28%
General partner's tax rate	28%
Selling expenses	5%

a. Determine an estimated return ($ATIRR_e$) for a limited partner. (*Hint:* Consider all 35 limited partners as a single investor.)

b. Determine an estimated return ($ATIRR_e$) for the general partner.

c. Why do the returns differ for the general and limited partners?

3. A and B form a partnership where A, the limited partner, contributes $500,000 and B, the general partner, contributes no cash. The partnership secures a $2 million (10% interest only) nonrecourse loan and acquires AB Apartments for $2.5 million. Assume that the results from the first year of operations of AB Apartments are as follows:

Net operating income	$ 250,000
Less debt service (interest only)	−200,000
Before-tax cash flow	$ 50,000

Assume that tax depreciation the first year is $250,000.

The partnership agreement provides that 90 percent of all taxable income, loss, and cash flow from operations is to be allocated to A and 10 percent to B. At resale, taxable gains or losses are to be split 50–50 between A and B, and cash proceeds are distributed first to A in an amount equal to his original investment less any cash distributions previously received, and then split 50–50 between A and B.

a. What are the capital account balances for A and B after one year?

b. Assume that AB Apartments is sold after year 1 for $3 million with no expenses of sale. How much cash is available (before tax) from sale?

c. How much cash would be distributed to A and B upon sale of the property?

d. How much capital gain would be allocated to A and B upon sale of the property?

e. Calculate the capital account balances for A and B after sale.

www.mhhe.com/bf15e

4. **Excel.** Refer to the "Ch18 Partner" tab in the Excel Workbook provided on the Web site. Suppose that the split between the limited and general partner is 99 percent for the limited partner and 1 percent for the general partner for equity contributions, income, and allocation of gain. How does this change the expected return to each partner?

19

The Secondary Mortgage Market: Pass-Through Securities

Introduction

We begin this chapter with a brief description of the evolution of the secondary market. Particular attention is paid to the need for this kind of market and the major organizations that participate in it. We then describe the various types of mortgage-backed securities that have evolved in recent years and provide a framework for analyzing their investment characteristics. Although mortgage-related securities may be offered on many types of mortgage pools, we generally limit our discussion to residential mortgage-backed pools. The chapter concludes with a section on "pricing" two types of mortgage-related securities and provides an evaluation of characteristics that differentiate these more important security types. The next chapter is a continuation of this one. It provides a detailed analysis of collateralized mortgage obligations (CMOs) and "derivative" securities. It also contains an introduction to commercial mortgage-backed securities.

Evolution of the Secondary Mortgage Market

The **secondary mortgage market,** as we know it today, evolved as a result of a combination of the following influences:

1. A need existed for a market in which specialized mortgage originators, such as mortgage banking companies, could sell mortgages and thereby replenish funds with which new loans could be originated.

2. A need also existed for a market mechanism to facilitate a geographic flow of funds. Such a market would allow lenders located in regions where the demand for housing and mortgage financing far exceeded the availability of deposits to sell mortgages to other intermediaries in regions with a surplus of savings.

3. Beginning in the late 1960s, many innovations in securitization occurred in response to the trend toward deregulation of depository-type financial institutions. Because of this trend, savers were no longer limited to traditional methods of saving, such as savings accounts and certificates of deposit. Further, with the passage of legislation giving individual retirement accounts (IRAs) favorable tax treatment, and the aging of the U.S. population increasing the flow of funds to pension accounts, the market for investable funds became much broader. Hence, mortgage lenders, with the aid of organizations specializing in underwriting and selling securities to the public and institutional investors, were faced with the challenge of attracting savings from the public in different ways so as to replenish funds for new mortgage loans. There has been a long-standing commitment on the part of the federal government to encourage home ownership and to provide support for a strong system of housing finance.

Early Buyers of Mortgage Loans

There has always been a secondary mortgage market of some type. Prior to the mid-1950s, primary mortgage originators included mortgage companies and, to a lesser extent, thrift institutions. Investors, including large life insurance companies and eastern thrifts with a surplus of funds, purchased mortgages from mortgage companies or from thrifts in regions where housing demand was great relative to funds available for lending. By purchasing mortgages, these institutional investors helped to replenish funds necessary for the housing boom during the postwar era.

One major factor enhancing the early development of the secondary market was that the federal government, through programs initiated with the Federal Housing Administration (FHA) and later the Veterans Administration (VA), protected mortgage investors from losses by providing either default insurance (FHA) or loan guarantees (VA). One outcome of these programs was a system of minimum underwriting standards for borrower qualifications, appraisals, and building specifications. Uniform administrative procedures required by the FHA and VA were followed by mortgage companies and helped to accommodate significant volumes of FHA and VA originations and facilitated servicing activities. Given (1) the availability of default insurance and loan guarantees, (2) the development of standardized loan underwriting, processing, and servicing, and (3) the availability of hazard and title insurance, investors in mortgages could acquire a large quantity of loans and expect to receive interest and principal payments with little or no risk. Administrative problems regarding defaults, late payments, and so forth were usually handled for a fee by the servicer, making mortgage investments resemble those of a bond or fixed-income security. With funds acquired from sales of mortgages to institutional investors, originators (primarily mortgage companies) replenished funds with which they could originate new loans.

The Secondary Market after 1954

In 1954, Congress rechartered the **Federal National Mortgage Association (FNMA),** now commonly known as "Fannie Mae," assigning it three separate and distinct activities: (1) enhancement of secondary market operations in federally insured and guaranteed mortgages, (2) management of direct loans previously made and, where necessary, liquidation of properties and mortgages acquired by default, and (3) management of special-assistance programs, including support for subsidized mortgage loan programs. Each function was carried out as though it was operated as a separate corporation.

Throughout this and earlier periods, interest rates on FHA and VA mortgages were *regulated* by those agencies. Instead of deregulating interest rates on FHA and VA mortgages, Congress, in its attempt to keep mortgage interest rates as low as possible to would-be home buyers, preferred to maintain a system under which FHA-VA interest rates would remain regulated. FNMA's role would be to raise capital by issuing debt when necessary to purchase mortgages, thereby replenishing capital to originators during periods of rising interest rates. It was thought that those mortgages would be sold at a gain when interest rates declined, thereby providing FNMA with funds to retire debt that was previously issued to acquire mortgages. FNMA was thus viewed as a vehicle that would provide liquidity to the home finance system when needed, and would assume the interest rate risk associated with its role as an intermediary between mortgage originators (primary originators of FHA and VA loans) and investors in its bonds. Ostensibly, over many periodic cycles of interest rate movements, it was hoped that FNMA would, on the average, earn a "spread" between interest earned on mortgages and interest paid on its bonds, while providing liquidity to the home finance system.[1]

FNMA's Changing Role

As market interest rates gradually increased and FHA-VA mortgage interest rates lagged, the "spread" referred to above became more problematic for FNMA to maintain. These influences prompted Congress to review the operations of FNMA and culminated in the Charter Act of 1954. Among the provisions in the act, however, was an additional provision that governmental participation in the operation of the principal secondary market facility should be gradually replaced by a private enterprise. The act included a procedure, whereby FNMA would, over a period of time, be transformed into a privately owned and managed organization. By converting FNMA to a private operation rather than setting up a new one, FNMA's years of experience in the secondary market could be utilized during the transition period and eventually would concentrate the whole operation in private hands.

To provide a financial base to operate FNMA, the Charter Act also authorized issuance of nonvoting preferred and common stock for the financing of secondary market operations. The preferred stock was issued to the secretary of the treasury. Sellers of mortgages to FNMA were required to purchase FNMA stock as a condition of sale, which provided additional capital for operations and resulted in widespread ownership of FNMA. Additional funding for FNMA came from its issuance of notes and debt instruments. The act provided that, if necessary, the U.S. Treasury would be permitted to acquire up to $2.25 billion of these notes. This "backstop" was intended to provide assurance of liquidity to FNMA bond and note purchasers and a price support for such securities, should FNMA's profitability or inability to issue more of these obligations ever come into question. It also provided FNMA with a distinct advantage when borrowing in capital markets to finance its activities. FNMA could now borrow at lower rates of interest than it otherwise could have in the absence of the Treasury backstop.

In 2008, due to concerns about FNMA's viability in light of the subprime mortgage crisis, the Federal Housing Finance Agency (FHFA) was appointed as conservator of FNMA, thus placing FNMA under federal government control (FHLMC was likewise placed under federal government control). Additionally, the U.S. Treasury agreed to provide up to $100 billion of capital as needed to ensure that FNMA continues to provide liquidity to the housing and mortgage markets. Given the continuing economic uncertainty, more changes to FNMA in the future would not be unexpected.

The Government National Mortgage Association

The **Government National Mortgage Association (GNMA)** was organized as part of the Housing and Urban Development Act of 1968 to perform three principal functions: (1) management and liquidation of mortgages previously acquired by FNMA—the

[1]Obviously, the risk of such a strategy is that the *net* cost of bonds and notes used to raise funds over periods of rising and falling interest rates could exceed the *net* interest income from mortgages held in a portfolio. This could occur if, over several cycles, net purchases of mortgages exceeded net sales.

liquidation of the portfolio acquired from FNMA at the time of its partition comes through regular principal repayments and sales; (2) special-assistance lending in support of certain federal subsidized housing programs; GNMA, also known as "Ginnie Mae," is authorized to guarantee mortgages that are originated under various housing programs designed by FHA, to provide housing in areas where it cannot be provided by conventional market lending; and (3) provision of a guarantee for FHA-VA mortgage pools, which would provide a timely payment of principal and interest guarantee for mortgage-backed securities. Its operations are financed through funds from the U.S. Treasury and from public borrowing.

Mortgage-Backed Securities and the GNMA Payment Guarantee

The guarantee program provided for in 1968 was one of the most significant provisions in the development of the secondary mortgage market as we know it today. Essentially, GNMA was empowered to guarantee the timely payment of principal and interest on securities backed or secured by pools of mortgages insured by the FHA and the Farmers Home Administration (FmHA) or guaranteed by the VA. One of the problems in the secondary mortgage market prior to this time was that even though FHA-insured mortgages could be purchased by investors who received monthly payments of principal and interest (less servicing fees), investors often experienced delays in payments when borrower defaults occurred. In these cases, servicers would have to make a claim for any payments in arrears plus remittance of the loan balance from FHA or the guarantee from VA. Settlement of these claims could be time consuming and required additional administrative effort on the part of investors.

Many investors in mortgage packages disliked this waiting period, which resulted in unpredictable cash flows and a reduction in investment yields. By providing the buyer with a guarantee of timely payment of interest and principal, GNMA was, in essence, guaranteeing monthly payments of interest and principal from amortization. The guarantee also included repayment of outstanding loan balances, should mortgages be prepaid before maturity or should borrowers default. GNMA would make timely payments to the security purchaser, and then take responsibility for settling accounts with the servicer. This would relieve investors from administrative problems and delays in receiving mortgage payments. For this guarantee, the buyer was charged a guarantee fee, which provided GNMA with operating funds to perform this function.

As a result of this GNMA guarantee program, a virtual explosion in the secondary market occurred. This guarantee enabled originators of FHA and VA mortgages to pool or package mortgages and to *issue securities,* called *pass-through securities,* which were collateralized by the mortgages and were based on the notion of investors buying an undivided security interest in a pool of mortgages with interest and principal passed through to investors as received from borrowers. These securities would be underwritten by investment banking firms and sold to investors in markets that were not reached prior to this innovation. Funds received by originators from the sales of pass-through securities would be used to originate new mortgages.

Investors were attracted to these securities because default risk on them was minimized as a result of either FHA insurance or a VA guarantee. Securities issued against such pools were viewed by investors as virtually riskless or very similar to an investment in a government security. With the added guarantee of timely payment of interest and principal by GNMA, these securities also took on the repayment characteristics of a bond, although repayment of the outstanding principal could occur at any time. Repayment could occur when a borrower defaulted, refinanced, or repaid the outstanding loan balance.[2]

---

[2] Repayment could also occur if a property was sold and the loan was not assumed by the buyer, or, in the event of a hazard (fire, etc.), if proceeds from hazard insurance were used to repay the mortgage rather than to reconstruct the improvement.

The Federal Home Loan Mortgage Corporation

By the early 1970s, the mortgage-backed securities market based on pools of FHA-insured and VA home mortgages was well established under the operation of FNMA and GNMA. However, no such secondary market existed for the resale of *conventional* loans originated by thrifts. These mortgages have historically accounted for the vast majority of residential loan originations. For example, conventional mortgage originations accounted for approximately 79 percent of total residential loans, while FHA and VA mortgages accounted for only 21 percent of the total. Thrifts originated the majority of conventional loans (58%), and mortgage companies originated the majority of FHA-VA mortgages (80%). Hence, finding a way to securitize conventional loans was very important if funds were to continue to flow to originators.

Periods of intermittent interest rate volatility, particularly during the mid- and late-1960s, was also causing liquidity problems that plagued thrifts.[3] This resulted in a reduction in the flow of funds to the conventional mortgage market and prompted Congress, under Title III of the Emergency Home Finance Act of 1970, to charter the **Federal Home Loan Mortgage Corporation (FHLMC),** more commonly known as "Freddie Mac." Its primary purpose was to provide a secondary market and, hence, liquidity for conventional mortgage originators just as Fannie Mae and Ginnie Mae did for originators of FHA-VA mortgages.

Initially, Freddie Mac was authorized to purchase and make commitments to purchase first lien, fixed rate conventional residential mortgage loans and participations. This bill also allowed Fannie Mae to purchase conventional mortgages, and Freddie Mac was given the authority to purchase FHA-VA loans as well. This provision would, in essence, allow both organizations to *compete* for all mortgage loans. However, the vast majority of Freddie Mac's business was, and continues to be, conventional mortgages, and FNMA continues to be the dominant purchaser of FHA-VA mortgages, although its acquisition of conventional loans now exceeds its FHA-VA acquisition volume.

Concerns about Freddie Mac's solvency in the midst of the subprime mortgage crisis of 2008 caused the federal government to assume control of Freddie Mac, just as it did with FNMA. The Federal Housing Finance Agency (FHFA) was appointed as conservator of Freddie Mac in September of 2008. Given the continuing economic uncertainty, more changes to Freddie Mac in the future would not be unexpected.

Operation of the Secondary Mortgage Market

To understand how the secondary mortgage market functions, remember that the primary function of this market is to provide a mechanism for replenishing funds used by mortgage originators. This, in turn, enables them to maintain a flow of new mortgage originations during periods of rising and falling interest rates. They may accomplish this by selling mortgages directly to Fannie Mae, Freddie Mac, or other private entities. Or they may form mortgage pools and issue various securities, thereby attracting funds from investors who may not otherwise make investments directly in mortgage loans. Hence, much like any corporation raising funds for doing business, the primary goal of mortgage originators in today's market is to replenish funds by reaching broader investor markets.

[3] Prior to the era of interest rate deregulation (on savings deposits), the small investor would deposit funds in a thrift or bank, which would in turn originate and retain the mortgage as an investment. During this period of regulated interest rates, savers withdrew deposits and began investing directly in financial securities. This change, as well as legislation allowing individuals to open individual retirement accounts (outside of savings institutions), forced thrifts to find a way to compete for funds that they once had been able to acquire by offering savings accounts.

Direct Sale Programs

Exhibit 19–1 illustrates the direct sale approach used by mortgage originators to replenish funds. As previously indicated, prior to the mid-1950s, the secondary market was utilized by mortgage companies and some thrifts who originated FHA and VA mortgages, which were in turn sold to life insurance companies and some large eastern thrifts. These institutions utilized funds obtained from policyholder reserves and savings deposits, respectively, to acquire mortgage packages. This market changed during the mid-1950s as FNMA became the predominant purchaser of FHA-VA mortgages from mortgage bankers. The FHLMC entered the market by 1970, offering savings and loan associations the opportunity to sell conventional and FHA-VA mortgages.

FNMA's current commitment program is divided into two parts: mandatory and optional. Under the mandatory commitment option, Fannie Mae is obligated to purchase a certain amount of mortgages at a certain price at a certain time, and mortgage originators are *obligated* to deliver the mortgages. Originators pay a commitment fee to Fannie Mae for the privilege of selling mortgages under the commitment program. Under the optional delivery program, originators pay Fannie Mae a fee (the amount is higher than the corresponding commitment fee under the mandatory commitment program) for the *option* to deliver their mortgages to Fannie Mae. Under the mandatory commitment program, mortgage originators will benefit if market interest rates rise, but they could lose if market interest rates fall because they could have received a higher price elsewhere. On the other hand, the optional delivery commitment program gives the mortgage originator the "right but not the obligation" to sell the mortgages to Fannie Mae. Hence, if interest rates increase, originators can sell mortgages to Fannie Mae, but if rates fall, they retain the option to sell mortgages to another party for a better price (or even to renegotiate a price with Fannie Mae). With the advent of these commitment programs, mortgage originators were able to continue to shift most interest rate risk to Fannie Mae; however, this can now only be done for a fee. The program became so successful for Fannie Mae that Freddie Mac instituted a similar program in 1970.

The Development of Mortgage-Related Security Pools

As discussed previously, in addition to direct sales of mortgages from originators to investors, many large mortgage originators found that they could place mortgages in pools and sell securities of various types, using the mortgages in these pools as collateral. With the aid of investment bankers, large originators could issue securities in small denominations which would be purchased by many more investors. Firms with smaller mortgage origination volumes could continue to sell mortgages directly to FNMA and

EXHIBIT 19–1
Funds Flow Analysis (Direct Purchase Programs)

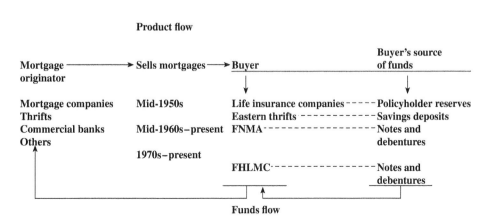

FHLMC, who in turn would create large pools of their own and issue securities. Creation of mortgage pools for securitization has clearly changed the previous pattern of thrifts *originating and holding* mortgages in their own portfolios and mortgage companies originating and selling mortgages directly to life insurance companies or large thrifts in regions where a surplus of savings existed. As we will see, many originators are no longer willing to take the interest rate risk associated with originating loans with funds obtained from deposits and have found a way, through securitization, to raise funds and shift interest rate risk to various classes of investors who are willing to take that risk.

Many types of mortgage-related securities have been developed in recent years. The number and types of securities are continuing to increase as mortgage originators, investment bankers, and the three federally related institutions discussed thus far (FNMA, FHLMC, and GNMA) continue to innovate and reach investor markets that provide the ultimate sources for many of the funds used in new mortgage originations. In this chapter and the next, we will deal in depth with the major types of mortgage-backed securities currently in use:

1. Mortgage-backed bonds (MBBs).
2. Mortgage pass-through securities (MPTs).
3. Mortgage pay-through bonds (MPTBs).
4. Collateralized mortgage obligations (CMOs).

Mortgage-Backed Bonds

One approach to mortgage securitization that has been used by private mortgage originators such as mortgage companies, commercial banks, and savings and loans to replenish funds for new originators has been to issue **mortgage-backed bonds (MBBs).** When issuing MBBs, the issuer establishes a pool of mortgages—this pool usually includes residential mortgages, but commercial mortgages and other mortgage-related securities may also be used—and issues bonds to investors. The issuer retains ownership of the mortgages, but they are pledged as security and are usually placed in trust with a third-party trustee. This trustee makes certain that the provisions of the bond issue are adhered to on behalf of the security owners. Like corporate bonds, MBBs are usually issued with fixed-coupon rates and specific maturities.

To assure investors that the income from mortgages will be sufficient to pay interest on the bonds and to repay principal on the maturity date, the issuer usually "overcollateralizes" the bond issue. This is done by placing mortgages in the pool with outstanding loan balances in excess of the dollar amount of the securities issued. Historically, issuers have pledged from 125 percent to 240 percent in mortgage collateral in excess of the par value of securities issued. This practice is followed because some borrowers may default or fall behind in payments on mortgage loans in the pool. In this case, the overcollateralization ensures that interest payments promised to security holders will continue even though some mortgages may be in default. Further, some loans may be prepaid either before the maturity date of the mortgage or before the bond maturity date. Because mortgage-backed bonds are issued for a specified number of years, overcollateralization ensures that, as mortgages are prepaid, others will still be in the pool to replace them. Another reason for overcollateralization is that bond issues usually provide that the trustee "mark all mortgage collateral to the market." This is done periodically to make sure that the market values of mortgages used for over-collateralization are maintained at the level agreed upon at the time of issue (e.g., 125% or 240%) or at other levels agreed upon throughout the life of the bond issue. Should the market value of the mortgages in trust fall below the agreed-upon level of overcollateralization or be reduced because of an excessive number of defaults or prepayment on mortgages in the pool, the issuer must *replenish* the pool with additional mortgages of the same quality. If the issuer does not replenish or does not abide by the provisions of the security issue, the trustee may sell all collateral in the trust to protect the security owners.

Mortgage-backed bonds, like all mortgage-related securities, are usually underwritten by investment banking companies, given an investment rating by an independent bond-rating agency,[4] and sold through an underwriting syndicate.[5] The investment rating depends on (1) the quality of the mortgages in the underlying pool, which is a reflection of the types of mortgages and their loan-to-value ratios, and whether they are insured or guaranteed against default, either fully or partially; (2) the extent of geographic diversification in the mortgage security; (3) the interest rates on mortgages in the pool; (4) the likelihood that mortgages will be prepaid before maturity; (5) the extent of overcollateralization; and (6) in the case of commercial mortgages, the appraised value and debt coverage ratio.

Obviously, for mortgage pools containing FHA-VA mortgages or conventional mortgages with private mortgage insurance, the risk of default losses would be lower than if such mortgages were not insured or guaranteed. In some cases, however, the issuer may include some additional types of credit enhancement from a third party as additional security against default losses to bondholders. This enhancement could be a letter of credit from a bank, based on the issuer's credit standing and deposit requirements maintained at the bank issuing the letter, or some types of surety in the form of an insurance or other agreement negotiated with a creditworthy third party for a fee. When credit enhancements are used, the investor must also evaluate the ability of the third party to perform on the guarantee or to evaluate the terms and conditions of letters of credit when provided by the issuer or third parties. The quality of the enhancement will generally affect the amount of overcollateralization required or the coupon rate offered on the bonds.

In summary, the quality and types of mortgages in the pool are the primary determinants of whether the cash flows used to pay interest on the bonds and to eventually retire them will be adequate. These characteristics will affect the ability of the issuer to meet the requirements of the bond issue and, hence, affect the risk to investors. This risk will determine the yields required by investors on such bonds and, hence, the price that the issuer will receive for them. This pricing issue is considered next.

Pricing Mortgage-Backed Bonds

To illustrate how mortgage-backed bonds are priced by issuers when negotiating with underwriters, we assume that $200 million of MBBs will be issued against a $300 million pool of mortgages, in denominations of $10,000 for a period of 10 years. The bonds will carry a coupon, or interest rate, of 8 percent, payable annually,[6] based on the quality of the mortgage security in trust, the overcollateralization, and the creditworthiness of the issuer (and/or credit enhancement provided by the issuer). We assume that the securities receive a rating of Aaa or AAA.[7] To determine the *price* at which the security will be offered on the *date of issue,* we must discount the present value of the future interest payments and return of principal at the market rate of return demanded by investors (who will purchase them from underwriters). This rate is obviously a reflection of the riskiness of the bond relative to other securities and the yields on comparable securities in the marketplace.

---

[4] Such agencies might be Moody's or Standard & Poor's Corporation.

[5] Prominent underwriters of mortgage-related securities have included Lehman Brothers, Morgan Stanley, and Goldman Sachs & Co.

[6] Most bonds pay interest semiannually. We are simplifying the analysis here.

[7] This is the highest rating obtainable. An explanation of the meaning and determination of ratings can be obtained from Moody's or Standard & Poor's.

In our example, the price of the security is determined by finding the present value of a stream of $800 interest payments (made annually for 10 years, plus the return of $10,000 in principal at the end of the 10th year). Assuming that the issuer, in concert with the underwriters, agrees that the rate of return that will be required to sell the bonds is 9 percent, then the price will be established as follows:

Solution:

$$i = 9\%$$
$$n = 10$$
$$PMT = \$800$$
$$FV = \$10,000$$
Solve for PV $= \$9,358$

Function:

$$PV (i, n, PMT, FV)$$

Hence, the bond would be priced at a discount of $642, or at 93.58 percent of par value ($10,000), resulting in a yield to maturity of 9 percent.[8] The issuer would receive $187,160,000 from the underwriter,[9] less an underwriting fee, in exchange for the securities. On the other hand, if the yield was deemed to be 7 percent, then the present value of the bonds would be $10,702 or they would sell at a premium of $702 and the issuer would receive $214,400,000. Hence, the price of the issue will depend on the relationship between the coupon rate on the bond and prevailing required rates of return. When market rates exceed the coupon rate, the price of the bond will be lower, and vice versa. Exhibit 19–2 shows the relationship between price and the market yield or rate of return at the time that the 8 percent MBB is issued. Note the inverse relationship between prices and demanded rates of return.

EXHIBIT 19–2
Prices for an 8 Percent Coupon versus a Zero Coupon MBB at Varying Interest Rates

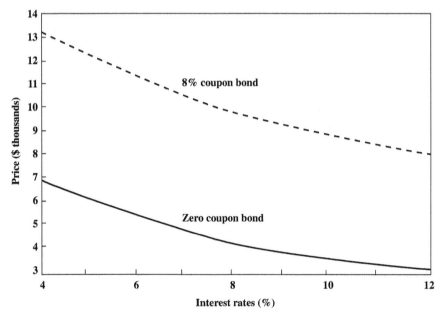

[8] *Yield to maturity* is a term used by bond investors that is identical to the internal rate of return. It is calculated upon whether the coupon (interest) payments are made semiannually, quarterly, and so on.

[9] We assume that the underwriter makes a firm commitment to purchase the entire offering from the originator for an agreed-upon price. The underwriter then forms a syndicate with other underwriters, who then take the risk of reselling securities to the public and institutional investors through a network of securities dealers.

Subsequent Prices

The bonds referred to will be traded after they are issued and, although the prices at which they trade will no longer affect funds received by the issuer, these prices are important to investors as well as issuers who plan to make additional security offerings. For example, if we assume that two years after issue the required rate of return is again 9 percent, then the bond price would be:

Solution:	Function:
$i = 9\%$	$PV\,(i, n, PMT, FV)$
$n = 8$	
$PMT = \$800$	
$FV = \$10,000$	
Solve for PV $= \$9,447$	

Hence, we can see that the price of the security would now be 94.47 percent of par value. The discount is now lower than at the time of issue because the remaining number of years to maturity is now 8 instead of 10. Alternatively, if the demanded return was 7 percent after two years, then the premium would be $10,597, or a price 105.97 percent of par. Hence, the extent of premium and discount when the maturity period is 10 years is different from the pattern illustrated when the remaining maturity is eight years. However, regardless of the remaining maturity period, when the market rate of return is 8 percent, or equal to the coupon rate, the security will always sell at par value. The student should verify this.

Zero Coupon Mortgage-Backed Bonds

In some cases, bonds issued against mortgages will carry zero coupons or will not pay any interest. These MBBs accrue interest until the principal amount is returned at maturity. To illustrate, we assume the bond in our previous example is to be issued with a zero coupon, but interest is to be accrued at 8 percent until maturity. At maturity, the *par value* of the security will be redeemed for $10,000. If, however, at the time of issue, the rate of return demanded by investors in these securities is 8 percent, then the security will be *priced* as follows:

Solution:	Function:
$i = 8\%$	$PV\,(i, n, PMT, FV)$
$n = 10$	
$PMT = \$0$	
$FV = \$10,000$	
Solve for PV $= \$4,632$	

Based on this result, the security would be priced to sell at $4,632, or 46.32 percent of par value at maturity ($10,000). Should market rates of interest be 7.5 percent at the time of issue, the security would be priced at $4,852, or 48.52 percent of par. Exhibit 19–2 also shows the relationship between prices and various market rates of return for a zero coupon MBB with a 10-year maturity period at the time of issue. When compared with the 8 percent coupon bond, the price sensitivity of a zero coupon bond, as a percentage of par value, is far greater than that of the more standard bonds that pay interest currently. For example, if the required return were 4 percent, the 8 percent interest-bearing coupon bond would sell at 130 percent of par, while the zero coupon bond would sell at about 68 percent of par. The greater price sensitivity for zero coupon bonds relative to interest-bearing bonds occurs because all income is deferred until maturity with the zero coupon bond. Therefore, its present value will always be more sensitive to changes in interest rates than that of investments returning some cash flows during the investment period.

Marking the Mortgage Portfolio to Market

As mentioned previously, the trustee selected to oversee that the provisions of the bond issue are carried out must ascertain periodically whether the market value of the mortgages placed in trust is equal to the agreed-upon level of overcollateralization. The pricing techniques used by the trustee to establish the market value of the pledged mortgages are very complex because (1) there are generally many different interest rates on mortgages placed in trust, (2) those mortgages will be amortizing principal, (3) many of the mortgages in the pool may be prepaid because many of them may allow the borrower to repay the outstanding loan balance at any time, and (4) some borrowers may default on loans. These latter two factors would obviously reduce the amount and number of mortgages in the pool.

To make an estimate of the value of mortgages in the pool (referred to as *marking the mortgages to market*), the trustee must value each of the mortgages in the pool by first establishing the number and outstanding balance of each mortgage in trust. Estimates must then be made of the current market yield demanded by investors for each type of mortgage based on assumptions about the period that each mortgage is expected to be outstanding (not the contract maturity period, because most mortgages on single-family residential properties are prepaid as properties are sold, loans are refinanced, borrowers default, etc.).[10] Hence, the valuation of the underlying security is a more complex undertaking, particularly when the prepayment patterns are considered. Many of the techniques that must be considered in evaluating such securities are also important when valuing mortgage pass-through securities.

Mortgage Pass-Through Securities

In 1968, Ginnie Mae initiated the mortgage-backed guarantee program. This program represented an attempt to create a mortgage-backed investment capable of competing with corporate and government securities for investment funds. As previously pointed out, one of the most serious objections that had to be overcome with this type of security was the issue of safety. Because mortgage-related securities would represent loans made by many individual borrowers with different income and household characteristics, an investment vehicle had to be created whereby the collateral underlying the mortgage security could be easily understood and yet be comparable to other securities.

We know that mortgages are subject to default risk and interest rate risk. Although fixed interest rate mortgage securities, like corporate and government bonds, would also be subject to interest rate risk, default risk could be eliminated by FHA insurance or dramatically reduced with a VA guarantee. Another characteristic of concern to potential investors in mortgage-related securities was the predictability of the income stream. Substitute investments, such as noncallable bonds, have very predictable interest payment schedules. As pointed out previously, mortgage payments can be delayed because of a household's inability to keep payments current or because of default. To overcome this lack of

---

[10] Other methods of principal repayment may also be used, such as sinking fund retirements and call provisions. For a discussion, see any basic text dealing with investments.

timeliness in payments, Ginnie Mae guaranteed the full and timely payment of principal and interest. GNMA's position as guarantor was that of a surety, with securities carrying the GNMA guarantee having the full faith and credit of the U.S. government behind them. This full faith and credit guarantee meant that GNMA could borrow without limit from the Treasury. This unique guarantee made the GNMA security the most liquid of all secondary mortgage market securities.

Before the advent of the first mortgage-backed security, the pass-through, the only way an originator could sell a package of mortgage investments was to sell whole loans, which involved the transfer of ownership in addition to all of the investor concerns mentioned above. The mortgage pass-through overcame many of these problems. **Mortgage pass-through securities (MPTs)** are issued by a mortgage originator (e.g., mortgage company, thrift) and represent an undivided ownership interest in a pool of mortgages. The pool may consist of one or many mortgages. However, the usual minimum size of such a pool is $100 million, which could represent 1,000 or more residential mortgages. Each mortgage placed in the pool continues to be serviced by its originator or an approved servicer. A trustee is designated as the owner of the mortgages in the pool and ensures that all payments are made to individual security owners. Cash flows from the pool, which consist of principal and interest, less servicing and guarantee fees, are distributed to security holders. That is why the securities are called pass-throughs, because cash flows are "passed-through" to the investors by the mortgage servicer.

Exhibit 19–3 presents a flowchart showing how mortgage pass-through securities are originated and sold. Essentially, mortgages are originated by lenders and are pooled by them or sold to FNMA or FHLMC. If pooled by the originator, the originator will work with a securities underwriter to issue securities. These securities are then sold through security dealers to mutual funds, individuals with individual retirement accounts (IRAs), trust and pension fund administrators, life insurance companies, or even thrifts and commercial banks in geographic areas with a surplus of savings. This pattern of securitization enables originators of mortgages to ultimately reach the relatively small investor, who can now purchase an interest in a Ginnie Mae pass-through or another pass-through security by investing in a mutual fund or buying it directly.[11]

EXHIBIT 19–3   **Mortgage Pass-Through Securities: Issuance and Funds Flow**

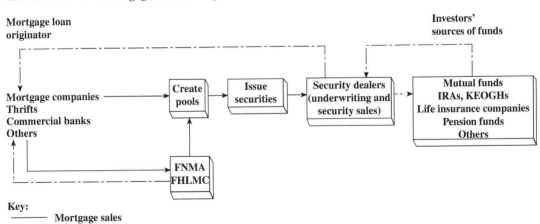

[11] In addition to the pass-through process shown in Exhibit 19–3, there are a number of other programs related to this process that have evolved over time. These include the participation certificate (PC) program and the "swap" program, among others.

Important Characteristics of Mortgage Pools

Exhibit 19–4 provides information on the most important types of pass-through securities that have been used. Although all pass-through securities have the same underlying structure, some major differences between them should be pointed out. These differences are extremely important to issuers when creating mortgage pools and are equally important to investors when evaluating the possibility of investing in a mortgage pass-through security as opposed to a government bond, corporate bond, or another interest-bearing security.

Not all mortgage-backed securities are alike. When you are reviewing the characteristics listed in Exhibit 19–4, pay particular attention to how the market value of a pass-through security, which is backed by an underlying pool of mortgage loans made to borrowers, will respond to general changes in market interest rates. The change in market value of a particular security depends on the characteristics of the mortgages in the underlying pool, the response of borrowers to changes in interest rates, and the changes in borrower behavior in response to changes affecting their demand for housing, employment opportunities, and other influences. Borrowers may choose to refinance or repay their loans in response to changes in interest rates. As economic conditions change, they may sell their present house to buy another or to take a job transfer to another region. In these cases, they would very likely prepay their outstanding mortgages. These factors are extremely important to investors who must evaluate the timing of the receipt of cash flows when estimating value.

Security Issuers and Guarantors

The first security type listed in Exhibit 19–4 is referred to as a GNMA pass-through, which is usually issued by mortgage companies, thrifts, commercial banks, and other organizations that originate FHA and VA mortgages. The remaining two security types, participation certificates and mortgage-backed securities, are securities issued by FHLMC and FNMA, respectively. As previously mentioned, the latter two securities are backed by pools of mortgages that are purchased from originators by FHLMC and FNMA, which,

EXHIBIT 19–4   **Selected Characteristics of Mortgage Pass-Through Securities**

Issuer	Mortgage companies, thrifts, others: GNMA pass-throughs	FHLMC: participation certificates	FNMA: mortgage-backed securities
Guarantor against default on mortgages	FHA,VA, FmHA	Private mortgage insurance, FHA/VA	FHA/VA, private mortgage insurance
Types of mortgages in pool*	FRM, GPM, MH, ARM seconds	FRM, GPM, ARM, MF, seconds	FRM, GPM, ARM, MF,
Interest rate on mortgages in underlying pools allowed to vary?	Yes	Yes	Yes
Seasoned mortgages allowed in pools?	Yes	Yes	Yes
Nature of payment guarantee	Timely payment of P & I and prepayments	Timely payment of P & I and eventual prepayments	Timely payment of P & I and prepayments
Guarantor	GNMA and credit of U.S. government	FHLMC only	FNMA only

*Key
FRM = 1–4 single-family, 30-year fixed rate mortgages.
GPM = Graduated payment mortgages.
ARM = Adjustable rate mortgages.

MH = Manufactured housing mortgages.
MF = Multifamily housing mortgages.
Seconds = Mortgage pools secured by second mortgages.

in turn, provide a timely payment guarantee. In these cases, FNMA and FHLMC act as intermediaries, purchasing smaller quantities of mortgages from many originators, and then accumulating larger pools against which they issue securities.

Default Insurance

GNMA pass-through securities are backed with FHA-VA mortgages that carry either insurance or a guarantee against default losses. When it first began, this program was limited to FHA-VA pools because private mortgage default insurance on conventional mortgages was not generally available. Even today, with the availability of private mortgage insurance, major issuers of pass-through securities usually do not mix *both* FHA-VA and conventional mortgages in the same pool because of the greater depth of FHA default insurance coverage and the VA guarantee compared with conventional default coverage. As shown in Exhibit 19–4, GNMA pass-throughs still contain mortgages with FHA-VA backing, whereas FNMA and FHLMC pass-throughs may be based on separate pools of either FHA-VA backing or conventional mortgages. In their conventional mortgage-backed programs, both FNMA and FHLMC require conventional mortgages with loan-to-value ratios greater than 80 percent to carry private mortgage insurance.

Payment Patterns and Security for Mortgages in Pools

As Exhibit 19–4 indicates, most mortgage varieties may be individually pooled for a pass-through security issue. This is true for mortgages with adjustable payment patterns such as adjustable rate mortgages (ARMs); graduated payment mortgages (GPMs); mortgages secured by single family, multifamily, and mobile homes; and even second-lien mortgages. However, the vast majority of mortgages used in the pass-through security market are fixed interest rate loans secured by mortgages on single-family houses.

The rule about not mixing FHA-VA and conventional mortgages in the same pool generally applies to payment patterns and the nature of loan security and loan maturity. In other words, mortgage pools are usually grouped according to (1) payment patterns (e.g., ARMs), (2) maturity (e.g., second mortgages with 10-year terms), or (3) security (e.g., single-family homes, mobile homes). The reason this is done is that investors must be able to predict the cash flow pattern that they can expect to receive in a pass-through security with some confidence. If pools contained mortgages with many different payment patterns, investors would have a more difficult time assessing the likely cash flow pattern that they could expect to receive. The payment pattern of individuals making fixed interest rate loans may vary considerably from those making ARMs, second liens, and so on. As we will see in the material on pricing securities, expected prepayment patterns dramatically affect expected yields on mortgage securities. Hence, a general rule followed thus far has been to keep mortgage pools as homogeneous as possible so that their prepayment patterns are somewhat easier for investors to assess.

Coupon Rates, Interest Rates, and Number of Seasoned Mortgages in Pools

Pass-through securities issues guaranteed by Fannie Mae and Freddie Mac have allowed for a mixture of *interest rates* on mortgages included in a pool to enable a faster accumulation of larger pools for securitization. This pattern has been followed by security issuers, who believe that the variation in cash flows caused by mixing such mortgages is not large enough to offset the lower issuance costs on very large mortgage pools (i.e., economies of scale).

When Freddie Mac began its PC pass-through program, it allowed a variation of 200 basis points (from highest to lowest) in interest rates on mortgages packaged in the same pool. Fannie Mae allowed a 200-basis-point range with its first mortgage-backed security offering in 1981. The GNMA pass-through programs provide that some pools contain mortgages with the same interest rate, while others allow a variation of 100 basis points on mortgages in the underlying pool. These ranges are subject to revision by the guarantors from time to time.[12]

The variation in interest rates on a mortgage pool may be very important for investors to consider, because in each case the *coupon rate* promised to investors purchasing securities is generally based on the *lowest* interest rate on *any* mortgage in the pool, less servicing and guarantee fees. This means that for two security issues bearing the same coupon rate, expected cash flows to investors in the pool containing mortgages with different rates will be less variable than cash flows to investors in the pool with the same interest rates. This occurs because each mortgage included in a pool with different interest rates will have a lower likelihood of prepayment than pooled mortgages with the same interest rate. This likelihood exists because mortgages with one interest rate are *all* more likely to be prepaid, should interest rates decline. This would obviously make the pattern of expected cash flows more variable.

Another important factor relating to the amount and timing of cash flows received by investors is the maturity distribution of mortgages and the extent to which "seasoned" mortgages are included in a pool. *Seasoning* is a term used to describe the age, or number of years, that a loan has been outstanding before it is placed in a pool. The scheduled maturity date for a pass-through security issue is generally the date on which the mortgage with the longest remaining maturity in the pool is scheduled to be repaid, assuming no prepayment. Each guarantor listed in Exhibit 19–4 places limitations on the number of seasoned mortgages allowed in a pool. Most GNMA-insured mortgage pools generally contain mortgages made within one year of pool formation. Fannie Mae and Freddie Mac generally allow for more variation in seasoning in pools that they guarantee. The concern over seasoning is important because the more seasoned a mortgage is, the greater the likelihood of prepayment. The likelihood that borrowers will sell houses, change job locations, and so on increases with the length of time the mortgage has been outstanding.

On the other hand, the risk of default is usually greatest in the early years of the life of a mortgage. Hence, seasoned mortgages tend to reduce the possibility of prepayment because of default. However, to the extent seasoning reduces or increases the likelihood of prepayment, more variation in cash flows results, which makes evaluation of the security more difficult for investors. This will, in turn, affect the price investors are willing to pay for the security.

Number of Mortgages and Geographic Distribution

Other factors relating to mortgages in the underlying pool that may affect the predictability and, hence, the variability of the monthly cash flows on pass-through securities are the *number* and *geographic* distribution of mortgages in the pool.

Both of these factors may be critical when estimating the yield on a pass-through security because they influence the expected repayment of principal. Generally, the larger the dollar amount of the pool issue, the more individual mortgages will be contained in the pool; and the larger the number of mortgages in the pool, all else being equal, the more predictable the monthly cash flow. This means that the likelihood of a major change in cash flows owing to default or prepayment of one or a few individual mortgages will not significantly affect future cash flows paid to investors. Most mortgage pools underlying pass-throughs are in minimum denominations of $100 million. If the average mortgage size is about $100,000, most pools of residential mortgages will contain at least 1,000 mortgages. This may be enough to assure investors that changes in cash flows caused by a small number of mortgages are minimal.

Geographic factors are important because they may affect the likelihood of prepayment and default. Certain regions of the country may be affected more by economic downturns

---

[12] The GNMA I pass-through program requires all mortgages in a pool to have the same interest rate.

and resulting unemployment than others and, hence, may have higher default rates. Prepayment rates, because of mobility by borrowers due to their age and family status, may be higher in some areas than others. A mortgage pool with more geographic diversity tends to insulate investors from cash flow irregularities.

Borrower Characteristics and Loan Prepayment

Perhaps more important than any of the other explicit pool characteristics discussed in conjunction with Exhibit 19–4 are borrower characteristics, or the socioeconomic makeup of individuals who have made the mortgage loans and are the ultimate source of cash flows for the mortgage pool. These characteristics are important because (1) households prepay existing mortgage loans as they adjust their consumption of housing over time in response to changes in income, family size, and tastes; (2) like other economic entities, households respond to changes in interest rates by refinancing their loans when interest rates fall and postponing adjustments in housing consumption when interest rates rise; and (3) households may default on loan obligations because of loss of employment, divorce, and so on, and although most pools have default insurance, the mortgage balance is prepaid upon default. Therefore, changes in borrower behavior with respect to these characteristics will affect the expected cash flows on loans and expected maturities. Indeed, depending on borrower behavior, the expected maturity of a loan may vary significantly, therefore affecting the expected yield on the mortgage. Unfortunately, not much information about borrower characteristics for individual loans in an underlying mortgage pool is made available to investors in pass-through securities. Hence, even though it is an important variable affecting cash flows on mortgage securities, no reliable source of information is generally available to investors.

Nuisance Calls

Where the prepayment rate reaches the point where a diminishing number and amount of mortgages remain in the pool, say about 10 percent of the initial pool amount, the servicer may call the remainder of the securities. This call is referred to as a *nuisance* or *cleanup call* and is used when the cost of servicing begins to become large relative to servicing income.

Mortgage Pass-Through Securities: A General Approach to Pricing

As we have seen, many things influence the pricing of a mortgage pass-through security (or any mortgage-backed security). We can summarize these influences as follows:

1. *Interest rate risk*—Reductions in market value due to an unanticipated rise in interest rates. This risk is generally greatest for pools containing fixed interest rate loans.
2. *Default risk*—Losses due to borrower default. For single-family loans, the likelihood of default losses is lowest for FHA-insured mortgages, slightly greater for VA-guaranteed mortgages, and generally greater for privately insured mortgages. This source of risk is also generally higher for ARMs and variable payment mortgages.
3. *Risk of delayed payment of principal and interest*—This source of risk can be evaluated in relation to the financial strength of the guarantor because the guarantee of *timely payment* is only as good as the ability of the guarantor to perform on the guarantee. GNMA is backed by the full faith and credit of the U.S. government, and presumably so are FNMA and FHLMC now that they are both under federal government control.
4. *Prepayment risk*—Loss in yield because of greater-than-anticipated loan repayments. In general, most mortgage loans are prepaid before the stated maturity date. Hence, when investing in a pass-through, an investor must estimate expected cash flows by including an assessment of the prepayment rate on loans in the underlying pools.

In the case of fixed interest rate mortgage pools, the impact of prepayment on cash flows passed through to investors will vary according to the:

a. Number of mortgages in the pool.

b. Distribution of interest rates on such mortgages.

c. Number of seasoned mortgages included in the pool.

d. Geographic location of borrowers.

e. Household (borrower) characteristics.

f. Unanticipated events (e.g., flood, earthquake).

Although the above sources of risk are important to issuers and investors, information available on mortgage pools is usually limited to very general borrower and mortgage characteristics. Information usually available on mortgage pools is discussed in the following sections.

Pass-Through Rates, Yields, and Servicing Fee

The pass-through rate is the coupon rate of interest promised by the issuer of a pass-through security to the investor. The yield to maturity, or internal rate of return, on such a security is equal to this rate only when it is issued at par value.

The coupon rate on pass-throughs is lower than the lowest rate of interest on any mortgage in the pool. The difference between the two rates is known as the *servicing fee*. The GNMA I, which allows no variance in interest rates in the underlying pool, has a total servicing fee of .5 percent, or 50 basis points below the interest rates on all mortgages in the pool. The servicing fee is divided between the guarantor fee and the loan services fee and is calculated as a percentage of the outstanding principal balance of the pool. As an example, GNMA takes .06 percent or 6 basis points of the outstanding principal balance of the pool as its fee for guarantee of timely payment of principal and interest, while the remaining 44 basis points of the servicing fee are retained by the servicer. For mortgage pass-through securities that allow a range of interest rates on mortgages in the pool (e.g., GNMA II), the coupon rate will be set lower than the lowest mortgage rate in the pool.

Weighted Average Coupon

The **weighted average coupon** (WAC) is a measure of the homogeneity of the coupon rates on mortgages in a pool. It is calculated as the average of the underlying mortgage interest rates weighted by the dollar balance of each mortgage as of the security issue date. WACs are meaningful only for pools that allow a variance in interest rates on mortgages. In most instances, the servicing and guarantee fee can be approximated as the difference between the WAC and the pass-through coupon rate.

Stated Maturity Date of Pool

The stated maturity date of the pass-through pool is the longest maturity date for any mortgage in the pool, assuming that no prepayments occur. For example, if 75 percent of the pool contained 15-year mortgages and the remaining 25 percent contained 20-year mortgages, the stated pool maturity would be 20 years. GNMA generally imposes more restrictions on the variance in mortgage maturities allowed in pools. FNMA and FHLMC pools may contain more seasoned loans with a wider range in stated maturity dates.

Weighted Average Maturity

Because the remaining term to stated maturity of mortgages in a pool may affect the prepayment rate of mortgages and, consequently, the yield of securities issued against the pool, the concept of a **weighted average maturity** was developed. The weighted average maturity is calculated as the average remaining term of the underlying mortgages as of the pass-through issue date, with the principal balance of the mortgage as the weighting factor.

Payment Delays by Servicer

Payment delay is the time lag between the time that the homeowners make their mortgage payments and the date that the servicing agent actually pays the investors holding the pass-through securities. This delay may range from 14 to 55 days. As with other securities, the timing of cash flows is important. Delays in payments received by investors obviously reduce yields.

Pool Factor

The **pool factor** is the outstanding principal balance divided by the original pool balance. This balance changes every month as mortgages are amortized and balances prepaid. The pool factor starts out as 1 and usually declines. (However, it may increase above 1 if the pool includes mortgages that allow negative amortization.) The pool factor is used to determine the current principal balance of the pool based on the outstanding balance of all mortgages remaining in the pool at any point in time. For example, if the pool factor is .9050 and the pool initially contained mortgages with $50,000 in balances outstanding, the current principal balance of the pool would be $50,000 $\times$ .9050 = $45,250. This factor is particularly important when securities are traded *after* the issue date, when subsequent buyers are considering how much to pay for a security. For example, as the pool factor becomes smaller, the remaining balances on mortgages in the pool are also becoming smaller; hence, the likelihood of prepayment becomes greater (holding all else constant).

Mortgage Pass-Through Payment Mechanics Illustrated

Exhibit 19–5 illustrates cash flow patterns that are important when evaluating mortgage pass-through securities. In this exhibit, it is assumed that $1,000,000 of 10 percent fixed interest rate mortgages have been pooled as security for an issue of pass-through securities. The pass-through will carry a coupon, or pass-through, rate of 9.5 percent. The difference between the pooled mortgage rates and coupon rate, or .5 percent, is the servicing fee, which is assessed on the outstanding loan balances. To simplify the discussion, we have assumed that all mortgages in the pool have a maturity of 10 years and that mortgage payments, or cash flows and outflows in and out of the pool, occur annually.[13]

The cash flows passed through to individual security holders (column g) are based on annual mortgage payments for a 10 percent, 10-year mortgage on the initial pool balance of $1,000,000, resulting in total principal and interest payments generated by the pool (column c).[14] The servicing fee of .5 percent (column e) is then assessed on the outstanding loan balance at the end of each previous period and subtracted from total principal and interest payments. This results in actual payments to be made to all investors (column f). Because of the way servicing fees are calculated, payments passed through to investors (column f) are not the same from year to year, even though payments into the pool (column d) are level.[15] If no mortgages in the pool are prepaid (column c)—that is, all mortgages remain outstanding for their stated maturities—the principal balance in the pool will not reach zero until the end of the 10th year.

---

[13] For most pass-through issues, payments are made to investors monthly.

[14] Because all mortgages in the pool are 10 percent, 10-year loans, the constant payment in column (c) is computed as one annual payment on a $1,000,000 loan.

[15] If there are any prepayments (column c), this will also cause payments passed through to investors to vary from year to year.

EXHIBIT 19–5 Cash Flows from Mortgage Pass-Through Security (Constant Payment, Fixed Rate, 10-Year Mortgage Pool, Interest Rate = 10%, Prepayment Assumed to Be 0%, Coupon Rate = 9.5%, Rounded)

	(a)	(b)	(c)	(d)	(e)	(f)	(g)
					Guarantee		Payment to
				Total	and	Total PMTs	Individual
End of	Pool	P&I	Principal	Payments*	Service Fees	to Investors	Investor
Period	Balance	Payment	Prepayment	(b) + (c)	(0.5%)†	(d) − (e)	(f) ÷ 40
0	$1,000,000						$(25,000)
1	937,255	$162,745	$0	$162,745	$5,000	$157,745	3,944
2	868,235	162,745	0	$162,745	4,686	158,059	3,951
3	792,313	162,745	0	$162,745	4,341	158,404	3,960
4	708,799	162,745	0	$162,745	3,962	158,784	3,970
5	616,933	162,745	0	$162,745	3,544	159,201	3,980
6	515,881	162,745	0	$162,745	3,085	159,661	3,992
7	404,724	162,745	0	$162,745	2,579	160,166	4,004
8	282,451	162,745	0	$162,745	2,024	160,722	4,018
9	147,950	162,745	0	$162,745	1,412	161,333	4,033
10	0	162,745	0	$162,745	740	162,006	4,050

A.
Value of cash flows to issuer if required rate is 9.50%   = $1,000,000
Value of cash flows to individual investors at 9.50   = $ 25,000
B.
Value of cash flows to issuer if required rate is 8.50%   = $ 1,045,219
Value of cash flows to individual investors at 8.50   = $ 26,130
C.
Value of cash flows to issuer if required rate is 10.50%   = $ 957,754
Value of cash flows to individual investors at 10.50   = $ 23,944

*Payments calculated on an annual basis.
†Based on pool balance at the end of the previous year.

The amount of cash that will be received by an issuer when this type of pool is formed and securitized depends on the prevailing market rate of return that investors demand on the investment. If it is assumed that, based on the pool characteristics discussed above, the market, or desired, rate of return is *equal* to the coupon rate (9.5%), then the amount to be received (paid) by the issuers (investors) will be $1,000,000 (or 40 securities with a face value of $25,000 will be sold). This is based on the stream of annual cash flow payments in the exhibit, discounted at 9.5 percent. In this instance, the securities would be sold at par value, or $25,000 each.

It is rarely ever true, however, that the rate of return demanded by investors is *exactly* equal to the coupon rate on a security. As we know, market interest rates change continually; hence, it would only be coincidental that interest rates on mortgages originated at some previous time and placed in a pool would bear interest rates exactly equal to the market rate demanded by investors at the time the securities were issued. Inasmuch as the annual cash flows into the pool based on payments received by borrowers are known at the time of issue and passed through to investors, the price received by the issuer will depend on the present value of all payments received by investors, discounted at the prevailing market rate of return. As discussed earlier, the latter rate is determined by the real rate of interest, inflationary expectations, and a premium for the various sources of risk. It is also based on yields available on alternative investments. We shall see that the periods that mortgages are expected to remain outstanding is also very important in the determination of the prices that investors are willing to pay for pass-through securities.

To illustrate the effect that market interest rates have on the price of pass-through securities, note that if the stream of cash flows paid to investors (column g) in Exhibit 19–5 is discounted at a market rate of 8.5 percent, the securities will sell at a premium or $26,130 (part B), the result of discounting payments in column (g) by 8.5 percent. If market rates were to rise to 10.50 percent at the time of issue, the security prices would reflect a *discount* of $23,944 (part C). Both of these calculations assume, however, that the expected maturity of the pass-through security is equal to the stated maturity of mortgages in the pool (10 years). Hence, the amortization of principal is assumed to occur over the full 10-year period; that is, no prepayment is assumed.

To provide some idea of the effect of the sensitivity of security prices to changes in market interest rates, Exhibit 19–6 shows the effect of rising and falling interest rates on the issue *price* of the mortgage pass-through securities in our example. (Keep in mind that the assumption regarding repayment of principal over the 10-year period remains the same.) Results show that for all rates of return desired by investors in excess of 9.5 percent, the pass-through is issued at a discount; when required rates decrease, the security is sold at a premium. Note that only when the required rate of return is *equal* to the promised coupon rate (9.5%) does the security sell at par value (an amount equal to the initial pool balance of $1,000,000, or $25,000 per security).

Prepayment Patterns and Security Prices

One problem that affects how securities are priced and is unique to the mortgage-backed securities market is the option that most borrowers have to prepay or repay the outstanding mortgage balance at any time.[16] This topic is important because when investors make

EXHIBIT 19–6

Relationship between Security Price and Required Rates of Return (Prepayment Rate Assumed to be 0%)

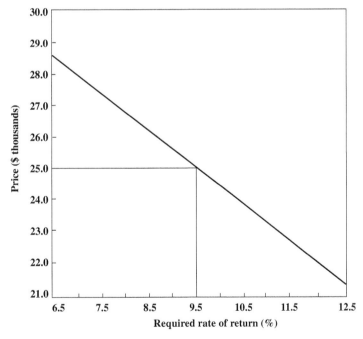

[16] There are some exceptions and additional facts that should be mentioned that affect mortgage prepayment. FHA and VA mortgages are assembled by buyers of properties. Hence, they are not always repaid when a property is sold. Conventional mortgages may contain a due-on-sale clause, which prohibits assumptions; hence, they would be more likely to be repaid if a property is sold. Some older conventional fixed interest rate mortgages may also contain prepayment penalties, which tend to discourage early repayment. Conventional mortgages made more recently and ARMs generally do not include such penalties.

comparisons between pass-throughs, corporate bonds, U.S. government bonds, and various state and local bond issues, the *expected* maturity period for pass-throughs is usually more difficult to estimate relative to the other investments. For example, when corporate bonds are issued, an *option to call* the outstanding principal is usually made explicit in the indenture agreement by specifying the price at which the bond may be called by the corporation each year that the bond issue is outstanding. Such options to call are usually included in the event that interest rates decline and the company wants to refinance the debt at a lower interest rate.[17]

As an alternative to call provisions, bond indentures issued by both corporations and state and local issuers may specify that a *scheduled* number of bonds will be called and retired in specific years after issue, regardless of what the current level of interest rates is at that time. This is not an option but a requirement of the indenture agreement.[18] The vast majority of U.S. government securities are issued for a stated maturity and are generally not callable. In other words, they are generally issued to run until maturity.[19]

The point is that other fixed interest rate securities are generally more predictable with respect to when repayment of principal can be expected. This is not true for mortgage pass-through securities. Hence, when comparing yields on pass-throughs with other securities, there is definitely some additional uncertainty regarding the rate of repayment of principal that investors must take into account.

Prepayment Assumptions

Because some prepayments by borrowers are likely to occur over time, as outstanding balances on mortgages contained in pools are repaid, proceeds are passed through to investors in pass-through securities. Pass-throughs of mortgage balances can be zero in months when interest rates increase and can accelerate rapidly when market interest rates decline. During the latter periods, many households choose to refinance. Mortgages are then paid off and removed from the pool as principal is passed through to investors.

When issuing pass-through securities, the issuer generally specifies both a coupon rate of interest (9.5% in our preceding example) *and* an offering price on the securities being issued. This offering price may be above or below par value. This specification is made because investors may demand a rate of return that is different from the coupon rate of 9.5 percent as market conditions vary at the time of issue. Even when no prepayments are assumed, the range in security prices may vary considerably, depending on the market rate of return demanded by investors (see Exhibit 19–6). However, because investors realize that there is also a strong likelihood that some prepayments will occur while they own these securities, issuers usually take into account some *assumed prepayment pattern* when pricing these securities. This is necessary to provide a more accurate estimate of cash flows (hence, yield to investors), rather than assuming that all borrowers will repay loans in accordance with a stated amortization schedule.

---

[17] To include this option in the agreement with investors, however, the issuer usually includes a schedule of premiums in excess of par value that will be paid to bondholders if the option to call is exercised by the corporation. This premium is paid because (1) the market value of the bonds will have increased if market rates have fallen and calling in the bond would deprive bondholders of an increase in market value and (2) if investors expect to own the bonds for the entire maturity period, refinancing by the company may represent an unanticipated interruption in cash flows, and bondholders would have to reinvest at lower interest rates.

[18] These retirements amount to an implicit method of amortization (e.g., a mortgage) and are usually accomplished with a sinking fund that is used (1) to call bonds as scheduled, by serial number at either a premium or par value, (2) to call a percentage of the original issue at random by serial number at either par value or a premium, or (3) to use sinking funds to enter the market and repurchase bonds at market value.

[19] A limited number of U.S. government bond issues are callable for a specified number of years prior to maturity.

Methods that issuers use to include prepayment assumptions when pricing securities fall into four broad classes:

1. *Average maturity.* This method assumes, for example, that a pool of 10-year mortgages is scheduled to amortize principal based on a 10-year maturity, but the pool is totally paid off after some average period of time, such as the fifth year. Hence, when calculating yields or pricing securities, issuers assume that regular mortgage payments will be made for five years, and the principal due at that time will amount to a balloon payment. This method has the advantage of simplicity because an average prepayment rate is chosen to represent all mortgages in the pool. Further, choosing an average maturity has the effect of facilitating comparison with traditional bonds.

The disadvantages of this technique far outweigh its advantages. There is considerable evidence that the so-called five-year-average-life convention is not an adequate method of handling the prepayment problem and will usually result in under- or overestimation of yield. As previously explained, prepayments are the product of numerous factors, including interest rate changes and household characteristics. Hence, using an average maturity may not reflect changes underlying these characteristics.

2. *Constant rates of prepayment.* This method of handling prepayment assumes that a constant percentage of the total mortgages in the pool will be paid off every year. The advantages of the **constant prepayment assumption** are that it is simple to understand and prepayments are easy to compute. However, empirical evidence suggests that prepayments due to defaults occur more frequently early in the life of most mortgages. Hence, most constant prepayment rates tend to understate prepayment in earlier years and overstate it in later years. While this method may be preferable to an average maturity, it is also not likely to reflect underlying pool characteristics.

3. *FHA prepayment experience.* Prepayment assumptions based on empirical evidence from actual prepayment experience collected by the FHA over several decades have been suggested as a guide for making more accurate prepayment assumptions. The FHA has developed an extensive database on mortgage terminations as a part of its insurance program. This database contains the total number of mortgage terminations during a single policy year, including information on the number resulting from defaults and repayments. Many argue that prepayment assumptions could be based on this FHA "experience." For example, if slower or faster prepayment on pools of mortgages is expected because of differences in investor expectations, those rates could be adjusted to be less than 100 percent or greater than 100 percent of FHA experience, and yields could be disclosed to investors.

However, the FHA data on prepayment experience are not without shortcomings. Major problems are encountered when applying historic FHA experience to current mortgage pools because the precise causes of prepayment (e.g., changes in interest rates, borrowers' employment) over time are difficult to determine. There is no assurance that this pattern will repeat in the future; the FHA does not keep enough detailed data on each mortgage and borrower to enable a systematic investigation into the causes of prepayment behavior.

4. *The PSA prepayment model.* The **PSA prepayment model** was developed by the Public Securities Association to simplify the FHA prepayment experience model. Even though it suffers from the same shortcomings as the FHA prepayment experience model, it has become an industry standard for prepayment assumptions used by most issuers of mortgage-backed securities. Simply put, the model is based on monthly prepayment rates, which vary during the life of a mortgage pool underlying the security. At present, the standard PSA prepayment rate curve (referred to as *100% PSA*) begins at .2 percent per month for the first year, and then increases by .2 percent each month until month 30. It then remains at .5 percent per month, or 6 percent per year, for the remaining stated maturity period of the pool. The model combines both FHA experience and the constant rate of repayment approach.

Because investors and issuers are aware that yields are likely to be affected by the rate of loan repayment, the PSA assumption is widely used to convey both price and yield information to investors at the time of issue. To provide prospective security buyers with additional information about the sensitivity of yields to different prepayment rates at the time of issue, a series of yield quotes based on various PSA repayment rates (e.g., 75% PSA, 150% PSA) are placed on the prospectus.

The Effects of Prepayment Illustrated

To illustrate the effects of prepayment on cash flows to investors in mortgage pass-through securities, a schedule of payments is shown in Exhibit 19–7. The rate of prepayment is assumed to be 10 percent each year based on the pool balance at the end of the preceding period. Payments in column (g) should be compared to those in Exhibit 19–5, which are based on a zero prepayment rate. However, in spite of these differences, when cash flows in column (g) of both exhibits are discounted at 9.5 percent, the present value in both cases equals $1,000,000, or $25,000 per investor. This result occurs because even though the 10 percent prepayment assumption results in more cash flows early in the life of the pool, interest is still calculated at 9.5 percent on the outstanding balance at all times. Therefore,

EXHIBIT 19–7   Cash Flows from Mortgage Pass-Through Security (Constant Payment, Fixed Rate, 10-Year Mortgage Pool, Interest Rate = 10%, Prepayment Assumed to Be 10%, Coupon Rate = 9.5%, Rounded)

www.mhhe.com/bf15e

	(a)	(b)	(c)	(d)	(e)	(f)	(g)
End of Period	Pool Balance	P&I Payment	Principal Prepayment	Total Payments* (b) + (c)	Guarantee and Service Fees (0.5%)†	Total PMTs to Investors (d) − (e)	Payment to Individual Investor (f) ÷ 40
0	$ 1,000,000						$(25,000)
1	837,255	$ 162,745	$ 100,000	$ 262,745	$ 5,000	$ 257,745	6,444
2	691,873	145,381	83,725	229,107	4,186	224,921	5,623
3	562,186	129,688	69,187	198,875	3,459	195,415	4,885
4	446,710	115,476	56,219	171,695	2,811	168,884	4,222
5	344,142	102,568	44,671	147,239	2,234	145,005	3,625
6	253,358	90,784	34,414	125,198	1,721	123,477	3,087
7	173,431	79,927	25,336	105,263	1,267	103,996	2,600
8	103,692	69,739	17,343	87,082	867	86,215	2,155
9	43,946	59,746	10,369	70,115	518	69,597	1,740
10	0	48,340	0	48,340	220	48,120	1,203

A.

Value of cash flows to issuer if required rate is 9.50%	= $1,000,000
Value of cash flows to individual investors at 9.50	= $ 25,000

B.

Value of cash flows to issuer if required rate is 8.50%	= $1,033,908
Value of cash flows to individual investors at 8.50	= $ 25,848

C.

Value of cash flows to issuer if required rate is 10.50%	= $ 967,970
Value of cash flows to individual investors at 10.50	= $ 24,199

*Payments calculated on an annual basis.
†Based on pool balance at the end of the previous year.

even though the investor is receiving *principal* on the pass-through faster, interest continues on the outstanding balance at 9.5 percent. Hence, the present value of both columns (g) in Exhibits 19–5 and 19–7, when discounted at 9.5 percent, equals $25,000.

Exhibit 19–8 depicts cash flows from a pool assuming 0 percent, 10 percent, and 50 percent prepayment rates. Obviously, the cash flow to investors will vary dramatically, depending on the repayment rate. Also, as previously discussed, in the unlikely event that the market rate of return demanded by investors is equal to the coupon rate on the pass-through security, the security will always sell at par value, or $25,000, regardless of the prepayment rate. (Think about why this result is true.)

Security Prices and Expected Yields

As previously pointed out, when mortgage pass-through securities are priced by the issuer (with the advice of security underwriters), some assessment of yields expected by investors *at the time of issue* must be made. Further, this yield is likely to be different from the coupon rate on securities at the time of issue. This assessment is usually made by (1) establishing the extent of the premium that investors expect in excess of current yields on government securities with maturities in the same expected maturity range or (2) considering the current yields on other pass-throughs currently trading in the market. Establishing the premium may be difficult in the former case because of the uncertainty in repayment rates on pass-throughs. It may be difficult in the latter case because pricing of other pass-throughs assumes that the characteristics underlying both pools are the same. Nonetheless, the securities must be priced to sell to investors at the time of issue.

Let us turn back to our example. If we *assume* after considering all current market conditions and future expectations regarding repayment that the issuer decides that an expected yield of 8.5 percent will be required to successfully sell all securities to investors *and* that the prepayment rate will be 10 percent, then the security price will be equal to the present value of cash flows in column (g) of Exhibit 19–7 discounted at 8.5 percent. This yields a price of $25,848, or a premium of $848 over the $25,000 par value (see part B of Exhibit 19–7). The security is now said to be "priced at 103.39 percent of par ($25,848 ÷ $25,000) to yield 8.5 percent." However, the issuer will usually provide yield information to the investor by assuming *faster* and *slower prepayment rates.* This is accomplished by taking the offering price for the security ($25,848) and setting it equal to the expected cash flows that would occur above and below 10 percent prepayment, and then solving for the internal rate of return. Faster (or slower) rates of prepayment will cause the yield to be lower (or higher) in this example. The investor is willing to pay a premium of $848 in this example because the coupon rate is

EXHIBIT 19–8
Mortgage Pass-Through Security Cash Flow Payments to Individual Investors at Various Prepayment Rates

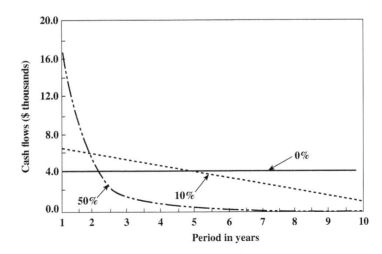

higher than the investor's required yield. But because the mortgages in the pool are likely to be prepaid sooner than expected, the investor will not benefit from the higher coupon rate for very long because of the increase in prepayments. Hence, the premium must reflect not only the relationship between the coupon rate on the security and the market yield on similar investments demanded by investors, but also the expected rate of repayment by homeowners. On the other hand, if market yields indicated that at the time of issue the security should be priced to yield 10.5 percent at 10 percent prepayment, it would be issued at a discount, or at a price of $24,199 (see part C of Exhibit 19–7). In this case, mortgages are not likely to be prepaid so quickly by homeowners; hence, the expected rate of repayment decreases and the discount paid on the security must reflect this as well as coupon rates and market yields.

Market Interest Rates and Price Behavior on Mortgage Pass-Throughs

To illustrate the very important relationships between changes in interest rates and varying rates of prepayment, Exhibit 19–9 shows that if the market rate of interest were to fall to 7.5 percent, investors having a 9.5 percent coupon rate pass-through security would expect an *increase* in its *price* because of the decline in interest rates. Further, if there were no prepayment assumed (i.e., 0%), the price of the pass-through would increase from $25,000 to approximately $27,500. However, if interest rates decline and the prepayment rate accelerates because more borrowers choose to refinance or pay off loans, the price will not rise to the extent that it would have if no increase in prepayments occurred. This can be seen by comparing prices at extreme rates of repayment, such as prices at 0 percent PSA (no prepayment), with prices at 50 percent for interest rates less than 9.5 percent. Note that even if interest rates *decline,* if the prepayment rate accelerates to 50 percent, the price at a 7.5 percent demanded yield would now be only slightly in excess of $25,000 compared with about $27,500 assuming no prepayment. On the other hand, when market interest rates are *greater* than the coupon rate, prices of mortgage pass-throughs (MPTs) will fall, and by a greater amount as repayments slow. This can also be seen by comparing prices for interest rates greater than 9.5 percent at 0 percent and 50 percent. Hence, prices of mortgage pass-throughs (MPTs) are *inversely* related to interest rates; however, they are less sensitive to declines in interest rates and more sensitive to increases in interest rates because rates of repayment are likely to accelerate as interest rates fall and slow as interest rates rise. This asymmetry affects the duration of the investment and its convexity. **Convexity** is a measure of the sensitivity of duration to changes in interest rates. For example, because prepayments may decelerate with rising interest rates, MPTs usually exhibit negative convexity resulting from an increase in duration. This limit on premiums is referred to as **price compression.**

EXHIBIT 19–9

Mortgage Pass-Through Security Prices at Various Required Rates of Return and Prepayment Rates

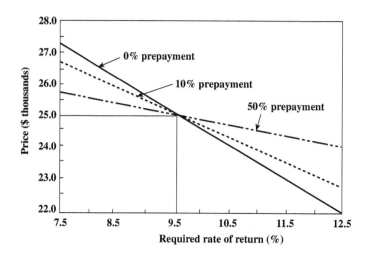

Web App

Go to the Government National Mortgage Association (Ginnie Mae) Web site (**www.ginniemae.gov**). What has the average rate been on Ginnie Mae mortgage- backed securities in recent years?

Further, as interest rates decline and prepayments accelerate, all cash flows received by investors must be reinvested at lower interest rates. This prospect is perhaps the most serious problem that investors perceive when investing in mortgage pass-through securities. It is this problem, coupled with other factors, that has given rise to collateralized mortgage obligations (CMOs), one of the mortgage-related securities that we will cover in the next chapter.

A Note on MBBs and MPTs

We previously indicated that the trustee is required to periodically "mark the mortgage collateral to the market" to determine whether the overcollateralization requirements of bond issues are being maintained. The methodology just outlined for pricing MPTs is the methodology that a trustee would generally follow to establish the market value of the mortgage pool for an issue of mortgage-backed bonds (MBBs). Further, with MBBs, *issuers bear prepayment risk* by virtue of the overcollateralization requirement. In other words, as prepayments accelerate and mortgages are prepaid, more mortgages must be replaced in the pool. With MPTs, *security holders bear prepayment risk* because all prepayments are passed through to investors. This means that (1) MBBs should be priced to provide lower yields than MPTs because the MBB issuer bears prepayment risk and (2) as market interest rates change, the price of MBBs will not reflect accelerated prepayment rates. As shown in Exhibit 19–9, this is not the case for MPTs. If all other terms of the MPT offering described in our examples were exactly the same for an MBB offering, the price behavior for the MBB would be represented by the 0 percent curve.

Key Terms			
	constant prepayment assumption, *643*	Government National Mortgage Association (GNMA), *624*	price compression, *646*
	convexity, *646*		PSA prepayment model, *643*
	Federal Home Loan Mortgage Corporation (FHLMC), *626*	mortgage-backed bonds (MBBs), *628*	secondary mortgage market, *622*
		mortgage pass-through securities (MPTs), *633*	weighted average coupon, *638*
	Federal National Mortgage Association (FNMA), *623*	pool factor, *639*	weighted average maturity, *638*

Useful Web Sites

www.fanniemae.com—Fannie Mae/Federal National Mortgage Association (privately owned) provides information about becoming a homeowner.

www.ginniemae.gov—Ginnie Mae/Government National Mortgage Association is within HUD and ensures mortgage funds are available throughout the United States, especially in rural and urban areas where it is harder to borrow money. Ginnie Mae guarantees securities backed by pools.

www.hud.gov—U.S. Department of Housing and Urban Development.

www.fha.gov—Federal Housing Administration.

www.freddiemac.com—Federal Home Loan Mortgage Corporation.

www.va.gov—Veteran's Administration. See www.homeloans.va.gov/ for information on VA guaranteed loans.

Questions

1. What is the secondary mortgage market? List three reasons why it is important.
2. What were the three principal activities of FNMA under its 1954 charter? What is its principal function now?
3. Name two ways that FNMA currently finances its secondary mortgage operations.
4. When did GNMA come into existence? What was its original function? What is its main function now?
5. Why was the formation of FHLMC so important?
6. What is a mortgage-related security? What are the similarities and differences between mortgage securities and corporate bonds?
7. Name the principal types of mortgage-related securities. What are the differences between them?
8. There are several ways that mortgages can be sold in the secondary market. Choose two and compare and contrast their length of distribution channel, relative ease of transaction, and efficiency as they relate to maximizing funds flow from sale.
9. What is the function of the optional delivery commitment?
10. What is a mortgage swap certificate?
11. Name five important characteristics of mortgage pools. Tell why each is important.
12. In general, would a falling rate of market interest cause the price of an MPT security to increase or decrease? Would the increase or decrease be greater if the security was issued at a discount? Would an increase in prepayment be likely or unlikely? Describe with an example.

Problems

1. Two 25-year maturity mortgage-backed bonds are issued. The first bond has a par value of $10,000 and promises to pay a 10.5 percent annual coupon, while the second is a zero coupon bond that promises to pay $10,000 (par) after 25 years, including accrued interest at 10 percent. At issue, bond market investors require a 12 percent interest rate on both bonds.

    a. What is the initial price on each bond?

    b. Assume that both bonds promise interest at 10.5 percent, compounded semiannually. What will be the initial price for each bond?

    c. If market interest rates fall to 9.5 percent at the end of five years, what will be the value of each bond, assuming annual payments as in (*a*) (state both as a percentage of par value and actual dollar value)?

2. The Green S & L originated a pool containing 75 ten-year fixed interest rate mortgages with an average balance of $100,000 each. All mortgages in the pool carry a coupon of 12 percent. (For simplicity, assume that all mortgage payments are made *annually* at 12% interest.) Green would now like to sell the pool to FNMA.

    a. Assuming a constant annual prepayment rate of 10 percent (for simplicity, assume that prepayments are based on the pool balance at the end of the preceding year and begin at the *end* of year 1), what is the price that Green could obtain if market interest rates were (1) 11 percent? (2) 12 percent? (3) 9 percent?

    b. Assume that five years have passed since the date in (*a*). What will the pool factor be? If market interest rates are 12 percent, what price can Green obtain now?

    c. Instead of selling the pool of mortgages in (*a*), Green decides to securitize the mortgages by issuing 100 pass-through securities. The coupon rate will be 11.5 percent and the servicing and guarantee fee will be .5 percent. However, the current market rate of return is 10.5 percent. How much will Green obtain for this offering of MPTs? What will each purchaser pay for an MPT security, assuming the same prepayment rate as in (*a*)?

    d. Assume now that immediately after purchase in (*c*), interest rates fall to 9 percent and that the prepayment rates are expected to accelerate to 20 percent per year, beginning at the end of the first year. What will the MPT security be worth now?

3. **Excel.** Refer to the "Ch19 MPS" tab in the Excel Workbook provided on the Web site.

    a. Find the value of the cash flows to the issuer and to individual investors based on a required rate of return of 7.5 percent.

    b. Find the value of the cash flows to the issuer and to individual investors based on a required rate of return of 11.5 percent.

20

The Secondary Mortgage Market: CMOs and Derivative Securities

Introduction

In this chapter, a continuation of Chapter 19, we continue to explore the secondary mortgage market, focusing in particular on two additional securities that have been introduced to securitize mortgage pools. The first is referred to as a mortgage pay-through bond (MPTB). It contains elements of mortgage-backed bonds and mortgage pass-through securities. The second security, referred to as a collateralized mortgage obligation (CMO), was developed in conjunction with investment underwriters by Freddie Mac in 1983 and adopted by Fannie Mae in 1987. These securities should be viewed as a natural outgrowth of the initial success of the mortgage-backed bond and pass-through security programs. Recall that many risks and investor concerns with purchasing whole mortgages discussed in the previous chapter were alleviated to some extent by mortgage pass-throughs. However, several key concerns with prepayment risk and reinvestment risk remained for some investors. Innovators of mortgage-backed securities believed that in addition to CMOs, new product types, called **derivative securities,** or simply "derivatives," had to be developed to address these concerns.

Mortgage Pay-Through Bonds (MPTBs)

These bonds can be best described as hybrid securities or ones containing elements of both mortgage pass-throughs and mortgage-backed bonds. **Mortgage pay-through bonds (MPTBs)** are issued against mortgage pools and, like MPTs, cash flows from the pool (i.e., principal and interest) are passed through to security holders. However, unlike an MPT, this security is a *bond* and not an undivided *equity* ownership interest in a mortgage pool. Like the MBB, the MPTB is a debt obligation of the issuer, who retains ownership of the mortgage pool. However, like the MPT, cash flows paid to bondholders are based on a coupon rate of interest while principal is passed through as it is received from normal amortization and prepayment of loans in the pool. Hence, an MPTB can be viewed as an MBB with the pass-through of principal and prepayment features of an MPT.

Most pay-through issues are based on residential pools and, like MBBs, will generally be overcollateralized by including (1) more mortgages in the pool than the sum of the securities issued against it or (2) additional collateral in the form of U.S. government bonds or other agency obligations. The income from this additional collateral is used as added assurance that sufficient cash flows will be available to service the bonds. Again, like MBBs, MPTBs may be issued either with a coupon rate or on a zero coupon basis.

An MPTB credit rating depends on (1) the riskiness of mortgages in the pool, (2) the extent of overcollateralization, and (3) the nature of any government-related securities constituting the excess collateral. Emphasis is placed on the extent of cash flow that will be produced by the pool, the reinvestment period that the issuer faces between receipt of principal and interest from the mortgage pool and periodic (usually semiannual) payments to bondholders, the securities making up the overcollateralization, and its relationship to promised coupon payments. All of these features are evaluated relative to prepayment risk. Because of the pass-through of amortization and prepayments, the market value of the collateral is not as important as it is with MBBs. Hence, there is usually no need to mark the collateral to the market or to provide for replenishment of collateral as long as the amount of overcollateralization is adequate. Because of the pass-through of principal, overcollateral requirements are not as great as for MBBs. Credit enhancements in the form of letters of credit and third-party guarantees or insurance are used by MPTB issuers to acquire higher credit ratings. In the absence of these enhancements, the creditworthiness of the issuer is very important because, should the mortgage pool experience a high rate of default losses and prepayments, the issuer must be looked to for satisfaction by the debt security holders.[1]

Although we do not provide a detailed analysis of MPTBs, the cash flow patterns are similar to those shown in the illustrations used for MBBs and MPTs in Chapter 19. However, contrary to the MBB, the issuer of MPTBs does not bear prepayment risk. It is borne by the investor. Hence, when MPTBs are priced, the risks that are so important when evaluating MPT prepayment patterns and reinvestment rates are equally important to MPTBs. This uncertainty regarding cash flows from prepayments has resulted in yet another security type, one that provides more protection against prepayment risk than MPTs and MPTBs, but less than that of an MBB. This security, referred to as the collateralized mortgage obligation (CMO), is the subject of the next section.

Collateralized Mortgage Obligations

To understand how **collateralized mortgage obligations (CMOs)** help to alleviate some of the reinvestment and prepayment risk for investors, we must understand the concept of a CMO and how it differs from MPTs and MPTBs. CMOs are debt instruments (like MBBs) that are issued using a pool of mortgages for collateral. In the pass-through, investors own an individual interest in the entire pool. In contrast, the issuer of a CMO offering *retains the ownership* of the mortgage pool and issues the bonds as debt against the mortgage pool. However, like the MPT and MPTB, the CMO is a pay-through security in that all amortization and prepayments flow through to investors. This means that the *security holder* continues to assume prepayment risk. However, the CMO modifies how the risk is allocated. Like both the MBB and MPTB, the difference between assets pledged as security and the amount of the debt issued against the pool constitutes the equity position of the issuer.

[1] Like other mortgage-related securities, default risk can be reduced by using FHA-VA mortgages or conventional loans with private mortgage insurance.

The major difference between CMOs and the other mortgage-backed securities is that CMOs are securities issued in multiple classes against the same pool of mortgages. These securities may have a number of maturity classes, such as three, five, or seven years. Such maturities are chosen by the issuer to meet the investment needs of various classes of investors. By issuing multiple classes of securities, each with a different maturity, the issuer is effectively creating different securities with maturity and payment streams that are vastly different from the underlying mortgage pool.

There are several fundamental differences between CMOs and MPTs. To reduce prepayment risk (and the coincident reinvestment risk), a mechanism had to be developed for an entity other than the investor to assume this risk while retaining the basic procedure of issuing securities against a mortgage pool. This was accomplished by the *issuer* retaining the ownership of the mortgage pool and prioritizing the payment of interest and principal among the various classes of debt securities issued against the pool. This prioritization is accomplished by issuing CMOs in classes referred to as **tranches** with different stated maturity dates. To achieve the desired number and maturity of these tranches, a prioritization of interest, principal, and prepayment proceeds from the mortgage pool to bondholders is made. Based on this prioritization, some classes of CMO investors receive cash flows like investors in conventional debt securities, while other investors agree to defer cash flows to later periods. This allocation was designed to appeal to more investor groups than would be willing to invest in MPTs, but who also were willing to bear some prepayment risk at yields that would be higher than those earned on MBBs. A CMO can also be referred to as a *multiple security class, mortgage pay-through security.*

Since its inception in 1983, the CMO has evolved into an extremely complex investment alternative. Although the sequential pay structure (see Exhibit 20–1) was used extensively during the initial years of CMO offerings and did much to stimulate investor interest, high demand and rather specific investor needs have led to the creation of a wide array of tranche alternatives. By slightly modifying either the method of principal repayment or coupon calculation, investment bankers have created a multitude of unique derivative investment vehicles that dominate the current CMO market.[2]

CMOs Illustrated

Exhibit 20–1 shows provisions that a very simplified offering of a CMO security might contain. On the "asset" side of the exhibit, the pool used for the bond collateral is assumed to be either FHA, VA, or conventional mortgages with interest rates fixed at 11 percent interest over a 10-year maturity. As with pass-throughs, mortgages placed in CMO pools are generally secured by very similar kinds of real estate and have equally similar payment patterns. It is also possible to pool GNMAs or other pass-through securities for a CMO offering.[3] The latter securities can be used in a pool because they ultimately represent securities based on a pool of mortgages.

On the "liability" side of the exhibit, three classes of bonds are created with different maturities and coupon rates. The amount of CMOs issued against the $75 million pool is $72 million. The difference ($3 million) is overcollateral, which is the equity contribution made by the issuer. The need for the overcollateralization will be apparent as the structure

---

[2] The term *derivative* refers to any investment with an underlying value that is dependent upon another security, index, or pool of securities. For example, if an investor purchased a call option in the S&P 500 index, that option would be classified as a derivative because its price would be dependent on changes in the value of the S&P 500 index. Many derivative-type investments have been created with prices that are dependent on the changes in the cash flows from mortgages in an underlying pool. These derivatives are discussed later in this chapter.

[3] CMOs can be created based on many different mortgage pools (e.g., ARMs, GPMs), such as those discussed in the previous chapter.

EXHIBIT 20–1 Contents of a CMO Security Offering with Sequential Pay Tranches

Assets:		Liabilities:	Estimated Maturity (years)	Coupon Rate (%)	Amount Issued	Weight	Weighted Average Coupon (%)
Mortgages	$75,000,000	Class A bonds	2–5	9.25%	$27,000,000	0.375	3.47%
(11-year interest)		Class B bonds	4–7	10.00	15,000,000	0.208	2.08
10-year maturity		Class Z bonds	6–10	11.00	30,000,000	0.417	4.58
		Total bonds			72,000,000	1.000	10.14%
		Equity:			3,000,000		
Total assets	$75,000,000	Total debt and net worth			$75,000,000		

Major investors:

Class A—Thrifts, commercial banks, money market funds, corporations

Class B—Insurance companies, pension funds, trusts, international investors

Class Z—Pension funds, trusts, international investors, and hedge funds

of the CMO issue is explained. Another observation that can be made in our example is that the 11 percent rate to be earned on the asset pool exceeds the coupon rates promised to each class of bondholders except the Z class. The difference between the 11 percent earned on the $75 million pool, or $8,250,000, and the *weighted average rate of interest* promised to security holders, or 10.14 percent on $72,000,000, which is an interest cost of $7,297,500, represents the source of profit at about $956,400 to be earned by the issuer. This residual cash flow will represent a return on the $3 million in overcollateral, or equity, invested in the venture. The issuer earns a profit on the equity that is used for creating the security issue. Fees may also be earned for providing any credit enhancements, managing, and administering the mortgage pool.

To achieve the desired maturity pattern for the CMOs shown in Exhibit 20–1, the conditions of the issue are such that the coupon rate of interest is not paid currently on all tranches. This structure, which is one of many possible payout possibilities, is referred to as a *sequential payout tranche* structure and is used to achieve the desired maturity pattern. For example, interest is paid currently on tranches A and B, but it is not paid on tranche Z until principal on the other tranches is repaid. For securities in tranche Z, interest will be accrued and accumulated into the investment balance. To ensure that the maturity of tranche A securities is kept relatively short, all interest accrued on the portion of the security offering contributed by the tranche Z is also allocated first to the tranche A security holders as additional principal. Further, all current amortization of principal and prepayments from the *entire* mortgage pool will also be allocated *first* to tranche A. Hence, tranche A investors, representing $27 million of the CMO issue, will receive principal on all mortgages in the pool (including prepayments), plus interest that would have been paid to tranche Z until the $27 million tranche is repaid, in addition to a coupon rate of 9.25 percent on their outstanding investment balance. Their investment balance is reduced by all principal payments from the pool plus the interest not currently paid but accrued on the Z class investment balance. As to the spread in stated maturities for tranche A securities (two to five years), it represents (1) the maximum number of years that it would take for class A investors to recover their principal, *assuming that no prepayments* occurred on the underlying mortgage pool and (2) an *estimate* of the minimum number of years (two) that it would take them to recover their investment. Of course, this latter estimate could be longer or shorter, depending on the *actual* rate of prepayment.

Until tranche A is repaid, tranche B receives "interest-only" payments. After class A is repaid, all principal allocations are made to B, and so on. As pointed out, the Z class of security holders receives no interest payments or principal payments, while the A and B tranches are being repaid. Instead, interest is accrued on the $30 million invested by this class of investors and is compounded at the 11 percent coupon rate. The accrued interest is then added to the amount owed. After classes A and B are repaid, cash interest payments are made to the Z class, and all principal payments from the pool are then directed toward this class.

The $3,000,000 in extra mortgages placed in the pool, which represents *over-collateralization* or equity invested in the issue, is required for several reasons. First, in addition to the cash flow patterns described, most CMO issues promise payments to investors quarterly or semiannually; we know, however, that payments into the mortgage pool occur monthly. Because monthly mortgage payments may be reinvested by the issuer until semiannual payments are due to investors, the issuer promises a minimum rate of interest on these investable funds *in addition to* promised coupon payments and priority repayment of principal. Hence, in addition to the risk of prepayment, a reinvestment risk exists in the event that market interest rates fall dramatically. In this event, prepayments into the pool would accelerate, thereby repaying all tranches *much faster* than expected. Further, the issuer may not be able to earn the promised rate of return on interim cash flows as interest rates fall (reinvestment risk). In this event, any cash shortfall to CMO investors will be paid from the $3 million of additional mortgage collateral. Hence, as with MBBs and MPTBs, the extent of overcollateralization is an important consideration that investors must make when evaluating a CMO investment. Obviously, the greater the amount of overcollateralization, the more likely that promised coupon rates and rates on interim cash flows will be paid. However, lower risk also implies that the coupon rate and rate on reinvested funds promised to the shorter-term tranches may also be lower.

Another important consideration with these securities is whether the CMO issuer is liable beyond the $3 million of equity. Usually issued by a corporation, CMOs are debt instruments that can be made with or without recourse to the issuer. Hence, like an issue of corporate bonds, CMO security owners may have recourse against the assets of the issuing corporation, should the issuer become bankrupt and not perform as promised and liability exceed $3 million.

CMO Mechanics

Some idea of cash flow patterns from a CMO offering is given in Exhibit 20–2, in which the data from Exhibit 20–1 are used to produce cash flows. To simplify this analysis, we have assumed that payments into the pool from mortgage borrowers occur annually. Consequently, we do not consider any reinvestment of interim cash flows between receipt of mortgage payments into the pool and payment to the various tranches of securities. We begin by assuming a rate of prepayment equal to 0 percent. Essentially, the exhibit details the source and composition of cash flows into the mortgage pool backing the CMO offering. Exhibit 20–3 provides a breakdown of cash flows for the various tranches of securities. Based on the assumption that no prepayments occur, tranche A security holders would be paid (1) interest at 9.25 percent of $27,000,000, or $2,497,500, (2) all principal repayments of $4,485,107 flowing into the pool (see column 3 in Exhibit 20–2), plus (3) the $3,300,00 in interest that would have been paid to the Z class of securities, or a total of $10,282,607 at end of the first year (see Exhibit 20–3). The cash flow pattern just described continues each year until the class A securities are repaid, which occurs at the end of the fourth year.

EXHIBIT 20–2
Annual Cash Flows
into CMO Mortgage
Pool (prepayment
rate = 0%)

Period	(1) Total Mortgage Pool: 10-Year Term 11% Fixed Rate	(2) Principal and Interest Payments into Pool	(3) Amount Amortization Excluding Prepayments	(4) Interest	(5) Owed to Security Holders
0	$75,000,000				$72,000,000
1	70,514,893	$12,735,107	$ 4,485,107	$8,250,000	67,514,893
2	65,536,424	12,735,107	4,978,469	7,756,638	62,536,424
3	60,010,324	12,735,107	5,526,100	7,209,007	57,010,324
4	53,876,352	12,735,107	6,133,971	6,601,136	50,876,352
5	47,067,644	12,735,107	6,808,708	5,926,399	44,067,644
6	39,509,978	12,735,107	7,557,666	5,177,441	36,509,978
7	31,120,968	12,735,107	8,389,009	4,346,098	28,120,968
8	21,809,168	12,735,107	9,311,801	3,423,307	18,809,168
9	11,473,069	12,735,107	10,336,099	2,399,008	8,473,069
10	0	12,735,107	11,473,069	1,262,038	0

Note again that class Z investors receive no current cash payments because interest is being accrued in that class.

Exhibit 20–3 provides a similar breakdown for class B and Z security holders. Note that class B securities receive current interest payments from years 1 to 3, but they do not receive any repayment of principal until class A is repaid. They then receive current interest plus all amortization flowing into the pool and interest from the tranche Z accrual. Note that when no prepayment is assumed, the B class would have a maturity period of five years based on normal amortization of the underlying mortgage pool. Note that the Z tranche accumulates interest until year 5 when investors in this tranche begin to receive cash flow.

Exhibit 20–4 provides detail on what is referred to as the cash flow to the **residual,** or equity, position in the CMO offering. Recall in our example that the firm that issues the CMO securities had collateralized the issue by $3 million, which represents the equivalent of an equity investment in the CMO offering. Hence, the issuer is entitled to retain any excess cash flow after payments are made to all security owners, and servicing fees and so on are paid. These cash flows represent the source of any return to the residual, or equity, position. Note that the cash flows are simply the sum of all cash flows into the pool, less all cash flows paid out to all tranches according to the CMO agreement. The cash flow available to the residual equity depends on how much interest is earned on the mortgage pool relative to the amount of interest paid to the A, B, and Z security holders. In our example, cash flow residuals are received by the equity investor each year, even when the Z class of securities does not receive any cash flows.[4] Also, the $952,500 initial cash flow to the residual interest represents a very small margin (less than 1%) relative to the $75 million security issue. This residual cash flow includes any servicing fees that are earned by the issuer, who we assume also retains the servicing responsibility for the mortgage pool. This margin is important because, for example, if $10 million of the mortgage pool was to unexpectedly prepay immediately after the securities were issued, this large amount of prepayments would significantly reduce the interest flow into the pool. Further, these unanticipated

---

[4] Some CMO provisions may require that this payment be placed in reserve until termination of the issue. In this event, the internal rate of return shown at the bottom of the exhibit would be lower because residual cash flows would not be realized by the issuer until mortgages in the pool are completely amortized.

EXHIBIT 20–3   **Cash Flows to Class A, B, and Z Investors* (prepayment rate = 0%)**

	Tranche A (coupon rate = 9.25%; amount invested = $27,000,000)			
Period	Amount Owed to Security Holder at End of Period	All Principal from Pool and Interest from Z Class	Coupon Interest	Total Payments
0	$27,000,000			
1	19,214,893	$7,785,107	$2,497,500	$10,282,607
2	10,573,424	8,641,469	1,777,378	10,418,846
3	981,394	9,592,030	978,042	10,570,072
4	0	981,394	90,779	1,072,173
5	0	0	0	0
6	0	0	0	0
7	0	0	0	0
8	0	0	0	0
9	0	0	0	0
10	0	0	0	0

	Tranche B (coupon rate = 10.00%; amount invested = $15,000,000)			
Period	Amount Owed to Security Holder at End of Period	All Principal from Pool and Interest from Z Class	Coupon Interest	Total Payments
0	$15,000,000			
1	15,000,000	0	$1,500,000	$ 1,500,000
2	15,000,000	0	1,500,000	1,500,000
3	15,000,000	0	1,500,000	1,500,000
4	5,334,240	$9,665,760	1,500,000	11,165,760
5	0	5,334,240	533,424	5,867,664
6	0	0	0	0
7	0	0	0	0
8	0	0	0	0
9	0	0	0	0
10	0	0	0	0

	Tranche Z (coupon rate = 11.00%; amount invested = $30,000,000)			
Period	Amount Owed to Security Holder at End of Period	Interest	Accrued Interest	Principal Allocation	Total Payments
0	$30,000,000				
1	33,300,000	$3,300,000	$3,300,000		
2	36,963,000	3,663,000	3,663,000		
3	41,028,930	4,065,930	4,065,930		
4	45,542,112	4,513,182	4,513,182		
5	44,067,644	5,009,632		$ 1,474,468	$ 6,484,101
6	36,509,978	4,847,441		7,557,666	12,405,107
7	28,120,968	4,016,098		8,389,009	12,405,107
8	18,809,168	3,093,307		9,311,801	12,405,107
9	8,473,069	2,069,008		10,336,099	12,405,107
10	0	932,038		8,473,069	9,405,107

*Cash distributions to investors in Tranches A, B, and Z have come to be known as the "waterfall."

prepayments must be reinvested to compensate for the loss in interest and to pay the class A tranche at the end of the year. Consequently, the $952,500 cash flow to the residual would have to be used to offset the difference between interest lost because of prepayment and any interest earned on interim reinvestment.

EXHIBIT 20–4
Residual Cash Flows (prepayment rate = 0%)

	Residual Equity Class ($3,000,000 Invested)		
Period	Total Cash Flows into Pool	Total Payments to A, B, and Z Classes	Residual Cash Flows to Equity Class
0			$(3,000,000)
1	$12,735,107	$11,782,607	952,500
2	12,735,107	11,918,846	816,261
3	12,735,107	12,070,072	665,035
4	12,735,107	12,237,933	497,174
5	12,735,107	12,351,765	383,342
6	12,735,107	12,405,107	330,000
7	12,735,107	12,405,107	330,000
8	12,735,107	12,405,107	330,000
9	12,735,107	12,405,107	330,000
10	12,735,107	9,405,107	3,330,000

Residual *IRR* = 20.19%

The possibility of unanticipated prepayment and the potential problem with reinvesting in a period of declining interest rates (which is also likely to cause even more prepayments) should clarify why the $3 million overcollateralization is required. Further, we have assumed that the mortgages used to form the pool for the CMO issue are FHA, VA, or conventional fixed rate mortgages. In any case, we have assumed that there is adequate insurance protection against default losses. Where there are no limited or no full guarantees against default losses (e.g., where CMOs are issued against commercial mortgages or second mortgages), the investor would have to consider the possibility of greater losses because of the impact of default on cash flows. Hence, in the latter instances we would expect to see (1) larger amounts of overcollateralization, and/or (2) pool insurance purchased by the issuer from a third party who is willing to insure investors against part or all default loss, or (3) a provision referred to as a *calamity call,* which allows the issuer to recall all securities for a specified time after issue in the event interest rates decline sharply, prepayments accelerate, and reinvestment rates fall below rates promised to investors. However, if cash flows were to occur as shown in Exhibit 20–4, the issuer would earn a *BTIRR* of 20.19 percent on the $3 million in equity (servicing and other fees not removed from residual cash flows). This rate obviously exceeds the rates earned by each security class, which has a prior claim on all cash flows paid into the pool.

CMO Cash Flows and Prepayment Assumptions

Because there will always be some prepayment of principal from mortgages in an underlying pool, the expected maturity for each security class will affect profitability to the issuer. To illustrate this effect, we now assume that prepayment will occur at approximately 10 percent instead of zero as illustrated in the preceding exhibits.

Cash payments from the pool to each of the classes of security holders are shown in Exhibit 20–5. Note that in addition to normal amortization payments into the pool, prepayments are assumed to occur at 10 percent per year. As shown in Exhibit 20–6, investors in tranche A receive their promised coupon payments, $2,497,500, plus the tranche Z portion of interest in $3,300,000, plus all amortization of $4,485,107 and prepayments of $7,500,000 flowing into the pool during the first year, or a total of $17,782,607. Based on this accelerated pattern of cash flows, class A investors would now be repaid after two years. This compares with four years when no prepayment was assumed. For this reason, class A securities are sometimes referred to as the "fast pay tranche." After two years, class

EXHIBIT 20–5   Annual Cash Flows into CMO Mortgage Pool (Prepayment Rate = 10%)

Period	(1) Mortgage Pool: 10-Year Term 11% Fixed Rate	(2) Principal and Interest Payment into Pool	(3) Assumed Prepayments* (10%)	(4) Total Amortization Excluding Prepayments	(5) Interest	(6) Amount Owed to Security Holders	(7) Total Available for Distribution (2) + (3)
0	$75,000,000					$72,000,000	
1	63,014,893	$12,735,107	$7,500,000	$4,485,107	$8,250,000	60,014,893	$20,235,107
2	52,264,447	11,380,595	6,301,489	4,448,956	6,931,638	49,264,447	17,682,084
3	42,631,009	10,156,083	5,226,445	4,406,993	5,749,089	39,631,009	15,382,527
4	34,010,368	9,046,951	4,263,101	4,357,540	4,689,411	31,010,368	13,310,052
5	26,311,218	8,039,254	3,401,037	4,298,113	3,741,141	23,311,218	11,440,291
6	19,455,296	7,119,034	2,631,122	4,224,800	2,894,234	16,455,296	9,750,156
7	13,378,894	6,270,955	1,945,530	4,130,872	2,140,083	10,378,894	8,216,484
8	8,037,865	5,474,818	1,337,889	4,003,140	1,471,678	5,037,865	6,812,708
9	3,424,664	4,693,580	803,786	3,809,415	884,165	424,664	5,497,366
10	0	3,801,377	0	3,424,664	376,713	0	3,801,377

*Based on pool balance at the end of the preceding year.

B investors, who receive current interest-only payments, would begin receiving the interest accrued on tranche Z plus all principal from mortgages paid into the pool during the third year. Based on this pattern of cash receipts, tranche B would now be repaid after one additional year, or a total of three years from the date of issue. This compares to five years with no prepayment.

As indicated earlier, tranche Z security holders do not receive interest or principal payments until the A and B tranches are repaid. Exhibit 20–6 shows that during the first three years, interest would be accrued on the Z class by compounding the $30 million invested at 11 percent. Interest is calculated at the coupon rate (11%) on the accumulated investment balance, which contains $30 million plus all accrued interest. In year 3, the Z class begins to receive some payments but it is not enough to cover the interest until year 4 when all other securities have been paid off. All principal payments flowing into the pool at this point are also allocated to the Z class. The Z class, based on our prepayment assumptions, will now be repaid in the 10th year.

Finally, the issuer retains residual cash flows remaining after all cash payments are made to each tranche of securities. This residual amounts to, in essence, the spread earned by the issuer for investing equity (overcollateralization) and for managing the provisions of the CMO issue. Exhibit 20–7 shows the residual cash flows, or the difference between total payments into the pool and cash payments made to all of the investor classes (based on all preceding exhibits). Recall that these residuals are based on the assumption that the repayment rate remains at 10 percent. Obviously, these residuals would vary considerably at different rates of repayment. When the residual cash flows received over 10 years by the issuer are set equal to the $3 million in equity invested at the time of issue, a yield, or internal rate of return, of 17.25 percent results. As expected, this yield still represents a higher return than is earned on the A, B, or Z tranches. Further, this yield would obviously increase if the amount of equity used to finance the CMO issue were reduced (because of the use of financial leverage).[5]

[5] The reader may think of leverage in the financial structure of a CMO issue much like that of leveraging any income-producing asset with debt. Similarly, the risk assumed by the various classes of bondholders and the issuer will vary based on the amount of overcollateralization.

EXHIBIT 20−6   Cash Flows to Class A, B, and Z Investors (prepayment rate = 10%)

	Tranche A (coupon rate = 9.25%; amount invested = $27,000,000)			
Period	Amount Owed to Security Holder at End of Period	All Principal from Pool and Interest from Z Class	Coupon Interest	Total Payments
0	$27,000,000			
1	11,714,893	$15,285,107	$2,497,500	$17,782,607
2	0	11,714,893	1,083,628	12,798,521
3	0	0	0	0
4	0	0	0	0
5	0	0	0	0
6	0	0	0	0
7	0	0	0	0
8	0	0	0	0
9	0	0	0	0
10	0	0	0	0

	Tranche B (coupon rate = 10.00%; amount invested = $15,000,000)			
Period	Amount Owed to Security Holder at End of Period	All Principal from Pool and Interest from Z Class	Coupon Interest	Total Payments
0	$15,000,000			
1	15,000,000	0	$1,500,000	$ 1,500,000
2	12,301,447	$ 2,698,553	1,500,000	4,198,553
3	0	12,301,447	1,230,145	13,531,592
4	0	0	0	0
5	0	0	0	0
6	0	0	0	0
7	0	0	0	0
8	0	0	0	0
9	0	0	0	0
10	0	0	0	0

	Tranche Z (coupon rate = 11.00%; amount invested = $30,000,000)				
Period	Amount Owed to Security Holder at End of Period	Interest	Accrued Interest	Principal Allocation	Total Payments
0	$30,000,000				
1	33,300,000	$3,300,000	$3,300,000		
2	36,963,000	3,663,000	3,663,000		
3	39,631,009	4,065,930	2,668,009		$ 1,397,921
4	31,010,368	4,359,411		$8,620,641	12,980,052
5	23,311,218	3,411,141		7,699,150	11,110,291
6	16,455,296	2,564,234		6,855,922	9,420,156
7	10,378,894	1,810,083		6,076,402	7,886,484
8	5,037,865	1,141,678		5,341,029	6,482,708
9	424,664	554,165		4,613,201	5,167,366
10	0	46,713		424,664	471,377

Also note that in the case of faster prepayment, the *BTIRR* (Exhibit 20–7) will fall to 17.25 percent from the slower prepayment example (Exhibit 20–4), where the *IRR* was 20.19 percent. This occurs because the total interest collected from the pool will be lower if prepayment accelerates; therefore, the dollar spread between interest inflow and outflow becomes smaller.

EXHIBIT 20–7
Residual Cash
Flows (prepayment
rate = 10%)

	Residual Equity Class ($3,000,000 invested)		
Period	Total Cash Flows into Pool	Total Payments to A, B, and Z Classes	Residual Cash Flows to Equity Class
0			$(3,000,000)
1	$20,235,107	$19,282,607	952,500
2	17,682,084	16,997,073	685,011
3	15,382,527	14,929,513	453,014
4	13,310,052	12,980,052	330,000
5	11,440,291	11,110,291	330,000
6	9,750,156	9,420,156	330,000
7	8,216,484	7,886,484	330,000
8	6,812,708	6,482,708	330,000
9	5,497,366	5,167,366	330,000
10	3,801,377	471,377	3,330,000

Residual *IRR* = 17.25%

CMOs: Pricing and Expected Maturities

Exhibit 20–8 provides additional insight into how the patterns of cash flow payments to each tranche of securities vary with prepayment rates. The graph in panel A shows the expected cash flows to each class of CMO investors based on a 0 percent prepayment rate. In panel B, four very distinct cash flow patterns emerge. This is exactly the goal of the CMO issuer: that is, to reach different *market segments* of investors who have more specific maturity requirements than a mortgage pass-through security provides, but who may not need the exact maturity requirements that an MBB provides. As indicated, however, the CMO does not completely eliminate prepayment risk. Indeed, if mortgage interest rates decline substantially, these securities may provide investors with only slightly more prepayment protection than a pass-through security. To illustrate what cash flows and the maturity of security classes may look like assuming a significant increase in prepayment, Exhibit 20–9 shows results assuming a 10 percent prepayment rate.

By placing a priority on the distribution of cash flows to various classes of security owners, the CMO generally provides more predictability with respect to expected maturity periods and cash flows than a mortgage pass-through. Recall that in our simplified example in Chapter 19, MPT investors could be committed for a period of up to 10 years, with substantial variation in cash flows received from period to period, depending on the repayment rate.

CMO securities, when based on a pool of FHA, VA, or conventionally insured mortgages, should provide a yield in excess of U.S. Treasury securities with equivalent maturity classes[6] because of added cash flow uncertainty. In any case, if no significant decline in interest rates is expected by security holders, the pattern of cash flows shown in Exhibit 20–9 may be appealing to some investors who would otherwise be interested in a pass-through security. This may be particularly true for the class A, or fast-pay, tranche, which would compete with short-term Treasury bills and notes and may be attractive to managers of money market funds. Tranche B may be more appealing to insurance companies and pension funds, while tranche Z may be preferred by either long-term or hedge-type

[6] Because the investor in a CMO is dealing with an *expected* range in maturity, that expected maturity must be used as a basis of comparison for maturities of alternative investments.

EXHIBIT 20–8
Annual Cash Flows to CMO Tranches and Residual Equity (prepayment rate = 0%)

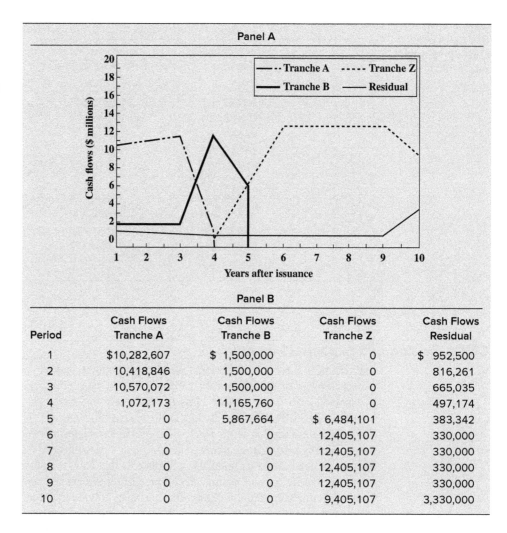

Panel B

Period	Cash Flows Tranche A	Cash Flows Tranche B	Cash Flows Tranche Z	Cash Flows Residual
1	$10,282,607	$ 1,500,000	0	$ 952,500
2	10,418,846	1,500,000	0	816,261
3	10,570,072	1,500,000	0	665,035
4	1,072,173	11,165,760	0	497,174
5	0	5,867,664	$ 6,484,101	383,342
6	0	0	12,405,107	330,000
7	0	0	12,405,107	330,000
8	0	0	12,405,107	330,000
9	0	0	12,405,107	330,000
10	0	0	9,405,107	3,330,000

mutual funds. Hence, prioritization of cash flows does create the possibility of reaching a broader class of investors with more specific maturity requirements than would be the case with MPTs.[7]

To establish some idea of the sensitivity of expected *maturity* to expected rates of prepayment, Exhibit 20–10 shows the outstanding amount owed for each tranche under the prepayment assumption of 0 percent PSA (panel A) and 10 percent. As expected, the balances shown for tranche A in panel A begin to amortize immediately, and tranche B amortizes in accordance with the priority allocation of cash flows. However, the amount owed to the Z class increases sharply as interest accrues (like that on a GPM mortgage). In the event that the repayment rate increases sharply (as in panel B), the amounts owed to each security class will decrease significantly and all investors in the CMO offering will be repaid within 10 years.

[7] The reader may have reached the conclusion that a CMO issue with its various classes of expected maturities resembles tax-exempt serial bonds, which are frequently issued by state and local municipalities. Recall that bond issues with serial and sinking fund provisions call for the retirement of specific amounts of bonds at specific time intervals. This pattern of different maturities appeals to many investor groups that have a specific need to match liabilities coming due on specific dates with an interest-bearing asset with the same maturity. The different pattern of CMO maturities does emulate such bond issue offerings in this respect. However, the use of a Z class of security and residual, or equity, interest is the truly innovative aspect of this type of offering.

EXHIBIT 20–9
Annual Cash Flows to CMO Tranches and Residual Equity (prepayment rate = 10%)

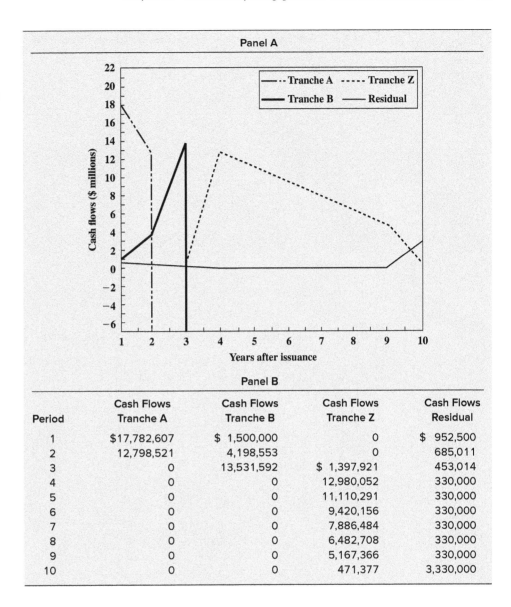

Panel A

Panel B

Period	Cash Flows Tranche A	Cash Flows Tranche B	Cash Flows Tranche Z	Cash Flows Residual
1	$17,782,607	$ 1,500,000	0	$ 952,500
2	12,798,521	4,198,553	0	685,011
3	0	13,531,592	$ 1,397,921	453,014
4	0	0	12,980,052	330,000
5	0	0	11,110,291	330,000
6	0	0	9,420,156	330,000
7	0	0	7,886,484	330,000
8	0	0	6,482,708	330,000
9	0	0	5,167,366	330,000
10	0	0	471,377	3,330,000

CMO Price Behavior and Prepayment Rates

As with MPTs, CMO prices will vary with both changes in interest rates and prepayment rates. The relationship for 0 percent PSA is shown in panel A of Exhibit 20–11. An important characteristic of the prices is their relatively narrow range (vertical axis) that results from changes in demanded market rates of return (interest rates, horizontal axis) for the A and B tranches. The reason is the prioritization of cash flows, which has a "smoothing effect" on prices. However, with respect to prices for tranche Z and the present value of the residual interest, these two classes exhibit more volatility in price behavior than tranches A and B. This volatility is a by-product of the market segmentation chosen for this CMO security issue.

Even when an extremely significant increase in the prepayment rate occurs, as shown in panel B of Exhibit 20–11, the range in prices tends to narrow for all tranches in the CMO issue. This can be seen by comparing the ranges in panels A and B. However, also keep in mind that the *expected maturity period* also declines significantly as rate of prepayment

EXHIBIT 20–10
**Maturity of CMO
Tranches at Various
Prepayment Rates**

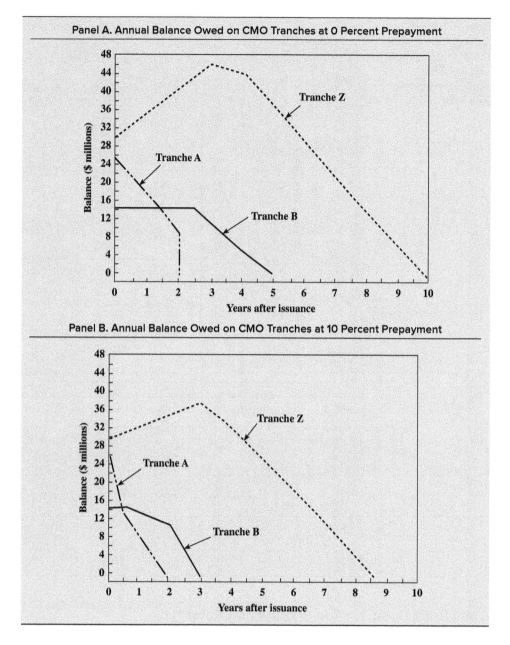

increases (see Exhibit 20–10). Hence, this CMO structure makes a trade-off in price stability from the Z and residual classes to the A and B tranches as the maturity period contracts for all classes. However, relative to mortgage pass-through securities, the A and B tranches of CMOs receive some additional prepayment and price protection not given to MPT security holders. Investors in MPTs would receive an increase in cash flows as the rate of prepayment increases, but not necessarily as dramatic a reduction in maturity (although the cash flows in the later years may be relatively small). Consequently, structuring a CMO offering with a maturity and cash flow pattern for one Z tranche, while retaining shorter maturities for the A and B tranches, may make it possible to appeal to investors who have a preference for shorter maturities and a strong dislike for the MPT. One measure that is often used to measure the relationship between price, yield, and maturity for tranches with

EXHIBIT 20–11
CMO Price Behavior
in Response
to Changes in
Interest Rates and
Prepayment Rates

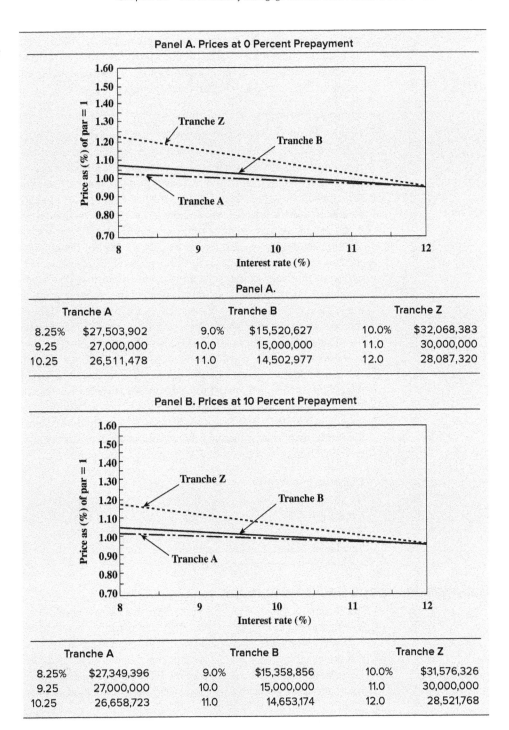

Panel A. Prices at 0 Percent Prepayment

Panel A.

Tranche A		Tranche B		Tranche Z	
8.25%	$27,503,902	9.0%	$15,520,627	10.0%	$32,068,383
9.25	27,000,000	10.0	15,000,000	11.0	30,000,000
10.25	26,511,478	11.0	14,502,977	12.0	28,087,320

Panel B. Prices at 10 Percent Prepayment

Tranche A		Tranche B		Tranche Z	
8.25%	$27,349,396	9.0%	$15,358,856	10.0%	$31,576,326
9.25	27,000,000	10.0	15,000,000	11.0	30,000,000
10.25	26,658,723	11.0	14,653,174	12.0	28,521,768

sequential payment and other structures is called *duration*. This measure is discussed in considerable detail in the appendix to this chapter.

CMO Tranche Variations

Although the preceding illustration is useful in gaining a basic understanding of the mechanics of a CMO, the elementary structure used in this example reflects only a small portion of today's CMO market. In today's market, up to 20 different CMO tranches may be used to create many derivative security types from a single mortgage pool. What follows is a discussion of a select number of other classes that, because of their importance in the multiclass mortgage-backed security market, deserve further discussion.

Principal Repayment Variations

Instead of the *sequential pay tranches* used to construct the previous CMO example, issuers may use a sinking fund structure to redeem the securities' principal balance. This method of principal repayment allows issuers to create tranches with more cash flow certainty. In a sinking fund structure, two or more tranches are eligible to receive paydowns of principal on a payment date. The actual amount of payment to each depends on the sinking fund schedule for the structure and the amount of prepayments received.

Under a sinking fund structure, a **planned amortization class (PAC) tranche** offers the greatest degree of cash flow certainty. Instead of being allocated all principal repayments from the underlying pool, the PAC receives *fixed payments* over a predetermined period of time under a range of prepayment scenarios. This range, or *PAC band,* is delineated by a minimum and maximum constant payment speed under which the PAC scheduled repayment will remain unchanged. A **targeted amortization class (TAC)** schedule, on the other hand, corresponds to a single "targeted" prepayment speed (e.g., 150% PSA). This targeted prepayment speed is often referred to as the TAC's *pricing speed.* For either of these classes, prepayments in excess of the amounts specified in the sinking fund schedule will be applied to one or more of the non-PAC and non-TAC tranches in the structure, which are often called *companion* or *support tranches* because they are issued in tandem with PACs and TACs and absorb any significant variation in prepayments. As a consequence, when PACs and TACs are present, an attempt to insulate the security holder from the prepayment risk of the underlying pool is desired. However, the prepayment risk must be transferred to the other non-PACs or non-TACs in the structure.

Coupon Variations

As shown in the earlier example, class Z tranches, also known as *accrual* or *accretion bonds,* provide for the unpaid coupon to be added to the outstanding principal balance, resulting in automatic reinvestment at the coupon rate. Since the interest that accrues on Z tranches is used to pay down principal on other tranches, the issuer can offer shorter average life securities as companions.

Subprime Mortgage-Backed Securities

Traditionally, the CMO structure described above included either FHA-insured or VA-guaranteed mortgages or conventional mortgages that were designed to attract "prime" borrowers who had a good credit rating. Also, the securities often had GNMA guarantees that protected investors against default. Unfortunately, during the early to mid-2000s, lenders increasingly made loans to borrowers who were *not* prime borrowers. Rather, they were what we refer to as "subprime" borrowers, people who had poor credit ratings and for whom it was questionable whether they really could afford the mortgage payments. Many subprime borrowers were lured into believing they could afford the payments because the mortgages were ARMs with a "teaser" rate, as discussed in Chapter 5. That is, the initial interest rate was below what the rate would be once it was fully indexed—whether interest rates changed or not. So even though these borrowers could afford the payments at first, when rates rose they could not. If home prices had not declined, they may have been able to refinance and use equity from the home to help cover the mortgage payments. But when home prices fell as the housing boom turned to bust, defaults on subprime mortgages mushroomed.

The securities backed by these subprime mortgages were not GNMA guaranteed, so investors were exposed to default risk. As borrowers began to default on their subprime mortgages, the lower-rated CMO tranches lost value. And to make things worse, many of the lower-rated CMO securities were used as collateral for creation of another security called a *collateralized debt obligation,* or CDO (discussed later in this chapter). As a result, many investors that held securities backed by subprime mortgages lost a considerable amount of money—including banks that had issued and sold the mortgages but purchased mortgage-backed securities as an investment. This caused severe problems in the banking system.

In retrospect, it appears that the risk of mortgages backed by subprime mortgages was not fully understood by investors or the rating agencies that rated the securities. Perhaps they believed that the risk would be reduced because the mortgages were well diversified, there being thousands of different mortgages from borrowers throughout the United States. But when home prices fell on a national basis, it affected virtually all of the subprime mortgages.

The basic concept of having multiple classes of securities backed by a pool of mortgages is still valid, but it is likely that, in the future, lenders will be more careful in regard to the types of mortgages they make and investors will be more wary of securities backed by subprime mortgages. The rating agencies are also likely to be more stringent in their requirements when granting a high credit rating to securities backed by subprime mortgages.

Derivatives Illustrated

Floating rate tranches are generally attractive to institutional investors seeking assets to match floating rate liabilities. The **floater tranche,** as it is often called, has coupon rates that adjust periodically to a fixed spread over an index. For example, if a floater's corresponding index fell from 7 percent to 6.75 percent and the tranche offered a spread of 75 basis points, the coupon rate of the floating rate tranche would adjust from 7.75 percent to 7.5 percent on its reset date. The indexes currently used in the CMO market include the **LIBOR,**[8] the 11th district cost of funds (COF), the one-year Treasury rate, and the certificate of deposit (CD) rate. Reset intervals for these tranches typically range from one to six months.

To offset the variable payout for the floating rate tranche, an *inverted floating rate tranche* is often used in the same CMO issue. The **inverse floater tranche** has a coupon interest rate that adjusts in the *opposite* direction to its index. By setting the ratio of the floating rate tranche to inverted floating rate tranche equal to 1, the CMO issuer can ensure that the weighted average rate of interest for the two classes will be stabilized with respect to changes in the index.

An illustration of the floater–inverse floater structure is as follows: Assume that in our example, a portion of one tranche is subdivided into equal amounts of $10 million. Each subdivided amount is now referred to as a floater (F) and inverse floater (IF) tranche. If we assume that the F tranche is tied to LIBOR, with coupon interest on the floater portion *increasing* with increases in LIBOR and the inverse floater portion *decreasing* with declines in LIBOR, and on the day of issue LIBOR is 6 percent, then the interest allocation

---

[8] LIBOR, or the London Interbank Offer Rate, is a very important deposit rate that is quoted daily among banks that do business in the Eurocurrency market. This interest rate is widely used throughout the world as an index upon which interest rates on many financial instruments are based.

to each tranche within this portion of the mortgage pool on the date of issue is as shown in case 1.

Case 1:

Interest due to the (F) and (IF) tranches on *date of issue,* LIBOR = 6%:

$$(F) \text{ floater } \$10,000,000 = .50 \times .06 = \$\ \ 600,000$$
$$(IF) \text{ inverse floater } \$10,000,000 = .50 \times .06 = \underline{\ \ \ 600,000}$$
$$\text{Interest payable} = \underline{\underline{\$1,200,000}}$$

If, after the issue date, LIBOR *increased* by 1 percent, the interest payable to *both* classes of investors would be as shown in case 2.

Case 2:

Interest due if LIBOR increases by 1 percent to 7 percent:

$$(F) \text{ floater } \$10,000,000 = .50 \times .07 = \$\ \ 700,000$$
$$(IF) \text{ inverse floater } \$10,000,000 = .50 \times .05 = \underline{\ \ \ 500,000}$$
$$\text{Interest payable} = \underline{\underline{\$1,200,000}}$$

Note that total interest payable remains at $1,200,000 and that the relative share received by (F) and (IF) investors changes in case 2. Investors in the floaters would now receive $700,000, or $100,000 more than they received in case 1. IF investors would receive $100,000 *less* than they received in case 1. Also, if LIBOR were ever to increase by 6 percent to 12 percent, the F tranche would receive *all* interest available for distribution, or $1,200,000, and IF investors would receive nothing. Since IF investors cannot receive negative interest payments, this implies that a cap for F tranche investors must always be specified at the time of issue. The *maximum* cap would be equal to $1,200,000 divided by $20,000,000, or LIBOR = 12%. However, depending on investor demand for F and IF securities at the time of issue, caps may be set at various levels below 12 percent. Conversely, if LIBOR were to *decline* by 2 percent when payments were due, then IF tranche investors would receive base LIBOR of 6 percent plus 2 percent, or a total of 8 percent, and F tranche investors would receive 6 percent minus 2 percent, or 4 percent. Again, interest payments must sum to $1,200,000, the total available to both investor classes. A minimum, or *floor,* must also be set for IF investors. In this case, it happens to be a 6 percent decline from base LIBOR. However, floors may also be set at other levels between base LIBOR and zero. This is essentially the purpose of the floater/inverse floater structure. If LIBOR increases, the share of interest that F tranche investors receive increases by the amount of the increase in LIBOR and the share of total interest received by IF investors declines by a like amount. When LIBOR declines, the opposite pattern applies.

Using these basic relationships, we can show how underwriters may change the above investment structure to meet whatever investor preferences are relative to prevailing market conditions. This can be done by **scaling** the ratio of the relative composition of interest to be received by the F and IF tranche investors. For example, if the F investors and the IF investors in the example accounted for 60 percent and 40 percent of the tranche, respectively, then the scale of F to IF would be 60 percent divided by 40 percent, or 1.5. In this case, we would have the following relationship at the time of issue:

Total interest allocation at time of issue:

$$
\begin{array}{lllll}
\text{(F) tranche} & 60\% & = 12{,}000{,}000 \times .06 = \$ & 720{,}000 \\
\text{(IF) tranche} & \underline{40} & = \underline{8{,}000{,}000} \times .06 = & \underline{480{,}000} \\
& 100\% & = 20{,}000{,}000 & \$1{,}200{,}000
\end{array}
$$

Note that even though the scale of F to IF has changed, the total interest payable is still $1,200,000. However, because the relative share that results from scaling the F and IF tranches is 1.5, if LIBOR were to increase by 1 percent to a level of 7 percent, we would have:

$$
\begin{array}{lllll}
\text{(F) tranche} & 60\% & = 12{,}000{,}000 \times .070 = \$ & 840{,}000 \\
\text{(IF) tranche} & \underline{40} & = \underline{8{,}000{,}000} \times .045 = & \underline{360{,}000} \\
& 100\% & = 20{,}000{,}000 & \$1{,}200{,}000
\end{array}
$$

Note that interest due to F tranche investors is tied directly to increases in LIBOR, which is now 6 percent plus 1 percent, or 7 percent. Therefore, F investors must now receive $840,000. However, because the total interest payment on both tranches must sum to $1,200,000, or the total available for distribution, the inverse floater tranche will earn only 4.5 percent, or the original LIBOR rate of 6 percent less the 1 percent increase in LIBOR times 1.5. The 1.5 multiple, times the inverse of the *change* from the base LIBOR, is also specified at the time of issue. Therefore, IF investors will always receive interest based on the scale of 1.5 times the inverse of the change from base LIBOR. As pointed out above, a *cap* for the maximum increase in LIBOR must also be included. The maximum cap would be an increase of 4 percent, at which point LIBOR equals 10 percent. At that level, the F tranche would receive $1,200,000 and the IF tranche would receive nothing. The theoretical floor for IF investors would be the point where IF investors receive all interest available to both investor classes, or $1,200,000 divided by $8,000,000, which equals 15 percent.

Returning to our example, if base LIBOR *decreased* by 4 percent from 6 percent to a level of 2 percent, we would have:

$$
\begin{array}{lllll}
\text{(F) tranche} & 60\% & = 12{,}000{,}000 \times .02 = \$ & 240{,}000 \\
\text{(IF) tranche} & \underline{40} & = \underline{8{,}000{,}000} \times .12 = & \underline{960{,}000} \\
& 100\% & & \$1{,}200{,}000
\end{array}
$$

In this case, the 4 percent *decline* in LIBOR from its initial 6 percent level to 2 percent would result in interest to IF tranche investors equal to 4 percent times 1.5, or 6 percent. When added to the base LIBOR of 6 percent, a total of 12 percent results. The total interest payment of $960,000 would now be distributed to IF tranche investors. Clearly, with a 4 percent decline from base LIBOR, the total interest payable to IF investors would increase by 100 percent from the allocation determined on the date of issue.

From this simple example, it should be clear that the ratio of F to IF can be scaled and both floors and caps can be set for specified maximum increases or decreases in LIBOR. Also, the greater the scale used to differentiate interest payable to F and IF investors, the greater the "leverage" applied to the IF investors. Our examples show that when such leverage is applied, it increases the potential volatility (hence, risk) in cash flows to F and IF investors. In practice, the scale that will be used depends on how much potential volatility versus return F and IF investors want to buy at the time the securities are offered for sale. Underwriters and issuers also must decide then what structure will be most marketable to investors.

Why would investors ever purchase an F or IF derivative investment in the first place? They do so if they believe that interest rates are likely to rise or fall and if they have *liabilities* that must be paid at some future date based on interest rates that prevail on the date that these liabilities are payable. Derivatives may be purchased to protect the yield on another portfolio of mortgages or bonds. For example, assume that an investor holds a portfolio of fixed interest rate bonds with a current market value of $1,000,000, which are being used as *collateral* for a business loan that matures in *six months*. The value of the collateral *must* remain $1,000,000 at all times. If interest rates rise, the value of the collateral will fall. In this event, the investor is required to *add* more collateral to the portfolio. Instead of buying more bonds to add to the collateral, an investor might consider purchasing a floating rate (F) tranche CMO with an expected maturity corresponding to either the maturity of the business loan or six months. This approach may be less costly than purchasing more bonds that have to be sold after six months at a gain or loss.[9]

Given the changing amounts of interest payments that are to be received, the *range in prices* for F or IF tranche securities is likely to be extremely volatile. Indeed, derivative securities generally exhibit greater price volatility, or a much greater high or low trading range, than is the case when the underlying security (e.g., mortgage) is purchased directly. Consequently, the potential for greater gains (and losses) exists for investors seeking riskier investments.

Yield Enhancement

It also should be apparent that instead of hedging, investors may want to purchase F and IF securities to enhance yields on a portfolio. For example, if an investor holds a portfolio of lower-risk investments (e.g., short-term U.S. Treasury bills), declines in interest rates will not materially affect the *value* of the portfolio because of its very short-term nature. As these securities rapidly mature, proceeds are also being reinvested at *current, lower interest rates.* By purchasing an IF tranche CMO investment with a relatively short-term expected maturity, an investor may offset the loss in income in the base portfolio from falling interest rates by the increasing interest payment from the IF investment. Of course, the opposite effect occurs if interest rates suddenly rise.

A *super floating rate tranche* incorporates the characteristics of the standard floating rate tranche along with the scaling factor found in inverted floating rate tranches. The result is that the coupon rate on this type of security floats in the same direction as, but has much more volatility than, its associated index.

IO and PO Strips

Principal-only (PO) tranches are created with a coupon set at zero, producing a "principal-only" security that resembles a zero coupon bond. Payment patterns are generally slow in early years and increase over time as amortization and prepayment increase. If a CMO structure contains both a PAC (or a TAC) and a PO class, the PO is often referred to as a super PO because the prepayment risk that is directed from the PAC causes the *companion* super PO to become far more volatile than its generic counterpart.

Interest-only (IO) tranches are created to allocate interest to investors that is generally high in the beginning years and then declines over time as amortization and prepayments of underlying principal increase. These are usually issued with PO tranches and are referred to as "stripped" mortgage-backed security issues. These derivative securities have increased in importance in recent years. To illustrate IO and PO strip tranches, consider the following greatly simplified example.

Exhibit 20–12 shows that the two security types are created by "stripping" interest and principal from one segment, or tranche, of the mortgage pool; hence, the terms **IO strips**

[9] Obviously, there are many other ways to hedge this kind of risk. An investor desiring to hedge could produce a financial futures contract on T-bills, which could also be sold short as a hedge against collateral loss. Similarly, a put option could be purchased on an interest rate futures contract against interest increases. This alternative may also be suitable if the investor is not concerned about receiving interest income in the interim. When an F or IF CMO is purchased, interest income is also received in addition to a price hedge against increases or decreases in collateral value. This may also be important to the investor.

EXHIBIT 20–12
Pool Segment Used to
Create IO/PO Strips

Pool characteristics: $1,000,000 mortgages
11% interest annually
10-year maturity

Panel A. Cash Flow to the IO and PO Strip Investors at 0% Prepayment Rate

Period	Beginning Balance	Interest IO/Strip	Principal PO/Strip	PO Prepayment	Ending Balance
1	$1,000,000	$110,000	$ 59,801	0	$940,199
2	940,199	103,422	66,380	0	873,819
3	873,819	96,120	73,681	0	800,138
4	800,138	88,015	81,786	0	718,351
5	718,351	79,019	90,783	0	627,569
6	627,569	69,033	100,769	0	526,800
7	526,800	57,948	111,853	0	414,946
8	414,946	45,644	124,157	0	290,789
9	290,789	31,987	137,815	0	152,974
10	152,974	16,827	152,974	0	0
			$1,000,000	0	
PV at 11% =		$461,248	$ 538,752		

Panel B. Cash Flow to the IO and PO Strip Investors at 20% Prepayment Rate

Period	Beginning Balance	Interest IO/Strip	Principal PO/Strip	PO Prepayment	Ending Balance
1	$1,000,000	$110,000	$ 59,801	$200,000	$740,199
2	740,199	81,422	52,259	148,040	539,900
3	539,900	59,389	45,525	107,980	386,395
4	386,395	42,503	39,495	77,279	269,620
5	269,620	29,658	34,074	53,924	181,623
6	181,623	19,978	29,163	36,325	116,135
7	116,135	12,775	24,658	23,227	68,249
8	68,249	7,507	20,421	13,650	34,178
9	34,178	3,760	16,198	6,836	11,144
10	11,144	1,226	11,144	0	0
			$332,738	$667,261	
PV at 11% =		$276,200	$222,403	$501,397	

and **PO strips.** Note that if no prepayment occurs on any of the mortgages in the pool and if investors demand an 11 percent return on each strip, which is equal to the interest rate on all mortgages in the pool, the present value (PV) of the IO strip is $461,248, while that of the PO strip is $538,752. Obviously, the sum of the two present values must equal $1,000,000 when the discount rate that investors demand equals 11 percent. In practice, this will rarely occur.

However, there are very specific risks regarding prepayment that must be taken into account when making IO and PO strip investments. As discussed many times before, in the event that interest rates decline significantly after issuance, there is a high probability that a number of mortgages in the pool will be *prepaid.* When this occurs, holders of the PO strip will receive cash flows from repayments sooner than expected. This unexpected increase in the rate of cash flow, coupled with the decline in interest rates, will tend to drive the price of the PO strips higher. Conversely, when prepayments increase, IO strip holders receive less cash flow as the pool gets smaller because they receive "interest only" from the pool; when mortgages are paid off, interest ceases altogether. In the limit, if *all* mortgages are paid off, the *value of the IO strip becomes zero.* Therefore, the investment return to IO strip investors consists of interest *only.* If we assume that prepayment *accelerates* from 0 percent to 20 percent per year, the cash flow pattern of panel B in Exhibit 20–12 results. IO strip investors will receive far less cash flow; when discounted by 11 percent, the present value of those floors falls from $461,248 in panel A to $276,200 in panel B, a decline of $184,048, or about 40 percent in value. The PO strip, on the other hand, with receipt of accelerated prepayments (see PO prepayment in panel B), receives *more* cash flow much sooner. When the PO strip is discounted to present value at 11 percent, it shows an increase of 34 percent from panel A (normal amortization of $222,403 + prepayments of $501,397 = $723,806). Note that the PO strip receives the same *total* cash flow ($1,000,000) regardless of prepayment.

In Exhibit 20–13, we see the combined effects of prepayment and changing interest rates on IO and PO prices. Note that the present value of the IO strip *declines* dramatically from a 10-year normal amortization to a 20 percent prepayment throughout the range of discount rates. The PO strip, on the other hand, *increases* in value because more cash flow is recovered *sooner* than if interest rates had remained stable.

This comparison points out the *potentially volatile price behavior* of IO and PO strips. It also implies that, in practice, when investors consider IOs and POs, they must take into account or form expectations about likely future movements in mortgage interest rates (either up or down) *and* the rate of repayment from the mortgage pool (faster or slower).

EXHIBIT 20–13
IO and PO Prices at Various Discount Rates: Prepayment Rate (PPR) at 0 percent and 20 percent

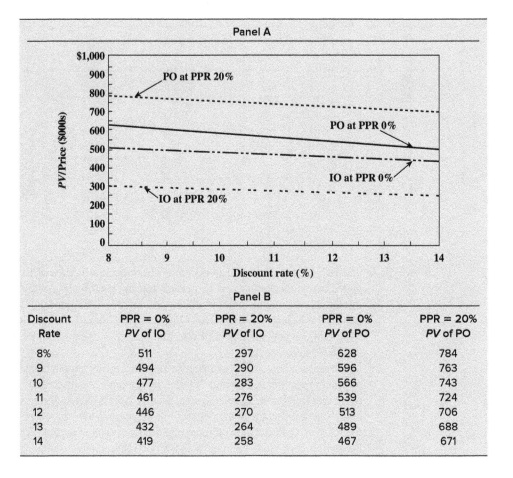

Discount Rate	PPR = 0% PV of IO	PPR = 20% PV of IO	PPR = 0% PV of PO	PPR = 20% PV of PO
8%	511	297	628	784
9	494	290	596	763
10	477	283	566	743
11	461	276	539	724
12	446	270	513	706
13	432	264	489	688
14	419	258	467	671

In addition to investment considerations, these derivative-type investments, like the F and IF investments discussed earlier, may also be purchased when investors expect interest rate volatility to occur and choose to hedge against it.

Convexity

Another useful way to describe the present value patterns shown in panels A and B of Exhibit 20–13 is to say that the curve representing the PO strip exhibits greater **convexity** than the IO curve. This can be seen by examining the range in *PVs* when the PPR = 0. Note that at PPR = 0, the PO curve has a greater slope than the IO curve over the range of discount rates. This means that the price of the PO in our example is *more sensitive* than the IO to changes in market rates of interest (discount rates). In other words, the PO has greater price convexity. However, note that when the prepayment rate increases to 20 percent, the price of the PO *rises* because mortgages are repaid sooner. However, note that the price of the IO *declines*. The IO declines in price because interest payments *cease* on 20 percent of the mortgage portfolio. In the latter case, the prepayment rate must be taken into account when estimating prices of IOs at various discount rates. The resulting prices for IOs will show much greater sensitivity to prepayment and interest rate changes.

Residential Mortgage-Related Securities: A Summary

We now briefly summarize some of the major characteristics of the four major types of securities covered thus far. Exhibit 20–14 contains a summary of some important terms and definitions used in the mortgage-backed securities (MBS) business. Exhibit 20–15 is a classification of some of the more important aspects of these securities that should aid you in understanding cash flow and risk-bearing patterns associated with each type.

With the exception of MPTs, which represent an undivided ownership equity interest in a pool of mortgages, all other securities discussed in the chapter are actually debt. An MPT should be viewed as a stand-alone investment that is placed in trust after it is sold to investors in a securitized form. Because the mortgage pools backing the issue are usually FHA/VA or conventionally insured mortgages and a timely payment guarantee is usually provided by the issuer or GNMA, MPTs can be a stand-alone investment; that is, there is no need for overcollateralization or credit enhancements. The success of the investment is based solely on the income produced by mortgages in the pool, and the recovery of investment by investors depends on how amortization and prepayments from the mortgage pool occur. However, because of the pass-through of principal, investors bear all prepayment and reinvestment risk since they do not know exactly what cash flows will be from period to period, nor do they know when the security that they own will mature.

The debt securities listed in Exhibit 20–15 may be differentiated on the basis of (1) who bears prepayment risk and (2) the extent and type of overcollateralization or the use of credit enhancements. Issuers of MBBs bear all of this prepayment risk; hence, the extent of overcollateralization or credit enhancements for these securities must be greatest. Conversely, to the extent that the investor bears prepayment risk—or to the extent that the pass-through of principal flows directly to investors—the need for overcollateralization or credit enhancements is reduced somewhat (holding all else constant). This is true because, for example, as prepayments accelerate on MPTBs and CMOs, maturities are reduced, whereas the maturity for MBBs remains constant regardless of the prepayment rate on the underlying pool. Therefore, in anticipation of the possibility of prepayment in the latter case, the issuer will have to provide more collateral than with the other two debt securities. This means that in each case, the use of overcollateralization and credit enhancements and the extent to which the investor bears prepayment risk must all be taken into account when assessing the relative attractiveness of each security type.

EXHIBIT 20–14 **Summary of Important Terms Used in the Market for CMOs and Derivative Securities***

CMO

A collateralized mortgage obligation, or CMO, is a bond or debt obligation that is backed by mortgages or mortgage-backed securities. Its cash distributions from the mortgage pool are designed to provide mortgage pass-through (MPT) and CMO investors with a broader selection of cash flows and maturities risk.

Contraction risk

When mortgage market rates fall, homeowners tend to accelerate refinancing. Contraction risk affects the price of an MBS in two ways: (1) Because of the prepayment risk on an MBS, price will not increase as much as a noncallable alternative with an equivalent maturity such as a Treasury bond. (2) As MBS investors receive prepayments of principal, they must reinvest at prevailing lower market interest rates. The combination of these two effects is referred to as *contraction*.

Convexity

The rate of change in the price of an investment with respect to a change in market interest rates (investor discount rates).

Derivative security

A derivative security derives its value from another security, index, or financial claim. Because the values of mortgage-backed securities (MBSs), such as MPTs and CMOs, are based on pools of mortgages, both are referred to as derivatives. There are many other derivatives, such as options, swaps, and so forth.

Duration

When prepayment rates increase (decrease) in response to declining (increasing) interest rates, the expected maturity of an MBS becomes shorter (longer) as cash flows from amortization change. The present value of such investments obviously changes, but so does the maturity. Duration is a measure of the time-weighted pattern of the receipt of cash flow and is a companion tool that helps investors rank present values on the weight and timing of the receipt of cash flows.

Extension risk

Extension risk is the opposite of contraction risk. It is the risk investors face when interest rates increase. Rising rates affect MBS investors in two ways: (1) The price of the MBS security declines like other fixed-income securities; however, because the rate of prepayment slows with rising interest rates, cash flows to the investor decline and the expected maturity increases. This causes the price of the MBS to fall more than an equivalent noncallable alternative, such as a Treasury bond. (2) As prepayment rates decline, opportunities to reinvest greater cash flows at higher interest rates are lost. The combination of these two effects, MBS price declines and lower reinvestment returns, is referred to as *extension risk*.

IO/PO strips

IO and PO strips occur when mortgages are split ("stripped") into two securities. IO (interest only) strip investors receive only the interest payments from the mortgage pool. PO (principal-only) strip investors receive the principal payments. Declining interest rates cause the price of PO strip securities to increase because lower rates induce borrowers to refinance, thereby providing PO investors with an acceleration in cash flows. Rising interest rates are beneficial to IO investors because refinancing slows as homeowners prefer to keep their original mortgages. IO holders then receive interest payments for a longer time than expected, thereby increasing the cash flows over that time.

LIBOR

The London Interbank Offer Rate, LIBOR, is a widely quoted interest rate on deposit-based transactions between banks in the Eurocurrency market.

Prepayment risk

Because homeowners can choose to prepay or keep their original mortgages, MBS investors must forecast mortgage repayment rates when analyzing their investments. This is important because the timing of cash flows (i.e., investor returns) are affected by the rate of prepayment.

Tranche

Tranches are bond classes in a CMO that differ from one another either by priority of the receipt of cash flows or in some other way. The word comes from the French *trancher,* which means "to cut."

---

*For a review of terminology and a basic understanding of mortgage pass-throughs and derivatives, see R. S. Guttery and E. McCarthy, "Real Estate Derivative Assets: CMOs, IOs, POs and Inverse Floaters," *Real Estate Finance,* Winter 1995, pp. 18–29.

EXHIBIT 20–15

Summary of Important Investment Characteristics of Mortgage-Related Securities

		MBB	MPT*	MPTB	CMO
(a)	Type of security interest acquired	Debt	Equity	Debt	Debt
(b)	Number of security classes	One	One	One	Multiple
(c)	Pass-through of principal	None	Direct	Direct	Prioritized
(d)	Party bearing prepayment risk	Issuer	Investor	Investor	Investor
(e)	Overcollateralization?	Yes	No	Yes	Yes
(f)	Overcollateral marked to market?	Yes	NA	No	No
(g)	Credit enhancements used?	Yes	No	Yes	No
(h)	Maturity period known?	Yes	No	No	No
(i)	Call provisions?	Possibly	Cleanup	Possibly	Calamity and nuisance
(j)	Off-balance-sheet financing possible?	No	Yes	No	Yes

*Assumed to be a GNMA/MPT, FNMA/MBS, or FHLMC/PC.

Finally, with respect to the issuer, the use of MBBs and MPTBs should be viewed as a method of debt financing. Although the securitized mortgages are placed with a trustee, they are still carried as an asset on the issuer's balance sheet while the MBBs are categorized as debt. This would also apply to CMOs unless the issuer sells the residual interest to a third party, in which case the issuer would no longer retain an ownership interest and would not have to carry the mortgage pool as an asset or the CMO securities as liabilities. As an alternative to a CMO issue, the issuer could create a real estate mortgage investment conduit (REMIC) to achieve off-balance-sheet financing. With this vehicle, the issuer is selling the mortgage pool to investors and the transaction is completely off-balance-sheet financing. The issuer must only recognize a gain or loss on the sale of mortgages when they are securitized and sold.

Residential Mortgage-Related Securities: Some Closing Observations

Much of what has been discussed strongly suggests that there may exist some market segmentation among investors based on a strong preference for investments with specific maturities. This preference results from the demand by investment managers for interest-bearing assets with the same maturities as liabilities that come due at specified times (e.g., pension plan assets may be acquired with maturities that match liabilities coming due as a number of beneficiaries retire each year).

Finally, because of the different cash flow patterns that are likely to be encountered when choosing among an MBB, MPT, MPTB, or CMO, additional questions are related to receipt of cash flows and the measurement of yields that must be addressed. With an MBB, for example, a level stream of interest payments for a fixed maturity plus a lump-sum return of principal will be received, whereas an MPT may have more variable cash flows due to prepayments, and the Z tranche on a CMO issue may pay cash flows to the investor toward the end of a maturity period. If we assume that each security type is being offered at the same yield,[10] should an investor consider each as equivalent? Or, if all three investments exist in a portfolio and payments are to be used to pay liabilities coming due at specific time periods,

[10] Generally, the yield on the three security types would not be the same even if backed by the same pool of securities because the issuer of an MBB bears prepayment risk and the investor would earn a lower yield than with an MPT, where the investor bears that risk. A Z tranche security, such as the one demonstrated in the chapter, would yield more than an MPT because not only does that investor bear prepayment risk but interest is also accrued and paid later in the life of the security.

can we assess the relationship between the maturity periods over which cash inflows will be received and the rate at which liabilities mature? The appendix to this chapter develops a measure that combines both cash flows constituting the yields *and* maturity into a measure called *duration,* which may be useful in assessing these questions.

Commercial Mortgage-Backed Securities (CMBSs)

In this and the preceding chapter, we have dealt primarily with mortgage-related securities backed by *residential* mortgage pools. Essentially, the methods and structures used to issue *commercial* mortgage-backed securities are very similar. However, the nature of the mortgage collateral, its ability to produce income, and the risk associated with commercial mortgage pools differ from a residential pool in very important ways. These differences are elaborated and contrasted in this section.

Like residential mortgage-backed securities, most **commercial mortgage-backed security (CMBS)** offerings take the form of a mortgage-backed bond, pass-through security, or a collateralized mortgage obligation. The primary distinction between residential-backed and commercial-backed pools centers around the likelihood of losses due to **default risk.** Recall that in most residential offerings, mortgages in the pool are usually FHA insured or VA guaranteed, or are conventional mortgages with private mortgage insurance. In most cases, timely payment of principal and interest is usually guaranteed by a branch of the U.S. government (GNMA) or an agency (FNMA, FHLMC). While private entities have issued many mortgage-backed bonds and mortgage pay-through bonds with no government guarantees, the dollar volume of government-backed securities has been far greater in amount.

In contrast to residential-backed issues, commercial-backed securities are secured by mortgages on income-producing properties. Tenants in these properties sign lease agreements that provide the source of income from which mortgage payments are made. Hence, the quality of properties, geographic regions in which they are located, and the creditworthiness of the tenant must play some part in assessing the risk of a commercial-backed security offering. Clearly, *if tenants default on lease payments or if the geographic market in which the property is located becomes overbuilt and rents generally decline, the income stream used to make mortgage payments will become jeopardized.* Further, because such permanent mortgage loans are made on a nonrecourse basis, the lender may look only to proceeds from the sale of the property to satisfy the loan in the event of default. A CMBS offering has certain distinctive elements (see Exhibit 20–16). First, commercial mortgage assets in the pool are likely to have short maturities (5–15 years) and they are likely to be interest only. This means that—like a corporate or U.S. government bond—flows into the pool will consist of monthly interest only with the *full amount* of principal repaid by the borrowers at maturity. A second difference lies in the structure of the CMO securities. Two major classes of debt securities are usually offered as a part of a CMBS offering: *senior* and *subordinated* tranches. Sometimes these are referred to as the "A piece" and "B piece," respectively. In practice, there will be several subclasses within each of these major classes. The distinction between the two classes is largely based on the *priority of claims* on all payments flowing into the pool, with the **senior tranche** receiving highest priority and the **subordinated tranche** coming second. As before, any cash flow remaining after paying the senior and subordinated tranche is received by residual- or equity-class shareholders. In the example illustrated in Exhibit 20–16, we would say that the senior tranche is subordinated by 30 percent because the subordinate tranche is 30 percent of the securities. This means that there can be up to 30 percent loss in value of the mortgage pool before the senior tranche will incur any losses.

Another important aspect of these securities concerns repayment of principal. Repayments of residential loans are *expected* to occur long before most mortgages reach maturity,

EXHIBIT 20–16
Simplified Example of a Commercial Mortgage-Backed Security (CMBS) Offering

Pool Characteristics: $10,000,000 mortgages, 10% interest rate, 5-year maturity

Assets		Liabilities		
Commercial mortgages	$10,000,000	Senior securities: Class A bonds	Coupon 8%	$ 6,000,000
		Subordinated securities: Class B bonds	10%	3,000,000
		Total		9,000,000
		Net worth (residual)		1,000,000
Total	$10,000,000	Total		$10,000,000

as homeowners sell properties to pay off existing loans and buy new homes as they change employment, refinance, and so on. This is not likely to be true of commercial mortgages. Little or no principal payments or prepayments are likely to flow into the CMBS pool because of **lockouts** that prevent prepayment for a specified number of years. As a result, a *major* focus of CMBS–CMO investors centers on the likelihood of borrowers making full repayment of principal when mortgages mature.

Commercial mortgages often have a "balloon payment" that is due before the loan is fully amortized. When the balloon payment is due, there must be a source to refund or refinance the properties serving as security for the mortgages. This source may be the original lender who agrees to refinance, or "roll over," the mortgage at maturity. In this case, funds from refinancing are used to repay existing loans in the pool, and recovery of principal will flow through to commercial investors in the CMBS pool. The risk that borrowers can refinance their properties when the balloon payment is due may be significant for commercial real estate loans because *at the time of refunding, property markets may be poor, interest rates high,* and so on. As a result, original lenders may choose not to refinance loans at all or to refinance them only at a reduced loan amount. As a result, borrowers may not be able to fully repay loans or they may be able to refinance only a portion of the loan balance. This will pose problems for commercial mortgage-backed security holders who are expecting to be repaid when the underlying mortgages mature. If this happens, CMBS investors may have to wait for the trustee administering the pool to foreclose, negotiate loan extensions, and so forth, as most commercial mortgages in the pool will be nonrecourse mortgages against both the borrower and lender-issuer. The risk that borrowers will not be able to refinance their properties when the loan matures is called **extension risk.** If the borrower defaults and foreclosure results, the property may eventually be sold and the proceeds used to repay the loan balance. A deficiency results if the value of the property is *less* than the loan balance. In this event, some CMBS investors are not likely to recover all principal due at maturity, resulting in a loss. Therefore, considerable investor focus is centered on the *likelihood of borrower default* resulting in a full or partial loss in cash flows when the commercial mortgage matures.

Exhibit 20–17 illustrates the distribution of cash flows and potential risk associated with the CMBS offering shown in Exhibit 20–16. In panel A, cash inflows consisting of interest only are distributed first to the senior tranche, which is due 8 percent interest and accounts for 60 percent of the offering. The subordinated tranche then receives interest at a rate of 10 percent on its segment, or 30 percent of the offering. The remainder goes to the residual class, which contributed $1,000,000, or 10 percent of the offering. If no default occurs, investors in each security class receive cash flows as promised, plus recovery of the initial investment in year 5 when underlying mortgages mature and borrowers repay outstanding balances.

EXHIBIT 20–17
Cash Flows to CMBS Security Holders

	Panel A. No Default or Mortgage Prepayment			
End of Period	Cash Inflow to Pool	Senior	Subordinated	Residual
1	$ 1,000,000	$ 480,000	$ 300,000	$ 220,000
2	1,000,000	480,000	300,000	220,000
3	1,000,000	480,000	300,000	220,000
4	1,000,000	480,000	300,000	220,000
5	11,000,000	6,480,000	3,300,000	1,220,000
	IRR =	8%	10%	22%

	Panel B. Default Occurs at Maturity and Sale of Property is 80% of Outstanding Loan Balance			
End of Period	Cash Inflow to Pool	Senior	Subordinated	Residual
1	$1,000,000	$ 480,000	$ 300,000	$220,000
2	1,000,000	480,000	300,000	220,000
3	1,000,000	480,000	300,000	220,000
4	1,000,000	480,000	300,000	220,000
5	9,000,000	6,480,000	2,520,000	–0–
	IRR =	8%	5.33%	–4.92%

Panel B of Exhibit 20–17 illustrates what happens to the cash flow patterns if default and foreclosure occur when mortgages mature and the sale of properties brings only 80 percent of the total loan balances due at the end of year 5. Note that cash flows into the pool in year 5 total $9,000,000, or $1,000,000 in interest only plus $8,000,000, or 80 percent of the principal amount due at that time. From this cash flow, the senior tranche receives its full amount of interest, or $480,000 plus $6,000,000 on the total initial investment. However, the subordinated tranche investors receive interest due of $300,000 plus only $2,220,000 in loan repayments. This represents a $780,000 loss to subordinated investors because of default. Residual investors lose all their initial investment of $1,000,000. Based on these distributions, the internal rate of return earned by senior tranche investors remains at 8 percent; however, the *IRR* declines from 10 percent to 5.33 percent for the subordinated tranche investors. The residual class does not recover its investment; its return falls from a projected 22 percent (see panel A) to −4.92 percent.

Exhibit 20–17 illustrates the basic mechanics of a CMBS offering. Because of the potential for default loss, residual investors obviously take the greatest risk, while the subordinated tranche investors stand to lose their investment next. For this reason, the subordinated tranche is usually referred to as the **first loss position** among the bond investors. It should be obvious that the size of investment made by each security class and its priority in cash distributions relative to the likelihood of default are the critical variables that must be assessed by investors when evaluating a CMBS offering.

Because of the importance of default risk, the source for many mortgages used in forming mortgage pools comes from insurance companies and commercial banks that have previously originated loans on commercial (and multifamily) properties. These loans are usually seasoned and have a payment record spanning a number of years. This is useful information for potential investors. As the market value of these loans increases during periods of declining interest rates, many lenders want to sell them. However, the very thin secondary market for such individual loans, which tend to be relatively large in amount and are not standardized in terms of loan provisions, makes finding buyers difficult. Hence, by placing these mortgages in a pool and issuing securities against them, the lender may issue securities in smaller denominations which are ultimately sold to many investors, thereby converting the mortgages to cash and realizing gains because of lower interest rates. Other motivations for lenders to securitize may be simply to obtain more funds for operating requirements by converting previously originated loans.

The security for a commercial-backed mortgage pool, therefore, can range from one mortgage on a very large mixed use, multitenant property to a group of smaller income-producing properties on which mortgages have been made by a lender. In general, however, securities are issued based on mortgage pools owned by one lender. Further, properties serving as collateral for the mortgages are generally the same type (i.e., either office buildings or retail) and are geographically diverse.

Rating Commercial Mortgage-Backed Securities

Most security offerings backed by commercial mortgages are rated by independent credit rating firms. However, because of the nature of mortgage collateral in the pool, the criteria used for rating differ dramatically from those used in rating residential pools. Where the securities being rated are based on the credit standing of the issuer and do not contain guarantees or insurance from third parties, the cash flows expected to be earned on each mortgaged property in the pool are usually subjected to a worst-case scenario regarding rents, vacancy allowances, operating expenses, and so on, and a judgment about the property's ability to cover debt service is made. This is particularly important when only one or a few mortgages will make up the pool. Where several mortgages are in a pool, more emphasis is placed on the past underwriting record of the lender. In other words, losses due to defaults from previous loan originations (unrelated to the mortgage pool) are given serious consideration. To provide the worst-case scenario, data specific to the local market area are used as input to the cash flow projections. Generally, rating agencies will only give the senior tranche, or A piece, an investment-grade rating (e.g., AAA, AA, or A). The subordinated tranches will have a lower rating (BBB to B) or remain "unrated," which means that they are not investment-grade quality and therefore cannot be purchased by many pension and trust funds. Exhibit 20–18 illustrates the likely ratings for classes (bonds) with different levels of subordination. The exhibit also shows the loan-to-value (LTV) and debt service coverage ratio (DSCR) for each security.

For a commercial-backed offering to be successful, the issuer may have to provide enough credit enhancement to the investor to reduce default risk to an acceptable level. These enhancements may include one or more of the following types of support.

1. *Issuer of third-party guarantees.* These may include (*a*) a guarantee of timely payment and/or (*b*) a guarantee of payments to the security holder in the event of a cash flow

EXHIBIT 20–18
CMBS General Bond Risk Considerations

Rating	Subordination[*]	DSCR[†]	LTV[††]	Price	
AAA	30%	2.00	52.50%	102	*Premium*
AA	24%	1.84	57.00%	101	
A	18%	1.71	61.50%	100	
BBB	11%	1.57	66.75%	98	
BB	6%	1.49	70.50%	75	
B	3%	1.44	72.75%	65	*Discount*
NR	0%	1.40	75.00%	35	

Source: Diagram created by Mr. Josh Marston, Mass Financial Services, and provided by Charter Research.

[*]Note that the subordination is equal to $1 - (LTV/75\%)$, where 75 percent is the LTV for the underlying loan; for example for the AA class, we have $1 - (57\%/75\%) = 24\%$ subordination. This is how much loan loss can exist before the next highest rated class loses money. Therefore, AA investors will not lose money unless the loan has lost 24 percent of its value.

[†]Debt service coverage ratio.

[††]Loan-to-value ratio.

shortfall from the mortgage pool jeopardizing promised coupon payments, and/or (*c*) a guarantee of repayment of principal to the security holder. Such guarantees may be limited, and they may be provided in part by the issuer with a third-party guarantee for any losses in excess of some specified limit. In any case, the ability of the issuer or third party to perform on the guarantee must be considered by the investor.

2. *Surety bonds and letters of credit.* These are provided by banks and insurance companies for a fee and may be used to guarantee interest and principal payments. In this case, the third-party guarantor is assuming default risk. These guarantees may be made in addition to the guarantee provided in (1). The amount of the guarantee may also vary.

3. *Advance payment agreements.* These are timely payment guarantees made by the issuer and may be limited to a specified number of payments after default.

4. *Loan substitutions and repurchase agreements.* Some commercial-backed issues may provide that the issuer will substitute a defective mortgage with one of better quality, or that issuers stand ready to repurchase any nonperforming mortgages.

5. *Lease assignments.* This provision simply provides that the property owner will assign lease payments directly to the mortgage lender who, in turn, makes payments to the security holder (instead of loan payments being made first to a property manager, or owner, and then to the lender). In this way, the probability that cash flow would not be received by security holders is reduced should the property owner or manager ever become threatened with the possibility of bankruptcy.

6. *Overcollateralization.* As discussed previously, overcollateralization amounts to a lender providing a mortgage pool with a dollar value in excess of the value of securities being used against the pool. By doing this, more income flows into the pool from the larger amount of mortgages relative to required coupon payments to investors. Defaults would have to be approximately equal to the amount of overcollateralization before investors would suffer losses. The extent of overcollateralization necessary in commercial-backed issues is usually based on a desired debt coverage ratio (i.e., the number of mortgages needed to provide an adequate amount of income relative to the interest payment) to investors in the pool.

7. *Cross-collateralization and cross-default provision.* When a pool of mortgages is used for a security issue, the lender may be able to provide a blanket mortgage or cross-collateralization agreement for all mortgages in the pool. This can occur if the lender has made loans to one developer or investor. A cross-collateralization agreement provides that all properties serving as collateral for individual loans will serve to collateralize the entire debt as represented by the blanket mortgage. Hence, in the event that one mortgage defaults, the lender may accelerate prepayments on all mortgages that are a part of the agreement. This means that any loss on one mortgage in a pool because of default may be made up by the security provided by the properties, which may have appreciated in value and are now a part of the blanket mortgage security. By also accelerating on the notes secured by the appreciated properties, the owner-borrower will generally find a way (e.g., second lien, syndication) to raise additional equity and make up any payments on a defaulted loan rather than lose all of the properties.[11] Thus, a blanket mortgage or cross-collateralization agreement is usually beneficial to mortgage-backed security holders.

---

[11] Cross-collateralization is used by lenders when dealing with developers who pledge previously developed properties as security to obtain financing for new developments. They do this to reduce cash equity in new developments. Lenders may also insist on this additional security because most permanent mortgages are made on a nonrecourse basis; hence, lenders must look to the real estate pledged as security for loans in the event of default.

Perhaps the most important impediment to growth in this market is the refinancing risk associated with mortgages when the maturity date is reached. Contrary to the residential market, where there are frequent sales and refinancing is available (1) as households sell and purchase new homes and (2) default risk is minimized by the FHA or private insurance, this is not true in the commercial mortgage market. As a result, when a commercial mortgage matures and refinancing is not readily available, investors in the mortgage pool may have to extend financing beyond the original maturity date.

In the event that a third party provides a letter of credit or other guarantee of principal and interest on the mortgage pool, the ability of the third party to perform is more important than the mortgages in the underlying pool because default risk shifts from the issuer to the third party. Hence, the security holder will be more concerned with the creditworthiness of the insurer or guarantor.

Collateralized Debt Obligations (CDOs)

Collateralized debt obligations (CDOs) have been introduced in recent years to provide more flexibility in the types of collateral that may be included in the pool for securities backed by debt. Commercial mortgage-backed securities (CMBSs), discussed earlier in this chapter, use commercial mortgages as collateral. However, CDOs use a much broader range of collateral such as debt issued by real estate investment trusts (REITs) and other kinds of debt that would be considered too risky to include in collateral for a CMBS. Including riskier debt from several different mortgages in a CDO provides diversification for investors willing to invest in this higher-risk debt. That is, the mortgage assets of the CDO include a diversified mix of different types of debt, which will be elaborated on below. Different classes of securities are then issued by the CDO in the same way that securities are issued by a CMBS (A class, B class, etc.) with a similar payment principal and default priority structure, as we have discussed previously.

Riskier second mortgages are sometimes included in CDOs but it is more common to include subordinate debt by creating and selling junior portions of first mortgages. The subordinated position of the secured mortgage is structured by requiring it to assume the first loss position for the entire mortgage loan. For example, the holder of the first mortgage might carve out what is referred to as an **A note** and a **B note,** both secured by the first mortgage. The B note is subordinate to the A note, which means that it absorbs any losses before the A note is allocated any losses. The riskier B note is often put in a CDO, whereas the A note secured by the same mortgage would be included as collateral for a lower-risk CMBS.

Other collateral for a CDO may include the lower-rated bonds from a CMBS. For example, as discussed earlier in the chapter, a CMBS may be issued which includes class A and class B securities. Rather than sell the Class B CMBS securities directly to investors, the class B securities can be sold to the issuer of a CDO that includes the class B securities along with other types of mortgages as collateral for the CDO.

Another type of debt that might be included in a CDO is a **mezzanine loan.** A mezzanine loan bridges the gap between the first mortgage debt on the property and the equity investment. It is similar to a second mortgage; however, it is not secured by a mortgage on the property. Rather, it is secured by the investor's equity in the property. This means that in the event of default, rather than following the normal foreclosure procedure, the mezzanine lender would exercise a conversion option that gives the lender an equity interest in the property. The mezzanine lender also would normally have an intercreditor agreement with the first-mortgage lender to have the right to take over the first mortgage in the event of default. The first-mortgage lender is willing to enter into this agreement because it provides another party to look to for payment on the first mortgage. The combination of being able to convert from debt to equity and having the intercreditor agreement usually gives the mezzanine lender more rapid and total control of the property. This is because equity in the corporation or partnership is personal property; thus, ownership can be obtained through a legal process that is not as lengthy as foreclosure on a mortgage in default.

Finally, a CDO may also include **preferred equity** as one of the assets. Preferred equity is an equity interest in the property but has debtlike characteristics because it has a superior claim on cash flows produced by the property relative to the **common,** or **residual, equity** investors. For example, the preferred equity may receive an 8 percent preferred return on equity invested, which means that preferred investors receive an 8 percent return on their investment before the common equity investors receive any distribution of cash flow. This return may be cumulative, which means that if the preferred investors do not receive their 8 percent return in a given year, any shortfall carries over to succeeding years and must be paid before the regular equity holders receive any cash distributions. After payment of the preferred return, the remaining cash flows are often split between the preferred equity investors and the residual equity investors. Thus, preferred equity is somewhat analogous to mortgages with participations, discussed in previous chapters. By combining preferred equity from several different properties along with the other types of debt discussed above, a well-diversified asset structure for the CDO can be created. This makes it possible for the A class securities issued by a CDO to receive good credit ratings (e.g., AAA or AA) by the rating agencies even though the individual debt investments in the pool are riskier than mortgages that may be included in a typical CMBS pool.

Managed CDO

Managed CDOs were designed to provide even more flexibility to the issuer of the CDO. In managed CDOs, the issuer may (1) substitute collateral backing the CDO and (2) reinvest the principal payments received on mortgages. Substitution of collateral may occur when one or more mortgages in the pool is repaid. The CDO may provide that funds from the repayment be reinvested in a mortgage of similar quality. Reinvestment of principal may apply when monthly payments are received from borrowers, and rather than paying principal to investors in the CDO securities, the issuer may reinvest the principal into other mortgages. This allows the CDO issuer to find opportunities to make additional investments after the initial issuance of the CDO that may be more profitable for the CDO investors, who would not have to reinvest principal payments distributed to them. Managed CDOs may provide for a wide variety of reinvestment possibilities, such as construction and development loans.

Exhibit 20–19 illustrates the structure of a CDO using the various debt instruments discussed above. In this example, $500 million property has a $400 million first-mortgage loan from a commercial investment bank and $100 million of equity. The investment bank carves out a $300 million A note and a $100 million B note from the $400 million mortgage loan. The equity in the property consists of $25 million of mezzanine debt, $25 million of preferred equity, and $50 million of common equity. (Recall that the mezzanine debt is a claim that may be converted to equity and is not secured by the mortgage.)

The $300 million A note is put into a CMBS that has an A class and a subordinate B class. The B class of the CMBS, the B note carved out of the mortgage, the mezzanine debt, and the preferred equity may all be contributed as collateral for a CDO. The CDO would then issue its own securities (e.g., A class, B class, and C class). For simplicity, only three classes of securities are shown in the exhibit. In reality, there would typically be additional classes of securities with different ratings. Exhibit 20–20 shows a typical CDO capital structure.

In more recent years, it has become painfully clear that there are problems with the CDO structure. From the discussion above, we can see that higher-risk assets, such as B notes, lower-rated CMBS bonds, mezzanine debt, and so on, were used as collateral

EXHIBIT 20-19 **Illustration of CDO Structure**

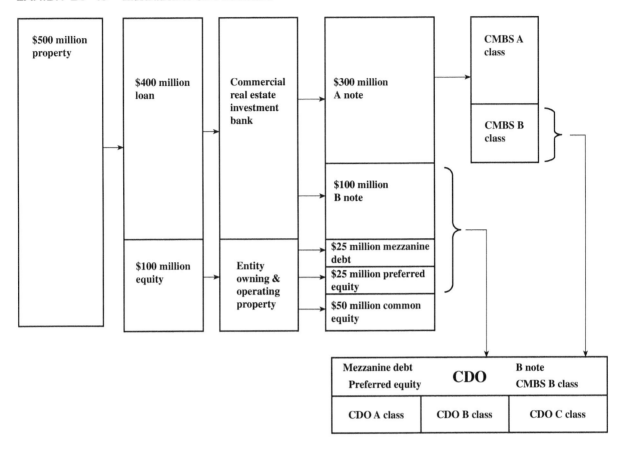

EXHIBIT 20-20
Typical CDO Capital Structure

Investor Class	Amount ($)	Rating	Annual Return (%)	Annual Return (%)
Class A	$ 75,000,000	AAA	5.60%	4.20%
Class B	3,000,000	AA	5.84	0.18
Class C	4,000,000	BBB	6.84	0.27
Class D	7,000,000	BB	7.70	0.54
Class E	2,000,000	B	8.72	0.17
Total debt	91,000,000			5.36
Equity	9,000,000	Not rated	15.00	1.35
Service and transactional charges				0.85
Total capital raised	$100,000,000			7.56%

for issuing a CDO where the higher priority classes of the CDO received an A credit rating. Because these assets came from many different sources (e.g., CMBS BBB-rated bonds from several different CMBS issues), it may have appeared that they were well diversified. However, when property values fell in the late 2000s and borrowers started defaulting on the underlying loans, many of the lower-rated CMBS securities started to lose value because they would not receive all of their principal back. Because the CDOs were backed by these securities, they also lost value, and in many cases became worthless. While it is easy to look back in history and find fault, it is clear that many investors and the rating agencies they depended on did not fully understand the systematic risk that CDO investors faced.

Mortgage-Related Securities and REMICs

Prior to the creation of CMOs, most mortgage-related securities would have been issued as mortgage-backed bonds or mortgage pass-through securities. The federal tax treatment of these securities is relatively straightforward. For MBBs and MPTs, a grantor trust is generally utilized on which mortgages are usually placed under the administration of a trustee who oversees the provision of the trust agreement on behalf of security owners. While such provisions may vary, if federal income tax regulations defining a qualified trust are met, the trust avoids taxation, and interest that flows through to investors is taxed only at the investor level. The primary conditions that such a trust has to meet are that: (1) it must have a limited life, (2) it must be self-liquidating, and (3) it must need no substantive amount of management after the assets are placed in trust. In essence, to avoid classification as an association doing business as a corporation and thus becoming subject to taxation, investment income from the trust has to be passive in nature. Hence, for MBBs and MPTs, the payment of principal and interest from a pool of mortgages under the maintenance of a trustee would generally be sufficient to avoid tax at the entity level. This means that only interest received by investors (or beneficiaries of the trust) would be taxed.

When CMOs were first offered, the IRS ruled mortgage-backed securities with multiple tranches and an equity or residual ownership interest retained by an issuer were too similar to a corporation retaining control of the vehicle used to raise funds. In effect, the issuing entity could use a CMO offering as financing for a business purpose, as opposed to creating a passive investment entity. Further, it required more active management than a pass-through offering. This would be particularly true with respect to selecting securities when reinvesting interim cash flows between the date of receipt from the mortgage pool and disbursement to CMO security holders. Hence, the IRS took the position that if a mortgage-related security offering had more than one class of securities issued against a pool, it ran the risk of being classified as a corporation for tax purposes, resulting in double taxation of income, at both the entity and investor levels. If this tax treatment were applied, CMOs could obviously not compete effectively with MPTs and MBBs, the income from which was generally taxable only at the individual level.

As part of the Tax Reform Act of 1986, Congress passed legislation creating **real estate mortgage investment conduits** (**REMICs**, pronounced "remmicks"). This legislation provided regulations that, if adhered to, allowed mortgage-backed offerings with multiple security classes to be issued without the risk of taxation at the entity level. The intent of the legislation was to provide the issuer some flexibility in managing a mortgage pool and its income, while retaining the basic passive character of the trust and the flow of income to security holders.

Regulatory Provisions

Generally, an REMIC is considered to be a tax entity (not necessarily a legal form of organization such as a corporation or partnership) that can be created by simply selecting an

REMIC tax status and maintaining separate records relative to the mortgage pool and the management of funds related to the pool. A corporation, partnership, trust, or association may also elect REMIC status. To retain REMIC status, very stringent rules must be followed by the issuer. For example, substantially all assets must consist of "qualified mortgages," foreclosure property, cash flow investments, and a qualified reserve fund. These may be summarized as follows:

1. *Qualified mortgages* generally include any mortgages secured directly or indirectly by an interest (full or partial) in real estate (residential, commercial, and all other real estate). This definition is very broad and encompasses virtually all first mortgages, participations, seconds, other pass-through securities, and so on. Mortgages must be placed in the pool prior to its creation or within three months thereafter. New mortgages may not be acquired or sold by the REMIC after its creation; however, the REMIC is allowed to substitute new mortgages for defective mortgages up to two years after its creation.

2. *Foreclosure property* may include real estate, the title to which is retained only by virtue of defaults of a mortgage in the pool.

3. Additional *cash flow investments* are limited to short-term, passive, interest-bearing assets that may be used to reinvest interim cash flows received from mortgages but not yet paid out to investors (e.g., T-bills or guaranteed investment contracts, or GICs).

4. A *qualified reserve fund* may contain longer-term investments, the income from which may be used to pay expenses for managing the REMIC pool because it may be used as added assurance to investors against losses from defaults on mortgages in the pool. These reserves may take the form of passive investments, letters of credit, mortgage pool insurance, and other forms of credit enhancement. This fund is generally more important for commercial mortgage-backed securities or other mortgages that are not backed by the FHA, VA, or private mortgage default insurance.

REMICs: Other Considerations

Because of the pass-through nature of an REMIC, owners of residual interests (usually the issuers) may avoid including REMIC assets, liabilities, and residual interests in REMICs and may avoid taxes at the entity level. Also, if regulations pertaining to REMICs are followed, the owner of the residual interests does not have to participate in balance-sheet reporting to the public because REMICs are intended to be more like a passive, stand-alone entity. In theory, creation of an REMIC is akin to a sale of assets from an origination to the REMIC with a gain or loss on sale realized by the seller and subject to taxation either immediately or over the life of the REMIC.

As such, the seller no longer carries the assets or liabilities created by the REMIC on its balance sheet. However, if the seller chooses not to recognize gain or loss when the sale of assets to the REMIC occurs, the value of the residual interest owned in the REMIC as an asset will be reported. Generally, this off-balance-sheet accounting treatment has been allowed on issues of mortgage-related securities only if the residual interest was sold or transferred by the issuer to a third party.

Web App

The Government National Mortgage Association (Ginnie mae) Web site (**www.ginniemae.gov**) has prospectuses for current REMIC offerings. Obtain a prospectus for an REMIC and summarize the offering in terms of the number of classes of securities and the rates being offered.

In summary, by providing for REMICs, Congress has created a tax-exempt conduit through which CMOs may be issued. This allows for the creation of mortgage-backed securities with multiple maturity classes and other investment choices that would not be available with mortgage pass-through securities. This should provide more choices to more investors and broaden the participation in mortgage-related securities.

Conclusion

The explosion in the market for mortgage-backed securities (MBSs) has led to some of the most significant capital market innovations in recent history. This market began with relatively simple mortgage pass-through securities in which mortgages were pooled, securities were issued, and investors received a pro rata share of principal and interest less servicing fees. Investor concerns over unanticipated cash flow due to borrower prepayment prompted investment bankers and underwriters to innovate and develop the collateralized mortgage obligation (CMO). Rather than simply "passing through" cash flow, the new CMO structure provided for debt securities secured by a mortgage pool. Cash flows were prioritized according to different security classes. Investors in CMOs usually receive a coupon rate of interest and select a priority for the receipt of cash flow from amortization and prepayments on mortgages in the pool. The latter allocation effectively allows investment bankers to pool longer-term mortgages with higher interest rates as security for debt securities that range from short-term, lower interest rate securities to longer-term, higher interest rate securities. More investors can be reached in this structure, with its greater variety of securities, than in a simple pass-through structure. More recent innovations in this market include stripped securities and inverse floaters. These "derivatives" are intended to broaden the market even further as well as to offer investors the opportunity to hedge and manage interest rate risk.

Key Terms

A note, *679*
B note, *679*
collateralized debt obligation (CDO), *679*
collateralized mortgage obligation (CMO), *650*
commercial mortgage-backed security (CMBS), *674*
common (residual) equity, *680*
convexity, *671*
default risk, *674*
derivative securities, *649*
extension risk, *675*

first loss position, *676*
floater tranche, *665*
inverse floater tranche, *665*
IO strips, *668*
LIBOR, *665*
lockouts, *675*
managed CDOs, *680*
mezzanine loan, *679*
mortgage pay-through bonds (MPTBs), *649*
planned amortization class (PAC) tranche, *664*

PO strips, *669*
preferred equity, *680*
real estate mortgage investment conduit (REMIC), *682*
residual, *654*
scaling, *666*
senior tranche, *674*
subordinated tranche, *674*
targeted amortization class (TAC), *664*
tranches, *651*

Useful Web Sites

www.freddiemac.com—Freddie Mac/Federal Home Loan Mortgage Corporation works to stabilize the nation's mortgage markets for homeowners and maintain affordable rental housing by ensuring there is a continuous flow of funds to mortgage lenders. Freddie Mac purchases mortgages from lenders and provides families with even more affordable mortgage financing. This site offers single and multifamily info as well as business tools.

www.frbservices.org—The Federal Reserve Financial Services Web site provides transaction capabilities and service information.

www.investinginbonds.org—Information about investing from the Bond Market Association.

www.fanniemae.com—Fannie Mae/Federal National Mortgage Association (privately owned) provides information about becoming a homeowner.

www.ginniemae.gov—Ginnie Mae/Government National Mortgage Association is within HUD and ensures mortgage funds are available throughout the United States, especially in rural and urban areas where it is harder to borrow money. Ginnie Mae guarantees securities backed by pools.

www.hud.gov—U.S. Department of Housing and Urban Development.

www.fha.gov—Federal Housing Administration.

www.va.gov—Department of Veteran Affairs—see **www.homeloans.va.gov** for information on VA guaranteed loans.

www.nasdbondinfo.com—This Web site contains transaction information on investment grade, noninvestment grade, and convertible corporate bonds as reported to NASD TRACE (Trade Reporting and Compliance Engine). In addition, basic descriptive information and credit ratings on individual corporate bonds are available. The transaction data are updated and available on a real-time basis, except for certain transactions in new issues and large transactions ($1MM+) in less active high-yield bonds.

www.intex.com—This Web site provides information about the latest deals in real estate derivative markets. It also provides software to estimate required cash flows for CDO modeling.

Questions

1. What is a mortgage pay-through bond (MPTB)? How does it resemble a mortgage-backed bond (MBB)? How does it differ?
2. Are the overcollateralization requirements for mortgage pay-through bonds the same as for mortgage-backed bonds?
3. Name two different ways that MPTBs can be overcollateralized.
4. What is a CMO? Explain why a CMO has been called as much of a marketing innovation as a financial innovation.
5. What is meant by a derivative investment?
6. Name the four major classes of mortgage-related securities. As an issuer, explain the reasons for choosing one type over another.
7. What is the major difference between a CMO and the other types of mortgage-related securities?
8. Why are CMOs overcollateralized?
9. What is the purpose of the accrual tranche? Could a CMO exist without a Z class? What would be the difference between the CMO with and without the accrual class?
10. Which tranches in a CMO issue are least subject to price variances related to changes in market interest rates? Why?
11. What is the primary distinction between mortgage-related securities backed by residential mortgages and those backed by commercial mortgages?
12. Name the major types of credit enhancement used for commercial-backed mortgage securities.
13. What is a "floater"/"inverse-floater" tranche in a CMO offering?
14. What is the role of the "scale" in structuring an F and IF structure?
15. Why would anyone want to purchase an F or IF derivative type of investment?
16. What are IO and PO strips? Which tends to be more volatile in price? Why?
17. In what ways is a CMBS structure different from a CMO backed by residential mortgages? Why is default F risk in a CMBS offering given more attention?
18. How do CDOs differ from CMBSs?

Problems

1. The MZ Mortgage Company is issuing a CMO with three tranches. The A tranche will consist of $40.5 million with a coupon of 8.25 percent. The B tranche will be issued with a coupon of 9.0 percent and a principal of $22.5 million. The Z tranche will carry a coupon of 10.0 percent with a principal of $45 million. The mortgages backing the security issue were originated at a fixed rate of 10 percent with a maturity of 10 years (annual payments). The issue will be overcollateralized by $4.5 million, and the issuer will receive all net cash flows after priority payments

are made to each class of securities. Priority payments will be made to the class A tranche and will include the promised coupon, all amortization from the mortgage pool, and interest that will be accrued to the Z class until the principal of $40.5 million due to the A tranche is repaid. The B class securities will receive interest-only payments until the A class is repaid, and then will receive priority payments of amortization and accrued interest. The Z class will accrue interest at 10 percent until both A and B classes are repaid. It will receive current interest and principal payments at that time.

a. What will be the weighted average coupon (WAC) on the CMO when issued?

b. What will be the maturity of each tranche assuming no prepayment of mortgages in the pool?

c. What will be the WAC at the end of year 3? year 4? year 8?

d. If class A, B, and Z investors demand an 8.5 percent, 9.5 percent, and 9.75 percent yield to maturity, respectively, at the time of issue, what price should MZ Mortgage Company ask for each security? How much will the company receive as proceeds from the CMO issue?

e. What are the residual cash flows to MZ? What rate of return will be earned on the equity overcollateralization?

f. *Optional.* Assume that the mortgages in the underlying pool prepay at the rate of 10 percent per year. How will your answers in (b)–(e) change?

g. *Optional.* Assume that immediately after the securities are issued in case (f), the price of all securities suddenly trades up by 10 percent over the issue price. What will the yield to maturity be for each security?

2. An investor is considering the purchase of either an IO or PO strip from a CMO offering. The portion of the mortgage pool backing this tranche consists of $1,000,000 in mortgages with a remaining maturity of 10 years and an 8 percent interest rate.

a. Assuming annual payments and a zero prepayment rate, prepare a schedule showing the IO and PO cash flows that would be payable to investors in this tranche. If the interest rate demanded by investors on this investment is also 8 percent, what would be the prices of the IO and PO strips?

b. If interest rates *increased* to 10 percent and prepayments remained at a zero rate, how would the price of the IO and PO strips change? Which security, the IO or PO, exhibits the greatest price change from (a)? Why?

c. Investor interest rates now *decline* to 6 percent. What is the price of the IO? PO? Prepayments now increase to a rate of 20 percent per year because mortgage borrowers in the pool begin to refinance at lower interest rates. What would prices for the IO and PO be now? (Assume that the 20% prepayment received at the end of each year is based on the outstanding loan balances at the end of the preceding year.) Which security, the IO or PO, exhibits the greatest change in price when compared to (a) and (b) above? Why? What does this pattern suggest about the relative risk of each security?

3. An issuer is trying to structure a floating rate tranche in a CMO offering. The tranche will be backed by mortgages with an 8 percent interest rate and a current balance of $2,000,000. Interest payable to investors in the floating rate securities (F) and inverse floater securities (IF) will be based on an initial, or base, market rate of 8 percent. Investors in the F portion of the tranche will benefit to the extent of any *increases* from the base rate of interest and IF investors will benefit to the extent of any *decreases* from the base rate.

a. Assuming that the F and IF portions of the tranche are equal (50% each), what will the share of interest be for each class of investors on the day of issue? A maximum cap must be set on increases in the base rate of interest for the F investors. What would such a cap be? What would be the floor for the IF portion of the offering?

b. Assume that the IF buyers prefer a leveraged offering. If the terms in (a) were altered to a ratio of 60 percent to F investors and 40 percent to IF investors, what would the interest allocation be on the day of issue? What would the cap and floor be?

c. Compare the terms in (*a*) and (*b*). Assume now that a 2 percent *increase* from the base rate of 8 percent occurs immediately after the CMO offering. What happens to the cash distributions to the F and IF investors? Assume that a 2 percent *decrease* from the base rate occurs. What happens to cash distributions? Which class of investors experiences more volatility in cash flow and, therefore, price volatility? Why?

4. **Excel.** Refer to the "Ch20 CMO" tab in the Excel Workbook provided on the Web site. What is the return on the residual class for prepayment rates of 15 percent, 20 percent, 25 percent, and 30 percent?

5. **Excel.** Refer to the "Ch20 Floater" tab in the Excel Workbook provided on the Web site. Assume that $15,000,000 in floaters and $5,000,000 in inverse floaters are issued. How does this change the returns for the inverse floater when LIBOR is 2 percent, 4 percent, and 6 percent?

6. **Excel.** Refer to the "CH20 IO_PO" tab in the Excel Workbook provided on the Web site. What is the return on the IO and PO at prepayment rates of 25 percent and 30 percent?

7. **Excel.** Refer to the "Ch20 CMBS" tab in the Excel Workbook provided on the Web site. Suppose that there is default at maturity and the property sells for 90 percent of the loan balance. What are the returns to the subordinate tranche and residual?

www.mhhe.com/bf15e

Appendix

Duration—An Additional Consideration in Yield Measurement

We have presented many examples of mortgage-related or derivative securities in this chapter. Recall that most mortgage-backed bonds (MBBs) are very much like corporate bonds in that they promise a coupon rate of interest and repayment of principal at maturity. Mortgage pass-throughs (MPTs) also promise an interest payment; however, principal is also passed through to the investor from the mortgage pool as it is received from borrowers. Hence, repayment of principal is received over the life of the MPT security. Collateralized mortgage obligations (CMOs) differ from both of the above securities. They promise a coupon rate of interest but also promise priority to some tranches of securities concerning receipt of interest and principal payments as they are made into the pool. Interest on some tranches may be deferred and distributed after repayment of principal on other tranches with a higher priority.

The very different patterns of cash flows on the securities just described raise significant problems when investors are comparing yields. These problems come about because if the yield to maturity (*IRR*) is the tool used to measure return on investment, it is possible for the investments to have the same yield but drastically different cash flow patterns. How should two securities with the same yield but different cash flows be compared? Should the magnitude and timing of each cash flow be taken into account as an additional consideration when comparing the investments?

One measure that has been developed to aid in the analysis is *duration*. Recall that it is a measure that takes into account *both* size of cash flows and timing of receipt. Specifically, it

is a measure of the *weighted-average* time required before all principal and interest are received on an investment.

Duration (*D*) is defined mathematically as:

$$D = \sum_{t=1}^{n} w_t(t)$$

where *t* is the time period in which a payment is received, *n* is the total number of periods during which payments will be received, and *w* is a weight representing the annual proportion of the investment's present value received each year. If we assume that security A has a current price of $10,000 and a coupon of 10 percent, that its maturity is five years and interest only is to be paid to investors annually, the yield to maturity, or *IRR*, would be calculated for the investment as follows:

Solution:	Function:
n = 5 years	*i* (*n, PV, PMT, FV*)
PV = $10,000	
PMT = $1,000	
FV = $10,000	
Solve for *i* = 10%	

Hence, we know that the yield to maturity on the bond is 10 percent.

Alternatively, if we assume that investment B is also priced at $10,000, and that five payments of principal and interest equal to $2,637.97 are to be received annually at the end of each year for five years, the yield to maturity would also be 10 percent. This can be seen as follows:

Solution:	Function:
$n = 5$ years	$i\,(n, PV, PMT, FV)$
$PV = \$10,000$	
$PMT = \$2,637.97$	
$FV = \$0$	
Solve for $i = 10\%$	

Hence, by construction, both yields are 10 percent. However, when cash flows are compared, they differ dramatically. Duration provides us with a measure that can be used to determine the weighted-average time to full recovery of principal and interest payments. More specifically, for a required rate of return (i), the weight (w) for each period (t) is computed as:

$$w_t = t\left[\frac{\dfrac{R_t}{(1+i)^t}}{PV}\right] \text{ where } PV = \sum_{t=1}^{n}\frac{R_t}{(1+i)^t}$$

Given the above defined terms, we calculate duration for any asset (j) as :

$$D_j = (1)\left[\frac{\dfrac{R_t}{(1+i)^1}}{PV}\right] + (2)\left[\frac{\dfrac{R_2}{(1+i)^2}}{PV}\right]$$

$$+ \dots (n)\left[\frac{\dfrac{R_n}{(1+i)^n}}{PV}\right]$$

Note in this equation that the proportion that each cash flow received in each period (R_t) bears to the present value (or price) of the investment is calculated and multiplied by the year in the sequence during which each cash flow is received. In our example, we would have for investment A:

$$D_A = (1)\left[\frac{\dfrac{1,000}{(1+.10)^1}}{10,000}\right] + (2)\left[\frac{\dfrac{1,000}{(1+.10)^2}}{10,000}\right]$$

$$+ (3)\left[\frac{\dfrac{1,000}{(1+.10)^3}}{10,000}\right] + (4)\left[\frac{\dfrac{1,000}{(1+.10)^4}}{10,000}\right]$$

$$+ (5)\left[\frac{\dfrac{\$11,000}{(1+.10)^5}}{10,000}\right]$$

$$= .0909 + .1653 + .2254 + .2732 + 3.4151$$

$$= 4.170 \text{ years}$$

For investment B, we have:

$$D_B = (1)\left[\frac{\dfrac{2,637.97}{(1+.10)^1}}{10,000}\right] + (2)\left[\frac{\dfrac{2,637.97}{(1+.10)^2}}{10,000}\right]$$

$$+ (3)\left[\frac{\dfrac{2,637.97}{(1+.10)^3}}{10,000}\right] + (4)\left[\frac{\dfrac{2,637.97}{(1+.10)^4}}{10,000}\right]$$

$$+ (5)\left[\frac{\dfrac{2,637.97}{(1+.10)^5}}{10,000}\right]$$

$$= .2398 + .4360 + .5946 + .7207 + .8190$$

$$= 2.810 \text{ years}$$

From the preceding calculations, we can see that the duration (D) for investment B is lower than the duration for investment A. This implies that although the yields and maturities on the two investments are identical, the weighted-average number of years required to realize total cash flows from investment B is far less than that for A. Hence, depending on the likelihood of better reinvestment opportunities as cash flows are received each year, the investor may choose investment B over A. For example, if the yield curve is expected to take on a more steep, positive slope, the larger cash flows from investment B may be viewed as more favorable, as it may be possible to reinvest them at higher rates of interest.

Duration is also a measure of the extent to which different investments expose investors to interest rate risk. For example, if interest rates were to increase suddenly, it is clear that the price of investment A, with its longer duration, is likely to decline by a greater amount than that of B. For example, if interest rates suddenly increased to 15 percent, the likely percentage change in the prices of the two securities can be approximated as follows:

$$\% \text{ decline in price} = -D\left(\frac{\Delta i}{1+i_t}\right) \text{ when } \Delta i > 0 \text{ and}$$
of investment

$$D\left(\frac{\Delta i}{1+i_t}\right) \text{ when } \Delta i < 0$$

In our example for A, we have:

$$\% \text{ decline} = -4.170\left(\frac{.05}{1.10}\right)$$

$$= -.1895, \text{ or an } 18.95\% \text{ decline}$$
in price to $8,105

For B, we have:

$$\% \text{ decline} = -2.180\left(\frac{.05}{1.10}\right)$$

$$= -.1278, \text{ or a } 12.78\% \text{ decline}$$
$$\text{in price to } \$8,722$$

Other applications of duration may involve a portfolio, or pool, of assets and liabilities where each component of the portfolio may have different cash flow patterns and the same or different maturities. When assessing exposure to interest rate risk, duration provides a better measure of risk exposure than reliance on a simple weighted-average maturity for assets and liabilities because it takes into account the magnitude and timing of cash flows. To illustrate, if investment A represented an asset and B represented a liability, even though the maturities for both investments are equal (five years), if there were an interest rate change to 15 percent, the market value of our asset A ($8,105) would be less than that of liability B ($8,722). Depending on the circumstances, this imbalance could cause serious problems for a portfolio manager of an investment fund or an asset-liability manager of a financial institution. Hence, in addition to making yield comparisons, duration may provide an alternative approach to matching assets and liabilities that fluctuate in value when interest rates change.

Effective Duration

When dealing in the world of mortgage pools and derivative investments, the notion of *effective duration* is used. Because prepayment rates are estimated when analyzing these investments, the above, or standard, measure of duration is modified to take into account various rates of prepayments on cash flows. The standard duration formula detailed above is modified to take account of changes in cash flow (faster or slower repayment at various interest rates). An estimate of duration is made for a range of various assumptions regarding prepayment and is referred to as "effective" duration.

Problem

A–1. The Provincial Insurance Company has the choice of investing $100,000 in either a mortgage bond with annual payments based on a 10-year amortization schedule with a maturity of five years at 10 percent or a five-year corporate bond with annual interest payments and a final principal payment also yielding 10 percent.

   a. Find the duration of each instrument if they are issued at par.

   b. If the market rate of interest on each bond fell from 10 percent to 7 percent and the durations found in part (*a*) remained constant, what would be the new price for each bond?

Chapter

21

Real Estate Investment Trusts (REITs)

Introduction

The concept of the real estate investment trust dates back to the 1880s. In the early years, trusts were not taxed if trust income was distributed to beneficiaries. In the 1930s, however, a Supreme Court decision required all passive investment vehicles that were centrally organized and managed like corporations to be taxed as corporations. This included real estate investment trusts.

Stock and bond investment companies, also affected by the same Supreme Court decision, promptly secured legislation (in 1936) that exempted regulated investment companies, including mutual funds, from federal taxation. At this time, real estate trusts were not organized to press for equal consideration, and the trust did not develop into importance as a legal form for investing in real estate.

After World War II, however, the need for large sums of real estate equity and mortgage funds renewed interest in more extensive use of the **real estate investment trust,** which also became known as the **REIT** (pronounced "reet"), and a campaign was begun to achieve for the REIT special tax considerations comparable to those accorded to mutual funds. In 1960, Congress passed the necessary legislation.

Legal Requirements

A real estate investment trust is basically a creation of the Internal Revenue Code. It is a real estate company or trust that has elected to qualify under certain tax provisions to become a pass-through entity that distributes to its shareholders substantially all of its taxable earnings in addition to any capital gains generated from the sale or disposition of its properties. In accordance with the tax provisions under which it was established, the real estate investment trust can deduct distributions to shareholders when calculating taxable income. Because REITs distribute most if not all of their income to shareholders, this means they generally pay little or no federal income tax. The distributed earnings do represent dividend income to its shareholders and are taxed accordingly. Similarly, any distributed capital gains are taxed at the shareholder's applicable tax rate.

Effective January 1, 1961, special income tax benefits were accorded a new type of investment institution by an amendment to the Internal Revenue Code (Sections 856–858). Under this amendment, a real estate investment trust meeting prescribed requirements during the taxable year may be treated simply as a conduit with respect to the income distributed to beneficiaries of the trust. Thus, the unincorporated trust or association ordinarily taxed as a corporation is not taxed on distributed taxable income when it qualifies for the special tax benefits. Only the beneficiaries pay the tax on the distributed income. To qualify as a real estate investment trust for tax purposes, the trust must satisfy the following requirements:

Asset Requirements

- At least 75 percent of the value of a REIT's assets must consist of real estate assets, cash, and government securities.
- Not more than 5 percent of the value of the assets may consist of the securities of any one issuer if the securities are not includable under the 75 percent test.
- A REIT may not hold more than 10 percent of the outstanding voting securities of any one issuer if those securities are not includable under the 75 percent test.
- Not more than 25 percent of its assets can consist of stocks in taxable REIT subsidiaries.

Income Requirements

- At least 95 percent of the entity's gross income must be derived from dividends, interest, rents, or gains from the sale of certain assets.
- At least 75 percent of gross income must be derived from rents, interest on obligations secured by mortgages, gains from the sale of certain assets, or income attributable to investments in other REITs.

Distribution Requirements

- Distributions to shareholders must equal or exceed the sum of 90 percent of REIT taxable income.

Stock and Ownership Requirements

- The REIT must be taxable as a corporation.
- The REIT must be managed by a board of directors or trustees.
- Shares in a REIT must be fully transferable.
- Shares in a REIT must be held by a minimum of 100 persons.
- No more than 50 percent of REIT shares may be held by five or fewer individuals during the last half of a taxable year.

Prior to 1986, a management activity restriction existed to ensure the passive nature of REITs. Trustees, directors, or employees of a REIT were not permitted to actively engage in managing or operating REIT property, rendering services to tenants of REIT property, or collecting rents from tenants. These functions were generally performed by an independent contractor. In 1986, the Tax Reform Act relaxed the management limitations, allowing REITs to render normal and customary maintenance and other services for tenants, eliminating the need for an outside independent contractor for property-related functions like property management. The result of this change is that REIT managers now have the ability to internalize these functions, creating vertically integrated operating companies and fundamentally altering the REIT vehicle.

In the pre-1986 era, many REITs were organized or sponsored by a financial institution, such as an insurance company, a commercial bank, or a mortgage banker. The sponsoring institution also served as an advisor to the REIT, either directly or through an affiliate. Responsibility was delegated to the advisor for managing the operations of the REIT, including management of the REIT's assets and liabilities. Following the 1986 Tax Act, the REIT became a more attractive vehicle for real estate developers who had not been interested in a passive investment vehicle. Real estate developers and operators have become the dominant sponsors of REITs, particularly for larger companies.

Two landmark initial public offerings helped shape the modern REIT industry. The first was the 1991 Kimco Realty offering, which was the first offering of a modern vertically integrated REIT, providing its own property and asset management. Although some existing REITs adapted following the 1986 Act, Kimco Realty was the first significant REIT initial public offering designed to be internally managed and advised. The second significant offering was the Taubman Realty offering, which launched the public **umbrella partnership REIT,** or UPREIT.

An **UPREIT** is a REIT that owns a controlling interest in a limited partnership that owns the real estate, as opposed to a traditional structure in which the REIT directly owns the real estate. This structure was created in 1992 as a tax-deferred mechanism through which real estate developers and other real estate owners could transfer their properties to the REIT form of ownership. Since the transfer is an exchange of one partnership interest for another, it is not a taxable event. These partnership interests, known as operating partnership units, or OP units, are generally convertible into shares of the REIT, offering voting rights and dividend payments matching those of the REIT shares.

In 1992, traditional real estate capital sources were largely absent from the market, creating a credit crunch. In these conditions, the "modern" REIT structure featuring active management and tax-deferred exchanges of assets was attractive to owners and investors alike. The result was massive growth in REIT equity market capitalization.

In 2007 and 2008, the U.S. financial system was rocked by the fallout of the subprime mortgage crisis, resulting in a very severe credit crunch in which many REITs were unable to refinance corporate debt or property-level debt when it came due, irrespective of operating performance. REIT pricing declined dramatically, and as of December 31, 2008, there were 136 REITs registered with the Securities and Exchange Commission that were trading on one of the major stock exchanges, with the majority trading on the New York Stock Exchange. These REITs had a combined equity market capitalization of $192 billion, as compared to 183 REITs with a combined equity market capitalization of $438 billion as of December 31, 2006. The growth of the REIT industry and the impact of the global credit crisis on REITs are shown in Exhibit 21–1.

As the U.S. financial system recovered from the subprime mortgage crisis, REITs recovered strongly. As of June 30, 2014, there were 210 REITs registered with the Securities and Exchange Commission trading on the major stock exchanges, with 182 of these REITs trading on the New York Stock Exchange. These REITs have a combined equity market capitalization of $816 billion, as compared to $192 billion at December 31, 2008.

EXHIBIT 21–1

Market Capitalization of Publicly Traded REITs

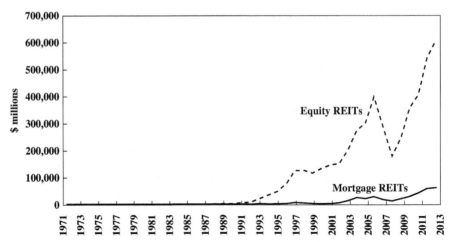

Source: See: "Data and Research" at the NAREIT website: www.nariet.org.

The vast majority of today's equity REITs are self-advised, vertically integrated operating companies. They actively manage their portfolios in an effort to grow their cash flow and their portfolios, a fundamentally different entity from the earlier "passive" REIT. They also actively manage their capital structure, securing capital through public equity and debt offerings, property- and portfolio-level debt, and joint ventures with institutional and foreign investors. The industry continues to change in response to real estate market dynamics, capital market dynamics, and investor preferences.

Tax Treatment

One area of importance in accounting for REITs is the treatment of depreciation for financial reporting and the determination of taxable income. For example, a REIT may use an accelerated method of depreciation in its determination of taxable income, but when determining income available for dividends it is required to use a 40-year asset life. The use of inconsistent methods of income calculation sometimes results in shareholders receiving dividends in excess of the REIT's calculated taxable income. However, to the extent that the distribution represents a return on investment, these dividends will be taxed as ordinary income. In May 2003, the U.S. Congress passed the Jobs and Growth Tax Relief Reconciliation Act, which cut income tax rates on most dividends to a 15 percent maximum, subject to certain income tests. Because REITs do not generally pay corporate taxes, the majority of REIT dividends continue to be taxed as ordinary income at prevailing tax rates. Any additional amounts distributed, such as those representing depreciation, will be considered a return of original capital and thus will simply reduce the shareholder's tax basis. REITs report the breakdown of their distribution annually on Form 1099 and investors may choose to hold specific REITs in taxable or nontaxable accounts based on the breakdown of their distribution.

Violation Penalties and Status Termination

In the event that an entity fails to qualify as a REIT or voluntarily revokes its REIT status, the entity's election to be taxed as a REIT terminates for that and subsequent years. Once this termination has occurred, the entity cannot make a new election to be taxed as a REIT until five years after the termination date. However, if the entity's REIT status was terminated as a result of a failure to satisfy the qualifying requirements, the entity may reelect REIT status within the five-year time period if it can prove to the IRS that its failure to qualify was due to reasonable cause and not willful neglect. In October 2004, a corporate tax reform bill was signed into law which provided the IRS with the ability to impose monetary penalties in lieu of loss of REIT status for reasonable-cause violations, reducing the risk of loss of REIT status through errors of omission and protecting shareholders from the negative consequences associated with loss of REIT status.

Taxable REIT Subsidiaries

In 1999, the REIT Modernization Act (RMA) was signed into law. The RMA contains several provisions designed to allow REITs to compete more effectively with other owners of commercial real estate. Prior to the RMA, there were restrictions that prohibited REITs from providing services to tenants beyond those "usual and customary" to their industry. For example, an office REIT might lease furniture to tenants. A shopping center REIT might offer its own credit card to customers. If REITs provided services beyond "usual and customary," the income from the property where the services were provided was treated as not being qualifying real estate income. As the real estate industry continued to evolve, "usual and customary" became more difficult to define and monitoring compliance became very expensive. Given the risk associated with large amounts of nonqualifying income (possible loss of REIT status), some REITs were reluctant to provide services, limiting their ability to compete.

The RMA also provides for the establishment of the taxable REIT subsidiary (TRS) that can be 100 percent owned by a REIT. Under the new law, a TRS can provide services to REIT tenants and others, pay any associated income tax, and pass the income up to the REIT as qualifying income. Taxable REIT subsidiaries were designed to replace a previous structure under which REITs owned partial interests in non-REIT C corporations. Those C corporation structures had significant conflicts of interest. The TRS structure eliminates many of those conflicts. The RMA also provides for limitations on debt and rental payments between the REIT and the TRS and a 100 percent excise tax on any transaction between the TRS and an affiliated REIT not negotiated as an arm's-length transaction.

Types of REITs

The two principal types of publicly traded real estate trusts are *equity trusts* and *mortgage trusts*. Prior to 2010, there was a third classification, hybrid REITs, which generally consisted of REITs with a mix of equity and debt real estate investments. As of December 17, 2010, NAREIT discontinued tracking these REITs, as only four hybrid REITs remained at that time. There are also REITs that are public companies but are not listed on an exchange or traded over the counter, which are generally called "private" REITs. Up until the 1970s, the equity trust was the most prevalent type of REIT, but during the mid-1970s, the mortgage trust became more important. More recently, the equity trust has again grown in importance and is now the dominant REIT type by both number and market capitalization figures. As of June 30, 2014, 81 percent of REITs were equity REITs and 19 percent were mortgage REITs.

The difference between assets held by the equity trust and those held by the mortgage trust is fairly obvious. The equity trust acquires property interests, while the mortgage trust purchases mortgage obligations and thus becomes a creditor with mortgage liens given priority to equity holders.

Equity REITs

Most REITs specialize by property type; some specialize by geographic location. Others specialize by both property type and location. Not all REITs specialize; some diversify by both property type and geographic location. Specialization implies a concentration of effort to create a comparative advantage. REITs and analysts generally use the term *specialization* to cover a fairly broad range of concentration. In reality, specialization is a matter of degree. The extent to which a REIT is specialized impacts the risks associated with ownership of the REIT. Therefore, it is important to determine how specialized an individual REIT is in comparison with other REITs, in order to assess relative risks. For purposes of description, equity trusts have generally been broken down by property type specialization. The National Association of Real Estate Investment Trusts (NAREIT) divides equity REITS into the following property types:

1. **Industrial/Office.** These REITs are further subdivided into those that own industrial, office, or a mix of office and industrial properties. Some analysts further segregate these REITs by property location (i.e., whether they are in central business district [CBD] or suburban locations, whether they specialize in medical office properties).
2. **Retail.** These REITs are further subdivided into those that own strip centers, regional malls, and free-standing retail properties.
3. **Residential.** These REITs are further subdivided into those that own multifamily apartments and manufactured home communities. Some analysts further segregate those REITs that own student and military housing.

4. **Diversified.** These REITs own a variety of property types, or own properties of one type that is not otherwise categorized, such as single-family rental housing, data centers, or prisons.

5. **Lodging/Resorts.** These REITS primarily own hotels, motels, and resorts.

6. **Health Care.** These REITs specialize in owning hospitals, seniors housing, medical office and related health care facilities that are leased back to private health care providers who operate such facilities. This is a highly specialized form of REIT and one which many do not consider to be a "true, real estate–backed" security.

7. **Self-Storage.** These REITs specialize in ownership of self-storage facilities.

8. **Timber.** These REITs specialize in owning timberland.

9. **Infrastructure.** The REITs specialize in owning various types of infrastructure, including railroads, electric and gas transmission and distribution, cell towers, and other forms of infrastructure.

The distribution of REIT ownership by property type changes over time. In September 1991, residential properties accounted for more than half of all total publicly traded REIT real estate investments, followed by office, retail, health care, industrial, hotels, and other properties. By mid-year 2003, industrial/office REITs represented the largest sector at just over one-quarter of the total, followed by retail, residential, diversified, lodging/resorts, health care, self-storage, and specialty properties. As of June 30, 2014, the office/industrial sector and the retail sector each account for approximately 22 percent of REITs, followed by the diversified, residential, lodging, health care, timber, self storage, and infrastructure sectors. Concept Box 21.1 lists the largest U.S. REITs as of July 2014.

REITs may also be categorized by other variables, including duration of the trust, or finite-life versus nonfinite-life REITs. A finite-life (or self-liquidating) REIT is undertaken with the goal of disposing of its assets and distributing all proceeds to shareholders by a specified date. These REITs were instituted in response to the criticism of many investors that the prices of REIT shares tended to behave more like shares of common stock; that is, they were based on current and expected future earnings instead of the underlying real estate value of the REIT. Hence, by the establishment of a terminal distribution date, it is argued that REIT share prices would more closely match asset values because investors could make better estimates of the terminal value of the underlying properties. This, it is argued, is not the case with nonfinite-life REITs, which reinvest any sale and financing proceeds in new or existing properties and tend to operate more like a going concern, as opposed to an investment conduit. One potential problem with finite-life REITs has to do with general market conditions at the time the REIT plans to dispose of assets. If interest rates are high and occupancies and rents are low, the timing of such disposition activity may not be good and distribution dates may have to be extended. Most new REITs are nonfinite-life REITs, and several existing finite-life REITs have amended their articles of incorporation to become nonfinite-life REITs. Finite-life REITs are not publicly traded on exchanges.

The Investment Appeal of Equity REITs

The equity-oriented real estate investment trust has provided investors with opportunities to (1) invest funds in a diversified portfolio of real estate under professional management and (2) own equity shares that trade on organized exchanges, thus providing more liquidity than if a property were acquired outright. Because the individual investor has the opportunity to pool his or her resources with those of persons of like interests, funds are assembled to permit purchase of buildings, shopping centers, and land in whatever proportion seems to offer the most attractive returns. Investments must be approved and

Company	Ticker	Type	Market Capitalization (billions)
Simon Property Group, Inc.	SPG	Equity	52,250
American Tower Corporation	AMT	Equity	37,438
Public Storage	PSA	Equity	29,204
Crown Castle International Corp.	CCI	Equity	24,781
Equity Residential	EQR	Equity	23,273
General Growth Properties, Inc.	GGP	Equity	20,652
Prologis, Inc.	PLD	Equity	20,333
Vornado Realty Trust	VNO	Equity	19,735
Health Care REIT, Inc.	HCN	Equity	19,546
AvalonBay Communities, Inc.	AVB	Equity	19,157
HCP, Inc.	HCP	Equity	19,023
Ventas, Inc.	VTR	Equity	18,684
Boston Properties, Inc.	BXP	Equity	18,113
Host Hotels & Resorts, Inc.	HST	Equity	16,438
Weyerhaeuser Company	WY	Equity	16,395
American Realty Capital Properties, Inc.	ARCP	Equity	11,904
Essex Property Trust, Inc.	ESS	Equity	11,791
Annaly Capital Management, Inc.	NLY	Mortgage	10,514
SL Green Realty Corp.	SLG	Equity	10,226
Realty Income Corporation	O	Equity	9,532
Macerich Company	MAC	Equity	9,136
Kimco Realty Corporation	KIM	Equity	9,083
Digital Realty Trust, Inc.	DLR	Equity	8,715
American Capital Agency Corp.	AGNC	Mortgage	8,235
Federal Realty Investment Trust	FRT	Equity	8,159
Plum Creek Timber Company, Inc.	PCL	Equity	7,319
UDR, Inc.	UDR	Equity	7,276
W.P. Carey Inc.	WPC	Equity	6,508
DDR Corp.	DDR	Equity	6,301
Camden Property Trust	CPT	Equity	6,139

Source: Brad Case, NAREIT.

management activities reviewed by a board of trustees who are accountable to shareholders and are ordinarily well qualified to make such decisions. The REIT shares are usually readily salable in the over-the-counter market or on major stock exchanges. Investments in REITs may also be made through mutual funds specializing in REIT securities. There are also a number of real estate and REIT exchange-traded funds (ETFs) and closed-end funds.

The REIT market is continually evolving as new investment alternatives emerge and mature. A recent development has been the emergence of international REIT investments. Capital flows have increased substantially as investors explore and invest in global real estate opportunities in an effort to diversify their portfolios. International REIT investment has occurred in two major ways: via cross-border investment in U.S. and foreign REITs and via existing U.S. REITs that are building international portfolios. It is now relatively easy for investors to find alternative mechanisms that allow them to get exposure to international real estate. The worldwide credit crisis that began in 2007 resulted in a decline in capital flows to all types of real estate investment, including international real estate investment. As capital market conditions recovered, investor interest and investment in international real estate have continued to grow.

The introduction of REITs and similar vehicles in over 30 countries has eased the flow of capital in and out of international markets. As of December 31, 2012, the FTSE

EPRA/NAREIT[1] Developed Market Real Estate Index included more than 290 listed companies in 20 countries across the globe. On an equity market capitalization basis, approximately 50 percent of the index's value was in North America, approximately 36 percent was in Asia, and approximately 14 percent was in Europe. See Concept Box 21.2 for an overview of international REITs.

Caveats

As described above, when an equity REIT is created, existing properties or projects to be developed will be acquired as investments. In addition, during the life of the REIT, management fees, advisory fees, and commissions will be paid to affiliates and other parties doing business with the trust. Typically, a real estate owner working with an investment banker can form a REIT that is capitalized through a public securities offering. The REIT may then use the funds it has raised to acquire the owner's properties. The prices that prevail in these transactions are generally not based on arm's-length negotiations and there is generally no appraisal or other independent indication of value.

Obviously, the formation transactions and the close association of REITs with other real estate organizations or individuals who sponsor them can create potential conflicts of interest. These conflicts can come in several forms, including preferential treatment given to properties owned by management but not owned by REIT investors, and so on. Investors have reacted harshly to REITs perceived as "holding out" properties of exceptional value and have forced management to make provision for the REIT to acquire all noncontributed properties. Other conflicts include managers negotiating an excessive price for their contributed real estate operating companies, including third-party management contracts. The UPREIT form adds more potential conflicts, including the fact that OP units holders, often the managers, have a different tax position relative to contributed properties, and a sale or refinancing of properties they contributed may be taxable. A number of safeguards attempt to protect investors against the problems of such conflicts, including the provision in the articles of incorporation of most REITs that a *majority* of the trustees or directors may not be affiliated with the sponsors of a REIT. Some REITs also engage independent appraisers to determine whether the purchase prices of properties acquired from the sponsors are at fair market value and that "fees paid to the REIT's management and advisory companies are reasonable." Many REITs are "self-advised" and avoid many of these conflicts by not using external advisors. Self-advised REITs will disclose and identify specific managers, their responsibilities, compensation, and so on, thereby providing information that investors can use when evaluating the shares. Additional safeguards have been put in place via the Sarbanes-Oxley regulations regarding disclosures by publicly traded companies.

Public nonlisted REITs

Although most REITs trade on one of the established securities markets, there is no requirement that REITs be publicly traded. REITs that are not listed on an exchange or traded over-the-counter are called public nonlisted REITs. These REITs are public companies, but are not listed.

The National Association of Real Estate Investment Trusts (NAREIT) classifies three typical types of private REITs as follows: (1) REITs targeted to institutional investors that take large financial positions, (2) REITs syndicated to investors as part of a package offered by a financial consultant, and (3) "incubator" REITs that are funded by venture capitalists with the expectation that the REIT will develop a sufficient track record to launch a public offering in the future.

[1] European Public Real Estate Association/National Association of Real Estate Investment Trusts.

The real estate investment trust (REIT) system was born in the United States in 1960 and REIT markets later opened in the Netherlands, Australia, and Puerto Rico. The Japanese REIT market was launched on the TSE in March 2001, making Japan the thirteenth country in the world to launch a REIT market.

After the Japanese REIT market was launched, REIT structures were introduced in South Korea, Hong Kong, Taiwan, and other Asian countries. Later, in Europe, France launched a system in 2003. The United Kingdom and Germany adopted REITs in 2007 and they were adopted in Finland and Spain in 2009 followed by Hungary in 2011 and Ireland in 2013. In total there are now 31, counting Hong Kong and China as the same country.

This chapter focuses on REITs, which have become the dominant fund real estate securitization product in the world today. The following is a summary of overseas REIT structures that are currently being used and analyses

of characteristics, common areas, and differences of the respective systems.

This chapter presents overseas REITs from the eight countries of America (REIT), Canada (C-REIT), the Netherlands (FBI), Belgium (SICAFI), France (SIIC), Australia (LPT), Singapore (S-REIT), and South Korea (K-REIT). The table below presents a direct comparison between the various REIT systems and also includes Japan (J-REIT), Malaysia (PTF), Hong Kong (H-REIT), and Turkey (REIC).

For ease of comparison between the world's primary REITs, the table below has organized the REIT comparison by the four categories of (1) date established, (2) legal system, (3) fund format, and (4) REIT requirements.

The structures of REITs are largely dependent on the tax law of each country as it is essential for REITs to serve as nontaxable conduits for tax purposes and that there be no double taxation at the REIT level and investor level specifically for the REIT investment. REITs can be broadly

Comparison of REIT Systems

	1	2	3	4	5
Country	United States	Canada	The Netherlands	Belgium	France
System	Real Estate Investment Trusts (REIT)	Real Estate Investment Trusts (C-REIT)	Fiscale Beleggingsinstelling (FBI)	Sociètè d'Investissement á Capital Fixe Immobilière (SICAFI)	Sociètè d'Investissements Immobiliers Cotèes (SIIC)
1 Data Established	1960	1993	1969	1995	2003
2 Legal System					
2-(1) Tax law	Internal Revenue Code (IRC)	Income Tax Law	Corporation Tax Law	Income Tax Law	Income Tax Law tax bulletins
2-(2) Related laws	Corporate law of each state, Trust Law, Securities Act of 1933, Securities and Exchange Act of 1934	Trust law of each province and securities law of each province	Act on the Supervision of Collective Investment Schemes	Act of December 4, 1990, Royal Decree of April 10, 1995	2003 Budget Law
2-(3) Stock exchange	New York (NYSE), NASDAQ	Toronto (TSX)	Euronext Amsterdam	Euronext Brussels	Euronext Paris
2-(4) Competent regulatory authorities	Securities and Exchange Commission	Securities and Exchange Commission of each province	Netherlands Authority for the Financial Markets (AFM)	Banking, Finance and Insurance Commission (BFIC)	Financial Market Authority (AMF)
2-(5) Collective Investment Scheme	No	Yes	Yes	Yes	No
3 Fund Format					
3-(1) Listed/Unlisted	Both	Both	Both	Only listed	Only listed
3-(2) Closed-end/Open-end	Closed-end	Both types exist	Closed-end	Closed-end	Closed-end
3-(3) Externally managed/Internally managed	Both (most internally managed)	Large internally managed, small externally managed	Both	Both	Internally managed
3-(4) Fund vehicle	Corporation, Trust	Corporation, Trust	Corporation, Trust	Corporation, etc.	Corporation
4 REIT Requirements					
4-(1) Organizational requirements	Not financial Institution or insurance company: taxed as domestic company: managed by more than one officer or trustee	Canada resident unit trust, business objective is limited to the acquisition, ownership, maintenance, renovation and management of real estate	Approval from AFM	Permission from the Belgian BFIC; after initial registration, 30% or more of stocks with voting rights must be publicly placed within one year	Main business objective is the acquisition and construction of rental property (including direct and indirect ownership of other corporations with the same objectives)
4-(2) Minimum paid-in capital			BV 180,000 euros, NV 450,000 euros	1.2 million euros	15 million euros
4-(3) Minimum number of stockholders	100	150			
4-(4) Public offering requirements				Public offering of 30% or more of stocks with voting rights	
4-(5) Specific stockholder shareholder ownership regulations (including foreign ownership)	Five people or less must not hold more than 50%	Foreign ownership up to 49%	Specific foreign stockholders cannot hold more than 25% directly or indirectly; retail investor must not hold more than 25% of B1 stocks		

Source: Reprinted from pages 178 and 179 of the *Real Estate Securitization Handbook 2005*, with permission from the Association for Real Estate Securitization (ARES), In Tokyo, Japan.

categorized into those systems that are purely based on the taxation system such as in America and the Netherlands and those that are based on an investment trust law where real estate investments have been incorporated into collective investment structures and the taxation system.

Although REITs are based on either the American structure (tax) or Australian structure (trust law), most countries base their structure on the closed-end Australian style that uses a trust as the vehicle to collect the investors' investments and is externally managed by an asset management company. However, there is a clear trend toward the American style of external management rather than internal management, and from just being engaged in passive investment rental real estate to also include development properties.

There are many methods for securing the pass-through nature of the investment entity, the most popular being either pay-through or pass-through. The most common method employed is pay-through: this allows paid dividends to be deducted as expenses. Each country has established different requirements for being recognized as a REIT including dividend requirements, various organizational requirements, asset and income requirements, and liability limitations. A structure is recognized as a REIT when the organizational requirements are met. These include minimum capital amounts, minimum number of stockholders, public placement requirements, listing requirements, asset and income requirements such as the content and ratio of owned assets, investor restrictions' business content, and limits on debt ratios. Almost all of the countries require a certain level of dividend to be paid as a minimum dividend requirement.

The capital gains from selling the real estate are handled very differently between countries. There are countries that make the capital gains tax free, others that make them tax free if reinvested, others that do not include them in dividend requirements, and others that tax the capital gains by including them in ordinary income.

	6	7	8	9	10	11	12
	Australia	Japan	Singapore	Korea	Malaysia	Hong Kong	Turkey
	Listed Property Trust (LPT)	Real Estate Investment Trust (J-REIT)	S-REIT	K-REIT (Ordinary REIT, CR-REIT)	Property Trust Funds (PTF)	H-REIT	Real Estate Investment Company (REIC)
	1971	2000	1999	2001	1986	2003	1985
	Income Tax Law	Corporation Tax Law	Income Tax Act, individual bulletins	Corporation Tax Law	Income Tax Act	Income Tax Law	Income Tax Law
	Corporate Act, MIA Law	Investment Trusts and Investment Corporations Law, Securities and Exchange Law	Securities and Futures Act 2001, Guidelines for Property Funds	Real Estate Investment Company Law	Securities Commission Act 1993, Guidelines on Property Trust Funds	Securities and Futures Ordinance, Code on Real Estate Investment Trusts	Capital Market Law, communiqués
	Australia (ASX)	Tokyo (TSE)	Singapore (SGX)	Korea	Kuala Lumpur (KSE)	Hong Kong	Istanbul (ISE)
	Australian Securities and Investments Commission (ASIC)	Financial Services Agency	Monetary Authority of Singapore (MAS)	Ministry of Construction and Transportation, Financial Supervisory Commission (CR)	Securities Commission (SC)	Securities and Futures Commission (SFC)	Capital Markets Board (CMB)
	Yes	Yes	Yes	No	Yes	Yes	No
	Both	Both	Both	Both	Both	Only listed	Only listed
	Closed-end	Both (only closed-end exists)	Closed-end	Closed-end	Closed-end	Closed-end	Closed-end
	Externally managed	Externally managed	Externally managed	Internally managed (general), externally managed (CR)	Externally managed	Externally managed	Internally managed
	Trust	Corporation, Trust	Corporation, Trust	Corporation	Trust	Trust	Corporation
	Register with ASIC: managed by external management company (RE)	Investment corporation registered with Financial Services Agency, investment corporation that satisfies the following "Minimum number of stockholders" or "Public offering requirements"	Management by management company approved by MAS; the management company must be a listed firm established in Singapore	At establishment, the stockholders shall own at least 10% of stocks (limit of 30%)	Management company must be a listed firm established in Malaysia; management company shall be a subsidiary of a financial institution or subsidiary of a developer	Management company must be certified by SFC	Use the "real estate investment trust" trade name: stockholders must have a certain income and satisfy asset ownership requirements; must not be involved in business, industry and agriculture outside of legally allowed transactions; must not be involved in capital market activities other than for managing its own portfolio; must not be involved in construction activities
		100 million yen		50 billion won	100 million ringgit		1 trillion Turkish lira
		Ownership by more than 50 individuals or qualified institutional investor			1,250 (each stockholder must own at least 1,000 stocks)		
		On establishment, publicly offered and total amount of at least 100 million yen		Public offering of at least 30% on establishment (general)	Public offering of at least 25%		Publicly place 49% or more
		Three or fewer stockholders may not own more than 50% of the total stock value: More than 50% of stock must be placed domestically (written in bylaws)		Specific stockholders limited to 10% ownership of stocks (general)	Foreign ownership of up to 30%		

While there are some prominent REITs that are targeted to institutional investors or formed as an incubator, REITs syndicated to investors have experienced rapid growth and have become a major factor in property markets. In the low interest rate environment that has accompanied the recovery of the financial markets, public unlisted REITs have experienced very large inflows of cash as investors have purchased their securities in part due to their high dividends relative to alternative investments. Robert A. Stanger & Company, which tracks the unlisted REIT Industry, reported $10.3 billion in funds raised in 2012, followed by a record $19.8 billion raised in 2013. They have become major players in prominent markets, largely in response to their need to invest this new capital.

Unlisted REITs typically sell subscriptions of shares through financial planners to investors at a fixed price. Some portion of that initial price is paid out to the financial planner as a "marketing" fee, and some portion of that price is paid to the unlisted REIT's advisor. The remaining funds are then used to purchase assets that fit within the unlisted REIT's stated investment policy. In most cases, the fees are well in excess of 10 percent, leaving less than 90 cents on the dollar to be invested in properties.

Critics suggest that unlisted REITs are very expensive and illiquid compared to listed REITs. Proponents suggest that unlisted REITs are not subject to short-term market price volatility and that there are generally provisions in their prospectuses that lead to liquidity. Generally, unlisted REITs have "list or liquidate" provisions under which the REIT must liquidate the assets and return the net proceeds of the liquidation if the stocks are not listed by a particular date. This adds additional risk to these investments in that these companies may be forced to liquidate at a very disadvantageous point in time. There were several very well-publicized collapses in the unlisted REIT industry in the wake of the subprime crisis.

There are significant differences among listed and unlisted REITs. Investors and their advisors should be familiar with these differences and incorporate all associated risks in making investment decisions or recommendations.

Importance of FFO (Funds from Operations)

FFO stands for **funds from operations,** which most analysts consider the REIT equivalent of earnings in industrial stocks. FFO is used by analysts and investors as a measure of the cash flow available to the REIT for distributions (dividends) to shareholders. Most investors are familiar with the use of earnings per share in this capacity. However, for REITs, earnings are not the best measure of cash flow, largely due to the element of depreciation. Because REITs own real estate assets that are subject to large depreciation allowances, the reader should be aware of the difference between REIT earnings per share (EPS) and funds from operations (FFO) per share. The distinction between the two can best be made with a simple example:

	REIT Income Statement	REIT FFO
Rent	$100	$100
−Operating expenses	40	40
Net operating income	60	60
−Depreciation	40	—
+Gains on sale of property	20	—
Net income	40	—
Cash flow	—	60
EPS	$ 4	—
FFO per share	—	$ 6

Assuming that the REIT above has 10 shares of stock outstanding, its earnings per share (EPS) would be reported as $4.00 per share. However, its funds from operations (FFO) per share would be $6.00. *Generally accepted accounting principles* (GAAP) provide for depreciation of assets over time as their useful life is expended. Depreciation is assumed to occur in a predictable fashion and the time periods and rates of depreciation for different types of assets are well established. Most people are familiar with the concept and logic of depreciation based on their experiences with automobiles and other durable goods. As these goods get older, their mechanical parts break down and function less efficiently, decreasing their value. Real estate values tend to rise and fall over time based more on market conditions than physical conditions, although physical conditions can and do play a role in value. The result is that GAAP earnings calculations that use historical cost depreciation do not provide an accurate or meaningful picture of REIT financial performance.

The National Association of Real Estate Investment Trusts (NAREIT) recognized this problem and has worked to develop and promulgate FFO as a more representative measure of REIT performance. In 1991, NAREIT adopted a definition of FFO that was refined slightly in 2002 as follows:

> *Funds from operations* means net income (computed in accordance with generally accepted accounting principles), excluding gains (or losses) from sales of property, plus depreciation and amortization, and after adjustments for unconsolidated partnerships and joint ventures. Adjustments for unconsolidated partnerships and joint ventures will be calculated to reflect funds from operations on the same basis.

The definition was well accepted in the industry and FFO has become a standard measure of REIT performance. FFO provides analysts and investors with an "apples to apples" measure for comparing performance among REITs. NAREIT suggests that the adoption of the FFO measure has made it easier for investors to understand REIT operations. It claims that increased understanding has facilitated the growth in REITs as an ownership form, a claim that has some merit.

As REITs have grown, FFO and its reporting have emerged as an important issue. The definition adopted by NAREIT was, of necessity, rather broad. It left considerable room for interpretation. During the IPO boom in 1992 and 1993, REIT initial pricing was generally couched in terms of a **dividend yield** supported (at least in theory) by a projected FFO. The value of management's ownership position was a function of the initial price, so there was a strong incentive to project FFO at maximum levels. By mid-1993, the page of the prospectus dealing with the projected FFO had become known as the "magic page." The implication was that FFO was being created to support overly aggressive initial pricing.

Many analysts and investors have gone beyond the FFO to look at adjusted funds from operations (AFFO), funds available for distribution (FAD), or cash available for distribution (CAD). AFFO, FAD, and CAD are largely interchangeable, with different analysts using the term they prefer. The major difference between FFO and these supplementals relates to the issue of capital improvements, particularly ongoing capital improvements. To understand the difference, consider a multifamily apartment building. There are several major expenditures, such as painting and replacement of carpets, that have to be made on a recurring basis. For example, carpeting may be replaced every five years, and painting redone every three years. Accounting policies vary from REIT to REIT on how to handle these expenses. The most conservative treatment is to classify them as expenses, counting them against the current year's income. Others choose to classify them as capital improvements, capitalizing them on the balance sheet and amortizing them over time. In the latter case, the amount spent for capital expenditures will not affect FFO because amortization is added back to EPS when calculating FFO. Thus, although either treatment is valid, the variation causes difficulty in comparing income and expense figures across REITs. NAREIT has encouraged REITs to provide supplemental disclosure to FFO in several areas, including capital improvements, straight-line rents, and results of discontinued operations.

REIT Expansion and Growth

Because of the requirement that 90 percent of earnings be paid out as dividends, REITs have limited opportunities to retain earnings or cash flow to acquire additional real estate assets. Stated another way, REITs have very little free cash flow. Consequently, most REITs must plan for expansion by reserving the right to issue additional stock at some future time. This is referred to as a secondary, or follow-on, stock offering to raise more equity capital, which may in turn be used to acquire additional real estate assets. Analysts may view eventual issuance of these shares as a potential source of *dilution* of future earnings. The general tendency in the industry is to evaluate the use of funds from follow-on offerings to determine if they will generate an increase in cash flow that more than offsets the dilution. In the industry, this is referred to as an *accretive* transaction. This is particularly important when looking at the period just after additional shares are issued and before additional cash flow is realized from the newly acquired assets. Furthermore, any interim problems with developing, leasing, managing, and renovating the new real estate assets could require time to correct and thus serve as a potential drag on earnings. The dilution of earnings from issuing additional shares might also have a depressing effect on the stock price of the REIT, through the impact on the dividend.

REITs also make use of significant amounts of debt financing, including individual property mortgages, mortgage pools, secured debt, unsecured debt, and corporate lines of credit. Many REITs have been assigned investment ratings by the various ratings agencies and use multiple sources of debt capital for growth. Proceeds from debt financing may be used to finance additional asset acquisitions. In some cases, lines of credit or unsecured debt financing can be used as an interim source of funds until long-term mortgage financing or a supplemental stock offering can be accomplished. In any event, because REITs are "asset-intensive" entities with a considerable restriction on earnings retention, their ability to finance any future expansion must be planned with great care. Because real estate investments are long-lived assets, it is important for REITs to balance their capital structure to avoid large concentrations of risk, particularly with respect to timing of refinancing. Concept Box 21.3 discusses the impact that the recent global credit crisis has had on REIT distributions and capital structure decisions.

There are five ways in which a REIT can grow income and increase funds from operations, thus securing its dividend and making dividend increases possible. These five methods are (1) growing income from existing properties, (2) growing income through acquisitions, (3) growing income through development, (4) growing income through provision of services, and (5) financial engineering. The relative balance among these areas is a strategic decision, as are the mechanisms for operations within the areas.

Growing Income from Existing Properties

The most obvious method for growing income in an existing portfolio is increasing occupancy by renting more space. The second is by raising rents. Obviously, the two are intrinsically related and both are dependent on the supply and demand conditions in the market. Redevelopment offers a third alternative. Redevelopment primarily refers to remodeling of space to meet changing tenant needs. This can result in income growth because it results in either more aesthetically appealing space or space that is more suitable for prospective tenants, both of which can result in higher rents. Redevelopment may address other physical problems, such as the lack of an elevator in a three-story office building. Expansion can increase income by providing more physical space for rental purposes and is fairly

In traditional finance, evaluation of refinancing risk includes the risks associated with the cost of debt and the availability of capital. Prior to 2008, most analysis of REIT capital structure risks focused on the *cost* of capital, as opposed to the *availability* of capital. In 2007 and 2008, the U.S. financial system and the global financial system were rocked by the fallout of the subprime mortgage crisis, resulting in a very severe credit crunch in which many REITs were unable to refinance corporate debt or property-level debt when it came due, irrespective of operating performance. In some cases, cost was not an issue as replacement debt capital was, in a practical sense, nonexistent. Analysts and rating agencies began to talk about REITs in terms of "sustainable" capital structures, focusing on the availability of capital to refinance debt maturing in the short or intermediate term. The focus of discussion became the topic of "survivability." Not surprisingly, many REIT investors were troubled by these changes to the REIT market, and there was a massive sell-off in REIT shares.

REIT pricing declined dramatically, and one very high-profile REIT, General Growth Properties, which had been one of the largest REITs in existence, sought bankruptcy protection. Other REITs, including REITs that had previously been viewed as "best in class" operating companies, faced similar pressures due to capital structure issues. In most cases, these REITs had substantially greater capital structure risk than analysts, ratings agencies, and investors recognized prior to the credit crisis.

REIT capital structures have changed substantially since 1992. At the inception of the modern REIT era, most REITs' capital structures consisted of a combination of common equity and individual property-level debt. As REITs gained greater market acceptance, common equity offerings were supplemented with preferred equity issues and property-level debt was replaced or supplemented by debt secured by larger portfolios. REITs increasingly began to issue debt at the corporate level, making use of bonds, lines of credit, and unsecured debt. Over time, the percentage of unsecured debt and floating-rate debt used by REITs increased substantially. At the same time, debt maturities shortened, as REITs increasingly relied on intermediate term notes, typically three to five years in duration. While the interest rates on this debt were initially lower than those offered on longer term fixed rate debt, the risks attendant on refinancing increased. In an era of plentiful capital, these risks seemed small relative to the perceived benefits, but there was a fundamental mismatch of long-lived assets being financed with short-term capital.

In dealing with the limitations on their ability to secure debt financing, the boards of directors of some REITs were forced to consider measures for securing capital that would not have been seriously considered under more "normal" capital market conditions. When debt comes due and similar replacement debt is not available, the primary alternatives are to seek alternative debt (i.e., replacing unsecured debt with secured debt) or secure additional equity capital.

In 2008, many REITs facing liquidity constraints found it difficult to distribute 90 percent of their taxable income in the form of cash dividends, risking their qualification as a REIT. On December 10, 2008, the Internal Revenue Service issued Revenue Procedure 2008-68, which provides that a stock distribution by a REIT may be treated as a taxable dividend for tax years ending on or before December 31, 2009, which provided that a stock distribution by a REIT could be treated as a taxable dividend for tax years if certain requirements are met. Essentially, this measure allows REITs to meet mandatory distribution requirements through the issuance of a stock dividend. While this measure allowed REITs to suspend cash dividends and retain cash to meet liquidity needs, it also created a debate in the REIT industry. In essence, a stock dividend results in existing shareholders making a required additional equity investment. Many shareholders invest in REITs as a means of securing regular cash flow, and stock dividends represent a "double whammy" to these investors, as they do not receive any cash associated with the distribution but incur the tax liability associated with that distribution, and the tax liability is required to be paid in cash. As a result, the investor is forced to either pay the tax from other cash resources or sell the stock and use a portion of the proceeds to

[1]Contributed by Ron Donohue, Ph.D.

pay the tax obligation, incurring trading costs in the process. Some in the industry view the ability to issue stock dividends as a valuable and essential capital management tool, while others view REITs making distributions in the form of stock dividends as breaking an implied contract with REIT investors with potential long-term negative consequences.

Some REITs elected to deleverage their capital structure by issuing new equity, despite the fact that some of those offerings were at stock prices substantially below the net asset value of the company's assets, resulting in substantial dilution. Market reception of these offerings was very positive, largely because these offerings, while dilutive, provided replacement capital for maturing debt at a critical juncture, removing the "survivability" question facing many REITs. Other companies elected to sell properties despite declining prices and difficult marketing conditions and have used the proceeds to pay down debt.

In the short term, these capital structure changes, along with improving global credit market conditions resulted in stabilization and as markets improved there has been significant recovery in REIT market pricing. REITs that had been viewed as seriously at risk of bankruptcy gained time to allow markets to recover. In many cases, these REITs have recovered to pricing levels and market capitalizations in excess of those in place prior to the credit crisis.

---

common in retail facilities, where an anchor tenant may expand, or outlying parcels may be developed to generate additional rental income. Office and industrial REITs, particularly those that specialize in industrial/office parks, often hold substantial amounts of land in close proximity to their existing parks. This land, which is usually permitted and approved, is simply held in anticipation of growing demand for space. Where the demand does not emerge, the property can be sold and the assets reallocated to more productive areas. Another means of growing income is in altering the market segments addressed. A mall might shift to a fashion focus, essentially developing a retenanting focus. Marketing and policies may also change, as is the case in eliminating a no-pets policy at an apartment community. REITs may also grow net income by controlling expenses. For example, many apartment REITs have provided sub-metering at the individual apartment level, transferring utility costs and associated volatility directly to tenants.

Growing Income through Acquisitions

There are two methods of growing the portfolio through acquisitions. These two methods are (1) purchasing properties with cash at positive spreads, utilizing the arbitrage between cost of capital and the yield of the property and (2) swapping shares in the REIT or operating partnership units for interests in properties, taking advantage of the tax and form benefits. Positive spread acquisitions are fairly common in periods when REITs are trading at low cap rates relative to the underlying real estate, but they are more difficult to achieve as REIT yields come closer to or exceed the cap rates on the underlying properties. Another way of looking at this is in terms of **net asset value (NAV).** Net asset value is the net "market value" of all of a company's assets, including but not limited to its properties, after subtracting all its liabilities and obligations. When a REIT is trading above NAV, it is more likely to find attractive spreads than when it is trading below NAV. When yields (prices) are very close, it may not be wise to acquire properties in this fashion because of the costs associated with securing capital.

Swapping shares in the REIT or operating partnership units for interests in properties has the advantage of a minimal cash requirement. As a general rule, operating partnership swaps are the more attractive of the two options because of the potential for tax timing. Existing shareholders can benefit because the swaps are generally done at favorable cap rates, with the owners of the acquired property willing to accept a discount for their properties in exchange for liquidity. In some cases, these swaps also include other business enterprises or personnel that are beneficial to the acquiring REIT. For example, an existing REIT with limited development capacity might work out a swap with a private company in the REIT IPO pipeline that has development capacity. The acquiring REIT gets the benefits associated with a larger portfolio and a set of skills that it did not have before the transaction. The owners of the acquired properties satisfy some of their goals that led to the consideration of going public, without incurring the substantial costs associated with the legal process of becoming a REIT.

Growing Income through Development

REITs may also choose to grow their income through development of properties. Risk is generally higher than in redevelopment or acquisition, but can be mitigated. For example, the risks associated with build-to-suit development of properties subject to long-term net leases with quality credit tenants are considerably lower than those associated with speculative development. In either case, thorough market analysis is an absolute necessity. Development offers an opportunity to secure entrepreneurial profits and increase funds from operations significantly. However, the returns are offset by a series of risks. There are always risks of construction delays, cost overruns, and lease-up problems. In the market, many investors are extremely concerned with quarterly performance, a focus where it probably does not make a great deal of sense to invest in a long-term asset like real estate, but which can influence pricing. As acquisition opportunities decline, REITs may shift to a development orientation. In some cases, the REITs have a long and distinguished development history and are capitalizing on in-house expertise. In other cases, the REIT does not have the expertise in-house and is forced to acquire it through acquisition of operating companies or through hiring. A third alternative is to develop a relationship with an existing developer and act as the take-out on its construction projects.

Growing Income through Provision of Services

REITs may also derive a portion of their income from provision of services to related and unrelated third parties. The income from these activities varies substantially across REITs. Some companies derive a significant portion of their income from these activities, while others do not produce any external income. These services may include property management, development, licensing agreements, or provision of other real estate–related services to related parties and unrelated third parties. In many cases, REITs enter into joint-venture arrangements with institutional investors under which the REIT owns a minority interest in a joint venture that owns a portfolio of properties. The REIT acts as the property and asset manager for the joint venture and is generally compensated at competitive market rates for its efforts. REITs may also provide real estate–related services to unrelated third parties, for which they receive competitive market rates. Increasingly, REITs are marketing telecommunication, financial, and other services to their tenants and their tenants' customer base. The result is that REITs have an opportunity to leverage off their real estate expertise and human capital to generate additional earnings, often through taxable REIT subsidiaries.

Financial Engineering

A fifth alternative is to grow the funds from operations through financial engineering. Financial engineering includes a variety of accounting treatments and uses of leverage that tend to magnify the funds from operations, which many view as the best short-term measure of the REIT's income-producing ability. Financial engineering also includes the ability to secure favorable rates, financing terms, and sources of capital. These factors can influence the long-term cost of capital for the REIT. Essentially, the idea is that REIT management can manipulate the capital structure in order to maximize distributions. Some of the risks and rewards of various financial engineering alternatives are discussed next.

Accounting treatments can be used to magnify funds from operation (FFO). Since REITs have tended to trade at some multiple of funds from operations, magnifying funds from operations often results in higher stock prices. The risk is that the REIT will be unable to meet its shareholders' expectations based on magnified FFO numbers. The shareholders may view these magnified numbers as indicative of future growth and expect corresponding increases in dividends. REITs that fail to meet FFO projections or sustain high growth levels have been treated harshly by investors.

As an example of the influence of accounting treatments, some recurring expense items can be either expensed or capitalized. In some property types, particularly multifamily residential properties, recurring expenses are cyclical, impacting the REITs' ability to distribute funds on a regular basis. REITs vary as to their treatment of these expenses, making comparisons among REITs difficult. As a result, many analysts have moved to **cash available for distribution (CAD),** as discussed earlier. Cash available for distribution treats recurring expenses as expenses rather than capital items, providing a more conservative estimate of the potential stream of income available for dividend purposes. The problem is that CAD calculation is not standardized, and the information necessary for standardization is often not available.

REITs can also use leverage to magnify FFO in the short term. One way is for the REIT to use short-term variable-rate loans to acquire properties. The rates on this type of loan are lower than those that can be obtained for long-term fixed rate debt, so the rate of return on the investment is higher, at least in the short run. Higher return on the investment leads to higher FFO and dividends, which in an ideal situation will lead to an increased multiple, making it feasible to replace the debt with attractively priced equity. Unfortunately, the higher rates of return are accompanied by greater risks and the leverage can reverse, magnifying losses and moving prices in the other direction. The result can be an inability to replace debt with equity and a need to refinance at a less-than-opportune time. This refinancing risk needs to be evaluated and priced.

REITs can also alter payout ratios. The payout ratio is the percentage of FFO, or alternatively CAD, that is used to pay out the dividend. The payout ratio is an important indicator of the financial flexibility of an organization and its ability to maintain its dividend. As an example, consider two REITs. REIT 1 has FFO of $1.00 per share and pays a dividend of $0.85, resulting in a payout ratio of 85 percent. REIT 2 has FFO of $0.93 and a dividend of $0.85, resulting in a payout ratio of 91.4 percent. If both REITs were subject to a $0.10 per share drop in income, then the resulting payout ratios at the same dividend rate would be 94.4 percent and 102.4 percent, respectively. While REIT 1 can maintain its dividend without dipping into cash reserves, REIT 2 is required to dip into cash reserves, essentially giving the shareholders their money back. While this type of distribution can be maintained for short periods under unusual circumstances, it cannot be maintained indefinitely without hampering growth prospects.

Important Issues in Accounting and Financial Disclosure: Equity REITs[2]

When analyzing financial statements, one must understand that REITs, like other economic entities, have considerable latitude when accounting for their operations. This section covers some issues and interpretations that REIT investors should bear in mind when

---

[2] The authors thank Eric Hemel and Neil Barsky for providing them with the report, "Do You Believe in Magic? Understanding a REIT IPO's Pro Forma Funds from Operation" (Morgan Stanley: *U.S. Investment Research*, January 24, 1994).

performing a financial analysis based on financial statements and other documents. These issues are widely covered in various industry reports provided by investment bankers and other REIT market analysts. The following presents some of the basic issues and explains their significance in evaluating REITs and their financial statements.

Tenant Improvements and Free Rents: Effects on FFO

When markets are soft and vacancies are above normal, tenants may be induced by owners to sign leases with free rent or improvements provided by REIT management. This possibility is important to understanding REIT revenue, particularly where leases are long term. Occupancy and revenues are obviously important items when reporting income for industrial, office, and retail properties. Occupancy rates can be raised and rental revenues increased by providing important concessions to tenants, often in the form of tenant improvements. Generally, new commercial tenants must always incur some costs to reconfigure the space and make it suitable for their operations. Landlord allowances for some tenant improvements are a common practice in much of the real estate industry, but concessions could be a concern if they are very large relative to what other owners are offering. Tenant improvements paid by the landlord are often capitalized and then depreciated. Thus, the cash flows for tenant improvements are not included in FFO calculations because FFO represents earnings before depreciation. Therefore, the investor should be aware that this cash outflow may be occurring currently but accounted for in depreciation expense *over time.* Investors should also pay particularly close attention to any notes to FFO estimates that include "signed leases scheduled to commence." This may indicate that the REIT is currently including the effect of leases not taking effect until a future date.

One way investors can evaluate the implications of new leases is to determine the "cost" per square foot and the extent that tenant improvements and free rent are included in the leases. This determination may be particularly important when the REIT is about to go public with an initial public offering (IPO). For example, suppose that tenant improvement costs averaged $7 per square foot of newly leased space during the three years before the IPO. However, the company spent $20 per square foot *in the year prior* to the IPO. The additional amounts spent on tenant improvements could suggest that the company was preparing for the impending IPO by attempting to boost its occupancy rates and nominal rent levels to make itself more attractive to investors. Many companies do not explicitly disclose the cost per square foot of tenant improvements, but they may disclose enough information about historical leasing activity and aggregate tenant improvement levels so that investors can make their own estimates.

Leasing Commissions and Related Costs

A number of REITs pay outside leasing brokers a commission to solicit tenants. These commissions are usually paid in cash, and the cost is capitalized over the life of the lease. These costs are included in depreciation and amortization expense. Because investors traditionally measure REIT profitability according to funds from operations (earnings before depreciation and amortization), any deferred leasing costs may be overlooked. There is no single, accepted standard for disclosing deferred leasing costs. Many REITs do their own leasing and pay their employee-brokers salaries or commissions, or both. These REITs may then either expense or capitalize and defer the costs. The deferral of leasing costs raises two issues: (1) Leasing costs are an ongoing source of operating expense; omitting them as an operating expense reduces expenses and increases FFO. (2) In rare instances, brokers are paid commissions over the life of the leases instead of up front. In that case, investors in a REIT that is about to embark on an IPO will be paying commissions incurred on leases signed *prior* to the IPO; this means that the REIT may have to pay out cash in the future for leases signed in previous periods.

Use of Straight-Line Rents

Another accounting issue arises when a REIT relies on long-term leases with rent increases contractually stipulated over the life of the lease. This is rarely a factor in apartment companies, which usually have year-to-year or month-to-month leases, but it can be important for REITs with long-term leases, and this includes virtually every category of commercial and industrial property.

To understand the potential problem, consider a simple situation in which a tenant signs a 10-year lease with step-ups: The lease is $8 per square foot in years 1 through 3, $10 per square foot in years 4 through 7, and $12 per square foot in years 8 through 10. If revenue recognition is based on "straight-line" reporting, the rent will be averaged over the full lease term, which in this case is $10 per square foot. Thus, rental revenues in year 1 are counted as $10 even though the actual cash flow is $8. Since FFO is calculated as earnings before depreciation, a pro forma FFO may use $10 instead of the actual $8, unless the assumptions underlying the pro forma calculation clearly specify otherwise. Obviously, the FFO estimate will be lower than the actual revenue in the later years of the lease, when $12 of cash flow exceeds the $10 average. However, in an IPO, considerable attention is given to the initial or near-term estimates of FFO. In this case, investors may want to bend the straight line of the rental stream. Management should provide clear guidance to investors about the cash flow without the straight-line rent adjustment in year 1. In this way, investors can better assess the dividend-paying ability of the REIT and accurately evaluate the company on the basis of potential cash flow growth resulting from contractual rent adjustments well into the future. This is one of the primary reasons that many analysts have moved to estimating adjusted FFO, CAD, and other supplemental measures of cash flow as previously discussed.

FFO and Income from Managing Other Properties

As noted previously, a number of REITs receive third-party management income, or income in exchange for managing other properties not owned by the REIT. While third-party management income may provide additional earnings, its associated revenue stream is likely to vary more than the underlying rental income from REIT-owned properties because many management contracts may be cancelable by third-party owners on short notice. Moreover, other events might affect this source of income: Many REITs have sold off portions of their portfolio in joint ventures with institutional investors, often retaining a minority interest in the portfolio (20% is typical) and deriving fee income from managing the properties while freeing equity capital for other corporate purposes. The joint-venture partner's control over properties and right to replace the REIT as manager is typically established in the joint-venture agreement, so it makes sense for investors and analysts to be familiar with the terms of these agreements. Other properties managed by the REIT may be sold, or the management of REIT-owned properties could suffer if the REIT gives too much attention to managing third-party properties. As a result, many REIT security analysts assign a lower multiple to the portion of FFO produced by management income. Investors should always be aware of any fee based on other sources of income that the REIT reports because a large portion of these fees may be short-term. The character of the third-party relationship is also important, in that the REIT's managers may have a partnership interest that effectively locks in the contracts. It is important to understand the nature of third-party management contracts and other sources of income. In addition, some sources of income may not constitute income from real properties and may jeopardize the REIT's tax status if in excess of allowable levels. Taxable REIT subsidiaries were designed and implemented largely to "clean" the income from these activities.

Types of Mortgage Debt and Other Obligations

When one examines a REIT investment, it is important to consider the terms of the company's mortgage debt. Mortgages may be either short- or long-term, floating rate or fixed, and nonamortizing or amortizing. As a practical matter, most REITs do not amortize much of their debt. The result is a continual return to the debt market to replace maturing debt. By using short-term, floating-rate debt, the REIT borrower may enjoy a lower mortgage rate in exchange for assuming some portion of the risk of inflation and increasing interest rates. The use of a short-term floating rate may be favorable in the near term because of low interest charges, but it exposes the REIT to significantly greater risk. The REIT can hedge this risk through the use of interest rate "caps" or "swaps," the extent and cost of which should be disclosed to shareholders. REITs may also issue corporate debt of varying terms, both secured and unsecured.

Existence of Ground Leases

As the name suggests, ground leases encumber the land underneath buildings. They are typically made for long periods of time, sometimes up to 99 years. Ground leases tend to be "net" leases, which means the tenant pays for all costs associated with operating the building, including utilities, taxes, renovations, and so on. The landowner, or "fee" owner, plays no operating role other than to collect land rents from the building owner or operator. At the time the lease expires, the landowner owns residual rights to all buildings and improvements situated on the land.

Two basic arrangements of ground leases are likely to apply to REITs. First, the REIT *owns buildings subject to* a ground lease owned by another party. The REIT may have a potential advantage if the ground-lease payments are *fixed.* In this event, the REIT is using the equivalence of leverage because, if the cash flow from the building rental income continues to grow relative to the fixed ground-lease payments, a higher return on equity will be achieved. The universal disadvantage of the ground lease is that the REIT will give up ownership of the buildings at the time of lease expiration or it must renegotiate the lease prior to its expiration. In their valuation process, investors should heavily discount the cash flow from any buildings on a ground lease with an approaching expiration date. In addition, some ground leases may call for the lessor to participate in revenue growth. This is similar to a participating debt and may be negative from a REIT investor's perspective. Obviously, the terms and conditions of all ground leases should probably be renegotiated *long before* the lease term expires.

The second case applies to a REIT that *owns a ground lease* that it has acquired from the landowner. Ground leases are allowable investments for REITs, which simply put the REIT between the landowner, who retains all rights of reversion, and the building owner. This arrangement is known as "spread investing," where the REIT takes the risk of collecting a stream of rents from the building owner and pays a lower and perhaps fixed payment to the landowner. Ground leasing to third parties, depending on their credit, can be a safe and reliable way to assure an income stream.

Some ground leases are important and complex enough to warrant detailed financial analysis. Many *retail* REITs, for example, own shopping malls subject to ground leases. In this case, lessors and landowners usually enjoy a substantial share of the cash flow once certain retail revenue thresholds are exceeded, but payments to the ground lease may reduce the ultimate growth prospects of the REIT.

Lease Renewal Options and REIT Rent Growth

Investors should review the lease rollover schedules of REITs. This is particularly important for REITs that concentrate in sectors with long-term leases: regional malls, industrial properties, and offices. Most initial public offerings for these REITs should disclose the average rent of recently expired leases as well as the new rents. Following the initial public offerings, most REITs disclose a schedule of aggregate annual lease expirations in the supplemental materials to their financial statements. This, combined with notes and management's discussion and analysis, should enable investors to determine how many new leases are being made at or below previous rents and how much or how little growth is occurring from lease rollovers.

Expected lease rollovers should be examined to determine the amount of space subject to *renewal options* and the range of rent levels at which those options are set. Rents could be far below the prevailing rents at the time of lease expiration. Investors should also question the likelihood that some tenants will elect not to renew their leases. This may occur because tenants find that the existing space is inadequate for their expanding operations, or for any one of a number of reasons. Therefore, investors must consider the probability that the space will be leased to new tenants, and how long it will take and how much it will cost a REIT (lease commissions and finish-out) to attract new tenants.

Occupancy Numbers: Leased Space or Occupied Space?

When discussing occupancy numbers, nearly all REITs use the term *occupied space* in notes to financial statements and operating results. Like other disclosure issues, this at first appears innocuous, but on closer examination it opens the way for potential distortion. Occupied space quantifies the space for which tenants are now paying rent. *Leased space* includes all space for which leases are signed, even if the lease does not go into effect for another 6 to 12 months. The amount of leased space is often several percentage points higher than occupied space. Investors who compare occupied space in one REIT against leased space in another may be using two different—and noncomparable—methods of counting occupancy. For example, one REIT may report space as occupied that is currently leased but that has been, or is about to be, vacated by tenants, while another may report that space as vacant. There is also variation by property sector, largely due to differences in the structure and length of leases. To be conservative, REITs should either not claim credit for occupied space that it has reason to believe will be vacant in the immediate future or disclose the impending vacancy.

Retail REITs and Sales per Square Foot

There is no standard way to measure retail sales per square foot of a small store. Several methods of calculation have evolved, but investors should beware of the implications of each. For example, one method excludes sales per square foot from "in-line stores in regional malls." Another method uses "mall store sales" but excludes sales of "large space users" where space is used less intensively or where a portion of the total space is owned by the tenant or governed by a highly restricted operating agreement. The problem with both definitions is that total retail sales and sales per square foot in a mall are affected by excluding large space users. Even though many large space users may own their space in a mall or have a very strict operating agreement that gives them considerable control over their space, investors are in a sense paying for the lease portfolio or tenant roster and "sales power" of all tenants. A better approach may be to report total sales per square foot rather than to exclude large space users. Some REITs separate anchor tenant sales from in-line tenant sales.

One legitimate defense of excluding large space users from financial statements is that many older malls have large variety-type stores that bring down average sales per square foot. Lease rollovers may provide the mall with significant opportunities for sales and revenue growth, particularly if the leases of variety-type stores are about to expire. Consequently, the more inclusive definition of sales per square foot may tend to understate the long-term sales potential of a mall.

A third definition of sales per square foot is based on "mall store tenants that reported 12 months of sales for the operating period." This definition may exclude tenants that reported less than 12 months of sales, possibly because of bankruptcy or deliberate lease terminations. This measure may suffer from "tenant survivorship bias," or the counting of only those tenants that survived and the exclusion of those that did not. The excluded tenants probably experienced lower sales per square foot than their healthier counterparts; if included, they would have pulled down the average. Alternatively, the measure leaves off sales of seasonal "kiosk" or "cart" operators that sell goods in common areas during holidays and other periods of heavy demand. These operators can contribute significantly to income, as they typically have percentage rent provisions in their leases, and income can be highly variable.

Additional Costs of Being a Public Company

REITs typically have to purchase insurance for directors and officers, pay directors' fees, pay for listings on the stock exchanges, and file annual and quarterly reports with the Securities and Exchange Commission. While these costs are usually included in general and administrative costs, the actual amounts may be considerably more than a REIT initially estimated.

A major recent development is the Sarbanes-Oxley law of 2002, the congressional act designed to prevent financial scandals like those at Enron and WorldCom. The law amended the regulatory provisions of the Securities Commission Act of 1934. The Securities Exchange Commission (SEC) is the principal governing body charged with making the rules to enforce the Sarbanes-Oxley changes. Sarbanes-Oxley set forth or revised several standards for corporate boards of publicly traded companies and required rule making by the national stock exchanges to impose additional standards. Parts of the law have taken effect already, like rules for audit committees, reporting supplemental financial information, and auditor independence. Other parts will be phased in over the course of the year, like including accelerated filing requirements for periodic reports. The final standards for still other parts of the law dealing with additional disclosure requirements are still being written. The cost of complying with the regulations enacted so far does not vary proportionally with the size of the company, so the reality is that smaller REITs face a disproportionate burden in meeting the requirements. Some smaller REITs that merged with other companies or which been taken private subsequent to the act cited the act as one of the reasons it felt a business combination or sale was necessary.

The Investment Appeal of Mortgage REITs

The mortgage real estate investment trust is unlike the equity trust in that it does not own the real property. Rather, it owns mortgage paper secured by the underlying real property. Income generated by the mortgage paper is affected by the interest rate on the mortgage note, the discount (or premium) at which the obligation is acquired, and the amount of funds outstanding on the loans. REIT expenses applicable against this income are the interest paid for the funds to make payments on loans, management company costs, and other lesser expenses incident to the operations of this kind of investment company.

During the late 1960s and early 1970s, the mortgage REIT was used as a source of loans, particularly for construction and development that were beyond the legal or policy limits of the highly regulated banks, savings and loans, insurance companies, or other real estate–oriented financing institutions. Because their lending policies were relatively unregulated and because they had access to public securities markets, mortgage REITs were in a position to fill a void in the real estate financing market. Even though their cost for short-term borrowed funds was relatively high, there was always the reasonable expectation that the trust could make construction or development loans at rates 3.5 percent to 4 percent higher than rates available from other lending sources. The spread between borrowing costs and loan income thus held the promise of increasing earnings on the shareholders' equity as the loan portfolio grew. This earnings growth would support further sales of shares in the trust at higher prices, and so on. Following this pattern, the expansion of mortgage trusts during the early 1970s was spectacular.

However, during 1974 a general economic recession set in, and the prime bank lending rate rose to unprecedented heights. Because of the unanticipated rise in their cost of funds, many mortgage trusts were forced into an operating loss position because they were not able to pass on a sufficient amount of these higher costs to borrowers. Further, many advance mortgage commitments had already been made at lower rates with inadequate flexibility for upward rate adjustments. During this period of rising interest rates, many developers were unable to sell completed units or could not complete projects because of rapidly inflating construction costs. Consequently, they were thrown into default on their construction loans. The share values of mortgage trusts fell dramatically, thus reducing the possibilities for further stock offerings as a source of funds.

Because of loan default expectations, the commercial paper market also dried up for trusts and forced them to rely almost exclusively on bank credit lines. As the defaults continued to increase during 1975, many large commercial banks were forced to extend the maturities on notes taken pursuant to these credit lines, which had usually been extended by banks as a group under a revolving credit agreement. The extensions were granted to avoid the cumulative impact on the total financial system if the trusts were forced to undertake mass foreclosures during a serious business recession. When credit became so tight that commercial bank lines could no longer be reasonably renewed, a number of bank sponsors took large blocks of mortgages out of the trust portfolios and put them into their own loan and liquidation accounts to reduce trust debts. These actions had an impact on overall commercial bank liquidity and removed the mortgage trusts generally from the construction and development loan markets as a supplier of funds for the foreseeable future. As a practical matter, many mortgage REITs invested in commercial mortgage-backed securities (CMBS) of pools of residential mortgages rather than whole loans. Increasingly, mortgage REITs are engaging in more diversified investment, including mezzanine loans and construction loans.

During the global credit crisis that began in 2007, mortgage REITs were severely impacted by capital limitations, higher than expected default rates, and short-term interest rate fluctuations. These factors, along with general market conditions, led investors in mortgage REITs to demand greatly increased risk premiums. Meanwhile, stock prices declined dramatically and companies were forced to declare bankruptcy when they were unable to refinance their debt. In some cases, mortgage REITs were able to sell some portion of their loan portfolio to repay their debt, but those sales typically occurred at dramatically reduced pricing, resulting in a loss of value to shareholders.

Mortgage REITs faced difficult market conditions following the subprime crisis and underperformed other REIT sectors as Federal Reserve policies contributed to historically low interest rates over an extended period of time. As the Federal Reserve has tapered its quantitative easing, mortgage REITs saw some growth and recovery. Mortgage REITs raised $16.2 billion in total equity offerings in 2012 and $7.3 billion in 2013. As of December 31, 2013, there were 26 listed residential Mortgage REITs with a market capitalization of $42.3 billion and 19 listed commercial Mortgage REITs with a market capitalization of $19.7 billion.

Caveats

As was the case with equity REITs, the potential for a conflict of interest exists when sponsors and affiliates of mortgage REITs (e.g., mortgage companies, thrifts, commercial banks) are also originators of mortgage loans. In these instances, there may be incentives to sell the submarginal loans of REITs while charging fees for servicing them. As indicated earlier, the rules governing the appointment of nonaffiliated trustees and the use of outside appraisers must also be followed in the creation and operation of mortgage REITs. In addition, CMBS portfolios often contain fairly high risk tranches, known as "B" pieces, that offer significantly higher risks and returns than other tranches. Mortgage REITs, under pressure to grow income, were at one time prime buyers of "B" pieces. Investors should review a mortgage REIT's investment policy and the quality of its loans as carefully as an equity REIT's properties. Many mortgage REITs focus much of their attention on managing interest rate risk. Essentially, they are purchasing long-lived assets using short-term financing. As a result, income streams can be very volatile, particularly relative to equity REITs.

Financial Analysis of an Equity REIT Illustrated

What follows is an analysis of an equity REIT that a prospective investor or shareholder might make. The financial statement for Midwestern America Property Trust is provided in Exhibit 21–2. Midwestern America (MA) owns and manages approximately five million square feet of suburban office, office-warehouse, and specialty office/distribution space, which it has assembled over the years in three Midwestern states. The cost basis for these assets is $300 million; the REIT has made or assumed mortgages totaling $80 million as part of financing its asset acquisitions. Midwestern America's stock is currently trading at $75 per share, making its current market value worth $375 million.

When you analyze an equity REIT, two key financial relationships must be understood: (1) the judgment of investment performance and risk and (2) the comparison of the prospective equity REIT with other equity REITs. Referring to Exhibit 21–2, we see that MA earned $13,600,000 in net income or $2.72 per share, during the past year. However, additional data (see Exhibit 21–3) indicate that other interesting and important

EXHIBIT 21–2   **Financial Statement Midwestern America Property Trust**

Panel A. Operating Statement Summary

Net revenue	$ 70,000,000
Less:	
Operating expenses	30,000,000
Depreciation and amortization	15,000,000
General and administrative expenses	4,000,000
Management expense	1,000,000
Income from operations	$ 20,000,000
Less:	
Interest expense	6,400,000
Net income (loss)	$ 13,600,000
Net income (loss) per share	$2.72

Panel B. Balance Sheet Summary

Assets			Liabilities	
Cash		$ 500,000	Short term	$ 2,000,000
Rents receivable		1,500,000	Mortgage debt	80,000,000
Properties @ cost	$300,000,000		Total	$ 82,000,000
Less: Acc. depr.	130,000,000		Shareholders' equity	90,000,000
Properties—net		170,000,000		
Net assets		$172,000,000	Total liabilities and equity	$172,000,000

EXHIBIT 21-3
Summary Indicators of Financial Performance: Midwestern America Property Trust

I. General Summary:

Properties: 5 million sq. ft.

Original cost: $300 million

Depreciated cost: $170 million

Mortgage debt: $80,000,000

Avg. interest 8%, 10 year maturity

Number of common shares: 5 million

II. Profit Summary:

	$ Amount	Per Share
Earnings per share (*EPS*)[1]	13,600,000	$2.72
Income from operations plus depreciation and amortization (*NOI per share*)[2]	35,000,000	$7.00
Funds from operations (*FFO per share*)[3]	28,600,000	$5.72

III. Other Important Financial Data:

Market price per share of common stock	$75.00
Dividend per share	$4.00
Shareholder recovery of capital (*ROC per share*)[4]	$1.28
Cash retention per share (*CRPS*)[5]	$1.72
Earnings yield[6]	3.62%
FFO yield[7]	7.62%
Dividend yield[8]	5.33%
Current **earnings multiple**[9]	27.6x
Current **FFO multiple**[10]	13.1x
Net assets per share (*NAPS*)[11]	$34.00
Equity or **book value per share** (*BVPS*)[12]	$18.00

IV. Explanation and Calculations:

[1]*EPS:* Net income $13,600,000/5,000,000 shares outstanding = $2.72

[2]*NOI:* Income from operations plus depreciation and amortization ($20,000,000 + $15,000,000)/5,000,000 shares outstanding = $7.00

[3]*FFO:* Net Income + Depreciation & Amortization ($13,600,000 + $15,000,000)/ 5,000,000 shares outstanding = $5.72

[4]*ROC:* Dividend per share − EPS = $4.00 − $2.72 = $1.28

[5]*CRPS:* FFO − Dividend per share $5.72 − $4.00 = $1.72

[6]EPS/Market price per share = $2.72/$75 = 3.62%

[7]FFO/Market price per share = $5.72/$75 = 7.62%

[8]Dividend per share/Market price per share = $4.00/$75 = 5.33%

[9]Current price per share/EPS = $75/$2.72 = 27.6x

[10]Current price per share/FFO = $75/$5.72 = 13.1x

[11]*NAPS:* Net assets $172,000,000/5,000,000 = $34.00

[12]*BVPS:* (Assets − Liabilities)/shares = $90,000,000/5,000,000 = $18.00

relationships must be understood. As is always the case with real estate investment, considerable emphasis is given to *cash flow*. For example, section II of Exhibit 21–3 includes additional performance measures. **Net income from operations** is the income before interest or depreciation deductions. It is somewhat analogous to net operating income (*NOI*), which we have discussed in earlier chapters for the income before taxes and before financing for individual properties. However, this is the net income from operations of the entire REIT, and it includes deductions for expenses associated with operating the REIT, such as general and administrative expenses and REIT management expenses. In order to calculate the *NOI* from all of the individual properties, we would deduct the operating expenses for the properties from the net revenue received from properties. This would be $70,000 − $30,000 = $40,000 for Midwestern America Property Trust. Net income from operations represents the operating cash flow exclusive of interest, which was $7.00 per share for the past year. The second measure, funds from operations (FFO), is analogous to net cash flow per share. As you may recall, it is derived by adding all noncash expense items to net income (loss). Noncash accounting charges generally include depreciation and amortization. Most industry analysts rely heavily on FFO when making judgments and comparisons among REITs. We can see that the FFO per share for MA was $5.72 during the past year versus **earnings per share (EPS)** of $2.72. The difference in this simplified example is due to the $15 million depreciation allowance.

One REIT regulation previously detailed indicates that 90 percent of taxable income must be paid out as dividends. Therefore, another very important relationship shown in section III of Exhibit 21–3 is the dividend payment per share. In our example, the payment of $4.00 per share meets the 90 percent requirement, but this amount is also greater than the earnings per share; thus, MA paid dividends of $4.00 per share even though EPS was only $2.72. This can occur because FFO, or *cash flow* per share, was $5.72, which exceeded earnings per share. Indeed, MA could have paid dividends of $5.72 per share even though it was required to pay only 90 percent of $2.72 or only $2.45 per share. By paying a $4.00 dividend, Midwestern America met the 90 percent of earnings requirement and retained cash of $1.72 per share for operations and acquisitions of new assets.

The difference between REIT earnings and dividends has a very important effect on the taxes that shareholders pay. Tax regulations provide that even though investors in Midwestern America receive $4.00 per share, only $2.72 of earnings are reported as a taxable dividend. The remaining $1.28 is treated as **recovery of capital (ROC)** and serves to reduce the cost basis of the stock acquired by the investor. For example, if a share of MA stock was purchased for $75 prior to the dividend declaration date, the investor would reduce the investment basis of the stock by $1.28, from $75.00 to $73.72. When the stock is eventually sold, the investor would then calculate any gain or loss based on the sale price, less $73.72, or the reduced basis of the stock. If the stock has been owned for one year or more and results in a gain, it would be taxed at the prevailing capital gains tax rate. This also means that if there is a difference between ordinary and capital gains tax rates, the investor saves taxes in the amount of $1.28 times the difference in the two tax rates. Consequently, this treatment allows investors to receive a portion of the dividend ($1.28) "tax free" until the stock is sold or the REIT is liquidated. At that point, if the investor has owned the stock long enough to qualify for capital gains treatment and capital gains tax rates are lower than tax on ordinary income, the investor will also save taxes.

When REITs report operating losses, none of the losses can be passed through to investors. Instead, losses must be carried forward to offset income in future periods. The passive loss limitation provision does not materially affect REITs because their losses cannot be passed through to investors. REIT dividends are considered to be *portfolio income* and thus do not qualify as passive income to offset passive losses.

With respect to capital gains from the sale of property, REITs may either (1) retain the gain and defer its distribution to shareholders, in which case the gain is taxed at the appropriate corporate capital gains rate, or (2) distribute the gain as a dividend to shareholders. In the latter case, the REIT is not taxed on the distributed gain; however, the REIT is required to designate such dividends as a capital gain distribution to shareholders, who must recognize it as a capital gain in their individual taxes. Capital losses cannot be passed through to individual investors but must be carried forward by the REIT and offset against any future capital gains.

Also important in section III of Exhibit 21–3 is cash flow retention, or the difference between FFO per share and dividends per share, which amounts to $1.72. Midwestern America may have retained this amount as a cash reserve or to acquire properties during the past year. As pointed out, MA could have paid this amount as a dividend and been taxed at ordinary income rates. However, because it was not paid currently, the cash flow retention is converted eventually into a capital gain if the *price* of MA stock responds favorably to management's decision to retain and invest these funds instead of paying dividends. Unlike corporations that may choose not to pay any dividends and retain all earnings for future expansion, MA must pay at least 90 percent of $2.72 or $2.45 per share. In other words, MA has far less discretion than corporations with respect to paying a minimum dividend—a major difference between REITs and corporate entities, which affects REIT dividend reinvestment and expansion policy in very important ways.

Valuing REITs as Investments

In previous chapters we have discussed how to estimate the value of individual properties. Estimating the value of a REIT is much more challenging because REITs tend to own and operate large, geographically diversified real estate portfolios. Thus, we need to estimate the value of a portfolio of properties in different locations and also consider the value of the REIT management and any goodwill established by the REIT as a going concern. Furthermore, as was the case when valuing individual properties, estimating the value of a REIT requires an understanding of both real estate space and capital market fundamentals.

There are analysts that publish investment research and recommendations with respect to REITs, but this information is not often available to the general investing public on a timely basis. Also, there is considerable variation in terms of methodology and content across analysts. Some analysts look at REITs from a real estate perspective, while other analysts focus on the analysis of financial statements and ratios. Other analysts take a blended approach, looking at the real estate, capital structure, management, and technical stock market factors.

REIT public filings provide a great deal of information, but they do not typically provide estimates of the value of the real estate owned by the REIT. The Financial Accounting Standards Board (FASB) has been active over recent years in its efforts to require fair value accounting of real assets as part of its efforts to bring U.S. financial reporting in line with the standards prevailing internationally. While there is no policy in place requiring fair value accounting for U.S. REITs currently, there is some chance that U.S. REITs will either elect to be required to the value of its assets on a fair value basis in the future. In the absence of this type of reporting, investors need to develop their own estimates of the value of the real estate owned by REITs. In this section we describe different methods that can be used to estimate the value of a REIT using Midwestern America Property Trust (introduced earlier in this chapter) as an example.

Valuation of Midwestern America Property Trust

Our previous analyses of Midwestern America Property Trust focused on the company and its performance at a specific point in time. To estimate the value of Midwestern America Property Trust, we need to make some assumptions about future performance. These assumptions will be added as we discuss the various approaches to valuation of the REIT.

Gordon Dividend Discount Model

A REIT security is a stock that can be valued using methods typically used to value other stocks. One simple and commonly accepted way of valuing stocks is the **Gordon dividend discount model.** This traditional model assumes a constant dividend growth rate for the stock. The model assumes that the value of a stock is the present value of expected future dividends, and it is particularly applicable for REITs because they tend to pay a relatively high dividend rate. The model states that the value (V) of the stock equals the dividend to be paid in the next year (D_1) divided by the difference between the required rate of return (K) and the dividend growth rate (g), or

$$V = D_1/(K - g)$$

In regard to our analysis of Midwestern America, let's assume the following:

- The current dividend of $4.00 per share is projected to increase by 5 percent to $4.20 next year and continue to increase by 5 percent per year thereafter.
- The required rate of return for a REIT like Midwestern America Trust is 10.5 percent, which is a reasonable long-term rate of return for REITs.

Applying the above assumptions to the constant dividend growth stock valuation model, we can conclude that the stock value should be $4.20/(10.5% − 5%) = $76.36 per share.

Income (FFO) Multiple

Another valuation method analysts apply is to estimate income and then multiply that income by an appropriate multiple of income or price-to-earnings ratio. Analysts often look at multiples for comparable companies and then select an appropriate multiple for the company being valued based on its characteristics relative to the comparable companies.

In the case of developing income multiples for REITs, the most common practice is to use FFO for income for the reasons we discussed earlier (one being FFO is a better measure of the cash flow that a REIT can generate than earnings per share). Next, comparable REITs that own the same general type of properties in developing the multiples would be selected. In the case of Midwestern America Property, the FFO is $5.72 per share, and the current FFO multiple is approximately 13.1×, resulting in a share price of $75.00.

Suppose that we find that there are four comparable REITs in the market, trading at FFO multiples ranging from 12× to 15×. Thus, we see that Midwestern currently trades at a multiple slightly below the midpoint of the range of the comparable REITs.

If we believe that Midwestern is expected to improve its performance relative to the comparables, it is possible that a higher multiple would be appropriate. In the final analysis, determining the appropriate multiple is a subjective process, although objective data play an important role in the process. However, it is common to rank REITs on a relative basis and assign a multiple that reflects a REIT's placement in that ranking. So, we might elect to apply a 14× multiple to the FFO for Midwestern because we believe the market will eventually recognize that it has improved its performance relative to the comparables. Applying the 14× multiple to the $5.72 in FFO results in an expected share price of $80.08.

Net Asset Value

The final valuation method we will consider is based on analyzing a REIT's net asset value (NAV). A REIT's primary asset is real estate and a REIT's primary liability is the debt associated with that real estate. Logically, if one can estimate the total current value of the real estate and other assets owned by a REIT, then subtract the total debt and other liabilities owed by the REIT, the remainder will be the REIT's net asset value (NAV), which is an indication of shareholders' equity.

REITs report real estate holdings at book value, which can differ substantially from current market value for various reasons. What we want is an estimate of the current market value of the real estate. Unfortunately, REITs do not routinely provide NAV estimates, so the analyst needs to do that.[3]

A significant divergence between the NAV and the market value of a REIT stock may indicate a difference between what public market investors are willing to pay for properties versus what private market investors are willing to pay for those properties. If private market investors are willing to pay more, the REIT may elect to go private, or it may be taken over by a private company. Alternatively, if public market investors are willing to pay a premium, more private companies may decide to go public.

To estimate NAV, we estimate the net operating income (*NOI*) for the entire REIT and then divide that by a **blended capitalization rate** that would be applicable to the entire REIT. A blended capitalization rate means one that is an average of the capitalization rates that would be used for the individual properties in the portfolio if we were valuing each property separately.[4] The problem is that we do not typically have the *NOI* on each individual property. Thus, we need to try to value all the properties at once by applying a blended capitalization rate to an estimate of the aggregate *NOI* from all the properties held by the REIT. Thus, we have

$$NAV = NOI/r$$

where *NOI* is for all the properties held by the REIT and *r* is the blended cap rate.

To estimate the NAV of the real estate assets, we need to look at the properties separately from the entity. We do this by using net operating income from the property operations, using property level income and expenses, and not including entity level expenses such as general and administrative expenses, depreciation, and interest expense. Midwestern has rental revenue of $70,000,000 ($14.00 per share) less operating expenses of $30,000,000 ($6 per share), resulting in real estate *NOI* of $40,000,000 ($8 per share). At an implied 8.75 percent capitalization rate, the total value of Midwestern's assets is approximately $457,000,000 ($91.40 per share). We then subtract debt of $82,000,000 ($16.40 per share), resulting in a net asset value for Midwestern's real estate of $375,000,000 ($75 per share).

If the REIT is doing a significant amount of development, it may be more appropriate to use a projected stabilized *NOI* rather than the current *NOI* to estimate the value and then perhaps adjust that value down slightly, because there will be some rent loss until the properties are leased up.

Summary of Value Estimates

To summarize the estimates we found using the above valuation methods, we have:

Gordon dividend growth model	$76.36/per share
FFO multiple	$80.08/per share
Net asset value (NAV)	$75.00/per share

In this case, the NAV estimate is a little lower than the others and is where the stock price is currently trading. But REITs often trade at premiums or discounts to their NAV depending on how the market views the management and its ability to identify good investment and development opportunities in the future. The FFO multiple approach assumed that the market would recognize that Midwestern is better than reflected in its current stock price and that it would start to trade at a price more in line with the better comparables.

---

[3] There are also companies like Green Street Advisors (**www.greenstreetadvisors.com**) that provide NAV estimates for REITs to subscribers.

[4] The average would be weighted toward those locations that had the most properties.

Web App

Go to the NAREIT Web site (**www.reit.com**) and find the most recent value of the FTSE NAREIT Equity REIT Index for Equity REITs. Then go to the Web site for any REIT and find the following information: Full Company Name, Stock Symbol, Exchange, Property Type, Portfolio Composition (number of properties, units or square feet, and major markets), Current Price, Current Dividend, and Current Yield. Finally, go to the Dividend Discount Model site and value the REIT you selected using an appropriate discount rate. (One way to select a discount rate is to see what the expected return is for REIT indexes on the site.)

The Gordon dividend growth model approach resulted in a stock price of $76.36, which is between the other two estimates. All things considered, we may conclude that a price of around $76 to $77 is appropriate. This suggests that the REIT might be slightly undervalued by the market at its current price of $75.

Further Considerations

The above analysis provides us with an estimate of the range in which we might expect the stock price for a REIT to fall. But of course, estimating stock prices is far from an exact science. All stocks tend to rise and fall with the overall market, and REITs are no exception. As will be discussed in Chapter 22, REITs are not highly correlated with the overall market so they do provide some diversification benefits. But they will still tend to be pulled in the direction of the rest of the market, so investors must also consider the likely direction of the overall stock market when valuing a REIT.

Another consideration is where the property types held by the REIT are in their investment cycle, as discussed in Chapter 10. For example, if the REIT invests in office properties and office properties are in a downward cycle in the areas where the REIT owns properties, this may impact their ability to generate the *NOI* or FFO we had projected—especially if the REIT relies on income from newly developed properties.

Finally, an investor should try to determine whether there are reasons that the stock price should sell for more or less than the value of its underlying real estate based on the NAV calculations. REITs are not just a portfolio of properties. REITs are companies that buy, sell, develop, finance, operate, and renovate the properties. So keep in mind that the investment is a business—not just real estate. Factors such as the strength of the management, the "trade name" of the REIT, the loyalty of its tenants, and other factors that can affect a business must all be considered.

Conclusion

The resurgence of real estate investment trusts (REITs) in the early 1990s is another indication of the extent that real estate has become "securitized." Compared with traditional methods of investing, real estate–backed securities appear to be gaining in importance because of their marketability, the public accountability of management, and numerous other reasons. REITs allow investors to participate in a portfolio of properties that may be geographically diversified and professionally managed. REITs own assets that consist of commercial properties, supplies, and intellectual capital, and manage those assets to maximize profit. Mutual funds, in contrast, own claims on the earnings produced by assets that are entirely under the management of others. Further, REITs usually pay no taxes so long as they pass through as dividends to investors most of the cash flow produced from managing the portfolio. Accounting practices for depreciation and amortization and the resultant effects on net income may allow a portion of the tax on REIT dividends to be deferred. Today the market value of REITs exceeds $816 billion, and many of the premier real estate operators in the United States are operating within the REIT format, so market research and analysis for individual REITs and the industry are widely available from investment banks and other investment firms.

Key Terms

book value per share, *714*
blended capitalization rate, *718*
cash available for distribution
(CAD), *706*
dividend yield, *701*
earnings multiple, *714*
earnings per share (EPS), *715*
earnings yield, *714*

FFO multiple, *714*
FFO yield, *714*
funds from operations
(FFO), *700*
Gordon dividend discount
model, *716*
net asset value (NAV), *704*

net income from
operations, *714*
real estate investment trust
(REIT), *690*
recovery of capital (ROC), *715*
umbrella partnership REIT
(UPREIT), *692*

Useful Web Sites

www.reit.com—The Web site for the National Association of Real Estate Investment Trusts (NAREIT). It provides programs, statistics, publications, and research, as well as information about REITs and REIT investing.

www.investopedia.com—This site is a complete, unbiased, easy-to-understand educational guide to investing and personal finance. It provides the biggest financial dictionary on the Web, hundreds of articles and tutorials, and an investing simulator where you can practice managing a portfolio without putting your money at risk.

www.riskgrades.com—RiskGrade™ Measure is an open and transparent benchmark to measure the risk of the world's financial assets.

www.snl.com/sectors/real-estate—This Web site provides fundamental financial data on more than 230 REITs, REOCs, and homebuilders. It gives detailed, descriptive property data, cost and performance data, and property mapping. It also is a good source for analyst coverage, FFO estimates, proprietary AFFO, and NAV consensus estimates.

www.iirealestate.com/reitcafe_talk.aspx—This Web site provides numerous podcast programs focused on the REIT industry, consensus NAV estimates, REIT company conference calls in podcast format, and up-to-the-minute news on the industry.

Questions

1. What are the general requirements regarding income, investments, and dividends with which a REIT must comply to maintain its qualification to be taxed as a REIT?

2. What are the two principal types of REITs?

3. List and characterize equity REITs based on their property types.

4. What is the difference between earnings per share (EPS), funds from operations (FFO), adjusted funds from operations (AFFO), and dividends per share?

5. Explain how an investor in an equity REIT may receive a current dividend, part of which may be tax-deferred.

6. What are some important lease provisions which investors should be aware of when analyzing the financial statements of REITs?

7. What is a mortgage REIT?

Problems

1. You have been presented with the following set of financial statements for National Property Trust, a REIT that is about to make an initial stock offering to the public. This REIT specializes in the acquisition and management of warehouses. Your firm, Blue Street Advisors, is an investment management company that is considering the purchase of National Property Trust shares. You have been asked to prepare a financial analysis of the REIT.

National Property Trust

Panel A. Operating Statement Summary

Net revenue	$100,000,000
Less:	
Operating expenses	40,000,000
Depreciation and amortization	22,000,000
General and administrative expenses	6,000,000
Management expense	3,000,000
Income from operations	29,000,000
Less:	
Interest expense*	6,400,000
Net income (loss)	$ 22,600,000

*At 8% interest only.

Panel B. Balance Sheet Summary

Assets	
Cash	$ 51,500,000
Rents receivable	2,500,000
Properties @ cost	700,000,000
Less: Accumulated depreciation	450,000,000
Properties—net	250,000,000
Total net assets	$304,000,000

Liabilities	
Short term	$ 12,000,000
Mortgage debt*	80,000,000
Total	92,000,000
Shareholder equity†	212,000,000
Total liabilities and equity	$304,000,000

*At 8% interest only.
†10,000,000 shares outstanding.

> a. Develop a set of financial ratios that will provide Blue Street Advisors with useful informa-
> tion in the evaluation and comparison of National Property Trust with other REITs.
>
> b. Your research also indicates that the shares of comparable REITs specializing in warehouse
> acquisitions in the same regions are selling at dividend yields in the range of 8 percent. Price
> multiples for these REITs are about 12× current FFO. What price range does this suggest
> for National shares? What does this price range imply about the amount of dividend that
> National would have to pay to be in line with comparable REITs?
>
> c. What is the NAV for National Property Trust assuming that a blended capitalization rate of
> 10 percent would be applicable for the properties owned by Blue Street Advisors?

2. Robust Properties is planning to go public by creating a REIT that will offer 1 million shares
of stock. It is currently trying to develop a pro forma set of financial statements. Robust is
faced with a number of questions about its handling of some accounting and financial disclosure issues.

Robust Properties

I. Major Financial Information:
a. Assets—properties (actual cost)	$100,000,000
b. Depreciable basis—buildings only	$80,000,000
c. Useful life	40 years
d. Operating expenses	38% of rents
e. Management expenses—third parties	5% of rents
f. General and administrative expenses	3% of rents
g. Mortgage @ 8% interest only, 10 years	$30,000,000
h. Financing fees	$900,000

II. Lease Information:
a. Average lease term	5 years
b. Leasable space	1,000,000 sf.
c. Base rents (year 1)	$15 psf.
d. Escalation factor—rents per year	5%
e. Lease commissions	4% of year 1 rent
f. Tenant improvements	$10 psf.

The management of Robust Properties has asked you to prepare preliminary pro forma financials for the next *three years*. Specifically, you should have (1) a *beginning* balance sheet, (2) operating statements for each of the next three years, and (3) all relevant financial ratios for year 1 results only. Robust will pay all financing fees, tenant improvements, and lease commissions upon commencing operations. It would like to pay a minimum dividend of $4.00 per share.

In preparing your pro forma operating statements, Robust wants you to consider the effects of reporting in the following two ways:

a. What would EPS, FFO, and ROC be under both approaches? How should Robust think about its accounting policy?

Approach	(1)	(2)
Lease commissions	Amortize, 5 years	Expense in year 1
Finance fees	Amortize, 10 years	Expense in year 1
Tenant improvements	Depreciate, 40 years	Depr. over 5-year lease term
Buildings	Depreciate, 40 years	Depr., 40 years

3. Atlantis REIT expects an income of $8.00 per share. This includes a deduction of $2.00 per share for depreciation. Atlantis did not have any gains from the sale of real estate. Its properties are mainly apartments, and you believe that apartments are currently selling on average at about an 8 percent cap rate. Atlantis has 1 million shares outstanding and its balance sheet shows liabilities of $40 million. Comparable REITs have FFO multiples of about 10. Atlantis is expected to pay a dividend during the next fiscal year of $6.00 per share and to increase those dividends at about 2 percent per year in the future. Investors in REITs like Atlantis usually expect a return of about 12 percent.

a. What is the FFO and value per share based on an FFO multiple?

b. What value per share is indicated using a dividend discount model?

c. What is the value per share implied by the net asset value of the properties?

Chapter

22

Real Estate Investment Performance and Portfolio Considerations

Introduction

Thus far, our discussion of risk and required rates of return has stressed a methodology or an approach that should be used when evaluating a specific project or mortgage financing alternative. In this chapter, we provide some insight into the measurement of return and risk for various real estate investment vehicles and investment portfolios.

We will apply concepts and methodologies based on financial theory and demonstrate possible applications to real estate investments. The use of many of these applications is gaining in importance to institutional investors, such as life insurance companies, investment advisors, consultants to pension funds, bank trust departments, and other entities that manage portfolios with real estate assets. Portfolio managers must be able to measure the performance of real estate assets and be able to compare it to the performance of stocks, bonds, and other investments. Also, many portfolio managers are interested in knowing how well investment portfolios perform when real estate investments are *combined* with other securities. In the following chapter, we will extend these concepts to discuss how to compare the performance of a portfolio with benchmarks and try to determine why there was any difference in performance.

The Nature of Real Estate Investment Data

When measuring the investment performance of something as broadly defined as real estate, one must keep many things in mind. Ideally, to measure real estate investment performance, we would like to have data on prices for all investment property transactions—ranging from hotels to warehouses to apartment units—taking place in the economy, a detailed description of the land, improvements, and cash flows produced by these properties. We would also like to have data on repeated sales of the same properties over time. We could then calculate various measures of return on investment over time. Unfortunately, such a data series, or even an adequate sample of transactions in the many areas of real estate, is not available because the market is one in which the price for a relatively nonhomogeneous asset is negotiated between two parties. Generally, this price does not have to be disclosed to any public or private agency. Hence, unlike securities markets, there is no centralized collection of real estate transactions and operating income data.[1]

Because of these limitations, current attempts to measure real estate investment performance are based on limited data that are made available from a few select sources. The available data may not be representative of (1) the many types of properties, (2) the many geographic areas in which commercial real estate is located, or (3) the frequency of transactions indicative of real estate investment activity in the economy as a whole. Consequently, you must be careful when making generalizations about real estate performance.

Sources of Data Used for Real Estate Performance Measurement

In this section, we provide information on two sources of real estate data that are used to a limited extent when measuring real estate investment performance. We also consider investment returns from data that are available on common stocks, corporate bonds, and government securities. Exhibit 22–1 summarizes the data available for these investments. We rely on two sources for real estate returns in this chapter. The first is security prices as represented by real estate investment trust (REIT) shares. The second data source is based on estimates of value of individual properties owned by pension plan sponsors. Note that the primary differences in these data is that one source is based on real estate–backed securities and the other is based on estimates of individual properties.

REIT Data: Security Prices

One of the two sources of data used to produce investment returns on real estate in this chapter is based on REITs. The National Association of Real Estate Investment Trusts REIT Share Price Index (**NAREIT Index**) is a monthly index based on ending market prices for shares owned by REIT investors. Data for this series are available beginning with January 1972 and include all REITs actively traded on the New York NYSE MKT LLC Stock Exchange as well as the Nasdaq National Market System.[2]

The data used in this chapter are based on only those REITs that *own* real estate, or equity REITs. NAREIT compiles a monthly index for equity REITs based on month-end prices and dividends on securities owned by investors in each equity REIT contained in the index. Hence, the prices of REIT shares are determined by how successful investors believe the trustees of an individual REIT will be in finding properties at favorable prices, managing them, and then selling them. While equity REIT share prices certainly reflect investors' perceptions of the quality, diversity, and risk of real estate assets owned, investors are also evaluating the effectiveness of trustees in their valuation of equity REIT securities. Further, when purchasing shares, investors do not give up as much liquidity as they would if they acquired and managed real estate assets directly, because a continuous auction market (e.g., NYSE) exists in which shares are traded. Thus, investing in an equity REIT may be less risky than investing directly in real estate.

---

[1] In some states, actual transaction prices must be disclosed to property tax assessors. However, other data relating to property characteristics and operating cash flows are generally not available.

[2] Obtained from various publications of the National Association of Real Estate Investment Trusts, Washington, DC.

Hybrid and Mortgage REITs

A mortgage REIT investment return series and a hybrid REIT return series are also shown in Exhibit 22–1. The mortgage REIT index is based on security prices of shares outstanding in REITs that specialize in acquiring various types of mortgage loans on many types of properties. Hence, when investing in a mortgage REIT, an investor is buying equity shares in an entity whose assets are primarily mortgage loans. Hybrid REITs operate by buying real estate *and* by acquiring mortgages on both commercial and residential real estate.

EXHIBIT 22–1

Common Sources of Data Used for Measuring Investment Performance

Real Estate–Equity Returns	Description of Data
NAREIT—Equity REIT Share Price Index and Dividend Yield Series	Monthly index computed based on share prices of REITs that own and manage real estate assets. Security prices used in the index are obtained from the New York Stock Exchange (NYSE), NYSE MKT LLC, and National Association of Security Dealers Automated Quotation (Nasdaq) system. Divided data are collected by NAREIT. Properties owned may be levered or unlevered. Index values are available from 1972 to the present.
NAREIT—Mortgage REIT Share Price Index and Dividend Yield Series	Monthly index computed on share price data of REITs that make primarily commercial real estate loans (construction, development, and permanent), although some make or purchase residential loans (both multifamily and single family). Prices obtained from NYSE, NYSE MKT LLC and Nasdaq market system. Dividend data are collected by NAREIT. Monthly index data available from 1972 to the present.
NAREIT—Hybrid REIT Index	Monthly index compiled by NAREIT from share prices and dividends for REITs that (1) own properties and (2) make mortgage loans. Sources of data are the same as for equity and mortgage REITs. Index values are available from 1972 to the present.
NCREIF Property Index—National Council of Real Estate Investment Fiduciaries	NCREIF members contribute data based on about 5,000 properties, with an aggregate market value of about $200 billion, that are owned by pension fund plan sponsors through investment managers. An index is calculated quarterly and data consist of (1) net operating income and (2) beginning- and end-of-quarter appraised values for all properties. Actual sale prices are used, as available. Quarterly index values are available from 1978 to the present.
Common stocks— Standard & Poor's (S&P) 500	Daily index based on common stock prices for the 500 corporations with the highest market value of common stock outstanding. Data available from the financial press. Dividend data compiled by Wilshire and Associates and included in a monthly and annual total return index by Ibbotson Associates, Chicago. Daily index data available from 1926 to the present.
Corporate bonds— Barclays Capital U.S. Aggregate Bond Index	The U.S. Aggregate Bond Index covers the USD-denominated, investment-grade, fixed-rate, taxable bond market of SEC-registered securities. The index includes bonds from the Treasury, government-related, corporate, MBS (agency fixed-rate and hybrid ARM pass-throughs), ABS, and CMBS sectors. The U.S. Aggregate Bond Index is a component of the U.S. Universal Index in its entirety. The index was created in 1986, with index history backfilled to January 1, 1976.
Government securities	U.S. Treasury bills and bonds. Price data obtained from *The Wall Street Journal.* A monthly total return series compiled by Ibbotson Associates, Chicago. Daily index data available from 1926 to the present.

NCREIF Property Index: Property Values

The NCREIF Property Index measures the historic performance of income-producing properties either (1) acquired by open-end or commingled investment funds that sell investment units owned by qualified pension and profit-sharing trusts, or (2) acquired by investment advisors and managed on separate account bases. The data incorporated in the **NCREIF Index** are based on the performance of properties managed by members of the National Council of Real Estate Investment Fiduciaries (NCREIF).[3] Quarterly rates of return are calculated for all properties included in the index and are based on two distinct components of return: (1) net operating income less capital expenditures and (2) the quarterly change in property market value (appreciation or depreciation). The NCREIF Index contains data on five major property categories: apartment complexes, office buildings, industrial (warehouses, office/showrooms/research and development facilities), retail properties (including regional, community, and neighborhood shopping centers as well as freestanding store buildings), and hotels. Property values are based on either appraised values or, for properties that are sold, net sales proceeds, which are entered as the final market value in the quarter in which the property is sold. The index returns represent an aggregate of individual property returns calculated quarterly before deduction of investment advisory fees. The quarterly series is calculated by summing the increase or decrease in the value of each property plus its net operating income less capital expenditures for the quarter. To obtain changes in value, *quarterly appraisals* are made, and when sales occur, actual transaction prices negotiated by the buyer and seller are a part of the index.

Data Sources for Other Investments

In contrast to the scarcity of real estate return data, data on financial assets are plentiful and easy to obtain. In this chapter, we will also develop measures of investment performance for common stocks from the Standard & Poor's 500 Index of Common Stocks (S&P 500), U.S. Treasury bills (T-bills), longer term U.S. Treasury bonds, and long-term corporate bonds contained in the Barclays Capital U.S. Aggregate Bond Index. These indexes (see Exhibit 22–1) are generally computed daily, weekly, monthly, quarterly, and annually and are published regularly in the financial press.

Cumulative Investment Return Patterns

A series of historic total return indexes (see Exhibit 22–2) have been developed to begin the discussion of real estate equity investment performance. We have included three equity indexes: the S&P 500, EREIT (equity REITs), and NCREIF Property Index. Debt securities are represented by indexes for T-bills and government bonds (for sources, see Exhibit 22–1). These indexes are cumulative total returns based on quarterly data for each security: Each series is indexed at 100 beginning in 1985 (1Q) and is compiled through 2009 (2Q) and includes reinvestment of dividends, income, or interest as appropriate.[4]

The patterns indicate that $100 invested from the end of 1985 through 2009 would have produced the greatest total return (based on quarterly price changes and reinvestment of all dividends, interest, or income) if it had been invested in securities comprising the S&P 500 index. Total return rankings of the other indexes were as follows: Equity REITs, NCREIF Index, Bond index, and T-bills. We stress, however, that although these return patterns are informative, it should not be implied that each investment is equivalent in *risk*. When we

---

[3] See the *NCREIF Real Estate Performance Report,* various issues, published by the National Council of Real Estate Fiduciaries (Chicago), www.NCREIF.org.

[4] Dividends are included for the S&P 500 and EREITs. Net operating income is included in the NCREIF Index. Interest is included in the corporate bond index. T-bills include price changes only as no interest is paid on these instruments. They are bought and sold at discounts to maturity.

EXHIBIT 22–2   Cumulative Total Returns for REITs, S&P 500, NCREIF, Bonds, and T-Bill Indexes, 1985–2014

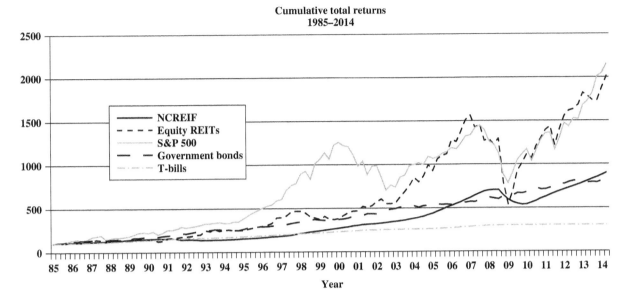

attempt to compare different securities, cumulative return data must be broken down into an appropriate time series so that various measures of volatility can be calculated to provide some idea about the relative risk of each security. It should be stressed that when we analyze investments, returns provide us with only one-half of the information that we need. Information on the risk characteristics of investment are equally important.

Computing Holding Period Returns

While the cumulative total returns shown in Exhibit 22–2 are useful information, additional insight into the risk-return characteristics of each security can be obtained by examining returns over shorter time periods. The most fundamental unit of measure used by portfolio managers to measure investment returns for individual securities, or a class of securities in a portfolio, is the **holding period return (*HPR*).** This is generally defined as follows:

$$HPR = \frac{P_t - P_{t-1} + D_t}{P_{t-1}}$$

where P_t is the end-of-period price for the asset, or value of an index for an investment, or index representing a class of investments, whose performance is being assessed; P_{t-1} is the beginning-of-period value; and D represents any dividends or other cash payouts that may have occurred during the period over which the *HPR* is being measured.

An example of how holding period returns are calculated for a hypothetical security index is demonstrated in Exhibit 22–3. The first quarter's return was calculated by subtracting the end-of-period value and dividing by the beginning-of-period value. This example assumes that any dividends have been reinvested so that the *HPR* is only affected by price changes. The following chapter goes into more detail into the calculation of *HPRs* for real estate when there are cash flow distributions during the quarter. The arithmetic mean, variance, standard deviation, and coefficient of variation have also been calculated. These measures will be used in our discussion of risk later in the chapter. The *HPR* for the first quarter in the series was 13.49 percent. The mean *HPR*, or, $\overline{HPR}$ of all quarterly returns in the series was 1.09 percent.

An alternative way of considering these return data is to calculate the **geometric mean return.** This return is calculated by finding the *n*th root of the product of each quarterly

EXHIBIT 22–3
Sample Computation of Holding Period Returns (*HPRs*) and Related Statistics: Hypothetical Security Index

www.mhhe.com/bf15e

Period Ending	Index	HPR	HPR − $\overline{HPR}$	(HPR − $\overline{HPR}$)²
Quarter				
1	673.7	—	—	—
2	764.6	0.1349	0.1240	0.0154
3	787.6	0.0301	0.0192	0.0004
4	803.6	0.0203	0.0094	0.0001
5	802.5	−0.0014	−0.0123	0.0002
6	886.3	0.1044	0.0935	0.0087
7	890.6	0.0049	−0.0061	0.0000
8	855.3	−0.0396	−0.0505	0.0026
9	773.1	−0.0961	−0.1070	0.0115
10	844.3	0.0921	0.0812	0.0066
11	867.8	0.0278	0.0169	0.0003
12	878.5	0.0123	0.0014	0.0000
13	874.4	−0.0047	−0.0156	0.0002
14	895.6	0.0242	0.0133	0.0002
15	948.5	0.0591	0.0482	0.0023
16	982.6	0.0360	0.0250	0.0006
17	952.5	−0.0306	−0.0415	0.0017
18	914.5	−0.0399	−0.0508	0.0026
19	911.8	−0.0030	−0.0139	0.0002
20	780.7	−0.1438	−0.1547	0.0239
21	804.9	0.0310	0.0201	0.0004
		Σ0.2181		Σ0.0779

$$\text{1st quarter } HPR = (764.6 - 673.7) \div 673.7 = 0.1349$$
$$\text{Mean } HPR = \overline{HPR} = \Sigma HPR \div n = 0.2181/20 = 0.0109$$
$$\text{Variance} = \sigma^2 = \Sigma (HPR - \overline{HPR})^2 \div n = 0.0779/20 = 0.0039$$
$$\text{Standard deviation} = \sigma = \sqrt{\sigma^2} = \sqrt{.0039} = 0.0624$$
$$\text{Coefficient of variation} = 0.0624 \div 0.0109 = 5.7219$$
$$\text{Geometric mean return} = \sqrt[n]{(1 + HPR_1)(1 + HPR_2)\cdots(1 + HPR_n)} - 1 = .0089$$

HPR in series multiplied together, minus 1 (see bottom of Exhibit 22–3). The geometric mean return was equal to .89 percent, a measure of the quarterly *compounded* rate of return that an investor would have earned on $1 invested in the index during the period.

Although the values of the arithmetic mean and geometric mean are sometimes very close, this will not always be the case, particularly if values in the series rise and fall sharply or the series is longer than the sample shown in the exhibit. There is a distinct conceptual difference between the arithmetic and geometric mean returns. The geometric mean is used by portfolio managers when considering the performance of an investment and is expressed as a compound rate of interest from the beginning to the end of a specific period of time. **Arithmetic mean returns** are simple averages (not compounded) and are widely used in statistical studies spanning very long periods of time.[5]

[5] The geometric mean is considered superior to the arithmetic mean when the past performance of an investment is being considered for a specified period of time, say, from the date of purchase until the present time, or for an investment portfolio where funds are flowing in and out and the investment base is changing. For example, suppose the price of a security is 100, 110, 100 at the end of each of three consecutive years. The *HPRs* are 10 percent and −9.09 percent. The arithmetic mean is .45 percent; however, the geometric mean is zero. The latter result occurs because the beginning and ending security prices are equal. This return better represents the performance of a security from the time of purchase until the present. Arithmetic mean returns are used in statistical studies where some inference about the future is based on averages of past performance. In these cases, an entire series of returns may be used to justify a long-term future decision and no specific time interval is considered any more important than another.

EXHIBIT 22–4
Summary Statistics of Performance Measures for Investment Alternatives

	CPI	Govt Bond	S&P 500	T-Bills	NCREIF	EREIT
Arithmetic mean	0.70%	1.85%	3.06%	0.95%	1.92%	3.11%
Standard deviation	0.79%	2.50%	8.25%	0.63%	2.21%	9.29%
Coefficient of variation	0.56	1.35	2.70	0.66	1.15	2.99
Geometric mean	0.69%	1.82%	2.71%	0.95%	1.90%	2.66%

Exhibit 22–4 contains summary statistics for various investments that we have chosen to include in the chapter. Note that for each of the return series, we have calculated quarterly arithmetic mean and geometric mean returns and related statistics. The exhibit also includes data for the consumer price index (CPI).

Comparing Investment Returns

We can now begin to compare total returns for the various investment categories contained in Exhibit 22–4. A number of patterns should be apparent from the data. The geometric mean returns (also called *time-weighted returns* by many portfolio managers) show that from 1985 to 2014, stocks constituting the Standard & Poor's 500 Index (S&P 500) produced quarterly returns of 2.71 percent. Equity REIT (NAREIT) returns were 2.66 percent, which were slightly below the S&P 500 returns. Returns for government bonds were 1.82 percent, followed by returns on the NCREIF Index, which were 0.95 percent, and T-bills (1.82%).

HPRs and Inflation

All returns shown in Exhibit 22–4 may also be compared with the quarterly rate of inflation, as represented by the CPI, which was 0.69 percent. The comparison with the CPI provides some insight into whether returns from each investment category exceeded the rate of inflation (thereby earning *real* returns).

Comparing Risk Premiums

In addition to returns, risk premiums may be calculated for each investment class relative to T-bills. Risk premiums may also be calculated for each investment relative to all other investments. For example, during the 1985–2014 period, EREITs earned an average *risk premium* of 1.71 percent per quarter, in excess of T-bills (2.66%−0.95%). T-bills are generally used to represent a riskless investment; hence, T-bill returns provide a measure of a risk-free return. Investors in EREITs would also have earned a premium of 0.84 percent relative to returns on government bonds (2.66%−1.82%). When compared to the NCREIF Index, which provided returns of 1.90 percent compounded quarterly, EREIT returns were higher by 0.76 percent. We should recall, however, that the NCREIF Index is compiled on an *unleveraged* basis; that is, the properties in the index were purchased on an all-cash basis, or "free and clear" of debt. Hence, a more appropriate comparison for the NCREIF Property Index would be relative to equity REITs that purchase properties on an all-cash basis, or unleveraged basis, because EREIT returns include the effects of leverage, while the NCREIF Index does not. Hence, EREITs are more risky. Therefore, holding all else constant, a premium should be earned on EREIT shares relative to returns based on the NCREIF Index.

Risk, Return, and Performance Measurement

While comparing investment returns is an important starting point in evaluating investment performance, it represents only one part of the analysis. We know from material presented earlier that investments that produce higher returns usually exhibit greater price volatility and are generally *riskier* than investments that produce lower returns. In cases involving *individual real estate* investments, such risks may be a function of the type of property, its location, design, lease structure, and so on. Those attributes, and the attendant risks associated with those attributes, can be thought of as a type of *business risk*.

Another source of risk occurs when real estate investments are leveraged. In these cases, *default risk* is present. Finally, because of the relative difficulty and time required to sell property, *liquidity risk* is certainly present. As we know, when these three major sources of risk are compared among properties or among alternative investments, when more risk is taken by investors, a risk premium, or higher investment return, should be earned by investors who bear that additional risk. One way of considering this risk-return relationship is to compute risk premiums, as we did above. A subjective assessment can then be made about whether risk premiums earned on riskier assets are adequate relative to the additional risk taken. An investor may then judge whether the premium earned on EREITs is sufficient to compensate for their added risk taken if EREITs are purchased instead of government bonds.

Another way of looking at the risk-return relationship is to think about the way in which business, default, and liquidity risks affect the pattern of returns that investors expect to earn. Over time, returns (dividends and price changes) on investments with more of these risks present are likely to exhibit more *variation* than investments with fewer of these risks. Recalling our earlier discussions on investment risk, we would expect a property with more risk to provide higher, but more variable, investment returns than a property with less risk. The point is that greater variability in market prices and cash flows can be thought of as commensurate with increased risk because an investor owning a risky asset with a highly variable price pattern (up and down) faces having to sell it for a more unpredictable price than a less risky asset. *The assumption that variability in asset returns represents risk and that premiums over what could be earned on a riskless investment represent the price of risk is the foundation for modern finance theory.* It is also a premise that must be understood if the techniques for risk-adjusting returns that are described next are to be used.

Risk-Adjusted Returns: Basic Elements

Given that the combined effects of the sources of risk described above will be reflected in the variability in investment returns, one way of taking into account investment risk when evaluating performance is to consider the variability of returns. The variability of holding period returns for specific assets or classes of assets enables one to make a better comparison among investments exhibiting different risk.

One approach that may be used to consider risk and returns is to compute the **coefficient of variation** of the returns. This is defined as the standard deviation of returns divided by the mean return (this can be based on either the arithmetic or geometric mean returns for a given investment or investment index). This concept is sometimes referred to as a *risk-to-reward ratio* and is intended to relate total risk, as represented by the standard deviation, to the mean return with the idea of determining how much return an investor could expect to earn relative to the total risk taken if the investment was made. For example, if an investor holds a portfolio containing securities with a mean return of 2 percent and a standard deviation of 3 percent, the coefficient of variation is 1.5. This may be interpreted as taking 1.5 units of risk for every unit of return that is earned.[6]

---

[6] This calculation also assumes that the risk premium, or return, is proportional to the risk taken on all investments by all investors. This assumption clearly *does not hold* for all investors, some of whom are more risk-averse than others. Even for the same investor, risk aversion cannot be considered for individual assets independently of one another. Rather, risk must be assessed in terms of the additional risk assumed relative to the total portfolio of assets owned. More will be said about this later.

An interesting comparison may now be made between the investment performance of EREITs and the NCREIF Index. Recall from Exhibit 22–4 that the NCREIF Index produced a lower mean return compared with EREITs. However, when mean returns for both investment categories are risk-adjusted, the NCREIF Index appears to have outperformed the EREIT index on a risk-adjusted basis. When the coefficients of variation for EREITs and the NCREIF Index are compared, the NCREIF had a lower coefficient of variation than the EREITs. A lower coefficient of variation suggests less risk relative to the return. Or conversely, higher return relative to the risk—thus, a higher *risk-adjusted* return.

It has already been pointed out that the NCREIF Index (1) does not include the effect of leverage in investment returns and (2) property values used to compute the NCREIF Index are based largely on quarterly appraisals plus a relatively small number of actual sale transactions. Using appraisals may have a smoothing effect on returns and reduce variability. If property appraisals (1) differ significantly from actual market values and (2) affect the variation in the index, then the NCREIF Index may not be representative of true real estate returns or volatility in those returns. For example, results in Exhibit 22–4 for EREITs indicate that the geometric mean return was 2.66 percent and the standard deviation of returns was 9.29 percent, resulting in a coefficient of variation of 2.99. This compares to a mean return of 1.90 percent and a standard deviation of 2.99 percent for the NCREIF Index and a coefficient of variation of 1.15. These results indicate a material difference in both return and risk for the two indexes. This difference may also be due to considerable differences in the types of properties (e.g., office, retail, apartment), in the geographic distribution of their locations (e.g., north, south, east, or west and suburban or urban sites), and in the investment strategies employed by investment managers (e.g., investing in raw land in predevelopment stages or in fully leased properties only). Such differences may affect the relative risk of investments in each index. Further, equity REIT shares are bought and sold in an *auction* market with continuous trading, whereas the individual properties that make up the NCREIF Index are bought and sold in a much more limited, *negotiated* market between parties. Premiums for liquidity and transaction costs when making such comparisons are really not well understood, nor have such premiums been isolated in research studies. Finally, the definition of income used in calculating the holding period returns for both indexes may not be exactly comparable because of advisory and other management fees that are deducted from REIT income, but not for properties in the NCREIF Index. More research must be done before the nature of risk and return for investments made in REIT shares versus direct investment in real estate, as represented by the NCREIF Index, is well understood.

Elements of Portfolio Theory

The preceding section dealt with one approach that may be used to compare investments by considering the investment's mean return and the standard deviation of those returns. The standard deviation was used as a measure of risk when making comparisons among investments. In addition, investors must consider the extent to which the acquisition of an investment affects the risk and return of a *portfolio* of assets. This question is very important because of the interaction between returns when investments are *combined* in a portfolio. This interaction may cause the variance of return on a portfolio to be less than the average of the individual investments. When investors add to an existing portfolio, it is important to understand how the acquisition of new assets may *impact* the return and risk of the entire portfolio.

Building a portfolio by considering the return and standard deviation of returns for *individual* investments will not always ensure that an optimum portfolio will be obtained. Indeed, any new asset that is being considered as an addition to a portfolio should be

EXHIBIT 22–5 Computation of the Mean *HPR* and Standard Deviation for a Hypothetical Portfolio Containing Stocks *i* and *j* in Equal Proportions

Quarter	Stock *i* HPR	Stock *j* HPR	$HPR_p = .5(HPR_i) + .5(HPR_j)$	$(HPR_p - \overline{HPR}_p)$	$(HPR_p - \overline{HPR}_p)^2$
1	0.1350	0.1407	0.1379	0.1145	0.0131
2	0.0301	0.0591	0.0446	0.0212	0.0004
3	0.0202	−0.0697	−0.0247	−0.0481	0.0023
4	−0.0013	0.0540	0.0264	0.0030	0.0000
5	0.1044	0.2133	0.1588	0.1354	0.0183
6	0.0048	0.0514	0.0281	0.0047	0.0000
7	−0.0396	0.0662	0.0133	−0.0101	0.0001
8	−0.0961	−0.2263	−0.1612	−0.1846	0.0341
9	0.0921	0.0587	0.0754	0.0520	0.0027
10	0.0279	0.0660	0.0469	0.0235	0.0006
11	0.0123	0.0039	0.0081	−0.0153	0.0002
12	−0.0047	0.0310	0.0132	−0.0102	0.0001
13	0.0242	0.0703	0.0472	0.0238	0.0006
14	0.0591	0.0880	0.0735	0.0501	0.0025
15	0.0360	0.1065	0.0713	0.0478	0.0023
16	−0.0307	0.0205	−0.0051	−0.0285	0.0008
17	−0.0399	−0.0302	−0.0351	−0.0585	0.0034
18	−0.0029	0.0629	0.0300	0.0066	0.0000
19	−0.1438	−0.1378	−0.1408	−0.1642	0.0270
20	0.0310	0.0895	0.0603	0.0369	0.0014
n = 20	0.2181	0.7180	0.4681		0.1100

$$\text{Stock } i \text{ holding period return } \overline{HPR}_i = 0.2181 \div 20 = 0.0109$$
$$\text{Stock } i \text{ variance} = \sigma^2_i = 0.0779 \div 20 = 0.0039$$
$$\text{Stock } i \text{ standard deviation} = \sigma_i = \sqrt{\sigma^2_i} = 0.0624$$
$$\text{Stock } j \text{ holding period return } \overline{HPR}_j = 0.7180 \div 20 = 0.0359$$
$$\text{Stock } j \text{ variance} = \sigma^2_j = 0.1741 \div 20 = 0.0087$$
$$\text{Stock } j \text{ standard deviation} = \sigma_j = \sqrt{\sigma^2_j} = 0.0933$$
$$\text{Portfolio}_p \text{ holding period return } \overline{HPR}_p = 0.4681 \div 20 = 0.0234$$
$$\text{Portfolio variance} = \sigma^2_p = (HPR_p - \overline{HPR}_p)^2 \div n = 01100/20 = 0.0055$$
$$\text{Portfolio standard deviation} = \sigma_p = \sqrt{\sigma^2_p} = 0.0742$$

judged on the grounds of "efficiency," that is, whether its addition to an existing portfolio will increase expected portfolio returns while maintaining, or lowering, portfolio risk. Alternatively, an investor may also judge whether the portfolio efficiency of an asset will lower portfolio risk while maintaining or increasing the expected portfolio return.[7]

To illustrate how the interaction between investment returns occurs, we consider the data in Exhibit 22–5. Returns in column 1 are calculated on quarterly *HPR*s for stock *i*, abbreviated as HPR_i. Returns in column 2 are the quarterly returns computed for stock *j* over the same time period. The statistics presented at the bottom of the exhibit indicate that the quarterly mean return for stock *j* was 3.59 percent and the standard deviation was 9.33 percent. The mean return for stock *i* was 1.09 percent, and the standard deviation of the return was 6.24 percent (calculations not shown). Obviously, risk and returns for these two investments are very different. Stock *j* produced both a higher mean return and higher standard deviation

---

[7] The basis for modern portfolio theory was developed by Harry Markowitz, "Portfolio Selection," *Journal of Finance* 7, no. 1 (March 1952), pp. 77–91.

(risk) when compared with the returns from stock *i*. Assuming that an investor was holding a portfolio *composed only* of stock *j* at the beginning of the investment period, the question to answer is, how would the addition of another investment (as represented by real estate stock *i*) affect the quarterly mean *portfolio* return and its standard deviation? Would the investor have been better off adding real estate securities to this portfolio?

Calculating Portfolio Returns

To demonstrate an approach that may be used to answer these questions, we will assume that both stocks *i* and *j* were *weighted equally* in one portfolio at the beginning of the period. We will then compute the mean return and standard deviation for the *combined portfolio* (see Exhibit 22–5). The mean return for the portfolio, $\overline{HPR}_p$, is calculated as

$$\overline{HPR}_p = W_i(\overline{HPR}_i) + W_j(\overline{HPR}_j)$$

$$= .5(.0109) + .5(.0359)$$

$$= .0055 + .0179$$

$$= .0234$$

where *W* represents the weights that securities *i* and *j* represent as a proportion of the total value of the portfolio (i.e., $W_i + W_j = 1.0$). Based on this calculation, we see that the *portfolio* return would have been 2.34 percent quarterly, which is less than what would have been earned on stock *j* alone. However, we cannot really conclude much from this result until we consider how portfolio *risk* may have been affected when the two investments were combined.

Portfolio Risk

To consider how total portfolio risk would have been affected by the *addition* of stock *i* to an existing portfolio consisting only of stock *j*, the standard deviation of the *new portfolio* returns is calculated (see Exhibit 22–5). Those results indicate that the portfolio standard deviation is 7.42 percent, which is far less than the standard deviation of stock *j*, which was 9.33 percent.

However, it is important to note that unlike the mean *HPR* for the portfolio, the *standard deviation of portfolio returns* for the two indexes is not equal to the simple weighted average of the individual standard deviations of the two indexes; that is, [(.5)(6.24%)] + [(.5)(9.33%)] does *not* equal the standard deviation of the portfolio returns. This is because when the returns of the two assets are combined, a greater-than-proportionate reduction in the variance in portfolio returns is achieved. In other words, there is *interaction* between the two returns in the sense that the pattern, or direction of movement, in each of the individual *HPR*s is not the same in each period.[8] Indeed, in some quarters, the *HPR*s for EREITs are positive and the *HPR*s for the stocks are negative. Hence, when combined in one portfolio, the returns on the portfolio are less volatile than the individual assets. The nature of this interaction is important to understand when measuring the risk of an investment portfolio because it demonstrates whether a portfolio investor will benefit from diversification.

---

[8] As shown in Exhibit 22–5, the portfolio standard deviation can be calculated each time weights for stocks change. Another method of computation for the two-security case can be made by simply changing the weights W_E and W_S for stocks *E* and *S* in the following equation: $[(W_E)^2(S_E)^2 + (W_S)^2(S_S)^2 + 2(W_S)(W_E)(S_S)(S_E)\rho_{SE}]^{1/2}$ = portfolio standard deviation, where *W* = weight of security types *E*, *S* (all *WS* must total 1), *S* = standard deviation of security, and ρ_{SE} is the coefficient of correlation between *S* and *E*. Exhibit 22–6 shows the calculations for the standard deviation for each security as well as the correlation between the securities.

EXHIBIT 22-6 Computation of Covariance for Stocks *i* and *j*

Period Ending Quarter	HPR Stock i	HPR Stock j	$HPR_i - \overline{HPR}_i$	$HPR_j - \overline{HPR}_j$	$(HPR_i - \overline{HPR}_i) \times (HPR_j - \overline{HPR}_j)$	Stock i $(HPR_i - \overline{HPR}_i)^2$	Stock j $(HPR_j - \overline{HPR}_j)^2$
1	0.1350	0.1407	0.1241	0.1048	0.0130	0.0154	0.0110
2	0.0301	0.0591	0.0192	0.0232	0.0004	0.0004	0.0005
3	0.0202	−0.0697	0.0093	−0.1056	−0.0010	0.0001	0.0111
4	−0.0013	0.0540	−0.0122	0.0181	−0.0002	0.0001	0.0003
5	0.1044	0.2133	0.0935	0.1774	0.0166	0.0087	0.0315
6	0.0048	0.0514	−0.0061	0.0155	−0.0001	0.0000	0.0002
7	−0.0396	0.0662	−0.0505	0.0303	−0.0015	0.0026	0.0009
8	−0.0961	−0.2263	−0.1070	−0.2622	0.0281	0.0115	0.0687
9	0.0921	0.0587	0.0812	0.0228	0.0019	0.0066	0.0005
10	0.0279	0.0660	0.0170	0.0300	0.0005	0.0003	0.0009
11	0.0123	0.0039	0.0014	−0.0320	−0.0000	0.0000	0.0010
12	−0.0047	0.0310	−0.0156	−0.0049	0.0001	0.0002	0.0000
13	0.0242	0.0703	0.0133	0.0344	0.0005	0.0002	0.0012
14	0.0591	0.0880	0.0482	0.0521	0.0025	0.0023	0.0027
15	0.0360	0.1065	0.0251	0.0706	0.0018	0.0006	0.0050
16	−0.0307	0.0205	−0.0416	−0.0154	0.0006	0.0017	0.0002
17	−0.0399	−0.0302	−0.0508	−0.0661	0.0034	0.0026	0.0044
18	−0.0029	0.0629	−0.0138	0.0270	−0.0004	0.0002	0.0007
19	−0.1438	−0.1378	−0.1547	−0.1737	0.0269	0.0239	0.0302
20	0.0310	0.0895	0.0201	0.0536	0.0011	0.0004	0.0029
$n = 20$	0.2181	0.7180			0.0940	0.0779	0.1741

$COV_{ij} = \Sigma[HPR_i - \overline{HPR}_i][HPR_j - \overline{HPR}_j] \div n$
$= 0.0940 \div 20$
$= 0.0047$

Correlation between stocks i and j
$= [COV_{ij}] \div [\sigma_i \, \sigma_j] = 0.8070$

Covariance and Correlation of Returns: Key Statistical Relationships

One important aspect of individual investment returns to consider is how the return on a prospective new asset will vary with returns on an existing portfolio. Clearly, if the asset is producing returns that move up and down in a pattern that is very *similar* to movements in portfolio returns, the inclusion of that asset in the portfolio will not reduce total variation (*risk*) by very much. This pattern, when considered with the mean of portfolio returns and mean return of the prospective asset, will give us an indication of how efficient the acquisition of an asset will be when combined with another asset or with an existing portfolio. Two statistics provide a numerical measure of the extent to which returns tend to either move together, in opposite directions, or have no relationship to one another. These statistics are the *covariance* and *correlation* between the two return series.

The **covariance** between returns on two assets is an *absolute* measure of the extent to which two data series (*HPR*s) move together over time. It is calculated for our example in Exhibit 22–6. Essentially, the covariance is computed for two investments by first finding the deviation of each investment's *HPR* from its mean ($\overline{HPR}$). These deviations for each security in each period are then multiplied and summed. The summed deviations are divided by the number of observations in each series. The result is the *covariance* or statistic that provides an *absolute* measure of the extent to which returns between two securities move together. In our example, the covariance between i and j is .47 percent.

Because the covariance was positive, the returns on the two securities tended to move *together,* or in the same direction, during the period over which we made the calculation. Hence, we have *positive covariance* between the two stocks. It is also possible to have *negative covariance,* indicating that returns tend to move in opposite directions. While the covariance measure is useful, it is somewhat difficult to interpret because it is an *absolute* measure of the relationship between returns. We would expect that very large covariance values may indicate a very strong relationship (either positive or negative) between investment returns. However, the covariance statistic can take on values ranging from $+\infty$ to $-\infty$, and, as a result, it is difficult to know when a covariance value is "large" or "small." Because of this problem, we need a method to gauge the importance of the statistic on a *relative* scale of importance. The coefficient of **correlation** (ρ) is used to obtain this *relative* measure or the extent to which one set of numbers moves in the same or opposite direction with another series. The formula for the correlation statistic ρ is

$$\rho_{ij} = COV_{ij} \div (\sigma_i \, \sigma_j)$$

In our example we have

$$\rho_{ij} = .0047 \div (.0624)(.0933)$$

$$= .8070$$

The correlation statistic may only range between $+1$ and -1; therefore, it is a much easier way to interpret the extent to which returns are related. For example, as the coefficient of correlation approaches $+1$, two series are said to move very closely together, or be highly correlated. Hence, given a change in one of the series, there is a high likelihood of a change in the other series in the same direction.[9] Conversely, as the coefficient approaches -1, the series are negatively correlated because they move in exactly opposite directions. Hence, given a change in one series, the other would be expected to move in the opposite direction. If the correlation coefficient is close to zero, the implication is that no relationship exists between the two series. In our example, a correlation coefficient of .8070 indicates a strong positive correlation between stocks i and j over the period considered because the coefficient has a positive sign and is much closer to $+1.0$ than it is to zero.[10]

What are some other important relationships at this point? It should be clear that if two investments are *highly positively correlated,* the reduction in the variance in portfolio returns (hence, risk) is likely to be smaller than if there is no correlation or negative correlation because, in the latter case, the distribution of two returns will be either unrelated or negatively related, and the interaction between returns will not be reinforced. If returns are negatively correlated, they will be offsetting and the sum of the deviations from the portfolio mean will be smaller after the security is added; hence, the standard deviation of portfolio returns will be lower (i.e., lower risk). Consequently, it should be stressed that anytime the correlation between returns on two assets is less than $+1$, *some* reduction in risk (standard deviation) may be obtained by combining investments, as opposed to holding one investment

---

[9] Obviously there would have to be an underlying cause-and-effect relationship between the two series to make an assertion that any past relationship can be used to predict a future relationship.

[10] When the coefficient of correlation has a value greater than .5, the association between two series is considered high. There are also statistical tests of significance that enable us to say with more confidence whether two series are correlated or whether the correlation statistic calculated between the series resulted from an unrepresentative sample taken from the underlying distribution of returns. For a discussion of correlation, normal distribution assumptions, and related statistics, see a standard college textbook on elementary statistics.

(or one portfolio) with higher standard deviation than the prospective investment. However, the potential for risk reduction is much greater as the correlation approaches −1.

Based on the foregoing analysis, it should be clear why the standard deviation of portfolio returns in our example is not equal to a simple, weighted average of the standard deviation of the two individual investment returns. Further, if variation in security returns is a reasonable representation of risk to investors, then it should become apparent that there may be some benefit, in the form of risk reduction, by *diversifying* an investment portfolio to include assets with returns that are negatively correlated, or assets with returns showing little or no correlation. Of course, the other critical dimension that has to be considered is how the *mean return* of the portfolio will be affected when the individual securities are combined. For example, if two securities have the *same* positive mean returns and these returns are perfectly, negatively correlated (e.g., −1), then it may be inferred that an investor can earn a positive portfolio return with zero risk if both investments are purchased (the standard deviation of the combined returns is zero). The possibility that this will ever occur is slight, however, because the likelihood of finding perfectly negatively correlated (−1) securities is small. However, many investments with returns that are negatively correlated, uncorrelated, or less than perfectly positively correlated may be candidates for addition to a portfolio on the grounds of efficiency outlined above. These basic elements of portfolio analysis should make the reader aware of a framework that may be used to consider many questions regarding risk and returns.

Portfolio Weighting: Trading Off Risk and Return

In our hypothetical example, we have seen that adding stock *i* to a portfolio containing stock *j* would have reduced portfolio risk (standard deviation) by a lesser amount (%) than the reduction in portfolio mean return. This implies that a portfolio containing both stocks (indexes) would not have been more efficient than a portfolio containing only one stock. However, in our computations, we assumed that *both assets were equally weighted.* Could a more optimal portfolio, that is, one containing some other combination of stocks that would have either increased returns relative to an increase in risk or maintained returns while decreasing risk, been attained by *varying the weight (proportion) of the two securities in the portfolio?* To answer this question, we first consider the *sample* of NCREIF and S&P 500 returns from Exhibit 22–4, or those returns that comprised the *period* 1985–2014. The arithmetic quarterly mean *HPR* for the S&P 500 index was 2.71 percent with a standard deviation of 8.25 percent, and the *HPR* for NCREIF was 1.90 percent with a standard deviation of 2.21 percent. The correlation between both return series was 0.1344 (see Exhibit 22–7).[11] Because the correlation coefficient was less than 1, some reduction in risk would have been possible by combining the two assets.

EXHIBIT 22–7
Correlation Matrix for Investment Alternatives: Quarterly Returns, 1978–2014

	CPI	Bonds	S&P 500	T-Bills	NCREIF	REITs
			1978–2014			
CPI	1					
Bonds	−0.2078	1				
S&P 500	0.0014	0.1047	1			
T-Bills	0.4764	0.1815	0.0375	1		
NCREIF	0.2980	−0.1212	0.1344	0.2895	1	
REITs	0.0818	0.2091	0.6169	0.0684	0.1525	1

[11] The correlations are calculated over a longer time period to capture the long-run correlation between the different assets.

Second, we want to understand the importance of weighting securities in a portfolio. To determine the optimal *weighting, all combinations* of both assets must be considered. In our example, the weight of each security was changed in increments of 10 percent, and the mean portfolio return and standard deviation were calculated for each weighting. The result is shown in Exhibit 22–8. The diagram shows all values lying between the two extreme cases, that is, the case where the portfolio would be composed entirely of S&P 500 stocks and no NCREIF properties and the case where the portfolio would be composed of 100 percent NCREIF properties and no S&P shares. Hence, the curve in the exhibit shows the *trade-off* between return and risk for the portfolio as the two asset classes are combined in varying proportions.

Note that even though the NCREIF Index had a lower mean *HPR* during this period, when compared with the S&P index (see Exhibit 22–4), diversification benefits may be realized by *combining* assets as opposed to holding only S&P 500 or NCREIF properties. This is illustrated in Exhibit 22–8.

In Exhibit 22–8, note that having a portfolio of 100 percent NCREIF has a lower return but greater risk than holding some S&P with NCREIF. This results from the diversification benefits of including both stocks (S&P) and properties (NCREIF) in a portfolio. The portion of the curve with a positive slope (returns increase as risk increases) is known as the *efficient frontier.* It represents the most efficient combination of securities that provides investors with maximum portfolio returns as portfolio risk increases. Returns below the efficient frontier (or in the interior of the ellipse) are *inferior* because there is always a better combination of securities that will increase returns for a given level of risk. Investors will choose the combination of securities along the efficient frontier in accordance with their willingness to take risk. Investors who are risk-averse would tend to hold a mix with more properties (NCREIF) in this example. Less risk-averse investors would tend to weigh stocks (S&P) more heavily in their portfolio. Holding all stocks (100% S&P) has the greatest expected return but also the greatest risk.

EXHIBIT 22–8 **Portfolio Returns of NCREIF and S&P 500 Stocks, 1978–2009**

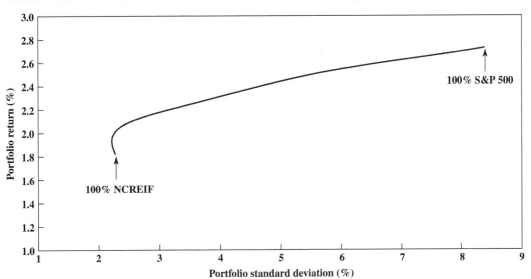

Real Estate Returns, Other Investments, and the Potential for Portfolio Diversification

From the preceding analysis, it should be clear that there are many different assets that have the potential to be combined efficiently in a portfolio that will provide an optimal risk-return relationship for investors. Clearly, our example consisting of only NCREIFs and S&P 500 assets shows this potential. However, many other assets can be considered by investors when selecting assets. One of the key relationships that indicate the potential for combining assets in a portfolio is the correlation between asset returns. Exhibit 22–7 is a *correlation matrix,* or table, that contains the coefficient of correlation for returns on all securities listed in Exhibit 22–4. The purpose of calculating these coefficients is to consider how various *investment vehicles* might be combined efficiently with various other assets when building a portfolio.

We can gain some insight into the question of whether portfolios containing certain securities would be more efficient if *real estate investment vehicles* were added. We will focus on this more narrow question, because to consider the question of what *the* optimum portfolio *should* contain would have to include an examination of the risk and returns for the global, or worldwide, set of securities and assets that are available to investors. Such a portfolio might contain bonds, stock, real estate, gold, jewelry, coins, stamps, and virtually any asset that can be owned by investors. Based on mean standard deviation of returns and covariance between returns, investors would hold portfolios containing the optimum combination of available investments. An efficient frontier, such as the one shown in our two-investment case in Exhibit 22–8, would also exist for this larger, diversified "market portfolio." If all investors made decisions based on whether or not the ratio of risk to return for the total portfolio would be improved, all investor portfolios would tend to be diversified and efficient. Returns on any additional investments would be evaluated on the basis of any incremental increases or decreases in total portfolio risk, and the risk premium paid by investors for these securities would reflect that incremental risk. In short, risk premiums for investments would be determined on the basis of the expected addition or reduction in portfolio risk and all investments would be priced in accordance with that relationship.[12]

In this section, we consider the question of portfolio performance, diversification, and real estate. Portfolio managers have seriously considered real estate as an investment class for only about 20 years. Only in recent years has equity ownership in real estate become widely available in a "securitized" form such as a REIT share or in ownership "units" in open- and closed-ended commingled investment funds. Also, regulatory restrictions governing pension funds have been relaxed to include real estate as an acceptable investment. However, many institutions, which heretofore considered only government securities, corporate bonds, and common stocks, have shown increasing interest in real estate.

We now consider the question of whether real estate investments are likely to provide **diversification benefits** to investors with portfolios consisting of some government securities, stocks, and bonds. In other words, we begin with some assumptions about the nature of existing investment portfolios. We then consider whether these portfolios could have benefited from diversifying by acquiring real estate investments over the period 1985–2009.

Portfolio Diversification: EREITs and Other Investments

Looking again at Exhibit 22–7, we can see what the historical (or ex-post) correlation in quarterly returns was for each investment relative to all others for the period 1978–2009.

---

[12] For additional information regarding capital market theory and efficient markets, see Z. Bodie, A. Kane, and A. Marcus, *Investments,* 8th ed. (Burr Ridge, IL, McGraw-Hill, 2009).

Focusing our attention on equity investments in real estate, we note, for example, that returns on EREITs tended to be positively correlated with common stocks (0.6169), bonds (0.2091), and T-bills (0.0684). This relationship suggests that because EREITs have less-than-perfect correlation with the S&P 500 and bonds and the correlation coefficient between both EREITs and T-bills is very low, there is a good chance that if this real estate investment were combined in a portfolio containing common stock, bonds, and T-bills, diversification benefits could be achieved. Furthermore, NCREIF has a negative coefficient with bonds (–0.1212), but a positive but low correlation with the S&P 500 (0.1344) and T-bills (0.2895). This suggests that adding direct investment in properties may provide more diversification benefits than just adding REITs.

To illustrate the diversification benefits of adding equity real estate to a portfolio of stocks and bonds, we will use the mean (arithmetic) returns from Exhibit 22–4 and the correlations from Exhibit 22–7.[13] Exhibit 22–9 shows two efficient frontiers. The lower frontier consists of only stocks (S&P 500) and bonds. The upper frontier includes stocks, bonds, and private real estate investments (NCREIF Index). Note that the frontier that includes real estate has higher returns at each level of risk (standard deviation). The only exception is the highest risk/highest return portfolio, which in both cases consists entirely of stocks. Including private real estate with stocks and bonds also provides a wider spectrum of risk-return combinations at the lower end of the frontier (i.e., where there is less return but lower levels of risk).

It should be noted that these results are based on historical returns over a specific time period and may not be indicative of future performance. Investors make investment decisions based on future or expected risks and returns. This example has used ex-post, or

EXHIBIT 22–9 **Efficient Frontiers**

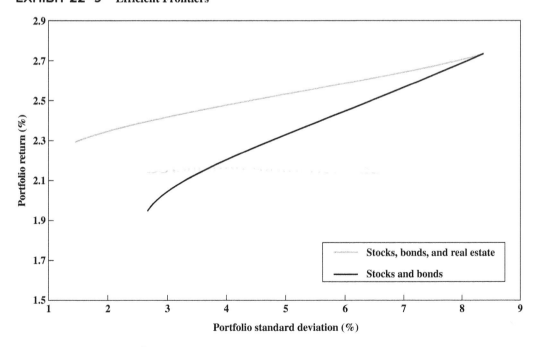

[13] In practice, we might use expected future returns rather than historical returns for this type of analysis. We use historic returns to illustrate the diversification benefits based on what was actually achieved for each asset.

past, returns to illustrate concepts. There is no assurance that these results will be repeated in the future. In practice, investors often use historic correlations as was done in this example unless there is evidence that there has been a significant change in the correlation between different assets. Similarly, historic standard deviations for securities are used unless there is a reason to believe that the underlying risk of the asset has changed. But expected future rather than historic returns are used for each asset. Historic returns are only used as one indication of what might be realistic to expect in the future.

We also used the NCREIF Index as an indication of the return and risk (standard deviation) for private real estate. The NCREIF Index has a very low mean return and standard deviation of returns. As noted in the beginning of this chapter, this index may not fully capture the true variability in returns for private real estate because it is based on appraised values rather than transaction prices. Some have argued that the use of appraised values may reduce or "smooth" the variation in returns. This does not mean that the estimates of value are erroneous. Rather, the appraisal process is such that sudden shifts in the market, as reflected in a few transactions, are not fully captured in appraised values until the change in market conditions can be sufficiently confirmed by additional market evidence. Thus, indexes based on appraised values may not fully capture quarterly changes in property values in an index like the NCREIF Index.

Public versus Private Real Estate Investments

We saw previously that the performance of private real estate as reflected in the NCREIF Index and the performance of REITs as reflected in the NAREIT Index were quite different in terms of historic returns, standard deviations, and correlations with other assets. For example, the standard deviation of the NAREIT Index is higher than that of the NCREIF Index. One explanation for this might be that the NCREIF Index does not capture all of the variability of returns because it is based on appraised values, as discussed earlier. An alternative explanation, however, is that when real estate is owned by publicly traded REITs, it takes on more of the risk of public markets in general. As we saw in Exhibit 22–7, REITs have a much higher correlation with the S&P 500 than NCREIF. Also, we saw that the NCREIF Index has a higher correlation with the CPI, indicating that it may be a better inflation hedge than REITs.

There is likely to be truth in both arguments—that appraisals reduce the variance of the true returns in the NCREIF Index but publicly traded REITs take on additional variance because they trade in more active markets that are influenced more by short-term flows of capital into and out of the stock market. To see what the difference in variability is between NCREIF and NAREIT, we have plotted the historic returns for each in Exhibit 22–10. Note that in order to better compare the returns over time, we have used a different scale for the NCREIF returns (-10% to $+8\%$) than for NAREIT returns (-50% to $+40\%$). The NAREIT Index clearly has more volatility in its returns than the NCREIF Index and the two indexes perform quite differently during many time periods.

Although some people argue about which index is a better indication of the performance of equity real estate, it is quite possible that the conclusion should be that both private real estate investments (represented by the NCREIF Index) and public real estate investments (represented by the NAREIT Index) could play a role in a portfolio. Both provide diversification benefits to a pure stock and bond portfolio, and there are advantages and disadvantages of each as an investment alternative. For example, REITs are more liquid than private real estate but the investor does not have control over decisions as to when to sell individual properties as he or she would by owning properties instead of shares of stock. The purpose of this chapter is not to suggest which type of investment is better for a particular investor, but rather to illustrate what tools an investor can use to evaluate the role of either one or both ways of including equity real estate in a portfolio.

Web App

Go to the Web site for the National Council of Real Estate Investment Fiduciaries (**www.ncreif.org**). Find the quarterly returns for the nation during the past year. (See data—NPI Returns on the Web site.) What is the recent trend in the returns for real estate? How does this compare with the trend in returns for stocks based on the S&P 500 or Dow Jones Industrial Average?

EXHIBIT 22–10   **NCREIF versus NAREIT Quarterly Returns, 1985–2014**

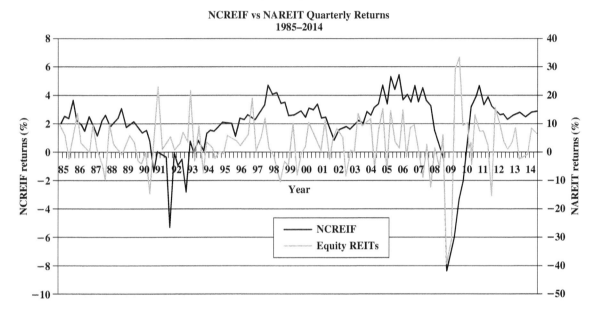

Real Estate Performance and Inflation

One final comparison of interest to portfolio managers is the relationship between real estate performance and *inflation.* More specifically, did real estate returns exceed the rate of inflation? To provide some insight into this question, we recall our earlier comparisons between the EREIT and NCREIF indexes and the CPI. In all cases, the real estate indexes exceeded the rate of growth in the CPI. This implies that at least for the period 1985–2009, real estate investments, as represented by the data used in Exhibit 22–4, exceeded the rate of inflation and produced real investment returns. Another question of importance is whether real estate returns are *correlated* with inflation. If we use the correlation matrix in Exhibit 22–7, it would appear that direct investment in properties represented by NCREIF provides a better inflation hedge. In this context it is important to realize that a *positive* correlation with inflation is desirable because it indicates that the asset is an inflation hedge. That is, if inflation increases, then returns also increase, which preserves the real rate of return.

Diversification by Property Type and Location

We have seen that when individual properties are combined in a portfolio, the risk of the portfolio is reduced when the properties are not correlated. Therefore, investors want to find properties that are not highly correlated with each other. This is often done by

Investors have long been interested in "socially responsible" or "ethical" investing. Seeking to follow their values and influence corporate behavior, socially responsible investors select investments that combine financial objectives with a commitment to social justice, economic development, or environmental quality. Today, an increasing number of institutional and individual property investors are doing the same, because property is at the leading edge of many social and environmental concerns. For example, according to the UN/World Meteorological Society, just over one-half of the greenhouse gas emissions produced worldwide come from operating residential and commercial buildings and the road transport of people and goods between them. Indeed, as much as 80 percent of the environmental impact per employee of service sector companies is associated with the design, location, and operation of their premises.

Today, a viewpoint is emerging among property investors that social and environmental issues—from poverty and crime to global warming and natural hazards—can have significant material consequences for their investment portfolios. Shifting consumer preferences, environmental risks, government regulations, legal liabilities, expensive resource and material inputs, and pressure from affected stakeholders are converging to make it both financially risky to ignore social and environmental concerns and financially beneficial to address them in the process of real estate investing.

This view has led to the emergence of *Responsible Property Investing (RPI)*, or portfolio, asset, and property management activities that go beyond compliance with minimum legal requirements to better manage the risks and opportunities associated with environmental and social issues in property investing. RPI encompasses a variety of efforts to address ecological integrity, community development, and human fulfillment in the course of profitable real estate investing. It seeks to reduce risk and pursue opportunities while helping to address the challenging issues facing present and future generations.

RPI is neither philanthropy nor altruism. While it is true that some investors and executives are motivated by ethics and values, most RPI investors are primarily driven by concern for risk and return and the opportunity to outperform. Today there are investment funds focused on brownfields, green buildings, affordable housing, urban revitalization, historic preservation, student learning, fair labor practices, and other strategies that have social and environmental merit and can generate competitive returns. Meanwhile, asset managers with more conventional portfolios are implementing eco-efficiency strategies, fair labor practices, and stakeholder engagement programs without harming, and sometimes even helping, the bottom line.

Economists have begun to research the financial consequences of RPI. So far, they're finding that it can improve rents, net operating incomes, market values, and investment returns. Although much more work remains to be done, studies so far suggest that investors can do well and do good with RPI.

There are two types of financially sound RPI strategies: no cost and value added. With *no cost strategies*, managers find ways to improve the social or environmental performance of their properties at zero added expense. Turning out the lights in unoccupied areas, for example, fights global warming and reduces energy bills. *Value-added strategies*, on the other hand, require some initial outlay, but pay for themselves by either increasing net incomes (via higher rents or lower costs) or reducing risk premiums (by lower environmental, depreciation, or marketability risk). Designing a socially beneficial child care facility into a new project may cost more, but the added costs may be offset by higher rents and occupancy.

Because so many factors contribute to the social and environmental performance of buildings, RPI touches upon literally dozens of property location, design, management, and investment strategies. They can be grouped, however, into 10 elements:

[1] Contributed by Professor Gary Pivo, University of Arizona.

1. *Energy conservation:* Green power generation and purchasing, energy-efficient design, conservation retrofitting.
2. *Environmental protection:* Water conservation, solid waste recycling, habitat protection.
3. *Voluntary certifications:* Green building certification, certified sustainable wood finishes, and so on.
4. *Less auto-dependent development:* Transit-oriented development, walkable communities, mixed-use development.
5. *Urban revitalization and adaptability:* Infill development, flexible interiors, brownfield redevelopment.
6. *Health and safety:* Site security, avoidance of natural hazards, first-aid readiness.
7. *Worker well-being:* Plazas, onsite child care, indoor environmental quality, barrier-free design.
8. *Corporate citizenship:* Regulatory compliance, sustainability disclosure and reporting, independent boards, adoption of voluntary codes of ethical conduct, stakeholder engagement.
9. *Social equity and community development:* Fair labor practices, affordable/social housing, community hiring and training.
10. *Local citizenship:* Quality design, minimum neighborhood impacts, considerate construction, community outreach, historic preservation, no undue influence on local governments.

The growth of RPI could be very consequential. All forms of socially responsible investment (SRI) in the United States encompassed $2.71 trillion in 2007, according to the Social Investment Forum. If just 10 percent of the SRI market was committed to real estate, it would equal nearly 90 percent of the total market capitalization of the U.S. REIT industry.

Today, with so many private real estate investment funds committed to green buildings and many more committed to social issues such as affordable housing, community development, and fair wages and benefits, it seems clear that RPI has become a major trend in property development and finance.

To read more about Responsible Property Investing, visit:

Responsible Property Investing Center (*www.responsibleproperty.net*)

UNEP Finance Initiative Property Working Group (*www.unepfi.org*)

Urban Land Institute, Responsible Property Investment Council (*www.uli.org*)

Professor Pivo's homepage (*www.u.arizona.edu/~gpivo*)

U.S. Green Building Council (*www.usgbc.org*)

BREEAM (BRE Environmental Assessment Method) (*www.breeam.org*)

U.S. Environmental Protection Agency—Energy Star (*www.energystar.gov*)

Green Globes Assessment and Rating System (*www.greenglobes.com*)

National Association of Home Builders Green Building Program (*www.nahbgreen.org*)

investing in different property types and different locations. Different property types are affected by different economic fundamentals that affect the demand for space in that property type, as we have learned in earlier chapters. Similarly, properties in different locations are affected by different economic fundamentals affecting the economic base of the area. Exhibit 22–11 shows the returns for office, retail, industrial, and apartment properties from 1979 through 2014. Although the business cycle and certain economic events (such as the real estate recession of the early 1990s) tend to affect all properties, there are certainly times when one property type is doing better than another and they

EXHIBIT 22–11 **NCREIF Returns by Property Type**

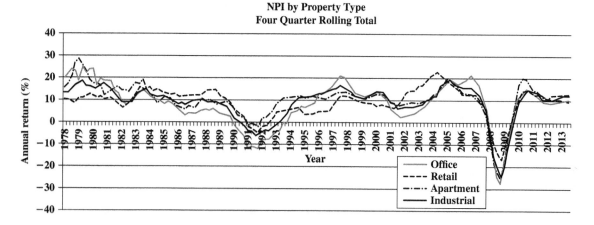

NPI by Property Type
Four Quarter Rolling Total

are not perfectly correlated. For example, retail had the lowest returns in the early 1980s, it had the highest returns during the latter part of the 1980s, the lowest return in the late 1990s, and then the highest return again in the early 2000s. Portfolio risk is reduced by investing across all four property types.

Exhibit 22–12 shows the performance of five selected MSAs. We see that different metropolitan areas behaved differently over time. For example, Boston was the best performer during some time periods and the worst during others. Diversifying across the different MSAs reduces overall portfolio risk.

Global Diversification

In recent years there has been an increasing interest among investors, especially large institutional investors, to invest on a global basis. There are several reasons for this. First, the number of investment opportunities around the globe is increasing. We saw in the last chapter that many countries have adopted REIT structures similar to what we have in the United States. These countries are also developing commercial mortgage-backed securities (CMBS) and other instruments that make it easier to invest in these countries. Exhibit 22–13 shows a breakdown of the global real estate market, and Exhibit 22–14 shows the countries with the largest commercial real estate markets and the size of the market.

Second, indexes measuring the historic returns for commercial real estate are being developed in other countries, allowing investors to have a benchmark for the performance of real estate in those countries like we have with the NCREIF index in the United States. For example, the Association for Real Estate Securitization (ARES) in Japan recently introduced the first index of the performance of real estate in Tokyo based on the same methodology as the NCREIF index.

A third reason for investing globally is that there are diversification benefits that result from including real estate from other countries in a portfolio. We have seen that there are diversification benefits of including real estate in a portfolio with stocks and bonds because real estate is not highly correlated with stocks and bonds. We have also seen that there are benefits from diversifying by property type and geographic area. Similarly, it should not be surprising that there are diversification benefits from investing in different countries. Exhibit 22–15 shows the performance of real estate in several countries based on GDP growth rates. (Because indexes of the returns were not available historically for all of the countries, gross revenue growth was used, which was available.)

EXHIBIT 22–12   **NCREIF Returns by Selected MSA**

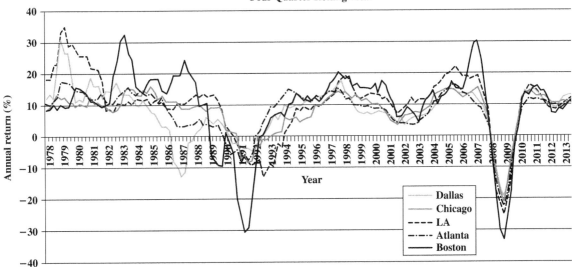

NCREIF Returns by Selected MSA
Four Quarter Rolling Total

EXHIBIT 22–13
Global Real Estate Universe by Region, 2013

Institutional Real Estate Total = $7.4 trillion

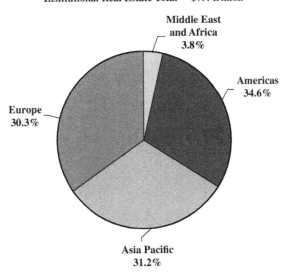

Source: LaSalle Investment Management As of 3Q 2012

Note: The Listed Real Estate Universe includes all publicly listed property companies, primarily REITs and REOCs. Vertically integrated development companies that hold real estate are included in emerging markets, but homebuilders are excluded. The Institutional Real Estate Universe includes all institutional investor-owned property, public, and private.

We see that there are differences in the performance of real estate in different global cities. This suggests that there are low correlations between the returns of the real estate in the cities, which leads to diversification benefits. Exhibit 22–16 shows the correlations between the revenue growth rates for the different global cities. Note that New York, Washington, DC, and San Francisco all have negative correlations with Tokyo, suggesting a lot of diversification benefits for U.S. investors by including Tokyo real estate in their portfolio. Similarly, there are negative correlations between these U.S. cities and Hong

EXHIBIT 22–14
Largest Commercial Real Estate Markets

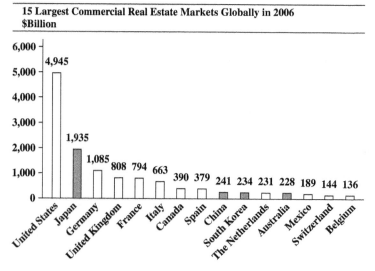

Largest Commercial Real Estate Markets

15 Largest Commercial Real Estate Markets Globally in 2006
$Billion

Source: Prudential Real Estate Investors.

EXHIBIT 22–15
GDP Growth Rates for Different Global Cities

GDP Growth Rates
Year-over-Year%

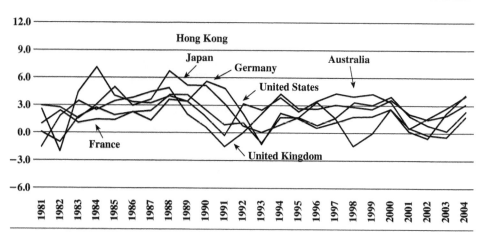

Source: Morgan Stanley.

Kong. Even where the correlations are not negative, such as between the U.S. cities and London, Paris, and Sydney, there are still diversification benefits, and portfolio risk can be reduced if the expected returns in these countries are favorable.

Risks of Global Investment

We have found that there are many reasons to consider investing on a global basis. However, this approach carries with it certain risks that are not necessarily reflected in the measures of portfolio risk we have discussed in this chapter. First, there is currency risk because exchange rates may change in a way that makes the dollar worth less relative to the

EXHIBIT 22-16
Correlations of Gross Revenue Growth in Global Cities

Correlations of Property Gross Revenue Growth 1990 to 2004

City	New York	Wash DC	San Fran	London	Paris	Frankfurt	Tokyo	Hong Kong	Sydney
New York	1.00	0.92	0.72	0.94	0.54	0.26	(0.59)	(0.54)	0.84
Wash DC		1.00	0.46	0.82	0.45	0.04	(0.63)	(0.64)	0.78
San Fran			1.00	0.69	0.29	0.24	(0.43)	(0.13)	0.57
London				1.00	0.68	0.39	(0.39)	(0.51)	0.91
Paris					1.00	0.78	0.33	(0.47)	0.52
Frankfurt						1.00	0.49	(0.20)	0.19
Tokyo							1.00	0.10	(0.44)
Hong Kong								1.00	(0.57)
Sydney									1.00

currency of the country where the investment is located. As cash flows from operating and eventual sale of the property are converted back to dollars, there could be a loss because of an unfavorable change in exchange rates. Second, although indexes and information sources are developing in many countries, the data may not be as reliable in all cases or as extensive as in the United States. This adds risk because investors may be acting on incomplete information. Third, there are different tax laws and property rights to deal with when investing globally. This can add additional legal risks. Fourth, there could be political instability in the country, which may increase risk because of uncertainty as to how the political situation will affect attitudes about foreign investment in the country. Fifth, there are the obvious communication barriers and cultural differences. To try to mitigate many of these risks, U.S. investors often try to find a joint venture partner based in the country where they want to invest. It can be a challenge to find the right partner, but doing so can significantly reduce the risks and allow the expertise and financial resources of the U.S. investor to be combined with the local-country operating knowledge of the local joint venture partner, who knows the culture, language, and legal considerations specific to that country. Global investment is likely to continue to grow as there are increasing opportunities to invest in developing countries with attractive returns and diversification benefits for U.S. investors.

Use of Derivatives to Hedge Portfolio Risk

In recent years we have seen the introduction of derivatives based on the NCREIF Property Index, discussed previously in this chapter. Derivatives allow investors to take a position in real estate or hedge a position without actually buying or selling properties. They receive or pay a return based on the performance of the NCREIF Property Index or an index based on one of the property types shown earlier in the chapter.

Derivatives can be used as a way to enter the real estate market for the first time. An investor might purchase a derivative that has a return based on the NCREIF Property Index. This would be a "long" position in the index. At the same time, another investor, who feels overexposed to the commercial real estate market, may decide to "sell," or "short," the index rather than sell individual properties, which the investor may want to continue to own and manage. This reduces real estate risk exposure without requiring sale of the properties. This especially makes sense if the investor expects to earn above-average returns on the properties currently owned.

Another important use of derivatives is to adjust exposure to different property types. We have seen that there are benefits of diversifying across property types. An investor may feel overexposed to a particular property type and underexposed to another. For example, the investor may believe she has too much retail and not enough office properties. She could enter into a swap where the parties agree to pay returns on retail properties and receive returns on office properties, with both returns based on the performance of the respective NCREIF Property Index. They would be "short" the retail index and "long" the office index. Again, this allows them to adjust the risk of the portfolio without selling any properties.

Example—Swap Office for Retail

To illustrate the use of derivatives to hedge portfolio risk, consider the following example. ABC Investors decided to enter into a derivative transaction on January 1, 2000, that swapped office returns for retail returns. That is, it agreed to *pay* the return on the NCREIF office index but *receive* the returns on the NCREIF retail index. The term of the contract was five years terminating December 31, 2004. What return did ABC Investors earn on this strategy?[14]

Retail returns outperformed office returns over this particular five-year period. The NCREIF office index increased at an 8.15 percent average annual return. Over the same period the retail index increased at an average annual return of 13.67 percent. Thus, the investor who swapped office for retail would have earned an average annual return of 13.67 percent while paying 8.15 percent for a net return of 5.52 percent.

Note that the investor is not taking the risk of the returns on real estate as reflected by the NCREIF Index in this case. The investor is taking the risk related to the *relative* performance of retail versus office—in this case, betting that retail will outperform office. If the investor had been overexposed to office and underexposed to retail, then she would have earned a return that was closer to the NCREIF return by using this strategy and hedged her portfolio risk.

Concept Box 22.2 summarizes the types of derivatives based on the NCREIF Index that are available through Credit Suisse, which was the first investment bank in the United States to offer derivatives for commercial real estate based on an index. This market is certain to grow in the United States and in other countries because derivatives provide an important tool for adjusting portfolio risk and helping to make the real estate market more efficient.

Conclusion

This chapter has introduced the measurement of investment performance and the basic elements of portfolio theory. We have also dealt with the question of whether real estate investments tend to provide diversification benefits to portfolios that have traditionally consisted of government securities, common stocks, and corporate bonds.

We have stressed that the nature of real estate investment return data is very limited and may not be representative of a broad measure of real estate returns. Further, some of the data are based on a group of properties owned by investment advisors. In this case, an index is calculated on reported net operating income and appraised property values with very few actual transaction prices.

Results from the portfolio simulations conducted and reported in the last part of the chapter indicate that there appeared to be significant gains available from portfolio diversification into real estate during the period 1985–2009 based on these limited data sets. In all simulations, real estate increased portfolio efficiency. Of course, these results are based on historical data from a limited sample of real estate investments and may not be indicative of future results or apply generally to all real estate investments.

---

[14] For simplicity we assume that at the time the investor enters into the swap, the expected return for office and retail is the same. In practice, there may be a difference in expected return which would require the investor who swaps for a property type with a higher expected return to pay a fixed amount to adjust for the difference in expected returns. Similarly, if the investor is swapping for a property type that would have a lower expected return, she would receive a payment to adjust for this difference.

NCREIF Index Derivatives Issued by Credit Suisse

1. Price Return Swap: A swap transaction where an investor receives (or pays) the quarterly capital value return component published by NCREIF and in return pays (or receives) a fixed spread.

Quarterly Settlement Flow Funds

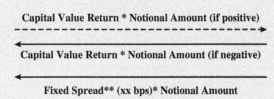

2. Property Type Swap: A swap transaction in which an investor receives the total return for one property type and pays the total return on a different property type for the same notional amount. Depending on the property type swap that is entered into, an investor will either pay or receive a fixed spread as part of such a property type swap.

Quarterly Settlement Flow Funds (ex. Retail/Office Swap)

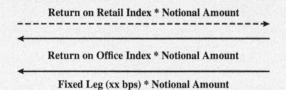

3. Total Return Swap: A swap transaction where an investor receives (or pays) the quarterly total return published by NCREIF and in return pays (or receives) three-month LIBOR plus spread.

Quarterly Settlement Flow Funds

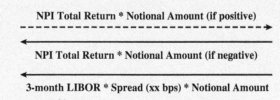

- Depending on market conditions, it is possible that fixed spread will be flat or negative (i.e., payer of index would pay a fixed spread in order to pay index).
- Trades are notional-based and the only up-front cost to enter trades is the margin requirements necessary to manage counterparty risk.

Key Terms

arithmetic mean returns, *728*
coefficient of variation, *730*
correlation, *735*
covariance, *734*

diversification benefits, *738*
geometric mean return, *727*
holding period return
  (*HPR*), *727*

NAREIT Index, *724*
NCREIF Index, *726*

Useful Web Sites

www.ncreif.com—The National Council of Real Estate Investment Fiduciaries (NCREIF) is an association of institutional real estate professionals who share a common interest in their industry. This site provides real estate information standards, indexes, membership, and resource information.

www.allegiancecapital.com—A site designed for institutional investors and high-net-worth individuals. Provides information on various investment alternatives.

www.wilshire.com—Wilshire Associates produces a number of indexes including a real estate index.

www.reit.com/news/realestateportfoliomagazine/tabid/74/default.aspx—Real Estate Portfolio contains comprehensive coverage and analysis of specific market issues and trends, sector analysis, company and executive profiles, and statistical data and forecasts pertaining to the publicly traded real estate industry.

www.demographia.com—This site is a very good resource for finding relevant demographic information about different markets spread across the world. Some of the main features of this site are that it gives international housing affordability rankings, different surveys, different economic reports, and different trends related to real estate. It's also a good source to find regulations and policies related to real estate.

www.realtyrates.com—This Web site is a good resource for real estate investment and development news, trends, analytics, and market research reports. It also provides survey reports that include national mortgage term and interest rates, financial indicators, and demographic information for seven core commercial property types. Some of the content provided by this site is not free.

www.snl.com/sectors/real-estate—This Web site provides fundamental financial data on more than 230 REITs, REOCs, and homebuilders. It gives detailed, descriptive property data, cost and performance data, and property mapping. It also is a good source for analyst coverage, FFO estimates, proprietary AFFO, and NAV consensus estimates.

Questions

1. What are some of the difficulties in obtaining data to measure real estate investment performance?
2. What are the distinguishing characteristics between REIT data and the NCREIF Property Index?
3. What is the difference between arithmetic and geometric mean returns?
4. What statistical concept do many portfolio managers use to represent risk when considering investment performance?
5. When NCREIF returns and REIT returns are compared, NCREIF returns exhibit a much lower pattern of variation. Why might this be the case?
6. Mean returns for portfolios are calculated by taking the weighted average of the mean returns for each investment in the portfolio. Why won't this approach work to calculate the standard deviation of portfolio returns?
7. What is the difference between covariance and correlation? Why are these concepts so important in portfolio analysis?
8. Results reported in the chapter show that by including either REITs or the NCREIF Index in a portfolio containing S&P 500 securities, corporate bonds, and T-bills, diversification benefits result. Why is this true? Do those benefits come about for the same reason for each category of real estate investment?
9. Results presented in the chapter are based on historical data. Of what use are these results to a portfolio manager who may be making an investment decision today? Elaborate.
10. Why should an investor consider investing globally?
11. What are the risks of global investment?

12. How can a derivative security be used to hedge portfolio risk?

Problems

1. As an investment advisor for MREAF (Momentum Real Estate Advisory Fund), you are about to make a presentation to the portfolio manager of the ET&T pension fund. You would like to show what would have happened had ET&T made an investment in MREAF during the past 13 quarters. The ET&T manager has provided you with historical data on the performance of its portfolio, which is made up entirely of common stock. Historical data for the ET&T portfolio and MREAF are as follows:

	ET&T Common Stock Fund		MREAF Real Estate Fund	
Period Ending	Unit Value	Quarterly Dividend	Unit Value	Quarterly Dividend
Quarter				
1	$ 701.00	$ 8.28	$ 70.00	$2.17
2	752.50	8.11	80.05	2.14
3	850.52	10.30	90.80	2.01
4	953.75	9.81	100.50	2.01
5	1,047.57	12.05	99.14	1.87
6	1,221.70	14.17	95.50	1.81
7	1,443.90	17.18	93.77	1.79
8	1,263.31	14.91	80.31	1.54
9	1,258.56	13.84	77.34	1.49
10	1,526.72	18.32	76.53	1.44
11	1,616.81	19.73	78.42	1.51
12	1,624.08	19.98	79.01	1.53
13	1,560.25	18.88	81.75	1.55

a. Calculate the quarterly *HPR* for each investment.

b. Calculate the arithmetic mean *HPR*, the standard deviation of the *HPR*s, and the geometric mean for each fund. Which fund contained more risk per unit of return?

c. Was there any correlation between returns on the ET&T fund and MREAF?

d. Would a portfolio that contained equal amounts of ET&T securities and MREAF have provided any investment diversification? Why?

e. *Optional.* Assume each investment could have been combined in a portfolio with weights ranging from 0 percent to 100 percent. What pattern of risk and return would result if each investment were added (deleted) in increments of 10 percent (remember that the sum of the two proportions must always sum to 100%)? What combination of securities would have constituted the "efficient frontier" (if any)?

f. If the manager of ET&T is considering making an investment in MREAF, of what use is this analysis?

www.mhhe.com/bf15e

2. **Excel.** Refer to the "Ch22_Frontier" tab in the Excel Workbook provided on the Web site. Suppose the correlation between NCREIF and the S&P 500 is −20 percent. How does this change the standard deviation of the portfolio when 50 percent of the portfolio is allocated to each investment?

23

Real Estate Investment Funds: Structure, Performance, Benchmarking, and Attribution Analysis

Previous chapters have provided an extensive discussion of commercial real estate investment. Most of the chapters focused on individual properties, leases, valuation, financial metrics, as well as accounting and tax considerations. Chapter 22 added the dimension of including real estate investments in a portfolio to provide diversification benefits. To maximize diversification benefits, however, a sufficient number of properties must be in the portfolio to eliminate most of the volatility in returns due to factors unique to a particular property type, a specific location, or even an individual property.

Most investors, even wealthy individuals, as well as many endowments and pension funds, do not have sufficient capital or expertise to construct a portfolio that is well diversified by property type and geographic location. Thus, investors whose strategy is to have a well-diversified portfolio of real estate often rely on various real estate funds to fill that need. These funds are created by investment management firms that have the expertise in acquiring and managing large portfolios geared to the needs of a particular type of investor.

This chapter discusses many important characteristics of these *private real estate investment funds*. These funds include a range of privately structured investment vehicles that have grown considerably in importance, particularly to institutional investors. A limited partnership structure, similar to that discussed in Chapter 18, is widely used by these investment funds. However, funds discussed in this chapter differ in that they tend to invest in many properties resulting in a large total value. Typically, these large, private funds are created by real estate investment managers who develop an investment strategy involving (1) the types of properties to be acquired and markets where acquisitions will be made, (2) how the fund will be operated, (3) when properties are to be sold, and

(4) how the fund strategy will align with the real estate investment requirements of investors. These funds are then marketed to institutional investors (public and private pension funds, sovereign wealth funds, nonprofit entities such as the endowments of research and educational institutions), family offices, as well as high net worth individuals. These investment entities are typically long-term investors who want to invest directly in a portfolio of commercial real estate.

Generally, registered investment advisors[1] create and market these funds stressing various objectives that are consistent with the investment objectives of investors. It also should be pointed out that investments in many of the funds are held "in trust" on behalf of pension plan beneficiaries. This means that the **fiduciary** duties and responsibilities of pension plan sponsors to pension beneficiaries "carry over" to managers of these real estate investment funds.[2] In addition, both investment managers and pension plan sponsors are accountable to, and regulated by, the U.S. Department of Labor.[3]

		Top 25 Private Real Estate Fund Companies in 2014		
2014 Rank	Movement	Name of Firm	Capital Raised ($bn)	2013 Rank
1	↔	The Blackstone Group	32,129	1
2	↑	Lone Star Funds	12,500	3
3	↓	Starwood Capital Group	8,661	2
4	↔	Colony Capital	7,454	4
5	↑	Brookfield Asset Management	6,928	9
6	↔	Tishman Speyer	5,757	6
7	↑	Angelo, Gordon & Co	4,606	15
8	↑	Westbrook Partners	4,532	13
9	↑	Oaktree Capital Management	4,496	21
10	*	Global Logistic Properties	4,400	–
11	↑	Walton Street Capital	4,189	23
12	↑	GI Partners	3,524	38
13	↑	Orion Capital Managers	3,523	29
14	↓	The Carlyle Group	3,434	7
15	↑	Fortress Investment Group	3,159	19
16	↑	TA Associates Realty	3,055	20
17	↑	CapitaLand	2,895	18
18	↑	Cerberus Capital Management	2,650	39
19	↓	LaSalle Investment Management	2,557	5
20	↑	Beacon Capital Partners	2,541	28
21	↑	Hines	2,471	37
22	↑	Northwood Investors	2,381	24
23	↑	Rockpoint Group	2,330	34
24	↓	Prudential Real Estate Investors	2,315	16
25	↑	GTIS Partners	2,287	40

Source: Real Capital Analytics

[1] These investment advisers must "register" and comply with regulations as promulgated by the U.S. Securities and Exchange Commission and/or State Securities Commissions. For a list of advisors, see Money Market Directory, Standard and Poor's published by McGraw Hill & Co.

[2] Fiduciaries are in a position of trust and must (1) place the interest of beneficiaries of the trust above their own and (2) eliminate and/or disclose any potential conflict of interests to beneficiaries of the trust.

[3] Pension plans and investment advisors are subject to regulation by the DOL under the Employee Retirement Income Security Act (ERISA), as amended.

Investor Goals and Objectives

When evaluating which private real estate investment funds to invest in, investors have to keep in mind their investment objectives, that is, what do they want to accomplish with their real estate allocation and what role will real estate fulfill within their overall investment portfolio. These goals are generally expressed in terms of risk that investors are willing to assume and the investment returns (reward) that they expect to earn for risk-taking. Investors in funds must evaluate whether properties to be acquired by the fund are consistent with their portfolio objectives. This typically includes a desired level of diversification that will result after combining real estate investments with other asset classes such as public securities (stocks), fixed income (bonds), and other investments as discussed in Chapter 22. Also, investors must assess whether such properties can be acquired, managed, and sold profitably by the fund manager. This requires extensive due diligence and an analysis that includes the fund manager's past performance, personnel and organization structure, and their expertise and execution ability to accomplish the objectives of the fund that they market. As to the operation of the fund, there are many factors that must be incorporated into fund offerings. *These provisions are included in the fund agreement which is used to document, identify, and disclose to investors the investment strategies, the types of properties and locations where acquisitions will occur, exit strategies, and so on. It also provides guidance to investors as to the discretion that managers will have when acquiring, managing, and selling real estate assets as they operate the fund.*

Exhibit 23–1A provides a list (not all-inclusive) of some of the more important provisions that are usually considered by fund managers when creating a fund and marketing to potential investors. Fund provisions typically include a description of how the fund will be operated, limits on manager discretion, manager fees, and other provisions that enable investors to better assess the risk being taken by fund managers. Depending on the objectives of the fund, various combinations of these provisions may be used in the development of the fund agreements. The exhibit is used only to describe some of the many possible combination of fund provisions.

General Explanation of Possible Provisions in Fund Offerings

What follows is a brief discussion of the items included in Exhibit 23–1.

Section A. Many real estate investment funds are categorized by their investment styles, which are identified by the status or condition of the properties to be acquired on the basis of fund strategy. Typically, funds are identified as (1) core funds, (2) **value-added funds,** or (3) opportunity funds. These strategies were introduced in Chapter 11. Core funds primarily invest in stabilized existing operating properties with current cash flows, low vacancy, and located in major metropolitan areas. They usually invest in a wide variety of property types and use very limited financial leverage. Thus, they are relatively low risk. Value-added funds take on more risks by purchasing properties that either have some current vacancies or have upcoming major tenant rollovers and/or are in need of some renovation and capital improvement so the funds can create value by renovating and leasing up the property. They typically also use more financial leverage compared to the core funds. Opportunity funds take on even more risks by doing ground up development projects that expose the funds to additional construction risks, such as entitlements, construction delays, cost overruns, complex JV management issues, and so on. These funds typically use a relatively high degree of financial leverage. They may also be less diversified and concentrate in certain geographic areas or property types that the fund managers think will outperform the rest of the market. Their strategy often involves purchasing "distressed property assets." They then add value by

EXHIBIT 23–1A   **Examples of Possible Provisions in Real Estate Investment Fund Offerings**

A. Properties/Markets/Acquisitions

(A.1) Property Fund Strategy	(A.2) Possible Markets	(A.3) Possible Sub-Markets	(A.4) Possible Property Categories
Core	Global	CBD	Multifamily
Core-Plus	Domestic	Suburban	Retail
Value-Added	Gateway Cities	Urban	Office
New	Secondary Cities	Infill/Uptown/In Town	Industrial/Distribution
Existing	Tertiary Cities	Undeveloped Land	Hotel
Opportunistic		Other	Mixed-Use
Other			Other

B. Fund Structures/Characteristics

(B.1) Fund Structures	(B.2) Investor Entry/Exit	(B.3) Debt/Leverage	(B.4) $ Size and Values of Properties In Fund
Commingled	Minimum Investment	Leverage Restrictions:	Expected $ Size of Fund
Open End	Requirements	Acquisitions	Maximum % Value for
Closed End	Admission of new	Assumption of Debt	any Single Property to Total
Expected Life of Fund	Investors	% Maximum L/V for	Fund Value (i.e., Single
Finite Life	Redemptions:	any Single Property	Asset Exposure)
Fund Renewal Options	Queuing Policy	% Maximum Total	Maximum % Value for
Fund Liquidation	Reinvestment Policy	Debt to Total	any Property
	Property Appraisals:	Fund Value	Classification (A.4) to
	Annually, Quarterly,		Total Fund Value (i.e., Single
	Internal, External		Property Type Explore)
	Transfer of Interests		

C. Fund Management/Performance/Reporting

(C.1) Additional Fund Management Provisions	(C.2) Manager Fees	(C.3) Performance Reporting	(C.4) Performance Benchmarks
Advisory Committee	Acquisition Fees	Operating Results	NCREIF Index
Disclosures	Management Fees	Income	ODCE Index
Investor Capital:	Disposition Fees	Appreciation	"Minimum Real Return"
Commitments	Promotes	Returns	
Contributions	"Catch-Ups"	Distributions	
	Carried Interests	IRR and TWR	
		Investment Multiple	

repositioning or re-leasing properties to enhance property value. In some cases, these funds may purchase at a discount, mortgage debt which is in default. Properties are acquired at foreclosure sales, then resold at a later date. These funds are not designed for long-term investment and will tend to sell properties that are purchased within a relatively short time.

Fund managers typically obtain commitments from investors to invest in the funds. Capital is "called" from the investors as investment opportunities are identified and ready for funding. Core funds tend to be open end (discussed below) as the properties are stable and investors generally can get in and out of the fund with relative ease. The funds will continue to make new acquisitions as more capital is committed. Value-added and

opportunistic funds, on the other hand, tend to be held in closed end (discussed below) form because of the time needed to execute the investment strategy. As a result, many of these funds will have a lock-up period (typically one to two years during the initial stage of the fund) where investors' exit from the fund is not permitted. In addition, the funds typically have a limited investment period when new acquisitions can be made.

Fund managers may or may not have **full discretion** to invest in properties without permission of the investors. In some cases, the investors may reserve the right to approve the investments.

Generally, funds will focus investment activity on one of these strategies so investors know what to expect when investing in the fund. In limited instances, however, some flexibility is accorded to the fund manager. For example, a core property fund may acquire a core property that includes some undeveloped land that will be developed at a future date. This could be referred to as a "core-value-added," or a "build to core" property investment. Also, commonly referred to as "a B property in an A location," a core property may be acquired with high occupancy in a good location but it may be in need of *minor* improvements and modernization to bring it on par with the area competition. These are sometimes referred to as "Core Plus" properties which would be a minor component of a core fund. However, because these investments would be *exceptions* to the primary focus of the fund and typically are subject to a percentage limit as to their composition within a fund, the fund would probably continue to be identified as a "core property fund."

The investment strategy of a fund also may identify its target markets, submarkets, and property categories in which investments will be made. For example, a fund could include certain geographic areas and may specifically exclude certain markets (e.g., properties in non-U.S. countries). To further clarify the fund strategy, metro markets in which properties may be acquired may also be identified. (For example, investments could be limited to "Gateway Cities." As such, investments may be restricted to cities such as Seattle, San Francisco, Los Angeles, San Diego, Chicago, Boston, New York, Washington DC, Miami, Houston, Dallas, Atlanta.) Submarkets within metro markets in which investments may be acquired also may be identified. For example, only properties in CBDs and urban infill locations may be acquired within metro markets.

Depending on the fund strategy, investments may be limited as to categories of property types. For example, investments may be limited to one or more specific categories, such as retail, office, multifamily, and industrial/warehouse properties. However, depending on the strategy, this list could be expanded to include hotel, mixed-use properties, and possibly investments into student housing, medical offices, seniors' housing, healthcare facilities, parking structures, and even light manufacturing properties.

Section B.   In addition to categories of properties and markets, *fund structure* is also very important. When a very large fund is created and expected to contain a large number of properties in many locations, a **commingled fund** structure is often used by mangers and then marketed to many institutional investors. These large, commingled funds are typically *open-end funds.* This means that after the initial offering and after the fund commences operation, new investors may be admitted on the basis of the values of unit shares in the fund at that time. Similarly, the open-end structure also allows investors to exit the fund and redeem their unit interests. Some funds may also allow existing investors to transfer (sell) their unit interests to other investors. These transfers may be made to investors who are already in the fund, or in some cases to new investors. Open-end funds typically follow a core strategy.

Another fund structure used by investment managers is the ***closed-end fund.*** Closed-end funds seek to raise a specific amount of capital over a specific period of time, after which the fund is closed to new investors. These funds usually require a significant minimum investment amount per investor. This tends to limit the number of investors in the fund. The closed structure may be important to fund managers trying to create a fund in

EXHIBIT 23–1B   Real Estate Investment Styles

	Core	Value-Added	Opportunistic
Fund Structure	Generally Open-Ended	Primarily Closed-End; Few Open-Ended	Closed-End
Indices	NPI	NPI + 400 BP	NPI + 600 BP
Return Projections	Less than 10%	10%–14%	15%+
Income Return (% of Total Return)	70%+	40%–60%	0%–50%
Property Types	Industrial, Multifamily, Office, Retail	Expanded (e.g., seniors housing, student housing, and medical office)	All
Property Life Cycle	Stabilized, Leased	Identifiable Deficiency	Distressed, Development
Occupancy	80%+	N/A	N/A
Development	None	Modest	Significant
Leverage	<35%	Up to 75%	Up to 100%
Markets	Primary/Secondary, Domestic	Primary/Secondary/Tertiary, Domestic	Primary/Secondary/Tertiary, Domestic & International

a relatively short period of time. These funds also tend to restrict exit, or redemptions, by investors. The focus of closed-end funds tends to be more specific than open-end funds. In many cases, the closed-end structure is used for value-added or opportunistic property fund strategies. Closed-end funds also tend to have finite lives (typically 5 to 7 years with limited extension options) and provide procedures for liquidation when the goal of the fund is achieved, or when the time allotted for the operations of the fund expires.

Exhibit 23–1B summarizes the main investment strategies (styles) and structures that tend to be used for each style. Once a fund has selected a particular investment strategy (style), it is important to investors that the manager follows this style when acquiring properties. Investors select funds that meet their particular needs, including their risk tolerance and how that fund will fit into their overall investment strategy. Thus, investors do not want the fund to deviate from the style they indicated would be followed. When fund managers deviate from their stated strategy and acquire properties that do not conform to the stated objectives of the fund, this is called **"style drift"** and can be a concern for investors. For example, if the fund promotes itself as a **core fund** but begins to undertake development projects, this would represent a major change in investment style. In some cases, the fund manager may be trying to achieve a higher return to outperform an index, or making riskier investments to compensate for poor investments made previously. When there is an incentive fee based on the manager beating an index, they may also be tempted to take on riskier projects in the hope of earning the incentive fee. In essence, the fund may be trying to achieve a higher return but may be taking on more risk—this subjecting investors to more risk than they agreed to when they invested in the fund.

Appraisals.   The reader should realize that real estate investment funds are *unlike* stock and bond funds in many ways. One very important difference is that the latter funds can be valued more easily. This is because stocks and bonds are traded very frequently and prices for these securities are usually available. Private real estate values cannot be determined as easily, or as often. This is because properties are bought and sold less frequently and differ with respect to size, quality, and location. As a result, price discovery for real estate is more complicated.

Regardless of the type of fund created for investing in real estate, fund managers must provide investors with periodic information on values for properties in the

In addition to the fund structures shown in Section B of Exhibit 23–1, another "fund-like" vehicle that may be used by investment managers is what is referred to as a "separate account." **Separate accounts** are single-client investment vehicles set up for one investor versus commingled funds where multiple investors pool their investment capital together. Separate account agreements are usually made between one individual investor (institutional or not) and individual fund managers. (However, one investor may have several separate account relationships with several different, individual managers.) A partnership structure is generally used and provisions in separate account agreements may be very similar to those found in open-end funds. However, important differences lie in the area of fund manager *discretion* and transfer of ownership interests. When creating a separate account, the investor does not want its investment commingled with funds contributed by other investors. These investors usually desire more control and want a more significant role in major decisions regarding acquisition, operation, leasing, financing/refinancing, and transfer/disposition of properties. This reduces the discretion of the fund manager. Also, by not commingling funds with those of other investors, separate account provisions usually give investors the option to terminate fund agreements with fund managers and to transfer all properties to a new fund manager.

fund, as well as investment performance during the life of the fund. As pointed out, price discovery for real estate assets can be somewhat complicated. When reporting investment performance, fund managers frequently use property appraisals to estimate value. Fund documents typically disclose (1) how frequent (quarterly, annually, etc.) properties in portfolios are to be appraised, (2) to what extent such appraisals may be performed internally by the fund manager, or if and when they are to be done by external (third-party) appraisers. While fund managers may be allowed to provide investors with estimates of value (internal appraisals) from time to time, external appraisals done by third-party appraisers are usually required at specific time intervals. External appraisals are done periodically to provide a third-party opinion of value. This adds some objectivity when determining property values and tends to reduce possible conflicts faced by fund management when reporting property values to investors in the fund. For commingled, open-end funds, these appraisals also help establish unit values for new investors and for existing investors desiring to redeem their unit interests, should they desire to exit the fund. A **redemption policy** is usually provided in the fund documents specifying conditions under which redemptions can be accomplished. This policy may be important because some properties in the fund may have to be sold in order to provide the needed liquidity and capital for those investors wanting to exit. Many funds adopt a redemption policy to establish the exit order (queue) to deal with the possible situation where multiple investors choose to exit at the same time.

Debt/Leverage.   Depending on the expected risk profile of the fund, the use of debt and financial leverage by the fund when acquiring properties may be restricted, or not allowed at all. When acquiring properties provides an opportunity to assume debt with attractive terms, management may be allowed to do so on a limited basis. Some funds may allow the use of debt but may specify (1) a maximum loan-to-value ratio for any one property and/or (2) a maximum percentage of total debt to total fund value. These limitations are included to restrict discretion of fund managers as to the amount of leverage and financial risk to be taken by the fund.

Other restrictions on the discretion of fund managers may include (1) limit on single-asset exposure, that is, a maximum percentage value of any one property to the total value of the fund (e.g., no property may represent more than 10 percent of total fund value) and (2) limit on single property type exposure, that is, maximum value of one property classification to total fund value (e.g., the value of all office properties may not exceed 30 percent of total fund value). Again, these provisions are intended to limit the discretion of fund managers and are included to assure investors of some minimum amount of diversification in the portfolio of the investment fund.

Section C. Fund Management. Some funds (especially the open-end commingled structures) may provide for the formation of an investor advisory committee that will provide some guidance to fund management. Generally fund management will have **full discretion** as to property selection, management, and sale. However, in some cases, funds will use an advisory committee for input as to the operation of the fund. Fund managers will disclose to the advisory committee any potential conflicts of interest as the fund operates. For example, property management is usually not done by the fund manager. When possible, the property management is usually performed by third-party firms. Deviations from this policy and any potential conflicts would generally be disclosed to the Fund Advisory Committee. In some cases, the advisory committee also may be asked to exercise "rights of first refusal" options on some property acquisitions. For example, should a property be under consideration for purchase by a commingled fund and also be under consideration for possible acquisition by another fund (e.g., separate account) that is sponsored by the same fund manager, a rotation policy may be included in the fund agreement. This policy establishes the order in which funds that are involved in negotiations investing the same property may exercise the option to purchase, or pass, on the acquisition of that property.

Most funds also differentiate between investor capital commitments and investor capital contributions. The former usually relates to the time during which investors have made capital *commitments* to the fund but before the fund has commenced actual property acquisitions. The former usually refers to the amount of capital allocation that the investor commits to the fund manager to be deployed in making property acquisitions. As the fund begins to acquire properties, it will make a "capital call" to investors, who then make *capital contributions*. Capital committed versus capital contributed can be two very different things, complicated by a number of factors, such as whether the funds are successful in deploying the capital within its specified investment period, or if additional capital may be required in the later years of the fund's life after the initial commitment has been fulfilled which could increase total capital contributed. The difference between capital commitments and capital contributions is important, as it may affect how fund management fees will be determined and paid by investors.

Investment Management Fees. Fees charged by investment fund managers generally fall into one or more of the following categories:

- Acquisition fees
- Disposition fees
- Management fees
- Performance fees (aka incentive fees, "promotes" and "carried interests")

Acquisition fees are charged when each property is acquired and is typically a percent of the acquisition cost. Disposition fees are charged when the asset is sold.

Management fees are charged to investors during the entire term of the fund. As funds are created and managers compete for business, the determination of fees to be charged by fund managers may vary. For example, core property funds usually base fees on equity capital (property value less any debt). It is generally expressed annually, as a percent (or as basis points). Fees to some investors may be lower than others depending on the amount of equity committed. For very large equity commitments and/or lead investors of the fund, fees may be reduced (discounted).

A typical cycle for raising a fund can be thought about in three phases. During the first phase (capital-raising phase) the fund management obtains **commitments** from a number of investors who agree to make investments in the fund. After the fund manager has received a sufficient number of commitments and management is ready to acquire properties the second phase referred to as the **investment period** begins. This is the official start of the fund term. Capital calls are made to investors for capital contributions during this period. This can last for several years with a maximum time period usually specified in the fund prospectus. Capital calls are made as investments are identified for acquisition by the fund. After the completion of the investment period, phase 3 involves the continued management of the investments and ultimately sale of assets, and a return of capital to investors (unless the fund has an option to reinvest). Closed-end funds usually have a fixed term after which all the investments are to be sold, although there may be several extension options to provide more time for dispositions if needed by the fund manager. Open-end funds will typically reinvest the funds in other investments and do not have a finite life for the fund.

Management fees may vary during each phase. They would typically start at the beginning of the investment period and fees are often initially based on **committed capital,** which is the maximum amount investors have agreed to contribute to the fund when investments are found. After the investment period, fees may change and be based on **invested capital** (either at cost or market value), which, if at cost, is the amount actually invested in properties, although some funds may continue to base fees on committed capital. The amount invested could be less than the commitments if the fund manager did not find enough investments that meet the fund's criteria to use the entire amount of committed capital. But the fund cannot require investors to provide more than the amount that they committed.

Example—Fees on Capital Committed versus Invested

Fees for a fund will be 35 basis points (0.35%) on all *committed* capital during the investment period and then 50 bps on *invested capital* after the end of the investment period. In our example, investors' **commitments** will be $100 million, which will be called in over a two-year investment period. After the two-year investment period, the fee will be based on all capital invested. It is anticipated that during years 4 and 5, the fund will begin to sell properties and will return capital to investors.

Year	Contributed Capital	Capital Returned	Invested Capital	Fee on Committed Capital	Fee on Invested Capital	Total Fee
1	$50,000,000	$ 0	$ 50,000,000	$350,000		$350,000
2	$50,000,000	$ 0	$100,000,000	$350,000		$350,000
3		$ 0	$100,000,000		$ 500,000	$500,000
4		$50,000,000	$ 50,000,000		$ 250,000	$250,000
5		$40,000,000	$ 10,000,000		$ 50,000	$ 50,000

Note that the fees on committed capital are paid on the entire commitment of $100 million during the two-year investment period. But after that, fees are only based on capital still invested and not returned to investors. This is just one example of how fees might be structured. Many variations are found in practice.

As indicated, fees are often based on investor equity, that is, property value less any mortgage debt. This is because investors may not want to pay fees on any debt used by fund managers when they acquire properties. In some cases, however, fees may be based on the total value of the assets under management, including both debt and equity. However, in this case, the management fee as a percentage of asset value would generally be lower than fees that would be charged as a percentage of equity capital invested.

Management fees/rates also may be graduated (tiered) on the basis of the size of the portfolio. Also, in some cases, fees may be based on the initial **cost** of assets acquired. This approach is more commonly used in joint ventures and for value-added funds where value is being added to properties that are being improved by management over time. Because a value-added strategy takes time to implement, interim estimates of property values may be difficult to make.

Other Fund Management Fee Structures:
Other ways fund management fees might be calculated include:

- A percentage of net operating income
- A percentage of cash flow distributions
- Project Revenues (sometimes used on residential land development projects)
- Project Costs (sometimes used on commercial development projects).

Example: Fees Based on NOI:

Assume the fee is structured as follows:

> 6 percent up to $15 million in annual NOI
> 5 percent for next $10 million in annual NOI
> 4 percent for all over $25 million in annual NOI
> If actual NOI = $35 million annually, fees paid to fund managers will be:
> First $15 million NOI × 6% = $ 900,000
> Next $10 million NOI × 5% = $ 500,000
> Next $10 million × 4%   = $ 400,000
> Total Fee   = $1,800,000

Performance Fees:

In some cases, most notably, for "value-added" and "opportunity" funds, the fund manager may receive what is referred to as a **"promote."** This fee is paid to fund managers as an added incentive to enhance fund performance. The fee is usually charged toward the end of the life of fund, or until 100 percent of investor's capital has been returned. The fee is usually based on the extent to which the fund manager earns a return that exceeds a "hurdle rate of return" that is agreed to by the fund manager and investors at the inception of the fund. Typically, incentive fees for managers of these funds is to compensate them for taking on additional and appropriate risks in developing or "turning properties around" by repositioning, redeveloping, and/or improving assets. Therefore, it may require time for these strategies to be executed and the full market value on such properties may not be realized until they are sold. It is at the time of sale that fund managers are typically compensated/rewarded with a "promote" because they have successfully completed the "property turnaround" and/or other goals of the fund.

Example
- Assumptions
  - Initial Investment = $1,000,000
  - Hurdle = 10%; Promote Percentage to Fund Manager = 20%
  - Annual Cash Flow from Property Operations = $80,000
  - 3-Year Hold Period
  - Net Proceeds from Sale of Properties = $1,500,000
  - Annual Asset Management (AM) Fee of 1% of $1,000,000 or $10,000

	Investment Cash Flows (CF)	Less AM Fees	CF Net of AM Fees	CF Applied to Achieve Hurdle	Remaining Cash Flow	Promote to Manager	Remaining Cash Flow to Investor	Final CF to Investor
Time 0	$−1,000,000		$−1,000,000	$−1,000,000				$−1,000,000
Year 1	$ 80,000	$−10,000	$ 70,000	$ 70,000				$ 70,000
Year 2	$ 80,000	$−10,000	$ 70,000	$ 70,000				$ 70,000
Year 3	$ 1,580,000	$−10,000	$ 1,570,000	$ 1,169,300	$400,700	$80,140	$320,560	$ 1,489,860
IRRs				10%				18.7%

The amount of cash flow in year 3 required to achieve a 10 percent target IRR for investors can be determined as

$$\$1,000,000 = (\$70,000)\, \frac{1}{(1 + .10)^1} + (\$70,000)\, \frac{1}{(1 + .10)^2} + (X)\, \frac{1}{(1 + .10)^3}$$

Solving for (X) = $1,169,300

Note that in year 3, a total of $1,570,000 is available to distribute to investors and to pay fund management fees. Of that amount, $1,169,300 is the total cash flow (including $70,000 in asset management fees) required to provide investors with the hurdle IRR of 10 percent over the three-year life of the fund. After paying investors $1,169,300 from the available cash flow, $400,700 remains. Investors will receive an 80 percent share, or $320,560 of that remaining cash flow. This produces total cash flow to investors of $1,489,860 and a net after-fee IRR of 18.7 percent. The fund manager will retain 20 percent of $400,700 or $80,140 as the "Promote."

Reporting Fund Performance

An example of the quarterly financial results from a hypothetical real estate fund is provided in Exhibit 23–2. The reader should be aware that in addition to properties, results at the "fund level" are affected by many other items that are necessary to operate the fund. For example, fund managers may need access to liquidity in the form of cash balances, or marketable short-term investments. Sources of short-term debt (e.g., lines of credit) are also used. Fund managers must manage net cash inflows or income received from property operations, as well as cash inflows from additional equity contributions from new investors. Managers then accumulate funds with which to make property acquisitions. Managers also must sell properties and make cash distributions to investors. As a result, when considering performance at the fund level, there are many activities in addition to buying and selling properties that must be performed continuously by the manager during the period.

Measuring and Reporting Investment Returns

One challenge faced by fund managers is how to report periodic results for the performance of a fund. For example, Exhibit 23–2 contains a financial summary of activities for a hypothetical open-end, commingled real estate investment fund. Looking closely at the exhibit, we can see that during the reporting period, the market value (MV) of equity increased from $200 million at the beginning of the quarter (Section A) to market value of $425 million at the end of the quarter (Section C). We also see (Section B) that during the quarter, properties in the portfolio produced net operating income of $10 million. Additional property acquisitions totaled $220 million as investors provided $225 million of additional equity. This could be new investors or existing investors funding their undrawn commitments. The fund also reported a distribution of $5 million to equity investors, while the cash balance in the fund increased to $18 million in anticipation of possible future acquisitions.

EXHIBIT 23-2   Summary of Funds Flow—Hypothetical Real Estate Investment Fund (in million $)

A. Market Value of Fund (Beginning of Quarter)				B. Operating and Capital Flows During Quarter		C. Market Value of Fund (End of Quarter)			
Assets		**Liabilities**		**Property Operations**		**Assets**		**Liabilities**	
Cash Balance	$ 10	ST Debt	$ 10	NOI	$ 10	Cash Balance	$ 18	ST Debt	$ 10
ST Investments	$ 20	Total Debt	$ 10	Less: Fund Mgt Fees	$ 2	ST Investments	$ 20	Total Debt	$ 10
Properties @ MV	$ 200	**MV Equity**	**$ 220**	Plus: Interest Income	$ 1	Properties @ MV	$ 425	**MV Equity**	**$ 453**
Total Assets @ MV	$ 230	Total D+E	$ 230	Less: Interest Expense	$ 1	Total Assets @ MV	$ 463	Total D+E	$ 463
				=Funds Avail for Distrib	$ 8				
				Less: Distributions	$ 5				
				=Cash Retained	$ 3				
				Capital Flows					
				Investor Contributions	$ 225				
				Property Acquisitions	$ 220				
				Property Dispositions	$ 0				
				Cash Retained	$ 5				

Summary of Major Activity during Quarter:

Beginning of Period:

- Fund contains $30 million in cash + short-term (ST) investments
- The fund also includes properties with a market value (MV) of $200 million
- MV Total Assets = $230 million
- Short-Term Debt = $10 million
- MV of equity = $220 million

During Quarter:

- Cash inflow from property operations (NOI) = $10 million
- Fund management fees paid totaled $2 million
- Fund distributed $5 million to investors
- Investor contributions to the fund during quarter totaled $225 million
- Properties acquisition totaled $220 million
- No long-term debt was used for acquisitions
- No properties were sold (i.e., no dispositions)
- Cash balance increased during quarter by $8 million ($3 from property operations and $5 from net investor contributions)

End of Period:

- Fund-level cash totals $18 million and ST Investments total $38 million
- MV properties at end of quarter = $425 million

The question that we must now answer is how should performance and investment returns for the fund be calculated and reported to investors for the quarter? This is somewhat complicated by the fact that cash flows from property operations may be occurring daily during the quarter, some cash flows may occur monthly, while property acquisitions may occur at any time during the period. Finally, we should recall that MV of equity is based, in large part, on appraised property values. Exhibit 23–3 provides a diagram of the many

EXHIBIT 23–3
**Real Estate
Investment Funds
Flow**

Real estate investment funds flow

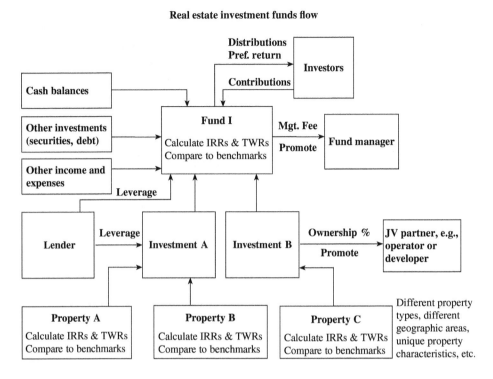

functions and cash flows involved in the operation of a commercial real estate investment fund. How will fund management provide guidance to investors regarding fund performance? How will these cash flow activities be converted into a single rate of return on investment?

When trying to answer this question, several other factors also must be kept in mind. The majority of properties in the fund have not been sold and continue to comprise most of the fund's investment equity portfolio. As a result, the $425 million shown as MV of equity at the end of the quarter is based largely on appraised values. The $5 million in property appreciation for the quarter is, therefore, a gain that is "unrealized." Consequently, the financial information being reported to investors should be thought of as an estimate of the performance, assuming all the properties could have been sold at their appraised value. When there are sudden changes in market values, appraised values can sometimes lag values reflected in transaction prices because it can take a quarter or two for appraisers to see enough evidence to feel confident that the market has actually changed.

Performance returns (realized or unrealized) are very important to all parties involved with the operation of the fund because investors use return data to assess how well their investments and the fund manager are performing. Furthermore, as we have discussed, fee compensation paid to fund managers may be partially dependent on property fund performance. Manager fees may depend on whether reported returns exceed the target return that fund managers indicated that they expect to achieve in the fund offering document and when the fund was marketed to investors. (We will discuss performance targets/benchmarks in the next section.) Industry consultants may also use performance data to make "peer group comparisons" when recommending investment funds to clients.

Calculating Returns

Typically, investment results are computed and reported by fund managers in the context of industry standards and practice. During the past 30+ years, there has been much discussion regarding the development of performance metrics that capture and present an accurate picture of results for commercial real estate funds. We have pointed out that cash flows from operations, property sales, capital contribution, acquisitions, and cash distributions to investors may occur throughout the period. Managers also must have liquidity (cash balances, etc.) to pay expenses, make additional property acquisitions, and so on. Because these fund flows usually occur within a quarterly reporting period, they are often referred to as "intra-period" cash flows.

For computational purposes, it would be preferable if all cash flows occurred at either the beginning or end of a period. This way, we could calculate an IRR as we have done numerous times in the preceding chapters. To illustrate using our fund example in Exhibit 23–2, if all cash flows occurred at the end of a quarter, we **could** characterize cash flows as follows, then solve for the internal rate of return:

$$(MVBE) = [MVEE + CF - CC] \times \frac{1}{(1 + i)^1}$$

Solving for i we have:

$$i = ([MVEE + CF - CC]/MVBE) - 1$$

Taking values from Exhibit 23–3:

$$i = ([\$453 + \$5 - \$225]/\$220) - 1 = 5.91\%$$

Note:
MV = Market Value
BE = Beginning Equity
EE = Ending Equity
CF = Cash Distributions (CD) and all Net Cash Flows (all inflows − outflows)
CC = Capital Contributions
i = Internal Rate of Return

Unfortunately this simplified, single-period IRR is inadequate because we know that the fund included several intra-period cash flows. In other words, not all cash flows occur at the beginning, or end, of the period. Furthermore, intuitively we know that if a significant amount of all net positive cash flows occurred early in the period, the IRR in our example is likely to be understated. How can we improve our estimate of returns that will reflect funds flow during the reporting period more accurately?

One approach would be to use the XIRR function in Excel. This function allows for specification of the exact date for each cash flow during each quarter also considering the number of days in the quarter. The resulting IRR can be then converted to an effective quarterly and annual rate (if desired) for comparison purposes.

A second approach to calculating returns would be to use a more simple approximation to the IRR called the "Modified Dietz" return formula.[4] The "Modified Dietz" (R_D) formula may be used to approximate an IRR when intra-period cash flows occur during the quarter. It does not require a computer using Excel and was developed before the XIRR function was available. The modified Dietz method weights each net cash inflow by the remaining number of days in the reporting period that cash flows is held in the investment fund. This formula is as follows:

$$R_D = \frac{MVEE - MVBE + \Sigma CFj}{MVBE - CFW}$$

[4] This formula evolved from an original formula proposed by Peter O. Dietz (late professor at the University of Oregon and President of the Frank Russell Company). The original Dietz formula had all intra-period cash flows occurring at the *midpoint* during the quarter. Later, the "modified Dietz" formula was introduced, which considers the exact day of the quarter each cash flow occurs. This is more accurate, as it weights cash flows in the fund by the remaining days in the reporting period after any cash flow occurs. This "day weighting" of cash flows provides a more accurate estimate of the IRR for the quarter. The modified Dietz approach is now used extensively when reporting performance by real estate funds in the United States.

MVEE is the market value of fund at the end of the period.

MVBE is the market value of fund at the beginning of the period.

CFj is the net positive cash flow received by investors in the fund (distributions less contributions) during the *j*th day.

ΣCFj is the sum of all net positive cash flow during all days in the period.[5]

CFW is the time-weighted cash flow calculated as $\Sigma CFj\,(N-j)/N$. The net positive cash flow for each day is weighted by the remaining days in the period.

N = total number of days in the period.

The denominator shown in the R_D formula can be thought of as adjusting the initial equity value (*MVBE*) by net cash inflows or outflows (*CFW*) each day during the period. Net cash flows into the fund are weighted by the number of days remaining in the reporting period to adjust for the time value of money. So the entire denominator can be interpreted as the day-weighted investment during the quarter. In essence, if positive cash flows occur early during the quarter, *CFW* increases. A larger *CFW* in the formula reduces the denominator, thereby increasing the return (R_D).

To illustrate further, in our example if we assume (1) all cash distributions (CD) occurred equally on the 30th, 60th, and 90th days during the quarter and (2) that the quarter was 90 days in length, focusing on CFW, we have:

$$CFW = [1/3CD \times (90 - 30)/90] + [1/3CD \times (90 - 60)/90] + [1/3CD \times (90 - 90)]$$

Note that the last distribution is assumed to occur at the very end of the last month of the quarter and therefore is weighted by zero. Consequently, it does not affect *CFW*.

Substituting from our example in Exhibit 23–2, we have distributions to investors of $5 million during the quarter, or $1.67 million at the end of three equal 30-day intervals during the quarter, therefore:

$$CFW = [\$1.67 \times (90 - 30)/90] + [\$1.67 \times (90 - 60)/90]$$
$$+ [\$1.67 \times (90 - 90)/90] = \$1.67 \text{ million}$$

In this case, *CFW* coincidently turns out to be one month's cash flow of $1.67 million

$$\Sigma CFj = \$5 - \$225 = -\$220$$

Now using the modified Dietz formula we have

$$R_D = \frac{MVEE - MVBE + \Sigma CFj}{MVBE - CFW}$$

$$R_D = (\$453 - \$220 - \$225)/(\$220 - \$1.67) = .0595, \text{ or } 5.95\%$$

Note that 5.95 percent is very close to the same answer that we calculated using the IRR, which was 5.91 percent. Again, the reason for the higher 5.95 percent Dietz return is because some cash flows available for distribution to investors occurred early in the quarter. Results using the Modified Dietz formula will not always equal IRRs for the same period, but it is usually a good approximation. It has become a standard among institutional investors to measure and report performance to investors. Also note:

Income Return (after fees)	$8/($220−$1.67)	=	3.66%
Appreciation Return	$5/($220−$1.67)	=	2.29%
Total Return			5.95%

[5] The sign would be negative if *CF* was defined as net investment, that is, contributions to the fund by investors.

Calculating Returns at the "Property Level"

In the previous section, we examined the returns reported at the **"fund level"** and described the way that investment returns are calculated when intra-period cash flows occur.

We now turn to the examination of investment performance at the **"property level."** This means that we want to focus only on the performance of the **properties in the fund.** In this case, we do not want to consider the effects of any debt (leverage), cash retention, short-term investments, or short-term liabilities. While these items are very important to managers operating the **fund,** we want to focus here only on how the **properties** acquired for the investment fund performed. We will also ignore debt that was obtained to finance individual properties because we want to calculate a return that only reflects the performance of the property independent of financial structuring.

Turning back to our previous example in Exhibit 23–2, we see in Section (A) that the beginning market value for properties in the fund was $200 million. During the period, investors contributed new equity of $225 million, and $200 million was expended for property acquisitions. At the end of the period, all properties in the fund were valued at $425 million. The property portfolio also generated NOI of $10 million during the period. How well did the **property portfolio** perform? How do we evaluate intra-period cash flows, the property appreciation of $5 million and the receipt of cash from NOI of $10 million during the period?

To accomplish this we can turn once again to the approximation of the IRR for the quarter by using the Modified Dietz calculation.

$$R_D = \frac{MVEE - MVBE + \Sigma CFj}{MVBE - CFW}$$

Values in millions for the terms in Modified Dietz formula are:

$$MVEE = \$425$$
$$MVBE = \$200$$
$$NOI = \$\ 10$$
$$CF = \$220$$

We can calculate returns as follows:

$$R_D = \frac{\$425 - \$200 + (\$10 - \$220)}{\$220 - CFW}$$

Assuming again that $CFW = \$3.33$ million or $10 million in distributions received in three equal amounts every 30 days by investors, then we calculate R_D as follows:

$$[\$3.33 \times (90 - 0)/90] + [\$3.33 \times (90 - 60)/90] + [\$3.33 \times (90 - 90)/90] = \$3.33$$

$$R_D = \frac{\$425 - \$200 + (-\$220 + \$10)}{\$220 - \$3.33} = 7.62\%$$

Also note that:

$$\text{Income Return (before fees)} = \frac{\$10}{\$200 - \$3.33} = 5.08\%$$

$$\text{Appreciation Return} = \frac{\$5}{\$200 - \$3.33} = \underline{2.54\%}$$

$$\text{Total Return} = \underline{\underline{7.62\%}}$$

Comparing Returns: Fund Level versus Property Level

In the previous two sections, we provided calculations for returns at the **fund level** and the **property level** when intra-period cash flows occurred. At the fund level, the return for the quarter was estimated to be 5.95 percent while at the property level, the return was 7.62 percent (both returns were calculated with the "Modified Dietz" formula to approximate the quarterly IRR). The difference between the two returns, or 1.67 percent, has been referred to as the **"cash drag"** and/or **"administrative drag"** on fund-level returns because of the need for some cash balances and short-term investments that may not be earning much of a return as well as the fund administrative fees. Most fund managers try to minimize the "drag" on fund returns by managing these items as cost-effectively as possible. It should also be noted that because we ignored leverage, the property return could also be lower than the fund return regardless of any cash or administrative drag.

Returns: Before and After Fees

In a previous section of this chapter, we included a discussion of management fees. In practice, returns at the fund level are often calculated "before and after fees." Looking back to our hypothetical example in Exhibit 23–2, we show that management fees of $2 million were paid during the quarter. We also calculated returns at the "fund level" to be 5.95 percent, which was computed "after fees." In order to calculate returns "before fees" we would have to add back fees of $2 million to the distributions shown in Exhibit 23–2. This would increase the amount available for distribution from $5 million to $7 million, or $2.33 million monthly. We would then recalculate returns by increasing CF by $2 million and CFW by $2.33 million in the R_D computations. Before fee returns would then be calculated as

$$CFW = (\$2.33 \times (90 - 30)90) + \$2.33 \times (90 - 60)/90) = \$2.33 \text{ million and}$$

$$R_D = (\$453 - \$220 + \$225) + \$7)/(\$220 - \$2.33) = 6.89\%$$

This calculation indicates that the return **before fees** at the fund level would have been 6.89 percent, while the return **after fees** was 5.95 percent. This implies a reduction in investor returns of 94 basis points (BP) or .94 percent due to management fees. This is often referred to as the "fee loss" in investor returns.

Calculating Historical Returns

Some real estate investment funds have existed for many years. Some well-known open-end, commingled, core property funds have existed for well over 20 years. Consequently, investors and analysts are very interested in how well funds have performed historically, as they use these returns to make forecasts and projections of future returns.

There are generally two ways that historical returns are calculated for real estate investments. The first approach is to calculate what is referred to as a **time-weighted return** (TWR). This approach requires having an estimate of value at the *beginning* and *end* of **each time interval** in the time series. Recall that in the previous chapter we illustrated the calculation of holding period returns (HPR) for a series of time period. As we have pointed out, in commercial real estate transaction prices are generally not available on a periodic basis. This may require the use of appraised values for beginning and ending values each quarter.

The second approach is an IRR, which is the same calculation as we have done many times in previous chapters of this book. Generally, this approach considers the acquisition price the property was initially purchased, all cash flows realized by investors from property operations, then all cash flow received when the property is sold, or based on an end of period value as if it was sold for its appraised value.

Time-weighted returns are a very important and a commonly used measure of performance for real estate funds. These returns are particularly important when investors and analysts need an indicator that (1) captures how well a fund has performed over time and

(2) can be compared with results of other funds or indices over the same time period. TWRs have the added advantage that calculations are (a) independent of the dollar size of investment that is being made or being redeemed and (b) returns can be broken down into any number of sub periods that an analyst desires.

Internal rates of return are generally used by **investors** to measure what rate of return has, or will, be earned on their particular investment. This usually is based on the specific date that an investment was made, dates that cash contributions were made and cash distributions were received, and a specific date of sale. Unlike TWRs, these dates may not coincide with the beginning and/or end of any particular investment reporting period. IRRs are also influenced significantly by the dollar magnitude of cash flows. (Consequently, IRRs are also called "dollar-weighted returns.") In some cases, when properties are not sold, estimates of IRR may be made on the basis of appraised values for properties. In other words, IRRs can be based on appraised values if the investor believes that appraised values are an accurate reflection of property prices and when the investor needs an estimate of the IRR.

Time-Weighted Returns

When returns (HPRs) are reported for fixed time intervals (e.g., quarterly), most analysts will "chain link" them and then calculate geometric returns for various cumulative time intervals (e.g., 1, 3, 5 years). The result is referred to as a "time-weighted return" (TWR). This is because the return reported for each period (e.g., quarterly) **within** the cumulative time period being analyzed (e.g., a year) carries the same weight in the calculation of the return. That is, returns from cash flows during the first period that the property was owned has the same impact on the TWR calculation as cash flows received in the last period. Recall that in the previous chapter we calculated these geometric means for a hypothetical portfolio and for several indices.

Given that returns from each time period has the same weight on the TWR, a very important aspect of the calculation is that it doesn't matter if more or less capital is invested **during** a particular time period. For example, if a fund has $100 million invested in properties at the beginning of the first period, and then earns $5 million during the period and the value of the properties increase to $105 million by the end of the period, then the return for the first period will be (105 + 5 − 100)/100 = 10%. Then suppose that at the very beginning of the second period an additional $95 million of capital inflows occurs from investors. Also assume that the $95 million is invested by the fund manager in additional properties. The fund then earns $15 million from operations during the second period and the total value of the fund at the end of the second period increases to $215 million. The return for the second period is (215 + 15 − 200)/200 = 15%. Then to get a TWR for the two periods, we would have 1.10 × 1.15 − 1 = 26.5%. The reader should note that the return for each quarterly period had the same weight in determining the total returns. This is true even though twice as much money was invested in period two relative to period one. The **geometric mean** is 12.47 percent, which reflects an equal weighting of both period's returns. We will elaborate on the rationale for the use of time-weighted returns later in this chapter.

In the example above, it should be noted that we added 1 to each return before chain-linking them. This is done to capture the compounding effect of returns that are carried over from period to period. To calculate the average return for the entire period, we then take the geometric mean of the chain-linked returns.

If we wanted to evaluate returns for all four periods, we would chain link these returns as follows:

$$(1 + R1) \times (1 + R2) \times (1 + R3) \times (1 + R4)$$

where R1 is the return for the first year, R2 is the return for the second year, and so on.

To determine the average return for the four periods, we then calculate the fourth root of the chain-linked quarterly returns and subtract 1. The result is the time-weighted return

(TWR), which is the geometric mean of the chain-linked returns. Chain linking the returns and then taking the geometric mean is very important. Why the geometric mean is important can be shown by comparing it to an **arithmetic mean,** which is determined by simply adding the returns and taking the arithmetic mean. The difference is summarized below:

$$\text{Arithmetic average return over 4 years} = (R1 + R2 + R3 + R4)/4$$

$$\text{Geometric average return over 4 years} = [(1+R1) \times (1+R2) \times (1+R3) \times (1+R4)]^{(1/4)} - 1$$

The geometric mean, or TWR, is considered the most relevant for performance measurement by most industry professionals. To illustrate why, consider the following example. A property begins the year with a value of 100 and ends five years later with a value of 100. We assume that there is no intra-period cash flow. The example shows that the arithmetic mean is slightly positive. But how can this be if the investor begins and ends with $100 or exactly what he or she started with? In contrast, the geometric mean is exactly zero, which represents the true performance of the investment.

Arithmetic versus Geometric Mean			
Year	Value	Return	Return + 1
0	100		
1	105	5.00%	1.0500
2	110	4.76%	1.0476
3	115	4.55%	1.0455
4	107	−6.96%	0.9304
5	100	−6.54%	0.9346
		Σ.81	1.0000

Arithmetic Mean: .81/5 = 0.16%

Geometric Mean: $\sqrt[5]{1.000} - 1 = 0.00\%$

When the returns are calculated quarterly, it is a common industry practice to "annualize" the returns for reporting purposes. Consider the following example with returns calculated over 3 years or 12 quarters.

Annualized Returns Example			
Quarter	Return	(1 + Return)	Chain Link
1	2%	1.02	1.0200
2	3%	1.03	1.0506 ← (1.02) × (1.03)
3	4%	1.04	1.0926
4	2%	1.02	1.1145
5	0%	1.00	1.1145
6	−2%	0.98	1.0922
7	−4%	0.96	1.0485
8	1%	1.01	1.0590
9	2%	1.02	1.0802
10	4%	1.04	1.2267
11	5%	1.05	1.1795
12	4%	1.04	1.2267

An Index

$(1.2267)^{(1/12)} - 1 = .017175$ or 1.7175% average quarterly return
$(1.017175)^4 - 1 = .0705$ or 7.05% annualized
Shortcut: $(1.2267)^{(4/12)} - 1 = .0705$ or 7.05% annualized

Again, we can chain link the quarterly returns and then take the geometric mean to get an average quarterly return. In this case, the average quarterly return is 1.7175 percent. To annualize this average quarterly return, we must compound it over four quarters. We have $(1.017175)^4 - 1 = 7.05\%$ as the average annual return (TWR) for the 12 quarters.[6]

Internal Rates of Return

Exhibit 23–4A below shows the calculation of the IRR for an investment over the past five years. As we know from prior chapters, the IRR is the rate that makes the present value of the cash flows including the resale price equal to the initial purchase price. Alternatively, it makes the net present value equal to zero. In this example, it considers the cash flows over all five years. In the example, a property was acquired for $500,000 and actual cash flows were $50,000, $40,000, $30,000, $50,000, and $60,000 in years 1–5, respectively. The property was then sold for $600,000 at the end of the fifth year. The resulting IRR is 11.22 percent. So we can say that an investor who purchased the property and sold it after five years earned 11.22 percent on his or her outstanding capital investment each year. (We should also note that, if the *estimated selling price* at the end of year 5 was based on an *appraised value* of $600,000, then 11.22 percent would be the *estimated IRR* because the $600,000 sale price would be unrealized.)

Comparing IRR and TWR

It is useful to see how the calculation of the IRR compares with that of the TWR discussed previously over an investment time period. In the previous example we calculated the IRR for a five-year period assuming annual cash flows. To calculate a time-weighted return (TWR) over the same time period, we would need to have estimated values at the end of each year in order to calculate yearly holding period returns (HPRs) and then take the geometric mean of the five HPRs to get the average annual TWR for the five years.

In Exhibit 23–4B, we add assumed appraised values at the end of years 1 through 4. The HPR is shown for each year, which varies considerably depending on how the values are changing over time. The TWR is the geometric mean of the five HPRs, which is 13.49 percent. The IRR for the same time period is 12.22 percent. Again, the difference reflects the fact that the TWR treats each period equally (each year in this case) in its impact on the geometric mean, whereas the IRR reflects the exact timing of each cash flow and gives more weight to cash flows received in early periods.

EXHIBIT 23–4A
IRR Example

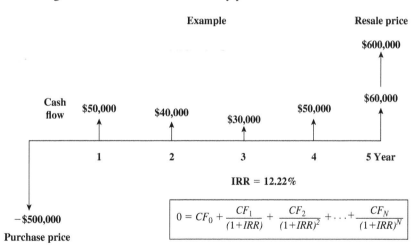

$$0 = CF_0 + \frac{CF_1}{(1+IRR)} + \frac{CF_2}{(1+IRR)^2} + \ldots + \frac{CF_N}{(1+IRR)^N}$$

The single rate that discounts all the net cash flows back to a zero NPV.

[6] The average annual return could be computed more directly by taking the 12/4, or third root, of the chain-linked returns.

EXHIBIT 23–4B
TWR versus IRR

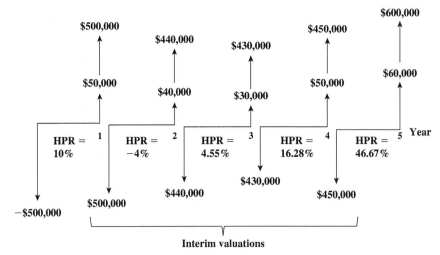

Each HPR is like an IRR for the interim
period, for example, one year in this example.

TWR (Geo Mean of HPR) = 13.49%
IRR = 12.22% (for the 5 years)

Choosing IRR versus TWR for Performance Measurement

Given the discussion in the previous section, a relevant question becomes: "What is the best measure of fund performance?" When the manager has control over the amount of funds available to invest each period, then the IRR is an appropriate measure of the manager's performance. But when the manager does NOT have control over the flow of funds available to invest each period, then the TWR is a better measure of how the investment or fund manager performed.

Whether the manager has control over the amount of funds invested often depends on the type of fund. For example, as we have pointed out, an *open-end fund* provides considerable latitude over how often investors can either make investment or redemptions. These funds are often used for investing in relatively large well-diversified portfolios of "core" properties. As we have discussed, these funds are often "core" open-end commingled funds. They are (1) relatively low risk, (2) generally use relatively low amounts of leverage, and (3) properties are usually in good locations with high occupancy. In general, under normal conditions, investors have considerable flexibility as to how much capital they choose to keep in the fund.[7] Consequently, in this case, a fund manager has little, if any, control of the amount of capital invested in the fund. In this case, the TWR would be the best measure of the fund manager's performance. This is because time-weighted returns are not affected by the magnitude of cash flows in the calculation; therefore, the manager's performance is not influenced by the investor's decisions to get in or out of the fund, which could trigger significant capital decisions involving either acquisitions or dispositions or partial sales.

In the case of closed-end, value-added and opportunistic funds, restrictions on the ability of investors to add or withdraw capital from funds are much more common. These funds are often used for more specialized investment strategies and generally make riskier investments on properties in lifecycles that are not stable yet. For example, investments may be made in properties that are not performing well with a strategy of creating value by increasing occupancy or making improvements. Properties might also be purchased that require significant renovation. Finally, these funds generally use higher amounts of

[7] There will generally be restrictions on investors' ability to withdraw funds if the market becomes extremely weak and/or a lot of investors are making redemption requests from the fund at the same time.

leverage. When funds use this investment strategy, they may be referred to as "value-added funds." Or in cases where they use considerable amount of leverage and also do development in addition to major renovations, they may be considered "opportunity funds."

Value-added and opportunistic funds are usually closed end. In these cases, it is more likely that the fund manager will decide when to request funds from investors and when to make distributions by selling properties and liquidating the fund. Furthermore, closed-end fund managers are less likely to value every property in the fund on a regular basis. Given that investors are not adding capital and taking capital out of the fund on a regular basis, managers may not want the fund to incur the costs of appraisals every quarter or even every year. In conclusion, in cases when managers have more control over when capital is invested and when capital is returned to investors, the IRR may be a better measure of the investment manager's performance. Exhibit 23–5 summarizes the relationship between (1) the extent of manager control over cash flows into and out of the fund, (2) the frequency that property valuation may be required, and (3) whether an IRR or TWR may be more appropriate for measuring investment performance.

Target Returns and Benchmarks

When marketing to potential investors, an estimate of the rate of return that investors may expect to earn is usually provided by fund managers. This "expected return" is sometimes referred to as a "**target return** for the fund."

This target return may be a specific return, for example, "the fund is expected to produce a 10 percent return on investment after fees." However, in many cases, the target return may change with economic conditions. Consequently, the expected return will be tied to a "benchmark" that is readily determined from a well-known market index, adjusted by a "margin" or spread. Using an analogy from the mutual fund industry as an example: For a diversified fund of large cap growth stocks, a manager could set target returns using the S&P 500 as a benchmark, then add a spread as a premium for "active management" of a portfolio constructed to outperform the S&P 500.[8]

EXHIBIT 23–5
When to Use IRR versus TWR

When to Use IRR versus TWR

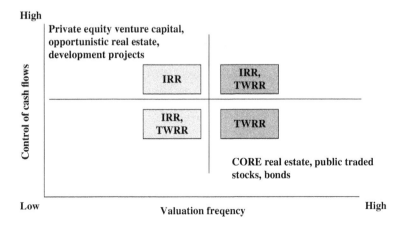

[8] "Active management" describes cases where a fund manager is actually doing research, actively asset managing, buying and selling assets in an attempt to outperform a benchmark. A "passive" investment could be made by an investor without a fund manager. In the case of common stocks, an investor could make a "passive investment" by purchasing the S&P Index (SPDRs) without any active management (of picking and choosing individual stocks). Therefore, to justify fees charged by active fund managers, it would be expected that these actively managed funds should achieve a target return in excess of the S&P benchmark.

EXHIBIT 23–6
Real Estate
Investment Styles

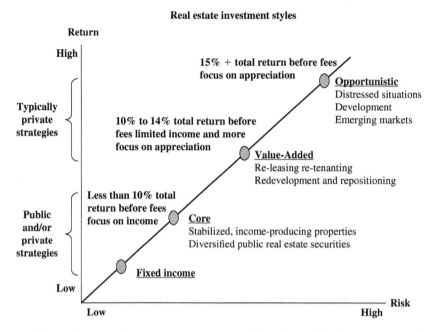

Real estate investment styles

Return

High

15% + total return before fees
focus on appreciation

Opportunistic
Distressed situations
Development
Emerging markets

Typically
private
strategies

10% to 14% total return before
fees limited income and more
focus on appreciation

Value-Added
Re-leasing re-tenanting
Redevelopment and repositioning

Less than 10% total
return before fees
focus on income

Core
Stabilized, income-producing properties
Diversified public real estate securities

Public
and/or
private
strategies

Fixed income

Low

Low

Risk

High

How are benchmarks or target returns usually estimated by fund managers for real estate investment funds? First, it may be helpful to think about the risk and return profiles for the various fund types discussed in Exhibit 23–1 (Section A). We show a conceptual diagram for these real estate investment funds in Exhibit 23–6.

In Concept Box 23–2 we list some of the benchmarks that may be used for real estate investment funds. For core funds, a common **benchmark** that is used for open-end, commingled funds is the ODCE fund-level index produced by NCREIF. For core separate accounts, the NCREIF-NPI (property level) index may serve as a benchmark. Property funds may then add a "spread" or premium to the benchmark when indicating what expected or target returns may be achieved by investors in the fund. The extent of this spread will depend on how focused or specialized the property fund being marketed compares to properties making up the benchmark. For example, while a core property fund strategy may be to invest only in core properties, management may believe that it has superior skills in selecting properties and locations for investment properties, and it may indicate that it expects to earn some premium above the ODCE index. Similarly, if a fund was created to invest only in core office properties in the Western half of the United States, the fund manager may use ODCE as a benchmark but then add a premium because they expect investment performance for the fund to be greater because of its specialized focus and limited diversification.

Investment Multiple

We have discussed IRRs and TWRs as important ways of measuring the performance of a fund. Another measure that is relatively simple to calculate but also useful to investors is the **investment multiple.** It is also sometimes called the equity multiple. The equity multiple is calculated as follows:

$$\text{Equity Multiple} = (\text{Current Net Asset Value of Fund} + \text{Cumulative Distributions}) / \text{Contributions}$$

The current net asset value of the fund is what investors could, in theory, receive as of the current date and the cumulative distributions is money they have already received. This is divided by the amount that investors have contributed to the fund. Obviously, the extent to which the ratio exceeds one the more investors have received relative to what they invested.

NFI-ODCE

The National Council of Real Estate Investment Fiduciaries (NCREIF) Fund Index: Open-End Diversified Core Equity (ODCE) is a *fund-level index* for commingled funds pursuing a core investment strategy. Returns include quarterly cash distributions and beginning and ending equity values. Fund returns also include cash balances and leverage (returns also reflect any partial ownership positions in properties/assets). Quarterly returns are time-weighted. Returns are reported both gross and net of fees. As of second quarter 2014, ODCE reported gross real estate assets of $150 billion and net real estate market value of $117 billion with 22 funds reporting on 2,156 investments. The index composition is as follows: 36.0 percent office, 25.3 percent apartment, 19.3 percent retail, 14.7 percent industrial, 1.9 percent hotel, and 2.9 percent other. Additional information can be found at www.ncreif.org.

NCREIF-NPI

The National Council of Real Estate Investment Fiduciaries (NCREIF) Property Index (NPI) is a *property-level index* for individual properties based on data collected from its members. Most properties have been acquired on behalf of tax-exempt institutions and are held in a fiduciary environment. The properties include both wholly owned and joint venture investments but data is reported to NCREIF as if the property was 100 percent owned by the manager. It is restricted to operating properties only (not development properties) and includes only investment grade, nonagricultural, income-producing properties. These include apartment, hotels, industrial, office, and retail. The NCREIF Property Index is unleveraged and is compiled before the deduction of acquisition, asset management, and disposition fees. As of second quarter 2014, NPI reported 7,141 properties with a total market value of $382.5 billion. Additional information can be found at www.ncreif.org.

10-YEAR U.S. TREASURY YIELD (NOMINAL CONSTANT MATURITY)

One frequently used benchmark is the 10-year Treasury Yield. This yield represents the current market interest rate on U.S. Treasury bonds that will mature 10 years from the date of purchase. This rate is established daily by the Board of Governors of the Federal Reserve System. Closing market bids used to calculate yields are based on actively traded Treasury securities in the over-the-counter market. Yields are calculated on the basis of closing quotations obtained by the Federal Reserve Bank of New York.

CPI ADJUSTED—REQUIRED REAL RETURNS

Portfolio returns are calculated and then deflated by the Consumer Price Index: Urban Consumer (CPI).The CPI(U) is published by the U.S. Bureau of Labor Statistics (BLS).

Attribution Analysis

In the previous section, we provided a brief description of benchmarks and expected, or target, returns. We pointed out that the majority of real estate investment funds tend to be "actively managed." In many cases, these managers indicate that investment results for their fund will exceed (outperform) the benchmarks (some managers estimate the spread that they expect to earn in excess of the benchmark). When actual results either over- or underperform expected returns, investors and analysts may want to determine why. This question may be answered by using **attribution analysis.**

Benchmarks are often used to perform what is referred to as "attribution analysis." The term "Attribution Analysis" refers to explaining why the performance of a fund may be higher or lower than the benchmark return. Attribution analysis involves the *decomposition* of the total investment performance into additive components so as to "attribute" the total performance to sources that may reflect various "active" investment management *functions.* For example, an investment manager may earn a rate of return of 10 percent on a fund. This return may be acceptable; however, if the ODCE index (benchmark) reported a return of 12 percent for the same time period, investors would probably think that the manager did not perform as well as the investor would have expected.

To elaborate, an investment manager adds value in two ways: (1) Choosing superior property investments, which is referred to as "selection" and (2) executing a superior strategy as to how a fund invests in different market segments and geographic locations. This is referred to as "allocation."

Superior *selection* is value added by a transactions team, superior asset/property management practices and executing an effective disposition policy.

Superior *allocation* is value added from buying and selling in the right market locations.

Exhibit 23–7 shows that a fund earned 2.75 percent while its benchmark earned 2.50 percent. Thus, the fund *outperformed* the benchmark. But the return for the *benchmark was higher* in the two property sectors. How could the fund have performed better than the benchmark? The answer is that the fund had more capital allocated to sector A, which performed better than sector B. So although the fund did a poor job at "selection" of individual properties, they did a superior job at "allocation" across property sectors. In this case, superior allocation more than offsets inferior property selection.

In the example shown in Exhibit 23–8, the fund *underperformed* the benchmark. However, the fund did better than the benchmark in both sectors. How could this happen? In this case, the fund manager did a good job of selecting properties but did a poor job allocating across sectors (property types, regions, MSAs). The fund allocated too much capital to sector B, which was the worst performing sector. Poor allocation offset good property selection.

It should be clear that *both* individual property selection and allocation across sectors is important for superior fund performance. Identifying the area (selection or allocation) that caused the fund to underperform is important for fund managers when trying to improve future performance.

EXHIBIT 23–7
Example 1–Attribution Analysis

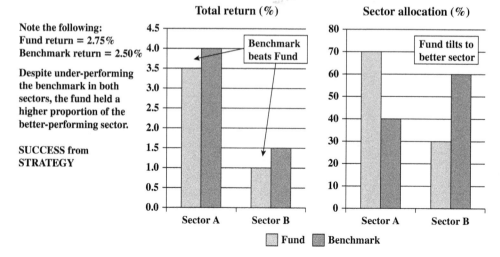

Example 1

Weak property selection, good sector allocation strategy

Note the following:
Fund return = 2.75%
Benchmark return = 2.50%

Despite under-performing the benchmark in both sectors, the fund held a higher proportion of the better-performing sector.

SUCCESS from STRATEGY

EXHIBIT 23–8
Example 2–Attribution
Analysis

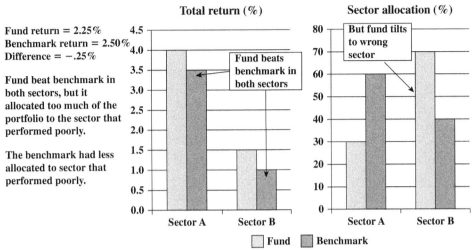

Example 2

Good property selection, poor sector allocation strategy

Fund return = 2.25%
Benchmark return = 2.50%
Difference = −.25%

Fund beat benchmark in both sectors, but it allocated too much of the portfolio to the sector that performed poorly.

The benchmark had less allocated to sector that performed poorly.

☐ Fund   ▨ Benchmark

Attribution Analysis Mathematics

In this section we look more closely at the math used in attribution analysis.

First, we define the following terms for an individual sector:

R_f Fund return for sector i
R_b Benchmark return for sector i
W_f Fund weight of sector i
W_b Benchmark weight of sector i

There are four key terms for each sector:

$W_f R_f$ Sector i contribution to total fund return
$W_b R_b$ Sector i contribution to total benchmark return
$W_b R_f$ Fund proportion of sector i
$W_f R_b$ Benchmark proportion of sector i

Summing over all of the sectors we get:

$R = \Sigma W_f R_f$ Fund total return
$B = \Sigma W_b R_b$ Benchmark total return
$S = \Sigma W_b R_f$ Fund return if diversified like the benchmark
$A = \Sigma W_f R_b$ Benchmark return if diversified like the fund

A tabular form of the above is summarized as follows:

	Fund weights	Benchmark weights
Fund returns	$R = \Sigma W_f R_f$	$S = \Sigma W_b R_f$
Benchmark returns	$A = \Sigma W_f R_b$	$B = \Sigma W_b R_b$

Our objective is to explain why the fund return (R) differs from the benchmark (B). The calculation of this difference, $R - B$, is shown in Exhibit 23–9.

Note that $R - B$ can be decomposed into the **selection effect,** the **allocation effect,** and a "cross product" term that results from the interaction of the two effects. Some analysts include the cross product term in either the selection or allocation term but, in theory, it is a separate term that results from the interaction between selection and allocation. In most cases, it tends to be relatively small and may even be zero. This is summarized in Exhibit 23–9.

EXHIBIT 23–9
Sector Attribution—
The Basic Math

R − B =	Total excess return	
S − B $\Sigma W_b \cdot (R_f - R_b)$	Selection effects	Benchmark weight applied to return difference
+A − B $\Sigma (W_f - W_b) \cdot R_b$	Allocation effects	Benchmark return applied to weight difference
+R − S −A − B $\Sigma (W_f - W_b) \cdot (R_f - R_b)$	Cross product terms	Difference in weights × difference in returns

*Source: Lieblich (1995)

Example

Using the previous example, we now use the following formulas to calculate the allocation effect, selection effect, and any cross product term.

Using Previous Example 2		
R − B =	Total excess return	2.25% − 2.50% = −.25%
S − B $\Sigma W_b \cdot (R_f - R_b)$	Selection effects	= .60 × (4% − 3.5%) + .40 × (1.5% − 1%) = .5%
+A − B $\Sigma (W_f - W_b) \cdot R_b$	Allocation effects	= (.30 − .60) × 3.5% (.7 − .4) × 1% = −.75%
+R − S −A − B $\Sigma (W_f - W_b) \cdot (R_f - R_b)$	Cross product terms	= (.3 − .6) × (4% − 3.5%) + (.7 − .4) × (1.5% − 1%) = 0%

Summary for Previous Example 2	
Selection effects	.50%
+Allocation effects	−.75%
+Cross Product	.00%
=Total excess return	−.25%

As we can see, attribution analysis helps explain why returns for a fund differs from the benchmark. Differences in performance can be due to the following:

- Differences in risk.
- Differences in the ability to select individual properties.
- Differences in the allocation of the portfolio by sector (property type or location) compared to the benchmark.
- The attribution analysis we have examined so far implicitly assumes that the benchmark and the investment fund have the *same level of risk*. We will consider how to handle differences in risk in the next section.

Evaluating Risk Differences[9]

Portfolio performance, in part, consists of compensation for taking on risk. Total performance can be decomposed into risk-adjusted and risk premium segments. Modern capital market and portfolio theory indicates that investors should receive a return premium

[9] Much of the discussion in this section is also covered in finance textbooks on investments. The reader may be interested in reviewing relevant materials on stocks, bonds and other investment that parallel this discussion. For example, see: *Investments* by Bodie, Kane and Marcus, 10th Edition, McGraw Hill, 2013.

EXHIBIT 23–10
Frequently Used
Measures of Fund
Risk

Fund Risk Measures	
Measure	Definition
Sharpe Ratio	(Avg. fund return − risk-free rate)/std. dev. of (fund returns − risk free rate)
Beta	(Covariance between fund returns and benchmark returns)/(Variance of benchmark returns)*
Treynor Ratio (T_i)	(Avg. fund return − risk-free rate)/beta
Tracking Error	Std. dev. of *difference* in returns for fund versus benchmark
Information Ratio	Avg. of difference in returns for fund vs. benchmark/tracking error
Jensen's Alpha	Difference between actual fund return and fund return expected from CAPM**

* Also calculated by the coefficient of a linear regression of the fund returns against the benchmark returns.
** Capital Asset Pricing Model (CAPM): Expected Return = Risk-Free Rate + Beta × (Market Rreturn − Risk-Free Rate)

for each unit of risk taken. Because investment risk usually involves some level of expected volatility in returns, there are various ways to measure fund risk. Many of these measures are summarized in Exhibit 23–10.

To illustrate these various risk measures, we use a hypothetical data series in Exhibit 23–11. This data set includes yearly returns for the fund, the benchmark returns, and the risk-free rate. Although the risk-free rate could vary from year to year, for simplicity we keep it constant. Some additional calculations useful in calculating these various risk measures are also included in the exhibit.

EXHIBIT 23–11   Data for Risk Measures

Year	Fund Return	Benchmark Return	(Fund − Benchmark)	Risk-Free Rate	Fund Excess Return*	Benchmark Excess Return
1	14.00%	8.00%	6.00%	3.00%	11.00%	5.00%
2	9.00%	10.00%	−1.00%	3.00%	6.00%	7.00%
3	16.00%	12.00%	4.00%	3.00%	13.00%	9.00%
4	12.00%	13.00%	−1.00%	3.00%	9.00%	10.00%
5	16.00%	14.00%	2.00%	3.00%	13.00%	11.00%
6	20.00%	14.00%	6.00%	3.00%	17.00%	11.00%
7	14.00%	12.00%	2.00%	3.00%	11.00%	9.00%
8	15.00%	11.00%	4.00%	3.00%	12.00%	8.00%
9	12.00%	10.00%	2.00%	3.00%	9.00%	7.00%
10	13.00%	9.00%	4.00%	3.00%	10.00%	6.00%
11	6.00%	8.00%	−2.00%	3.00%	3.00%	5.00%
12	8.00%	5.00%	3.00%	3.00%	5.00%	2.00%
13	−6.00%	3.00%	−9.00%	3.00%	−9.00%	0.00%
14	−8.00%	1.00%	−9.00%	3.00%	−11.00%	−2.00%
15	−6.00%	2.00%	−8.00%	3.00%	−9.00%	−1.00%
16	6.00%	3.00%	3.00%	3.00%	3.00%	0.00%
17	2.00%	5.00%	−3.00%	3.00%	−1.00%	2.00%
18	8.00%	8.00%	0.00%	3.00%	5.00%	5.00%
19	18.00%	10.00%	8.00%	3.00%	15.00%	7.00%
20	12.00%	12.00%	0.00%	3.00%	9.00%	9.00%
Variance	0.62%	0.16%	0.22%		0.62%	0.16%
Std dev	7.86%	3.97%	4.74%		7.86%	3.97%
Mean	9.05%	8.50%	0.55%		6.05%	5.50%

* Excess return is return over the risk free rate.

Sharpe Ratio. The Sharpe ratio is calculated as the excess return for a fund divided by the standard deviation of fund excess returns. It is a measure of excess return relative to risk. An alternative ratio that is sometimes calculated uses the standard deviation of the excess returns (returns in excess of the risk-free rate) in the denominator. The Sharpe ratio is a measure of how much excess return was earned per unit of risk. In our example, the excess return for the 20 years averaged 6.05 percent. The standard deviation of the fund returns was 7.86 percent. Because we assume that the risk-free rate is constant in this example, the standard deviation of the excess returns for the fund would also be 7.86 percent. Dividing the excess return 6.05 percent by the standard deviation of the returns 7.86 percent results in a Sharpe Ratio of .7693. This could be compared to the Sharpe Ratio for the benchmark, or the ratio calculated for other funds to compare risk.

Beta. Beta is a measure of risk that considers how the returns for a particular fund tend to increase or decrease as the returns for the benchmark increase or decrease. A beta of 1.0 means that the return for the fund tends to increase or decrease by the same amount as increases or decreases in the benchmark. So if the benchmark return increases by 100 basis points, the fund return will also go up by 100 basis points and vice versa. A beta greater than 1.0 would mean that the return goes up or down by more than the change in the return for the benchmark. Conversely, a beta less than 1.0 would mean that the return goes up or down by *less* than that of the benchmark.

Beta for the fund can be determined by the following formula:

Beta = Covariance (Fund Return, Benchmark Return)/Variance (Benchmark Return)

In our example, the covariance between the fund returns and the benchmark returns is .00276 (see Exhibit 23–6 for the covariance formula). The variance of the benchmark return is .001575. Dividing the two results in a beta of 1.75. This suggests that if the benchmark increases (or decreases) by 100 basis points, the fund return will increase (decrease) by 175 basis points. Thus, investments in the fund are more volatile or risky than those comprising the benchmark.

It should be noted that when a fund has higher risk, this is not necessarily bad. The question is whether the investors can expect to be compensated for the extra risk by earning a higher return. The strategy of the fund may be to seek higher beta investments, an attempt to earn higher returns for investors. For example, the fund may use higher amounts of leverage or make investments in underperforming properties that could be leased up or require renovations. This would be a higher risk strategy and thus has a higher beta, but will hopefully produce higher returns. What is important is that investors understand what the risk strategy is for the fund when deciding to invest.

It is also informative to know that Beta can be found by the slope of a linear regression of the fund return against the benchmark return. This would be the coefficient for the independent variable in a simple linear regression (with the dependent variable being the fund return and the independent variable being the benchmark return). Exhibit 23–12 shows the results of this regression with our example data. The regression equation is

$$\text{Fund return} = (1.7508 \times \text{benchmark return}) - .0583.$$

The slope of the regression line (coefficient of the benchmark return variable) is 1.7508, which is the beta of the fund.

Capital Asset Pricing Model. We have seen that beta is a measure of the riskiness of an asset relative to the risk of a benchmark. The capital asset pricing model (CAPM) is a theoretical model that expresses the expected return for any investment as a function of its beta where the benchmark used to calculate the beta is what is referred to as the "market

EXHIBIT 23–12
Beta from Regression

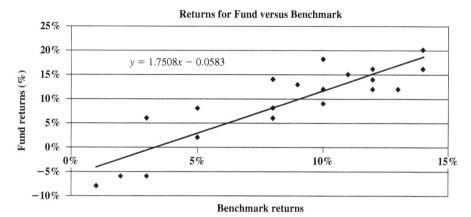

Returns for Fund versus Benchmark

$y = 1.7508x - 0.0583$

portfolio" or a portfolio that, in theory, consists of all possible investments. In practice, the market portfolio is usually thought of as a broad market index like the S&P 500, which includes some real estate investments in the form of REITs. So the beta of a property fund may be based on its covariance with the S&P 500. Because the beta for the market portfolio is theoretically 1, investment fund with a beta greater than 1 is riskier than the market portfolio and vice versa.

The expected return for a fund based on the CAPM would be as follows:

$$R_{fund} = R_{free} + (R_{Market} - R_{free}) \times Beta$$

where
R_{free} is the risk-free rate.
R_{Market} is the return for the market portfolio.
Beta is the beta for the fund relative to the market.
We will return to the CAPM after discussing Jensen's alpha.

Treynor Ratio.   Also known as the reward to volatility ratio, the Treynor ratio is similar to the Sharpe ratio but divides excess returns earned by the fund by beta instead of the standard deviation. The reason for this difference is that beta may be a more relevant measure of risk than the standard deviation. This is because the standard deviation for a fund doesn't take into account that investors may be offsetting some of the variation in fund returns from year to year by holding a diversified portfolio of different funds with different types of investments. Beta, on the other hand, tends to capture the risk that is inherent in the fund being evaluated. Thus, the Treynor ratio measures how much excess return the investors get relative to the fund's beta. The Treynor ratio in our example is (.0605/1.75) or .0346. The Treynor ratio would be compared to the Treynor ratio for the benchmark and the ratio of other funds to be used for evaluation purposes. This would allow investors to see how the fund compares in delivering return relative to risk.

Tracking Error.   The tracking error measures how closely a portfolio performs compared to its benchmark and how much the fund returns differ from the benchmark returns over time. It is calculated as the standard deviation of the difference in returns between the fund and the benchmark. To illustrate, if a fund tends to have a return that is persistently 100 basis points higher than the benchmark, it will have a very low tracking error as it tracks the index closely in its movement. On the other hand, if the fund return is more volatile and is, at times, higher than the benchmark and, at other times, lower than the benchmark then the fund will have a higher tracking error. If the benchmark is appropriate for the fund and the manager is doing a good job, returns would tend to be consistently above the benchmark and have a relatively low tracking error. It should be noted, however, that the tracking error could also be low if the fund returns are consistently lower than the benchmark by a particular amount. So a low tracking error does not always indicate that the manager is beating the benchmark. But it does suggest that the risk of the fund is very similar to that of the benchmark. The tracking error for our fund example is 4.74 percent, as shown at the bottom of Exhibit 23–11.

Information Ratio.   The information ratio addresses the issue mentioned above regarding the possibility of a low tracking error when fund is underperforming, that is, returns are persistently less than the benchmark. The information ratio is calculated as follows:

$$\text{Information Ratio} = \text{Average (Fund Return} - \text{Benchmark Return)/Tracking Error}$$

Information ratio measures two things: (1) whether a fund manager is generating excess returns relative to a benchmark, and (2) whether this over-/underperformance is a consistent behavior. The information ratio will only be positive if the fund is earning on average a higher return than the benchmark. This also means that the lower the tracking error, the higher the information ratio. For our example, the average difference in returns between the fund and the benchmark is .5500 percent. This average is then divided by the tracking error of 4.74 percent, which give a positive information ratio, or .5500%/4.74% = .1160.

Jensen's Alpha

The final risk measure that we will consider, Jensen's Alpha, also uses beta. Recall that if the beta for a fund is greater than the beta for the benchmark, then as the benchmark return increases, the fund return should increase even more to a greater extent. However, if a fund produces a higher return than the benchmark, it could mean that the manager did nothing more than taking on more risk. What investors ultimately want to know is whether or not the fund manager was able to generate returns that are greater than would be expected, given the level of risk for the fund. Exhibit 23–13 illustrates what a fund

EXHIBIT 23–13
The Relationship between Fund Performance (Return) for a Specific Level of Beta

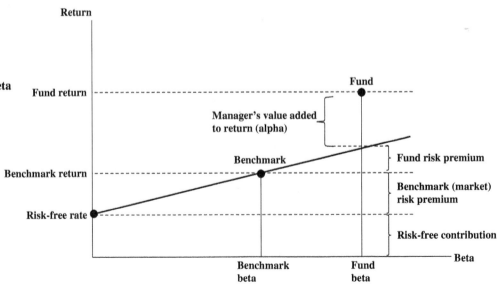

expected return should be given its beta. It also shows the "extent of value added" by the fund.

In this illustration, the fund has a higher beta than the benchmark. The benchmark return is what should be earned given the beta for the benchmark. Because the fund has a beta that is higher than the benchmark, it should earn a higher return than the benchmark for taking on incremental risk in excess of the benchmark risk. This can be thought of as the fund risk premium relative to its benchmark. Finally, because in this case the manager was able to earn a return that was even higher than what we would expect from its beta, this can be attributable to active management of the fund. The excess return, above the amount attributable to the fund's beta, represents what the manager should be compensated for. This additional return is referred to as "alpha."

We could say that there are two ways a manager can try to achieve higher returns. First, the manager can make investments that result in the fund having a higher beta. Secondly, the manager can try to generate alpha by doing a good job at executing investment strategies through selecting investments and managing the operations of the fund such that the returns are greater than what would be expected on the basis of the amount of risk taken by the fund.

As discussed previously, the CAPM is a model that gives you the expected return for an investment given its beta relative to the market portfolio as a benchmark. For a fund, we can express this as

$$R_{fund} = R_{free} + (R_{Market} - R_{free}) \times Beta$$

For the sample data we have been evaluating in Exhibit 23–11, the return on the fund should be

$$R_{fund} = 3\% + (8.5\% - 3\%) \times 1.751 = 12.63\%$$

Given that the mean return for the fund was 9.05 percent, the return was *less* than what it should have been based on the risk. Furthermore, Jensen's alpha would be

$$Jensen's\ Alpha = Actual\ Fund\ Return - Fund\ Return\ from\ CAPM$$
$$= 9.05\% - 12.63\% = -3.58\%$$

Thus, again, the fund did not do as well as what would be expected given its beta on a risk-adjusted basis. In summary, we can conclude that although the fund produced returns that were higher than returns based on the benchmark returns, it did not achieve enough returns to appropriately cover the additional risks it took on as reflected by its beta.

Conclusion

This chapter focused on commercial real estate investment funds that consist of a portfolio of properties and available to institutional investors and high net worth individuals. We discussed various ways these funds are structured and the different strategies that they may follow to appeal to different investor clienteles. Investors want to know how funds they have invested in (or might invest in) have performed relative to other funds and industry benchmarks. The chapter included a discussion of the different measures of return used for performance measurement of funds such as time-weighted returns. We then discussed how attribution analysis can evaluate why a fund may have performed differently than a benchmark to determine if "active fund management" was effective. We concluded with a detailed description of risk measurement techniques used to determine how much risk a fund may have taken relative to other funds and benchmarks. When fund performance exceeds its benchmark index, this analysis can be done to determine whether fund managers achieved superior performance by making better investment decisions than the typical fund manager or by simply taking additional risk.

Key Terms

allocation effect, *777*
arithmetic mean, *770*
attribution analysis, *775*
benchmark, *774*
cash drag, *768*
closed-end fund, *756*
commingled fund, *756*
committed capital, *760*

core fund, *757*
fiduciary, *753*
geometric mean, *769*
invested capital, *760*
investment period, *760*
investment multiple, *774*
opportunistic fund, *756*
promote, *761*

redemption/queueing
  policy, *758*
selection effect, *777*
separate account, *758*
style drift, *757*
target return, *773*
time-weighted return, *768*
value-added fund, *754*

Useful Web Sites

www.irei.com—Institutional Real Estate Investor. Articles and news regarding pension and other fund investors.

www.pionline.com—Pension and Investments. Source of articles, announcements and reviews of studies of issues involving the pension fund industry.

www.mmdwebaccess.com—Money Market Directory. Published by Standard and Poor's. Lists contact information for all Public and Private Pension Funds.

www.ncreif.org—National Council of Real Estate Investment Fiduciaries. Source of the NCREIF and ODCE indices discussed in the chapter.

www.swfinstitute.org—Provides a list and contact information for sovereign wealth funds throughout the world.

Questions

1. What are the primary differences between an open-end and closed-end fund? Why would an investor choose to invest in one or the other?

2. What is the difference between a time-weighted return and an internal rate of return? When reporting historical investment performance to investors in a core fund, which return would be more likely to be reported? What return would likely be used for an opportunity fund?

3. Which fund, core or opportunistic, would you expect to have higher returns? Why? Which would be expected to have greater volatility in returns? Why?

4. What is meant by a target return? How does it relate to an investment benchmark?

5. When comparing investment funds, what is the difference between committed capital and invested capital? Why may this matter for investors?

6. When evaluating investment funds, what is meant by performance at the "fund level" and at the "property level"? What would generally cause a difference between the two? What is this difference called?

7. When thinking about the extent of discretion that fund managers have when making property acquisitions, under which fund structures would a manager tend to have the greatest discretion? Under which structures would they tend to have the least discretion? Why?

8. When reporting property values to investors in funds, which fund types would generally require more frequent appraisals than others? Why?

9. What are the objectives of performing an attribution analysis? How could fund managers be evaluated by using an attribution analysis?

10. When evaluating fund performance, what is meant by "style drift"? How might style drift impact investment returns and volatility?

Problems

1. An institutional investor is comparing management fees for two competing real estate investment funds. Both funds expect to begin operations and are accepting capital commitments. When the funds begin acquiring properties, capital call will be made to investors for capital contributions during the investment period. Fund A will charge a fee of 45 BP on capital committed

and 60 BP on capital invested after the investment period ends. Fund B will charge a fee of 50 BP on capital committed and 55 BP on capital invested after the investment period ends. Both funds expect to have $500,000,000 in capital commitments and project a five-year cycle for startup and acquisitions. Capital flows are expected as follows:

Fund A

Year	Contributed Capital	Capital Returned	Invested Capital
1	$200,000,000	$ 0	$200,000,000
2	$300,000,000	$ 0	$500,000,000
3		$ 0	$500,000,000
4		$100,000,000	$400,000,000
5		$ 50,000,000	$350,000,000

Fund B

Year	Contributed Capital	Capital Ceturned	Invested Capital
1	$300,000,000	$ 0	$300,000,000
2	$200,000,000	$ 0	$500,000,000
3		$ 0	$500,000,000
4		$ 50,000,000	$450,000,000
5		$100,000,000	$350,000,000

a. What will total fees be for Fund (A)? For Fund (B)?

b. What may the pattern of capital commitments/contributions indicate about the expectations of the respective fund managers?

2. A closed-end, commingled opportunity fund is being created with an expected three-year life. It expects to acquire properties that it expects to "turnaround" and sell at the end of three years for a gain. It also plans a minimum "target return" of 10 percent to investors, which will be based on cash distributions from operations *and* from the sale of properties at the end of the life of the fund. The opportunity fund manager expects to receive a "promote" equal to 25 percent of cash flows remaining after sale of the assets and after equity investors receive their minimum 10 percent target return. Cash flows are expected as follows:

Year	Equity Investment	Cash Distributions from Operations to Equity Investors (After Management Fees)	Expected Sale Proceeds
0	$2,000,000		
1		$50,000	
2		$50,000	
3			$3,000,000

a. What must be the cash flows to equity investors at the end of year 3 in order to achieve their total target 10 percent return on equity investment?

b. How much of the proceeds from property sales must the fund manager receive in order to earn its 25 percent "promote"?

c. After the equity investors earn their 10 percent target return (IRR) and the fund manager earns the 25 percent promote, how much will be distributed to equity investors?

d. After the "promote" is paid to the fund manager in year 3, what will be the IRR to equity investors for the three-year investment period?

3. A commercial real estate investment fund must report its quarterly investment performance to investors. A summary of its (1) beginning and end-of-quarter assets and equity, and (2) cash inflows and outflows during the quarter are as follows:

Beginning of Quarter		During Quarter	
$40 million	Cash + ST investments	$15 million	NOI from operations
$220 million	Market value of props	$2 million	Paid management fees
$10 million	Short-term debt	$8 million	Distributions to investors
		$200 million	Investor contributions
		$150 million	Property acquisitions
		$0	Property distributions

Assume any interest on short-term investments is offset by interest paid on short-term debt.

   a. What would be the beginning equity value?

   b. What would be the MVEE?

   c. Assuming that all cash flows from operations, equity contributions, acquisitions, and distributions occurred at the end of the quarter, what would be the quarterly return (IRR)?

   d. Assuming that all cash distributions to investors occurred equally in 30-day intervals during the quarter. What would be an approximation to the IRR using the Modified Dietz approach?

   e. Assuming the same cash flows in (d) what would the return be before fees?

   f. Assuming this same cash flows in (d) what would be return at the "property level"?

   g. How would (f) change if the value of properties was $400 million at the end of the quarter?

4. An investor is evaluating the historical performance of an investment fund. The following annual returns are provided to the investor:

Year	Fund Value
0	100
1	103
2	107
3	110
4	105
5	100

   a. Calculate the investment returns for each year.

   b. Compute the arithmetic mean return.

   c. Calculate the geometric mean return.

   d. Why is there a difference between (b) and (c)?

5. You have been asked to evaluate returns from your commercial real estate investment fund (Bluestone Fund) against an industry benchmark index to determine how successful your "active" investment strategy has been. Specifically, a potential client wants you to compare the performance of your portfolio strategy against a "passive" strategy of simply investing based on the same proportions of properties and locations comprising the index.

During the most current quarter, the following information has been provided to you based on property type and location:

A.

Property Type	Bluestone Fund % of Fund Value	Return	Weighted Return	Industry Index % of Index Value	Return	Weighted Return
Apartments	14.4%	13.0%	1.8%	20.4%	8.9%	1.8%
Hotel	0.0%	0.0%	0.0%	2.1%	8.5%	0.2%
Industrial	13.5%	8.5%	1.2%	16.0%	7.0%	1.1%
Office	44.1%	12.7%	5.6%	37.2%	7.6%	2.8%
Retail	28.3%	8.6%	2.4%	24.3%	9.7%	2.4%
Total	**100.0%**	—	**11.0%**	**100.0%**	—	**8.3%**

B.

	Bluestone Fund			Industry Index		
Location Type	% of Fund Value	Return	Weighted Return	% of Index Value	Return	Weighted Return
North	6.3%	4.5%	0.3%	11.0%	6.1%	0.6%
South	27.6%	8.6%	2.4%	18.0%	7.8%	1.4%
East	43.3%	14.0%	6.1%	34.0%	9.0%	3.1%
West	22.7%	9.9%	2.2%	37.0%	8.8%	3.2%
Total	**100.0%**	—	**11.0%**	**100.0%**	—	**8.3%**

a. Calculate the extent to which the Bluestone Fund is over- or (under)weighted by *property type* relative to the industry index.

b. Calculate the extent to which the Bluestone Fund is over- or (under)weighted by *location/ region* relative to the industry index.

c. To what extent was the superior performance by Bluestone attributable to property selection and allocation in (A)?

d. To what extent was the superior performance by Bluestone attributable to property selection and allocation in (B)?

e. Assuming that the standard deviation of returns for its Bluestone Fund was 10.0 and 9.0 for index returns, what may be said about the relative risk for the two funds?

Index

Words in **bold** indicate key words